TENTH EDITION

INTERNATIONAL BUSINESS

ENVIRONMENTS AND OPERATIONS

John D. Daniels
UNIVERSITY OF MIAMI

Lee H. Radebaugh
BRIGHAM YOUNG UNIVERSITY

Daniel P. Sullivan
UNIVERSITY OF DELAWARE

PEARSON
Education

Credits and acknowledgments borrowed from other sources and reproduced, with permission, in this textbook appear on appropriate page within text.

ISBN 81-297-0411-0

First Indian Reprint, 2004
Second Indian Reprint, 2004

This edition is manufactured in India and is authorized for sale only in India, Bangladesh, Bhutan, Pakistan, Nepal, Sri Lanka and the Maldives.

Published by Pearson Education (Singapore) Pte. Ltd., Indian Branch, 482 F.I.E. Patparganj, Delhi 110 092, India

Printed in India by Baba Barkha Nath Printers.

BRIEF CONTENTS

CONTENTS

Part Two

COMPARATIVE ENVIRONMENTAL FRAMEWORKS   42

CHAPTER 4   The Economic Environment   102

Part Three

THEORIES AND INSTITUTIONS: TRADE AND INVESTMENT   138

Government Influence on Trade   170

7 Regional Economic Integration and Cooperative Agreements 202

8　Factor Mobility and Foreign Direct Investment　234

Part Four

WORLD FINANCIAL ENVIRONMENT　262

9　The Foreign-Exchange Market　262

**CASE　Foreign Travels, Foreign-Exchange Travails:
Excerpts from the Travel Journal of Lee Radebaugh　263**

10   The Determination of Exchange Rates   288

Part Five

THE DYNAMICS OF INTERNATIONAL BUSINESS-GOVERNMENT RELATIONSHIPS 316

11 Government Attitudes Toward Foreign Direct Investment   316

14 Collaborative Strategies 410

15 Control Strategies   438

Part Seven

OPERATIONS: MANAGING BUSINESS FUNCTIONS
INTERNATIONALLY   470

16   Marketing   470

17 Export and Import Strategies   504

18 Global Manufacturing and Supply Chain Management 536

21 Human Resource Management 628

PREFACE

We examined the text offerings in business and economics from five leading publishers and discovered that only about five percent of texts have carried on to a tenth edition. We are gratified to be a part of this select group. On the one hand, the longevity illustrates that we have given students and professors a pedagogically sound approach to relevant material through nine editions. On the other hand, we worried if we could present sufficiently fresh content and approaches for a tenth edition. With this worry in mind, we added Daniel P. Sullivan as a third co-author. Not only is he younger than the other two co-authors (John D. Daniels and Lee H. Radebaugh), his background and academic publications illustrate the fresh and contemporary ideas that he brings to this text. In addition, we vowed to relate all relevant business and environmental changes since the ninth edition to the current study of international business.

A perusal of our end-of-chapter references shows that most are post-20th century. Further, they cite not only works by international business scholars, but also the latest work by disciplinary and functional specialists.

The tenth edition includes 12 new cases, including cases on such topical companies as Carrefour, Cisco, Johnson & Johnson, and Vivendi. Some of our new cases illustrate how companies' foreign activities affected their home-country operations, such as the new case dealing with Enron's foreign accounting practices that contributed to its failure. Some illustrate how companies struggled to adapt to a deteriorating foreign environment, such as the new case on HSBC's adjustments to the collapse of the Argentine peso. Those cases that are carry-overs from the ninth edition have been substantially updated and restructured, some by collecting information on location—such as in Chile for Cranchile and in Hungary for GE Hungary.

Since our ninth edition was published, a number of global occurrences have impacted international business. Among these are the emergence of Russia as the world's number one oil exporter, the terrorist attack in New York on September 11, 2001, the failure of some formerly significant companies, like Enron and WorldCom, the Argentine financial crisis, the U.S. west coast dock strike, the institution of the Euro, and the accession of China to the World Trade Organization. We now relate all of these to specific chapter discussions. For example, we discuss the post September 11th situation in chapter 3 regarding confidence in governmental institutions, in chapter 4 about the economic shock it caused, in chapter 8 concerning changes in foreign investment flows, and in chapter 21 on the hassles of international travel for international business managers.

We haven't just updated by looking at events since the ninth edition. We have also strengthened coverage of areas that we had previously included. For example, because of the continued concern about the piracy of industrial property, we have added a case on global software piracy. Because of growing concern, especially by non-governmental organizations, about foreign investment and privatization, we have added a case on Newmont Mining in Indonesia. We have also re-titled chapter 8 to Factor Mobility and Foreign Direct Investment to reflect content change as we substantially increased coverage of migration as it affect international business.

In addition to looking backward, we also look forward to the many discussions that could harbinger changes in the international business environment, such as U.S.-Cuban trade relations, a possible Free Trade Area of the Americas, the expansion of the European Union, and efforts to establish global accounting standards.

Although our discussion has emphasized the changes we made between the ninth and tenth editions, we have maintained the basic philosophy and pedagogical techniques that sustain student interest to read and master the important chapter lessons. For example, we still open each chapter with a short non-fictional descriptive case that illustrates points that are discussed throughout the chapter. We end each chapter with a short discussion case so that students can apply lessons from the chapter to their own analysis. Throughout the book, we illustrate points with what are probably more up-to-date real examples than in any other competitive text. We list learning objectives at the beginning of each chapter, summarize major chapter points at the end, place marginal notes to abridge major points, and put new terms in bold lettering the first time they are used. Each chapter has a section dealing with ethical dilemmas pertaining to the chapter's subject matter. Finally, each chapter has a section outlining future scenarios that may unfold. Hopefully, professors will enjoy teaching from the text and students will enjoy learning from it.

ACKNOWLEDGEMENTS

We have been fortunate since the first edition to have colleagues who have been willing to make the effort to critique draft materials, react to coverage already in print, advise on suggested changes, and send items to be corrected. Because this is the culmination of several previous editions, we would like to acknowledge everyone's efforts. However, many more individuals than we can possibly list have helped. To those who must remain anonymous, we offer our sincere thanks.

Special thanks go to the faculty members who made detailed comments that contributed to the planning of this edition:

Behnam Nakhai, Millersville University

Stanley Flax, St. Thomas University

R. Boyd Johnson, Indiana Wesleyan University

Namgyoo K. Park, University of Miami

Ralph F. Jagodka, Mt. San Antonio Community College

Douglas K. Peterson, Indiana State University

Carol A. Howard, Oklahoma City University

Aseem Prakash, University of Washington

Tunga Kiyak, Michigan State University

We would also like to thank the staff who have helped to research and prepare the manuscript for this edition: Melanie Hunter, Paul Marer, Gordon B. Swanson, Charles Buckwalter, Jean Boddewyn, Andrew Gross, Amber Benson (Chapters 3, 4, 7, 9, 10, 17, and 18), John Benson (Chapter 20), and Ervin Black (Chapter 19).

Supplements

Instructor's Manual with Video Guide. Designed to guide the educator through the text, each chapter in the instructor's manual includes chapter objectives, a chapter overview, a detailed chapter outline that includes teaching tips and additional tips regarding the boxed features, answers to case questions and discussion questions in the text, and one to two new additional exercises.

Test Item File. Each chapter contains multiple-choice, and short answer/essay questions. Because the test item file is a critical component of the supplements package, the test item file author worked closely with the authors to craft questions that are relevant to the text and will challenge students. All of the test questions were based upon a list of study questions generated by the authors, to ensure that the test item file covers all of the important topics in the text.

TestGen-EQ Test Generating Software. The print Test Bank is designed for use with the TestGen-EQ test generating software. This computerized package allows instructors to custom design, save, and generate classroom tests. The test program permits instructors to edit, add, or delete questions from the test banks; edit existing graphics and create new graphics; analyze test results; and organize a database of tests and student results. This new software allows for greater flexibility and ease of use. It provides many options for organizing and displaying tests, along with a search and sort feature.

PowerPoint Electronic Transparencies. A comprehensive package, these PowerPoint transparencies are designed to aid the educator and supplement in-class lectures. They are available both online (**www.prenhall.com/daniels**) or on the Instructor's Resource CD-ROM.

Instructor's Resource CD ROM. All of the resources for your text are available in one place! On the IRCD, you will find the electronic files for the Instructor's Manual and Test Item File, the TestGen-EQ software, and the complete set of PowerPoints.

Companion Website. The format of our Websites has been updated, and includes the same great features in a more user-friendly format. Here you will find password-protected Instructor's Resources, as well as a student section, which features sample true/false, multiple choice, and Internet essay questions. The CW site also includes *In the News* articles, which are updated during the course of the year. The articles are provided by XanEdu, and are supported by exercises and activities for the student. The Website for *International Business, 10/e,* can be found at **www.prenhall.com/daniels.**

CultureⓆuest **Exciting feature for the 10th Edition! Culture Quest Global Business Videos.** The CultureQuest series of products deliver engaging, high-quality culture, country, and business programs to help people better understand the world around them. These videos run from 7-17 minutes in length.

The CultureQuest Global Business videos include the following timely and exciting topics:

- **The Debate on Globalization**—While globalization clearly appears inevitable, it has both critics and advocates. See and hear how the debate on global trade is evolving through a review of the key issues. (Chapter 1, p. 27)

- **Impact of Culture on Business: Spotlight on Latin America**—Many think that Latin America is one big homogenous culture. In reality, each country has its own local history, religion, values and practices which have created a diverse and colorful mosaic of cultures that make up the region. Whether in business or as part of the vibrant society, the culture of Latin America continues to have a deep and meaningful impact on people throughout the region. (Chapter 2, p. 75)

- **Understanding the Foreign Exchange Markets: Spotlight on Argentina and Ecuador**—Explore how the global financial exchange markets work. Learn more about the Argentine financial crisis and how countries like Ecuador have avoided the same currency fate. (Chapter 10, p. 314)

- **Understanding Foreign Direct Investment: Spotlight on South Africa**—Learn how government policies directly encourage or restrict multinational enterprise operations and their global investments. Explore the factors that challenge the South African government efforts to attract and retain foreign direct investment. (Chapter 11, p. 342)

- **Global Business and Ethics**—Learn how ethics and diplomacy impact global business. See how the local culture in a country can influence business negotiations and ethical standards. (Chapter 12, p. 373)

- **Understanding Entry Modes into the Chinese Market**—Learn how companies navigate a land of 1.3 billion consumers and one of the most unwieldy bureaucracies. Explore the best ways to enter the Chinese market and, identify the options and local factors that foreign companies have to consider as they start to do business in China. (Chapter 14, p. 436)

Chapter Opening and Closing Cases

In addition to the chapter opening cases, Daniels, Radebaugh, and Sullivan's closing cases pose questions that students must answer based on what they have learned in the chapter. These closing cases contain questions that are answered in the instructor's manual.

Maps

Designed to help improve students' geographic literacy, the book's many maps add interest and illustrate facts and topics discussed in the text. Many case maps zero in on the case company's home country to give students a close-up look at foreign locales.

A complete atlas with index is available following Chapter 1.

About the Authors

Three respected and renowned scholars show your students how dynamic, how real, how interesting the study of international business can be.

John D. Daniels, the Samuel N. Friedland Chair of Executive Management at the University of Miami, received his Ph.D. at the University of Michigan. His dissertation won first place in the award competition of the Academy of International Business. Since then he has been an active researcher. His articles have appeared in such leading journals as Academy of Management Journal, California Management Review, Columbia Journal of World Business, Journal of Business Research, Journal of International Business Studies, Strategic Management Journal, and Weltwirtschaftliches Archiv. On its thirtieth anniversary, Management International Review referred to him as "one of the most prolific American IB scholars." He has also served as president of the Academy of International Business and dean of its Fellows. He also served as chairperson of the international division of the Academy of Management. He has worked and lived a year or longer in seven different countries, worked shorter stints in about thirty other countries on six continents, and has traveled in many more. His foreign work has been a combination of private sector, governmental, teaching, and research assignments. He was formerly director of the Center for International Business Education and Research (CIBER) at Indiana University and holder of the E. Claiborne Robins Distinguished Chair at the University of Richmond.

Lee H. Radebaugh, is the KPMG Professor at Brigham Young University, the executive director of the BYU-University at Utah Center for International Business Education and Research, and the director of the School of Accountancy and Information Systems.

He received his MBA and doctorate from Indiana University. He taught at the Pennsylvania State University from 1972 to 1980. He also has been a visiting professor at Escuela de Administracion de Negocios para Graduados (ESAN), a graduate business school in Lima, Peru. In 1985, Professor Radebaugh was the James Cusator Wards visiting professor at Glasgow University, Scotland. His other books include International Accounting and Multinational Enterprises (John Wiley and Sons, 4th Edition) with S.J. Gray; Introduction to Business: International Dimensions (South-Western Publishing Company) with John D. Daniels; and seven books on Canada-U.S. trade and investment relations, with Earl Fry as co-editor. He has also published several other monographs and articles on international business and international accounting in journals such as the Journal of Accounting Research, the Journal of International Financial Management and Accounting, the Journal of International Business Studies, and the International Journal of Accounting. His primary teaching interests are international business and international accounting. He is an active member of the American Accounting Association, the European Accounting Association, and the Academy of International Business, having served on several committees as the president of the International Section of the AAA and as the secretary-treasurer of the AIB. He is a member of the Fellows of the Academy of International Business.

He is also active with the local business community as past president of the World Trade Association of Utah and member of the District Export Council. In 1998, he was named International Person of the Year in the State of Utah and Outstanding International Educator of the International Section of the American Accounting Association.

Daniel P. Sullivan, an Associate Professor of Management at the Alfred Lerner College of Business of the University of Delaware, received his Ph.D. from the University of South Carolina. He researches a range of topics, including Globalization and Business, International Management, Global Strategy, Competitive Analysis, and Corporate Governance. His work on these topics has been published in leading scholarly journals, including the *Journal of International Business Studies, Management International Review, Law and Society Review,* and *Academy of Management Journal.* In addition, he served on the editorial boards of *Journal of International Business Studies* and *Management International Review.* He has been honored for both his research and teaching, receiving grants and winning awards for both activities while at the University of Delaware and, his former affiliation, the A.B. Freeman School of Business of Tulane University. He has been awarded numerous teaching honors at the undergraduate, MBA, and EMBA levels—most notably, he was voted the Outstanding Teacher by the students of seven consecutive Executive MBA classes at the University of Delaware and Tulane University. He has taught, designed, and administered a range of graduate, undergraduate, and non-degree courses on topics spanning Globalization and Business, International Business Operations, International Management, Strategic Perspectives, and Corporate Strategy. In the United States, he has delivered lectures and courses at several university sites and company facilities. In addition, he has led courses in several foreign countries, including Bulgaria, the Czech Republic, France, Switzerland, and the United Kingdom. Finally, he has worked with many managers and consulted with several multinational enterprises on issues of international business.

PART ONE

Background for International Business

CHAPTER 1

INTERNATIONAL BUSINESS: AN OVERVIEW

The world is a chain, one link in another.

—MALTESE PROVERB

OBJECTIVES

- To define international business and describe how it differs from domestic business
- To explain why companies engage in international business and why its growth has accelerated
- To introduce different modes a company can use to accomplish its global objectives
- To illustrate the role social science disciplines play in understanding the environment of international business
- To provide an overview of the primary patterns for companies' international expansion
- To describe the major countervailing forces that affect international business

CASE

Star Wars: Episode II—Attack of the Clones[1]

Lucasfilm's *Star Wars: Episode II—Attack of the Clones*, which was released in 2002, had the third highest opening weekend of revenue in movie history. Within a few weeks, *Attack of the Clones* joined its four *Star Wars* predecessors (*Star Wars, The Empire Strikes Back, Return of the Jedi*, and *Star Wars-The Phantom Menace*) among the 15 highest grossing movies of all time.

The intergalactic aspect of the *Star Wars* quintet is obvious. Less obvious, though, are the international dimensions, right here on the planet Earth, that contributed to the success.

The deal to produce *Star Wars* in the 1970s was international from the start. George Lucas, the American producer, used his last $2,000 to buy a ticket to the Cannes (France) Film Festival, in the hope of gaining some backing. There, he made a production agreement with Twentieth Century Fox executives who thought that *Star Wars* was too high a risk to warrant giving Lucas their customary signing bonus of about a half million dollars. Instead, the studio gave him all sequence and merchandising rights, which it has regretted ever since.

George Lucas used multicountry production locations for each movie in the *Star Wars* quintet. He used British studios for the first four movies, but he switched to Australian ones for *Attack of the Clones* because they could provide comparable quality at a lower cost. The lower cost of Australian technicians more than offset the additional cost of transporting actors and other production personnel to Australia. Further, the Australian government promotes large-scale movie making in Australia by assessing a low tax on the movies' earnings. Additionally, for *Attack of the Clones*, Lucasfilm used locations in Italy, Tunisia, Spain, the United Kingdom, and the United States. For example, Italy is the site for scenes of the planet Naboo; interiors of Queen Amidala's palace were shot in Caserta and exteriors of gardens in Lake Como. Scenes of the desert planet Tatooine were shot in the Sahara Desert of Tunisia. Because of transportation and communications advances, such global production of movies is now commonplace. These advances enable us to see more realistic-looking scenes than were possible only a few years ago.

The cast and crew of *Attack of the Clones* are as multicountry as its production locations. For example, Ewan McGregor (Obi-Wan Kenobi) is from Scotland, Natalie Portman (Padmé Amidala) from Israel, Hayden Christensen (Anakin Skywalker) from Canada, Pernilla August (Shmi Skywalker) from Sweden, Temuera Morrison (Jango Fett) from New Zealand, Oliver Lee (Count Dooku) from England, and Jimmy Smits (Senator Bail Organa) from the United States. John Williams, from the United States, composed the music, but he performed it with the London Symphony Orchestra and Choir.

The distribution of the *Star Wars* quintet has been truly international. The expectation of receiving both domestic and foreign income is necessary to justify the risky investment. About 40 percent of revenues have come from outside the United States; however, there have been some formidable obstacles. For example, some countries, such as Haiti and Mali, have such poor economies that few people can afford to attend movies. Even if Lucasfilm could generate attendance, the moviegoers would pay in gourdes and francs, respectively. Because the governments are also poor, especially in ownership of other currencies, they would be hard-pressed to convert the gourdes and francs to a currency that the producers can use. *The Phantom Menace* emulated this problem when the Tatooine merchant would not accept the heroes' galactic currency. Lucasfilm has made separate agreements with each country that shows one of the *Star Wars* movies so that it will receive revenues in U.S. dollars.

All the *Star Wars* films have been well attended almost everywhere they have been screened. For example, the debut of *Attack of the Clones* set attendance records in Australia. The popularity has been due at least in part to shrewd marketing and extraordinary special effects, yet many movies that share these attributes still fail to become international hits. What these movies did, which was probably the critical factor in their success, was to portray universal themes. The noted French anthropologist Claude Levi-Strauss has studied widespread cultures and observed common threads in their myths, tragedies, and fairy tales. He attributed this commonality to the fact that the mind classifies by opposing absolutes, such as good versus evil. Another explanation may be that there is a bit of the child in all of us, all over the world, and George Lucas says he makes movies for children and wants to teach them about goodness.

In spite of the films' widespread acceptance, they have not been identical everywhere. Censors in each country must review and approve them. In some cases, they required Lucasfilm to remove scenes they considered too violent for children. For example, the British Board of Film Classification feared that children might copy the head-butt inflicted on Obi-Wan Kenobi in *Attack of the Clones*. Rather than accept a PG rating that would preclude attendance by moviegoers under the age of 12 (about 15 percent of the potential audience), Lucasfilm cut the scene for the British version.

Lucasfilm has made other operating adjustments because of national technical differences. For instance, it made *Attack of the Clones* digitally (hence it was taped instead of filmed); however, not all movie houses are equipped to screen movies digitally. Lucasfilm decided to debut the movie only in movie houses with digital projection capabilities so that professional and word-of-mouth reviewers would observe the best projection of special effects. This meant that *Attack of the Clones* debuted in only 3,161 movie houses compared with 8,100 for the popular *Harry Potter* a year earlier. It also meant a delay for screenings in nondigital movie houses and, in turn, delayed screenings in some countries. For example, there was a two-and-a-half-month delay before the movie was shown in El Salvador. In addition, studios must convert movies to various home-viewing systems because there is no worldwide standard for either televisions or videocassette systems. Further, in some countries, people primarily watch movies at home on videocassettes, but in other countries they mainly use another medium, such as CD-ROMs.

Next, there was a problem of translation. Lucasfilm has made its *Attack of the Clones* logos visually similar for different parts of the world even though the information on those logos is in different languages and alphabets. Figure 1.1 shows some of these logos. Lucasfilm also had to go through the costly process of dubbing or adding subtitles to appeal to the mass clientele who do not understand English. It dubbed *Attack of the Clones* into 18 foreign languages (French, Italian, German, Castilian Spanish, French Canadian, Latin American Spanish, Catalan, Thai, Cantonese, Hindi, Hungarian, Russian, Czech, Slovak, Polish, Turkish, Japanese, and Brazilian Portuguese). (The release in Portugal used subtitles instead of Brazilian Portuguese.) For many countries, *Attack of the Clones* was shown either in English or in one of six subtitled versions. Lucasfilm auditioned and hired native-speaking actors in about 30 countries to do the dubbing. It hired sound technicians (to tweak the words to fit mouth movements more closely) in each of the 18 countries where it did the dubbing.

Lucasfilm released *Attack of the Clones* on the same day in nine countries and a day later in another large group of countries. Its decision for a simultaneous domestic and foreign release was based on two factors. First, Lucasfilm wanted to placate fans in many countries who had complained about having to wait to see earlier *Star Wars* movies. Second, Lucasfilm realized the difficulty of preventing unauthorized copying (piracy) of its movies, an activity that yields no revenue to Lucasfilm. Because Lucasfilm had to make so many copies of *Attack of the Clones*, it was almost inevitable that some copies would slip out of its security and be reproduced. Thus, Lucasfilm sought to minimize attacks on its revenues from cloned copies by making *Attack of the Clones* quickly available in theaters. Nevertheless, many people have seen unauthorized versions of the movie, especially in countries where laws against copying are not well enforced. For example, a Taiwanese downloading site (Movie88.com) has sometimes made new movies available on the Internet before studios ever released them. Lucasfilm believes that about one million people chose to download *Attack of the Clones* before it was ever officially distributed. Even in war-torn Afghanistan, where the Taliban had recently forbidden television and videos, video stores were renting *Attack of the Clones* before its debut in the United States.

One of the big revenue sources for all of the *Star Wars* movies has been the sale of rights to companies worldwide to produce and sell products with characters and scenes from the movies. *Attack of the Clones* has

FIGURE 1.1   Attack of the Clones: International Titles

Latin America

Bulgaria

Taiwan

Denmark

Estonia

Finland

France

Germany

Greece

Hungary

India

Italy

Japan

Turkey

Portugal

Romania

Russia

Spain

Sweden

Thailand

Selling globally usually requires translations.
Courtesy of Lucasfilm Ltd.

been no exception. For example, Master Replicas from the United States is making miniature reproductions, such as reproductions of guns. One of its customers, Styles on Video Japan, bought rights from Master Replicas to sell them in Japan, South Korea, China, and Taiwan. Titon Publishing in the United Kingdom is producing an *Attack of the Clones* comic book. Lego, a Danish company, is producing a variety of construction toys, such as Jedi Defense figures. Hasbro received marketing rights for action figures, such as Jedi Defense figures, which it is making in China.

In making and distributing *Star Wars: Episode II—Attack of the Clones*, Lucasfilm is demonstrating a global mindset—one that sees the whole world as an opportunity for finding the best inputs for production and for subsequently selling that production. To take advantage of these opportunities, Lucasfilm has sometimes had to adapt its methods of operations to the needs and circumstances of different countries.

INTRODUCTION TO THE FIELD OF INTERNATIONAL BUSINESS

International business is all commercial transactions—private and governmental—between two or more countries. Private companies undertake such transactions for profit; governments may or may not do the same in their transactions. These transactions include sales, investments, and transportation.

The goal of private business is to increase or to stabilize profits, which partly depend on

- Foreign sales
- Foreign resources

Government business may or may not be profit motivated.

Not only is business spreading globally, it is extending beyond the confines of any country, such as to outer space, non-territorial ocean areas, and Antarctica. The photo shows a large array of satellite tracking devices in New Mexico (United States). Satellites are used in international business for such activities as communications and weather forecasting.

Why should you study international business? A simple answer is that international business comprises a large and growing portion of the world's total business. Today, global events and competition affect almost all companies—large or small—because most sell output to and secure supplies from foreign countries. Many companies also compete against products and services that come from abroad.

A more complex answer is that a company operating internationally will engage in modes of business, such as exporting and importing, that differ from those it is accustomed to domestically. To operate effectively, managers must understand these different modes, which we'll discuss shortly.

The conditions within a company's external environment (the conditions outside a company as opposed to its internal ones) affect the way business functions such as marketing are carried out. These conditions are physical, societal, and competitive. When a company operates internationally, it adds foreign conditions to its domestic ones, making its external environment more diverse. Figure 1.2 shows the relationship's among influences in the external environment—physical, societal, and competitive—and a firm's operations.

Even if you never have direct international business responsibilities, you may find it useful to understand some of its complexities. Companies' international operations and governmental regulation of international business affect company profits, employment security and wages, consumer prices, and national security. A better understanding of international busi-

FIGURE 1.2   International Business: Operations and Influences

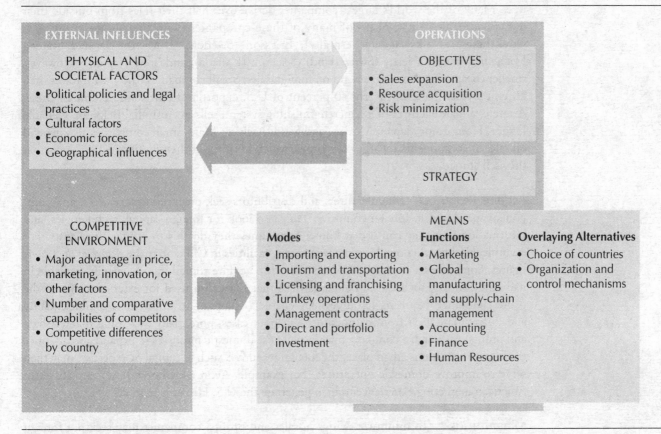

The conduct of international operations depends on companies' objectives and the means with which they carry them out. The operations affect and are affected by the physical and societal factors and competitive environment.

ness may help you to make more informed decisions, such as where you want to work and what governmental policies you want to support.

Why Companies Engage in International Business

When operating internationally, a company should consider its mission (what it will seek to do and become over the long term), its objectives (specific performance targets to fulfill its mission), and strategy (the means to fulfill its objectives). Figure 1.2 shows three major operating objectives that may induce companies to engage in international business. They are

- To expand sales.
- To acquire resources.
- To minimize risk.

Expand Sales   Companies' sales are dependent on two factors: the consumers' interest in their products or services and the consumers' willingness and ability to buy them. The number of people and the amount of their purchasing power are higher for the world as a whole than for a single country, so companies may increase the potential market for their sales by pursuing international markets.

Ordinarily, higher sales mean higher profits, assuming that each unit sold has the same markup. For example, *Attack of the Clones* cost millions of dollars to produce, but as more people see it, the average production (fixed) cost per viewer decreases.

So increased sales are a major motive for a company's expansion into international business. Many of the world's largest companies derive over half their sales from outside their home countries. You've heard of many of these companies (with their home country in parentheses)—Volkswagen (Germany), Ericsson (Sweden), IBM (the United States), Michelin (France), Nestlé (Switzerland), Seagram (Canada), and Sony (Japan).[2] However, smaller companies also may depend on foreign sales. Small companies (those with fewer than 20 employees) make up nearly 70 percent of U.S. exporters.[3] For example, one of these, Artcrete, a manufacturer of a concrete finishing system, sells in Australia, Belgium, Canada, France, Hong Kong, Japan, Mexico, and Saudi Arabia.[4] Many small companies also depend on sales of components to large companies, which in turn put them in finished products that they sell abroad.

Acquire Resources   Manufacturers and distributors seek out products, services, and components produced in foreign countries. They also look for foreign capital, technologies, and information that they can use at home. Sometimes they do this to reduce their costs. For example, Hasbro relies on cheap manufacturing facilities in China to make *Attack of the Clones* figures. Sometimes a company operates abroad to acquire something not readily available in its home country, such as the Italian gardens that Lucasfilm used for exterior scenes of the planet Tatooine. Acquiring resources may enable a company to improve its product quality and differentiate itself from competitors—in both cases, potentially increasing market share and profits. Although a company may initially use domestic resources to expand abroad, once the foreign operations are in place, the foreign resources, such as capital or expertise, may then serve to improve domestic operations. For example, Avon used know-how from its Latin American marketing experience to help penetrate the U.S. Hispanic market.[5]

Minimize Risk   To minimize swings in sales and profits, companies may seek out foreign markets to take advantage of business cycle—recessions and expansions—differences among countries. Sales decrease or grow more slowly in a country that is in a recession and increase or grow more rapidly in one that is expanding economically. For example, in 2001, Nestlé experienced slower growth in Western Europe and the United States, but this slow growth was offset by higher growth in Asia, Eastern Europe, and Latin America.[6] By obtaining supplies of the same product or component from different countries, companies may be able to avoid the full impact of price swings or shortages in any one country.

Many companies enter into international business for defensive reasons. They want to counter advantages competitors might gain in foreign markets that, in turn, could hurt them domestically. For example, Company A and Company B compete in the same domestic market. Company A may fear that Company B will generate large profits from a foreign market if left alone to serve that market. Company B may then use those profits in various ways (such as additional advertising or development of improved products) to improve its competitive position in the domestic market. Companies harboring such a fear may enter foreign markets primarily to prevent a competitor from gaining advantages.

Reasons for Recent International Growth— from Carrier Pigeons to the Internet

It's hard to determine just how much international business has occurred at different times in history. Shifting boundaries may cause what were domestic transactions to become international transactions, or vice versa. For example, when the former Soviet Union disbanded, business transactions between Russia and Ukraine changed from domestic to international.

Regardless, international business has grown in most recent years at a faster pace than global production. However, during the global economic downturn of 2001, it grew much slower than in the preceding years.[7]

It seems the reasons companies pursue international business—to expand sales, acquire resources, and minimize risk—would have applied in earlier periods as well. So what has happened in recent decades to bring about the increased growth in international business? The answer lies in the following four, sometimes interrelated, factors:

1. Rapid increase in and expansion of technology
2. Liberalization of government policies on cross-border movement of trade and resources
3. Development of institutions that support and facilitate international trade
4. Increased global competition

Expansion of Technology It was only a century and a quarter ago that Jules Verne fantasized about people traveling around the world in only 80 days. Much of what we take for granted today results from recent advances that have been accelerating at a dizzying rate. Tremendous strides in communications and transportation technology enable people in one part of the world to know about and demand products and services developed in another part of the world. Today's senior citizens can remember when there was no Internet as we know it today, no commercial transatlantic jet or supersonic travel, no faxing or e-mailing, no teleconferencing or overseas direct-dial telephone service, and no sales over the Internet (e-commerce sales). Moreover, the cost of improved communications and transportation has risen more slowly than costs in general. A three-minute phone call from New York to London cost $10.80 in 1970 but less than $.20 in 2003.

By increasing the demand for new products and services, technology has had and continues to have a tremendous impact on international business. As demand increases, so do the number of international business transactions. On the one hand, conducting business on an international level usually involves greater distances than does conducting domestic business, and greater distances increase operating costs and make control of a company's foreign operations more difficult. On the other hand, improved communications and transportation speed up interactions and improve a manager's ability to control foreign operations. Lucasfilm could control its far-flung production of *Attack of the Clones* because it was able to move actors quickly from country to country and transfer videos overnight from a shooting location in one country to a shooting or dubbing location in another country. When Lucasfilm completed production, transportation permitted it to distribute the movie efficiently worldwide.

Liberalization of Cross-Border Movements Every country restricts the movement across its borders of goods and services and the resources, such as workers and capital, to produce both. Such restrictions make international business more expensive to undertake. Because the regulations may change at any time, international business is also riskier.

Generally, governments today impose fewer restrictions on cross-border movements than they did a decade or two ago. They have lowered them for the following reasons:

1. Their citizens have expressed the desire for easier access to a greater variety of goods and services at lower prices.
2. They reason that their domestic producers will become more efficient as a result of foreign competition.
3. They hope to induce other countries to reduce their barriers to international movements.

Fewer restrictions enable companies to take better advantage of international opportunities. However, with more competition, people have to work harder. Figure 1.3 shows this humorously.

The liberalization of cross-border movements isn't without controversy, however. Recently, large groups have protested globalization at meetings of international organizations and heads of state because they fear they will be better off with more, rather than

Business is becoming more global because

- Transportation is quicker
- Communications enable control from afar
- Transportation and communications costs are more conducive for international operations

Lower government barriers to the movement of goods, services, and resources enable companies to take better advantage of international opportunities.

FIGURE 1.3   A Downside of Competition Caused by Globalization

Although global competition brings more efficiency, it also requires companies and workers to expend more effort.

Supporting services

- Are made by business and government
- Ease the flow of goods
- Reduce risk

fewer, cross-border restrictions. These protests could influence governments to enact more, rather than fewer, restrictions.

Development of Supporting Services   Companies and governments have developed services that ease international business. For example, banks have developed efficient means that allow companies to receive payment for their foreign sales. As soon as a *Star Wars* film arrives in French customs, a bank in Paris can collect the distribution fee, in euros, from the French distributor and then make payment to Lucasfilm, in U.S. dollars, at a bank in the United States. In contrast, if business were still being conducted as in the era of early caravan traders, Lucasfilm probably would have to accept payment in the form of French merchandise, such as perfume or wine, which it would ship back to the United States and sell before receiving U.S. dollars.

Although companies do barter internationally, it can be cumbersome, time-consuming, risky, and expensive.[8] Today, most producers can be paid relatively easily for goods and services sold abroad because of, for example, bank credit agreements, clearing arrangements that convert one country's currency into another's, and insurance that covers damage en route and nonpayment by the buyer.

Consider the transport of mail internationally. Until the sixteenth century, when France and part of what is now Germany established an agreement on carrier pigeon service, there was no postal system as we know it today. Citizens had to make separate arrangements for payment and shipment of each letter for each country through which it would pass. Today, because of postal agreements among countries, you can mail a letter to any place in the world using only stamps from the country where you mail it, regardless of how many countries the letter must pass through and regardless of the nationality of the company carrying it. For example, Lucasfilm can use U.S. postage stamps for a letter or package sent to its French distributors, even though the letter might be carried on an Indian airline that makes a stop en route in the United Kingdom. Or Lucasfilm can send its correspondence via any of the international package service companies, such as UPS or DHL, by simply paying them in U.S. dollars.

Consumer Pressures   Because of innovations in transportation and communications, consumers know about products and services available in other countries. Further, global discretionary income has risen to the point that there is now widespread demand for products and services that would have been considered luxuries in the past. Thus, consumers want more, new, better, and differentiated products. This development has spurred companies to respond by spending on research and development and by searching worldwide—via the Internet, industry journals, trade fairs, and trips to foreign countries—for innovations and differentiated products that they can sell to ever-more-demanding consumers.

Increase in Global Competition   The pressures of increased foreign competition can persuade a company to expand its business into international markets. Today, companies can respond rapidly to many foreign sales opportunities. They can shift production quickly among countries if they're experienced in foreign markets and because they can transport goods efficiently from most places.

Once a few companies respond to foreign market and production opportunities, other companies may see the foreign opportunities as well. For example, after Lucasfilm demonstrated the advantage of producing part of *Star Wars* in Tunisia, other studios followed suit, such as filming *The English Patient* there.[9] Many other firms have to become more global to maintain competitiveness; failure to do so could be catastrophic for them.

More companies operate internationally because

- New products quickly become known globally
- Companies can produce in different countries
- Domestic companies' competitors, suppliers, and customers have become international

MODES OF INTERNATIONAL BUSINESS

When pursuing international business, private enterprises and governments have to decide how to carry out the business, such as what mode of operation to use. Figure 1.4 shows that a company can choose from a number of operating modes.

Merchandise Exports and Imports

Companies may export or import either goods or services. More companies are involved in exporting and importing than in any other international mode. This is especially true of smaller companies, even though they are less likely than large companies to engage in exporting. (Large companies are also more apt to engage in other forms of foreign operations in addition to exporting and importing.) **Merchandise exports** are tangible products—goods—sent out of a country; **merchandise imports** are goods brought into a country. Because these goods can be seen leaving and entering a country, they are sometimes called visible exports and imports. The terms *exports* and *imports* frequently apply to merchandise, not to a service. When a Chinese contractor sends *Attack of the Clones* action figures from China to Hasbro in the United States, the contractor exports and Hasbro imports. The action figures are exports for China and imports for the United States. For most countries, exporting and importing of goods are the major sources of international revenue and expenditures.

Merchandise exports and imports usually are a country's most common international economic transaction.

Service Exports and Imports

Service exports and imports generate nonproduct international earnings. The company or individual receiving payment is making a **service export**. The company or individual paying

Services are nonproduct auxiliary functions.

- Examples of services are travel and transportation.
- They are very important for some countries.
- They include many specialized international business operating modes.

FIGURE 1.4   Means of Carrying Out International Operations

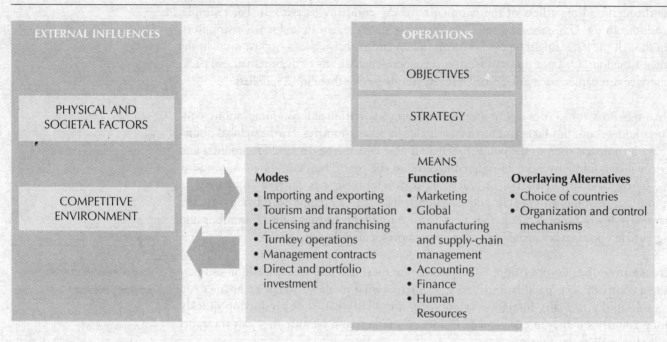

Companies may choose from a number of modes for conducting international business.

---

is making a **service import**. Service exports and imports take many forms. In this section, we discuss the following sources of such earnings:

- Tourism and transportation
- Performance of services
- Use of assets

Tourism and Transportation   When Lucasfilm exports films from the United States, the films travel internationally, as do Lucasfilm employees when they go abroad to promote the films. Let's say that Lucasfilm sends its employees and films to Germany on Lufthansa, a German airline, and that its employees stay in Germany for a few days. Their payments to Lufthansa and their expenses in Germany are service exports for Germany and service imports for the United States. International tourism and transportation are important sources of revenue for airlines, shipping companies, travel agencies, and hotels. Some countries' economies depend heavily on revenue from these economic sectors. For example, in Greece and Norway, a significant amount of employment, profits, and foreign-exchange earnings comes from foreign cargo that is carried on ships owned by citizens of those countries. Earnings from foreign tourism are more important for the Bahamian economy than are earnings from the export of merchandise. Similarly, in recent years, the United States has earned more from foreign tourism than from its exports of agricultural goods.

Performance of Services   Some services—banking, insurance, rentals (such as of *Attack of the Clones*), engineering, management services, and so on—net companies earnings in the form of fees (i.e., payments for the performance of those services). On an international level, for example, companies pay fees for engineering services that are often handled through **turnkey operations**—construction, performed under contract, of facilities that are transferred to the owner when they are ready to begin operating. Companies also pay fees for **management contracts**—arrangements in which one company provides personnel to perform general or specialized management functions for another company. Disney receives management fees from managing theme parks in France and Japan.

Use of Assets   When companies allow others to use their assets, such as trademarks, patents, copyrights, or expertise under contracts, also known as **licensing agreements**, they receive earnings called **royalties**. On an international level, for example, Lucasfilm has licensed The Lego Group from Denmark to use its trademarked *Attack of the Clones* figures in construction toys. Royalties also come from franchise contracts. **Franchising** is a mode of business in which one party (the franchisor) allows another party (the franchisee) to use a trademark that is an essential asset for the franchisee's business. The franchisor also assists on a continuing basis in the operation of the business—for example, by providing components, management services, and technology.

Dividends and interest paid on foreign investments are also treated as service exports and imports because they represent the use of assets (capital). However, countries treat the investments themselves separately in the international economic statistics they report.

Investments

Foreign investment means ownership of foreign property in exchange for a financial return, such as interest and dividends. Foreign investment takes two forms: direct and portfolio.

Direct Investment   A **direct investment** is one that gives the investor a controlling interest in a foreign company. Such a direct investment is also a **foreign direct investment** (**FDI**), a term common to this text. Control need not be a 100-percent or even a 50-percent interest. If a company holds a minority stake and the remaining ownership is widely dispersed, no other owner may be able to counter the company effectively. When two or more companies share ownership of an FDI, the operation is a **joint venture**. When a government joins a company in an FDI, the operation is called a **mixed venture**, which is a type of joint venture.

Companies may choose FDI as a way to access certain resources or reach a market. Today, about 63,000 companies worldwide have FDIs that encompass every type of business function—extracting raw materials from the earth, growing crops, manufacturing products or components, selling output, providing various services, and so on.[10] FDI is not the domain of large companies only. For example, many small firms maintain sales offices abroad to complement their export efforts, which are FDI along with the real estate they own abroad. However, because large companies tend to have larger foreign facilities and operate in more countries, the value of their FDI is higher.

Portfolio Investment   A **portfolio investment** is a noncontrolling interest in a company or ownership of a loan to another party. A portfolio investment usually takes one of two forms: stock in a company or loans to a company or country in the form of bonds, bills, or notes that the investor purchases.

Foreign portfolio investments are important for most companies that have extensive international operations. Companies use them primarily for short-term financial gain—that is, as a means that allows a company to earn more money on its money with relative safety. Company treasurers routinely move funds among countries to earn higher yields on short-term investments.

International Companies and Terms to Describe Them

Many of the terms in international business are confusing because writers, both in the popular media and in government and academic reports, use them to define different things.

Companies benefit from direct investment by

- Control
- Access to foreign markets
- Access to foreign resources
- Partial ownership (sometimes)

Key components of portfolio investment are

- Noncontrol of a foreign operation
- Financial benefit (for example, loans)

Although an international company is any company operating internationally, there are many terms that differentiate their types of operations.

There are numerous ways that companies may work together in international operations, such as through joint ventures, licensing agreements, management contracts, minority ownership in each other's company, or long-term contractual arrangements. An all-encompassing term to describe these operations is **collaborative arrangements**. Another term, **strategic alliance**, can sometimes mean the same thing, but more narrowly—to indicate an agreement that is of critical importance to the competitive viability of one or more partners. We shall use strategic alliance only in its narrower meaning.

The **multinational enterprise (MNE)** is a company that takes a global approach to foreign markets and production. It is willing to consider market and production locations anywhere in the world. The true MNE usually uses most of the modes discussed thus far. However, it can be difficult to determine whether a company takes this global approach, so narrower definitions of the term *multinational enterprise* have emerged. For example, some say a company, to qualify as an MNE, must have production facilities in some minimum number of countries or be of a certain size. Under this definition, an MNE usually would have to be a giant company. However, a small company also can take a global approach within its resource capabilities and might use most of the operating forms we have discussed; therefore, most writers today use the term to include any company that has operations in more than one country—the way that we use the term in this text.

The term **multinational corporation (MNC)** is also commonly used in the international business arena and often is a synonym for MNE. We prefer the MNE designation because there are many internationally involved companies, such as accounting partnerships, that are not organized as corporations. Another term sometimes used interchangeably with MNE, especially by the United Nations, is **transnational company (TNC)**. However, this term also has two other meanings. The first (and earliest) is "a company owned and managed by nationals in different countries." For example, Royal Dutch Shell is a company whose owners and corporate management are split between the United Kingdom and the Netherlands. However, this type of company is uncommon, so we don't often use the term in this way. Today, the most common use of the term has come from writers on international business strategy. They use the term to mean "an organization in which capabilities and contributions may differ by country but are developed and integrated into its worldwide operations." This type of organization learns from all of its operating environments and uses that knowledge throughout its global operations.[11]

Companies with international operations can be global or multidomestic. A **global company**, sometimes called a **globally integrated company**, integrates its operations that are located in different countries. For example, it might design a product or service with a global market segment in mind. Or it might depend on its operations in different countries to produce the components used in its products and services. In this type of company, the development of capabilities and the decisions to diffuse them globally are essentially made in the company's home country. A **multidomestic company**, sometimes called a **locally responsive company** and sometimes a multinational company, allows each of its foreign-country operations to act fairly independently—for example, by designing and producing a product or service in Australia for the Australian market and in Japan for the Japanese market. Thus, a global company and a multidomestic company differ in the degree of integration among company operations in different countries. However, a company's operations may have elements of both. For example, its production may be global, while its marketing is multidomestic. The TNC is like the global company insofar as it leverages the capabilities of both the home country and the foreign countries where it operates, but its main location of power within the organization may be geographically dispersed.

A company that has a worldwide approach to markets and production is known as an MNE or TNC. It usually undertakes nearly every type of international business practice.

EXTERNAL INFLUENCES ON INTERNATIONAL BUSINESS

A company should not form its strategies—or the means to implement them—without examining its external environment. Figure 1.5 shows that the external environment includes physical factors, such as a country's geography, and societal factors, such as a country's politics, law, culture, and economy. It also includes competitive factors, such as the number and strength of suppliers, customers, and rival firms. A company faces different external environments in each country where it operates.

Managers in international business must understand social science disciplines and how they affect all functional business fields.

Understanding a Company's Physical and Societal Environments

To operate within a company's external environment, its managers should have, in addition to knowledge of business operations, a working knowledge of the basic social sciences: political science, law, anthropology, sociology, psychology, economics, and geography.

Politics helps shape business worldwide because the political leaders control whether and how international business takes place. For example, Lucasfilm cannot distribute *Attack of the Clones* in Cuba because political conflict between Cuba and the United States has led to trade restrictions. Political disputes, particularly those that result in military conflicts, can disrupt trade and investment. Even small conflicts can have far-reaching effects.

Domestic and international law determines largely what the managers of a company operating internationally can do. Domestic law includes regulations in both the home and host countries on such matters as taxation, employment, and foreign-exchange transactions. For example, Japanese law determines how Lucasfilm revenues from Japanese screenings are taxed and how they can be exchanged from yen to U.S. dollars. U.S. law, in turn, determines how and when the losses or earnings from Japan are treated for tax purposes in the United States. International law in the form of legal agreements between two countries governs how the earnings are taxed by both. International law may also determine how and whether companies can operate in certain locales. For example, companies from most countries suspended sales to Iraq because of U.N. trade sanctions over Iraq's failure to allow access to weapons inspectors.[12] How laws are enforced also affects operations. For example, U.S. movie companies estimate

Each country has its own laws regulating business. Agreements among countries set international law.

FIGURE 1.5   Physical and Societal Influences on International Business

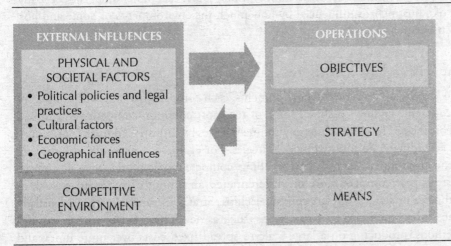

Companies affect and are affected by their external environments.

that they lose $3 billion a year to pirated copies of their films. This fact influenced Lucasfilm's decision to debut *Attack of the Clones* in so many countries simultaneously.[13] Companies should understand the treaties among countries and the laws of each country in which they want to operate, as well as how laws are enforced, to operate profitably abroad.

The related sciences of *anthropology, sociology*, and *psychology* describe, in part, people's social and mental development, behavior, and interpersonal activities. By studying these sciences, managers can better understand societal values, attitudes, and beliefs concerning themselves and others. This understanding can help them function better in different countries. For example, recall that Lucasfilm cut scenes of *Attack of the Clones* for British distribution because of British concerns about the effects of violence in movies on impressionable youthful audiences.

Economics explains, among other concepts, why countries exchange goods and services with each other, why capital and people travel among countries in the course of business, and why one country's currency has a certain value compared to another's. By studying economics, managers can better understand why, where, and when one country can produce goods or services less expensively than another can. In addition, managers can obtain the analytical tools needed to determine the impact of an international company on the economies of the host and home countries and the effect of a country's economic policies and conditions on the company.

Managers who know *geography* can better determine the location, quantity, quality, and availability of the world's resources, as well as the best way to exploit them. The uneven distribution of resources results in different products and services being produced or offered in different parts of the world. Geographical barriers such as high mountains, vast deserts, and inhospitable jungles affect communications and distribution channels for companies in many countries. The probability of natural disasters and adverse climatic conditions such as hurricanes, floods, or freezing weather make it riskier to invest in some areas than in others. These factors also affect the availability of supplies and the prices of products. For example, New Zealand's droughts in 2001 and 2002 caused farmers there to reduce their stocks of sheep, which led to global shortages and rising prices of lamb and wool.[14] In addition, population distribution around the world and the impact of human activity on the environment exert a strong influence on international business. For example, concern about destruction of the world's rain forests may lead to regulations or to other pressures on companies, forcing them to change the place or method of their business activities.

The political, legal, social, economic, and geographic environments affect how a company operates and the amount of adjustment it must make to its operations in a particular country, such as how it produces and markets its products, staffs its operations, and maintains its accounts. In fact, the external environment may affect each function of the company. The amount of adjustment is influenced by how much the environments of home and host countries resemble each other.

The Competitive Environment

A company's situation may differ among countries by

- Its competitive ranking
- The competitors it faces

In addition to its physical and societal environments, each company operates within its competitive environment. Figure 1.6 shows some of the most common competitive factors in international business. The competitive environment varies by industry, company, and country—and so, accordingly, do international strategies. For example, companies in industries with homogeneous products, such as copper tubing, compete more on price than do companies in industries that compete more on differentiated and innovative products, such as branded toothpaste or state-of-the-art computer chips. Strategies for the former are usually more influenced than the latter by cost savings, such as developing better equipment and operating methods, producing on a large scale to spread fixed costs over more units, and locating to secure cheap labor and materials.

FIGURE 1.6   The Competitive Environment and International Business

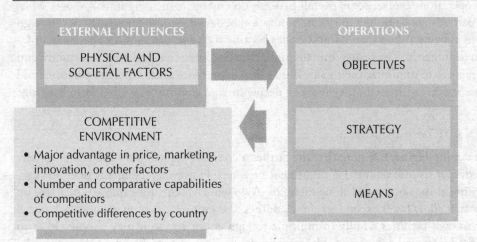

Companies face different competitive environments depending on the products, strategies, and countries where they operate.

Companies within the same industry also differ in their competitive strategies. Honda's greater concern about reducing automobile costs than BMW helps explain why the former has recently moved much of its automobile production to China to take advantage of lower labor costs while the latter has not. Still another competitive factor is the size of the company and the resources it has compared to its competitors. For example, a market leader, such as Coca-Cola, has resources for many more international options than does a smaller competitor, such as Royal Crown. But being a leader in one market does not guarantee leadership in all. For example, in most markets, Coca-Cola is the leader, with Pepsi-Cola in a strong second position; however, Coca-Cola is number three in the Indian market, after Pepsi-Cola and Thums Up, a locally owned soft drink.[15]

The competitive environment also varies in other ways among countries. For example, the domestic market in the United States is much larger than the one in Sweden. Swedish producers have had to become more highly dependent than U.S. producers are on foreign sales to spread fixed costs of product development and production. The Swedish company Electrolux, for instance, had to promote exports very early in its history and depends much more on foreign sales of household appliances than do its main U.S. competitors, GE and Whirlpool. Another result of the larger U.S. market is that foreign companies have to invest much more money to gain national distribution in the United States than they do in Sweden, because there are more places to sell their products.

Still another competitive factor is whether companies face international or local competitors at home and in foreign markets. On the one hand, Boeing and Airbus compete with each other everywhere they try to sell commercial aircraft. Therefore, what they learn about each other in one country is useful in predicting the other's strategies and actions in other countries. On the other hand, Tesco, a British grocery chain, faces different retailers as competitors in each of the foreign countries where it operates.

EVOLUTION OF STRATEGY IN THE INTERNATIONALIZATION PROCESS

When we think of multinational enterprises, we often think of giant companies like IBM or Nestlé, which have sales and production facilities in scores of countries. But companies do not start out as giants, and few think globally at their inception. As we discuss strategies, we shall note that companies are at different levels of internationalization and that their status

Strategies for heavy international commitments usually evolve gradually from

- Passive to active pursuit of opportunities
- External to internal handling of the business
- Limited to extensive modes of operations
- Few to many foreign locations
- Similar to dissimilar environments

affects the strategic alternatives available to them. Although there are variations in how international operations evolve, some overall patterns do emerge, which Figure 1.7 shows. Most of these patterns are a product of risk minimization behavior—most companies view foreign operations as being riskier than domestic ones because such companies must operate in unfamiliar environments. Thus, they initially undertake international activities reluctantly and follow practices to minimize their risks. But as they learn more about foreign operations and experience success with them, they move to deeper foreign commitments that seem less risky.

Patterns of Expansion

As you examine Figure 1.7, note that the farther a company moves from the center on any axis, the deeper its international commitment becomes. However, a company does not necessarily move at the same speed along each axis. A slow movement along one axis may free up resources that allow faster expansion along another. For example, a company may lack initial capacity to own facilities wholly in multiple foreign countries, so it may choose either to limit its foreign capital commitment by moving slowly along Axis C in order to move rapidly along Axis D (to multiple foreign countries), or vice versa.

Passive to Active Expansion   The impetus of strategic focus is shown on Axis A in Figure 1.7. Most new companies are established in response to domestic needs, and they frequently think only of domestic opportunities until a foreign opportunity presents itself to them. For example, companies commonly receive unsolicited export requests because someone has seen or heard of their products. Often these companies have no idea of how their products became known abroad, but at this juncture, they must make a decision to export or not. Many decide not to do so because they fear they will not be paid or they know too little about the mechanics of foreign trade. Those that do so may then see opportunities available to them abroad, thus making it more likely that they will seek out other markets to sell their goods. Even large companies may move from passive to active expansion with aspects of their business.

External to Internal Handling of Operations   A company commonly uses intermediaries to handle foreign operations during the early stages of international expansion because such a strategy minimizes risk. A company can then commit fewer resources to international endeavors, instead relying on intermediaries that already know how to operate in the foreign market. But if the business grows successfully, the company will usually want to handle the operations with its own staff. This is because it has learned more about foreign operations, considers them less risky than at the onset, and realizes that the volume of business may justify the development of internal capabilities such as hiring trained personnel to maintain a department for foreign sales or purchases. This evolution is shown on Axis B in Figure 1.7.

Deepening Mode of Commitment   Axis C shows that importing or exporting is usually the first mode a company undertakes to become an international firm. At an early stage of international involvement, importing and exporting require the least formal commitment and pose the least risk to the company's resources, such as capital, personnel, equipment, and production facilities. A company could, say, use excess production capacity to produce more goods, which it would then export. By doing this, it would limit its need to invest more capital in such additional production facilities as plants and machinery and in such functions as managing a foreign workforce.

A company often moves into some type of foreign production after successfully building an export market. Initially, this foreign production is apt to minimize the use of a company's resources by licensing another company to handle production abroad, by sharing ownership in the foreign facility, or by limiting the amount of manufacture, such as assembling output abroad. Nevertheless, this foreign production usually requires a greater international com-

FIGURE 1.7   The Usual Pattern of Internationalization

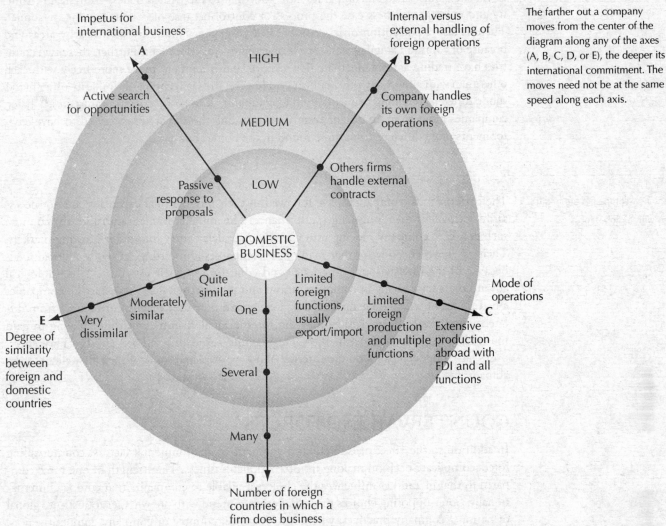

The farther out a company moves from the center of the diagram along any of the axes (A, B, C, D, or E), the deeper its international commitment. The moves need not be at the same speed along each axis.

mitment of the company's resources than exporting or importing because the company has to send qualified technicians to the foreign country to establish and help run the new operation. Further, the company must be responsible for multifunctional activities abroad, such as sales and production. Later, the company might make an even higher commitment through foreign direct investments to produce abroad. Its infusion of capital, personnel, and technology are highest for these operations.

A company typically does not abandon its early modes of operating abroad, such as importing and exporting, when it adopts other means of operating internationally. Rather, it usually either continues them by expanding its trade to new markets or complements them with new types of business activities.

Geographic Diversification   When companies first move into the international realm, they are most apt to do business in only one or very few foreign locations. Axis D in Figure 1.7 shows that over time, the number of countries in which they operate increases. The initial narrow geographic expansion parallels the low early commitment of resources abroad. The choice of countries in this geographic expansion also tends to follow certain patterns, as Axis E indicates. Initially, companies tend to go to those locations that are similar and geographically close. For example, when beginning foreign operations, most U.S. companies have gone first to Canada, and Canadian companies have gone first to the United States.[16] Physical proximity and cultural closeness ease the process of control because of ease in moving personnel. There is also a perception of less risk because of greater familiarity with nearby areas and because of common languages and levels of economic development. Further, these two countries have trading agreements that allow exports and imports to move more freely with each other than with almost any other countries. However, this perception of similarity often masks subtle differences among countries, lulling companies into costly operating mistakes.[17] Later, companies move to more distant countries, including those that are perceived to have environments more different from those found in the home country.

Leapfrogging of Expansion

Many new companies are beginning with a global focus.

The patterns most companies have followed in their international expansion are not necessarily optimal for their long-range performance. The initial movement into a nearby country, such as a U.S. company moving into Canada, may delay entry into faster-growing markets. There is, however, evidence that many new companies are starting out with a global focus because of the international experience and education of their founders.[18] Technological advancements, especially in communications and the Internet, give these start-up companies a better idea of where their markets are globally and how they may gain resources from different countries.[19] Further, they may tap international customers without having to gain much knowledge about those markets. For example, some inns and bed-and-breakfast enterprises have put Web pages on the Internet and have attracted some of their first clients from abroad.[20]

COUNTERVAILING FORCES

In addition to the effect of external and competitive environmental factors, countervailing forces complicate decision making in international business. The strength of one force compared to that of another influences the choices available to companies that compete internationally. Some opposing choices that companies contend with are whether to institute global or national company practices, whether to focus on country or company competitiveness, and whether to develop sovereign or cross-national relationships.

Globally Standardized Versus Nationally Responsive Practices

Globally standardized practices tend to lower costs.

Nationally responsive practices enable companies to adjust to unique local conditions.

Any company operating internationally must decide between the advantages of globally standardized practices and those practices that respond to different national preferences. These advantages may vary by product, function, and country of operation.

The trends that have influenced the recent worldwide growth in international business—rapid expansion of technology, liberalization of government trade policies, development of the institutions and services needed to support and facilitate international trade, and increased global competition—also usually favor a global strategy, specifically one that has a great deal of standardized practices from one country to another. One advantage is that the company can reduce costs. For example, by designing a product or service to suit multiple countries, a company can avoid duplicating developmental expenses. It also may reduce manufacturing costs by serving multiple markets from a single production unit. In either case, the company gains from economies of scale—that is, the cost per unit is lowered as output increases because fixed costs are allocated over more units of production.

However, when a company goes abroad, it faces conditions very different from those it encounters at home. The company may need to engage in national responsiveness, meaning it makes operating adjustments where it does business to reach a satisfactory level of performance. In such cases, a multidomestic approach often works better than a global one because the company managers abroad are best able to assess and deal with the environments of the foreign countries in which the company operates. As a result, they are given a great deal of independence in running facilities in those countries.

Country Versus Company Competitiveness

Thus far, we have addressed competition from the viewpoint of companies. Companies, at least those that are not government owned, may compete by seeking maximum production efficiency on a global scale. To accomplish this goal, a company's production would use the best inputs for the price, even if the production location moved abroad. The company would then sell the output wherever it would fetch the best price. Such practices should lead to maximum performance for the company.

But countries also compete with each other. They do so in terms of fulfilling economic, political, and social objectives. Countries are concerned not only with the absolute achievement of these objectives but also with how well they do compared to other countries. Keep in mind that competition among countries is the means to an end—the end being the well-being of a country's citizens. However, there is no consensus on how to measure well-being, and accepted indicators of current prosperity actually may foretell longer-term problems. For example, high current consumption may occur at the expense of investment for future production and consumption.

At one time, the performance of a country and that of companies headquartered in that country were considered mutually dependent and beneficial—that is, they rose and fell together. For example, consider the once-popular U.S. expression "What's good for General Motors is good for the country." The idea was that if General Motors (GM) performed well, the United States would benefit also—from more automobile sales, tax collections, and jobs, both production and managerial. This benefit was considered possible because almost all of the company's production and sales at the time were in the United States. But today, the relationship between country performance and company performance is not as clear-cut. GM could elect to improve its global or even its domestic performance by producing more cars in its foreign manufacturing units and fewer in the United States. What would this mean for the U.S. competitive performance?

In answering this question, some people would argue that the important indicator is the location of **high-value activities**; that is, activities that either produce high profits or are done by high-salaried employees such as managers. Therefore, GM's move to produce more cars abroad could improve the U.S. competitive position by increasing high-value activity at headquarters (e.g., in the form of more jobs for managers and executives), while reducing low-value activity in production (e.g., in the form of fewer jobs for U.S. assembly-line workers). In fact, there is evidence that the demand and income for higher-paid employees in the United States has increased as a result of U.S. companies' outsourcing to low-labor-cost countries.[21] However, other people argue that the U.S. well-being has deteriorated because the loss of assembly-line jobs has resulted in more income inequality.[22]

Closely related to this debate is another regarding whether a government should be concerned if its production facilities are owned by foreigners. For example, should it matter whether U.S. auto production is owned by Honda in Japan instead of GM in the United States? Some would argue that it would make no difference because the United States gains the jobs and production either way; others would argue that the high-value activity jobs would more likely be in Japan if Honda were the owner.[23] In actuality, there is little hard evidence to support any conclusion regarding the relationship between company and country performance.

Regardless of these ongoing debates, countries continue to entice companies to locate headquarters and production facilities within their borders. They do this through regulations

Countries moderate companies' fulfillment of global efficiency objectives because of those countries' rivalry with other countries.

Sorting Through the World of Right and Wrong in International Business

During the early part of the twenty-first century, several U.S. companies faced severe financial prob-lems and even dissolution because of their managers' unethical or illegal actions. Some of these com-panies hid their illicit actions for a number of years through their international operations. The exposés caused public outrage, investor anxiety, and a heightened interest in companies' ethical and socially responsible behavior.

There are many actions that elicit almost universal agreement on what is right or wrong.[24] However, managers face many situations that are less clear. We all have beliefs about what is right and wrong based on family and religious teachings, the laws and social pressures of our societies, our observations and experiences, and our own economic circumstances. Our ethical beliefs tend to be deep-seated, so our debates with people who hold opposing viewpoints tend to be emotional. Even within a country, vastly opposing viewpoints frequently exist. This is demonstrated in the United States by the controversies on abortion, gay rights, capital punishment, gun control, euthanasia, organ trans-plants, marijuana use, and welfare payments. To further complicate matters, our own values on given issues may differ from our employers' policies, and any of these values may differ from the prevalent societal norms or laws. As managers, we face domestic dilemmas on what we should do to be ethical and socially responsible. Internationally, the dilemmas are even greater.

An MNE can operate in foreign markets in which it has either narrower or greater latitude in mak-ing decisions than in its home country. Normal practices in a given foreign country will depend on that country's ethics and opinions about social responsibility, which may conflict with the company's domestic practices or with the beliefs of its domestic constituencies. For example, U.S. companies must contend with child labor laws at home that they probably wouldn't encounter in, say, Bangladesh.

In the international arena, companies, whether they know it or not, have two basic views about cul-tural practices that contradict those in their home countries. On the one hand, *relativism* affirms that ethical truths depend on the groups holding them, making intervention unethical. Adherence to other cultures is itself a Western cultural phenomenon, one that goes back at least as far as St. Ambrose's fourth-century advice: "When in Rome, do as the Romans do." On the other hand, *normativism* holds that there are universal standards of behavior (based on people's own values) that all cultures should follow, making nonintervention unethical.

A company can face pressures to comply with a country's norms. These pressures may include laws that permit or even require certain practices, competitive advantages for rivals who adapt to local norms, or accusations of meddling if a company tries to impose its home-country practices in the for-eign country. However, companies can face pressures not to comply. These pressures can come from a company's own ethical values, its home-country government, or constituencies that threaten to boycott its products or to spread adverse publicity about it or its products.

Many individuals and organizations have laid out minimum levels of business practices that they say a company (domestic or foreign) must follow regardless of the legal requirements or ethical norms prevalent where it operates.[25] They argue that legal permission for some action may be given by un-educated or corrupt leaders who either do not understand or do not care about the consequences, such as permission to import toxic wastes. They argue further that MNEs are obligated to set good examples that may become the standard for socially responsible behavior.

From a business standpoint, two possible objectives are to create competitive advantages through socially responsible behavior and to avoid being perceived as irresponsible. In terms of the former, it is argued that responsible acts create strategic and financial success because they lead to trust, which leads to commitment.[26] Further, philanthropic practices may gain loyal customers. In terms of the latter, nongovernmental organizations (NGOs) have become very active in monitoring and publicizing companies' international practices. For example, the Interfaith Center on Corporate Responsibility (ICCR) represents about 275 religious institutions. It has sponsored shareholder resolutions and has threatened to pull its $110 billion in pension funds from investments in companies whose practices it considers irresponsible. It has prodded many companies to change their practices, such as ExxonMobil to deal with global warming and Disney to outline new labor standards for its foreign suppliers.[27]

Another complicating factor is that both societies and companies often must choose between the lesser of two evils. For example, the pesticide DDT is dangerous for the environment (especially to birds), and high-income countries have banned its use. Companies from those countries subsequently have been chided for selling DDT to lower-income countries that need it to fight malaria, which is one of the world's biggest killers of humans.[28]

Social responsibility requires human judgment, which makes it subjective and ambiguous. Many multilateral agreements exist that can help companies make ethical decisions. These agreements deal primarily with employment practices, consumer protection, environmental protection, political activity, and human rights in the workplace. Despite this growing body of agreements and codes, no set of workable corporate guidelines is universally accepted and observed. For one thing, there are so many codes that companies have difficulty deciphering them. For example, there are more than 50 international codes of conduct dealing just with the use of child labor.[29]

Clearly, many aspects of international business raise ethical questions. We'll discuss these ethical dilemmas and social responsibility issues in each chapter.

and enticements. In spite of growing cooperation among governments, their behavior very much reflects what they see as their own national interests.[30] In the GM example, the U.S. government might enact regulations to prevent GM from expanding abroad—for example, by limiting the capital it could send out of the country. Or the government could restrict imports of foreign-produced automobiles so that GM could sell more only by producing in the United States. It might try to persuade GM by holding out the possibility of future defense contracts (for companies acting in the "national interest") or by appealing to nationalism. To improve the country's investment-worthiness, the U.S. government might improve the availability and quality of education, build roads and port facilities, or lower taxes. Any of these incentives could apply only to U.S.-based companies or to any company, regardless of nationality.

Business managers need to understand these complexities so that they can debate logically and effectively regarding legislation that may affect their operations. At the same time, they must balance dual roles: In one, they are managers with global efficiency objectives; in the second, they are members of a given society that has national rather than global objectives.

Sovereign Versus Cross-National Relationships

Countries compete. They also cooperate. Countries sometimes cede sovereignty (freedom from external control) reluctantly because of coercion and international conflicts. However,

Countries reluctantly cede some sovereignty because of

• Coercion
• International conflicts

they willingly cede sovereignty through treaties and agreements with other countries for the following reasons:

1. To gain reciprocal advantages
2. To attack problems jointly that one country acting alone cannot solve
3. To deal with areas of concern that lie outside the territory of all countries

Countries want to ensure that companies headquartered within their borders are not disadvantaged by foreign-country policies. Thus, such countries enter into treaties and agreements with other countries on a variety of commercial activities, such as transportation and trade. Treaties and agreements may be bilateral (involving only two countries) or multilateral (involving a few or many). Countries commonly enter into treaties in which each allows the other's commercial ships and planes to use certain seaports and airports in exchange for reciprocal port use. They may enact treaties that cover commercial aircraft safety standards and flyover rights or treaties that protect property, such as direct investments, patents, trademarks, and copyrights in each other's territory. They also may enact treaties for reciprocal reductions of import restrictions (and then retaliate when others interfere with trade flows by, for example, raising barriers of their own or cutting diplomatic ties).

Countries also enact treaties or agreements to coordinate activities along their shared borders, such as building connecting highways and railroads or hydroelectric dams that serve all parties. They also enact treaties to solve problems they either cannot or will not solve alone because of one or both of two reasons:

1. The problem is too big or will benefit from joint inputs.
2. The problem results from conditions that spill over from another country.

In the first case, the resources needed to solve the problem may be too large, or one country does not want to pay all the costs for a project that also will benefit another country. For example, countries may enact a treaty whereby they share the costs of joint technology development, such as the cooperation between Japan and the United States on ballistic missile defense technology.[31] In the second case, one country's economic and environmental policies may affect another country or countries. For example, high real-interest rates in one country can attract funds from countries in which interest rates are lower, which can disrupt economic conditions in the latter countries because there will be a shortage of funds available for investment. This is why eight economically important countries (known as the G8 countries)—Canada, France, Germany, Italy, Japan, Russia, the United Kingdom, and the United States—meet regularly to coordinate economic policies.[32] In fact, because information can flow rapidly, particularly over the Internet, an event in one country can have almost instantaneous effects in another. Further, competitive locations may more easily shift.[33] In addition, most environmental experts agree that there must be cooperation among most countries to institute environmental policies. So far, most countries have made agreements with some other countries on such issues as restricting harmful emissions, keeping waterways unpolluted, preserving endangered species, and banning the use of certain pesticides. Despite these agreements, however, discussions among countries continue on these and other issues.

Three areas remain outside the territories of countries—the noncoastal areas of the oceans, outer space, and Antarctica. Until their commercial viability was demonstrated, these areas excited little interest in multinational cooperation. The oceans contain food and mineral resources. They also are the surface over which much international commerce passes. Today, treaties on the use of oceans specify the amounts and methods of fishing allowed, international discussion attempts to resolve who owns oceanic minerals, and agreements detail how to deal with pirates (yes, even today, pirates are a problem).[34] Much disagreement exists on who should reap commercial benefits from space. For example, com-

LOOKING TO THE FUTURE

Seizing that Window of International Business Opportunity

At this juncture, there is much doubt about the future growth of international business. Although most governments are embracing openness to international trade and investment, antiglobalization sentiments are strong and vocal. Growing numbers are demonstrating at meetings of international organizations, such as the World Bank and the World Trade Organization (WTO).[35] They argue that globalization makes people vulnerable to adverse conditions far from their homes and that the benefits of globalization have gone to few people rather than to the masses.[36] Another argument is that international organizations and institutions cannot adequately deal with the dislocations that occur as economies open internationally. Thus, they aggravate crises rather than resolve them.[37]

Only time will tell, but a company wanting to capitalize on international opportunities can't wait too long to see what happens on political and economic fronts. Investments in research, equipment, plants, and personnel training can take many years to complete.

Forecasting foreign opportunities and risks correctly is persistently challenging. However, by envisioning different ways in which the future may evolve, a company's management may better avoid unpleasant surprises. Each chapter of this text contains a section that discusses foreseeable ways in which topics covered in the chapter may develop in the future.

mercial satellites pass over countries that receive no direct benefit from them but that believe they should. Antarctica, with minerals and abundant sea life along its coast, attracts thousands of tourists each year. Consequently, a series of recent agreements limit its commercial exploitation.

In general, countries whose companies are technologically able to exploit ocean, space, and Antarctic resources believe that their companies should reap all the benefits from exploitation. However, other countries (generally the poorer ones) feel that commercial benefits from such exploitation should be shared among all countries. Until this debate is settled, companies will face uncertainty as to whether and how they can commercialize these new frontiers.

Summary

- Companies engage in international business to expand sales, acquire resources, and to diversify or to reduce their risks.

- International business has been growing rapidly in recent decades because of technological expansion, the liberalization of government policies on cross-border movements (goods, services, and the resources to produce them), the development of institutions needed to support and facilitate international transactions, consumer pressures to buy foreign products and services, and increased global competition. Because of these factors, foreign countries increasingly are a source of both production and sales for domestic companies.

- When operating abroad, companies may have to adjust their usual methods of carrying on business. This is because foreign conditions often dictate a more suitable method and because

the operating modes used for international business differ somewhat from those used on a domestic level.

- A company can engage in international business through various operating modes, including exporting and importing merchandise and services, direct and portfolio investments, and collaborative arrangements with other companies.

- Multinational enterprises (MNEs) take a global approach to markets and production. They sometimes are referred to as multinational corporations (MNCs) or transnational corporations (TNCs).

- International companies might allow their different countries' operations to be fairly autonomous from each other (a multidomestic strategy), might integrate different country operations through their headquarters' control (a global strategy), or might integrate different countries' operations while dispersing the location of control (a transnational strategy).

- To operate within a company's external environment, its managers must have not only knowledge of business operations but also a working knowledge of the basic social sciences: political science, law, anthropology, sociology, psychology, economics, and geography.

- A company's competitive strategy influences how and where it can best operate. Likewise, from one country to another, a company's competitive situation may differ in terms of its relative strength and in terms of which competitors it faces.

- Few companies include a high commitment to international operations as part of their start-up strategy. Typically, the

inclusion of this commitment within their growth and operating strategies evolves over time.

- More start-up companies are becoming international very early in their lives because of managerial knowledge about foreign locations and because of advancements in communications.

- Countervailing forces influence the conditions in which companies operate and their options for operating internationally. A company's quest for maximum global profits is inhibited by rivalry among countries, cross-national treaties and agreements, and ethical dilemmas.

- Although governments act in their own self-interests, they, nevertheless, cooperate with other governments and even cede some sovereignty to gain reciprocal advantages, tackle big problems, and deal with problems outside anyone's territory.

CASE

Disney Theme Parks[38]

The Walt Disney Company is the world's largest amusement park operator. It runs all its parks as theme parks, which are amusement parks that focus on a particular motif, such as cartoon characters or animals, in addition to the traditional offerings of rides, food, and games. Map 1.1 shows that Disney operates seven of the world's ten most attended amusement parks.

In 2002, Disney had four theme parks in operation outside the United States. These were Tokyo Disneyland, Tokyo DisneySea, Disneyland Paris, and Walt Disney Studios (a movie theme park adjacent to Disneyland Paris). Disney also had one park under construction (Hong Kong Disneyland, scheduled to open in 2005) and had signed a letter of intent to build another in Shanghai, China, to be ready in time for the Olympics there in 2008. When all of them are operating, Disney's theme park attendance outside the United States will exceed that inside the country.

Tokyo Disneyland opened in 1983 and is now the world's most visited amusement park. The Oriental Land Company of Japan proposed the park to Disney, which accepted the concept but did not

MAP 1.1   The Ten Most Visited Amusement Parks

Seven of the ten most visited amusement parks in the world (those shown with mouse ears) are Disney or Disney-related parks. All ten parks are easily reached from highly populated areas. The five parks in the United States are more suitable, climatewise, for yearlong outside activities than the other locations are.

Source: Figures are 2001 estimates of attendance by the International Association of Amusement Parks and Attractions, accessed July 16, 2002: http://www.iaapa.org/media/mk-attendance.htm.

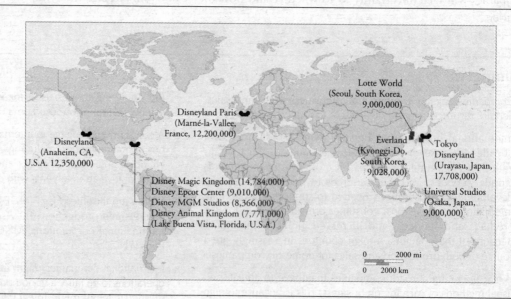

Lotte World (Seoul, South Korea, 9,000,000)

Disneyland Paris (Marné-la-Vallee, France, 12,200,000)

Disneyland (Anaheim, CA, U.S.A. 12,350,000)

Everland (Kyonggi-Do, South Korea, 9,028,000)

Tokyo Disneyland (Urayasu, Japan, 17,708,000)

Disney Magic Kingdom (14,784,000)
Disney Epcot Center (9,010,000)
Disney MGM Studios (8,366,000)
Disney Animal Kingdom (7,771,000)
(Lake Buena Vista, Florida, U.S.A.)

Universal Studios (Osaka, Japan, 9,000,000)

0   2000 mi
0   2000 km

want to provide any financing. Therefore, the Oriental Land Company owns the park. Disney provided the master planning, design, manufacturing, and training services during construction as well as consulting services after completion of the facility. Disney received fees for its efforts during the construction phase, and it now receives royalties from admissions and from merchandise and food sales. The Oriental Land Company also owns Tokyo DisneySea, which opened in 2001, and Disney receives licensing royalties from the operation.

The Tokyo park is in some ways a paradox. Although such firms as Lenox China and Mister Donut had to adapt to Japanese sizes and tastes, Tokyo Disneyland is nearly a replica of Disneyland and the Magic Kingdom in the United States. Signs are in English, and most food is U.S.-style. The management of the Oriental Land Company demanded this because it wanted visitors to feel that they were getting the "real thing" and because the company had noted the enormous success that such franchises as McDonald's had in Japan as Japanese youths embraced U.S.-style culture. Yet Disney made a few adaptations, such as the addition of a Japanese restaurant and a big-screen attraction showing Japanese history.

Because of Tokyo Disneyland's success and research showing that droves of Europeans were visiting Disney's U.S. parks, Disney announced in 1985 that it would open a theme park in either France or Spain. A location near Paris had advantages because its central location enabled a large population to drive there easily. Paris is the most visited European city, and the French are the largest European consumers of Disney products, such as comic books. Nevertheless, because the park would employ thousands of people and attract large numbers of tourists, Disney acted like Scrooge McDuck as it played France against Spain to get incentives. Eventually, the French government offered to extend the Paris railway to the park (linking the park to the rest of Europe) at a cost of almost $350 million, to make available cheap land on which to build the park, and to lend Disney 22 percent of the funds needed to build it.

Disney invested only $140 million to take a 49-percent ownership in a $5 billion operation, which also includes hotels, shopping centers, campgrounds, and other facilities. An international syndicate of banks and security dealers sold the remaining 51 percent to other investors, mainly in France and the United Kingdom. In addition, Disney contracted to receive a management fee and a royalty payment on admissions and food sales.

Even before Disney signed an agreement with the French government, it began to have problems in France because people believed the park would contribute to the destruction of French culture. Disney's chairman was pelted by eggs in Paris, and a French magazine showed a giant Mickey Mouse stepping on the rooftops of Parisian buildings. Disney sought to preempt criticism by agreeing to make French the first language in the park even though all employees had to speak another European language as well. (See Figure 1.8.) It also added some attractions to cater to French tastes, such as an exhibit based on the science-fiction stories of Jules Verne. Nevertheless, when Disneyland Paris opened in 1992, French farmers blocked transportation to and entry to the park because the French government had forced them to sell their land to Disney and because the United States was limiting importation of French agricultural products. Many potential customers instead visited the 1992 Olympics and World's Fair in Spain or other European amusement parks that sprang up or were refurbished as soon as Disney announced its plan to locate in France. At the time, the values of European currencies were fluctuating greatly, and many Europeans were wary that prices might be unexpectedly high once they got to the park. Although Disney put in fireplaces, protected waiting lines, and placed a glass dome over the teacup ride, the Parisian climate was too much colder than California's and Florida's to attract many winter visitors to the park. Finally, Disney put in a no-alcohol policy in the park to maintain its family image, but German and U.K. visitors balked, claiming that wine is part of the French experience.

The early problems almost bankrupted Disneyland Paris. But a Saudi Arabian investor put up almost $400 million for about a 25 percent stake, while Disney's share went down to 39 percent and that of the general public fell to 36 percent. In the meantime, Disney lowered prices, eliminated its no-alcohol policy, and promoted the park more heavily while putting a moratorium on receipt of its royalty payments. Disneyland Paris now has more than twice as many visitors as the Louvre and is making a small profit. Disney put up 39 percent of the funds to build the movie theme park, Walt Disney Studios. The company learned from its early experience with Disneyland Paris and is using European actors like Jeremy Irons, Isabella Rossellini, and Natasha Kinski (speaking in their native languages) as the virtual tour guides. It is also emphasizing European films.

Disney is interested in Asia because it accounts for about half the world's population and is becoming affluent enough so that more people can afford to take trips and pay for leisure activities. Further, China has had a one child per family policy, which has increased family disposable incomes and made parents reluctant to deny anything to their only child, such as a visit to a theme park.

Disney considered a number of Asian locations, mainly in China, before deciding on Hong Kong. Although Hong Kong has only 6.8 million people, it is Asia's largest tourist destination, getting about 10 million visitors per year. Further, Hong Kong has a better infrastructure (roads, airport, and utilities) and higher family incomes than does mainland Chinese cities. Finally, since Hong Kong reverted from British to Chinese control, Asians have not found it as appealing a tourist destination, so the government of Hong Kong was eager to attract Disney to bolster its tourist industry. Disney expects that its park will attract another 1.4 million outside visitors in the first year of operations and 2.9 million outside visitors within 15 years. Further,

FIGURE 1.8

At Tokyo Disneyland, signs are in English. At Disneyland Paris, French is the first language.

Source: © The New Yorker Collection 1987 Frank Modell from cartoonbank. com. All Rights Reserved. Reprinted by permission.

Hong Kong is presently not a family-oriented destination, and the Hong Kong government thinks that a Disney theme park can change that condition, thus bringing in a type of tourist who would not visit otherwise. Finally, Disney expects that it will create 18,400 direct and indirect jobs in its first year of operation and 35,800 in later years.

Disney also saw a theme park in Hong Kong as a way to improve its relationship with and business opportunities in mainland China. The Chinese government suspended distribution of Disney films after Disney released *Kundun* in 1996, a movie about the exiled Dalai Lama, whom the Chinese government considers to be a threat to its control over Tibet. Building a park in Hong Kong, which is a Chinese territory, showed Disney's willingness to cooperate with China.

Disney and the Hong Kong government negotiated for nearly a year. The final agreement is for a joint venture: Hong Kong International Theme Parks, owned 57 percent by the government of Hong Kong and 43 percent by Disney. The joint venture will own the theme park and other developments adjacent to it, such as hotels and restaurants. The Hong Kong government insisted that Disney invest money ($300 million) in addition to contributing expertise and the aura of its attractions and cartoon characters. In the end, the cost of the park and related projects—roads and a rail link to connect the park to the rest of Hong Kong—will probably exceed $4 billion.

The success of the park is far from assured. The cost of air transport and hotels may preclude visits from many Southeast Asian tourists. The only link by land to Hong Kong is China. Disney is obviously counting on Chinese visitors. Mainland Chinese must get exit visas from China and entry visas from Hong Kong to travel to Hong Kong. The Chinese government gives these visas sparingly, and the Hong Kong government issuance takes time. The Hong Kong government has indicated that it might eliminate the visa requirement for Chinese visitors coming for less than a week. Competition is another factor. Between 1994 and 1999, China built more than 2,000 amusement parks, ranging from lavish to shoddy. But most of them have not done well. Disney bets that the Chinese are not disinterested in amusement parks, only in the bad ones. Finally, there is the question of affordability. The joint venture is planning to build smaller, more affordable hotels to cater to Chinese visitors in an area almost as large as the park.

Given the financial problems of Disneyland Paris, Hong Kong Disneyland will be on a smaller scale than Disneyland Paris—needing 5 million annual visitors rather than 10 million to break even. The park itself will incorporate an exhibit center modeled after Epcot, along with the amusements. Disney does not expect that there will be a cultural backlash from the park like the one that it encountered in France because people in Hong Kong are reputedly more interested in making money than in preserving culture. Disney says it plans to give the hotels and restaurants a strong Chinese flavor, but the Magic Kingdom portion will be "ruled by Mickey Mouse, not Chairman Mao."

Given the large investment being made in Hong Kong, especially the one by the Hong Kong government, the letter of intent in 2002 to build a park in Shanghai surprised most analysts. The government of Hong Kong worries that a park in Shanghai will siphon potential tourists from visiting Hong Kong. Disney's authorities have countered that concern by saying the parks will attract different potential visitors. Disney says it has made no definite commitment to build the park in Shanghai, and some analysts feel Disney is really using the negotiations to make other inroads into China, such as by introducing a Disney television channel there.

QUESTIONS

1. What do you think motivated Disney to set up parks abroad, and what might be the pros and cons from the standpoint of the Walt Disney Company?
2. Why do you suppose Disney made no financial investment in Japan, one of $140 million in France, and then one of over $300 million in Hong Kong?
3. What factors in the external environment have contributed to Disney's success, failure, and adjustments in foreign theme park operations?
4. Should Disney set up a park in Shanghai? If so, what types of operating adjustments might it make there?

VIDEO: THE DEBATE OF GLOBALIZATION

This first chapter introduced the concept of globalization and its role for both businesses and people around the world. Based on viewing the accompanying video and materials in the chapter, please answer the following questions:

1. In your opinion, is globalization inevitable? Are the overall benefits of globalization positive? What are the gains and losses from globalization?
2. What external influences does a company encounter when determining how and where to conduct business globally?
3. What is the evolution of stages that a company goes through, as its operations become more global?

Chapter Notes

1 The information in this case is from the following sources: "Attack of the Clones," *The Grocer* (April 6, 2002): 60; Jonah Goldberg, "Send in the Clones," *National Review Online* (May 20, 2002): n.p.; Jose Martinez, "Fears Spears Clones," *Daily News* [New York] (June 3, 2002): 4; Guyon Espiner, "No Butts, Star Wars Fight Had to Be Tamed," *The Times* [London] (June 13, 2002): n.p.; "Star Wars Episode II: Attack of the Clones," *Intertec Publishing Corporation* (June 2002): 7; John Donnelly, "Fighting Terror a New Climate/New Era; Star Wars CD Debuts in Kabul," *Boston Globe* (May 19, 2002): A24; Bobbie Johnson, "Cybervillains," *The Guardian* [London] (May 20, 2002): 40; Bob Longino, "Clones Has Third Best Debut Ever," *Atlanta Journal and Constitution* (May 20, 2002): 1D; Lawrie Zion, "New Star Wars Prequel Breaks Box Office Records," *The Age* [Melbourne] (May 21, 2002): 2; Josh Grossberg, "Clones Attacking Early," *Eonline*: (November 14, 2001) www.eonline.com (accessed April 8, 2002); "Where Did They Film Star Wars: Episode II?" *Star Wars Kids*: www.starwarskids.com; "Wizards of the Coast," *Business Wire* (January 2, 2002): n.p.; "Japan Firm to Sell Star Wars Prop Replicas," *Asia Pulse* (April 2, 2002): n.p.; Lew Irwin, "Lucasfilm to Confront a Tower of Babel" (January 13, 2002): www.Hollywood.com/news/detail/article/ 109978; Michael Bodey, "PM to Hollywood: May Tax Breaks Be with You," *Daily Telegraph* [Sydney] (September 5, 2001): 7; and "Top 50+ All Time Highest Grossing Movies" July 18, 2002: http://movieweb.com/movie/alltime.html.

2 United Nations Conference on Trade and Development, *World Investment Report 2001: Promoting Linkages* (New York and Geneva: United Nations, 2001), 90–92.

3 Office of Trade and Economic Analysis, "Small and Medium-Sized Enterprises Play an Important Role," *Export America* 2, no. 11 (September 2001): 26–29.

4 Erin Butler, "Building Products Supplier Shares Exporting Secrets," *Export America* 3, no. 3 (March 2002): 6–7.

5 Nery Ynclan, "Avon Is Opening the Door to Spanglish," *Miami Herald* (July 23, 2002): E1.

6 Suzanne Kapner, "Nestlé Says Emerging Markets Help It Show Rise in Profits," *New York Times* (August 23, 2001): W1.

7 See "World Trade Growth Slower in 1998 After Unusually Strong Growth in 1997," *World Trade Organization Press Release* (April 16, 1999); "Developed Countries Boost Foreign Direct Investment by 46 Percent to New Record," *UNCTAD Press Release*, TAD/INF/2826 (September 23, 1999); and United Nations Conference on Trade and Development, *Trade and Development Report, 2002* (New York and Geneva: United Nations, 2002).

8 See Alister Foye, "Money Is Sunny, Barter's Smarter," *Daily Telegraph* (London) (January 24, 2002): 67; "Romania Offset Laws to Change," *Jane's Defence Weekly* (July 3, 2002): Section 1,

18; Loretta Leung, "Barter Trade Tackles Inventory Surplus," *South China Morning Post* (June 21, 2002): 4; and Nancy Dunne, "Barter Grows as Trade Deals Hit Problems," *Financial Times* (September 17, 1998): 7.

9 John Westbrooke, "Let's Go Where the Film Stars Go," *Financial Times* (October 6, 2001): 16.

10 United Nations Conference on Trade and Development, op. cit., 1.

11 Christopher A. Bartlett and Sumantra Ghoshal, *Transnational Management*, 3rd ed. (Boston: Irwin McGraw Hill, 2000).

12 Mariam Shahin, "When Will Iraq Take Its Place in the 21st Century?" *Middle East* 309 (February 2001): 16–18.

13 Ronald Grover, "The Emperor Strikes Back," *Business Week* (May 6, 2002): 38–40.

14 Terry Hall, "New Zealand Seeks Lost Sheep," *Financial Times* (March 28, 2002): 36.

15 Edward Luce, "Hard Sell to a Billion Consumers," *Financial Times* (April 25, 2002): 14.

16 There are many historical studies on this. For a fairly recent anecdotal example, see Jim Cramer, "Car Care Product Manufacturer 'Cleans-Up' Internationally," *Export America* 3, no. 2 (February 2002): 6–7.

17 See Shawna O'Grady and Henry W. Lane, "The Psychic Distance Paradox," *Journal of International Business Studies* 27, no. 2 (Second Quarter 1996): 309–33; and Jody Evans, Alan Treadgold, and Felix Mavondo, "Explaining Export Development Through Psychic Distance," *International Marketing Review* 17, no. 2 (2000): 164–68.

18 See Rodney C. Shrader, Benjamin M. Oviatt, and Patricia Phillips McDougall, "How New Ventures Exploit Trade-offs Among International Risk Factors: Lessons for the Accelerated Internationalization of the 21st Century," *Academy of Management Journal* 43, no. 6 (December 2000): 1227–247; and Ian Fillis, "The Internationalization Process of the Craft Microenterprise," *Journal of Developmental Entrepreneurship* 7, no. 1, April 2002, 25–43.

19 S. Tamer Cavusgil, "Extending the Reach of E-Business," *Marketing Management* 11, no. 2 (March–April 2002): 24–29.

20 Terri R. Lituchy and Anny Rail, "Bed and Breakfasts, Small Inns, and the Internet: The Impact of Technology on the Globalization of Small Business," *Journal of International Marketing* 8, no. 2 (2000): 86–97.

21 Robert C. Feenstra and Gordon H. Hanson, "The Impact of Outsourcing and High-Technology Capital on Wages: Estimates for the United States, 1979–1990," *Quarterly Journal of Economics* 114, no. 3 (August 1999): 907–40.

22 Jay Mazur, "Labor's New Internationalism," *Foreign Affairs* 79, no. 1 (January–February 2000): 79–93. For a refutation of that position, see David Dollar and Aart Kraay, "Spreading the Wealth," *Foreign Affairs* 81, no. 1 (January–February 2001): 120–33.

23 John Canavan, "Should Foreign Ownership of U.S. Telecom Infrastructure Be Restricted?" *Telecommunications* 33, no. 10 (October 1999) 94–96.

24 Ronald Berenbeim, "The Search for Global Ethics," *Vital Speeches of the Day* 65, no. 6 (January 1, 1999) 177–78.

25 S. Prakash Sethi, "Standards for Corporate Conduct in the International Arena: Challenges and Opportunities for Multinational Corporations," *Business and Society Review* 107, no. 1 (Spring 2002): 20–39.

26 David J. Vidal, *The Link Between Corporate Citizenship and Financial Performance* (New York: Conference Board, 1999).

27 Elizabeth Wine, "Ethical Crusaders Resolve to Redeem the Corporate Sinners," *Financial Times* (March 30–31, 2002): 24.

28 See "Indonesia's Plague," *Far Eastern Economic Review* 164, no. 27 (July 12, 2001): 8; and John Danley, "Balancing Risks: Mosquitos, Malaria, Morality, and DDT," *Business and Society Review* 107, no. 1 (Spring 2002): 145–70.

29 Ans Kolk and Rob van Tulder, "Child Labor and Multinational Conduct: A Comparison of International Business and Stakeholder Codes," *Journal of Business Ethics* 36, no. 3 (March 2002): 291–301.

30 Stanley Hoffmann, "Clash of Globalization," *Foreign Affairs* 81, no. 4 (July–August 2002): 104–15.

31 Kerry Gildea, "U.S., Japan Review Options For Future Sea-based Missile Defense Work," *Defense Daily International* 2, no. 36 (July 12, 2002): 1–2.

32 Traditionally, there have been seven countries, the G7 countries; however, Russia now attends meetings, making the group the G8 countries.

33 Thomas L. Friedman, "Moving with the Herd," *Computerworld* 35, no. 3 (January 15, 2001): 41–43; and Daniele Archiburgi and Bengt-Ake Lundvall, eds., *The Globalizing Learning Economy* (Oxford: Oxford University Press, 2001).

34 See, for example, "Malacca Strait Piracy Plummets," *Financial Times* (July 23, 2002): 6.

35 James Harding, "Globalisation's Children Strike Back," *Financial Times* (September 11, 2001): 4.

36 Duane Windsor, "The Future of Corporate Social Responsibility," *Journal of Organizational Analysis* 9, no. 3 (2001): 225–56.

37 Joseph E. Stiglitz, *Globalization and Its Discontents* (New York: W. W. Norton, 2002).

38 The information in this case is from the following sources: "Disney's New Japan Theme Park Hosts 10 Million Visitors in Shortest Time," AP News Wire (July 7, 2002); "Disneyland Unveils Pan-Euro Ads for Second Theme Park," *Euromarketing* via E-mail (March 15, 2002); Zach Coleman, "Disney Signs Letter of Intent to Build Shanghai Theme Park," *Wall Street Journal* (July 22, 2002): A3; Paulo Prada and Bruce Orwall, "A Certain 'Je Ne Sais Quoi' at Disney's New Park," *Wall Street Journal* (March 12, 2002): B1 +; Rahul Jacob,

"Disney Seals HK Park Deal," *Financial Times* (November 2, 1999): 4; Rahul Jacob, Christopher Parkes, and Ho Swee Lin, "Mickey Mouse to Fill Role Left Empty by Empire," *Financial Times* (November 3, 1999): 7; Mark Lander, "Mickey and Minnie Go to Hong Kong," *New York Times* (November 3, 1999): C1; Jon E. Hilsenrath and Zach Coleman, "Disney-Park Deal May Not Wave a Magic Wand Over Hong Kong," *Wall Street Journal* (November 4, 1999): A26; Mark Lander, "After Protracted Talks, a Disneyland Will Rise in Hong Kong," *New York Times* (November 1, 1999): C1; Mahon Meyer, "Mickey Goes to China," *Newsweek* (November 15, 1999): 42; "Fantasyland," *The Economist Newspaper* (November 6, 1999): n.p.; Christopher Parkes, "Disney's Sea Theme Park in Tokyo Gets Go-ahead," *Financial Times* (November 27, 1997): 1; Charles Fleming, "Euro Disney to Build Movie Theme Park Outside Paris," *Wall Street Journal* (September 30, 1999): A18; "Euro Disney to Open New Park," *Financial Times* (September 30, 1999): 26; Michael Dobbs, "Mickey Mouse Storms the Bastille," *Across the Board* 23, no. 4 (April 1986): 9–11; "Trouble at Magic Kingdom," *Business Week* (September 26, 1992): 8; Peter Gumbel and David J. Jefferson, "Disney Continues Drive to Expand Worldwide," *Wall Street Journal* (November 20, 1992): B4; and Sharon Waxman, "Le Mouse That Roared Back," *Washington Post* (July 27, 1995): B9.

An Atlas

Satellite television transmission now makes it commonplace for us to watch events as they unfold in other countries. Transportation and communication advances and government-to-government accords have contributed to our increasing dependence on foreign goods and markets. As this dependence grows, updated maps are a valuable tool. They can show the locations of population, economic wealth, production and markets; portray certain commonalities and differences among areas; and illustrate barriers that might inhibit trade. In spite of the usefulness of maps, a substantial number of people worldwide have a poor knowledge of how to interpret information on maps and even of how to find the location of events that affect their lives.

We urge you to use the following maps to build your awareness of geography.

WEB CONNECTION
We also encourage you to visit our Web page for links to key resources for you in your study of international business.

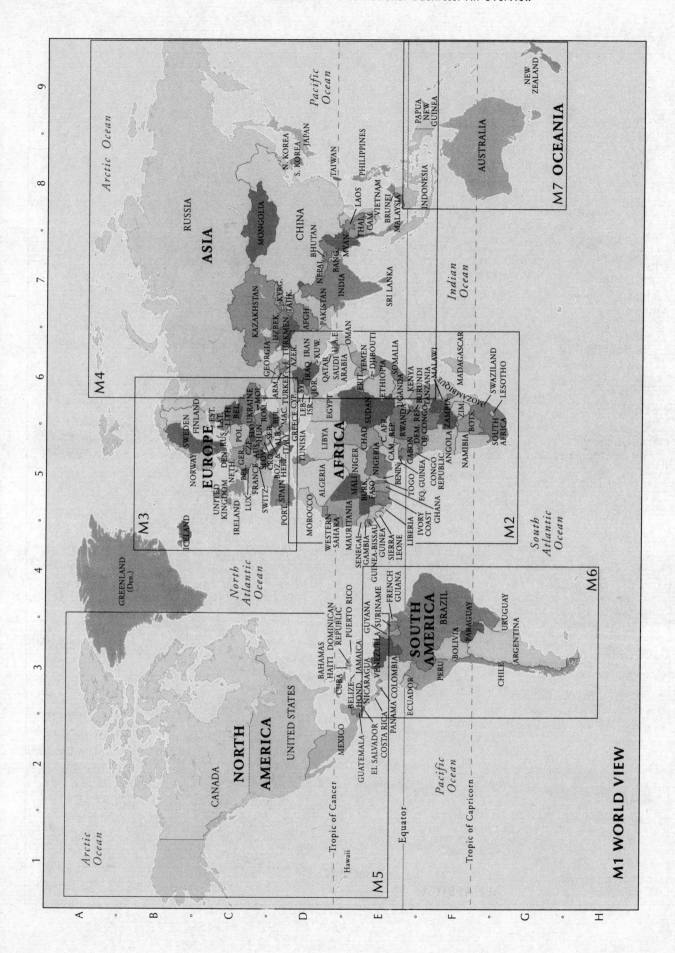

M1 WORLD VIEW

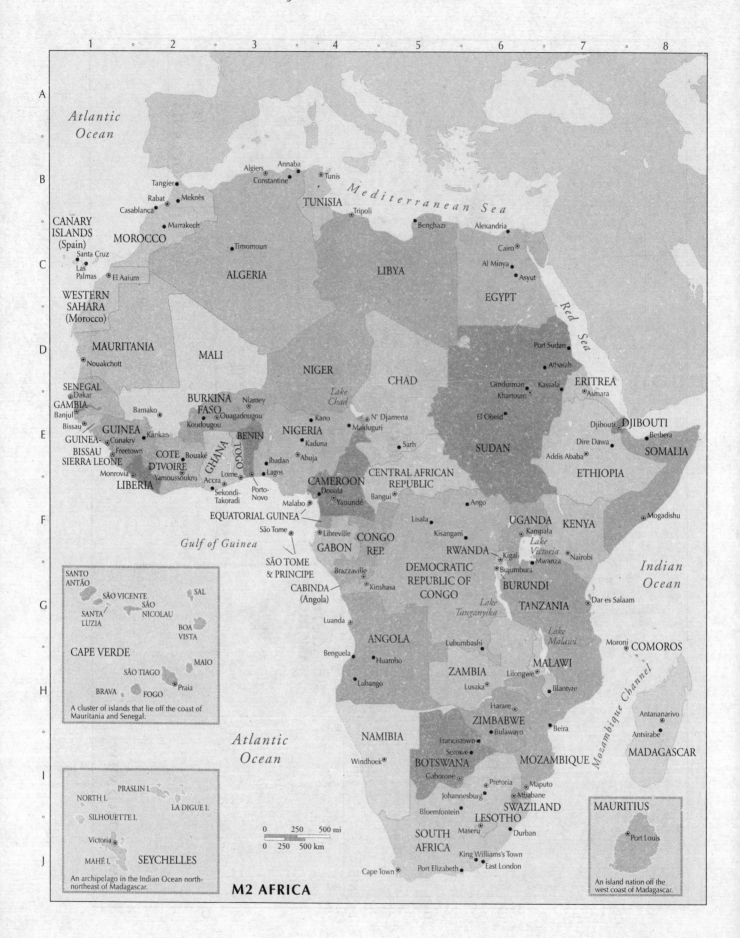

M2 AFRICA

M3 EUROPE

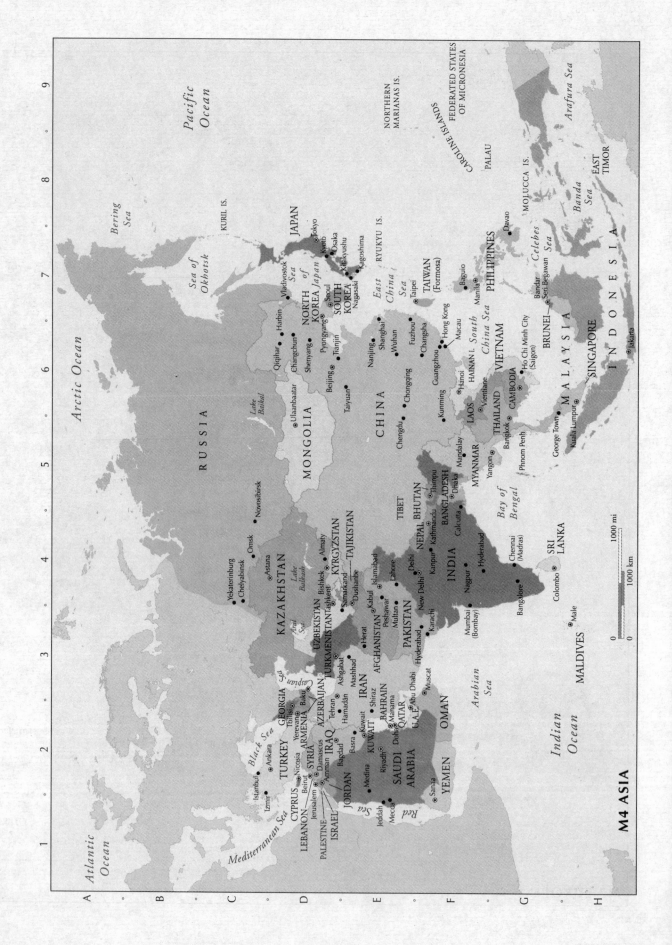

M4 ASIA

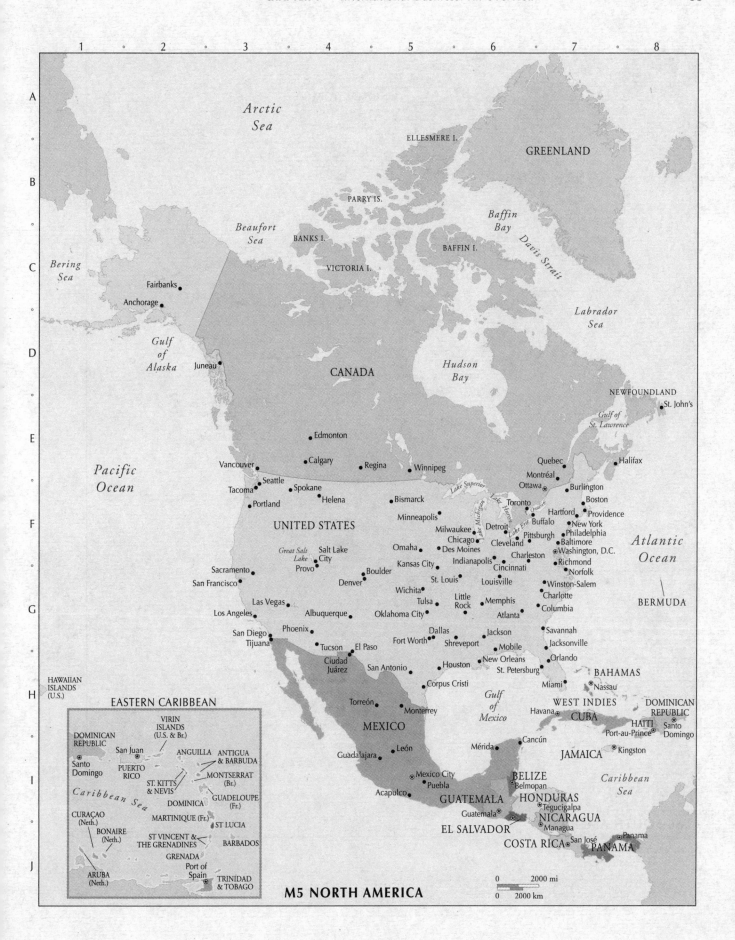

M5 NORTH AMERICA

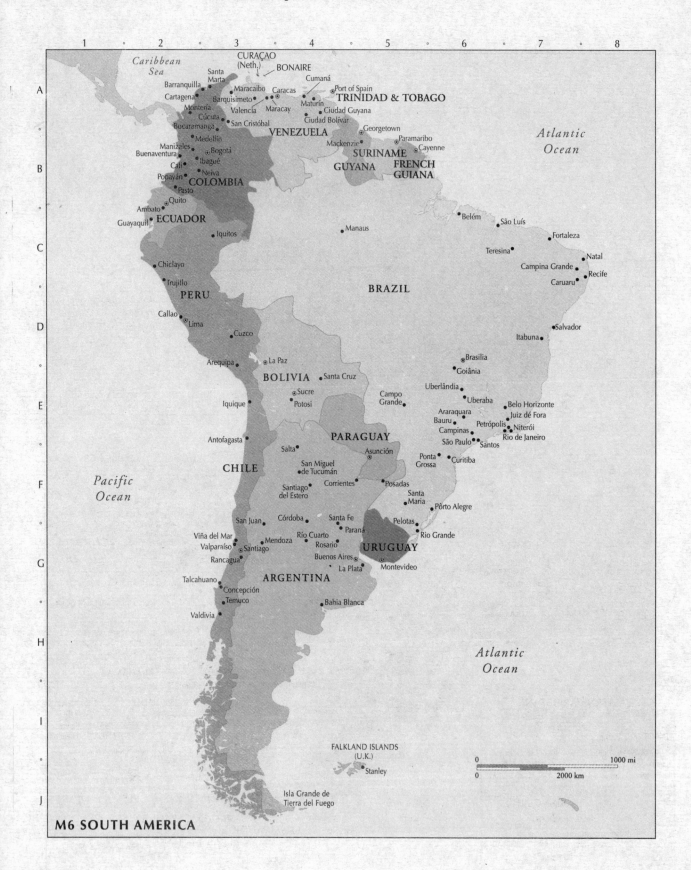

M6 SOUTH AMERICA

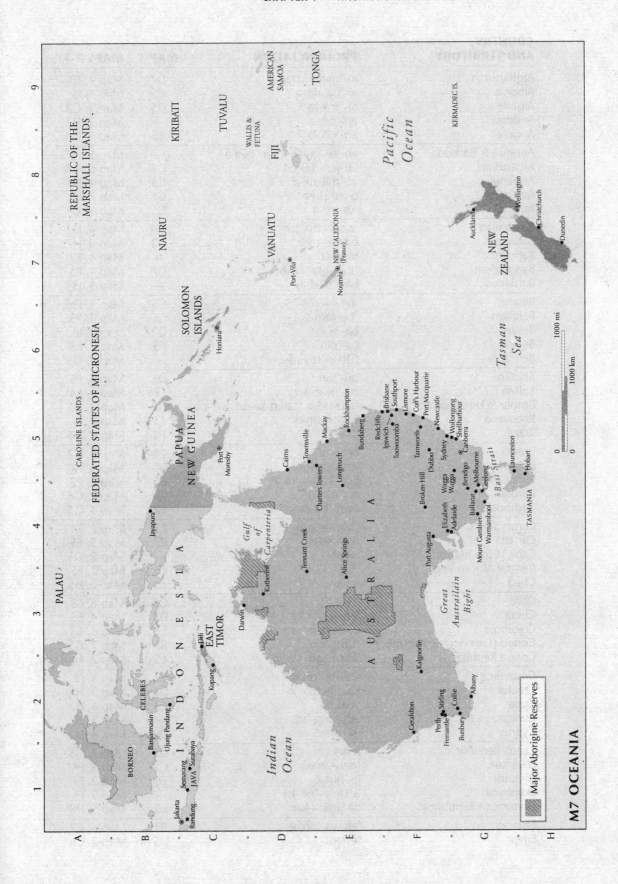

M7 OCEANIA

COUNTRY AND TERRITORY	PRONUNCIATION	MAP 1	MAPS 2-7
Afghanistan	af-'gan-ə-,stan	D7	Map 4, E3
Albania	al-'bā-nē-ə	C5	Map 3, I5
Algeria	al-'jir-ē-ə	D5	Map 2, C3
Andorra	an-'dȯr-ə	—	Map 3, H2
Angola	an-'gō-lə	E5	Map 2, G4
Antigua & Barbuda	an-'tē-g(w)ə / bär-'büd-ə	—	Map 5, I3
Argentina	,är-jen-'tē-nə	G3	Map 6, G3
Armenia	är-'mē-ne-ə	C6	Map 4, D2
Australia	ȯ-'strāl-yə	G8	Map 7, E4
Austria	'ȯs-trē-ə	C5	Map 3, G4
Azerbaijan	,az-ər-,bī-'jän	D6	Map 4, D2
Bahamas	bə-hä'-məz	D3	Map 5, H7
Bahrain	bä-'rān	—	Map 4, E2
Bangladesh	,bäŋ-glə-'desh	D7	Map 4, F5
Barbados	bär-'bäd-əs	—	Map 5, J3
Belarus	,bē-lə-'rüs	C5	Map 3, F6
Belgium	'bel-jəm	C5	Map 3, F3
Belize	bə-'lēz	D2	Map 5, I6
Benin	bə-'nin	E5	Map 2, E3
Bermuda	(,)bər-'myüd-ə	—	Map 5, G8
Bhutan	bü-'tan	D7	Map 4, F5
Bolivia	bə-'liv-ē-ə	F3	Map 6, E4
Bosnia & Herzegovina	'bäz-nē-ə / ,hert-sə-gō-'vē-nə	D5	Map 3, H5
Botswana	bät-'swän-ə	F5	Map 2, I5
Brazil	brə-'zil	F3	Map 6, D6
Brunei	broo-nī'	E8	Map 4, G7
Bulgaria	,bəl-'gar-ē-ə	D5	Map 3, H6
Burkina Faso	bur-'kē-nə-'fȧ-sō	E5	Map 2, E2
Burundi	bu-'rün-dē	E6	Map 2, G6
Cambodia	kam-'bd-ē-ə	E7	Map 4, G5
Cameroon	,kam-ə-'rün	E5	Map 2, F4
Canada	'kan-əd-ə	C2	Map 5, E5
Cape Verde Islands	'vard	—	Map 2, G1
Central African Rep.		E5	Map 2, E5
Chad	'chad	E5	Map 2, D5
Chile	'chil-ē	G3	Map 6, F3
China	'chī-nə	D8	Map 4, E5
Colombia	kə-'ləm-bē-ə	E3	Map 6, B3
Congo (Democratic Republic)	'käŋ(,)gō	E5	Map 2, G5
Congo Republic	'käŋ(,)gō	E5	Map 2, F4
Costa Rica	,käs-tə-'rē-kə	E2	Map 5, J7
Croatia	krō-'ā-sh(ē)ə	D5	Map 3, H5
Cuba	'kyü-bə	E3	Map 5, H7
Curaçao	'k(y)ür-ə-'sō	—	Map 5, J1
Cyprus	'sī-prəs	D6	Map 4, D2
Czech Republic	,chek	C5	Map 3, G5
Denmark	'den-,märk	C5	Map 3, E4
Djibouti	jə-'büt-ē	E6	Map 2, E7
Dominica	,däm-ə-'nē-kə	—	Map 5, I3
Dominican Republic	də-,min-i-kən	E3	Map 5, H8
Ecuador	'ek-wə-,dȯ(ə)r	E3	Map 6, C2
Egypt	'ē-jəpt	D5	Map 2, C6

COUNTRY AND TERRITORY	PRONUNCIATION	MAP 1	MAPS 2-7
El Salvador	el-'sal-və-,dȯ(ə)r	E2	Map 5, I6
Equatorial Guinea	ē-kwa'-tōr-ē al ġi-nē	E5	Map 2, F4
Eritrea	,er-ə-'trē-ə	E6	Map 2, E6
Estonia	e-'stō-nē-ə	C5	Map 3, E6
Ethiopia	,ē-thē-'ō-pē-ə	E6	Map 2, E7
Falkland Islands	'fȯ(l)-klənd	—	Map 6, J4
Fiji	'fē-jē	—	Map 7, D8
Finland	'fin-lənd	B5	Map 3, C6
France	'fran(t)s	C5	Map 3, G3
French Guiana	gē-'an-ə	E3	Map 6, B5
Gabon	ga-'bōⁿ	E5	Map 2, F4
Gambia	'gam-bē-ə	E4	Map 2, E1
Georgia	'jȯr-jə	C6	Map 4, D2
Germany	'jerm-(ə-)nē	C5	Map 3, F4
Ghana	'gän-ə	E5	Map 2, E2
Greece	'grēs	D5	Map 3, I6
Greenland	'grēn-lənd	A4	Map 5, E7
Grenada	grə-nā'də	—	Map 5, J3
Guatemala	,gwät-ə-'mäl-ə	E2	Map 5, I6
Guinea	'gin-ē	E4	Map 2, E1
Guinea-Bissau	,gin-ē-bis-'au̇	E4	Map 2, E1
Guyana	gī-'an-ə	E3	Map 6, B4
Haiti	'hāt-ē	E3	Map 5, H8
Honduras	hän-'d(y)u̇r-əs	E2	Map 5, I7
Hong Kong	'häŋ-,käŋ	—	Map 4, F6
Hungary	'həŋ-g(ə)rē	C5	Map 3, G5
Iceland	'ī-slənd	B4	Map 3, B1
India	'in-dē-ə	D7	Map 4, F4
Indonesia	,in-də-'nē-zhə	E8	Map 4, H7; Map 7, B3
Iran	i-'rän	D6	Map 4, E3
Iraq	i-'räk	D6	Map 4, D2
Ireland	'ī(ə)r-lənd	C5	Map 3, F1
Israel	'iz-rē-əl	D6	Map 4, D2
Italy	'it-ᵊl-ē	D6	Map 3, H4
Ivory Coast	ī 'və-rē	E5	Map 2, E2
Jamaica	jə-'mā-kə	E3	Map 5, I7
Japan	jə-'pan	D8	Map 4, D7
Jordan	'jȯrd-ᵊn	D6	Map 4, D2
Kazakhstan	kə-,zak-'stan	D7	Map 4, D4
Kenya	'ken-yə	E6	Map 7, F7
Kiribati	kîr-ĭ-bǎs'	—	Map 7, B8
Korea, North	kə-'rē-ə	D8	Map 4, D7
Korea, South	kə-'rē-ə	D8	Map 4, D7
Kuwait	kə-'wāt	D6	Map 4, E2
Kyrgyzstan	kîr-gē-stän'	D7	Map 4, D4
Laos	'lau̇s	D7	Map 4, F5
Latvia	'lat-vē-ə	C5	Map 3, E6
Lebanon	'leb-ə-nən	D6	Map 4, D2
Lesotho	lə-'sō-(,)tō	F6	Map 2, J6
Liberia	lī-'bir-ē-ə	E5	Map 2, F2
Libya	'lib-ē-ə	D5	Map 2, C4

COUNTRY AND TERRITORY	PRONUNCIATION	MAP 1	MAPS 2-7
Liechtenstein	lĭk'tən-stīn'	—	Map 3, G4
Lithuania	,lith-(y)ə-'wā-nē-ə	C5	Map 3, E6
Luxembourg	'lək-səm-,bərg	C5	Map 3, G3
Macedonia	,mas-ə-'dō-nyə	D6	Map 3, I6
Madagascar	,mad-ə-'gas-kər	F6	Map 2, I8
Malawi	mə-'lä-wē	F6	Map 2, H6
Malaysia	mə-'lā-zh(ē-)ə	E8	Map 4, G6
Maldives	môl'dīvz	—	Map 4, H3
Mali	'mäl-ē	D5	Map 2, D2
Malta	'mȯl-tə	—	Map 3, J5
Marshall Islands	mär'shəl	—	Map 7, A8
Mauritania	,mȯr-ə-'tā-nē-ə	D5	Map 2, D1
Mauritius	mô-'rĭsh'əs	—	Map 2, J8
Mexico	'mek-si-,kō	D2	Map 5, I5
Micronesia	mī 'krō-nē'zhə	—	Map 7, A5
Moldova	mäl-'dō-və	D6	Map 3, G7
Mongolia	män-'gōl-yə	D8	Map 4, D5
Morocco	mə-'räk-(,)ō	D5	Map 2, B2
Mozambique	,mō-zəm-'bēk	F6	Map 2, H6
Myanmar	'myän-,mär	E7	Map 4, F5
Namibia	nə-'mib-ē-ə	F5	Map 2, I4
Naura	nä'-ü-rü	—	Map 7, B7
Nepal	nə-'pȯl	D7	Map 4, E4
Netherlands	'neth-ər-lən(d)z	C5	Map 3, F3
New Caledonia	,kal-ə-'dō-nyə	—	Map 7, E7
New Zealand	'zē-lənd	G9	Map 7, H7
Nicaragua	,nik-ə-'räg-wə	E3	Map 5, I7
Niger	'nī-jər	E5	Map 2, D4
Nigeria	nī-'jir-ē-ə	E5	Map 2, E4
Norway	'nȯ(ə)r-,wā	C5	Map 3, D3
Oman	ō-'män	E6	Map 4, F2
Pakistan	,pak-i-'stan	D7	Map 4, E3
Palau	pä-lou'	—	Map 7, A3
Palestine	pa-lə-'stī n	—	Map 4, D1
Panama	'pan-ə-,mä	E3	Map 5, J8
Papua New Guinea	'pap-yə-wə	F9	Map 7, C5
Paraguay	'par-ə-,gwī	F3	Map 6, E4
Peru	pə-'rü	F3	Map 6, D2
Philippines	,fĭl-ə-'pēnz	E8	Map 4, F7
Poland	'pō-lənd	D5	Map 3, F5
Portugal	'pōr-chi-gəl	D5	Map 3, I1
Puerto Rico	,pōrt-ə-'rē(,)kō	E3	Map 5, I2
Qatar	'kät-ər	D6	Map 4, E2
Romania	rō-'mā-nē-ə	D5	Map 3, H6
Russia	'rəsh-ə	C7	Map 3, D7; Map 4, C5
Rwanda	rü-'än-də	E6	Map 2, F6
St. Kitts & Nevis	'kits / 'nē-vəs	—	Map 5, I3
St. Lucia	sā nt-'lü-shə	—	Map 5, I3
St. Vincent and the Grenadines	grĕn'ə-dē nz'	—	Map 5, J3
San Marino	săn mə-rē'nō	—	Map 3, H4

COUNTRY AND TERRITORY	PRONUNCIATION	MAP 1	MAPS 2-7
São Tomé and Príncipe	soun tōō -mě 'prēn'-sēpə	—	Map 2, F3
Saudi Arabia	,saüd-ē	E6	Map 4, E2
Senegal	,sen-i-'gȯl	E4	Map 2, D1
Serbia & Montenegro	'sər- bē -ə / ,män-tə-'nē -grō	D5	Map 3, H2
Seychelles	sā-shě lz'	—	Map 2, J1
Sierra Leone	sē -,er-ə-lē -'ō n	E4	Map 2, E1
Singapore	'siŋ-(g)ə-,pō (ə)r	—	Map 4, H6
Slovakia	slō -'väk-ē -ə	C5	Map 3, G5
Slovenia	slō -'vē n-ē -ə	C5	Map 3, H5
Solomon Islands	'säl-ə-mən	—	Map 7, C6
Somalia	sō -'mäl-ē -ə	E6	Map 2, F8
South Africa	'a-fri-kə	F6	Map 2, J5
Spain	'spā n	C5	Map 3, I1
Sri Lanka	(')srē -'läŋ-kə	E7	Map 4, G4
Sudan	sü-'dan	E6	Map 2, E6
Suriname	sȯr-ə-'näm-ə	E3	Map 6, B5
Swaziland	'swäz-ē -,land	F6	Map 2, I6
Sweden	'swē d-ᵊn	B5	Map 3, C5
Switzerland	'swit-sər-lənd	C5	Map 3, G4
Syria	'sir-ē -ə	D6	Map 4, D2
Taiwan	'tī -'wän	D8	Map 4, E7
Tajikistan	tä-,ji-ki-'stan	D7	Map 4, E4
Tanzania	,tan-zə-'nē -ə	F6	Map 2, G6
Thailand	'tī -land	E8	Map 4, F5
Togo	'tō (,)gō	E5	Map 2, E3
Tonga	'tän-gə	—	Map 7, D9
Trinidad & Tobago	'trin-ə-,dad / tə-'bā -(,)gō	—	Map 5, J3
Tunisia	t(y)ü-'nē -zh(ē -)ə	D5	Map 2, B4
Turkey	'tər-kē	D6	Map 4, D2
Turkmenistan	tûrk'-men-i-stǎ n'	D6	Map 4, D3
Tuvalu	tü'-vä-lü	—	Map 7, C9
Uganda	(y)ü-'gan-də	E6	Map 2, F6
Ukraine	yü-'krā n	C6	Map 3, F7
United Arab Emirates	yoo-nī 'tid ǎ r'əb i-mîr'its	D6	Map 4, E2
United Kingdom	king'dəm	C5	Map 3, F2
United States	yȯ-,nī t-əd-'stā ts	D2	Map 5, F5
Uruguay	'(y)ȯr-ə-gwī	G3	Map 6, G5
Uzbekistan	(,)ȯz-,bek-i-'stan	C6	Map 4, D3
Vanuatu	van-ə-'wät-(,)ü	—	Map 7, D7
Vatican City	vǎ t'ǐ -kən	—	Map 3, H4
Venezuela	,ven-əz(-ə)-'wā -lə	E3	Map 6, A4
Vietnam	vē -'et-'näm	E8	Map 4, G6
Western Sahara	sə-hâr'ə	D4	Map 2, C1
Yemen	'yem-ən	E6	Map 4, F2
Zambia	'zam-bē -ə	F5	Map 2, H5
Zimbabwe	zim-'bäb-wē	F6	Map 2, H6

* in thousands
+ in millions of U.S. dollars
** in U.S. dollars   [NA = Not Available]

PART TWO

Comparative Environmental Frameworks

CHAPTER

2

THE CULTURAL ENVIRONMENTS FACING BUSINESS

To change customs is a difficult thing.

—LEBANESE PROVERB

OBJECTIVES

- To discuss the problems and methods of learning about cultural environments
- To explain the major causes of cultural difference and change
- To examine behavioral factors influencing countries' business practices
- To examine cultural guidelines for companies that operate internationally

CASE

Adjusting to Saudi Arabian Culture[1]

For most outsiders, Saudi Arabia is a land of contrasts and paradoxes. (Map 2.1 shows its location.) It has supermodern cities, but its strict Islamic religious convictions and ancient social customs, on which its laws and customs depend, often clash with modern economic and technical realities. Saudi Arabians sometimes employ latitude in legal formation and enforcement to ease these clashes and sometimes accommodate different behaviors from foreigners. Nevertheless, many foreigners misunderstand Saudi laws and customs or find them contrary to their own value systems. Foreign companies have had mixed success in Saudi Arabia, due in large part to how well they understood and adapted imaginatively to Saudi customs.

Companies from countries with strict separation between state and religion or where few people actively engage in religion find Saudi Arabia's pervasiveness of religion daunting. Religious decrees have sometimes made companies rescind activities. For example, an importer halted sales of the children's game Pokémon because the game might encourage the un-Islamic practice of gambling, and a franchisor was forced to remove the face under the crown in Starbucks' logo because Saudi authorities felt the public display of a woman's face was religiously immoral. However, most companies know the requirements in advance. For instance, Coty Beauty omits models' faces on point-of-purchase displays that it depicts in other countries. Companies know that they must remove the heads and hands from mannequins and must

MAP 2.1 Saudi Arabia

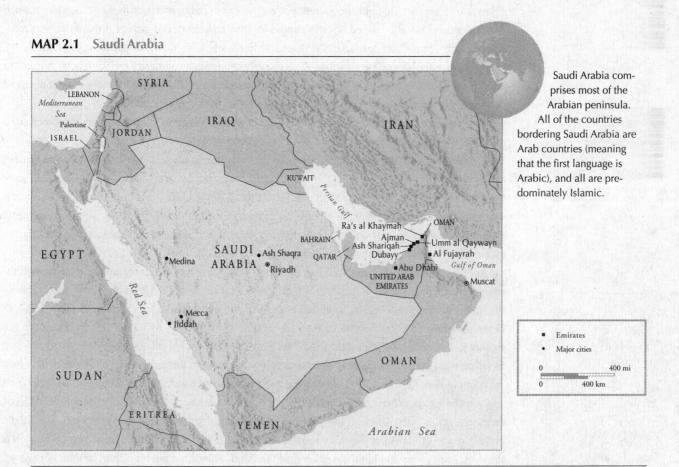

Saudi Arabia comprises most of the Arabian peninsula. All of the countries bordering Saudi Arabia are Arab countries (meaning that the first language is Arabic), and all are predominately Islamic.

not display them scantily clad. Companies, such as McDonald's, dim their lights, close their doors, and stop attending to customers during the five times per day that men are called to pray. Companies also adjust voluntarily to gain the goodwill of customers—for example, by converting revenue-generating space to prayer areas. (Saudi Arabian Airlines does this in the rear of its planes, and the U.K.'s Harvey Nichols does this in its department store.) During the holy period of Ramadan, people are less active during the day because they fast, so many stores shift some operating hours to the evenings when people prefer to shop.

In 2000, Saudi Arabia ratified an international agreement designed to eliminate the discrimination of women; however, its prescribed behaviors for women appear paradoxical to outsiders. On the one hand, women now outnumber men in Saudi Arabian universities and own about 20 percent of all Saudi businesses. (There are separate male and female universities, and female-owned businesses can sell only to women.) Women also comprise a large portion of Saudi teachers and doctors. On the other hand, women account for only about 7 percent of the workforce. They cannot have private law or architectural firms, nor can they be engineers. They are not permitted to drive, because this may lead to evil behavior. They must wear *abayas* (robes) and cover their hair completely when in public. They cannot work alongside men except in the medical profession, and they cannot sell directly to male customers. If they are employed where men work, they must have separate work entrances and be separated from males by partitions. They must be accompanied by an adult male relative when dealing with male clerks.

The female prescriptions have implications for business operations. For example, the Saudi American Bank established branches for and staffed only by women. Pizza Hut installed two dining rooms—one for single men and one for families. (Women do not eat there without their families.) Both Harvey Nichols and Saks Fifth Avenue have created women-only floors in their department stores. On lower levels, there is mixed shopping, all male salespeople (even for products like cosmetics and bras), and no change rooms or places to try cosmetics. On upper floors, women can check their *abayas* and shop in jeans, spandex, or whatever. The stores have also created drivers' lounges for their chauffeurs. A downside is that male store managers can visit upper floors only when the stores are closed, which limits their observations of situations that might improve service and performance. Similarly, market research companies cannot rely on discussions with family-focused groups to determine marketing needs. Because men do much more of the household purchasing, companies target them more in their marketing than in other countries.

Why do high-end department stores and famous designers operate in Saudi Arabia where women cover themselves in *abayas* and men typically wear *thobes* (long robes)? Simply, the many very rich people in Saudi Arabia are said to keep Paris couture alive. Even though Saudi Arabia prohibits fashion magazines and movies, this clientele knows what is in fashion. (The government also prohibits satellite dishes, but some estimates say that two-thirds of Saudi homes have them.) Women buy items from designers' collections, which they wear abroad or in Saudi Arabia only in front of their husbands and other women. Underneath their *abayas*, they often wear very expensive jewelry, makeup, and clothing. Wealthy men also want the latest high-end fashions when traveling abroad.

Another paradox is that about 60 percent of the Saudi private workforce is foreign, even though the unemployment rate is about 30 percent. Changing economic conditions are at least partially responsible for this situation. In the early 1980s, Saudi oil revenues caused per capita income to jump to about $28,000, but this plummeted below $7,000 by the early 2000s. When incomes were high, Saudis brought in foreigners to do most of the work. At the same time, the government liberally supported university training, including study abroad. Saudis developed a mentality of expecting foreigners to do all the work or at least some of the work for them. The New Zealand head of National Biscuits & Confectionery said that Saudis now want only to be supervisors and complain if they have to work at the same level as people from Nepal, Bangladesh, and India. Although the government has taken steps to replace foreign workers with Saudis, prevailing work attitudes impede this transition. For example, the acceptance by a Saudi of a bellboy job at the Hyatt Regency hotel in Jidda was so unusual that Saudi newspapers put his picture on their front pages.

Saudi Arabian legal sanctions seem harsh to many outsiders. Religious patrols may hit women if they show any hair in public. The government carries out beheadings and hand-severances in public and expects passers-by to observe the punishments, some of which are for crimes that would not be offenses in other countries. For example, the government publicly beheaded three men in early 2002 for being homosexuals. However, there are inconsistencies. For example, religious patrols are more relaxed about women's dress codes in some Red Sea resorts, and they are more lenient toward the visiting female executives of MNEs than toward Saudi women. Whereas they don't allow Saudi women to be flight attendants on Saudi Arabian Airlines, because they would have to work alongside men, they permit women from other Arab countries to do so. Further, in foreign investment compounds, where almost everyone is a foreigner, these religious patrols make exceptions to most of the strict religious prescriptions.

Interesting situations concern the charging of interest and the purchase of accident insurance, both of which are disallowed under strict Islamic interpretations of the Koran. In the case of interest, the Saudi government gives interest-free loans for mortgages. This worked well when Saudi Arabia was awash with oil money, but borrowers must now wait about 10 years for a loan. In the case of accident insurance (by strict Islamic doctrine, there are no accidents, only preordained acts of God), the government eliminated prohibitions because businesses needed the insurance.

Personal interactions between cultures are tricky, and those between Saudis and non-Saudis are no exception. For example, Parris-Rogers International (PRI), a British publishing house, sent two salesmen to Saudi Arabia and paid them on a commission basis. They expected that by moving aggressively, the two men could make the same number of calls as they could in the United Kingdom. They were used to working eight-hour days, to having the undivided attention of potential clients, and to restricting conversation to the business transaction. To them, time was money. However, they found that appointments seldom began at the scheduled time and most often took place at cafés where the Saudis would engage in what the salesmen considered idle chitchat. Whether in a café or in the office, drinking coffee or tea and talking to acquaintances seemed to take precedence over business matters. The salesmen began showing so much irritation at "irrelevant" conversations, delays, and interruptions from friends that they caused irrevocable damage to the company's objectives. The Saudi counterparts considered them rude and impatient.

Whereas businesspersons from many countries invite counterparts to social gatherings at their homes to honor them and use personal relationships to cement business arrangements, Saudis view the home as private and even consider questions about their families as rude and an invasion of privacy. In contrast, Saudi businessmen seldom regard business discussions as private; they thus welcome friends to sit in. The opposite is true in many countries.

In spite of contrasts and paradoxes, foreign companies find ways to be highly successful in Saudi Arabia. In some cases, legal barriers to some products, such as to alcoholic beverages and pork products, have created boons for other products, such as soft drinks and turkey ham. In addition, some companies have developed specific practices in response to Saudi conditions and have later benefited from them in their home countries. For example, companies, such as Fuji and Kodak, created technology for while-you-wait photo development for Saudi Arabia because customers wanted to retrieve photos without anyone else seeing them. They transferred this technology to the United States several years later.

INTRODUCTION

The opening case illustrates how important it is for companies to adjust when entering different cultures. PRI's lack of adjustment led to its failure; Harvey Nichols's adjustments are leading to its success. The major problems of cultural collision in international business are when

- A company implements practices that work less well than intended.
- A company's employees encounter distress because of an inability to accept or adjust to foreign behaviors.

Business employs, sells to, buys from, is regulated by, and is owned by people. Because international business includes people from different cultures, every business function—

Technology, especially in transportation and communications, brings traditional and contemporary cultures in greater contact, sometimes creating cultural clashes and sometimes creating cultural changes. The photo shows a traditional aborigine at a modern store in Sydney, Australia.

managing a workforce, marketing output, purchasing supplies, dealing with regulators, securing funds—is subject to potential cultural problems. An international company must be sensitive to these cultural differences in order to predict and control its relationships and operations. Further, it should realize that its accustomed way of doing business may not be the only or best way. When doing business abroad, a company should first determine what business practices in a foreign country differ from those it's used to. Management then must decide what, if any, adjustments are necessary to operate efficiently in the foreign country.

In Chapter 1, you learned that companies need to understand external environments to operate efficiently abroad. Figure 2.1 illustrates that **culture**—the specific learned norms based on attitudes, values, and beliefs that exist in every nation—is an integral part of external environments. This chapter will first examine cultural awareness, especially the need for building it. Second, the chapter will discuss the causes of cultural differences, rigidities, and changes. Third, the chapter will describe behavioral factors that affect the conduct of business internationally. Finally, the chapter will explore why businesses and individuals adjust—or don't adjust—to another culture.

FIGURE 2.1   Cultural Influences on International Business

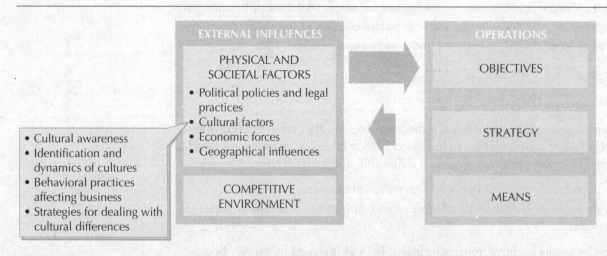

CULTURAL AWARENESS

Building cultural awareness is not an easy task, and no foolproof method exists for doing so.[2] As we just said, culture consists of specific learned norms based on attitudes, values, and beliefs, all of which exist in every nation. Visitors remark on cultural differences, experts write about them, and international businesspeople find that they affect operations. Yet controversy surrounds these differences because people disagree on what they are, whether they are widespread or exceptional differences, and whether the differences are deep-seated or superficial. Further, culture cannot easily be isolated from such factors as economic and political conditions. For example, an opinion survey of a country's citizens that measures, say, attitudes toward buying a new product may reflect a response to temporary economic conditions rather than basic values and beliefs that will have lasting effects on the product's acceptance.

Some differences, such as those regarding acceptable attire, are discerned easily; others may be more difficult to perceive. All people have culturally ingrained responses to given situations and sometimes expect that people from other cultures will respond the same way as people in their own culture do. For example, in the opening case, the British salesmen for PRI budgeted their time and so regarded drinking coffee and chatting about nonbusiness activities in a café as "doing nothing," especially if there was "work to be done." In fact, their compensation system did not give them the privilege of spending much time on each business transaction. The Arab businessmen had no compulsion to finish at a given time, viewed time spent in a café as "doing something," and considered "small talk" an indication of whether they could get along with potential business partners. Because the Englishmen believed "you shouldn't mix business and pleasure," they became irritated when friends of the Arab businessmen joined their conversations. In contrast, the Arabs felt "people are more important than business" and saw nothing private about business transactions.

Some people seem to have an innate ability to do and say the right thing at the right time, and others offend unintentionally or misrepresent what they want to convey. Nevertheless, there is general agreement that businesspeople can improve their awareness and sensitivity and that training about other cultures will enhance the likelihood of succeeding in those cultures.

Researching descriptions of a specific culture can be instructive. But managers must carefully assess the information they gather because it sometimes presents unwarranted stereotypes, offers an assessment of only a segment of the particular country, or reports outdated information. In a given society, managers can also observe the behavior of those people who have the respect they would like themselves. Of course, it helps to study the overseas market directly.

There are so many cultural variations that businesspeople cannot expect to memorize all of them for every country. Wide variations exist even in addressing people. For example, it may be difficult to know whether to use a given name or surname, which of several surnames to use, and whether a wife takes her husband's name. Making a mistake may be construed by foreign businesspeople as ignorance or rudeness, which may jeopardize a business arrangement. Fortunately, there are guidebooks for particular geographical areas, based on the experiences of many successful international managers. A manager may also consult with knowledgeable people at home and abroad—from governmental offices or in the private sector.

Not all companies need to have the same degree of cultural awareness. Nor must a particular company have a consistent degree of awareness during the course of its operations. As we discussed in Chapter 1, companies usually increase foreign operations over time. They may expand their cultural knowledge as they move from one to multiple foreign functions or locations, from similar to dissimilar foreign environments, and from external to internal handling of their international operations. A company that is new to international business may need only a minimal level of cultural awareness, but a highly entrenched company needs a high level of awareness because of its multifunctional operations in multiple countries.

Businesspeople agree that cultural differences exist but disagree on what they are.

Problem areas that can hinder managers' cultural awareness are

- Subconscious reactions to circumstances
- The assumption that all societal subgroups are similar

A company's need for cultural knowledge increases as

- Its number of foreign functions increases
- The number of countries of operations increases
- It moves from external to internal handling of operations

When a company engages in few foreign functions—for example, when it just exports its home-country production—it must be aware of only those cultural factors that may influence its marketing program. Consider advertising, which may be affected by the target market's perception of different words and images. A company undertaking a purely resource-seeking foreign activity by manufacturing abroad can ignore the effects of cultural variables on advertising but must consider factors that may influence management of a foreign workforce, such as the management styles and operational practices most likely to motivate its workforce. For multifunctional activities, such as producing and selling a product in a foreign country, a company must be concerned with a wide array of cultural relationships. The more countries in which a company does business, the more cultural nuances it must consider.

A company may handle foreign operations on its own or contract with another company to handle them. The risk of making operating mistakes because of cultural misunderstandings goes down if it turns foreign operations over to another company at home or abroad that is experienced in the foreign country. If the operations are contracted to a company abroad, then each company needs some cultural awareness to anticipate and understand the other company's reactions.

IDENTIFICATION AND DYNAMICS OF CULTURES

Cultures are elusive objects of study. There is no universally satisfactory definition of the domain of a culture. Cultures consist of people with shared attitudes, values, and beliefs; people simultaneously belong to national, ethnic, professional, and organizational cultures. At the same time, individual and group attitudes, values, and beliefs evolve. In the following discussion, we will first explain why nations are a useful, but not perfect, cultural reference for international business. Next, we'll discuss why cultures develop and change. Finally, we'll show the role of language and religion as stabilizing influences on culture.

The Nation as a Point of Reference

The nation is a useful definition of society because

• Similarity among people is a cause and an effect of national boundaries

• Laws apply primarily along national lines

The nation provides a workable definition of a culture for international business because the basic similarity among people is both a cause and an effect of national boundaries. The laws governing business operations also apply primarily along national lines. Within the bounds of a nation are people who share essential attributes, such as values, language, and race. There is a feeling of "we," whereas foreigners are "they." National identity is perpetuated through rites and symbols of the country—flags, parades, rallies—and a common perception of history results from the preservation of national sites, documents, monuments, and museums. These shared attributes do not mean that everyone in a country is alike. Nor do they suggest that each country is unique in all respects. In fact, nations usually include various subcultures, ethnic groups, races, and classes, some of which transcend national boundaries (e.g., the ethnic Chinese in various Asian countries are hybrids of Chinese and local cultures).[3] However, the nation legitimizes itself by being the mediator of the different interests.[4] Failure to serve adequately in this mediating role may cause the nation to dissolve. Nevertheless, each nation possesses certain human, demographic, and behavioral characteristics that constitute its national identity and that may affect a company's methods of conducting business effectively in that country.

Managers find country-by-country analysis difficult because

• Not everyone in a country is alike

• Variations within some countries are great

• Similarities link groups from different countries

Similarities can link groups from different nations more closely than groups within a nation. For instance, regardless of the nation examined, people in urban areas differ in certain attitudes from people in rural areas, and managers have different work attitudes than production workers do. Thus, managers in countries A and B may hold more similar values with each other than either person holds with production workers in his or her own country. When international businesspeople compare nations, they must be careful to examine relevant groups,—for example, by differentiating between people in rural and urban areas of a country when predicting what will be accepted. Nevertheless, these groups may differ because of organizational cultures. For example, scientists at Cambridge and MIT set up a well-funded joint institute to enhance the impact of teaching and research on economic success. However, the institute worked poorly because of different attitudes toward links with businesses.[5]

Cultural Formation and Dynamics

Culture is transmitted in various ways—from parent to child, teacher to pupil, social leader to follower, and one peer to another. The parent-to-child route is especially important in the transmission of religious and political affiliations. Developmental psychologists believe that by age 10, most children have their basic value systems firmly in place, after which they do not make changes easily. These basic values include such concepts as evil versus good, dirty versus clean, ugly versus beautiful, unnatural versus natural, abnormal versus normal, paradoxical versus logical, and irrational versus rational.[6]

However, individual and societal values and customs may evolve over time. Examining this evolution and its causes may reveal something about the process by which the new practices are accepted, thus aiding international companies that would like to introduce changes into the culture. Change may come about through choice or imposition. Change by choice may take place as a reaction to social and economic changes that present new alternatives. For example, when rural people choose to accept factory jobs, they change their customs by working regular hours that don't allow the social interaction with their families during work hours that farmwork allowed. Change by imposition, sometimes called **cultural imperialism**, has occurred, for example, when countries introduced their legal systems into their colonies by prohibiting established practices and defining them as criminal. The introduction of some, but not all, elements of an outside culture often is called *creolization, indigenization,* or *cultural diffusion.* International business increases changes in cultures, and governments have often limited such business to protect their national cultures. However, such protection is less successful as people access foreign information through better international communications.[7]

Language as a Cultural Stabilizer

In addition to national boundaries and geographical obstacles, language is a factor that greatly affects cultural stability. Map 2.2 approximates the world's major language groups. When people from different areas speak the same language, culture spreads easily. That helps explain why more cultural similarity exists among English-speaking countries or among Spanish-speaking ones than between English-speaking and Spanish-speaking countries. Map 2.2 does not include most of the world's approximately 6,000 languages spoken in small areas by few people. When people speak only a language with few speakers, especially if those speakers are concentrated in a small geographic area, they tend to adhere to their culture because meaningful contact with others is difficult. For example, in Guatemala, the official language is Spanish. However, there are 22 ethnic groups, three main ethnic languages, and derivations of those three.[8] The ethnic differences in Guatemala (and in some other countries) have led to political strife that undermines a company's ability to conduct business. The language diversity has also made it difficult for companies to integrate their workforces and to market their products on a truly national level.

The English, French, and Spanish languages have such widespread acceptance (they are spoken prevalently in 44, 27, and 20 countries, respectively) that native speakers of these languages don't generally try to learn other languages as much as do speakers of languages that are official in only one country, such as Finnish and Greek. Commerce can occur more easily with other nations that share the same language because expensive and time-consuming translation is unnecessary. When people study a second language, they usually choose one that is useful in

Cultural value systems are set early in life but may change through

- Choice or imposition
- Contact with other cultures

A common language within countries is a unifying force.

MAP 2.2   Major Languages of the World

Thousands of languages are spoken globally, but a few dominate. This map shows 12 major ones. Note that English, French, or Spanish is the primary language in a significant portion of the world's countries. Some other languages, such as Mandarin and Hindi, are prevalent in only one country but are important to international business because of the number of speakers.

Source: http://www.udon.de/ sprachk.htm. The number of native speakers is taken from *World Almanac and Book of Facts* (Mahwah, NJ: Primedia Reference, 2002).

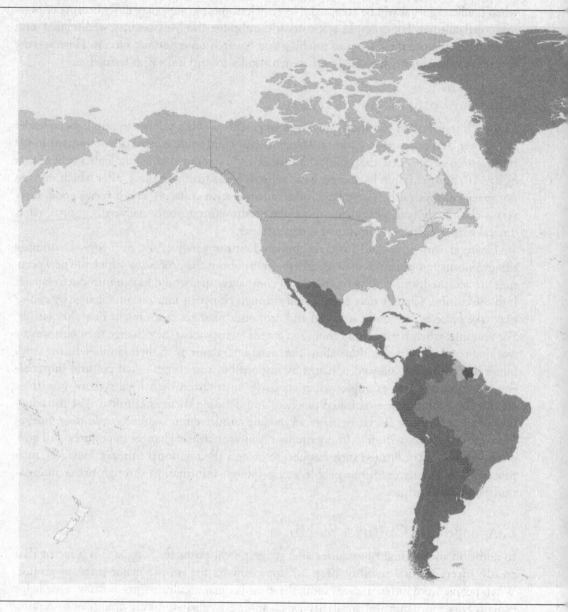

dealing with other countries, especially in commerce. Figure 2.2 shows the share of world output accounted for by major language groups. It is easy to see why English is the most important second language and why much of the world's business is conducted in English.

English, especially American English, words are making their way into languages worldwide, partly because the United States originates so much new technology as well as so many products and services. When a new product or service enters another language area, it may take on an Anglicized name. For example, Russians call tight denim pants *dzhinsi* (pronounced "jeansy"), and the French call a self-service restaurant *le self.* An estimated 20,000 English words have entered the Japanese language. As English has entered other languages, we see the development of hybrids, such as Spanglish (Spanish and English) and Chinglish (Mandarin Chinese and English), that may ultimately become separate languages.[9] However, some countries, such as Finland, have largely developed their own new words rather than use Anglicized versions. Because countries see language as an integral part of their cultures, they sometimes regulate their languages—for example, by requiring that all business transactions be conducted and all "Made in _____" labels be printed in their languages.

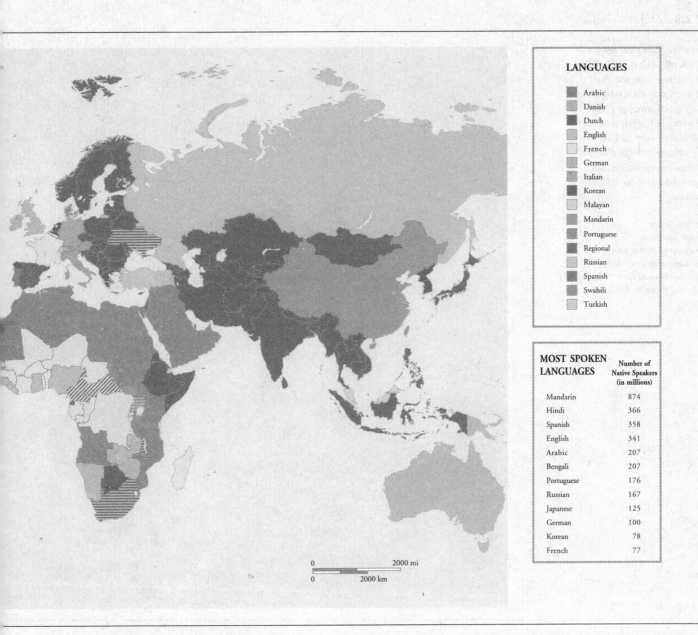

LANGUAGES
Arabic
Danish
Dutch
English
French
German
Italian
Korean
Malayan
Mandarin
Portuguese
Regional
Russian
Spanish
Swahili
Turkish

MOST SPOKEN LANGUAGES	Number of Native Speakers (in millions)
Mandarin	874
Hindi	366
Spanish	358
English	341
Arabic	207
Bengali	207
Portuguese	176
Russian	167
Japanese	125
German	100
Korean	78
French	77

FIGURE 2.2   Portion of World Output Accounted for by Major Language Groups

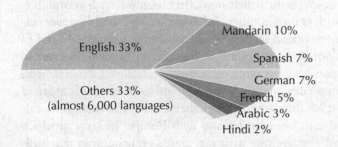

English 33%

Mandarin 10%

Spanish 7%

German 7%

French 5%

Arabic 3%

Hindi 2%

Others 33%
(almost 6,000 languages)

The portion of world output (the value of goods and services produced) from language groups differs substantially from the portion of people in each language group that Map 2.2 shows. People tend to learn a second language because of their need to communicate where output takes place.

Source: Data were taken from estimates by Brian Reading, "Speaking in Tongues Won't Do at Work," *Financial Times* (January 17–18, 1998): p. xxi

MAP 2.3   Major Religions of the World

Almost all regions have people of various religious beliefs, but a region's culture is most influenced by its dominant religion. Some religions' areas of dominance transcend national boundaries. The dominant religion usually influences legal and customary business practices, such as required days off for religious observance.

Source: http://www.warmware.com/world-religions/map.gif. The numbers for adherents are taken from *World Almanac and Book of Facts* (Mahwah, NJ: Primedia Reference, 2002).

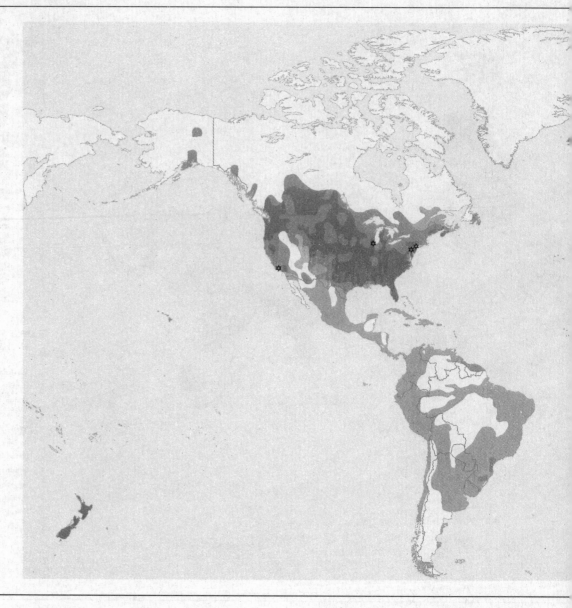

Religion as a Cultural Stabilizer

Religion is a strong shaper of values. Map 2.3 shows the approximate distribution of the world's major religions. Within these religions—Buddhism, Christianity, Hinduism, Islam, and Judaism—are many factions whose specific beliefs may affect business, such as prohibiting the sale of certain products or work at certain times. For example, McDonald's serves neither beef nor pork in India so as not to offend its Hindu and Muslim populations,[10] and El Al, the Israeli national airline, does not fly on Saturday, the holy day in Judaism. But not all nations that practice the same religion have the same constraints on business. For example, Friday is normally not a workday in predominantly Muslim countries because it is a day of worship; however, Turkey is a secular Muslim country that adheres to the Christian work calendar in order to be more productive in business dealings with Europe. In areas in which rival religions vie for political control, the resulting strife can cause so much unrest that business is disrupted through property damage, difficulty in getting supplies, and the inability to reach customers. In recent years, violence among religious groups has erupted in India, Northern Ireland, and Yugoslavia.

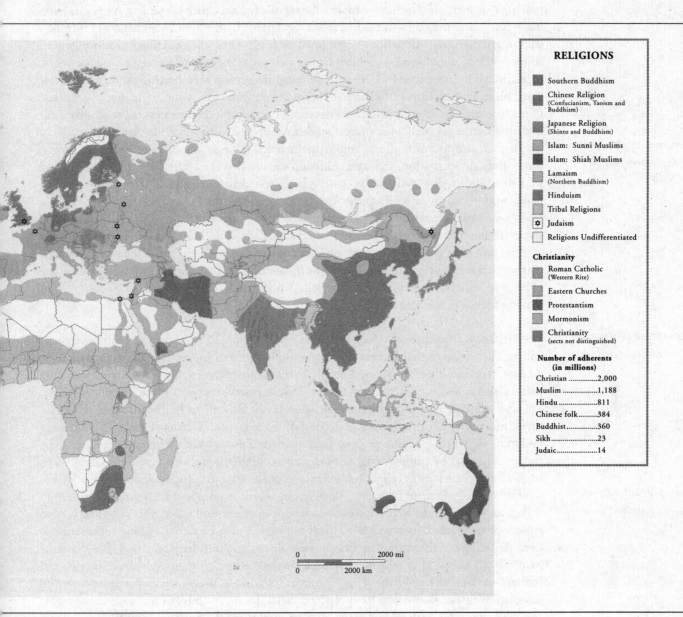

RELIGIONS

Southern Buddhism

Chinese Religion
(Confucianism, Taoism and Buddhism)

Japanese Religion
(Shinto and Buddhism)

Islam: Sunni Muslims

Islam: Shiah Muslims

Lamaism
(Northern Buddhism)

Hinduism

Tribal Religions

Judaism

Religions Undifferentiated

Christianity

Roman Catholic
(Western Rite)

Eastern Churches

Protestantism

Mormonism

Christianity
(sects not distinguished)

**Number of adherents
(in millions)**

Christian 2,000
Muslim 1,188
Hindu 811
Chinese folk..........384
Buddhist...............360
Sikh 23
Judaic...................14

0   2000 mi
0   2000 km

BEHAVIORAL PRACTICES AFFECTING BUSINESS

Attitudes and values affect business behavior, from what products to sell to how to organize, finance, manage, and control operations. Researchers define cultural variables differently, attaching different names to slightly different and sometimes overlapping attitudes and values. Similarly, businesspeople define business functions differently. The result is that there are thousands of possible ways of relating culture to business—too many to discuss exhaustively in one chapter. The following discussion merely highlights those that international managers and academic researchers have most noted as influencing different business practices from one country to another. We shall further discuss the effect of these and other cultural variables in later chapters.

Social Stratification Systems

Every culture values some people more highly than others, and such distinctions dictate a person's class or status within that culture. In business, this might mean valuing members of managerial groups more highly than members of production groups. However, what determines the

Group affiliations can be

• Ascribed or acquired
• A reflection of class and status

ranking—or social stratification—varies substantially from country to country. A person's ranking is partly determined by individual factors and partly by the person's affiliation or membership in given groups. Affiliations determined by birth—known as **ascribed group memberships**—include those based on gender, family, age, caste, and ethnic, racial, or national origin. Affiliations not determined by birth are called **acquired group memberships** and include those based on religion, political affiliation, and professional and other associations. Social stratification affects such business functions as marketing. For example, companies choose to use people in their advertisements that their target market admires or with whom they associate.

Further, stratification affects employment practices. A study comparing banks' hiring, promotion, compensation, and staff reduction showed that they differed by nationality on all four dimensions. For example, when the banks needed to make staff reductions, British banks were most prone to discharge on the basis of performance-to-salary (for example, a middle-age manager with high salary and average performance) and German banks to discharge young managers (regardless of performance) who could find jobs more easily.[11]

The following discussion centers on some of the characteristics and group memberships that influence a person's ranking from country to country. In addition, two other factors are often very important—education (especially where it was received) and social connections (having friends in the highest places).[12]

Performance Orientation   Some nations reward people for performance improvement and excellence more than others do, for example more so in the United States and New Zealand than in Greece or Japan.[13] People in the United States value performance so highly that legislative and judicial actions aim to prevent discrimination on the basis of sex, race, age, and religion, even though such legislation is not fully effective. But in some other cultures, individual performance is of secondary importance. Whatever factor has primary importance—whether seniority, as in Japan (where the workplace is characterized more by cooperation than by compeition), or humaneness (kindness and tolerant of mistakes)—will largely influence a person's eligibility for certain positions and compensation.[14]

The more egalitarian, or open, a society, the less difference ascribed group membership makes for receiving rewards. However, in less open societies, laws sometimes are a way to enforce or are a means to overcome distinctions on the basis of ascribed group memberships. Laws requiring racial or ethnic quotas usually aim to counter discrimination. For example, Malaysia has long had employment quotas for three ethnic groups—Malays, Chinese, and Indians—to protect employment opportunities for Malays. Brazil, which has more than 300 terms to designate skin color, has proposed racial quotas in universities, government jobs, and television soap operas.[15] (It plans no such quotas for the national football team, where only competence counts.) However, critics argue that quotas favor less competent over more competent people and are, therefore, discriminatory. In other cases, group memberships prevent large numbers of people from getting the preparation that would equally qualify them for jobs. For example, in the Middle Eastern and North African countries, the mean years of schooling for women is two to three years lower than for men.[16] Companies face very different workforces from one country to another in terms of who is qualified and who among the qualified they can and do hire. In some places, such as Malaysia, they must also maintain expensive record-keeping systems.

Even when individuals qualify for certain positions and there are no legal barriers to hiring them, social obstacles, such as public opinion in a company's home country against the use of child labor, may make companies wary of employing them abroad. Further, other workers, customers, local stockholders, or government officials may oppose certain groups, making it even more difficult for companies to hire them.

Gender-Based Groups   There are strong country-specific differences in attitudes toward males and females. In China and India, there is an extreme degree of male preference. Because

Managers must consider local stratification systems when hiring personnel.

Businesses reward performance highly in some societies.

Egalitarian societies place less importance on ascribed group memberships.

Country-by-country attitudes vary toward
• Male and female roles
• Respect for age
• Family ties

of both their governmental and economic restrictions on family size as well as the desire to have a son to carry on the family name, the practices of aborting female fetuses and killing female babies are widespread despite government opposition.[17] However, many Chinese and Indian females have been successful in business and government positions. In some countries, such as Egypt and Qatar, there is a strong preference against gender equality.[18] Recall in the opening case the practices prescribed for women in Saudi Arabia.

Even among countries in which women constitute a large portion of the working population, vast differences exist in the types of jobs regarded as "male" or "female." For example, in the United States, women fill a higher percent of administrative and managerial positions, than in Japan.

Barriers to employment based on gender are easing substantially in many parts of the world. Statistical and attitudinal studies from even a few years ago may be considered unreliable. One change has been the growing numbers of women and men in the United States employed in occupations previously dominated by the other gender. Even in Saudi Arabia, women now work at some hotel reception desks.[19]

Age-Based Groups   Many cultures assume that age and wisdom are correlated. These cultures usually have a seniority-based system of advancement. But in the United States, retirement at age 60 or 65 was mandatory in most companies until the 1980s, revealing that youth has the professional advantage. For example, U.S. television scriptwriters complain of an inability of finding jobs after age 30. The emphasis on youth also explains the big U.S. market for products that are designed to make people look younger. However, this esteem for youth has not carried over into the U.S. political realm where there is no mandatory retirement age. This difference in attitude toward age between business and government illustrates the issue's complexity. Clearly, companies need to examine reference groups when considering whom they may hire and how best to promote their products.

Family-Based Groups   In some societies, the family is the most important group membership. An individual's acceptance in society largely depends on the family's social status or respectability rather than on the individual's achievement. Because family ties are so strong, there also may be a compulsion to cooperate closely within the family unit while distrusting relationships with others. In societies in which there is low trust outside the family, such as in China and southern Italy, small family-run companies are more successful than large business organizations. But the difficulty of expanding family-run companies retards these countries' economic development because large-scale operations are often necessary for many products.[20]

Occupation   In every society, people perceive certain occupations as having greater economic and social prestige than others. This perception usually determines the numbers and qualifications of people who will seek employment in a given occupation. Although some perceptions are universal (for example, professionals outrank street cleaners), there are some international differences. For instance, university professors are more influential as opinion leaders in Korea and Japan than in the United States and the United Kingdom.[21]

Another international difference is citizens' desire to work as entrepreneurs rather than for an organization. For example, the Belgians and the French, more than most other nationalities, prefer, if possible, to go into business for themselves. Thus, Belgium and France have more retail establishments per capita than most other countries. Owning a small or medium-size enterprise—rather than earning more income—is a means for Belgian and French people to move up socially from the working class. Further, psychological studies show that Belgian and French workers place a greater importance on personal independence from the organizations employing them than do workers in many other countries.[22] An implication is

The perception of what jobs are "best" varies somewhat among countries.

that foreign retailers operating in Belgium and France encounter competition much more from small local retailers than in most other countries.

Jobs with low prestige usually go to people whose skills are in low demand. In the United States, occupations such as baby-sitting, delivering newspapers, and carrying groceries traditionally go to teenagers, who leave these jobs as they age and gain additional training. In most poor countries, these are not transient occupations but are filled by adults who have very little opportunity to move on to more rewarding positions.

Motivation

Employees who are motivated to work long and hard are normally more productive than those who are not. On an aggregate basis, this influences economic development positively. For example, a study on why some areas of Latin America, such as Antioquia in Colombia, developed a higher economic level than others attributed differences to an early development of a strong work ethic.[23] International companies are concerned about economic development because markets for their products grow as economies grow. They are also interested in motivation because higher productivity normally reduces production costs. Studies show substantial country-to-country differences in how much people are motivated to work and why. The following discussion summarizes the major differences.

Materialism and Leisure   Max Weber, an early twentieth-century German sociologist, observed that the predominantly Protestant countries were the most economically developed. Weber attributed this fact to an attitude he labeled "the Protestant ethic." According to Weber, the Protestant ethic—an outgrowth of the Reformation—reflected the view that work is a way to gain salvation. Adhering to this view, people preferred to transform productivity into material gains rather than into leisure time. Historically, there is strong evidence that the desire for material wealth is a prime incentive for the work that leads to economic development.[24]

Some societies take less leisure time than others, which means they work longer hours, take fewer days for holidays and vacation, and spend less time and money on leisure. For example, on average, the Japanese take less leisure than do people in any other wealthy country. In the United States, another country where incomes probably allow for considerably more leisure time than most people use, there is still much disdain, on the one hand, for the millionaire socialite who contributes nothing to society and, on the other hand, for the person who receives unemployment benefits. People who are forced to give up work, such as retirees, complain of their inability to do anything useful. This view contrasts with views in some other societies. In much of Europe, people have been more prone than in the United States to take added productivity in the form of leisure rather than income.[25] In parts of some poor countries, such as in rural India, living a simple life with minimum material achievements is a desirable end in itself. When there are productivity gains, people are prone to work less rather than earn and buy more.[26]

However, most people today consider personal economic achievement to be commendable regardless of whether they live in wealthy or poor countries. Most people believe they would be happy with just "a little bit more," until they have that "little bit more," which then turns out to be "not quite enough." Nevertheless, countries differ in their degree of materialism. For example, some leaders in poor countries are rejecting the labels of *traditional* for themselves and *progressive* for the higher-income countries, as they stress the need for a culture that combines material comforts with spirituality.[27]

Expectation of Success and Reward   One factor that motivates a person's behavior toward working is the perceived likelihood of success and reward. Generally, people have little enthusiasm for efforts that seem too easy or too difficult, where the probability of either

In the most economically developed countries, most people work to satisfy materialistic needs.

Good international managers know that the motives for working vary in different countries.

Employees' work attitudes may change as they achieve economic gains.

People are more eager to work if
- Rewards for success are high
- There is some uncertainty of success

success or failure seems almost certain. For instance, few of us would be eager to run a foot race against either a snail or a racehorse because the outcome in either case is too certain. Our highest enthusiasm occurs when the uncertainty is high—in this example, when racing another human of roughly equal ability. The reward for successfully completing an effort, such as winning a race, may be high or low as well. People usually will work harder at any task when the reward for success is high compared with that of failure.

The same tasks performed in different countries will have different probabilities of success, different rewards for success, and different consequences for failure. In cultures in which the probability of economic failure is almost certain and the perceived rewards of success are low, there is a tendency to view work as necessary but unsatisfying. Because people see little self-benefit from their efforts, this attitude may exist in harsh climates, in very poor areas, or in subcultures that are the objects of discrimination. In areas such as Cuba, where public policies distribute output from productive to unproductive workers, enthusiasm for work is low. The greatest enthusiasm for work exists when high uncertainty of success is combined with the likelihood of a very positive reward for success and little or none for failure.[28]

Assertiveness   The average interest in career success varies substantially among countries. For example, one study compared the attitudes of employees from 50 countries on a masculinity index. Employees with a high masculinity score were those who admired the successful achiever, had little sympathy for the unfortunate, and preferred to be the best rather than on a par with others. They had a money-and-things orientation rather than a people orientation, a belief that it is better "to live to work" than "to work to live," and a preference for performance and growth over quality of life and the environment. The countries with the highest masculinity scores were Japan, Austria, Venezuela, and Switzerland. Those with the lowest scores were Sweden, Norway, the Netherlands, and Denmark.[29] Similarly, countries differ in the degree that individuals are assertive, confrontational, and aggressive in their relationships with others.[30] These attitudinal differences help explain why local managers typically react in different ways from country to country, sometimes in ways that an international manager may neither expect nor wish. For instance, a typical purchasing manager from a low masculinity country has a high need for smooth social relationships that transforms into more concern with developing an amiable and continuing relationship with suppliers than with, say, reducing costs or speeding delivery. Or local managers in some countries may place such organizational goals as employee and social welfare ahead of the foreign company's priorities for growth and efficiency.

Need Hierarchy   The hierarchy of needs is a well-known motivation theory. According to the theory, people try to fulfill lower-order needs sufficiently before moving on to higher ones.[31] People will work to satisfy a need, but once it is fulfilled, it is no longer a motivator. The Calvin and Hobbes cartoon in Figure 2.3 ties the hierarchy of needs theory to materialism theory humorously. Because lower-order needs are more important than higher-order ones, they must be nearly fulfilled before any higher-order need becomes an effective motivator. For instance, the most basic needs are physiological, including the needs for food, water, and sex. One needs to satisfy or nearly satisfy (say, 85 percent satisfied) a physiological need before a security need becomes a powerful motivator. Then one must satisfy the security need, centering around a safe physical and emotional environment, before triggering the need for affiliation, or social belonging (peer acceptance). After filling the affiliation need, a person may seek an esteem need—the need to bolster one's self-image through recognition, attention, and appreciation. The highest-order need is that for self-actualization, which means self-fulfillment, or becoming all that it is possible for one to become.

FIGURE 2.3

A fulfilled need is no longer a motivator. Materialism motivates work, which leads to productivity and economic growth.

Source: CALVIN AND HOBBES ©

The ranking of needs differs among countries.

The hierarchy of needs theory is helpful for differentiating the reward preferences of employees in different countries. In very poor countries, a company can motivate workers simply by providing enough compensation for food and shelter. Elsewhere, other needs will motivate workers. Researchers have noted that people from different countries attach different degrees of importance to needs and even rank some of the higher-order needs differently. Figure 2.4 illustrates these differences.

Relationship Preferences

We have discussed two categories of behavioral practices affecting business—social stratification systems and motivation. Within social stratification systems, not everyone within a reference group is necessarily an equal. Further, there may be strong or weak pressures for conformity within one's group. In both cases, there are national differences in norms that influence management styles and marketing behavior. The following section discusses the values underlying these differences.

FIGURE 2.4   The Hierarchy of Needs and Need-Hierarchy Comparisons

The lower hierarchy on the right has a wider affiliation bar (3) and a narrower self-actualization bar (5) than the upper one. People represented by the lower hierarchy require more affiliation needs to be fulfilled before a self-esteem need (4) will be triggered as a motivator. These people would be less motivated by self-actualization than would those represented by the upper hierarchy.

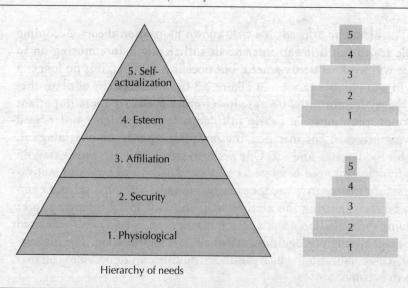

Power Distance   Employee preferences in how to interact with their bosses, subordinates, and peers varies substantially internationally. There is considerable anecdotal evidence that they perform better when their interactions fit their preferences. Therefore, companies may need to align their management styles to those preferences.

There are national variations in preference for autocratic or consultative management.

Power distance is a term describing the relationship between superiors and subordinates. Where power distance is high, people prefer little consultation between superiors and subordinates—usually wanting and having an autocratic or paternalistic management style in their organizations. Where power distance is low, people prefer and usually have consultative styles.[32]

If an international company transferred typical Dutch managers (typically low-power distance) to Morocco (typically high-power distance), these managers might consult with their subordinates in an attempt to improve their work. However, these efforts might make subordinates feel so uncomfortable that their performance deteriorates rather than improves.

It is interesting that those employees preferring an autocratic style of superior–subordinate relationship are also willing to accept decision making by a majority of subordinates. What they don't accept is the interaction between superiors and subordinates in decision making. Clearly, it may be easier for organizations to initiate certain types of worker-participation methods in some countries than in others.

Individualism Versus Collectivism   Studies have compared employees' inclinations toward *individualism* or *collectivism*. Attributes of individualism are low dependence on the organization and a desire for personal time, freedom, and challenge. Attributes of collectivism are loyalty and/or dependence on the organization. In those countries with high individualism, self-actualization will be a prime motivator because employees want challenges. However, in countries with high collectivism, the provision of a safe physical and emotional environment (security need) will be a prime motivator.[33]

"Safe" work environments motivate collectivists. Challenges motivate individualists.

The degree of individualism and collectivism also influences how employees interact with their colleagues. Japan has a much more collectivist culture than the United States does, especially concerning the work group, and this causes contrasts at work. For example, a U.S. scientist invited to work in a Japanese laboratory was treated as an outsider until he demonstrated his willingness to subordinate his personal interests to those of the group. He did so by mopping the lab floor for several weeks, after which he was invited to join the group.[34] In contrast, Levi's introduced team-based production for U.S. plants because its management had observed high productivity from that system in Asian plants. U.S. employees—especially the faster, more skilled ones—detested the system, productivity decreased, and Levi's abandoned the team-based production system.[35]

However, measuring country differences in terms of individualism versus collectivism is complex and controversial.[36] As a result, people may vary their individualism depending on circumstances. For example, although China and Mexico are characterized as collectivist cultures, they differ from Japan insofar as the collectivism is based on kinship and does not carry over to the workplace.[37] Further, the concept of family in China and Mexico includes not only a nuclear family (a husband, wife, and minor children) but also a vertically extended family (several generations) and perhaps a horizontally extended one (aunts, uncles, and cousins). This difference affects business in several ways. First, material rewards from an individual's work may be less motivating because these rewards are divided among more people. Second, geographical mobility is reduced because relocation means other members of a family also have to find new jobs. Even in cases in which extended families do not live together, mobility may be reduced because people prefer to remain near relatives. Third, purchasing decisions may be more complicated because of the interrelated roles of family members. Fourth, security and social needs may be met more extensively at home than in the workplace.

Where collectivism is high, companies find their best marketing successes when emphasizing advertising themes that express group (rather than individual) values. For example,

Marlboro cigarettes have had better success in Asian markets than Camel cigarettes, partially because their marketing campaigns have used group themes more.[38]

Risk-Taking Behavior

Nationalities differ in how happy people are to accept things the way they are and how they feel about controlling their destinies. The following discussion examines four aspects of risk-taking behavior—uncertainty avoidance, trust, future orientation, and fatalism—across nations.

Uncertainty Avoidance   Studies on uncertainty avoidance show that in countries with the highest scores on uncertainty avoidance, employees prefer set rules that are not to be broken even if breaking them is sometimes in the company's best interest. Further, these employees plan to work for the company a long time, preferring the certainty of their present positions over the uncertainty of better advancement opportunities elsewhere.[39] When uncertainty avoidance is high, superiors may need to be more precise and assured in the directions they give to subordinates because the subordinates are not motivated to figure out what they need to do to advance the company's interests.

In countries characterized by high uncertainty avoidance, few consumers are prepared to take the risk of trying a new product first. This is very important when it comes time for firms to choose where to introduce new products. For example, 40 percent of Gillette's sales come from products it has introduced in the last five years. It may be advantageous for Gillette to enter markets with low uncertainty avoidance before entering those with high uncertainty avoidance.[40]

Trust   Surveys that measure trust among countries by having respondents evaluate such statements as "Most people can be trusted" and "You can't be too careful in dealing with people" indicate substantial international differences. For example, a much higher percentage of Norwegians than Brazilians think most people are trustworthy. Where trust is high, there tends to be a lower cost of doing business because managers do not have to spend time foreseeing every possible contingency and then monitoring every action for compliance in business relationships. Instead, they can spend time investing and innovating.[41] Norwegians and Brazilians may actually be responding to the conditions existing in their respective countries. A Norwegian businessperson going to Brazil may act too naively, whereas a Brazilian going to Norway may act too cautiously.

Future Orientation   Countries also differ in the extent to which individuals live for the present rather than the future because they see risks in delaying gratification and investing for the future. For example, the future orientation is higher in Switzerland, the Netherlands, and Canada than in Russia, Poland, and Italy.[42] Where future orientation is higher, companies may be able to better motivate workers through delayed compensation, such as retirement programs.

Fatalism   If people believe strongly in self-determination, they may be willing to work hard to achieve goals and take responsibility for performance. But a belief in fatalism, that every event is inevitable, may prevent people from accepting this basic cause-and-effect relationship. The effect on business in countries with a high degree of fatalism is that people plan less for contingencies. For example, they may be reluctant to buy insurance. In this regard, religious differences play a part. Conservative or fundamentalist Christian, Buddhist, Hindu, and Muslim societies tend to view occurrences as "the will of God."

Information and Task Processing

The nineteenth-century author Margaret Hungerford wrote, "Beauty is altogether in the eye of the beholder." People do perceive and reach conclusions differently. So do cultures. Further, once people have what they perceive as accurate information, they handle this information in different ways. The following discussion examines how people from different cultures perceive, obtain, and process information.

Perception of Cues   We perceive cues selectively. We may identify what things are by means of any of our senses (sight, smell, touch, sound, or taste) and in various ways within each sense. For example, through vision, we can sense color, depth, and shape. The cues people use to perceive things differ among societies. The reason is partly physiological. For example, genetic differences in eye pigmentation enable some groups to differentiate colors more finely than others can. It also is partly cultural. For example, a richness of descriptive vocabulary can allow people to express very subtle differences in color. Further, this difference in richness allows each culture to perceive some subjects more precisely than other cultures. For example, Arabic has more than 6,000 different words for camels, their body parts, and the equipment associated with them.[43] Arabic speakers can note things about camels that are most likely overlooked by other speakers.

Obtaining Information   In spite of vast differences within countries, some, such as the United States and those in northern Europe, are categorized as being **low-context cultures**—that is, most people consider relevant only firsthand information that bears directly on the decision they need to make. In business, they spend little time on small talk and say things directly. However, other countries—for example, those in southern Europe—are **high-context cultures** (i.e., most people believe that peripheral information is valuable to decision making and infer meanings from things said indirectly). When managers from the two types of cultures deal with each other, the low-context individuals may believe the high-context ones are inefficient and time wasters. The high-context individuals may believe the low-context ones are too aggressive to be trusted. (Recall the opening case in which the English salesmen had problems dealing with their Saudi counterparts.)

Information Processing   Information processing is universal insofar as all cultures categorize, plan, and quantify. All cultures also have ordering and classifying systems. However, sometimes cultures do this differently from one another. In U.S. telephone directories, the entries appear in alphabetical order by last (family) name. In Iceland, entries are organized by first (given) names. Icelandic last names are derived from the father's first name: Jon, the son of Thor, is Jon Thorsson, and his sister's last name is Thorsdottir (daughter of Thor). One needs to understand the different ordering and classifying systems to perform efficiently in a foreign environment. Further, the different ordering and classifying systems create challenges that make it difficult for companies to use global data effectively. Even the use of global personnel directories is problematic because of different alphabetizing systems. Information processing also includes ordering tasks. Cultures, such as those in northern Europe, are called **monochronic**; in such cultures, people prefer to work sequentially (people will finish with one customer before dealing with another). Conversely, **polychronic** southern Europeans are more comfortable when working simultaneously on all the tasks they face. For example, they feel uncomfortable when not dealing immediately with all customers who need service.[44] Imagine the potential misconceptions that can occur. Scandinavian businesspeople might erroneously believe their Italian counterparts are uninterested in doing business with them if they fail to give them their undivided attention.

Some cultures tend to focus first on the whole and then on the parts, whereas others do the opposite. For example, when asked to describe an underwater scene in which one large fish swam among smaller fish and other aquatic life, most Japanese first described the overall picture and most Americans first described the large fish.[45] Similarly, some cultures will determine principles before they try to resolve small issues (idealism), while other cultures will focus more on details rather than principles (pragmatism). From a business standpoint, the differences manifest information processing in a number of ways. For example, in a

All languages are complex and reflective of environment. Without knowing the language of the area, a manager may not perceive the subtleties of that environment.

It helps managers to know whether cultures favor

- Focused or broad information
- Sequential or simultaneous handling of situations
- Handling principles or small issues first

society of pragmatists such as the United States, labor disputes tend to focus on specific issues—for example, increase pay by a dollar per hour. In a society of idealists such as Argentina, labor disputes tend to lead to less precise demands and depend instead on mass action, such as general strikes or support of a particular political party, to publicize their principles.

STRATEGIES FOR DEALING WITH CULTURAL DIFFERENCES

After a company identifies cultural differences in the foreign country where it intends to do business, must it alter its customary practices to succeed there? How can it avoid misrepresenting its intent? Can individuals overcome adjustment problems when working abroad? What strategies can a company follow to get host cultures to accept the innovations it would like to introduce? There are no easy answers to these questions.

Making Little or No Adjustment

Host cultures do not always expect foreigners to adjust to them.

Although the opening case illustrates the advantages of adjusting, such as Harvey Nichols providing drivers' lounges and prayer rooms in its Saudi Arabian department store, international companies sometimes have succeeded in introducing new products, technologies, and operating procedures to foreign countries with little adjustment. That's because some of these introductions have not run counter to deep-seated attitudes or because the host society is willing to accept foreign customs as a trade-off for other advantages. Bahrain has permitted the sale of pork products (otherwise outlawed by religious law) as long as they are sold in separate rooms of grocery stores where Muslims can neither work nor shop.

Often local society looks on foreigners and its own citizens differently. For example, Western female flight attendants are permitted to wear jeans and T-shirts in public when staying overnight in Jidda, Saudi Arabia, even though local women cannot.[46] Members of the host society may even feel they are being stereotyped in an uncomplimentary way when foreigners adjust too much.[47] Moreover, Western female managers in Hong Kong say local people see them primarily as foreigners, not as women. There and elsewhere, foreign women are accepted as managers more readily than local women are.[48]

Some countries are relatively similar to one another, usually because they share many attributes that help mold their cultures, such as language, religion, geographical location, ethnicity, and level of economic development. Map 2.4 groups 58 countries by middle managers' attitudes and values about leadership. A company should expect fewer differences (and have to consider fewer adjustments) when moving within a cluster (an Ecuadorian company doing business in Colombia) than when moving from one cluster to another (an Ecuadorian company doing business in Thailand). However, there still may be significant differences within similar countries that could affect business dealings. Managers may expect that seemingly similar countries (those within clusters) are more alike than they really are; a company may be lulled into a complacency that overlooks important subtleties. For example, women's roles and behaviors differ substantially from one Arab country to another.[49]

Communications

Cross-border communications do not always translate as intended.

Thus far, we've seen how language affects culture—and international business. We now look at problems of communications—translating spoken and written language. These problems occur not only in moving from one language to another but also in communicating from one country to another that has the same official language. Second, we discuss communications outside the spoken and written language, the so-called "silent language."

Spoken and Written Language   Translating one language directly into another can be difficult, making international business communication difficult. First, some words do not have a direct translation. For example, there is no one word in Spanish for everyone who works in a business (i.e., *employees*). Instead, there is a word, *empleados*, which means "white-collar workers," and another, *obreros*, which means "laborers." This distinction shows the substantial class difference that exists between the groups, and it affects international business because there may be miscommunication when managers in Spanish-speaking and English-speaking countries come together. Second, languages and the common meaning of words are constantly evolving. For example, Microsoft purchased a thesaurus code for its Spanish version of Word 6.0, but the meaning of many synonyms had changed and become insulting. The company corrected the software after newspapers and radio reports denounced the program, but by then, Microsoft had alienated many potential customers.[50] Third, words mean different things in different contexts. One company described itself as an "old friend" of China. However, it used the word for *old* that meant "former" instead of "long-term."[51] Finally, grammar and pronunciation are complex, and a slight misuse of vocabulary or word placement may change meanings substantially. Consider the following examples of signs in English observed in hotels around the world.

France: "Please leave your values at the desk."

Mexico (to assure guests about the safety of drinking water): "The manager has personally passed all the water served here."

Japan: "You are invited to take advantage of the chambermaid."

Norway: "Ladies are requested not to have children in the bar."

Switzerland: "Because of the impropriety of entertaining guests of the opposite sex in the bedroom, it is suggested that the lobby be used for this purpose."

Greece (at check-in line): "We will execute customers in strict rotation."

The above examples offer a humorous look at language barriers, and, in fact, the wrong choice of words usually is just a source of brief embarrassment. However, a poor translation may have tragic consequences. For example, inaccurate translations have caused structural collapses and airplane crashes, such as the collision between aircraft from Air Kazakhstan and Saudia Air over India.[52] In contracts, correspondence, negotiations, advertisements, and conversations, words must be chosen carefully. There is no foolproof way of handling translations. However, good international business managers use rules such as the following.

- Get references on the people who will do the translation for you.

- Make sure your translator knows the technical vocabulary of your business.

- Do a back translation for written work by having one person go, say, from English to French and a second person translate the French version back into English. If it comes back the same way it started, it is probably satisfactory.

- Use simple words whenever possible, such as *ban* instead of *interdiction*.

- Avoid slang. Such U.S. phrases as *blue chip stocks* and *ballpark figures* are likely to be meaningless to most businesspeople outside the United States.

- When you or your counterpart is dealing in a second language, clarify communications in several ways (such as by repeating in different words and asking questions) to assure that all parties have the same interpretation.

- Recognize the need for and budget from the start for the extra time needed for translation and clarification.

When dealing with someone from another country that shares your official language, don't assume that communication will go smoothly. For example, between the United States

MAP 2.4   A Synthesis of Country Clusters

This map based on the GLOBE study, shows that middle managers in certain countries share similar cultural attitudes and values concerning leadership that may affect business practices. Not all countries have been studied sufficiently to determine how similar they are to other countries. Note that the names for clusters are based on the majority of countries in each cluster; for example, Turkey is in the Arab group, although its language is not Arabic. Costa Rica and Guatemala are in the Latin American group although their attitudes are more similar to the Latin European group.

Source: Vipin Gupta, Paul J. Hanges, and Peter Dorfman, *Journal of World Business* 37, no. 1 (Spring 2002): 13.

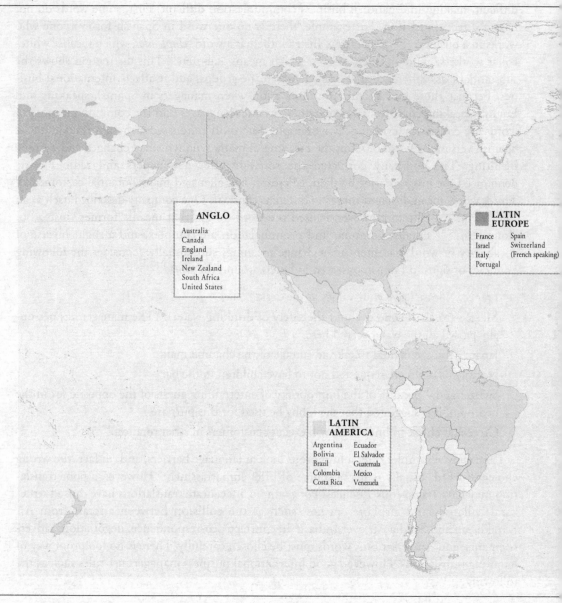

ANGLO

Australia
Canada
England
Ireland
New Zealand
South Africa
United States

LATIN EUROPE

France   Spain
Israel   Switzerland
Italy   (French speaking)
Portugal

LATIN AMERICA

Argentina   Ecuador
Bolivia   El Salvador
Brazil   Guatemala
Colombia   Mexico
Costa Rica Venezuela

Silent language includes color associations, sense of appropriate distance, time and status cues, and body language.

and the United Kingdom, approximately 4,000 words have different meanings. Table 2.1 shows some common business terms that differ in the two countries.

Silent Language   Of course, spoken and written language is not our only means of communicating. We all exchange messages through a host of nonverbal cues that form a silent language.[53] Colors, for example, conjure up meanings that come from cultural experience. In most Western countries, black is associated with death. White has the same connotation in parts of Asia and purple in Latin America. For products to succeed, their colors must match the consumers' frame of reference. For example, United Airlines promoted a new passenger service in Hong Kong by giving white carnations to its best customers there. The promotion backfired because people in Hong Kong give white carnations only in sympathy for a family death.

Another aspect of silent language is the distance between people during conversations. People's sense of appropriate distance is learned and differs among societies. In the United States, for example, the customary distance for a business discussion is 5 to 8 feet. For

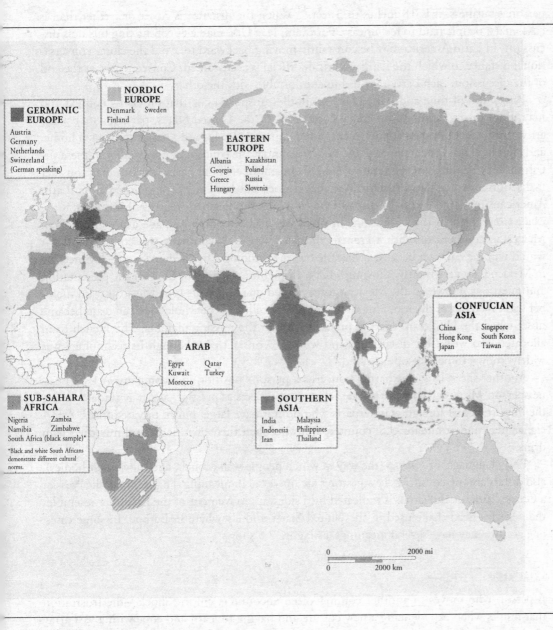

GERMANIC
EUROPE
Austria
Germany
Netherlands
Switzerland
(German speaking)

NORDIC
EUROPE
Denmark   Sweden
Finland

EASTERN
EUROPE
Albania   Kazakhstan
Georgia   Poland
Greece   Russia
Hungary   Slovenia

CONFUCIAN
ASIA
China   Singapore
Hong Kong   South Korea
Japan   Taiwan

ARAB
Egypt   Qatar
Kuwait   Turkey
Morocco

SUB-SAHARA
AFRICA
Nigeria   Zambia
Namibia   Zimbabwe
South Africa (black sample)*

*Black and white South Africans
demonstrate different cultural
norms.

SOUTHERN
ASIA
India   Malaysia
Indonesia   Philippines
Iran   Thailand

0   2000 mi
0   2000 km

● **TABLE 2.1**

BUSINESS LANGUAGE DIFFERENCES

Below are a few of the approximately 4,000 words whose common U.S. and U.K. meanings differ. Although we usually expect comprehension problems when people from two different languages communicate, we may erroneously not expect miscommunication between people from two countries that share the same language.

UNITED STATES	UNITED KINGDOM
turnover	redundancy
sales	turnover
inventory	stock
stock	shares
president	managing director
paperback	limp cover

personal business, it is 18 inches to 3 feet.[54] When the distance is closer or farther than is customary, people tend to feel uneasy. For example, a U.S. manager conducting business discussions in Latin America may be constantly moving backward to avoid the closer conversational distance to which the Latin American official is accustomed. Consequently, at the end of the discussion, each party may feel uncomfortable with the other.

Perception of time and punctuality is another unspoken cue that differs by context and may differ across cultures and create confusion. In the United States, participants usually arrive early for a business appointment, a few minutes late for a dinner at someone's home, and a bit later for a cocktail party. In another country, the concept of punctuality in these situations may be different. For example, a U.S. businessperson in Latin America may consider it discourteous if a Latin American manager does not keep to the appointed time. Latin Americans may find it equally discourteous if a U.S. businessperson arrives for dinner at the exact time given in the invitation. In one case, a U.S. company made a presentation in Mexico in competition with a French company. The U.S. company was confident that it would win the contract because it had the better technology. It scheduled a one-day meeting in Mexico City very tightly, allowing what it thought was plenty of time for the presentation and questions. However, the Mexican team arrived one hour late. One Mexican team member was called out of the room for an urgent phone call, and the whole Mexican team became upset when the U.S. team tried to proceed without the missing member. The French team allocated two weeks for discussions and won the contract even though its technology was widely known to be less sophisticated.[55]

Another silent language barrier concerns a person's position in a company. A U.S. businessperson who tends to place a great reliance on objects as prestige cues may underestimate the importance of foreign counterparts who do not have large, plush, private offices. A foreigner may underestimate U.S. counterparts who open their own doors and mix their own drinks.

Body language, or *kinesics* (the way in which people walk, touch, and move their bodies), also differs among countries. Few gestures are universal in meaning. For example, the "yes" of a Greek, Turk, or Bulgarian is indicated by a sideways movement of the head that resembles the negative head shake used in the United States and elsewhere in Europe. In some cases, one gesture may have several meanings, as Figure 2.5 shows.

Culture Shock

A person who moves to another country often encounters culture shock—the frustration that results when experiencing a new culture and having to learn and cope with a vast array of new cultural cues and expectations. People working in a very different culture may pass through stages. First, like tourists, they are elated with quaint differences. Later, they may feel

Managers should know that perceptual cues—especially those concerning time and status—differ among societies.

Some people get frustrated when entering a different culture.

FIGURE 2.5   Kinesics Are Not Universal

Few gestures are universal. This figure shows that a common and similar gesture has different connotations internationally. The meaning in Germany also prevails in most Latin American countries.

Source: The meanings have been taken from descriptions in Roger E. Axtell, *Gestures* (New York: John Wiley, 1998).

United States
It's fine

Germany
You lunatic

Greece
An obscene symbol for a body orifice

France
Zero or worthless

Japan
Money, especially change

ETHICAL DILEMMA

To Intervene or Not to Intervene

Neither international companies nor their employees are always expected to adhere to a host society's behavioral norms. In fact, exposure to certain practices may be traumatic to foreigners. For example, many practices that Western culture considers wrong are customary elsewhere, such as slavery, polygamy, concubinage, child marriage, and the burning of widows. Some companies have avoided operating in locales in which such practices occur, whereas others have pressured a host country to change the "wrong" behaviors.

A thorny ethical question concerns international business practices that do not clash with foreign values directly but that, nevertheless, may undermine the host country's long-term cultural identity. Consider the use of a company's home-country language or cultural artifacts and the introduction of products and work methods that cause changes in social relationships. Host countries have sometimes reacted negatively to such use. For example, Finns have criticized MNEs for introducing non-Finnish architecture, and France fined Bodyshop for using English in its French stores.[57]

The Society for Applied Anthropology, which advises government and nongovernment agencies on how to institute change in different cultures, has adopted a code of ethics to protect foreign cultures with which such agencies interact. The code considers whether a project or planned change actually will benefit the target population. Because the definition of what constitutes a benefit depends on cultural value systems, implementing this code is a challenge. Further, there may be balances to consider, such as a trade-off between economic gains for the target population and ending a way of life that gives that population great satisfaction. We often hear of "spiritual poverty in the midst of plenty"—a phrase that means that aesthetic, philosophical, and human dimensions suffer in favor of economic prosperity. Further, the concept of "quality of life" varies substantially among cultures. The result is that an international company may be criticized as being socially irresponsible if it ignores the total spectrum of human needs for each place in which it operates.

Companies often lack complete information that they can use to guide them in advance of taking action abroad. For example, consider the area of human rights. In 1948, before many of today's nations were in existence, the United Nations adopted a Universal Declaration of Human Rights. Government and academic leaders from many countries have criticized the declaration for having too Western an orientation. Some provisions that lack universal acceptance include the right to individual ownership of property, the right to governance through universal secret elections, and the implicit statement that the nuclear family is the fundamental unit of society. In fact, not all countries have explicitly declared their concept of human rights. Without such a declaration, the accuracy of descriptions of the human rights sentiments of many countries is uncertain.[58]

depressed and confused—the culture shock phase—and their usefulness in a foreign assignment may be greatly impaired. Fortunately for most people, culture shock begins to ebb after a month or two as optimism grows and satisfaction improves.[56] Interestingly, some people also encounter culture shock when they return to their home countries—a situation known as reverse culture shock—because they have learned to accept what they have encountered abroad. Dealing with transfers to a foreign country is a significant concern for companies and transferees, a concern covered in Chapter 21, "Human Resource Management."

Company and Management Orientations

Whether and how much a company and its managers adapt to foreign cultures depends not only on the conditions within the foreign cultures but also on the attitudes of the companies and their managers. The following sections discuss three such attitudes or orientations—polycentrism, ethnocentrism, and geocentrism.

Polycentrism   In polycentric organizations, control is decentralized so that "our manager in Rio" is free to conduct business in what he or she thinks is the Brazilian way. In other words, business units in different countries have a significant degree of autonomy from the home office and act very much like local companies. Because many discussions of international business focus on the unique problems that companies have experienced abroad, it is understandable that many companies develop a polycentric orientation. Polycentrism may be, however, an overly cautious response to cultural variety.

A company that is too polycentric may shy away from certain countries or may avoid transferring home-country practices or resources that may, in fact, work well abroad. When practices do not work abroad, management may point to the unique foreign environment. If the foreign environment is not the cause, the company might erroneously take a more polycentric orientation. For example, American Express assembled its worldwide personnel managers for an exchange of views on performance evaluation. The complaints from the overseas managers centered on certain corporate directives that they claimed did not fit "their" countries. These managers claimed that foreign operations were unique and that each overseas office should develop its own procedures. Further talks, however, revealed that the complaints really focused on one particular personnel evaluation form. If the company had delegated procedural control, as these overseas managers were suggesting, it would have risked not introducing abroad some of its other standard forms and procedures that would work reasonably well. Furthermore, it would have risked duplicating efforts by having each country's managers develop their own forms, which might have been more costly than trying to administer the ill-suited form. Personnel managers in U.S. offices indicated that they too had just as many problems with the form as their foreign counterparts did. The problematic evaluation form, which managers originally attributed to cultural differences, was not a cultural problem at all.

To compete effectively with local companies, an international company usually must perform some functions in a distinct way, such as by introducing new products or ways to produce and sell them. Polycentrism, however, may lead to such extensive delegation of decision making or such extensive imitation of proven host-country practices that the company loses its innovative superiority. Furthermore, the company may lose overall control as managers within each country foster local rather than worldwide objectives.

Ethnocentrism   Ethnocentrism is the belief that one's own culture is superior to others. In international business, it describes a company or individual so imbued with the belief that what worked at home should work abroad that it ignores environmental differences. Ethnocentrism takes three general forms.

1. Managers overlook important cultural factors abroad because they have become accustomed to certain cause-and-effect relationships in the home country. To combat this type of ethnocentrism, managers can refer to checklists of cultural variables, such as those discussed in this chapter, to assure themselves that they are considering all the major factors.
2. Management recognizes the environmental differences but still focuses on achieving home-country rather than foreign or worldwide objectives. The result may be diminished long-term competitiveness because the company does not perform as well as its competitors and because opposition to its practices develops abroad.

Margin notes:

Polycentrist management is so overwhelmed by national differences that it won't introduce workable changes.

Ethnocentrist management overlooks national differences and

• Ignores important factors
• Believes home-country objectives should prevail
• Thinks change is easy

3. Management recognizes differences but assumes that the introduction of its new products or ways to produce and sell them is both necessary and easy to achieve when it is really a complex process. Ethnocentrism is not entirely bad. Much of what works at home will work abroad. However, excessive ethnocentrism may cause costly business failures.

Geocentrism   Between the extremes of polycentrism and ethnocentrism are business practices that are neither the home operation's nor the host-country company's but a hybrid of the two. For example, Toyota has purposely blended Japanese and French cultures in its French plant.[59] When the host-country environment is substantially different from the one at home, the international company must decide whether to persuade people in that country to accept something new (in which case, the company would be acting as a change agent) or to make changes in the company itself. Geocentrism exists when a company bases its operations on an informed knowledge of home- and host-country needs, capabilities, and constraints. This is the preferred approach to business dealings with another culture because it increases the introduction of innovations and decreases the likelihood of their failures.

Geocentric management often uses business practices that are hybrids of home and foreign norms.

Strategies for Instituting Change

As we have indicated, companies may need to transfer new products or operating methods from one country to another if they are to have competitive advantages. How they make such introductions is important for assuring success. Fortunately, substantial change-agent literature exists that deals with overcoming resistance in the international arena. Further, we can gain insights from the international experiences of businesses and not-for-profit organizations. We discuss these approaches and experiences in the following sections and conclude with a discussion on the importance of learning as a two-way process, one in which companies transfer knowledge abroad from their home countries and to their home countries from abroad.

Value System   It is much easier to adapt to things that do not challenge our value systems than to things that do. For example, Eritreans eat only 175 grams of fish per capita per year (compared with 20,000 grams in the United States and 70,000 grams in Japan) despite having a long coastline rich in seafood and having had endured past famines. The Eritrean government and the United Nations World Food Program have faced formidable opposition in trying to persuade Eritrean adults to eat more seafood because their value system is too set. Many have religious taboos about eating insectlike sea creatures (such as shrimp and crayfish) and fish without scales, and most grew up believing that seafood tasted putrid. But there is little opposition to eating seafood among Eritrean schoolchildren. Simply stated, their value system and habits are not yet set.[60] The business lesson here is that the more a change disrupts basic values, the more the people affected will resist it. When changes do not interfere with deep-seated customs, accommodation is much more likely.

The more a change upsets important values, the more resistance it will engender.

Cost Benefit of Change   Some adjustments to foreign cultures are costly to undertake, whereas others are inexpensive. Some adjustments result in greatly improved performance, such as higher productivity or sales. Other changes may improve performance only marginally. A company must consider the expected cost-benefit relationship of any adjustments it makes abroad. For example, Cummins Engine shuts down its plant in Mexico each December 12 so workers may honor the Virgin of Guadalupe. The company throws a celebration in its cafeteria for employees and their families that includes a priest who offers

The cost of change may exceed its benefit.

prayers to the Virgin at an altar.[61] The cost is worth the resultant employee commitment to the company.

Resistance to Too Much Change   When German company Gruner + Jahr bought the U.S. magazine *McCall's*, it quickly began to overhaul the format. Gruner + Jahr changed its editor, eliminated long stories and advice columns, increased coverage on celebrities, made the layouts more dense, started using sidebars and boxes in articles, and refused discounts for big advertisers. But employee turnover began to increase because of low morale, and revenues fell because the new format seemed too different to advertisers.[62] Employee and advertiser acceptance might have been easier to obtain had Gruner + Jahr made fewer demands at one time and phased in other policies more slowly.

Participation   One way to avoid problems that could result from change is to discuss a proposed change with stakeholders in advance. By doing so, the company may learn how strong resistance to the change will be, stimulate in the stakeholders a recognition of the need for improvement, and ease their fears of adverse consequences resulting from the change. For example, employees may be satisfied that management has listened to their viewpoints, even though management makes decisions contrary to what the employees suggest.[63] Managers sometimes think that stakeholder participation is unique to countries where people have educational backgrounds that enable them to make substantial contributions. Experience with government-to-government economic development and population-control programs, however, indicates that participation may be extremely important to companies even in countries where power distance and uncertainty avoidance are high. However, stakeholder participation is limited to the extent that proposed actions do not violate conditions in the prevailing value system and to the extent that participants are not so fatalistic that they believe they can have no control over the outcomes.

Reward Sharing   Sometimes a proposed change may have no foreseeable benefit for the people who must support it. For example, production workers may have little incentive to shift to new work practices unless they see some benefits for themselves. A company's solution may be to develop a bonus system for productivity and quality based on using the new approach. In one case, a U.S.-Peruvian gold-mining venture donated sheep to the Andean villagers, who initially opposed the operation because they saw no benefit for themselves.[64]

Opinion Leaders   By discovering the local channels of influence, an international company may locate opinion leaders who can help speed up the acceptance of change. Opinion leaders may emerge in unexpected places. For example, AES, the world's largest independent power producer, enlisted the help of local shamans in Uganda to appease spirits and remove local opposition to a dam on the Nile.[65] Such actions achieve the desired result without destroying important social structures. Ford sends Mexican operatives, rather than supervisors, from its plants in Mexico to one in the United States to observe operating methods. Their Mexican peers are more prone to listen to them than to their supervisors.[66] Characteristics of opinion leaders may vary by country—for example, they are generally older people in India and Korea, but not in Australia.[67]

Timing   Many good business changes fall flat because they are ill-timed. For example, a labor-saving production method might make employees fear that they will lose their jobs regardless of management's reassurances. However, less employee fear and resistance will occur if management introduces the labor-saving method when there is a labor shortage. A culture's attitudes and needs may change slowly or rapidly, so keeping abreast of these

LOOKING TO THE FUTURE

The Globalization of Culture

Contact across cultures is becoming more widespread than ever. This should lead to a leveling of cultures, which, on the surface, is occurring. People around the world wear similar clothes and listen to the same recording stars. Competitors from all over the world often buy the same production equipment, the use of which imposes more uniform operating methods on workers. This globalization of culture is illustrated by Japanese tourists listening to a Philippine group sing a U.S. song in an Indonesian hotel.

However, below the surface, people continue to hold fast to their national differences. In other words, although some tangibles have become more universal, how people cooperate, attempt to solve problems, and are motivated have tended to remain the same. Religious differences are as strong as ever. Language differences continue to bolster separate ethnic identities. These differences fragment the globe into regions and stymie the global standardization of products and operating methods.

One factor that inhibits the leveling of cultures is nationalism. Without perceived cultural differences, people would not see themselves so apart from other nationalities; cultural identities are thus used to mobilize national identity and separateness. This is done by regulating and encouraging the so-called national culture.

International companies, therefore, are likely to continue to face diverse cultures in different parts of the world and for different parts of their operations. In some areas, diversity will decrease as small cultural groups are absorbed into more dominant national ones. For example, such absorption in recent years has led to the extinction of many languages. Only 5 percent of languages are safe, meaning at least a million people speak them.[69] At the same time, there is evidence of more powerful subcultures within some countries because of immigration, the global rise in religious fundamentalism, and the growing belief among ethnic groups that they should be independent from dominant groups.

All of these factors might lead to future problems in defining culture along national lines. Subcultures may transcend national boundaries, and the distinct subcultures within a country may have less in common with each other than they do with subcultures in other countries. Examples of transnational subcultures are the Inuits that transcend country boundaries in Arctic lands and the Kurds that do the same in the Middle East.

Cultures are becoming more similar in some respects but not in others.

Two scenarios for future international cultures are

- Smaller cultures will be absorbed by national and global ones
- Subcultures will transcend national boundaries

changes helps in determining timing. However, a crisis may stimulate acceptance of change. For example, family members dominate business organizations in Turkey. In some cases, poor company profits have stimulated a rapid change from "a family running the business" to a "family only on the board." But in other cases, family members continue to exert substantial influence on companies' practices even after they have no official responsibilities.[68]

Learning Abroad   The discussion so far has centered on cultural differences among countries. As companies operate abroad, they affect the host society and are affected by it. The company may learn things that will be useful in its home country or in other operations. This last point is the essence for undertaking transnational practices in which the company seeks to capitalize on diverse capabilities among the countries in which it operates. Basically, companies believe natural intelligence exists in just about the same proportion throughout the world and that innovations and good ideas may come from anywhere.

International companies should learn things abroad that they can apply at home.

Summary

- Culture includes norms of behavior based on learned attitudes, values, and beliefs. Businesspeople agree that there are cross-country differences but disagree as to what they are.

- International companies must evaluate their business practices to ensure that they take into account national norms in their behavioral characteristics.

- A given country may encompass very distinct societies. People also may have more in common with similar groups in foreign countries than with groups in their own country.

- Companies can build awareness about other cultures. The amount of effort needed to do this depends on the similarity between countries and the type of business operation undertaken.

- Cultural change may take place as a result of choice or imposition. Isolation from other groups, especially because of language, tends to stabilize cultures.

- People fall into social stratification systems according to their ascribed and acquired group memberships. These memberships determine a person's degree of access to economic resources, prestige, social relations, and power. An individual's affiliations may determine his or her qualifications and availability for given jobs.

- Some people work far more than is necessary to satisfy their basic needs for food, clothing, and shelter. People are motivated to work for various reasons, including their preference for material items over leisure, the belief that work will bring success and reward, and the desire for achievement.

- Nationalities differ as to whether they prefer an autocratic or a consultative working relationship, whether they want set rules, and how much they compete or cooperate with fellow workers.

- Nationalities differ in the degree to which people trust one another, believe in fate, and forego present for future gratification.

- Host cultures do not always expect companies and individuals to conform to their norms. They sometimes accommodate foreign companies and have different standards for foreigners.

- People communicate through spoken, written, and silent language, based on culturally determined cues.

- Information processing is greatly affected by cultural background. The failure to perceive subtle distinctions in behavior can result in misunderstandings in international dealings.

- People working in a foreign environment should be sensitive to the dangers of excessive polycentrism and excessive ethnocentrism. They should try to become geocentric.

- In deciding whether to try to bring change to home- or host-country operations, an international company should consider how important the change is to each party, the cost and benefit to the company of each alternative, the use of opinion leaders, and the timing of change.

- Although increased contact among people is evoking more widespread cultural similarity among nations, people nevertheless tend to hold on to their basic values. These values are bolstered by efforts to protect cultural separateness and national identity.

CASE

John Higgins[70]

Leonard Prescott, vice president and general manager of Weaver-Yamazaki Pharmaceutical of Japan, believed that John Higgins, his executive assistant, was losing effectiveness in representing the U.S. parent company because of an extraordinary identification with the Japanese culture. (Map 2.5 shows Japan and Table 2.2 shows Japan's work customs.)

The parent company, Weaver Pharmaceutical, had extensive international operations and was one of the largest U.S. drug firms. Its competitive position depended heavily on research and development (R&D). Sales activity in Japan started in the early 1930s, when Yamazaki Pharmaceutical, a major producer of drugs and chemicals in Japan, began distributing Weaver's products. World War II disrupted sales, but Weaver resumed exporting to Japan in 1948 and subsequently captured a substantial market share. To prepare for increasingly keen competition from Japanese producers, Weaver and Yamazaki established in 1954 a jointly owned and operated manufacturing subsidiary to produce part of Weaver's product line.

Through the combined effort of both parent companies, the subsidiary soon began manufacturing sufficiently broad lines of products to fill the general demands of the Japanese market. Imports from the United States were limited to highly specialized items. The subsidiary

MAP 2.5 Japan

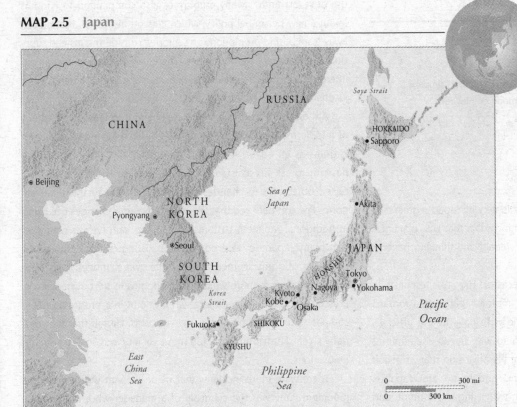

Japan is a nation consisting of islands. Its four main islands are Kyushu, Shikoku, Honshu, and Hokkaido. Japan's island status makes it less prone to cultural borrowing. Foreign companies doing business in Japan must try to adapt to Japanese culture, although Japan does have a certain fascination with foreign cultures.

conducted substantial R&D on its own, which was coordinated through a joint committee representing both Weaver and Yamazaki to avoid unnecessary duplication of efforts. The subsidiary turned out many new products, some marketed successfully in the United States and elsewhere. Weaver's management considered the Japanese operation to be one of its most successful international ventures and felt that the company's future prospects were promising, especially given the steady improvement in Japan's standard of living.

Shozo Suzuki headed the subsidiary, but, as executive vice president of Yamazaki and president of several other subsidiaries, he limited his participation in Weaver-Yamazaki to determining basic policies. Prescott, assisted by Higgins and several Japanese directors, managed daily operations.

Weaver Pharmaceutical had a policy of moving U.S. personnel from one foreign post to another with occasional tours in the home-office international division. Each assignment generally lasted for three to five years. There were a limited number of expatriates, so company personnel policy was flexible enough to allow an employee to stay in a country for an indefinite time if he or she so desired. A few expatriates had stayed in one foreign post for over 10 years. Prescott replaced the former general manager, who had been in Japan for six years. An experienced international business-

man who had spent most of his 25-year career at Weaver abroad, Prescott had served in India, the Philippines, and Mexico, with several years in the home-office international division. He was delighted to be challenged with expanding Japanese operations, and after two years, he felt a sense of accomplishment in having developed a smoothly functioning organization. Born in a small Midwestern town, Higgins entered his state university after high school. Midway through college, however, he joined the army. Because he had shown an interest in languages in college, he was able to attend the Army Language School for intensive training in Japanese. Fifteen months later, he was assigned as an interpreter and translator in Tokyo and took more courses in Japanese language, literature, and history. He made many Japanese friends, fell in love with Japan, and vowed to return there. After five years in the army, Higgins returned to college. Because he wanted to use Japanese as a means rather than an end in itself, he finished his college work in management, graduating with honors, and then joined Weaver. After a year in the company training program, Weaver assigned him to Japan, a year before Prescott's arrival.

Higgins was pleased to return to Japan, not only because of his love for the country but also because of the opportunity to improve the "ugly American" image held abroad. His language ability and

● TABLE 2.2

JAPANESE WORK CUSTOMS

Low employee turnover

Advancement based primarily on longevity with the company

Considerable after-work socializing among employees

Group work assignments and rewards

Bottom-up consensus building for decisions

interest in Japan enabled him to intermingle with broad segments of the Japanese population. He noted with disdain that U.S. managers tended to impose their value systems, ideals, and thinking patterns on the Japanese.

Under both Prescott and his predecessor, Higgins's responsibilities included troubleshooting with major Japanese customers, attending trade meetings, negotiating with government officials, conducting market research, and helping with day-to-day administration. Both general managers sought his advice on many difficult and complex administrative problems and found him capable. Prescott became concerned, however, with Higgins's attitude and thinking. He felt that Higgins had taken to the Japanese culture to such a degree that he had lost the U.S. point of view. He had "gone native," resulting in a substantial loss of administrative effectiveness.

Prescott mentally listed a few examples to describe what he meant by Higgins's complete emotional involvement with Japanese culture. The year before, Higgins had married a Japanese woman. At that time, Higgins had asked for and received permission to extend his stay in Japan indefinitely. According to Prescott, this marked a turning point in Higgins's behavior. Higgins moved to a strictly Japanese neighborhood; relaxed in a kimono at home; used the public bath; and was invited to weddings, neighborhood parties, and even Buddhist funerals. Although Weaver had a policy of granting two months of home leave every two years, with paid transportation for the employee and his family, Higgins declined to take trips, preferring instead to visit remote parts of Japan with his wife.

At work, Higgins also had taken on many characteristics of a typical Japanese executive. He spent considerable time listening to the personal problems of his subordinates, maintained close social ties with many men in the company, and had even arranged marriages for some of the young employees. Consequently, many employees sought out Higgins to register complaints and demands. These included requests for more liberal fringe benefits, such as recreational activities and the acquisition of rest houses for employees to

use at resort areas. Many employees also complained to Higgins about a new personnel policy, which Prescott instituted, that moved away from basing promotions on seniority, considering instead superiors' evaluations of subordinates. The employees asked Higgins to intercede on their behalf. He did so, insisting their demands were justified.

Although Prescott believed it was helpful to learn the feelings of middle managers from Higgins, he disliked having to deal with Higgins as an adversary rather than as an ally. Prescott became hesitant to ask his assistant's opinion because Higgins invariably raised objections to changes that were contrary to the Japanese norm. Prescott believed that there were dynamic changes occurring in traditional Japanese customs and culture, and he was confident that many Japanese were not tied to existing cultural patterns as rigidly as Higgins seemed to think they were. Indeed, Japanese subordinates were more willing than Higgins to try out new ideas. Prescott also thought that there was no point in a progressive U.S. company's merely copying the local customs. He felt that the company's real contribution to Japanese society was in introducing innovations.

There were more incidents that made Prescott doubt Higgins's judgment. One was the dismissal of a manager who, in Prescott's opinion, lacked initiative, leadership, and general competency. After two years of continued prodding by his superiors, including Prescott, the manager still showed little interest in improvement. Both Higgins and the personnel manager objected vigorously to the dismissal because the company had never fired anyone before. They also argued that the employee was loyal and honest and that the company was partially at fault for having kept him on for the last 10 years without spotting the incompetency. A few weeks after the dismissal, Prescott learned that Higgins had interceded on behalf of the fired employee, so that Yamazaki Pharmaceutical transferred him to its own operation. When confronted, Higgins said that he had done what was expected of a superior in any Japanese company by assuring a subordinate's continued employment.

Prescott believed these incidents suggested a serious problem. Higgins had been an effective and efficient manager whose knowledge of the language and the people had proved invaluable. Prescott knew that Higgins had received several outstanding offers to go with other companies in Japan. On numerous occasions, Prescott's friends in U.S. companies said they envied him for having a man of Higgins's qualifications as an assistant. However, Prescott felt Higgins would be far more effective if he had a detached attitude toward Japan. In Prescott's view, the best international executive was one who retained a belief in the fundamentals of the home point of view while also understanding foreign attitudes.

QUESTIONS

1. How would you describe Higgins's and Prescott's attitudes toward implementing U.S. personnel policies in the Japanese operations?

2. What are the major reasons for the differences in attitude?

3. If you were the Weaver corporate manager responsible for the Japanese operations and the conflict between Higgins and Prescott came to your attention, what would you do? Be sure to identify some alternatives first and then make your recommendations.

Culture Quest

VIDEO: THE IMPACT OF CULTURE ON BUSINESS: SPOTLIGHT ON LATIN AMERICA

Although there are many cultural differences among the many countries in Latin America, Map 2.4 in the chapter indicates that many of the Latin American countries share similar cultural attitudes and values that affect business practices. Based on viewing the accompanying video on Latin America and materials in the chapter, answer the following questions.

1. List some aspects of Latin American culture and indicate the influences on their development.

2. What current factors might cause cultural change to occur in Latin America? What are the likely changes?

3. Explain some cultural contrasts or differences within Latin America. How might they impact international business operations?

Chapter Notes

1 Data for this case were taken from Rachel Miller, "How to Exploit Pop Around the Globe," *Marketing* (August 8, 2002): point-of-purchase section, 27; Neil MacFarquhar, "Leisure Class to Working Class in Saudi Arabia," *New York Times* (August 26, 2001): A1+; Roula Khalaf, "Saudi Women Carve a Place in the Future of Their Country," *Financial Times* (January 25, 2002): 3; Steve Jarvis, "Western-Style Research in the Middle East," *Marketing News*: International section, 37; Nadim Kawach, "Job Nationalisation to Gain Peace," *Financial Times Global News Wire* (July 12, 2002); John A. Quelch, "Does Globalization Have Staying Power?" *Marketing Management* 11, no. 2 (March–April 2002): 18–27; Andy Fry, "Pushing into Pan Arabia," *Haymarket Publishing Services* (June 8, 2001): worldwide advertising section, 21; Ali Kanso, Abdul Karim Sinno, and William Adams, "Cross-cultural Public Relations," *Competitiveness Review* 11, no. 1 (2001): 65; "Culture Shock," *Design Week* (August 25, 2000): 17; "Saudi Consumers Face Changing Environment," *Financial Times Global News Wire* (March 1, 2000): n.p.; Edward Pilkington, "Like Dallas Policed by the Taliman," *The Guardian* [London] (July 2, 2002): sec. G2, 2; James Sherwood, "Fashion: Your Highness, Is

That Gucci or Diro Under Your Veil?" *The Independent* [London],: Features section, 9; Barbara Slavin, "U.S. Firms' Saudi Offices Face Manpower Issues," *USA Today* (May 13, 2002): 5A; Susan Taylor Martin, "Inside Saudi Arabia," *St. Petersburg Times* (July 21, 2002): 1A; Susan Taylor Martin, "Hanging Out at the Mall, Saudi Style," *St. Petersburg Times* (July 24, 2002): 8A; Colbert I. King, "When in Saudi Arabia . . . Do as Americans Do," *Washington Post* (February 2, 2002): A25; Donna Abu-Nasr, "Saudis Begin to Show Wear and Tear of Life Under Feared Religious Police," *AP Worldstream* (April 28, 2002): n.p.; and Parris-Rogers International (PRI) case in John D. Daniels and Lee H. Radebaugh, *International Business: Environments and Operations*, 9th ed. (Upper Saddle River, NJ: Prentice-Hall, 2001), 45–46.

2 Tomasz Lenartowicz and Kendall Roth, "Cultural Assessment Revisited: The Selection of Key Informants in 1B Cross-Cultural Studies," paper presented at the Annual Meeting of the Academy of International Business, Sydney, Australia (November 2001).

3 See Aihwa Ong, *Flexible Citizenship: The Cultural Logics of the Transnationality* (Durham, NC: Duke University Press, 1999); and Leo

Paul Dana, *Entrepreneurship in Pacific Asia* (Singapore: World Scientific, 1999).

4 Robert J. Foster, "Making National Cultures in the National Ecumene," *Annual Review of Anthropology* 20 (1991): 235–60, discusses the concept and ingredients of a national culture.

5 "The Lively Chemistry of Transatlantic Enterprise," *Financial Times* (November 1, 2001): 13.

6 Harry C. Triandis, "Dimensions of Cultural Variation as Parameters of Organizational Theories," *International Studies of Management and Organization* (Winter 1982–1983): 143–44.

7 Philip H. Gordon and Sophie Meunier, *The French Challenge: Adapting to Globalization* (Washington, DC: The Brookings Institute, 2002); and Robert Graham, "Air France Drops English Ruling," *Financial Times* (April 7, 2000): 14.

8 A 1999 referendum required the use of Spanish in schools. See "Guatemalan Indians Lament Recognition Measure's Defeat," *New York Times* (May 18, 1999): A5.

9 "Experts: English Language Faces Increasing Corruption," *Miami Herald* (March 25, 2001): 21A.

10 Paul Taylor, "McDonald's Learns the Ropes of Being an American Icon Abroad," *Financial Times* (April 18, 2002): 22.

11 Michael Segalla, "National Cultures, International Business," *Financial Times* (March 6, 1998): mastering global business section, 8–10.

12 Fons Trompenaars, *Riding the Waves of Culture* (Burr Ridge, IL: Richard D. Irwin, 1994), 100–16.

13 Gyula Bakacsi et al, "Eastern European Cluster: Tradition and Transistion," *Journal of World Business,* Vol. 37, (2002): 69–80; Neal M. Ashkanasy, Edwin Trevor-Roberts, and Louise Earnshaw, "The Anglo Cluster: Legacy of the British Empire," *Journal of World Business,* Vol. 37, 2002, 28–39; and Neal M. Ashkansy, "Leadership in the Asian Century: Lessons from GLOBE," *International Journal of Organisational Behaviour,* Vol. 5, No. 3, (2002): 150–163.

14 "When Culture Masks Communication: Japanese Corporate Practice," *Financial Times* (October 23, 2000): 10; and Robert House et al, "Understanding Cultures and Implicit Leadership Theories Across the Globe: An Introduction to Project GLOBE," *Journal of World Business,* Vol. 37, (2002): 3–10.

15 Larry Rohter, "Multiracial Brazil Planning Quotas for Blacks," *New York Times* (October 2, 2001): A3.

16 Valentine M. Moghadam, "Responses to Jean Bonvin's Globalization and Linkages: Challenges for Development Policy," *Development* 40, no. 3 (1997): 62–69.

17 Miriam Jordan, "Brief Lives," *Wall Street Journal* (May 9, 2000): A1+.

18 Hayat Kabasakal and Muzaffer Bodur, "Arabic Cluster: A Bridge between East and West," *Journal of World Business,* Vol. 37 2002, 40–54.

19 Steve Liesman, "Driven to Distraction, Saudi Women May Soon Take the Wheel," *Wall Street Jounal* (March 1, 1999): A10.

20 Francis Fukuyama, *Trust: The Social Virtues and the Creation of Prosperity* (New York: Free Press, 1995).

21 Mary Jordan, "Respect Is Dwindling in the Hallowed-Halls," *Washington Post* (June 20, 1994): A3, citing data collected by the Carnegie Foundation for the Advancement of Teaching in a survey of 20,000 professors in 13 nations and Hong Kong.

22 Jean J. Boddewyn, "Fitting Socially in Fortress Europe: Understanding, Reaching, and Impressing Europeans," *Business Horizons* (November–December 1992): 35–43; and Geert Hofstede, "National Cultures in Four Dimensions," *International Studies of Management and Organization* (Spring–Summer 1983): 46–74.

23 Everett E. Hagen, *The Theory of Social Change: How Economic Growth Begins* (Homewood, IL: Richard D. Irwin, 1962), 378.

24 See, for example, David S. Landes, *The Wealth and Poverty of Nations* (New York: W. W. Norton, 1998).

25 Martin Wolf, "Hard Work Versus Joie de Vivre," *Financial Times* (February 20, 2002): 15.

26 David Gardner, "Indians Face 10m Rupee Question: Do You Sincerely Want to Be Rich?" *Financial Times* (July 15–16, 2000): 24.

27 See R. Inden, "Tradition Against Itself," *American Ethnologist* 13, no. 4 (1986): 762–75; and P. Chatterjee, *Nationalist Thoughts and the Colonial World: A Derivative Discourse* (London: Zed Books, 1986).

28 Triandis, op cit., 159–60.

29 Geert Hofstede, *Cultures and Organizations: Software of the Mind* (New York: McGraw-Hill, 1997), 79–108.

30 House et al, loc. cit.

31 Abraham Maslow, *Motivation and Personality* (New York: Harper & Row, 1954).

32 Hofstede, op. cit., 26; and House et al, loc cit.

33 Hofstede, op. cit., 49–78; and House et al, loc cit.

34 Book review of Patricia Gercik, *On the Track with the Japanese* (Kodansha, 1992), by James B. Treece, *Business Week* (December 28, 1992): 20.

35 Ralph T. King, "Jeans Therapy," *Wall Street Journal* (May 20, 1998): A1.

36 Maxim Voronov and Jefferson A. Singer, "The Myth of Individualism–Collectivism: A Critical Review," *The Journal of Social Psychology* 142, no. 4 (August 2002): 461–81.

37 See John J. Lawrence and Reh-song Yeh, "The Influence of Mexican Culture on the Use of Japanese Manufacturing Techniques in Mexico," *Management International Review* 34, no. 1 (1994): 49–66; P. Christopher Earley, "East Meets West Meets Mideast: Further Explorations of Collectivistic and Individualistic Work Groups," *Academy of Management Journal* 36, no. 2 (1993): 319–46.

38 Marieke De Mooij, *Global Marketing and Advertising* (Thousand Oaks, CA: Sage, 1998).

39 Hofstede, op. cit., 113.

40 See Jan-Benedict E. M. Steenkamp, Frenkel ter Hofstede, and Michel Wedel, "A Cross-National Investigation into the Individual and National Cultural Antecedents of Consumer Innovativeness," *Journal of Marketing* 63 (April 1999): 55–69; and Hellmut Schütte, "Asian Culture and the Global Consumer," *Financial Times* (September 21, 1998): mastering marketing section, 2–3.

41 See Stephen Knack, "Low Trust, Slow Growth," *Financial Times* (June 26, 1996): 12; and Francis Fukuyama, *Trust: The Social Virtues and the Creation of Prosperity* (London: Hamish Hamilton, 1995).

42 The examples are all taken from the GLOBE project. See Bakacsi et al, loc cit; Ashkansy et al, loc cit; Szabo, Erna et al, "The Germanic Europe Cluster: Where Employees Have a Voice," *Journal of World Business,* Vol. 37, 2002, 55–68; and Jorge Correia Jesino, "Latin Europe Cluster: From South to North," *Journal of World Business,* Vol. 37, 2002, 81–89.

43 Benjamin Lee Whorf, *Language, Thought and Reality* (New York: Wiley, 1956), p. 13.

44 For an examination of subtle differences within northern Europe, see Malene Djursaa, "North Europe Business Culture: Britain vs. Denmark and Germany," *European Management Journal* 12, no. 2 (June 1994): 138–46.

45 Richard E. Nisbett et al., "Culture and Systems of Thought: Holistic Versus Analytic Cognition," *Psychological Review* 108, no. 2 (April 2001): 291–310.

46 Daniel Pearl, "Tour Saudi Arabia: Enjoy Sand, Surf, His-and-Her Pools," *Wall Street Journal* (January 22, 1998): A1.

47 June N. P. Francis, "When in Rome? The Effects of Cultural Adaptation on Intercultural Business Negotiations," *Journal of International Business Studies* 22, no. 3 (1991): 421–22.

48 R. I. Westwood and S. M. Leung, "The Female Expatriate Manager Experience," *International Studies of Management and Organization* 24, no. 3 (1994): 64–85.

49 Carla Power, Scott Johnson, and Amanda Bernard, "The New Arab Woman," *Newsweek* (June 12, 2000): 22; and Kabasakal and Bodur, loc cit.

50 Don Clark, "Hey, #@*% Amigo, Can You Translate the Word 'Gaffe'?" *Wall Street Journal* (July 8, 1996): B6.

51 Rene White, "Beyond Berlitz: How to Penetrate Foreign Markets Through Effective Communications," *Public Relations Quarterly* 31, no. 2 (Summer 1986): 15.

52 Mark Nicholson, "Language Error 'Was Cause of Indian Air Disaster,'" *Financial Times* (November 14, 1996): 1.

53 Much of the discussion on silent language is from Edward T. Hall, "The Silent Language in Overseas Business," *Harvard Business Review* (May–June 1960). He included five variables—time, space, things, friendships, and agreements—and was the first to use the term *silent language.*

54 Ibid.

55 Trompenaars, op. cit., 130–31.

56 Adrian Furnham and Stephen Bochner, *Culture Shock* (London: Methuen, 1986), 234.

57 See Pirkko Lammi, "My Vision of Business in Europe," in eds. Jack Mahoney and Elizabeth Vallance, *Business Ethics in a New Europe* (Dordrecht, Netherlands: Kluwer Academic, 1992), 11–12; and Andrew Jack, "French Prepare to Repel English Advance," *Financial Times* (January 7, 1997): 2.

58 See Alison Dundes Renteln, "The Concept of Human Rights," *Anthropos* 83 (1988): 343–64; and Ingrid Mattson, "Law, Culture, and Human Rights: Islamic Perspectives in the Contemporary World," summary of a conference at Yale Law School (November 5–6, 1993) in *The American Journal of Islamic Social Sciences* 11, no. 3 (1994): 446–50.

59 John Tagliabue, "At a French Factory, Culture Is a Two-Way Street," *New York Times* (February 25, 2001): BU4.

60 Geraldine Brooks, "Eritrea's Leaders Angle for Sea Change in Nation's Diet to Prove Fish Isn't Foul," *Wall Street Journal* (June 2, 1994): A10.

61 Marjorie Miller, "A Clash of Corporate Cultures," *Los Angeles Times* (August 15, 1992): A1.

62 Patrick M. Reilly, "Pitfalls of Exporting Magazine Formulas," *Wall Street Journal* (July 24, 1995): B1.

63 Mzamo P. Mangaliso, "Building Competitive Advantage from Ubuntu: Management Lessons from South Africa," *Academy of Management Executive* 15, no. 3 (August 2001): 23–34.

64 Sally Bowen, "People Power Keeps Peru's Investors in Check," *Financial Times* (February 6, 1998): 6.

65 Marc Lacey, "Traditional Spirits Block a $500 Million Dam Plan in Uganda," *New York Times* (September 13, 2001): B1–B2.

66 Roberto P. Garcia, "Learning and Competitiveness in Mexico's Automotive Industry: The Relationship Between Traditional and World-Class Plants in Multination Firm Subsidiaries," unpublished Ph.D. dissertation (Ann Arbor, MI: University of Michigan, 1996).

67 Roger Marshall and Indriyo Gitosudarmo, "Variation in the Characteristics of Opinion Leaders Across Cultural Borders," *Journal of International Consumer Marketing* 8, no. 1 (1995): 5–21.

68 "Business Must Come Before Family," *Euromoney* (Febuary 1999): 92–96.

69 "Cultural Loss Seen as Languages Fade," *New York Times* (May 16, 1999): 12.

70 The case is a condensed version from *Case: John Higgins* by M. Y. Yoshino. Reprinted with permission of Stanford University Graduate School of Business, ©1963 by the Board of Trustees of the Leland Stanford Junior University

3

THE POLITICAL AND LEGAL ENVIRONMENTS FACING BUSINESS

Half the world knows not how the other half lives.

— ENGLISH PROVERB

OBJECTIVES

- To discuss the different functions that political systems perform
- To compare democratic and totalitarian political regimes and to discuss how they can influence managerial decisions
- To describe how management can formulate and implement strategies to deal with foreign political environments
- To study the different types of legal systems and the legal relationships that exist between countries
- To examine the major legal issues in international business

CASE

The Hong Kong Dilemma[1]

Swire Pacific Ltd., one of the major *hongs,* or family-controlled trading houses prominent in Hong Kong business circles, must learn to operate successfully in Hong Kong now that the city has reverted from British to Chinese rule. In addition, Swire management must cope with the unstable economic environment initiated by the Asian financial crisis of 1997 and significantly worsened by the world economic downturn beginning in 2001.

Swire Pacific Ltd. is a publicly quoted company (a company whose shares are listed on a stock exchange) with diversified interests under the control of five operating divisions: property, aviation, beverages, marine services, and trading and industrial. Swire's profits in 2001 were marginally higher than in 2000, but its aviation and property divisions suffered due to the global economic downturn, which was complicated by the terrorist events of September 11, 2001 and by the resulting drop-off in airline traffic. The major contributor to Swire's overall profits, Cathay Pacific Airways of the aviation division, experienced a 90 percent decrease in profits over the course of the year.

How could Hong Kong's new political status be a problem for Swire? Until the mid-seventeenth century, China sought to minimize its contact with foreigners by restricting foreign trade to the port at Macao, which is 75 miles south of Canton, now known as Guangzhou. These restrictions resulted from a long history of mutual distrust and misunderstanding between the Chinese and foreigners. In the late eighteenth century, the Chinese opened more of their ports, but by the middle of the nineteenth century, they again sought to restrict foreign trade, this time to Canton.

Despite the history of restrictions, trade between China and the West had been flourishing, especially with Britain. The British wanted Chinese tea; the Chinese wanted the opium that British traders shipped in from India. Although opium was illegal in China, its use was widespread, so the Chinese government sought to halt its importation. Not surprisingly, the British protested. The results were three Opium Wars between the two countries within a period of 21 years (1839–1860). In all three, China emerged the loser. The first Opium War gave the British permanent ownership of the island of Hong Kong and its harbor. From the Third Opium War, they gained Kowloon. The New Territories, which comprise 90 percent of the land area of Hong Kong, came under British control in 1898 under the terms of a 99-year lease that expired on June 30, 1997. Map 3.1 shows the region. Until the early 1980s, the issue of the 99-year lease's expiration was dormant. However, real estate in Hong Kong tends to be leased on a 15-year basis. So in 1982, nervousness on the part of the Hong Kong business community led the British government to initiate talks with the Chinese government about what would become of Hong Kong in 1997.

After prolonged negotiations, the British and Chinese signed the Sino–British Joint Declaration in 1984. Under the terms of the agreement, China assumed control over Hong Kong on July 1, 1997; at that time, Hong Kong became a Special Administrative Region of China, which allows Hong Kong to operate under a different legal, political, and economic system from the rest of China. The agreement called for "one country, two systems," meaning that Hong Kong and China—together, "one country"—will have two government systems. China will continue its current economic structure, which means heavy governmental control. Hong Kong will retain its separate political and economic status for 50 years (until 2047) and continue to enjoy the free-wheeling, free-market economy that has flourished there. The Joint Declaration along with the Basic Law, the post-1997 Hong Kong constitution that China developed, provides a sense of direction for economic and political change.

MAP 3.1 Hong Kong

Hong Kong, situated at the mouth of the Pearl River, is now a Special Administrative Region in China.

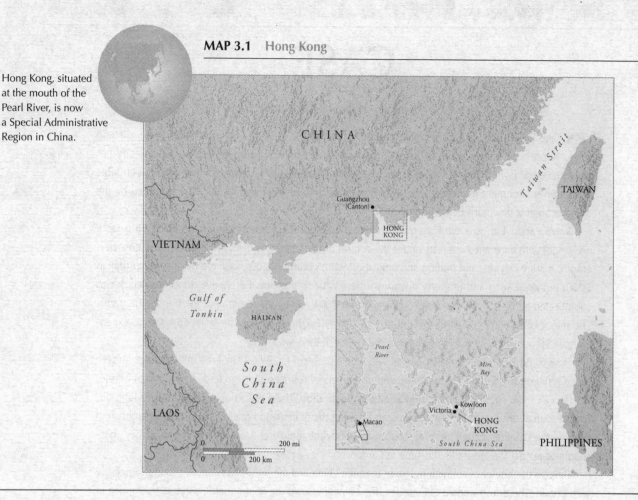

Democracy has never been a major part of the political landscape in Hong Kong. Only once in the first 140 years of British rule did Hong Kong consider representative rule, and that was quashed by the local business elite. Until Hong Kong reverted back to China, it was considered a British colony, presided over by a governor appointed by the queen of England. Once the Joint Declaration of 1984 established a date for the turnover of Hong Kong to China, the British began to push for democracy.

In 1990, political parties began to form, and in 1991 for the first time, the parties won the right to be represented in Hong Kong's Legislative Council (Legco). The people of Hong Kong directly elect only a small percentage of Legco's members, and China appoints the rest. The Basic Law provides that 50 percent of the legislature may be directly elected by the people by 2004 and that full democratization should be discussed in 2007.

In 1996, a 400-person committee appointed by the Chinese government voted for Hong Kong shipping magnate C. H. Tung as the first chief executive to run Hong Kong beginning July 1, 1997. Under direction from China, Mr. Tung has been slow to make sweeping changes in Hong Kong that will align it more closely with China. Rather, they have made small gradual changes that ensure a stable transition. Freedom of speech and demonstration still exist, and businesses have a free hand to run as they always have. On the political front, although China has encouraged a new era of democracy in Hong Kong, no one dared run against China's favorite Mr. Tung in the 2002 elections, ensuring him another five-year term beginning in July 2002. Many believe that Mr. Tung is unable to help Hong Kong's deteriorating economy because his interests lie with pleasing Beijing instead of acting in Hong Kong's best interest. Hong Kong has been hit with a recession and record unemployment because of the collapse of the local property market, the fall of the dollar, and competition from China's emerging cargo ports. On July 1, 2002, the largest measure of change in political structure was enacted when policy makers established a ministerial system of political appointees to replace the civil servants. Some fear this development nicks away at the freedom in place by putting more power in the chief executive position and in the appointees that Beijing will choose.

Companies are taking different approaches to deal with the transition in Hong Kong. Swire has chosen to establish a close working relationship with China by entering into partnerships and selling division stakes to Chinese firms. One of its rival *hongs,* Jardine Matheson group, has resisted attempts at Chinese ownership and even moved its legal headquarters to Bermuda to reduce its exposure to Hong Kong's uncertainty, significantly reducing its influence in China and its ability to grow as China's economy expands.

Swire is cooperating directly with China in a significant way. Swire even removed the Union Jack from its Cathay Pacific aircraft and repainted the aircraft an oriental jade color. The Swire family and its British-based parent company, John Swire & Sons, have some 90 percent of their assets in China and are involved in many Chinese joint ventures. Western investors who want to do business in China constantly approach Swire. However, Swire management is clearly concerned about Swire's future in Hong Kong and China. China could seize its businesses, just as it did in Shanghai many years ago. More important, however, Chinese partners could become more influential and sophisticated and might rely less on Swire's partnership. Will Swire management be able to negotiate the political environment that is arising in Hong Kong? Will the trend toward democracy reduce Swire's influence and control, or will Swire's top management and the other business leaders in Hong Kong still have significant influence? Is Swire management correct in pegging its future to the future of China, a country that is stable politically but searching for the best accommodation between a market economy and a totalitarian political regime? And as China continues to position Shanghai as a major business center in China, will that lessen Hong Kong's importance?

INTRODUCTION

Multinational enterprises (MNEs) like Swire must operate in countries with different political and legal conditions. For the company to succeed, its management must carefully analyze whether its corporate policies will fit a desirable political and legal environment. Can it operate successfully in China doing the same things it does in Hong Kong, or must it adapt its operating strategies to fit the political and economic climate in China? This chapter discusses the political and legal systems that managers encounter and the factors they need to consider when operating in different countries.

THE POLITICAL ENVIRONMENT

Figure 3.1 shows how political and legal factors are part of the external environment that influences managerial decisions. A political system integrates the parts of a society into a viable, functioning unit. A major challenge of the political system is to bring together people of different ethnic or other backgrounds and to allow them to work together to govern themselves. A country's political system influences how business is conducted domestically and internationally. In Hong Kong, for example, the political change that resulted when China took control in 1997 worried many managers because they believed that China would change the relationship between government and business, with the government exerting more influence and control in the business environment.

Figure 3.2 illustrates the development of political policies and their implementation. Political policies are established by aggregating, or bringing together, different points of view that are articulated by key constituencies, such as politicians, individuals, businesses, or other special-interest groups.[2] In the case of Hong Kong, business has always been the key constituency regarding decisions about what government policies are to be established. However, that is beginning to change; other interest groups are emerging to balance off the needs of business. Given the interests of different constituencies, governments identify policy alternatives and then choose a specific policy that it will pursue. The policy is then implemented,

The role of the political system is to integrate society.

Political process functions include

- Interest articulation
- Interest aggregation
- Policy making
- Policy implementation and adjudication

Political change or validation may come in many forms. The photo shows throngs of people waiting to vote in Zimbabwean elections. Note that males and females wait in separate lines.

Interest aggregation is the collection of interests in the political system.

MNE management tries to influence governments on policies that affect it through lobbying.

and it may be altered depending on the reactions of political parties, government bureaucracies, legislatures, courts, and other constituencies. Normally, the chief executive officer (CEO) of an MNE watches policies as they develop and makes sure that the company voices its concerns in the interest articulation stage. Then the CEO may want to work closely with a country's key decision makers in the policy formulation stage, which entails lobbying activities. Finally, the CEO may voice the company's stance on policies once they have been implemented. The key is to make sure that the company doesn't look as if it's trying to influence laws inappropriately. Sometimes a CEO will try to influence the home-country government on policies that affect countries in which the firm is operating. Prior to 2000, when the United States granted permanent normal trade relations to China, that decision had to be made annually. The United States–China Business Council, an organization of over 250 companies doing business in China, lobbies on behalf of its members for stable and expanded U.S.–China economic links.[3] The council includes companies such as Philip Morris, AT&T, Federal Express, BellSouth, and Lockheed Martin Company.

FIGURE 3.1   Political and Legal Influences on International Business

EXTERNAL INFLUENCES

OPERATIONS

PHYSICAL AND SOCIETAL FACTORS

- Political policies and legal practices
- Cultural factors
- Economic forces
- Geographical influences

OBJECTIVES

- Basic political ideologies
- The impact of the political system on management decisions
- Formulating and implementing political strategies
- The legal environment

STRATEGY

COMPETITIVE ENVIRONMENT

MEANS

FIGURE 3.2   The Political System and Its Functions

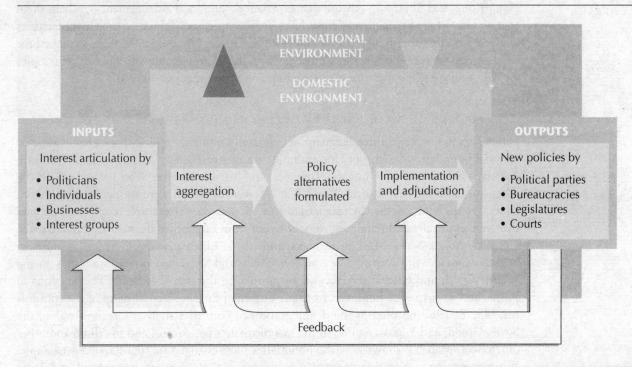

Governments formulate policy alternatives based on the inputs of different foreign and domestic entities and then implement the policies. The market-place then tests the outputs of these policies and revises them as necessary.

Source: From *Comparative Politics Today: A World View,* 3rd ed., by Gabriel A. Almond and G. Bingham Powell, Jr. Copyright © 1984 Gabriel A. Almond and G. Bingham Powell, Jr. Reprinted by permission Addison-Wesley Educational Publishers.

BASIC POLITICAL IDEOLOGIES

A **political ideology** is the body of constructs (complex ideas), theories, and aims that consti-tute a sociopolitical program. The liberal ideology of the Democratic Party and the conservative ideology of the Republican Party in the United States are examples of political ideologies. Most modern societies are **pluralistic** politically, meaning that different ideologies coexist within them because there is no one ideology that everyone accepts. Pluralism arises because groups within countries often differ significantly from each other in language (e.g., India), ethnic back-ground (e.g., South Africa), tribal groups (e.g., Afghanistan), or religion (e.g., the former Yugoslavia). These and other cultural dimensions strongly influence the political system. Managers from the United States, where there are only two key political parties, might find it difficult to understand the political environment in a country where there are many different ideologies even within the political parties themselves. This makes it difficult for the manager to determine how to articulate the firm's interests and how to influence policy making.

The ultimate test of any political system is its ability to hold a society together despite pressures from different ideologies that tend to split it apart. The more different and strongly held the ideas are, the more difficult it is for a government to formulate policies that every-one can accept. Differing ideologies in countries such as Yugoslavia and the Soviet Union already broke those countries apart during the 1990s. The resulting political instability has made it difficult for them to attract foreign investment and for managers to feel comfortable operating in and committing resources to them.

However, ideologies also help to bring countries together. One reason China wants Hong Kong back is because of ethnic Chinese ties. The belief is that a common Chinese heritage will enable Hong Kong and China to merge together faster than countries with very different eth-nic ties. In fact, the U.S. government calls mainland China, Taiwan, Hong Kong, and

Political ideology—a body of constructs (complex ideas), theories, and aims that consti-tute a sociopolitical program.

Pluralism—the coexistence of different ideologies.

The ultimate test of any political system is its ability to hold a society together despite pres-sures from different ideologies.

Singapore the Chinese Economic Area. Foreign companies that have had experience in Taiwan, Hong Kong, and Singapore can use that experience—and local management—to help them operate successfully in mainland China. Nike, for example, uses Taiwanese shoe manufacturers to invest in China and to manufacture shoes using Chinese labor. Because of the strong ethnic Chinese ties between Taiwan and China, political disagreements notwithstanding, it is easier for Nike to use its Taiwanese partners than to manufacture shoes on its own.

The Impact of Ideological Differences on National Boundaries

Differences in history, culture, language, religion, and political ideology have greatly affected national boundaries. In Europe, for example, the Austro-Hungarian Empire broke up into Austria, Czechoslovakia, Hungary, Romania, and Yugoslavia after World War I. With the advent of communist rule after World War II, countries often were formed from different ethnic groups held together by totalitarian rule. Yugoslavia, for example, comprised peoples that were ethnically and religiously very different from each other (Roman Catholic Croats, Greek Orthodox Serbs, Muslim Bosnians, and ethnic Albanians who lived in the southern Yugoslav province of Kosovo). The country's Croats and Serbs were on opposite sides during World War II, and Croats were accused of murdering thousands of Serbs. The Muslims in Bosnia and Kosovo were holdovers from the Ottoman Empire. The breakup of the communist bloc in 1989 resulted in the disintegration of countries such as Czechoslovakia, the Soviet Union, and Yugoslavia due to the loss of totalitarian control and to ethnic and other differences. Map 3.2 shows how the boundaries have changed in Yugoslavia, for example. When operating in a foreign country, it is important that managers understand its history and the present ethnic groups that could cause political tension and instability.

A Political Spectrum

The two extremes on the political spectrum are democracy and totalitarianism.

Figure 3.3 presents a general schematic of the various forms of government. An example of a conservative democracy is the United States during the presidency of George Bush. An example of a liberal democracy was the United States during the presidency of Bill Clinton. China is an example of a communist totalitarian government, and Myanmar is an example of a fascist totalitarian government. MNEs may be able to operate equally effectively in democratic and totalitarian regimes, but democracies usually have economic freedom and legal rules that safeguard individual (and corporate) rights. Let's now learn about the world's major political ideologies.

Democracy

Democratic systems involve wide participation by citizens in the decision-making process.

Former British Prime Minister Winston Churchill once called democracy the worst form of government—except for all the others.[4] The ideology of pure democracy derives from the ancient Greeks, who believed that all citizens should be equal politically and legally, should enjoy widespread freedoms, and should actively participate in the political process. In reality, society's complexity increases as the population increases, and so full participation by citizens in the decision-making process has become impossible in these modern times. Consequently, most democratic countries practice various forms of representative democracy; in such circumstances, citizens elect representatives to make decisions rather than vote on every specific issue themselves. Contemporary democratic political systems share the following traits:

Representative democracy—majority rule is achieved through periodic elections.

1. Freedom of opinion, expression, press, and freedom to organize
2. Elections in which voters decide who is to represent them
3. Limited terms for elected officials
4. An independent and fair court system, with high regard for individual rights and property
5. A nonpolitical bureaucracy and defense infrastructure
6. An accessibility to the decision-making process[5]

MAP 3.2   Boundary Changes in Yugoslavia

Since the breakup of the communist bloc in 1989, the boundaries of the former Yugoslavia have changed due to the loss of totalitarian control and ethnic differences.

Political Rights and Civil Liberties   A key element of democracy is freedom in the areas of political rights and civil liberties. Each year since 1941, Freedom House, a New York not-for-profit organization that monitors political rights and civil liberties around the world, has published a list of countries ranked according to the degree to which these freedoms exist. The major indicators for political rights are

- The degree to which fair and competitive elections occur.
- The ability of voters to endow their elected representatives with real power.
- The ability of people to organize into political parties or other competitive political groupings of their choice.
- The existence of safeguards on the rights of minorities.

The major indicators for civil liberties are

- The existence of freedom of the press.
- Equality under the law for all individuals.
- The extent of personal social freedoms.
- The degree of freedom from extreme governmental indifference or corruption.

Factors for evaluating freedom

- Political rights
- Civil liberties

FIGURE 3.3   The Political Spectrum

Although purely democratic and totalitarian governments are extremes, there are variations to each approach. For example, democratic governments range from radical on one side (advocates of political reform) to reactionary (advocates of a return to past conditions). The majority of democratic governments, however, lie somewhere in between.

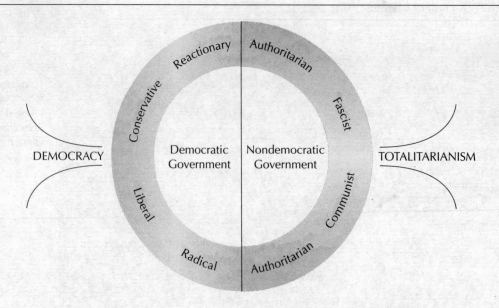

Figure 3.4 illustrates that countries high in both political rights and civil liberties are free, that countries quite low in both political rights and civil liberties are not free, and that countries in between are partly free. In 2002, 86 of the world's 192 countries were classified as free, whereas 58 countries were partly free and 48 were not free. "Partly free" countries enjoy limited political rights and civil liberties, often in the context of corruption, weak rule of law, ethnic strife, or civil war. "Not free" countries deny their citizens basic rights and civil liberties.[6] The Freedom House survey identifies the number of countries in each category as well as the percentage of the world's population in each category. In 2002, it noted that there were 121 electoral democracies, more than double the number of countries that were called democracies in the early 1970s. The 121 electoral democracies represented 63 percent of the world's countries.[7] What some call the "third wave" of democratization started in the early 1970s and is still underway.[8] The following identifies the percentage of the total population living in free, partly free, and not free conditions in 1981, 1990, 1998 and 2002.[9]

	1981	1990	1998	2002
Free	35.9%	38.9%	21.7%	41.4%
Partly free	21.6	21.8	39.1	23.2
Not free	42.5	39.3	39.2	35.4

Source: Adrian Karatnycky, *Freedom in the World 2001–2002: The Democracy Gap*

The problem facing international business managers is the democracies that have emerged since the early 1970s are fragile and unstable. Indonesia and many of the former republics of the former Soviet Union are examples. Their instability stems from internal division, corruption, militaries and oligarchies (ruling power in the hands of a few), and destabilization from abroad. There is still concern over whether these democracies will continue on the path to freedom in political rights and civil liberties.

In some democracies, such as the presidential form in the United States, people directly elect a president and a legislature. In other democracies, people vote for their representatives—or ruling party—and the ruling party selects the prime minister, who is the chief executive of the country. The parliamentary form of democracy in the United Kingdom is an example. There are also hybrids of each form. For example, Israel has a parliamentary government like that of the United Kingdom, but people vote directly for the prime minister as well.

The trend toward democracy is increasing, but many new democracies are fragile and unstable.

In a parliamentary system, the party with the most votes forms a government outright (if it has a majority) or through coalitions (if it has less than a majority).

FIGURE 3.4   Comparative Measures of Freedom

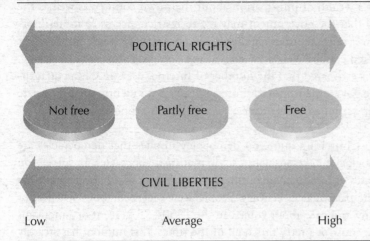

Countries classified as "free" in a political sense have a high degree of political rights and civil liberties. Those classified as "partly free" tend to be average to just below average in political rights and civil liberties. Those classified as "not free" tend to be quite low in both political rights and civil liberties. Examples of free countries include Australia, Bahamas, Belgium, Canada, Chile, Czech Republic, Estonia, Japan, Mexico, South Africa, and South Korea. Partly free countries include Albania, Brazil, Burkina Faso, Ethiopia, Malaysia, Nigeria, and Russia. Not free countries include Algeria, Cambodia, China, Egypt, Iraq, Kenya, North Korea, Saudi Arabia, and Zimbabwe.

Source: Original art based on Freedom House survey. Adnan Karatnycky, *Freedom in the World* (New York: Freedom House 1995).

Many democracies have only a few dominant parties, so it usually is not difficult for them to form a government. However, Israel is an example of a democracy in which there are so many political parties that the government in power is usually a minority government (it has earned less than a majority of the votes) that is formed from a coalition of several minority parties. Minority governments tend to be unstable because the coalition can fall apart, forcing a new governing alliance to form. For example, Ariel Sharon was elected Prime Minister of Israel in 2001, establishing a broad unity government with representatives from at least eight different parties. But the Labor Party withdrew its support in November 2002 and forced new elections to be called in early 2003, adding to the economic and security problems Israel faces. This inherent instability in the political environment in Israel is a product of the need to form a coalition government of political parties with divergent interests in the absence of an outright victory in the elections.

Democracies differ not only in the amount of citizen participation in decision making but also in the degree of centralized control. Canada, for example, gives significant political power to the provinces at the expense of its federal government. A major difficulty in negotiating the Canada–U.S. Free Trade Agreement (FTA) was that many provinces had their own trade barriers. The United States also considers states, rights important as a counterweight to encroaching intervention and control by the central government, even though it has a stronger federal government than Canada does.

Companies may have difficulty determining how to act in decentralized democratic systems because such companies face many (sometimes conflicting) laws. For example, because of different state tax systems in the United States, foreign companies need to locate their U.S. headquarters carefully. In contrast, the political and legal systems of France and Japan are more highly centralized. Companies consequently find it easier to deal with those countries' systems because there is less variation from one part of the country to another.

The Internet is having a big effect on government, both democratic and totalitarian. The essence of politics is communication, and the Internet has made communicating that much easier and cheaper. Government documents that used to be available only through hard copy or CD-ROM are now available on the Internet, giving managers instant access to a lot of information that can help them in the decision-making process. Not only are companies using the Internet to get their message across to potential investors and customers, so are politicians and lobbyists. The United States–China Business Council has an Internet site with special services for its members. The Internet will not replace elected representatives, because democracy still needs specialists who can interpret and compromise, but the Internet makes it easier to find the information on which to base an informed decision, and it allows elected representatives to keep more in touch with constituents.

The Internet allows politicians and government to communicate more effectively with constituents and provide information to managers.

In addition, the Internet has an impact on totalitarian societies. Where people have access to the Internet, they can get a wealth of information about their own country as well as the outside world—information that the government may try to restrict. Access to more information could reduce the power of totalitarian regimes. China has struggled to control access to the Internet and has blocked certain Web sites, such as the homepage for *Time* magazine. Between 2000 and 2002, it is estimated that the number of Internet users in China quadrupled to 38.5 million, and the government moved more aggressively to identify inappropriate Web sites and to monitor the activities of cybercafés, a very difficult proposition.[10]

Stability in Democracies   Churchill's quote on democracy implies that democracies are not perfect. Just as new democracies have problems, so do mature democracies. In surveys on democracy in the United States, it is clear that confidence in politicians and government has continued to decline over the past quarter century. People are concerned about whether or not politicians are trustworthy and care about voters. In the 1950s, 75 percent of Americans trusted the U.S. government most or pretty much all of the time. This number has steadily dropped to a low of 26 percent in 1998.[11] In addition, the percentage of people who vote is declining. The loss of faith in political institutions and the feeling that professional pressure groups and lobbying organizations are increasingly more influential than individuals are causes of concern in democracy. In spite of this, 75 percent of people in democracies strongly feel that democracy is the best form of government.[12] The public's confidence in the U.S. government rose after the September 11 attacks to 55 percent, its highest level in 30 years.[13]

Totalitarianism

As Figure 3.3 showed, democracy is at one end of the political spectrum, and totalitarianism is at the other. Totalitarian governments are usually theocratic or secular. In theocratic totalitarianism, religious leaders are also the political leaders. This form is best exemplified in Islamic countries such as Iran. In secular totalitarianism, the government often imposes order through military power. Examples of this form are found in Cambodia, Afghanistan (before the overthrow of the Taliban regime in 2001), and Iraq (under the rule of Saddam Hussein). In a totalitarian state, a single party, individual, or group of individuals monopolizes political power and neither recognizes nor permits opposition. Only a few individuals participate in decision making. All countries considered not free and many considered partly free in Figure 3.4 are totalitarian.

Totalitarianism takes several forms, including fascism, authoritarianism, and communism. Mussolini (Italy's dictator from 1924 to 1943) defined *fascism* as follows: "The Fascist conception of the state is all-embracing; outside of it no human or spiritual value may exist, much less have any value. Thus understood Fascism is totalitarian and the Fascist State, as a synthesis and a unit which includes all values, interprets, develops and lends additional power to the whole life of a people."[14] Examples of fascist totalitarianism in the past include Italy under Mussolini, Germany under Hitler, Portugal under Salazar, and Spain under Franco. Examples of authoritarian totalitarianism include Chile under Pinochet and South Africa prior to the end of apartheid and the initiation of black rule. Authoritarianism differs from fascism in sofaras the former simply desires to rule people, whereas the latter desires to control people's minds and souls, to convert them to its own faith.[15]

Communism is a form of secular totalitarianism in which political and economic systems (and philosophies) are virtually inseparable. Communists believe in the equal distribution of wealth, which entails total government ownership and control of resources. Communism has failed in most parts of the world. The Eastern European countries and the former Soviet Union have moved away from communism to various degrees of democracy. As communism moves toward democracy, the link between economics and politics in communist countries has been weakened, making countries such as Estonia, Latvia, and Lithuania free. China,

Confidence in democracies in general is waning, but people in democratic countries still believe democracy is the best form of government.

Theocratic totalitarianism—religious leaders are the political leaders.

Secular totalitarianism—control is enforced through military power.

In a totalitarian system, decision making is restricted to a few individuals.

Communism—a form of secular totalitarianism that combines political and economic systems into a sociopolitical agenda.

North Korea, and Vietnam, however, are still communist countries with strong centralized authoritarian control over the political process.

As noted earlier, totalitarian regimes fit primarily in the "not free" category in Figure 3.4. Freedom House notes that 90 percent of the "not free" countries share one or more of the following characteristics.

1. They have a majority Muslim population and are frequently forced to confront the pressures of fundamentalist Islam.
2. They are multiethnic societies in which power is not held by a dominant ethnic group (one that represents over two-thirds of the population).
3. They are neocommunist or postcommunist transitional societies.[16]

With few exceptions, most totalitarian governments have been opening up and liberalizing since 1989 when the Berlin Wall fell and the Soviet bloc broke apart. As these countries move from totalitarian to democratic states, the degree of instability increases, creating problems for foreign companies interested in doing business there. Accompanied by political changes are economic changes as these countries move more toward the market model. We'll discuss those economic issues in Chapter 4, but for now, let's see how political systems affect international management.

THE IMPACT OF THE POLITICAL SYSTEM ON MANAGEMENT DECISIONS

Political Risk

As managers evaluate a country as a potential place to do business and as they struggle to succeed once they have committed resources, they need to be aware of **political risk**. Political risk is when international companies fear that the political climate in a foreign country will change in such a way that their operating position will deteriorate. Although political risks can occur in democratic as well as in totalitarian political regimes, they tend to be more prevalent in totalitarian regimes.

Political risk—a risk that occurs because of political instability.

Types and Causes of Political Risk   Political actions that may affect company operations adversely are government takeovers of property, either with or without compensation, operational restrictions that impede the company's ability to take certain actions, and agitation that disrupts sales or causes damage to property or personnel. Although one usually thinks of political risk as a situation in which one is not able to operate in a specific country because of political instability in that country, there are other ways that political risk can affect a company. For example, during the period of apartheid in South Africa, many U.S. companies with investments in South Africa faced boycotts in the United States by groups that were morally opposed to apartheid. Similarly, groups opposed to doing business with Myanmar have put up Internet sites criticizing U.S. policy and U.S. companies doing business in that country, hoping to exert the same kind of pressure that forced many companies out of South Africa.

Political risk may occur for the following reasons:

1. *Opinions of political leadership.* Political leaders' opinions may change over time, and the leaders could be replaced by force or election with politicians whose views toward business and foreign investment are much less positive. Changes may result in adverse operating regulations, such as limits on remittances or discriminatory taxes. Such changes may lead to the breaching of existing contracts or the takeover of the investors' property.
2. *Civil disorder.* Unrest may occur because of economic conditions, human rights violations, or group animosity within the society. A good example of this risk took place in

Causes of political risk
• Changing opinions of political leadership
• Civil disorder
• External relations

Argentina at the beginning of 2002 during the height of its economic crisis, when the government froze withdrawals from bank accounts to prevent complete depletion of cash from the banking sector. Groups of street protesters and rioters started targeting and attacking mainly foreign-owned banks. Many banks operated with wooden and steel plates covering their windows. The manager of London-based HSBC's Argentina subsidiary mentioned that he felt about as popular as a serial killer.[17] Further, widespread crime, such as the kidnapping of personnel, may result from inadequate police control. Conditions may result in procurement difficulties, work stoppages, shipment delays, and property damage. If carried to an extreme, the nation itself may break apart, leaving the investor to operate in a smaller market or forcing him or her to leave the market.

3. *External relations.* Animosity between the host country and the foreign investor's home country may result in work-stoppage protests, the forced divestment of operations, and the loss of supplies and markets. Animosity, especially war, between the host country and any other country may result in property damage and the inability to get supplies or to deliver goods.

Micro political risk—political actions are aimed at specific foreign investments.

Micro and Macro Political Risks   If political actions are aimed only at specific foreign investments, they are known as **micro political risks**. For example, after the beginning of the U.S. bombing of Afghanistan in October 2001, anti-American protesters in Pakistan burned a KFC restaurant, a McDonald's restaurant, and a Shell gas station.

Companies most likely to be affected by micro political risk are those that may have a considerable and visible impact on a given country because of their size, monopoly position, importance to their home country's national defense, and dependence of other industries on them. If agitation's cause is animosity between factions in the host country and the government of a foreign country, protesters may target only the most visible companies from that foreign country, like McDonald's. There is also evidence that firms are apt to face adverse political situations if they act in a socially irresponsible manner.

Macro political risk—political actions affect a broad spectrum of foreign investors.

If political actions affect a broad spectrum of foreign investors, they are **macro political risks**. For example, after the communist revolution in Cuba, the takeover of property was aimed at all foreign investors regardless of industry or nationality, or of whether or not the investors' past behavior had been socially responsible. This is not as much an issue now as it was in the 1960s, when a number of countries declared their independence from previous colonial powers. Today, most countries realize that they need the stability of foreign direct investment in order to grow.

Government Intervention in the Economy

As companies move abroad, management must deal with governments that influence the economy in different ways. There are two ideological paradigms on the role of governments: *individualistic* and *communitarian*.[18]

Individualistic—minimal government intervention in the economy.

The **individualistic paradigm** believes in minimal intervention in the economy. Individualistic states believe in regulation, and they are likely to be democratic and economically free. They will handle market defects, such as entry barriers and insufficient consumer knowledge and power, but they will not intervene too much. They believe in the limited role of government as well as in checks and balances, and they have a high distrust of central government power. Government is essentially separate from business.

Communitarian—the government defines needs and priorities and partners with business in a major way.

In a **communitarian paradigm**, government tends to be prestigious, authoritative, and sometimes authoritarian. It is very hierarchical and may be either democratic, as in the case of Japan, or autocratic, as in the case of China. It thrives on a respected, centralized bureaucracy with a stable political party or coalition in power.

Individualistic countries bring business activity into line with the needs of the community by promoting marketplace competition and by regulating the marketplace in those instances in which competition by itself is unreliable or unacceptable, such as when a company might be able to establish a monopoly position or degrade the environment. Communitarian countries may do the same, but they also establish a partnership with business. The communitarian concept has spread to other Asian countries more anxious to mirror the examples of Japan and China than the more individualistic example of the United States.

Japan is a good example of how the communitarian philosophy can affect business. After World War II, Japan had to rebuild its economy. It focused on recovery rather than reform of its basic system. Because there was no need to focus on military and defense, it could put its efforts into infrastructure and the economy. It had good political stability and a highly educated workforce. At the time, Japan decided to insulate its economy from outside competition, even though it was highly competitive inside. However, that decision made it difficult for foreign companies to establish a market position in Japan, a condition that is still true today. The government told companies to focus on scale (large size, which permits large production runs and lower costs per unit) and concentration (few competitors in an industry or at least lots of cooperation among competitors) rather than on small entrepreneurial activities. It also encouraged companies to focus on export to high-income countries. Government's role was to establish a broad vision of the future and then set incentives and sanctions to accomplish these objectives. Japan's key government institutions were the Ministry of International Trade and Industry (MITI), the Ministry of Finance, the Bank of Japan, and the Economic Planning Agency. These institutions funded preferred industries and controlled access to technology, foreign exchange, and imports. In response, the Keidanren, an organization of the top companies in Japan, helped establish a consensus within the business community. Its main objective was to influence the government on policies responsive to its wishes.[19]

In addition to understanding government functions, managers also must realize that governmental action is not always consistent. In the United States, for example, significant conflict exists within government regarding how and to what extent it should regulate international business activities for U.S. firms operating outside of the United States. No specific government agency deals with international issues, so conflicting policies can exist. For example, at least three different U.S. government agencies share responsibility for regulating nonagricultural exports: the State Department, the Department of Defense, and the Department of Commerce. State is responsible for the overall political relationships between the United States and other countries, Defense is responsible for national defense, and Commerce is responsible for facilitating commercial—including export—activities. These agencies often have different viewpoints on how to regulate exports. For example, it might seem perfectly logical from a commercial standpoint to sell satellite technology to China, but the Defense Department might veto such sales in the name of national security.

If a U.S. company moves from the United States to Germany, Japan, or South Korea, three very communitarian countries, it may have to develop new strategies for its relationships with government, suppliers, customers, and competitors. In the United States, relationships may be arm's length, competitive, and adversarial, while in Germany, Japan, and South Korea, they may be much more cooperative.

FORMULATING AND IMPLEMENTING POLITICAL STRATEGIES

Formulating political strategies often is more complicated for managers than formulating competitive marketplace strategies. When dealing in the political arena, managers need to know how decisions are made that could influence their ability to operate. Then they need to know what the rules are for trying to influence political decisions.

There are certain steps that a company must follow if it wants to establish an appropriate political strategy in its countries of operation.

Government action isn't always consistent—different agencies may have different attitudes toward business issues.

Formulating political strategies is complicated by the wide range of participants in the decision-making process, by differences in logic, and by institutional power.

1. *Identify the issue*. What is the specific issue facing a firm—trade barriers, environmental standards, worker rights?
2. *Define the political aspect of the issue*. Does the government feel strongly about the specific issue, or is it of minimal concern? Is there a political dimension to the issue, or is it something that can be dealt with outside of politics?
3. *Assess the potential political action of other companies and special-interest groups*. Who are the parties that are affected and able to generate political pressure? What are their strategies likely to be?
4. *Identify important institutions and key individuals*. Are they legislatures, regulatory agencies, courts, important personalities?
5. *Formulate strategies*. What are the key objectives, the major alternatives, and the likely effectiveness of alternative strategies?
6. *Determine the impact of implementation*. What will be the public relations fallout in the home and host countries if the action taken is unpopular?
7. *Select the most appropriate strategy and implement it.*[20]

Implementing a strategy means marshaling whatever resources are necessary to accomplish the company's political objectives. For example, in the United States, companies—domestic or foreign—hire lobbyists to educate and persuade government decision makers about the merits of their position. In a representative democracy, lobbyists represent constituencies and perform the important role of aggregating ideas and communicating them to decision makers. Without the freedom of expression—such as lobbying—democracy could not exist. As the ethics of government-business relationships have become more important—even in totalitarian countries—companies have greater reason to examine carefully their policy formulation and implementation strategies.

A company also can attempt to influence government action from consumers and others by using a grassroots campaign or by building coalitions of different groups that share the company's interests. As noted earlier in the chapter, the United States–China Business Council is a lobbying organization that represents the interests of its members to the appropriate people in the U.S. government. Because of both its size and the importance of its members, the council is able to wield a degree of influence that would not be possible for a single company.

Part of the problem in establishing a global political strategy is that democracies and totalitarian regimes deal with companies differently. In general, foreign companies can influence democracies through lobbying. However, companies sometimes abuse their power by engaging in bribery and other illicit activities. Sometimes a totalitarian regime might seem more stable because it doesn't have to deal with the pressures of democracy. But when such a regime is overthrown, the changes for business tend to be larger and more rapid than change typically is within a democracy. For example, when the Soviet Union broke up, foreign companies that had entered into contracts with the former central government found that these contracts were not binding on the individual republics' governments. Companies had to renegotiate the contracts or pull out of the country. In another example, Mozambique was a colony of Portugal. When it declared its independence in 1988, it forced Portuguese investors out of the country, telling them to abandon their investments. Even though the colony might have seemed stable, a change in government caused significant change in investment strategies. Since then, however, Mozambique has invited back many former Portuguese investors in an effort to rebuild the economy.

THE LEGAL ENVIRONMENT

Closely related to the political system, the legal system is another dimension of the external environment that influences business. Managers must be aware of the legal systems in the countries in which they operate; the nature of the legal profession, both domestic and international; and the legal relationships that exist between countries. Legal systems differ in terms of the nature of the system—common law, civil law, and theocratic law—and the degree of independence of the judiciary from the political process. As noted in the opening case, for example, there was some concern in 1999 that Hong Kong was moving away from the legal traditions established by the British toward the influence of Beijing. Also, some of the totalitarian countries that are going through a transition to democracy and to a free-market economy don't have a legal system in place that deals with business transactions in a global market context.

Kinds of Legal Systems

Legal systems usually fall into one of three categories: common law, civil law, and theocratic law.

Common Law   The United States and the United Kingdom are examples of countries with **a common law system**. Common law is based on tradition, precedent, and custom and usage. The courts fulfill an important role by interpreting the law according to those characteristics. Because the United Kingdom originated common law in the modern setting, its former and current colonies, such as Hong Kong, also have common law systems.

Civil Law   The **civil law system**, also called **a codified legal system**, is based on a detailed set of laws that make up a code. Rules for conducting business transactions are a part of the code. Over 70 countries, including Germany, France, and Japan, operate on a civil law basis.

The two legal systems differ mostly because common law is based on the courts' interpretations of events, whereas civil law is based on how the law is applied to the facts. An example of an area in which the two systems differ in practice is contracts. In a common law country, contracts tend to be detailed, with all contingencies spelled out. In a civil law country, contracts tend to be shorter and less specific because many of the issues that a common law contract would cover already are included in the civil code. So when entering into contracts abroad, it is important for the manager to understand which type of legal system will establish the contract. Civil law also tends to be less adversarial than common law because judges rely on detailed legal codes rather than on precedent when deciding cases. This is one reason why British and U.S. law firms encounter so much resistance when they enter civil law countries. They are used to the competitive, adversarial approach that the common law system engenders.

Theocratic Law   The third type of legal system is the **theocratic law system**, which is based on religious precepts. The best example of this system is Islamic law, which is found in Muslim countries. Islamic law, or Shair'a, is based on the following sources

- The Koran, the sacred text
- The Sunnah, or decisions and sayings of the Prophet Muhammad
- The writings of Islamic scholars, who derive rules by analogy from the principles established in the Koran and the Sunnah
- The consensus of Muslim countries' legal communities[21]

Given that 25 percent of the world's population is Islamic, it is important to understand how Islam is translated into rules that govern economic transactions. This is true for Islamic countries—such as Iran, Sudan, and Pakistan, which have banned traditional commercial banking and adopted Islamic banking models—and for Muslims who live in non-Islamic countries.[22] Since the tenth century A.D., Islamic law has remained frozen—it cannot change, modify, or extend with changing times. Islamic law is a moral rather than a commercial law and was intended to govern all aspects of life. Many Muslim countries have legal systems that are a unique blend of the Islamic law system and a common or civil law system derived from

Countries in transition struggle to develop a legal system consistent with the global market economy.

A common law system is based on tradition, precedent, custom and usage, and interpretation by the courts.

A civil law system also called a codified legal system, is based on a detailed set of laws organized into a legal code.

A theocratic legal system is based on religious precepts, such as Islamic law.

previous colonial ties. Even though Islamic law is fixed, Islamic jurists and scholars are constantly debating its application in different modern settings. The key is to adhere to the constants of Islam while maintaining sufficient flexibility to operate in a modern economy.

An example of how Islamic law influences international business can be found in banking. According to Islamic law, banks cannot charge interest or benefit from interest.[23] Instead, banks have to structure fees into their loans to allow them to make a profit. For example, assume that a company needs to borrow money to purchase merchandise. It can approach a bank, which would buy the goods and sell them to the company, which will pay the bank at a future date at an agreed-upon markup.[24] Also, banks can structure loans so that they share in the profits of a venture rather than receive interest. The underlying principle is that money can earn a return by being employed productively, but not by being earned in financial markets.[25] There are approximately 250 Islamic banks in 27 Muslim and 16 non-Muslim countries, which manage funds of $200 billion.[26] Many Western banks, such as Citibank, J. P. Morgan, Deutsche Bank, and ABN AMRO Bank of the Netherlands, have Islamic units.[27]

Consumer Safeguards

A major challenge that companies face in the global environment is how to deal with product liability issues. Different legal systems provide different safeguards for consumers. For example, it appears that Japanese consumers have less access to and assistance from the legal community in Japan than American consumers do in the United States, given that they have fewer lawyers per capita than does the United States. Also, the Japanese legal system differs from the U.S. system in a variety of ways. The Japanese Federation of Bar Associations sets legal fees, foreign lawyers are prohibited from advising clients on Japanese law or from hiring local Japanese lawyers to do so, and advertising restrictions limit consumer information about legal services. In addition, the high cost of legal services and the long delays in the legal process discourage consumers from filing civil suits.

The Legal Profession

MNEs must use lawyers for a variety of services, such as negotiating contracts and protecting intellectual property. Lawyers and their firms vary among countries in terms of how they practice law and service clients.

Law firms that service international clients have changed over the years. In general, most law firms are quite small. There are still large firms servicing multinational clients, but many MNEs, concerned about upward-spiraling legal fees, have established in-house legal staffs. Smaller companies in international business still rely on outside legal counsel for help with a wide variety of issues, such as agent–distributor relationships and protecting intellectual property.

Just as MNEs have invested abroad to take advantage of expanding business opportunities, law firms have expanded abroad to service their clients. Laws vary from country to country, and legal staffs need to understand local practices. Also, law firms have had to overcome significant barriers as they have expanded. Those barriers include restrictions on foreign firms from hiring local lawyers, from forming partnerships with local law firms, or even from entering the country to practice law. However, there are countries that allow foreigners to practice law and to open offices within their borders. Some countries even allow law firms to merge—an aggressive move. In 1999, senior lawyers at Clifford Chance in London and Rogers & Wells in New York voted to join forces in what would be the first overseas merger of large law firms. The merger took place to service multinational clients better and to counter the competition of the global public accounting firms, such as KPMG, that had begun to move into the legal business. Although there have been complications when trying to unify the payment systems and conflicts of interest in certain growth areas, the joint company brought in revenues of $1.4 billion in 2001, a 24 percent increase in the aggregate revenues of the individual companies.[28]

Is "When in Rome, Do as the Romans Do" the Best Approach for Global Ethics?

Ethical dilemmas entail balancing means and ends. Means are the actions one takes, which may be right or wrong; ends are the results of the actions, which may also be right or wrong. Ethics teaches that "people have a responsibility to do what is right and to avoid doing what is wrong."[29] Some people argue that cultural relativism, or the belief that behavior has meaning only in its specific cultural or ethical context, implies that no method exists for deciding whether any behavior is ever appropriate. However, we contend that it is possible to measure whether behavior is appropriate. Individuals must seek justification for their behavior, and that justification is a function of cultural values (many of which are universal), legal principles, and economic practices.

Some people also argue that the legal justification for ethical behavior is the only important one. By this standard, a person or company can do anything that is not illegal. However, there are five reasons why the legal argument is insufficient.

1. The law is not appropriate for regulating all business activity because not everything that is unethical is illegal. This would be true of many dimensions of interpersonal behavior, for example.
2. The law is slow to develop in emerging areas of concern. Laws take time to be legislated and tested in courts. Further, they cannot anticipate all future ethical dilemmas; basically, they are a reaction to issues that have already surfaced. Countries with civil law systems rely on specificity in the law, and there may not be enough laws passed that deal with ethical issues.
3. The law often is based on moral concepts that are not precisely defined and that cannot be separated from legal concepts. Moral concepts must be considered along with legal ones.
4. The law is often in need of testing by the courts. This is especially true of case law, in which the courts establish precedent.
5. The law is not very efficient. A reliance on legal rulings on every area of ethical behavior would not be in anyone's best interests.[30]

In spite of the pitfalls of using the law as the major basis for deciding ethical disputes, there also are good reasons for at least complying with it.

1. The law embodies many of a country's moral beliefs and is an adequate guide for proper conduct.
2. The law provides a clearly defined set of rules. Following those rules at least establishes a good precedent. Some people are afraid to go beyond the law because of the potential legal liability that could result if they did.
3. The law contains enforceable rules that all must follow. It puts everyone on an equal footing. For example, everyone working for a company established in the United States must comply with the Foreign Corrupt Practices Act, which prohibits bribery of foreign government officials for business purposes. As long as everyone complies with the law, no one will have an edge due to bribery. However, laws are still subject to interpretation and often contain loopholes.
4. The law represents a consensus derived from significant experience and deliberation. It should reflect careful and wide-ranging discussions.[31]

The problem for companies that use a legal basis for ethical behavior is that laws vary among countries. For example, a major area of contention between industrial and developing countries is the protection of intellectual property, such as computer software. The industrial countries, which have strong laws concerning intellectual-property rights, argue that developing countries need to strengthen such laws and their enforcement. U.S. software manufacturers note that in some Asian countries, it is possible to buy a heavily discounted pirated version of new software in one store and then to go next door and purchase a photocopy of the documentation for the legal version. Using a legal basis for ethical behavior would mean that such purchases are ethical because they occur in countries that either do not have laws on intellectual-property rights or do not enforce the laws. Although international trade agreements provide for better protection of intellectual property, it is up to the member countries to implement the provisions, and that is proceeding at a very slow pace. One could argue that the moral values that cross cultures will be embodied in legal systems, but as the software example demonstrates, that is too simplistic. Not all moral values are common to every culture. In addition, strong home-country governments may try to extend their legal and ethical practices to the foreign subsidiaries of domestically headquartered companies—an action known as extraterritoriality. For example, a subsidiary of a U.S. company operating in China might be forced to follow some U.S. laws, even though China has no comparable laws and other companies operating there are not subject to the U.S. laws. In some cases, such as with health and safety standards, extraterritoriality should not cause problems. In other cases, such as with restrictions on trade with enemies of the United States, extraterritoriality may cause tension between the foreign subsidiary and the host-country government.

As noted earlier, the law provides a clearly defined set of rules, which companies often follow strictly because of concerns about potential legal liability. However, a company may seek a loophole to accomplish an objective. Evaluating potential liability and the legality of actions varies between countries with civil law systems and those with common law ones. Civil law countries tend to have a large body of laws that specify the legality of various behaviors. Common law countries tend to rely more on cases and precedents than on statutory regulations. A company must pay attention to laws to ensure the minimum level of compliance in each country in which it operates. When faced with conflicting laws, however, management must decide which applies.

A far less aggressive move overseas is for law firms to establish correspondent relationships with firms in other countries. For example, a law firm in the United States would refer clients looking to do work in France to a French law firm.

The manager doing business overseas has a number of ways to get legal work done in different countries. The key is to choose a law firm that has connections overseas and to do so through the company's own offices, a merger, or correspondent relationships. The laws in each country differ so much that it is important to have some representation in the local environment.

Legal Issues in International Business

Impact of laws on international business:

- National laws affect all local business activities
- National laws affect cross-border activities
- International treaties and conventions may govern some cross-border transactions

National laws affect business within the country or business among countries. Some national laws on local business activity influence both domestic and foreign companies, especially in the areas of health and safety standards, employment practices, antitrust prohibitions, contractual relationships, environmental practices, and patents and trademarks. For example, the maximum workweek in Thailand is 84 hours, and that applies to domestic and foreign firms. Nike subcontracts its shoe manufacturing to a local Thai company. However, because of pressures from labor and consumer groups to follow better employment practices, Nike has established its own maximum of 60 hours, which the local contractor must follow. If Nike wanted to follow the Thai law, it could do so, but that would be in violation of its own code of conduct.

LOOKING TO THE FUTURE

Will Democracy Survive?

The terrorist attacks of September 11, 2001, in New York City were aimed at destroying the very democracy that much of the world prospers on. As the U.S. Democratic National Committee Chairman Terry McAuliffe said, "Democracy itself was attacked on September 11. The terrorists sought to destroy not just American lives and American buildings; they were aiming straight for the American way of life. There is only one way to withstand such an attack—by reaffirming the very freedoms that our enemies resent."[32]

What will the world's political makeup look like in the next decade? Will democracy continue to grow, will terrorist groups erode democracy's fundamentals, or will totalitarianism creep back? The next decade will test whether the 40 or so countries that have become democratic in the past two decades will remain democratic or slip back into totalitarianism.

Some people argue that democracy has certain preconditions, such as economic development. Indeed, most high-income or upper-middle-income countries are democratic, while most nondemocracies are poor, non-Western, or both. Others argue that democracy is the product of political leaders with the will and skill to see democratization occur.[33] These people say that the move toward democracy in Russia occurred because of two men: Mikhail Gorbachev and Boris Yeltsin. When Gorbachev went as far as he could, Yeltsin was there for the next steps. Now Vladamir Putin is taking Russia to the next democratic plateau.

Democracy does not necessarily mean stability. The newer democracies of the 1990s, especially those in the former Soviet bloc countries, are still unstable enough to possibly threaten war. Terrorism is also a threat to the stability of democracy. As U.S. President George Bush commented, "Terror, unanswered, can not only bring down buildings, it can threaten the stability of legitimate governments."[34] Managers ought not to assume that just because they are operating in a democratic country, there is no political risk. They still need to monitor the political environment just as they might in a less free country.

Asia is testing an alternative to democracy. With the exception of Japan—and, to a lesser extent, India and South Korea—most Asian countries are not democracies, and their leaders do not appear to want democracy. Instead, they are attempting to link strong economic growth and totalitarian political systems. This is clearly the case with China—and to a slightly lesser extent, Singapore. In some respects, the elimination of strong central controls with the advent of democracy has created problems in some countries—problems such as the removal of individual moral constraints, resulting in crime, corruption, and an atmosphere of amoralism.[35]

The threat to democracy could come from a return to communism, from terrorism and electoral victories of antidemocratic forces (such as Islamic fundamentalism), or from the concentration of power in a leader. The key, then, is to define democracy in different national contexts. It could be argued, as totalitarian governments do, that democracy is not appropriate for all countries. Who is to say that China would fare any better if it held elections or allowed free speech. However, there is a clear link between political and economic freedom and economic growth. So as the emerging democracies liberalize politically, they may loosen up economically, setting the stage for solid economic growth.

Laws also exist that govern cross-border activities, such as the investment of capital, the payment of dividends to foreign investors, and customs duties on imports. International laws, such as treaties governing the cross-border transfer of hazardous waste, can also determine how a firm operates when transporting shipments across borders.

Because laws affect so many aspects of international business, several subsequent chapters discuss legal issues in more depth. For example, we'll discuss laws governing the regulation of trade and investments, taxes, intellectual-property protection, the regulation of financial flows and of ownership, reporting requirements, contractual relationships, extraterritoriality (the extension by a government of the application of its laws to foreign operations of companies), international treaties, and dispute resolution.

Summary

- The political process involves inputs from various interest groups, articulation of issues that affect policy formulation, aggregation of those issues into key alternatives, development of policies, and implementation and adjudication of the policies.

- The ultimate test of any political system is its ability to hold a society together despite pressures from different ideologies.

- In democracies, there is wide participation in the decision-making process. In totalitarian regimes, only few citizens participate, although some regimes are beginning to allow greater participation in the decision-making process. Totalitarian regimes can be either theocratic or secular.

- Factors considered in measuring freedom include the degree to which fair and competitive elections occur, the extent to which individual and group freedoms are guaranteed, and the existence of freedom of the press.

- Political risk occurs because of changing opinions of political leadership, civil disorder, or external relations between the host country and the foreign investor's home country.

- Individualistic political regimes believe in minimal intervention in the economy by government; communitarian regimes believe that a government's role is to define a nation's needs and priorities and to ensure that they are met through a close cooperation between government and business.

- Companies try to educate government officials on specific actions that will benefit the companies' ability to compete through lobbying efforts.

- In formulating political strategies, managers must consider the possible political actions that could affect the company, the different constituencies that might influence those political actions, the political strategies that would be in the best interests of the company, and the costs of implementing those strategies.

- Common law systems are based on tradition, precedent, and custom and usage. Civil law systems are based on a detailed set of laws organized into a code. Theocratic legal systems are based on religious precepts, as exemplified by Islamic law.

- Many law firms have increased their size through mergers to better service corporate clients in domestic and international mergers and acquisitions.

- There are national laws that govern local business activity of both domestic and foreign firms, national laws that govern cross-border activities, and international laws that govern cross-border activities.

- Although there is legal justification for some ethical behavior, the law is not an adequate guide for all such behavior. The legality of an action is one element that should be considered, but not the only one.

CASE

Newmont Mining in Indonesia[36]

Paul Lahti, the director of the Minahasa Raya mine for Newmont Mining Corp. in Indonesia, was both disappointed and relieved about Newmont's latest decision. Faced with a changing political and legal landscape, illegal miners, environmental protests, and decreasing gold reserves, Newmont decided to close the Minahasa Raya mine in 2003.

Newmont Mining, headquartered in Denver, Colorado, is the second biggest gold producer worldwide. Beginning Indonesian operations in 1996, it now has two mining operations—Batu Hijau on the island of Sumbawa and Minahasa Raya on the island of Sulawesi. Newmont's involvement in Indonesia has been one of frustrations and struggles yet also great success. To understand its situation in

Indonesia, it is necessary to first understand the political history of the country.

POLITICAL HISTORY OF INDONESIA

Indonesia is the fourth largest country in the world in population, with 210 million people, and 87 percent of the population is Muslim, making it the largest Muslim country in the world. Indonesia is an archipelago stretching more than 3,000 miles and comprising 17,000 islands, 6,000 of which are inhabited. Sixty percent of the population resides on the island of Java, where the capital city of Jakarta is located. Indonesians fight extreme poverty, with per capita income at $570 and a 15-to-20 percent unemployment rate.

For many years prior to World War II, Indonesia, known as the Dutch East Indies, was governed under autocratic rule by the Netherlands. During World War II, the Japanese invaded the country and took control for the next three years. During this time and prior to the Japanese invasion, an independence movement by many Indonesian nationalists began forming. Although suppressed by the ruling government, the main party—the Indonesian Nationalist Party—was run by Ahmed Sukarno. The Japanese withdrew from the country upon their surrender to the Allies, and Indonesia claimed independence on August 17, 1945.

Ahmed Sukarno emerged as the country's first president and quickly established his authoritarian regime, labeled "Guided Democracy." In the mid-1960s, a failed coup begun by the Indonesian Communist Party (PKI), which Sukarno empathized with, was stamped out by the national military that was led by the army chief of staff, General Suharto. In an effort to rid the country of a communist presence, Suharto's forces killed hundreds of thousands of suspected communists.

Never able to regain support, Sukarno passed political and military powers to Suharto. Suharto established his political "New Order" by massing power in the central government and military. The economy improved dramatically under Suharto's rule, although corruption filtered through the military, government, and legal system. He is known for using an iron fist to impose his will on the country's vast array of religious and ethnic groups.

When the Asian financial crisis of 1997 hit, Indonesia's flawed economic structure and corruption sent the country spiraling downward. Inflation hit 80 percent at one point, and the economy contracted by 14 percent. Demonstrators turned against ethnic Chinese, and conflicts arose between Christians and Muslims. Companies owned by ethnic Chinese or foreign companies using ethnic Chinese in management positions were the targets of demonstrators and incurred serious property damage. Protesters and rioters demanded Suharto's resignation, and he eventually gave in after 32 years of rule.

On October 20, 1999, Abdurrahman Wahid was elected by the Indonesian legislature to be president, and Megawati Sukarnoputri,

the daughter of Sukarno, became vice president. Both leaders were faced with the daunting tasks of restoring the economy, ridding the country of its corruption, and trying to establish policies to govern the vast array of religions and ethnicities. Although known for his political acumen, Wahid was not able to restore the country and avoid corruption. He was impeached for alleged corruption in April 2001, and Megawati became Indonesia's President.

Another political issue facing Indonesia was the independence movement by East Timor, an island situated between Indonesia and Australia. Since 1975, when Portuguese rule left the territory, East Timor engaged in a civil war between advocates of integration with Indonesia and those who wanted an independent nation. After UN intervention, the Indonesian military withdrew from the territory, and East Timor became the world's newest nation on May 20, 2002.

Major Challenges Facing Newmont Mining   Newmont Mining is faced with many problems in Indonesia, including a changing political and legal landscape, illegal mining, environmental protests, and declining gold prices and reserves.

Although Suharto caused many problems in Indonesia, his policies helped stabilize the mining industry. Newmont worked directly with the central government rather than deal with the different local governments. All this changed once Suharto resigned.

Indonesia's current leaders have been struggling to grant power and decision-making responsibilities to the provinces and regions. Wahid was unwilling to use Suharto's same tough tactics on local governments, and as a result the central government has lost much of its power to the regions. This has caused confusion among the business and industry sectors. They don't know whether to follow the central or the regional government's laws and policies.

It is not enough that the political spectrum is going through dramatic change; Indonesia's legal system is in turmoil too. The corruption of the Suharto era filtered into the courts, making it even riskier for foreign firms like Newmont to operate. There is a deterioration of the court system, stemming from the political conflicts between local regulations, parliamentary decrees, ministerial decisions and presidential orders. Local authorities engage in political and legal battles with many western MNEs, like Newmont, because they feel the contracts drafted in the Suharto era are corrupt and benefit only the MNE. The abject poverty in most of these regions only fans the flames.

Newmont was hit head-on from the defective court system and local aggression in September 1999, when the local Minahasa district demanded $8.2 million in back pay of taxes for waste material. Newmont's contract, established with the central government of Suharto, exempted Newmont from paying any tax on mining waste materials, including topsoil and rock. However, Minahasa's local parliament passed a law allowing it to collect levies from local companies.

After forcing the mine to shut down a number of times, Minahasa's local courts, under pressure from Indonesia's Supreme

Court, agreed to settle with Newmont for $500,000, and it paid another $2.5 million to be added into employee programs and community development projects. This will help to reduce the resentment of the community, which faces extreme poverty and unemployment.

President Wahid passed new autonomy laws in hopes of solving some of the political and legal conflict. Some people fear that these laws, which took effect at the beginning of 2001, will just escalate the problems. The laws are intended to hand more of the central government's power to the regions, but neither Wahid nor Megawati have passed any regulations to implement them.

With the government's move toward democracy and decentralization, local groups have found it the perfect time to demand more from companies operating in their regions. Labor activists, environmental protesters, and local social groups are demanding that corporations improve their social responsibility programs if they are to receive popular local acceptance. Under Suharto's regime, corporations could turn to the central government to brush aside any uprisings from local groups. These companies are now finding it necessary to implement social programs, engage in better labor relations, and meet local environmental regulations.

Local problems have caused Newmont to close down its Minahasa Raya mine several times for short periods since its opening. In the last quarter of 2000, former landowners blockaded the entrance to the mine at least three times, demanding more money for the land Newmont now mines on. Newmont argues that it compensated the landowners fairly when it initially purchased the land.

Another major difficulty for Newmont is the fact that illegal miners are stealing gold from the mine. The number of illegal miners has tripled since 1997 because of the large number of unemployed which the recession has created. In the Minahasa mine alone, there are 3,000 illegal miners. Mr. Lahti took a creative approach to ridding the mine of illegal miners. He developed and signed a memorandum of understanding with the local government that Newmont would give a portion of its mine to the illegal miners if the government cleared them out of the rest of the mine.

The deal fell through because the government failed to implement its side of the bargain. Although he lobbied and pleaded with local and national authorities, Mr. Lahti was unable to rid the mine of the looters.

Ever since the opening of the Minahasa mine, Newmont has been under environmental scrutiny, with mounting evidence of pollution problems. Environmental groups claim that the tailings, or waste material, that Newmont disposes into the ocean contain toxic levels of mercury and arsenic. Studies have found that the number of fish has drastically decreased in the area and the health of the local people has been affected.

Because of these studies, the environment minister required Newmont to conduct an environmental risk assessment and to detoxify its tailings before dumping them into the ocean. Despite these efforts, environmentalists continue to protest.

Some, however, believe the environmental problems are mainly the result of the illegal miners, who use antiquated mining practices to extract the gold. They also use mercury to separate the gold from the ore and then dump the waste into rivers. Local officials don't want to upset the local miners though. Sam Kindangen, who heads the environmental control office of the North Sulawesi government, worries about the dangers of illegal mining. But he says, "Under the reform era, we have to consider the people. We don't want the people to demonstrate against us."

On top of all these problems, the price of gold and gold reserves in the mine has been declining. From February 2000 to March 2001, the price of gold declined 13 percent and has devalued a third since 1997. There are only about one-fifth of the reserves of gold left in the mine. Once they are gone, the mine will be forced to shut down.

Managers of foreign firms in Indonesia like Mr. Lahti wonder if all the risk involved with operating in the country is worth it. They have been working with local and national authorities to change some of the laws and policies governing business in the country, yet there is still much that needs to be done to reduce the political and legal uncertainty. Mr. Lahti wonders what he could have done differently to continue operations in Minahasa Raya. He wonders if Newmont's other mines will suffer the same fate Minahasa Raya has, or if things will change for businesses in Indonesia.

QUESTIONS

1. What were the key political problems facing Mr. Lahti and Newmont Mining in Indonesia?
2. How has the legal situation in Indonesia contributed to Newmont Mining's dilemma?
3. What are the environmental dimensions to gold mining in Indonesia, and whose responsibility is it to protect the environment?
4. Evaluate Mr. Lahti's approach to solving Newmont's problems. Could he have done anything differently?

Chapter Notes

1 The major sources for the case are as follows: "The Dragon's Embrace," *The Economist* (August 26, 1989): 51–52; John Newhouse. "Tweaking the Dragon's Tail," *The New Yorker* (March 15, 1993): 89–103; "Pattern Sets the Path," *The Economist* (October 10, 1992): 35–36; "The Noble Houses Look Forward," *The Economist* (October 1, 1994): 77–78; "The Taipan and the Dragon," *The Economist* (April 8, 1995): 62; "The Swire Group: Thin Ice?" *The Economist* (September 23, 1995): 58; Joyce Bamathan and David Lindorff, "Hong Kong's New Boss," *Business Week* (December 23, 1996): 50; "Superman versus the Hong," *The Economist* (August 7, 1997): http://www.economist.com; Rahul Jacob and Louise Lucas, "Redefining the Territory: Businessmen Find That Hong Kong's Problem Since the Handover to China Is Not Too Little Political Freedom but Too Much," *Financial Times* (February 1, 1999): 12; "Tung's Cosmetic Ministers," *The Economist* (June 27, 2002): http://www.economist.com; "Could Be Worse. Was Better," *The Economist* (June 27, 2002): http://www.economist.com; Matt Pottinger, "Hong Kong Turns to Beijing for Help with Listless Economy," *Wall Street Journal* (June 28, 2002): http://www.wsj.com.

2 Gabriel A. Almond and G. Bingham Powell,x Jr., eds., *Comparative Politics Today: A World View*, 3rd ed. (Boston: Little, Brown, 1984), 1–9.

3 The United States–China Business Council (June 11, 2002): http://www.uschina.org.

4 "Politics Brief: Is There a Crisis?" *The Economist* (July 17, 1999): 49

5 Robert Wesson, *Modern Government–Democracy and Authoritarianism*, 2nd ed (Upper Saddle River, NJ: Prentice Hall, 1985). 41–42.

6 Adrian Karatnycky, *Freedom in the World 2001–2002: The Democracy Gap* (New York: Freedom House, 2002). http://www.freedomhouse.org.

7 Ibid.

8 Samuel Huntington, "Democracy for the Long Haul," *The Strait Times* (September 10, 1995): 1, available: Nexis Library: News Curnws.

9 Adrian Karatnycky, *Freedom in the World 2001–2002: The Democracy Gap*

10 Hannah Beech, "China Unplugged." *Time Asia* online, 160, no. 1 (July 15, 2002).

11 Alexander Stille, "Suddenly, Americans Trust Uncle Sam," *New York Times* (November 3, 2001): http://www.nytimes.com.

12 "Politics Brief: Is There a Crisis?" *The Economist* (July 17, 1999): 49.

13 Stille, op. cit.

14 Jaroslaw Piekalkiewicz and Alfred Wayne Penn, *Politics of Ideocracy* (Albany: State University of New York Press, 1995), 4.

15 Ibid., 17.

16 Adrian Karatnycky. *Freedom in the World* (New York: Freedom House, 1999), 6–7.

17 "Argentina's Collapse." *The Economist* (February 28, 2002): http://www.economist.com.

18 George C. Lodge, "Roles and Relationships of Business and Government," *Harvard Business School* Case 9-388-159, 1–48.

19 Audrey T. Sproat and Bruce R. Scott, "Japan D1: A Strategy for Economic Growth," *Harvard Business School* Case 9-378-106, 1–35.

20 David P. Baron, *Business and Its Environment* (Upper Saddle River, NJ: Prentice Hall, 1993), 177–79.

21 Ray August, *International Business Law: Text, Cases, and Readings* (Upper Saddle River, NJ: Prentice Hall, 1993), 51.

22 Kirk Albrecht, "Turning the Prophet's Words into Profits," *Business Week* (March 16, 1998) 46.

23 Aline Sullivan "Westerners Look at Risks and Rewards of Islamic Banking." *International Herald Tribune* (January 30, 1993): 1

24 Albrecht, *op. cit.*, 46.

25 Shaun Harris, "Making Money the Muslim Way," *Africa News* (September 17, 1999): Lexis/Nexis News: Curnws.

26 "Stats of Islamic Banking," *The Institute of Islamic Banking and Insurance* (July 17, 2002): http://www.islamic-banking.com.

27 Albrecht, *op. cit.*, 46.

28 Krysten Crawford, "A Marriage of Convenience," *The American Lawyer* (October 30, 2001): http://www.law.com.

29 Alfred Marcus, *Business & Society: Ethics, Government, and the World Economy* (Homewood, IL Irwin, 1993), 49–52.

30 John R. Boatright, *Ethics and the Conduct of Business* (Upper Saddle River, NJ: Prentice Hall, 1993), 13–16.

31 Ibid., 16–18.

32 Terry McAuliffe, "United We Stand," Democratic National Committee (July 2002): http://www.democrats.org/sept11.

33 Huntington, op. cit.

34 George W. Bush, "Address to a Joint Session of Congress and the American People" (September 20, 2001): http://www.whitehouse.gov.

35 Huntington, op. cit.

36 The material for the case was taken from the following sources: "Still Living Dangerously," *The Economist* (February 10, 2000): http://www.economist.com.; Jose Manuel Tesoro, "Indonesia Courts Trouble," *Asiaweek Magazine* (May 12, 2000) 26, no 18; "Devolve, but Do It Right," *The Economist* (July 6, 2000): http://www.economist.com; "Background Note: Indonesia," U.S. Department of State (October 2000): http://www.state.gov/r/pa/ei/bgn/2748.htm; *The World Factbook* (January 1, 2001): http://www.cia.gov/cia/publications/factbook/index.html; Jane Lee, "Newmont to Shut Indonesian Gold Mine as Illegal Mining Rises," *Bloomberg* (March 9, 2001): "Minahasa Mine Closure in Indonesia Is Scheduled for 2003," *Newmont* Mining Corporation News (March 9, 2001): Michael Schuman, "Vein of Discontent: Big Mining Loses Fortune in Indonesia: Illegal Operators Take Over Newmont and Aurora Sites, Troubles Reflect Political Breakdown," *Wall Street Journal Europe* (May 17, 2001): online edition, "Companies in Conflict Situations: Extractive Companies in Indonesia," *Changing Corporate Roles and Responsibilities* (Oxford: Oxford Analytica, January 2002): Series 2, issue 2; "Getting Ready for Statehood," *The Economist* (April 11, 2002): http://www.economist.com; "History of Indonesia," *World History Information* (June 2002): http://www.countryreports.org/history/indonhist.htm; "Indonesia: History and Government," *WorldTravelGuide.net* (June 2002): http://www.travel-guide.com/data/idn/idn580.asp.

CHAPTER 4

THE ECONOMIC ENVIRONMENT

Poverty does not destroy virtue, nor does wealth bestow it.

—SPANISH PROVERB

OBJECTIVES

- To learn the criteria for dividing countries into different economic categories
- To learn the differences among the world's major economic systems
- To discuss key economic issues that influence international business
- To assess the transition process certain countries are undertaking in changing to market economies—and how this transition affects international firms and managers

CASE

McDonald's Corporation in Emerging Markets[1]

Nearly everyone has an opinion about McDonald's, including Jerry Seinfeld. In one of his live standup acts, he relayed the following observations.

Why is McDonald's still counting? How insecure is this company? 40 million, 80 jillion, billion, zillion, killion, tillion. . . . Is anyone really impressed anymore? "Oh, 89 billion sold. . . . alright, I'll have one. I'm satisfied." . . . Who cares?

I would love to meet the chairman of the board of McDonald's and just say to him, "Look, We all get it. OK, you've sold a lot of hamburgers, whatever the number is. Just put on the sign, 'McDonald's—We're doing very well.' We are tired of hearing about every dang one of them."

What is their ultimate goal, to have cows just surrendering voluntarily or something? Showing up at the door: "We'd like to turn ourselves in. We see the sign. We realize we have very little chance out there. We'd like to be a Happy Meal® if that's at all possible."

With 30,000 outlets in 121 countries, McDonald's Corporation *is* "doing very well" by many measures. It has taken an aggressive growth stance by entering into risky emerging markets and riding on the economic growth spurt of the 1990s. But as the world slipped into an economic recession in 2001, McDonald's has felt the blow, showing six consecutive quarters of declining results. Although prosperous in some emerging markets, like Russia and China, it has done poorly in others, like Turkey, Malaysia, and the Philippines, where it closed 163 unproductive stores at a cost of $91 million in 2001. As the world economy has taken a downward turn, McDonald's is facing risks and challenges that raise questions and doubts about the future of its worldwide operations.

McDonald's entry into Russia in 1990 exemplifies the process and difficulties it has encountered in most developing countries where it has begun operations. During the 1976 Olympics in Montreal, George A. Cohon, president of McDonald's Canadian subsidiary, made the first contact with Soviet officials. They began lengthy negotiations, which lasted until 1988 when a formal agreement was signed. In the meantime, McDonald's had opened restaurants in Hungary and Yugoslavia, thus providing the company with valuable experience in operating in communist countries. By the mid-1980s, the company was expanding more rapidly outside the United States than inside, and company executives reasoned that if they were to meet the company's rapid growth objectives, that trend must continue.

Although the Moscow City Council was a partner of McDonald's in the Russian joint venture, the company repeatedly ran into negative responses, such as "Sorry, you're not in my five-year plan," when it attempted to obtain such materials as sand or gravel to build the restaurant. The company had to negotiate to ensure it would be allocated, in the then-Soviet Union central plan, sufficient sugar and flour, which were in chronically short supply. Even for some products in sufficient supply, such as mustard, government regulations prevented Soviet manufacturers from deviating from standard recipes in order to comply with McDonald's needs. In other cases, strict allocation regulations dictated that Soviet plants sell all output to existing Soviet companies, thus leaving them no opportunity to produce products for McDonald's. Yet another problem was that some supplies simply were not produced or consumed in the Soviet Union, including iceberg lettuce, pickling cucumbers, and the Russet Burbank potatoes that are the secret behind McDonald's French fries.

To handle these problems, McDonald's scoured the country for supplies, contracting for such items as milk, cheddar cheese, and beef. To help ensure ample supplies of the quality products it needed, it undertook to educate Soviet farmers and cattle ranchers on how to grow and raise those products. In addition, it built a $40 million food-processing center about 45 minutes from its first Moscow restaurant.

One problem McDonald's did not encounter was attracting employees and customers. The company placed one small help-wanted ad and received about 27,000 Russian applicants for its 605 positions. McDonald's did no advertising prior to its Moscow opening. However, Russian television covered the upcoming event extensively. When the restaurant's doors opened for the first time in January 1990, it was almost impossible to accommodate the crowd, even though it was the largest McDonald's in the world. An estimated 30,000 people were served the first day, eclipsing the previous daily record of 9,100 set in Budapest. The crowds continued to arrive, even though the price of a Big Mac, French fries, and soft drink equaled a Russian worker's average pay for four hours of work. In contrast, lunch at a state-run or private sector cafe cost 15 to 25 percent as much as a meal at McDonald's.

The entry of McDonald's into China in 1990 resembled its experience in Russia. However, the Chinese government moved faster and was more accommodating than the Russian government had been. China's government wanted to establish its fast-food market and felt that Western companies like McDonald's could take the risks in proving its success. McDonald's encountered similar roadblocks in China, such as lack of quality supplies and distribution difficulties, and it has found analogous benefits, like high volumes of customers and employees.

In 1997, the Asian financial crisis hit, devastating most of the economies in Asia. However, China's economy, including its catering industry, kept growing. In fact, the Chinese government in 1998 designated the catering industry as a new economic growth sector, growing at an annual rate of 20 percent in the 1990s. Because China avoided most of the economic turmoil its neighboring countries experienced, McDonald's prospered. Much of this growth is attributed to increases in individual's income, changing consumer patterns, development of the tourism sector, and overall growth in the fast-food industry—all signs of a growing economy.

McDonald's success in China has continued into the twenty-first century. In the first six months of 2001, McDonald's opened 96 restaurants in China, totaling 430 restaurants altogether. It plans to open 100 stores each year from 2003 to 2013. McDonald's record of success in Russia did a turnaround in 1998 when the Russian economy collapsed because of the devaluation of the ruble. However, with sales and growth on the rebound in Russia, McDonald's had 73 stores by the end of 2001. In fact, it is McDonald's success in China, Russia, and a couple of European countries that is one of the few positive notes in McDonald's 2001 annual report. The 2001 letter to shareholders written by the chairman and CEO of McDonald's opens by saying, "From many different perspectives, 2001 was one tough year." He goes on to say, "Our 2001 performance was hampered by the strong U.S. dollar and weak economies in many countries in which we operate." The continued economic crisis in Asia and Latin America and the economic recession in the United States led to reduced profits. In 2001, McDonald's was forced to close down 163 unproductive stores in countries whose economies are struggling.

When questioned about how world economic situations affect the company's expansion plans, Matt Paull, the chief financial officer (CFO) of McDonald's replied,

When planning openings, we consider each market's current economic conditions, long-term demographic and lifestyle trends, competitive environment and stage of development, as well as the potential effect on existing McDonald's restaurants and returns.

Based on these criteria, we reduced the number of restaurant additions over the past few years and expect to add 1,300 to 1,400 McDonald's restaurants in 2002. About 60 percent of these openings will be in the U.S., Europe, and Canada, where economies are relatively stable and returns are strong. We also are adding restaurants in China, where the near- and long-term growth potential is enormous.

At the same time, we are reducing openings in markets with weak economic environments until we see signs of improvement. Since we already have a clear competitive lead in these countries, this temporary slowdown makes good business sense.

What will be the future of McDonald's worldwide operations? Will it continue to focus more on the United States, Canada, and Europe as stated earlier, or will it return to the emerging markets where growth is higher, although more unstable? Will McDonald's management be able to choose the right countries, commit the right amount of resources, and provide a strategy for sound economic growth for the future?

INTRODUCTION

Understanding the economic environments of foreign countries and markets can help managers predict how trends and events in those environments might affect their companies' future performance there. In this chapter, we discuss the economic environments of the countries in which an MNE may want to operate. An MNE such as McDonald's knows how to operate in its home-country economic system. However, when such a company wants to do business in another country for the first time, it needs answers to questions such as these:

1. Under what type of economic system does the country operate?
2. What are the size, growth potential, and stability of the market?
3. Is the company's industry in that country's public or private sector?
4. If it is in the public sector, does the government also allow private competition in that sector?
5. If the company's industry is in the private sector, is it moving toward public ownership?
6. Does the government view foreign capital as being in competition with or in partnership with public or local private enterprises?
7. In what ways does the government control the nature and extent of private enterprise?
8. How much of a contribution is the private sector expected to make in helping the government formulate overall economic objectives?

These questions appear simple to answer. However, because of the dynamic nature of political and economic events, the answers are complex—or yet to be seen. For example, foreign companies have continued to invest in Hong Kong since the United Kingdom returned Hong

Company managers need to understand economic environments to predict trends that might affect their performance.

A global concern is the growing gap between rich and poor, especially in many developing countries. The photo shows the stark contrast between urban slums and upper-income housing in Caracas, Venezuela.

Kong to China in 1997, even though the business world is wondering whether China will stifle some of Hong Kong's economic freedoms. Companies like McDonald's, which invest in emerging markets, are experiencing enormous difficulties because the changes taking place in those countries are so rapid and unpredictable. The question is whether today's global companies can keep up with the world's changing economic landscape.

As Figure 4.1 notes, economic forces are an important part of the physical and societal factors that help comprise the external influences on company strategy. Economic forces include such issues as the general economic framework of a country, economic stability, the existence and influence of capital markets, factor endowments, the size of the market, and the availability of a good economic infrastructure, such as transportation and communications. Managers need to understand the nature of the world's economies if they are going to make wise investment decisions. To provide them with a frame of reference, we will first describe countries by income level, location, and economic system. Then we will look at key economic indicators, such as economic growth, inflation, and surpluses and deficits that affect the decision of management on where to commit MNE resources and efforts. Finally, we will examine the potential of the major geographic regions in the world, with special emphasis on countries in economic transition.

AN ECONOMIC DESCRIPTION OF COUNTRIES

There are 207 countries in the world with populations of more than 30,000.[2] Which of those countries are the ones where managers should commit resources? Although the answers vary by company, it is true that companies do business abroad for a variety of reasons, such as access to factors of production or demand conditions. **Factor conditions**, or production factors, include essential inputs to the production process, such as human resources, physical resources, knowledge resources, capital resources, and infrastructure.[3] Physical resources include weather, the existence of waterways to get goods to and from market, and the availability of crucial minerals and agricultural products. Knowledge resources are best represented by research and development conducted by companies and governments. For example, the Silicon Valley in the United States is a hotbed of high-tech research. The U.S. government has also poured significant resources into the U.S. aviation industry for the development of military aircraft, and this technology has been helpful in developing the civilian aircraft industry as well. Capital resources include the availability of debt and equity capital that firms can use to expand. Infrastructure includes roads, port facilities, energy, and communications.

Key economic forces include

- *The general economic framework of a country*
- *Economic stability*
- *The existence and influence of capital markets*
- *Factor endowments*
- *Market size*
- *Availability of economic infrastructure*

Factor conditions—inputs to the production process, such as human, physical, knowledge, and capital resources and infrastructure.

FIGURE 4.1   Physical and Societal Influences on International Business

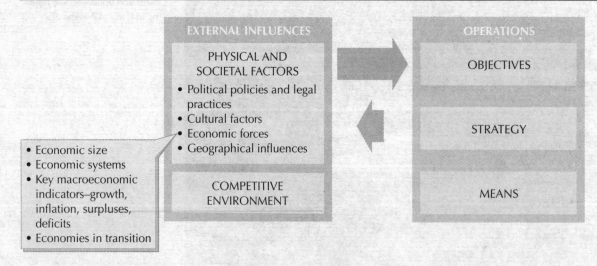

Demand conditions, also known as market potential, include three dimensions: the composition of home demand (or the nature of buyer needs), the size and pattern of growth of home demand, and the internationalization of demand.[4] The composition of demand is known as the *quality of demand*, and size is known as the *quantity of demand*. Factor conditions are especially crucial for investments made for the production of goods, but demand conditions are crucial for market-seeking investments. The combination of factor and demand conditions, along with other qualities, makes up the **location-specific advantage** that a country has to offer domestic and foreign investors.

Countries Classified by Income

Although we can classify countries along any of the dimensions mentioned earlier, the key dimension we use to distinguish one country from another is the size of demand, or **gross national income** (GNI), formerly referred to as **gross national product** (GNP). In particular, we classify countries according to per capita GNI, or the size of GNI of a nation divided by its total population. Those countries with high populations and high per capita GNI are most desirable in terms of market potential. Those with low per capita GNI and low populations are least desirable, and the other countries fit somewhere in between.

What is GNI? It is the broadest measure of economic activity. It is the market value of final goods and services newly produced by domestically owned factors of production.[5] For example, the value of a Ford car manufactured in the United States and the portion of the value of a Ford manufactured in Mexico using U.S. capital and management counts in U.S. GNI. However, the portion of the value of a Japanese Toyota manufactured in the United States using Japanese capital and management would not be counted in U.S. GNI, but it would be counted in Japanese GNI. The World Bank and other institutions now use GNI, but the definition and measurements remain the same as GNP used previously. An alternative to GNI is **gross domestic product** (GDP), the value of production that takes place within a nation's borders, without regard to whether the production is done by domestic or foreign factors of production.[6] So both a Ford and a Toyota manufactured in the United States would be counted in U.S. GDP, but a Ford produced in Mexico would not be.

Why do we use GNI to describe countries? The **World Bank** (www.worldbank.org), a multilateral lending agency, uses per capita GNI as a basis for its lending policies. The World Bank Group was founded in 1944 by the United Nations. It consists of five closely associated institutions: the International Bank for Reconstruction and Development (IBRD), the International Development Association (IDA), the International Finance Corporation (IFC), the Multilateral Guarantee Agency (MIGA), and the International Center for Settlement of Investment Disputes (ICSID). The World Bank is comprised of 183 countries, and its major objective is to provide development assistance to countries, especially the poorest of the poor. It uses the measure *per capita income* to identify those countries that need the most help. In particular, its programs include

- Investing in people, particularly through basic health and education.
- Focusing on social development, inclusion, governance, and institution-building as key elements of poverty reduction.
- Strengthening the ability of the government to deliver quality services, both efficiently and transparently.
- Protecting the environment.
- Supporting and encouraging private business development.
- Promoting reforms to create a stable macroeconomic environment, one that is conducive to investment and long-term planning.[7]

The activities of the World Bank are important to MNEs, because they build infrastructure and promote economic growth and stability, thus improving the quality and quantity of

---

Demand conditions

- Composition of home demand (quality of demand)
- Size and growth of demand (quantity of demand)
- Internationalization of demand

Gross national income

- The market value of final goods and services newly produced by domestically owned factors of production
- Per capita GNI—GNI divided by total population

Gross domestic product (GDP)—the value of production that takes place within a nation's borders.

The World Bank—a multilateral lending institution that provides investment capital to countries.

demand. In particular, the World Bank is most interested in eliminating poverty and its demand-reducing influences. The World Bank classifies economies into one of the following categories according to per capita GNI.[8]

Low income	$755 or less in 1999
Middle income	$756–$9,265
Lower middle income	$756–$2,995
Upper middle income	$2,996–$9,265
High income	$9,266 or more

The World Bank refers to the low- and middle-income countries as **developing countries**, even though it recognizes that not all "developing" countries are alike—nor are they all "developing." Developing countries are also known as **emerging countries**, a term also used to distinguish the capital markets (debt and equity markets) in those countries from the capital markets in the more advanced countries. In addition, the World Bank's terminology does

Per capita income classifications

- Low income ($755 or less)
- Middle income ($756–$9,265)
- High income ($9,266 or more)

Developing countries

- Low- and middle-income countries
- Also called emerging economies

MAP 4.1   *The World's Wealth Measured in Per Capita GNI*

High-income countries are clustered in a few geographic areas of the world, whereas the developing countries are scattered throughout. The low-income countries are located mostly in Africa and Asia. Per capita GNI is GNI divided by midyear population.

Note: No data available for Western Sahara.

Source: From *The World Bank Atlas 2001,* p. 41. Reprinted by permission of The World Bank.

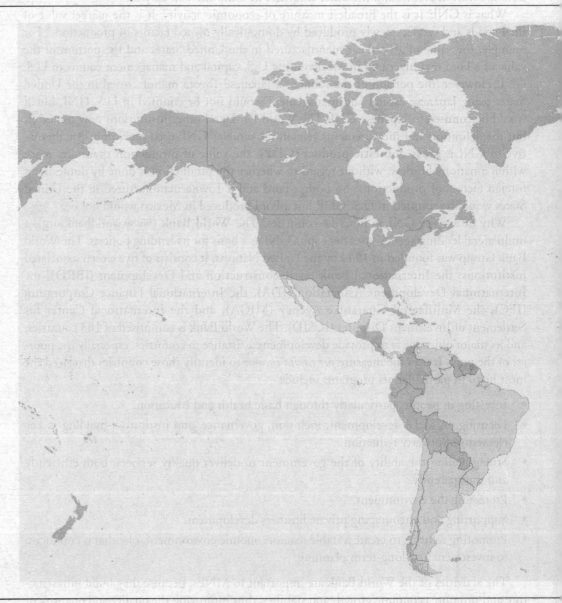

not imply that the high-income countries have reached some preferred or final stage of development. High-income countries are also sometimes called **developed countries** or **industrial countries**. Initially, this was because those countries had a relatively high percentage of their GNP and employment from industry rather than from agriculture. Now, however, these countries have a larger percentage of their GNP and employment tied up in services rather than industry. But the term *industrial countries* is still popular. The developing countries include different types of countries—some with large populations, such as China (1.2 billion people) and India (997 million people), and others with small populations, such as Guyana (697,181 people). These countries also include countries in economic transition to a market economy, such as China, Poland, Russia, and Vietnam. Some developing countries, especially those in Asia and Latin America, are generally moving forward, whereas others, especially some in Africa, are not making much progress.

Map 4.1 shows the geographic location of these countries (also see www.worldbank.org/html/extdr/regions.htm for individual country data). The high-income countries are clustered in just a few geographic areas, whereas the developing countries are found in all areas of the world. Table 4.1 illustrates the relative imbalance among the low-, middle-, and high-income

High-income countries—also known as developed or industrial countries.

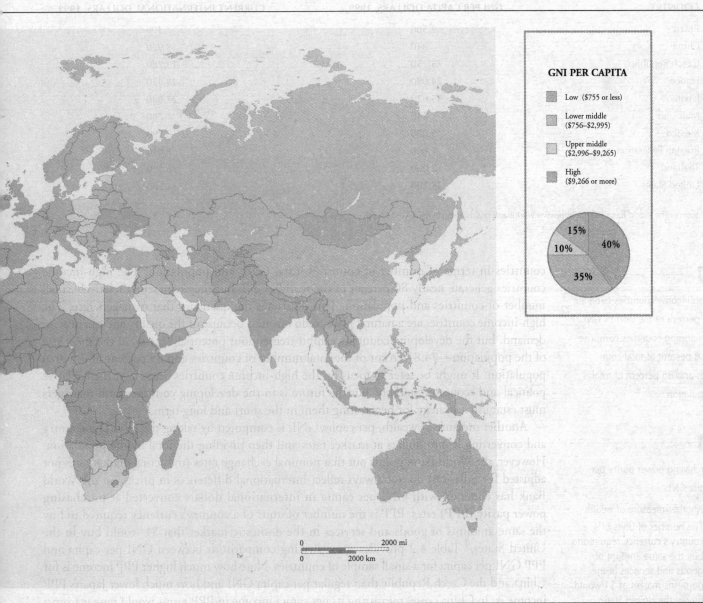

GNI PER CAPITA

Low ($755 or less)

Lower middle ($756–$2,995)

Upper middle ($2,996–$9,265)

High ($9,266 or more)

15%

10%

40%

35%

0   2000 mi

0   2000 km

● **TABLE 4.1**

RELATIVE SIZE AND WEALTH OF THE WORLD'S ECONOMIES IN PERCENT OF TOTAL

	NUMBER OF COUNTRIES	GNI $MILLIONS, 2000	POPULATION MILLIONS, 1999
Low (64)	30.9	3.4	40.4
Middle (93)	44.9	17.6	44.6
High (50)	24.2	79.0	15.0
Total (207)	100.0	100.0	100.0

Source: From *The World Bank Atlas 2001.* p. 40. Reprinted by permission of The World Bank.

● **TABLE 4.2**

PER CAPITA INCOME MEASURED TWO WAYS

COUNTRY	GNI PER CAPITA DOLLARS, 1999	PPP ESTIMATES OF GNI PER CAPITA CURRENT INTERNATIONAL DOLLARS, 1999
Brazil	3,580	7,300
China	840	3,920
Czech Republic	5,250	13,780
France	24,090	24,420
Japan	35,620	27,080
Mali	240	780
Mexico	5,070	8,790
Russian Federation	1,660	8,010
Thailand	2,000	6,320
United States	34,100	34,100

Source: The World Bank (2000): http:www.worldbank.org/data/databytopic/GNPPC.pdf.

High-income countries generate 80 percent of the world's GNI. Developing countries comprise 74.8 percent of total countries and 85 percent of total population.

Purchasing power parity per capita GNI

• Another measure of wealth
• The number of units of a country's currency required to buy the same amount of goods and services in the domestic market as $1 would buy in the United States

countries in terms of number of countries, total GNI, and population. The high-income countries generate nearly 80 percent of the world's GNI, but they represent a relatively small number of countries and population. This illustrates the quandary that managers face. The high-income countries are a natural place to do business because of the quality and quantity of demand, but the developing countries exhibit tremendous potential because of the sheer size of the population—74.8 percent of the total number of countries and 85 percent of the total population. It might be safer to focus on the high-income countries because of their relative political and economic stability, but the future is in the developing countries, and managers must establish a strategy for penetrating them in the short and long term.

Another measure of wealth, per capita GNI, is computed by taking the GNI of a country and converting it into dollars at market rates and then dividing the total by the population. However, the World Bank points out that nominal exchange rates (the actual market rates not adjusted for inflation) do not always reflect international differences in prices. So the World Bank has come up with GNI per capita in international dollars converted at **purchasing power parity (PPP)** rates. PPP is the number of units of a country's currency required to buy the same amounts of goods and services in the domestic market that $1 would buy in the United States.[9] Table 4.2 provides some striking comparisons between GNI per capita and PPP GNI per capita for a small sample of countries. Note how much higher PPP income is for China and the Czech Republic than regular per capita GNI and how much lower Japan's PPP income is. In China's case, measuring its per capita income in PPP terms would raise it from a lower-middle-income country to an upper-middle-income country, which is more consistent with people's perceptions of economic improvements in China.

The United Nations publishes an annual report, the Human Development Report, that ranks countries according to the Human Development Index. The index measures a country's achievements by looking at life expectancy, education, and income per person. The index does not include political freedom or inequality measures. The index for 2002, as shown in Table 4.3, shows that the United States ranks second in per capita GDP but only sixth in the Human Development Index; it is outranked by neighboring country Canada.

Countries Classified by Region

Much of the World Bank data for developing countries is provided by geographic region, and this factor will be especially important as we discuss economic growth in a later section of the chapter. As noted in Map 4.2 on pages 112–113, the major regions are

> East Asia and Pacific
>
> Latin America and the Caribbean
>
> The Middle East and North Africa
>
> South Asia
>
> Sub-Saharan Africa

These designations are important to MNEs, which tend to organize their operations along geographic lines. Managers can use the data compiled and disclosed by the World Bank to spot trends in key markets. Investors can use the data to analyze where potential growth and risks exist in the regions where their companies operate.

Importance of regional groupings of countries

- Similar economic conditions
- Mirrors the way companies organize their firms geographically

● TABLE 4.3

HUMAN DEVELOPMENT INDEX, 2002

COUNTRY	INDEX RANK	GDP PER PERSON RANK
Norway	1	3
Sweden	2	17
Canada	3	7
United States	6	2
Japan	9	11
France	12	18
United Kingdom	13	20
Germany	17	15
Hong Kong, China	23	14
Czech Republic	33	39
Mexico	54	55
Russian Federation	60	58
Brazil	73	60
Uzbekistan	95	119
South Africa	107	51
Pakistan	138	131
Burundi	171	171
Niger	172	168
Sierra Leone	173	173

Source: United Nations, *Human Development Report 2002* http://hdr.undp.org/reports/global/2002/en/, p. 149.

Ownership

- Who owns the resources engaged in economic activity
- Can be public sector, private sector, or both

Countries Classified by Economic System

A final way of classifying countries is by their economic system. Every government struggles with the right mix of *ownership* and *control* of the economy, as illustrated in Figure 4.2. Ownership means those who own the resources engaged in economic activity—the public sector, the private sector, or both. Public sector ownership of economic activity refers to the existence of state-owned enterprises. A good example would be China prior to the reforms initiated in 1978 by Chinese leader Deng Xiaoping. At that time, all enterprises in the country were owned by the state. Private enterprise was neither permitted nor encouraged. The same could be said of all the countries under the control of the Soviet Union, such as Poland and Czechoslovakia (now the countries of the Czech Republic and Slovakia), where state-owned enterprises generated most of the economic activity of the country. However, state-owned enterprises are not just a phenomenon of the communist countries. Countries like Brazil in South America, India in South Asia, and France in Europe also have large state-owned enterprises that are an important part of the overall economy.

MAP 4.2   The World by Region

Countries in different regions of the world, such as Argentina and Chile in Latin America, are often more similar to each other than they are to countries in other regions of the world, such as Thailand and Indonesia in East Asia. Because they are proximate geographically, they trade with each other, so it is interesting to examine factors such as growth in per capita income on a regional basis. However, there are differences within regions. For example, Japan and Malaysia are in East Asia (although Japan is classified as an OECD* country), but they are very different from each other in terms of ethnic makeup, history, politics, and economics. OECD countries—those in the Organization for Economic Cooperation and Development—are considered high-income countries.

*Organization for Economic Cooperation and Development

Source: From *The World Bank Atlas 2001*, pp. 2–3, 41. Reprinted by permission of The World Bank.

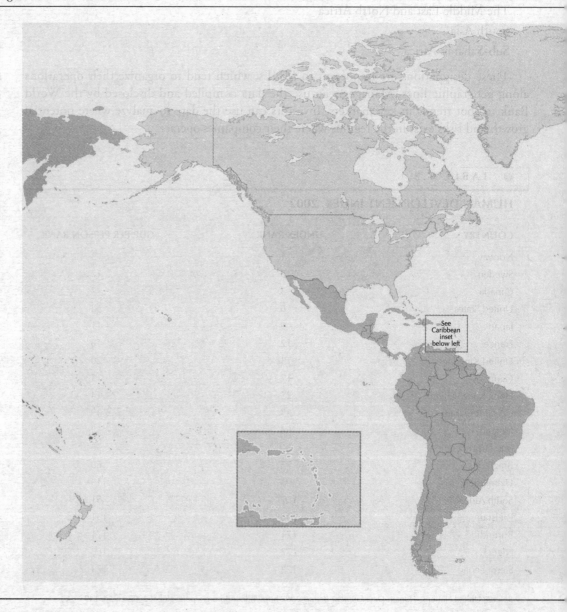

Hong Kong and the United States are examples of the absence of state ownership in major economic activity. Although there are extremes, most countries are a mixture of public and private ownership of economic activity. The degree varies, but most countries with significant state-owned enterprises, such as those mentioned earlier, are moving toward less, not more, ownership of enterprises. This is known as the process of *privatization*, which we will discuss later in the chapter.

Control of economic activity refers to the fact that resources may be allocated and controlled by the public or the private sector. Each year, the Heritage Foundation and the *Wall Street Journal* publish an index of economic freedom in which they rate countries according to 50 variables organized into 10 economic factors: trade policy, fiscal burden of government, government intervention in the economy, monetary policy, capital flows and investment, banking and finance, wages and prices, property rights, regulation, and black markets. The study is helpful insofar as it identifies ways that governments control economic activity and the degree to which they do so.

Control—whether resources are allocated and controlled by the public or the private sector.

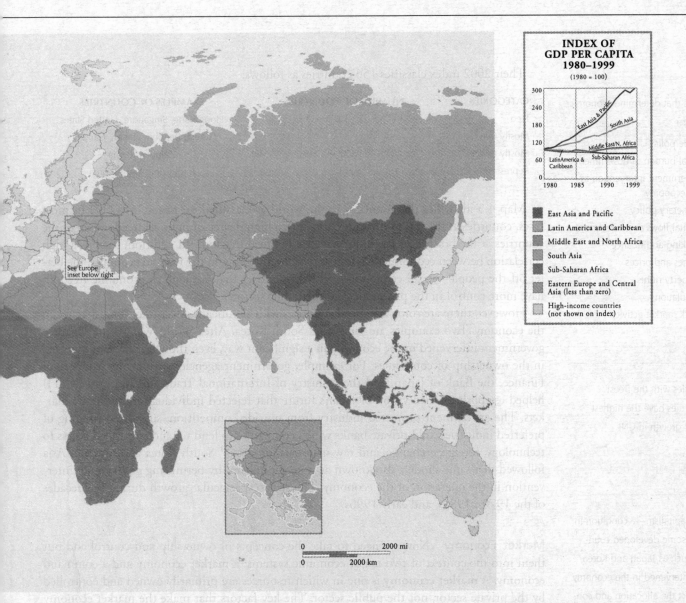

INDEX OF GDP PER CAPITA 1980–1999

(1980 = 100)

East Asia & Pacific

South Asia

Middle East/N. Africa

Latin America & Caribbean

Sub-Saharan Africa

East Asia and Pacific

Latin America and Caribbean

Middle East and North Africa

South Asia

Sub-Saharan Africa

Eastern Europe and Central Asia (less than zero)

High-income countries (not shown on index)

See Europe inset below right

0   2000 mi

0   2000 km

FIGURE 4.2   Relationships Between Control of Economic Activity and Ownership of Production Factors

Although the most logical combinations of ownership and control are sectors A and I, most countries in the world have mixed economies with a variety of combinations of ownership and control.

	OWNERSHIP OF PRODUCTION		
CONTROL OF ECONOMIC ACTIVITY	Private	Mixed	Public
Market	A	B	C
Mixed	D	E	F
Command	G	H	I

Control/Ownership	Control/Ownership	Control/Ownership
A. Market/Private	D. Mixed/Private	G. Command/Private
B. Market/Mixed	E. Mixed/Mixed	H. Command/Mixed
C. Market/Public	F. Mixed/Public	I. Command/Public

Factors that determine economic freedom

- Trade policy
- Fiscal burden of government
- Government intervention in the economy
- Monetary policy
- Capital flows and investment
- Banking and finance
- Wages and prices
- Property rights
- Regulation
- Black market activity

Countries with the freest economies have the highest annual growth in GNI.

State capitalism—a condition in which some developed countries, such as Japan and Korea, have intervened in the economy to direct the allocation and control of resources.

Their 2002 index classifies 156 countries as follows:

CATEGORIES	NUMBER OF COUNTRIES	EXAMPLES OF COUNTRIES
Free	14	Hong Kong, Singapore, United States
Mostly free	57	Czech Republic, Japan, Canada
Mostly unfree	72	Zambia, Russia
Repressed	13	Iraq, Cuba, North Korea

Map 4.3 identifies the countries in the world as classified on pages 116–117. In most cases, countries at the top of the index also have a high degree of political freedom; all of the countries at the bottom of the index have no political freedom. In addition, there is a high correlation between economic freedom and economic growth: the freer an economy, the better off the people—at all economic levels.[10] Countries that are high in economic freedom have more control in the private than in the public sector.

However, there are some advanced countries with significant government interference in the economy. Two examples are Japan and South Korea. After World War II, the Japanese government intervened in the economy in a significant way, even though it was not involved in the ownership of companies. For example, government agencies such as the Ministry of Finance, the Bank of Japan, and the Ministry of International Trade and Industry (MITI) helped establish a broad vision of Japan's future that rejected individualism and open markets. The government protected industry from outside competition; supported funding of preferred industries; told private banks which companies to lend to; and controlled access to technology, foreign exchange, and raw materials imports.[11] South Korea and much of Asia followed that same model, also known as **state capitalism**, by permitting government intervention in the operation of the economy. This led to spectacular growth during the decades of the 1970s, 1980s, and early 1990s.

Market Economy   Now we need to take the concepts of ownership and control and put them into the context of two major economic systems: a market economy and a command economy. A **market economy** is one in which resources are primarily owned and controlled by the private sector, not the public sector. The key factors that make the market economy work are **consumer sovereignty**—that is, the right of consumers to decide what to buy—and freedom for companies to operate in the market. Prices are determined by supply and demand. In a market economy, for example, the price of gasoline rises during holidays because of the excess of demand over supply. Rising prices bring supply and demand into balance. At higher prices, consumers will eventually consume less, resulting in a drop in demand to match existing supply.

Command Economy   In a **command economy**, also known as a **centrally planned economy**, all dimensions of economic activity, including pricing and production decisions, are determined by a central government plan. The government owns and controls all resources. The government sets goals for all business enterprises in the country—how much they produce and for whom. In this type of economy, the government considers itself a better judge of resource allocation than its businesses or citizens. To use the gasoline example described earlier in the market context, the price of gasoline always stays the same in a command economy, because the government determines its price. When supply becomes tight, people line up and buy gasoline until the supply is exhausted, so supply is allocated by the queue rather than by price. Before prices were freed in Russia, people used to say that if they ever saw a line, they just stood in it. When they got to the front of the line, they bought whatever was being sold. Even if they didn't need the item, they figured that someone in their extended family did, so they just bought it. When the supply ran out, there wouldn't be any more left, no matter what price you were willing to pay.

Mixed Economy   In actuality, no economy is purely market or completely command. Most market economies have some degree of government ownership and control, whereas most command economies are moving toward a market economy and away from command concepts. If you think of economic systems as a spectrum with market on one end and command on the other, Hong Kong and the United States would represent two of the countries at the market end of the spectrum, and Vietnam and North Korea would represent two countries at the command end of the spectrum. In Hong Kong and the United States, the government plays a very small role in economic activity, desiring instead to provide a stable environment in which economic activity can take place. In communist countries such as Vietnam and North Korea, the government still owns and controls most aspects of economic activity. China is an example of a communist country that is trying to move from command to market.

Another example of a mixed economy is **market socialism**, in which the state owns significant resources, but in which allocation of the resources comes from the market-price mechanism.[12] France, as mentioned earlier, is a good case in point. Although the government owns significant economic resources, it allows supply and demand—rather than government fiat—to set prices. Sweden is a country that owns few economic resources, but it levies heavy taxes to fund an aggressive social program. Although the market determines prices, a lot of economic activity is controlled by government fiscal policies.

As mentioned in the eight questions raised at the beginning of the chapter, managers need to be aware of both the type of economic system in which they are doing business and what the role of their companies is and is likely to become. Many Western managers complain about the government bureaucracy in China and the degree of influence of the Chinese government in economic decision making. However, China is going through a transition, so it is important for managers to understand the direction and speed of change and how their own industries will be affected by these changes. The same is true of any country, especially those going through transition, so managers need to understand the context of the ownership and control of resources of the countries where they wish to operate. In addition, the degree of interference by the government may vary by state within a country, especially those that are quite decentralized.

Market economy—resources are allocated and controlled by consumers.

Command economy—all dimensions of economic activity are determined by a central government plan.

Mixed economy—different degrees of ownership and control best describe most countries.

Market socialism—the state owns significant resources, but allocation comes from the market price mechanism.

MAP 4.3   Countries Ranked According to Economic Freedom

Economic freedom is measured according to 50 variables organized into 10 economic factors: trade policy, fiscal burden of government, government intervention in the economy, monetary policy, capital flows and investment, banking and finance, wages and prices, property rights, regulation, and black markets. Countries are classified as free, mostly free, mostly unfree, and repressed, according to the degree to which governments intervene in these factors. There is a high correlation between economic freedom and economic growth: The freer an economy, the better off the people—at all economic levels.

Source: The 2002 Index of Economic Freedom (The Heritage Foundation and *Wall Street Journal*, 2002), http://www.heritage.org/index/2002/world.html. Reprinted by permission.

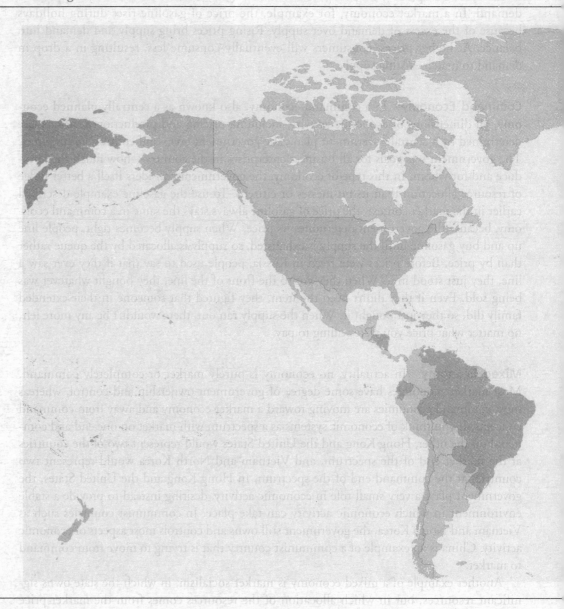

KEY MACROECONOMIC ISSUES AFFECTING BUSINESS STRATEGY

In the *2001 Annual Report to Shareholders*, the CEO of Hewlett-Packard stated:

> In terms of economic growth and stability, 2001 was one of the toughest years on record, particularly for the IT [information technology] industry. Triggered in part by the collapse of the hyperinflated dot-com sector, in Q3 of calendar 2001, the U.S. economy softened considerably. A dramatic slowdown in business investment, compounded by the events of September 11, tipped the United States into its first recession in a decade. During 2001, the world's three leading economies slowed simultaneously for the first time since 1974. The European economy stalled, and Japan struggled to fight deflation and recession. Information technology spending plummeted. The telecommunications and manufacturing industries—two of HP's largest customer sectors—were hit especially hard by the global economic slowdown. These factors had a significant impact on HP's fiscal 2001 results.[13]

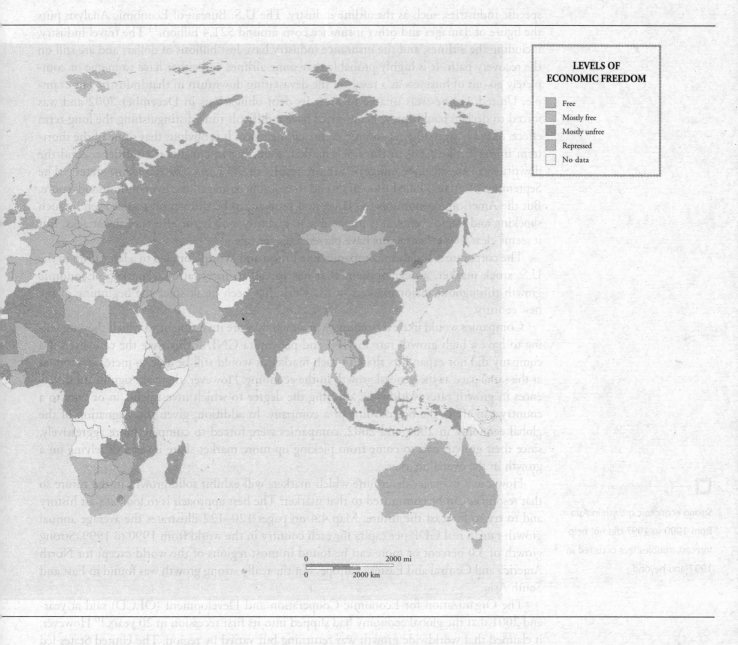

LEVELS OF
ECONOMIC FREEDOM

- Free
- Mostly free
- Mostly unfree
- Repressed
- No data

0   2000 mi
0   2000 km

This is an example of the impact of the global economy on company profits and operating strategy. Management must learn to scan the environment to determine market conditions in the countries where it is either doing business or contemplating entering the market. We will discuss three key issues in the following pages: economic growth, inflation, and surpluses and deficits. Then we will follow with a section discussing the unique challenges facing countries in transition from a command to a market economy.

The global economy can affect company profits and operating strategy.

Economic Growth

Just as the world was recovering from the Asian financial crisis of 1997, the dot-com (Internet-based companies) bubble burst in 2000, thus triggering the slowdown in economic growth in the United States that has filtered throughout the world, particularly in Japan and the euro zone. The terrorist attacks of September 11 compounded this economic slowdown by eroding consumer and business confidence. The (IMF) listed the *direct impact* as one of the impacts of the attacks—that is, the destruction of life and property and the downturn of specific industries, such as the airline industry. The U.S. Bureau of Economic Analysis puts the figure of damages and other insurance costs around $21.4 billion.[14] The travel industry, including the airlines, and the insurance industry have lost billions of dollars and are still on the recovery path. It is highly probable that some airlines will either have to merge or completely go out of business as a result of the devastating downturn in that industry. For example, United Airlines was unable to meet its debt obligations in December 2002 and was forced to declare bankruptcy. Economists have a difficult time distinguishing the long-term effects of 9/11 from other economic events taking place. It is obvious that some of the short-term impacts, like a fall in the stock market, a decline in consumer confidence, and the downturn in the airlines industry, are the results of 9/11. As *The Economist* states, "The September 11 attacks killed thousands and irrevocably damaged the lives of thousands more. But the American economy is too large, and resilient, to be thrown off course even by such shocking and tragic events. It is impossible to quantify exactly the effects of the attacks. But it seems clear that other factors have played a bigger role."[15]

The corporate scandals in companies like Enron and WorldCom led to a large drop in the U.S. stock market, a development that has spread to international markets. Economic growth throughout major markets in the world has been bleak since the beginning of the new century.

Companies would like every country in which they are investing or to which they are selling to have a high growth rate in GNI and per capita GNI. If this were the case, even if a company did not expand its share in each market, it would still be able to increase revenues at the same pace as the general growth in the economy. However, there are significant differences in growth rates worldwide, affecting the degree to which investments in or sales to a country can affect the bottom line of a company. In addition, given the stagnation of the global economy in 2001 and 2002, companies were forced to compete more aggressively, since their growth had to come from picking up more market share instead of relying on a growth in the overall market.

How can a manager determine which markets will exhibit solid growth in the future so that resources can be committed to that market? The best approach is to look at past history and to try to forecast the future. Map 4.4 on pages 120–122 illustrates the average annual growth rate in real GDP per capita for each country in the world from 1990 to 1999. Strong growth of 3.0 percent or more can be found in most regions of the world except for North America and Central and Eastern Europe, but the really strong growth was found in East and South Asia.

The Organization for Economic Cooperation and Development (OECD) said at year-end 2001 that the global economy had slipped into its first recession in 20 years.[16] However, it claimed that worldwide growth was returning but varied by region. The United States led the recovery with stronger growth after the end of 2001. The euro area recovered more gradually, with growth still slow in mid-2002. Japan's recovery was also slow, but global demand for exports began to pick up. The rest of Asia has shown surprising resilience to the global downturn, with growth in China continuing around 7 percent and growth in the Asia-Pacific region strengthening in 2002 as the tech sector turned up.[17] However, future growth is bound to be unpredictable and variable by region.

As illustrated by McDonald's in emerging markets, a drop in economic growth can have detrimental effects on investment. New investors are hesitant to put money into emerging markets, whereas existing investors are forced to cut back operations and maybe even pull out of the market. As noted in Chapter 3, the developing countries with high growth rates are often unstable politically or offer other challenges.

Many companies, including Intel, have been hurt by the recent slowdown. Intel's net income for 2001 fell 70 percent from the previous year as a result of weak PC sales, a slowdown in the economy, and weak consumer confidence. Many companies built up technology inventory with the boom of the late 1990s because they expected continued growth; but

Strong economic growth in Asia from 1990 to 1997 did not help forecast troubles that occurred in 1997 and beyond.

when the recession hit, most companies cut technology spending and used up inventory. Although Intel hoped sales would pick up in 2002, they have continued to be low, particularly in Europe.[18]

The new century, which has tended to be very unstable economically, is proving to be a huge challenge for managers trying to determine where to invest. Even the high-income countries have proven to be a challenge. However, managers need to continue to monitor economic news and to try to predict where the growth areas will be in the future. The added dimension of global terrorism and its ability to quickly affect the global economy has forced companies to be much more cautious in predicting the future and in committing significant resources, especially in unstable areas.

Inflation

Another economic factor that management needs to consider is inflation. **Inflation** means that prices are going up. The inflation rate is the percentage increase in the change in prices from one period to the next, usually a year. Economists use different types of indices to measure inflation, but the one they use the most is the **consumer price index (CPI)**. The CPI measures a fixed basket of goods and compares its price from one period to the next. A rise in the index results in inflation. Inflation occurs because aggregate demand is growing faster than aggregate supply. The demand can occur because of government spending in which spending is rising faster than the tax revenues that are used to fund the spending or because of increases in the money supply. Inflation affects interest rates, exchange rates, the cost of living, and the general confidence in a country's political and economic system.

High inflation often results in an increase in interest rates for two reasons. The first reason is that interest rates must be higher than inflation so that they can generate a real return on interest-bearing assets. Otherwise, no one would hold those assets. Second, monetary authorities such as the Federal Reserve Bank in the United States or the European Central Bank use high interest rates to bring down inflation. When interest rates rise, companies are more hesitant to borrow money, and this tends to slow down economic growth. In addition, consumers are hesitant to incur consumer debt because of the higher cost of repayment. As demand falls, prices should stabilize or fall.

Inflation is also the most significant factor that influences exchange rates, as will be discussed in more detail in Chapter 10. Basically, the higher the inflation in a country, the more likely that that country's currency will fall. Countries with low inflation should have stable or relatively strong currencies. Inflation also affects the cost of living. As prices rise, consumers find it more difficult to purchase goods and services unless their incomes rise the same or faster than inflation. During periods of rapid inflation (e.g., in Brazil in the early 1990s, when inflation was rising at a rate of 1 percent per day), consumers have to spend their paychecks as soon as they get them, or they won't have enough money to buy goods and services later. Finally, inflation also affects confidence in the government. Because of the devastating effects of inflation on the consumer, governments are always under pressure to bring inflation back under control. If governments have to raise interest rates and slow down the economy to slow down inflation, social unrest could occur. This would also occur if governments control wages while other prices are spiraling out of control, leading to animosity in the population.

A good example of the impact of inflation on corporate strategy is Pizza Hut in Brazil in the early 1990s. When inflation was running wild, no one really knew how to compare prices. Prices were changing daily, and salaries were going up as well, so people did not have a good reference point. After the new currency was implemented in 1994 and prices stopped rising, people began to compare prices and make more informed decisions. Consumers began to wonder if the relatively higher price of a Pizza Hut pizza was worth the price, given local alternatives. In the case of purchases, Pizza Hut used to collect sales immediately (the stores operated on a cash and carry basis) and delay the payment of supplies. Because Pizza

Inflation—a condition in which prices are going up.

Consumer price index—an index that measures a fixed basket of goods and compares its price from one period to the next.

High inflation results in higher interest rates for two reasons.

- Banks need to offer high interest rates to attract money.
- Governments raise interest rates to slow down economic growth.

High inflation results in weaker currencies because increasingly expensive exports eventually drop and relatively cheaper imports rise.

MAP 4.4   GDP Per Capita Growth Rate

This map shows the average annual percentage change in a country's real GDP per capita. The growth rate excludes the effects of inflation. In spite of the economic problems in Asia that were manifest after the first half of 1997, the East and South Asian economies showed the fastest growth in the decade of the 1990s. The slowest growth was exhibited in the former Soviet Union and in the countries in Africa.

Source: From *The World Bank Atlas 2001*, p. 41. Reprinted by permission of The World Bank.

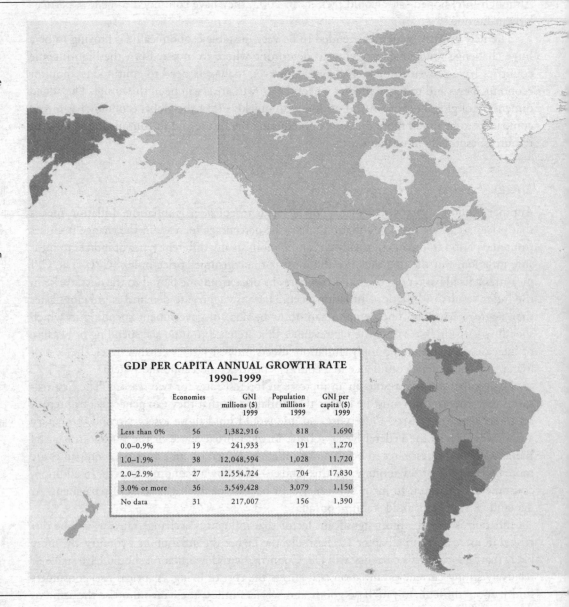

GDP PER CAPITA ANNUAL GROWTH RATE 1990–1999

	Economies	GNI millions ($) 1999	Population millions 1999	GNI per capita ($) 1999
Less than 0%	56	1,382,916	818	1,690
0.0–0.9%	19	241,933	191	1,270
1.0–1.9%	38	12,048,594	1,028	11,720
2.0–2.9%	27	12,554,724	704	17,830
3.0% or more	36	3,549,428	3,079	1,150
No data	31	217,007	156	1,390

Hut was constantly increasing prices, it was generating more than enough cash flow to pay for supplies once they came due. In effect, it was paying expenses in one period that were incurred in a prior period, and the money it was using was worth less than it was at the beginning of the period, even though the company had more of it to spend. So Pizza Hut was paying for supplies with inflated sales revenues. However, this benefit disappeared once inflation slowed down. Pizza Hut was forced to control costs better and to price more aggressively in order to remain competitive. High inflation also creates problems for companies that deal in exports. If inflation is going up but the exchange rate is staying the same, the products will gradually become more expensive in export markets. For example, assume that a British exporter is trying to sell a product to a U.S. distributor for 100 pounds when the exchange rate is $1.59 per British pound. That means the product would cost the U.S. distributor $159.00. If due to inflation in the United Kingdom, the price were to rise to 110 pounds, it would now cost $174.90 (110 × $1.59). At that new price, U.S. consumers might start looking for substitutes. However, one would expect the exchange rate to eventu-

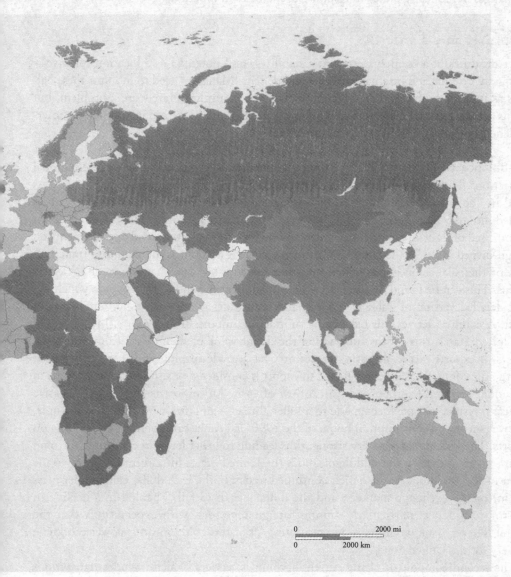

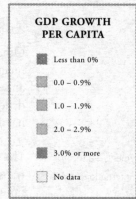

GDP GROWTH PER CAPITA

Less than 0%

0.0 – 0.9%

1.0 – 1.9%

2.0 – 2.9%

3.0% or more

No data

ally change, causing the British pound to become weaker. If the rate falls to $1.47 per pound, the new dollar cost of the product would be $161.70 (110 × $1.47), which is only a slight rise over the previous price. If the demand by U.S. consumers is very sensitive to changes in prices, an increase in prices would result in a fall in demand. So without a change in the exchange rate, inflation in Britain would take a toll on U.S. demand.

Through the 1990s and continuing into the present, the world has witnessed diminishing inflation. When the 1990s began, inflation was around 4 percent in advanced economies, and 100 percent in emerging economies. In emerging economies, inflation decreased to double digits by the mid-1990s and single digits (around 5 percent) by 2000. In advanced economies, inflation decreased to 2.5 percent by 2000. During the Asian financial crisis, inflation rates stayed surprisingly low—except in Indonesia. Russia experienced high inflation rates during its financial crisis of 1998–1999, but it has made strong progress in lowering inflation rates. Inflation is still high in Turkey, Venezuela, Indonesia, and Argentina.[19] Managers need to monitor trends in inflation to determine how inflation could affect their

The latter part of the 1990s and into 2002 resulted in lower inflation worldwide, with the exception of a few countries.

company's cost structure and competitiveness in world markets as well as to anticipate possible changes in monetary policy in response to increases in inflation.

Surpluses and Deficits

Other measures of a country's economic stability—and potential as a location for investment—are external and internal surpluses and deficits. Managers need to monitor these balances as indicators of economic strength or weakness. Surpluses rarely are a problem, but deficits are. An external deficit is when a country's cash outflows exceed its inflows. An internal deficit is when government expenditures exceed government revenues.

The Balance of Payments The **balance of payments** records a country's international transactions. These can be transactions between companies, governments, or individuals. As noted in Table 4.4, "U.S. International Transactions 2001," the balance of payments is divided into the current account and the capital and financial account. The **current account** is comprised of trade in goods and services and income from assets abroad and payments on foreign-owned assets in the country. Part of the current account is **merchandise trade balance**, or the balance on goods which measures the country's merchandise trade deficit or surplus. This can be found on line 71 of the Appendix at the end of the chapter, which is a more detailed version of Table 4.4. Merchandise includes goods such as automobiles and wheat. A country derives this balance by subtracting imports from exports. In the case of the United States, this means subtracting the dollar value of its imports from that of its exports. If exports exceed imports, the country has a trade surplus, and if imports exceed exports, the country has a trade deficit. An export is considered positive because it results in a payment received from abroad—an inflow of cash. An import is considered negative because it results in a payment made to a seller abroad—an outflow of cash. For example, the investment and consumption boom of the 1990s led Americans to increase spending on imports. The U.S. dollar was very strong, thus leading to lower levels of exports. This trend became so great that by the middle of 2002, the United States hit a record monthly trade deficit of $35.9 billion. As the deficit continued to climb, the U.S. dollar came under pressure in foreign-exchange markets, and the dollar began to fall. This led to a decline in investor confidence, particularly among foreign investors, with expectations that the Federal Reserve Bank would raise interest rates. All of this could mean a slower economic recovery for the United States.[20]

The second component of the current account is services, which includes transactions such as travel, passenger fares, and other transportation, as well as royalties and fees on licensing agreements with foreign customers. Although the popular definition of the trade balance usually refers just to merchandise trade, it is probably more accurate to measure the goods and services trade balance together. For some economies, like that of the United States, which generates a large percentage of its GNI from services, the balance on goods and services is a more accurate measure than just goods. In 2001, for example, the United States had a merchandise trade deficit of $427.165 billion, whereas it had a slightly lower goods and services deficit of $358.290 billion due to a services surplus of $68.875 billion.[21]

The third component of the current account is income receipts—payments on assets. This includes items such as receipts from foreign direct investments abroad. A final category, unilateral transfers, is typically not a significant component of the current account balance, but it includes government and private relief grants and income transferred abroad by guest workers, such as Turkish workers in Germany sending money back to their families in Turkey. The current account balance is an important long-run and comprehensive measure of a country's transactions with the rest of the world.

The **capital account** shows transactions in real or financial assets between countries. For example, when the Turtle Bay Hilton Hotel on the north shore of Oahu, Hawaii, was sold to

Balance of payments—a record of a country's international transactions.

Current account—trade in goods and services and income from assets abroad.

Merchandise trade balance—the net balance of exports minus imports of merchandise.

Deficit—imports exceed exports; surplus—exports exceed imports.

Capital account—transactions in real or financial assets between countries, such as the sale of real estate to a foreign investor.

● **TABLE 4.4**

U.S. INTERNATIONAL TRANSACTIONS, 2001 (ABRIDGED VERSION)

For updated information, click on www.bea.doc.gov and select "Balance of payments and related data" from the Bureau of Economic Analysis's economic accounts. Then select "Interactive Access" for a list of tables. Table 1 is "U.S. International Transactions." the table which we selected. You can then choose annual or quarterly data for any time period of interest. For a full table, see the appendix at the end of the chapter.

[IN MILLIONS OF DOLLARS]

(CREDITS + DEBITS −)	2001
CURRENT ACCOUNT	
Exports of goods and services and income receipts	1,281,793
Exports of goods and services	998,022
Goods, balance of payments basis	718,762
Services	279,260
Income receipts	283,771
Income receipts on U.S.-owned assets abroad	281,389
Compensation of employees	2,382
Imports of goods and services and income payments	−1,625,701
Imports of goods and services	−1,356,312
Goods, balance of payments basis	−1,145,927
Services	−210,385
Income payments	−269,389
Income payments on foreign-owned assets in the United States	−260,850
Compensation of employees	−8,539
Unilateral current transfers, net	−49,463
CAPITAL AND FINANCIAL ACCOUNT	
Capital Account	
Capital account transactions, net	826
Financial Account	
U.S.-owned assets abroad, net (increase/financial outflow (−)	−370,962
U.S. official reserve assets, net	−4,911
U.S. government assets, other than official reserve assets, net	−486
U.S. private assets, net	−365,565
Foreign-owned assets in the United States, net (increase/financial Inflow (+)	752,806
Foreign official assets in the United States, net	5,224
Other foreign assets in the United States, net	747,582
Statistical discrepancy (sum of above items with sign reversed)	10,701

Source: Bureau of Economic Analysis, "U.S. International Accounts Data 2001" (September 26, 2002): www.bea.doc.gov.

Japanese investors, the transaction was recorded as an inflow of capital to the United States, which is a positive transaction in the capital account. Other examples of capital account transactions include foreign direct investments, such as the purchase of Chrysler (United States) by Daimler Benz (Germany); the purchase and sale of securities, such as the purchase of Brazilian stocks by an American investor; and the purchase of U.S. treasury bonds by a Japanese investor. Also measured in financial assets are changes in the official reserve assets of a country, such as gold, special drawing rights (which we'll discuss in Chapter 10), and foreign currencies.

Companies monitor the balance
of payments to watch for factors
that could lead to currency instability or government actions to
correct an imbalance.

What difference does it make to companies whether a country has a current account surplus or deficit? There probably is no direct effect. However, the events that comprise the balance-of-payments data influence exchange rates and government policy, which, in turn, influence corporate strategy. As a manager is monitoring the investment climate of a country where the company has invested or is considering investing assets, it is important to watch for factors that might lead to currency instability. One of the problems leading up to the Argentine financial crisis was the large current account deficit that it accumulated throughout the 1990s. This deficit led Argentina's foreign debt to grow to about one-half of one year's GDP. A popular fiscal policy that can be used to combat a growing account deficit is to devalue the currency, making exports more popular to the rest of the world. Argentina was unwilling to devalue its currency, the peso, because Argentine policy kept the peso pegged to the U.S. dollar. The dollar—and thus, the peso—was very strong at the end of 2001, making Argentine exports unattractive and imports more appealing. Eventually, the recession and high interest payments on foreign debt took their toll, and Argentina defaulted on its $155 billion of foreign debt. In January 2002, the president of Argentina decided that the best course of action would be to let the peso float. By February 1, 2002, the peso had lost half its value, making it worth only 0.494 U.S. dollars. Foreign companies have lost all interest in expanding into Argentina until its economic climate stabilizes. By monitoring trends in the balance of payments, a manager can add one more piece of data when deciding whether or not to do business in a country.[22]

External debt

- The amount of money borrowed from foreign public or private sector banks
- Major debtor nations—Brazil, Mexico, Indonesia, China, Argentina, and Russia
- African countries have the highest debt as a percentage of GNI in the world

External Debt   Many developing countries—in both the public and private sector—borrowed heavily abroad during the 1990s to fuel expansion. This external debt can be measured in two ways—as the total amount of the debt and as debt as a percentage of GDP. The larger these two numbers become, the more unstable the economies of those countries become. Foreign investors need to monitor debt to determine if the government will need to take corrective action to reduce its debt, normally by slowing down economic growth.

The most heavily indebted countries in the world in terms of total debt are Brazil ($238.0 billion), Russia ($160.3 billion), Mexico ($150.3 billion), China ($149.8 billion), Argentina ($146.2 billion), and Indonesia ($141.8 billion).[23] However, all of these countries are large in terms of GDP, so debt as a percentage of GDP was comparitively small. In the case of Brazil, external debt is 40 percent of GDP. However, many African countries have external debt in excess of 100 percent of GDP. The plight of the African countries is severe, because the only way to get access to foreign capital is to borrow it from international banks and institutions like the World Bank. They are not able to attract foreign investment because of small market conditions and political instability, so they must turn to foreign debt to expand. This is going to make it virtually impossible for them to pay off their debt. Most of the foreign exchange they earn from exports must be used to service the external debt (make principal and interest payments).

Because Argentina's currency was pegged to the U.S. dollar, many foreign investors willfully lent money to the country because they felt there was no risk of currency devaluation. Yet even when the economy started dropping in 1996, investors kept on pouring money into Argentina believing things would pick up, and Argentina kept spending heavily. As noted earlier, in January 2002, Argentina defaulted on its $155 billion in external debt, the largest default by any country in history.[24]

Internal Debt and Privatization   External debt results from borrowing money abroad. Internal debt results from an excess of government expenditures over revenues. The government budget deficits each year contribute to the overall debt. In the case of the European Union (EU), the target is to have annual deficits no greater than 3 percent of GDP and total debt no greater than 60 percent of GDP. In contrast, India has had serious problems with its internal debt. The general government deficit (central and state budget deficit) was estimated in 2002 to be 10.25 percent of GDP. Including state-owned enterprises, the public sector deficit was estimated to have exceeded 11.7 percent of GDP, and the public sector gross debt was over 90 percent of GDP.[25]

Government internal deficits occur for one of several reasons: The tax system is so poorly run that the government cannot collect all the revenues it wants to, government programs such as defense and welfare are too big for revenues to cover, and state-owned enterprises run huge deficits. All governments, including those in transition from command to market, struggle with several issues, such as "rightsizing" government, setting spending priorities, working toward better expense control and budget management, as well as improving tax policy.[26] Sometimes, however, governments may work hard to control expenditures but fall short due to a recession, which reduces the amount of taxes it collects.

As countries move to control expenditures and reduce their budget deficits, one important strategy to pursue is the **privatization** of state-owned enterprises. Privatization reduces debt by removing the need of the government to subsidize the state-owned enterprises. When the government owns enterprises, it often feels an obligation to keep the enterprises afloat to preserve jobs. Once it is free from ownership, the enterprises can succeed or fail on their own merits.

However, privatization is not easy. It is a political as well as an economic process, and political objectives do not always result in the best economic results. Many state-owned enterprises, such as Pemex, the state-owned oil company in Mexico, are considered to be the crown jewels of a country, and it is difficult to allow them to be sold off to private investors, especially foreign investors. In addition to political objectives are political impediments, such as the obstructive attitudes of existing managers and employees of state-owned enterprises.[27] Thus, consider again the example of India cited earlier, in which the deficits of state-owned enterprises raised the overall government debt from 10.25 percent to 11.7 percent of GDP and the stock of government debt from 80 percent to 90 percent of GDP.

In most countries, the problem with privatization is selling the inefficient, unproductive enterprises—not those that have a chance to survive. Where permitted, the privatization process enables foreign companies to pick up assets and gain access to markets through acquisition. In Eastern Europe, Latin America, and East Asia, the number of foreign investors purchasing state-owned enterprises has been increasing, particularly in sectors like telecommunications, banking, oil, and gas. Foreign purchases account for about 76 percent of the total.[28]

TRANSITION TO A MARKET ECONOMY

So far, we've been learning about economic systems with the assumption that countries are in one economic system or another and that they were not in transition from one classification to another. However, many countries are undergoing transition from command economies to market economies because of the failure of central planning to generate economic growth. The process of transition has made the world of international business very interesting indeed.

The breakup of the Berlin Wall and the overthrow of Eastern European communist dictatorships in 1989 renewed Western interest in doing business in countries throughout Eastern Europe as well as in the former Soviet Union that previously had been off limits. These countries were classified as command economies. Most of the command economies are in the process of transition to a market economy. Command economies in transition are typically grouped into East Asian (such as China and Vietnam) and European. Some have shown consistent economic growth since the transition process began, some have experienced growth reversals, and others have shown little or no growth.

What does transition mean? In general, transition implies:

Liberalizing economic activity, prices, and market operations, along with reallocating resources to their most efficient use.

Developing indirect, market-oriented instruments for macroeconomic stabilization.

Internal deficits are the excess of government expenditures over tax receipts; debt is the accumulation of deficits over time.

Privatization—the sale of state-owned enterprises to the domestic or foreign private sector; this process helps governments reduce internal debt.

Most command economies are going through the process of transition to market economies; transition economies are in Asia, Europe, or Latin America (e.g., Cuba).

Transition includes liberalizing economic activity, reforming business activity, and establishing legal and institutional frameworks.

Achieving effective enterprise management and economic efficiency, usually through privatization.

Imposing hard budget constraints, which provide incentives to improve efficiency.

Establishing an institutional and legal framework to secure property rights, the rule of law, and transparent market-entry regulations.[29]

The process of transformation to a market economy differs from country to country—no single formula applies to all. In addition, the various economies in transition differ greatly in their commitment to and progress toward transformation into market economies. Figure 4.3 identifies some of the key policies that must be pursued for countries to have successful reform leading to economic progress. Figure 4.3 also points out the factors that retard reforms and economic progress.

Why do these changes bring renewed Western interest in doing business with economies in transition? The answer is partly political and partly economic. Most economies in transition experienced slow economic growth during the Cold War years of the 1970s and 1980s. Consequently, the outlook for foreign investors who wanted to do business in those countries seemed bleak. But with the end of the Cold War came the hope that the governments of these countries would eliminate their trade barriers, thus encouraging economic growth and increased business opportunities. However, there is still significant volatility in the midst of change. As the Russian economic crisis in 1998 showed, the transition is not smooth. Russia is one of the countries in transition that is experiencing extreme volatility. Since the economic crisis, it has achieved macroeconomic stability, but weak institutional and structural systems leave companies facing a great deal of risk.

As countries continue the transition process, more opportunities for trade and investment should open up for MNEs.

FIGURE 4.3   Reforms and Economic Progress

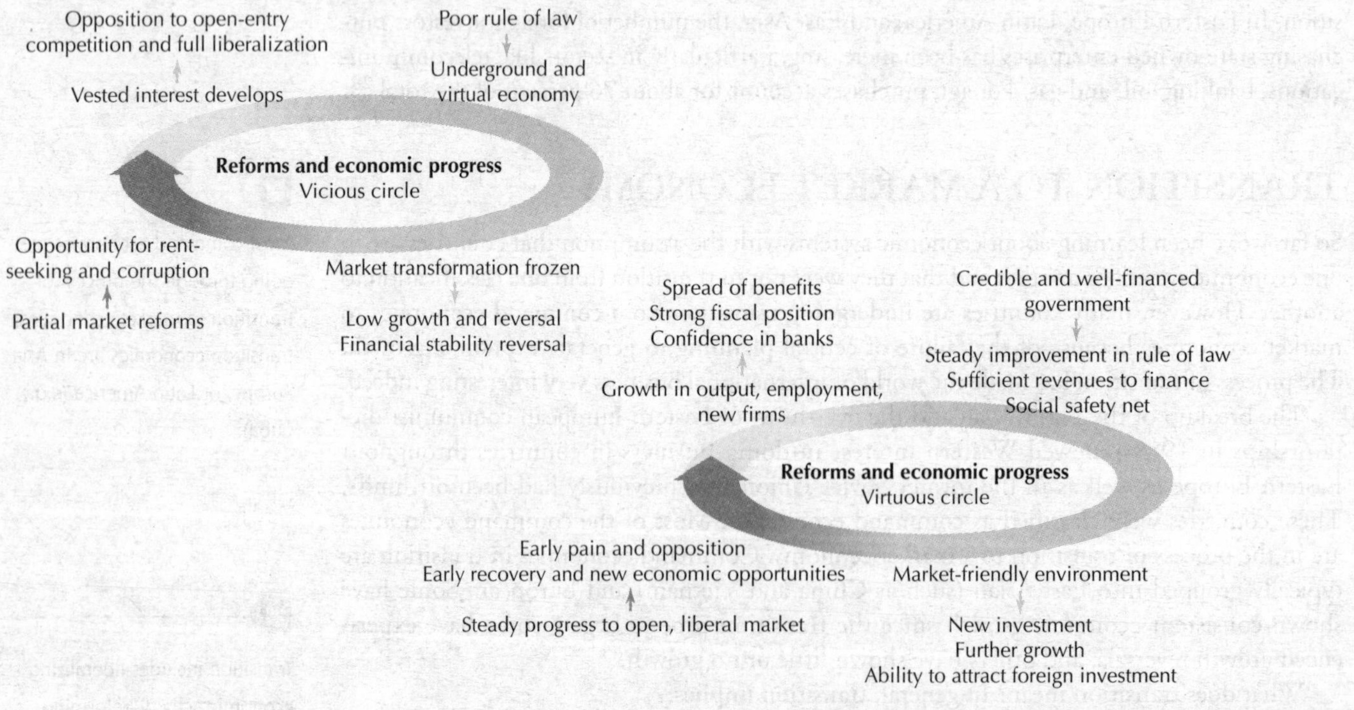

There are several reforms that are necessary to achieve economic progress, but there are also factors that retard economic progress.

Source: Reprinted by permission of the International Monetary Fund © International Monetary Fund, Finance & Development, June 1999, Volume 36, Number 2.

The Process of Transition

The transition process has provided significant opportunities for MNEs. As the countries in transition have liberalized and opened their doors to the outside world, many foreign companies have increased their exports to them. In addition, the privatization process has provided many opportunities for foreign companies to acquire state-owned companies and enter the market through acquisition.

For Russia, the transition to a market economy has been difficult because the government has been trying simultaneously to change the country's economy and its political system. The resulting political turmoil is exacerbated by the battle between conservatives who are afraid of moving too fast and reformers who want to install capitalism quickly through privatization and price decontrol.

The Soviet economy was cumbersome, inefficient, and corrupt, but somehow it seemed to work. However, the breakup of the central Soviet government and the loss of the relationship Russia had with the other 14 Soviet republics and the former Eastern bloc countries has resulted in a contraction of the economy every year since 1989. Although government statistics are not very reliable, it is estimated that the Russian economy by the end of 1996 was half the size of the economy in 1989, which is a steeper contraction than the Great Depression in the United States.[30]

The transition to a market economy in Russia has included massive privatization. However, most of the companies ended up in the hands of the former managers under communist rule.[31]

The economic crisis in Russia in August 1998 exposed a number of serious weaknesses. Under the socialist system that existed prior to 1989, the economy operated under soft budget constraints and hard administrative constraints. The focus was not on profits but on meeting the goals established by the state. Managers knew that they would receive subsidies, loans on easy terms, and a delay in tax payments to make up for a deficit in the bottom line.[32] However, Russian managers were under the control of the state and had to behave. They might have skimmed some profits for their private gain, but they had to meet the requirements of the central plan and take care of the workers. Any shortcomings in these areas were dealt with severely.[33]

Now Russia is trying to adjust to the market economy. Soft budgets have not been done away with entirely, but administrative constraints have disappeared. In their place is "old boy" cronyism and corruption.[34] The allegations of corruption, money laundering, and capital flight by key Russian businesspeople, officials, and family members of high government officials became evident in the aftermath of the crisis of 1998 when the ruble was devalued.[35]

The economy has also had a difficult time with fiscal and monetary reform. It has suffered large budget deficits for two major reasons. The first is that it was not collecting taxes. Second, the government was having trouble curtailing spending, two problems which are not unique to countries in transition, as noted in the earlier section on internal deficits.

In 1978, China's government launched reforms designed to move the Chinese economy away from central planning, government ownership, and import substitution policies (the favoring of local production over imports) and toward greater decentralization and an opening up of the Chinese economy. Since then, the Chinese economy has grown dramatically. From 1990 to 1999, the economy grew at an average annual rate of 10.7 percent.[36]

The Chinese approach to transformation differs significantly from that of the former Soviet Union, since the Chinese leadership is not at all interested in democratic reform. It continues to hold tight to totalitarian political control. Initially, privatization was not an issue, but China has moved to liberalize its economy and allow private investment while not completely giving up control of the economy. However, every year, the Chinese government loosens the economy a little bit more. Chinese growth in GDP has exceeded that of the industrial countries, the world in general, and East Asia and the Pacific. However, China's

Russian transition

- Includes political and economic transition at the same time
- Initial transition steps resulted in steep economic declines
- The transition has involved massive, although not altogether effective, privatization
- Soft budgets—subsidies and other government-supporting activities—have continued
- Hard administrative constraints have disappeared and are being replaced with connections and corruption
- Debts and deficits—both internal and external—are a real challenge

China's transition

- Chinese growth has been far stronger than for other countries in transition
- China has maintained totalitarian political control while loosening the economy
- A major challenge is privatizing state-owned enterprises

growth initially was internal rather than export-led in contrast to other East Asian countries like Korea, Japan, and Taiwan. But China struggles with its state-owned enterprises (SOEs). Although the SOEs are becoming less influential in the Chinese economy, they are still huge and a source of concern because of the large numbers of people they employ. Most of China's government subsidies have shifted from daily necessities to covering enterprise losses, which is the same as the soft budget constraints mentioned earlier in the example of the former Soviet Union. Although China has borrowed from abroad, it has financed over 75 percent of its growth from domestic sources, but it has some of the largest foreign-exchange reserves in the world to back up current and future international borrowing.

The Future of Transition

In its report on economic transition in Eastern Europe and the former Soviet Union, the World Bank noted that many of the challenges of the first five years of reform continue.[37] Some of the major challenges that the countries in transition will have to resolve are:

1. *Continued macro stability.* The crisis of 1998 helped Russia achieve basic macroeconomic stability (in terms of controlling inflation), fiscal stability, and a more stable exchange rate. But continued efforts need to be made to keep these areas in control.

2. *Maintaining economic growth.* The boost to the Russian economy from the devaluation of 1998 and the rise in oil prices has helped spur economic growth, but growth in domestic demand continues to be a challenge. This is definitely not a problem in China, where domestic demand has been especially strong.

3. *Continued improvement in institutional and structural areas.* This includes the protection of property rights, the functionality of the legal system, the liberalization of new enterprise entry and the reduction of administrative barriers to enterprises, and the development of an effective banking structure in which people can have confidence.

4. *The solution of social issues, such as poverty, child welfare, and HIV/AIDS.*

The challenge facing the Chinese leadership is how to maintain economic growth as the country continues to transition to a market economy while resisting the growing pressures to liberalize politically. The key is the reform of the SOEs. Although the Chinese government is supporting them so as not to have massive unemployment during transition, it is moving to privatize more of them each year so that it is not burdened with them in the future. In addition, now that China has joined the World Trade Organization (WTO), it must also open up its economy even more, exposing its enterprises to foreign competition.

Many of the issues identified earlier are not unique to economies in transition. Within the next 5 to 10 years, as the legacy of communism and a command economy grows fainter, the challenges of countries in transition will be virtually the same as those of other developing countries.

The future of transition

- Continued macro stability
- Maintaining economic growth
- Continued improvement in institutional and structural areas
- The solution of social issues such as poverty, child welfare, and HIV/AIDS

How Much Economic Assistance Is Too Much?

A major issue of economic social responsibility is the obligation of high-income countries to assist developing ones. Some of the areas in which the high-income countries might have an ethical obligation to provide support are access to markets for emerging economies' exports, foreign aid, and repayment of loans.

First, emerging economies must have access to markets in high-income countries in order to sell products. Many emerging economies have domestic markets of limited size, and their trade with each other is not significant. However, politicians in high-income countries are sensitive to increased imports, which could lead to unemployment. That could lead to protectionist measures to limit imports from low-wage developing countries. If high-income countries discriminate against exports from emerging economies, they are hurting those countries' prospects for further development and the ability to develop into future markets.

Second, there has been increasing pressure in the United States to cut down on the amount of foreign aid and to use the funds to improve the domestic economy. However, the United States and other high-income countries benefit from trade with emerging economies not only because they gain access to those new markets but also because they can use the resources of those markets. Some high-income countries view foreign aid as a means of putting resources back into emerging economies. For example, high-income European countries, such as Germany and the Netherlands, provide funding to their developing neighbors, Spain and Portugal, in order to help them improve their infrastructure. In contrast, when the United States and Mexico were debating the North American Free Trade Agreement (NAFTA) in 1993, much of the opposition to the agreement came from people who wondered how it was going to be funded rather than how the United States could help Mexico develop its economy.

A third ethical issue is the repayment of loans. Because of the overwhelming size of the external debt of many emerging economies, one possible solution is forgiveness of some or all of such debt. Another possibility is to restructure repayment so it is less burdensome to an emerging economy's economic growth. Forgiveness might be more appropriate for loans made by governments of high-income countries than for those made by private sector banks. But in any case, some feel the high-income countries need to make an effort to be part of the solution to the debt crisis. Yet it is unlikely that banks are going to forgive loans to developing countries. When Argentina defaulted on $155 billion in debt in January 2002, borrowers were willing to receive a few cents on the dollar in repayment. Most of Argentina's debt is owned by individual bondholders rather than by large institutions, thus making the Argentine situation very different from that of Russia in 1998 and from many of the Asian countries during their own economic crises.[38] It is unlikely that individuals or institutions will be willing to loan money to Argentina for some time. In fact, the IMF, has been reluctant to provide a loan package to Argentina unless it completes some reform measures. It is clear that developing countries that default on their debts will have a more difficult time raising capital in the future. That will place more strain on the banks, both public and private, to determine how they will deal with heavily indebted countries in the future.

LOOKING TO THE FUTURE

A Global Economy in the New Millennium

As the twenty-first century began, the global economy was strengthening. Led by economic growth in the United States and accompanied by low inflation and low interest rates, economic growth was beginning to pick up in Asia, Latin America, Africa, and Europe. But then a serious economic downturn in the 2001–2002 period threatened to grind the global economy to a halt. What will be the keys to the future? Will the global economy recover, providing opportunities for MNEs?

Although the United States closed the millennium on a strong note, there was some concern about its growing trade deficit and what many believed to be a large inflation in the stock market. Most of the growth of the U.S. economy in the latter part of the 1990s was consumer-led, which itself was fueled by strong growth in the stock market. When the technology bubble burst in 2000, the NASDAQ and New York Stock Exchange both took a dive. Then the terrorist attacks of September 11, along with a run-up of oil prices and the war in Iraq, caused a further drop in the stock market and in consumer confidence. Companies started failing, and unemployment began to rise—the U.S. economy was in a full-blown recession.

Because the United States makes up about a third of the total global economy, the rest of the world's major economies followed in its footsteps. Europe's recession happened almost as quickly and to the same extent as the recession in the United States due primarily to the commonality of shocks and the ties the two areas have with each other. Although Japan, the second largest economy in the world, experienced economic turmoil before the U.S. recession, Japan's situation is now worse because of the U.S. downturn. The contraction in Japan and, to a lesser extent, the one in the United States, has led to a slowdown in the Asia-Pacific region as well. Latin America is not without its problems. Argentina has led the movement with a political and economic crisis that has spread to its neighboring countries. Africa is making positive strides in ridding itself of civil and political conflicts, but the continent is still burdened by large amounts of debt and other economic problems.

Although the last few years have been bleak, the future is looking up for most parts of the world. Most of the world is looking to the United States to lead the recovery. The U.S. stock market will continue to be very volatile as reports emerge of new accounting scandals among corporations and as a result of the war in Iraq and possibly North Korea. The market will stabilize as new accounting laws are passed and enforced, as the GDP continues to rise, and as consumers regain their confidence. If the dollar remains low and if foreign investors continue to put their money elsewhere, the recovery in the United States, and hence the rest of the world, will be slow. Some fear a double-dip recession, but others believe the United States is well on its way to recovery. However, a drop in consumer confidence and a widening of the war against terrorism could have a damaging effect on the economy.

Europe is also on its way to recovery, but its recovery is slower than the one in the United States. The transition to the euro has been very smooth thus far. But many policies and measures are still needed to ensure the currency's success. Although many companies are hurt by the price transparency that the euro has brought, it will make the euro zone more competitive worldwide. Europe's rising labor costs will stall growth unless consumer confidence and spending increase. As growth continues to pick up in Europe, the European countries should be able to reduce unemployment. However, Europe's inability to maintain economic growth in the face of market socialism is a real challenge. European countries refuse to adopt Anglo-American capitalism, which is much more market-based and less reliant on a social welfare state than their own brand of capitalism, but they feel that their more humanitarian form of a market economy is superior.[39]

Some believe that Japan's economy has bottomed out, but there has been no real sign of recovery yet. Japan will not fully recover until it fixes its decade-long banking crisis. If one of Japan's $1 trillion banks defaults, that event could send shudders throughout the world. Japanese banks need to solve the debt crisis by writing off bad loans and allowing failing financial institutions to go bankrupt or merge with other institutions. The rest of Asia, led by South Korea, will recover more quickly, especially as the IT sector picks up again and as demand for exports increases. China and India, which have not been as affected by the downturn, will continue to grow, particularly in the manufacturing sector, as they attract MNEs with cheap labor. As a whole, Asia's recovery will be slowed by Japan's recession.

In Latin America, many believed that only Uruguay would be affected by Argentina's crisis, but other countries have felt the effects. Uruguay, Brazil, and Paraguay will look to the United States and the IMF for help, and other countries may follow suit. Latin America must solve many of its problems, including an ineffective political class, heavy central governments, and high dependence on foreign capital. Exports need to rise and government spending fall. Although Brazil increased exports, they are still only 10 percent of GDP. The United States will probably be more willing to help Brazil and less willing to help Argentina because of the large number of U.S. companies invested in the former country, because of the large size of the market and because Brazil's economic policies are more sound. Many wonder whether an effective trade bloc will ever emerge in that hemisphere.[40]

Africa leads the world in debt as a percent of GDP and in the number of countries in the low-income category. However, sub-Saharan Africa has been growing at a relatively stable rate since the mid-1990s, and its growth should continue. African countries are saddled with numerous problems, including small populations—and, therefore, small markets, ethnic warfare, political instability, and huge debt burdens. However, an IMF official notes "Many parts of Africa have made great progress in lowering inflation, liberalizing markets, and resuming growth."[41] The problem is that Africa is far more reliant on external forces, such as commodity prices, global interest rates, and international aid, than are most countries in the world, so there are major elements over which it has no control. In spite of that, African countries need to continue to reform internally if they are to have a chance to succeed.

Summary

- Understanding the economic environments of foreign companies and markets can help managers predict how trends and events in those environments might affect their companies' future performance there.

- Companies enter foreign markets because of factor conditions—essential inputs to the production process—or demand conditions—the composition, size and growth potential of the market.

- Gross national income is a broad measure of national income, that is the market value of final goods and services produced by domestically owned factors of production. Per capita GNI is used to rank countries in terms of their individual wealth.

- Economic freedom is the degree to which governments intervene in economic activity. Free countries tend to have higher economic growth; people generally are better off than those in unfree or repressed countries.

- The economic system determines who owns and controls resources. In a market economy, private sector companies and individuals allocate and control resources, whereas in a command economy, the government owns and controls resources.

- Economic growth, which refers to growth in GNI from one year to the next, is a good measure of the well-being of a country.

- Inflation, a condition in which prices are going up, can be devastating to a country. It can result in high interest rates, which slow down economic growth and make a country less desirable as a place to do business. It can also result in a loss of confidence in the government.

- An excess of imports over exports causes external deficits. External deficits result in an outflow of capital.

- The trade balance measures exports less imports of goods. The current account measures exports less imports of goods and services, plus the net income earned from investments abroad and net unilateral transfers (e.g., the transfer abroad of money by foreign workers and public and private relief efforts).

- External debt occurs when countries borrow money from foreign public or private banks or other financial institutions. The biggest borrowers are Brazil, Russia, Mexico, China, Argentina, and Indonesia, but many African countries have borrowed a larger amount as a percentage of GDP.

- Internal deficits occur because governments spend more than they collect in tax revenues. The accumulation of deficits over time results in internal debt. Privatization of state-owned enterprises is one way to reduce internal deficits.

- The transition to a market economy is one in which former command economies liberalize their economic policies and move from ownership and control of the economy by government to reliance on market forces to control economic activity.

CASE

The Daewoo Group and the Asian Financial Crisis[42]

In 1999, Daewoo Group (www.daewoo.com), Korea's second-largest *chaebol*, or family-owned business conglomerate, collapsed under $57 billion in debt and was forced to split into independent companies. The Asian financial crisis and its aftermath finally took its toll on the expansion-minded Daewoo and forced both Daewoo and the Korean government to decide how to dissolve the *chaebol*.

Kim Woo-Choong started Daewoo in 1967 as a small textile company with only five employees and $10,000 in capital. In just 30 years, Mr. Kim had grown Daewoo into a diversified company with 250,000 employees worldwide as well as over 30 domestic companies and 300 overseas subsidiaries that generated sales of more than $100 billion annually. However, some estimated that Daewoo and its subcontractors employed 2.5 million people in Korea. Although Daewoo started in textiles, it quickly moved into other fields, first heavy and chemical industries in the 1970s, and then technology-intensive industries in the 1980s. By the end of 1999, Daewoo was organized into six major divisions:

- Trading Division
- Heavy Industry and Shipbuilding
- Construction and Hotels
- Motor Vehicle Division
- Electronics and Telecommunications
- Finance and Service

However, Daewoo was struggling. Its $50 billion debt was 40 percent greater than in 1998, equaling 13 percent of Korea's entire GDP. A good share of that total, about $10 billion, was owed to overseas creditors. Its debt-to-equity ratio (total debt divided by shareholders' equity) in 1998 was 5 to 1, which was higher than the 4 to 1 average of other large *chaebol*, but it was significantly higher than the U.S. average, which usually is around 1 to 1 but which rarely climbs above 2 to 1. Of course, there is no way of knowing the true picture of Daewoo's financial information because of the climate of secrecy in Korean companies. In addition, it is possible that Daewoo's estimated debt might be greatly underestimated because no one knows whether or not the $50 billion figure included debt of foreign subsidiaries.

How did Daewoo get into such a terrible position, and how much did the nature of the Korean economy and the Asian financial crisis affect Daewoo?

KOREAN ECONOMY

The impact of the Asian financial crisis on Korea was partly a result of the economic system of state intervention adopted by Korea in the mid-1950s. Modeled after the Japanese economic system, the Korean authoritarian government targeted export growth as the key for the country's future. Initially, the government adopted a strategy of import substitution, and that later gave way to a strategy of "export or die." Significant incentives were given to exporters, such as access to low-cost money (often borrowed abroad in dollars and loaned to companies at below-market interest rates in Korean won), lower corporate income taxes, tariff exemptions, tax holidays for domestic suppliers of export firms, reduced rates on public utilities, and monopoly rights for new export markets. Clearly, the government wanted Korean companies to export.

The *chaebol*, of which the four largest were Hyundai, Daewoo, Samsung, and the LG Group, became the dominant business institutions during the rise in the Korean economy. They were among the largest companies in the world and were very diversified, as can be seen by Daewoo's investment and business choices. They were held together by ownership, management, and family ties. In particular, family ties played a key role in controlling the *chaebol*. Until the 1980s, the banks in Korea provided most of the funding to the *chaebol*, and they were owned and controlled by the government. Because of the importance of exporting, the *chaebol* were all tied to general trading companies. The *chaebol* received lots of support from the government, and they were also very loyal to the government, giving rise to charges of corruption.

Most *chaebol* were initially involved in light industry, such as textile production, but the government realized that companies needed to shift first to heavy industry and then to technology industries. Daewoo transitioned to heavy industry in 1976 when the Korean government asked President Kim to acquire an ailing industrial firm rather than let the firm go out of business and create unemployment.

ASIAN FINANCIAL CRISIS AND ITS IMPACT ON KOREA

The country continued to liberalize, and democracy finally came into being in 1988 with the introduction of a new constitution and the election of Kim Young-Sam, the first democratic president in Korea's history. The economy also continued to grow at 5 to 8 percent annually during the early to mid-1990s, led primarily by exports, and the World Bank predicted that Korea would have the seventh largest economy in the world by 2020. However, the Asian financial crisis brought that growth to a halt. After the Thai baht was devalued on July 2, 1997, the Korean won soon followed, and the Korean stock market crashed as well. By the end of 1997, the South Korean won was 46.2 percent lower than its predevaluation rate. At the time the crisis hit, Korea's external debt was estimated to be $110 billion to $150 billion, 60 percent of it maturing in less than one year. In addition, Korea had another $368 billion of domestic debt.

Korea's banks had been a tool of state industrial policy, with the government ordering banks to make loans to certain companies even if they were not healthy. Banks borrowed money in dollars and lent them to firms in won, shifting the burden of the foreign exchange from the firms to the banks. Hanbo Steel and Kia Motors went bankrupt, leaving some banks with huge losses. The Korean won fell in the fall of 1997, causing the government to raise interest rates to support the won and resulting in more problem loans. Bad loans at the nine largest financial institutions in Korea ranged from 94 percent to 376 percent of the banks' capital, making the banks technically insolvent.

The *chaebol* were also very overextended. The top five *chaebol* were in an average of 140 different businesses, ranging from semiconductor manufacture to shipbuilding to auto manufacturing. This was happening during a time when most other companies in the industrial world were selling off unrelated businesses and focusing on their core competencies. Twenty-five of the top 30 *chaebol* had debt-to-equity ratios of 3 to 1, and 10 had ratios of over 5 to 1, as noted earlier. Compare this to Toyota Motor of Japan, which had a debt-to-equity ratio in 1998 of 0.7 to 1.

During this crisis, Korea began to negotiate with the IMF for help. The IMF agreed to help, but only if Korea raised interest rates to support its currency, reduced its budget deficits, reformed its banks, restructured the *chaebol*, improved financial disclosure, devalued the currency (to stimulate exports even more), promoted exports, and restricted imports. In return for a pledge to introduce the reforms, the IMF released funds to Korea to help it pay off its foreign debt and to keep its banks from going bankrupt. This in turn brought in more money from foreign banks that were encouraged by Korea's pledge to reform itself.

One of the IMF's key areas was banking reform. The IMF encouraged Korea to open up its banking sector to foreign investment, hoping that an infusion of foreign banking expertise might help the Korean banks make better loans. Of course, foreign banks had made a sizable number of bad loans in Asia as well. In addition, the IMF encouraged the Korean government to pass good bankruptcy laws to allow bad companies, including banks, to fail. However, the IMF hoped that Korean banking institutions would merge, forming fewer but stronger banks. In addition, the IMF encouraged banking reform in order to cut the links between bankers and politics, tighten supervision and regulation of the banking industry, and improve accounting and disclosure.

IMPACT OF THE CRISIS ON DAEWOO

While the financial crisis was going on, Daewoo's President Kim ignored the warning signs and continued to expand. In 1998, a year when the Daewoo Group lost money, it added 14 new firms to its existing 275 subsidiaries. While Samsung and LG were cutting back, Daewoo added 40 percent more debt.

Finally, Korean President Kim Dae Jung had had enough. He ordered the banks to stop lending to the *chaebol* until they came up with and began to execute a plan to sell off businesses and to focus on their core competencies. But that didn't stop Daewoo. To get access to more money to feed its growth, Daewoo issued corporate bonds, which were purchased by Investment Trust Companies (ITCs), finance companies associated with the *chaebol*. The ITCs purchased nearly $20 billion in corporate bonds.

In early 1999, Daewoo announced a plan to sell off some of its businesses to comply with government restructuring requirements before the government took more drastic action, such as nationalization. However, the plans limped along until July 1999. At that point, with Korea still in a deep recession, Daewoo announced that it would go bankrupt unless its Korean creditors backed off. It basically could not even service its interest payments of $500 million a month, let alone its principal. The government immediately stepped in and froze Daewoo's loans until November 1999. This shock rippled through Korea, because nobody thought a *chaebol* would ever be allowed to collapse. That had never happened before, and the close ties between government and business were such that it was never expected to happen. The shock of Daewoo's announcement negatively affected the corporate bond market, and the ITCs came under pressure because of their huge exposure to Daewoo. Negotiations in

Korea involved 60 banks, some owned by the government, others in the private sector. On September 16, 1999, Daewoo asked its foreign creditors for a moratorium on interest payments until March 2000, so the instability spread to the international markets.

DAEWOO'S FUTURE

By the end of 1999, Daewoo's President Kim was left with few options to solve Daewoo's problems. One possibility was to dismantle Daewoo and let it have only auto-related businesses. All of the other businesses would be sold off to domestic or foreign investors, and the name would be changed to something other than Daewoo. Another option for President Kim was to sell some of Daewoo's auto assets. Ford, DaimlerChrysler, and General Motors showed interest, but selling Daewoo Motor, the second largest automaker in Korea, would be a big blow to the country.

As the Korean economy began to recover in 1999, some felt that the *chaebol* should weather the storm and not allow themselves to be broken up. However, President Kim Dae Jung had mandated that the *chaebol* get their debt-to-equity ratios from 5 to 1 to 2 to 1 by the end of 1999, and that goal seemed impossible unless there was a huge infusion of equity capital or either a write-off of debt through debt restructuring with the banks or a selling off of debt-laden businesses to others. Under immense pressures caused by the debt and by accusations of fraud and embezzlement, President Kim Woo-Choong abandoned his company and fled the country. The government separated the Daewoo subsidiaries and worked with creditors to convert the debt to equity, to set up subsidiaries on debt workout programs, and to look for buyers.

After a year of negotiations, General Motors purchased a portion of the $1.2 billion Daewoo Motor in April 2002 for $400 million. It agreed to keep only three manufacturing plants—two in Korea and one in Vietnam—leaving creditors scrambling to sell its other plants in Eastern Europe, Asia, and the Middle East. By mid-2002, the Korean economy was showing promising signs of recovery and reform. In 2001, the economy grew by 3 percent and was expected to grow by 5 to 6 percent in 2002. The government has done away with debt-based management of the large *chaebol* and is working to dissolve the large conglomerates to better compete internationally. Of the top-30 *chaebol* that existed prior to the economic crisis, only 14 remain.

The improving economy helped General Motors make its decision to purchase Daewoo Motor, but GM is faced with a new decision: how to market Daewoo cars and reduce the $830 million of Daewoo debt. Should GM continue selling Daewoo cars in the United States and Europe and compete with its own brands? Without increasing its debt, will it be able to restore Daewoo's 37 percent share of the market in Korea?

QUESTIONS

1. How would you describe Korea's economic system? What are the key elements in that system? How would you describe the interaction between politics and economics in Korea?
2. Does Korea look like a good place to invest? Why or why not?
3. What are the key mistakes Kim Woo-Choong made in formulating and implementing Daewoo's strategy, and how did the economic crisis in Korea and in the rest of Asia affect that strategy?
4. What risks does GM face in taking over Daewoo Motor?

Chapter Notes

1   The information in this case is from the following sources: Erich E. Toll, "Hasabburgonya, Tejturmix and Big Mac to Go," *Journal of Commerce* (August 24, 1988): 1A; Vincent J. Schodolski, "Moscovites Stand in Line for a 'Beeg Mak' Attack," *Chicago Tribune* (February 1, 1990): sec. 1, p. 1; Bill Keller, "Of Famous Arches, Beeg Maks, and Rubles," *New York Times* (January 28, 1990): A1; "McDonald's," *The Economist* 313, no. 7629 (November 18, 1989): 34; Peter Gumbel, "Muscovites Queue Up at American Icon," *Wall Street Journal* (February 1, 1990): A12; Ann Blackman, "Moscow's Big Mak Attack," *Time* (February 5, 1990): 51, 80–91; Celestine Bohlen, "How Do You Spell Big Mac in Russian?" *New York Times* (May 25, 1993): B1; Oleg Vikhanski and Sheila Puffer, "Management Education and Employee Training at Moscow McDonald's," *European Management Journal* (March 1993): 102–7; Jerry Seinfeld, "I'm Telling You for the Last Time," Universal Records (1999): Track 10; Aviva Freudmann, "Supplying Big Mac's: A Lesson in Logistics," *Journal of Commerce* (May 19, 1999): 1A; Bloomberg News, "McDonald's Is Slowing Its Expansion in Russia," *New York Times* (February 20, 1999): C3; Natalia Olynec, "Big Mac Blues in Russia," *Chicago Sun Times* (February 28, 1999): 58; "Fast Food and Organized Catering in China: A Market Analysis," *Access Asia* (August 2001): 1;

"Restaurants Feeding on Success," *China Daily* (February 20, 2002): http://service.china.org.cn/link/wcm/Show_Text?info_id=27181&P_qry= mcdonalds; *McDonald's Corporation 2001 Summary Report* (March 12, 2002): http://www.mcdonalds.com; "McDonald's Stock Rises 76 Cents to Rally Market," *QSR Magazine* (June 17, 2002): http://www.qsrmagazine.com/shells/full.phtml?id=1324; http://www.mcdonalds.com (July 2002).
2   The World Bank Group (2002): www.worldbank.org/data/databytopic/class.htm.
3   Michael E. Porter, *The Competitive Advantage of Nations* (New York: Free Press, 1980), 74–75.
4   Ibid., 86.
5   Andrew B. Abel and Ben S. Bernanke, *Macroeconomics* (Reading, MA: Addison-Wesley, 1992), 30.
6   Ibid., 32–33.
7   The World Bank Group, "About Us" (2002): www.worldbank.org.
8   Data is from The World Bank, Data and Statistics (August 2002): http://www.worldbank.com/data/databytopic/class.htm.

9   Data is from The World Bank, *World Development Indicators 2001* (Washington, DC: The World Bank, 2001), 293.

10 Bryan T. Johnson, Kim R. Holmes, and Melanie Kirkpatrick, "Freedom Is the Surest Path to Prosperity," *Wall Street Journal* (December 1, 1998): A22; also see www.heritage.org/index for more details.

11 Bruce R. Scott and Audrey T. Sproat, "Japan D1: A Strategy for Economic Growth," *Harvard Business School Case 9-378-106*, rev. (September 26, 1994): 1–35.

12 Michael P. Todaro, *Economic Development*, 6th ed. (Reading, MA: Addison-Wesley, 1996), 705.

13 *Hewlett-Packard Annual Report 2001* (2002): http://www.hp.com/hpinfo/investor/financials/annual/2001/text_only_10k.pdf, 2001.

14 The International Monetary Fund, "World Economic Outlook 2001: The Global Economy After September 11th" (December 2001): http://www.imf.org/external/pubs/ft/weo/2001/03/index.htm, p. 16.

15 "Counting the Cost," *The Economist* (September 11, 2002): www.economist.com.

16 Organization for Economic Cooperation and Development, "OECD Economic Outlook," no. 71 (June 2002): http://www.oecd.org/pdf/M00028000/M00028752.pdf, p. 1.

17 "OECD Slashes Growth," CNN (November 20, 2001): www.cnn.com.

18 "Letter to Shareholders," *Intel Annual Report 2001* (2002): www.intel.com.

19 International Monetary Fund, "The Decline of Inflation in Emerging Markets: Can It Be Maintained?" (2001): http://www.imf.org/External/Pubs/FT/weo/2001/01/pdf/Chapter4.pdf.

20 Robert Gavin, "Leading Indicators Advance, But Trade Gap Hits a Record," *Wall Street Journal* (June 21, 2002): www.wsj.com.

21 Douglas B. Weinberg, "U.S. International Transactions, First Quarter 2002," Bureau of Economic Analysis (July 2002): http://www.bea.gov/bea/ARTICLES/2002/07July/0702ITA.pdf.

22 Andrew B. Abel and Ben S. Bernanke, *Macroeconomics* (Reading, MA: AW Higher Education, 2003), Ch. 13.

23 Information from the World Bank Group, *Topic Indicators* (2000): http://devdata.worldbank.org/external/dgcomp.asp?rmdk=110&smdk=473880&w=0.

24 "A Decline without Parallel," *The Economist* (February 28, 2002): www.economist.com.

25 International Monetary Fund, "IMF Concludes 2002 Article IV Consultation with India," *Public Information Notice* (PIN) 2/95 (August 29, 2002): http://www.imf.org/external/np/sec/pn/2002/pn0295.htm.

26 The World Bank, *World Development Report 1996* (Washington, DC: World Bank, 1996), 113–20.

27 International Finance Corporation, *Privatization Principles and Practice* (Washington, DC: IFC, 1995), 1.

28 Sunita Kikeri and John Nellis, "Privatization in Competitive Sectors: The Record to Date," The World Bank (June 2002): 6.

29 Oleh Havrylyshyn and Thomas Wolf, "Determinants of Growth in Transition Economics," *Finance & Development* (June 1999): 12.

30 "Russia Survey: The Makings of a Molotov Cocktail," *The Economist* (July 12, 1997): 5.

31 Ibid., 12.

32 Yegor Gaidar, "Lessons of the Russian Crisis for Transition Economies," *Finance & Development* (June 1999): 6–7.

33 Ibid., 7.

34 Ibid.

35 Timothy L. O'Brien, "Follow the Money, If You Can," *New York Times* (September 5, 1999): Money & Business section, p. 1.

36 The World Bank, *World Development Indicators 2001*, op. cit., 194.

37 The World Bank, *Transition–The First Ten Years: Analysis and Lessons for Eastern Europe and the Former Soviet Union* (Washington DC: The World Bank Group, January 1, 2002), 164.

38 Alan Beattie, "Rhodes Urges Banks to Hold on in Argentina," *Financial Times* (May 2, 2002): www.ft.com.

39 International Monetary Fund, "World Economic Outlook" (April 2002): http://www.imf.org/external/pubs/ft/weo/2002/01/index.htm.

40 Matt Moffett, "Going South: Old Demons Return to Haunt Latin American Progress," *Wall Street Journal* (July 25, 2002): www.wsj.com.

41 "Managing the World's Economy," *The Economist* (August 1, 2001): http://www.economist.com/displayStory.cfm?Story_ID=1259312.

42 The information in this case is from the following sources: Benjamin Gomes-Casseres, "State and Markets in Korea," *Harvard Business School Case 9 387–181*, rev. (August 16, 1995); www.daewoo.com; John Burton, "Daewoo to Cut Debts with Shipbuilding Sale," *Financial Times* (April 20, 1999): 22; John Burton, "Seoul Threatens Industry Giants," *Financial Times* (April 28, 1999): 4; John Burton, "Taming the Titans," *Financial Times* (April 28, 1999): 16; Jane L. Lee and Michael Schuman, "South Korea's Daewoo Gets Debt Reprieve from Creditors," *Asia Wall Street Journal* (July 19, 1999): http://www.wsj.com; Michael Schuman, "Daewoo's Woes Spark Jitters in South Korea," *Wall Street Journal* (August 3, 1999): http://www.wsj.com; David Roche, "The Daewoo Litmus Test," *Wall Street Journal* (August 3, 1999): http://www.wsj.com; Jennifer Veale, Larry Armstrong, and Joann Muller, "How Daewoo Ran Itself off the Road," *Business Week* (August 30, 1999): 48; "The Sting of Death," *The Economist* (September 18, 1999): 82; "The Death of Daewoo," *The Economist* (August 21, 1999): 55, 58–59; "GM May Have Landed a Dandy Daewoo Deal," *Business Week* (October 8, 2001): www.businessweek.com; "Daewoo Corruption Scandal Deepens," BBC News (February 2, 2002): http://news.bbc.co.uk/hi/english/business/newsid_1149000/1149061.stm; Hae Won Choi, "GM-Daewoo Agreement Signals Korea Is Receptive to Outsiders," *Wall Street Journal* (April 23, 2002): www.wsj.com; Joseph B. White, "GM Reaches Final Agreement to Acquire Control of Daewoo," *Wall Street Journal* (April 30, 2002): www.wsj.com; Kim Ki-tae, "Feelings Mixed at Daewoo's Overseas Arms," *Korea Times* (May 1, 2002): http://www.times.hankooki.com; Peter Green and Don Kirk, "Daewoo Leaves Foreign Plants Adrift," *New York Times* (May 15, 2002): www.nytimes.com; Lee Ki-ho, "Korea's Reform and Economic Rebound," *Korea Times* (May 21, 2002): http://www.times.hankooki.com; "GM Won't Inject More Funds Into Korea Daewoo Motor—Exec," *Dow Jones Newswires* (May 23, 2002): www.wsj.com; "Cool Korea," *Business Week* (June 10, 2002): www.businessweek.com.

Appendix

●	**TABLE 4.1**

U.S. INTERNATIONAL TRANSACTIONS, 2001—FULL TABLE

For updated information, click on www.bea.doc.gov and select "Balance of payments and related data" from the Bureau of Economic Analysis's economic accounts. Then select "Interactive Access" for a list of tables. Table 1 is "U.S. International Transactions," the table that we selected. You can then choose annual or quarterly data for any time period of interest.

U.S. INTERNATIONAL TRANSACTIONS
[MILLIONS OF DOLLARS]

LINE	(CREDITS + DEBITS –)	2001
	CURRENT ACCOUNT	
1	**Exports of goods and services and income receipts**	**1,281,793**
2	Exports of goods and services	998,022
3	Goods, balance of payments basis	718,762
4	Services	279,260
5	Transfers under U.S. military agency sales contracts	12,220
6	Travel	73,119
7	Passenger fares	18,007
8	Other transportation	28,306
9	Royalties and license fees	38,668
10	Other private services	108,109
11	U.S. government miscellaneous services	831
12	Income receipts	283,771
13	Income receipts on U.S-owned assets abroad	281,389
14	Direct investment receipts	125,996
15	Other private receipts	151,832
16	U.S government receipts	3,561
17	Compensation of employees	2,382
18	**Imports of goods and services and income payments**	**−1,625,701**
19	Imports of goods and services	−1,356.312
20	Goods, balance of payments basis	−1,145,927
21	Services	−210,385
22	Direct defense expenditures	−15,198
23	Travel	−60,117
24	Passenger fares	−22,418
25	Other transportation	−38,823
26	Royalties and license fees	−16,359
27	Other private services	−54,588
28	U.S. government miscellaneous services	−2,882
29	Income payments	−269,389
30	Income payments on foreign-owned assets in the U.S.	−260,850
31	Direct investment payments	−23,401
32	Other private payments	−156,784
33	U.S government payments	−80,665
34	Compensation of employees	−8,539
35	**Unilateral current transfers, net**	**−49,463**
36	U.S. government grants	−11,628

LINE	(CREDITS + DEBITS –)	2001
37	U.S. government pensions and other transfers	−5,798
38	Private remittances and other transfers	−32,037
	CAPITAL AND FINANCIAL ACCOUNT	
	Capital Account	
39	**Capital account transactions, net**	**826**
	Financial Account	
40	**U.S.-owned assets abroad, net (increase/financial outflow (–))**	**−370,962**
41	U.S federal reserve assets, net	−4,911
42	Gold	....
43	Special drawing rights	−630
44	Reserve position in the International Monetary Fund	−3,600
45	Foreign currencies	−681
46	U.S. government assets, other than official reserve assets, net	−486
47	U.S. credits and other long-term assets	−4,431
48	Repayments on U.S. credits and other long-term assets	3,873
49	U.S foreign currency holdings and U.S. short-term assets, net	72
50	U.S. private assets, net	−365,565
51	Direct investment	−127,840
52	Foreign securities	−94,662
53	U.S. claims on unaffiliated foreigners reported by U.S nonbanking concerns	−14,358
54	U.S claims reported by U.S. banks, not included elsewhere	−128,705
55	**Foreign-owned assets in the United States, net (increase/financialinflow (+))**	**752,806**
56	Foreign official assets in the United States, net	5,224
57	U.S government securities	31,665
58	U.S. Treasury securities	10,745
59	Other	20,920
60	Other U.S. government liabilities	−1,882
61	U.S liabilities reported by U.S banks, not included elsewhere	−30,278
62	Other foreign official assets	5,719
63	Other foreign assets in the United States, net	747,582
64	Direct investment	130,796
65	U.S. Treasury securities	−7,670
66	U.S. securities other than U.S. Treasury securities	407,653
67	U.S currency	23,783
68	U.S liabilities to unaffiliated foreigners reported by U.S. nonbanking concerns	82,353
69	U.S liabilities reported by U.S banks, not included elsewhere	110,667
70	**Statistical discrepancy (sum of above items with sign reversed)**	**10,701**
70a	*Of which:* Seasonal adjustment discrepancy	
	Memoranda:	
71	Balance on goods (lines 3 and 20)	−427,165
72	Balance on services (lines 4 and 21)	68,875
73	Balance on goods and services (lines 2 and 19)	−358,290
74	Balance on income (lines 12 and 29)	14,382
75	Unilateral current transfers, net (line 35)	−49,463
76	Balance on current account (lines 1, 18, and 35 or lines 73, 74, and 75)	−393,371

Source: Bureau of Economic Analysis, "U.S. International Accounts Data 2001" (September 26, 2002): www.bea.doc.gov.

PART THREE

Theories and Institutions: Trade and Investment

CHAPTER

5

INTERNATIONAL TRADE THEORY

A market is not held for the sake of one person.
—AFRICAN (FULANI) PROVERB

OBJECTIVES

- To explain trade theories
- To discuss how global efficiency can be increased through free trade
- To introduce prescriptions for altering trade patterns
- To explore how business decisions influence international trade

CASE

Sri Lankan Trade[1]

S ri Lanka, an island country of nearly 20 million people off the southeast coast of India (see Map 5.1), received its independence from the United Kingdom in 1948. Known as Ceylon from the early sixteenth century until 1972, Sri Lanka is typical of most emerging economies. It has a low per capita income (about $3,250 per year based on purchasing power parity), high dependence on primary products (minerals and agricultural products) and manufactured products that use high inputs of cheap labor for its foreign-exchange earnings, and insufficient foreign-exchange earnings to purchase all desired consumer and industrial imports. In many other ways, however, Sri Lanka is atypical. On various measurements comparing the quality of life among countries, Sri Lanka ranks fairly high. Its literacy rate, standards of nutrition, health care, equality of income distribution, and life expectancy are some of the highest among developing countries. Its recent population growth rate is one of the lowest.

Sri Lanka has a long history of international trade. For example, Ionian merchants set up shop in the middle of the third century B.C., and myth says that King Solomon purchased Sri Lankan gems, elephants, and peacocks, which he used to woo the Queen of Sheba. One by one, European powers came to dominate the island in order to acquire products unavailable at home. The Portuguese, for example, sought such products as cinnamon, cloves, and cardamom. The English developed the island's economy with tea, rubber, and coconuts, all of which replaced rice as the major agricultural crops.

MAP 5.1   Sri Lanka

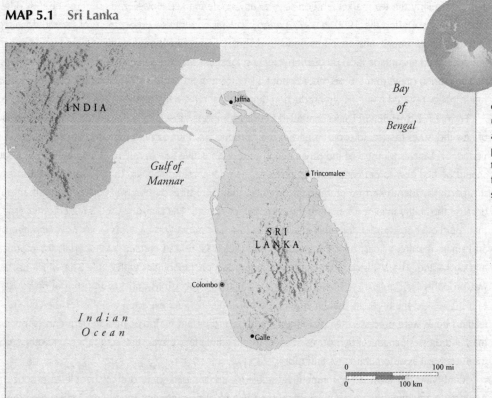

The island nation of Sri Lanka lies off the southeast coast of India. Like other countries, Sri Lanka uses trade policy to help achieve its economic and political objectives. To these ends, it has followed four different trade policies since its independence in 1948.

Since gaining its independence, Sri Lanka has looked to international trade to help it solve such problems as (1) shortage of foreign exchange, (2) overdependence on tea exports, (3) overdependence on the British market, and (4) insufficient growth of output and employment. First, foreign exchange is needed to buy imports, and the Sri Lankan desire for foreign products or foreign machinery has grown more rapidly than the foreign-exchange earnings needed to buy them. Second, until 1975, more than half of the country's export earnings were from tea. Wholesale tea prices fluctuate by as much as 90 percent from one year to the next because of a bumper crop or natural disaster in any tea-exporting country. This fluctuation makes planning for long-term business or government projects difficult. Third, because Sri Lanka is a former British colony, many Sri Lankans also have been concerned that the country cannot be politically and economically independent as long as trade centers on the British market. At the time of independence, for example, one-third of Sri Lankan exports went to the United Kingdom. Fourth, world demand for Sri Lanka's traditional mining and agricultural products has not grown as rapidly as that for many other products, particularly manufactured ones. So Sri Lanka has not met its economic objectives for growth and employment.

To help solve these interrelated problems, Sri Lanka has basically followed four different trade policies since gaining its independence in 1948. These policies have reflected views of different political leaders and changes in Sri Lankan conditions. They are:

- 1948 to 1960, liberal trade regime (minimal government interference in trade)
- 1960 to 1977, import substitution (seeking local production of goods and services that would otherwise be imported)
- 1977 to 1988, strategic trade policy (government actions to develop specific industries with export potential) along with import substitution
- 1988 to present, strategic trade policy along with openness to imports

During the 1948 to 1960 period, over 99 percent of Sri Lanka's exports were of primary products—mainly tea. Throughout the last three trade periods, Sri Lanka has become less dependent on primary product markets, particularly the tea market, and on sales to any single market. However, these three periods differ in other respects. During the 1960 to 1977 period, Sri Lanka sought to export more of its traditional commodities—tea, rubber, and coconuts—and to diversify its production by restricting imports. Restricting imports would encourage local production, creating jobs and saving foreign exchange. During that period, manufacturing grew from 5.6 percent to about 11 percent of Sri Lanka's GDP. However, this import substitution policy resulted in inefficient production that could survive only if imports were prohibited.

From 1977 to 1988, Sri Lanka continued to restrict imports substantially but shifted to the development of new industries that could export a part of their production, thus earning more foreign exchange. In this period, Sri Lanka's Ministry of Industries began to take an active role in determining what those products should be and how to get companies to produce them for foreign markets. The Ministry of Industries did this partly by identifying nontraditional products that were already being exported in small amounts, because the ability to export indicated the potential for growth. The Ministry also identified other products that could offer Sri Lanka a potential advantage in foreign competition by using inexpensive and abundant Sri Lankan resources—particularly semiskilled and skilled labor and certain raw materials for production and packaging. The Ministry further matched its production capabilities with markets in which Sri Lanka was probably best able to sell because of special market concessions and low transportation costs. The Ministry ranked the products that emerged by export potential and expected benefits for the country. The leading items were processed tea (packaged tea bags and instant tea); ready-made garments (shirts, pajamas, and dresses); chemical derivatives of coconut oil, edible fats, bicycle tires and tubes, and other rubber products, such as automobile tires and tubes.

Identifying the most likely competitive industries encouraged some businesspeople to produce new products. In addition, the government established industrial development zones. Companies that produced in and exported production from these zones could qualify for lower taxes on their earnings. They could also defer taxes on imported goods and components until the resulting products were sold domestically. If the products were exported, there were no import taxes. The first producers to take advantage of the incentives were textile and footwear companies that had special access to the U.S. and European markets. Since then, the company base has become more diverse and includes companies making PVC film, carpets, and companies entering information into computerized databanks.

Since 1988, the Sri Lankan government has continued to target industries that it deems to have export potential for example, by offering tax and investment incentives for ceramic and light engineering industries, for companies doing software development, and for companies using only locally derived raw materials. Sri Lanka also has encouraged the export of services, particularly earnings from its workers abroad and from foreign tourists visiting the country. For example, several hundred thousand Sri Lankans work in foreign countries and send remittances to their families. The government has promoted visits by foreign tourists for example, by legalizing gambling casinos and betting centers that are open only to foreigners.

What has differentiated the period since 1988 from the previous one is the use of more open markets (fewer import restrictions) to foster competition. Consequently, many companies and industries that started up when local production was protected have gone out of business. But the open economy has permitted Sri Lankan companies to more easily import materials, such as bulk rubber, so that they can process them for domestic and foreign sales. It has also permitted Sri Lanka to grow economically despite a civil war and heavy military expenditures.

The move to establish new export industries has allowed Sri Lanka to achieve many of its objectives. Manufacturing now accounts for over 70 percent of Sri Lankan exports, and textiles and garments account for about two-thirds of the manufacturing. Tea, though still an important export (about 16 percent of exports), is increasingly going out in value-added forms, such as instant tea and tea bags. The value-added forms create Sri Lankan jobs and do not fluctuate in price as much as bulk tea. In addition, Sri Lanka's export markets have become more dispersed, with such countries as the United States, Saudi Arabia, Germany, and India gaining in importance.

Sri Lankan trade policies have evolved in response to different objectives and conditions, both within and outside Sri Lanka. They will undoubtedly continue to evolve in the future.

A combination of resource availability and market demands influence where products and services are produced. The photo shows the harvesting of saffron, a popular condiment in Spanish food, in La Mancha, Spain.

Trade theory helps managers and government policy makers focus on these questions:

- What products should we import and export?
- How much should we trade?
- With whom should we trade?

Some theories explain trade patterns that exist in the absence of government interference.

Some theories explain what government actions should strive for in trade.

INTRODUCTION

Why study trade theory? Figure 5.1 shows that trade in goods and services is one of the means by which countries are linked economically. Authorities in all countries wrestle with the questions of what, how much, and with whom their country should import and export. Once they make decisions, officials enact policies to achieve the desired results. These policies have an impact on business because they affect which countries can produce given products more efficiently and whether countries will permit imports to compete against their own domestically produced goods and services. In turn, a country's policies influence which products companies might export to given countries, as well as what and where companies can produce in order to sell in the given countries. This was demonstrated in the case of Sri Lanka, where officials created policies to achieve trade objectives. Some countries take a more laissez-faire approach, allowing market forces to determine trading relations on the premise that government policies lead to less optimum results for economies. Whether taking activist or laissez-faire approaches, countries rely on trade theories to guide policy development.

Two general types of theories about trade pertain to international business: *descriptive* and *prescriptive* theories (see Table 5.1). Descriptive theories deal with the natural order of trade. They examine and explain trade patterns under laissez-faire conditions. Theories of this type pose questions about what happens in the absence of restrictions: Which products are traded? How much is traded? With whom will a country trade? For descriptive theories in Table 5.1. a check indicates the question pertains to the specific theory and a dash means it does not.

The second type of theory prescribes whether governments should interfere with the free movement of goods and services among countries to alter the amount, composition, and direction of trade. Not all theories deal with whether governments should or should not interfere. Those that do not pertain have a dash in Table 5.1 under the question, "Should government control trade?" Those that do pertain have a "yes" or "no" under this question, which is followed by check marks to indicate whether the prescription covers the categories "how much," "what products," or "with whom to trade."

FIGURE 5.1   Companies' International Operations Link Countries Economically

To meet their international objectives, companies' strategies require them to trade and transfer means of production internationally, such as between countries A and B in the figure. This trading and transferring links countries economically. This chapter focuses on the trade linkages.

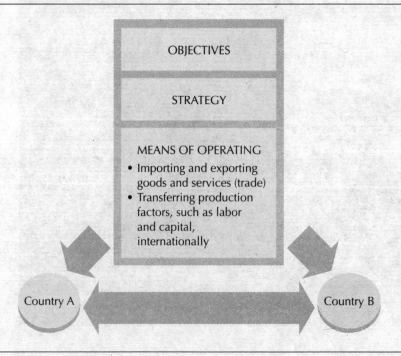

● **TABLE 5.1**

EMPHASES OF MAJOR THEORIES

Trade theories have different emphases. Some theories are descriptive whereas others are prescriptive. A check mark indicates that a theory deals with the question for the column, and a dash indicates that it does not. In column 4, the "yes" or "no" answers the question at the head of the column, and a dash indicates that the theory does not address the question.

THEORY	DESCRIPTION OF NATURAL TRADE			PRESCRIPTIONS OF TRADE RELATIONSHIPS			
	HOW MUCH IS TRADED?	WHAT PRODUCTS ARE TRADED?	WITH WHOM DOES TRADE TAKE PLACE?	SHOULD GOVERNMENT CONTROL TRADE?	HOW MUCH SHOULD BE TRADED?	WHAT PRODUCTS SHOULD BE TRADED?	WITH WHOM SHOULD TRADE TAKE PLACE?
Mercantilism	—	—	—	yes	✔	✔	✔
Neomercantilism	—	—	—	yes	✔	—	—
Absolute advantage	—	✔	—	no	—	✔	—
Comparative advantage	—	✔	—	no	—	✔	—
Country size	✔	✔	—	—	—	—	—
Factor proportions	—	✔	✔	—	—	—	—
Product life cycle (PLC)	—	✔	✔	—	—	—	—
Country similarity	—	✔	✔	—	—	—	—
Dependence	—	—	—	yes	—	✔	✔
Strategic trade policy	—	✔	—	—	—	✔	—
Porter diamond	—	✔	—	—	—	—	—

Both the descriptive and prescriptive types of theories influence international business. They provide insights about favorable market locales for exports as well as potentially successful export products. They also help companies determine where to locate their production facilities because, in the absence of government trade restrictions, exports of given products will move from lower-cost to higher-cost production locations. However, trade restrictions may diminish export capabilities and cause companies to locate some production in the restricting countries. The theories also increase understanding about government trade policies and predict how those policies might affect companies' competitiveness.

Because no single descriptive theory explains all trade patterns under laissez-faire conditions and because all prescriptive theories influence government policies, this chapter examines specific trade theories whereas the next chapter covers government interference in trade.

MERCANTILISM

Why has Sri Lanka been so dependent on raw materials rather than on manufactured products? Perhaps the answer lies in **mercantilism**, the trade theory that formed the foundation of economic thought from about 1500 to 1800.[2] Mercantilism held that a country's wealth was measured by its holdings of treasure, which usually meant its gold. According to the theory, countries should export more than they import and, if successful, receive gold from countries that run deficits. Nation-states were emerging during the period from 1500 to 1800, and gold empowered central governments that invested it in armies and national institutions. These nation-states sought to solidify the people's primary allegiances to the new nation and lessen their bonds to such traditional units as city-states, religions, and guilds. One can see why mercantilism flourished.

To export more than they imported, governments imposed restrictions on most imports, and they subsidized production of many products that could otherwise not compete in domestic or export markets. Some countries used their colonial possessions, such as Sri

According to mercantilism, countries should export more than they import.

Lanka under British rule, to support this trade objective. Colonies supplied many commodities that the mother country might otherwise have had to purchase from a nonassociated country. Second, the colonial powers sought to run trade surpluses with their own colonies as an additional way to obtain revenue. They did this not only by monopolizing colonial trade but also by preventing the colonies from engaging in manufacturing. The colonies had to export less highly valued raw materials and import more highly valued manufactured products. Mercantilist theory was intended to benefit the colonial powers. The imposition of regulations based on this theory caused much discontent in the British colonies and was one cause of the American Revolution.

As the influence of the mercantilist philosophy weakened after 1800, the governments of colonial powers seldom aimed directly to limit the development of industrial capabilities within their colonies. However, their home-based companies had technological leadership, ownership of raw material production abroad, and usually some degree of protection from foreign competition. This combination continued to make colonies dependent on raw material production and to tie their trade to their industrialized mother countries.

Running a favorable balance of trade is not necessarily beneficial.

Some terminology of the mercantilist era has endured. A **favorable balance of trade**, for example, still indicates that a country is exporting more than it is importing. An **unfavorable balance of trade** indicates the opposite, which is known as a deficit. Many of these terms are misnomers. For example, the word *favorable* implies "benefit," and *unfavorable* suggests "disadvantage." In fact, it is not necessarily beneficial to run a trade surplus nor is it necessarily disadvantageous to run a trade deficit. A country that is running a surplus, or a favorable balance of trade, is, for the time being, importing goods and services of less value than those it is exporting.[3] In the mercantilist period, the difference was made up by a transfer of gold, but today it is made up by holding the deficit country's currency or investments denominated in that currency. In effect, the surplus country is granting credit to the deficit country. If that credit cannot eventually buy sufficient goods and services, the so-called favorable trade balance actually may turn out to be disadvantageous for the country with the surplus.

A country that practices neomercantilism attempts to run an export surplus to achieve a social or political objective.

Recently, the term **neomercantilism** has emerged to describe the approach of countries that try to run favorable balances of trade in an attempt to achieve some social or political objective. For instance, a country may try to achieve full employment by setting economic policies that encourage its companies to produce in excess of the demand at home and to send the surplus abroad. Or a country may attempt to maintain political influence in an area by sending more merchandise to the area than it receives from it, such as a government granting aid or loans to a foreign government to use for the purchase of the granting country's excess production.

ABSOLUTE ADVANTAGE

Thus far, we have intentionally ignored the question of why countries need to trade at all. Why can't Sri Lanka (or any other country) be content with the goods and services produced within its own territory? In fact, many countries, following mercantilist policy, did try to become as self-sufficient as possible through local production of goods and services.

According to Adam Smith, a country's wealth is based on its available goods and services rather than on gold.

In 1776, Adam Smith questioned the mercantilists' assumption that a country's wealth depends on its holdings of treasure.[4] Rather, he said, the real wealth of a country consists of the goods and services available to its citizens. Smith developed the theory of **absolute advantage**, which holds that different countries produce some goods more efficiently than other countries; thus, global efficiency can increase through free trade. Based on this theory, he questioned why the citizens of any country should have to buy domestically produced goods when they could buy those goods more cheaply from abroad.

Smith reasoned that if trade were unrestricted, each country would specialize in those products that gave it a competitive advantage. Each country's resources would shift to the efficient industries because the country could not compete in the inefficient ones. Through specialization, countries could increase their efficiency because of three reasons:

- Labor could become more skilled by repeating the same tasks.
- Labor would not lose time in switching from the production of one kind of product to another.
- Long production runs would provide incentives for the development of more effective working methods.

A country could then use its excess specialized production to buy more imports than it could have otherwise produced. But in what products should a country specialize? Although Smith believed the marketplace would make the determination, he thought that a country's advantage would be either *natural* or *acquired*.

NATURAL ADVANTAGE

A country may have a natural advantage in producing a product because of climatic conditions, access to certain natural resources, or availability of certain labor forces. The country's climate may dictate, for example, which agricultural products it can produce efficiently. Sri Lanka's climate supports the production of tea, rubber, and coconuts. Climate also is a factor in Sri Lanka's export of services because foreign tourists visit its beaches. Sri Lanka imports wheat and dairy products. If it were to increase its production of wheat and dairy products, for which its climate is less suited, it would have to use land now devoted to the cultivation of tea, rubber, or coconuts, thus reducing the output of those products. Conversely, the United States could produce tea (perhaps in climate-controlled buildings) but at the cost of diverting resources away from products such as wheat, for which its climate is naturally suited. Trading tea for wheat and vice versa is a goal more easily achieved than if these two countries were to try to become self-sufficient in the production of both. The more the two countries' climates differ, the more likely they will favor trade with one another.

Most countries must import ores, metals, and fuels from other countries. No one country is large enough or sufficiently rich in natural resources to be independent of the rest of the world except for short periods. Sri Lanka, for example, exports graphite but must import nitrates. Another natural resource is soil, which, when coupled with topography, is an important determinant of the types of products a country can produce most efficiently.

Variations among countries in natural advantages also help to explain in which countries certain manufactured or processed products might be best produced, particularly if by processing an agricultural commodity or natural resource prior to exporting, companies can reduce transportation costs. Recall that Sri Lankan authorities sought to identify industries that could use the country's primary commodities such as tea. Processing tea into instant tea reduces bulk and is likely to reduce transport costs on tea exports. Producing canned liquid tea could add weight, lessening the industry's internationally competitive edge.

ACQUIRED ADVANTAGE

Most of the world's trade today is of manufactured goods and services rather than agricultural goods and natural resources. Countries that produce manufactured goods and services competitively have an **acquired advantage**, usually in either product or process technology. An advantage of product technology is that it enables a country to produce a unique product or one that is easily distinguished from those of competitors. For example, Denmark exports silver tableware, not because there are rich Danish silver mines but because Danish

Natural advantage considers climate, natural resources, and labor force availability.

Acquired advantage consists of either product or process technology.

companies have developed distinctive products. An advantage in process technology is a country's ability to produce a homogeneous product (one not easily distinguished from that of competitors) efficiently. For example, Japan has exported steel in spite of having to import iron and coal, the two main ingredients for steel production. A primary reason for Japan's success is that its steel mills encompass new labor-saving and material-saving processes.

Rapid technological changes have created new products, displaced old ones, and altered trading-partner relationships. The most obvious examples of change are new products and services, such as computers and software, which make up a large portion of international business. Products that existed in earlier periods have increased their share of world trade because of technological changes in the production process. For example, early hand-tooled automobiles reached only elite markets, but a succession of manufacturing innovations—from assembly lines to robotics—have enabled automobiles to reach an ever-widening mass market. In other cases, new uses have been found for old products, such as the use of aloe in sunscreen. Other products have been at least partially displaced by substitutes, such as cotton, wool, and silk by artificial fibers, and hydrogen fuel cell technology may displace much of the world's petroleum trade in the near future. Some products that were once major exports have been displaced by mechanically made products. For example, U.S. companies used to export natural ice to Jamaica, but Jamaicans now produce mechanically made ice. However, new product and process technologies usually create trading advantages for the countries where they are developed.

Because most technological advances have emanated from the most industrialized (richer) countries, companies from these countries control a greater share of the trade and investment in manufacturing, which has been the major growth sector. Consequently, many poorer countries have been accounting for a proportionately smaller share of the world's international trade.

Resource Efficiency Example

We'll demonstrate absolute trade advantage by examining two countries (Sri Lanka and the United States) and two commodities (tea and wheat). Because we are not yet considering the concepts of money and exchange rates, we shall define the cost of production in terms of the resources needed to produce either tea or wheat. This example is realistic because real income depends on the output of goods compared to the resources used to produce them.

Start with the assumption that Sri Lanka and the United States are the only existing countries and that each has the same amount of resources (land, labor, and capital) to produce either tea or wheat. Using Figure 5.2, let's say that 100 units of resources are available in each country. In Sri Lanka, assume that it takes 4 units to produce a ton of tea and 10 units per ton of wheat. This is shown with the Sri Lankan production possibility line, whereby Sri Lanka can produce 25 tons of tea and no wheat, 10 tons of wheat and no tea, or some combination of the two. In the United States, it takes 20 units per ton of tea and 5 units per ton of wheat. This is shown in the U.S. production possibility line, whereby the United States can produce 5 tons of tea and no wheat, 20 tons of wheat and no tea, or some combination of the two. Sri Lanka is more efficient (that is, takes fewer resources to produce a ton) than the United States in tea production, and the United States is more efficient than Sri Lanka in wheat production.

To demonstrate how production can be increased through specialization and trade, we need first to consider a situation in which the two countries have no foreign trade. We could start from any place on each production possibility line; for convenience, however, we assume that if Sri Lanka and the United States each devotes half of its 100 resources or 50 to producing tea and half or 50 to producing wheat, Sri Lanka can produce $12\frac{1}{2}$ tons of tea (divide 4 into 50) and 5 tons of wheat (divide 10 into 50). These values are shown as point A

FIGURE 5.2   Production Possibilities with Absolute Advantage

ASSUMPTIONS
for Sri Lanka
1. 100 units of resources available
2. 10 units to produce a ton of wheat
3. 4 units to produce a ton of tea
4. Uses half of total resources per product
   when there is no foreign trade

ASSUMPTIONS
for United States
1. 100 units of resources available
2. 5 units to produce a ton of wheat
3. 20 units to produce a ton of tea
4. Uses half of total resources per product
   when there is no foreign trade

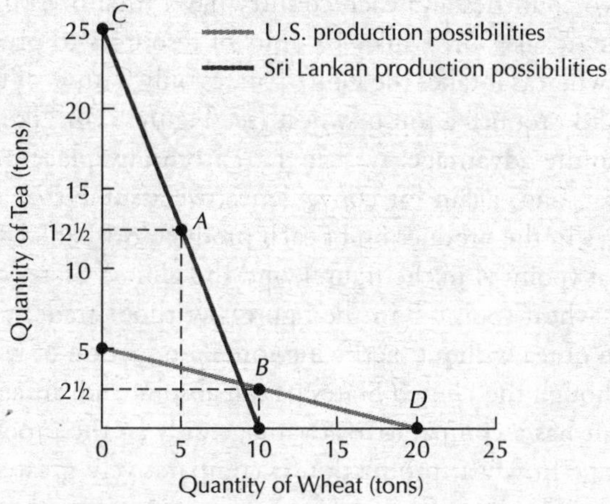

Output will increase through specialization.

PRODUCTION	Tea (tons)	Wheat (tons)
Without Trade:		
Sri Lanka (point A)	12½	5
United States (point B)	2½	10
Total	15	15
With Trade:		
Sri Lanka (point C)	25	0
United States (point D)	0	20
Total	25	20

in Figure 5.2. The United States can produce $2\frac{1}{2}$ tons of tea (divide 20 into 50) and 10 tons of wheat (divide 5 into 50). These are shown as point *B* in Figure 5.2. Because each country has only 100 units of resources, neither can increase wheat production without decreasing tea production, or vice versa. Without trade, the combined production is 15 tons of tea ($12\frac{1}{2}$ + $2\frac{1}{2}$) and 15 tons of wheat (5 + 10). If each country specialized in the commodity for which it had an absolute advantage, Sri Lanka then could produce 25 tons of tea and the United States 20 tons of wheat (points *C* and *D* in the figure). You can see that specialization increases the production of both products (from 15 to 25 tons of tea and from 15 to 20 tons of wheat). By trading, global efficiency is optimized, and the two countries can have more tea and more wheat than they would without trade.

COMPARATIVE ADVANTAGE

What happens when one country can produce all products at an absolute advantage? In 1817, David Ricardo examined this question and expanded on Adam Smith's theory of absolute advantage to develop the theory of **comparative advantage**. Ricardo reasoned that there may still be global efficiency gains from trade if a country specializes in those products that it can produce more efficiently than other products—regardless of whether other countries can produce those same products even more efficiently.[5]

Gains from trade will occur even in a country that has absolute advantage in all products because the country must give up less efficient output to produce more efficient output.

An Analogous Explanation of Comparative Advantage

Although this theory may seem initially incongruous, an analogy should clarify its logic. Imagine that the best physician in town also happens to be the best medical secretary. Would it make economic sense for the physician to handle all the administrative duties of the office? Definitely not. The physician can earn more money by working as a physician, even though that means having to employ a less skilled medical secretary to manage the office. In the same manner, a country will gain if it concentrates its resources on producing the commodities it can produce most efficiently. It will then trade some of those commodities for those commodities it has relinquished. The following discussion clarifies why this theory is true.

Production Possibility Example

In this example, assume that the United States is more efficient in producing both tea and wheat than Sri Lanka is. The United States has an absolute advantage in the production of both products. As in the earlier example of absolute advantage, again assume that there are only two countries and each country has a total of 100 units of resources available. In this example, it takes Sri Lanka 10 units of resources to produce either a ton of tea or a ton of wheat, whereas it takes the United States only 5 units of resources to produce a ton of tea and 4 units to produce a ton of wheat (see Figure 5.3). Like our production possibility example for absolute advantage, we can start from any place on each production possibility line. However, once again for convenience, we assume that if each country uses half (50) of its resources in the production of each product, Sri Lanka can produce 5 tons of tea and 5 tons of wheat (point A in the figure), and the United States can produce 10 tons of tea and $12\frac{1}{2}$ tons of wheat (point B in the figure). Without trade, neither country can increase its production of tea without sacrificing some production of wheat, or vice versa.

Although the United States has an absolute advantage in the production of both tea and wheat, it has a comparative advantage only in the production of wheat. This is because its advantage in wheat production is comparatively greater than its advantage in tea production. Thus, by using the same amounts of resources, the United States can produce $2\frac{1}{2}$ times as much wheat as Sri Lanka but only twice as much tea. Although Sri Lanka has an absolute disadvantage in the production of both products, it has a comparative advantage (or less of a comparative disadvantage) in the production of tea. This is because Sri Lanka is half as efficient as the United States in tea production and only 40 percent as efficient in wheat production.

FIGURE 5.3   Production Possibilities with Comparative Advantage

There are advantages to trade even though one country may have an absolute advantage in the production of all products.

ASSUMPTIONS for Sri Lanka	ASSUMPTIONS for United States
1. 100 units of resources available	1. 100 units of resources available
2. 10 units to produce a ton of wheat	2. 4 units to produce a ton of wheat
3. 10 units to produce a ton of tea	3. 5 units to produce a ton of tea
4. Uses half of total resources per product when there is no foreign trade	4. Uses half of total resources per product when there is no foreign trade

PRODUCTION	Tea (tons)	Wheat (tons)
Without Trade:		
Sri Lanka (point A)	5	5
United States (point B)	10	12½
Total	15	17½
With Trade (increasing tea production):		
Sri Lanka (point C)	10	0
United States (point D)	6	17½
Total	16	17½
With Trade (increasing wheat production):		
Sri Lanka (point C)	10	0
United States (point E)	5	18¾
Total	15	18¾

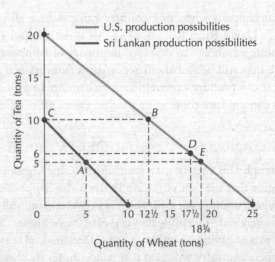

Without trade, the combined production is 15 tons of tea (5 in Sri Lanka plus 10 in the United States) and $17\frac{1}{2}$ tons of wheat (5 in Sri Lanka plus $12\frac{1}{2}$ in the United States). By trading, the combined production of tea and wheat within the two countries can be increased. For example, if the combined production of wheat is unchanged from when there was no trade, the United States could produce all $17\frac{1}{2}$ tons of wheat by using 70 units of resources ($17\frac{1}{2}$ tons times 4 units per ton). The remaining 30 U.S. units could be used for producing 6 tons of tea (30 units divided by 5 units per ton). This production possibility is point D in Figure 5.3. Sri Lanka would use all its resources to produce 10 tons of tea (point C in the figure). The combined wheat production has stayed at $17\frac{1}{2}$ tons, but the tea production has increased from 15 tons to 16 tons.

If the combined tea production is unchanged from the time before trade, Sri Lanka could use all its resources to produce tea, yielding 10 tons (point C in Fig. 5.3). The United States could produce the remaining 5 tons of tea by using 25 units of resources. The remaining 75 U.S. units could be used to produce $18\frac{3}{4}$ tons of wheat (75 divided by 4). This production possibility is point E in the figure. Without sacrificing any of the tea available before trade, wheat production has increased from $17\frac{1}{2}$ tons to $18\frac{3}{4}$ tons.

If the United States were to produce somewhere between points D and E in Figure 5.3, both tea and wheat production would increase over what was possible before trade took place. Whether the production target is an increase of tea or wheat or a combination of the two, both countries can gain by having Sri Lanka trade some of its tea production to the United States for some of that country's wheat output.

The comparative advantage theory is accepted by most economists and is influential in promoting policies for freer trade. Nevertheless, many government policy makers, journalists, managers, and workers confuse comparative advantage with absolute advantage and do not understand how a country can simultaneously have a comparative *advantage* and absolute *disadvantage* in the production of a given product. This misunderstanding helps to explain why managers face uncertain government trade policies that affect where they choose to locate their production.

SOME ASSUMPTIONS AND LIMITATIONS OF THE THEORIES OF SPECIALIZATION

Both absolute and comparative advantage theories are based on specialization. They hold that output will increase through specialization and that countries will be best off by trading the output from their own specialization for the output from other countries' specialization. However, these theories make some assumptions that are not always valid.

Full Employment

The physician–secretary analogy we used earlier assumed that the physician could stay busy full time practicing medicine. If we relax this assumption, then the advantages of specialization are less compelling. The physician might, if unable to stay busy full time with medical duties, perform secretarial work without having to forgo a physician's higher income. The theories of absolute and comparative advantage both assume that resources are fully employed. When countries have many unemployed or unused resources, they may seek to restrict imports to employ or use idle resources.

Full employment is not a valid assumption of absolute and comparative advantage.

Economic Efficiency Objective

The physician–secretary analogy also assumed that the physician who can do both medical and office work is interested primarily in maximization of profit, or maximum economic efficiency. Yet there are a number of reasons why physicians might choose not to work full

Countries' goals may not be limited to economic efficiency.

time at medical tasks. They might find administrative work relaxing and self-fulfilling. They might fear that a hired secretary would be unreliable. They might wish to maintain secretarial skills in the somewhat unlikely event that administration, rather than medicine, commands higher wages in the future. Countries also often pursue objectives other than output efficiency. They may avoid overspecialization because of the vulnerability created by changes in technology and by price fluctuations. Recall Sri Lankan concerns about price fluctuations of tea. Or they may have noneconomic objectives. For example, a Sri Lankan journalist said. "Our unique set of cultural values cannot fit into any sort of twisted, hybrid economic culture, haphazardly devised in the name of development and economic progress."[6]

Division of Gains

Although specialization brings potential benefits to all countries that trade, the earlier discussion did not indicate how countries will divide increased output. In the case of our wheat and tea example, if both the United States and Sri Lanka receive some share of the increased output, both will be better off economically through specialization and trade. However, many people, including government policy makers, are concerned with relative as well as absolute economic growth, relative meaning in comparison to trading partners. If they perceive that a trading partner is gaining too large a share of benefits, they may forgo absolute gains for themselves so as to prevent relative losses.[7]

Two Countries, Two Commodities

For simplicity's sake, Smith and Ricardo originally assumed a simple world composed of only two countries and two commodities. Our example made the same assumption. Although unrealistic, this assumption does not diminish the theories' usefulness. Economists have applied the same reasoning to demonstrate efficiency advantages in multiproduct and multicountry trade relationships.

Transport Costs

If it costs more to transport the goods than is saved through specialization, then the advantages of trade are negated. For example, geographically isolated countries such as Fiji and Mauritius, trade less than would be expected from their sizes because transportation costs increase the price of traded goods substantially.[8] In other words, in our example of Sri Lanka and the United States, the countries would need to divert workers from tea or wheat production to ship tea and wheat between them. However, as long as the diversion reduces output by less than what the two countries gain from specialization, there are still gains from trade.

Mobility

Resources are neither as mobile nor as immobile as the theories of absolute and comparative advantage assume.

The theories of absolute and comparative advantage assume that resources can move domestically from the production of one good to another—and at no cost. But this assumption is not completely valid. For example, a steelworker in the eastern part of the United States might not move easily into a software development job on the West Coast. That worker probably would have difficulty working in such a different industry and might have trouble moving to a new area. The theories also assume that resources cannot move internationally. Increasingly, however, they do. For example, thousands of Sri Lankans go to the Middle East to work. The movement of resources such as labor and capital is clearly an alternative to trade, a topic that we'll discuss in Chapter 8. However, it is safe to say that there is more domestic mobility of resources than there is international mobility.

Statics and Dynamics

The theories of absolute and comparative advantage address countries' advantages by looking at them at one point in time. Thus, the theories view the advantages statically. However, the relative conditions that give countries advantages or disadvantages in the production of given products are dynamic (constantly changing). For example, the resources needed to produce tea or wheat in either Sri Lanka or the United States could change substantially because of advancements in genetically modified crops.[9] Further, our opening case showed how Sri Lanka's competitive advantage has improved in the production of apparel items. Thus, one should not assume that future absolute or comparative advantages will remain as they are today.

Services

The theories of absolute and comparative advantage deal with commodities rather than services. However, an increasing portion of world trade is in services. This fact does not render the theories obsolete, because resources must go into producing services, too. For instance, some services that the United States sells extensively to foreign countries are education (many foreign students attend U.S. universities) as well as credit card systems and collections. However, the United States buys more foreign shipping services than foreigners buy U.S. shipping services. To become more self-sufficient in international shipping, the United States might have to divert resources from its more efficient use in higher education or in the production of competitive products.

THEORY OF COUNTRY SIZE

The theories of absolute and comparative advantage do not deal with country-by-country differences regarding how much and what products will be traded through specialization. However, research based on country size helps explain these differences.

Bigger countries differ in several ways from smaller countries. They

- Tend to export a smaller portion of output and import a smaller part of consumption
- Have higher transport costs for foreign trade
- Can handle large-scale production

Variety of Resources

The theory of country size says that countries with large land areas are apt to have varied climates and an assortment of natural resources, making them more self-sufficient than smaller countries. Most large countries, such as Brazil, China, India, the United States, and Russia, import much less of their consumption needs and export much less of their production output than do small countries, such as Uruguay, the Netherlands, and Iceland.

Transport Costs

Although the theory of absolute advantage ignores transport costs in trade, these costs affect large and small countries in different ways. Normally, the farther the distance, the higher the transport costs. Thus, as we have discussed, more geographically isolated countries tend to depend less on trade with other countries than do less geographically isolated countries. However, among countries that border each other, the smaller country tends to depend more on trade than the larger country because of transportation costs. Assume, for example, that the normal maximum distance for transporting a given product is 100 miles because, beyond that distance, prices increase too much. Almost any place in Belgium is within 100 miles of a foreign country; however, this is not true for its two neighbors, France and Germany. Thus, Belgium's trade involves a higher percentage of its production and consumption than the comparable figures in either France or Germany.

Size of Economy and Production Scales

Although land area is the most obvious way of measuring a country's size, countries also can be compared on the basis of economic size. Countries with large economies and high per capita incomes are more likely to produce goods that use technologies requiring long production runs. This is because these countries develop industries to serve their large domestic markets, which, in turn, tend to be competitive in export markets.[10] However, companies may locate long production runs in small countries if they expect few barriers in other countries to the export of their output.[11] In industries where long production runs are important for gaining competitive advantages, companies tend to locate their production in few countries, using these locations as sources of exports to other countries. Where long production runs are unimportant, companies are more apt to minimize exporting. Instead, they produce in most countries where they sell. In addition, high expenditures on research and development create high fixed costs for companies. Therefore, the technologically intensive company from a small nation may have a more compelling need to sell abroad than would a company with a large domestic market. In turn, this pulls resources from other industries and companies within the company's domestic market, causing more national specialization than in a larger nation.[12]

FACTOR-PROPORTIONS THEORY

According to the factor-proportions theory, factors in relative abundance are cheaper than factors in relative scarcity.

Smith's and Ricardo's theories did not help to identify the types of products that would most likely give a country an advantage. Those theories assumed that the workings of the free market would lead producers to the goods they could produce more efficiently and away from those they could not produce efficiently. About a century and a quarter later, Eli Heckscher and Bertil Ohlin developed the **factor-proportions theory,** a theory that is based on countries' production factors—land, labor, and capital (funds for investment in plant and equipment). This theory said that differences in countries' endowments of labor compared to their endowments of land or capital explained differences in the cost of production factors. These economists proposed that if labor were abundant in comparison to land and capital, labor costs would be low relative to land and capital costs. If labor were scarce, labor costs would be high in relation to land and capital costs. These relative factor costs would lead countries to excel in the production and export of products that used their abundant—and, therefore, cheaper—production factors.[13]

Land–Labor Relationship

Production factors are not homogeneous, especially labor.

On the basis of the factor-proportions theory, Sri Lankan authorities reasoned that their country had a competitive advantage in products that used large numbers of abundant semi-skilled workers. The factor-proportions theory appears logical. In countries in which there are many people relative to the amount of land—for example, Hong Kong and the Netherlands—land price is very high because it's in demand. Regardless of climate and soil conditions, neither Hong Kong nor the Netherlands excels in the production of goods requiring large amounts of land, such as wool or wheat. Businesses in countries such as Australia and Canada produce these goods because land is abundant compared to the number of people.

Casual observation of manufacturing locations also seems to substantiate the theory. For example, the most successful industries in Hong Kong are those in which technology permits the use of a minimum amount of land relative to the number of people employed: Clothing production occurs in multistory factories where workers share minimal space. Hong Kong does not compete in the production of automobiles, however, which requires much more space per worker.

Labor–Capital Relationship

In countries where there is little capital available for investment and where the amount of investment per worker is low, managers might expect to find cheap labor rates and export competitiveness in products that require large amounts of labor relative to capital. These managers can anticipate the opposite when labor is scarce. For example, Iran (where labor is abundant in comparison to capital) excels in the production of handmade carpets that differ in appearance as well as in production method from the carpets produced in industrial countries by machines purchased with cheap capital.

However, because the factor-proportions theory assumes production factors to be homogeneous, tests to substantiate the theory have thus been mixed.[14] Labor skills in fact, vary within and among countries because people have different training and education. Training and education require capital expenditures that do not show up in traditional capital measurements, which include only plant and equipment values. When the factor-proportions theory accounts for different labor groups and the capital invested to train these groups, it seems to explain trade patterns.[15] For example, because industrial-country exports embody a higher proportion of professionals such as scientists and engineers than emerging economies' exports, those countries are using their abundant production factors to maintain their lead in exports. Exports of emerging economies, though, show a high intensity of less skilled labor.[16] This variation in labor skills among countries has led to more international specialization by task to produce a given product. For example, a company may locate its research activities and management functions primarily in countries with a highly educated population, and it may locate its production work to countries where less skilled—and less expensive—workers can be employed.

Technological Complexities

The factor-proportions analysis becomes more complicated when the same product can be produced by different methods, such as with labor or capital. Canada produces wheat with a capital-intensive method (high expenditure on machinery per worker) because of its abundance of low-cost capital relative to labor. In contrast, India produces wheat by using a much smaller number of machines in comparison to its abundant and cheap labor. In the final analysis, managers must compare the cost in each locale based on the type of production that will minimize costs there.

THE PRODUCT LIFE CYCLE THEORY OF TRADE

Raymond Vernon's international product life cycle (PLC) theory of trade states that the location of production of certain kinds of products shifts as they go through their life cycles, which consists of four stages—introduction, growth, maturity, and decline.[17] Table 5.2 highlights the stages.

Changes Through the Cycle

Companies develop new products because there is a nearby observed need and market for them. This means that a U.S. company is most apt to develop a new product for the U.S. market, a French company for the French market, and so on. At the same time, almost all new technology that results in new products and production methods originates in industrial countries because of a combination of factors—competition, demanding consumers, the availability of scientists and engineers, and high incomes.[18]

Once a company has created a new product, theoretically it can manufacture that product anywhere in the world. In practice, however, the early production (introductory stage)

According to the PLC theory of trade, the production location for many products moves from one country to another depending on the stage in the product's life cycle.

The introduction stage is marked by

- Innovation in response to observed need
- Exporting by the innovative country
- Evolving product characteristics

● TABLE 5.2

INTERNATIONAL CHANGES DURING A PRODUCT'S LIFE CYCLE

Overall, production and sales shift from industrial countries to emerging economies during a product's life cycle.

	LIFE CYCLE STAGE			
	1: INTRODUCTION	2: GROWTH	3: MATURITY	4: DECLINE
Production location	• In innovating (usually industrial) country	• In innovating and other industrial countries	• Multiple countries	• Mainly in developing countries
Market location	• Mainly in innovating country, with some exports	• Mainly in industrial countries • Shift in export markets as foreign production replaces exports in some markets	• Growth in developing countries • Some decrease in industrial countries	• Mainly in developing countries • Some developing country exports
Competitive factors	• Near-monopoly position • Sales based on uniqueness rather than price • Evolving product characteristics	• Fast-growing demand • Number of competitors increases • Some competitors begin price-cutting • Product becoming more standardized	• Overall stabilized demand • Number of competitors decreases • Price is very important, especially in developing countries	• Overall declining demand • Price is key weapon • Number of producers continues to decline
Production technology	• Short production runs • Evolving methods to coincide with product evolution • High labor input and labor skills relative to capital input	• Capital input increases • Methods more standardized	• Long production runs using high capital inputs • Highly standardized • Less labor skill needed	• Unskilled labor on mechanized long production runs

generally occurs in a domestic location so that the company can obtain rapid market feedback as well as save on transport costs. At this stage, companies may sell a small part of their production to customers in foreign markets, mainly in other industrial countries, because those customers have incomes to spend on newer products.

The production process is apt to be more labor-intensive in the introductory stage than in later stages. Because the product is not yet standardized, its production process must permit rapid changes in product characteristics, as market feedback dictates. This implies high labor input as opposed to more capital-intensive automated production. Further, the capital machinery necessary to produce a product on a large scale usually develops later than product technology, only when sales begin to expand rapidly enough (Stage 2—growth) to warrant the high development costs of the machines for the new process. Although the early production is most apt to occur in industrial countries, which have high labor rates, this labor tends to be highly educated and skilled so that it is adept and efficient when production is not yet standardized. Even if production costs are high because of expensive labor, companies can often pass costs onto consumers who are unwilling to wait for possible price reductions later.

As sales of the new product grow (Stage 2—growth), competitors enter the market. At the same time, demand is likely to grow substantially in foreign markets, particularly in other industrial countries. In fact, demand may be sufficient to justify producing in some foreign markets to reduce or eliminate transport charges, but the output at this stage is likely to stay almost entirely in the foreign country with the additional manufacturing unit. Let's say, for example, that the innovator is in the United States and the additional manufacturing unit is in Japan. The producers in Japan will sell mainly in Japan for several reasons:

Growth is characterized by

• Increases in exports by the innovating country

• More competition

• Increased capital intensity

• Some foreign production

1. There is increased demand in the Japanese market for the product.

2. Producers need to introduce unique product variations for Japanese consumers.

3. Japanese costs may still be high because of production start-up problems.

Because sales are growing rapidly at home and abroad, there are incentives for companies to develop process technology. However, *product* technology may not yet be well developed because of the number of product variations introduced by competitors that are also trying to gain market share. So the production process may still be labor intensive during this stage, although it is becoming less so. The original producing country will increase its exports in this stage but lose certain key export markets in which competitors commence local production.

In Stage 3, maturity, worldwide demand begins to level off, although it may be growing in some countries and declining in others. There often is a shakeout of producers such that product models become highly standardized, making cost an important competitive weapon. Longer production runs become possible for foreign plants, which, in turn, reduce per unit cost for the producer's output. The lower per unit cost creates demand in emerging markets. Because markets and technologies are widespread, the innovating country no longer commands a production advantage. There are incentives to begin moving plants to developing countries in which unskilled, inexpensive labor is efficient for standardized (capital-intensive) processes. Exports decrease from the innovating country as foreign production displaces it.

As a product moves to Stage 4, decline, those factors occurring during the mature stage continue to evolve. The markets in industrial countries decline more rapidly than those in developing countries as affluent customers demand ever-newer products. By this time, market and cost factors have dictated that almost all production is in developing countries, which export to the declining or small-niche markets in industrial countries. In other words, the country in which the innovation first emerged—and exported from—then becomes the importer.

> Maturity is characterized by
>
> - A decline in exports from the innovating country
> - More product standardization
> - More capital intensity
> - Increased competitiveness of price
> - Production start-ups in emerging economies

> Decline is characterized by
>
> - A concentration of production in developing countries
> - An innovating country becoming net importer

Verification and Limitations of PLC Theory

The PLC theory holds that the location of production facilities that serve world markets shifts as products move through their life cycle. Such products as ballpoint pens and portable calculators have followed this pattern. They were first produced in a single industrial country and sold at a high price. Then production shifted to multiple industrial country locations to serve those local markets. Finally, most production is located in emerging markets, and prices have declined. However, if transportation costs are very high, there is little opportunity for export sales, regardless of the stage in the life cycle. Additionally, there are many types of products for which shifts in production location do not usually take place. In these cases, the innovating country maintains its export ability throughout the product's life cycle. These exceptions include

1. Products that, because of very rapid innovation, have extremely short life cycles, a factor that makes it impossible to achieve cost reductions by moving production from one country to another. For example, product obsolescence occurs so rapidly for many electronic products that there is little international diffusion of production.

2. Luxury products for which cost is of little concern to the consumer.

3. Products for which a company can use a differentiation strategy, perhaps through advertising, to maintain consumer demand without competing on the basis of price.

4. Products that require specialized technical labor to evolve into their next generation. This seems to explain the long-term U.S. dominance of medical equipment production and German dominance in rotary printing presses.[19]

In addition, changes in technology and demand might lead to all kinds of permutations. For example, microchip production began in the United States, at which time the United

ETHICAL DILEMMA

Values, Free Global Trade, and
Production Standards—A Hard Trio to Mix

There is usually heated debate over laissez-faire versus activist government trade policies as well as the independence versus dependence of countries. Why? Because different country values underlie different positions.

For example, the argument for free-trade policy is based on the achievement of global economic efficiency. However, some countries may not be content with only global economic efficiency. In addition, some people argue that free trade, although leading to lower production costs, does not take into account differences in individual countries' standards—such as requirements for worker safety, disposal of wastes, and worker conditions. These standards reflect the social and environmental values of the countries' citizens. Because standards vary among countries, the costs producers incur vary as well, and producers who must adhere to more stringent standards argue against free trade. For example, environmental compliance costs are much lower in many countries than in the United States. Thus, some U.S. companies have home-country cost disadvantages when compared to production abroad. However, if other countries eventually establish and enforce standards similar to those in the United States, U.S. companies may have gained first-mover advantages because those companies had to develop technologies and gained experience with them.[20] In another case, the European Union's threat to ban fur imports from countries using steel-jawed leg-hold traps, which reduce trapping costs but cause the animals great pain and a slow death, led Canada to abolish use of the traps.[21] The European Union (EU) now threatens to limit imports of cosmetics tested on animals.[22] Opponents of free trade in the United States have argued that imports should be disallowed from Malaysia because of its antiunion directives and from China when jailed workers produce their exports.

Ethical questions center on whether all countries should have similar production standards, whether countries should limit imports of competing products because of differences in standards, and whether companies should locate production to wherever they can capitalize on less stringent standards that allow them to lower their costs.

States was an exporter. But then production moved largely abroad, as would be predicted by PLC theory, and the United States became an importer. But then most production returned to the United States in response to additional product innovations and changing market conditions, and the United States became an exporter again.

Regardless of the product type, there has been an increased tendency on the part of MNEs to introduce new products at home and abroad almost simultaneously. In other words, instead of merely observing needs within their domestic markets, companies develop products and services for observable market segments that transcend national borders. In so doing, they eliminate delays as a product is diffused from one country to another, and they choose a production location that will minimize costs for serving markets in multiple countries. Further, companies sometimes produce abroad simply to take advantage of production economies rather than in response to growing foreign markets. Ericsson, for example, produces in Sri Lanka primarily to sell in export markets, not to supply the Sri Lankan market.

COUNTRY-SIMILARITY THEORY

Thus far in this chapter, the theories explaining why trade takes place have focused on the differences among countries. These theories tend to explain most of the trade among dissimilar countries, such as trade between an industrial country and an emerging economy or trade between a temperate country and a tropical one. On the basis of these theories, you would expect that the greater the dissimilarity among countries, the greater the potential for trade. For example, great differences in climatic conditions will lead to highly differentiated agricultural products. Countries that differ in labor or capital intensities will differ in the types of products they can produce efficiently. National differences in innovative abilities will affect how production of a product will move from one country to another during the product's life cycle.

Most trade theories emphasize differences among countries in
- Climate
- Factor endowment
- Innovative capability

Economic Similarity of Industrial Countries

Observations of trade patterns reveal that most of the world's trade occurs among countries that have similar characteristics, specifically among industrial, or developed, countries. For example, the United States is the world's largest trader, and 8 of its 10 largest trading partners are either industrialized or newly industrialized countries.[23] Globally, 11 of the 12 largest traders are industrialized or newly industrialized countries.[24] Overall trade patterns seem to be at odds with the traditional theories that emphasize country-by-country differences.

Most trade today occurs among apparently similar countries.

The fact that so much trade takes place among industrial countries is due to the growing importance of acquired advantage (product technology) as opposed to natural advantage (agricultural products and raw materials) in world trade (see Figure 5.4). The **country-similarity theory** says that once a company has developed a new product in response to observed market conditions in the home market, it will turn to markets it sees as most similar to those at home.[25] In addition, markets in industrial countries can support products and their variations. Thus, companies from different countries produce different product models, and each may gain some markets abroad. This theory helps explain why both road vehicles (automobiles and small trucks) and passenger jet aircraft comprise large categories of U.S. imports and U.S. exports.[26]

Although the markets within the industrial countries might have similar demands, countries also specialize to gain acquired advantage—for example, by apportioning their research efforts more strongly to some sectors than to others. Germany is traditionally strong in machinery and equipment, Switzerland in pharmaceutical products, and Denmark in food products.[27]

The importance of industrial countries in world trade is due, in addition to specialization, to these countries' economic size. In other words, these countries produce so much that there is more to sell—both domestically and internationally. In addition, because these countries produce so much, incomes are high and people buy more—from both domestic and foreign sources. At the same time, little of the trade of developing countries is with other developing countries. Instead, the developing countries mainly export primary products and labor-intensive mature products to industrial countries in exchange for new and technologically advanced products.

Similarity of Location

Although the theories regarding country differences and similarities help to explain broad world trade patterns, such as those that link industrial countries and developing countries, they do little to explain specific pairs of trading relationships. Why, for example, will a particular industrial country buy more from one developing country than another? Why will it buy from one industrial country rather than another? Although there is no single answer to explain all product flows, the geographic distance between two countries accounts for many of these world trade relationships. For example, Finland is a major exporter to Russia because its transport costs are cheap and fast compared to its transport costs to other countries. Acer, a Taiwanese computer maker, built a plant in Finland to serve Russia

Trading partners are affected by
- Distance
- Competitive capabilities
- Cultural similarity
- Relations between countries

FIGURE 5.4   World Trade by Major Product Category as Percentage of Total World Trade for Selected Years

Manufactured products continue to be the largest product category traded (as a percentage of total world trade).

Source: From World Trade Organization, *Annual Report,* 2001, (Geneva: World Trade Organization, 2001); 95–96 Reprinted by permission of World Trade Organization.

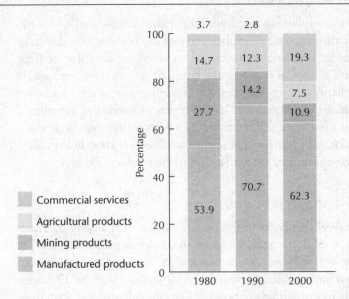

because it realized savings by shipping from Finland rather than from Asia and because a Finnish plant provided more secure storage and ease of operations than a Russian one.[28]

But transport cost is not the only factor in trade partner choice. For example, New Zealand competes with Chile, Argentina, and South Africa for out-of-season sales of apples to the Northern Hemisphere—but with a disadvantage in freight costs. It has countered this disadvantage by increasing yields, developing new premium varieties, bypassing intermediaries to sell directly to supermarkets abroad, and consolidating efforts through a national marketing board. However, such methods to overcome distance disadvantages are difficult to maintain. For example, both Chinese and Chilean orchardists have smuggled new strains of apple tree cuttings out of New Zealand.[29]

Cultural Similarity

Cultural similarity, as expressed through language and religion, also helps explain much of the direction of trade. Importers and exporters find it easier to do business in a country they perceive as being similar to their home countries. Likewise, historic colonial relationships explain much of the trade between specific industrial countries and developing countries. For instance, the colonial history of France in Africa has given an edge to Air France in serving those former colonies' international air passenger markets.[30] Likewise, much of the lack of trade among nations in the Southern Hemisphere is due to the absence of historic ties. Importers and exporters find it easier to continue business ties than to develop new distribution arrangements in countries in which they are less experienced.

Similarity of Political and Economic Interests

Political relationships and economic agreements among countries may discourage or encourage trade between them or their companies. An example of trade discouragement is the political animosity between the United States and Cuba that has caused mutual trade to be almost nonexistent for the last four decades. The United States replaced Cuban sugar imports with imports from such countries as Mexico and the Dominican Republic. An example of trade encouragement is the agreement among EU countries to remove all trade barriers with each other. This agreement has caused a greater share of countries' total trade to be conducted within the group.

Military conflicts disrupt traditional international business trade patterns as participants divert their transportation systems and much of their productive capacity to the war effort. In addition, political animosity and transport difficulties may interfere with trading channels. For example, Iraq's international trade fell sharply after its 1990 invasion of Kuwait as other countries either severed trade relations or disrupted supply lines. The composition of trade changes from consumer goods to industrial goods, which the warring countries use to meet military objectives.

DEGREE OF DEPENDENCE

The theories of independence, interdependence, and dependence help to explain world trade patterns and countries' trade policies. They form a continuum, with independence at one extreme, dependence on the other, and interdependence falling in the middle. No countries are located at either extreme of this continuum, but some tend to be closer to one extreme than the other.

No country is completely dependent or independent economically, although some are closer to one extreme or the other.

Independence

In a situation of independence, a country would have no reliance on other countries for any goods, services, or technologies. However, because all countries need to trade, no country has complete economic independence from other countries. The most recent instances of economic near-independence have been the Liawep tribe, found in Papua New Guinea in 1993, and Bhutan during the latter part of the twentieth century.[31] Isolation from other societies brought certain advantages to the Liaweps and Bhutanese. They did not have to be concerned, for example, that another society might cut off their supply of essential foods or tools. Of course, the price of independence for both societies is having higher priced products or to do without goods they could not produce themselves. An additional disadvantage of independence is that it hinders a country's ability to borrow and adapt technologies already in existence. Such borrowing and adaptation can add significantly to a country's economic growth. In most countries, government policy has focused on achieving the advantages of independence without depriving its citizens. Governments try to forge trade relationships that are minimally vulnerable to foreign control of supply and demand. For example, the U.S. government maintains stocks of essential minerals so that its citizens will have access to them for a prolonged period if foreigners cut off supplies.

Too much economic independence means doing without certain goods, services, and technologies.

Interdependence

One way a country limits its vulnerability to foreign changes is through interdependence: the development of trade relationships on the basis of mutual need. France and Germany, for example, have highly interdependent economies. Each depends about equally on the other as a trading partner, and so neither is likely to cut off supplies or markets for fear of retaliation. Such interdependence sometimes spurs international companies to pressure their governments to sustain trade relations. For example, about a third of world trade is intracompany trade—that is, companies export components and finished products between their foreign and home-country facilities. Any trade cessation would adversely affect these companies. For example, Ford buys and produces different components in different countries and would be severely affected if supplies from any one were to be suddenly disrupted.

Interdependence is mutual dependence.

Dependence

Many developing countries have decried their dependence because they rely so heavily on the sale of one primary commodity or on one country as a customer and supplier. Although most

Too much dependence causes a country to be vulnerable to events in other countries.

developing countries depend on one commodity for over 25 percent of their export earnings, Iceland is the only industrialized country that depends on one product (fish) for over a quarter of its export earnings. While about one-quarter of developing countries depend on one country (almost always an industrial one) for more than half of their export earnings, Canada is the only industrialized country with this high a dependence (on the United States). Because the developing countries have low levels of production, they tend to be much more dependent on a given industrial country than the industrial country is dependent on them. Mexico, for example, depends on the United States for over 80 percent of its exports, but the United States depends on Mexico for less than 15 percent of its exports. U.S. policies can affect Mexico much more than Mexican policies can affect the United States. Further, developing countries primarily depend on production that competes on the basis of low-wage inputs. This sort of dependence has led to concern among many economists that dependence will delay emerging economies' development.

Although theorists and policy makers wishing to lower dependency have proposed a number of different approaches, they all suggest that developing countries intervene in foreign trade markets. As shown in the opening case, Sri Lanka has attempted to diversify its exports by developing nontraditional products that its policy makers believe can ultimately compete in world markets. But some developing countries see little opportunity to diversify production away from a basic commodity for which there is global oversupply.

STRATEGIC TRADE POLICY

Given the importance of acquired advantage in world trade, it is understandable that governments have debated what their roles should be in affecting the acquired advantage of production within their borders. At the same time, government influence is seldom neutral, so even though government decisions and policies may not seek to affect world trade, they nevertheless have that effect. For example, U.S. government efforts to improve agricultural productivity and defense capabilities have undoubtedly helped the U.S. exports of farm and aerospace products. Further, a government's decision to help certain industries may hurt others. For example, European airlines have argued that their governments' support for high-speed rail traffic in Europe has hurt their ability to be competitive on international routes with U.S. air carriers, which profit from not having to compete much with railroads for passenger traffic in the United States.

From the standpoint of national competitiveness, the issue revolves around the development of successful industries. Of particular importance are emerging growth industries, because they offer the possibility of adding value (from high profits and wages) within the country in which most of the industry is headquartered. Further, by being first, there are marketing and production cost advantages that retard competition from other countries. But to be internationally competitive, governments and companies must have the right resources that are needed for the targeted industry. Governments may try to alter their absolute and comparative advantages so that there is a fit, such as by importing and developing the specific skills they need.

There are two basic approaches to government policy: (1) alter conditions that will affect industry in general, (2) alter conditions that will affect a targeted industry. Regardless of whether a government takes a general or specific approach, it may alter the competitive positions of specific companies and production locations. The first approach means altering conditions that affect factor proportions, efficiency, and innovation. A country may upgrade production factors by improving human skills through education, providing infrastructure (transportation, communications, capital markets, utilities), promoting a highly competitive environment so that companies must make improvements, and inducing consumers to demand an ever higher quality of products and services. This approach is general insofar as it creates conditions that may affect a variety of industries.

Countries seek to improve their trade capabilities by
- Altering conditions for industries in general
- Targeting conditions for a specific industry

The second approach is to target specific industries. This approach has usually resulted in no more than small payoffs, largely because governments find it difficult to identify and target the right ones.[32] For example, a country may target an industry for which global demand never reaches expectations, such as France's support for supersonic passenger aircraft. Or the companies in the targeted industry do not become competitive: Consider, for example, Thailand's support of the steel companies, which have had high costs because of poorly trained managers and rising labor costs in relation to other nearby countries.[33] Moreover, there has been a tendency for too many countries to identify the same industries, so excessive competition has led to inadequate returns.[34] Finally, relative conditions change, causing relative capabilities to change as well. For instance, Singapore successfully attracted companies that were involved in mature consumer electronics production and was able to compete globally because of its low wages in comparison to its productivity. However, in recent years, Singapore has been losing its competitive advantage because of its rising labor costs. It has also seen many companies move their production elsewhere, such as to Malaysia. Singapore is now trying to attract more research and development facilities for new products with higher profit margins.[35]

Nevertheless, there are some notable government successes. For example, the Indian Ocean country of Mauritius increased its adult literacy rate from 60 percent to 100 percent within three years. It successfully targeted textile manufacturing and a variety of service exports (such as tourism, banking, and phone betting) and was thus able to transform its dependence on sugar production. The growth rate in the 1990s was one of the world's highest.[36]

WHY COMPANIES TRADE INTERNATIONALLY

Now that we know some *country* trade theories, let's see why *companies* trade. Regardless of the advantages a country may gain by trading, international trade ordinarily will not begin unless companies within that country have competitive advantages that enable them to be viable traders—and they must foresee profits in exporting and importing. Only if they perceive that the international opportunities might be greater than the domestic ones will they divert their resources to the foreign sector. To understand why trade takes place, it is useful to understand the competitive advantages and trade opportunities that accrue to individual businesses.

The Porter Diamond

Why do specialized competitive advantages differ among countries—for example, why do Italian companies have an advantage in the ceramic tile industry and Swiss companies have one in the watch industry? Figure 5.5, the **Porter diamond**, shows that four conditions are important for competitive superiority: demand conditions; factor conditions; related and supporting industries; and firm strategy, structure, and rivalry. We have already discussed all four of these conditions in the context of other trade theories, but how they combine affects the development and continued existence of competitive advantages. The framework of the diamond is, therefore, a useful tool for understanding how and where globally competitive companies develop. Usually, but not always, all four conditions need to be favorable for an industry within a country to attain global supremacy.

Points and Limitations of the Porter Diamond Both PLC theory and country-similarity theory show that new products (or industries) usually arise from companies' observation of need or demand, which is usually in their home country. *Demand conditions* are the first point in the diamond. Companies then start up production near the observed market. This was the case for the Italian ceramic tile industry after World War II: There was a postwar housing boom, and consumers wanted cool floors because of the hot Italian climate. The second point of the Porter diamond—*factor conditions* (recall natural advantage within absolute advantage theory and the factor-proportions theory)—influenced both the choice of tile to meet

Companies' development of internationally competitive products depends on their domestic

- Demand conditions
- Factor conditions
- Related and supporting industries
- Firm strategy, structure, and rivalry

LOOKING TO THE FUTURE

Companies Adjust to Changing Trade Policies and Conditions

When countries have few restrictions on foreign trade, companies have greater opportunities to gain economies of scale by servicing markets in more than one country from a single base of production. They also can pursue global, as opposed to multidomestic, strategies more easily. But government trade restrictions vary from one country to another, from one point in time to another, and from one product or service to others within the same economies. Nevertheless, it is probably safe to say that trade restrictions have been diminishing, primarily because of the economic gains that countries foresee through freer trade. However, critics claim that freer trade accentuates the gap between the rich and poor because not everyone fairly shares in the economic benefits of free trade.[37] Thus, there are uncertainties as to whether the trend toward the freer movement of trade will endure. Groups worldwide question whether the economic benefits of more open economies outweigh some of the costs, both economic and noneconomic. Although the next chapter will discuss import restrictions (protectionism) in detail, it is useful at this point to understand the overall issues of evolving protectionist sentiment.

One key issue is the trade between industrial and developing countries. At the same time that trade barriers are being lowered, many developing countries, in which wage rates are very low, are increasing productivity more rapidly than are industrial countries. The result could mean certain shifts in production to developing countries and the displacement of many jobs within industrial countries. There is uncertainty as to how fast new jobs will replace old ones in industrial countries and how much tolerance industrial countries will have for employment shifts that would be less likely to occur within protected markets.

A second key issue results from the concept of national sovereignty.[38] Separate nations exist because of differences in culture and in economic and political priorities. The more interdependent economies become due to trade, the more difficult it is for a country to maintain differences from its major trading partners. For example, two neighboring countries may differ in preferences for income equality, on whether to place the major tax burden on companies or individuals, on the level of required employee safety provisions, and on how much the environment should be protected. Such differences create production cost differences. With unrestricted trade, a country with more stringent (expensive) requirements may either have to relax those requirements or face production adjustments as products enter easily from abroad. Presently, there is evidence that many countries may invoke national sovereignty by preventing trade that may undermine their own priorities and objectives, even though such moves may have certain negative economic costs for them.

Companies must try to predict whether there will be freer or more restrictive trade in those industries in which they operate. Restrictive trade limits companies' options. Restrictions also may cause companies to make some decisions about where to locate and sell that are different from the choices they would otherwise make. If present trends continue, relationships among factor endowments (land, labor, and capital) will continue to evolve. For example, the population growth rate is much higher in developing countries than in developed countries. Two possible consequences of this growth are continued shifts of labor-intensive production to developing countries and of agricultural production away from densely populated areas. At the same time, the finite supply of natural resources may lead to price increases for these resources, even though oversupplies have generally depressed prices for some time. The limited supply may work to the advantage of developing countries because supplies in industrial countries have been more fully exploited.

Four factors are worth monitoring, because they could cause product trade to become relatively less significant in the future.

1. There are some indications that protectionist sentiment is growing. For example, major trading countries have recently squabbled over trade for a number of products, including genetically altered agricultural products, bananas, steel, and passenger aircraft. These sorts of disputes could prevent competitively produced goods from entering foreign countries.

2. As economies grow, efficiencies of multiple production locations also grow, which may allow country-by-country production to replace trade in many cases. For example, most automobile producers have moved into Thailand or plan to do so as a result of Thailand's growing market size.

3. Flexible, small-scale production methods, especially those using robotics, may enable even small countries to produce many goods efficiently for their own consumption, thus eliminating the need to import those goods. For example, steel production used to take larger capital outlays that needed enormous markets before the development of efficient minimills that can produce on a small scale.

4. Services are growing more rapidly than products as a portion of production and consumption within industrial countries. Consequently, product trade may become a less important part of countries' total trade. Further, many of the rapid-growth service areas, such as home building and dining out, are not easily traded, so trade in goods plus services could become a smaller part of total output and consumption.

consumer demand and the choice of Italy as the production location. Wood was less available and more expensive than tile, and most production factors (skilled labor, capital, technology, and equipment) were available within Italy on favorable terms. The third condition—the existence of nearby *related and supporting industries* (enamels and glazes)—was also favorable. (Recall discussions of the importance of transport costs in the theory of country size, in assumptions of specialization, and in the limitation factors of PLC theory.)

The combination of three conditions—demand, factor conditions and related and supporting industries—influenced companies' decisions to initiate production of ceramic tiles in postwar Italy. The ability of these companies to develop and sustain a competitive advantage required favorable circumstances for the fourth condition—*firm strategy, structure*, and

FIGURE 5.5 Determinants of Global Competitive Advantage

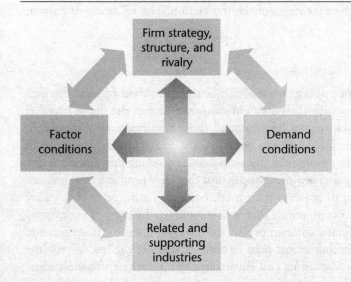

The Porter diamond shows the interaction of four conditions that usually need to be favorable if an industry in a country is to gain a global competitive advantage.

Source: Adapted with the permission of The Free Press, a Division of Simon & Schuster, Inc., from *The Competitive Advantage of Nations* by Michael E. Porter. Copyright © 1990, 1998 by Michael E. Porter.

rivalry. Barriers to market entry were low in the tile industry (some companies started up with as few as three employees), and hundreds of companies initiated production. Rivalry became intense as companies tried to serve increasingly sophisticated Italian consumers. These circumstances forced breakthroughs in both product and process technologies, which gave the Italian producers advantages over foreign producers and enabled them to gain the largest global share of tile exports.

The existence of the four favorable conditions does not guarantee that an industry will develop in a given locale. Entrepreneurs may face favorable conditions for many different lines of business. In fact, comparative advantage theory holds that resource limitations may cause companies in a country to avoid competing in some industries even though an absolute advantage may exist. For example, conditions in Switzerland would seem to have favored success if companies in that country had become players in the personal computer industry. However, Swiss companies preferred to protect their global positions in such product lines as watches and scientific instruments rather than to downsize those industries by moving their highly skilled people into a new industry.

A second limitation of the diamond concerns the increased ability of companies to attain market information, production factors, and supplies from abroad. At the same time, they face more competition from foreign production and foreign companies. The absence of any of the four conditions from the diamond domestically, therefore, may not inhibit companies and industries from becoming globally competitive. First, take the existence of demand conditions. We have already discussed how observations of foreign, rather than domestic, demand conditions have spurred much of the recent growth in Asian exports. In fact, such Japanese companies as Uniden and Fujitech target their sales almost entirely to foreign markets.[39] Second, domestic factor conditions can change. For example, capital and managers are now internationally mobile. Much of Singapore's recent global export growth of high-tech components has depended on the importation of these two factors. Third, if related and supporting industries are not available locally, materials and components are now more easily brought in from abroad because of advancements in transportation and the relaxation of import restrictions. In fact, many MNEs now assemble products with parts supplied from a variety of countries. Finally, companies react not only to domestic rivals but also to foreign-based rivals with which they compete at home and abroad.

COMPANIES' ROLE IN TRADE

Every trade transaction is an export for one party and an import for another. So both the exporter and importer must see the advantages of the transaction. The following discussion will describe these advantages.

Strategic Advantages of Exports

Most companies would prefer to concentrate on domestic rather than foreign markets because of their greater familiarity with their own environments and of the desire to avoid trade regulations and converting currencies. However, all those advantages we discussed in Chapter 1 for engaging in international business apply for trade. For example, companies may export to utilize their capacities more fully than is possible by selling only domestically. When they sell more, they usually decrease the cost per unit that they produce, thus increasing their profits or enabling them to improve their market shares. Thus, the market leader may garner cost advantages over its competitors that even discourage the entry of other companies into the industry. In fact, many companies that are not the leaders in their domestic markets may be more active in seeking export sales in order to counter the leaders' volume advantage. For example, in Japan, Matsushita and Toyota are their industries' market leaders. However, Sony and Sanyo as followers of Matsushita as well as Nissan and Honda as follow-

Most trade theories are based on a national perspective, but decisions to trade are usually made by companies.

Managers' incentives to export include

- Use of excess capacity
- Reduced production costs per unit
- Increased markup
- Spread of risk

ers of Toyota are more active in export markets.[40] However, the gains that result by reducing the per unit production cost must be weighed against additional costs arising from exporting, such as those for product adaptation, management time, inventory increases, and more credit extension. These costs may outweigh the advantages of developing foreign markets.

A producer might also be able to sell the same product at a greater profit abroad than at home. This may happen because the competitive environment in the foreign market is different, possibly because in that market, the product is in a different stage of its life cycle. A mature stage at home may force domestic price-cutting, whereas a growth stage abroad may make foreign price reductions unnecessary. Greater profitability also may come about because of different government actions at home and abroad that affect profitability—for example, differences in the taxation of earnings or the regulation of prices. If, however, companies must divert efforts from domestic sales to service foreign markets, they may lack the resources to sustain their overall growth objectives.

By spreading sales over more than one foreign market, a producer might be able to minimize the effects of fluctuations in demand. Business cycles and product life vary among countries. Another factor in spreading risk through exportation is that a producer might be able to develop more customers, reducing its vulnerability to the loss of a single customer or a few.

Strategic Advantages of Imports

The impetus for trade may come from either the importer or the exporter. Impetus may come from an importer because that company is seeking out cheaper or better-quality supplies, components, or products to use in its production facilities. Or a company may be seeking new foreign products that complement its existing lines, giving the importer more to sell.

If international procurement of supplies and components lowers costs or improves the quality of finished products, the procuring company may then be better able to combat import competition for the finished products. Or it may be able to compete more effectively in export markets. The automobile industry exemplifies global competition that depends on subcontractors, including foreign ones, to reduce production costs.

An importer, like an exporter, might be able to spread its operating risks. By developing alternative suppliers, a company is less vulnerable to the dictates or fortunes of any single supplier. For example, many large U.S. steel customers, such as the automobile industry, have diversified their steel purchases to include European and Japanese suppliers. This strategy has reduced the risk of supply shortages for the U.S. automobile industry in case of a strike among U.S. steelworkers. At the same time, however, it has contributed to the U.S. steel industry's problems. This is an industry with high fixed-production costs; its loss of domestic market share increases its unit cost of steel. Its profits suffer because of fewer sales and lower per unit profits on the remaining sales.

Managers' incentives to import include

- Cheaper supplies
- Additions to product line
- Reduction of risk of no supply

Summary

- Trade theory is useful because it helps explain what might be produced competitively in a given locale, where a company might go to produce a given product efficiently, and whether government practices might interfere with the free flow of trade among countries.

- Some trade theories examine what will happen to international trade in the absence of government interference. Other theories prescribe how governments should interfere with trade flows to achieve certain national objectives.

- Mercantilist theory proposed that a country should try to achieve a favorable balance of trade (export more than it

imports) to receive an influx of gold. Neomercantilist policy also seeks a favorable balance of trade, but its purpose is to achieve some social or political objective.

- Adam Smith developed the theory of absolute advantage, which says that consumers will be better off if they can buy foreign-made products that are priced more cheaply than domestic ones.

- According to the theory of absolute advantage, a country may produce goods more efficiently because of a natural advantage (e.g., raw materials or climate) or because of an acquired advantage (e.g., technology or skill for a product or process advantage).

- David Ricardo's comparative advantage theory says that total global output can increase through foreign trade, even if one country has an absolute advantage in the production of all products.

- Policy makers have questioned some of the assumptions of the absolute and comparative advantage theories. These assumptions are that full employment exists, that output efficiency is always a country's major objective, that there are no transport costs among countries, that countries are satisfied with their relative gains, that advantages appear to be static, and that resources move freely within countries but are immobile internationally. Although the theories use a two-country analysis of products, the theories hold for multicountry trade and for services as well.

- The theory of country size holds that because countries with large land areas are apt to have varied climates and natural resources, they are generally more self-sufficient than smaller countries are. A second reason for this greater self-sufficiency is that large countries' production centers are more likely to be located at a greater distance from other countries, raising the transport costs of foreign trade.

- The factor-proportions theory holds that a country's relative endowments of land, labor, and capital will determine the relative costs of these factors. These factor costs, in turn, will determine which goods the country can produce most efficiently.

- The international product life cycle (PLC) theory states that companies will manufacture products first in the countries in which they were researched and developed. These are almost always industrialized countries. Over the product's life cycle, production will shift to foreign locations, especially to developing countries as the product reaches the stages of maturity and decline.

- According to the country-similarity theory, most trade today occurs among industrial countries because they share similar market segments and because they produce and consume so much more than developing countries.

- Manufactured products comprise the bulk of trade among industrialized countries. This trade occurs because countries apportion their research and development differently among industrial sectors. It also occurs because industrial country consumers want and can afford to buy products with a greater variety of characteristics than are produced in their domestic markets.

- Some developing countries are concerned that they are overly vulnerable to events in other countries because of their high dependence on one export product or one trading partner. As developing countries try to become more independent of the external environment, however, they face the risk that their own consumers may have to pay higher prices or do without some goods.

- Countries seek to improve their national competitiveness by developing successful industries. They do this by altering conditions that affect industry in general or by targeting the development of specific industries (a strategic trade policy).

- Although most trade theories deal with cross-country benefits and costs, trading decisions usually are made at the company level, where both an exporter and importer see advantages from trade. Companies must have competitive advantages to be viable exporters. These may come from domestic demand and factor conditions, availability of related and supporting industries, and strong competitive situations. They may seek trading opportunities to use excess capacity, lower production costs, sell at higher prices, or spread risks. Importers seek cheaper or better-quality supplies and products that complement their existing lines.

CASE

The Indian Cashew Processing Industry.[41]

Even though the cashew tree grows fruit, it is best known for its nuts. India is the world's largest producer, processor, and exporter. In 2000, that country accounted for 65 percent of the $208 million in total global exports.

The fruit of the tree (known as the cashew apple), however, drew the earliest attention. The Tupi Indians of Brazil first harvested the cashew apple in the wild. They later introduced it to early Portuguese traders, who, in turn, propagated the tree in other tropical countries. But attempts to grow the tree on plantations proved unsuccessful because it was vulnerable to insects in the close quarters of plantations. Instead, some of the abandoned plantation trees propagated new trees in the wild forests of India, East Africa, Indonesia, and Southeast Asia.

Two other factors inhibited early harvest of the cashew nut. First, cashew fruit matures before the nut, and the fruit will keep only

about 24 hours after harvesting the nut. So the fruit is usually discarded in pursuit of the nut, which, if dried, can last a year or longer. Second, the processing of cashew nuts is tedious and time-consuming. In the 1920s, however, India developed a cashew-processing industry in response to the growing demand for cashew nuts among Indian consumers.

The processing required much manual dexterity and low wage rates because the nut is contained beneath layers of shell and thin skin. To remove the shell, workers must place the nut in an open fire for a few minutes and then tap it (while still hot) with a wooden hammer. If the nut breaks from the tapping, its value decreases considerably. Once workers remove the shell, they place the nut in an oven for up to 10 hours, after which they remove the skin by hand while the nut is still warm—without the use of fingernails or any sharp objects that can mark or break the surface. The workers then sort the nuts into

33 grades, based mainly on size and wholeness. The highest grades sell for several times the price of the lowest grades, which are sold almost entirely to the confectionary industry.

India maintained a virtual monopoly on cashew processing until the mid-1970s. This monopoly was due to three factors.

1. India was the largest producer of cashews.
2. Early demand occurred largely in India, meaning that any other country would have to incur added transport charges to reach the Indian market.
3. Most important, the Indian workers were particularly adept at the process technology.

Through the years, other factors threatened India's prominence as a cashew producer. First, a shortage developed when demand for the nuts grew in the United States and the United Kingdom. Second, because the nuts were ill suited for plantation growth, India could not produce enough and thus turned to East Africa, especially Mozambique, Tanzania, and Kenya, for supplies. Those countries were experiencing high unemployment and were at first eager to sell the raw nuts, which grew in the wild. But by the 1950s, they began to realize they could bypass India by processing the raw nuts themselves. Cashew-processing methods were well known and did not require the East Africans to invest in expensive machinery, so there was no technological obstacle. Mozambique became the world's largest cashew grower by the mid-1970s, and processed cashews became the country's leading export. However, because the Indian labor force worked on making handicrafts at home as children, by the time they were employed in cashew processing, they could perform delicate hand operations efficiently. Without such training, the East Africans were at a fatal disadvantage. Further, the Mozambique government neglected reinvestments in the state-owned processing plants, and many of the trees became diseased and too old to be productive. By the twenty-first century, Mozambique was no longer a major player in the industry.

Although the Africans' inability to compete granted a reprieve to the Indian industry, it put it on notice that it was vulnerable to supply cutoffs. The Indian Council for Agricultural Research, the International Society for Horticultural Sciences, and the Indian Society for Plantation Crops expanded their efforts to increase India's production of raw nuts. Concomitantly, three different companies developed mechanical equipment to replace hand processing. They sold equipment to East African countries and Brazil in the 1970s. These countries reduced their exports of raw nuts to India to maintain supplies for their own processing.

MAP 5.2 Major Export Markets for Indian Processed Cashew Nuts, 2000–2001

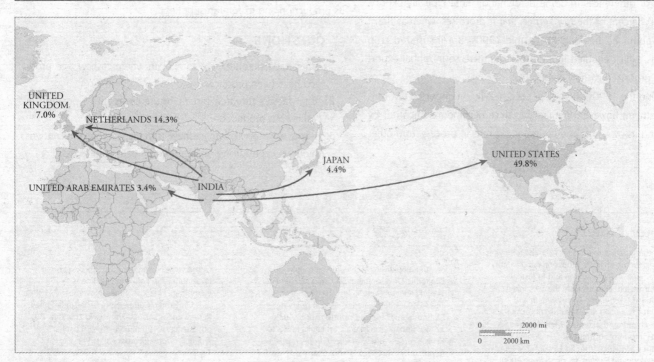

The United States accounts for almost half of India's exports of processed cashew nuts, and India's top-five markets account for 79 percent of its exports.

Source: The figures were taken from the Web site of the Cashew Export Promotion Council of India (September 7, 2002): http://www.cashewindia.org/html/c0300com.htm.

Three factors have kept India's hand-processing industry afloat.

1. The machinery breaks many cashew nuts, so Indian processors have had an advantage in the sale of higher-grade nuts. At any time, however, newer machinery might solve the breakage problem, again threatening the approximately 200 Indian processors and their 300,000 employees. Moreover, there is increased competition for the lower-grade output.

2. Indian processors have been able to obtain increased supplies of raw nuts, partially as a result of Indian production increases. Pesticide technology now makes cashew tree plantations feasible, increasing the number of trees per acre. Nevertheless, about 97 percent of nuts come from trees in the wild. Indian experimentation in hybridization, vegetative propagation, and grafting and budding techniques promises to increase the output per tree to five times what it was in the wild. Further, India has been increasing its imports of raw nuts substantially, primarily from Tanzania.

3. India uses fewer fertilizers than Brazil, the biggest export competitor, and the lack of fertilizer apparently gives Indian nuts a better flavor.

Because its exports consist of a higher portion of higher-grade nuts and because of flavor differences, Indian exports sell for a premium in comparison with those of competitors—for example, about 15 percent more than nuts from Brazil. However, yields are usually higher in Brazil, and Brazilian processors pay only between 30 and 36 percent of the price the Indian processors pay for raw nuts. Further, because of differences in domestic demand, India typically exports about 50 percent of the raw kernels that it processes, whereas Brazil exports about 85 percent. In the mid-1990s, Brazil suffered crop problems, which enabled India to gain an increase in global export share of processed cashew kernels.

During the 1990s, India depended heavily on imported raw nuts from Vietnam; however, Vietnam has since become a competitor by processing its own nuts and by importing nuts to process from other countries. The Vietnamese government is spending heavily to introduce high-tech strains into production in order to improve both quantity and quality. Vietnamese exports are of high quality, and so the country's exporters are not only targeting India's largest export market, the United States, but also emerging markets such as China, Saudi Arabia, and Russia. (Map 5.2 shows the location of India's main export markets.) If Vietnam's growth in exports continues at the same rate, it will surpass India as the largest exporter by 2010.

There is potential for an excess supply of cashew nuts, which might result from plantation techniques and improved technology in India and elsewhere. To find outlets for a possible nut glut, the All-India Coordinated Spices and Cashew Nut Improvement Project has focused its efforts on increasing nut sales in small markets and on finding new markets for products from the cashew tree. For example, experimentation is going on to harvest both the fruit and the nut. The fruit is also being studied for commercial use in candy, jams, chutney, juice, carbonated beverages, syrup, wine, and vinegar. Another area of research is in the use of cashew nutshell liquid (oil), which was once discarded as a waste product. It is now used extensively in industrial production of friction dusts for formulation in brake linings and clutch facings. Thus far, however, the extraction of cashew nutshell liquid has been too costly to make the product fully competitive with some other types of oils. There is also a potential for short-term cashew shortages, such as occurred in 1999 because of unfavorable climatic conditions. This has led India to try to increase its production and its foreign supplies.

QUESTIONS

1. What trade theories help to explain where cashew tree products have been produced historically?

2. What factors threaten India's future competitive position in cashew nut production?

3. If you were an Indian cashew processor, what alternatives might you consider to maintain future competitiveness?

Chapter Notes

1   The information in this case is from the following sources: Prema-chandra Athukorala and Sarath Rajapatirana, "Liberalization and Industrial Transformation: Lessons from the Sri Lankan Experience," *Economic Development and Cultural Change* 48, no. 3 (April 2000): 543–72; Prema-chandra Athukorala, "Manufactured Exports and Terms of Trade of Developing Countries: Evidence from Sri Lanka," *The Journal of Development Studies* 36, no. 5 (June 2000): 89–104; *The CIA World Factbook* August 26, 2002 http://www.cia.gov/cia/publications/factbook/geos/ce.html; P. Murugasu, "Selecting Products for Export Development," *International Trade Forum* (October–December 1979): 4–7;

Sarath Rajapatirana, "Foreign Trade and Economic Development: Sri Lanka's Experience," *World Development* 16, no. 10 (October 1988): 1143–58; Vinita Piyaratna, "A Year of Living Optimistically," *Asian Business* (April 1993): 37–38; Rohan Gunaskera, "Sri Lanka Seeks to Revive Port Fortunes," *Reuter European Business Report* (July 24, 1996); Rahul Sharma, "New Sri Lanka Government to Boost Local Industry," Reuters World Service (August 22, 1994); Rohan Gunaskera, "Sri Lankans Pore Over Instant Tea Exports," *Reuter Asia-Pacific Business Report* (March 24, 1996); John Zarocostas, "Sri Lanka Receives Praise for Its Trade Reforms," *Journal of*

Commerce (November 13, 1995): A3; Amal Jayasinghe, "Sri Lanka to Legalize Gambling," *Financial Times* (November 7, 1996): 6; A.G. (Sandy) Cuthbertson, "The Trade Policy Review of Sri Lanka," *The World Economy* 20, no. 5 (August 1999): 633–48; "Sri Lanka," *Financial Times* (February 3, 1998): 21; Paul Taylor, "Sri Lanka," *Financial Times* (June 2, 1999): South Asian Software Services section, p. ii; and Amal Jayasinghe, "The Tea Industry," *Financial Times* (February 3, 1998): 23. For up-to-date information through the Internet on Sri Lanka, the address is www.lanka.net/cgi-bin/index2.html.

2 The mercantilist period is not associated with any single writer. A good coverage is in Gianni Vaggi, *A Concise History of Economic Thought: From Mercantilism to Monetarism* (New York: Palgrave Macmillan, 2002).

3 For reviews of the literature, see Jordan Shan and Fiona Sun, "On the Export-Led Growth Hypothesis for the Little Dragons: An Empirical Reinvestigation," *Atlantic Economic Review* 26, no. 4 (December 1998): 353–71; and George K. Zestos and Xiangnan Tao, "Trade and GDP Growth: Causal Relations in the United States and Canada," *Southern Economic Journal* 68, no. 4 (April 2002): 859–74.

4 Many publishers have subsequently printed his 1776 book. See, for example, Adam Smith, *An Inquiry into the Nature and Causes of the Wealth of Nations* (Washington: Regnery Publishing, 1998).

5 *On the Principles of Political Economy and Taxation*, originally published in London in 1817, has since been reprinted by a number of publishers. See, for example, David Ricardo, *On the Principles of Political Economy and Taxation* (Amherst, NY: Prometheus Books, 1996.)

6 Gaston de Rosayro, "Sri Lanka in the Doldrums," *South China Morning Post* (June 1, 1995): 21.

7 For a good discussion of this paradoxical thinking, see Paul R. Krugman, "What Do Undergraduates Need to Know About Trade?" *American Economic Review Papers and Proceedings* (May 1993): 23–26. For a discussion of some developing countries' views that monopolistic conditions keep them from gaining a fair share of gains from international trade, see A. P. Thirwell, *Growth and Development* 6th ed. (London: Macmillan, 1999).

8 Jeffrey A. Frankel and David Romer, "Does Trade Cause Growth?" *The American Economic Review* 89, no. 3 (June 1999): 379–99.

9 See David Adams, "UN Attempts to Boost Biosafety in Developing World," *Nature* 415, no. 6870 (January 24, 2002): 353; and Hemel Hempstead, "World-wide Project to Assess Safety of GM Crops," *Appropriate Technology* 29, no. 1 (January–March 2002): 37–38.

10 See Paul Krugman, "Scale Economies, Product Differentiation, and the Patterns of Trade," *The American Economic Review* 70 (December 1980): 950–59; and James Harrigan, "Estimation of Cross-Country Differences in Industry Production Functions," *Journal of International Economics* 47, no. 2 (April 1999): 267–93.

11 Drusilla K. Brown and Robert M. Stern, "Measurement and Modeling of the Economic Effect of Trade and Investment Barriers in Services," *Title Review of International Economics*, 9, no. 2 (May 2001): 262–86 discuss the role of economies of scale and trade barriers.

12 See Gianmarco I. P. Ottaviano and Diego Puga, "Agglomeration in the Global Economy: A Survey of the 'New Economic Geography,'" *The World Economy* 21, no. 6 (August 1998): 707–31; and Gianmarco Ottaviano, Takatoshi Tabuchi, and Jacques-François Thisse, "Agglomeration and Trade Revisited," *International Economic Review* 43, no. 2 (May 2002): 409–35.

13 Eli J. Heckscher, *Heckscher-Ohlin Trade Theory* (Cambridge, MA: MIT Press, 1991).

14 For a discussion of how the theory does not fit the reality of trade, see Antoni Estevadeordal and Alan M. Taylor, "A Century of Missing Trade?" *The American Economic Review* 92, no. 1 (March 2002): 383–93.

15 See, for example, Donald R. Davis and David E. Weinstein, "An Account of Global Factor Trade," *The American Economic Review* 91, no. 5 (December 2001): 1423–53; and Oner Guncavdi and Suat Kucukcifi, "Foreign Trade and Factor Intensity in an Open Developing Country: An Input-Output Analysis for Turkey," *Russian & East European Finance and Trade* 37, no. 1 (January–February 2001): 75–88.

16 See, for example, P. Krugman and A. J. Venables, "Globalization and the Inequality of Nations," *Quarterly Journal of Economics* 110 (1995): 857–80.

17 See Raymond Vernon, "International Investment and International Trade in the Product Life Cycle," *Quarterly Journal of Economics* (May 1996): 190–207; and David Dollar, "Technological Innovation, Capital Mobility, and the Product Cycle in North–South Trade," *American Economic Review* 76, no. 1, (March 1986): 177–90.

18 This is true by various indicators. See, for example, International Bank for Reconstruction and Development, "Science and Technology," *The World Development Indicators* (Washington, DC: 2000): 300.

19 David Dollar and Edward N. Wolff, *Competitiveness, Convergence, and International Specialization* (Cambridge, MA: MIT Press, 1993).

20 Chad Nehrt, "Maintainability of First Mover Advantages When Environmental Regulations Differ Between Countries," *Academy of Management Review* 23, no. 1 (1998): 77–97.

21 Nicholas Read, "Steel-Jawed Leghold Traps Now Banned in Canada," *Vancouver Sun* (May 5, 2001): A17.

22 Rory Watson, "Slap in Face for Cosmetic Firms," *The Herald* [Glasgow] (April 4, 2001): 9.

23 "U.S. International Transactions, Fourth Quarter and Year 2001," *Survey of Current Business* (April 2002): 29–57.

24 "World Trade Slows Sharply in 2001 Amid the Uncertain International Situation," *WTO News: 2001 Press Releases* (October 19, 2001): 1–7.

25 Stefan B. Linder, *An Essay on Trade Transformation* (New York: Wiley, 1961).

26 Two discussions of intra-industry trade are Don P. Clark, "Determinants of Intraindustry Trade Between the United States and Industrial Nations," *The International Trade Journal* XII, no. 3 (Fall 1998): 345–62; and H. Peter Gray, "Free International Economic Policy in a World of Schumpeter Goods," *The International Trade Journal* XII, no. 3 (Fall 1998): 323–44.

27 Dirk Pilat, "The Economic Impact of Technology," *The OECD Observer*, no. 213, (August–September 1998): 5–8.

28 "That's Snow-biz," *The Economist* (April 13, 1996): 58.

29 Terry Hall, "NZ Finds Pirated Varieties in Chile," *Financial Times* (January 21, 1999): 24.

30 Daniel Michaels, "Landing Rights," *Wall Street Journal* (April 30, 2002): A1+.

31 See "New Tribe Found in New Guinea," *Herald-Times* [Bloomington, IN] (June 28, 1993): 1; Rose George, "Outrageous Beauty and a Constant Puzzle," *Financial Times* (August 10, 2002): 17; and "Bhutan Edges Towards Economic Self-Reliance", BBC Worldwide Monitoring (June 28, 2002).

32 Paul Krugman and Alasdair M. Smith, eds., *Empirical Studies of Strategic Trade Policies* (Chicago: University of Chicago Press, 1993).

33 Paul M. Sherer, "Thailand Trips in Reach for New Exports," *Wall Street Journal* (August 27, 1996): A8.

34 Richard Brahm, "National Targeting Policies, High-Technology Industries, and Excessive Competition," *Strategic Management Journal* 16 (1995): 71–91.

35 James Kynge and Elisabeth Robinson, "Singapore to Revise Trade Priorities," *Financial Times* (January 21, 1997): 6.

36 Helene Cooper, "Trade Wins," *Wall Street Journal* (July 14, 1998): A1.

37 Jagdish Bhagwati and T. N. Srinivasan, "Trade and Poverty in the Poor Countries," *The American Economic Review* 92, no. 2 (May 2002): 180–83.

38 Kyle Bagwell and Robert Staiger, "National Sovereignty in the World Trading System," *Harvard International Review* 22, no. 4 (Winter 2001): 54–59.

39 Kiyohiko Ito and Vladimir Pucik, "R&D Spending, Domestic Competition, and Export Performance of Japanese Manufacturing Firms," *Strategic Management Journal* 14, (1993): 61–75.

40 Ito and Pucik, op. cit.

41 Data for this case were taken from Jean-Pierre Jeannet, "Indian Cashew Processors, Ltd.," ICH Case 9-378-832 (Boston: Harvard Business School, 1977); Jean-Pierre Jeannet, "Note on the World Cashew Nut Industry," ICH Case 9-378-834 (Boston: Harvard Business School, 1977); Steven Jaffee, *Private Sector Response to Market Liberalization: The Experience of Tanzania's Cashew Nut Industry* (Washington, DC: World Bank, 1994); "Cashewnuts," *Handbook of Indian Agriculture* (New Delhi: Vikas Publishing House, 1995); U.S. Department of Commerce, Bureau of the Census, "Merchandise Trade—U.S. Imports by Commodity, Cashew Nuts," document 0801300000 (September 8, 1999); "World Cashew Meet May Help Curb Falling Exports—Rajagopal," *Indian Express Newspapers* [Bombay], (February 26, 2001): n.p.; "How Cashew Production in Mozambique Came to an End: www.afrol.com/countries/Mozambique/background_cashew.htm; "Vietnam Stalks India on Global Cashew Exports," *Businessline* [Islamabad], (July 13, 2002): 1; "The Cashew Export Promotion Council of India" (September 7, 2002): www.cashewindia.org; "Cashew Facts" (September 7, 2002): www.beer-nuts.com/cashew.htm; and G. K. Nair, "India: Cashew Exports May Drop by Rs 150 cr," *Businessline* [Islamabad], (December 28, 2001): 1.

CHAPTER 6

GOVERNMENT INFLUENCE ON TRADE

A little help does a great deal.

—FRENCH PROVERB

OBJECTIVES

- To evaluate the rationale for government policies that enhance and restrict trade
- To examine the effects of pressure groups on trade policies
- To compare the protectionist rationales used in developed countries with those used in developing countries
- To study the potential and actual effects of government intervention on the free flow of trade
- To give an overview of the major means by which trade is restricted, regulated, and liberalized
- To profile the GATT and the World Trade Organization
- To show that government trade policies create business uncertainties and business opportunities

CASE

European and U.S. Trade Relations[1]

E urope and the United States trade a growing range of goods and services, and their respective gains highlight the benefits of free trade. Still, disagreements regularly disturb their relationship. For example, in 1993, the European Union (EU) adopted a trade policy that directly favored the small banana growers in various countries in Africa, the Caribbean, and Pacific. Consequently, this policy indirectly imposed trade barriers on the cheaper bananas grown in Latin America. Nine years later, the EU and United States declared the so-called banana war over and decreed a new sprit of trade cooperation. Between these two points, the banana war took on major political and economic significance that both involved national trade authorities and targeted industries, producers and distributors, transnational institutions, and political parties.

The banana war is a notable saga because it testified to the hope that, like good friends who occasionally disagree, the United States and Europe could interpret aspects of trade in different ways that did not threaten their broader trade relationship. This belief was important given the number of simmering transatlantic trade disputes. Specifically, the United States and the EU disagreed on matters like the import of hormone-treated beef, the labeling and licensing of genetically modified foods, data protection and privacy, aerospace subsidies, the standards for a new generation of cellular phones, and agricultural subsidies. This situation seemed to tip to an extreme when the United States moved to protect its $80 billion steel market. The United States said it would assign a tax of up to 30 percent on the imported value of foreign steel in order to give its domestic steel industry three years of protection. The EU Trade Commissioner called the act "a blatant call for protectionism" and "a clear violation of World Trade Organization (WTO) rules." The EU, along with Japan, China, and others, complained to the WTO, the institution that arbitrates trade disputes among countries, and it threatened to counter with retaliatory tariffs. As this and other trade battles escalated, some wondered whether the EU-U.S. banana war was the odd exception or a workable blueprint. Table 6.1 reports significant aspects of the trade relations between the EU and United States.

The formation of the Single European Market in 1992 meant that the EU had to unify the existing differential arrangements in Europe for the import of many products, including bananas. For instance, Germany had no import tax on bananas, whereas the United Kingdom gave special treatment to imports from its former Caribbean colonies. In 1993, the EU passed a communitywide banana import policy that gave specific countries privileged access to the European market. Essentially, this system preserved market share for bananas grown within the EU by politically powerful farmers—that is, Greece and the off-continent areas of the Canary Islands (Spain), Martinique and Guadeloupe (France), and Madeira (Portugal). In addition, it awarded preferential market access to "traditional bananas" from African, Caribbean, and Pacific countries, many of which were former British or French colonies. The EU claimed that small banana growers in these countries would suffer without such help. The lower-priced banana imports from Latin America and South America, produced largely under the direction of U.S. multinational food companies, were penalized with volume restrictions and higher import taxes.

There were three sales quotas, each of which had subquotas. The EU's quota system affected competitive rivalry and product prices. First, since it allocated market share by country of production, it eliminated the incentive for exporters to use price as a competitive strategy. Instead, the quota system set European banana prices in terms of the high-cost producers in the eastern Caribbean—Dominica, Grenada, St. Lucia, and St. Vincent—whose higher wages and lower efficiency made the cost of their bananas more than three times that of bananas produced in Latin America. To prevent low-cost producers

● **TABLE 6.1**

U.S.-EU TRADE, 2000

	IN U.S. $BILLIONS	% CHANGE FROM 1999
U.S. Exports of Goods to the EU	159	+9.1%
U.S. Imports of Goods from the EU	220	+13.0%
U.S. Exports of Services to the EU	93	+5.0%
U.S. Imports of Services from the EU	82	+18.5%
Total of U.S. Exports of Goods and Services from the EU	255	+7.6%
Total of U.S. Imports of Goods and Services from the EU	302	+14.4%
Top 5 U.S. Goods Exports to the EU		
Computers & electronic products	43.2	+2.7%
Transportation equipment	30.3	+3.9%
Chemicals	22.6	+2.7%
Nonelectric machinery	19.8	−0.7%
Manufactured commodities	7.5	+13.8
Top 5 U.S. Goods Imports from the EU		
Nuclear reactors, boilers & machinery	39.5	−1.5%
Vehicles	27.7	+3.0%
Organic chemicals	19.3	+8.3%
Electric machinery	16.4	+2.7
Optic instruments	11.6	+3.1

Source: European Union (November 7, 2002): http://www.eurunion.org/profile/EUUSStats. htm.

from reaping windfall gains from now higher market prices, the EU assigned higher tariffs to their banana imports and required that they also pay special surcharges. Second, few companies handle the transportation, ripening, and distribution of banana exporting. In 1993, three companies accounted for two-thirds of world banana logistics. Since the EU's quota system prevented them from increasing market share, they had little incentive to improve efficiency or lower prices. Consequently, their costs were much higher for the EU market than for the United States, thereby inflating prices even more for European consumers. The World Bank estimated that European consumers paid about $2 billion a year in higher prices because of the quota system. Moreover, the quota system meant that EU consumers spent $13.25 for each $1 that made it to those producing countries that had been granted privileged access. Essentially, $150 million of the $2 billion in higher taxes went to those countries targeted for help. The rest generated tariff revenue for the EU and inflated profits for intermediaries. Third, the higher cost for European consumers dampened their demand for bananas, thereby leading to excess supplies elsewhere. This further reduced revenue and profits for banana producers that had lost market share because of the EU quotas.

Although the most popular fruit in the world, the value of the banana trade was trivial to the total trade between the EU and the United States. Still, the humble banana triggered a full-scale trade war. Immediately, multinational banana companies, notably Chiquita Brands and Dole Food Company, protested the EU's quota system because it illegally restricted their expansion. Chiquita, the largest banana distributor in Europe, had invested millions in plantations and ships in the early 1990s in anticipation that a unified Europe would be more open to trade. Chiquita pushed the United States to challenge the EU's decision. This, in itself, fueled the notoriety of the banana war. Carl Lindner, president of Chiquita Brands, was a major financial backer of President Clinton, had been an overnight guest of President Clinton in the Lincoln Bedroom in 1995, and had let U.S. Senator Bob Dole use his family's aircraft. Mr. Linder lobbied

Democratic and Republican officials to initiate WTO proceedings against the EU and to pressure Latin American countries to challenge the EU quotas. On the larger stage, though, the United States maintained that the EU used import quotas to protect European banana importers and Europe's farm sector while punishing its customers, other countries, and companies. More fundamentally, the United States argued that the EU banana policy opposed governments' efforts to liberalize world trade.

In 1995, the United States, backed by Mexico, Guatemala, Ecuador, and Honduras, took its case to the WTO. In 1997, the WTO ruled the EU banana import regime illegal because it discriminated against bananas from Latin America. The EU was given until January 1999 to comply, pay damages, or face retaliation. On January 1, 1999, the EU announced amendments to its banana policy that it stated complied with the WTO directive. The United States and its allies claimed that the revised EU policy contained trivial changes and asked the WTO to reject it.

In April 1999, the WTO ruled that the EU reforms were still unfair and ordered the EU to revise its policy again. Accusing Europe of stalling, the United States said that it planned to retaliate by raising the tax, or tariff, it charged on European goods when they entered the United States by 100 percent. The United States targeted $520 million worth of European luxury goods because this was the value that U.S. companies, such as Chiquita Brands and Dole, estimated they had lost because of the EU's banana quota. The European products targeted for the tariff hike included French wine, Belgian biscuits, Scottish cashmere sweaters, Italian cheese, and Spanish leather goods that heavily depended on the U.S. market. While far removed from the world of bananas, these were high-profile products in those countries that were believed to support the EU's banana quotas. The United States hoped that distressed European producers would pressure their governments to reform the banana policy. Products from Denmark and the Netherlands were exempt because they opposed the EU banana policy.

The U.S. punitive tariffs promised minuscule economic gains—the $520 million represented less than one-quarter of 1 percent of U.S. imports from Europe in 1998. The political impact, though, was enormous. The European Trade Commissioner called it an "unacceptable and unlawful act that fanned the flames of this dispute." President Clinton replied, "We cannot maintain an open trading system, which I am convinced is essential for global prosperity, unless we have rules that are abided by." The U.S. trade representative noted that the 100 percent tariff sanctions ensured that when "the arbitrators reach their final decision, we will be in the same position as if they had rendered their final decision yesterday."

The EU complained to the WTO about the U.S. punitive tariffs. The WTO ruled them permissible, but only for $191.4 million of EU exports. Although the sum was reduced, the tariff hike of 100 percent on selected EU exports was permitted. Hard hit companies scrambled for solutions. Arran Aromatics, the largest employer on a Scottish island, blamed the British government for its need to fire employees. The head of a British packaging company, Beamglow, said it might have to relocate to the Netherlands. Some other companies sought exemptions from the U.S. tariffs for their own products. Representatives of the Scottish cashmere industry got cashmere removed from the list of punitive products after meeting with President Clinton and other U.S. officials. However, this was not before the industry's reduced imports of raw cashmere had already caused unemployment in Mongolia's second biggest export segment. Meanwhile, some U.S. companies grumbled about the rising costs of supplies. For example, Exide makes batteries and employs 18,000. Its CEO said the increase in the price of gel lead from Germany for its battery production "would cause a severe hardship."

In 1999, the EU adopted a new regulation designed to set a WTO-compatible banana import regime. This system required companies to declare their intention to import a specified quantity of bananas, and the EU would then use a "first-come, first-served" pre-allocation principle. Dole, which had diversified its sourcing of bananas and branched out into other lines of fruit, endorsed this proposal. So did Ecuador, which supplied many of Dole's bananas. The United States rejected this plan outright and stated it would file a new complaint with the WTO if it were implemented. The EU withdrew this proposal.

In 2001, the EU and the United States jointly declared the banana war over. Both parties agreed to a new regime for importing bananas into the EU. Specifically, until 2006, the EU would follow a system whereby countries would be allowed to ship the amount of bananas that they had shipped to Europe from

1994 through 1996. Thereafter, the EU will apply the same tariff on all banana imports. Although not perfect, the agreement complied with WTO rulings and ensured fair access to the European market for bananas from all origins and all traders. The EU and the United States symbolized their revived spirit of trade cooperation by stating, "The banana disputes of the past nine years have been disruptive for all the parties involved—traders, Latin American, African, and Caribbean producers, and consumers. We are confident that today's agreement will end the past friction and move us toward a better basis for the banana trade." A few months later, the United States suspended the punitive tariffs on select EU exports.

As the banana war faded, attention turned to the growing confrontation over steel. Already, Europe had blasted the United States for violating free trade principles and WTO directives. The EU had little sympathy for the U.S. claim that the tariffs on imported steel were a crucial crutch for the struggling American industry to restore its international competitiveness. In April 2002, the EU proposed applying $336 million of trade sanctions on an odd assortment but politically sensitive U.S. products. That is, the EU planned to "hit the U.S. where it hurts" by targeting exports from states crucial to U.S. President George W. Bush's reelection in 2004—exports include citrus fruits from Florida, apples and pears from Washington and Oregon, and steel from Pennsylvania,

Workers affected negatively by import competition are apt to be more vocal than consumers who want lower priced imports. The photo shows steelworkers in the United States protesting the rising tide of cheap steel imports.

Ohio, and West Virginia. In mid-2003, the WTO ruled that the steel tarrifs imposed by the United States were illegal. The Bush administration said it would appeal the decision. If the United States loses, European and other nations could impose trade sanctions of comparable value against the United States.

INTRODUCTION

At some point, you may work for or own stock in a company whose performance—or even survival—depends on government policies that affect the competitive moves of foreign producers or that create opportunities or reduce risks abroad. Likewise, government measures may limit your ability to sell abroad—for example, by prohibiting the export of certain products to certain countries or by making it difficult for you to buy what you need from foreign suppliers. Collectively, these government measures are known as **protectionism**. In the opening case, EU protectionism helped the competitive position of some countries, such as the Windward Islands of Dominica, Grenada, St. Lucia, and St. Vincent, while helping some companies, such as European banana distributors. At the same time, it harmed the competitive position of some other countries, such as Panama, and some other companies, such as Chiquita Brands. The EU also affected individuals, as consumers and taxpayers, by increasing the prices of and taxes on bananas in Europe. Similarly, government expenses rose in many countries due to the need to administer the banana import regulations.

In Chapter 5, we showed that the trade of goods and services is a major means of linking countries economically and that more linkages improve global efficiency. However, the variety of restrictions illustrated in the EU-U.S. trade relations case is not atypical. In principle, no country allows an unregulated flow of goods and services across its borders. (Figure 6.1 illustrates the effect of government regulations on companies' competitive positions.) Rather, governments routinely influence the flow of imports and exports. Also, governments directly or indirectly subsidize domestic industries to help them engage foreign producers at home or challenge them abroad. This chapter begins by reviewing the economic and noneconomic rationales for trade protectionism, followed by an explanation of the major forms of trade controls and a profile of the WTO.

All countries seek to influence trade, and each has

- Economic, social, and political objectives
- Conflicting objectives
- Interest groups

FIGURE 6.1   Physical and Societal Influences on Protectionism and Companies' Competitive Environment

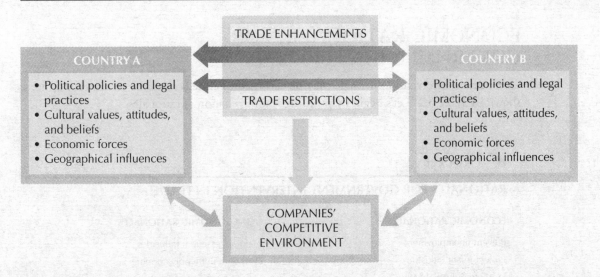

In response to physical and societal influences, governments enact measures that enhance or restrict companies' international trade. These measures affect competition because they improve or hinder companies' abilities and needs to compete internationally. Companies likewise influence governments to adopt trade policies that benefit them.

CONFLICTING RESULTS OF TRADE POLICIES

The discussion of trade theory in Chapter 5 explained the gains from free trade. Despite these benefits, all countries interfere with international trade to varying degrees. Governments intervene in trade to attain economic, social, or political objectives. It is important to note, however, that governments pursue political rationality when trying to regulate trade. Government officials apply trade policies that they believe will have the best chance to benefit the nation and its citizens—and, in some cases, their personal political longevity. Determining the best way to influence trade is complicated by frequent conflicts among objectives. For example, the EU banana policy was intended to help former colonies economically while preserving low prices to consumers; in actuality, it helped the former yet hurt the latter. Governments would also like to help struggling companies and industries without penalizing those that are doing well. This goal is often impossible—especially if other countries retaliate against a government's protectionist actions. For example, the EU banana policy helped EU banana distributors but penalized other EU companies when the United States retaliated by restricting imports of various luxury goods from various European markets.

Proposals for trade regulation reform often spark fierce debate among people and groups that believe they will be affected. Of course, those that are most directly affected (so-called stakeholders) are most apt to speak out. For example, EU stakeholders whose livelihood depended on the export of cashmere wool to the United States (workers, owners, suppliers, and local politicians) complained about losses due to the U.S. restrictions. Displaced workers saw themselves as being forced to take new jobs in new industries, perhaps even in new towns. They feared prolonged unemployment, reduced incomes, uncertain work conditions, and unstable social surroundings. People threatened in this way tend to object often and loudly. In contrast, individual consumers often misinterpret how much retail prices rise because of import restrictions. Typically, the economic costs are spread out. For example, the $2 billion a year in higher EU banana costs was significant in total but trivial for each banana. Similarly, current U.S. tariffs on peanut products from Mexico range from 140 percent to 160 percent. By 2008, peanut products will be permitted to be imported from Mexico without a tariff. Until then, however, the cost of this tariff protection adds about 33 cents to a typical jar of peanut butter in the United States.[2] Even if consumers knew about this surcharge, few would likely see enough incentive to band together and push their government leaders to rectify the situation.

ECONOMIC RATIONALES FOR GOVERNMENT INTERVENTION

Government intervention in trade may be classified as either economic or noneconomic, as shown in Table 6.2. Let's begin by profiling leading economic rationales.

TABLE 6.2

RATIONALES FOR GOVERNMENT INTERVENTION IN TRADE

ECONOMIC RATIONALES	NONECONOMIC RATIONALES
Prevent unemployment	Maintain essential industries
Protect infant industries	Deal with unfriendly countries
Promote industrialization	Maintain spheres of influence
Improve position compared to other countries	Preserve national identity

Unemployment

Pressure groups, whether workers, consumers, or some mix of stakeholders, often question government policy makers and businesspeople. Policy makers must decide which conflicting pressure groups to heed. Businesspeople must lobby policy makers to counter groups whose proposals might penalize them. There is probably no more effective pressure group than the unemployed; no other group has the time and incentive to picket companies, contact government representatives, and confront organizations. For example, unemployed U.S. steelworkers pressured U.S. lawmakers to apply tariffs and quotas to restrict steel imports in order to preserve their jobs and pensions.

One difficulty with restricting imports to create jobs is that other countries normally retaliate with their own restrictions. That is, trade restrictions designed to support domestic industries typically trigger a drop in production in some foreign country. For example, EU banana import restrictions led the United States to restrict the import of battery gel. One country's plan to "export unemployment" to a trade partner has usually triggered quick retaliation from the latter. Often, retaliations cause more job losses than the gains in industries protected by the new restrictions.[3]

Two factors can ease the effects of retaliation. First, there may be a lower tendency to retaliate against a small country (in terms of economic might) that restricts imports. For example, Peruvian automobile import restrictions provoked no Japanese retaliation because of the trivial loss of sales to Japanese car makers. Second, retaliation that reduces employment in a capital-intensive industry but increases it in a labor-intensive industry may indirectly achieve overall employment objectives. For example, the United States limits imports of apparel, typically a labor-intensive good. Any resultant foreign retaliation against, say, U.S.-produced semiconductors of the same value as displaced apparel sales would threaten fewer U.S. jobs than would be gained from maintaining apparel production because fewer people are needed to produce the same value of semiconductors. Even if no country retaliates, the restricting country may gain jobs in one sector only to lose jobs elsewhere. For example, lower imports of a product means fewer import-handling jobs.

Government policy makers must consider the conflicting effects of protectionism on different industries and companies. In other words, imports may also help create jobs in other industries, and these industries may champion free trade. Imports also stimulate exports, although less directly, by increasing foreign income and foreign-exchange earnings, which are then spent on new imports by foreign consumers. If import restrictions do increase domestic employment, fellow citizens must face higher prices or higher taxes. In addition, if managers believe trade protection is a long-term policy, they may see no competitive urgency to invest in technological innovation, thus further depriving consumers of higher-quality products at lower prices.

Government officials should compare the costs of higher prices with the costs of unemployment and displaced production that would result from free trade. In addition, they must consider the costs of policies that are designed to ease the plight of displaced employees—for example, unemployment benefits or retraining expenses. These are challenging tasks that involve difficult economic and social questions. For example, it is hard to put a price on the distress suffered by people who lose their jobs due to increasing imports. It is also difficult for working people to understand that they may be better off financially (because of lower prices) even if they must then pay higher taxes to support unemployment or welfare benefits for people who lost their jobs due to rising imports.

The employment issue can slow trade liberalization because displaced workers are often the ones who are least able to find alternative work at a comparable salary. On average, trade-displaced workers in the United States earned about 13 percent less in their new jobs than they did on their old jobs—more than a third suffered a 30 percent drop in wages.[4] Similar effects have been found in Germany, Canada, and France.[5] In addition, displaced

The unemployed can form an effective pressure group for import restrictions.

Import restrictions to create domestic employment

- May lead to retaliation by other countries
- Are less likely to be met with retaliation if implemented by small economies
- May reduce the number of export jobs because of price increases for components

Possible costs of import restrictions include

- Higher prices
- Higher taxes

Such costs should be compared with those of unemployment.

workers often spend their unemployment benefits on living expenses rather than on retraining in the hope that they will be recalled to their old jobs. When they do seek retraining, many workers, especially older ones, lack the educational background needed to gain the required skills. Worse still, some train for jobs that do not materialize.

In summary, persistent unemployment pushes many groups to call for protectionism. However, evidence suggests that efforts to reduce unemployment through import restrictions are usually ineffective.[6] Unemployment, in and of itself, is better dealt with through fiscal and monetary policies. Further, as the rest of the chapter shows, governments can use other rationales to justify trade protectionism.

The infant-industry argument says that production becomes more competitive over time because of

• Increased economies of scale
• Greater worker efficiency

Infant-Industry Argument

In 1792, Alexander Hamilton presented what has become one of the oldest arguments for protectionism. The infant-industry argument holds that a government should shield an emerging industry from foreign competition by guaranteeing it a large share of the domestic market until it is able to compete on its own. Many developing countries use this argument to justify their protectionist policies. The infant-industry argument presumes that the initial output costs for a small-scale industry in a given country may be so high as to make its output noncompetitive in world markets. Eventual competitiveness is not the reward for endurance but the consequence of the efficiency gains resulting from the economies of large-scale production. Therefore, the host government needs to protect an infant industry long enough for its fledgling companies to gain economies of scale and for their employees to translate experience into higher productivity. These achievements will enable a company to manufacture efficiently, thereby positioning it to compete internationally. At this point, the government can then recoup the costs of trade protection through benefits like higher domestic employment, lower social costs, and higher tax revenues.

Although it is reasonable to expect production costs to decline over time, they may never fall enough to create internationally competitive products. This risk poses two problems for governments trying to protect an infant industry. First, they must identify those industries that have a high probability of success. Some industries grow to be competitive because of government protection; automobile production in Brazil and South Korea are good examples. However, in many other cases—for example, automobile production in Malaysia and Australia—the protected industries remain inefficient even after years of government aid. If infant-industry protection goes to an industry that fails to reduce costs enough to compete against imports, chances are that its owners, workers, and suppliers will constitute a formidable pressure group that may prevent the importation of competing, lower-priced products. In addition, the security of government protection against import competition may deter managers from adopting the innovations needed to compete globally.

Second, even if policy makers can determine those infant industries likely to succeed, it does not necessarily follow that companies in those industries should receive government assistance. There are many examples of entrepreneurs who endured early losses to achieve future benefits without public help. Still, policy makers regularly contend that governments should assist new companies facing high entry barriers and efficient foreign rivals.

Infant-industry protection requires some segment of the economy to incur the higher cost of inefficient local production. Typically, consumers end up paying higher prices for the protected companies' products. A government can subsidize companies so that consumer prices do not increase; still, taxpayers indirectly pay this subsidy. In addition, production subsidies reduce government revenue, a serious consideration in developing countries. Ultimately, the validity of the infant-industry argument rests on the expectation that the future benefits of an internationally competitive industry will exceed the costs of the associated protectionism.

Industrialization Argument

Countries with a large manufacturing base generally have higher per capita incomes than those that do not. Moreover, a number of countries, such as the United States and Japan, developed an industrial base while largely regulating imports from foreign producers. Many developing countries try to emulate this strategy, using trade protection to spur local industrialization. Specifically, they believe:

1. Surplus workers can more easily increase manufacturing output than agricultural output.
2. Inflows of foreign investment in the industrial area promote sustainable growth.
3. Prices and sales of agricultural products and raw materials fluctuate very much.
4. Markets for industrial products grow faster than markets for agricultural products.
5. Local industry reduces imports and promotes exports.
6. Industrial activity helps the nation-building process.

We now review each of these beliefs.

Use of Surplus Workers   A large portion of the population in many developing countries live and farm in rural areas. Usually, agricultural output per person is low. Consequently, many people can migrate from the agricultural to the industrial sector without significantly reducing total agricultural output. Like the infant-industry argument, the industrialization argument presumes that the unregulated importation of lower-priced products prevents the development of a domestic industry. However, unlike the infant-industry argument, the industrialization rationale asserts that industrial output will increase even if domestic prices do not become globally competitive, because local consumers must buy goods from local producers.[7]

Shifting people out of agriculture, however, can create problems:

1. Workers' high expectations of industrial jobs may be unfulfilled, leading to an increasing demand for social services. A major problem facing developing countries is the migration to urban areas of people who then cannot find suitable jobs, housing, and social services. For example, China's move toward industrialization has spurred millions of people to move to cities. Most have prospered, but many have not. Some estimate that China's urban unemployment rate runs 3 to 5 times the officially reported rate.[8] Many struggle to find work because the industrialization process has proceeded slowly, few jobs are created in traditional industries, or individuals lack the skills and work habits required for manufacturing jobs.
2. Improved agriculture practices, not a drastic shift to industry, may be a better means of achieving economic success. Typically, few developing countries farm their land efficiently—doing so can create great benefits at low cost.[9] In addition, industrialization is not the only means of growth. The United States, Canada, and Argentina grew during the nineteenth century, largely because of their comparative advantage in agricultural exports. Even today, they continue to profit from the export of food products. Similarly, Australia, New Zealand, and Denmark maintain high per capita income with a mix of industry and agricultural specialization.
3. Rapid migration from rural to urban areas may abruptly reduce agricultural output, further jeopardizing a country's self-sufficiency. It is interesting that most of the world's agricultural production and exports come from industrial countries because their efficient and capital-intensive agricultural sectors enable them to transfer resources into the manufacturing sector without reducing agricultural output.

Promoting Investment Inflows   Import restrictions that are applied to spur industrialization may also increase foreign direct investment. Barred from an attractive foreign market by trade restrictions, foreign companies may transfer manufacturing to that country to avoid

Countries seek protection to promote industrialization because that type of production

- Brings faster growth than agriculture
- Brings in investment funds
- Diversifies the economy
- Brings more income than primary products do

When a country shifts from agriculture to industry

- Demands on social and political services in cities may increase
- Output increases if the marginal productivity of agricultural workers is very low
- Development possibilities in the agricultural sector may be overlooked

If import restrictions keep out foreign-made goods, foreign companies may invest to produce in the restricted area.

the loss of a lucrative or potential market. The resulting influx of foreign companies may speed a country's industrialization. For example, Thailand's automobile import restrictions prompted foreign automakers like GM, Ford, and BMW to invest there. Foreign investment inflows may also add to local employment, which is attractive to policy makers.

Diversification   The export prices of many primary products fluctuate markedly.[10] Price variations due to uncontrollable factors—for example, weather affecting supply or business cycles abroad affecting demand—can wreak havoc on economies that depend on the export of primary products. This is especially true when an economy must rely on a few commodities for job creation and export earnings. Moreover, many developing countries depend on just one primary commodity for export earnings. Frequently, they are caught in a feast or famine cycle—they can afford foreign luxuries one year but they are unable to find the funds for replacement parts for essential equipment the next.[11] Contrary to expectations, a greater dependence on manufacturing does not guarantee diversification of export earnings. The GDPs of many developing countries are small; a move to manufacturing may shift dependence from one or two agricultural products to one or two manufactured commodities.

Terms of trade for developing countries may deteriorate because

- Demand for primary products grows more slowly
- Production cost savings for primary products will be passed on to consumers

Greater Growth for Manufactured Products   The **terms of trade** is the quantity of imports that a given quantity of a country's exports can buy—that is, how many bananas must Country A sell to Country B to purchase one refrigerator from Country B. Historically, the prices of raw materials and agricultural commodities do not rise as fast as the prices of finished products. Hence, over time, it takes more primary products to buy the same amount of manufactured goods. Further, the quantity of primary products demanded does not rise rapidly, so most developing countries have become increasingly poorer relative to industrial countries. Therefore, their governments try to support up-and-coming manufacturing companies that use traditional raw materials and agricultural commodities to produce higher-value finished products. For instance, Sri Lankan officials helped local companies move from harvesting tea leaves to making tea bags and instant tea. The declining terms of trade for developing countries is partly explained by the slowing consumer demand for agricultural products and by changes in technology that have reduced the need for many raw materials. A further explanation is that competitive rivalry transfers many of the benefits of lower production costs of primary products to consumers. In contrast, cost savings for manufactured products go mainly to higher profits and wages.

Industrialization emphasizes either

- Products that can be sold domestically or
- Products that can be exported

Import Substitution Versus Export Promotion   Traditionally, developing countries promoted industrialization by restricting imports in order to boost local production for local consumption. This policy is known as import substitution. In recent years, many countries have come to believe that import substitution is not the ideal approach to develop new industries. If the protected industries do not become efficient, an all-too-frequent outcome, local consumers may have to support them by paying higher prices or higher taxes. In addition, the fact that most industries must usually import capital equipment and other supplies reduces foreign-exchange savings. In contrast, some countries, such as Taiwan and South Korea, have achieved rapid economic growth by promoting the development of industries that export their output. This approach is known as export-led development. Recent studies confirm that export promotion programs boost companies' performance.[12] In reality, it is not easy to distinguish import substitution from export promotion. Industrialization may result initially in import substitution, yet export development of the same products may be feasible later. For example, India restricts the importation of automobiles and their parts, thereby letting local production capture those sales. In all likelihood, India will eventually promote the export of cars. Finally, the fact that a country concentrates its industrialization activities on products for which it would seem to have a comparative advantage does not guarantee that those products will necessarily become competitive exports. There are various trade barriers, discussed later in this chapter, that interfere with the export of manufactured goods from developing countries.

Nation Building   The performance of free markets suggests a strong relationship between industrialization and aspects of the nation-building process. Industrialization helps countries to build infrastructure, advance rural development, enhance rural peoples' social lives, and boost the skills of the workforce. For example, Ecuador and Vietnam maintain that industrialization has helped them move from feudal economies suffering chronic food shortages to nations with improved food security and budding export competitiveness.[13]

Economic Relationships with Other Countries

Countries monitor their absolute economic welfare as well as track how their performance compares to other countries. Governments impose trade restrictions to improve their relative trade positions. They might buy less from other countries than those countries buy from them. They might try to charge higher export prices while keeping import prices low— though not so low as to penalize their domestic producers. Among the many motivations, three stand out:

Balance-of-Payments Adjustments   The trade account is a major part of the balance of payments for most countries. If the exports of a country exceed its imports, the country is said to have a favorable balance of trade. Conversely, if imports exceed exports, an unfavorable balance of trade exists. A trade deficit creates problems for countries with low foreign exchange reserves—the funds that help a country to finance the purchase of foreign goods and to maintain its export trade. Governments can improve their balance of payments by improving their balance of trade. So if balance-of-payments difficulties arise and persist, a government may restrict imports or encourage exports to balance its trade account. For example, since the 1970s, the United States has imported more from Japan than it has exported there. Trade in automobiles makes up most of the imbalance. At times, the U.S. government has tried to correct the imbalance by regulating the value and number of Japanese vehicles imported into the United States, persuading Japanese automotive companies to locate more production within the United States, and negotiating with the Japanese government to ease the entry of U.S.-made cars into Japan.

Comparable Access or "Fairness"   Companies and industries often argue that they are entitled to the same access to foreign markets as foreign industries and companies have to their markets. Economic theory supports this idea, since it assumes that producers that operate in industries in which increased production leads to steep cost declines but that lack equal access to a competitor's market will struggle to gain enough sales to be cost-competitive. The comparable-access argument has been used in the semiconductor, chemicals, aircraft, softwood lumber, energy, and telecommunications industries.[14]

The argument for equal access is also presented as one of fairness. For example, the U.S. government permits foreign financial service companies to operate in the United States, but only if their home governments allow U.S. financial service companies equivalent market access. However, some reject using the idea of fairness to justify comparable market access. First, tit-for-tat market access can lead to restrictions that may deny one's own consumers lower prices. Second, countries' imposition of additional import restrictions to coerce other countries to reduce their entry barriers may escalate trade frictions. For example, France prohibited the entry of U.S. hormone-treated beef. The United States countered by placing additional taxes on such French products as Roquefort cheese and foie gras in an effort to prod France to rescind its restrictions. Not only did the French government maintain the restrictions, but French farmers also protested at McDonald's restaurants by dumping manure at entryways and throwing potatoes at its customers.[15] Third, governments would find it impractical to negotiate and monitor separate agreements for each of the thousands of different products and services that might be traded.

Price-Control Objectives   Countries sometimes withhold goods from international markets in an effort to raise prices abroad. This action is most feasible when a few countries hold monopoly or near-monopoly control of certain resources. They can then limit the supply so consumers must pay a higher price. This policy often encourages smuggling. Consequently, these countries must incur high prevention costs or else risk a price collapse. For example, Colombia incurs great expense to patrol its borders to try to prevent emeralds from flooding world markets. Export controls are especially ineffective if a product can be digitized—such as music, images, video, and text. In addition, if prices are too high or supplies too limited, people will seek substitutes. Iranian controls on carpet exports have led to Iran's loss of market share because of lower-priced carpets from China, India, and Pakistan.[16]

A country may limit exports of a product that is in short supply worldwide in order to favor domestic consumers. Typically, greater supply pushes local prices beneath those in the intentionally undersupplied world market. India, for instance, has done this with rice.[17] Favoring consumers usually disfavors producers. Lower prices at home often prompt companies to boost foreign output at the expense of local production.

Countries also fear that foreign producers will price their exports so artificially low that they drive domestic producers out of business. High entry barriers, the reasoning goes, let the surviving foreign producers charge exorbitant prices abroad or limit exports so that companies in their own countries gain better access to supplies. However, competition among foreign producers limits their ability to charge exorbitant prices as well as encourages them to forgo selling abroad. For example, low import prices have eliminated most U.S. production of consumer electronics. Still, the United States has some of the lowest prices in the world for consumer electronics. Therefore, the ability to price low abroad may result from high domestic prices due to a lack of competition at home or from home-country government subsidies.

Companies sometimes export below cost or below their home-country price. This practice is called dumping. Most countries prohibit imports of dumped products, but enforcement usually occurs only if the imported product disrupts domestic production. If there is no domestic production, then host country consumers get the benefit of lower prices. Companies may dump products because they cannot otherwise build a market abroad—essentially, a low price encourages consumers to sample the foreign brand. Companies can afford to dump products if they can charge high prices in their home market or if their home-country government subsidizes them. They may also opt to incur short-term losses abroad, presuming that they can recoup those losses when, after they eliminate their rivals or gain brand loyalty, they can then raise their prices. Ironically, home-country consumers or taxpayers seldom realize that paying high prices locally often results in lower prices for foreign consumers. A company that believes it is competing against dumped products may appeal to its government to restrict those imports. However, determining a foreign company's cost or domestic price is difficult because of limited access to the foreign producers' accounting statements, fluctuations in exchange rates, and the passage of products through layers of distribution before reaching the end-consumer. The result is that governments allegedly restrict imports arbitrarily through the antidumping provisions of their trade legislation and are slow to dispose of the restrictions if pricing situations change. Companies caught in this situation often lose the export market they had labored to build.[18]

Another price argument for government influence on trade is the **optimum-tariff theory**. This theory states that a foreign producer will lower its prices if the importing country places a tax on its products. If this occurs, benefits shift to the importing country because the foreign producer lowers its profits on the export sales. For example, assume that an exporter has costs of $500 per unit and is selling to a foreign market for $700 per unit. With the imposition of a 10 percent tax on the imported price, the exporter may choose to lower its price to $636.36 per unit, which, with a 10 percent tax of $63.64, would keep the price at $700 for the importer. The exporter may feel that a price higher than $700 would result in lost sales and that a profit of $136.36 per unit instead of the previous $200 per unit is better than no profit at all. Consequently, an amount of $63.64 per unit has shifted to the importing country. As long as the foreign producer lowers its price by any amount, some shift in revenue goes to the importing country and the tariff is deemed an optimum one. There are many examples of products whose prices did not rise as much as the amount of the imposed tariff; however, it is difficult to predict when and which exporters will voluntarily reduce their profit margins.

NONECONOMIC RATIONALES FOR GOVERNMENT INTERVENTION

Economic rationales help explain many government actions on trade. However, governments sometimes use noneconomic rationales, such as the following:

- Maintenance of essential industries (especially defense)
- Prevention of shipments to unfriendly countries
- Maintenance or extension of spheres of influence
- Protecting activities that help preserve the national identity

Let's look at each rationale.

Maintaining Essential Industries

Governments apply trade restrictions to protect essential domestic industries during peacetime so that a country is not dependent on foreign sources of supply during war. This is called the **essential-industry argument**. For example, the U.S. government subsidizes the domestic production of silicon so that domestic computer chip producers will not need to depend on foreign suppliers. This argument for protection has much appeal in rallying support for import barriers. However, in times of real crisis or military emergency, almost any product could be deemed essential. Because of the high cost of protecting an inefficient industry or a higher-cost domestic substitute, the essential-industry argument should not be (but frequently is) accepted without a careful evaluation of costs, needs, and alternatives. Once an industry receives protection, it is difficult to turn off this protection because the affected companies and their employees support politicians who defend their continued protection—even when the rationale for the subsidies long ago disappeared. This is why the United States, for example, continues to subsidize its mohair producers more than 20 years after mohair was deemed no longer essential for military uniforms.[19]

In protecting essential industries, countries must

- Determine which ones are essential
- Consider costs and alternatives
- Consider political consequences

Dealing with "Unfriendly" Countries

Groups concerned about security often use national defense arguments to prevent the export, even to friendly countries, of strategic goods that might fall into the hands of potential enemies or that might be in short supply domestically. For example, the FBI and Justice Department successfully prevented U.S. exports of data-encryption technology (data-scrambling hardware and software) until a group of U.S. high-tech companies allied themselves with privacy advocate groups to convince the U.S. government to relax the export curbs. U.S. companies now can export any encryption product to the members of the EU and other European and Pacific Rim allies without first getting permission.[20] Export constraints may be valid if the exporting country assumes there will be no retaliation that prevents it from securing even more essential goods from the potential importing country. Even then, the importing country may find alternative supply sources or develop a production capability of its own. In this situation, the country that limits exports is the economic loser.[21]

Trade controls on nondefense goods also may be used as a weapon of foreign policy to try to prevent another country from meeting its political objectives. For example, the United States imposed trade sanctions on nine Chinese companies and an Indian businessperson that it found had sold technology to Iran that was then put to use by that country's chemical and conventional weapons programs. The two-year sanctions barred these firms from doing business with the U.S. government, forbade them from exporting goods into the United States, and prevented U.S. companies from exporting certain items to them.[22] Still, there is potential for gains from trade as countries become friendlier. For example, in an exception to its stringent trade restrictions on Cuba, the United States passed a law allowing humanitarian shipments to Cuba following damage inflicted by Hurricane Michelle in 2001.[23]

Maintaining Spheres of Influence

There are many examples of government actions on trade designed to support that government's spheres of influence. Governments give aid and credits to—and encourage imports from—countries that join a political alliance or vote a preferred way within international bodies. For example, our opening case showed the EU's preferential treatment of bananas from certain former colonies. Similarly, the EU and the 77 members of the African, Caribbean, and Pacific group of states signed the Cotonou Agreement to formalize preferential trade relationships by offering members of the latter group privileged access to European markets.[24]

A country's trade restrictions may coerce governments to follow certain political actions or punish companies whose governments do not. For example, China delayed permission for Allianz, a German insurance group, to operate in China after Germany gave a reception for the Dalai Lama, the exiled Tibetan spiritual leader.[25] Many interest groups in the United States have called for trade restrictions on Chinese products because of China's controversial human rights record, as Figure 6.2's cartoon points out.[26]

FIGURE 6.2

The general public seldom understands how trade restrictions are carried out, or their ramifications.

"DO WE WANT TAKE-OUT CANTONESE, MANDARIN, OR SZECHUAN-- OR DO WE BOYCOTT UNTIL HUMAN RIGHTS QUESTIONS ARE SOLVED?"

Source: Reprinted by permission of Harley Schwadron Cartoons.

Preserving Cultures and National Identity

Countries are held together partially through a unifying sense of identity that sets their citizens apart from those of other nations. To sustain this collective identity, countries limit foreign products and services in certain sectors. For many years, Japan, South Korea, and China maintained an almost total ban on rice imports, largely because rice farming has been a historically cohesive force in each country. Recent pressures from the WTO have led them to relent.[27] Canada relies on a cultural sovereignty argument to prohibit foreign ownership or control of publishing, cable TV, and bookselling.[28] Similarly, France protects its cinema industry out of fear that, if unregulated, the resulting invasion of the English language and Anglo-Saxon culture will weaken its cultural identity. The French government subsidizes activities in the filmmaking and dubbing industries and limits the percentage of foreign films shown on French television.[29]

INSTRUMENTS OF TRADE CONTROL

Governments use many rationales and seek a range of outcomes when they try to influence exports or imports. We now profile the instruments that governments use to try to do so. Because a country's trade policy has repercussions abroad, retaliation from foreign governments looms as a potential obstacle to achieving the desired objectives. Therefore, the choice of the instrument of trade control is crucial because each type may incite different responses from domestic and foreign groups. One way to understand the types of instruments is to distinguish between those that indirectly affect the amount traded by directly influencing the prices of exports or imports versus those that directly limit the amount that can be traded.

Tariffs

A common distinction is between tariff barriers and nontariff barriers. Tariff barriers affect prices; nontariff barriers may affect either price or quantity directly. A **tariff** (sometimes called **duty**) is the most common type of trade control and is a tax that governments levy on a good shipped internationally. That is, governments charge a tariff on a good when it crosses an official boundary—whether it be that of a country, say Mexico, or a group of countries, like the EU, that have agreed to impose a common tariff on goods entering their bloc. Tariffs collected by the exporting country are called an **export tariff**; if collected by a country through which the goods have passed, it is a **transit tariff**; if collected by the importing country, it is an **import tariff**. The import tariff is by far the most common.

Figure 6.3 illustrates how tariff and nontariff barriers affect both the price and the quantity sold, although in a different order and with a different impact on producers. Parts (a) and (b) both have downward-sloping demand curves (*D*) and upward-sloping supply curves (*S*). In other words, the lower the price, the higher the quantity that consumers demand; the higher the price, the more that suppliers make available for sale. The intersection of the *S* and *D* curves illustrates the price (P_1) and quantity sold (Q_1) without government interference. When a tax (tariff) raises the price from P_1 to P_2 in part (a), the amount consumers are willing to buy will fall from Q_1 to Q_2. Producers do not benefit because the price increase goes to the government as taxes rather than to them as profits. Part (b) shows a restriction in available supply; therefore, a new supply curve (S_1) is imposed. The quantity sold now falls from Q_1 to Q_2. At the lower supply, sellers raise the price from P_1 to P_2, which is shown in the intersection of the *D* and S_1 curves. The major difference in the two forms of trade control is that sellers raise the price in (b), which helps compensate them for the decline in quantity sold. In (a), producers sell less and are unable to raise their price because the tax has already done so.

Tariffs may be levied

- On goods entering, leaving, or passing through a country
- For protection or revenue
- On a per unit or a value basis

FIGURE 6.3   Comparison of Trade Restrictions

In (a), the tax on imports ($P_2 -$ P_1) raises the price, which reduces the quantity demanded from Q_1 to Q_2. In (b), the quantity limit on imports ($Q_1 - Q_2$) reduces the supply available and raises prices from P_1 to P_2. The price rise in (b) is charged by producers.

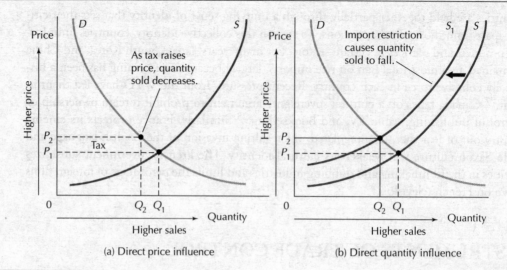

(a) Direct price influence   (b) Direct quantity influence

Import tariffs raise the price of imported goods, thereby giving domestically produced goods a relative price advantage. A tariff may be protective even though there is no domestic production in direct competition. For example, a country that wants its residents to spend less on foreign goods and services may raise the price of some foreign products—even though there are no close domestic substitutes—in order to curtail demand for imports.

Tariffs also serve as a source of government revenue. Generally, import tariffs are of little importance to industrial countries; for example, the EU spends about the same to collect duties as the amount it collects.[30] Tariffs, however, are a major source of revenue in many developing countries. This is because government authorities in developing countries may have more control over determining the amounts and types of goods crossing their borders and collecting a tax on them than they do over determining and collecting individual and corporate income taxes. Although revenue tariffs are most commonly collected on imports, many countries that export raw materials charge export tariffs.[31] Transit tariffs were once a major source of revenue for countries, but government treaties have nearly abolished them.

A government may assess a tariff on a per-unit basis, in which case it is applying a **specific duty**. It may assess a tariff as a percentage of the value of the item, in which case it is an **ad valorem duty**. If it assesses both a specific duty and an ad valorem duty on the same product, the combination is a **compound duty**. A specific duty is straightforward for customs officials who collect duties, because they do not need to determine a good's value on which to calculate a percentage tax.

A tariff controversy concerns industrial countries' treatment of manufactured exports from developing countries that seek to add manufactured value to their exports of raw materials (like making tea bags from tea leaves). Raw materials frequently enter industrial countries free of duty; however, if processed, industrial countries then assign an import tariff. Because an ad valorem tariff is based on the total value of the product, meaning the raw materials and the processing combined, developing countries argue that the effective tariff on the manufactured portion turns out to be higher than the published tariff rate. For example, a country may charge no duty on tea leaves but may assess a 10 percent ad valorem tariff on instant tea. If $5 for a package of instant tea bags covers $2.50 in tea leaves and $2.50 in processing costs, the $0.50 duty is effectively 20 percent on the manufactured portion, because the tea leaves could have entered duty free. This anomaly further challenges developing countries to find markets for their man-ufactured products. At the same time, the governments of industrial countries cannot easily remove barriers to imports of developing countries' manufactured products largely because these imports affect unskilled or unemployed workers who are least equipped to move to new jobs.

Nontariff Barriers: Direct Price Influences

We have shown how tariffs raise prices and influence trade. We now turn to how govern-ments alter the price of products to influence their trade.

Subsidies Countries sometimes make direct payments to domestic companies to com-pensate them for losses incurred from selling abroad, such as U.S. subsidies to cotton exporters.[32] However, they provide other types of assistance to make it cheaper or more profitable to sell overseas. For example, most countries offer potential exporters many business development services, such as market information, trade expositions, and foreign contacts. From the standpoint of market efficiency, these sorts of subsidies are more justi-fiable than tariffs because they seek to overcome, rather than create, market imperfections. There are also benefits to disseminating information widely because governments can spread the costs of collecting information among many users. Finally, other countries are less likely to complain about business development assistance than direct subsidies.

Trade frictions result from disagreement on the definition of a subsidy. For instance, did Canada subsidize exports of fish because it gave grants to fishermen to buy trawlers? Similarly, did India subsidize insurance when the government-owned insurance carrier incurred severe losses? Questions also surround governments' support of R&D, as well as tax programs that directly or indirectly affect export profitability. One interesting subsidy case involves commercial aircraft. The United States indirectly subsidizes Boeing through payments for developments in military aircraft that also have commercial applications. The EU subsidizes Airbus Industrie directly. In response, the United States and the EU have set up a bilateral agreement to allow subsidies on commercial aircraft production but to limit the subsidy amounts.[33]

Aid and Loans   Governments also give aid and loans to other countries. If the recipient is required to spend the funds in the donor country, which is known as tied aid or tied loans, some products can compete abroad that might otherwise be noncompetitive. Tied aid helps win large contracts for infrastructure, such as telecommunications, railways, and electric-power projects. However, there is growing skepticism about the value of tied aid. Tied aid can slow the development of local suppliers in developing countries, and it can shield suppliers in the donor countries from competition. These concerns led the members of the OECD to untie financial aid to developing countries, thus freeing aid-recipient countries from having to purchase equipment from suppliers in the donor country.[34]

Customs Valuation   The temptation exists for exporters and importers to declare a low price on invoices in order to pay a lower ad valorem tariff. For example, the U.S. Customs Department levied more than $22 million in penalties over a six-month span in 2000 for custom valuation violations, ranging from minor discrepancies in the classification or valua-tion of merchandise to a willful intent to defraud the government.[35] Generally, most coun-tries have agreed on preventive procedures for assessing values when their customs agents levy tariffs. First, customs officials must use the declared invoice price. If there is none or if they doubt its authenticity, agents must then assess on the basis of the value of identical goods. If not possible, agents must assess on the basis of similar goods arriving in or about the same time. For example, there is no sales invoice when imported goods enter for lease rather than purchase. Customs officials must then base the tariff on the value of identical or similar

Government subsidies may help companies be competitive.

- Subsidies to overcome market imperfections are the least controversial.
- There is little agreement on what a subsidy is.
- There has been increased effort to assist companies' export plans.

Because it is difficult for customs officials to determine if invoice prices are honest

- They may arbitrarily increase value
- Valuation procedures have been developed

goods. If this basis cannot be used, officials may compute a value based on final sales value or on reasonable cost. Argentine customs authorities, using this method, revalued a shipment of 2,000 bicycles that the exporter had invoiced for $1.78 each.[36] Similarly, sometimes agents use their discretionary power to assess the value too high, thereby preventing the importation of foreign-made products.[37]

The fact that so many different products are traded creates valuation problems. It is easy (by accident or intention) to misclassify a product and its corresponding tariff. Administering more than 13,000 categories of products means a customs agent must use professional discretion to determine if, say, silicon chips should be considered "integrated circuits for computers" or "a form of chemical silicon." Similarly, the U.S. Customs Service had to determine whether sport utility vehicles, such as the Suzuki Samurai and the Land Rover, were cars or trucks. It assessed the 25 percent duty on trucks instead of the 2.5 percent duty on cars. Later, a federal trade court ruled that SUVs should be regarded as cars. Finally, automobile parts are assessed about half the duty assessed on automobiles in Poland. But what is an automobile part? Many Poles have discovered that they can travel to neighboring Germany to buy cars, dismantle them just enough so that each section can be classified as a part, and bring the sections into Poland at the lower duty rate.[38]

Other Direct Price Influences   Countries use other means to affect prices, including special fees (such as for consular and customs clearance and documentation), requirements that customs deposits be placed in advance of shipment, and minimum price levels at which goods can be sold after they have customs clearance.

Nontariff Barriers: Quantity Controls

Governments use other nontariff regulations and practices to affect directly the quantity of imports and exports. Principal forms of quantity controls include the following:

Quotas   The quota is the most common type of quantitative import or export restriction. An import quota prohibits or limits the quantity of a product that can be imported in a given year. Quotas raise prices just as tariffs do but, being defined in physical terms, they directly affect the amount of imports by putting an absolute ceiling on supply—say, for example, three million DVD players from a particular country in a given year. Therefore, quotas usually increase the consumer price because there is little incentive to use price competition to increase sales. A notable difference between tariffs and quotas is their direct effect on revenues. Tariffs generate revenue for the government. Quotas generate revenues for those companies that are able to obtain a portion of the intentionally limited supply of the product that they can then sell to local customers.

Sometimes governments allocate quotas among countries based on political or market conditions. This choice can create problems because goods from one country might be transshipped, or deflected, to another country to take advantage of the latter's unused quota.[39] Similarly, the product may be converted into one for which there is no quota. Import quotas are not necessarily imposed to protect domestic producers. Japan maintains quotas on many agricultural products that are not produced within the country. It then allocates import rights to competing suppliers as a means of bargaining for sales of Japanese exports as well as to prevent excessive dependence on any one country for essential foods in the event that adverse climatic or political conditions abruptly halt supply.

A variation of an import quota is the so-called **voluntary export restraint** (VER). Essentially, the government of Country A asks the government of Country B to reduce its companies' exports to Country A voluntarily. The term voluntarily is somewhat misleading; typically, either Country B volunteers to reduce its exports or else Country A may impose tougher trade regulations. For example, in the 1980s, the United States pressed the

A quota may

• Set the total amount to be traded

• Allocate amounts by country

ETHICAL DILEMMA

Do Trade Sanctions Work?

Some argue that countries should use trade policy to pressure other countries to change objectionable policies. For example, countries have limited trade with North Korea in order to weaken its repressive leadership, with India to protest its nuclear tests, with Myanmar because of its human rights policies, with Malaysia so that it will prohibit the employment of child labor, with Taiwan so that it will curtail the trade of endangered animals, and with Brazil so that it will restrict the destruction of Amazon forests. Sanctions against a country's overall trade may prevent an MNE from exporting from that country even though the company may not be engaged in the so-called undesirable practices.

Although these causes enjoy public support, countries wrestle with the basic question of whether to use trade policy to try to promote change in other countries. The principal dilemma is the issue of relativism versus normativism—or simply, whether or not to intervene. There are other complications. Some challenge the practicality of making sanctions work, especially if they aim to topple repressive regimes. The targeted country can often get what it wants from other countries. For example, the United States maintained a 20-year trade embargo on Vietnam. Still, Vietnamese consumers were able to buy U.S. consumer products, such as Coca-Cola, Kodak film, and Apple computers, through other countries that did not enforce the sanctions.[40] Others note that sanctions can actually inspire nationalism, as has happened in Iran and Iraq, and rally the populace to support the government. Still, few doubt that trade sanctions on South Africa and Haiti significantly damaged their political regimes.[41]

Overall, trade sanctions aimed at changing policies in foreign countries seldom work as intended; they can even cause job and economic losses in the sanctioning country.[42] In fact, it appeared that the liberalization of trade, not oppressive sanctions, more effectively destabilized the leaders and systems of the former communist countries.

Other arguments include:

- *The costs of sanctions on innocent people.* This occurred in Iraq, where there were widespread reports of children's deaths because of inadequate supplies of food and medicine due to the sanctions.[43]
- *The inability of sanctions to induce a change in leadership.* For instance, Fidel Castro of Cuba has withstood a U.S. trade embargo that has lasted more than 40 years.
- *The unevenness with which policies are applied among countries.* For example, the United States at one point considered trade sanctions against Taiwan but not against China in order get the former to curtail its trade in rhino horns and tiger bones, which are ingredients in traditional medicines.
- *The need to look at a country's overall record rather than at just its unpopular policy.* Some critics have suggested using trade policies to press Brazil to restrict the cutting of Amazon forests even though its overall environmental record, particularly its limiting of adverse exhaust emissions by converting automobile engines to use methanol instead of gasoline, is quite good.
- *The lack of agreement about the cause being protested.* Consider, for example, the argument that trade sanctions should be placed on countries permitting child labor, whereas others argue that the use of children on family farms is a way to promote strong family ties.

Ultimately, some proponents of trade sanctions say it is irrelevant whether they provoke change or not. The purpose of sanctions, they argue, is to make a meaningful social or moral declaration.

Japanese to limit "voluntarily" their exports of automobiles to the United States to no more than 1.85 million vehicles per year. Therefore, like a quota, a VER limits the quantity of trade between countries and, therefore, raises the prices of imported goods to consumers. For example, the U.S. Federal Trade Commission (FTC) estimated that U.S. consumers overpaid nearly $5 billion for Japanese automobiles between 1981 and 1985 due to the automobile industry VER. Procedurally, VERs have unique advantages. A VER is much easier to switch off than an import quota. In addition, the appearance of a "voluntary" choice by a particular country to constrain its exports to another country tends not to damage political relations between those countries as much as an import quota does.

A country may establish export quotas to assure domestic consumers of a sufficient supply of goods at a low price, to prevent depletion of natural resources, or to attempt to raise export prices by restricting supply in foreign markets. To restrict supply, some countries band together in various commodity agreements, such as those for coffee and petroleum, which then restrict and regulate exports from the member countries. The typical goal of an export quota is to raise prices to importing countries.

A specific type of quota that prohibits all forms of trade is an **embargo**, which works like a quota. Countries—or groups of countries—may place embargoes on either imports or exports, on whole categories of products regardless of destination, on specific products to specific countries, or on all products to given countries. Governments impose embargoes in an attempt to use economic means to achieve political goals.

Through "buy local" laws

- Government purchases give preference to domestically made goods
- Governments sometimes legislate preferences for domestically made goods

"Buy Local" Legislation   Another form of quantitative trade control is "buy local" legislation. Government purchases are a large part of total expenditures in many countries; typically, governments favor domestic producers. In the United States, for example, "buy American" legislation requires government procurement agencies to favor domestic goods. Sometimes governments specify a domestic content restriction—that is, a certain percentage of the product must be of local origin. Sometimes they favor domestic producers by establishing price mechanisms. For example, a government agency may buy a foreign-made product only if the price is at some predetermined margin below that of a domestic competitor. Many countries prescribe a minimum percentage of domestic content that a given product must have for it to be sold legally in their country. In addition, they may prod foreign producers to add local content with the threat of import restrictions. Such programs have proven successful. For example, U.S. trade pressures against Japan-based auto parts exporters spurred Japanese automakers in the United States to purchase more parts from U.S.-based suppliers; some Japanese branded cars now have the same level of domestic content as vehicles made by General Motors and Ford.[44]

Other types of trade barriers include

- Arbitrary standards
- Licensing arrangements
- Administrative delays
- Reciprocal requirements
- Service restrictions

Standards   Countries can devise classification, labeling, and testing standards to allow the sale of domestic products but obstruct that of foreign-made ones. Take product labels, for instance. The requirement that companies indicate on a product where it is made provides information to consumers who may prefer to buy products from certain countries. This technicality adds to a firm's production costs, particularly if the label must be translated for each export market. Further, raw materials, components, design, and labor increasingly come from many countries, so most products today are of mixed origin. For example, the United States stipulated that any cloth substantially altered (woven, for instance) in another country must identify that country on its label. Consequently, designers like Ferragamo, Gucci, and Versace must declare "Made in China" on the label of garments that contain silk from China.[45]

The professed purpose of testing standards is to protect the safety or health of the domestic population. However, some foreign companies argue that testing standards are just another means to protect domestic producers. For example, EU standards keep some United States and Canadian products out of the European market completely. This is the case with genetically engineered corn and canola oil even though the worldwide scientific community reports that the genetic engineering poses no human health risk and France grows and sells a small amount of genetically engineered corn itself.[46]

Specific Permission Requirements   Some countries require that potential importers or exporters secure permission from government authorities before conducting trade transactions. This requirement is known as an **import license**. A company may have to submit samples to government authorities to obtain an import license. This procedure can restrict imports or exports directly by denying permission or indirectly because of the cost, time, and uncertainty involved in the process. A **foreign-exchange control** is a similar type of control. It requires an importer of a given product to apply to a government agency to secure the foreign currency to pay for the product. As with an import license, failure to grant the exchange, not to mention the time and expense of completing forms and awaiting replies, obstructs foreign trade.

Administrative Delays   Closely akin to specific permission requirements are intentional administrative delays, which create uncertainty and raise the cost of carrying inventory. For example, United Parcel Service (UPS) provisionally suspended its ground service between the United States and Mexico because of burdensome Mexican customs delays. Competitive pressure, however, moves countries to improve their administrative systems. Chinese trade authorities, for example, cut the time taken for goods manufactured by Hong Kong firms in Guangdong to pass through internal customs checks from one week to one day. Improved processes, such as electronic submission of cargo manifests, affected 68,000 non-mainland firms and reduced administration costs more than $70 million.[47]

Reciprocal Requirements   Governments sometimes require exporters to take actual merchandise in lieu of money or to promise to buy merchandise or services in place of cash payment in the country to which they export. This requirement is common in the aerospace and defense industries—sometimes because the importer does not have enough foreign currency. For example, Russia's commercial airline, Aeroflot, has exchanged Russian crude oil for Airbus aircraft.[48] More frequently, however, reciprocal requirements are made between countries with ample access to foreign currency that want to secure jobs or technology as part of the transaction.[49] For example, McDonnell Douglas sold helicopters to the British government but had to equip them with Rolls-Royce engines (made in the United Kingdom) as well as transfer much of the technology and production work to the United Kingdom.[50] These sorts of barter transactions are called **countertrade** or **offsets**. They often require exporters to find markets for goods outside their lines of expertise or to engage in complicated organizational arrangements that require them to relinquish some operating control. All things being equal, companies avoid countertrade.[51] However, some companies have developed competencies in these types of arrangements.

Restrictions on Services   Many countries depend on revenue from the foreign sale of such services as transportation, insurance, consulting, and banking. Services like these account for about 20 percent of the value of all international trade but are growing much faster than the trade of goods. Countries restrict trade in services for three reasons:

Three main reasons for restricting trade in services are

- Essentiality
- Standards
- Immigration

1. *Essentiality.* Countries judge certain service industries to be essential because they serve strategic purposes or because they provide social assistance to their citizens. These countries sometimes prohibit private companies, foreign or domestic, in some sectors because they believe the services should not be sold for profit. In other cases, they set price controls for private competitors or subsidize government-owned service organizations, creating disincentives for foreign private participation. Postal, education, and hospital health services are not-for-profit sectors in which few foreign firms compete. When a government privatizes these industries, its customary preference for local ownership and control

of essential services precludes foreign firms. For example, most countries, including the United States, restrict foreign airline companies from transporting cargo and passengers over their domestic routes. Other essential services in which foreign firms are sometimes excluded are media, communications, banking, and utilities. Service companies sometimes pressure their home governments to negotiate deregulation abroad when they believe they have competitive advantages. For example, the American International Group, the largest industrial insurer in the world, and other insurance corporations pressured and relied on the U.S. government to open the Indian insurance sector to foreign insurance companies, which had been restricted to government-owned companies.[52]

2. *Standards.* Governments limit foreign entry into many service professions to ensure practice by qualified personnel. The licensing standards of these personnel varies by country and includes such professionals as accountants, actuaries, architects, electricians, engineers, gemologists, hairstylists, lawyers, physicians, real estate brokers, and teachers. At present, there is little reciprocal recognition in licensing from one country to another because occupational standards and requirements differ substantially. This means, for example, that an accounting or legal firm from one country cannot easily do business in another country, not even to service the local needs of its home-country clients. The company must hire professionals within each foreign country or else try to earn certification where required. The latter option can be difficult because examinations will be in a foreign language and likely emphasize materials different from those in the home country. Further, there may be lengthy prerequisites for taking an examination, such as internships and course work at a local university.

3. *Immigration.* Satisfying the standards of a particular country does not guarantee that a foreigner can then work there. Earlier discussion noted that countries protect the job opportunities and security of their citizens. In addition, government regulations often require that an organization—domestic or foreign—search extensively for qualified personnel locally before it can apply for work permits for personnel it would like to bring in from abroad. Even if no one from domestic sources of labor is available, hiring a foreigner is still difficult.[53]

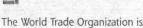

The World Trade Organization is the major body for

- Reciprocal trade negotiations
- Enforcement of trade agreements

THE WORLD TRADE ORGANIZATION (WTO)

So far, we have discussed the motives and methods that governments use to regulate trade. At the same time, governments actively cooperate with each other to remove trade barriers. The following discussion looks at the WTO. Before doing so, we look at GATT, the philosophical and organizational predecessor of the WTO.

GATT: The Predecessor

In 1947, 23 countries formed the General Agreement on Tariffs and Trade (GATT) to abolish quotas and reduce tariffs. By the time the WTO replaced GATT in 1995, 125 nations were members. Many believe that GATT's contribution to trade liberalization made possible the expansion of world trade in the second half of the twentieth century.

The fundamental principle of GATT was that each member nation must open its markets equally to every other member nation—any sort of discrimination was prohibited. The principle of "trade without discrimination" was embodied in GATT's **most-favored-nation (MFN)** clause—once a country and its trading partners had agreed to reduce a tariff, that tariff cut was automatically extended to every other country irrespective of whether they were a signatory to the agreement. GATT held several major conferences (eventually referred to as rounds) from 1947 to 1993 to address trade issues. These sessions led to many multilateral reductions in tariffs and nontariff barriers. Table 6.3 identifies these sessions.

● TABLE 6.3

GATT MILESTONES

DATE	SITE/ROUND	NUMBER OF MEMBER NATIONS	OUTCOME
1946	London, England	—	Fifty countries met to discuss creating an international trade organization as a third world economic pillar alongside the World Bank and IMF. These discussions failed.
1947	Havana, Cuba	—	Twenty-three countries reconvened and negotiated more than 45,000 reductions in their customs duties that affected $10 billion of trade, then about one-fifth of the world's total. These agreements were codified into the General Agreement on Tariffs and Trade (GATT).
1947	Geneva, Switzerland	23	First official meeting of founding members of GATT.
1949	Annecy, France	13	Negotiated more than 5,000 tariff concessions.
1951	Torquay, England	38	Additional tariff reductions and concessions.
1956	Geneva, Switzerland	26	Additional tariff reductions and concessions.
1960–1961	The Dillon Round,	26	Additional tariff reductions and concessions. GATT now formally named each Geneva, Switzerland session.
1964–1967	The Kennedy Round, Geneva, Switzerland	62	Expanded discussion to review new trade rules and passed an anti-dumping agreement.
1973–1979	The Tokyo Round	102	Reduced customs duties. Reached series of agreements on various non tariff barriers. However, these agreements were only signed by some participants. Failed to reform agricultural trade and stopped short of new agreement on emergency import measures.
1986–1994	The Uruguay Round	123	Session began in Uruguay to reflect the fact that developing countries had become the majority in GATT. Expanded discussion to review tariffs, nontariff measures, trade rules, services, intellectual property, dispute settlement, textiles, and agriculture. Created the World Trade Organization (WTO) and its mandate to cover new areas of trade.

Over time, GATT grappled with the issue of nontariff barriers in terms of industrial standards, government procurement, subsidies and countervailing duties (duties in response to another country's protectionist measures), licensing, and customs valuation. In each area, GATT members agreed to apply the same product standards for imports as for domestically produced goods, treat bids by foreign companies on a nondiscriminatory basis for most large contracts, prohibit export subsidies except on agricultural products, simplify licensing procedures that permit the importation of foreign-made goods, and use a uniform procedure to value imports when assessing duties on them.

GATT slowly ran into problems. Its success led some governments to devise craftier methods of trade protection. Some countries began to negotiate bilateral trade deals while others gave subsidies to local companies. Similarly, world trade grew more complex, and trade in services—not covered by GATT rules—grew more important. Procedurally, GATT's institutional structure and its dispute settlement system seemed increasingly overextended. Some countries objected that nonmembers, under the umbrella of the most-favored-nation clause, gained freer foreign entry for their products without making any concessions—the so-called free-rider problem. In addition, GATT could not enforce compliance with agreements; it depended on its members' commitment to cooperate with each other. These market trends and organizational challenges made trade agreements harder to work out. The Uruguay Round, the final GATT session, spanned more than seven years and accomplished less than envisioned. Restoring an effective means for trade liberalization led officials to create the WTO in 1995.

LOOKING TO THE FUTURE

The Prospects for Freer Trade

Countries prefer to act independently; however, they cede authority on trade when they perceive cooperation to be in their net interest. For example, countries have surrendered elements of their sovereignty to the binding dispute-settlement provisions of the WTO. They have also banded together on other trade issues, such as multilateral treaties on ivory trade to protect elephants. In any situation, though, a country has the inalienable right to withdraw. At some point, a country might withdraw from the WTO rather than accept its reprimand in a trade dispute. Such action could greatly hamper trade liberalization, particularly if the United States or the EU were to withdraw.

The issue of environmental standards for products and their production defy swift resolution. Countries with strict environmental regulations will undoubtedly consider assigning "green countervailing duties" to penalize those firms that opt to operate where regulations are lax. Producers facing these import restrictions undoubtedly will claim that altruistic environmental standards are really a ruse to protect inefficient domestic producers. Further, governments of developing countries suspect that stricter product standards, largely advocated by industrial countries, will impose yet another non-tariff trade barrier.[54]

Ultimately, trade policy depends to a great extent on public opinion Groups that believe they have been adversely affected by imports, especially if due to unfair practices, are apt to be more vocal and persuasive at shaping public opinion than people who benefit from trade. What is more worrisome, recent surveys report that a majority of people in the United States feel that foreign trade has been bad for the U.S. economy.[55] These surveys were taken during the boom years of the late 1990s. One doubts that the economic trials of the early twenty-first century have improved Americans' outlooks. Such negative sentiment threatens to slow foreign trade liberalization, especially in the face of a prolonged economic downturn.

Nonetheless, there are many positive indications that international trade will become freer and fairer. Global trade has grown rapidly for decades. Prevailing attitudes and arrangements suggest that it should continue to do so. Consumers around the world have grown fond of being able to buy higher-quality products for lower prices. Companies have invigorated their operations and developed innovative management methods. Institutions like the WTO continue to refine the administrative infrastructure of international trade. Governments, fearful of seeing their countries left behind, privatize companies, rethink regulations, open import markets, and advise companies to innovate or perish. These movements know no bounds, affecting consumers, companies, and countries everywhere.

Major decision-making units of the WTO include

- Ministerial Conference
- General Council
- Goods Council
- Services Council
- Intellectual Property Council

The WTO

The WTO adopted the principles and trade agreements reached under the auspices of GATT but expanded its mission to include trade in services, investment, intellectual property, sanitary measures, plant health, agriculture, and textiles, as well as technical barriers to trade. Currently, the WTO has more than 140 members that collectively account for more than 90 percent of world trade. More than 30 other countries are currently in negotiations to become members. The entire membership makes significant decisions by consensus. However, there are provisions for a majority vote in the event of a nondecision by member countries. Agreements then must be ratified by the governments of the member nations.

The highest-level decision-making body in the WTO's structure is the Ministerial Conference; it meets at least once every two years. The next level is the General Council (usually ambassadors and the director of a country delegation) that meets several times a year. The General Council also meets as the Trade Policy Review Body and the Dispute Settlement Body. At the next level are the Goods Council, Services Council, and Intellectual Property Council. Specialized committees, working groups, and working parties deal with the individual agreements and other areas, such as the environment, development, membership applications, and regional trade agreements. WTO members deal with these areas separately and on an ongoing basis.

Normal Trade Relations   The WTO replaced the most-favored-nation clause of GATT with the concept of normal trade relations. (Terminology changes slowly, and *normal trade relations* are still often called *most-favored-nation*, or *MFN*.) The WTO restricts this privilege to official members in order to eliminate earlier objections to free-rider countries. Still, governments have made the following exceptions:

1. Developing countries' manufactured products have been given preferential treatment over those from industrial countries. For example, most industrial countries grant tariff preferences to developing countries under the Generalized System of Preferences (GSP) in the belief that developing countries must export more to develop their economies.[51]
2. Concessions granted to members within a regional trading alliance, such as the EU or the North American Free Trade Agreement (NAFTA) have not been extended to countries outside the alliance. The rationale for regional trading arrangements is discussed in Chapter 7.
3. Exceptions are made in times of war or international tension. For example, since the early 1960s, the United States and Cuba have denied normal trade relations to each other due to political hostility. Similarly, India and Pakistan have curtailed their trade relations due to ongoing political tension.

Settlement of Disputes   Countries may bring charges of unfair trade practices to a WTO panel, and accused countries may appeal. There are time limits on all stages of deliberations, and the WTO's rulings are binding. If an offending country fails to comply with the panel's judgment, its trading partners have the right to compensation. If this penalty is ineffective, then the offending country's trading partners have the right to impose countervailing sanctions (such as the tariff duties the United States put on EU products in response to the EU's reluctance to repeal its banana import restrictions). Thus far, the WTO's dispute-settlement body has had a heavier caseload than GATT had. Rather than suggesting growing trade misunderstandings, it indicates countries' confidence in the effectiveness of the WTO dispute-resolution process.

DEALING WITH GOVERNMENT TRADE INFLUENCES

Government intervention in trade affects the flow of import and exports of products between countries. Companies have several options for dealing with this situation. Four stand out: (1) Move operations to a lower-cost country, (2) Concentrate on market niches that attract less international competition, (3) Adopt internal innovations (i.e., greater efficiency or superior products), or (4) Try to get government protection.

There are costs and risks with each option. Nevertheless, the record of many companies shows that success is possible. For example, competition from Japanese imports spurred the U.S. automobile industry to move some production abroad, develop the ideas of the minivan and suburban utility vehicle, subcontract with foreign companies to supply cheaper parts, and adopt lean-production techniques to improve efficiency and product quality.

When facing import competition, companies can

- Move abroad
- Seek other market niches
- Make domestic output competitive
- Try to get protection

Collectively, these moves have once again made the United States the center of the global auto industry.[56] Granted, these methods are not realistic for every industry. Companies may lack the managerial, capital, or technological resources to shift production abroad. They may not be able to identify more profitable product niches. In addition, even if they manage to improve efficiency, the innovation may be quickly copied by foreign competitors. In such situations, companies often ask their governments to restrict imports or to open export markets. In the case of automobiles, the U.S. industry sought and received protection from Japanese imports in the form of VERs. Our opening case showed that Chiquita and Dole's inability to increase their EU market share through fair competition led them to lobby the United States successfully to pressure the EU with retaliatory tariffs. Finally, similar events are underway in the U.S. steel industry; the United States has proposed using high tariffs to give the American steel industry more time to restore its competitiveness.

It is impossible for governments to try to help every company that faces tough international competition. Inevitably, the burden falls upon companies to convince government officials that their situation warrants public assistance. Doing so begins with identifying the key decision makers, whether they are an official of the executive branch, a member of parliament, or a career civil servant. Trade policies in the United States, for example, are often championed by members of Congress who are especially sensitive to employment and company conditions in their home districts.[57] In any situation, companies must convey to public officials that voters and stakeholders support their position. Managers can and do use the economic and noneconomic arguments presented in this chapter.

Companies improve the odds of success if they can ally most, if not all, companies in their industry. Otherwise, officials may feel that a particular company's problems are due to its specific inefficiencies rather than the general challenge of imports. Similarly, it helps to involve many stakeholders. When the U.S. auto industry sought relief from Japanese auto competition, for example, company managers and union representatives worked together. Managers may also identify other groups that may have a common objective—even though for different reasons. For example, the International Brotherhood of Teamsters worried about U.S. job losses because of citrus imports from Brazil. It then allied with activist groups concerned about the use of child labor in Brazil to marshal support for citrus import restrictions.[58] Companies often build public support by advertising their positions to stakeholders. Finally, companies can lobby decision makers and endorse the political candidates who understand their situations.

Companies can take different approaches to deal with changes in the international competitive environment. Frequently, companies' attitudes toward protectionism are a function of the investments they have made to develop their international strategy. Companies that depend on freer trade and those that have integrated their production and supply chains among countries tend to oppose protectionism. In contrast, companies with single or multidomestic production facilities, such as a plant in Japan to serve the Japanese market and a plant in Taiwan to serve the Taiwanese market, have less to lose from protectionism. Companies also differ in their perceived abilities to compete against imports. In nearly half the cases over the last 60 years in which U.S. firms proposed protecting a U.S. industry, one or more companies in that industry opposed it. The latter typically commanded competitive advantages in terms of scale economies, supplier relationships, or differentiated products. Hence, they reasoned that not only could they successfully battle international rivals, but they also stood to gain even more as their weaker domestic competitors failed to do so.[59]

Chapter 5 showed that countries attempt to become more competitive by upgrading factors of production. However, governments' political objectives often oppose economic proposals to improve market efficiency and international competitiveness. Ultimately, government officials must resolve this dilemma. This chapter shows that companies should prepare for those situations in which a government chooses politics over economics and intervenes in the flow of imports and exports.

Summary

- Despite the documented benefits of free trade, no country permits an unregulated flow of goods and services across its borders.

- It is difficult to determine how protecting an industry affects employment due to the likelihood of retaliation and the fact that imports as well as exports create jobs.

- Policy makers continue to struggle with the problem of income redistribution due to changes in trade policy.

- The infant-industry argument holds that governments must try to prevent import competition in order to help certain industries move from high-cost to low-cost production.

- Government interference, it is often argued, is beneficial if it promotes industrialization, given the positive relationship between industrial activity and economic development.

- Trade controls are used to regulate prices of goods traded internationally. The objectives of such controls include protection of monopoly positions, prevention of foreign monopoly prices, greater assurance that domestic consumers get low prices, and lower profit margins for foreign producers.

- Considerable government interference in international trade is motivated by political rather than economic concerns, including maintaining domestic supplies of essential goods and preventing potential enemies from gaining goods that would help them achieve their objectives.

- Many developing countries seek export markets within the industrialized world for their manufactured products; they commonly argue, however, that the effective tariffs on their products are excessive.

- Tariffs raise the cost of imported products. The gains from tariffs go directly to the government, in the form of increased tax revenues, and to producers, who are protected from foreign competition. The costs of tariffs go to consumers who must pay more for imports.

- Tariffs affect prices whereas nontariff barriers may affect either price or quantity.

- Trade controls that directly affect price and indirectly affect quantity include tariffs, aids and loans, VERs, subsidies, arbitrary customs-valuations methods, and special fees.

- Trade controls that directly affect quantity and indirectly affect price include quotas, "buy local" legislation, arbitrary standards, special permission requirements, administrative delays, requirements to take goods in exchange, and restrictions on services.

- The General Agreement on Tariffs and Trade (GATT), begun in 1947, created a continuing means for countries to negotiate the reduction and elimination of trade barriers and to agree on simplified mechanisms for the conduct of international trade.

- The World Trade Organization (WTO) replaced GATT in 1995 as a continuing means of trade negotiations that aspires to foster the principle of trade without discrimination and to provide a better means of mediating trade disputes and of enforcing agreements.

- A company's development of an international strategy will greatly determine whether that company will benefit more from protectionism or from some other means for regulating international competition.

CASE

U.S.-Cuban Trade[60]

The U.S. embargo of Cuba has been a resilient foreign policy, able to weather a variety of political leaders, economic events, and historical eras. However, signs point to a showdown on the question of how the United States ought to deal with its trade relationship with Cuba. Various events indicate that it is increasingly possible that the United States might lift its long running embargo and redefine its Cuba policy with Fidel Castro still in power. Map 6.1 shows the proximity of Cuba to the United States.

In the 1950s, more than two-thirds of Cuban foreign trade took place with the United States. After Castro overthrew the Batista government in 1959, he threatened to incite revolutions elsewhere in Latin America. The United States countered by canceling its agreements to buy Cuban sugar, and Cuba retaliated by seizing U.S. oil refineries. When the oil companies refused to supply Cuba with crude oil, Cuba then turned to the Soviet Union for replacement supplies. This conflict occurred at the height of the Cold War tension between the United States and the Soviet Union. In 1962, the United States severed diplomatic relations and initiated the full trade embargo of Cuba through a presidential directive issued under the 1917 Trading with the Enemy Act. In 1963, the Treasury Department set forth the Cuban Asset Control Regulations, which prohibited all unlicensed financial transactions, forbade direct or indirect imports from Cuba,

MAP 6.1   Cuba

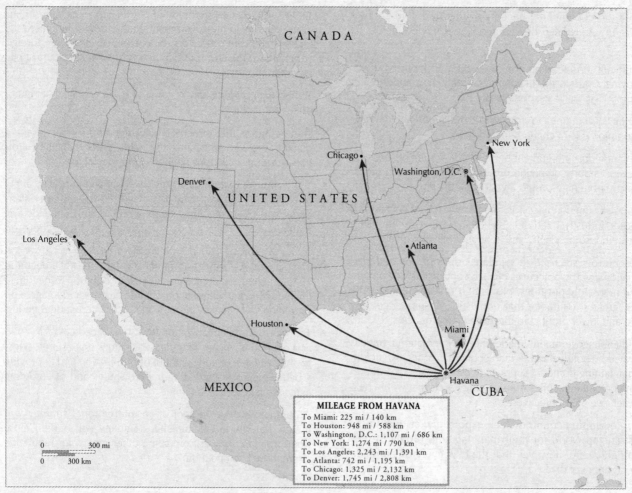

Politically, Cuba and the United States have been as "far apart" as any countries have been since the 1960s. Geographically, though, Cuba is surprising close to the Untied States—only about 90 nautical miles south of Key West, Florida and anywhere from an hour to a few hours air travel from most U.S. cities.

and imposed a total freeze on Cuban government assets held in the United States. Trade between the United States and Cuba stopped.

The incidents that strained relations during the next three decades are too numerous to detail. Some threatened peace; others bordered on the absurd. They included the U.S. sponsorship of an invasion by Cuban exiles at the Bay of Pigs, the placement and removal of Soviet missiles in Cuba, the deployment of Cuban forces to overthrow regimes that the United States supported (such as in Nicaragua and Angola), and exposés that the CIA had tried to airlift someone to assassinate Castro and had spent thousands of dollars to develop a powder to make his beard fall out. Figure 6.4 gives a time line of major events in U.S.-Cuban relations.

During this period, the U.S. trade embargo endured as originally set. However, spurred by the collapse of communism in the early 1990s, the U.S. Congress passed the Cuban Democracy Act in 1992. This policy codified the ban on American travel to Cuba and

extended the embargo to the foreign subsidiaries of U.S. companies operating abroad—there would be no trade, direct or otherwise, between the United States and Cuba. The act also required Cuba to hold democratic elections before the U.S. executive branch could repeal the embargo.

The Helms-Burton Act in 1996 reinforced many of these provisions and added stipulations for penalizing foreign companies that did business in Cuba. This act provided for legal action (the seizing of U.S. assets) against non-U.S. companies using expropriated property in Cuba that U.S. citizens (including Cuban exiles) had owned. It prohibited executives of these companies and their families the right to visit the United States and forbade normal U.S. relations with any future Cuban government that included Castro.

The embargo has had an immense effect on Cuba. In 1999, the Cuban National Assembly declared that the United States had violated the 1948 United Nations convention against genocide because

FIGURE 6.4   Major Events in U.S.-Cuban Relations

There have been many significant events affecting U.S.-Cuban relations during the last hundred years.

of the cumulative suffering imposed by the embargo. Over time, the U.S.-Cuban drama has played to a less sympathetic audience worldwide. Initially, many countries supported the U.S. embargo. All members of the Organization of American States (OAS) except Mexico agreed in 1964 to endorse it. Gradually, countries began trading with Cuba anyway. In 1995, the United Nations voted 117 to 3 against the U.S. embargo. Only Israel and Uzbekistan voted with the United States, and both of these countries traded with Cuba. By 2001, some 150 nations had normal trade relations with Cuba.

Pro-embargo supporters urged a relentless tightening of the embargo in order to spur the collapse of Cuban communism. Their reasoning was straightforward—the Cuban economy was so weak that a demoralized population would overthrow Castro if economic conditions deteriorated just a little more. This movement scored notable success with the Cuban Democracy and Helms-Burton Acts. This pro-embargo viewpoint, while recently diminished, had not faded. In 2001, U.S. Secretary of State Colin Powell ruled out the possibility of lifting the Cuba embargo until Castro departed. In addition, President George W. Bush directed the Treasury Department to limit remittances as well as to toughen enforcement of trade and travel prohibitions. The U.S Congress debated the Cuba Solidarity Act of 2001—essentially, sending $100 million in fax machines, telecommunications equipment, and other forms of aid to "voices of liberty" in Cuba in an attempt to mimic the Solidarity approach that helped bring about Poland's liberation from communism in the early 1990s.

Events increasingly undermined the rationale for continuing the embargo. The fall of the Berlin Wall and end of the Cold War in the early 1990s triggered many changes. The attendant collapse of the Soviet Union deprived Cuba of the estimated $3.5 to $4.5 billion in annual subsidies that sustained its feeble economy. Around this time, the U.S. Congress took a leadership role as the primary arbiter of the

U.S. Cuba policy. It promptly legislated the Cuban Democracy Act and Helms-Burton Act.

The U.S. public seemed increasingly divided on the usefulness of the embargo on Cuba. At the very least, hardline policies had failed for more than 40 years to dislodge Castro from power while causing adversity for some 11 million Cubans. Advocates of normal relations with Cuba argued that tighter restrictions on U.S. firms and reprisals on foreign companies would not weaken Castro's political power. Further, they warned that the latter policies would likely invite retaliation and aggravate U.S. immigration tensions with Cuba. Growing numbers of leaders in the United States (including heads of major firms, Democratic and Republican members of Congress, and labor leaders) publicly favored normalization of U.S.-Cuban trade rather than a tightening of the economic noose. For example, former U.S. Secretary of State Lawrence Eagleburger reasoned that U.S. trade actions gave Castro something, other than his inept policies, to blame for his economic blunders. Eagleburger added, "The worst thing that could happen would be for the U.S. to open the gates of trade and travel." Increasing exposure to the United States, not embargo, seemed a more promising force of change.

Repealing the embargo would help many U.S. industries and companies. Cuba had already attracted investments from many businesses from other countries, largely drawn by its highly qualified workforce, high literacy rate, and demand for foreign products and services. Groups in the United States noted the market potential of Cuba; California, for example, estimated that its farmers could sell some $90 million worth of agricultural products to Cuba annually if the embargo were lifted. Others cited the potential gains for U.S. tourism and transportation companies.

Finally, there was a debate over the basis for the pro-embargo position. Some argued that in an age when China is a member of the WTO and countries like North Korea are trading with the United

States, the Cuban embargo looked like a Cold War relic. Moreover, besides being far tougher than the U.S. economic blockades of Iran, Iraq, Libya, and North Korea, the Cuban embargo is the longest and harshest embargo by one state against another in modern history. In addition, some questioned the politics of U.S. policy. Officially, President George W. Bush's administration opposed any easing of the embargo until Cuba adopted principles of democracy and halted human rights abuses. However, there seemed to be a strong personal dimension; Vice President Cheney observed that "as soon as (Castro, then 75 years old) is gone from the scene, there is no reason in the world why we can't have a really first-class normalized set of relationships with Cuba."

Calls to normalize relations with Cuba steadily gained volume. In 2001, Congress passed a law allowing humanitarian shipments to Cuba, an exception to the U.S. embargo in response to damage inflicted by Hurricane Michelle. The 107th U.S. Congress introduced several anti-embargo bills, including the U.S.-Cuba Trade Act, the Free Trade with Cuba Act, the Cuba Humanitarian Trade Act, the Cuba Food and Medicine Access Act, and the Bridges to the Cuban People Act. In 2002, former U.S. President Jimmy Carter made a goodwill visit to Cuba; he called on the United States to take the first step to normalize relations by ending the embargo. Similarly, members of the U.S. Congress also toured Cuba; they suggested that the time had come to replace tension and hostility with trade and travel.

QUESTIONS:

1. Should the United States seek to tighten the economic grip on Cuba? If so, why?

2. Should the United States normalize business relations with Cuba? If so, should the United States stipulate any conditions?

3. Assume you are Fidel Castro. What kind of trade relationship with the United States would be in your best interest? What type would you be willing to accept?

4. How does the structure of and relationships within the American political system influence the existence and specification of the trade embargo?

Chapter Notes

1   Data for this case were taken from the following sources: Justine Newsome and James Wilson, "Latin American Banana Growers Hail WTO Ruling," Financial Times (April 9, 1999): 4; Holman W. Jenkins, Jr., "Business World," Wall Street Journal (February 10, 1999): A23; Quentin Peel, "Banana Republican," Financial Times (November 14–15, 1998): 7; Martin Wolf, "Going Bananas," Financial Times (March 24, 1999): 14; Oswaldo Ramirez-Landazuri, "What Banana Trade Means to Ecuador," Financial Times (April 16, 1999): 16; Canute James and James Wilson, "The Big Place of the Banana in a Small Part of the World," Financial Times (March 19, 1999): 7; Mireya Navarro, "An Outpost in the Banana and Marijuana Wars," New York Times (March 4, 1999): A2; Canute James and George Parker, "U.S. Faces Caribbean Threat to Quit Drugs Treaty," Financial Times (March 8, 1999): 1; Guy de Jonquières, "WTO Puts Skids Under Banana Regime," Financial Times (March 20, 1999): 7; Frances Williams, "WTO Ruling Could Ruin Poor Banana Economies," Financial Times (September 10, 1996): 4; David Rosenbaum, "U.S. Threatens Europe with 100% Tariffs," New York Times (November 11, 1998): C4; Andrew Harig, "Far More Is at Stake Than Bananas and Beef," Journal of Commerce (June 16, 1999): 8; Charles Ogletree and Randall Robinson, "The Banana War's Missing Link—Campaign Funding," Christian Science Monitor (March 31, 1999): 11; Daniel Dombey, "EU Finds Bananas a Slippery Case," Financial Times (January 16, 1998): 5; Rachel Simpson, "Banana War Victims Make Plea," The Guardian (June 19, 1999): 21; Annette McCann and Lucy Patton, "Split in Banana Dispute Tactics," The Herald (March 18, 1999): 2; Heidi Przybyla, "U.S. Firms Slipping on EU Banana Tariff," Journal of Commerce (April 6, 1999): 1A; David Sanger, "Miffed at Europe, U.S. Raises Tariffs for Luxury

Goods," New York Times (March 4, 1999): A1+; Guy de Jonquières, "Trade Goes Bananas," Financial Times (January 26, 1999): 15; Teresa Poole, "Goatherds Hit Hard by Row Over Bananas," The Independent (April 10, 1999): 16; Clive Crook, "The Great Banana Trade War—and Why It Matters," National Journal (March 13, 1999): 663; "U.S. Lifts 'Banana War' Sanctions," European Report (July 4, 2001): 513; Michael Mann and Edward Alden, "Europe Plans $300m Sanctions Retaliation on US," Financial Times (April 19, 2002); "A Fruity Peace: An End to the Banana War," The Economist (April 21, 2001): 2; "This Banana War Is No Laughing Matter," Business Week (March 22, 1999): 39; Daniel Altman, "Yes, Bananas They Handle, But Steel . . . Is It Too Hot?" New York Times (May 2, 2002); statement by EU trade Commissioner Sir Leon Brittan, Agra Europe (March 5, 1999): 5; "U.S. Imposes 100% Duties as EU Banana War Erupts," Business Week (March 22, 1999): 39; statement by U.S. Trade Representative Peter Scher, Agra Europe (March 5, 1999): 5; Joint statement by European Trade Commissioner Pascal Lamy, European Agriculture Commissioner Franz Fischler, U.S. Trade Representative Robert Zoellick, and U.S. Commerce Secretary Don Evans reported in "EU/U.S.: Transatlantic Deal Settles Banana War," European Report (April 12, 2001): 506.

2   Hans S. Nichols, "Taking the Fix out of Farm Subsidies," Insight on the New 17, (August 13, 2001): 20.

3   Nancy Dunne, "U.S. Shoots Itself in the Foot," Financial Times (August 22, 1995): 6.

4   Lori Kletzer, Job Loss from Imports: Measuring the Costs (Washington, DC: Institute for International Economics, 2001).

5   See Kenneth A. Couch, "Earnings Losses and Unemployment of Displaced Workers in Germany," Industrial and Labor Relations Review

54 (April 2001): 559; and David Margolis, "Worker Displacement in France," mimeograph (Paris: Universite de Paris, Pantheon-Sorbonne, 90, Rue de Tolbiac, 1999).

6   Fuat Sener, "Schumpeterian Unemployment, Trade And Wages," Journal of International Economics 54 (June 2001): 119.

7   This argument is most associated with the writings of Raul Prebisch, Hans Singer, and Gunnar Myrdal in the 1950s and 1960s. For a recent discussion, see John Waterbury, "The Long Gestation and Brief Triumph of Import-Substituting Industrialization," World Development 27, no. 2 (1999): 323–41.

8   Jiang Xueqin, "Letter from China," The Nation (March 4, 2002): 23.

9   Steve Padgitt, Peggy Petrzelka, Wendy Wintersteen, and Eric Imerman, "Integrated Crop Management: The Other Precision Agriculture," American Journal of Alternative Agriculture 16 (January 2001): 16.

10 Sergio Lence and Dermot Hayes, "U.S. Farm Policy and the Volatility of Commodity Prices and Farm Revenues," American Journal of Agricultural Economics 84 (May 2002): 335–52.

11 Craig R. Whitney, "Protesters Just Say No to 'McDo,' " New York Times (September 15, 1999): A17.

12 Esra F. Gencturk and M. Kotabe, "The Effect of Export Assistance Program Usage on Export Performance: A Contingency Explanation," Journal of International Marketing 9 (Summer 2001): 51–73.

13 See Hou Hexiang, "Vietnam to Accelerate Industrialization and Modernization of Rural Areas," Xinhua News Agency (June 2, 2002): 1008; "Pushing Ecuador into the 21st Century," LatinFinance (March 2002): 30, retrieved on July 17, 2002, from http://web.lexis-nexis.com/universe/; and "Is Inequality Decreasing? Debating

the Wealth and Poverty of Nations," *Foreign Affairs* (August 2002): 178.

14 See Gerald K. Helleiner, "Markets, Politics, and Globalization: Can the Global Economy Be Civilized?" *Global Governance* (July–Sept 2001): 243; Marina Murphy, "EU Chemicals Need Flexibility: A Level Playing Field Should Be Established Between the EU and US Chemicals Industries," *Chemistry and Industry* (July 1, 2002): 9; and Lisa Schmidt, "How U.S. Sees Trade Rows," *Calgary Herald* (June 25, 2002): A2.

15 Whitney, op. cit.

16 Harry Maurer and Afshin Molavi, "Carpet Merchants Need Some Magic," *Business Week*, (June 7, 1999): 4.

17 Kunai Bose, "India Set to Abandon Rice Export Curbs," *Financial Times* (September 8, 1999): 22.

18 See Wilfried Pauwels, Hylke Vandenbussche, and Marcel Weverberg. "Strategic Behaviour Under European Antidumping Duties," *International Journal of the Economics of Business* 8 (February 2001): 75; and Greg Mastel, "The U.S. Steel Industry and Antidumping Law," *Challenge* 42 (May–June 1999): 84.

19 Stephen Moore, "Tax Cut and Spend: The Profligate Ways of Congressional Republicans," *National Review* 53 (October 2001): 19.

20 George Leopold, "U.S. Eases Regulations on Cryptography Exports," *Electronic Engineering Times* (July 24, 2000): 43.

21 Michael Hirsh, "The Great Technology Giveaway?" *Foreign Affairs* 77, no. 5 (September–October 1998): 2–9.

22 James Dao, "U.S. to Punish 10 Businesses for Iran Sales," *New York Times* (July 20, 2002): D1.

23 Kathleen Parker, "Exposure, Not Embargoes, Will Free Fidel's Cuba," *Seattle Times* (March 14, 2001): B6.

24 "EU/Latin America/Caribbean: Leaders Aim to Revive Ties," *European Report* (May 15, 2002): 501.

25 See Tony Walker, "China Warns Australia over Dalai Lama Visit," *Financial Times* (September 18, 1996): 1; and Ying Ma, "China's America Problem," *Policy Review* (February 2002): 43–57.

26 Ann Kent, "States Monitoring States: the United States, Australia, and China's Human Rights, 1990–2001," *Human Rights Quarterly* 23 (August 2001): 583–625.

27 Gail L. Cramer, James M. Hansen, and Eric J. Wailes, "Impact of Rice Tariffication on Japan and the World Rice Market," *American Journal of Agricultural Economics* 81 (December 1999): 1149.

28 Matthew Fraser, "Foreign Ownership Rules Indefensible: And There Appears to be Appetite for Change," *Financial Post* (May 28, 2001): C2.

29 C. Christopher Baughn and Mark A. Buchanan, "Cultural Protectionism," *Business Horizons* 44 (November–December 2001): 5–16.

30 Guy de Jonquières, "Report Says EU's Tariffs No Longer Cost Effective," *Financial Times* (April 15, 1996): 3.

31 Bernard Hoekman and Kym Anderson, "Developing-Country Agriculture and the New Trade Agenda," *Economic Development & Cultural Change* 49 (October 2000): 171.

32 Nicholas Elliot, "U.S. Farm Subsidies Under Fire: Benefits Will Spread," *Barron's* (January 28, 2002): 10.

33 "EU, U.S. Agree to Work on Issue of Subsidies to Boeing, Airbus," Associated Press (January 18, 2002).

34 See Chi-Chur Chao and Eden S. H. Yu, "Import Quotas, Tied Aid, Capital Accumulation, and Welfare," *Canadian Journal of Economics* 34 (August 2001): 661; and Mark Rice, "Australia Must Join Other Countries in Untying Overseas Aid," *Australian Financial Review* (April 4, 2002): 59.

35 Bill Mongelluzzo and Jack Lucentini, "October Surprise," *Journal of Commerce* (October 23, 2000): 10.

36 David Pilling, "First, Bribe Your Customs Officer," *Financial Times* (October 31, 1996): 6.

37 Mohsin Habib and Leon Zurawicki, "Corruption and Foreign Direct Investment," *Journal of International Business Studies* 33 (Summer 2002): 291–308.

38 See Douglas Harbrecht and James B. Treece, "Tread Marks on Detroit," *Business Week* (May 31, 1993): 30; and Judy Dempsey, "Car Importers Take Apart Customs Regulations," *Financial Times* (June 29–30, 1996): 2.

39 Peter J. Buckley, Jeremy Clegg, Nicolas Forsans, and Kevin T. Reilly, "Increasing the Size of the 'Country': Regional Economic Integration and Foreign Direct Investment in a Globalised World Economy," *Management International Review* 41 (July 2001): 251–75.

40 Philip Shenon, "In Hanoi, U.S. Goods Sold But Not by U.S.," *New York Times* (October 3, 1993): A1.

41 G. Scott Erickson, "Low-Level Trade Sanctions," *Global Competitiveness* 7 (1999): 375.

42 See Kimberly Ann Elliott and Gary Clyde Hufbauer, "Same Song, Same Refrain? Economic Sanctions in the 1990s," *AEA Papers and Proceedings* 89 (May 1999): 405–20, and Richard N. Haass, "Sanctioning Madness," *Foreign Affairs* 76 (November–December 1997): 74–85.

43 Stephen Zunes, "Foreign Policy by Catharsis: The Failure of U.S. Policy Toward Iraq," *Arab Studies Quarterly* 23 (Fall 2001): 69–87.

44 L. Chapell, "Japanese Carmakers Still Search for More U.S. Vehicle Content," *Automotive News* (May 24, 1999).

45 Blaise J. Bergiel and Erich B. Bergiel, "Country-of-Origin as a Surrogate Indicator: Implications/Strategies," *Global Competitiveness* 7 (1999): 187.

46 Judy Steed, "Caution the Law with GMOs in Europe," *Toronto Star* (June 10, 2002): D2.

47 Peggy Sito, "Guangdong to Slash Internal Customs Delays," *South China Morning Post* (May 16, 2002): 1.

48 Jonathan Bell, "Plane Trading," *Airfinance Journal* (June 1998): 34–36.

49 Chong Ju Choi, Soo Hee Lee, and Jai Boem Kim. "A Note on Countertrade: Contractual Uncertainty and Transaction Governance in Emerging Economies," *Journal of International Business Studies* 30 (Spring 1999): 189.

50 "McDonnell and Partner Win $4 Billion British Copter Deal," *New York Times* (July 14, 1995): C5.

51 Chong Ju Choi, Soo Lee, and Jai Kim, op. cit.

52 Prabhakar Sinha, "New Vistas Open up for Insurance Agents," *The Times of India* (January 23, 2002).

53 Sara Robinson, "Workers Are Trapped In Limbo by I.N.S.," *New York Times* (February 29, 2000): A12.

54 Diana Tussie, "The Environment and International Trade Negotiations: Open Loops in the Developing World," *The World Economy* 22, no. 4 (June 1999): 535–45.

55 Two surveys of note include Program on International Policy Attitudes, "Americans on Globalization: A Study of US Public Attitudes" (March 28, 2000). This survey found that just 41 percent of Americans, when asked to rate the benefits of the "growth of international trade" on a zero to 10 scale, viewed it as more positive than negative. (See http://www.pipa.org/OnlineReports/Globalization /appendixc/appendixc.html.) Similarly, a poll by *The Wall Street Journal* and NBC reported that 58 percent of the people in the United States felt that trade is bad for the economy, 32 percent believed that it is good, and 10 percent had no opinion. See Jackie Calmes, "Despite Buoyant Economic Times, Americans Don't Buy Free Trade," *Wall Street Journal* (December 10, 1998): A10.

56 Joann Muller, "Autos: A New Industry; Yes, Detroit is Losing Market Share. But America is a Big Winner as Foreign Companies Turn the U.S. into the Center of a Global Industry," *Business Week* (July 15, 2002): 98.

57 Ralph G. Carter and Lorraine Eden, "Who Makes U.S. Trade Policy?" *The International Trade Journal* XIII, no. 1 (Spring 1999): 53–100.

58 Matt Moffett, "Citrus Squeeze," *Wall Street Journal* (September 6, 1998): A1.

59 Eugene Salorio, "Trade Barriers and Corporate Strategies: Why Some Firms Oppose Import Protection for Their Own Industry" (Unpublished DBA dissertation, Harvard University, 1991).

60 Data for the case were adapted from Alan Burchardt, "Containing Cuba" (graphic), *Indiana Daily Student* [Indiana University student newspaper, Bloomington, IN] (August 1, 1996): 4; Pascal Fletcher, "US Anti-Cuba Law Feeds Businessmen's Paranoia," *Financial Times* (July 2, 1996): 5; Lionel Barber, "Europe Vows to Act on US Anti-Cuba Law," *Financial Times* (July 16, 1996): 1; William M. Leo Grande, "From Havana to Miami: U.S. Cuba Policy as a Two-Level Game," *Journal of Interamerican Studies and World Affairs* 40, no. 1 (Spring 1998): 67–86; Albert R. Hunt, "End the Anachronistic Embargo Against Cuba," *Wall Street Journal* (April 22, 1999): A23; Pascal Fletcher, "Cuba Brands US Sanctions 'Genocide,'" *Financial Times* (September 14, 1999): 6; Mark Fineman, "Carter Visit May Boost Growing Cuba Trade," *Los Angeles Times* (May 17, 2002); Daniel P. Erikson, "The New Cuba Divide," *The National Interest* (Spring, 2002); Kathleen Parker, "Exposure, Not Embargoes, Will Free Fidel's Cuba," *Seattle Times* (March 14, 2001): B6; Stephen Handelman, "Will Bush Try to Refreeze Cuban Thaw?" *Toronto Star* (January 30, 2001); "Carter's Cuba Trip Stirs Storm of Debate," *Deutsche Presse-Agentur* (May 12, 2002); Albor Ruiz, "Shifts Start in U.S.-Cuban Relations," *Daily News* (January 14, 2002): 3; Keith Suter "U.S. Should Lift Failed Sanctions on Cuba," *Canberra Times* (May 23, 2002); and Michael Doyle, "State Eyeing Cuban Trade: Lawmakers are Seeking to Lift the Longtime Embargo," *Sacramento Bee* (July 30, 2002).

CHAPTER 7

REGIONAL ECONOMIC INTEGRATION AND COOPERATIVE AGREEMENTS

Marrying is easy, but housekeeping is hard.

—GERMAN PROVERB

OBJECTIVES

- To define different forms of economic integration and to describe how each form affects international business
- To describe the static and dynamic effects of as well as the trade creation and diversion dimensions of economic integration
- To present different regional trading groups, such as the European Union (EU), the North American Free Trade Agreement (NAFTA), and Asia-Pacific Economic Cooperation (APEC)
- To describe the rationale for and success of commodity agreements
- To discuss the effects of economic integration on the environment

CASE

Ford Europe[1]

T he year 2001 was one of the toughest ones that Ford Motor Company has ever faced. The Firestone tire recall, the global economic downturn, and tough competition led to a loss of $5.45 billion for the year. However, the outcome in Europe was different. Ford is facing several challenges in Europe, such as the continued integration of the euro, higher competition from Japanese automakers because of the elimination of quotas, and a fiercely competitive market. But in 2001, Ford's European management was able to pull off the biggest turnaround in Ford history—it was able to break even in 2001 after a $1.1 billion loss in 2000. What did Ford do to turn this ailing business around? Will it be able to continue its success amidst the dramatically changing environment in Europe?

FORD IN EUROPE—AN HISTORICAL OVERVIEW

Ford's first foray into Europe occurred in 1903, only six months after the company was founded, and this happened when the company sold its first export to a customer in the United Kingdom. This development was followed by the opening of Ford's first European sales branch in Paris in 1908 and a branch in the United Kingdom in 1909. Production began in a U.K. assembly plant in 1911, followed by a French assembly operation in 1913 and the establishment of a French company in 1916. Ford did not begin operations in Germany until 1925, and it established an assembly plant only a year later. During the next several decades, Ford's European operations ran as separate subsidiaries that reported to U.S. headquarters, but they did not coordinate their policies in any meaningful way. This development occurred because individual countries had different environments, different consumer tastes and preferences, and unique tariff and nontariff barriers to trade.

In time, Ford came to consider Europe as one common market rather than a collection of individual markets. In 1967, Ford changed its management structure to include its European operations under one regional umbrella organization known as Ford Europe Incorporated. Its two large U.K. and German manufacturing centers remained an important dimension of the new strategy, but they were no longer considered separate, independently operating companies. Despite nationalistic tendencies on the part of host-country management, Ford decided that, from the company's perspective, it was best to obliterate national boundaries, thus allowing the company to cut engineering costs and achieve economies of scale in purchasing and manufacturing. Ford began designing and assembling similar automobiles throughout Europe rather than engineer separate cars in each market, a strategy that resulted in such models as the Escort, the Capri, and the Fiesta.

In 1994, Ford announced a new program called Ford 2000, which led Ford to merge the North American Automotive Operations and European Automotive Operations a year later into a single organization, Ford Automotive Operations. The major reason for the restructuring was to cut costs and be more competitive. As stated in the 1994 annual report, "We can't allow human and financial resources to be wasted duplicating vehicle platforms, power trains and other basic components that serve nearly identical customer needs in different markets." In 1995, Ford announced that it was reducing the number of engine and transmission combinations used worldwide and the number of basic vehicle platforms. In addition, Ford replaced its regional profit centers after having adopted a product-line focus. Five vehicle centers were established within Ford Automotive Operations, "each with responsibility for worldwide development of the cars or trucks assigned to [it]." Europe took responsibility for the development of small and midsize cars.

Despite all of the reorganizing, it was obvious by 1998 that Ford 2000 was not working, especially in Europe. Profits were down, market share was slipping—Ford finally fell behind both Volkswagen and General Motors—and people complained about how Ford's products were old and tired and not well positioned in the market. Europe is considered by many to be the toughest car market in the world, one with very demanding car buyers. Even so, Europe provides significant market opportunity for Ford. The reduction of barriers and integration of the different country markets in Europe caused Ford to shift its strategy from multidomestic to regional, and then Ford 2000 shifted its focus to align with the United States. Price competition in Europe forced down Ford's profits, and its centralized strategy pushed it too far away from the local markets. For example, the small and compact car segment is small in the United States, but 60 percent of the cars sold in Europe are in this segment. Volkswagen, Renault, and even Toyota seem to understand this car segment better than Ford does.

THE TRANSFORMATION STRATEGY

In an attempt to bring greater autonomy to Europe, Ford's European management replaced Ford 2000 with its "transformation strategy" in early 2000; this strategy included tough cost cutting and the goal of launching 45 new brands within five years. After losing $1.1 billion in 2000, Ford's goal for Europe was to break even in 2001 and to make a profit in 2002. Management slimmed down operations by closing some factories and turning other factories into "flex factories," which can produce multiple cars on one production line. Capacity utilization has increased because the company can produce new models more quickly and in numbers that better meet demand. Because Europe's national boundaries are continuing to loosen, Ford can easily sell cars produced in the flex factories to multiple countries. The flex factories have helped Ford respond more quickly to Europe's unique local demand.

The transformation strategy has been a great success. Although Ford lost $5.45 billion worldwide in 2001, its market share increased in Europe, and Ford Europe has returned to profitability. Ford's U.S. operations plan to implement flex factories with hopes that Ford will see some of the success its European operations have enjoyed. But will Ford's success in Europe last? The European Union has required its countries to drop quotas on Japanese cars, and Honda, Toyota, and Nissan are making inroads quickly. In 2002, the euro strengthened, and this led to lower profits when restated into U.S. dollars. And with the drastic cost cutting Ford did in 2000 and 2001, there is little room for additional cost cutting in order to increase profitability. When examining Ford's changing strategy in Europe and its resulting success, how much is due to the European Union itself? Would Ford have done what it did in Europe had there been no EU?

INTRODUCTION

In some respects, the United States is the perfect example of economic integration—the largest economy in the world comprised of 50 states in the continental United States plus Alaska and Hawaii, a common currency, and perfect labor and capital mobility. However, it is just one country. What about the rest of the world? In Chapter 6, we discussed the efforts of the World Trade Organization to reduce tariff and nontariff barriers, with the eventual goal of global free trade. But the WTO is moving slowly. Faster progress is occurring at the regional level, where countries close together already engage in a significant amount of trade. Is this the more important movement? What does regional economic integration hope to accomplish, and where will it go in the new millennium?

In the mid- to late-1940s, countries decided that if they were going to emerge from the wreckage of World War II and promote economic growth and stability within their borders, they would have to assist—and get assistance from—nearby countries. This chapter discusses some of the important forms of economic cooperation, such as regional economic integration and commodity agreements. Regional economic integration is the political and economic agreements among countries that give preference to member countries to the agreement. For example, regional economic groups might reduce tariffs for member countries while keeping tariffs for nonmember countries. The lowest level of cooperation usually involves at least trade, although higher forms of regional economic integration go beyond trade. But trade is usually the cornerstone of any form of regional economic integration. Commodity agreements result in cooperation among producers of commodities, such as the oil-producing countries, or between producers and consumers of commodities such as coffee and tin.

Why do you need to understand the nature of these agreements? Regional trading groups are an important influence on MNEs' strategies. Such groups can define the size of the regional market and the rules under which companies must operate. Companies in the initial stages of foreign expansion must be aware of the regional economic groups that encompass countries with good manufacturing locations or market opportunities. As companies expand internationally, they must change their organizational structure and operating strategies to take advantage of regional trading groups. As noted in the opening case, Ford changed from being a multidomestic to a regional company in Europe; then it centralized its operations worldwide, and more recently it decentralized back to Europe in order to be responsive to national differences. The development of European integration forced Ford to look at its operations more carefully so that it could operate successfully in the market.

As noted in Chapter 6, WTO members are required to grant the same favorable trade conditions to all WTO members. However, the WTO also allows a departure from this principle in the case of regional trade agreements. Nearly all of the WTO members have concluded regional trade agreements (RTAs) with other countries. As noted on the WTO's Web site (www.wto.org/english/tratop_e/region_e/region_e.htm), over 150 RTAs were in existence as of the end of 2002. Over 50 percent of the RTAs involve the EU, and 60 percent are bilateral agreements. We focus on the European Union and the North American Free Trade Agreement because of the high level of integration in both areas—and especially the size and degree of integration in the EU. That is not to minimize the importance of other groups to their member countries, but we will use the groups that follow to illustrate different types of regional integration. Internet links will be provided to those groups with homepages. The most important thing is to understand how these organizations and agreements affect company strategy.

Companies need to adjust organizational structure and operating strategy to take advantage of regional trade groups.

Many of the regional trade agreements (RTAs) registered with the WTO are bilateral RTAs.

Commodity producing countries have sought to increase both the price of their commodities and their share of revenues from the final sales. For example, coffee farmers receive less than 10 percent of the price charged for coffee at retailers in high-income countries. The photo shows workers sorting coffee beans in Guatemala.

REGIONAL ECONOMIC INTEGRATION

It's logical that most trade groups contain countries in the same area of the world. Neighboring countries tend to ally for several reasons:

- The distances that goods need to travel between such countries is short.
- Consumers' tastes are likely to be similar, and distribution channels can be easily established in adjacent countries.
- Neighboring countries may have a common history and interests, and they may be more willing to coordinate their policies.[2]

There are four basic types of regional economic integration.

1. **Free trade area (FTA)**. The goal of an FTA is to abolish all tariffs between member countries. Free trade agreements usually begin modestly by eliminating tariffs on goods that already have low tariffs, and there is usually an implementation period during which all tariffs are eliminated on all products. At the same time tariffs are being eliminated, the members of the FTA might explore other forms of cooperation, such as the reduction of nontariff barriers or trade in services and investment, but the focus is clearly on tariffs. In addition, each member country maintains its own external tariff against non-FTA countries.

2. **Customs union**. In addition to eliminating internal tariffs, member countries levy a common external tariff on goods being imported from nonmembers. For example, the North American Free Trade Agreement between Canada, the United States, and Mexico has eliminated tariffs on trade among the three countries, but each country maintains a separate tariff with the outside world. If a British company exports a product to the United States, it likely will enter the country at a different tariff rate than if the product were exported to Canada or Mexico because each NAFTA country can set its own external rate. But if a U.S. company were to export a product to the United Kingdom and France, two members of the EU, which is also a customs union, the product would enter both countries at the same tariff rate. There would be no tariff advantage to the U.S. company to enter the EU by exporting to the United Kingdom versus France.

3. **Common market**. A common market, such as the European Union, has all the elements of a customs union but it also allows free mobility of production factors such as labor and capital. This means that labor, for example, is free to work in any country in the common market without restriction. In the absence of the common market arrangement, workers would have to apply to immigration for a visa, and that might be difficult to come by.

4. **Economic integration**. Countries create even greater social and economic harmonization by adopting common economic policies. Such as fiscal or monetary policies. For example, the EU has established a common currency complete with a common Central Bank, which discussed in more detail in Chapter 10. This level of cooperation creates a degree of political integration among member countries, which means they lose a bit of their sovereignty. No region has attained complete economic integration, although the EU—which we'll read about shortly—comes the closest.

The Effects of Integration

Regional economic integration can affect member countries in social, cultural, political, and economic ways. For example, prior to the NAFTA accord, Canada had a small but successful film industry. However, the reduction of trade barriers would have meant that U.S. films would have overrun the Canadian market. The provinces control film distribution in Canada, and one province—Quebec—requires that foreign (including U.S.) films bear a

Canadian government issue classification sticker before being sold or distributed in Canada. During the NAFTA negotiations, the Canadian government wanted to retain these restrictions in order to protect its film industry. The added regulatory restrictions by Quebec mean that fewer U.S. films are being distributed there than would be the case in a free trade environment.

MNEs are especially concerned with the economic effects of integration. As we noted in Chapter 6, the imposition of tariff and nontariff barriers disrupts the free flow of goods, affecting resource allocation. Regional economic integration reduces or eliminates those barriers for member countries. It produces both **static effects** and **dynamic effects**. Static effects are the shifting of resources from inefficient to efficient companies as trade barriers fall. Dynamic effects are the overall growth in the market and the impact on a company caused by expanding production and by the company's ability to achieve greater economies of scale. Static effects may develop when either of two conditions occurs.

1. **Trade creation**—production shifts to more efficient producers for reasons of comparative advantage, allowing consumers access to more goods at a lower price than would have been possible without integration. Companies that are protected in their domestic markets face real problems when the barriers are eliminated and they then attempt to compete with more efficient producers. The strategic implication is that companies that might not have been able to export to another country—even though they might be more efficient than producers in that country—are now able to export when the barriers come down. Thus, there will be more demand for their products, and the demand for the protected, less efficient products will fall.

2. **Trade diversion**—trade shifts to countries in the group at the expense of trade with countries not in the group, even though the nonmember companies might be more efficient in the absence of trade barriers.

For example, assume that U.S. companies are importing the same product from Mexico and Taiwan. If the United States enters into an FTA with Mexico but not with Taiwan, these companies might be more likely to import goods from Mexico than from Taiwan due to lower tariffs. This does not mean, however, that Mexican products are any better or cheaper (in the absence of integration) than the Taiwanese goods, but the lower tariff gives them a competitive edge in the market.

Dynamic effects of integration occur when trade barriers come down and the size of the market increases. For example, Argentina, a country of 37.4 million people, is a member of MERCOSUR, a common market encompassing Argentina, Brazil, Paraguay, and Uruguay. The size of that market is 221 million people. Argentine companies could export to the country's neighbors in the absence of a trade agreement, but high tariffs would probably limit their ability to compete. When the trade barriers come down, however, the market size confronting the Argentine company increases dramatically. Because of the larger size of the market, Argentine companies can increase their production, which will result in lower costs per unit, a phenomenon we call **economies of scale**. Companies can produce more cheaply, which is good because they must become more efficient to survive.

Another important dynamic effect is the increase in efficiency due to increased competition. Many MNEs in Europe have attempted to grow through mergers and acquisitions to achieve the size necessary to compete in the larger market.

Major Regional Trading Groups

There are two ways to look at different trading groups: by location and by type. There are major trading groups in every region of the world. It is impossible to cover every group in every region, so we will cover a few of the major groups. However, it is important to understand that each regional group fits into one of the types defined above: free trade area, customs

Static effects of integration—the shifting of resources from inefficient to efficient companies as trade barriers fall. Dynamic effects of integration—the overall growth in the market and the impact on a company caused by expanding production and by the company's ability to achieve greater economies of scale.

Trade creation—production shifts to more efficient producers for reasons of comparative advantage, allowing consumers access to more goods at a lower price than would have been possible without integration.

Trade diversion—trade shifts to countries in the group at the expense of trade with countries not in the group.

Economies of scale—the cost per unit falls as the number of units produced rises; occurs in regional integration because of the growth in the market size.

Regional integration:

* By location—Europe, North America, Asia, Africa
* By type—free trade area, customs union, common market, economic integration
* Offers location-specific advantages to foreign investors due to increased market size

union, common market, or economic integration, with most of them being an FTA or a customs union.

Companies are interested in regional trading groups for their markets, sources of raw materials, and production locations. The larger and richer the new market, the more likely it is to attract the attention of the major investor countries and companies.

THE EUROPEAN UNION

The largest and most comprehensive of the regional economic groups is the European Union. It began as a customs union, but the formation of the **European Parliament** and the establishment of a common currency, the euro, make the EU the most ambitious of all the regional trade groups. For detailed information on the history, structure, and function of the EU, visit its Web site at http://europa.eu.int/index_en.htm. The key milestones for the **European Union** are summarized in Table 7.1. Map 7.1 identifies the members of the European Union and other key European groups.

Because of the economic and human destruction left by World Word II, European political leaders realized that greater cooperation among their countries would help speed Europe's recovery. Many organizations were formed, including the **European Economic Community (EEC)**, which eventually emerged as the organization that would bring together the countries of Europe into the most powerful trading bloc in the world. The EEC, later called the **European Community (EC)** and finally the European Union (EU), set about to abolish internal tariffs in order to more closely integrate European markets and hopefully allow economic cooperation to help avoid further political conflict.

The EU's Organizational Structure

The European Union encompasses many governing bodies, among which are the **European Commission**, **European Council**, European Parliament, and the **European Court of Justice**. In Chapter 3, we noted how important it is for MNE management to understand the political environment of every country where it operates. The same is true for the EU. To be successful in Europe, MNEs need to understand the governance of the EU, just as they need to understand the governance process of each of the individual European countries in which they are investing or doing business. These institutions, set parameters under which MNEs must operate, so management needs to understand the institutions and how they make decisions that could affect corporate strategy.

European Commission   The Commission provides the EU's political leadership and direction. The original intent was for the Commission to act as a supranational government for Europe. There are three distinct functions of the Commission:

1. Initiating proposals for legislation
2. Guardian of the treaties
3. Manager and executor of Union policies and of international trade relationships[3]

The Commission manages the annual budget of the EU, manages the EU, and negotiates trade agreements.

The Commission has always had a significant amount of power in the EU. However, in 1999, the Commission came under severe criticism, and its power was seriously curtailed. The power is now shifting to the Council, which more clearly represents the interests of the governments and is more likely to consider the interests of individuals in the EU.

European Council   The Council is also known as the Council of Ministers, which is composed of different ministers of the member countries. However, this doesn't mean that there

---

The Commission initiates proposals for legislation, is the guardian of the treaties, and is the manager and executor of Union policies and of international trade relationships.

The Commission has lost power vis-à-vis the Council of Ministers.

⬤ **TABLE 7.1**

EUROPEAN UNION MILESTONES

From its inception in 1957, the EU has been moving toward complete economic integration. However, it is doubtful that its initial adherents ever dreamed that European cooperation would have achieved such integration as to move to a common currency.

1946   Winston Churchill calls for a United States of Europe.

1947   The Marshall Plan for the economic revival of a Europe devastated by war is announced.

1948   The Organization for European Economic Cooperation (OEEC) is created to coordinate the Marshall Plan.

1949   The North Atlantic Treaty is signed.

1951   The Six (Belgium, France, Germany, Italy, Luxembourg, the Netherlands) sign the Treaty of Paris establishing the European Coal and Steel Community (ECSC).

1952   The ECSC Treaty enters into force.

1957   The Six sign the Treaties of Rome establishing the European Economic Community (EEC) and the European Atomic Energy Community (Euratom or EAEC). They become effective on January 1, 1958.

1958   The basis for the Common Agricultural Policy is introduced.

1959   The first steps are taken in the progressive abolition of customs duties and quotas within the EEC.

1960   The Stockholm Convention establishes the European Free Trade Association (EFTA) among seven European countries (Austria, Denmark, Norway, Portugal, Sweden, Switzerland, the United Kingdom). The OEEC becomes the Organization for Economic Cooperation and Development (OECD).

1961   The first regulation on free movement of workers within the EEC comes into force.

1962   The Common Agricultural Policy is adopted.

1965   A treaty merging the ECSC, EEC, and Euratom is signed. The treaty enters into force on July 1, 1967.

1966   Agreement is reached on a value-added tax (VAT) system; a treaty merging the Executives of the European Communities comes into force; and the EEC changes its name to European Community (EC).

1967   All remaining internal tariffs are eliminated, and a common external tariff is imposed.

1972   The currency "snake" is established in which the Six agree to limit currency fluctuations between their currencies to 2.25 percent.

1973   Denmark, Ireland, and the United Kingdom become members of the EC.

1974   The European Council sets up a European Regional Development Fund (ERDF) and Regional Policy Committee.

1979   European Monetary System comes into effect; European Parliament is elected by universal suffrage for the first time.

1980   Greece becomes tenth member of the EC.

1985   Commission sends the Council a White Paper on completion of internal market by 1992.

1986   Spain and Portugal become the eleventh and twelfth members of the EC. Single European Act (SEA) is signed, improving decision-making procedures and increasing the role of the European Parliament; comes into effect on July 1, 1987.

1989   Collapse of the Berlin Wall; German Democratic Republic opens its borders.

1990   The first phase of European Monetary Union (EMU) comes into effect. Unification of Germany.

1992   European Union signed in Maastricht; adopted by member countries on November 1, 1993.

1993   The Single European Market comes into force (January 1, 1993).

       Council concludes agreement creating European Economic Area, effective January 1, 1994.

1994   European Monetary Institute comes into effect.

1995   Austria, Finland, Sweden become the thirteenth, fourteenth, and fifteenth members of the EU.

1996   An EU summit names the 11 countries that will join the European single currency with all EU countries joining but Britain, Sweden, Denmark (by their choice), and Greece (not ready).

1999   The euro, the single European currency, comes into effect (January 1, 1999).

2001   Greece becomes the twelfth country to adopt the euro (January 1, 2001).

2002   The euro coins and notes enter circulation (January 1, 2002).

       The EU announces 10 new countries to join the EU in May 2004 (October 2002).

Source: Found on the Web site for the European Union, The History of the European Union, November 2002. http://europe.eu.int/abc/history/index_en.htm.

MAP 7.1   European Trade and Economic Integration

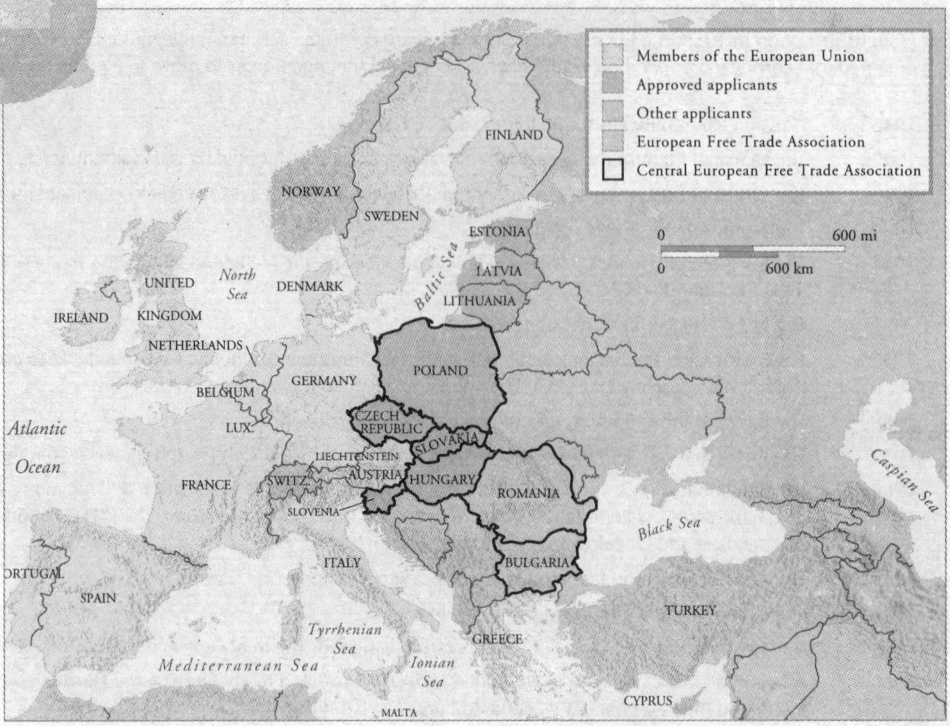

Although the EU remains the dominant trading bloc in Europe, the European Free Trade Association and Central European Free Trade Association are other regional trading blocs that promote free trade.

The Council of Ministers is a collection of 25 different councils representing the different ministries in each country, such as the Ministers of Agriculture. These councils have the final say over legislation in conjunction with Parliament.

The European Council or European Summit is comprised of the heads of state and government of each member country.

The three major responsibilities of the European Parliament are legislative power, control over the budget, and supervision of executive decisions.

is just one member of the Council for each EU member country. There are more than 25 different councils, such as Foreign Affairs, Economy and Finance, and Agriculture.[4] For example, the Agriculture Council of Ministers is comprised of the Ministers of Agriculture of all member countries. This specific council, whose members represent their member governments, decides issues dealing with agriculture. In many respects, the Council is much more democratic than the Commission because its members are elected officials in their home countries. The Council of Ministers is presided over by a presidency, which rotates between the member states every six months.

The Council has a tremendous amount of authority because it can adopt Commission-proposed legislation, amend it, or ignore it. The Council has the final say in legislative matters in cooperation with Parliament. The European Council is important because it sets priorities, gives political direction, and resolves issues that the Council of Ministers cannot resolve. The ascendancy of the European Council, or Council of Ministers, means that the efforts of the EU will have more influence and support by the individual countries, and this could hasten the integration process. Now the European Council will lead, the European Commission will be its servant and draftsman, and the European Parliament will be its sounding board.[5]

The European Parliament   The Parliament is composed of 626 members who are elected every five years, and its membership is based on country population. The three major responsibilities of the Parliament are legislative power, control over the budget, and supervision of executive decisions. The Commission presents community legislation to the Parliament. Parliament must approve the legislation before submitting it to the Council for adoption.[6]

The European Court of Justice   The Court of Justice ensures consistent interpretation and application of EU treaties. Member states, EC institutions, or individuals and companies may bring cases to the Court. The Court of Justice is an appeals court for individuals, firms, and organizations fined by the Commission for infringing Treaty Law.[7] The Court of Justice is relevant to MNCs because it deals mostly with economic matters. The Court is required to hear every case referred to it, even minor disputes over trade regulation and export issues. In recent cases, for example, the Court of Justice has taken up a high-profile case involving aviation agreements between the United States and Europe; it is deciding whether it is lawful for the EU to force a U.S.-based pharmaceutical company to share its data-collection process with its German competitors; and it is hearing an appeal by General Electric regarding the European Commission's refusal to allow GE to acquire Honeywell.[8]

The European Court of Justice ensures consistent interpretation and application of EU treaties.

THE SINGLE EUROPEAN MARKET

The European Union has been moving toward a single market since the passage of the Single European Act of 1987. Among other things, the act included the elimination of the remaining barriers to a free market, such as customs posts, different certification procedures, rates of **value-added tax**, and excise duties. Although progress is being made, a survey of the European business community at the end of 2001 revealed that trade would be improved with the easing of national and EU rules. Particularly, the study revealed that:

- a large number of companies are dissatisfied with the quality of their regulatory environment.
- most companies have not yet felt any impact from government's attempts to simplify legislation, particularly companies in France, Germany, and Denmark.
- at least €50 billion could be saved with better-quality legislation.
- Finland is regarded as the easiest member state to trade with, whereas the United Kingdom and Italy are the most difficult.[9]

The Single European Act was designed to eliminate the remaining nontariff barriers to trade in Europe. In spite of significant progress, there are still barriers to trade that need to be eliminated.

Common Trade and Foreign Policy

The EU Web site states, "The European Union is today the leading player in international trade, ahead of the United States and Japan. At a time of strong growth in international trade, it accounts for a fifth of world trade. The Union's influence on the international stage hinges on its ability to negotiate with its trade partners as a single entity."[10] As Table 7.2 shows, the EU membership in 2001 had a population and GNI just behind NAFTA (Canada, the United States, and Mexico), making it a formidable economic bloc.

The United States is the EU's largest trading partner. Relations between the two trading powerhouses worsened in early 2001 when the United States passed heavy steel tariffs and farm subsidies. Tensions have eased as the United States continues to add EU exemptions to the steel tariff and as the United States promises to ease agricultural protectionist measures. The EU also won a ruling by the WTO in August 2002 against the United States, which had been granting tax breaks to its companies that had a foreign presence. The WTO ruled this to be an illegal export subsidy, allowing the EU to impose sanctions on the United States of up to $4 billion. The EU will most likely wait to apply the sanctions, hoping that the United States will change its tax laws, thus helping to ease the trade tensions that already exist.[11] There are still barriers to trade with the United States, including tariffs, differences in legal and regulatory systems, and the absence of international standards.

The EU is currently working on trade agreements with Chile and the MERCOSUR trade group. An agreement was signed in June 2002 between Chile and the EU to improve political, economic, and trade relations. The EU will have negotiating rounds with MERCOSUR in 2002 and 2003, but things are moving slowly because of the economic crisis in Argentina and because of the political and economic problems in Brazil—the two largest players in MERCOSUR.[12]

● **TABLE 7.2**

COMPARATIVE DATA ON FIVE MAJOR TRADE GROUPS, 2001

	POPULATION (THOUSANDS)	GNI (MILLION US $)	PER CAPITA GNI (US $)
APEC	2,511,000	$16,305,089	$13,893
ASEAN	506,448	541,445	7,332
EU-15	385,400	8,307,426	23,815
EU-10 (to join in 2004)	75,093	329,131	10,795
EU Applicant-3	95,051	231,096	5,827
NAFTA	405,307	9,922,380	21,807
MERCOSUR	213,219	1,035,499	7,978

Source: World Bank, *World Bank Atlas 2001* (Washington, DC: The World Bank, 2001), *pp. 44–45.*

During the formation of the European Union, the organizing countries focused mainly on economic integration and left foreign policy to the individual countries. Realizing the benefits a common foreign policy would be to the EU, member countries began formalizing objectives in 1993 on armed conflicts, human rights, and other international foreign policy issues. Progress in this area has been slow, and the desire to incorporate an EU rapid-reaction force is constantly stalled due to differences in member opinion. National attitudes are currently the driving force behind European policy. Most European countries support the United States in the war on terror. However, countries are splintered in their views on the Middle East. Although Britain supports the United States in the war on Iraq, other countries oppose the views of the United States. The EU will continue to push toward a common foreign policy that will help align national differences and bring the member nations one step closer to complete integration.[13]

The Treaty of Maastricht sought to foster political union and monetary union.

EU countries that joined the new European Monetary Union had to converge their economic policies to reduce public deficits and debt as well as reduce inflation and interest rates.

The Euro

Not content with the economic integration envisaged in the Single European Act, the EU nations signed the Treaty of Maastricht in 1992, which set steps to accomplish two goals: political union and monetary union. The decision to move to a common currency in Europe has eliminated currency as a barrier to trade. To replace each national currency with a single European currency called the euro, the countries had to converge their economic policies first. It is not possible to have 15 different monetary policies and one currency. Those that met the criteria are part of the **European Monetary Union (EMU)**. Termed the stability and growth pact, the criteria outlined in the treaty and which continue for euro applicants today are the following:

Annual government deficit must not exceed 3 percent of GDP.

Total outstanding government debt must not exceed 60 percent of GDP.

Rate of inflation must remain within 1.5 percent of the three best performing EU countries.

Average nominal long-term interest rate must be within 2 percent of the average rate in the three countries with the lowest inflation rates.

Exchange rate stability must be maintained, meaning that for at least two years, the country concerned has kept within the "normal" fluctuation margins of the European Exchange Rate Mechanism.[14]

After a great deal of effort, 11 of the 15 countries in the EU joined the EMU on January 1, 1999. Greece joined on January 1, 2001. Those not yet participating in the euro are the

United Kingdom, Sweden, and Denmark (by their choice). Sweden announced in July 2002 that it has met all the criteria for joining the EMU, although it has not set a date for entry.[15] The euro is being administered by the **European Central Bank (ECB)**, which was established on July 1, 1998. The ECB has been responsible for setting monetary policy and for managing the exchange-rate system for all of Europe since January 1, 1999.

In its first year of operation, the euro fluctuated in value between a high of $1.1827 per euro to a low of nearly $1.00 per euro (and briefly lower in intraday trading). It fell in value compared to the U.S. dollar for most of 2000 and 2001 and began rising again in 2002. Some analysts believe it is still undervalued by 15 percent and will continue its upward swing.[16] The ECB began distributing actual banknotes, replacing individual national currencies on January 1, 2002.

The move to the euro has been smoother than predicted. It is affecting companies in a variety of ways. Banks had to update their electronic networks to handle all aspects of money exchange, such as systems that trade global currencies, that buy and sell stocks, that transfer money between banks, that manage customer accounts, or that print out bank statements. Deutsche Bank estimated that the conversion process cost several hundred million dollars.[17] Other companies feel that the euro will increase price transparency (the ability to compare prices in different countries) and eliminate foreign-exchange costs and risks. However, three years after the launch of the euro, large pricing gaps are prevalent among European countries. Although some price differences are due to shipping costs and the like, there are still wide differences in Europe that will have to narrow. For example, the Fiat Seicento is 63 percent more expensive in Britain than it is in Spain, and a bottle of Coca-Cola is twice as expensive in Denmark as it is in Germany.[18] Foreign-exchange costs are narrowing as companies operate in only one currency in Europe, and foreign-exchange risks between member states are also disappearing, although there are still foreign-exchange risks between the euro and non-member currencies, such as the U.S. dollar.

EU Expansion

One of the EU's major challenges is that of expansion. The next level of expansion, set for 2004, is to include Poland, Hungary, the Czech Republic, Slovenia, Slovakia, Latvia, Estonia, Lithuania, Malta, and Cyprus. Bulgaria and Romania have been given a date of 2007, and Turkey has been put on hold while it continues to improve its human rights record.[19] Map 7.1 shows the current countries of the EU and the expansion countries. On July 1, 1992, the Central European Free Trade Association (CEFTA) went into effect, with the Czech Republic, Slovakia, Hungary, and Poland as members. Since CEFTA's inception, Bulgaria, Romania, and Slovenia have joined the economic cooperation. CEFTA's goal was to establish a free trade area by 2000 that has the EU's basic trade structure.[20] Although some of these countries will join the EU in 2004, CEFTA countries continue to promote trade and prepare for accession to the EU.[21]

The acquisition of the 13 new countries will increase the EU's population by 100 million, enlarge its land by one-third, and add $400 billion to its economic output.[22] But the admission will bring many difficult problems to the zone. Most countries in Central and Eastern Europe are poor, have fledgling democracies, and depend greatly on agriculture—as much as 20 percent of GNI, compared with only 6 percent on average in the EU. They will thus strain the EU's financial resources. As noted in Table 7.2, in 2001, these 13 had a significantly lower per capita GNI ($9,648) than the existing 15 members of the EU ($23,815). Another problem of expansion is governance. Both geographically and economically large members of the EU, such as France and Germany, fear that the addition of so many new countries will weaken their control and influence. On the other hand, the addition of 10 new countries, and possibly 3 more later, will certainly move the EU ahead of NAFTA in total population and increase the EU's power as an international trading block.

The euro

- Is a common currency in Europe
- Is administered by the European Central Bank
- Initially involved all EU member countries except the United Kingdom, Denmark, Sweden, and Greece
- Was established on January 1, 1999
- Resulted in new bank notes in 2002

The EU is set to expand to at least 13 more countries, mostly from Central and Eastern Europe.

In addition, the EU has signed numerous free trade agreements with other countries around the world, making it the largest trading bloc in the world. This means that companies doing business in one EU country have access to a much larger market than anywhere else in the world.

Implications of the EU on Corporate Strategy

The EU is a tremendous market in terms of both population and income, and so it is one that companies cannot ignore. Merger and acquisition activity has really picked up in Europe. The market in Europe is still considered fragmented and inefficient compared with the United States, so most experts feel that mergers, takeovers and spinoffs will continue in Europe for years to come. U.S. companies are buying European companies to gain a market presence and to get rid of competition. An example was Staples' acquisition of the mail-order business of French retailer Pinault Printemps Redoute (PPR) SA in 2002. Staples was finding it difficult to expand its operations in Europe, but with the purchase of PPR, it will acquire stores in France, Belgium, Italy, Spain, and the United Kingdom and will increase sales by $600 million.[23]

European firms are also acquiring other European firms to improve their competitive advantage against U.S. companies and to expand their market presence. A good example is the purchase of Promodes Group, a French retailer, by Carrefour, another French retailer. That merger resulted in the creation of the number-one retailer in Europe.[24] Carrefour, in second place worldwide behind Wal-Mart, is still larger than Wal-Mart in foreign markets and is a formidable challenger to the number-one retailer in the world.

Due to the gloomy economic outlook in the EU and the strength of the euro, business confidence at the end of 2002 was low. Although the stronger euro proves its success amidst economic woes, it also has its downside for European business. Companies feel they are getting priced out of export markets and that U.S. demand for euro-priced goods is falling as goods become more expensive relative to the dollar. As the chief executive for Volvo Car Corp. put it, "I have to say, a stronger dollar helps the business."[25] Some companies feel they can't react quickly enough to the rise in the euro because of new EU regulations and strict employment protection laws. These external issues may force European regulators to sort out the EU's labor problems and force companies to lower costs to become more competitive— both beneficial moves in the long run.

Although Europe is moving closer together through the euro and the Single Market program, it is still not as homogeneous as is the U.S. market. Differences in languages, cultures, and governments still splinter Europe, and the eventual addition of the 13 new countries will create even more divisions in the market. Thus, companies need to develop a pan-European strategy without sacrificing different national strategies. Ford found this out, as noted in the opening case. National differences still mean something, even though it is important to establish pan-European strategies in areas where it makes sense.

Where Next for the EU?

The Economist identified five fundamental shifts that have occurred in the EU that will dramatically affect its future:

1. *The inversion of the Franco-German balance.* France had always had political control of the EU and could take the high road as a result of World War II. However, Germany's confidence has returned as a result of the reunification of the East and West, and Germany is now the largest and richest country in Europe. Germany may be the only country that can lead Europe in the future.

2. *A sense that the EU should possess a capacity for collective military action separate or separable from NATO.* This was confirmed in the Kosovo conflict in which the United States took control of a European conflict, and it could be an issue in the war on terrorism.

3. *The introduction of the euro.*

4. *The weakening of the European Commission and the ascendancy of national governments in controlling the destiny of the EU.*

5. *The planned enlargement of the EU.*[26]

There have been some proposal by some of Europe's leaders to take the EU even farther down the road of integration. Among the propositions are that the EU should:

- Abolish the right of individual EU countries to run their own foreign policies. Instead, as the head of the Commission says, the EU should "speak with one voice on all aspects of external relations."[27]

- Have the right to raise direct taxes.

- Use common border controls.

- Integrate the European police force.

- Influence the national governments' budgets much more strongly.

- Create a European president by allowing national leaders to elect a politician to run the Council of Ministers.[28]

The EU will move closer to a free-market, borderless economy as the European Court of Justice continues to remove obstacles to takeovers, thus making it easier to trade. As reported in the *Wall Street Journal*, "Soon the judges may go even further: opening the airline industry to consolidation; limiting the EU's power to force companies to share intellectual property; and further weakening the EU's ability to stop corporate deals."[29] EU nations are finding it difficult to meet the criteria of the stability and growth pact partially because of the recent downturn in the economy. Germany, France, Italy, and Portugal will likely fail to reach the target for government deficits by 2004, thus forcing the deadline to be moved to 2006. Changes will most likely be made to the stability and growth pact as a result of the entry of the 10 countries in 2004 or the future adoption of the euro by Britain.[30] Many issues face the EU as we move into the new millennium, but there are many opportunities for companies to expand their markets and sources of supply as the EU grows and encompasses more of Europe.

NORTH AMERICAN FREE TRADE AGREEMENT (NAFTA)

NAFTA, which includes Canada, the United States, and Mexico, went into effect in 1994. The United States and Canada historically have had various forms of mutual economic cooperation. They signed the **Canada–U.S. Free Trade Agreement** effective January 1, 1989, which eliminated all tariffs on bilateral trade by January 1, 1998. In February 1991, Mexico approached the United States to establish a free-trade agreement. The formal negotiations that began in June 1991 included Canada. The resulting North American Free Trade Agreement became effective on January 1, 1994.

NAFTA has a logical rationale, in terms of both geographic location and trading importance. Although Canadian-Mexican trade was not significant when the agreement was signed, U.S.-Mexican and U.S.-Canadian trade were. The two-way trading relationship between the United States and Canada is the largest in the world. As noted in Table 7.2, NAFTA is a powerful trading bloc with a combined population and total GNI greater than the 15-member EU. Table 7.3 shows the breakdown of population, GNI, and per capita GNI for the three NAFTA members. What is significant, especially when compared with the EU, is the tremendous size of the U.S. economy in comparison to those of Canada and Mexico. In addition, Canada has a much richer economy than that of Mexico, even though its population is about one-third that of Mexico.

The North American Free Trade Agreement

- Was preceded by free trade agreements between the United States and Canada
- Includes Canada, the United States, and Mexico
- Went into effect on January 1, 1994
- Is a large trading bloc but includes countries of different sizes and wealth

NAFTA rationale

- U.S.-Canadian trade is the largest bilateral trade in the world
- The United States is Mexico's and Canada's largest trading partner

⬤ **TABLE 7.3**

COMPARATIVE NAFTA DATA

		POPULATION (MILLIONS)	GNI (BILLIONS US $)	GNI PER CAPITA (US $)
NAFTA	Canada	30.491	$614,003	$25,440
	Mexico	96,586	428,877	8,070
	United States	278,230	8,879,500	31,910
		405,307	**9,922,380**	**21,807**

Source: World Bank, *World Bank Atlas 2001* (Washington, DC: The World Bank, 2001) pp. 44–45.

NAFTA calls for the elimination of tariff and nontariff barriers, the harmonization of trade rules, the liberalization of restrictions on services and foreign invest-ment, the enforcement of intel-lectual property, and a dispute settlement process.

NAFTA covers the following areas:

- *Market access*—tariff and nontariff barriers, rules of origin, and government procurement
- *Trade rules*—safeguards, subsidies, countervailing and antidumping duties, health and safety standards
- *Services*—provides for the same safeguards for trade in services (consulting, engineering, software, etc.) that exist for trade in goods
- *Investment*—establishes investment rules governing minority interests, portfolio invest-ment, real property and majority-owned or controlled investments from the NAFTA counties; in addition, NAFTA coverage extends to investments made by any company incorporated in a NAFTA country, regardless of country of origin
- *Intellectual property*—all three countries pledge to provide adequate and effective protec-tion and enforcement of intellectual property rights, while ensuring that enforcement measures do not themselves become barriers to legitimate trade
- *Dispute settlement*—provides a dispute-settlement process that will be followed; desired to keep countries from taking unilateral action against an offending party[31]

Most tariffs will be eliminated by 2004, some by 2008.

Mexico made significant strides in tariff reduction after joining GATT in 1986. At that time, its tariffs averaged 100 percent. Since then, it has reduced tariffs dramatically. As a result of NAFTA, most tariffs on originating goods traded between Mexico and Canada were eliminated immediately or phased in over a 10-year period that is to end on December 31, 2003. In a few exceptions, the phase-out period will be completed by the end of 2008. Tariffs between the United States and Mexico were, in general, either eliminated immediately or over a 5- or 10-year period that is to end on December 31, 2003. Although most tariffs will be eliminated in 5 or 10 equal annual stages, there are some exceptions. In the first five years of NAFTA, Mexico trimmed its average tariff on U.S. goods from 10 percent to 2 percent, while U.S. tariffs on Mexican products dropped to less than 1 percent.[32]

NAFTA provides the static and dynamic effects of economic integration discussed earlier in this chapter. For example, Canadian and U.S. consumers benefit from lower-cost agricul-tural products from Mexico, a static effect of economic liberalization. U.S. producers also benefit from the large and growing Mexican market, which has a huge appetite for U.S. products—a dynamic effect.

NAFTA is a good example of trade diversion; some U.S. trade with and investment in Asia has been diverted to Mexico.

In addition, NAFTA is a good example of trade diversion. Many U.S. and Canadian companies have established manufacturing facilities in Asia to take advantage of cheap labor. Now, U.S. and Canadian companies can establish manufacturing facilities in Mexico rather than in Asian countries to take advantage of relatively cheap labor. For example, IBM is mak-ing computer parts in Mexico that were formerly made in Singapore. In five years, IBM boosted exports from Mexico to the United States from $350 million to $2 billion. Had the subassemblies not been made in and exported from Mexico, they would have been made in Singapore and other Asian locations and exported to the United States. Gap Inc. and Liz Claiborne are increasingly buying garments from Mexican contractors, who can offer faster delivery than can Asian contractors.[33]

Rules of Origin and Regional Content

An important component of NAFTA is the concept of rules of origin and regional content. Because NAFTA is a free trade agreement and not a customs union, each country sets its own tariffs to the rest of the world. That is why a product entering the United States from Canada must have a commercial or customs invoice that identifies the product's ultimate origin. Otherwise, an exporter from a third country would always ship the product to the NAFTA country with the lowest tariff and then re-export it to the other two countries duty-free. "Rules of origin ensure that only goods that have been the subject of substantial economic activity within the free trade area are eligible for the more liberal tariff conditions created by NAFTA."[34]

According to regional content rules, at least 50 percent of the net cost of most products must come from the NAFTA region. The exceptions are 55 percent for footwear, 62.5 percent for passenger automobiles and light trucks and the engines and transmissions for such vehicles, and 60 percent for other vehicles and automotive parts.[35] For example, a Ford car assembled in Mexico could use parts from Canada, the United States, and Mexico, as well as labor and other factors from Mexico. For the car to enter Canada and the United States according to the preferential NAFTA duty, at least 62.5 percent of its value must come from North America.

Special Provisions of NAFTA

Most free trade agreements in the world are based solely on one goal: to reduce tariffs. However, NAFTA is a very different free trade agreement. Due to strong objections to the agreement by labor unions and environmentalists, two side agreements covering those issues were included in NAFTA. When first debating NAFTA, opponents worried about the potential loss of jobs in Canada and the United States to Mexico as a result of Mexico's cheaper wages, poor working conditions, and lax environmental enforcement. NAFTA opponents, particularly U.S. union organizers, thought companies would close down factories in the north and set them up in Mexico. As a result, the labor lobby in the United States forced the inclusion of labor standards, such as the right to unionize, and the environmental lobby pushed for an upgrade of environmental standards in Mexico and the strengthening of compliance.[36]

From a labor standpoint, the NAFTA side agreement "sets forth the following general objectives: improving working conditions and living standards, promoting compliance with and effective enforcement of labor laws, promoting the Agreement's principles through cooperation and coordination, and promoting publication and exchange of information to enhance mutual understanding of Parties' laws, institutions and legal systems."[37]

From an environmental standpoint, the NAFTA side agreement, "include[s] the promotion of sustainable development, cooperation on the conservation, protection and enhancement of the environment, and the effective enforcement of and compliance with domestic environmental laws. The Agreement promotes transparency and public participation in the development and improvement of environmental laws and policies."[38] Pollution levels in Mexico have increased since the signing of NAFTA partly because there is a strong positive correlation between pollution and economic growth. However, Mexican environmental standards are getting tougher, and enforcement of those standards is improving.

Labor and environmental activists were emboldened with their success at disrupting the WTO meetings in Seattle, Washington, in November 1999, so they are expected to continue

---

Rules of origin—goods and services must originate in North America to get access to lower tariffs.

Regional content

- The percentage of value that must be from North America for the product to be considered "North American" in terms of country of origin
- 50 percent for most products; 62.5 percent for most autos

Additional NAFTA provisions

- Workers' rights
- The environment
- Dispute resolution mechanism

to press for improvements in labor rights and the environment in NAFTA countries. The unions are disappointed with the results of the side agreement and recognize that enforcement to punish those who break labor and environmental standards is weak. President Bush agrees that he would like to improve such standards.

Impact of NAFTA on Trade, Investment, and Jobs

The test of any regional trading group is whether it creates trade and jobs. Since NAFTA has been in place, the United States, Canada, and Mexico have all tripled their business dealings, with trade among the countries equaling $1.7 billion per day. U.S. exports to Mexico have increased, but Mexican exports to the U.S. have surged even more—$135.9 billion in 2000 compared to $49.4 billion in 1994.[39]

The investment and employment pictures are far more complicated. One concern for U.S. workers was that investment would move to Mexico due to that country's lower wages and lax environmental standards. Wages are significantly lower in Mexico than they are in the United States and Canada, as noted in Table 7.4. In fact, they are lower than wages in many of the industrialized countries of Asia. When NAFTA was signed, companies like IBM and Canon began investing in Mexico instead of Asia for certain types of manufacturing. They could enjoy many tax and tariff exemptions, labor was plentiful and cheap, and high U.S. demand was just miles away. Foreign investment in Mexico rose from $4 billion per year in 1993 to $11.8 billion per year in 1999.[40] However, when NAFTA required Mexico to strip the *maquiladoras* (companies on the Mexican border) of their duty-free status in 2001, foreign companies started looking elsewhere. This was also compounded by the weakening U.S. economy and the stronger peso. Companies like Sanyo, Canon, and French battery producer Saft are leaving Mexico and relocating to China, Vietnam, and Guatemala, where labor is cheaper.[41]

However, only 2.6 percent of all U.S. foreign direct investment is in Mexico, compared with 10.6 percent in Canada. Mexico is only the twelfth most important location for U.S.

● **TABLE 7.4**

HOURLY COMPENSATION COSTS FOR PRODUCTION WORKERS IN MANUFACTURING, IN U.S. DOLLARS

Hourly compensation costs of manufacturing workers are significantly higher in the United States and Canada than in Mexico, where wages are also lower than in some of the newly industrialized countries in Asia.

COUNTRY	WAGE
Germany	$22.99
Japan	22.00
United States	19.86
Canada	16.16
Mexico	2.46
Hong Kong	5.53
Korea	8.13
Singapore	7.42
Taiwan	5.98

Source: United States Department of Labor, Bureau of Labor Statistics, "International Comparisons of Manufacturing Hourly Compensation Costs" (2000): http://stats.bls.gov/news.release/ichcc.toc.htm.

foreign direct investment, and it is not even the most important location for U.S. FDI in the Americas—Brazil is more important. However, in order to take advantage of NAFTA, countries like Germany and Japan are pouring a lot of FDI into Mexico.

NAFTA Expansion

When the United States began its discussions with Mexico and Canada, it perceived a future effort to pull together North, Central, and South America into an "Enterprise of the Americas." For the last seven years, representatives from 34 countries have been meeting to join the Americas into the Free Trade Area of the Americas (FTAA). Although negotiations have been slow, President Bush is a strong advocate of the agreement. With fast-track trade negotiating power under his belt, he will be a powerful force behind negotiations. If adopted, the FTAA will be the world's largest trade block, with a population of 800 million and $11 trillion in combined GDP.[42] In the meantime, Canada and Mexico have both entered into free trade agreements with Chile, perceived to be the next country that could join NAFTA, and the agreements were modeled after NAFTA. Free trade in the Americas will benefit companies greatly. An example is U.S.-based Caterpillar. When Caterpillar exports its motor graders to Chile, it must pay $15,000 in tariffs. If it manufactures the motor graders in Brazil and ships them to Chile, it only pays $3,700 in tariffs. However, Caterpillar's Canadian competitors can ship to Chile free of tariffs because of the Canada-Chile FTA.[43]

Mexico also entered into a free trade agreement with the European Union on July 1, 2001, that will end all tariffs on bilateral trade by 2007. EU officials feel that the FTA is important for them, because their share of trade with Mexico fell from 9 percent in 1993 to 6 percent in 2000.[44]

> Representatives from 34 countries are in negotiations to form the Free Trade Area of the Americas.

Implications of NAFTA on Corporate Strategy

Several predictions were made when NAFTA was signed. One prediction was that companies would look at NAFTA as one big regional market, allowing companies to rationalize production, products, financing, and the like (see Chapter 8 for more information on rationalized production). That has largely happened in a number of industries—especially in automotive products and in electronics (e.g., in computers). Each country in NAFTA ships more automotive products, based on specialized production, to the other two countries than any other manufactured goods. Employment has increased in the auto industry in the United States since NAFTA was established, even as it has declined in Mexico because of productivity.[45] Rationalization of automotive production has taken place for years in the United States and Canada, but Mexico is a recent entrant. Auto manufacturing has moved into Mexico from all over the world. Over 500,000 Mexicans make parts and assemble vehicles for all of the world's major auto producers. NAFTA's rules of origins requiring 62.5 percent regional content have forced European and Asian automakers to bring in parts suppliers and set up assembly operations in Mexico. In one case, a Canadian entrepreneur established a metal-stamping plant in Puebla, Mexico, to supply Volkswagen, the German auto manufacturer. The VW plant assembles the revitalized Beetle that is being supplied to the U.S. market.[46] DaimlerChrysler is producing 45,000 cars and 200,000 trucks in Mexico, between 80 and 90 percent of which are being exported to the United States and Canada. In 2000, DaimlerChrysler began producing a new model, the PT Cruiser, in Toluca, Mexico, for export to Canada, the United States, and Europe. It is using that one plant to manufacture that one model for the entire world. The story for DaimlerChrysler's production in the United States is similar. In 1993, Chrysler exported only 5,300 vehicles to Mexico. The following year, after the signing of NAFTA, it exported 17,500, and in 2000 it exported 60,000.[47] Because barriers to trade are next to zero in the NAFTA zone, companies can set

> NAFTA is causing MNEs to look at the region differently in terms of trade and investment.

up operations wherever it makes the most sense for them to do so and then easily ship their goods to any of the three countries.

The examples here describe how production is intertwined among the member countries. However, some companies are simply leaving the United States and Canada and moving to Mexico. General Electric divisions even told their suppliers that they had better move to Mexico as a way to cut costs or risk being dropped as a GE supplier. GE has gone through the process of globalizing its production, and in the process, it has reduced its U.S. domestic workforce by 50 percent since 1986 to 163,000 workers, while doubling its foreign employment to 130,000. At one time, GE employed 30,000 people in Mexico, and it has conducted seminars for suppliers on how to set up operations in Mexico, much to the chagrin of its U.S. workforce and union leaders.[48] The same can be said of apparel and furniture. However, NAFTA rules on apparel have caused the Mexican textile industry to bring jobs back from Asia, and U.S. textile companies are setting up operations in Mexico to supply both the Mexican and U.S. apparel markets. This is a good example of the concept of diversion being applied to investment—investment being diverted from Asia to NAFTA countries, especially Mexico. However, the labor cycle is turning again. Just as some companies left Asian countries like Malaysia and Singapore as labor rates increased, so too will they leave Mexico as wages increase. Mexico hopes that the benefits of a closer U.S. market due to NAFTA will keep companies interested in investing.

Although low-end manufacturing is moving south, more sophisticated manufacturing and services are increasing in the United States as a result of NAFTA, especially in the Southeast. European, Asian, and U.S. companies are using the area along Interstate Highway 85 through the Southeast to supply the NAFTA market. Although an estimated 35,000 jobs were lost in the traditional industries in the Southeast due to NAFTA, an estimated 65,000 more sophisticated manufacturing and high-tech jobs were created. The problem is that not all of those who lost traditional jobs were placed in the more sophisticated jobs. This is a real education and training problem for the region.

A second prediction was that sophisticated U.S. companies would run Canadian and Mexican companies out of business once the markets opened up. That has not happened. In fact, U.S. companies along the border of Canada are finding that Canadian companies are generating more competition for them than low-wage Mexican companies. Also, many Mexican companies have restructured to compete with U.S. and Canadian companies. The lack of protection has resulted in much more competitive Mexican firms. NAFTA has forced companies from all three countries to reexamine their strategies and determine how best to operate in the market.

A final prediction had to do with looking at Mexico as a consumer market rather than just a production location. Initially, the excitement over Mexico for U.S. and Canadian companies has been the low-wage environment. However, as Mexican income continues to rise—which it must do as more investment enters Mexico and more Mexican companies export production—demand is rising for foreign products. But U.S. and Canadian companies need to make the transition to Mexico as a significant final consumer market.

> In general, U.S. companies have not run Canadian and Mexican companies out of business.

> Mexico is being looked at more as a market for U.S. and Canadian exports than just a location for low-cost production.

REGIONAL ECONOMIC GROUPS IN LATIN AMERICA, ASIA, AND AFRICA

Other examples of regional integration can be found around the world, although the EU and NAFTA are the most successful, given the size of their respective economies and the degree of progress toward free trade. Economic integration in Latin America has changed over the years. Two of the original examples of regional economic integration in Latin America, the **Latin American Free Trade Association (LAFTA)** and the **Caribbean Free Trade Association (CARIFTA)**, changed their names to the **Latin American Integration Association (ALADI)** and the **Caribbean Community and Common Market (CARICOM)**. They also changed the focus of their activities. In spite of this evolution, the initial rationale for integration remains. The post–World War II strategy of import substitution to resolve balance-of-payments problems was doomed because of Latin America's small national markets. Therefore, some form of economic cooperation was needed to enlarge the potential market size so that Latin American companies could achieve economies of scale and be more competitive worldwide.

Latin countries rely heavily on the United States as their major export market. However, the size and scale of cooperation within Latin American trading groups is increasing. Map 7.2 identifies the major trading groups in Central America—the CARICOM and the Central American Common Market (CACM). Map 7.3 identifies the major trading groups in South America.

The major trade group in South America is **MERCOSUR**. In 1991, Brazil, Argentina, Paraguay, and Uruguay established MERCOSUR as a subregional group of ALADI. MERCOSUR is significant because of its size: The four original members generate 80 percent of South America's GNP. In addition, MERCOSUR has signed free trade agreements with Bolivia and Chile and is negotiating with the EU and other countries to do the same. MERCOSUR is also trying to become a customs union, but as of the end of 2002, that had not happened. Argentina's economic crisis in 2002 spilled over into Brazil and Uruguay and is threatening the stability of the entire region. The dramatic fall in the value of the Argentine peso changed the trading structure in MERCOSUR, making Argentine products cheaper but making it more difficult for Argentine tourists to travel to the resort areas in Brazil.

Although the Andean Common Market (ANCOM) is not as significant economically as MERCOSUR, it is the second-most important regional group in South America. As Map 7.3 shows, the **Andean Group** has been around since 1969. However, its focus has shifted from one of isolationism and statism (placing economic control in the hands of the state—the central government) to being open to foreign trade and investment.

Regional integration in Asia has not been as successful as the EU or NAFTA because most of the countries in the region have relied on the United States as major markets for

MERCOSUR is a customs union between Brazil, Uruguay, Paraguay, and Argentina. It has been slow in developing a common external tariff, and economic problems of member countries have hampered progress.

MAP 7.2 Economic Integration in Central America and the Caribbean

CENTRAL AMERICAN COMMON MARKET (CACM)	
Members	**Date of entry**
Costa Rica	Sept. 1963
El Salvador	May 1961
Guatemala	May 1961
Nicaragua	May 1961

CARIBBEAN COMMUNITY AND COMMON MARKET (CARICOM)	
Participating Members	**Date of entry**
Antigua and Barbuda	May 1974
Bahamas*	July 1983
Barbados	Aug. 1973
Belize	May 1974
Dominica	May 1974
Grenada	May 1974
Guyana	Aug. 1973
Jamaica	Aug. 1973
Montserrat	May 1974
St. Kitts and Nevis	May 1974
St. Lucia	May 1974
St. Vincent and the Grenadines	May 1974
Trinidad and Tobago	Aug. 1973

*The Bahamas is a member state of the community but is not a participant in the common market.

Countries in Central America and the Caribbean have shifted their forms of integration from free trade areas to common markets: the Central American Common Market (CACM) and the Caribbean Community and Common Market (CARICOM).

The Latin American Integration Association (ALADI) evolved from the Latin American Free Trade Association (LAFTA). The Andean Group and MERCOSUR are subgroups of ALADI that address special needs of member countries.

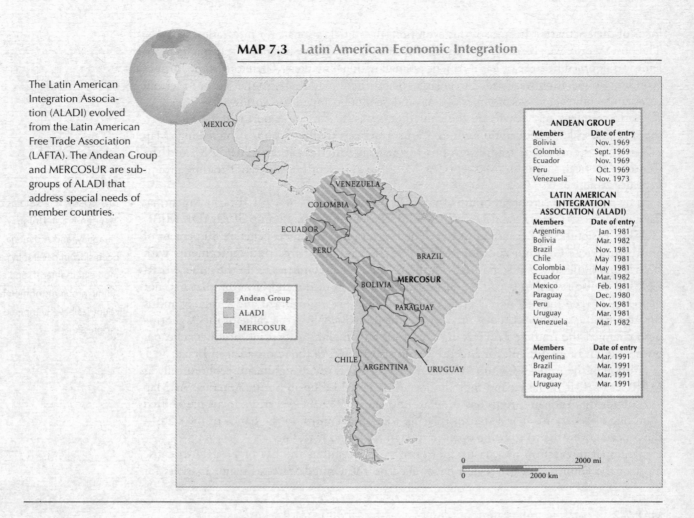

MAP 7.3   Latin American Economic Integration

ANDEAN GROUP	
Members	Date of entry
Bolivia	Nov. 1969
Colombia	Sept. 1969
Ecuador	Nov. 1969
Peru	Oct. 1969
Venezuela	Nov. 1973

LATIN AMERICAN INTEGRATION ASSOCIATION (ALADI)	
Members	Date of entry
Argentina	Jan. 1981
Bolivia	Mar. 1982
Brazil	Nov. 1981
Chile	May 1981
Colombia	May 1981
Ecuador	Mar. 1982
Mexico	Feb. 1981
Paraguay	Dec. 1980
Peru	Nov. 1981
Uruguay	Mar. 1981
Venezuela	Mar. 1982

Members	Date of entry
Argentina	Mar. 1991
Brazil	Mar. 1991
Paraguay	Mar. 1991
Uruguay	Mar. 1991

Andean Group
ALADI
MERCOSUR

ASEAN is a relatively successful free trade area in Southeast Asia that relies more on the U.S. market for exports than on each other.

their products. However, the Asian financial crisis of 1997 and 1998 demonstrated that weakness in one country resulted in contagion throughout the region. The **Association of South East Asian Nations (ASEAN)**, organized in 1967, comprises Brunei, Cambodia, Indonesia, Laos, Malaysia, Myanmar, the Philippines, Singapore, Thailand, and Vietnam (see Map 7.4). It promotes cooperation in many areas, including industry and trade. Member countries are protected in terms of tariff and nontariff barriers. Yet they hold promise for market and investment opportunities because of their large market size (500 million people). On January 1, 1993, ASEAN officially formed the **ASEAN Free Trade Area (AFTA)**. AFTA's goal is to cut tariffs on all intrazonal trade to a maximum of 5 percent by January 1, 2008. The weaker ASEAN countries would be allowed to phase in their tariff reductions over a longer period.

Many MNEs are hoping that ASEAN countries will work harder to loosen their borders. Companies such as BMW, Matsushita Electrical Industrial, Honda Motor, and Procter & Gamble have operations in the ASEAN countries but aren't able to expand to their full potential because ASEAN countries aren't cooperating with each other. Malaysia, Singapore, Thailand, and the Philippines are still passing protectionist measures which downgrade the effectiveness of AFTA and shrink trade. General Motors expanded heavily into Thailand in 1996, but in 2001 it built only 52,000 cars in a plant designed to build 130,000. Most of these cars were sent to the European market because barriers within ASEAN are too large. Unless ASEAN nations start cooperating, MNEs will move their operations to China. GM's sales doubled in China in 2001, and as GM's ASEAN chief put

MAP 7.4 The Association of South East Asian Nations

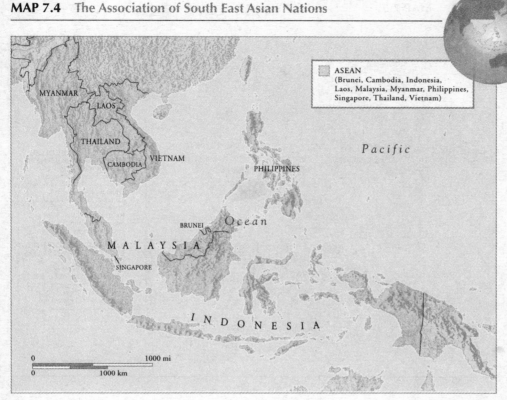

ASEAN
(Brunei, Cambodia, Indonesia, Laos, Malaysia, Myanmar, Philippines, Singapore, Thailand, Vietnam)

ASEAN is a regional group whose member countries have a total population greater than that of the EU (prior to 2004) or NAFTA, but their per capita GDP is smaller. However, economic growth rates of ASEAN members are among the highest in the world.

it, "It is growth like that, that makes it imperative for ASEAN nations to put aside their differences and embrace free trade."[49]

APEC, the Asia Pacific Economic Cooperation (http://www.apecsec.org.sg), was formed in November 1989 to promote multilateral economic cooperation in trade and investment in the Pacific Rim.[50] It is composed of 21 countries that border the Pacific Rim—both in Asia as well as the Americas.

To accomplish its objectives, APEC leaders committed themselves to achieving free and open trade in the region by 2010 for the industrial nations (which generate 85 percent of the regional trade) and by 2020 for the rest of the members.[51] The U.S. Department of State stated, "APEC has played an important role in promoting trade and investment liberalization in the region. As a result of these efforts, APEC markets are considerably more open today than they were 10 years ago, creating new opportunities for American business and creating new employment for American workers."[52]

APEC has the potential to become a significant economic bloc, especially because it generates such a large percentage of the world's output and merchandise trade. APEC is trying to establish "open regionalism," whereby individual member countries can determine whether to apply trade liberalization to non-APEC countries on an unconditional, most-favored-nation basis or on a reciprocal, free trade agreement basis. The United States prefers the latter approach. The key will be whether or not the liberalization process continues at a good pace.[53] The problem with APEC is its size. A major reason why regional integration like the EU and NAFTA work is because of close geographic proximity and a unity of purpose. APEC has too many countries with diverse interests, and it was established as a counterforce to NAFTA. It is hard to maintain serious progress for something borne out of a defensive rather than an offensive strategy.

APEC is comprised of 21 countries that border the Pacific Rim; progress toward free trade is hampered by the size of APEC and the geographic distance between member countries.

MAP 7.5

Although there are several regional economic groups in Africa, trade among their member countries is still quite small. African countries rely heavily on trading relationships with industrial countries to absorb regional exports.

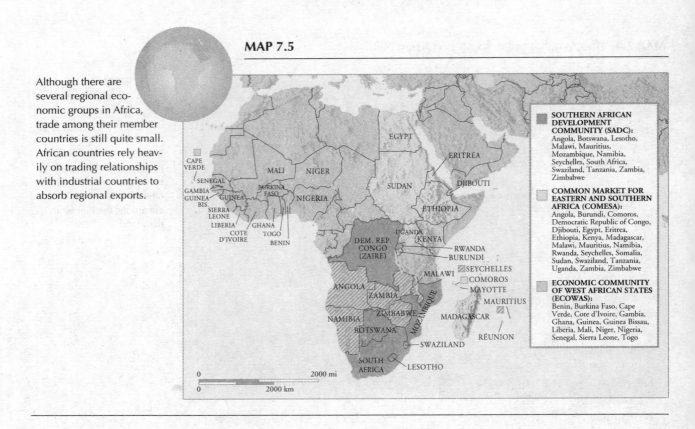

SOUTHERN AFRICAN DEVELOPMENT COMMUNITY (SADC): Angola, Botswana, Lesotho, Malawi, Mauritius, Mozambique, Namibia, Seychelles, South Africa, Swaziland, Tanzania, Zambia, Zimbabwe

COMMON MARKET FOR EASTERN AND SOUTHERN AFRICA (COMESA): Angola, Burundi, Comoros, Democratic Republic of Congo, Djibouti, Egypt, Eritrea, Ethiopia, Kenya, Madagascar, Malawi, Mauritius, Namibia, Rwanda, Seychelles, Somalia, Sudan, Swaziland, Tanzania, Uganda, Zambia, Zimbabwe

ECONOMIC COMMUNITY OF WEST AFRICAN STATES (ECOWAS): Benin, Burkina Faso, Cape Verde, Cote d'Ivoire, Gambia, Ghana, Guinea, Guinea Bissau, Liberia, Mali, Niger, Nigeria, Senegal, Sierra Leone, Togo

There are several African trade groups, but they rely more on their former colonial powers and other developed markets for trade than they do on each other.

Several African regional trade groups exist, and they are not necessarily mutually exclusive. The Ivory Coast, for example, is a member of several different organizations in Africa that promote political and economic development. Map 7.5 shows some of the major African groups such as Southern African Development Community, Common Market for Eastern and Southern Africa, and Economic Community of West African States. The problem is that African countries have been struggling to establish a political identity and are only recently adjusting to the freedom of South Africa. Civil war, corruption, and poor government infrastructures have hampered African countries and their ability to progress economically. Some African groups, such as the Organization for African Unity, have been preoccupied with political rather than trade issues. Most African countries rely on trade links with former colonial powers than with each other. African markets, with the notable exception of South Africa, are relatively small and undeveloped, making trade liberalization a relatively minor contributor to economic growth in the region.

COMMODITY AGREEMENTS

A commodity agreement is designed to stabilize the price and supply of a good; it takes the form of a producers' alliance or an international commodity control agreement.

Thus far, this chapter has focused on how countries cooperate to reduce trade barriers among themselves. However, producer and consumer countries of primary commodities have also come together to in an effort to stabilize commodity prices and supply. Primary commodity exports, such as crude petroleum, natural gas, copper, tobacco, coffee, cocoa, tea, and sugar, have become much less important to developing countries over the last decades except for Africa, which depends on these commodities for 80 percent of its exports.[54] Primary commodities are important to both consumers and producers. The slowdown in global growth in 2001 caused demand to fall for commodities, resulting in a fall in prices. The low commodity prices were a boon to consumer countries, because they helped companies keep down costs and, therefore, prices. But producer countries, especially developing countries, suffered because of low commodity revenues. This section deals with how countries use commodity agreements to stabilize the price and supply of selected commodities.

Producers' Alliances and ICCAs

Commodity agreements are of two basic types: *producers' alliances* and *international commodity control agreements* (ICCAs). Producers' alliances are exclusive membership agreements between producing and exporting countries. Examples are the Organization of Petroleum Exporting Countries (OPEC) and the Union of Banana Exporting Countries. ICCAs are agreements between producing and consuming countries. Examples of ICCAs are the International Cocoa Organization (ICCO) and the International Sugar Organization (ISO). Membership of the 1993 ICCO Agreement, for example, comprises 42 countries plus the European Union and represents over 80 percent of world cocoa production and over 70 percent of world cocoa consumption. The ISO helps its members by monitoring and publishing data on prices, production, consumption, trade, and stock developments. Similar tools are provided by most producers' alliances and ICCAs.

> Producers' alliances—exclusive membership agreements between producing and exporting countries, such as OPEC. ICCAs—agreements between producing and consuming countries.

Most developing countries traditionally have relied on the export of one or two commodities to supply the foreign currencies from industrial countries that they need for economic development. This is especially true of the African developing countries. However, commodity prices are not stable. Both consumers and producers prefer a stabilized pricing system that allows for planning of future costs and earnings. Unfortunately, many short-term factors, such as weather conditions and business cycles, cause sudden changes in supply and demand, thus resulting in price instability. In the face of strong market forces, countries try to counteract price instability through one of several different stabilization schemes:

  Stabilization of world commodity prices through the exercise of market power by a monopolistic producer or producer cartel or through international commodity agreements

  Stabilization of producer revenues through the use of risk-management instruments, such as commodities futures

  Stabilization of government revenues through precautionary savings funds Compensatory financing

  Stabilization of domestic producer and consumer prices through variable export taxes or tariffs, agricultural marketing boards, or domestic stockpiles and stabilization funds[55]

Another approach is a **quota system**, in which producing countries divide total output and sales to stabilize the price. For a quota system to work, participating countries must cooperate among themselves to prevent sharp fluctuations in supply. The quota system is most effective when a single country has a large share of world production or consumption because it is able to control supply much more easily. Three of the best examples of a quota system are oil, controlled by the OPEC countries; wool, controlled by Australia; and diamonds, controlled by the DeBeers Company in South Africa. Because DeBeers controls most of the diamond mining in the world, it can control price by determining how many diamonds to release on the world market. Not all commodity agreements work well. Countries in producers' alliances tend to disagree on the quotas allotted to them.

> Quota system—determines how producing and consuming countries divide total output and sales; used by OPEC.

The type of commodity also influences a commodity agreement's effectiveness. For some commodities, especially food, beverages, and agricultural raw materials, there are differences in substitutability. For example, tea can substitute for coffee, and sugar beets might substitute for cane sugar. This limits the ability of coffee and cane sugar producers to control price. However, not all commodities have a ready substitute, so those producers have more control over price. Cuba has recently decided to diversify out of sugar production because sugar prices are half what they were a decade ago. Although Cuba is ranked fourth in the world in sugar production, its inefficient industry can't compete. It is turning to tourism, cattle, and other grain production for more stable sources of income.[56]

The Organization of Petroleum Exporting Countries (OPEC)

OPEC is an example of a producer cartel. It is a group of commodity-producing countries that have significant control over supply and that band together to control output and price. OPEC is part of a larger category of energy commodities, which also includes coal and natural gas. OPEC is not confined to the Middle East. The members are Algeria, Indonesia, Iran, Iraq, Kuwait, Libya, Nigeria, Qatar, Saudi Arabia, the United Arab Emirates, and Venezuela. OPEC controls prices by establishing production quotas on member countries. Saudi Arabia has historically performed the role of the dominant supplier in OPEC that can influence supply and price. Periodically—at least annually—OPEC oil ministers gather together to determine the quota for each country based on estimates of supply and demand.

Politics are also an important dimension to OPEC deliberations. OPEC member countries with large populations need large oil revenues to fund government programs. As a result, they are tempted to exceed their export quotas to generate more revenues. A major reason for the invasion of Kuwait by Iraq in 1990 was because Kuwait was producing more than its quota, which depressed world oil prices. Iraqi President Saddam Hussein blamed Kuwait for low world oil prices, which reduced the amount of revenue Iraq could earn with its oil exports. Thus, he felt justified in invading Kuwait to gain control of its oil supplies so that he could increase his own oil revenues.

OPEC member countries produce about 41 percent of the world's crude oil and 15 percent of its natural gas. However, OPEC's oil exports represent about 55 percent of the oil traded internationally. Therefore, OPEC can have a strong influence on the oil market, especially if it decides to reduce or increase its level of production.[57] Sometimes OPEC policies work; sometimes they don't. In 1999, OPEC met and established strict production quotas to try to raise prices. It seemed to work so well that by the third quarter of the year, prices had nearly doubled and prices remained within OPEC's target band until the terrorist attacks of September 11.[58] Several factors seemed key: Countries actually stuck to their quotas, the Asian economies were beginning to recover, and the U.S. economy was remaining strong. The last two factors led to strong demand at the same time production was being trimmed, thus causing prices to rise.[59] External shocks such as September 11 and the U.S. attack on Iraq are harder for OPEC to manage and usually result in a spike in oil prices.

Keeping oil prices high has some downside for OPEC. Competition from non-OPEC countries increases because the revenues accruing to the competitors are higher. Because some OPEC countries are putting up roadblocks to production (they want things done their own way), major producers like BP, ExxonMobil, and Shell are investing heavily in areas like the Caspian Basin, the Gulf of Mexico, and Angola. Production in these areas is expected to grow twice as fast as the 1990s, and this growth should continue until 2010. Another problem is that higher oil prices depress growth in oil-thirsty economies like India and China and thus lower demand for oil. Also, because of OPEC's power, its countries have, for the most part, been able to avoid competitive pressures to improve their industries—and some are, therefore, decades out of date.[60] These problems have caused OPEC's market share to fall, and it will continue to do so unless some changes are made.

Because commodities are the raw materials used in the production process, it is important for managers of companies that use commodities to understand the factors that influence their prices. During the Asian financial crisis, when commodity prices collapsed, commodity exporters suffered but commodity importers benefited from the lower commodity costs.

The Environment

Pollution of the air, land, and sea clearly poses a threat to the future of the planet, and governments, companies, and individuals are concerned. Although many environmental problems are national in nature, they may have cross-national ramifications and require cross-national agreements. In addition, lax environmental rules and enforcement in one country could influence trade and investment flows, as noted in the discussion on NAFTA. Some of these cross-national agreements are tied to regional groups, such as the EU and NAFTA. These agreements tend to have a strong influence because of the commitment of group members to environmental issues. One example is the concern over water along the U.S.-Mexico border and the impact of acid rain in waters along the U.S.-Canadian border. It would make sense for countries to tackle those issues on a regional basis.

However, these regional agreements still do not solve problems on a global basis, and the major source of influence for global environmental agreements is the United Nations. The **United Nations** is a political organization composed of 189 countries (see www.un.org), and it is headquartered in New York City. The UN deals with a variety of political issues, such as security and world peace, but it also deals in social and economic issues. One of the key economic issues is that of the environment. In 1992, more than 100 heads of state met in Rio de Janeiro, Brazil, for the first international Earth Summit, which was convened to address urgent problems of environmental protection and socioeconomic development. The assembled leaders signed the Convention on Climate Change and the Convention on Biological Diversity, they endorsed the Rio Declaration and the Forest Principles, and they adopted Agenda 21, a 300-page plan for achieving sustainable development in the twenty-first century.[61] The Commission on Sustainable Development (CSD) was created to monitor and report on implementation of the Earth Summit agreements.

In 1997 the UN presented the Kyoto treaty that commits participant countries to reduce greenhouse gas emissions. Fifty-five countries, responsible for 55 percent of the world's emissions must ratify the treaty for it to take effect. President George Bush rejected the treaty because of the high costs it would bring to U.S. industry. This move brought international criticism because the United States is responsible for one-fourth of the world's carbon dioxide emissions. In December 2002, Canada signed the treaty, leaving only Russia to ratify the treaty for it to take effect.[62]

Major types of environmental degradation are ozone depletion, air pollution, acid rain, water pollution, waste disposal, and deforestation. Ozone depletion results from the burning of fossil fuels and the emission of ozone-depleting chemicals such as chlorofluorocarbons (CFCs). Ozone depletion may lead to global warming and the destruction of life as a result of excessive exposure to ultraviolet radiation.

The problem with international environmental agreements is that countries differ significantly in how they deal with environmental issues. This problem is especially acute in developing countries, where some of the worst environmental damage occurs and where laws tend to be the most lax. Some MNEs might be tempted to save costs by locating production facilities in countries in which environmental laws are weak. However, many MNEs are among the world's most environmentally responsible companies. They seek to reduce costs by redesigning manufacturing processes to use inputs more efficiently. More than 700 companies and 50 chief executives attended the UN Summit on Sustainable Development in Johannesburg, South Africa, in September 2002, and they all resolved to work with the United Nations and other regional groups to improve the environment. For example, "BMW is touting a car that will use hydrogen instead of petrol; South African mining companies are boasting of plans to give free health care (especially on AIDS) to their workers; oil companies such as Shell said they will now work closely with environmental groups like Greenpeace to see how to clean up their operations in poor countries.[63]

Corporate leaders say that cooperation with environmental agreements improves profits and helps them avoid criticism because they act more socially responsible in the countries where they are doing business. Initially, companies could perceive compliance as increasing the costs of doing business. However, the agreements put all companies on the same level, so environmental compliance should not disadvantage one company compared to another.

Many environmental problems require national solutions, but many involve cross-national boundaries and need to be solved through treaties and agreements.

The United Nations is a 189-member-country organization that deals with many social, political, and environmental issues.

ETHICAL DILEMMA

The Seattle WTO Protest Spotlights Free Trade's Effects on the Environment

In November 1999, the WTO met in Seattle, Washington, to set an agenda for the next round of trade talks. Everyone knew there would be protesters from all sides of the political spectrum, representing labor, environmental, and other groups. However, nobody but the anarchists dreamed that the demonstrations would turn so violent. In the aftermath of the demonstrations, the question remains, "What is the relationship between free trade and the environment?" What responsibility do groups like the EU and NAFTA have to push for improvements in the environment as they liberalize trade and investment flows?

Prior to the Seattle meetings, the WTO had largely ignored environmental issues. Its mandate was to liberalize trade, not protect the environment. However, environmental issues are important to both the EU and NAFTA. In the early 1990s, Mexico complained to GATT that the United States was unfairly banning imports of tuna caught in nets that kill dolphins. GATT ruled against the United States, stating that discriminatory trade practices shouldn't be used to protect dolphins but that the United States should require Mexican canners to label their tuna as dolphin-safe tuna so that consumers could make a choice.

In some ways, this galvanized the environmental lobby to oppose trade agreements that did not consider the environment. Presidential candidate Bill Clinton argued against NAFTA in the 1992 elections, but he ended up supporting NAFTA as president by including a side agreement on the environment. Since then, environmental issues have been an important—though not highly effective—part of NAFTA. The workers assumption of the WTO and all regional trade agreements is that free trade actually should help the environment. As trade increases, incomes rise, which results in a people who are both concerned about the environment and able to pay for cleaning it up. However, WTO also admits that increased trade can harm the environment. Instead of stopping trade, which extreme environmental groups advocate, WTO advocates increasing trade while dealing with the specific environmental issues. However, developing countries like Mexico are concerned that increased interest in environmental issues could just be an excuse for trade sanctions against them. Thus, the developing countries are not as anxious to pursue environmental issues in trade agreements. Several environmental proposals that regional and global trading groups will have to consider are

Eliminating environmentally damaging subsidies for farming, fishing, and fossil fuels.

Offering more scope for the labeling of eco-friendly products.

Assessing the environmental impact of the world trading system and of proposals for future liberalization.

Making agreements more transparent, accountable, and accessible to environmental NGOs—nongovernmental organizations.[64]

Although individual countries and regional trade groups have made it much more of a priority to deal with environmental issues since the protests of Seattle, opposition still exists. Protests have mellowed since Seattle, in part due to the sensitivities surrounding the events of 9/11, but the annual meetings of the IMF and World Bank in 2002 brought environmental protesters, and U.S. Secretary of State Colin Powell was heckled by protesters during his speech at the Earth Summit in 2002.

LOOKING TO THE FUTURE

How Much Territory Will Regional Integration Cover?

Will regional integration be the wave of the future, or will the WTO become the focus of global economic integration? The WTO's objective is to reduce barriers to trade in goods, services, and investment. Regional groups attempt to do that and more. Although the EU has introduced a common currency and is increasing the degree of cooperation in areas such as security and foreign policy, the WTO will never engage in those issues. Regional integration deals with the specific problems facing member countries, whereas the WTO needs to be concerned about all countries in the world. However, regional integration might actually help the WTO achieve its objectives in three major ways:

1. Regionalism can lead to liberalization of issues not covered by the WTO.
2. Regionalism, given that it typically involves fewer countries with more similar conditions and objectives, is more flexible.
3. Regional deals lock in liberalization, especially in developing countries.

NAFTA and the EU are the key regional groups in which significant integration is taking place. In the future, these groups will continue to develop stronger linkages, and then they will expand to include other countries. The key for NAFTA will be whether or not the U.S. Congress can avoid getting caught up in protectionist sentiment and allow expansion to take place. If it does not, Canada and Mexico will continue to engage in bilateral agreements with non-NAFTA countries in the region along the lines of the NAFTA agreement. The EU will continue to expand east until it meets Russia, and then its expansion will stop.

Regional integration in Africa will continue at a slow pace due to the existing political and economic problems there, but Asian integration, primarily in APEC, will pick up steam as the economies of East and Southeast Asia recover and open up. However, the key to their growth will continue to be non-APEC members Japan and the United States.

Summary

- Efforts at regional economic integration began to emerge after World War II as countries saw benefits of cooperation and larger market sizes. The major types of economic integration are the free trade area, the customs union, the common market, and complete economic integration.

- In its most limited form, economic integration allows countries to trade goods without tariff discrimination (a free trade area). In its most extensive form, all factors of production are allowed to move across borders, and some degree of social, political, and economic harmonization is undertaken (complete economic integration).

- The static effects of economic integration improve the efficiency of resource allocation and affect both production and consumption. The dynamic effects are internal and external efficiencies that arise because of changes in market size.

- Once protection is eliminated among member countries, trade creation allows MNEs to specialize and trade based on comparative advantage.

- Trade diversion occurs when the supply of products shifts from countries that are not members of an economic bloc to those that are.

- Regional, as opposed to global, economic integration occurs because of the greater ease of promoting cooperation on a smaller scale.

- The European Union (EU) is an effective common market that has abolished most restrictions on factor mobility and is harmonizing national political, economic, and social policies. As of 2002, it was composed of Austria, Belgium, Denmark, Finland, France, Germany, Greece, Ireland, Italy, Luxembourg, the Netherlands, Portugal, Spain, Sweden, and the United Kingdom. In 2004, 10 more countries will join the EU.

- Some of the EU's major goals are to abolish intrazonal restrictions on the movement of goods, capital, services, and labor; to establish a common external tariff; to achieve a common agricultural policy; to harmonize tax and legal systems; to devise a uniform policy concerning antitrust; and to establish a common currency and common monetary policy.

- On January 1, 1999, the EU introduced a common currency, the euro, with banknotes issued on January 1, 2002.

- The EU has several free trade agreements with countries and groups of countries, making it the world's largest and richest trading bloc. Ten countries have been targeted for the next phase of expansion set for 2004.

- The North American Free Trade Agreement (NAFTA) is designed to eliminate tariff barriers and liberalize investment opportunities and trade in services. Key provisions in NAFTA are labor and environmental agreements.

- There are key trade groups in other parts of the world, including Latin America, Asia, and Africa.

- Many developing countries rely on commodity exports to supply the hard currency they need for economic development. Instability in commodity prices has resulted in fluctuations in export earnings. Commodity agreements, using one of several stabilization schemes, seek to stabilize prices.

- Although many environmental issues can be solved at the national level, others require cross-national cooperation.

CASE

Wal-Mart de Mexico[65]

Comercial Mexicana S.A. (Comerci), one of Mexico's largest retail chains, is faced with a serious dilemma. Since Wal-Mart's aggressive entry into the Mexican retail market, Comerci has found it increasingly difficult to remain competitive. Wal-Mart's strong operating presence and low prices since NAFTA's lifting of tariffs have put pressure on Comerci, and now management must decide if it can improve Comerci's competitive position by remaining independent or by merging with either a local or foreign retailer. What has caused this intense competitive pressure on Comerci, and what is likely to be its future?

Mexico's retail sector has benefited greatly from the increasing trade liberalization the government has been pushing. After decades of protectionism, Mexico joined GATT in 1986 to help open its economy to new markets. In 1990, with Mexico's economy on the upswing and additional free trade negotiations with the United States and Canada taking place, the founder of Wal-Mart, Sam Walton, met with the president of Cifra, Mexico's leading retail store. Their meeting resulted in a 50/50 joint venture in the opening of Mexico's first Sam's Clubs, a subsidiary of Wal-Mart, in 1991 in Mexico City. It only took a couple of months after the opening to prove the store's success—it was breaking all of the U.S. records for Sam's Club. The joint venture evolved to incorporate all new stores, and by 1997, Wal-Mart purchased enough shares to have controlling interest in Cifra. In 2000, it changed the name to Wal-Mart de Mexico, S.A. de C.V., and the ticker symbol to WALMEX.

Prior to 1990, Wal-Mart had never made moves to enter Mexico or any country other than the United States. Once Wal-Mart started growing in Mexico, management created the Wal-Mart International Division in 1993. The company has expanded internationally to nine countries through new-store construction and acquisitions. It now operates in Argentina, Brazil, Canada, China, Germany, Korea, Mexico, Puerto Rico, and the United Kingdom. Wal-Mart's operations in Canada, the United States and Mexico's partners in NAFTA, began in 1994 with the acquisition of 122 Woolco stores. It now has 196 stores and has strong partnerships with Canadian suppliers.

With growth stalling in the United States, Wal-Mart is looking to international expansion for growth. In fiscal 2002, the international division increased sales by 10.5 percent—to $35.4 billion—and operating profit increased 31.1 percent—to $1.4 billion. The division accounts for 17 percent of sales and 11 percent of profits. Some forecasters believe Wal-Mart's growth outside of the United States will grow by an average of 26 percent for the foreseeable future. Wal-Mart's success internationally has varied by country. Although successful in countries like Mexico and Canada, where it has become the largest retailer, it has yet to prove itself in Germany and Argentina. It is learning from its past mistakes, and it is now adapting much better to local cultures and learning from partnerships formed in each country.

WAL-MART'S COMPETITIVE ADVANTAGE

Much of Wal-Mart's international success comes from the tested practices the U.S. division bases its success on. Wal-Mart is known for the slogan "Every Day Low Prices." It has expanded that internally to "Every Day Low Costs" to inspire employees to spend company money wisely and work hard to lower costs. Because of its sheer size and volume of purchases, Wal-Mart can negotiate with suppliers to drop prices to agreeable levels. It also works closely with suppliers on inventory levels using an advanced information system that informs suppliers when purchases have been made and when Wal-Mart will be ordering more merchandise. Suppliers can then plan production runs more accurately, thus reducing production costs, which are passed on to Wal-Mart and eventually the consumer.

Wal-Mart also has a unique distribution system that reduces expenses. It builds super warehouses in central locations that receive the majority of merchandise sold in Wal-Mart stores. It then transports the merchandise to the various stores, using its company-owned fleet or a partner. The central distribution center helps Wal-Mart negotiate lower prices with its suppliers because of the large purchasing volumes.

These strategies have resulted in great success for Wal-Mart. In 2001, it passed General Electric and ExxonMobil to become the largest company in the world, with sales of $217.8 million. It has the largest private-sector workforce, with 1.3 million people in 3,300 facilities throughout the world. And it even uses the second-most powerful computer in the world—behind the Pentagon's—to run its logistics.

WAL-MART IN MEXICO

In Mexico, Wal-Mart operates 573 units, including Sam's Clubs, Bodegas (discount stores), Wal-Mart Supercenters, Superamas (grocery stores), Suburbias (apparel stores), and VIPS restaurants. Wal-Mart encountered some difficulties with its opening in Mexico prior to the passage of NAFTA. One of the biggest challenges it faced was import charges on many of the goods sold in its stores, thus preventing Wal-Mart from being able to offer its "Every Day Low Prices." Unsure of local demand, Wal-Mart stocked its shelves with things like ice skates, fishing tackle, and riding lawnmowers—all unpopular items in Mexico. Rather than informing headquarters that they wouldn't need those items, local managers heavily discounted the items only to have the automatic inventory system reorder the products when the first batch sold. Wal-Mart also encountered logistics problems due to poor roads and the scarcity of delivery trucks. Yet another problem was the culture clashes between the Arkansas executives and the local Mexican managers. Some of these problems were solved by trial and error, but the emergence of the North American Free Trade Agreement in 1994 helped solve most of the problems. Among other things, NAFTA reduced tariffs on American goods sold to Mexico from 10 percent to 3 percent. Prior to NAFTA, Wal-Mart was not much of a threat to companies like Comerci, Gigante, and Soriana, Mexico's top retailers. But once the agreement was signed, the barriers fell and Wal-Mart was on a level playing field with its competitors—all it needed to become number one.

NAFTA encouraged Mexico to improve its transportation infrastructure, thus helping to solve Wal-Mart's logistical problems. The signing of NAFTA also opened the gates wider to foreign investment in Mexico. Wal-Mart was paying huge import fees on goods shipped to Mexico from areas like Europe and Asia. Foreign companies knew that if they built manufacturing plants in Mexico, they could keep costs low with Mexican labor but ship to NAFTA's free trade zone—Mexico, the United States, or Canada. As companies began to build manufacturing plants in Mexico, Wal-Mart could buy these products without paying the high import tariffs. An example of this tactic is Sony's flat-screen television line, Wega. Sam's Clubs in Mexico imported Wega TVs from Japan with a 23 percent import tariff plus huge shipping costs, resulting in a $1,600 sales price at Sam's Club. In 1999, Sony built a manufacturing plant in Mexico, thus allowing Sam's Club to purchase the Wegas without import tariffs; this tactic also yields much lower shipping fees. Sam's Clubs passed on the savings to customers—with a sales price of only $600.

The benefits of NAFTA, like lower tariffs and improved infrastructure, helped not only Wal-Mart but also its competitors, like Comerci. But Wal-Mart used the advantages of NAFTA better than anyone else. Rather than pocketing the differences the lower tariffs made, Wal-Mart reduced its prices. In 1999, it closed one of its Supercenters for a day to discount up to 6,000 items by 14 percent. Comerci and others have combated Wal-Mart's tactics by lowering their own prices, but on many items, they can't get the prices as low. Wal-Mart's negotiating power with its suppliers is large enough that it can get the better deal. Also, most of Mexico's retailers priced goods differently. They were used to putting certain items on sale or deep discount, a strategy known as "high and low," rather than lowering all prices. They are trying to adjust their pricing structure to match Wal-Mart's, but they are still frustrated with the continued cost cutting of Wal-Mart. Competitors and certain suppliers are so angry that they have gone to Mexico's Federal Competition Commission with complaints of unfair pricing practices.

Unable to compete with Wal-Mart using its current strategy, Comerci faces extinction. In 2001, Comerci's sales in new stores fell 3.3 percent and Wal-Mart's rose by 5.7 percent. Wal-Mart is the largest retailer in Mexico and owns about 50 percent of the market share in Mexico's supermarket sector. Comerci can look for possible foreign buyers, like France's Carrefour, or it can go to suppliers and make another attempt to get lower prices. The government may give Comerci a break if it rules against Wal-Mart's aggressive pricing, but as one analyst put it, "We do not believe the CFC will end up penalizing Wal-Mart for exercising its purchasing power in an attempt to get the best deals available in the marketplace, which is the goal of every retailer in the world, especially when [these savings] are ultimately passed on to consumers." Comerci may continue to lose its customers to Wal-Mart if it doesn't change something.

QUESTIONS

1. How has the implementation of NAFTA affected Wal-Mart's success in Mexico?
2. How much of Wal-Mart's success is due to NAFTA, and how much is due to Wal-Mart's inherent competitive strategy? In other words, could any other U.S. retailer have the same success in Mexico post-NAFTA, or is Wal-Mart a special case?
3. What do you think Comercial Mexicana S.A. should do, given the competitive position of Wal-Mart?

Chapter Notes

1 The information in this case is from the following sources: http://ford.com; various issues of the Ford Motor Company's *Annual Report*; "Tough at the Top," *The Economist* (March 13, 1993): 76; Richard A. Melcher and John Templeman, "Ford of Europe: Slimmer, but Maybe Not Luckier," *Business Week* (January 18, 1993): 44, 46; Timothy Aeppel, "Ford Reaches Fork in Road in Its European Operations," *Wall Street Journal* (October 6, 1992): 88; Richard A. Melcher, "Ford Is Ready to Roll in the New Europe," *Business Week* (December 12, 1988): 60; James B. Treece, Kathleen Kerwin, and Heidi Dawley, "Ford: Alex Trotman's Daring Strategy," *Business Week* (April 3, 1995): 94–104; Diana T. Kurylko, "European Profits Are a Priority; New Focus World Car Is Crucial," *Automotive News* (September 14, 1998): 41; Paul Einstein, "Ford Europe Still Struggling," *Automotive Industries* (October 1, 1998): 30; David Sumner Smith, "Ford's Global Potential with Luxury Brands," *Marketing* (April 1, 1999): 18; Bradford Wernele, "Ford Blames Aging Products for European Sales Slide," *Automotive News* (April 26, 1999): 6; Fara Warner, "Does Ford of Europe's Chief Face Impossible Mission?" *Wall Street Journal* (June 18, 1999): B4; Kathleen Kerwin and Jack Ewing, "Nasser: Ford Be Nimble," *Business Week* (September 27, 1999): 42–43; Kathleen Kerwin and Keith Naughton, "Remaking Ford," *Business Week* (October 11, 1999): 134–42; Robert Stevens, "Ford Europe Unveils Restructuring Strategy," World Socialist Web site (February 8, 2000): http://www.wsws.org/articles/2000/feb2000/ford-f18.shtml; Christine Tierney, "Ford: A Comeback in Europe Is Job One," *Business Week*, International Edition (May 29, 2000): www.businessweek.com; "Ford Europe Has Big Hope for New Fiesta," Auto.com (September 12, 2001): http://www.auto.com/industry/fiesta12_20010912.htm; Christine Tierney and Kathleen Kerwin, "Ford: Europe Has a Better Idea," *Business Week* (April 15, 2002): www.businessweek.com; "Ford Europe Sees No Need to Cut More Capacity Now," *Forbes* (June 25, 2002): http://www.forbes.com/.

2 Bela Balassa, *The Theory of Economic Integration* (Homewood, IL: Irwin, 1961), 40.

3 "The European Commission" (2002): http://europa.eu.int/inst-en.htm.

4 "The Council of the European Union" (2002): http://europa.eu.int/inst/en/cl.htm#function.

5 "City of Hypocrites," in a survey of Europe, *The Economist* (October 23, 1999): 4.

6 "The European Parliament" (2002): http://europa.eu.int/inst/en/ep.htm#intro.

7 "The European Court of Justice" (2002): http://europa.eu.int/inst/en/cj.htm.

8 Paul Hofheinz and Philip Shishkin, "Court Rulings Push the EU Closer to Borderless Economy," *Wall Street Journal* (August 8, 2002): www.wsj.com.

9 "Internal Market Business Survey Estimates Potential Savings of €50 Billion from Simpler Rules at EU and Member State Level," EU Internal Market Scoreboard (November 19, 2001): http://europa.eu.int/comm/internal_market/en/update/score/index.htm.

10 "External Trade: Introduction," Activities of the European Union: Summaries of Legislation, European Union Web site (August 2002): http://europa.eu.int/scadplus/leg/en/lvb/r11000.htm.

11 "WTO Grants EU $4 Billion In Sanctions Against U.S.," *Wall Street Journal* (August 30, 2002): www.wsj.com.

12 "Distant Friends," *The Economist* (May 16, 2002): www.economist.com.

13 "You Can Be Warriors or Wimps; Or So Say the Americans," *The Economist* (August 8, 2002): www.economist.com.

14 "Convergence Criteria for European Monetary Union," Bloomberg News (August 9, 2002): www.bloomberg.com.

15 "Prime Minister Says Sweden Fulfills Criteria to Adopt Euro," Dow Jones Newswires (August 19, 2002): www.wsj.com.

16 "Will the Rising Euro Smite Europe?" *Business Week* (July 8, 2002): www.businessweek.com.

17 Edmund L. Andrews, "On Euro Weekend, Financial Institutions in Vast Reprogramming," *New York Times* (January 2, 1999): www.nytimes.com.

18 "Car Prices in European Union: Still Substantial Price Differences, Especially in the Mass Market Segment," EU press releases (July 22, 2002): http://europa.eu.int/rapid/start/cgi/guesten.ksh?p_action.gettxt=gt&doc=IP/02/1109|0|RAPID&lg=EN.

19 "EU Sets Date for Historic Union," *The Economist* (October 9, 2002): www.economist.com.

20 Sandor Richter and Laszlo G. Toth, "After the Agreement on Free Trade Among Visegrad Group Countries," *Russian and East European Finance and Trade* (July–August 1994): 23–69.

21 "Declaration of Prime Ministers of the CEFTA Countries, "Taken from the Web site CEFTA: Summit of the Prime Ministers of the Central European Free Trade Agreement States (Sept. 14, 2002): http://www.government.gov.sk/temp/cefta_en/declaration.html.

22 John Rossant, "Commentary: The EU: Too Tough on Prospective Members?" *Business Week* (March 18, 2002): www.businessweek.com.

23 Joseph Pereira, "PPR Shares Skyrocket on Plan to Sell a Mail-Order Business," *Wall Street Journal* (August 23, 2002): www.wsj.com.

24 Carol Matlack, Inka Resch, and Wendy Zellner, "En Garde, Wal-Mart," *Business Week* (September 13, 1999): 54.

25 "Will the Rising Euro Smite Europe?" *Business Week*, op. cit.

26 "My Continent, Right or Wrong," in a survey of Europe, *The Economist* (October 23, 1999): 3.

27 "Romano Prodi, a Desperate Integrationist," *The Economist* (May 23, 2002): www.economist.com.

28 Ibid.

29 Hofheinz and Shishkin, op. cit.

30 "Farewell to the Stupidity Pact?" *The Economist* (October 21, 2002): www.economist.com.

31 See Linda M. Aguilar, "NAFTA: A Review of the Issues," *Economic Perspectives* (Federal Reserve Bank of Chicago, 1992), 14; and "OAS Overview of the North American Free Trade Agreement"

(2003): http://www.sice.oas.org/summary/nafta/naftatoc.asp, also on http://www.nafta.net.

32 Richard Lawrence, "NAFTA at 5: Happy Birthday?" *Journal of Commerce* (February 1, 1999).

33 Geri Smith and Elisabeth Malkin, "Mexican Makeover: NAFTA Creates the World's Newest Industrial Power," *Business Week* (December 21, 1998): 50–52.

34 "OAS Overview of the North American Free Trade Agreement, Chapter Four: Rules of Origin" (2003): http://www.sice.oas.org/summary/nafta/nafta4.asp.

35 Ibid.

36 "OAS Overview of the North American Free Trade Agreement, Chapter Twenty: Institutional Arrangements and Dispute Settlement Procedures" (2003): http://www.sice.oas.org/summary/nafta/nafta20.asp.

37 "Summary of the North American Agreement on Labor Cooperation" (2003): http://www.mac.doc.gov/nafta/3006.htm.

38 "Summary of the Agreement on Environmental Cooperation" (2003): http://www.mac.doc.gov/nafta/3005.htm.

39 "News and More," *Mexico Business* (August 30, 2002): http://www.mexicobusiness.com/news.htm.

40 Smith and Malkin, op. cit., 51.

41 "The Decline of the Maquiladora," *Business Week* (April 29, 2002): 59.

42 "Betting on Free Trade," *Business Week* (April 23, 2002): www.businessweek.com.

43 Robert B. Zoellick, "Speech on NAFTA Before the Foreign Trade Council," USTR (July 26, 2001): http://www.ustr.gov/speech-test/zoellick/zoellick_7.PDF, 7.

44 "Bilateral Trade Relations: Mexico," Europa Web site (August 2002): http://europa.eu.int/comm/trade/bilateral/mex.htm.

45 Sydney Weintraub, "A Politically Unpopular Success Story," *Los Angeles Times* (February 7, 1999): p. 2.

46 Smith and Malkin, op. cit., 51.

47 Zoellick, "Speech on NAFTA," op. cit., 3.

48 Aaron Bernstein, "Welch's March to the South," *Business Week* (December 6, 1999): 74, 78.

49 Jason Booth, "Southeast Asia Moves Haltingly Toward Single Consumer Market," *Wall Street Journal* (April 1, 2002): www.wsj.com.

50 Asia-Pacific Economic Cooperation (2003): http://www.apecsec.org.sg.

51 Fred Bergsten, "The Case for APEC," *The Economist* (January 6, 1996): 62.

52 "Why APEC Matters to Americans," United States APEC Index Web site (August 2002): http://www.apec.org.

53 http://www.apecsec.org.sg. op. cit.

54 "Trade to Pick Up Sharply in 2002 After Sharp Drop in 2001," World Trade Organization News (May 2, 2002): http://www.wto.org/english/news_e/pres02_e/pr288_e.htm.

55 Paul Cashin, Hong Liang, and C. John McDermott, "Do Commodity Price Shocks Last Too Long for Stabilization Schemes to Work?" *Finance & Development* 36, no. 3 (September 1999).

56 "Cuba Kisses Sugar Goodbye as a Main Export," CNN (August 10, 2002): http://www.cnn.com/2002/WORLD/americas/08/10/cuba.sugar/index.html.

57 "Frequently Asked Questions About OPEC" (2003): http://www.opec.org.

58 International Monetary Fund, "World Economic Outlook: The Information Technology Revolution" (October 2001): 52. http://www.imf.org/external/pubs/ft/weo/2001/02/index.htm.

59 "Oil: The Latest Shock," *The Economist* (September 18, 1999): 70.

60 "Does OPEC Have Sand in Its Eyes?" *Business Week* (July 1, 2002): 60.

61 "Earth Summit +5" (January 26, 2000): http://www.un.org/esa/earthsummit/ga97info.htm.

62 "Canadian PM Cretien Ratifies Kyoto Protocol," *Wall Street Journal* (December 16, 2002): www.wsj.com.

63 "Struggling to Agree," *The Economist* (September 2, 2002): www.economist.com.

64 "Embracing Greenery," *The Economist* (October 9, 1999): 89–90.

65 The information in this case is from the following sources: Gabriela Lopez, "Mexico Probes Retail Competition as Walmex Dominates," Reuters Company News (May 29, 2002); Gabriela Lopez, "Mexico's Retailers Launch Price War," *Forbes* (June 24, 2002): http://www.forbes.com/newswire/2002/06/24/rtr641092.html; "Wal-Mart Around the World," *The Economist* (December 6, 2001): http://www.economist.com/displayStory.cfm?Story_ID=895888; David Luhnow, "Crossover Success: How NAFTA Helped Wal-Mart Reshape the Mexican Market," *Wall Street Journal* (August 31, 2001): A1; and Alexander Hanrath, "Mexican Stores Wilt in the Face of US Group's Onslaught," *The Financial Times* (August 14, 2002): www.ft.com.

CHAPTER 8

FACTOR MOBILITY AND FOREIGN DIRECT INVESTMENT

Who moves, picks up; who stands still, dries up.

—ITALIAN PROVERB

OBJECTIVES

- ■ To show why the production factors of labor and capital move internationally
- ■ To evaluate the relationship between foreign trade and international factor mobility
- ■ To explain why investors and governments view direct investments and portfolio investments differently
- ■ To describe companies' motivations for and advantages from foreign direct investment
- ■ To demonstrate how companies make foreign direct investments
- ■ To show the major global patterns of foreign direct investment

CASE

LUKoil[1]

In 2001, LUKoil, Russia's largest oil company acquired 100 percent of Getty Petroleum in the United States, which gave it a retail network in the mid-Atlantic and northeastern states of about 1,300 gasoline stations. These are to be rebranded LUKoil-Getty. LUKoil has indicated it plans to make additional North American investments in both refining and distribution. Although the $71 million purchase price of Getty was small in comparison with many other international investments, this was the first Russian acquisition of a publicly held U.S. company. Given that Russia desperately needs capital, many analysts have wondered, "Why does a Russian company see advantages in investing abroad?" Before answering this question, we'll examine Russia's oil position along with LUKoil's competitive situation and strategy.

In recent years, so much oil has been discovered in Russia that the country now has 15 percent more proven reserves than Saudi Arabia. In addition, diplomatic negotiations to solicit Russian support for the war against the Taliban and al Queda in Afghanistan gained Russia's control over oil exports from oil-rich Azerbaijan and Kazakhstan in Central Asia. However, fierce rivalry in the global oil industry has meant that having large crude oil supplies is no guarantee of their sales at an acceptable margin. In essence, Russian oil companies can produce more crude oil than they can sell in Russia. Russia surpassed Saudi Arabia as the world's largest oil producer in 2001. Russian supplies are so large that the Moscow bureau chief of a New York- and London-based energy intelligence group said, "The country is choking on the crude it produces."

Thus, Russian oil companies must sell in foreign markets if they are to use their capacities adequately and if the plan to earn a profit. In the early part of the twenty-first century, Russia's export situation was favorable because the Organization of Petroleum Exporting Countries (OPEC), which Russia never joined, cut production to increase world crude prices. Further, many petroleum buyers sought Russian oil because they feared that political unrest would threaten Middle Eastern export supplies. The result was that Russian oil companies, such as LUKoil, could sell more oil outside Russia and at a higher price than they could a few years earlier. This favorable market situation enabled Russian oil companies to have enough capital to invest abroad if they reasoned that such investment would help their strategic positions. LUKoil believed that such investment met this test.

LUKoil was one of several companies created in 1991 out of the Russian state-owned petroleum monopoly. Since then, the Russian government has gradually reduced its LUKoil holdings to less than 10 percent. LUKoil became the first Russian oil company to integrate "from oil well to filling station." It has over 120,000 employees, about 1,100 Russian filling stations, and it produces about a quarter of Russia's crude oil production. It has one of the world's biggest proven oil reserves owned by a private company. (Some of the world's largest oil companies, such as Saudi Aramco from Saudi Arabia and Petroven from Venezuela, and their reserves are government owned.) By 2000, LUKoil was the world's fourth largest private oil company. Its president, Vagit Alexperov, a former deputy in the Soviet Oil & Gas Ministry, declared that his goal was to make LUKoil the world's largest oil company. He thinks that international expansion from both exports and foreign investments is the way to achieve that goal. One of his reasons for wanting foreign expansion is that the company can get bigger margins and more assurance of full on-time payment outside Russia. In fact, about two-thirds of LUKoil's sales are outside Russia, thus generating more capital to meet expansion goals than if the sales were domestic. However, why doesn't LUKoil simply export rather than make foreign investments? The answer lies in a combination of factors.

First, oil prices have fluctuated widely in the past; so has the ability to market Russian oil abroad. Figure 8.1 shows price fluctuations from 1970 through 2001. In fact, in the late 1990s, a global oil glut

FIGURE 8.1   World Oil Prices, 1970–2001

Note that prices sometimes increase by over 100 percent or decrease by over 50 percent from one year to another, mainly because of supply changes. The prices refer to the official price of Saudi Light oil.

Source: Energy Information Administration, "World Oil Market and Oil Price Chronologies: 1970–2001" (January 2002), http://www.eia.doe.gov/emeu/cabs/chron.

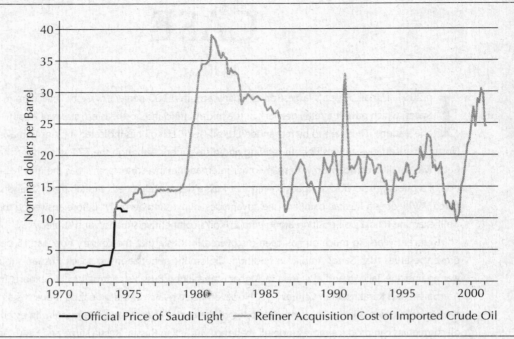

Official Price of Saudi Light   Refiner Acquisition Cost of Imported Crude Oil

and depressed world oil prices hampered LUKoil's ability to be profitable. So LUKoil emulated its larger Western competitors and embraced the idea of forward integration into ownership of foreign distribution. Its first foreign investments were in the former Soviet satellite countries of Bulgaria and Romania, because these countries were close, familiar, long-time customers of Russian oil, in which state-owned oil companies had been privatized. It has since expanded into more than 20 other countries, almost entirely by buying existing companies rather than through greenfield (start-up) operations. Simply stated, when producing companies invest in distribution, they capture markets that better enable them to sell their crude oil when there are global oversupplies. Further, this integration could potentially reduce LUKoil's operating costs because LUKoil will not have to negotiate and enforce agreements with any other company.

Second, despite having huge reserves in Russia and capturing foreign markets, where it sells some of the output from those reserves, LUKoil must depend primarily on oil sales to other companies. External and internal political relations could impair the future sales to these companies. Externally, an importing country could lower its purchases of Russian oil to protest some Russian political policy or simply to diversify its own supplies. Internally, the Russian government owns the pipeline system through which virtually all Russian oil exports pass. Because it allocates quotas among oil companies, a competitor might gain influence with Russian political decision makers to preempt part of LUKoil's quota. Thus, LUKoil sees the need to develop foreign oil supplies and aims to make them about 20 percent of its total supplies. It has seized the opportunity to invest in oil exploration in places where some non-Russian competitors are restricted, such as in Algeria, Iraq, Libya, and Sudan.

Third, to be a major global competitor, LUKoil must become as efficient as the major Western companies. To do so, it needs the latest petroleum technology, marketing skills, and operating efficiencies. For example, its administrative expenses and cost of capital have been high compared with Western competitors. Within Russia, these needs have created only minor problems because LUKoil's competition has been other Russian oil companies that also inherited operational inefficiencies from the former state-owned oil monopoly. However, new competitive threats within Russia have been gaining momentum. BP and TotalFinaElf bought interests in Russian companies in 2002, and the CEO of Russia's second largest oil company, Yukos, retorted that "within five years, only one or two major Russian oil companies will remain independent; the rest will be acquired by Western oil companies." Thus, LUKoil sees advantages in acquiring skills from foreign companies to help it compete better, both at home and abroad. With this outcome in mind, it has put independent directors from Western oil companies on its board. It also sees foreign acquisitions, such as the Getty acquisition in the United States, as a means of gaining experienced personnel, technology, and competitive know-how.

Fourth, LUKoil wants to place more of its assets outside Russia because Russia's political and economic policies historically have been unstable, unpredictable, and unfavorable to efficient business operations. Besides its communist heritage, Russia recently has endured inconsistent and unclear legislation along with a high tax structure. Further, Russia's currency (the ruble) has been weak, unreliable, and not easily exchanged into other currencies. Thus, LUKoil plans to reduce its risks by depending more on foreign operations. For example, LUKoil has recently been keeping about two-thirds of its cash and cash equivalents in nonruble accounts.

In summary, LUKoil's decision to invest abroad is due to a combination of company-specific, industry-specific, and global environmental conditions.

INTRODUCTION

Recall from Chapter 5 that factors of production increasingly move internationally. The LUKoil case illustrates both LUKoil's movement of capital from Russia, allowing it to make investments abroad, and BP's and TotalFinaElf's movement of capital into Russia, allowing them to make investments there. In addition to capital movements, there are people movements. Thus, a country's relative factor endowment may change because of factor movements. We'll briefly discuss the reasons for this mobility and explain its effect on international trade and global efficiency under different scenarios.

In Chapter 1, we defined a foreign direct investment (FDI) as a company controlled through ownership by a foreign company or foreign individuals. Gaining this control usually

High transportation costs often require companies to produce abroad if they are to sell abroad. Soft drinks are a good example because of the high cost of transportation relative to the price of the retail product. Fast food operations are another because of the impracticality of shipping prepared food great distances. The photo shows a variety of vending machines selling soft drinks from U.S. companies, along with a KFC outlet in Kuwait.

requires the international mobility of production factors. FDI is now the most important component of international business. For example, sales from foreign controlled facilities are now about double the value of world trade.[2] Given the importance of FDI both in international business and in factor mobility, we'll devote most of the chapter to its explanation. Figure 8.2 shows FDI's place in international business. In this chapter, we'll teach you what FDI is, how it is done, and what advantages companies gain by undertaking it. Yet no one theory or explanation encompasses all the reasons for FDI.[3]

The growth of FDI has resulted in a heightened interest in three questions that we'll cover in later chapters:

1. What effect does FDI have on a country's economic, political, and social objectives?
2. What is, or should be, a company's location pattern of foreign investment?
3. Should a company choose to operate abroad through some form other than direct investment, such as licensing?

Because of concerns raised in question 1, the Polish government rejected proposals by Russian oil companies to buy an oil refinery at Gdansk. We'll discuss question 1 in Chapter 11 ("Governmental Attitudes Toward Foreign Direct Investment"). In our opening case, we showed that LUKoil made its first FDI in former Soviet satellite countries, the location decision implied by question 2, which we'll discuss in Chapter 13 ("Country Evaluation and Selection"). Finally, we'll examine question 3 by illustrating different operating forms in Chapter 14 ("Collaborative Strategies").

FACTOR MOBILITY

In this section, we'll discuss why production factors move, what effects the movements have in transforming factor endowments, and the effect of international factor mobility on world trade.

Why Production Factors Move

Capital, especially short-term capital, is the most internationally mobile production factor. Companies and private individuals primarily transfer capital because of differences in expected return (accounting for risk). They find information on interest rate differences readily available,

Capital and labor move internationally to

- gain more income
- flee adverse political situations

FIGURE 8.2   The Place of FDI in International Business

FDI is a means by which international business is conducted.

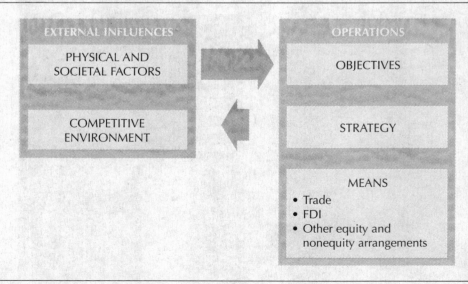

and they can transfer capital by wire almost immediately at a low cost. Short-term capital is more mobile than long-term capital, especially direct investment, because there is more likely to be an active market through which investors can quickly buy foreign holdings and sell them if they want to transfer capital back home or to another country. Further, investors feel more certain about short-term political and economic conditions in a foreign country than about long-term ones. These political and economic conditions affect investors' perceptions of risk and where they prefer to put their capital. However, not all capital movements occur because of risk to and expected returns on capital. Governments give foreign aid and loans. Not-for-profit organizations donate money abroad to relieve worrisome economic and social conditions. Individuals remit funds to help their families and friends in foreign countries.

People are also internationally mobile. Of course, some people travel to another country as tourists, students, and retirees; however, this travel does not constitute labor mobility unless they work there. Unlike funds that can be cheaply transferred by wire, people must usually incur high transportation costs to work in another country. If they move legally, they must get immigration papers, and most countries give these documents sparingly. Finally, such people may have to learn another language and adjust to a different culture away from their families and friends who serve as their customary support groups. Yet about two percent of the world's population has migrated to another country.[4] Since this two percent is spread unevenly, the impact is much greater on some countries than on others.

Of the people who go abroad to work, some move permanently and some move temporarily. For example, on the one hand, some people emigrate to another country, become citizens, and plan to reside there for the rest of their lives. On the other hand, MNEs assign managers to work abroad for periods ranging from a few days to several years, and some countries allow workers to enter for only short periods. New Zealand does this by giving three-to-six-months permits for workers from Tonga and Fiji. In many cases, workers leave their families behind in the hope of returning home after saving enough money while working in a foreign country. Some move legally and others move illegally (i.e., they are undocumented). People, whether professionals or unskilled workers, largely work in another country for economic reasons. For example, Indonesian laborers work in Malaysia because they can make almost 10 times as much per day as they can at home.[5] People also move for political reasons—for example, because of persecution or war dangers, in which case they are known as refugees. However, once they are refugees, they usually become part of the labor pool where they live. Sometimes it is difficult to distinguish between economic and political motives for international mobility because poor economic conditions often parallel poor political conditions. For example, in the three year period before 2002, about 600,000 Colombians left the country, fleeing both a civil war and unemployment.[6]

Effects of Factor Movements

Neither international capital nor population mobility is a new occurrence. For example, had it not been for historical masses of immigration, Australia, Canada, and the United States would have hardly any population today. Further, many immigrants brought human capital with them, thus adding to the base of skills that enabled those countries to be newly competitive in an array of products they might otherwise have imported. Finally, these same countries received foreign capital to develop infrastructure and natural resources, which further altered their competitive structures and international trade.

However, what about the more recent past? Evidence is largely anecdotal. Nevertheless, factor movements are substantial for many countries. For example, about 10 percent of the labor force in Austria is foreign,[7] and Singapore has transformed itself from a labor-intensive and low-wage country to a capital-intensive and high-wage country largely because of capital accumulation that has come from abroad.[8] Although labor and capital are different production factors, they are intertwined. For example, much of Singapore's capital accumulation has

Factor movements alter factor endowments.

been in human capital, i.e. import of skilled foreigners and the education of its own work-force. Further, countries lose potentially productive resources when factors leave, but they may gain from the foreign earnings on those factors. For example, Ecuador lost almost five percent of its population between 1999 and 2001, including 10,000 teachers and many other people with substantial work skills. However, many of these people are now sending remittances back to Ecuador. El Salvador and the Dominican Republic receive much more income from remittances that their citizens working abroad send home than they receive from their exports. Overall, Latin American and Caribbean countries are receiving more than three times as much from remittances as from the receipt of foreign aid.[9]

The Relationship of Trade and Factor Mobility

Factor movement is an alternative to trade that may or may not be a more efficient allocation of resources. If trade could not occur and production factors could not move internationally, a country would have to either forgo consuming certain goods or produce them differently; either scenario would usually result in lower worldwide output and higher prices. In some cases, however, the inability to gain sufficient access to foreign production factors may stimulate efficient methods of substitution, such as the development of alternatives for traditional production methods. For example, U.S. tomato farmers in California depended almost entirely on Mexican temporary workers (braceros) until the bracero program terminated in 1964. In 1960, it took 45,000 workers to harvest 2.2 million tons of tomatoes. By 1999, it took only 5,000 workers to harvest 12 million tons of tomatoes because the end of the bracero program spurred farmers to gain efficiency through mechanization. At the same time, the real cost of tomatoes fell 54 percent.[10]

Substitution   When the factor proportions vary widely among countries, pressures exist for the most abundant factors to move to countries with greater scarcity—where they can command a better return. In countries where labor is abundant compared to capital, laborers tend to be unemployed or poorly paid. If permitted, these workers will go to countries that have full employment and higher wages. Similarly, capital will tend to move away from countries in which it is abundant to those in which it is scarce. For example, Mexico gets capital from the United States, and the United States gets labor from Mexico.[11] If finished goods and production factors were both free to move internationally, the comparative costs of transferring goods and factors would determine the location of production. However, as is true of trade, there are restrictions on factor movements that make them only partially mobile internationally, such as both U.S. immigration restrictions that limit the legal and illegal influx of Mexican workers and Mexican ownership restrictions in the petroleum industry that limit U.S. capital investments in that industry.

A hypothetical example, shown in Figure 8.3, should illustrate the substitutability of trade and factor movements under different scenarios. Assume the following:

- The United States and Mexico have equally productive land available at the same cost for growing tomatoes.

- The cost of transporting tomatoes between the United States and Mexico is $0.75 per bushel.

- Workers from either country pick an average of two bushels per hour during a 30-day picking season.

The only differences in price between the two countries are due to variations in labor and capital cost. The labor rate is $20.00 per day, or $1.25 per bushel, in the United States and $4.00 per day, or $0.25 per bushel, in Mexico. The capital needed to buy seeds, fertilizers, and equipment costs the equivalent of $0.30 per bushel in the United States and $0.50 per bushel in Mexico.

Both finished goods and production factors are partially mobile internationally.

There are pressures for the most abundant factors to move to an area of scarcity.

FIGURE 8.3 Comparative Costs of Tomatoes Based on Trade and Factor Mobility Between the United States and Mexico

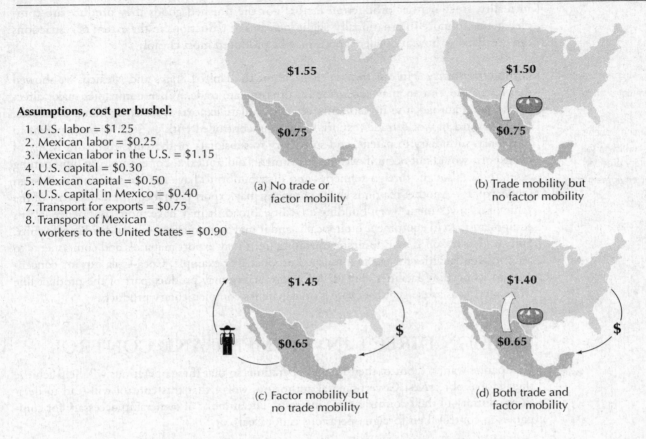

Assumptions, cost per bushel:

1. U.S. labor = $1.25
2. Mexican labor = $0.25
3. Mexican labor in the U.S. = $1.15
4. U.S. capital = $0.30
5. Mexican capital = $0.50
6. U.S. capital in Mexico = $0.40
7. Transport for exports = $0.75
8. Transport of Mexican workers to the United States = $0.90

(a) No trade or factor mobility

(b) Trade mobility but no factor mobility

(c) Factor mobility but no trade mobility

(d) Both trade and factor mobility

The lowest costs occur when trade and production factors are both mobile.

If neither tomatoes nor production factors can move between the two countries (see Figure 8.3[a]), the cost of tomatoes produced in Mexico for the Mexican market is $0.75 per bushel ($0.25 of labor plus $0.50 of capital), while those produced in the United States for the U.S. market cost $1.55 per bushel ($1.25 of labor plus $0.30 of capital). If the two countries eliminate trade restrictions on tomatoes between them (Figure 8.3[b]), the United States will import from Mexico because the Mexican cost of $0.75 per bushel plus $0.75 for transporting the tomatoes to the United States will be $0.05 less than the $1.55 per bushel cost of growing them in the United States.

Consider another scenario in which neither country allows the importation of tomatoes but both allow certain movements of labor and capital (Figure 8.3[c]). Mexican workers can enter the United States on temporary work permits for an incremental travel and living expense of $14.40 per day per worker, or $0.90 per bushel. At the same time, U.S. companies will invest capital in Mexican tomato production, provided the capital earns more than it would earn in the United States—say, $0.40 per bushel, which is less than the Mexican going rate. In this scenario, Mexican production costs per bushel will be $0.65 ($0.25 of Mexican labor plus $0.40 of U.S. capital) and U.S. production costs will be $1.45 ($0.25 of Mexican labor plus $0.90 of travel and incremental costs plus $0.30 of U.S. capital). Each country would reduce its production costs—from $0.75 to $0.65 in Mexico and from $1.55 to $1.45 in the United States—by bringing in abundant production factors from abroad.

With free trade and the free movement of production factors (Figure 8.3[d]), Mexico will produce for both markets by importing capital from the United States. According to the

The lowest costs occur when trade and production factors are both mobile.

above three assumptions, doing this will be cheaper than sending labor to the United States. In reality, since neither production factors nor the finished goods they produce are completely free to move internationally, slight increases or reductions in the extent of restrictions can greatly alter how and where goods may be produced most cheaply.

Complementarity   In our tomato example for the United States and Mexico, we showed that factor movements may substitute for or stimulate trade. When companies make direct investments abroad, the investments often stimulate exports from their home countries. About a third of world trade (exports) is among controlled entities, such as from parent to subsidiary, subsidiary to parent, and subsidiary to subsidiary of the same company. Many of the exports would not occur if overseas investments did not exist. For example, in our opening case, LUKoil bought foreign refineries and distribution to have captive sales for its Russian crude exports. Another reason is that a company may export capital equipment as part of the value of its investment when building a facility abroad. It may have more confidence in this equipment than in equipment built locally, and it may want maximum worldwide uniformity. Still another reason is that domestic operating units may export materials and components to their foreign facilities for use in a finished product. For example, Coca-Cola exports concentrate to its bottling facilities abroad. A foreign facility may produce part of the product line while serving as sales agent for exports of its parent's complementary products.

FOREIGN DIRECT INVESTMENT AND CONTROL

Companies want to control their foreign operations so that these operations will help achieve their global objectives. Governmental authorities worry that this control will lead to decisions contrary to their countries' best interests. The amount of ownership necessary for companies to control their foreign operations is not clear-cut.

The Concept of Control

For direct investment to take place, control must accompany the investment. Otherwise, it is a portfolio investment. If ownership is widely dispersed, then a small percentage of the holdings may be sufficient to establish control of managerial decision making. However, even a 100-percent share does not guarantee control. If a government dictates whom a foreign company can hire, what the company must sell at a specified price, and how the company must distribute its earnings, then control belongs to the government. Governments frequently do impose all or part of these decisions on foreign firms. But it is not only governments that may jeopardize the owners' control. If the company's owners do not regulate key resources the company needs, then those who control those resources may exert substantial influence on the company. Because direct investments can be difficult to define, governments have established arbitrary ownership minimums that they use when making policy and for reporting statistics. Usually, they stipulate that ownership of at least 10 or 25 percent of the voting stock in a foreign enterprise makes the investment direct. Because different governments and international organizations define direct investment differently, it is difficult to be definitive about FDI statistics on a global basis.[12]

The Concern About Control

Although defining direct investment is arbitrary, the concept is important. Both governments and companies are concerned with the issue of control.

Governmental Concern   Why should a government care whether an investment is controlled from abroad? Many critics of FDI worry that the host country's national interests will

---

Margin notes (left column):

Factor mobility via direct investment often stimulates trade because of

- the need for components
- the parent's ability to sell complementary products
- the need for equipment for subsidiaries

Direct investment usually implies an ownership share of at least 10 or 25 percent.

When foreign investors control a company, decisions of national importance may be made abroad.

suffer somewhat if a multinational company makes decisions from afar on the basis of its own global or national objectives. For example, GM, a U.S. company, owns a 100-percent interest in Vauxhall Motors in the United Kingdom. Such control means that GM's corporate management in the United States can make decisions about personnel staffing, export prices, and the retention and payout of Vauxhall's profits. This level of control concerns the British public because decisions that directly affect the British economy can come from the United States.

Investor Concern Control is also important to foreign companies. They may want to do what is best for their global operations rather than what is best for the operations in a specific country. For example, if LUKoil did not own 100 percent of Getty, its partner in the United States might argue that it should not buy oil from LUKoil, perhaps to save some transportation costs for the Getty operation. Companies are also reluctant to transfer vital resources—capital, patents, trademarks, and management know-how—to another organization. The company receiving these resources can use them to undermine the competitive position of the foreign company transferring them. For example, Samsung Electronics from South Korea leapfrogged to become the world's largest memory-chip maker mostly by acquiring technology from other companies.[13] For this reason, although Intel transfers nonvital resources to partnerships, it has strategically blocked other companies' access to its vital resources by handling them within its wholly owned operations.[14] This idea of denying rivals access to resources is called the **appropriability theory**.[15]

The control inherent in FDI may lower a company's operating costs and increase its rate of technological transfer because:

1. The parent and subsidiary usually share a common corporate culture.
2. The company can use its own managers, who understand its objectives and the nature of the sometimes difficult-to-teach processes that it wishes to transfer.
3. The company can avoid protracted negotiations with another company.
4. The company can avoid problems of enforcing an agreement.

This control through self-handling of operations (internal to the organization) is **internalization**.[16]

Despite the advantages of control, many circumstances exist in which companies transfer assets to noncontrolled entities. For example, a company may transfer its trademarks and technology through licensing agreements. In essence, companies lack resources to control all aspects of their production, supplies, and sales, so they funnel the resources that they do have to those activities that are most important to their strategies and their performance.

> Investors who control an organization
> - Are more willing to transfer technology and other competitive assets
> - Usually use cheaper and faster means of transferring assets

COMPANIES' MOTIVES FOR FDI

Foreign direct investment is a way to fulfill any one of the three major operating objectives we discussed in Chapter 1 that may lead companies to engage in international business:

1. To expand their sales
2. To acquire resources
3. To minimize competitive risk

In addition, governments may own FDI or influence their home-based companies to establish FDI because of political motives.

However, companies can pursue operating modes other than FDI, such as exporting, importing from another company, or collaborating with another company to handle operations on its behalf. These modes are less risky than FDI because a company has to expose fewer resources in a foreign country where it has a **liability of foreignness** (disadvantage

> Businesses and governments are motivated to engage in FDI in order to
> - Expand sales
> - Acquire resources
> - Minimize competitive risk
>
> Governments may additionally be motivated by some desired political advantage.

relative to local companies that understand how to better operate in the environment). Thus, companies must possess some advantage to compensate for the liability.[17] So why would a company risk operating in an environment less familiar than the one at home? Let's find out why, following Table 8.1's summary of the motivations for FDI.

Factors Affecting the Choice of FDI for Sales Expansion

One reason managers will risk operating abroad is to expand sales. In the sections that follow, we discuss how transportation, excess capacity, scale economies, product alterations, trade restrictions, country-of-origin effects, and changes in comparative costs affect companies' sales.

Transportation   When companies add the cost of transportation to production costs, some products become impractical to ship over great distances. A few of these products and their investing companies are newspapers (Thompson Newspapers, Canadian), margarine (Unilever, British-Dutch), dynamite (Nobel, Swedish), and soft drinks (PepsiCo, United States). These companies must produce abroad if they are to sell abroad. When companies move abroad to produce basically the same products they produce at home, their direct investments are **horizontal expansion**.

Excess Capacity   As long as a company has excess capacity, it may compete effectively in limited export markets despite high transport costs. This ability might occur if domestic sales cover fixed operating expenses, enabling the company to set foreign prices on the basis of variable rather than full (variable + fixed) costs. Such a pricing strategy may erode as foreign sales become more important or as output nears full plant capacity. Further, the company's average cost per unit decreases until it reaches full capacity. This helps explain why companies will export before establishing plants in more than one country. For example, Volkswagen placed its first plant to build the new Beetle at its facilities in Mexico, which served global markets. However, when demand pushed that plant toward capacity, Volkswagen announced it would build a second plant in Europe to serve the European market.[18]

This reluctance to expand total capacity while there is still substantial excess capacity is similar to the basis for a domestic-expansion decision. Internationally as well as domestically, growth is incremental. Most likely, a company will begin operations near the city in which its founders reside and will begin selling only locally. Eventually, sales may be expanded to a larger geographic market. As it reaches capacity, the company may build a second plant, warehouses, and sales offices in another part of the country to serve that region, save on

Margin notes:

Transportation may raise costs so much that it becomes impractical to export some products.

Excess capacity

- Usually leads to exporting rather than new direct investment
- May be competitive because of variable cost pricing

● TABLE 8.1

MOTIVATIONS FOR FDI AS AN ALTERNATIVE OR SUPPLEMENT TO TRADE

These objectives usually outweigh the risks of FDI.

SALES EXPANSION OBJECTIVES	RESOURCE ACQUISITION OBJECTIVES	RISK MINIMIZATION OBJECTIVES	POLITICAL OBJECTIVES
Overcome high transport costs	Savings through vertical integration	Diversification of customer base (same motivations as for sales expansion objectives	Influence companies, usually through factors under resource acquisition objectives
Lack of domestic capacity	Savings through rationalized production	Diversification of supplier base (same motivations as for resource acquisition objectives)	
Low gains from scale economies	Gain access to cheaper or different resources and knowledge	Following customers	
Trade restrictions	Need to lower costs as product matures	Preventing competitors' advantage	
Barriers because of country-of-origin effects (nationalism, product image, delivery risk)	Gain governmental investment incentives		
Lower production costs abroad			

transportation costs, establish closer contact with customers and suppliers, and attain lower delivery costs. In the pursuit of foreign business, not surprisingly, growing companies eventually find it advantageous to acquire assets abroad, which are FDIs.

Scale Economies and Product Alterations   The manufacture of some products necessitates a high fixed capital cost for plant and equipment. For such products, especially if they are standardized or undifferentiated from those of competitors, the cost per unit drops significantly as output increases. Products such as ball bearings, aluminum, and semiconductor wafers fall into this category. Companies can export large amounts of such products because the cost savings from scale economies overcome added transportation costs.

Companies that need to alter their products substantially for different foreign markets benefit less by scale economies. For these types of products, smaller plants to serve national rather than international markets will save transportation costs. This need to alter products affects company production in two ways. Initially, it means an additional investment, which might spur management to locate facilities abroad. Next, it may mean that certain economies from large-scale production will be lost, which may shift the least-cost location from one country to another. The more the product has to be altered for the foreign market, the more likely it is that production will shift abroad. Whirlpool, for example, finds that U.S. demand is for top-loading washing machines with large capacities using 110 electrical voltage, whereas European demand is for front-loading washing machines (more efficient in using energy and water) with smaller capacity using 220 voltage.[19] Given the differences in demand, Whirlpool produces in both the United States and Europe.

Trade Restrictions   Although governments have been reducing import barriers through the World Trade Organization (WTO), bilateral agreements, and regional trading groups, they still restrict many imports. Thus, companies may find that they must produce in a foreign country if they are to sell there. For example, Volkswagen decided to build Skoda cars in India because of India's 121 percent duty on the imports.[20]

Managers must view import barriers along with other factors, such as the market size of the country imposing the barriers. For example, import trade restrictions have been highly influential in enticing automobile producers to locate in Brazil because of its large market. Similar restrictions by Central American countries have been ineffective because of their small markets. However, Central American import barriers on products requiring lower amounts of capital investment for production and, therefore, smaller markets (for example, pharmaceuticals) have been highly effective at enticing direct investment.

Removing trade restrictions among a group of countries also may attract direct investment, possibly because the expanded market may justify scale economies and possibly because the output from a new location can be feasibly exported. For example, Israel has received an influx of high-tech direct investment to produce for markets in countries with which it has signed free trade agreements.[21]

Country-of-Origin Effects   Government-imposed legal measures are not the only trade barriers to competitive goods. Consumer desires also may dictate limitations. Consumers may prefer to buy goods produced in their own country rather than in another (perhaps because of nationalism).[22] If they feel strongly enough, they may even push for legislation requiring labels showing where products are made, such as U.S. labeling of agricultural products, or mandating the purchase of domestic goods when governments buy products, such as the state of Missouri's buy-American requirements.[23] Or they may believe that goods from a given country are superior, like German cars and French perfume, therefore preferring those countries' products. In actuality, consumers often view the quality of identical products differently on the basis of country of origin.[24] They may also fear that service and replacement parts for imported products will be difficult to obtain. Adding to this need to invest directly

---

In large-scale process technology, companies' exports reduce costs by spreading fixed costs over more units of output.

In small-scale process technology, companies' country-by-country production reduces costs by minimizing transportation expenses.

If imports are highly restricted, companies
- *Often produce locally to serve the local market*
- *Are more likely to produce locally if market potential is high relative to scale economies*

Consumers sometimes prefer domestically produced goods because of
- *Nationalism*
- *A belief that these products are better*
- *A fear that foreign-made goods may not be delivered on time*

is the global rise in just-in-time (JIT) manufacturing systems, which decrease inventory costs by having components and parts delivered as needed. These systems favor nearby suppliers who can deliver quickly.

In any of these cases, companies may find advantages in placing FDI where their output will have the best acceptance.

The least-cost production location changes because of inflation, regulations, transportation costs, and productivity.

Changes in Comparative Costs   A company may successfully compete from a production location within its home country. This success may be due to cost, which depends on its prices and the productivity of the individual production factors, the size of the company's operations, the cost of transporting finished goods, and any regulations on how to produce. None of these conditions is static, so the least-cost location may change from one country to another. For example, Honda is shifting some production and exports from Japan to China because Japanese costs of production have risen relative to those in China.[25]

Shifts in comparative production costs can be reasons for resource-seeking investments. A company may establish a direct investment to serve a foreign market but eventually export from that foreign market back to its home country. Production costs are discussed in the following section on resource-seeking investments.

Factors Affecting Motives to Acquire Resources Through FDI

A company may engage in international business to acquire goods or services from abroad. Of course, companies may obtain the goods and services from abroad by buying them from another company, but certain factors favor FDI as a way to gain these resources. Let's examine some reasons for using FDI to acquire resources from abroad.

In international vertical integration, raw materials, production, and marketing are often located in different countries.

Vertical Integration   **Vertical integration** is a company's control of the different stages (sometimes collectively called a value chain) of making its product—from raw materials through production to its final distribution. As products and their marketing become more complicated, companies need to combine resources that are located in more than one country. Let's take steel as an example. If one country has the iron, a second the coal, a third the technology and capital for making steel products, and a fourth the demand, there will be great interdependence among the four. The companies will need a tight relationship to ensure that production and marketing continue to flow. One way to help assure this flow is to gain a voice in the management of one or more of the foreign operations by investing in it. Much of the world's direct investment in petroleum, including those we discussed in the LUKoil case, may be partially explained by this concept of vertical integration. Because much of the petroleum supply is located in countries other than those with a heavy petroleum demand, the oil industry has become integrated vertically on an international basis.

Advantages of vertical integration may accrue to a company through either market-oriented (forward integration) or supply-oriented (backward integration) investments in other countries. Of the two, there have been more examples in recent years of supply-oriented investments designed to obtain raw materials in other countries. This is because of the growing dependence on emerging economies for raw material supplies and the lack of capital in those countries to exploit them fully. Nevertheless, forward integration has been increasing in many industries because margins have been better in distribution than in production.[26]

Companies may also gain certain economies through vertical integration. Because supply and/or markets are more assured, companies may be able to carry smaller inventories and spend less on promotion. They do not have to incur the costs of negotiating and enforcing contracts with other companies. By buying and selling within the family of companies, foreign direct investors also have considerably greater flexibility in shifting funds, taxes, and profits among countries. Despite these advantages, many companies have been moving away from vertical integration in order to concentrate their efforts on those links in the value chain in which they feel they have their best competencies.

Rationalized Production   Some companies produce different components or different portions of their product line in different parts of the world to take advantage of low labor costs, capital, and raw materials. This is **rationalized production**. For example, General Electric uses Mexico as a base for the manufacture and assembly of labor-intensive portions of its aircraft engine components.[27] As is the case with vertical integration, companies choose to own the production facilities in the different countries because of the need for a tight relationship to ensure a smooth production flow.

Many companies shrug off the possibility of rationalized production of parts. They fear work stoppages in many countries because of strikes or a change in import regulations in just one country. As an alternative to parts rationalization, a company can produce a complete product in a given country. However, only part of a company's product range is produced in that country. For example, a U.S. subsidiary in France may produce only product A, another subsidiary in Brazil only product B, and the home plant in the United States only product C. Each plant sells worldwide so that each can gain scale economies and take advantage of differences in input costs that may result in differences in total production cost. Each may get concessions to import because it can demonstrate that it can generate local jobs and incomes.

Another possible advantage of this type of rationalization is smoother earnings when exchange rates fluctuate. Consider the value of the Japanese yen compared to the U.S. dollar. Honda produces some of its line in Japan and then exports this production to the United States. Honda also produces some of its line in the United States and then exports this production to Japan. If the yen strengthens, Honda may have to cut its profit margin to stay competitive on its exports to the United States. But this cut may be offset by a higher profit margin on the exports from the United States to Japan. Given the multiple origins of products' components and the production of different product models in different countries, it is becoming harder to determine the nationality of a product, as Figure 8.4 shows.

Access to knowledge   The practice of seeking knowledge abroad that is not satisfactorily available in the home country closely resembles vertical integration and rationalized production, but it is different insofar as a company goes abroad to gain some capability for its organization as a whole. The search for knowledge as an FDI motive is becoming commonplace. For example, many non-U.S. companies have offices in New York City to gain better access to knowledge of what is happening within the U.S. capital market that can affect other worldwide capital occurrences. McGraw-Hill established an office in Europe to allow its personnel there to uncover European technical developments by visiting universities, trade associations, and companies. Two Indian software companies, Silverline Technologies and SSI, bought U.S. companies primarily to better understand the U.S. market where they already sold most of their Indian-developed software.[28]

The Product Life Cycle Theory   In Chapter 5, we explained the product life cycle (PLC) theory. This theory shows how, for market and cost reasons, production often moves from one country to another as a product moves through its life cycle. During the introductory stage, production occurs in only one (usually industrial) country. During the growth stage, production moves to other industrial countries, and the original producer may decide to invest in production facilities in those foreign countries to earn profits there. In the mature stage, production shifts largely to emerging economies, and the same company may decide to control operations there as well.

Governmental Investment Incentives   In addition to restricting imports, countries frequently encourage direct investment inflows by offering tax concessions or other subsidies.

In rationalized production, different components or portions of a product line are made in different parts of the world. The advantages are

- Factor-cost differences
- Long production runs

A company may establish a presence in a country in order to improve its access to knowledge.

The product life cycle theory explains why

- New products are produced mainly in industrial countries
- Mature products are more likely to be produced in emerging economies

---

Governmental incentives may shift the least-cost production location.

FIGURE 8.4

FDI, especially with vertical integration and rationalized production, obscures a product's nationality.

Source: By permission of Chip Bok and Creators Syndicate, Inc.

This subject is discussed in greater detail in Chapter 12, but briefly, such incentives affect the comparative cost of production among countries and entice companies to invest in a particular country to serve national or international markets. For example, Bermuda attacts large amounts of FDI by charging companies low tax rates on their earnings. So many U.S. companies, such as Columbia Laboratories, register their new patents in Bermuda so that foreign earnings from sales using the patents flow to Bermuda where they are almost tax-free.[29] In addition, many central and local governments offer direct-assistance incentives to gain jobs attracting FDI. For example, the state of Alabama (United States) gave the Korean company Hyundai over $250 million in incentives, including tax breaks, assistance in training personnel, site purchase, and road improvements.[30]

Risk Minimization Objectives

Companies may reduce risks by operating internationally, such as through sales diversification. Their choice of foreign direct investment as the means of reducing risk is due primarily to the same factors we have discussed for market expansion and resource acquisition motives. For example, Johnson Controls, a U.S. manufacturer of automobile parts and control systems for buildings, expanded into Europe largely to minimize its exposure to cyclical downturns in the United States.[31] One of LUKoil's FDI motives has been to move assets out of Russia. Further, much of the FDI by Latin American companies in the United States has been motivated by a desire to move funds from their risky home environments.[32] Transportation costs, foreign import restrictions, and foreign consumer desires for product alterations may make FDI the preferred operating mode for sales diversification. Let's now examine some specific reasons for using FDI to minimize risk.

Companies can keep customers by following them abroad.

Following Customers   Many companies' customers are other companies. They sell products, components, or services to those customers domestically, which then become embodied in a product or service that their customers sell. If an important customer makes a foreign direct investment, the supplier may have compelling reasons to make a foreign direct investment as well. First, it would like to get that customer's business. Second, if a competitor becomes the supplier in the foreign location, that competitor may improve its chances of serving the customer in the domestic market as well. Third, there may be prohibitions to serving the foreign market through exports. For example, Tredegar Industries sells plastic materials, primarily to Procter & Gamble (P&G), for use in paper diapers. When P&G decided to produce in China using JIT, Tredegar had little choice but to make an investment in China as well.[33]

Preventing Competitors' Advantage   Within oligopolistic industries (those with few sellers), several investors often establish facilities in a given country within a fairly short time of each other, and they thus often overcrowd the market.[34] For example, 10 different automobile companies have made investments in China, leading one analyst to say, "The number of entrants is so great, it's difficult to see where the profits could accrue."[35] In many industries, most companies experience capacity-expansion cycles concurrently. Thus, they would logically consider a foreign investment at approximately the same time. Externally, they might all be faced with changes in import restrictions or market conditions that indicate the wisdom of making a move to direct investment to serve consumers in a given country. In spite of the prevalence of these motivators, many movements by oligopolists seem better explained by defensive motives.

Much of the research in game theory shows that people often make decisions based on the "least-damaging alternative." Similarly, many companies ask, "Do I lose less by moving abroad or by staying at home?" Assume that some foreign market may be served effectively only by an investment in the market, but the market is large enough to support only one producer. To solve this problem, competitors could set up a joint operation and divide the profits among themselves if antitrust laws permit this kind of partnership. If only one company establishes a direct investment, it will have an advantage over its competitors by garnering a larger market, spreading its R&D costs, and making a profit it can reinvest elsewhere. Once one company decides to produce in the market, competitors are prone to follow quickly rather than let that company gain advantages. The company's decision to invest depends not so much on the benefits it gains but rather on what it could lose by not entering the field. In most oligopolistic industries (such as automobiles, tires, and petroleum), this pattern helps explain the large number of producers compared to the size of the market in some countries. Along these same lines, a company will sometimes invest in a foreign competitor's home market to prevent that competitor from using the high profits it makes in that market to invest and compete elsewhere.[36]

Political Motives

FDI sometimes depends on a country's political attempts to reduce security risk. For example, Chinese government-owned petroleum companies have been investing abroad so that China will be less dependent on foreign companies for its oil supplies.[37] The move may also help China hold down prices on the petroleum it receives. In the process of gaining control of resources, home countries also acquire much political control.

Control of resources is not necessarily the only political reason for direct investment. For example, during the early 1980s, the U.S. government instituted various incentives to increase the profitability of U.S. investment in Caribbean countries that were unfriendly to Cuba's Castro regime. The United States wanted to strengthen the economies of those friendly nations through the growth the FDI would bring and make it difficult for unfriendly leftist governments to gain control. But with the end of the Cold War, the United States ended investment incentives in the Caribbean region, and much investment was diverted to Mexico because of NAFTA.[38]

In oligopolistic industries, competitors tend to make direct investments in a given country about the same time.

Governments give incentives to their companies to make direct investments in order to

- Gain supplies of strategic resources
- Develop spheres of influence

Most successful domestic companies, especially those with unique advantages, invest abroad.

ETHICAL DILEMMA

Critics Debate the Ethics of FDI and Employment

NEC, a Japanese computer and electronics manufacturer, announced it was moving out of Scotland to gain cost advantages in China. These cost advanatages included not only labor, but also taxes, because the company would be operating within a special Chinese economic zone. The move stranded its Scottish employees, particularly since other companies in the area, such as Coats, Motorola, and Mayflower, had recently moved facilities from Scotland to China as well.[39] Similarly, two U.S. companies, Coastcast and Cast Alloys, moved golf club production from Mexico to China to reduce production costs.[40] Many critics of FDI argue that it is unethical for governments to lure companies away from existing locations by offering lucrative incentives. (Incentives are often much greater than the tax breaks offered by China.) These critics also argue that it is unethical for companies to accept them. Companies say that their response to more favorable conditions—such as incentives, taxes, and regulations—is necessary because competitors are bound to take advantage of these conditions. Do governments in countries where a company is already located have any ethical obligations—especially if their policies, such as environmental regulations or high taxes, burden producers? On the one hand, direct investment may lead to better global use of resources and will employ laborers from developing countries who otherwise may not find work. On the other hand, it is the newly unemployed workers who suffer if they lose their jobs and cannot easily find new ones. For these employees, there is little solace in the economic gains that go to previously unemployed workers abroad or the lower consumer prices or higher corporate earnings resulting from the foreign production. Some people argue that the plight of these newly unemployed workers is no different from the results of technological change, such as when workers in clothespin factories lost their jobs with the invention of the electric clothes dryer. Other people argue that displacement from FDI is different because the workers can seldom move abroad to take advantage of the new opportunities there and because their employers are responsible for the job losses. They argue that the company has an ethical obligation to give employees advance notice of the move and to provide training and help with job searches.

RESOURCES AND METHODS FOR MAKING FDI

Now that we've discussed why companies engage in FDI, we'll now look at how they actually acquire foreign direct investments.

Assets Employed

Direct investments usually, but not always, involve some capital movement.

Foreign direct investment is usually an international capital movement that crosses borders when the anticipated return (accounting for the risk factor and the cost of transfer) is higher overseas than at home. Although most FDI requires some type of international capital movement, an investor may transfer many other types of assets. For example, Westin Hotels has transferred very little capital to foreign countries. Instead, it has transferred managers, cost control systems, and reservations capabilities in exchange for ownership in foreign hotels.

There are other means of acquiring foreign investments that are not capital movements per se. A company may use funds it earns in a foreign country to establish an investment. For example, a company that exports merchandise but holds payment for those goods abroad can use the payment to acquire an investment. In this case, it has merely exchanged goods for equity. Although companies don't use this method extensively for initial investment, retained earnings are a major means of expanding abroad. Also, companies in different countries can trade equity—for example, through mergers. For example, Tabacalera in Spain acquired a share of Seita in France by giving Seita's owners stock in Tabacalera—a move that helped integrate the competitive strategies of the two tobacco companies.[41] (A peculiar twist to FDI statistics is that each country has both an inflow and outflow of FDI when there are cross-national mergers.) Finally, companies can borrow all (rarely) or part (frequently) of the funds in the host country to make an investment.

Buy-Versus-Build Decision

There are two ways companies can invest in a foreign country. They can either acquire an interest in an existing operation or construct new facilities. A company must consider both alternatives carefully because both have advantages and disadvantages.

Reasons for Buying   Whether a company makes a direct investment by acquisition or start-up depends, of course, on which companies are available for purchase. The large privatization programs occurring in many parts of the world have put hundreds of companies on the market, and MNEs have exploited this new opportunity to invest abroad. For example, foreign companies, such as Vivendi from France, bought many British utility companies when they were privatized.[42]

There are many reasons for seeking acquisitions. One is the difficulty of transferring some resource to a foreign operation or acquiring that resource locally for a new facility, especially if the company feels it needs to adapt substantially to the local environment or operate through a multidomestic strategy.[43] Personnel is a resource that foreign companies may find difficult to hire, especially if local unemployment is low. Instead of paying higher compensation than competitors do to entice employees away from their old jobs, a company can buy an existing company, which gives the buyer not only labor and management but also an existing organizational structure. This may be particularly important if the company is making an FDI to augment its capabilities, such as to acquire knowledge.[44]

Through acquisitions, a company may also gain the goodwill and brand identification important to the marketing of mass consumer products, especially if the cost and risk of breaking in a new brand are high. Further, a company that depends substantially on local financing rather than on the transfer of capital may find it easier to gain access to local capital through an acquisition. Local capital suppliers may be more familiar with an ongoing operation than with the foreign enterprise. In addition, a foreign company may acquire an existing company through an exchange of stock.

In other ways, acquisitions may reduce costs and risks—and save time. A company may be able to buy facilities, particularly those of a poorly performing operation, for less than the cost of new construction. If an investor fears that a market does not justify added capacity, acquisition enables it to avoid the risk of depressed prices and lower unit sales per producer that might occur if it adds one more producer to the market. Finally, by buying a company, an investor avoids inefficiencies during the start-up period and gets an immediate cash flow rather than the problem of tying up funds during construction.

Reasons for Building   Although acquisitions offer advantages, a potential investor will not necessarily be able to realize them. Companies frequently make foreign investments in sectors where there are few, if any, companies operating, so finding a company to buy may be difficult. In addition, local governments may prevent acquisitions because they want more competitors in the market and fear market dominance by foreign enterprises. Even if acquisitions are available, they often don't succeed. The acquired companies might have

---

The advantages of acquiring an existing operation include

- Adding no further capacity to the market
- Avoiding start-up problems
- Easier financing

Companies may choose to build if

- No desired company is available for acquisition.
- Acquisition will lead to carry-over problems
- Acquisition is harder to finance

substantial problems. Personnel and labor relations may be both poor and difficult to change, ill will may have accrued to existing brands, or facilities may be inefficient and poorly located. Further, the managers in the acquiring and acquired companies may not work well together, particularly if the two companies are accustomed to different management styles and practices or if the acquiring company tries to institute many changes.[45] Finally, a foreign company may find local financing easier to obtain if it builds facilities, particularly if it plans to tap development banks for part of its financial requirements.

INVESTORS' ADVANTAGES

Direct investment usually improves a company's performance.

Are companies profitable because they are multinational or multinational because they are profitable? Such a chicken-and-egg question has hounded direct investment theorists. On the one hand, evidence indicates that successful domestic companies (both large and small) are most likely to commit resources to FDI. On the other hand, ownership of FDI appears to improve a company's performance.[46] Let's take a look at companies' operating advantages before and after they become foreign direct investors.

Companies invest directly only if they think they hold some supremacy over similar companies in countries of interest. The advantage results from a foreign company's ownership of some resource—patents, product differentiation, management skills, access to markets—unavailable at the same price or terms to the local company. This edge is often called a monopoly advantage. Because of the increased cost of transferring resources abroad and the perceived greater risk of operating in a different environment, the company will not move unless it expects a higher return than it can get at home and unless it thinks it can outperform local firms.[47]

Companies from certain countries may enjoy a monopoly advantage if they can borrow capital at a lower interest rate than companies from other countries. Prior to World War I, Great Britain was the largest source of direct investment because of the strength of the pound sterling and the resulting lower interest rates on borrowing sterling funds. From World War II until the mid-1980s, the strength of the U.S. dollar gave an advantage to U.S. firms. After that, this advantage shifted to Japanese companies, until the Japanese yen weakened in 1997.[48] More recently, capital markets have become so international that companies can more easily borrow abroad if interest rates are lower there.

A similar advantage is when the foreign company's currency has high buying power. During the two and a half decades following World War II, the U.S. dollar was very strong. By converting dollars to other currencies, U.S. companies could purchase more in foreign countries than they could in the United States. This advantage was an incentive for U.S. companies to make foreign investments. They could add production capacity more cheaply abroad than at home. Further, non-U.S. companies could not as easily make FDIs in the United States. Currency values do not, however, provide a strong explanation for direct investment patterns because investors see a strong currency as an indicator of a strong economy that will enhance their sales.

To support the high costs necessary to maintain domestic competitiveness, companies frequently must sell on a global basis. To sell most efficiently, many companies establish direct investments abroad. In contrast to less internationally oriented companies, the advantage accruing to more internationally oriented companies from spreading out some of the costs of product differentiation, R&D, and advertising is apparent.

DIRECT INVESTMENT PATTERNS

Although foreign direct investment began centuries ago, its biggest growth has occurred since the middle of the twentieth century. Recent growth has resulted from several factors, particularly the more receptive attitude of governments to investment inflows, the process of privatization, and the growing interdependence of the world economy. By 2000, about 63,000 companies owned about 800,000 FDIs. These FDIs produced about 10 percent of global output.[49] Let's now look at where FDI is owned and located and the industries in which it exists.

Location of Ownership

The industrial countries account for a little over 90 percent of all direct investment outflows.[50] This is understandable, because more companies from those countries are likely to have the capital, technology, and managerial skills needed to invest abroad. Nevertheless, hundreds of firms from emerging economies have FDIs, although the holdings from individual developing countries remain small compared to investments from industrial nations. For example, of the 100 companies that own the most FDI, only five are from developing or newly industrialized countries, Hutchinson Whampoa (Hong Kong), Cemex (Mexico), LG Electronics (Korea), Petroven (Venezuela), and Petronas (Malaysia). Table 8.2 shows the top 25 foreign direct investors in terms of their foreign assets.

During much of the post–World War II period, the United States was the dominant investor. However, its share has been falling as the share from other industrial countries, especially the United Kingdom and Japan, has increased. Recently, FDI has been flowing more rapidly into the United States than out of it. Much of this development has resulted from the large foreign purchases of U.S. companies, such as British Petroleum's $61 billion acquisition of Amoco in 1998 and Vodaphone Group's (also from the United Kingdom) $58 billion acquisition of AirTouch in 1999.[51]

Location of Investment

The largest investors in the United States are the United Kingdom, Japan, and the Netherlands, accounting in 2001 for about 16, 12, and 12 percent, respectively, of FDI there.[52] The largest locations of U.S.-owned FDI in 2001 were in the United Kingdom, Canada, and the Netherlands, which held 18, 10, and 10 percent of the value of U.S.-owned FDI. Figure 8.5 shows the direction of recent global FDI inflows and outflows.

The major recipients of FDI are developed countries, which received about 79 percent of the world's total in 2001, as shown in Figure 8.5. However, for 2001 a larger share went to developing countries, primarily because of a drop in inflows to developed countries from 2000 to 2001 of more than half because of an economic slowdown.[53] Nevertheless, inflow to developing countries also fell, but not by as much. The small share going to emerging economies has caused concern about how those economies will meet their capital needs.

The interest in developed countries has come about for three main reasons:

1. More investments have been market seeking, and the markets are larger in developed countries.
2. Political turmoil in many emerging economies has discouraged investors.
3. The industrial nations, through the Organization for Economic Cooperation and Development (OECD), are committed to liberalizing direct investment among their members.

The OECD operates (with exceptions) under a principle that member countries should treat foreign-controlled companies no less favorably than domestic ones in such areas as taxes, access to local capital, and government procurement. The OECD member countries also have agreed on procedures through which direct investors can resolve situations that may result from conflicting laws between their home and host countries.

For worldwide FDI,

- Almost all ownership is by companies from developed countries

Most FDI occurs in developed countries because they have the

- Biggest markets
- Lowest perceived risk
- Least discrimination toward foreign companies

● TABLE 8.2

THE WORLD'S 25 LARGEST TNCS, RANKED BY FOREIGN ASSETS, 2000

(Billions of dollars and number of employees)

Note that all the companies are from developed or newly industrialized countries.

RANKING 2000 BY FOREIGN ASSETS	CORPORATION	COUNTRY	INDUSTRY	ASSETS FOREIGN	SALES FOREIGN	EMPLOYMENT FOREIGN
1	Vodaphone	United Kingdom	Telecommunications	221.2	7.4	24,000
2	General Electric	United States	Electronics	159.2	49.5	145,000
3	ExxonMobil	United States	Petroleum expl./ref./distr.*	101.7	143.0	64,000
4	Vivendi Universal	France	Diversified	93.3	39.4	210,084
5	General Motors	United States	Motor vehicles	75.2	48.2	165,300
6	Royal Dutch/Shell Group	The Netherlands/ United Kingdom	Petroleum expl./ref./distr.*	74.8	81.1	54,337
7	BP	United Kingdom	Petroleum expl./ref./distr.*	57.5	105.6	88,300
8	Toyota Motor	Japan	Motor vehicles	56.0	62.2	...
9	Telefónica	Spain	Telecommunications	56.0	12.9	71,292
10	Fiat	Italy	Motor vehicles	52.8	35.9	112,224
11	IBM	United States	Computers	43.1	51.2	170,000
12	Volkswagen Group	Germany	Motor vehicles	42.7	57.8	160,274
13	Chevron Texaco	United States	Petroleum expl./ref./dist.*	42.6	65.0	21,693
14	Hutchinson Whampoa	Hong Kong	Diversified	41.9	2.8	27,165
15	Suez	France	Diversified/utility	38.5	24.1	117,280
16	DaimlerChrysler AG	Germany/United States	Motor vehicles	...	48.7	83,464
17	News Corporation	Australia	Media	36.1	12.8	24,500
18	Nestlé S.A.	Switzerland	Food/beverages	35.3	48.9	218,112
19	Total Fina SA	France	Petroleum expl./ref./distr.*	33.1	82.5	30,020
20	Repsol YPF	Spain	Petroleum expl./ref./distr.*	29.8	9.1	...
21	BMW	Germany	Motor vehicles	31.2	26.1	23,759
22	Sony Corporation	Japan	Electronics	30.2	42.8	109,080
23	E.On	Germany	Electricity, gas and water	...	41.8	83,338
24	ABB	Switzerland	Electrical equipment	28.6	22.5	151,340
25	Phillips Electronics	Netherlands	Electrical & electronic equipment	27.9	33.3	184,200

Note: United Nations Conference on Trade and Development, *The World Investment Report* (Geneva and New York: United Nations, 2002), p. 86. Measurements are based on 10 percent ownership or more. Only nonfinancial companies are included. In some companies, foreign investors may hold a minority share of more than 10 percent.

*expl./ref./distr. = exploration, refining, and distribution

Economic Sectors of FDI

The highest recent growth in FDI has been in services.

Trends in the distribution of FDI generally conform to long-term economic changes in the home and host countries. Over time, the portion of FDI accounted for in the raw materials sector that includes mining, smelting, and petroleum has declined. The portion in manufacturing, especially resource-based production, grew steadily from the 1920s to the early 1970s, but it has since stabilized. Since then, FDI in the service sector (especially banking and finance) has growwn rapidly, as has FDI in technology-intensive manufacturing.

FIGURE 8.5   FDI Inflows and Outflows in Major World Regions, 2000 (in billions of U.S. dollars)

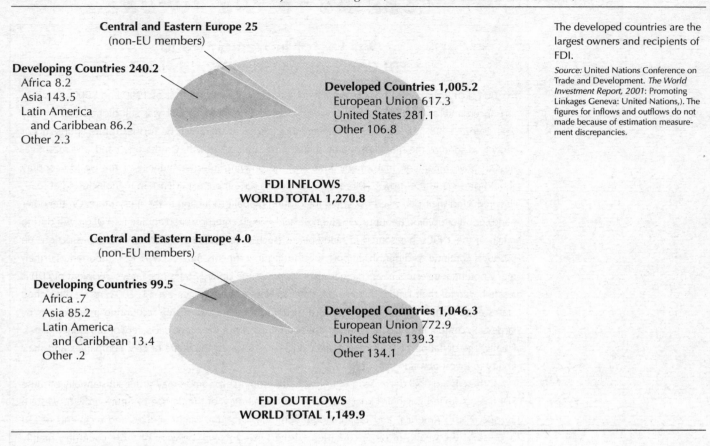

Central and Eastern Europe 25
(non-EU members)

Developing Countries 240.2
Africa 8.2
Asia 143.5
Latin America
    and Caribbean 86.2
Other 2.3

Developed Countries 1,005.2
European Union 617.3
United States 281.1
Other 106.8

FDI INFLOWS
WORLD TOTAL 1,270.8

Central and Eastern Europe 4.0
(non-EU members)

Developing Countries 99.5
Africa .7
Asia 85.2
Latin America
    and Caribbean 13.4
Other .2

Developed Countries 1,046.3
European Union 772.9
United States 139.3
Other 134.1

FDI OUTFLOWS
WORLD TOTAL 1,149.9

The developed countries are the largest owners and recipients of FDI.

Source: United Nations Conference on Trade and Development. *The World Investment Report, 2001*: Promoting Linkages Geneva: United Nations,). The figures for inflows and outflows do not made because of estimation measurement discrepancies.

FDI IN COMPANIES' STRATEGIES

Direct investment is an integral way to carry out global, multidomestic, and transnational strategies. Recall from Chapter 1 that multidomestic strategies differ from transnational and global strategies insofar as multidomestic strategies allow each foreign country operation to act somewhat independently. A transnational strategy allows each country to contribute ideas, resources, and direction so that the company's global operations are maximized. Global strategies integrate the company's operations, but most control and resources come from the country in which its headquarters is located.

Market-seeking direct investments—those that take place because companies must produce within the markets they serve (because of high costs of transportation or trade restrictions)—generally favor multidomestic strategies. Direct investments that are motivated by consumer or competitor moves are more likely to be global or transnational strategies. Resource-seeking investments that are designed to bring about vertical integration or rationalized production usually entail global or transnational strategies as well. Direct investment, because of its implied control, permits companies to make decisions to maximize global performance. When companies depend instead on licensing or foreign production contracts, the interests of their partner companies may constrain their ability to implement global or transnational strategies.

Direct investments help to serve the goal of global efficiency by transferring resources to where they can be used more effectively. However, countries distort movements of resources by restricting the inward or outward flow of direct investments. Although these distortions are less important in motivating investments and their locations than political conditions and natural economic forces are, managers must consider them. To the extent that countries give preferential treatment to domestically headquartered or state-owned firms, the environment in which companies compete internationally is further complicated.

LOOKING TO THE FUTURE

Will Factor Movements and FDI Continue to Grow Worldwide?

In 2001, FDI flows decreased substantially in relation to the record flows of 1999 and 2000, thus raising uncertainty about FDI's future growth. However, the flow for 2001 was still higher than for any year before 1998, leading many observers to expect that there will be further future spurts in FDI growth as soon as the global economy shows more signs of growth. On the one hand, the receptiveness of governments to investment flows and the growing interdependence of the world economy should presage future growth. Moreover, companies have more experience in manufacturing abroad, thus reducing their perceived risk when integrating global production in the near future. On the other hand, popular opinion about privatization of state-owned enterprises, an engine for FDI growth during much of the 1990s, has soured in many places (such as in Bolivia and Peru). As trade restrictions on products continue to diminish, import substituting investments may become less important. Further, many potential investors have changed their view that the United States (the largest recipient of FDI) is a safe haven for their funds. The terrorist attack in New York on September 11, 2001, made the United States appear more vulnerable to political risk. Subsequent exposés of accounting irregularities by large U.S. companies have raised additional questions about the economic safety of the United States. Finally, the deflation of U.S. stock market prices has lowered the value of U.S. companies and their ability to invest abroad.

If there is a global decrease in FDI growth, developing economies may suffer substantially because FDI has accounted for their largest capital inflow. Regardless of the degree of future growth, Western Europe, North America, and Japan should continue to be the major sources and recipients of FDI because of the wealth of those countries. Further, investors will be wary of those countries, mainly developing ones, in which corruption is rampant and in which there is high political uncertainty concerning the treatment of foreign direct investors. FDI in services may continue to grow in importance both because of the difficulty of removing protectionist barriers on the service trade and because of the need of service providers (such as investment bankers, advertising agencies, and insurance companies) to react quickly to the overseas needs of their clients.

There are also questions about the future of international labor mobility. On the one hand, the pressures to leave countries for economic and political reasons are likely to be as high as ever. On the other hand, there are indications that the industrial countries will be less receptive to accepting immigrants, whether they have high skills or not. For example, anti-immigration candidates have recently received surprisingly high numbers of votes in such countries as Australia, Denmark, and France. Part of the anti-immigration feeling stems from antiglobalization movements, because people fear that foreigners will take their jobs and undermine their accustomed ways of life. In addition, fears of terrorism may lead to greater border surveillance.

Summary

- Production factors and finished goods are only partly mobile internationally. The cost and feasibility of transferring production factors rather than exporting finished goods internationally will determine which alternative is best for the company.

- Although international mobility of production factors may be a substitute for trade, the mobility may stimulate trade through sales of components, equipment, and complementary products.

- Both countries and companies are concerned about the control of foreign investments—the former, because they fear decisions will be contrary to national interests; and the latter, because they want to safeguard their competitive positions.

- Companies may undertake FDI to expand foreign markets, to gain access to supplies of resources or finished products, and to reduce their operating risks. Home governments may encourage such investment for political purposes.

- The price of some products increases too much if they are exported. Therefore, foreign production is often necessary to tap foreign markets because it skirts import barriers and reduces transportation costs.

- As long as companies have excess domestic capacity, they usually try to delay establishing foreign production because their average cost per unit of output goes down until they reach capacity.

- The extent to which scale economies lower production costs influences whether production is centralized in one or a few countries or dispersed among many countries.

- Companies may establish FDI because consumers may prefer to buy domestically produced products and may demand that foreign companies alter products to fit their needs.

- FDI may enable companies to lower their operating expenses because they find cheaper locations and superior resources, rationalize their production, and integrate vertically.

- FDI sometimes has chain effects: When one company makes an investment, some of its suppliers follow with investments of their own, followed by investments by *their* suppliers, and so on.

- Within oligopolistic industries, several companies often invest in a foreign country at about the same time. This happens because they are responding to similar market conditions or because they wish to negate competitors' advantages in that market.

- There are advantages and disadvantages to FDI by either acquisition or start-up.

- Monopolistic advantages help explain why companies are willing to take what they perceive as higher risks of operating abroad. Certain countries and currencies have had such advantages, which helps explain the dominance of companies from certain countries at certain times.

- Most FDI originates from and goes to developed countries. The fastest recent growth of FDI has been in the service sector. This has happened because companies from those countries are more likely to have the needed resources and because developed countries have bigger markets and lower risks.

 CASE

Cran Chile[54]

Cranberries are native to North America, their claim to fame being a spot at the first Thanksgiving dinner in 1621. The first commercial crop was handpicked in 1817. Cranberries are so little known outside North America that few languages other than English have a word for the fruit. Cranberry sales have traditionally been seasonal due primarily to the ripening of North American berries in the fall and the berries' customary inclusion in U.S. Thanksgiving menus during November. The vulnerability to seasonal demand became apparent to cranberry growers in 1959, when the U.S. Secretary of Agriculture warned a few days before Thanksgiving that a new pesticide sprayed on cranberries could be carcinogenic. Even though the warning proved unfounded, sales plummeted. This spurred cranberry growers and processers to try to increase sales during other times of the year. Ocean Spray Cranberries, owned by more than 900 cranberry and grapefruit growers throughout the United States and

Canada, is the dominant competitor. Other competitors include Northland, a number of regional brands like Langers in California and Apple & Eve in New York, and a large and growing number of companies producing for the private label market, such as Cliffstar and Clement Pappas. Ocean Spray has done most of the work to build and diversify cranberry sales, especially by developing year-round sales of drinks using cranberry juice. Many other companies now buy cranberries, primarily from Ocean Spray and Northland, to use in some of their products. These include General Mills and Kellogg's for cereals; PepsiCo's Tropicana, Coke's Minute Maid, and Cadbury Schweppes' Snapple for drinks; and Nabisco and Pepperidge Farms for bakery products. When a Harvard study confirmed in the early 1990s that cranberries help combat urinary tract infections, sales increased significantly.

In addition to promoting new products using cranberries, U.S. companies have begun marketing cranberry products abroad.

Although some of these sales are aided by small grants from the U.S. Department of Agriculture's program that was established to stimulate exports, the exports by 2002 were less than one percent of the U.S. domestic consumption.

Continued growth in domestic and foreign sales is, of course, dependent on sufficient supplies of cranberries. A shortfall in supply prompted one man to make a foreign domestic investment to grow cranberries. Warren Simmons developed the Pier 39 retail complex in San Francisco and founded the Tia Maria and Chevys Mexican Restaurant chains. In 1992, his Chevys restaurants ordered a large shipment of fresh cranberries from Ocean Spray to make cranberry margaritas, but Ocean Spray could not fill the order. Simmons investigated the shortage and concluded that supplies could not grow fast enough in North America to fulfill the growing demand. Although production was increasing, demand was growing even faster.

He based his conclusion of inadequate future cranberry supplies from North America on the following factors:

1. *Regulations.* He assumed that most cranberries grew in bogs, which alternatively can serve as wetlands that provide a habitat for plants and wildlife, control flooding, and serve as a natural filter for ground pollutants. As U.S. wetland restrictions became more stringent, it became difficult, time-consuming, and costly to add land for cultivation.

2. *Yields.* Although research had been under way to increase yields, many bogs had become less fertile because of their many years of cultivation. Although new high-yielding varieties were available, growers were reluctant to lose current income from existing low-yielding beds while going through the costly and time-consuming process of planting the new varieties and awaiting their maturity.

3. *Land costs.* In some cranberry-growing regions, urbanization and land development had pushed land cost up so much that they were no longer profitable for cranberry cultivation. Further, many workers could not afford nearby accommodations from their earnings.

Mr. Simmons sold his Chevys Mexican Restaurants in 1992 to PepsiCo and used part of the proceeds to invest in foreign cranberry production. He hired one of the few horticulturists specializing in cranberries to advise him on where and how to grow berries. He chose an isolated area near Lanco, Chile (35 miles northeast of Valdivia and 450 miles south of Santiago), to invest in a new company called Cran Chile. (See Map 8.1.) He chose this area because of its fertile soil, climatic conditions, relatively stable government and

To Simmons, Lanco's soil, rain, and lack of enrironmental restrictions made it an attractive spot for cranberry production, although it is far from existing markets in the United States and potential markets in Europe and Asia.

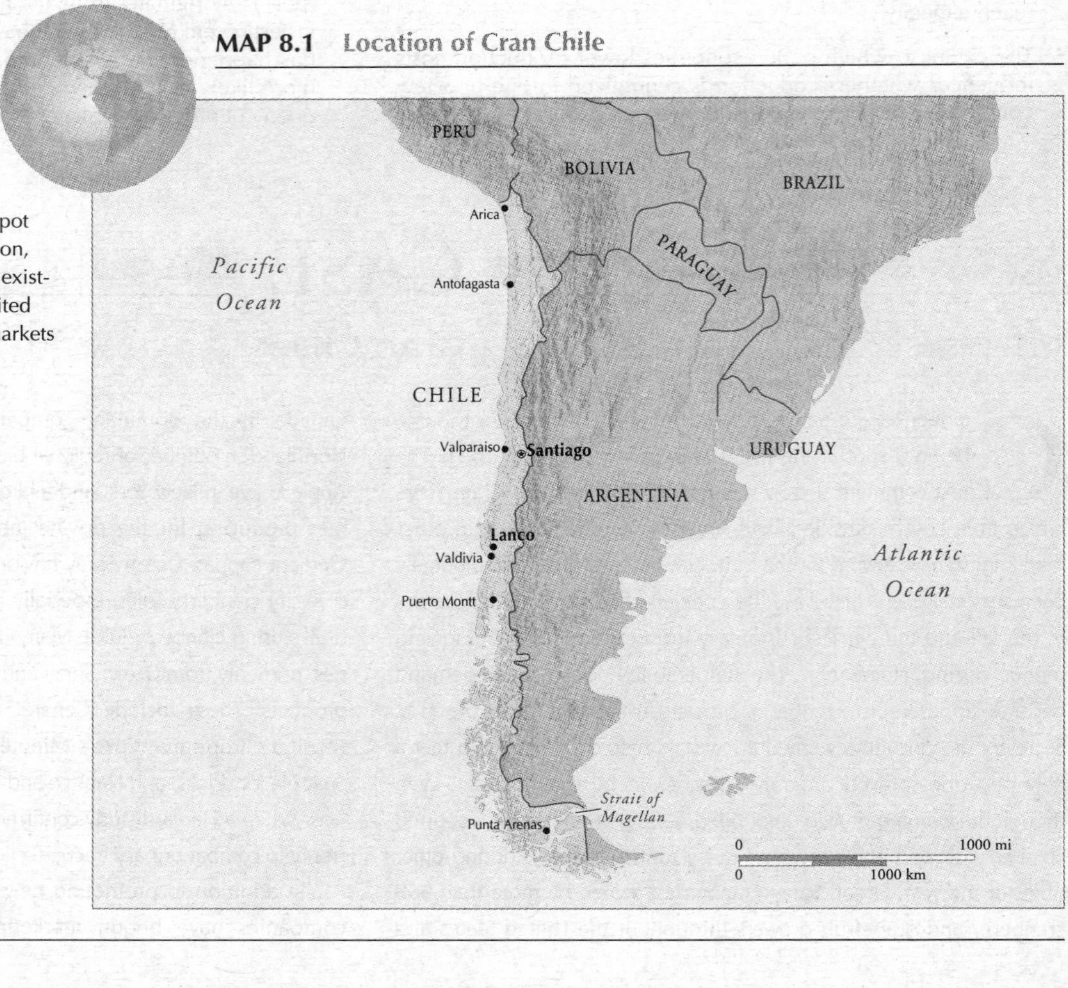

MAP 8.1   Location of Cran Chile

currency, strong legal system, and its ample water supply fed by exceptional amounts of rain and snow at higher elevations. The company was able to access its water from a number of well-located rivers that allowed the operation to use a gravity system for sprinkling and flooding the cranberry plants. By 1995, Simmons had invested about $20 million and planned eventually to have Cran Chile account for 10 percent of the world's cranberry land in cultivation.

In its first few years of operations, Cran Chile's managers made two major mistakes that almost caused the company's failure. First, the company failed to plant its limited planting material densely enough to overcome the growth of weeds. Second, although the industry's standard practice is to plant into soil with a layer of sand on top, Cran Chile omitted the sand because it was not readily available locally. In addition to the company's self-inflicted mistakes, the U.S. cranberry acreage increased about a third between 1994 and 2000, primarily in Wisconsin, where cranberries are largely grown in dry areas moistened with water from sprinklers. The result was an oversupply of cranberries that caused prices to fall from $60 a gallon to $12 a gallon, which was far below the break-even price of about $30-to-$35 per barrel (a barrel contains 100 pounds of cranberries).

Coincident with the company's mistakes and the precipitous drop in the price of cranberries, Simmons became ill. Simmons brought in a new CEO, whose management team downsized the company (in terms of hard assets and head count), made a number of senior management changes, and improved the company's balance sheet.

By 2002, Cran Chile had about 750 acres under cultivation, with expected yield-per-acre roughly double that of the fields in the United States. In addition to climatic conditions, this expected high productivity is due to several factors. Cran Chile has been able to hire Chilean technicians with about six years of formal training in agronomy. It also retained as a consultant a grower whose U.S. farm had one of the best yields in the United States. Cran Chile's agronomy team and its advisor decide on the use of fertilizer, watering (Cran Chile uses dry-land production rather than bogs), herbicides, and pesticides. They also decide when to hire part-time labor for hand-weeding and when to bring in bees for pollination. In addition, Cran Chile uses capital-intensive technology to increase yields and reduce costs. For example, Cran Chile plants cranberries in beds typically larger than those in the United States; thus, it must reposition watering and harvesting machinery less frequently. Cran Chile's farm is also significantly larger than the average farm in North America. This is shown in the accompanying photo.

One production problem Cran Chile faces is the great distance between Chile and customers in the United States. Because transportation costs preclude the export of whole cranberries from Chile, Cran Chile built a berry processing plant to make concentrate in Lanco. It sells the concentrate to companies making branded and private label drinks in the United States, Canada, and other parts of the world, including Japan, Australia and Europe. These companies have wel-

comed supplies from Cran Chile to supplement those they buy from Ocean Spray and Northland. (Since Ocean Spray and Northland produce their own brands of cranberry flavored drinks, Cran Chile's customers reason that Ocean Spray and Northland might use concentrate supplies themselves when there are shortages rather than sell the supplies to them.) Even if transportation costs were not a problem, Chilean crops are harvested about mid-February, which is not the right time to sell to the U.S. Thanksgiving market for whole cranberries. However, the year-round demand for cranberry drinks creates another problem for Cran Chile, whose crops and concentrate production are semiseasonal. Cran Chile's customers have developed production processes based on a just-in-time inventory system, whereby their plants keep only a few weeks' worth of supplies in inventory. Thus, Cran Chile must bear the cost of holding inventories until its customers need them. Further, these customers require Cran Chile to monitor and record the origin and dates of each concentrate batch (such as in which bed and when the berries were grown and picked and in which containers as well as on what dates they were stored, moved, and processed) in order to control for quality and to trace supplies in case of contamination.

Since Cran Chile's cranberry crops are seasonal, it processes concentrate for growers of other fruits, such as raspberries, in order to utilize its processing facilities more fully. Cran Chile's management is considering the possibility of contracting to sell these other fruit concentrates because its customers might prefer to buy from companies that can supply them with a variety of fruit concentrates, such as both cranberry and raspberry concentrates for cranberry and raspberry drinks.

When Simmons decided to invest in Chile, companies making cranberry juice products were projecting increased sales in Asia and Europe. Although there has been some increase, especially as more companies have developed cranberry drinks, the growth in these sales has been very slow. Ocean Spray's CEO summarized the difficulty, say-

The photo shows Cran Chile harvesting a flooded cranberry bed with a mobile bridge, which it also uses for fertilizing and pruning. Used with permission of Cran Chile.

ing, "We're introducing an unknown fruit in an unknown brand in a foreign market that's unknown to us." Ocean Spray's foreign expansion has already encountered some problems. For instance, the company started selling juice in Britain in bottles, but it had to change to small boxes because so many British families have small refrigerators. The introduction of cranberry juice in Japan was so disappointing that the company pulled out of the market temporarily. Although the children of Cran Chile's employees in Lanco enjoy cranberry juice, these employees agree that developing a viable market in Chile would require a long-term change in Chilean's distaste for the fruit.

In sum, Cran Chile represents a resource-seeking investment with a high risk but a potentially high return if production and marketing conditions go as its management anticipates.

QUESTIONS

1. What are the motivations and factors that influenced the foreign investment decision for Cran Chile? Compare these with those in the LUKoil case.
2. Relate Simmons's process of international expansion with companies' usual internationalization process (see Chapter 1).
3. Cran Chile is essentially a contractor that supplies components to other companies. What risks and opportunitiess does this relationship present to Cran Chile? Should Cran Chile begin marketing its own products to final consumers?
4. Simmons knew very little about cranberry production or marketing when he decided to enter the cranberry business. What did he do to overcome his deficiencies?

Chapter Notes

1 The information from this case is from the following sources: Sabrina Tavernise and Peter S. Green, "Oil Concerns in Russia Branch Out," *New York Times* (April 2, 2002): W1; Bhushan Bahree, "Western Oil Flirts with Russia Firms, Insider Says," *Wall Street Journal* (April 29, 2002): A13; Reuters, "Mobius and Chevron Exec Nominated for LUKoil Board" (January 17, 2002): http://biz.yahoo.com/rf/020117/117507998_1.html; Paul Starobin, "LUKoil Is Lonesome," *Business Week Online* (April 24, 2000): http://www.businessweek.com:2000/00_17/b3678229.htm?scriptFramed; OAO Lukoil, Interim Consolidated Financial Statements (March 31, 2001): "LUKoil Oil Company," http://www.lukoil.com/; "LUKoil Expands at Home and Abroad," *Hart's European Fuels News* 5, no. 5 (March 7, 2001); "Focus, the Russians Are Coming," *Petroleum Economist* (December 31, 2000); Andrew Jack and Arkady Ostrovsky, "LUKoil in U.S. Petro Deal," *Financial Times* (November 4, 2000): 8; David Ignatius, "The Russians Are Pumping," *Pittsburgh Post-Gazette* (December 28, 2001): A-21; Tina Obut, "Perspective on Russia's Oil Sector," *Oil & Gas Journal* (February 1, 1999): 20; and Anna Raff, Patricia Kranz, and Christopher Palmeri, "Russia: How Much of a Reserve Tank?" *Business Week* (October 29, 2001): 32.

2 United Nations Conference on Trade and Development, *World Investment Report 2000: Cross-border Mergers and Acquisitions and Development* (New York and Geneva: United Nations, 2000), xv–xvi.

3 John H. Dunning's eclectic theory is one treatment that covers most of the explanations. See, for example, John H. Dunning, "The Eclectic Paradigm as an Envelope for Economic and Business Theories of MNE Activity," *International Business Review* 9 (2000): 163–190; and John H. Dunning and John R. Dilyard, "Towards a General Paradigm of Foreign Direct and Foreign Portfolio Investment," *Transnational Corporations* 8, no. 1 (1999): 1–52. For a survey of the development and explanation of different theories, see Peter J. Buckley, "Is the International Business Research Agenda Running Out of Steam?" *Journal of International Business Studies* 33, no. 2 (2002): 365–73.

4 International Organization for Migration, *World Migration Report 2000*, www.iom.int.

5 John Salt, "The Future of International Labor Migration," *Migration Review* 26, no. 4 (Winter 2002): 1077.

6 "Making the Most of an Exodus," *Economist* (February 23, 2002): 41–42.

7 Geoff Winestock and Charles Fleming, "Le Pen Loses, but His Issues Linger," *Wall Street Journal* (May 6, 2002): A15, citing 1999 OECD data.

8 See C. Chris Rodrigo, "East Asia's Growth: Technology or Accumulation?" *Contemporary Economic Policy* 18, no. 2 (April 2000): 215–27; and Paul Krugman, "The Myth of Asia's Miracle," *Foreign Affairs* 73, no. 6 (1994): 62–78.

9 "Making the Most of an Exodus," *Economist* (February 23, 2002): 41–42.

10 Philip L. Martin and Michael S. Teitelbaum, "The Mirage of Mexican Guest Workers," *Foreign Affairs* 80, no. 6 (November–December 2001): 117–31.

11 See Frank D. Bean et al., "Circular, Invisible, and Ambiguous Migrants: Components of Differences in Estimates of the Number of Unauthorized Mexican Migrants in the United States," *Demography* 38, no. 3 (August 2001): 411–22; and United Nations Conference on Trade and Development, *World Investment Report 2000: Cross-border Mergers and Acquisitions and Development* (New York and Geneva: United Nations, 2000): 312.

12 Michael Stephan and Eric Pfaffmann, "Detecting the Pitfalls of Data on Foreign Direct Investment: Scope and Limits of FDI," *Management International Review* 41, no. 2 (Second Quarter, 2001): 189–218.

13 Linsu Kim, "The Dynamics of Samsung's Technological Learning in Semiconductors," *California Management Review* (Spring 1997): 86–100.

14 Allan Afuah, "Strategies to Turn Adversity into Profits," *Sloan Management Review* 40, no. 2 (Winter 1999): 99–109.

15 Internalization theory, or holding a monopoly control over certain information or other proprietary assets, builds on earlier market-imperfections work by Ronald H. Coase, "The Nature of the Firm," *Economica* 4 (1937): 386–405. It has

been noted by such writers as M. Casson, "The Theory of Foreign Direct Investment," *Discussion Paper No. 50* (Reading, England: University of Reading International Investment and Business Studies, November 1980); Stephen Magee, "Information and the MNC: An Appropriability Theory of Direct Foreign Investment," in *The New International Economic Order*, ed. Jagdish N. Bhagwati (Cambridge, MA: MIT Press, 1977), 317–40; C. W. Hill, L. P. Hwang, and W. C. Kim, "An Eclectic Theory of the Choice on International Entry Mode," *Strategic Management Journal* 11 (1990): 117–18; and Ashish Arora and Andrea Fosfuri, "Wholly Owned Subsidiary Versus Technology Licensing in the Worldwide Chemical Industry," *Journal of International Business Studies* 31, no. 4 (Fourth Quarter 2000): 555–72.

16 Alan M. Rugman, *Inside the Multinationals: The Economics of Internal Markets* (New York: Columbia University Press, 1981); David J. Teece, "Transactions Cost Economics and the Multinational Enterprise," *Berkeley Business School International Business Working Paper Series*, no. IB-3 (1985); B. Kogut and U. Zander, "Knowledge of the Firm and the Evolutionary Theory of the Multinational Corporation," *Journal of International Business Studies* 24, no. 4 (1993): 625–45; and Peter W. Liesch and Gary A. Knight, "Information Internalization and Hurdle Rates in Small and Medium Enterprise Internationalization," *Journal of International Business Studies* 30, no. 2 (Second Quarter 1999): 383–96.

17 See John M. Mezias, "Identifying Liabilities of Foreignness and Strategies to Minimize Their Effects: The Case of Labor Lawsuit Judgments in the United States," *Strategic Mangement Journal* 23, no. 3 (March 2002): 229–44; and Jose Mata and Pedro Portugal, "The Survival of New Domestic and Foreign-Owned Firms," *Strategic Management Journal* 23, no. 4 (April 2002): 323–43.

18 John Griffiths, "VW May Build Beetle in Europe to Meet Demand," *Financial Times*, (November 11, 1998): 17.

19 Peter Marsh, "The World's Wash Day," *Financial Times* (April 29, 2002): 6.

20 "Skoda Brings New Luxury Car, Octavia," *The Statesman* (India) (November 17, 2001): FT Asia Africa Intelligence Wire.

21 Aluf Benn, "Why Peace Doesn't Pay," *Foreign Policy* 124 (May–June 2001): 64–65.

22 Jill Gabrielle Klein, "Us Versus Them, or Us Versus Everyone? Delineating Consumer Aversion to Foreign Goods," *Journal of International Business Studies* 33, no. 2, (Second Quarter, 2002): 345–63.

23 See Lynda V. Mapes, "Food Fight Ensues Over Labeling," *Seattle Times* (April 25, 2002): A1; and Ken Leiser, "Toyota's Inroads with State Bypass 'Buy American' Law," (March 6, 2002): A1.

24 John S. Hulland, "The Effects of Country-of-Brand and Brand Name on Product Evaluation and Consideration: A Cross-Country Comparison," *Consumer Behavior in Asia: Issues and Market Practice* (New York: Haworth Press, 1999): 23–39.

25 Todd Zaun, Scott Miller, and Joseph B. White, "Honda Aims to Export Cars from China," *Wall Street Journal* (July 11, 2002): 12+.

26 Aneel G. Karnani, "Five Ways to Grow the Market and Create Value," *Financial Times* (October 18, 1999): mastering strategy section: 8.

27 Joel Millman, "Mexico Attracts U.S. Aerospace Industry," *Wall Street Journal* (January 23, 2002): A17+.

28 Joseph Pesta, "Indian Companies Book Passage to U.S.," *Wall Street Journal* (January 1, 2001): A16.

29 Glenn R. Simpson, "A New Twist in Tax Avoidance: Firms Send Best Ideas Abroad," *Wall Street Journal* (June 24, 2002): A1+.

30 Barbara Durr, "Korean Carmaker on Road to 'Detroit South,' " *Financial Times* (April 15, 2002): 22.

31 Peter Marsh, "Going International Can Spread Risks," *Financial Times* (January 13, 1998): viii, referring to a study by Arthur D. Little and Technische Hochschule, "Best Practice in Globalising Manufacturing: A Survey of Selected European Companies."

32 Jeffrey A. Krug and John D. Daniels, "Latin American and Caribbean Direct Investment in the United States: An Analysis of Investment Patterns and Implications for U.S. Policy," *Multinational Business Review* II, no. 1 (Spring 1994): 1–10.

33 G. George, D. Wood, and John D. Daniels, "Tredegar Industries: From Spin-off to Success," *Journal of Applied Case Studies* 2, no. 1 (2000): 47–58.

34 See Edward B. Flowers, "Oligopolistic Reactions in European and Canadian Direct Investment in the United States," *Journal of International Business Studies* (Fall–Winter 1976): 43–55; Frederick Knickerbocker, *Oligopolistic Reaction and Multinational Enterprise* (Cambridge, MA: Harvard University, Graduate School of Business, Division of Research, 1973).

35 David Murphy and David Lague, "As China's Car Market Takes Off, the Party Grows a Bit Crowded," *Wall Street Journal* (July 3, 2002): A8.

36 E. M. Graham, "Exchange of Threat Between Multinational Firms as an Infinitely Repeated Noncooperative Game," *The International Trade Journal* IV, no. 3 (Spring 1990): 259–77.

37 See Tony Walker and Robert Corzine, "China to Pay $4.3 bn for Kazakh Oil Stake," *Financial Times* (June 5, 1997): 16; and Keith Bradsher, "China Struggles to Cut Reliance on Mideast Oil," *New York Times* (September 3, 2002): A1+.

38 Larry Rohter, "Impact of NAFTA Pounds Economics of the Caribbean." *New York Times* (January 30, 1997): 1A.

39 See James Dow, "China to Phase Out Tax Breaks for Foreign Firms," *The Scotsman* (June 5, 2002): 3; and Brian Donnelly, "Fears for Jobs as NEC Switches Production." *The Herald* (Glasgow) (May 28, 2002): 2.

40 Joel Millman, "A Good Job Spoiled: The Golf Exodus," *Wall Street Journal* (July 24, 2002): A12.

41 "Spanish, French Tobacco Firms to Merge into Industry's Fourth-Biggest Company," *Wall Street Journal* (October 6, 1999): A18.

42 Andrew Taylor, "Overseas Groups Get on the UK Utility Map," *Financial Times* (June 17, 2002): 4.

43 Anne-Wil Harzing, "Acquisitions Versus Greenfield Investments: International Strategy and Management of Entry Modes," *Strategic Management Journal* 23, no. 3 (March 2002): 211–27.

44 Jaideep Anand and Andrew Delios, "Absolute and Relative Resources as Determinants of International Acquisitions," *Strategic Management Journal* 23, no. 2 (February 2002): 119–34.

45 See John Child, David Faulkner, and Robert Pitethly, *The Management of International Acquisitions* (Oxford: Oxford University Press, 2001.); and Peter Martin, "A Clash of Corporate Cultures," *Financial Times* (June 2–3, 2001): weekend section, xxiv.

46 See Jane W. Lu and Paul W. Beamish, "The Internationalization and Performance of SMEs," *Strategic Management Journal* 22, no. 6–7 (June–July 2001): 565–86; Marisa Ramirez-Aleson and Manuel Antonio Espita-Escuer, "The Effect of International Diversification Strategy on the Performance of Spanish-Based Firms During the Period 1991–1995," *Management International Review* 41, no. 3 (Third Quarter, 2001): 291–315; and Juha-Pekka Kallunki, Jorma Larimo, and Seppo Pynnonen, "Value Creation in Foreign Direct Investments," *Management International Review* 41, no. 4 (Fourth Quarter, 2001): 357–76.

47 See Stephen H. Hymer, *A Study of Direct Foreign Investment* (Cambridge, MA: MIT Press, 1976); Alan M. Rugman, "Internationalization as a General Theory of Foreign Direct Investment: A Re-Appraisal of the Literature," *Weltwirtschaftliches Archiv* 116, heft 2 (1980):

365–79; and Yojin Jung, "Multinationality and Profitability," *Journal of Business Research* 23 (1991): 179–87.

48 See Robert Z. Aliber, "A Theory of Direct Foreign Investment," in *The International Corporation*, ed. Charles P. Kindleberger (Cambridge, MA: MIT Press, 1970), 28–33; Robert Johnson, "Distance Deals," *Wall Street Journal* (February 24, 1988): 1; and Richard Waters, "Foreign Money for U.S. Slows," *Financial Times* (June 11, 1998): 7.

49 See United Nations Conference on Trade and Development, *World Investment Report 2000: Cross-border Mergers and Acquisitions and Development* (New York and Geneva: United Nations, 2000), xv–xvi; and United Nations Conference on Trade and Development, *World Investment Report 2001: Promoting Linkages* (New York and Geneva: United Nations, 2001), 1.

50 United Nations Conference on Trade and Development, *World Investment Report 2000: Cross-border Mergers and Acquisitions op. cit.*, 20.

51 "U.K. Firms Outrank U.S. in Investment for Foreign Firms," *Wall Street Journal* (January 18, 1999): A13.

52 "BEA Current and Historical Data—International Data." *Survey of Current Business* (March 2003): D59–D61.

53 www.oecd.org (July 13, 2002); and www.unctad.org/en/Press/pr0236en.htm (July 13, 2002).

54 Data for the case were taken from interviews at Cran Chile's facilities in Lanco, Chile, during December 2001 and from Calvin Sims, "Taking Cranberries to Chile, Where They Are Really an Acquired Taste," *New York Times* (November 22, 1995): C13; Joseph Pereira, "Unknown Fruit Takes On Unfamiliar Market," *Wall Street Journal* (November 9, 1995): B1; William R. Long, "U.S. Businessman in Chile Works from the Ground Up," *Los Angeles Times* (February 11, 1994): A6; Mark Shanahan, "Proposed Cranberry Operation in Alfred Moving Slowly Through Tangle," *Portland Press Herald* (June 9, 1996): 1B; Wisconsin State Cranberry Growers Association, "A History of Cranberry Growing," http://www.wiscran.org/history.html; Yahoo Finance, "Profile Northland Cranberries as of 1 July 2002," http://biz.yahoo.com/p/n/nrcna.ob.html; "U.S. to Restrict Cranberry Crop," *New York Times* (July 12, 2000): C7; Imogen Mark, "Chile Finds the Going Harder," *Financial Times* (August 16, 1996): 5; John Estrella, "Cranberry Growers Turn Wary Eye to Chile," *Standard Times* [Bedford, MA] (June 13, 1999): http://204.27.188.70/daily/03-96/03-06-96/01cranb.htm; John Estrella, "Frost Ruins Chile Cranberry Crop," *Standard Times* [Bedford, MA]: http://www.standardtimes.com/daily/03-97/03-06-97//c07lo186.htm; and "Cran Chile," http://www.cranchile.cl/cra.htm.

CHAPTER 9

THE FOREIGN-EXCHANGE MARKET

All things are obedient to money.

—ENGLISH PROVERB

OBJECTIVES

- To learn the fundamentals of foreign exchange
- To identify the major characteristics of the foreign-exchange market and how governments control the flow of currencies across national borders
- To understand why companies deal in foreign exchange
- To describe how the foreign-exchange market works
- To examine the different institutions that deal in foreign exchange

CASE

Foreign Travels, Foreign-Exchange Travails: Excerpts from the Travel Journal of Lee Radebaugh

One of the more daunting aspects of overseas travel for the business executive or the tourist is coping with currency. Recently, I traveled to Latin America (see Map 9.1) to visit alumni, interview candidates for our MBA program, and set up a foreign business excursion for graduate business students. I was in such a hurry to leave that I didn't even check the exchange rates in the *Wall Street Journal*—something I usually do. Even though the exchange rates in the *Journal* are the New York selling rates (my buying rates) for transactions of $1 million or more—and I didn't plan on exchanging $1 million—I could still have gotten a general idea of what to expect.

The first stop was Chile. I decided to carry a mixture of cash and traveler's checks, because on a trip to Brazil a few years earlier, I was attacked and nearly robbed in Rio de Janeiro. Traveler's checks provide security because they can be replaced. However, in that prior trip, the bank wouldn't cash traveler's checks at the Buenos Aires airport, so this time I came prepared for all possibilities. In addition, I like to use credit cards, as long as the local currency is stable. Credit card companies handle large volumes of currency daily, so they get favorable exchange rates.

When we cleared customs in Chile, the exchange rate was 350 pesos per dollar. I had no idea whether this was a good rate, so I waited until we arrived at the hotel in Santiago to cash in. When we got to the hotel, I asked the woman at the front desk if she could cash $100, and she said she was out of pesos but would have some in 30 minutes. This was no big deal because we needed to unpack and rest before having lunch. After a nap, we headed down to the front desk to get some cash. But still the answer was, "Sorry, no pesos." She did suggest an exchange house two blocks away. So off we headed. After getting lost, we finally asked directions and found a Casa de Cambio (Exchange House) next to the metro (subway or underground). To our pleasant surprise, the exchange rate was 450 pesos per dollar, and there was no service charge. Usually, when you convert currency at the airport, bank, or hotel, you have to pay a service charge on each transaction. We walked out of the Casa de Cambio with 45,000 pesos—10,000 more than if we had converted at the airport.

As we walked to lunch, I began to figure out how much things would cost. When I get foreign currency, I feel as if I'm spending Monopoly money—it just doesn't seem real for some reason. "Let's see, if I want to pay $10 for lunch, I should pay 4,500 pesos ($10 × 450 pesos, the exchange rate I got when I traded my dollars into pesos). That's easy. But what if lunch costs 7,800 pesos? How much is that? Never mind. It's more than $10 and less than $20 (between 4,500 and 9,000 pesos)." I said to myself that I might have to think about this some more.

After two wonderful days in Santiago, we checked out of the hotel—an experience in itself. Everyone was very pleasant, but the system was a little slow. The clerk said, "Do you want to keep the charges on your American Express?" "Of course," I said. I figured American Express could get a pretty good exchange rate for my room charge for two nights of 102,000 pesos. "That will be $255," he said. "Wait," I said. "What exchange rate are you using?" "Four hundred pesos," he replied. "That's a horrible rate," I said. "I got 450 pesos down the street." "That is not possible, Señor. Maybe you misunderstood. Perhaps 405, or maybe 415, but not 450." "I know what exchange rate I got and it was 450," I replied. "That is a very good exchange rate, Señor." Yeah, right, I thought. Not only did I not get the American Express rate, but the room cost me $127.50 per night! At my conversion rate of 450 pesos from the Casa de Cambio, I would have spent only $227 for two nights (102,000 pesos/450 pesos), thus saving $28. It wasn't enough

MAP 9.1   A Trip Through South America's Exchange Rates

Tourists and business travelers hope for favorable exchange rates when traveling abroad. By early 2003, the dollar had risen bringing the exchange rates to 713.78 Chilean pesos, 3.33 Argentine pesos, and 3.44 Brazilian reals per dollar. But the dollar began to drop again in mid-2003.

TRINIDAD & TOBAGO
VENEZUELA   GUYANA
SURINAME
COLOMBIA   FRENCH GUIANA
ECUADOR
PERU
BOLIVIA
PARAGUAY

SAO PAULO, BRAZIL
0.93 reals=U.S. $1.00

URUGUAY

SANTIAGO, CHILE
450 pesos=U.S. $1.00

BUENOS AIRES, ARGENTINA
1 peso=U.S. $1.00

0   1000 mi
0   1000 km

to cause an international incident, however, so I dropped it and thanked him for the lovely stay. I may be back, so I didn't want him to remember an ugly American.

When I got to the Santiago airport, I decided to exchange Chilean pesos for Argentine pesos, or "Argentino" for short, but only dollars were available. This was confusing without any additional complications, because both Chile and Argentina used the term *peso* for their currency even though the values are very different. I guess this is similar to the U.S.- Canadian situation—that is, both countries use the term *dollar* for their currencies. Then I noticed that the airport bank was selling dollars for 410 pesos per dollar and buying for 430. Because I had bought at 450 at the Exchange House and sold at 430 at the airport, I made about $0.11 on every 1,000 pesos. It didn't amount to much—but if only I could have traded $1 million at that spread. . . .

When we arrived at the Buenos Aires airport a few hours later, I cashed some more money at the bank in the airport. This time, the bank accepted traveler's checks, and I converted $100 for 93.95 pesos, which was a little surprising because I had read that the exchange rate was $1 = 1 peso. To my surprise, the bank charged me 5 percent to cash the traveler's checks and another 1.05 percent service fee—a total of 6.05 pesos.

Because everything was expensive in Buenos Aires, I ran out of pesos quickly, so I went to the American Express office the next day, and it converted $100 for 99.8 pesos. Next time, I'll ask before using traveler's checks. It can get confusing. At times, I've sold traveler's checks at a better rate than I got than if I'd been selling cash, and other times not. When we left Buenos Aires, the exchange rate was the same for buying and selling—1:1. There was a $0.15 service charge, so it cost almost nothing to change currency—$100 to buy 99.8 pesos at American Express and $100 for selling 99.85 pesos (100 pesos less $0.15).

After a delay at the airport in Buenos Aires, we finally headed for São Paulo, Brazil. The currency market in Brazil has always been the haven of the black marketer. No one ever has a clue to the real value, and it varies with personal checks, traveler's checks, or cash. Every hotel and shop has its own rate, which requires astute shopping around.

The last time I had been in Brazil, the country was in the process of locking the currency onto the U.S. dollar to eliminate these price differences and to stabilize its value, but the situation was still chaotic. Taxi drivers still preferred dollars, no matter what the exchange rate. Finally, the Brazilian government succeeded in stabilizing the currency in June 1994, and the Brazilian real (the name of the currency, pronounced hey-ALL) was fixed to the dollar (or pegged)—the rate was about 1:1. When I arrived at the airport, I changed dollars into reais (pronounced hey-ICE) at R$0.9300 = US $1.00. The bank demanded no service charge, but it sold dollars (or bought R$) for R$0.99 = US $1.00. What a change from the historical value! The first time I went to Brazil in 1964, the dollar was worth 1,200 cruzeiros, the name of the currency then. Since that time, the Brazilian currency has changed names seven times: cruzeiro (1942–1967), new cruzeiro (1967–1970), cruzeiro (1970–1986), cruzado (1986–1989), new cruzado (1989–1990), cruzeiro (again!) (1990–1993), cruzeiro real (1993–1994), and real (since 1994). Every change knocked three zeros off the currency. So 1,200 cruzeiros became 1.2 new cruzeiros, and so on. At an exchange rate of 1:1, it was obviously easier to figure out how much everything cost in dollars. But everything was more expensive compared to U.S. costs. When the Brazilian government fixed the rate at 1:1, it made the real a little too strong, so the dollar lost much of its purchasing power there.

It can be confusing to travel overseas—whether on a business trip or for pleasure—and the more countries you go to in a single trip, the more confusing it gets. And the worst part is that every time you travel, you need to get used to new exchange rates. For example, by early 2003, the Chilean peso was trading for 713.78 per U.S. dollar, the Argentine peso for 3.33 per dollar, and the Brazilian real for 3.44 per dollar—quite a change from my last trip to South America. ◥

INTRODUCTION

In the previous part of the book, we discussed some key theories underlying international trade and investment. Now let's move to global financial markets and see how the foreign-exchange market works in international business.

To survive, both MNEs and small import and export companies must understand foreign exchange and exchange rates. In a business setting, there is a fundamental difference between making payment in the domestic market and making payment abroad. In a domestic transaction, companies use only one currency. In a foreign transaction, companies can use two or more currencies. For example, a U.S. company that exports skis to a French distributor will ask the French store which buys skis to remit payment in dollars, unless the U.S. company has some specific use for euros (the currency France uses), such as paying a French supplier.

Assume you are a U.S. importer who has agreed to purchase a certain quantity of French perfume and to pay the French exporter 4,000 euros for it. Assuming you had the money, how would you go about paying? First, you would go to the international department of your local bank to buy 4,000 euros at the going market rate. Let's assume the euro/dollar exchange rate is 1.0314 euros per dollar. Your bank then would charge your account $3,878.22 (4,000/1.0314) plus the transaction costs and give you a special check payable in

Doing business in or traveling to another country usually means changing one currency for another. The photo shows an exchange booth in Tel Aviv, Israel, where a man is exchanging Israeli shekels for U.S. dollars.

euros made out to the exporter. The exporter would deposit it in a French bank, which then would credit the exporter's account with 4,000 euros. So, the *foreign-exchange* transaction would be complete. **Foreign exchange** is money denominated in the currency of another nation or group of nations.[1] The market in which these transactions take place is the foreign-exchange market. Foreign exchange can be in the form of cash, funds available on credit and debit cards, traveler's checks, bank deposits, or other short-term claims.[2]

An exchange rate is the price of a currency. It is the number of units of one currency that buys one unit of another currency, and this number can change daily. For example, on January 3, 2003, one euro could purchase U.S. $1.0417. Exchange rates make international price and cost comparisons possible.

The foreign-exchange market is made up of many different players. Some players buy and sell foreign exchange because they are exporters and importers of goods and services. Other players buy and sell foreign exchange because of foreign direct investments—both investing capital into and pulling dividends out of a country. Others are portfolio investors—they buy foreign stocks, bonds, and mutual funds, hoping to sell them at a more profitable exchange rate later. These players have different objectives for buying and selling foreign currencies, and in the meantime, they affect supply and demand for those currencies.

Foreign exchange—money denominated in the currency of another nation or group of nations

Exchange rate—the price of a currency

MAJOR CHARACTERISTICS OF THE FOREIGN-EXCHANGE MARKET

The foreign-exchange market has two major segments: the *over-the-counter* market (OTC) and the exchange-traded market. The OTC market is composed of banks, both commercial banks like Bank of America and investment banks like Merrill Lynch, and other financial institutions, and it is where most of the foreign-exchange activity takes place. The exchange-traded market is composed of securities exchanges, such as the Chicago Mercantile Exchange and the Philadelphia Stock Exchange, where certain types of foreign-exchange instruments, such as exchange-traded futures and options, are traded. These markets will be discussed in more depth later in the chapter.

Foreign-exchange market

• Over-the-counter (commercial and investment banks)

• Securities exchanges

Brief Description of Foreign-Exchange Instruments

Several different types of foreign-exchange instruments are traded in these markets, but the traditional foreign-exchange instruments that comprise the bulk of foreign-exchange trading are spot, outright forwards, and FX swaps. **Spot transactions** involve the exchange of currency the second day after the date on which the two foreign-exchange traders agree to the transaction. The rate at which the transaction is settled is the **spot rate. Outright forward** transactions involve the exchange of currency three or more days after the date on which the traders agree to the transaction. It is the single purchase or sale of a currency for future delivery. The rate at which the transaction is settled is the forward rate and is a contract rate between the two parties. The forward transaction will be settled at the forward rate no matter what the actual spot rate is at the time of settlement. In an **FX swap**, one currency is swapped for another on one date and then swapped back on a future date. Most often, the first leg of an FX swap is a spot transaction, with the second leg of the swap a future transaction. For example, assume that IBM receives a dividend in British pounds from its subsidiary in the United Kingdom but has no use for British pounds until it has to pay a British supplier in pounds in 30 days. It would rather have dollars now than hold on to the pounds for 30 days. IBM could enter into an FX swap in which it sells the pounds for dollars to a trader in the spot market at the spot rate and agrees to buy pounds for dollars from the trader in 30 days at the forward rate. Although an FX swap is both a spot and a forward transaction, it is accounted for as a single transaction.

In addition to the traditional instruments, which were the only foreign-exchange instruments traded until the 1970s, there are *currency swaps*, *options* and *futures*.[3] Currency swaps are OTC instruments, options are traded both OTC and on exchanges, and futures are exchange-traded instruments. **Currency swaps** deal more with interest-bearing financial instruments (such as a bond), and they involve the exchange of principal and interest payments. **Options** are the right but not the obligation to trade foreign currency in the future. A **futures contract** is an agreement between two parties to buy or sell a particular currency at a particular price on a particular future date, as specified in a standardized contract to all participants in that currency futures exchange.

The Size, Composition, and Location of the Foreign-Exchange Market

Before we examine the market instruments in more detail, let's look at the size, composition, and geographic location of the market. Every three years, the Bank for International Settlements (http://www.bis.org), a Basel, Switzerland-based central banking institution that is owned and controlled by 50 national central banks, conducts a survey of foreign-exchange activity in the world. In the 2001 survey, it estimated that $1.2 trillion in foreign exchange is traded every day.[4] Foreign exchange activity declined substantially in 2001 by 19 percent compared to 1998. This decline contrasts with previous survey results, which show a rapid increase in foreign-exchange activity. Some of the reasons for the decline are the consolidation of the banking industry, which has led to fewer trading desks, and the introduction of the euro, which has resulted in a declining number of foreign-exchange trades within the euro zone. Figure 9.1 illustrates the trends in foreign-exchange trading beginning with the 1989 survey. The $1.2 trillion daily turnover includes traditional foreign-exchange market activity only—spots, outright forwards, and FX swaps. In the OTC derivatives market, daily activity increased by 10 percent—to $1.4 trillion. This is also a significant slowdown in activity from the years between 1995 and 1998, when activity increased by 44 percent. In particular, spot transactions have decreased consistently since 1989.

The U.S. dollar is the most important currency in the foreign-exchange market; in 2001, it comprised one side (buy or sell) of 90 percent of all foreign currency transactions worldwide, as Table 9.1 illustrates. This means that almost every foreign-exchange transaction

---

Traditional foreign-exchange instruments

- Spot
- Outright forward
- FX swap

The spot rate is the exchange rate quoted for transactions that require delivery within two days.

Outright forwards involve the exchange of currency beyond three days at a fixed exchange rate, known as the forward rate.

An FX swap is a simultaneous spot and forward transaction.

Three other key foreign-exchange instruments

- Currency swaps
- Options
- Futures

Size of the foreign-exchange market

- $1.2 trillion daily in traditional instruments
- $1.4 trillion daily OTC derivative transactions

FIGURE 9.1   Average Daily Volume in World Foreign-Exchange Markets, 1989–2001

The average daily volume of foreign-exchange transactions was $1.5 trillion worldwide in April 1998, but it had declined slightly—to $1.2 trillion—in 2001.

Source: Bank for International Settlements, *Central Bank Survey of Foreign Exchange and Derivatives Market Activity 2001* (Basel, Switzerland: BIS, March 2002), 2.

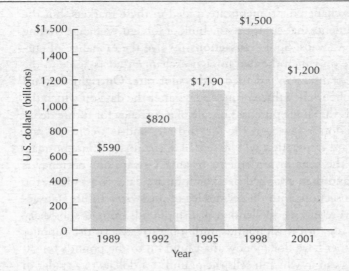

The dollar is the most widely traded currency in the world

- An investment currency in many capital markets
- A reserve currency held by many central banks
- A transaction currency in many international commodity markets
- An invoice currency in many contracts
- An intervention currency employed by monetary authorities in market operations to influence their own exchange rates

The dollar is part of four of the top seven currency pairs traded.

The dollar/euro is number one.

The dollar/yen is number two.

conducted on a daily basis has the dollar as one leg of the transaction. There are five major reasons why the dollar is so widely traded. It is

1. An investment currency in many capital markets.
2. A reserve currency held by many central bar.ks.
3. A transaction currency in many international commodity markets.
4. An invoice currency in many contracts.
5. An intervention currency employed by monetary authorities in market operations to influence their own exchange rates. [5]

Because of the ready availability of U.S. dollars worldwide, this currency is important as a vehicle for foreign-exchange transactions between two countries other than the United States. An example of how the dollar can be used as a vehicle currency for two other countries is when a Mexican company importing products from a Japanese exporter converts Mexican pesos into dollars and sends them to the Japanese exporter, who converts the dollars into yen. Thus, the U.S. dollar is one leg on both sides of the transaction—in Mexico and in Japan. There may be a couple of reasons to go through dollars instead of directly from pesos to yen. The first reason is that the Japanese exporter might not have any need for pesos, whereas it can use dollars for a variety of reasons. The second reason is that the Mexican importer might have trouble getting yen at a good exchange rate if the Mexican banks are not carrying yen balances. However, the banks undoubtedly carry dollar balances, so the importer might have easy access to the dollars. Thus, the dollar has become an important "vehicle" for international transactions, and it greatly simplifies life for a foreign bank because the bank won't have to carry balances in many different currencies.

Another way to consider foreign-currency trades is to look at the most frequently traded currency pairs. Four of the top seven currency pairs involve the U.S. dollar, with the top two pairs being the U.S. dollar and the euro (30 percent of total) and the U.S. dollar and Japanese yen (20 percent).[6] This reinforces the idea that the dollar is a vehicle currency for trading between other currencies, which is known as cross-trading.

The euro is also in four of the top seven currency pairs. Although the dollar is still more popular in most emerging markets, the euro is gaining ground, particularly in eastern European countries like the Czech Republic and Hungary. The Bank for International Settlements (BIS) believes the euro resembles the German mark in the exchange market in four ways: because of "its share in global foreign exchange trading, the tightness of spreads,

TABLE 9.1

CURRENCY DISTRIBUTION OF GLOBAL FOREIGN EXCHANGE MARKET ACTIVITY

	PERCENTAGE OF DAILY TURNOVER				
CURRENCY	APRIL 1989	APRIL 1992	APRIL 1995	APRIL 1998	APRIL 2001
U.S. dollar	90	82	83	87	90
Euro	—	—	—	—	38*
Japanese yen	27	23	24	21	23
Pound sterling	15	14	10	11	13
Swiss franc	10	9	7	7	6
All others	31	32	39	44	30

*The euro came into existence in 1999, after the April 1998 BIS survey, and only entered broad circulation on January 1, 2002.

Source: Bank for International Settlements, *Central Bank Survey of Foreign Exchange and Derivatives Market Activity 1998* (Basel, Switzerland: BIS, March 2002), 9.

its volatility vis-à-vis the dollar and the yen, and its role as an anchoring currency."[7] The 2001 BIS survey showed that the euro has not yet taken market share from any of the other currencies, such as the dollar or the yen. However, this could change as the euro becomes more popular and as more countries adopt the euro.

Given that the dollar is clearly the most widely traded currency in the world, that would seem to indicate that the biggest market for foreign-exchange trading would be in the United States. But as Figure 9.2 illustrates, the biggest market by far is in the United Kingdom. The four largest centers for foreign-exchange trading (the United Kingdom, the United States, Japan, and Singapore) account for slightly more than 62 percent of the total average daily turnover. The U.K. market is so dominant that more dollars are traded in London than in New York.[8] Why is London so important? There are two major reasons for London's prominence: 1. London, which is close to the major capital markets in Europe, is a strong international financial center where a large number of domestic and foreign financial institutions have operations. 2. London is positioned in a unique way because of the time zone it is situated in. In Map 9.2 on pages 272–273, note that at noon in London, it is 7:00 A.M. in New York and evening in Asia. The London market opens toward the end of the trading day in Asia and is going strong as the New York foreign-exchange market opens up. London thus straddles both of the other major markets in the world. Figure 9.3 illustrates the volume of foreign-exchange trading on a daily basis and illustrates how market activity is concentrated on the time period when Asia and Europe are open or when Europe and the United States are open, even though the market is really open 24 hours a day. Currencies trade in greater volume during the business time of the markets, even though there is the opportunity for trades 24 hours a day. You can get a better price for currencies when the markets are active and liquid.

The biggest market for foreign exchange is London, followed by New York, Tokyo, and Singapore.

London is open when Tokyo closes and when New York opens—it is centrally located in terms of time.

Key foreign-exchange terms
- Bid—the rate at which traders buy foreign exchange
- Offer—the rate at which traders sell foreign exchange
- Spread—the difference between bid and offer rates; the profit margin for the trader
- American terms—the number of dollars per unit of foreign currency (also called direct quote)
- European terms—the number of units of foreign currency per dollar (also called indirect quote)

MAJOR FOREIGN-EXCHANGE INSTRUMENTS

Now let's examine in more detail the major foreign-exchange instruments: spot, forward, options, and futures, as well as the convertability of currencies.

The Spot Market

Most foreign-currency transactions take place between foreign-exchange traders, so the traders who work for foreign-exchange brokerage houses or commercial banks quote the rates. The traders always quote a **bid** (buy) and **offer** (sell) rate. The *bid* is the price at which

FIGURE 9.2   Geographical Distribution of Global Foreign-Exchange Market Activity, April 2001.

The largest volume of foreign-exchange transactions occurs in the United Kingdom (London) due to its central location.

Source: Bank for International Settlements, *Central Bank Survey of Foreign Exchange and Derivatives Market Activity 2001* (Basel, Switzerland: BIS, March 2002). 12.

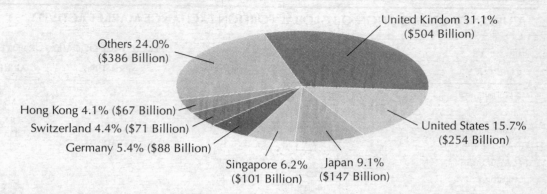

United Kindom 31.1% ($504 Billion)

Others 24.0% ($386 Billion)

Hong Kong 4.1% ($67 Billion)

Switzerland 4.4% ($71 Billion)

Germany 5.4% ($88 Billion)

Singapore 6.2% ($101 Billion)

Japan 9.1% ($147 Billion)

United States 15.7% ($254 Billion)

the trader is willing to buy foreign currency, and the *offer* is the price at which the trader is willing to sell foreign currency. In the spot market, the **spread** is the difference between the bid and offer rates, and it is the trader's profit margin. The rate a trader quotes for the British pound might be $1.5975/85. This means the trader is willing to buy pounds at $1.5975 each and sell them for $1.5985. Obviously, a trader wants to buy low and sell high.

In this example, the trader quotes the foreign currency as the number of U.S. dollars for one unit of that currency. This method of quoting exchange rates is called the **direct quote**, also known in the foreign-exchange industry as "**American terms.**" It represents a quote from the point of view of someone in the United States. The other convention for quoting foreign exchange is "**European terms,**" which means a direct quote from the perspective of someone from Europe. From a U.S. point of view, this means the number of units of the foreign currency per U.S. dollar. This is also sometimes called the **indirect quote** in the United States, although *American terms* and *European terms* are the most accurate ways to describe the quotes.

In European terms, exchange rates are quoted as the number of units of the foreign currency per U.S. dollar. The dollar is considered the **base currency**, also known as the *quoted, underlying,* or *fixed* currency, and the other currency is the **terms currency**. The terms currency is the numerator, and the base currency is the denominator. Thus, for an exchange rate of 105 yen per dollar (indirect or European terms), the yen is the numerator (terms currency) and the dollar is the denominator (quoted or base currency). Now most currencies, except for the British pound and Canadian dollar, are quoted in European terms in the United States[9].

When traders quote currencies to their customers, they always quote the base currency first, followed by the terms currency. A quote for "dollar/yen" means that the dollar is the base currency and the yen is the terms currency. If you know the dollar/yen quote, you can divide that rate into 1 to get the yen-dollar quote. In other words, the exchange rate in American terms is the reciprocal or inverse of the exchange rate in European terms.

For example, using the numbers in Table 9.2 (on pages 274–275), $\frac{1}{.008352} = 119.73$.

In a dollar-yen quote, the dollar is the denominator and the yen is the numerator. By tracking changes in the exchange rate, managers can determine whether the base currency is strengthening or weakening. For example, on June 20, 2002, the dollar-yen rate was ¥123/$1.00, and on January 3, 2003, the rate was ¥119.73/$1.00. As the numerator falls, the base currency—the dollar—is weakening or getting less expensive. If the rate were to rise to ¥125, the base currency would be strengthening or getting stronger.

Most large newspapers, especially those devoted to business or those having business sections, quote exchange rates daily. Because most currencies constantly fluctuate in value, many managers check the values daily. For example, the *Wall Street Journal* provides quotes in

FIGURE 9.3   The Circadian Rhythms of the FX Market

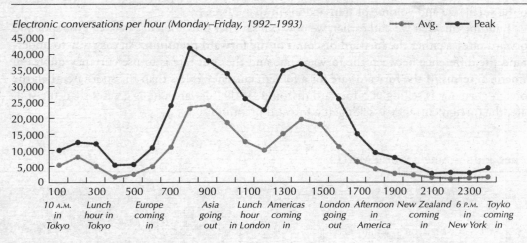

Electronic conversations per hour (Monday–Friday, 1992–1993)   ●— Avg.   ●— Peak

Market activity heightens when Europe and Asia are open and when Europe and the United States are open.

Source: Reuters.

100 / 10 A.M. in Tokyo
300 / Lunch hour in Tokyo
500 / Europe coming in
700
900 / Asia going out
1100 / Lunch hour in London
1300 / Americas coming in
1500 / London going out
1700 / Afternoon in America
1900 / New Zealand coming in
2100 / 6 P.M. in New York
2300 / Toyko coming in

Note: Time (0100–2400 hours, Greenwich Mean Time)

American terms (U.S. $ equivalent) and European terms (currency per U.S. $), as shown in Table 9.2. All of the quotes, except those noted as one-month, three-month, and six-month forward, are spot quotes. The spot rates are the selling rates for interbank transactions of $1 million and more. Interbank transactions are transactions between banks. Retail transactions, those between banks and companies or individuals, provide fewer foreign currency units per dollar than interbank transactions. If I were going on a business trip, I could check the *Wall Street Journal* to get an idea of the exchange rate in my destination country, just as I did in the opening case, but I would get fewer units of the foreign currency for my dollars than is quoted in the *Journal*. There are also a number of good Internet sources for exchange-rate quotes, such as CNN (http://money.cnn.com/markets/currencies/).[10]

A final definition that applies to the spot market is the **cross rate**. This is the exchange rate between non-U.S. dollar currencies. As an example, let's use the quotes for the Swiss franc and euro in European terms as given in Table 9.2 and figure the cross rate with the franc as the terms currency and the euro as the base currency. In Table 9.2, the spot rates for these currencies are 1.3990 francs per U.S. dollar and 0.9600 euro per U.S. dollar. The cross rate would be 1.3990/.9600 or 1.4573 Swiss francs per euro.

The *Wall Street Journal* also publishes a cross-rate table along with the dollar-exchange rates. Table 9.3 on page 275 identifies the cross rates for several key currencies. The rows are treated as the terms currency and the columns as the base currency. For example, starting in the Switzerland row and going to the euro column, we find that the exchange rate is 1.4573 Swiss francs per euro. The Swiss franc is the terms currency, and the euro is the base currency. You can also find cross rates of key currencies on the currency page of CNN online, and you can use the CNN currency converter to find out cross rates of more exotic currencies.

Cross rate—the relationship between two nondollar currencies.

The Forward Market

As noted earlier, the spot market is for foreign-exchange transactions that occur within two business days, but in some transactions, a seller extends credit to the buyer for a period that is longer than two days. For example, a Japanese exporter of consumer electronics might sell television sets to a U.S. importer with immediate delivery but payment due in 30 days. The U.S. importer is obligated to pay in yen in 30 days and may enter into a contract with a currency trader to deliver the yen at a *forward* rate—the rate quoted today for future delivery.

In addition to the spot rates for each currency, Table 9.2 shows the forward rates for the British pound, Canadian dollar, Japanese yen, and Swiss franc. These are the most widely traded currencies in the forward market. Many currencies do not have a forward market due to the small size and volume of transactions in that currency.

Building on what we said earlier, we now can say that the difference between the spot and forward rates is either the **forward discount** or the **forward premium**. An easy way to understand the difference between the forward rate and the spot rate is to use currency quotes in American terms. If the forward rate for a foreign currency is less than the spot rate, then the foreign currency is selling at a forward discount. If the forward rate is greater than the spot rate, the foreign currency is selling at a forward premium.

The forward rate is the rate quoted for transactions that call for delivery after two business days.

A forward discount exists when the forward rate is less than the spot rate.

A premium exists when the forward rate exceeds the spot rate.

MAP 9.2   International Time Zones and the Single World Market

The world's communication networks are now so good that we can talk of a single world market. It starts in a small way in New Zealand around 9:00 A.M., just in time to catch the tail end of the previous night's New York market. Two or three hours later, Tokyo opens, followed an hour later by Hong Kong and Manila, and then half an hour later by Singapore. By now, with the Far East market in full swing, the focus moves to the Near and Middle East. Bombay opens two hours after Singapore, followed after an hour and a half by Abu Dhabi and Athens, which Jidda and Beirut are an hour behind still. By this stage, trading in the Far and Middle East is usually thin as dealers wait to see how Europe will trade. Paris and Frankfurt open an hour ahead of London, and by this time Tokyo is starting to close down, so the European market can judge the Japanese market. By lunchtime in London, New York is starting to open up, and as Europe closes down, positions can be passed westward. Midday in New York, trading tends to be quiet because there is nowhere to pass a position to. The San Francisco market, three hours behind New York, is effectively a satellite of the New York market, although very small positions can be passed on to New Zealand

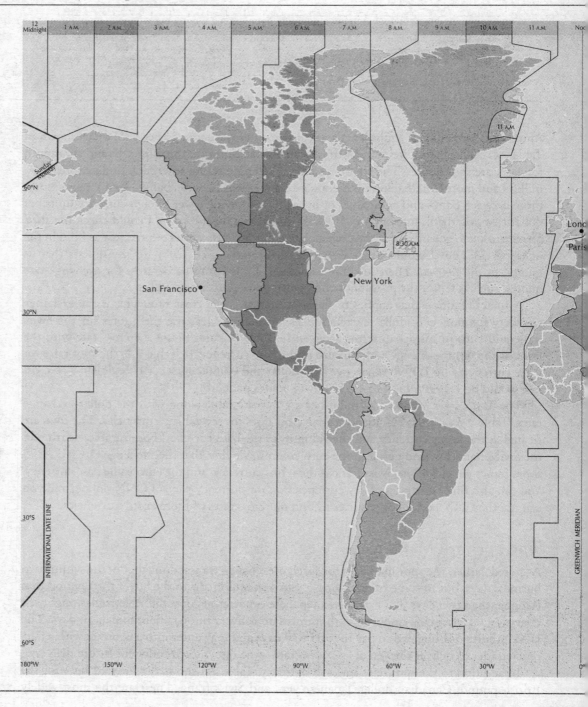

Options

An **option** is the right but not the obligation to buy or sell a foreign currency within a certain time period or on a specific date at a specific exchange rate. An option can be purchased OTC from a commercial or investment bank, or it can be purchased on an exchange, such as the Philadelphia Stock Exchange. For example, assume a company purchases an OTC option to buy Japanese yen at 120 yen per dollar (0.00833 dollars per yen). The writer of the option, the commercial or investment bank in this case, will charge the company a fee

An option is the right but not the obligation to trade a foreign currency at a specific exchange rate.

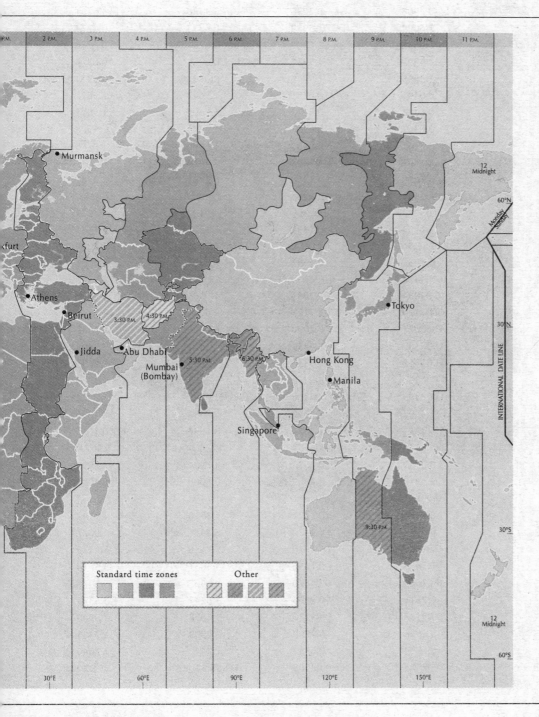

banks. (Note that in the former Soviet Union, standard time zones are advanced an hour. Also note that some countries and territories have adopted half-hour time zones, as shown by hatched lines.)

Source: Adapted from Julian Walmsley, *The Foreign Exchange Handbook* (New York: John Wiley, 1983), 7–8. Reprinted by permission of John Wiley & Sons, Inc. Some information taken from *The Cambridge Factfinders*, 3/e, edited by David Crystal (New York: Cambridge University Press, 1998), 440.

● TABLE 9.2

FOREIGN EXCHANGE RATES, FRIDAY, JANUARY 3, 2003

Because most currencies constantly fluctuate in value, many managers check values daily.

COUNTRY	U.S. $ EQUIV.		CURRENCY PER U.S. $	
	FRIDAY	THURSDAY	FRIDAY	THURSDAY
Argentina (Peso)	0.3003	0.2994	3.3300	3.3400
Australia (Dollar)	0.5676	0.5634	1.7618	1.7749
Bahrain (Dinar)	2.6526	2.6524	0.3770	0.3770
Brazil (Real)	0.2908	0.2836	3.4388	3.5261
Britain (Pound)	1.6094	1.5939	0.6213	0.6274
1 Month Forward	1.6058	1.5904	0.6227	0.6288
3 Months Forward	1.5993	1.5837	0.6253	0.6314
6 Months Forward	1.5895	1.5740	0.6291	0.6353
Canada (Dollar)	0.6391	0.6381	1.5647	1.5672
1 Month Forward	0.6383	0.6373	1.5667	1.5691
3 Months Forward	0.6367	0.6358	1.5706	1.5728
6 Months Forward	0.6343	0.6334	1.5765	1.5788
Chile (Peso)	0.001401	0.001392	713.78	718.39
China (Renminbi)	0.1208	0.1208	8.2781	8.2781
Colombia (Peso)	0.0003508	0.0003524	2,850.6	2,837.7
Czech Republic (Koruna) Commercial Rate	0.03322	0.03309	30.102	30.221
Denmark (Krone)	0.1403	0.1395	7.1276	7.1685
Ecuador (US Dollar)-e	1.0000	1.0000	1.0000	1.0000
Hong Kong (Dollar)	0.1282	0.1282	7.8003	7.8003
Hungary (Forint)	0.004427	0.004390	225.89	227.79
India (Rupee)	0.02084	0.02083	47.985	48.008
Indonesia (Rupiah)	0.0001120	0.0001121	8,928.6	8,920.6
Israel (Shekel)	0.2087	0.2090	4.7916	4.7847
Japan (Yen)	0.008352	0.008331	119.73	120.03
1 Month Forward	0.008362	0.008340	119.59	119.90
3 Months Forward	0.008380	0.008359	119.33	119.63
6 Months Forward	0.008409	0.008388	118.92	119.22
Jordan (Dinar)	1.4092	1.4092	0.7096	0.7096
Kuwait (Dinar)	3.3354	3.3320	0.2998	0.3001
Lebanon (Pound)	0.0006634	0.0006634	1,507.4	1,507.4
Malaysia (Ringitt)-b	0.2632	0.2632	3.7994	3.7994
Malta (Lira)	2.4947	2.4805	0.4008	0.4031
Mexico (Peso)	0.09622	0.09637	10.393	10.377
New Zealand (Dollar)	0.5286	0.5224	1.8918	1.9142
Norway (Krone)	0.1438	0.1427	6.9541	7.0077
Pakistan (Rupee)	0.01720	0.01720	58.139	58.139
Peru (New Sol)	0.2853	0.2856	3.5051	3.5014
Philippines (Peso)	0.01869	0.01870	53.505	53.476
Poland (Zloty)	0.2615	0.2606	3.8241	3.8373
Russia (Ruble)-a	0.03137	0.03130	31.878	31.949
Saudi Arabia (Riyal)	0.2666	0.2667	3.7509	3.7495
Singapore (Dollar)	0.5734	0.5734	1.7440	1.7440
Slovak Republic (Koruna)	0.02524	0.02505	39.620	39.920

South Africa (Rand)	0.1186	0.1178	8.4317	8.4890
South Korea (Won)	0.0008355	0.0008414	1,196.9	1,188.5
Sweden (Krona)	0.1146	0.1136	8.7260	8.8028
Switzerland (Franc)	0.7148	0.7131	1.3990	1.4023
1 Month Forward	0.7152	0.7136	1.3982	1.4013
3 Months Forward	0.7162	0.7146	1.3963	1.3994
6 Months Forward	0.7176	0.7160	1.3935	1.3966
Taiwan (Dollar)	0.02881	0.02883	34.710	34.686
Thailand (Baht)	0.02326	0.02317	42.992	43.159
Turkish (Lira)	0.00000061	0.00000060	1,639,344	1,666,667
United Arab (Dirham)	0.2723	0.2723	3.6724	3.6724
Uruguay (Peso) Financial	0.03670	0.03690	27.248	27.100
Venezuela (Bolivar)	0.0007110	0.0007190	1,406.5	1,390.8
Special Drawing Rights	1.3577	1.3546	0.7365	0.7382
Euro	1.04170	1.03610	0.9600	0.9652

Special Drawing Rights (SDR) are based on exchange rates for the U.S., German, British, French, and Japanese currencies. Source: International Monetary Fund.

a-Russian Central Bank rate. b-Government rate. d-Floating rate; trading band suspended on 4/11/00. e-Adopted U.S. dollar as of 9/11/00. f-Floating rate. eff. Feb 22.

● **TABLE 9.3**

KEY CURRENCY CROSS RATES, LATE NEW YORK TRADING FRIDAY, JANUARY 3, 2003

Many managers also examine currency cross rates, which are the exchange rates between non-U.S. dollar currencies.

	DOLLAR	EURO	POUND	SFRANC	PESO	YEN	CDNDLR
Canada	1.5647	1.6299	2.5182	1.1184	0.1506	0.0131	....
Japan	119.73	124.72	192.70	85.584	11.521	....	76.521
Mexico	10.393	10.826	16.726	7.4288	....	0.0868	6.6421
Switzerland	1.3990	1.4573	2.2515	....	0.1346	0.0117	0.8941
U.K.	0.6213	0.6473	....	0.4441	0.0598	0.0052	0.3971
Euro	0.9600	....	1.5450	0.6862	0.0924	0.0080	0.6135
U.S.	....	1.0417	1.6094	0.7148	0.0962	0.0084	0.6391

for writing the option. The more likely the option is to benefit the company, the higher the fee. The rate of 120 yen is called the *strike price* for the option. The fee or cost of the option is called the *premium*. On the date when the option is set to expire, the company can look at the spot rate and compare it with the strike price to see which is the better exchange rate. If the spot rate were 130 yen per dollar (0.00769 dollars per yen), it would not exercise the option because buying yen at the spot rate would cost less than buying them at the option rate. However, if the spot rate at that time were 110 yen per dollar (0.00909 dollars per yen), the company would exercise the option because buying at the option rate would cost less than buying at the spot rate. The option provides the company flexibility, because it can walk away from the option if the strike price is not a good price. In the case of a forward contract, the cost is usually cheaper than the cost for an option, but the company cannot walk away from the contract. So a forward contract is cheaper but less flexible than an option.

Futures

A futures contract specifies an exchange rate in advance of the actual exchange of currency, but it is not as flexible as a forward contract.

Residents and nonresidents of a country can exchange a convertible currency for other currencies.

A hard currency is a currency that is usually fully convertible and strong or relatively stable in value in comparison with other currencies.

A foreign currency future resembles a forward contract insofar as it specifies an exchange rate sometime in advance of the actual exchange of currency. However, a future is traded on an exchange, not OTC. Instead of working with a banker, companies work with exchange brokers when purchasing futures contracts. A forward contract is tailored to the amount and time frame that the company needs, whereas a futures contract is for a specific amount and specific maturity date. The futures contract is less valuable to a company than a forward contract. However, it may be useful to speculators and small companies that do not have a good enough relationship with a bank to enter into a forward contract or that need a contract for an amount that is too small for the forward market. The differences between the forward contract, which is traded OTC, and exchange-based contracts, such as futures and options, is summarized in Table 9.4.

Foreign-Exchange Convertibility

A key aspect of exchanging one currency for another is its convertibility. Fully convertible currencies are those that the government allows both residents and nonresidents to purchase in unlimited amounts. **Hard currencies**, such as the U.S. dollar and Japanese yen, are currencies that are fully convertible. They also are relatively stable in value or tend to be strong

---

● TABLE 9.4

COMPARISON OF MARKET FEATURES FOR EXCHANGE-BASED AND OTC OPTIONS IN FOREIGN MARKETS

	EXCHANGE-BASED (OPTIONS AND FUTURES)	OTC (FORWARD CONTRACTS)
Contract specifications	Standardized and customized	Customized
Regulation	Securities and Exchange Commission (SEC)	Self-regulated
Type of market	Open outcry, auction market	Dealer market
Counterparty* to every transaction	"AAA"-rated Options Clearing Corporation (OCC)	Bank on the contra-side
Transparency/Visible prices	Yes	No
Margin required for short positions**	Yes	No†
Orders anonymously represented in the market	Yes	No
Required to mark positions daily	Yes	No†
Audit trail	Complete sequential and second-by-second audit trail of each transaction	No
Participants	Public customers, as well as corporate and institutional users	Corporate and institutional users

*Counterparty means the person on the other side of the transaction. For example, if IBM enters into an option on the PHLX, the counterparty to the contract would be a registered broker. If it enters into an OTC option with Citibank, the counterparty would be the bank.
**A margin is a percentage of the contract value that the company, IBM, for example, would have to pay to enter into the contract. At the end of the day, the exchange marks the value of the option to the new market price. If the value has gone up, the margin requirement also rises. That is not required in the OTC market.
†Not a requirement, but available.

Source: From Philadelphia Stock Exchange. Reprinted by permission.

in comparison with other currencies. In addition, they are desirable assets. Currencies that are not fully convertible are often called **soft currencies**, or **weak currencies**. They tend to be the currencies of developing countries, also known as exotic currencies, a concept that will be discussed later in the chapter.

Most countries today have nonresident, or external, convertibility, meaning that foreigners can convert their currency into the local currency and can convert back into their currency as well. For example, travelers to Zimbabwe can convert U.S. dollars (USD) into Zimbabwe dollars (ZWD) and convert ZWD back into USD when they leave. However, they have to show receipts of all conversions into or from ZWD inside the country to make sure that all transactions took place on the official market. Whatever the travelers converted in the official market was the maximum they would have been allowed to convert back into USD when they left. In addition, they have to declare electronics products, such as cameras and stereos, upon entering the country and then prove they had them upon leaving. The government was afraid visitors would sell the products in the black market and then try to convert the proceeds into dollars and take them out of the country. Some countries limit nonresident convertibility.

To conserve scarce foreign exchange, some governments impose exchange restrictions on companies or individuals who want to exchange money. The devices they use include import licensing, multiple exchange rates, import deposit requirements, and quantity controls. As you will read in the concluding case, Argentina's government placed exchange restrictions on individuals and companies at the beginning of 2002.

Government licenses fix the exchange rate by requiring all recipients, exporters, and others who receive foreign currency to sell it to its central bank at the official buying rate. Then the central bank rations the foreign currency it acquires by selling it at fixed rates to those needing to make payment abroad for essential goods. An importer may purchase foreign exchange only if that importer has obtained an import license for the goods in question.

> Licensing occurs when a government requires that all foreign-exchange transactions be regulated and controlled by it.

Another way governments control foreign-exchange convertibility is by establishing more than one exchange rate. This restrictive measure is called **a multiple exchange-rate system**. The government determines which kinds of transactions are to be conducted at which exchange rates. Countries with multiple exchange rates often have a very high exchange rate (i.e., it takes more units of the local currency to buy dollars) for luxury goods and financial flows, such as dividends. Then they have a lower exchange rate for other trade transactions, such as imports of essential commodities and semimanufactured goods.

> In a multiple exchange-rate system, a government sets different exchange rates for different types of transactions.

Another form of foreign-exchange convertibility control is the **advance import deposit**. In this case, the government tightens the issue of import licenses and requires importers to make a deposit with the central bank, often for as long as one year and interest-free, covering the full price of manufactured goods they would purchase from abroad.

> Some governments require an import deposit—that is, deposit prior to the release of foreign exchange.

Governments also may limit the amount of exchange through quantity controls, which often apply to tourism. A quantity control limits the amount of currency that a local resident can purchase from the bank for foreign travel. The government sets a policy on how much money a tourist is allowed to take overseas, and the individual is allowed to convert only that amount of money.

> With quantity controls, the government limits the amount of foreign currency that can be used in a specific transaction.

In the past, these currency controls have significantly added to the cost of doing business internationally, and they have resulted in the overall reduction of trade. However, the liberalization of trade in recent years has eliminated a lot of these controls to the point that they are found to be a minor impediment to trade.[11]

HOW COMPANIES USE FOREIGN EXCHANGE

Most foreign-exchange transactions stem from the international departments of commercial banks, which perform three essential financial functions: (1) They buy and sell foreign exchange, (2) they collect and pay money in transactions with foreign buyers and sellers, and

> Commercial banks buy and sell foreign exchange, collect and pay money in transactions with foreign buyers and sellers, and lend money in foreign currency.

(3) they lend money in foreign currency. In performing collections, the bank serves as a vehicle for payments between its domestic and foreign customers. Lending usually takes place in the currency of the bank's headquarters, but the bank might be able to provide loans in a foreign currency if it has a branch in that country.

Commercial banks buy and sell foreign currency for many purposes. For one, travelers going abroad or returning from a foreign country will want to purchase or sell back its foreign currency. Also, residents of one country wanting to invest abroad need to purchase foreign currency from a commercial bank. Further, suppose a Canadian exporter receives payment from a U.S. importer in U.S. dollars and wants to use the dollars to buy raw materials in Norway. The bank in this case simultaneously serves as a collector and acts as a dealer in a foreign-exchange transaction.

There are a number of reasons why companies use the foreign-exchange market. The most obvious is for import and export transactions. For example, a U.S. company importing products from an overseas supplier might have to convert U.S. dollars into a foreign currency to pay that supplier. In addition, company personnel traveling abroad need to deal in foreign exchange to pay for their local expenses.

Companies also use the foreign-exchange market for financial transactions, such as those in FDI. Say a U.S. company decided to establish a manufacturing plant in Mexico. It would have to convert dollars into pesos to make the investment. After the Mexican subsidiary generated a profit, it would have to convert pesos to dollars to send a dividend back to the U.S. parent.

Sometimes companies—but mostly traders and investors—deal in foreign exchange solely for profit. One type of profit-seeking activity is **arbitrage**, which is the purchase of foreign currency on one market for immediate resale on another market (in a different country) in order to profit from a price discrepancy. For example, a trader might sell U.S. dollars for Swiss francs in the United States, then Swiss francs for British pounds in Switzerland, and then the British pounds for U.S. dollars back in the United States, the goal being to end up with more dollars. Assume the trader converts 100 dollars into 150 Swiss francs when the exchange rate is 1.5 francs per dollar. The trader then converts the 150 francs into 70 British pounds at an exchange rate of .467 pounds per franc and finally converts the pounds into 125 dollars at an exchange rate of .56 pounds per dollar. In this case, arbitrage yields $125 from the initial sale of $100.

Interest arbitrage is the investing in debt instruments, such as bonds, in different countries. For example, a trader might invest $1,000 in the United States for 90 days or convert $1,000 into British pounds, invest the money in the United Kingdom for 90 days, and then convert the pounds back into dollars. The investor would try to pick the alternative that would yield the highest return at the end of 90 days.

Investors can also use foreign-exchange transactions to speculate for profit or to protect against risk. **Speculation** is the buying or selling of a commodity, in this case foreign currency, that has both an element of risk and the chance of great profit. For example, an investor could buy euros in anticipation of the euro's strengthening against other currencies. If it strengthens, the investor earns a profit; if it weakens, the investor incurs a loss. Speculators are important in the foreign-exchange market because they spot trends and try to take advantage of them. They can create demand for a currency by purchasing it in the market, or they can create a supply of the currency by selling it in the market.

As protection against risk, foreign-exchange transactions can hedge against a potential loss due to an exchange-rate change. For example, a U.S. parent company expecting a dividend in British pounds in 90 days could enter into a forward contract to hedge the dividend flow. It could go to the bank and agree to deliver pounds for dollars in 90 days at the forward rate. That way, it would know exactly how much cash it is going to receive no matter what happens to the spot rate in 90 days. Foreign-exchange instruments such as outright forwards, FX swaps, options, and futures are used to hedge risks.

Companies need foreign exchange to settle imports and exports denominated in a foreign currency.

Arbitrage is the buying and selling of foreign currencies at a profit due to price discrepancies.

Interest arbitrage involves investing in interest-bearing instruments in foreign exchange in an effort to earn a profit due to interest-rate differentials.

Speculators take positions in foreign-exchange markets with the major objective of earning a profit. Speculators take a position on a currency and hope that the currency moves in such a way as to make them money.

THE FOREIGN-EXCHANGE TRADING PROCESS

When a company sells goods or services to a foreign customer and receives foreign currency, it needs to convert the foreign currency into the domestic currency. When importing, the company needs to convert domestic to foreign currency to pay the foreign supplier. This conversion takes place between the company and its bank, and most of these transactions take place in the OTC market. Originally, the commercial banks were the ones that provided foreign-exchange services for their customers. Eventually, some of these commercial banks in New York and other U.S. money centers such as Chicago and San Francisco began to look at foreign-exchange trading as a major business activity instead of just a service. They became intermediaries for smaller banks by establishing correspondent relationships with them. They also became major dealers in foreign exchange.

The left side of Figure 9.4 shows what happens when a U.S. company needs to sell euros for dollars. This situation could arise when a customer had to pay in euros or when a German subsidiary had to send a dividend to the U.S. company in euros. The right side of the figure shows what happens when a U.S. company needs to buy euros with dollars. This situation could arise when a company had to pay euros to a German supplier. However, there are other markets and institutions in which foreign exchange is traded. Most of the foreign-exchange activity takes place in the traditional instruments of spot, outright forward, and FX swaps, and commercial banks and investment banks or other financial institutions basically trade these instruments. However, companies could also deal with an exchange, such as the Philadelphia Stock Exchange to buy or sell an option contract and the Chicago Mercantile Exchange to deal in foreign-currency futures.

The Bank for International Settlements estimates that there are about 2,000 dealer institutions worldwide that make up the foreign-exchange market. Of these, about 100 to 200 are market-making banks, which means that they are willing to quote bid and offer rates to anyone in the currency or currencies in which they deal. Of this group, only a select few are major players, and they will be identified and discussed shortly in the section on commercial and investment banks.

As noted earlier, most of the foreign-exchange trades take place in the OTC market in which most of the dealers operate. These dealers operate more in the interbank market with

Companies work through their local banks to settle foreign-exchange balances, but they also use investment banks and exchanges.

An estimated 59 percent of the foreign-exchange trades took place among reporting dealers in 2001.

FIGURE 9.4   Structure of Foreign-Exchange Markets

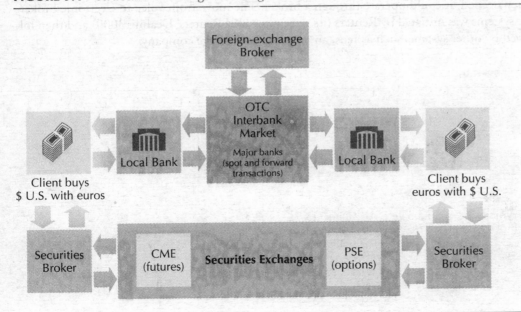

A company interested in exchanging currency can work with a commercial or investment bank in the OTC market or a broker on a securities exchange. Banks deal with each other in the interbank market, primarily through foreign-exchange brokers.

dealers of other banks than they do with corporate clients. The BIS estimated in 2001 that 59 percent of the foreign-exchange trades took place among reporting dealers. Fifty-seven percent of the business between dealers takes place across national borders, whereas 43 percent of the dealers' business with nonfinancial customers takes place in the domestic market. This number is declining rapidly, compared with 64 percent in 1998.[12]

When a company needs foreign exchange, it typically goes to its commercial bank for help. If that bank is a large market-maker, the company can get its foreign exchange fairly easily. However, if the company is located in a small market and uses a local bank, where does the bank get its foreign exchange? Figure 9.5 illustrates how foreign-exchange dealers at the banks trade foreign exchange. A bank, dealing either on its own account or for a client, can trade foreign exchange with another bank directly or through a broker. In the broker market, it can use a voice broker or an electronic brokerage system (EBS). In both the U.S. and U.K. markets, direct dealing is by far the most widely used method of trading currency; however, the use of electronic brokerages is increasing. An increase in electronic brokerage systems shows that dealers are directly trading less actively among themselves.[13] The share of electronic brokerages in interdealer trading volume was around 5 percent in 1992, 10 percent in 1995, 40 percent in 1998, and 60 percent in 2001.[14]

A foreign-exchange broker is an intermediary who matches the best bid and offer quotes of interbank traders. There are a number of brokerage houses around the world, such as the Martin Brokers Group in London, owned by Trio Holdings, Exco, Tullett & Tokyo Forex International, and Intercapital Group. These brokers have traditionally dealt in the market by voice, linking up interbank traders. According to the BIS survey in 1998, there were nine brokers in the United States, including the two major electronic brokerage systems, down from 17 in 1995.[15]

The use of brokers depends on a number of factors, such as the location of the market and the size and nature of the foreign-exchange transactions. Voice brokers are especially important for large foreign-exchange transactions. Brokers have filled an important role because of their ability to establish networks with a wide variety of banks, thus allowing banks to buy or sell currency from other banks faster than if they had to try to contact all the different potential banks themselves. However, the voice broker market has been rapidly giving way to electronic brokerage systems.

Historically, most trades took place by telephone. A dealer in one bank would call a dealer in another bank and execute a trade. If it did not have access to enough banks to get the currency needed, it could operate through a broker. The move from voice to electronic brokerage systems was initiated by Reuters (its system is called Reuters' Dealing 3000) and then followed by other systems such as Icos, an electronic brokerage company.

Dealers can trade foreign exchange

- Directly with other dealers
- Through voice brokers
- Through electronic brokerage systems

FIGURE 9.5   **Foreign-Exchange Transactions**

Companies get access to foreign exchange through dealers or the Internet. Dealers trade directly to an interbank counterparty or through voice brokers or automated brokers.

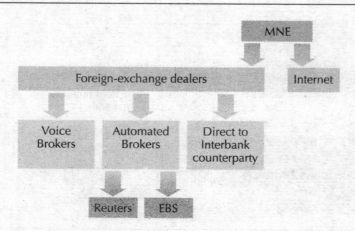

A bank gets access to the automated system by purchasing the service from Reuters by paying a monthly fee and receiving a link through telephone lines to the bank's computers. Then the bank can use the automated system to trade currency. The automated system is efficient, because it lists bid and sell quotes, allowing the bank to trade immediately. For large transactions, many dealers prefer the familiarity of a trusted voice broker to find a buyer or seller. Electronic dealers are efficient but too impersonal for the large transactions. Most electronic trades average in the $1 million to $2 million range, although a trade of $10 million to $20 million will occasionally show up.[16] Electronic brokerage systems are used in one-third of all transactions for the dollar, euro, and yen.[17] Many voice brokers are leaving the spot market and focusing more on derivatives, such as forwards and options.

A current trend in currency trading is the establishment of Internet currency trading. During the Internet boom of the 1990s, large banks and corporations started funding Internet start-ups that were aimed at facilitating Internet exchange trading. One example is a company called Atriax, which was formed by Citibank, JPMorgan Chase, and Deutsche Bank. When the bottom fell out of the stock market in 2000, many of these companies found themselves in trouble, including Atriax. Some companies survived, and Internet trading for foreign exchange is estimated to be around $14 billion a day. Many believe that in 10 to 20 years, there will be a variety of platforms that allow trading in multiple products. And as banks solve security issues associated with Internet trading, activity should pick up.[18]

Internet trades of currency are becoming increasingly popular and are competing with dealers.

Commercial and Investment Banks

At one time, only the big money center banks could deal directly in foreign exchange. Regional banks had to rely on the money center banks to execute trades on behalf of their clients. The emergence of electronic trading has changed that, however. Now even the regional banks can hook up to Reuters and EBS and deal directly in the interbank market or through brokers. In spite of this, the greatest volume of foreign-exchange activity takes place with the big banks.

There is more to servicing customers in the foreign-exchange market than size alone. Each year, *Euromoney* magazine surveys corporations and financial institutions to identify their customers' favorite banks and the leading traders in the interbank market. The criteria for selecting the top foreign-exchange traders include

The top banks in the interbank market in foreign exchange are so ranked because of their ability to

- *Trade in specific market locations*
- *Engage in major currencies and cross-trades*
- *Deal in specific currencies*
- *Handle derivatives (forwards, options, futures, swaps)*
- *Conduct key market research*

Ranking of banks by corporations and other banks in specific locations, such as London, Singapore, and New York.

Capability to handle major currencies, such as the U.S. dollar and euro.

Capability to handle major cross-trades—for example, those between the euro and pound or the euro and yen.

Capability to handle specific currencies.

Capability to handle derivatives (forwards, swaps, futures, and options).

Capability to engage in research.

Other factors often mentioned are price, quote speed, credit rating, liquidity, back office/settlement, strategic advice, trade recommendations, out-of-hours service/night desk, systems technology, innovation, risk appraisal, and e-commerce functions.[19]

For this reason, large companies may use several banks to deal in foreign exchange, selecting those that specialize in specific geographic areas, instruments, or currencies. For example, AT&T uses Citibank for its broad geographic spread and wide coverage of different currencies, but it also uses Deutsche Bank for euros, Swiss Bank Corporation for Swiss francs, NatWest Bank for British pounds, and Goldman Sachs for derivatives.

Table 9.5 identifies the top banks in the world in terms of foreign exchange trading. They are the key players in the OTC market and include both commercial banks (such as Citigroup and JPMorgan Chase) and investment banks (such as UBS Warburg—the

● TABLE 9.5

TOP OTC COMMERCIAL AND INVESTMENT BANKS IN FOREIGN-EXCHANGE TRADES

TRADING BANK	ESTIMATED MARKET SHARE %	BEST IN LONDON	BEST IN NEW YORK	BEST IN TRADING EURO/DOLLAR	BEST IN $/YEN
1. Citigroup	11.17	1	1	1	1
2. UBS Warburg	10.98	2	4	3	2
3. Deutsche Bank	9.97	3	3	2	3
4. Goldman Sachs	6.69	4	5	5	5
5. JPMorgan Chase	5.86	5	2	4	4
6. Credit Suisse First Boston	4.62	6	8	10	—
7. Morgan Stanley	3.70	—	9	—	—
8. ABN Amro	3.40	—		6	9
9. SEB	2.76	—		—	—
10. Barclays Capital	2.61	9=		—	—

= means bank tied for that place (example 6= means bank tied for (sixth place)

Source: "2002 Euromoney Foreign Exchange Poll," *Euromoney,* (May 2002): 58, 60, 62 Reprinted by permission of Euromoney PLC.

London-based investment banking division of Union Bank of Switzerland and Swiss Bank Corporation—and Goldman Sachs). Whether one is looking at overall market share of foreign-exchange trading, the ranking of best banks in specific locations, the best banks in the trading of specific currency pairs, or best dealers, these top 10 banks are usually at or near the top in every category.

One area that allows banks to develop niches is that of **exotic currencies**. An exotic is a currency from a developing country, such as the Russian ruble, the Malaysian ringgit, and the Mexican peso. Exotics are difficult for corporations to work with because the volume of activity in those currencies is pretty small, so the costs of dealing with those currencies are relatively high. It is hard to get a good price, and the bid/ask spread is usually higher than would be the case for a widely traded currency like the Japanese yen. In addition, local regulations governing the use of exotic currencies change daily, realignments of exchange rates are common, and the volume of activity in the currencies can be subject to wide swings.[20] Banks such as Citigroup help their clients with exotics by cutting through the regulations on buying and selling, dealing with difficult exchange-rate systems, working with exchange controls on investments, and getting information on potential changes in rates. The banks also help their clients manage positions and move funds. We discuss the specific financial instruments they use, such as bills of exchange and letters of credit, in Chapter 17.

In addition to the OTC market, there are a number of exchanges in which foreign-exchange instruments, mostly options and futures, are traded. Two of the best-known exchanges are the **Chicago Mercantile Exchange (CME)** and the Philadelphia Stock Exchange (PHLX). The CME offers futures and futures options contracts (contracts that are options on futures contracts rather than options on foreign exchange per se) in the euro, the Japanese yen, the Mexican peso, the Australian dollar, the British pound, the Canadian dollar, the Swiss franc, the Brazilian real, the South African rand, the New Zealand dollar, the Swedish krona, the Norwegian krone, and the Russian ruble. The CME hit record trading levels for futures contracts in 2002—with June and July the busiest months in history. When the economy turned down, investors flocked to the CME to purchase options in a move to hedge against falling portfolios. Also, electronic trading increased the ease and availability of trading.[21]

The **Philadelphia Stock Exchange** is the only exchange in the United States that trades foreign-currency options. The PHLX lists six dollar-based standardized currency option con-

An exotic currency is a currency of a developing country and is often unstable, weak, and unpredictable.

The Philadelphia Stock Exchange (PHLX) is the only exchange in the United States that trades foreign-currency options.

tracts: Australian dollars, British pounds, Canadian dollars, euros, Japanese yen, and Swiss francs. The PHLX has been growing faster than the CME. Much of the growth has come from MNEs. Although options cost more than futures, big companies prefer them to futures (the CME instrument) because of their greater flexibility and convenience. We will provide some examples in Chapter 20 of how companies use options to hedge against foreign-exchange risks. However, the exchange-traded instruments are still very small compared with the OTC trades.

ETHICAL DILEMMA

The Need for Checks and Balances

There are plenty of opportunities for a trader to make money illegally. One of the most publicized events in the derivatives markets in recent years involved 28-year-old Nicholas Leeson and 233-year-old Barings PLC. Leeson, a trader for Barings PLC, went to Singapore in the early 1990s to help resolve some problems Barings was having. Within a year, he was promoted to chief trader. The problem was that he was responsible for trading securities and booking the settlements. This meant that there were no checks and balances on his trading actions, thus opening the door to possible fraud. When two different people are assigned to trade securities and book settlements, the person booking the settlements can confirm independently whether or not the trades were accurate and legitimate. In 1994, Leeson bought stock index futures on the assumption that the Tokyo stock market would rise. Unfortunately, the market fell, and Leeson had to come up with cash to cover the margin call on the futures contract. A margin is a deposit made as security for a financial transaction that is otherwise financed on credit. When the price of an instrument changes and the margin rises, the exchange "calls" the increased margin from the other party—in this case Leeson.[22] However, Leeson soon ran out of cash from Barings, so he had to come up with more cash. One approach he used was to write options contracts and use the premium he collected on the contracts to cover his margin call. Unfortunately, he was using Barings' funds to cover positions he was taking for himself, not for clients, and he also forged documents to cover his transactions. As the Tokyo stock market continued to plunge, Leeson fell farther and farther behind and eventually fled the country, later to be caught and returned to Singapore for trial. Barings estimated that Leeson generated losses in excess of $1 billion, which put Barings into bankruptcy. Eventually, the Dutch bank ING purchased Barings. Leeson's activities in the derivatives market were illegal and a violation of solid internal controls.

Finally, Leeson went to prison in Singapore (where he was treated for colon cancer as well). On July 3, 1999, Leeson was released from prison, and he returned to his native Britain.[23]

Since the collapse of Barings, measures have been put into place in banks to prohibit such consequences, yet negative outcomes of rogue trading continue to happen. In February 2002, Allied Irish Banks discovered that an employee, John Rusnak, at its U.S. subsidiary, Allfirst Bank, lost $750 million in foreign-exchange derivatives. At the end of 2000, Rusnak's trading showed a gain of $224 million, but the profit was not investigated by the bank because it was making a great deal of money off his trades. But because of the volatility of the U.S. market at that time, Rusnak's leveraged gains quickly turned to huge losses. AIB suspects Rusnak was involved with fictitious trades and collusion inside or outside of Allfirst Bank. [24]

LOOKING TO THE FUTURE

Exchange Markets in the New Millennium

Significant strides have been made and will continue to be made in the development of foreign-exchange markets. The speed at which transactions are processed and information is transmitted globally will certainly lead to greater efficiencies and more opportunities for foreign-exchange trading. The impact on companies is that costs of trading foreign exchange should come down, and companies should have faster access to more currencies.

In addition, exchange restrictions that hamper the free flow of goods and services should diminish as governments gain greater control over their economies and as they liberalize currency markets. Capital controls still impact foreign investment, but they will continue to become less of a factor for trade in goods and services.

The introduction of the euro has allowed cross-border transactions in Europe to progress more smoothly. As the euro solidifies its position in Europe, it will reduce exchange-rate volatility and should lead to the euro taking some of the pressure off the dollar so that it is no longer the only major vehicle currency in the world.

Finally, technological developments may not cause the foreign-exchange broker to disappear entirely, but they will certainly cause foreign-exchange trades to be executed more quickly and cheaply. The growth of Internet trades in currency will take away some of the market share of dealers and allow more entrants into the foreign-exchange market. Internet trades will also increase currency price transparency and increase the ease of trading, thus allowing more investors into the market.

Summary

- Foreign exchange is money denominated in the currency of another nation or group of nations. The exchange rate is the price of a currency.

- The foreign-exchange market is divided into the *over-the-counter* market (OTC) and the exchange-traded market.

- The traditional foreign-exchange market is composed of the spot, forward, and FX swap markets. Other key foreign-exchange instruments are currency swaps, options, and futures.

- Spot transactions involve the exchange of currency on the second day after the date on which the two traders agree to the transaction.

- Outright forward transactions involve the exchange of currency three or more days after the date on which the traders agree to the transaction. An FX swap is a simultaneous spot and forward transaction.

- Approximately $1.2 trillion in foreign exchange is traded every day. The dollar is the most widely traded currency in the world (on one side of 90 percent of all transactions), and London is the main foreign-exchange market in the world.

- Foreign-exchange traders quote bid (buy) and offer (sell) rates on foreign exchange. If the quote is in American terms, the trader quotes the foreign currency as the number of dollars and cents per unit of the foreign currency. If the quote is in European terms, the trader quotes the dollar in terms of the number of units of the foreign currency. The numerator is called the "terms currency," and the denominator is called the "base currency."

- A cross rate is the exchange rate between two nondollar currencies.

- A convertible currency is one that companies can freely trade for other currencies. Some countries' currencies are partially convertible because residents are not allowed to convert them into other currencies although nonresidents are.

- If the foreign currency in a forward contract is expected to strengthen in the future (the dollar equivalent of the foreign currency is higher in the forward market than in the spot market), the currency is selling at a premium. If the opposite is true, it is selling at a discount.

- An option is the right but not the obligation to trade foreign currency in the future. Options can be traded OTC or on an exchange.

- A future is an exchange-traded instrument that guarantees a future price for the trading of foreign exchange, but the contracts are for a specific amount and specific maturity date.

- Companies use foreign exchange to settle transactions involving the imports and exports of goods and services, for foreign investments, and to earn money through arbitrage or speculation.

- Companies work with foreign exchange dealers to trade currency. Dealers also work with each other. Dealers can trade currency through voice brokers, electronic brokerage services, or directly with other bank dealers. Internet trades of foreign exchange are becoming more significant.

- The major institutions that trade foreign exchange are the large commercial and investment banks and securities exchanges. Commercial and investment banks deal in a variety of different currencies all over the world. The Chicago Mercantile Exchange specializes in futures contracts, and the Philadelphia Stock Exchange specializes in options.

CASE

HSBC and the Peso Crisis in Argentina[25]

HSBC Holdings plc, one of the world's largest banks, is faced with a difficult decision regarding its Argentine subsidiary. Argentina's economy collapsed at the end of 2001, leaving both local and foreign companies suffering from a shortage of cash, a devaluing peso, and a burden of growing debt. HSBC lost $1.1 billion in 2001 because of Argentina's problems, and its outlook for 2002 was not much better. If things don't improve soon in Argentina, HSBC may be forced to close its operations in the country.

London-based HSBC derives its name from its founding member, the Hongkong and Shanghai Banking Corporation Limited, which was established in 1865 to permit trade between China and Europe. Until the early twentieth century, Hongkong and Shanghai Banking Corporation set up offices and branches mainly in China and Southeast Asia—but also in India, Japan, Europe, and North America. As HSBC's Web site states, "In many of its branches, the bank was the pioneer of modern banking practice. From the outset, trade finance was a strong feature of the bank's business, with bullion, exchange, and merchant banking also playing an important part."

After World War II, Hongkong and Shanghai Banking Corporation expanded and diversified its business with acquisitions and alliances. Through the 1980s, it expanded into Canada, Australia, and the United States, and in the 1990s, it moved into Brazil and Argentina. In 1991, its member companies came together to form HSBC Holdings plc. HSBC pursues a balance of opportunities in developed economies and emerging markets and now has over 7,000 offices in 81 countries. It has stock market listings in London, Hong Kong, New York, and Paris.

HSBC's entry into Argentina began in 1997, when the bank acquired Roberts S.A. de Inversiones, changing its name to HSBC Argentina Holdings S.A. Along with the banking arm, HSBC bought into a general insurance agency with the purchase of Roberts. In 1994, HSBC united with New York Life to form a life and retirement insurance company, so the acquisition of Roberts was a strategic fit in both banking and insurance. HSBC Argentina has also acquired companies in pension fund management and medical care, thus creating a diversified portfolio in Argentina. HSBC is the eighth largest bank in Argentina and employs over 5,900 people in 183 offices. The banking arm of HSBC Argentina maintains commercial services with about 80 percent of the nation's top 200 companies and MNEs. The outlook for HSBC in Argentina looked good. In 1998, its first full year of operations, the bank had a pretax loss of $13 million but earned a profit of $67 million in 1999 and expected profits to continue growing at 100 percent.

To understand the decline of HSBC in Argentina, it is necessary to take a look at Argentina's economic history. Argentina's economy flourished in the beginning of the twentieth century, growing at an annual rate of 5 percent for three years. It attracted a flood of British and Spanish capital and was rated as one of the world's 10 richest countries—even ahead of France and Germany. However, it has been downhill since then. When Juan Perón ruled the country from 1946 to 1955, he instituted protectionist measures and printed money to finance generous benefits for workers. State intervention in all sectors led to poor productivity and structural weakness in the economy. Inflation plagued the country; there were two bouts of hyperinflation in the 1980s and two banking collapses. As a result, Argentines lost trust in the peso and invested in U.S. dollars or shipped their capital abroad.

In 1989, Carlos Menem took control of the country and set out to implement free-market reforms and to restructure monetary and economic policies. He privatized many state-run companies, tightened fiscal management, and opened up the country's borders to trade. Probably the most important policy he established was the Convertibility Law, which pegged the Argentine peso 1:1 with the U.S. dollar and restricted the money supply to its hard dollar currency reserves. This monetary arrangement was called a currency board and was established to impose discipline on the central bank. The new currency board accomplished what it set out to do: It halted inflation and attracted investment. Investors felt that there was little risk anymore in investing in the peso, since it was pegged to the dollar. The sentiment that "the peso is as good as the dollar" was strong throughout the country. Because there was a stable money supply, this reduced inflation to nearly 0 percent through the rest of the 1990s and kept the exchange rate at a constant value. Real GDP grew by 6.1 percent from 1991 to 1997 compared to 0.2 percent from 1975 to 1990.

In spite of these positive developments, the currency board also had its drawbacks. It reduced the Argentine government's ability to respond to external shocks by allowing its exchange-rate and monetary policy to be determined de facto by the United States. Interest rates were in reality set by the U.S. Federal Reserve; plus there was a risk-margin for investing in Argentina. This arrangement was put to the test in 1995, when the Mexican peso devalued. Investors got nervous about Latin America in general and pulled investments out of Argentina. Its economy shrank by 4 percent, and many banks collapsed. The government responded by tightening bank regulation and capital requirements, and some of the larger banks took over weaker ones. Argentina increased exports and investment, and the country returned to 5.5 percent growth.

Unfortunately, the government wasn't so lucky with its results at the end of the 1990s. Commodity prices, which Argentina relied heavily on, declined; the U.S. dollar strengthened against other currencies; Argentina's main trading partner, Brazil, devalued its currency; and emerging economies' cost of capital increased. Argentina soon fell into a recession, with GDP falling to 3.4 percent in 1999 and unemployment increasing into the double digits. Argentina, because of its hard link to the dollar, was unable to compete internationally, especially in Brazil, because of its high prices. One way to correct this problem would be to devalue the currency to bring the value closer to its fundamental value. Argentina couldn't devalue unless it canceled the currency board, a move it didn't want to take because of the currency board's popularity and past success. The only way for Argentina to become more competitive was for prices to fall. As deflation set in, the government (and some private companies) found it difficult to pay its debt because it was not collecting as much revenue. Banks had been lending dollars at 25 percent interest rates even though the risk was supposed to be low.

Argentina was acquiring a burgeoning public debt. When the recession hit, tax revenue fell and spending increased to pay for such things as higher unemployment. Tax evasion is extremely high in Argentina, but the government did little to tackle the problem. The budget went from a surplus of 1.2 percent of GDP in 1993 to a deficit of 2.4 percent in 2000. Increased interest rate payments also added to the increasing budget deficit. From 1991 to 2000, the amount of interest rate payments increased from $2.5 billion to $9.5 billion annually. This drained the economy more as most of this money went to overseas investors. This currency "mismatching," meaning most of the debt is taken out in one currency but assets are held in another, was large in Argentina and would later prove disastrous.

Politicians found little they could do to help the struggling economy. They fiddled with tariffs and finally the currency board. They pegged the peso half to the dollar and half to the euro for exporters. The idea of devaluation scared investors and caused interest rates to rise even more. Unable to pay its interest payments and unwilling to declare a debt default, the government turned to the banks. The Menem government had strengthened the banking system, particularly the central bank, but his successor, Fernando de la Rua, sent a crushing blow to the sector. He strong-armed the banks into buying government bonds. This triggered a bank run, and Argentines withdrew over $15 billion between July and November 2001. In a desperate attempt to save the industry, Mr. de la Rua imposed a ceiling of $1,000 a month on bank withdrawals on December 1. Within days, the country defaulted on $155 million in public debt, the largest such default in world history. As rioters and looters took to the streets, Mr. de la Rua resigned.

Argentina struggled to find a president who was fit for the job. It went through a total of five presidents in four months, ending finally with Eduardo Duhalde. The government abandoned the currency board in January 2002 and let the peso float against the dollar. The peso began falling quickly, so the government spent around $100 million a day—to a total of $1.2 billion—to prop up the value. More money was leaking out of the banking system too (around $50 million a day), because the courts had overturned the freeze on withdrawals.

In March 2002, Mr. Duhalde imposed new restrictions on the foreign exchange market. Individuals could buy no more than $1,000 a day and companies no more than $10,000 a day. Banks and businesses had restrictions on the number of dollars they could hold and on how much money could be shipped abroad. Currency exchanges could only operate three to four hours each day—versus the typical seven hours. However, the courts kept overturning policies set by the government and had police arrest bank managers who didn't follow their rulings. Still unable to prevent the increasing flow of money out of the system, Duhalde closed all banks for a week. In the meantime, he proposed to forcibly convert billions of dollars in bank deposits into low-interest bonds. The senate refused the president's bond proposal, thus sending him back to the drawing board.

As Argentina tries to repair its economy, it is waiting for help from the International Monetary Fund (IMF). However, the IMF continues to turn down Argentina's requests for help until it implements some sweeping changes in its exchange-rate policy, fiscal policy, and banking system. In an attempt to find someone to blame, Duhalde started criticizing foreign-owned banks, such as HSBC, for not infusing more cash into the system from their headquarters. The central bank has been printing pesos to keep banks solvent, but this has led to increased inflation. The national and provincial governments are also using bond notes, quasi-currency, to pay many of their debts. This note is being swapped in everyday transactions and has surprisingly held its value against the peso. Officials promise Argentines that once a deal is signed with the IMF, they will gather up this quasi-currency and swap it for pesos at face value.

Progress is slow with the IMF. Many of the measures required by the IMF are extremely unpopular with the provincial governors and the courts. As a result, Duhalde has had to abandon some of his required cost cutting in order to please the country. One of the last measures Duhalde has implemented is that of *pesification*, which turned bank's dollar assets and liabilities into devalued pesos. This again has put a severe strain on the banking system. People do not trust the banks anymore. They blame the banks for the bank freezes even though the government ordered them. Two foreign banks have left the country, and others are threatening to do the same.

Argentina's economy, though still deeply damaged, is starting to stabilize. The peso was trading around 27 cents in the latter half of 2002, inflation declined and the central bank's reserves increased a little (partly due to the fact that the nation's banks aren't paying their debts). Some economists believe that Argentina should go with full "dollarization" of its currency, not at 1 : 1 but more like 4 : 1. This would be even more binding than its previous policy, but it would bring confidence back to the economy. Others argue for a system of "managed floating plus" that would give the government flexibility to alter its monetary policy but still stay within certain targets and reduce its currency mismatching. The world is waiting to see what the IMF will do to support the country and what Argentina's next move will be.

HSBC's reaction to the crisis was similar to that of other banks in the country. It was forced to rethink loans and to decide if the political and economic instability of the country was worth the risk of continued operations. HSBC quickly cut its profit estimate for 2001 by 10 percent. Then when its annual report came out, the bank declared a $1.12 billion charge for provisions associated with Argentina and losses from foreign currency redenomination. A total of $520 million of this charge stems from the loss in value of the peso. In Latin America, HSBC lost $977 million in 2001, compared to a profit of $324 million in 2000. Overall, HSBC Holdings doubled its bad-debt charges to $2.4 billion, and pretax profits fell by 14 percent in 2001.

Because of the pesification instituted by the Argentine government, loan repayments to HSBC were deeply discounted. In June 2002, HSBC refused a loan payment by Perez Companc, an energy holding company, because the payment was in pesos. The original loan was for $101 million and Perez's offered payment of 104.57 pesos only equaled about $28 million at market rates. HSBC argued that debt was not covered by pesification. HSBC worked quickly to renegotiate all contractual agreements, but it hoped that the IMF would soon provide assistance to the battered country. Because the IMF was stalling, HSBC questioned whether it should continue to fight losses in Argentina or cease operations in the country. It injected $211 million into its Argentine operations to keep them stable, but if the situation continues to worsen in the country, HSBC may have no choice but to exit.

QUESTIONS

1. What are the major factors that caused the peso to fall in value against the dollar?
2. What should President Duhalde do to stabilize Argentina's currency?
3. What are HSBC's options in Argentina, and what do you think they should do?

Chapter Notes

1   Sam Y. Cross, *All About the Foreign Exchange Market in the United States* (New York: Federal Reserve Bank of New York, 2002),9.
2   Ibid.
3   Ibid., 31.
4   Bank for International Settlements, *Central Bank Survey of Foreign Exchange and Derivatives Market Activity 2001* (Basel, Switzerland: BIS, March 2002), http://www.bis.org/publ/rpfx02.htm.
5   Cross, op. cit., 19.
6   Bank for International Settlements, op. cit., 8
7   Gabriele Galati and Kostas Tsatsaronis, *The Impact of the Euro on Europe's Financial Markets*, Bank for International Settlements (Basel, Switzerland: BIS, July 2001), http://www.bis.org/publ/work100.pdf#xml=http://search.atomz.com/search/pdfhelper.tk?sp=o=33,100000,0
8   Cross op. cit., 12.
9   Cross, op. cit., 33.
10 See "Currencies" page in "Market Prices" page of the *Financial Times*, http://www.ft.com/. Also see "Currencies" page in "Markets & Investing" page in CNN Financial News, http://www.cnnfn.com/markets/currencies/; and Web links for Chapter 9 on the homepage for the textbook for more links.
11 Natalia T. Tamirisa, "Exchange and Capital Controls as Barriers to Trade," *IMF Staff Papers* 46, no. 1, (March 1999): 69.
12 Bank for International Settlements, op. cit., 7.
13 Ibid.
14 Bank for International Settlements, Alan Chaboud and Steven Weinberg, "Foreign Exchange Markets in the 1990s," *BIS Papers*, no 12, part 8 (August 2002): http://www.bis.org/publ/bppdf/bispap12h.pdf.

15 Ibid., 28.
16 Stephanie Cook, "Will Brokers Go Broke?" *Euromoney* (May 1996): 90.
17 Bank for International Settlements, "A Look at Trading Volumes in the Euro" (February 2000): http://www.bis.org/publ/r_qt0002e.pdf.
18 "Death of a Platform," *The Economist* (April 11, 2002): www.economist.com.
19 See "Foreign Exchange Results," *Euromoney* (May 2001): 79; and "Life After Execution," *Euromoney* (May 1999): 90.
20 Euan Hagger, "Handle Exotics with Care," *Euromoney* (October 1992): 71.
21 Kristina Zurla, "No Summer Doldrums at Chicago Futures Exchanges," Dow Jones Newswire (September 9, 2002): www.wsj.com
22 More specifically, Leeson did not actually buy the contracts outright but paid a certain percentage of the value of the contract, known as the "margin." When the stock market fell, the index futures contract became riskier, and the broker who sold the contract required Leeson to increase the amount of the margin.
23 See "The Collapse of Barings: A Fallen Star," *The Economist* (March 4, 1995): 19–21; Glen Whitney, "ING Puts Itself on the Map by Acquiring Barings," *Wall Street Journal* (March 8, 1995): B4; John S. Bowdidge and Kurt E. Chaloupecky, "Nicholas Leeson and Barings Bank Have Vividly Taught Some Internal Control Issues," *American Business Review* (January 1997): 71–77; "Trader in Barings Scandal Is Released from Prison," *Wall Street Journal* (July 6, 1999): A12; Ben Dolven, "Bearing Up," *Far Eastern Economic Review* (July 15, 1999): 47.

24 "The Ogre Returns," *The Economist* (February 14, 2002): www.economist.com.
25 Information for this case found on HSBC's Web site, www.hsbc.com, and the following: Dean Baker and Mark Weisbrot, "What Happened to Argentina," Center for Economic and Policy Research, January 31, 2002, http://www.cepr.net/IMF/what_happened_to_argentina.htm; "A Decline Without Parallel," *The Economist*, February 28, 2002, www.economist.com; "HSBC/Argentina –2: To Work With the Argentine Govt.," *Dow Jones*, March 4, 2002, http://216.239.37.100/search?q=cache:Nmw7jFQFeREC:sg.biz.yahoo.com/020304/15/2k8tv.html+hsbc+argentina&hl=en&ie=UTF-8; "Argentina Hits HSBC Profits," *BBC News*, March 4, 2002, http://news.bbc.co.uk/1/hi/business/1853342.stm; Larry Rohter, "Peso Down Steeply, Argentines Strengthen Currency Curbs," *New York Times*, March 26, 2002, www.nytimes.com; "Sympathy, But No Cash," *The Economist*, April 22, 2002, www.economist.com; Larry Rohter, "Argentine President Unveils Crisis Legislation," *New York Times*, April 23, 2002, www.nytimes.com; "Scraping Through the Great Depression," *The Economist*, May 30, 2002, www.economist.com; "Spoilt for Choice," *The Economist*, May 31, 2002, www.economist.com; "HSBC Rejects Perez Companc Peso Debt Payment," Reuters, June 21, 2002, www.reuters.com; "Carving Up the Scraps of Power," *The Economist*, September 5, 2002, www.economist.com; "Duhalde Sifts Budget Priorities, Raising Federal Wages, Benefits," *Wall Street Journal*, September 10, 2002, www.wsj.com; Andrew B. Abel and Ben S. Bernanke, *Macroeconomics*, (Reading, MA: Addison-Wesley, 2003), 20–22.

CHAPTER 10

THE DETERMINATION OF EXCHANGE RATES

A fair exchange brings no quarrel.

—DANISH PROVERB

OBJECTIVES

- To describe the International Monetary Fund and its role in the determination of exchange rates
- To discuss the major exchange-rate arrangements that countries use
- To identify the major determinants of exchange rates in the spot and forward markets
- To show how managers try to forecast exchange-rate movements using factors such as balance-of-payments statistics
- To explain how exchange-rate movements influence business decisions

CASE

The Chinese Renminbi[1]

China's currency is the renminbi (RMB), also known as the yuan. At the end of 1993, China announced it would adjust its exchange-rate system beginning January 1, 1994. After that date, rather than continuing to manage the system as a dual-track foreign-exchange system (we'll see what that is in a minute), it would allow the RMB to float according to market forces. Instead, however, the government locked the RMB onto the U.S. dollar and did all it could to keep the exchange rate fixed to the dollar. Eight years later, at the beginning of the twenty-first century, China was still trying to decide what to do with its currency. Should it devalue the currency and allow it to float according to market factors, or should it keep its value locked onto the dollar at basically the same rate that had existed since the devaluation of 1994?

The concept of a managed exchange rate as represented by the dual-track system was part of the centrally planned economy under which China had operated for decades. The People's Bank of China (PBC) is the country's central bank. The State Administration of Exchange Control (SAEC), operating under the PBC's control, is responsible for implementing exchange-rate regulations and controlling foreign-exchange transactions in accordance with state policy.

The dual-track system provided for two government-approved exchange rates: the official exchange rate and the swap-market rate. The SAEC set the official exchange rate for the renminbi based on China's balance of payments and the exchange rates of its major competitor countries, such as South Korea and Taiwan. When the SAEC first set the official rates in 1986, it set them at 3.72 RMB per dollar.

Government-owned companies primarily used the official exchange rate, and they did so mostly to purchase Foreign Exchange Certificates (FECs). FECs were a separate form of currency developed in 1980 for use by foreigners and foreign companies when paying for their expenses in China. However, the PBC decided to stop issuing FECs in 1994 and gradually withdrew them from circulation.

The other half of the dual-market system was the swap market, created in Shenzhen in 1985 for foreign and local businesses that had received official approval to exchange RMB and hard currency. The currency values in the swap market were based on supply and demand. By the end of 1993, there were around 100 swap centers, one in most major cities in China, the largest in Shanghai. By the end of 1993, 80 percent of the hard-currency transactions in China were occurring in the swap market. At that time, the swap rate was 8.7 RMB per U.S. dollar, a significant discount from the official rate of 5.8 RMB per dollar. This created challenges for foreign MNEs, which had to keep their books at the official rate even though the swap rate was a better indicator of the true value of the currency. In addition to the two government-approved markets—the official market and the swap market—a black market also existed. The black-market rate was at an even deeper discount than the swap market's.

As part of the move to the new exchange-rate system, the Chinese government closed the swap centers in early 1994. The swap center in Shanghai was replaced by the National Foreign Exchange Center, which is a national interbank center at which appointed banks can trade and settle foreign currencies. The remaining swap centers either became branches of the interbank system or economic information centers.

Even though China eliminated the dual exchange-rate system in 1994, there were still controls on both current and capital account transactions. After January 1994, companies in China could change renminbi into foreign currency to buy imports controlled by quotas if they had an import permit and an invoice. Foreign exchange for imports without quotas could be bought with just an import invoice. Foreign companies operated under conditions that were different from those of domestic companies. Foreign companies could buy and sell renminbi as long as they maintained a balanced foreign-exchange account—that is, as long as earnings in foreign exchange from exports balanced with the demand for foreign exchange for imports. However, the government decided to devalue the RMB in 1994, taking its value from about 5.8 yuan per dollar to just over 8.2 yuan per dollar, which was about the same as the old swap rate.

In 1996, the renminbi became fully convertible on a current account (trade in goods and services) but not a capital account (investment and income flows) basis. This means that Chinese citizens have a difficult time moving their money elsewhere and that foreigners can't invest in China's stock market (except for special stocks priced in foreign currency). In addition, the government allows the RMB to trade in a very narrow range against the U.S. dollar. The Asian financial crisis of 1997 did not affect the value of the RMB, although many experts predicted that the Chinese had no choice but to devalue the RMB to remain competitive in global markets.

In 2002, the renminbi's value was holding steady within the 0.3 percent band of around 8.277 to the U.S. dollar. Although the RMB has held to the dollar, the IMF figures that its real effective exchange rate has risen 6 percent since 1999 due largely both to the influx of foreign exchange from foreign investors and to rising exports. China has been under pressure, particularly from the IMF, to loosen its exchange-rate system in preparation for market liberalization. China is in a good position to adjust its exchange-rate policy. It made a bold move by joining the World Trade Organization in 2001, and there is currently an excess of dollars in China because of increased foreign direct investment and export revenue. China holds the second largest foreign-exchange reserves—at $246.5 billion.

There are certain steps China could take before letting its currency freely float. It could give Chinese citizens more access to the world's stock markets or permit foreign portfolio funds into local stocks. It could also gradually widen the RMB trading band with the dollar to 1 percent, then 5 percent, and up. Also, to reduce the RMB's dependence on the dollar, the government could base its currency on a basket of currencies. Although the leaders of the Chinese government admit that they are moving toward a floating exchange-rate policy, they are not planning any moves in the near future. The government feels it should first strengthen the central bank's ability to supervise foreign-exchange transactions and build up the exchange-rate market. In time, China will switch to a free-floating exchange-rate system—but when and how, only time will tell.

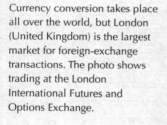

Currency conversion takes place all over the world, but London (United Kingdom) is the largest market for foreign-exchange transactions. The photo shows trading at the London International Futures and Options Exchange.

INTRODUCTION

As we learned in Chapter 9, an exchange rate represents the number of units of one currency needed to acquire one unit of another currency. Although this definition seems simple, it is important that managers understand how governments set an exchange rate and what causes the rate to change. Such understanding can help them both anticipate exchange-rate changes and make decisions about business factors that are sensitive to those changes, such as the sourcing of raw materials and components, the placement of manufacturing and assembly, and the choice of final markets.

THE INTERNATIONAL MONETARY FUND

In 1944, toward the close of World War II, the major Allied governments met in Bretton Woods, New Hampshire, to determine what was needed to bring economic stability and growth to the postwar world. As a result of the meetings, the International Monetary Fund (IMF) came into official existence on December 27, 1945, and began financial operations on March 1, 1947.[2]

Twenty-nine countries initially signed the IMF agreement. There were 184 member countries at the end of 2002. The IMF's major objectives are

- To promote international monetary cooperation.
- To facilitate the expansion and balanced growth of international trade.
- To promote exchange-rate stability.
- To establish a multilateral system of payments.
- To make its resources available to its members who are experiencing balance-of-payments difficulties.[3]

> The IMF was organized to promote exchange-rate stability and facilitate the international flow of currencies.

The Bretton Woods Agreement established a system of fixed exchange rates under which each IMF member country set a par value for its currency based on gold and the U.S. dollar. Because the dollar was valued at $35 per ounce of gold, the par value would be the same whether gold or the dollar was used as the basis for par value. This par value became a benchmark by which each country's currency was valued against other currencies. Currencies were allowed to vary within 1 percent of their par value (extended to 2.25 percent in December 1971), depending on supply and demand. Additional moves from par value and formal changes in par value are possible with IMF approval. As we'll see later, par values were done away with when the IMF moved to greater exchange-rate flexibility.

> The Bretton Woods Agreement established a par value, or benchmark value, for each currency initially quoted in terms of gold and the U.S. dollar.

Because of the U.S. dollar's strength during the 1940s and 1950s and its large reserves in monetary gold, currencies of IMF member countries were denominated in terms of gold and U.S. dollars. By 1947, the United States held 70 percent of the world's official gold reserves. Therefore, governments bought and sold dollars rather than gold. The understanding—though not set in stone—was that the United States would redeem dollars for gold. The dollar became the world benchmark for trading currency, and it has remained so, as noted in Chapter 9.

When a country joins the IMF, it contributes a certain sum of money, called a quota, relating to its national income, monetary reserves, trade balance, and other economic indicators. The quota is a pool of money that the IMF can draw on to lend to countries. It is the basis of how much a country can borrow from the IMF and the amount the country can receive from the IMF as the allocation of special assets called Special Drawing Rights, which will be discussed shortly. Finally, the quota determines the voting rights of the individual members. At the beginning of 2003, the total quota held by the IMF was SDR 213 billion. The United States has the largest quota, comprising 17.5 percent of the total. The next four countries are Japan (6.26 percent), Germany (6.11 percent), France (5.05 percent), and the

> IMF quota—the sum of the total assessment to each country, which becomes a pool of money that the IMF can draw on to lend to other countries. It forms the basis for the voting power of each country—the higher its individual quota, the more votes a country has.

United Kingdom (also 5.05 percent).[4] The Board of Governors, the IMF's highest authority, is composed of one representative from each member country. The number of votes a country has depends on the size of its quota. The Board of Governors is the final authority on key matters, but it leaves day-to-day authority to a 24-person Board of Executive Directors.[5]

IMF Assistance

The IMF lends money to countries to help ease balance-of-payments difficulties.

In addition to identifying exchange-rate regimes, which we'll discuss in more depth later, the IMF provides a great deal of assistance to member countries. When Brazil and Uruguay were facing severe economic challenges in the wake of the Argentine financial crisis, the IMF stepped in to provide some financial assistance. In September 2002, Brazil received $30.4 billion in standby credit, the largest loan in IMF history. Uruguay received $2.8 billion in August 2002. The loans are drawn out in stages as the two countries meet benchmarks and performance criteria established by the IMF. The IMF negotiates with a country to provide financial assistance if the country will agree to adopt certain policies to stabilize its economy. The IMF was more willing to loan to Brazil and Uruguay than to Argentina, because Argentina didn't meet the economic criteria. Argentina is trying to solve its economic and banking problems, in hope of receiving assistance from the IMF.[6] Often, as is the case with Argentina, the policies set out by the IMF are not very popular.

Special Drawing Rights (SDRs)

The SDR is

- An international reserve asset given to each country to help increase its reserves
- The unit of account in which the IMF keeps its financial records

Currencies making up the SDR basket are the U.S. dollar, the euro (previously the German mark and the French franc), the Japanese yen, and the British pound.

To help increase international reserves, the IMF created the **Special Drawing Right (SDR)** in 1969. The SDR is an international reserve asset created to supplement members' existing reserve assets (official holdings of gold, foreign exchange, and reserve positions in the IMF). SDRs serve as the IMF's unit of account and are used for IMF transactions and operations. By unit of account, we mean the unit in which the IMF keeps its records. For example, we noted earlier that the total quota the IMF holds is SDR 213 billion, which at current exchange rates (i.e., near the end of 2002) was about $280 billion. The value of the SDR is based on the weighted average of five currencies. On January 1, 1981, the IMF began to use a simplified basket of five currencies for determining valuation. At the end of 2002, the U.S. dollar made up 45 percent of the value of the SDR; the euro, 29 percent; the Japanese yen, 15 percent; and the British pound, 11 percent.[7] These weights were chosen because they broadly reflected the importance of each particular currency in international trade and payments. The value of the SDR can be found daily in key business publications, such as the *Wall Street Journal* and the *Financial Times* of London, as well as many online currency services. Unless the Executive Board decides otherwise, the weights of each currency in the valuation basket change every five years. The Board determined this rule in 1980. A new value was established in 2000 for the period 2001 to 2005, and the Board will decide whether or not to make a new determination in 2005 to become effective on January 1, 2006. One change to the basket in 2000 was an increase in the amount of the U.S. dollar as a move to take some of the weight off the euro, which was previously composed of the German mark and the French franc.

Although the SDR was intended to serve as a substitute for gold, it has not taken over the role of gold or the dollar as a primary reserve asset. In addition, several countries base the value of their currency on the value of the SDR.[8]

Evolution to Floating Exchange Rate

The IMF's system was initially one of fixed exchange rates. Because the U.S. dollar was the cornerstone of the international monetary system, its value remained constant with respect to the value of gold. Other countries could change the value of their currency against gold and the dollar, but the value of the dollar remained fixed.

On August 15, 1971, President Richard Nixon announced that the United States would no longer trade dollars for gold unless other industrial countries agreed to support a restructuring of the international monetary system. The resulting Smithsonian Agreement of December 1971 had several important aspects:

An 8-percent devaluation of the dollar (an official drop in the value of the dollar against gold)

A revaluation of some other currencies (an official increase in the value of each currency against gold)

A widening of exchange-rate flexibility (from 1 percent to 2.25 percent on either side of par value)

This effort did not last, however. World currency markets remained unsteady during 1972, and the dollar was devalued again by 10 percent in early 1973 (the year of the Arab oil embargo and the start of fast-rising oil prices and global inflation). Major currencies began to float (i.e., each one relied on the market to determine its value) against each other instead of relying on the Smithsonian Agreement.

Because the Bretton Woods Agreement was based on a system of fixed exchange rates and par values, the IMF had to change its rules to accommodate floating exchange rates. The Jamaica Agreement of 1976 amended the original rules to eliminate the concept of par values in order to permit greater exchange-rate flexibility. The move toward greater flexibility can occur on an individual-country basis as well as on an overall system basis. Let's see how this works.

EXCHANGE-RATE ARRANGEMENTS

The Jamaica Agreement formalized the break from fixed exchange rates. As part of this move, the IMF began to permit countries to select and maintain an exchange-rate arrangement of their choice, provided they communicate their decision to the IMF. The IMF has a surveillance program which allows it to monitor the economic policies of countries that would affect those countries' exchange rates. It also consults annually with countries to see if they are acting openly and responsibly in their exchange-rate policies. Each year, the countries notify the IMF of the exchange-rate arrangement they will use, and then the IMF uses the information provided by the country and evidence of how the country acts in the market to place each country in a specific category. There used to be three broad categories, but the IMF has now divided the countries into several categories, as Table 10.1 shows.

From Pegged to Floating Currencies

In the first three categories, countries lock the value of their currency onto another currency and allow the currency to vary by plus or minus 1 percent against that value. Several countries, especially those in the French franc zone in Africa, have basically adopted the franc as their currency, although the franc zone countries have now switched to the euro. That same concept was being considered in Latin America, especially in Brazil and Argentina, and it is called the dollarization of the economy. The idea would be to take all of their currency out of circulation and replace it with dollars. Basically, the U.S. Fed would make all monetary decisions instead of the governments of the local countries. Prices and wages would be established in dollars instead of in the local currency, which would disappear. The concern is that this would result in a loss of sovereignty and could lead to severe economic problems if the United States decided to tighten monetary policy at the same time those countries needed to loosen policy to stimulate growth. As seen in the Argentina case in Chapter 9, this is exactly what happened. Although Argentina's exchange-rate regime was not to the extreme of dollarization, its currency board regime was just a step away from dollarization. The currency

● TABLE 10.1

EXCHANGE-RATE REGIMES, END OF 2001

Exchange rates can be either fixed or pegged to another currency under very narrow fluctuations (exchange arrangements with no separate legal tender, currency board arrangements, or other conventional fixed peg arrangements), pegged to something else with a wider band of fluctuation (pegged exchange rates within horizontal bands), and floating, (crawling pegs, exchange rates within crawling bands, managed floating, or independently floating).

REGIMES	NUMBER OF COUNTRIES
Exchange arrangements with no separate legal tender	40
Currency board arrangements	8
Other conventional fixed peg arrangements	41
Pegged exchange rates within horizontal bands	5
Crawling pegs	4
Exchange rates within crawling bands	6
Managed floating with no pronounced path for exchange rate	42
Independently floating	40
Total	186

Exchange arrangements with no separate legal tender: The currency of another country circulates as the sole legal tender, or the member belongs to a monetary or currency union in which the members of the union share the same legal tender. An example would be the countries in the euro area.

Currency board arrangements: A monetary regime based on an implicit legislative commitment to exchange domestic currency for a specified foreign currency at a fixed exchange rate, combined with restrictions on the issuing authority to ensure the fulfillment of its legal obligation. Two examples would be Bosnia and Hong Kong.

Other conventional peg arrangements: The country pegs its currency (formal or de facto) at a fixed rate to a major currency or a basket of currencies in which the exchange rate fluctuates within a narrow margin of at most 1/21 percent around a central rate. For example, China pegs its currency to the U.S. dollar.

Pegged exchange rates within horizontal bands: The value of the currency is maintained within margins of fluctuation around a formal or de facto fixed peg that are wider than 1/21 percent around a central rate. Many countries that used to be considered managed floating are in this category because they basically peg their currency to something else. An example would be Denmark in the new Exchange Rate Mechanism in Europe, a country that was not part of the euro group in 2002, yet was still linking itself to the euro as much as possible but at a wider degree of flexibility.

Crawling pegs: The currency is adjusted periodically in small amounts at a fixed, preannounced rate or in response to changes in selective quantitative indicators. Costa Rica and Bolivia are two examples.

Exchange rates within crawling bands: The currency is maintained within certain fluctuation margins around a central rate that is adjusted periodically at a fixed preannounced rate or in response to changes in selective quantitative indicators. Romania, Israel, and Uruguay are three examples.

Managed floating with no pronounced path for the exchange rate: The monetary authority influences the movements of the exchange rate by actively intervening in the foreign-exchange market without specifying, or precommitting to, a preannounced path for the exchange rate. India and Azerbaijan are examples.

Independent floating: The exchange rate is market determined, with any foreign-exchange intervention aimed at moderating the rate of change and preventing undue fluctuations in the exchange rate rather than at establishing a level for it. Canada, the United States, and Mexico are three examples of countries in this category.

Source: International Monetary Fund, "*International Financial Statistics*" (November 1999): 2–3; and Andrea Bubula and Inci Otker-Robe, "The Evolution of Exchange Rate Regimes Since 1990: Evidence from De Facto Policies," IMF Working Page, (September 2002): http://www.imf.org/external/pubs/ft/wp/2002/wp02155.pdf.

board was tied closely enough to the dollar and to the decisions the U.S. Fed made that the government's ability to use monetary policy to strengthen its stalling economy was limited. However, this is the same problem facing the member countries in the euro area.[9]

The next category, pegged exchange rates within horizontal bands, contains only a few countries, and it is a slight variation of the first three categories. The countries in this pegged category simply have a wider band but are still locked onto something else, such as the euro for Denmark and Hungary, two of the countries in this category.

The last four categories have some degree of floating exchange-rate arrangements, either managed float or free float. Many countries that used to be managed floating countries have been reclassified into the fixed peg regime because they are so tightly linked to some type of anchor, like the dollar. In addition, countries are changing their regimes all the time. Chile, for example, was listed in the IMF survey as a country that keeps its exchange rate within a crawling band, which means that the exchange rate is adjusted periodically at a fixed pronounced rate or in response to changes in selective quantitative indicators, which, for Chile, is inflation. But in late 1999, Chile suspended the trading bands, which it had established around the peso, and moved to a floating rate regime in an effort to stimulate export-led economic growth. Likewise, in 2001, Iceland moved from a pegged regime, within a horizontal band, to a free-floating regime. Mexico did the same thing in 1994; so did Brazil in early 1999, and Turkey in 2001.[10]

Map 10.1 identifies the countries that fit into each category listed in Table 10.1. Because a country's classification is subject to change constantly, it is important for managers to frequently consult the most recent issue of the IMF's International Financial Statistics for updates. In addition, it is necessary to supplement the *International Financial Statistics* tables with current events, as illustrated in the earlier examples of regime changes in Chile and Iceland. It is important for MNEs to understand the exchange-rate arrangements for the currencies of countries in which they are doing business so that those MNEs can forecast trends more accurately. It is much easier to forecast a future exchange rate for a relatively stable currency that is pegged to the U.S. dollar, such as the Hong Kong dollar, than for a currency that is freely floating, such as the Japanese yen.

Countries may change the exchange-rate regime they use, so managers need to monitor country policies carefully.

Black Markets

Of the 186 IMF member countries, 92 have currencies that are reasonably flexible, 40 of which float independently. Many of the others control their currencies fairly rigidly. In many of these countries, a black market parallels the official market and is aligned more closely with the forces of supply and demand than is the official market. The less flexible a country's exchange-rate arrangement, the more there will be a thriving black market. A black market exists when people are willing to pay more for dollars than the official rate. As noted in the opening case, when China had an official exchange rate, the swap rate was significantly lower, indicating that the official rate was significantly overvalued. The movement to floating rates eliminates the need for a black market.

A black market closely approximates a price based on supply and demand for a currency instead of a government-controlled price.

The Role of Central Banks

Each country has a central bank that is responsible for the policies affecting the value of its currency. The central bank in the United States is the Federal Reserve System (the Fed), a system of 12 regional banks. The New York Fed, representing the Federal Reserve System and the U.S. Treasury, is responsible for intervening in foreign-exchange markets to achieve dollar exchange-rate policy objectives and to counter disorderly conditions in foreign-exchange markets. It makes such transactions in close coordination with the U.S. Treasury and Board of Governors of the Fed, and most often it coordinates with the foreign-exchange operations of other central banks. The Fed will sell dollars for foreign currency if the goal is to counter upward pressure on the dollar. If the goal is to counter downward pressure, it will purchase dollars through the sale of foreign currency. Further, the Federal Reserve Bank of New York serves as fiscal agent in the United States for foreign central banks and official international financial organizations. It acts as the primary contact with other foreign central banks. The services it provides for these institutions include the receipt and payment of funds in U.S. dollars; the purchase and sale of foreign exchange and Treasury securities; the custody of over

Central banks control policies that affect the value of currencies; the Federal Reserve Bank of New York is the central bank in the United States.

MAP 10.1   Exchange-Rate Arrangements, 2001

Over half of the countries in the world have a floating exchange rate, although only one-quarter of the countries' currencies are independently floating, like the U.S. dollar. Some countries have abandoned their currencies in favor of something else, such as the euro in many African countries, and others are considering adopting the dollar as their currency. See the International Monetary Fund's Web site for more information about countries and their exchange rates: www.imf.org/external/country/index.htm.

ANTIGUA & BARBUDA
ARUBA
BAHRAIN
BARBADOS
CAPE VERDE
COMOROS
DOMINICA
FIJI
GRENADA
KIRIBATI
MALDIVES
MALTA
MARSHALL ISLANDS
MAURITIUS
MICRONESIA
NETHERLANDS ANTILLES
PALAU
SAMOA
SAN MARINO
SÃO TOMÉ & PRÍNCIPE
SEYCHELLES
SOLOMON ISLANDS
ST. KITTS & NEVIS
ST. LUCIA
ST. VINCENT & THE GRENADINES
THE BAHAMAS
TONGA
TRINIDAD & TOBAGO
VANUATU

Source: "The Evolution of Exchange Rate Regimes Since 1990: Evidence from De Facto Policies," *IMF Working Paper* (September 2002): http://www.imf.org/external/pubs/ft/wp/2002/wp02155.pdf.

Central bank reserve assets are kept in three major forms; gold, foreign-exchange, and IMF-related assets. Foreign exchange was 84.4 percent of reserve assets worldwide in 2001.

$800 billion in currency, securities, and gold bullion credited to over 200 foreign accounts; and the storage of over $64 billion in monetary gold for about 60 foreign central banks, governments, and official international agencies (approximately one-third of the world's known monetary gold reserves).[11] In the European Union, the European Central Bank now coordinates the activities of each member country's central bank to establish a common monetary policy in Europe, much as the Federal Reserve Bank does in the United States.

Central bank reserve assets are kept in three major forms: gold, foreign-exchange reserves, and IMF-related assets. At the end of 2001, there were $2.4 trillion in reserves worldwide, of which 84.4 percent were in foreign exchange, followed by 11.6 percent in gold and 4 percent in IMF-related assets. The U.S. dollar was the most widely used currency as a reserve asset, with 68.3 percent of the total, up from 55.3 percent a decade earlier. It was followed by the

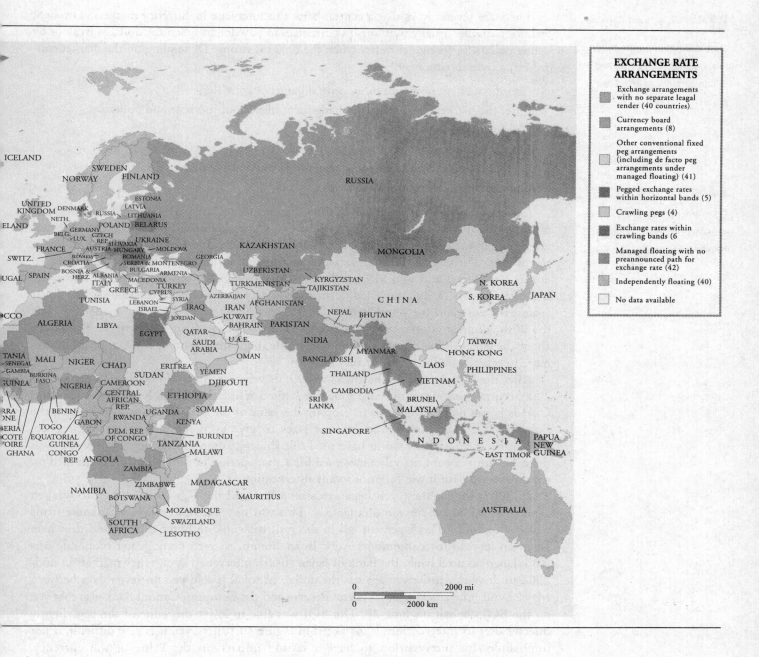

EXCHANGE RATE ARRANGEMENTS

- Exchange arrangements with no separate leagal tender (40 countries)
- Currency board arrangements (8)
- Other conventional fixed peg arrangements (including de facto peg arrangements under managed floating) (41)
- Pegged exchange rates within horizontal bands (5)
- Crawling pegs (4)
- Exchange rates within crawling bands (6
- Managed floating with no preannounced path for exchange rate (42)
- Independently floating (40)
- No data available

euro at 13 percent and the Japanese yen at 4.9 percent.[12] However, the mix of reserve assets varies from country to country. For example, in 2002, 98.3 percent of Singapore's reserves and 96.3 percent of Japan's reserves were in foreign exchange. However, only 49.7 percent of Germany's reserves and 42.4 percent of the U.S. reserves were in foreign exchange. European countries tend to be more heavily weighted toward gold as a reserve asset than are other countries in the world, even though they have more foreign exchange than gold as reserve assets.

Central banks are concerned primarily with liquidity to ensure that they have the cash and flexibility needed to protect their countries' currencies. The mix of currencies in a country's reserves is based on its major intervention currencies—that is, the currencies in which the country trades the most. The degree to which a central bank actively manages its reserves to earn a profit varies by country.

There are several ways that a central bank can intervene in currency markets. The U.S. Fed, for example, usually uses foreign currencies to buy dollars when the dollar is weak or by selling dollars for foreign currency when the dollar is strong. Depending on the market conditions, a central bank may

Coordinate its action with other central banks or go it alone.

Enter the market aggressively to change attitudes about its views and policies.

Call for reassuring action to calm markets.

Intervene to reverse, resist, or support a market trend.

Announce or not announce its operations, be very visible or very discreet.

Operate openly or indirectly through brokers.[13]

Government policies change over time, depending on the particular administration in office. In the first two and a half years of the first Clinton administration, the U.S. Treasury intervened in the market by buying dollars on only 18 days, spending about $12.5 billion in the process. The George Bush Sr. treasury/administration, in 1989 alone, bought and sold dollars on 97 days and sold $19.5 billion.[14] Since George W. Bush has been in office, the U.S. Treasury has rarely intervened in the market despite a decline in the value of the dollar against the euro and the yen. Former U.S. Treasury Secretary Paul O'Neill made very clear the Bush administration's views on currency intervention by saying, "There is a real doubt about the effectiveness of intervention and words about intervention. It is not possible anymore to actually fool markets for very long."[15]

After the introduction of the euro in 1999, its value continued to decline. In September 2000, central banks from the euro zone, the United States, the United Kingdom, Japan, and Canada began purchasing euros to prop up the value of the euro. Then two weeks later, the European Central Bank raised interest rates to give even more support to the euro. Governments around the world have used this strategy, often successfully. However, as was the case with the euro, its value increased for a short period of time and then continued on the downward path it was on prior to any intervention.[16]

In 2002, the Japanese yen began to strengthen and the U.S. dollar began to weaken against world currencies simultaneously. This was not welcome news to Japanese firms which, due to 2001's 15 percent fall in the yen, were able to boost exports and thus help Japan on its road to economic recovery. In an attempt to avert even greater economic turmoil, Japan's central bank, the Bank of Japan (BOJ), intervened in currency markets in mid-2002 to drive down the yen against the dollar. In total, it sold yen on seven days between May 22 and June 28. The U.S. Federal Reserve and the European Central Bank also sold yen on the BOJ's behalf on June 28. The BOJ was able to lower the value of the yen slightly directly after its interventions.[17] As noted in Figure 10.1, however, it is very difficult, if not impossible, for intervention to have a lasting impact on the value of the currency. Intervention may temporarily halt a slide, but it cannot force the market to move in a direction that it doesn't want to, at least for the long run.

The Central Bank of Russia intervenes in the market in a different way. To control the use of foreign currency, the Central Bank requires exporters to deposit 75 percent of the hard-currency proceeds with the Central Bank, but only during special trading sessions of interbank currency exchanges. The Central Bank's main objectives are to ensure that trading is conducted without interruptions and to prevent abrupt fluctuations of the exchange rate of the ruble. The Bank of Russia actively participates in drafting and refining rules to conduct currency trading on exchanges, taking into account the interests of different groups of foreign exchange market participants.[18]

Coordination of central bank intervention can take place on a bilateral or multilateral basis. The **Bank for International Settlements (BIS)** in Basel, Switzerland, links together the central banks in the world. The BIS was founded in 1930 and is owned and controlled by a

FIGURE 10.1   Intervention and the Japanese Yen

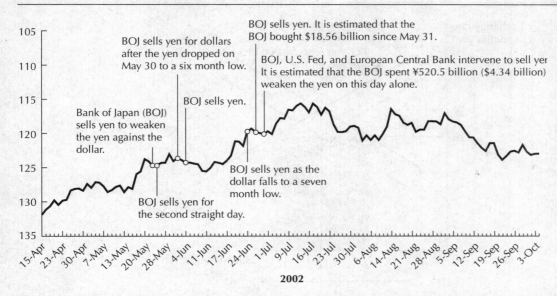

The yen is depicted daily in late New York trading. The graph gives the scale in terms of yen per dollar and inverts it to show the yen's strength. For example, the yen is stronger at 100 yen than at 130 yen per dollar. The size of the market and the volume of trading make it difficult for intervention to work effectively.

Source: "Chronology-History of Central Bank Interventions," Reuters Market News (July 31, 2002): data from x-rates.com, http://www.x-rates.com/d/JPY/USD/data120.html.

group of central banks. The major objective of the BIS is to promote the cooperation of central banks to facilitate international financial stability. Although only 50 central banks or monetary authorities are shareholders in the BIS—11 of which are the founding banks and are from the major industrial countries—the BIS has dealings with some 130 central banks worldwide.[19] The BIS acts as a central banker's bank. It gets involved in swaps and other currency transactions between the central banks in other countries. It also is a gathering place where central bankers can discuss monetary cooperation.[20]

THE DETERMINATION OF EXCHANGE RATES

One of the first steps in being able to forecast future values of a currency is to understand how exchange rates change in value. The exchange-rate regimes described earlier are either fixed or floating, with fixed rates varying in terms of how fixed they are and floating rates varying in terms of how much they actually float. However, currencies change in different ways depending on whether they are in floating rate or fixed rate regimes.

Floating Rate Regimes

Currencies that float freely respond to supply and demand conditions free from government intervention. This concept can be illustrated using a two-country model involving the United States and Japan. Figure 10.2 shows the equilibrium exchange rate in the market and then a movement to a new equilibrium level as the market changes. The demand for yen in this example is a function of U.S. demand for Japanese goods and services, such as automobiles, and yen-denominated financial assets, such as securities.

The supply of yen in this example is a function of Japanese demand for U.S. goods and services and dollar-denominated financial assets. Initially, the supply of and demand for yen in Figure 10.2 meet at the equilibrium exchange rate e_0 (for example, 0.008 dollars per yen, or 125 yen per dollar) and the quantity of yen Q_1.

Assume demand for U.S. goods and services by Japanese consumers drops because of, say, high U.S. inflation. This lessening demand would result in a reduced supply of yen in the foreign-exchange market, causing the supply curve to shift to S'. Simultaneously, the

Demand for a country's currency is a function of the demand for that country's goods and services and financial assets.

FIGURE 10.2   Equilibrium Exchange Rate

Comparatively high inflation in the United States compared with Japan raises the demand for yen but lowers the supply of yen, increasing the value of the yen in terms of U.S. dollars. If the Japanese government wants to keep the dollar/yen exchange rate at e_0, it needs to sell yen for dollars in order to increase the supply of yen in the market and therefore decrease the exchange rate.

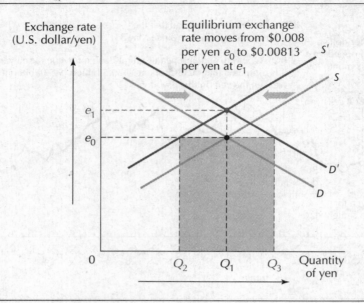

Exchange rate (U.S. dollar/yen)

Equilibrium exchange rate moves from $0.008 per yen e_0 to $0.00813 per yen at e_1

increasing prices of U.S. goods might lead to an increase in demand for Japanese goods and services by U.S. consumers. This, in turn, would lead to an increase in demand for yen in the market, causing the demand curve to shift to D' and finally leading to an increase in the quantity of yen and an increase in the exchange rate. The new equilibrium exchange rate would be at e_1 (for example, 0.00813 dollars per yen, or 123 yen per dollar). From a dollar standpoint, the increased demand for Japanese goods would lead to an increase in supply of dollars as more consumers tried to trade their dollars for yen, and the reduced demand for U.S. goods would result in a drop in demand for dollars. This would cause a reduction in the dollar's value against the yen.

Managed Fixed Rate Regime

A government buys and sells its currency in the open market as a means of influencing the currency's price.

In the preceding example, Japanese and U.S. authorities allowed changes in the exchange rates between their two currencies to occur so that the currencies could reach a new exchange-rate equilibrium. There can be times when one or both countries might not want exchange rates to change. Assume, for example, that the United States and Japan decide to manage their exchange rates. The U.S. government might not want its currency to weaken because its companies and consumers would have to pay more for Japanese products, which would lead to more inflationary pressure in the United States. Or the Japanese government might not want the yen to strengthen because it would mean unemployment in its export industries. But how can the governments keep the values from changing when the United States is earning too few yen? Somehow the difference between yen supply and demand must be neutralized.

In a managed fixed exchange-rate system, the New York Federal Reserve Bank would hold foreign-exchange reserves, which it would have built up through the years for this type of contingency. It could sell enough of its yen reserves (make up the difference between Q_1 and Q_3 in Figure 10.2) at the fixed exchange rate to maintain that rate. Or the Japanese central bank might be willing to accept dollars so that U.S. consumers can continue to buy Japanese goods. These dollars would then become part of Japan's foreign-exchange reserves.

The fixed rate could continue as long as the United States had reserves or as long as the Japanese were willing to add dollars to their holdings. Sometimes governments use fiscal or monetary policy—for example, by raising interest rates (as the European Central Bank did)—to create a demand for their currency and to keep the value from falling. Unless something changed the basic imbalance in the currency supply and demand, however, the New York Federal Reserve Bank would run out of yen and the Japanese central bank would stop accepting dollars because it would fear amassing too many. At this point, it would be necessary to change the exchange rate in order to lessen the demand for yen.

If a country determines that intervention will not work, it must adjust its currency's value. If the currency is freely floating, the exchange rate will seek the correct level according to the laws of supply and demand. However, a currency that is pegged to another currency or to a basket of currencies usually is changed on a formal basis—in other words, through a devaluation or revaluation, depending on the direction of the change.

Countries may be forced to revalue or devalue their currencies if economic policies and intervention don't work.

The earlier example used two currencies, the dollar and the yen. Often, however, a number of countries intervene in currency markets, sometimes in a coordinated fashion. The G7 comprises the finance ministers of seven key industrial countries: the United States, Canada, Japan, Germany, France, Italy, and the United Kingdom. Sometimes Russia is thrown in, resulting in the G7+1. However, the G7 is the most influential group of finance ministers in the world, and they meet periodically to discuss key economic issues, especially exchange rates. As was mentioned earlier, the countries from the G7 purchased euros in September 2000 to prop up its ailing value. Although this caused no immediate reversal in the value of the euro, it established a floor for investors, assuring them that the G7 would intervene if the euro's value fell below that level. Also, in June 2002, reports stated that there was a small possibility the G7 would intervene to prop up the falling U.S. dollar due to the possibility that the weak dollar would slow global economic recovery. This is unlikely to happen given the U.S. Treasury's strong stance against intervention.[21] In December 1999, a new group—the G20—met for the first time. The G20 is composed of the G7 plus Argentina, Australia, Brazil, China, India, Indonesia, Mexico, Russia, Saudi Arabia, South Africa, South Korea, and Turkey. The representatives of the European Union, including the European Central Bank, bring the tally to 20. This organization is considered important because it brings some developing countries into discussions previously held only by the industrial countries. The G20 will be discussing a wide variety of issues, including appropriate exchange-rate policies for member countries. Among the immediate concerns are the volatility of currency markets, corporate profitability and accounting standards, as well as the economic situations in Turkey and Argentina.[22]

The G7 group of industrial countries meets often to discuss global economic issues, including exchange-rate values. The G20 is an expansion of the G7 and includes some emerging economies.

Purchasing-Power Parity

Purchasing-power parity (PPP) is a well-known theory that seeks to define relationships between currencies. In essence, it claims that a change in relative inflation (meaning a comparison of the countries' rates of inflation) between two countries must cause a change in exchange rates in order to keep the prices of goods in two countries fairly similar. According to the PPP theory, if, for example, Japanese inflation were 2 percent and U.S. inflation were 3.5 percent, the dollar would be expected to fall by the difference in inflation rates. Then the dollar would be worth fewer yen than before the adjustment, and the yen would be worth more dollars than before the adjustment.

If the domestic inflation rate is lower than that in the foreign country, the domestic currency should be stronger than that of the foreign country.

An interesting illustration of the PPP theory for estimating exchange rates is the "Big Mac" index of currencies used by *The Economist* each year. Since 1986, *The Economist* has used the price of a Big Mac to estimate the exchange rate between the dollar and another currency (see Table 10.2). Because the Big Mac is sold in over 120 countries, it is easy to compare prices. PPP would suggest that the exchange should leave hamburgers costing the same in the United States as abroad. However, the Big Mac sometimes costs more and sometimes less, demonstrating how far currencies are under- or overvalued against the dollar. Looking at Table 10.2, a Big Mac in 2002 cost an average of $2.49 in the United States and Baht55.0 in Thailand. Dividing the baht price of the Big Mac by the dollar price of the Big Mac yields a

TABLE 10.2

THE HAMBURGER STANDARD

	BIG MAC PRICES				
	IN LOCAL CURRENCY	IN DOLLARS	IMPLIED PPP* OF THE DOLLAR	ACTUAL $ EXCHANGE RATE 04/23/02	UNDER (−)/OVER (+) VALUATION AGAINST THE DOLLAR, %
United States[†]	$2.49	2.49	—	—	—
Argentina	Peso2.50	0.78	1.00	3.13	−68
Australia	A$3.00	1.62	1.02	1.86	−35
Brazil	Real3.60	1.55	1.45	2.34	−38
Britain	£1.99	2.88	1.25[‡]	1.45[‡]	+16
Canada	C$3.33	2.12	1.34	1.57	−15
Chile	Peso1,400	2.16	562	655	−14
China	Yuan10.50	1.27	4.22	8.28	−49
Czech Rep	Koruna56.28	1.66	22.6	34.0	−33
Denmark	Dkr24.75	2.96	9.94	8.38	+19
Euro area	Euro2.67	2.37	0.93[§]	0.89[§]	−5
Hong Kong	HK$11.20	1.40	4.50	7.80	−42
Hungary	Forint459	1.69	184	272	−32
Indonesia	Rupiah 16,000	1.71	6,426	9,430	−32
Israel	Shekel12.00	2.51	4.82	4.79	+1
Japan	¥262	2.01	105	130	−19
Malaysia	M$5.04	1.33	2.02	3.80	−47
Mexico	Peso21.9	2.37	8.80	9.28	−5
New Zealand	NZ$3.95	1.77	1.59	2.24	−29
Poland	Zloty5.90	1.46	2.37	4.04	−41
Russia	Ruble39.00	1.25	15.7	31.2	−50
Singapore	S$3.30	1.81	1.33	1.82	−27
South Africa	Rand9.70	0.87	3.90	10.9	−64
South Korea	Won3,100	2.36	1,245	1,304	−5
Sweden	Skr26.00	2.52	10.4	10.3	+1
Switzerland	Sfr6.30	3.81	2.53	1.66	+53
Taiwan	NT$70.0	2.01	28.1	34.8	−19
Thailand	Baht55.0	1.27	22.1	43.3	−49
Turkey	Lira4,000,000	3.06	1,606,426	1,324,500	+21

*Purchasing-power parity: local price divided by price in United States
[†]Average of New York, Chicago, San Francisco, and Atlanta
[‡]Dollars per pound
[§]Dollars per euro

purchasing-power parity exchange rate of Baht22.1 per dollar. However, the actual exchange rate was Baht43.3 per dollar, so the baht was undervalued against the dollar by 49 percent. Based on the actual exchange rate, a Big Mac costs only $1.27 in Thailand (Baht55/43.3), so Big Macs are a real bargain in Thailand compared with the United States. (Of course, transportation costs to Thailand to buy the burger will eat up the difference.) European currencies outside of the euro zone were significantly overvalued against the dollar, whereas the euro zone currencies were only slightly undervalued. Most other currencies were undervalued against the dollar.[23]

There are supporters of the Big Mac index, also known as "McParity," but there also are detractors. Even though McParity may hold up in the long run, as some studies have shown, there are short-run problems that affect PPP:

The theory of PPP falsely assumes that there are no barriers to trade and that transportation costs are zero.

Prices of the Big Mac in different countries are distorted by taxes. European countries with high value-added taxes are more likely to have higher prices than countries with low taxes.

The Big Mac is not just a basket of commodities; its price also includes nontraded costs, such as rent, insurance, and so on.

Profit margins vary by the strength of competition. The higher the competition, the lower the profit margin and, therefore, the price.[24]

Interest Rates

Although inflation is the most important long-run influence on exchange rates, interest rates are also important. For example, a couple of articles on the foreign-exchange market in the *Wall Street Journal* note the impact of interest rates on exchange rates.

Among European currencies, the Swiss franc was moderately lower against the dollar after the Swiss National Bank's Bruno Gehrig, a member of the central bank's policy-making central directorate, said the central bank is prepared to cut interest rates if conditions warrant. "We will, if extraordinary shocks threaten our stability, react resolutely, and if necessary use even extraordinary measures," he said.

Elsewhere, the Canadian dollar gained ground against the U.S. currency, boosted by interest-rate differentials between the countries that favor Canada. All of the commodity-linked currencies—including the Australian, New Zealand, and Canadian dollars—are seeing [an] upside to rising interest rates, which make those countries more attractive for investment.[25]

To understand this interrelationship between interest rates and exchange rates, we need to understand two key finance theories: the Fisher Effect and the International Fisher Effect. The first theory links inflation and interest rates, and the second links interest rates and exchange rates. The **Fisher Effect** is the theory that the nominal interest rate r in a country (the actual monetary interest rate earned on an investment) is determined by the real interest rate R (the nominal rate less inflation) and the inflation rate i as follows:

$$(1 + r) = (1 + R)(1 + i)$$

According to this theory, if the real interest rate is 5 percent, the U.S. inflation rate is 2.9 percent, and the Japanese inflation rate is 1.5 percent, then the nominal interest rates for the United States and Japan are computed as follows:

$$r_{US} = (1.05)(1.029) - 1 = 0.08045, \text{ or } 8.045 \text{ percent}$$

$$r_J = (1.05)(1.015) - 1 = 0.06575, \text{ or } 6.575 \text{ percent}$$

So the difference between U.S. and Japanese interest rates is a function of the difference between their inflation rates. If their inflation rates were the same (zero differential) but interest rates were 10 percent in the United States and 6.575 percent in Japan, investors would place their money in the United States, where they could get the higher real return.

The bridge from interest rates to exchange rates can be explained by the **International Fisher Effect (IFE)**, the theory that the interest-rate differential is an unbiased predictor of future changes in the spot exchange rate. For example, the IFE predicts that if nominal interest rates in the United States are higher than those in Japan, the dollar's value should fall in

The nominal interest rate is the real interest rate plus inflation. Because the real interest rate should be the same in every country, the country with the higher interest rate should have higher inflation.

The IFE implies that the currency of the country with the lower interest rate will strengthen in the future.

the future by that interest-rate differential, which would be an indication of a weakening, or depreciation, of the dollar. That is because the interest-rate differential is based on differences in inflation rates, as we discussed earlier. The previous discussion on purchasing-power parity also demonstrated that the country with the higher inflation should have the weaker currency. Thus, the country with the higher interest rate (and the higher inflation) should have the weaker currency.

Of course, these issues cover the long run, but anything can happen in the short run. During periods of general price stability, a country (such as Germany) that raises its interest rates is likely to attract capital and see its currency rise in value due to the increased demand. However, if the reason for the increase in interest rates is because inflation is higher than that of its major trading partners and if the country's central bank is trying to reduce inflation, the currency will eventually weaken, until inflation cools down. Although the interest-rate differential is the critical factor for a few of the most widely traded currencies, the expectation of the future spot rate also is very important. Normally, a trader will automatically estimate the future spot rate using the interest-rate differential and then adjust it for other market conditions.

Other Factors in Exchange-Rate Determination

Various other factors can cause exchange-rate changes. One factor not to be dismissed lightly is confidence. In times of turmoil, people prefer to hold currencies considered safe. For example, during the Kosovo crisis, money flowed into the United States because of concern over the safety of Western Europe if a true crisis were to occur in Yugoslavia and involve the Russians.

In addition to basic economic forces and confidence, exchange rates may be influenced by such technical factors as the release of national economic statistics, seasonal demands for a currency, and a slight strengthening of a currency following a prolonged weakness, or vice versa. In the run-up to Brazil's presidential election of 2002, the real (Brazil's currency) hit all-time lows because of high poll ratings for a left-wing candidate whom investors feared would not be able to control the country's finances.[26] In the summer of 2002, the dollar lost value because of the aftershocks caused by the terrorist attacks of September 11, continued announcements of U.S. corporate scandals, and a swelling budget deficit.

FORECASTING EXCHANGE-RATE MOVEMENTS

The preceding section looked at the effect of the law of supply and demand on exchange rates, showed how governments intervene to manage exchange-rate movements, and explained how inflation and interest rates can be important determinants of exchange rates. This section identifies factors that managers can monitor to get an idea of what will happen to exchange rates.

Because various factors influence exchange-rate movements, managers must be able to analyze those factors to formulate a general idea of the timing, magnitude, and direction of an exchange-rate movement. However, prediction is not a precise science, and many things can cause the best of predictions to differ significantly from reality.

Fundamental and Technical Forecasting

Managers can forecast exchange rates by using either of two approaches: *fundamental forecasting* or *technical forecasting*. Fundamental forecasting uses trends in economic variables to predict future rates. The data can be plugged into an econometric model or evaluated on a more subjective basis. Technical forecasting uses past trends in exchange rates themselves to spot future trends in rates. Technical forecasters, or chartists, assume that if current exchange

Other key factors affecting exchange-rate movements are confidence and technical factors, such as the release of economic statistics.

Managers need to be concerned with the timing, magnitude, and direction of an exchange-rate movement.

Fundamental forecasting uses trends in economic variables to predict future exchange rates. Technical forecasting uses past trends in exchange-rate movements to spot future trends.

rates reflect all facts in the market, then under similar circumstances, future rates will follow the same patterns.[27]

However, all forecasting is imprecise. A corporate treasurer who wants to forecast an exchange rate—say, the relationship between the British pound and the U.S. dollar—might use a variety of sources, both internal and external to the company. Many treasurers and bankers use outside forecasters to obtain input for their own forecasts. Forecasters need to provide ranges or point estimates with subjective probabilities based on available data and subjective interpretation. Biases that can skew forecasts include:

Overreaction to unexpected and dramatic news events.

Illusory correlation, that is, the tendency to see correlations or associations in data that are not statistically present but that are expected to occur on the basis of prior beliefs.

Focusing on a particular subset of information at the expense of the overall set of information.

Insufficient adjustment for subjective matters, such as market volatility.

The inability to learn from one's past mistakes, such as poor trading decisions.

Overconfidence in one's ability to forecast currencies accurately[28]

Good treasurers and bankers develop their own forecasts of what will happen to a particular currency and use fundamental or technical forecasts of outside forecasters to corroborate them. Doing this helps them determine whether they are considering important factors and whether they need to revise their forecasts in light of outside analysis. However, it is important to understand that no matter how carefully prepared a forecast is, it is still an educated guess. As *The Economist* put it, "Currency forecasters have had it hard in recent years. Most expected the euro to rise after its launch in 1999, yet it fell. When America went into recession last year (2001), the dollar was tipped to decline; [yet] it rose."[29] Forecasting includes predicting the timing, direction, and magnitude of an exchange-rate change. The timing is often a political decision, and it is not so easy to predict. Although the direction of a change probably can be predicted, the magnitude is difficult to forecast. Toyota Motor Corporation estimated that the yen would rise from a level of 131 yen/dollar in the beginning of 2002. For its 2002 earnings forecast, the company predicted an exchange rate of 125 yen/dollar. This was accurate in terms of the direction but not the magnitude of the strengthening of the yen. The yen rose even farther in 2002—to levels around 116 yen to the dollar. This could translate to a loss of 150 billion yen, or $1.3 billion.[30] As noted in Figure 10.1, the Bank of Japan has been intervening in the market to try to weaken the yen and to provide some respite for companies such as Toyota.

It is hard to predict what will happen to currencies and to use those predictions to forecast profits and establish operating strategies. The problem with predicting the value of a freely floating currency like the yen is that you never know what could happen to its value. You might be tempted to think that a currency linked to the dollar, like the Hong Kong dollar, would be much easier to predict. But since political control of Hong Kong was handed over to China, there have been discussions concerning Hong Kong's adoption of the Chinese renminbi. Even rumors of this change spooked the region's financial markets. Hong Kong officials vow to stick with the 19-year-old currency system, but many economists think it makes more sense for Hong Kong to change to the RMB.[31] Which prediction is correct? How should a company position itself in these two different scenarios?

Factors to Monitor

For freely fluctuating currencies, the law of supply and demand determines market value. However, very few currencies in the world float freely without *any* government intervention. Most are managed to some extent, which implies that governments need to make political decisions about the value of their currencies. Assuming governments use a rational

Key factors to monitor—the institutional setting, fundamental analysis, confidence factors, events, technical analysis.

basis for managing these values (an assumption that may not always be realistic), managers can monitor the same factors the governments follow in order to try to predict values. These factors are

The institutional setting

- Does the currency float, or is it managed—and if so, is it pegged to another currency, to a basket, or to some other standard?
- What are the intervention practices? Are they credible? Sustainable?

Fundamental analysis

- Does the currency appear undervalued or overvalued in terms of PPP, balance of payments, foreign-exchange reserves, or other factors?
- What is the cyclical situation in terms of employment, growth, savings, investment, and inflation?
- What are the prospects for government monetary, fiscal, and debt policy?

Confidence factors

- What are market views and expectations with respect to the political environment, as well as to the credibility of the government and central bank?

Events

- Are there national or international incidents in the news; the possibility of crises or emergencies; governmental or other important meetings coming up (such as that of the G7, for example)?

Technical analysis

- What trends do the charts show? Are there signs of trend reversals?
- At what rates do there appear to be important buy and sell orders? Are they balanced? Is the market overbought? Oversold?
- What are the thinking and expectations of other market players and analysts?[32]

BUSINESS IMPLICATIONS OF EXCHANGE-RATE CHANGES

Why do we need to bother with predicting exchange-rate changes? As illustrated in the Toyota example, our operating strategies as well as translated overseas profits can be dramatically affected by exchange-rate changes. The Daiwa Institute of Research estimates that overall Japanese industry could lose 530 billion yen—or $4.4 billion—in 2002 because of exchange rate losses.[33] We will now look at how exchange-rate changes can affect companies' marketing, production, and financial decisions.

Marketing Decisions

A strengthening of a country's currency value could create problems for exporters.

Marketing managers watch exchange rates because they can affect demand for a company's products at home and abroad. If Sony were selling its new Plasma Wega TV set for 676,500 yen, it would cost $5,500 in the United States when the exchange rate was 123 yen to the dollar. At a forecast rate of 115 yen, the TV would cost $5,883. Suppose the yen rises even more—to 110—thus increasing the price of the TV to $6,150. At this point, would consumers be willing to pay $6,150 for a new TV set, or would they wait for the cost to come down? Should Sony pass on the new price to consumers or sell at the same price and absorb the difference in its profit margin? If the yen continues to strengthen beyond 110 yen, can it survive?

Production Decisions

Exchange-rate changes also can affect production decisions. For example, a manufacturer in a country where wages and operating expenses are high might be tempted to relocate production to a country with a currency that is rapidly losing value. The company's currency would buy lots of the weak currency, making the company's initial investment cheap. Further, goods manufactured in that country would be relatively cheap in world markets. For example, BMW made the decision to invest in production facilities in South Carolina because of the unfavorable exchange rate between the mark and the dollar. However, the company announced plans to use the facilities not only to serve the U.S. market but also to export to Europe and other markets.[34] The devaluation of the Mexican peso came shortly after the introduction of NAFTA. Although companies had already begun to establish operations in Mexico to service North America, the cheaper peso certainly helped their export strategies.

Companies might locate production in a weak currency country because

- Initial investment there is relatively cheap
- Such a country is a good base for inexpensive exportation

Financial Decisions

Finally, exchange rates can affect financial decisions, primarily in the areas of sourcing of financial resources, the remittance of funds across national borders, and the reporting of financial results. In the first area, a company might be tempted to borrow money in places where interest rates are lowest. However, recall that interest-rate differentials often are compensated for in money markets through exchange-rate changes.

Exchange rates can influence the sourcing of financial resources, the cross-border remittance of funds, and the reporting of financial results.

In deciding about cross-border financial flows, a company would want to convert local currency into its own home-country currency when exchange rates are most favorable so that it can maximize its return. However, countries with weak currencies often have currency controls, making it difficult for MNEs to do so.

Finally, exchange-rate changes can influence the reporting of financial results. A simple example illustrates the impact that exchange rates can have on income. If a U.S. company's Mexican subsidiary earns 1 million pesos when the exchange rate is 3.12 pesos per dollar, the dollar equivalent of its income is $320,513. If the peso depreciates to 8 pesos per dollar, the dollar equivalent of that income falls to $125,000. The opposite will occur if the local currency appreciates against that of the company's home country. This is the problem that Toyota faced in the earlier example. The yen equivalent of Toyota's dollar earnings in the United States continues to fall as the dollar falls against the yen.

It is important to learn about exchange rates and the forces that affect their change. Several years ago, a large U.S.-based telephone company was preparing a bid for a major telecommunications project in Turkey. The manager preparing the bid knew nothing about the Turkish lira, and he prepared his bid without consulting with the company's foreign-exchange specialists. He figured out the bid in dollars, then turned to the foreign-exchange table in the *Wall Street Journal* to see what rate he should use to convert the bid into lira. What he didn't realize was that the lira at that time was weakening against the dollar. By the time he received the bid, he had lost all of his profit to the change in the value of the lira against the dollar, and by the time he had finished the project, he had lost a lot of money. If he had talked to someone who knew anything about the lira, he could have forecast the future value and maybe entered into a hedging strategy to protect his receivable in lira. If managers don't understand how currency values are determined, they can make serious, costly mistakes.

Black Market Issues Aren't Black and White

Trading currency on the black market presents an ethical dilemma. If a host-country government has instituted currency controls and foreign management can't get its company's cash out of the country, can it deal in the black market? By using the black market to convert local currency into U.S. dollars, for example, the company would be operating outside of the banking system and would not be able to send cash back to headquarters through normal banking channels. Also, in the local black market, one can obtain more local currency for hard currency but less hard currency for local currency than in the official market. Moreover, the existence of a local black market usually means that it is very difficult, if not impossible, to obtain hard currency there.

It is always tempting to trade hard currency for local currency on the black market. The problem is that countries have varying attitudes—both ethical and legal—toward the black market. For example, all travelers to Mozambique in the late 1980s were warned by the government of Mozambique against dealing in the black market. Because of the civil war in that country and the virtual collapse of the economy following independence, hard currency was in high demand. To discourage black-market activity by foreigners and to defend its economy, the government cracked down on illegal currency trades.

In Zimbabwe during the same period, the government permitted visitors to convert foreign currency to local currency at approved currency-exchange centers; any excess local currency could be converted back to foreign currency when the visitors left the country. However, the government emphatically warned visitors that they must prove that their transactions took place at the approved centers. Clearly, the government was discouraging currency trading on the black market.

In contrast, at that time, Brazilian airport officials would meet visitors at their planes and offer to trade in currency. The Brazilian government basically looked the other way with respect to black-market currency trading. The point is that it is important to be aware of the prevailing official attitude toward black-market dealings in order to avoid serious trouble.

Black-market currency trading provides a test of the legal justification for ethical behavior, first discussed in Chapter 3. If trading on the black market is illegal and if the government's objections are emphatic, as was the case in both Mozambique and Zimbabwe, then companies should avoid dealing in that market since they should assume that the law will be enforced. However, the law might be more unevenly applied in other countries.

In 1999, China was trying to figure out what it needed to do to make its currency convertible on a capital account basis. The government had put controls into place to crack down on the illegal flow of hard currency. The reason for the controls is that during the Asian financial crisis, many individuals and companies were afraid that China would abandon its fixed exchange rate to the dollar and devalue the currency. So they engaged in a variety of fraudulent activities, including operating on the black market, to get money out of the country and into dollar accounts. The solution might be more controls, but in the long run, it will be preferable to allow the currency to float, eliminating the black market.

LOOKING TO THE FUTURE

Changing Times Will Bring Greater Exchange-Rate Flexibility

The international monetary system has undergone considerable change since the early 1970s, when the dollar was devalued the first time. New countries have been born with the breakup of the Soviet empire, and with them have come new currencies. As those countries have gone through transition to a market economy, the currencies have adjusted as well. The countries will continue to change over to a floating rate system as they get their economies under control.

It will be interesting to see what will happen to the currencies of Latin America. Since the collapse of the Argentine peso, economists across all ideologies have stepped up to the plate to predict what will happen with Argentina's exchange-rate regime. Likewise, in Brazil, the fall of the real has caused many to consider whether Brazil's government will need to make some currency changes. It could either dollarize or freely float. It is possible to have something in between, but as the economies of the Americas continue to merge, their currencies will come closer together as well. A decade ago, it was unthinkable that a currency union could develop in North and South America. Nationalism and economic differences might preclude that from happening, but it is not as far-fetched now as it once was. Trading relationships and a strong desire by Latin American governments to get their economies under control tend to lead to dollarization or at least some form of monetary union than ever before.

The euro will continue to succeed as a currency and will eventually take away market share from the dollar as a prime reserve asset. In addition, its influence will spread throughout Europe as non-euro zone countries adopt the euro or at least come into harmony with it. The 10 countries set to join the EU in 2004 and the other 3 countries waiting for acceptance have been pushing the EMU to allow them to switch to the euro. The EU is reluctant to allow this, but preparations are being made within the individual countries for such moves. Increasing trade links throughout Europe will dictate closer alliance with the euro.

For Asia, there is no Asian currency that can compare with the dollar in the Americas and the euro in Europe. The yen is too specific to Japan, and the inability of the Japanese economy to reform and open up will keep the yen from wielding the same kind of influence as the dollar and the euro, even though the yen is one of the most widely traded currencies in the world. In fact, it is far more likely that the dollar will continue to be the benchmark in Asia insofar as Asian economies rely heavily on the U.S. market for a lot of their exports.

The trend will continue to lead to greater flexibility in exchange-rate regimes. Even countries that lock onto the dollar will float against every other currency in the world as the dollar floats. Capital controls will continue to fall, and currencies will move more freely from country to country. As the Chinese government gets more control over its political and economic situation, it will open up its currency even more and make it convertible for capital flows as well as goods flows.

Summary

- The International Monetary Fund (IMF) was organized in 1945 to promote international monetary cooperation, to facilitate the expansion and balanced growth of international trade, to promote exchange-rate stability, to establish a multilateral system of payments, and to make its resources available to its members who are experiencing balance-of-payments difficulties.

- The Special Drawing Right (SDR) is a special asset the IMF created to increase international reserves.

- The exchange-rate arrangements of IMF countries can be either fixed or pegged to another currency under very narrow fluctuations, pegged to something else with a wider band of fluctuation, and floating.

- Many countries that strictly control and regulate the convertibility of their currency have a black market that maintains an exchange rate that is more indicative of supply and demand than is the official rate.

- Central banks are the key institutions in countries that intervene in foreign-exchange markets to influence currency values.

- The Bank for International Settlements (BIS) in Switzerland acts as a central banker's bank. It facilitates communication and transactions among the world's central banks.

- The demand for a country's currency is a function of the demand for its goods and services and the demand for financial assets denominated in its currency.

- A central bank intervenes in money markets by increasing a supply of its country's currency when it wants to push the value of the currency down and by stimulating demand for the currency when it wants the currency's value to rise.

- Some factors that determine exchange rates are purchasing-power parity (relative rates of inflation), differences in real interest rates (nominal interest rates reduced by the amount of inflation), confidence in the government's ability to manage the political and economic environment, and certain technical factors that result from trading.

- Major factors that managers should monitor when trying to predict the timing, magnitude, and direction of an exchange-rate change include the institutional setting (what kind of exchange-rate system does the country use), fundamental analysis (what is going on in terms of the trade balance, foreign-exchange reserves, inflation, etc.), confidence factors (especially political factors), events (like meetings of the G7 group of countries to discuss exchange rates), and technical analysis (trends in exchange-rate values).

- Exchange rates can affect business decisions in three major areas: marketing, production, and finance.

CASE

Pizza Hut and the Brazilian Real[35]

In 1994, Pizza Hut celebrated the opening of its 10,000th restaurant worldwide by featuring the former Brazilian soccer star Pele kicking an autographed soccer ball through a ceremonial ribbon to open a store in São Paulo, Brazil. This event was viewed by people in 12 countries in Europe as well as the United States via an international satellite broadcast. Over the next eight years, however, Pizza Hut came under increasing pressure in Brazil and was trying to decide if it should continue to operate there or pull out and invest in other countries.

Prior to October 7, 1997, Pizza Hut was part of the restaurants division of PepsiCo. However, poor operating performance forced PepsiCo to spin off its restaurant division into a new company, Tricon Global Restaurants, Inc., in 1997. In May 2002, Tricon changed its name to Yum! Brands, Inc. Yum! Brands has six major divisions: Pizza Hut, Taco Bell, KFC, A&W All-American Food Restaurants, Long John Silver's, and Yum! Restaurants International. There are 30,000 Yum! Brand restaurants in more than 100 countries, and they generate $7 billion in annual revenues and $22 billion in systemwide sales, making their total sales and revenues larger than those of McDonald's. Pizza Hut has more than 8,000 units in the United States and 4,200 units in more than 87 other countries. It operates through franchises (51.3 percent of total Pizza Hut sales and revenues), company-owned stores (25.9 percent), joint ventures (16.7 percent), and licenses (6.1 percent). However, Pizza Hut's earnings are flat; in contrast, Taco Bell and KFC are experiencing earnings growth.

What role will Brazil play in the growth of Pizza Hut worldwide? The three largest markets for Pizza Hut internationally are (1) the United Kingdom, (2) Canada, and (3) Australia. However, Pizza Hut's 10-year plan in the mid-1990s would have made Brazil the second or third largest market in the world by 2005. Brazil offers a number of location-specific advantages. First is its massive size. In 2000, Brazil was the ninth largest country in the world in GDP, but it ranked only 57th in per capita income. It was also the seventh largest country in the world in land mass. Brazil is very urbanized, with São Paulo and

Rio de Janeiro two of the largest cities in the world. The population is clustered in the major cities on the coast, so Brazil ranked only 175th in population density, even lower than that of the United States.

From an economic standpoint, Brazil is a land of tremendous opportunity. Historically, Brazil's governments pursued an economic policy based on import substitution and the transition from agriculture to industry. Protective tariffs and import quotas were essential to stimulate domestic industry. State-owned enterprises were established in steel, oil, infrastructure, and other industries, and they received subsidized, long-term credit to expand.

When the military took over in 1964, power was centralized from the states and from congress to the executive branch of government. As the economy began to heat up during the late 1960s and early 1970s, inflation also began to rise, averaging about 20 percent per annum. The government tried traditional means of slowing down inflation, such as raising interest rates, but the large concentration of industrial power resulted in price inflexibility, the indexing of prices above costs, and the passing on of higher interest rates as an additional cost. Due to this protection, foreign trade remained a small percentage of GDP.

The first oil shock in 1973 created problems for Brazil, because in spite of its wealth of natural resources, Brazil relies on imported oil. Economic growth expanded the demand for oil, and the rise in prices worsened Brazil's trade balance. However, import controls gave the government some breathing room. In spite of this, the government was forced to borrow money from abroad, and about 50 percent of the foreign debt was tied to state-owned enterprises. Inflation during the latter part of the 1970s increased to an annual rate of about 40 percent and the private sector began to show signs of significant resentment as a result of the favoritism shown to the state-owned enterprises. The second oil shock in 1979 was accompanied by rising interest rates on foreign debt, and Brazil went into more severe shock. The economy actually fell 2 percent in 1981, and Brazil was hit by recession, devaluation of the currency, rising real interest rates, real wage reductions, and a widening federal deficit.

The elected governments of 1985 and 1990 focused on foreign debt, inflation, and exchange-rate policies. Real per capita incomes actually fell 6 percent over the 1980s, and cumulative inflation during the 1980s reached 39,043,765 percent! Before he resigned from office in a corruption scandal in the early 1990s, President Collor had begun to tackle Brazil's serious economic problems, but he ran out of time. However, Fernando Henrique Cardoso instituted a new economic plan while he was finance minister that slowed down Brazil's inflation and stabilized the exchange rate. Prices that had been rising 30 to 50 percent per month suddenly slowed to single-digit figures, and Cardoso's popularity soared, allowing him to win the election in 1994 with 54 percent of the vote. However, Brazil continues to face serious economic and social problems. The state is still a dominant force in the economy, and privatization has been difficult. The vast gap between the rich and poor has widened in recent years, and there are problems with decent housing, clean water, and good sewage systems. However, trade restrictions have fallen, and Brazil is attracting a lot of foreign investment, both direct and portfolio.

Pizza Hut first entered Brazil in 1988 during a period of high inflation and economic instability through a franchisee who had contacted Pizza Hut. At that time, Pizza Hut did not have a specific strategy for Brazil. In 1989, Pizza Hut opened a mall unit in São Paulo, and in 1991, it set up an office in Brazil dedicated to establishing a plan for Brazil. In addition to Pizza Hut, KFC was also operating in Brazil. However, the two restaurants were operating under different strategies. KFC expanded in Brazil through unit-by-unit franchising, whereas Pizza Hut expanded through corporate franchises. In a unit-by-unit franchise, an individual restaurant is franchised to a particular franchisee. In a corporate franchise, the corporate franchisee is given a whole territory, generally the same as a state boundary (with the exception of São Paulo), and is not allowed to subfranchise (sell a franchise to someone else). The initial idea of using strong corporate franchises made sense to Pizza Hut, because it wanted franchisees with strong financial backing and experience in operating in an inflationary environment. However, the franchisees wielded a great deal of power, thus hampering Pizza Hut's implementation of a Brazilian strategy.

Pizza Hut established targets for all franchisees in terms of how they must grow the business in order to maintain the franchise. Because of its size, São Paulo was divided up into five different franchises. One of Pizza Hut's original franchisees in São Paulo, United Food Companies (UFC), also became a supplier of cheese products to the franchisees, thus allowing UFC to move down the value chain and the other franchisees to get access to cheese. Pizza Hut diversified to other suppliers, and it imported cheese from abroad.

By 1993, UFC had established 35 stores in São Paulo that generated sales-per-store-unit that were between 33 and 50 percent greater than at its U.S. counterparts. However, Brazil was also the only region in the world serviced solely by franchises—Pizza Hut had no equity interest in any of its stores. Management decided that it needed to own some stores in order to develop operating knowledge and expertise that it could share with its franchisees. The franchise value exists when the franchiser can make a valuable contribution to the franchisees, and Pizza Hut felt that it was lacking an important piece of operating knowledge. It was fairly easy to track the revenues and taxes of its franchisees, but it did not have a good understanding of the cost structure of the business. Therefore, Pizza Hut decided to buy UFC's 35 units in December 1993. Management soon found out that the restaurants were not very cost efficient, but it could get away with the restaurants' inefficiencies due to the high prices they were charging.

In the first six months of Pizza Hut's operations, several problems arose. The first was management culture. Store managers had been operating relatively independently, without any outside control, and now they had to adopt Pizza Hut's control process, not an easy thing to do. They rebelled against the outside control and did not appreciate having to manage differently and be held accountable for their actions. Second, the size of the staff at the stores was larger than Pizza Hut management realized. It was easy for the original franchisee to hide costs and employees during the initial negotiations, but Pizza Hut soon found out that the franchisee had hidden costs, and so Pizza Hut could not go back to the original owners and complain.

The third major problem was inflation. Between 1964 and 1993, when Pizza Hut bought its first 35 units, the annual increase in the consumer price index (CPI) in Brazil had been less than 20 percent only twice—in 1972 and 1973. In the 1990s, inflation had been out of control: 2,938 percent increase in 1990; 441 percent in 1991; 1,009 percent in 1992; and 2,148 percent in 1993. In early 1994, the CPI was rising at the rate of 1 percent a day. Then in June 1994, the government instituted the Real Plan, and inflation began to slow down. The new currency, the real, was pegged to the U.S. dollar, meaning that the government established an exchange rate between the real and dollar and would not allow the exchange rate to change as it had in the past. In addition, inflation dropped from an annual rate of 4,060 percent in the third quarter of 1994 to 33.4 percent by September 1995. The slowdown in inflation and implementation of the Real Plan affected business in many different ways. When the new currency came in and inflation slowed down, the stores took a big payroll hit. Although store managers had a fixed salary, they also received a bonus based on sales. Previously, the bonus was delayed 45 days. As a result, the price increases allowed stores to cover the bonuses with cheaper money, and inflated sales were immediately invested so that the store could generate interest income. However, the inflationary benefit disappeared, effectively increasing bonuses by the lost inflation—as much as 45 percent in that period. The same problem hit purchases and mall leases. In the case of purchases, Pizza Hut was used to collecting sales immediately, because the stores operated on a cash-and-carry basis and delayed the payment of supplies, thereby allowing the company to pay for supplies with inflated sales revenues. However, this benefit disappeared once inflation slowed down. Mall leases are based on 6 percent of sales and are typically delayed 30 to 45 days, thus allowing stores to use inflated revenues to pay for the leases. However, the drop in inflation meant that mall lease payments basically went up 30 to 45 percent.

In addition, the slowdown in inflation made consumers more knowledgeable. When inflation was running wild, no one really knew how to compare prices. Prices were changing daily, and salaries were going up as well, so people did not have a good reference point. With the implementation of the Real Plan, however, people—as well as franchises—were able to compare prices and make more informed decisions. At approximately $19 to $20 for a medium pizza, many consumers wondered if Pizza Hut was worth the price, given the alternatives.

Beginning in 1995, Pizza Hut Brazil was faced with the prospect of having to adapt to the new Brazilian operating environment. Because of the stabilization of prices and the exchange rate between the U.S. dollar and the Brazilian real, sales in Pizza Hut's São Paulo units dropped by nearly one-half from December 1994 to December 1995, even though the number of units increased. As people realized that the prices of Pizza Hut pizzas were high, store traffic fell. Although Pizza Hut's target increase in volume annually in Brazil was 19 percent, it was growing only 6 percent.

To stimulate sales, Pizza Hut tried two different strategies. Corporate management told the franchisees to reduce prices by 25 percent to be more price competitive. McDonald's, the leading fast-food chain in Brazil, increased prices by 40 percent in January 1992 to catch up to inflation but later reduced them by 20 percent and advertised the drop as a vote of confidence in Brazil. The campaign was successful and helped McDonald's to grow. Many Pizza Hut units, however, dropped prices in the last week of November and first week of December 1995, and it used the samba (a Brazilian dance of African origin) to announce the decision. However, the campaign failed. The press covered it as a desperation move to keep pace with McDonald's, and many felt that in adopting the samba, Pizza Hut adopted a strategy very inconsistent with the U.S. brand image that it had worked so hard to cultivate. One franchisee in Rio maintained that Pizza Hut would be better off putting more money into marketing than in dropping prices. Using that strategy, he was able to increase his volume, while those that dropped prices found that volume initially went up but then dropped back to the previous level.

In 1997, just as Tricon (Yum! Brands) came into being, the bottom fell out of the Brazilian economy. The Asian financial crisis put serious pressure on the Brazilian real, which had already weathered the Mexican peso crisis in 1994 and 1995. Although the real is considered to be an independently floating currency, it actually uses inflation to target its value. Since the implementation of the Real Plan in June 1994, the real has depreciated against the dollar at a very steady and predictable rate, as can be seen in Figure 10.3. When the Asian financial crisis hit in the fall of 1997, there was serious pressure against the real. Instead of devaluing the currency, the government decided to raise interest rates, making them more than 40 percent. That saved the real, but it threw the Brazilian economy into a recession. As economic activity slowed down, sales at Pizza Hut plummeted. Then by mid-1998, the global economy seemed to be on the verge of recovery, and the Brazilian government was able to lower interest rates and get the economy moving again. However, that development did not last long. In the summer of 1998, the Russian financial crisis, followed by a collapse in global capital markets, knocked the wind out of the sais of the Brazilian recovery. Interest rates went up again, but the real was still in trouble. In January 1999, the real collapsed again. The final straw was the refusal of the governor of the state of Minas Gerais to pay off state debt to the federal government, which led to a loss of confidence in the government's ability to control its debt. The governor of Minas Gerais, Itomar Franco, became the president of Brazil after Collor's impeachment and served during the time when Cardoso established the Real Plan. Cardoso defeated Franco in the election, so the events of January 1999 were political payback.

As noted in Figure 10.3, however, the one-time devaluation of the real did not turn into a full-fledged drop in the currency. The government was able to gain control of the economy quickly, and the steady, predictable trend line of the real started up again. In the fall of 1999, inflation began to pick up in Brazil, but the Brazilian government ruled out an increase in interest rates; instead it stated that it would be willing to intervene in currency markets to support the currency. That made sense until the Argentine crisis in 2001 and the fall in the Brazilian real in the run-up to the presidential elections in Brazil in October 2002.

Compounding the problems of inflation and exchange rate changes is the nature of the pizza business in Brazil. The pizza market is largely made up of small entrepreneurs, although there are some regional chains, such as Companhia de Pizzas in southern Brazil. In higher class pizzarias, pizzas are cooked in wood-burning ovens instead of in the gas-fired ovens that are more typical of the Pizza Hut store. In addition, pizzarias are used to selling *rodizio* pizza, which means that consumers pay one set price for all of the pizza they can eat. Waiters circulate in the restaurant with trays of different kinds of pizzas, and the consumer chooses a slice and keeps eating slices until he or she can't eat any more. Plus, the tastes are different—there are corn pizzas, stroganoff pizzas, 4-cheese pizzas and dessert pizzas, such as chocolate, chocolate/coconut, and banana pizza. Pizza Hut is trying to maintain its American image, but it has had to modify its product to fit the local tastes. It finally offered a chocolate dessert pizza in 2002, and it allows you to order a pizza with three or four different flavors, depending on the size of the pizza. This is Pizza Hut's attempt to counteract the variety in the rodizio pizza system.

QUESTIONS

1. Do you think it makes sense for Pizza Hut to get out of Brazil, or should it try to weather the storm and stay in? Justify your position.
2. Where does the Brazilian real fit in the exchange-rate regimes in Table 10.1? What does that imply in terms of how you would predict future values of the real?
3. Discuss whether or not you think the Brazilian government should dollarize its economy and get rid of the real.
4. What are some of the ways that instability in the real might be affecting Pizza Hut's operations in Brazil?

FIGURE 10.3 The Brazilian Real

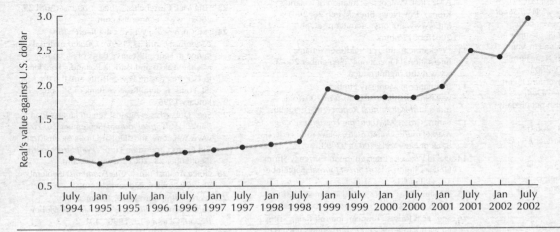

After the Brazilian government implemented the Real Plan in June 1994, the real depreciated steadily against the dollar.

Source: Exchange rates published on http://www.x-rates.com.

CultureQuest™

VIDEO: UNDERSTANDING THE FOREIGN MARKETS: SPOTLIGHT ON ARGENTINA AND ECUADOR

This chapter reviewed the core foreign exchange instruments and how currency markets operate. Based on viewing the accompanying video on Argentina and Ecuador, and materials in this chapter, please answer the following questions:

1. What factors contributed to the Argentine financial crisis?
2. In what ways have Argentina and Ecuador pursued different policies toward their currencies? Which have been more successful? Explain.
3. What are the currency risks for an American company operating in Argentina, and how might they best manage these risks?

Chapter Notes

1   The information in this case is from the following sources: "China's Financial Fix," *The Economist* (July 10, 1993): 69–70; James McGregor, "Reform in China Adds to Currency Woes," *Wall Street Journal* (June 2, 1993): A10; "China Needs Stable Currency Under Exchange Reform," *Agence France Paris* (January 31, 1994); "China Reforms Its Foreign Exchange System," Xinhua Foreign News Service (December 28, 1993); Dusty Clayton, "Confusion in Wake of Move to Make Yuan Convertible," *South China Morning Post* (November 14, 1995): Business Section, 5; Seth Faison, "Fearing Deflation, Chinese Set Limits on New Factories," *New York Times* (August 19, 1999): A1; Dexter Roberts, "Is It Cold Enough for You?" *Business Week* (March 29, 1999): 39; James Kynge, "Call to Widen Renminbi Band," *Financial Times* (November 3, 1999): 7; "China—Time Not Right for Renminbi Conversion," *China Daily* (November 2, 1999): 1; "Wrap: IMF Adjusts Advice to China on Currency Policy," *Wall Street Journal* (September 4, 2002): www.wsj.com; "Money Worries," *The Economist* (September 4, 2002): www.economist.com; "China Fin Min: No Plan to Move to Floating FX in Near Term," *Wall Street Journal* (September 10, 2002): www.wsj.com; "Central Bank Governor Dai on Financial Advances Made," *People's Daily* (September 17, 2002): www.english.peopledaily.com.cn.

2   "The IMF at a Glance" (August 21, 2002): http://www.imf.org/external/np/exr/facts/glance.htm.

3   Ibid.

4   "IMF Quotas, Governors, and Voting Power" (January 9, 2003): www.imf.org/external/np/sec/memdir/members.htm.

5   "The IMF at a Glance," op. cit.

6   See IMF "IMF Receives First Review and Approves New Increase on Uruguay Stand-by," (August 8, 2002): http://www.imf.org/external/np/sec/nb/2002/nb0287.htm; and "IMF Approves US $30.4 Billion Stand-by Credit for Brazil," IMF (September 6, 2002): http://www.imf.org/external/np/sec/pr/2002/pr0240.htm.

7   IMF "Special Drawing Rights: A Factsheet" (August 20, 2002): http://www.imf.org/external/np/exr/facts/sdr.htm.

8   See a current issue of International Financial Statistics for an example of a country that uses the SDR as a basis for the value of its currency.

9   See Guillermo A. Calvo and Carmen M. Reinhart, "Capital Flow Reversals, the Exchange Rate Debate, and Dollarization," *Finance & Development* 36, no. 3 (September 1999): http://www.imf.org/external/pubs/ft/fandd/1999/09/calvo.htm; "No More Peso?" *The Economist* (January 23, 1999): 69; Steve H. Hanke, "How to Make the Dollar Argentina's Currency," *Wall Street Journal* (February 19, 1999): A19; Michael M. Phillips, "U.S. Officials Urge Cautious Approach to Dollarization by Foreign Countries," *Wall Street Journal* (April 23, 1999): A4; and "A Decline Without Parallel," *The Economist* (February 28, 2002): www.economist.com.

10 Craig Torres, "Chile Suspends Trading Band on Its Peso," *Wall Street Journal* (September 7, 1999): A21; "IMF Welcomes Flotation of Iceland's Krona," IMF News Brief (March 28, 2001): http://www.imf.org/external/np/sec/nb/2001/nb0129.htm.

11 "Welcome to the Federal Reserve Bank: International Operations" (September 2002): www.ny.frb.org/introduce.

12 International Monetary Fund, www.imf.org/external/pubs/ft/nr/2001/org/index.htm *IMF Annual Report* (2001): 95–99.

13 Sam Y. Cross, *All About the Foreign Exchange Market in the United States* (New York: Federal Bank of New York, 2002), 92–93.

14 David Wessel, "Intervention in Currency Shrinks Under Clinton," *Wall Street Journal* (September 14, 1995): C1.

15 "Dollar Slides After O'Neill Testimony," BBC News (May 2, 2002): http://news.bbc.co.uk.

16 See "ECB Raises European Interest Rates," BBC News (October 5, 2000): http://news.bbc.co.uk; "Halting the Euro's Fall," *World Economics News* (December 10, 2000): http://www.worldgameofeconomics.com/EuroCurrencyIntervention.htm; and "Fasten Your Seatbelt," *The Economist* (May 24, 2002): www.economist.com

17 See "World Economic Outlook 2002," International Monetary Fund (2002): 23–25; and "Chronology: History of Central Bank Interventions," *Reuters Market News* (July 31, 2002): http://asia.news.yahoo.com/

18 Bank of Russia (2002): http://www.cbr.ru/eng/.

19 "Profile of the BIS: Organisation and Governance" (July 2002): www.bis.org/about/proforgan.htm.

20 "BIS History," Bank for International Settlements (July 2002): www.bis.org/about/history.htm.

21 See "Euro Broadly Lower as Friday's G7 Intervention Failed to Turn Sentiment," AFX (September 25, 2000): http://www.rbc.ru/afxnews/afxnewsdemo/general/20000925121344.shtml; and "Euro/U.S. Dollar Market Commentary," *Investica* (June 10, 2002): http://www.fxstreet.com/nou/content/2536/15-6-2002.asp.

22 "Background Information" and "Press Releases," G-20 Web Site (2002): http://g20.nic.in/indexe.html.

23 "Big Mac Currencies," *The Economist* (April 25, 2002): www.economist.com.

24 "McCurrencies: Where's the Beef?" *The Economist* (April 27, 1996): Quoted material contained in Federal Reserve Bank of St. Louis, Michael Pakko and Patricia Polland, "For Here or to Go? Purchasing Power Parity and the Big Mac (St. Louis: Federal Reserve Bank of St. Louis, January 1996).

25 See "Dollar Eases Against Yen on Japan's Plan for Bank," *Wall Street Journal* (September 26, 2002) www.wsj.com; and "Dollar Drops Against Yen But Gains Ground on Euro," *Wall Street Journal* (September 25, 2002): www.wsj.com.

26 "Race Against Time," *The Economist* (September 26, 2002): www.economist.com.

27 "Forecasting Currencies: Technical or Fundamental?" *Business International Money Report* (October 15, 1990): 401–2.

28 Andrew C. Pollock and Mary E. Wilkie, "Briefing," *Euromoney* (June 1991): 123–24.

29 "Big Mac Currencies," op. cit.

30 Because Toyota has sales in the United States, it risks losses in exchange rate translation when it records U.S. sales on its Japanese financial statements. Toyota estimated earnings for 2002 based on an exchange rate of 125 yen/dollar. If the yen strengthens to 116 against the dollar, Toyota's earnings translations will be much lower than at

the 125 yen/dollar exchange rate. See Akio
Hayashida and Junichi Maruyama, "Recovery
Hopes Hit by Fall in U.S. Dollar," *Daily Yomiuri*
(July 25, 2002): http://www.globalpolicy
.org/socecon/crisis/2002/0725yomiuri.htm.

31 Dominic Lau, "Market Jitters Making HK
Currency Peg Debate Taboo," Reuters News
Service (September 24, 2002):
http://asia.news.yahoo.com/.

32 Cross, op. cit., 114.

33 Hayashida and Maruyama, op. cit.

34 Oscar Suris, "BMW Expects U.S.-Made Cars to
Have 80% Level of North American Content,"
Wall Street Journal (August 5, 1993): A2.

35 The information in this case is from the following
sources: Various annual reports for PepsiCo and
Tricon Global Restaurants Inc.; "Pepsi-Cola Wins
Second Stadium Account," *Nation's Restaurant
News* (August 28, 1995): 46; J. R. Whitaker, "Fast
Food Francises Fight for Brazilian Aficionados,"
Brandweek (June 7, 1993): 20–24; "Pele Kicks
Open 10,000th Pizza Hut Restaurant," *Public
Relations Journal* (May 1995): 16; "Pizza Hut
Cooks in Brazil," *Advertising Age* (June 5,
1995):4; interviews with Pizza Hut employees in
Brazil by Lee Radebaugh: Peter Fritsch, "Brazil
Denies Fresh Speculation on Devaluation," *Wall
Street Journal* (December 2, 1998): A15; Peter
Fritsch, "Brazil's Devaluation Reignites Global

Fears of Spreading Malaise," *Wall Street Journal*
(January 14, 1999): A1; "Real Firms on IMF
Talks," CNNfn, Internet version (February 2,
1999): http://money.cnn.com/ Ian Katz, "Brazil's
Deepening Crisis," *Business Week* Online (March
22, 1999): www.businessweek.com; Ian Katz,
"Pulling Brazil Back from the Brink," *Business
Week* (May 10, 1999): 50; Peter Fritsch, "Brazil Is
Prepared to Support Local Currency," *Wall Street
Journal* (November 22, 1999): A17; Yum! Brand
(Tricon) Web site and *2002 Annual Report;*
United Nations, "Human Development Report
2002" (2002): http://hdr.undp.org/reports/
global/2002/en/default.cfm.

The Dynamics of International Business-Government Relationships

CHAPTER 11

GOVERNMENT ATTITUDES TOWARD FOREIGN DIRECT INVESTMENT

If a little money does not go out, great money will not come in.

—CHINESE PROVERB

OBJECTIVES

■ To examine the conflicting objectives of MNE stakeholders

■ To discuss problems in evaluating the activities of MNEs

■ To evaluate the major economic impacts—specifically, balance of payments and growth—of MNEs on home and host countries

■ To introduce major criticisms about MNEs

■ To provide an overview of the major political controversies surrounding the activities of MNEs

CASE

Foreign Direct Investment in China[1]

From 1949 to 1979, China had a nearly autarkic economy. During these 30 years of communist rule, China prohibited foreign investment and restricted foreign trade. Although its brand of communism stressed isolationism, China's policy also reflected its historical belief that contact with foreigners tended to corrupt its politics and harm its culture. However, fearing that it was falling farther behind other countries economically, China enacted the Law on Joint Ventures using Chinese and Foreign Investment in 1979.

Since then, China has experienced a dramatic rise in FDI. It has become the largest recipient of FDI among all developing countries, and since 1993, it has ranked second to the United States for FDI inflows among all countries. By mid-2002, total FDI in China had exceeded $700 billion and was invested in nearly 400,000 ventures. Japan, Taiwan, and the United States are China's most important sources of FDI. Map 11.1 shows the provinces of China.

While China steadily adopted the principles of free trade, it modified their practical aspects. As a rule, China restricted imports; foreign companies found FDI to be a more realistic way to serve the Chinese market. Moreover, while China let foreign investors propose their preferred mode of entry, it applied stringent criteria through an extensive review process. Specifically, the Chinese Ministry of Foreign Trade and Economic Cooperation (MOFTEC) or provincial-level authorities with jurisdiction over certain types of investments reviewed each foreign investment application to determine whether the investment was in the

MAP 11.1 China and Its Provinces

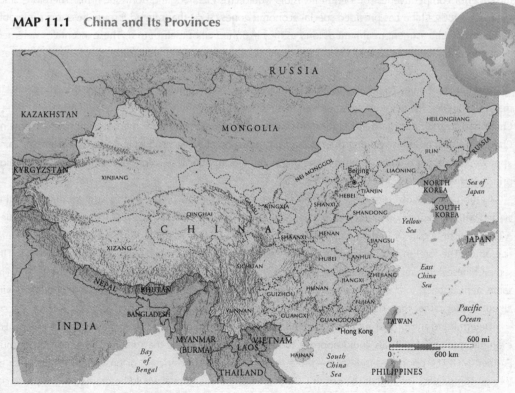

China is the world's third largest country in area and largest in population, which makes it attractive to market-seeking foreign direct investors. Early on, the provinces exercised considerable autonomy in approving FDI applications. Recently, the central government has taken a more active role in managing foreign investment flows.

best interests of China—that is, whether it helped capital formation, promoted exports, created jobs, or transferred technology. Chinese officials negotiated with each potential investor to try to improve its potential contributions. The Chinese rejected many proposals that offered insufficient benefits.

Foreign companies would endure protracted negotiations (often spanning several years) with Chinese companies and provincial authorities before presenting an application to MOFTEC. The growth of FDI in China in the face of the laborious entry process testified to companies' desire to operate in China. MNEs coveted China's market for several reasons, including:

- *Market potential*. China has about 1.3 billion inhabitants. A Monsanto spokesperson summed up this allure by stating, "You just can't look at a market that size and not believe that eventually a lot of goods are going to be sold there. One aspirin tablet a day to each of those guys, and that is a lot of aspirin."
- *Market performance*. China's purchasing power has been increasing because of its strong economic growth. This growth has translated into consumer spending on necessity and luxury products. Economists project that China will soon be the largest economy in the world as measured by purchasing power.
- *Infrastructure*. China is in the process of spending more than $1 trillion dollars on infrastructure projects, including dams, power plants, subway systems, highways, and railroads.
- *Resources*. China has an immense pool of inexpensive and productive labor as well as rich supplies of petroleum and minerals.
- *Strategic positioning*. Many companies see investment in China as a crucial part of a global strategy, particularly given its status as the world's final big growth market. Explained one analyst, "If you want to survive, you have to be global, and China is a part of the global economy."

Over time, the Chinese government has encouraged foreign investment—albeit only in certain sectors of the economy and only subject to evolving constraints. Early on, the Chinese government believed that the superior competitiveness of foreign investors would crush its fledgling domestic firms. Therefore, since the early 1980s, China has provided special economic zones (SEZs) that offered foreign investors preferable tax, tariff, and investment treatment as long as they exported all of their output. These incentives were necessary because the uncertainty of China's political environment made foreign companies wary about investing there.

Foreign companies could also establish joint ventures with Chinese companies to sell to the domestic market. However, the government approved these proposals only if they served a national priority for which China had to seek outside help. Chinese market-serving investments were made to improve an existing Chinese product or industry rather than to launch production of a new product in China. For example, China approved a number of joint ventures in the petroleum industry because it considered future oil sales a high priority for earning foreign exchange.

Getting permission to operate in China required companies to follow a long and winding road that started with an expression of interest and ended with extensive review by MOFTEC or provincial authorities. A foreign firm began by finding a Chinese organization to sponsor its application to establish a representative office. The foreign company might then be assigned a Chinese company with which it negotiated. This same Chinese company could negotiate with more than one foreign company to develop the best offer. The same steps applied to a wholly owned investment; however, the foreign company could deal directly with all authorities rather than have a proposed partner handle the arrangements.

Determining the proper authority depended on the priority of the particular type of investment. For example, provincial officials could approve those business operations that planned to export all output. Further, MOFTEC prioritized industries—those that it encouraged, restricted, or prohibited involvement by foreign companies. The higher the priority, the more likely that approval would be granted at the provincial level. The list of industries was quite detailed and specific. For example, the list applied in 1995 included industries within 18 categories.

Until the mid-1990s, China required most foreign firms to agree to an equity joint venture with a local partner as a precondition of market access. The Chinese government believed that equity joint ventures—versus other types of FDI—transferred capital, technology, and management skills yet did not dilute its own control. Theoretically, a foreign firm could establish a wholly foreign-owned venture in select industries. Such proposals, however, received greater scrutiny from Chinese authorities.

China had steadily increased its dependence on international business. Its trade (imports plus exports) as a percentage of GDP has risen; so too has the number of SEZs. It has gradually permitted wholly foreign-owned ventures; in 1997, such ventures surpassed equity joint ventures for the first time. By 1999, more than half of all foreign investments in China were in the form of wholly foreign-owned ventures. Further, Chinese companies could seek foreign joint venture partners on their own.

China joined the WTO in November 2001. Accession to the WTO required the Chinese government to agree to trade and investment liberalization. China's gradual integration into the WTO will change its economy by opening it to foreign products and firms. China must begin to accept a system of global trading rules—everything from lower tariffs to antidumping regulations to removal of rules restricting distribution and retailing as well as penalties for violating trademarks, patents, and copyrights.

There are benefits and costs to joining the WTO. Regarding the former, some forecast that China could double its exports by 2005, gain an extra percentage point of economic growth for the next decade, and double its FDI stock within the next five years. Regarding drawbacks, WTO membership requires the Chinese government to reform many business institutions and market practices. Some Chinese oppose such changes—for example, five independent bombings hit the operations of Western multinationals that were patronized by affluent Chinese, such as McDonald's, right after China joined the WTO.

Foreign firms welcome the changes required by the WTO. Foreign-invested enterprises make nearly half of all China's exports and three-quarters of its manufactured goods; a boost in exports directly benefits these firms. Operationally, WTO regulations give foreign firms the option to set up wholesale, retail, distribution, and after-sale networks in China. Similarly, foreign firms no longer must comply with local content requirements, deal with the previously high tariffs on imports, or submit investment proposals that involve technology transfers to MOFTEC. Moreover, China has agreed that its many state-owned enterprises may not discriminate against foreigners and that commercial considerations must apply when purchasing goods or services. Because trade and investment among WTO members must abide by a specified set of enforceable rules, the Chinese business environment should become more stable.

It remains to be seen how China interprets and enforces its WTO commitments. China jointed the WTO as a developing country, thereby gaining the right to comply with WTO regulations over several years. For example, Chinese import tariffs on automobiles, which in 2002 were slashed to between 44 and 51 percent (depending on engine size), are set to fall to 25 percent by mid-2006. Moreover, the Chinese government's system of import quotas and licenses for automobiles is not due to be phased out until 2006. Still, MNEs are optimistic about the wisdom of investing in China. Some noted that China's agreement when it joined the WTO reduced its political, legal, and economic risks to MNEs.

WTO membership seemed to be the latest step in China's long march toward an open-market economy. This march began in the spring of 1992, when veteran leader Deng Xiaoping, during his "southern tour," reiterated China's commitment to both an open-door policy and to movement to a market economy. The Fifteenth Communist Party Congress in 1997 marked the start of a new phase of market reform with its promise to transform the country's economic and business structure. In 1998, the Communist Party removed ideological barriers to private ownership by amending the state constitution to acknowledge the private sector. In 2001, President Jiang Zemin called on the Communist Party to allow entrepreneurs and business executives to join it, thereby legitimating the idea of private enterprise. Noted one observer, this proposal "basically turns the Party on its head. It means the Party will once and for all put aside all ideological reservations toward growing a private sector in China." However, party conservatives opposed President Jiang's proposal.

The contest between market economics and ideological legacies in China will play out over many years. During this time, foreign investors will play an increasingly prominent role in a country that historically has been wary of foreigners. Indeed, large segments of Chinese society are less than enchanted by an open market economy, growing exposure to foreign cultures, and increasing interdependence with other countries. This situation creates many challenges for managers. If history is any guide, the Chinese government's outlook on investments by foreign companies will largely influence their success. ◼

INTRODUCTION

For the most part, MNEs operate through FDI. Government policies encourage and restrict these operations. Figure 11.1 shows the major relationships. The principal concern about FDI is that MNEs' global orientation makes them insensitive to national interests and concerns. Although not all MNEs are huge, the sheer size of many of them troubles countries. For example, the sales of Wal-Mart, ExxonMobil, or Mitsubishi exceed the GNP of such countries as Argentina, Indonesia, Poland, and South Africa. Large MNEs have considerable power when negotiating business arrangements with governments; sometimes the outcomes of these contracts have greater consequences than do many treaties among countries. In fact, the executives of MNEs often deal directly with heads of state when negotiating the terms under which their companies may operate. Pressure groups in both home and host countries push their governments to devise policies that restrict or liberalize MNEs' movements. Growth in FDI suggests that these groups will more closely monitor MNEs. This chapter examines government attitudes toward FDI that derive from the major assertions about MNE practices. It also examines the evidence supporting or refuting those assertions.

The sheer size of MNEs is an issue

- Some have sales larger than many countries' GNPs.
- Some MNE executives deal directly with heads of state.

Pressure groups push to restrict MNEs' activities at home and abroad.

Although there is often a love-hate relationship to foreign ownership of domestic enterprises, most countries promote inflows of foreign direct investment. The photo shows Malaysian Prime Minister Mahatir Mohamad (in the right foreground) arriving in Entebbe, Uganda, for a meeting among nine countries to discuss ways to attract foreign investment.

FIGURE 11.1   Home- and Host-Country Influences on Companies' Use of FDI

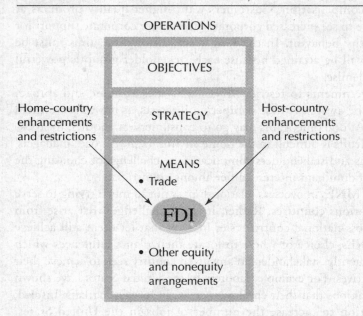

FDI is a major means for companies to conduct their international operations. Stakeholders influence how and whether companies operate through FDI.

EVALUATING THE IMPACT OF FDI

The opening case illustrates the changing attitude of the Chinese government toward FDI—from opposition to suspicion to cooperation. Other countries have similarly replaced obstacles with incentives for FDI.[2] Developing and industrial countries have deregulated their markets, privatized national enterprises, liberalized private ownership, and encouraged regional integration in an effort to create more favorable settings for foreign investments. Total worldwide FDI flows surged in this environment, rising from $202 billion in 1990 to a record $1.3 trillion in 2000.[3]

Others parts of this book specifically discuss how FDI benefits countries. FDI has come to be seen as a major contributor to growth and development, bringing capital, technology, management expertise, jobs, and wealth. However, FDI is not without controversy.[4] Many countries that opened their markets to FDI experienced economic and social disruptions; they also watched investments by MNEs constrain existing or potential domestic companies. MNEs have also run into problems; many made big foreign investments that have performed poorly. As a result, the first years of the twenty-first century saw declining volume of FDI worldwide.[5]

As MNE managers and as national citizens, we need to understand the costs and benefits of FDI. Companies, in the quest to optimize their performance, allocate resources among various countries. However, this allocation is influenced by governments' interpretation of the relative costs and benefits of FDI. As managers, we must be aware of these interpretations and, at times, try to clarify them. As citizens, we need to argue for government policies that will enhance national interests. Both responsibilities require understanding why countries would react to FDI, like China in our opening case, with opposition, suspicion, or cooperation.

The effort to create favorable investment environments has led many countries to replace obstacles to FDI with incentives for FDI.

The growing prevalence of FDI requires a better understanding of the views of home and host countries.

Trade-offs Among Constituencies

To prosper and survive, a company must satisfy different groups, which we call stakeholders. Stakeholders include stockholders, employees, customers, and society. In the short term, the aims of these groups conflict. Stockholders want additional sales and increased

Firms must satisfy
- Stockholders
- Employees
- Customers
- Society at large

productivity, which result in higher profits and higher returns for them. Employees want safer workplaces and higher compensation. Customers want higher quality products at lower prices. Society would like to see increased corporate taxes, more corporate support for social services, and trustworthy behavior. In the long term, all of these aims must be achieved adequately or none will be attained because each stakeholder group is powerful enough to cause a company's demise.

Pressure groups lobby governments to restrict MNEs' activities at home and abroad. Although management must be aware of these competing interests, it has to serve them unevenly at any given period. At one time, gains may go to consumers; at another, to stockholders. Making necessary tradeoffs is difficult in the home environment. Abroad, managers' poorer familiarity with customs and stakeholders complicates the challenge of choosing the best alternative—particularly if dominant interests differ among countries.

The principal difficulty for MNEs in overseas relationships is not so much trying to serve conflicting interests within various countries. Rather, it is the challenges that arise from MNEs' attempts to handle cross-national controversies in ways that let them still achieve global objectives. That is, MNEs' choice of where to locate their plants influences which countries will prosper. Consequently, stakeholders in any given country seek to achieve their own, rather than global, objectives. For example, laborers in the United States have shown little concern for the number of jobs that their employers create in foreign markets. Instead, they have pushed for legislation to increase the number of jobs in the United States. Managers' tasks, then, are complicated because the decisions they make in one country most likely have repercussions in another. The fact that these decisions determine the destination of jobs, profits, taxes, and capital flows attracts the interests of stakeholders and governments.

Management decisions made in one country have repercussions elsewhere.

Trade-offs Among Objectives

An MNE's actions may affect a country's economic, social, and political objectives. However, a positive effect on one objective, such as technology transfer, may accompany a negative effect on another objective, such as unemployment. Therefore, although a country hopes that an MNE can solve a given problem, it has to prepare for the costs created by the benefit. Naturally, governments want benefits with little or no costs; this, though, is seldom possible.[6] Therefore, countries must rank their objectives, somehow resolving the unavoidable tradeoffs among objectives.

The effects of an MNE's activities may be simultaneously positive for one national objective and negative for another.

Similar ideas influence how people see FDI. People sometimes mistakenly assume that if one stakeholder gains from FDI, then another must lose.[7] They might also assume that if there are gains in one country from FDI, then there must be losses in another country. Either may happen, but it is also possible that multiple stakeholders in more than one country will either gain or lose. In theory, no party would participate willingly in an FDI pact with the belief that the investment would harm its priorities. Controversies develop because agreements fail to work as planned, the weight given to the objectives changes, or disputes emerge over the distribution of gains even when these gains have benefited all the parties. The latter problem is at the heart of most controversies over FDI. China, as we saw in the opening case, encouraged foreign investment that transferred technology and management skills to its economy to try to manage this problem.

In an international transaction
- *Both parties may gain*
- *Both parties may lose*
- *One party may gain and the other lose*
- *Even when both parties gain, they may disagree over the distribution of the benefits*

Countries want a greater share of benefits from MNEs' activities.

Cause-Effect Relationships

Just because two factors move in relation to each other does not necessarily mean they are interdependent. Still, opponents of FDI try to link the actions of MNEs to matters like inequitable income distribution, political corruption, environmental debasement, and societal deprivation.[8] On the other hand, proponents link their actions to higher tax revenues, employment, innovation, and exports. These sorts of linkages often arise when governments

It is extremely hard to determine whether MNEs' actions cause societal conditions.

consider either restricting or encouraging FDI. Although the data presented by opponents or proponents of MNEs often are accurate and convincing, there is always the problem of speculating about what would have happened had MNEs gone elsewhere or followed different practices. Technological developments, competitors' actions, and government policies are just three of the variables that distort the analysis of cause and effect.

Individual and Aggregate Effects

One astute observer noted, "Like animals in a zoo, multinationals (and their affiliates) come in various shapes and sizes, perform distinctive functions, behave differently, and make their individual impacts on the environment."[9] Essentially then, it is ill advised to make general statements about the effects of MNEs. Much of the literature on the subject, from the viewpoints of both critics and defenders, takes isolated situations and presents them as exemplars. The anecdotes chosen usually make interesting reading because of their spectacular or extreme nature. Still, it is dangerous for governments to make policies based on exceptions rather than the routine.

Some countries have tried to evaluate MNEs and their activities individually. Although this process might lead to greater fairness and better control, it is time-consuming and costly. Therefore, many countries apply the same policies and control mechanisms to all MNEs. This approach eliminates some of the bureaucracy, but it risks throwing out some "good apples" along with the bad. Further, when examining foreign investments on an individual or an aggregate basis, governments have been far from perfect in predicting future impacts.

Potential Contributions of MNEs

The sheer scale of many MNEs makes them suspect to stakeholders. However, their scale also means they have assets that can contribute to a range of national objectives. MNEs control a large portion of the world's capital, a factor that increases production. They account for most of the world's exports of goods and services, thereby creating access to foreign exchange for a country's purchase of imports. They are the major producers and organizers of technology, which is crucial to improving national competitiveness and solving environmental problems.[10] Figure 11.2 shows the major assets of MNEs that can satisfy stakeholders' objectives. Nevertheless, critics argue that MNEs use their assets inadequately when trying to satisfy these objectives.

ECONOMIC IMPACT OF THE MNE

MNEs may affect countries' balance-of-payments, growth, and employment objectives. Under different conditions, these effects may be positive or negative for the host or home country.

Balance-of-Payments Effects

Countries want capital inflows because such inflows allow them to increase their imports. However, because FDI brings both capital inflows and outflows, countries fear that the net balance-of-payments effect may be negative.

Place in the Economic System   Recall from earlier discussion of the balance-of-payments that if a country runs a trade deficit, it must compensate for that deficit either by reducing its capital reserves or by attracting an influx of capital. The influx of capital may be from unilateral transfers (such as foreign aid), from the receipt of credit, or from the receipt of foreign investment.[11] Put another way, the more capital inflow a country receives, the more it can import and the more it can run a trade deficit. The capacity to run a trade deficit is especially important for

The philosophy, actions, and goals of each MNE are unique.

FIGURE 11.2   Resources and Possible Contributions of MNEs

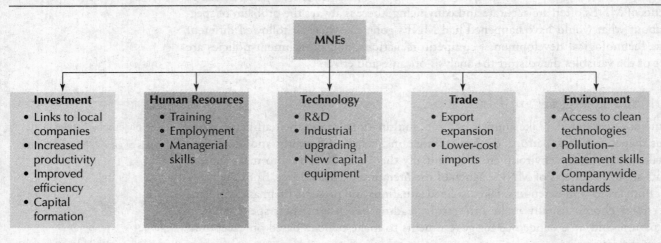

MNEs can contribute directly to investment, human resources, technology, trade, and the environment, thus contributing to host-country objectives.

Source: Adapted from Transnational Corporations and Management Division, *World Investment Report 1992: Transnational Corporations: Engines of Growth. An Executive Summary* (New York: United Nations, 1992), 13. Reprinted by permission.

developing countries because they typically have more goods and services available for their use than they produce themselves. The ability to use these additional resources helps them achieve their growth objectives. FDI has recently become a more crucial factor in the effort to contribute capital to developing countries, particularly in light of the stagnating contributions from foreign aid.[12] For example, China has been a large net receiver of FDI; it has also been running a trade surplus.[13] This capital accumulation has gone toward the buildup of Chinese reserves, which it holds largely in U.S. Treasury bills. These reserves will enable China to finance future trade deficits that will be necessary to fund infrastructure projects.

> One country's surplus is another's country's deficit; however, long- and short-term economic goals differ.

Like China, other countries attempt to regulate trade and investment movements and the capital flows that parallel those movements. They do this through incentives, prohibitions, and other types of government intervention.[14] An important aspect of the balance of payments is that gains are a zero sum game—one country's trade or capital surplus is another country's deficit. If both countries looked only at a fixed period, then one country might justifiably be described as a winner at the expense of the other. In fact, a country may be willing to forgo short-term surpluses in favor of long-term ones, or vice versa. As countries regulate capital flows, they influence companies' decisions on whether to invest in their local markets. These countries also constrain companies' ability to transfer income from FDI to other countries.

> The effect of an individual FDI may be positive or negative.

Effect of Individual FDI   Two extreme hypothetical scenarios of FDI highlight why countries need to evaluate the effect of each investment on their balance of payments. In the first example, a Mexican MNE makes an FDI when purchasing a Haitian-owned company by depositing dollars in a Bermudan bank for the former owners. The MNE makes no changes in management, capitalization, or operations, so profitability remains the same. However, dividends now go to the foreign owners rather than remaining in Haiti, so there is a drain on foreign exchange for Haiti and a corresponding inflow to Mexico. In the second example, a foreign MNE purchases idle resources (land, labor, materials, or equipment) in Haiti and converts them to the production of formerly imported goods. Rising consumer demand leads the MNE to reinvest its profits in Haiti. This import substitution increases Haiti's foreign exchange reserves.

Most investments or nonequity arrangements (such as licensing or management contracts) fall somewhere between these two extreme examples. Consequently, they are hard to evaluate, particularly when policy makers try to apply regulations to aggregate investment movements. Typically, problems arise from the difficulty of accurate measurement.[15] International business scholars continually refine the guidelines that government authorities use to evaluate companies' investments. Home and host governments follow these guidelines to determine whether to place outward and inward controls on FDI. A basic equation for making an analysis is:

$$B = (m - m_1) + (x - x_1) + (c - c_1)$$

where

B = balance-of-payments effect

m = import displacement

m_1 = import stimulus

x = export stimulus

x_1 = export reduction

c = capital inflow for other than import and export payment

c_1 = capital outflow for other than import and export payment

Although the equation is straightforward, determining the value for each variable is difficult. For instance, let's evaluate the effect of a Honda automobile plant in the United States, which would be an FDI by a Japanese MNE. To calculate the **net import change** $(m - m_1)$, we need to know how much the United States would import in the absence of the Honda plant. The amount that Honda makes and sells in the United States is only an indication of what the United States would import, because the selling price and product characteristics of those U.S.-made cars may differ from what otherwise would be imported from Japan. Moreover, some of the sales may have been at the expense of other automobile plants in the United States. By definition, the value of m_1 should include the equipment, components, and materials brought into the United States. For example, Honda buys many parts from suppliers that import them. The value of m_1 also should include estimates of the increase in U.S. imports due to increases in national income caused by the capital inflow from Japan. For instance, assume that U.S. national income rises $50 million because of Honda's investment; the **marginal propensity to import** principle says that the recipients of that income will spend some portion on imports. If this proportion is calculated to be 10 percent, imports should rise by $5 million.

The **net export effect** is the export stimulus minus the export reduction $(x - x_1)$. It is particularly controversial because conclusions vary widely depending on evaluators' assumptions. For the Honda example, we can argue that a U.S. plant merely substitutes for Japanese exports and production. By this assumption, there is no net export effect for the United States. For Japan, there is a negative net export effect because of Honda's export reduction. However, MNEs contend that their moves abroad are (largely) defensive. Under this assumption, Honda captures sales that would otherwise go to other carmakers in the United States. Thus, Honda's export reduction from Japan is only its export replacement (loss) caused by moving a production plant to the United States. It is neither the amount Honda would have lost anyway because of the U.S. government's trade restrictions nor shifts in cost advantages because of a strong yen relative to the dollar. MNEs have argued further that their investments stimulate home-country exports of complementary products that can be sold in host countries through their foreign-owned facilities. Again, we must make assumptions about the amount of these exports that could have materialized had the subsidiaries not been established.

The **net capital flow** $(c - c_1)$ is the easiest figure to calculate because of controls at most central banks. However, the problem with using a given year for evaluation is the time lag between an MNE's outward flow of investment funds and the inward flow of remitted earnings from the investment. What appears at a given time to be a favorable or unfavorable capital flow may prove over a longer period to be the opposite because companies plan eventually to take out more capital than they originally invested abroad. For example, the time it takes Honda to recoup the capital outflow is affected by things such as its need to reinvest funds in the United States, its ability to borrow locally, and its estimation of the future dollar-to-yen exchange rate. Given the number of variables, the capital flows will vary widely among companies and projects. Another complication arises because MNEs may try to manipulate the real returns on their investments by transferring funds in disguised forms, such as through transactions between the parent and a subsidiary at arbitrary rather than market prices.[16]

The equation presented earlier is useful in evaluating the broad balance-of-payments effects of MNEs' investments. Still, stakeholders should use it with caution. As noted earlier, there are measurement problems. In addition, an investment movement might have some indirect effects on a country's balance of payments that are neither readily or reliably quantifiable. For example, an investor might bring new technological or managerial efficiencies that other companies may copy. What these other companies do may affect the economic efficiency of the host country and the export ability of those companies.

Aggregate Assumptions and Responses   Generally, MNEs' investments are initially favorable to the host country and unfavorable to the home country. However, the situation reverses after some time.[17] This occurs because nearly all investors plan eventually to remit to the parent company more than they sent abroad. If the net value of the FDI continues to grow through retained earnings, dividend payments for a given year ultimately may exceed the total capital transfers that comprised the initial investment. The time before reversal can vary substantially, and there is disagreement as to the aggregate time span required.

From the standpoint of home countries, restrictions on capital outflow improve the availability of short-term capital. These restrictions, however, reduce future earnings inflows from foreign investments. In addition, host country restrictions may erode confidence in the economy because companies fear they cannot move their funds where they want them. This fear reduces capital inflows and spurs capital flight. Consequently, capital outflow restrictions are useful only in buying the time needed to institute other means for solving balance-of-payments difficulties.[18]

Governments also have sought to attract inflows of long-term capital as a means to develop production that will displace imports or generate exports. Countries, then, must determine how to benefit from FDI while minimizing the long-term adverse effects on their balance of payments. Many countries have approached this problem by strictly valuing new FDI based on contributions of freely convertible currencies, industrial equipment, and other physical assets—not on contributions of goodwill, technology, patents, trademarks, and other intangible assets. The basis of valuation helps determine the regulations on the maximum repatriation of earnings by the MNE, such as a percentage of the FDI valuation. Normally, the maximum is expressed as a percentage of the investment's value. Negotiating a lower stated value for the FDI lets the host government minimize the eventual repatriation of earnings. Doing so requires that governments strictly inspect the declared value of the equipment brought into their countries, especially when the investor is also the equipment supplier, to prevent inflated valuations. In addition, host governments often require part of the capital contribution to be in the form of loans. Whereas dividends from earnings on equity are capital outflows that can continue indefinitely, interest payments on loans are capital outflows that continue until the loans are repaid.

Growth and Employment Effects

In contrast to balance-of-payments effects, the effects of MNEs on growth and employment are not necessarily a zero-sum game (gains must equal losses) among countries. Classical

---

The balance-of-payments effects of FDI usually are

- Positive for the host country and negative for the home country initially
- Positive for the home country and negative for the host country later

---

Home and host countries make policies to try to improve short- or long-term effects

- Home countries establish outflow restrictions.
- Host countries impose repatriation restrictions, asset-valuation controls, and conversion to debt as opposed to equity.

Growth and employment effects are not a zero-sum game because MNEs may use resources that were unemployed or underemployed.

economists assumed that production factors were at full employment; consequently, a movement of any of these factors abroad would result in an increase in output abroad and a decrease at home. Even if this assumption were realistic, the gains in the host country might be greater or less than the losses in the home country.

The argument that both the home and the host countries may gain from FDI rests on two assumptions: (1) Resources are not necessarily fully employed, and (2) capital and technology cannot be easily transferred from one industry to another. For example, a soft-drink maker may be producing at maximum capacity for its domestic market but is limited in developing export sales due to high transportation costs. Further, the company may not simply move into other product lines or easily use its financial resources to increase domestic productivity. Establishing a foreign production facility, however, positions the company to develop foreign sales without reducing resource employment in its home market. In fact, it may wind up hiring additional domestic managers to oversee the international operations and receive dividends and royalties from the foreign use of its capital, brand, and technology.

Although stakeholders in both home and host countries may gain from FDI, some stakeholders argue that they are economic losers. Let's examine their arguments.

Home-country labor claims that jobs are exported through FDI.

Home-Country Losses   The United States is the home country for the largest amounts of foreign licensing and direct investment. Hence, its policies invite close examination. A leading detractor is organized labor, which argues that foreign production often displaces what would otherwise be jobs in the United States.[19] Figure 11.3 shows a wry view of this criticism. Detractors also cite examples of advanced technology that has been at least partially developed through government contracts and then transferred abroad. In fact, some U.S. MNEs move their newest technologies abroad and, in some cases, manufacture abroad before they do so in the United States. An example is Boeing's transfer of aerospace technology to China to produce aircraft parts. According to critics, if Boeing did not transfer the technology, China would have had to purchase the products in the United States, thereby increasing employment

FIGURE 11.3

"Great. You move to Mexico, and we all end up working at McDonald's."

Home-country stakeholders fear losses from outward flows of FDI.

Source: © The New Yorker Collection 1992 Dana Fradon from Cartoonbank.com. All Rights Reserved. Reprinted by permission.

and output there. These critics further argue that such technology transfer will speed the process of China's gaining control of future global aircraft sales. Alternatively, others counter that had Boeing not found a way to make the sale, then China might have bought aircraft from Airbus Industrie or independently developed the technology itself.[20]

Another question is whether outsourcing production causes wages to decline in the home country. Anecdotal evidence suggests it does. For example, call handlers' salaries are 85 to 90 percent lower in India than in the United Kingdom. Even though the costs of information technology infrastructure are higher in India, total operating costs in India are 35 percent lower than the United Kingdom. Consequently, British unions' attacks on declining wage levels in the U.K.'s 3,500 call centers met the warning that British operators must improve their service quality or else lose their jobs.[21] In contrast, evidence suggests that moving jobs to lower-wage countries increases the overall home-country demand and wages for skilled labor. MNEs can use the cost savings that result from producing abroad to lower prices that, in turn, generate more demand. For example, Nike uses inexpensive overseas labor to make its shoes and this lowers the price of its shoes and increases demand. Nike then needs more higher-skilled and higher-paid managerial personnel in the United States.[22]

Host-Country Gains   Most observers agree that an inflow of investment from MNEs can stimulate local development through the employment of idle resources. Companies will want to move resources, such as capital and technology, abroad when the potential return is high—especially to those markets where they are scarce. Certainly, the mere existence of resources in a country does not guarantee that they will contribute to output. MNEs, however, may enable idle resources to be used. Oil production, for instance, requires not only the presence of underground oil deposits but also the knowledge of how to find them, the capital equipment to extract it, and the facilities to refine it. Simply pumping oil is wasteful without markets and transportation facilities, which an international investor may be able to supply.

FDI by MNEs can initiate the upgrading of resources by educating local personnel to use equipment, technology, and new production methods.[23] Seemingly minor programs, such as promoting on-the-job safety, can reduce lost worker time and machine downtime. This occurred after the U.S. company Renbco acquired Doe Run Peru, a metallurgical complex.[24] The transfer of innovative work methods increases productivity, thereby freeing time for other activities. Further, additional competition may push existing companies to improve their efficiency. This happened with European retailers after Wal-Mart entered the European market and with Japanese retailers after Tower Records and Gap entered the Japanese market.[25]

Host-Country Losses   Critics argue that MNEs make investments that domestic companies otherwise would have made, thereby displacing potential local entrepreneurs. Similarly, foreign investors may bid up prices by competing with local companies for labor and other resources—such as when local companies in northern Indiana in the United States complained about Toyota's hiring its best workers by paying them higher wages (of course, the workers did not object).[26] Such critics argue, for example, that MNEs can raise lower-cost funds in different countries because they have operations in those countries and are known in those financial markets. Local companies, especially those operating only domestically in a developing country, do not have these options. Thus, MNEs can tap cheaper capital and reduce their capital cost relative to that of local companies. The MNEs can then pay more to attract the best personnel or use more promotions to lure customers from competitors and still earn profits. Evidence for these arguments is inconclusive. MNEs frequently pay higher salaries and spend more on promotion than local companies do. It is uncertain, however, whether these differences result from external advantages or represent the added costs of attracting workers and customers upon entering new markets. Higher compensation and promotion expenses may offset any external cost advantages obtained from access to cheaper

---

Host countries may gain through

- More optimal use of production factors
- The use of unemployed resources
- The upgrading of resource quality

Host countries may lose if investments by MNEs

- Replace local companies
- Take the best resources
- Destroy local entrepreneurship
- Decrease local R&D undertakings

foreign capital. Additionally, in many instances, the local competition can also raise funds in other countries.

Critics contend that FDI destroys local entrepreneurship, an outcome that affects national development. Because the reasonable expectation of success is necessary to inspire entrepreneurship, the collapse of small cottage industries in the face of MNEs' consolidation efforts may make the local population feel incapable of competing. A good deal of evidence questions this contention.[27] The presence of MNEs may increase the number of local companies in host-country markets because the MNEs serve as role models that local talent can then emulate. Moreover, an MNE buys many services, goods, and supplies locally that may stimulate local entrepreneurship. For example, automobile producers typically add less than half the value of an automobile at the factory, buying the remaining parts, subassemblies, and modules from suppliers, some of whom are local companies. In China, positive spillovers from FDI have contributed to Chinese companies' acquisition of financial resources, which has helped them become viable suppliers.[28] Finally, some maintain that true entrepreneurs will see large MNEs not as obstacles but as challenges.

There is evidence that local R&D can enhance a country's competitive capability.[29] However, a country needs a strong technological base if its R&D will create the foundation for product leadership. Therefore, governments seek technology from MNEs to establish their bases and then seek local R&D to build on those bases. At this point, some evidence suggests that dependence on FDI constrains host countries from developing workable R&D.[30] For example, Japan, Korea, Taiwan, and China have been much more restrictive on FDI inflows than have Malaysia, Singapore, and Thailand. The former countries spend much more on R&D as a percentage of gross domestic product than do the latter ones. China's original preference for FDI in the form of joint ventures with Chinese companies, for instance, reflected its desire to use foreign technology to develop local R&D capabilities. MNEs entered joint ventures with Chinese companies that had a base of product experience that positioned them to absorb the incoming technology. Ultimately, China reasoned that its home companies would build on the technology they absorbed through independent and indigenous R&D. This approach, though, is risky; a country that limits foreign ownership may discourage other companies from transferring their technologies.[31]

Another argument is that investors learn better ways of doing things abroad. By observing foreign competitive conditions, they may gain access to new technology that they can transfer to their home countries. Such early access, however, may prevent the original developers from fully exploiting their technologies. It may also prevent the originating country from fully capturing the economic benefits of the innovations developed by its residents. For example, foreign investment, especially from Japan, has grown rapidly in high-tech industries in California's Silicon Valley. This FDI may allow non-U.S. companies to develop competitive capacities in their home countries that are based on U.S. scientific and technical investments.[32] However, Japanese companies in Silicon Valley also spend heavily on R&D, and their results spillover to nearby U.S. companies.[33]

Critics assert that MNEs' use of local funds, by borrowing either locally or by receiving investment incentives, reduces the funds that are available to local companies.[34] This question then arises: Does this development necessarily mean that local companies lack access to funding sources? The answer is unclear.[35] For MNEs to have a material effect on capital availability in a country requires that the amount of funds diverted to those investors be larger than is typically the case. Further, few MNEs acquire all resources locally; capital transfers that are used to start up and then fund ongoing operations usually benefit the host economy. Still, some countries try to manage this risk, restricting local borrowing by MNEs and providing incentives for them to locate in depressed areas that have idle resources.

Many countries are alarmed when a foreign company buys a local firm. Debate persists over the employment effects of foreign acquisitions because of assumptions about what would have happened had the acquisition not taken place, particularly when the local company that is not doing well is then downsized. It is difficult to determine that there was more or less employment because of the acquisition. No matter what the circumstances are, it is ultimately speculation about what might have happened had the foreign acquisition not taken place.[36]

General Conclusions   Not all MNE activities will have the same effect on growth in the home or the host country. Complicating any analysis is the difficulty of identifying and reliably measuring the effects of MNEs' activities. The following observations help identify those situations in which foreign investment is likely to make a positive contribution to a host country:

1. *Developing countries and developed countries.* Developing countries are less likely than developed countries to have domestic firms capable of making investments like those made by foreign investors from developed countries. Therefore, foreign investment in developing countries is less likely to substitute for domestic investment; it tends to yield more growth than if it were located in developed countries.

2. *Degree of product sophistication.* When the foreign investor seeks to make highly differentiated products or to introduce new process technologies, local companies are less likely to undertake similar production on their own. The differentiation may derive from product style, quality, brand name, and technology.

3. *Access to resources.* A foreign investor with access to resources that local companies cannot easily acquire is more likely to generate local growth than merely substitute for what local companies would otherwise do. Some of these resources are capital and access to foreign markets.

4. *Degree of development of the country.* Foreign investors are more likely to transfer management processes and production technologies to the more economically advanced of the developing countries because such investors are better prepared to absorb these ideas.

POLITICAL AND LEGAL IMPACT OF THE MNE

The market power of many MNEs prompts concerns that they will undermine the sovereignty of host nations. The foremost concern is that an MNE will be a foreign-policy instrument of its home-country government.[37] Most MNEs have the majority of their sales and assets in their home countries and few foreigners on their executive boards.[38] Because the home countries of most MNEs are industrial countries, it is understandable that this concern is taken most seriously in developing countries. By no means, though, is it restricted to them.

Critics of MNEs raise two other concerns about sovereignty. One is that the MNE may become independent of both the home and the host countries, making it difficult for either country to regulate its actions. The second issue is that the MNE might become so dependent on its foreign operations that a host country can use it as a foreign-policy instrument against the company's home country or another country.

Extraterritoriality

Recall that extraterritoriality is when governments apply their laws to the foreign operations of their domestic companies. Generally, though, host countries abhor any weakening of their sovereignty over local business practices. MNEs fear that home-country and host-country laws will conflict, because settlement inevitably must be between governments, with companies caught in the middle. Laws need not be in complete conflict to trigger charges of

FDI is more likely to generate growth

- When the market is prepared to support business growth
- When the product or process is highly differentiated
- When the foreign investors have access to scarce resources
- In the more advanced developing countries

Countries are concerned that MNEs are

- Foreign-policy instruments of their home-country government
- Independent of any government
- Agents of their host-country government

Extraterritoriality occurs when governments apply their laws to their domestic companies' foreign operations.

extraterritoriality. Home-country laws that require companies to remit earnings or pay taxes at home on foreign earnings certainly have affected companies' foreign expansion and host governments' control over such expansion. Although extraterritoriality may result from legal differences between any two countries—and often does—the United States has been criticized the most for attempting to control what U.S. companies do abroad. Thus, we will primarily discuss the role of U.S. companies here.

Trade Restrictions   The primary focus of criticism has been the U.S. government's attempt to apply its Trading with the Enemy Act to the foreign subsidiaries of U.S. companies to prevent them from selling to unfriendly countries. At times, presidential orders have prevented foreign subsidiaries of U.S. companies from making sales to countries like Cuba, Libya, Nicaragua, South Africa, and Vietnam. These situations grow more complicated when the presidential orders violate the laws of some of the countries in which the subsidiaries were operating, such as France and Canada. Governments in these countries, in direct rejection of U.S. extraterritorially, required that the local subsidiary complete the sale. The Cuban embargo has been a thorny issue between Canada and the United States. Throughout most of the 1980s, the United States permitted foreign subsidiaries of U.S. companies to sell to Cuba. The Cuban Democracy Act of 1992, however, required that they stop doing so. This law led to discussions in Canada on whether Canada should impose trade or investment restrictions on the United States. Problems continued with the Helms-Burton Act's restrictions on individuals and business firms that maintain business relations with Cuba. This law has led to strong disapproval from other countries as a wrongful act of extraterritoriality.[39]

Antitrust Laws   A second focus of criticism has been the U.S. government's antitrust policies. The United States has acted against domestic firms' foreign investments whenever it has had concerns about those companies' participation in cartels that set prices or production quotas, about the granting of exclusive distributorships abroad, and about the formation of joint R&D or manufacturing operations in foreign countries. At various times, the U.S. government has:

> Governments are especially inclined to apply antitrust policies when concerned about possible harm to consumers.

- Delayed U.S. companies from acquiring facilities in foreign countries—for example, Gillette's purchase of Braun in Germany was held up because Braun made electric shavers and the acquisition would reduce the number of competitors in the shaving market.

- Prevented U.S. companies from acquiring facilities in the United States that were owned by a company they were taking over abroad—for example, Gillette's purchase of a division of Sweden's Stora Kopparbergs Bergslags could not include that division's subsidiary, U.S. Wilkinson Sword, because it would increase Gillette's share of the razor blade market.

- Stalled the alliance of American Airlines with British Airways because of the failure of the U.K. governments to agree to liberalize the aviation market between the two countries with an "open skies" deal that would allow more U.S. carriers to fly into Heathrow Airport, the popular gateway to London.

- Ordered U.S. companies to sell their interests in foreign operations—for example, Alcoa had to divest Alcan so that Alcan could compete against Alcoa.

- Restricted the entry of goods produced by foreign consortiums in which U.S. companies participated—for example, Swiss watches and parts.

- Pressured foreign companies to allow U.S. firms to make foreign sales using technology acquired from them—for example, the British company Pilkington licensed float-glass technology (used to make slate glass) to U.S. companies with the stipulation that they could sell the output only in the United States, but then it permitted U.S. companies to use the technology abroad after the U.S. Department of Justice brought suit against its U.S. subsidiary.[40]

In most cases, the actions these companies were restrained from taking were legal in the countries in which they would have occurred.

A recurring problem for U.S. companies has been the ambiguity of the U.S. Justice Department's antitrust policy regarding their relationships with other companies abroad. This ambiguity has been mitigated by the publication of foreign merger guidelines, including scenarios illustrating the application of antitrust enforcement principles. The United States also has several treaties with other countries that call for mutual consultation on restrictive business practices.[41]

Key Sector Control

Political concerns include fear of
• Influence over or disruption of local politics
• Foreign control of sensitive sectors of the local economy

Closely related to the extraterritoriality issue is the fear that if foreign-owned companies dominate key industries, then decisions made outside of the country may have adverse economic or political effects in the host country. This issue raises two questions: Are the important decisions actually made outside the host countries? If so, are these decisions different from those that would be made by local companies?

MNEs' home-country headquarters often decide on what, where, and how their foreign subsidiaries will produce and sell. These decisions might cause different rates of expansion in different countries and possible plant closings, leading to subsequent employment disruption in some of them. Further, by withholding resources or tolerating strikes, MNEs may affect other local industries adversely.

Some observers argue that governments generally have more control over those companies headquartered in their countries than over foreign companies' subsidiaries. Even MNEs with substantial operations abroad normally have primary loyalty to their home countries. This loyalty arises because most MNEs have a majority of their assets, sales, employees, managers, and stockholders in their home countries. They depend on their home countries for most of their R&D and other innovations that enable them to compete globally. In addition, the home-country government has access to their global financial records and can tax them on their global earnings, which host-country governments cannot do. Further, MNEs can ask their home-country government for help to resolve conflicts of interest but cannot expect a foreign government to intercede on their behalf with the home-country government.[42] Given these factors, companies tend to favor their home country's objectives over those of a host country during conflicts.

What if an MNE served as an instrument of foreign policy for its home-country government? What if it were powerful enough to disrupt or influence politics in a foreign country? These are crucial concerns for host countries. The former concern is a legacy of colonial periods, when such companies as Levant and the British East India Company often behaved as a political arm of their home-country government. The concern has resurfaced in the case of Japanese investment in the United States. Critics point out that the Japanese government and Japanese companies lobby strongly in an effort to affect U.S. government policy (e.g., to prevent new import restrictions on Japanese goods). Finally, a country that depends on foreign investment may be pressured to take actions that are unpopular locally.

Aside from establishing policies that restrict the entry of foreign investment, countries have selectively prevented foreign domination of key industries. This policy can affect a large segment of the economy or population by virtue of the scale or influence of the key industry. Different countries view key industries in different ways. For example, NAFTA specifies that foreign investors from its member countries generally be treated no less favorably than are domestic investors. However, because of different conceptions of what is "key," foreign ownership has been limited by Canada in cultural industries, by the United States in the airline and communications industries, and by Mexico in the energy and rail industries. In other cases, governments have required MNEs to manage local subsidiaries with local personnel to ensure that the companies can survive, if necessary, without foreign involvement. In the

United States, the President can halt any foreign investment that endangers national security. Although national security is not defined in the enabling legislation, enforcement has been extended to include economic security. In a few cases, governments have supported the development of local companies to fight foreign domination. These include consortia of computer manufacturers (such as ICL in the United Kingdom; as well as Siemens, CII, and Philips in Germany and the Netherlands) and consortia of aircraft producers (such as Messerschmitt-Boelkow-Blohm in Germany and Construcciones Aeronauticas in Spain).

Should host countries be concerned that foreign government-owned enterprises make direct investments within their borders? Although any MNE may in time of conflict favor home-country interests, the government-owned enterprise may be much more prone to do so.[43] Government officials in the home country may be able to quickly influence this type of company. Thomson Electronics, for example, a French state-owned MNE, announced it would shut down its U.S. assembly operation and shift its production to lower-cost Mexico. This tactic was impractical in France because of the French government's commitment to protect local jobs.

MNE Independence

Our discussion so far has centered on the concern that home-country governments unduly influence MNEs. However, observers worry that MNEs can play one country against another and thereby evade regulation by all countries. For instance, if MNEs dislike the wage rates, union laws, or pollution and safety codes in one country, they can move elsewhere or at least threaten to do so. In addition, they can develop ownership structures to minimize their payment of taxes anywhere.

This ability to play one country against another, especially if the countries are members of a regional trade association, is more likely when an MNE is negotiating initial permission to operate in a country. For example, Thailand and the Philippines, both members of ASEAN, vied with investment incentives to attract a GM car plant, whose output would be sold throughout the region.[44] Similarly, foreign companies often play one state against another when entering the United States—as seen by local officials' zeal to lure foreign car companies like Honda, BMW, or Hyundai to their state.[45] However, the fact that companies, once they are up and running, are generally reluctant to abandon fixed assets in one country to move abroad indicates that MNEs eventually face limits in getting countries to compete for them. Further, if sufficiently offended, the country from which a company departs can restrict importation of the goods that are now produced elsewhere.

Host-Country Captives

Critics allege that MNEs may become so dependent on foreign operations that they try to influence their home-country government to adopt policies favorable to the foreign countries even when those policies may not be in the best interests of the home country. Such assertions are difficult to test because there is always disagreement on what policies are in a country's best interests. However, there are many examples of lobbying efforts by MNEs seeking the adoption of policies that are more amenable to the foreign countries where they are doing business. For instance, many MNEs have lobbied against possible U.S. trade sanctions against China because they fear Chinese retaliation.[46]

Bribery

Since congressional investigations of U.S. MNEs in the 1970s, anecdotal information indicates that questionable payments to government officials by MNEs have been prevalent in both industrial and developing countries. Recent data give a sense of the proportions. The

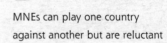

MNEs can play one country against another but are reluctant to abandon fixed resources.

Payments to government officials have been widespread and have been intended to

- Secure business from competitors
- Facilitate services
- Ensure the safety of employees and facilities

ETHICAL DILEMMA

Are Some Bribes Justifiable?

Companies have been criticized for bribing foreign officials. However, others object to the efforts to stop the bribes, such as through the FCPA or the OECD Bribery Convention. One complaint is that businesses cannot make payments but governments can. For example, the U.S. government frequently grants foreign aid as an implicit bribe, with the understanding that the host country will grant political concessions in return. Further, governments use high-level official visits and aggressive lobbying for their home-based companies to help them win foreign business. For example, the U.S. government has sometimes paid foreign government officials to get them to visit the United States when an American company is bidding on a contract. Similarly, it has given scholarships to family members of officials who can provide business to U.S. companies.[47] A second criticism is that some bribes are allowed, but others, like facilitation payments to expedite routine procedures, are not. Further, some argue that judging the morality of bribery should be weighed against interfering with a custom, such as bribery, that may be legally and culturally acceptable in some countries. Unilever, for example, explains that is does not condone facilitation payments and tries to avoid them, but it concedes that it makes such payments when they are based on local custom.[48]

Some defend bribes on the grounds that unethical "means" are justified to arrive at a desirable "end." For example, IBM and other U.S. companies claimed that the FCPA cost them a contract for air traffic control systems in Mexico. They argued that their inability to make payments to Mexican authorities led Mexico to install inferior technology.[49] It is debatable whether such an end would justify a bribe. Further, most MNE executives believe that bribes to government officials in developing countries are required to win contracts because most of their government officials are poorly paid and are immune from prosecution when accepting bribes.[50]

Given the fact that it is illegal for U.S. companies to pay government officials abroad to get business, U.S. companies have devised legal means to try to influence those officials. Many companies—for example, Hewlett-Packard in China—pay journalists to attend their news conferences, presumably so they will write favorably about the companies. So many companies finance foreign officials' visits to their plants in the United States, which include stops at popular tourist attractions, that a spokesperson for the industry-funded U.S.-China Business Council noted, "You'd think Disney World was a training site."[51]

Finally, there are strong pressures at work that push foreign companies to refrain from making payments to political parties in host countries. Still, some companies argue that avoiding local politics would be socially irresponsible. For example, British MNEs contributed millions of dollars in political donations to Democratic and Republican candidates in the 1996 and 2000 U.S. presidential elections. Although these payments are legal, since they came through the United States subsidiaries of the British MNEs, they have led to allegations of foreign influence. In response, Glaxo Wellcome, a British investor in the United States and one of the leading political contributors, explained that it had 9,000 U.S. employees, paid U.S. taxes, and had a substantial effect on the U.S. economy. It made donations to ensure that policies would be in the best interest of its U.S. operations and employees.[52]

United States reported that between 1994 and 2001, it learned of instances in which foreign firms from over 50 countries offered bribes to buyers in over 100 countries, and these cases involved over 400 competitions for contracts valued at $200 billion.[53] Figure 11.4 reports the propensity of companies from various countries to offer or pay bribes.

Bribery influences the performance of countries and companies. Higher levels of corruption are strongly associated with lower growth and lower levels of per capita income.[54] Also, corruption may erode the legitimacy of a government. Bribery scandals have led to the replacement of chiefs of state in Honduras, Italy, and Japan. Officials have been jailed in a number of countries, including Pakistan, Iran, and Venezuela, for accepting bribes. Executives in several companies have resigned, been fined, or gone to jail. Similarly, bribery inflates the costs of an MNE's operations and the prices of its products.

A common motive for bribery is to secure government contracts that otherwise might not be forthcoming or to obtain them at the expense of competitors. Another motive for bribery is to facilitate government services that companies are legally entitled to receive but that officials otherwise might delay, such as product registrations, construction permits, and import clearances. Other reported payments have been made to reduce tax liabilities, to keep a competitor from operating in a specific country (by General Tire in Morocco), and to gain government approval for price increases (by a group of rubber companies in Mexico). Some companies have made payments because of extortion. For example, Boise Cascade, IBM, and Gillette made payments to protect the safety of their employees.

Most reported payments have been in cash, but in some cases, they have included products made by the company, such as ITT's gift of a color TV set to a Belgian official. Some payments have been made directly to government officials by the companies; most, however, have been made via intermediaries and by diverse methods. For example, the relative of a person having influence over a purchasing decision sometimes has been put on the payroll as a consultant. In other cases, the person having influence has been paid as an intermediary at a fee exceeding normal commissions. Another common practice has been to overcharge a government agency and rebate the overcharge to an individual, usually in a foreign country.

In 1977, the United States passed the Foreign Corrupt Practices Act (FCPA), which outlaws the payment of bribes by U.S. firms to foreign officials, political parties, party officials, and candidates. In 1998, the overseas coverage of the FCPA was extended to include bribery by foreign firms operating in U.S. territory. The FCPA applies to companies registered in the

The U.S. legislation on bribery is controversial because

- Some payments to expedite compliance with law are legal, but others are not
- Extraterritoriality issues emerge
- Business may be lost

FIGURE 11.4   Likelihood of Paying Bribes Abroad by Nationality of Companies

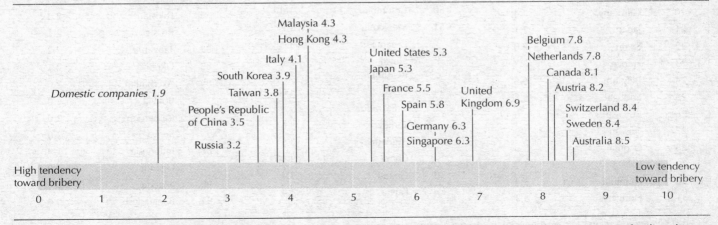

Transparency International asked 835 business experts in 15 countries the following: "In the business sectors with which you are most familiar, please indicate how likely companies from the following countries are to pay or offer bribes to win or retain business in this country?" The scale runs from 1 to 10, with higher scores indicating a lower propensity to pay or offer bribes.

Source: Transparency International (November 6, 2002): http://www.transparency.org.

United States and to any foreign companies that are quoted on any stock exchange in the United States.

An apparent inconsistency of the FCPA is that payments to officials to expedite their compliance with the law are legal (officially called facilitation payments but sometimes referred to as speed money or grease money), but payments to other officials who are not directly responsible for carrying out the law are not. Specifically, a 1988 amendment to the FCPA excluded facilitation payments from its definition of bribery. Facilitation payments take many forms. For example, payment to a customs official to clear legitimate merchandise is legal, whereas a payment to

● TABLE 11.1

INTERNATIONAL CORRUPTION: A SURVEY OF BUSINESS PERCEPTIONS

RANK	COUNTRY	2001 CORRUPTION PERCEPTIONS INDEX SCORE	RANK	COUNTRY	2001 CORRUPTION PERCEPTIONS INDEX SCORE	RANK	COUNTRY	2001 CORRUPTION PERCEPTIONS INDEX SCORE
1	Finland	9.9		Trinidad & Tobago	5.3	61	Malawi	3.2
2	Denmark	9.5					Thailand	3.2
3	New Zealand	9.4		Tunisia	5.3	63	Dominican Rep.	3.1
4	Iceland	9.2	34	Slovenia	5.2		Moldova	3.1
	Singapore	9.2	35	Uruguay	5.1	65	Guatemala	2.9
6	Sweden	9.0	36	Malaysia	5.0		Philippines	2.9
7	Canada	8.9	37	Jordan	4.9		Senegal	2.9
8	Netherlands	8.8	38	Lithuania	4.8		Zimbabwe	2.9
9	Luxembourg	8.7		South Africa	4.8	69	Romania	2.8
10	Norway	8.6	40	Costa Rica	4.5		Venezuela	2.8
11	Australia	8.5		Mauritius	4.5	71	Honduras	2.7
12	Switzerland	8.4	42	Greece	4.2		India	2.7
13	United Kingdom	8.3		South Korea	4.2		Kazakhstan	2.7
14	Hong Kong	7.9	44	Peru	4.1		Uzbekistan	2.7
15	Austria	7.8		Poland	4.1	75	Vietnam	2.6
16	Israel	7.6	46	Brazil	4.0		Zambia	2.6
	United States	7.6	47	Bulgaria	3.9	77	Ivory Coast	2.4
18	Chile	7.5		Croatia	3.9		Nicaragua	2.4
	Ireland	7.5		Czech Republic	3.9	79	Ecuador	2.3
20	Germany	7.4	50	Colombia	3.8		Pakistan	2.3
21	Japan	7.1	51	Mexico	3.7		Russia	2.3
22	Spain	7.0		Panama	3.7	82	Tanzania	2.2
23	France	6.7		Slovak Republic	3.7	83	Ukraine	2.1
24	Belgium	6.6	54	Egypt	3.6	84	Azerbaijan	2.0
25	Portugal	6.3		El Salvador	3.6		Bolivia	2.0
26	Botswana	6.0		Turkey	3.6		Cameroon	2.0
27	Taiwan	5.9	57	Argentina	3.5		Kenya	2.0
28	Estonia	5.6		China	3.5	88	Indonesia	1.9
29	Italy	5.5	59	Ghana	3.4		Uganda	1.9
30	Namibia	5.4		Latvia	3.4	90	Nigeria	1.0
31	Hungary	5.3				91	Bangladesh	0.4

2001 CPI Score—relates to perceptions of the degree of corruption as seen by businesspeople, risk analysts, and the general public, and it ranges between 10 (highly clean) and 0 (highly corrupt).

Source: Transparency International (November 6, 2002): http://www.transparency.org.

a government minister to influence the customs official is illegal. The FCPA allows the former payment because government officials in many countries delay compliance of laws indefinitely until they do receive payments, even though such payments may be illegal in those countries.[55]

Critics of the FCPA contend that U.S. companies lose business because firms from other countries not only have been permitted to make bribery payments but also have been able to take the expenses as tax deductions. Critics add that U.S. anticorruption laws might be seen as an extraterritorial attempt to meddle in other countries' domestic affairs.

Overall, the FCPA appears to be a useful deterrent.[56] For example, Procter & Gamble closed a Pampers plant in Nigeria rather than pay a bribe to a customs inspector.[57] The fear of penalty motivates greater compliance on the part of companies. IBM Argentina paid more than $4.5 million in bribes to officials of Banco de la Nacion Argentina in order to win a contract. The IBM parent company discovered the bribes and reported them to the U.S. government; IBM paid a civil penalty of $300,000. Similarly, Baker Hughes disclosed to U.S. officials that it had illegally authorized a $75,000 payment to an Indonesian tax official, plus illegal payments of $15,000 and $10,000 in India and Brazil. The United States did not impose any civil penalties, but it did require the company to sign a consent decree promising not to bribe foreign officials.[58]

Other efforts are under way to stop bribery. The CIA monitors bribery payments by non-U.S. companies so that the United States may put diplomatic pressure on foreign governments to stop the practice. The OECD's Bribery Convention obligates its 35 signatories to criminalize the bribery of foreign public officials in the conduct of international business.[59] Similar conventions against bribery have been passed by the Organization of American States (OAS), Global Coalition for Africa (GCA), and Council of Europe (COE).[60]

Various organizations also try to halt corruption. Transparency International, for instance, assists citizens in setting up national chapters to try to fight local corruption. It regularly compiles an international Corruption Perceptions Index (CPI) based on surveys of businesspeople, risk analysts, journalists, and the general public. Table 11.1 reports the ranking of 91 countries in terms of the perceived corruption in each.

There are several other efforts to stop bribery by:

- Government agencies
- Regional associations
- Private organizations

DIFFERENCES IN NATIONAL ATTITUDES TOWARD MNES

In theory, host countries may take completely restrictive or laissez-faire positions toward MNEs. In actuality, their policies are seldom completely restrictive or completely laissez-faire but rather ebb and flow over time. Currently, countries such as Bhutan and Cuba are close to the restrictive end, and countries such as the United States and the Netherlands are near the laissez-faire end of the continuum. Countries between these extremes adopt policies with varying degrees of restrictions as they attempt to attract investment and receive the most benefit from it. Presently, the effort to attract FDI has led more host governments to adopt policies that move their countries toward the laissez-faire end of the continuum.

The concern of home- and host-country stakeholders about MNEs' international operations increases with their international commitments. For example, home-country stakeholders are generally unconcerned when a company begins to export, but they are concerned when the company begins producing abroad because they fear that jobs, technology, and growth are being transferred. Likewise, host-country stakeholders pay more attention to foreign companies that are wholly owned direct investments than to those that share ownership locally or those that merely export into their market. Closer scrutiny occurs in such cases because the company now employs local personnel and—with full ownership—it may be able to pursue global or home-country objectives at the expense of local ones. Therefore, the need for companies to justify the benefit of their local operations grows in tandem with their international commitments.

LOOKING TO THE FUTURE

Will FDI Be Welcome as the Twenty-first Century Progresses?

In all likelihood, governments will continue to compete for a larger share of the benefits from the activities of MNEs. In the short term, most countries will probably work to create more favorable business environments for foreign investors. Investment inflows give developing countries ways to work around their debt burdens and capital accounts problems. Industrial countries struggling with trade-deficit problems, like the United States, are more inclined to take a positive stance toward receiving FDI. The EU, along with other regional trade associations, will probably continue to welcome foreign investment inflows to help it attain the growth that it seeks through unification.

However, FDI may be less welcome in the longer term. Historically, attitudes toward FDI have tended to vary, leaning toward more restrictions when economies are thriving and incentives when economies are struggling. Still, it is possible that if rapid growth does not occur in some developing countries after they have attracted substantial FDI, they may adopt the economic model used by such countries as Japan, South Korea, and China. The latter countries managed to grow on their own by extensively regulating both the flow of foreign investment and the behavior of foreign investors. Worse still, growing disappointment with the net benefits of foreign investment may lead some countries to fault FDI as the cause of their weaker sovereignty, their increasing poverty, and their cultural disintegration.

Where MNEs are controlled will continue to be an issue. Some MNEs (such as Nestlé, SKF, ABB, ICI, Coca-Cola, and Heinz) now have so many nationalities represented in their top management ranks that it is difficult to accuse them of favoring home-country interests. However, their internationalization leaves them open to the criticism of acting in their own corporate—rather than national—interest. Some MNEs, including Michelin, Matsushita, and United Technologies, have few shares held outside their home countries and practically no foreigners in high-level corporate positions.[61] In either situation, MNEs may need to heed the calls of home and host governments to make their decision making more transparent.

Countries tend to be more concerned about large companies than small ones because of the former's greater potential impact on national economic and political objectives. However, not all companies that operate internationally are large. Smaller companies generally have less significant foreign investments and have an easier time justifying their entry and operations. Because officials presume small companies have a smaller impact on host societies, countries often treat their FDIs differently. Further, the governments of many developing countries prefer smaller MNEs because such MNEs may be more willing to support host-country ambitions, increase local competition because of their numbers, and supply smaller-scale technology that is better suited to local needs.[62]

The perception of a company's operations in one country may have an effect on the perception of stakeholders in other countries. For example, a company's confrontation with labor, tax authorities, or environmental pressure groups in one country may cause similar stakeholders in another country to be warier of the company. Further, improving communications can widely publicize negative reports about company practices. As an MNE expands to more countries, the odds of negative perceptions about its impact increases.

The relationship between MNEs and societies has generated so many allegations and controversies that it is impossible to investigate all of them in this chapter. A number of them deal not so much with the legitimacy of the MNE but rather with the effect of certain business practices. In these cases, the targets are specific operational areas of management that we examine later in this book.

Summary

- Growing FDI increases the frequency and extent of relationships between MNEs and host governments.

- More governments have steadily replaced obstacles to FDI with incentives for FDI. Creating a more favorable investment environment, the reasoning goes, should have positive benefits for host countries. However, MNEs could face challenging times if host countries believe that the benefits fall short of expectations.

- Management must understand the need to compromise and satisfy the conflicting interests of stockholders, employees, customers, and society. For managers of MNEs, the problem is more complex because the strengths of these competing groups vary among countries.

- The economic and political effects of MNEs are difficult to evaluate because of conflicting influences on different countries' objectives, intervening variables that obscure cause-effect relationships, and differences among MNEs' practices.

- Countries are interested in their absolute gains or losses as well as their performance compared to other countries.

- Because a balance-of-payments surplus in one country must result in a deficit elsewhere, MNEs' trade and investment transactions have been scrutinized closely for their effects. However, countries often are willing to accept short-term deficits to achieve a long-term surplus or other economic gains.

- Managers and government officials can calculate how FDI will affect a country's balance of payments. However, so many assumptions underlie such calculations that there is ample room for disagreement. FDI projects differ so much that governments cannot easily make effective policies that apply to large groups of investors.

- Governments regulate FDI to improve their balance-of-payments positions by checking capital flows, requiring partial local ownership of FDI, limiting local borrowing by foreign investors, and stipulating that a part of capital inflows must be in the form of loans rather than equity.

- The growth and employment effects of MNEs do not necessarily benefit one country at the expense of another. Many of these effects come from the employment of resources with or without the MNEs' activities.

- MNEs may contribute to growth and employment by using idle resources, by using resources more efficiently, and by upgrading resource quality.

- The factors affecting countries' growth and employment include the location in which MNEs operate, product sophistication, competitiveness of local companies, government policies, and degree of product differentiation.

- Political concerns about MNEs are that they could be a foreign-policy instrument of home-country or host-country governments or that they may avoid the regulation of any government.

- Extraterritoriality is the application of home-country laws to the operations of companies abroad. It sometimes leads to conflicts between home and host countries and may put an MNE in the untenable position of having to disobey the laws of one country or the other.

- Countries most fear foreign control of key sectors in their economies because decisions made abroad may disrupt local economic and political stability. Foreign investors then may have enough power to affect local sovereignty adversely. Consequently, governments often restrict foreign ownership in key sectors of their economies.

- Bribery of government officials is a recurring problem in international business. Governments and international organizations have devised laws to stop corruption. Still, matters of facilitation payments, cultural norms, and company strategy complicate any regulations.

- The FCPA criminalizes bribery by U.S. companies in the conduct of international business; an important exception is facilitation payments.

- At any given point, some countries are more open to FDI than others are. However, countries' attitudes toward FDI change.

CASE

FDI in South Africa[63]

I n 1999, the South Africa's Reserve Bank declared, "Foreign direct investment inflows will be a prerequisite for faster economic growth and development." This verdict came five years after the end of apartheid, the system of minority white rule that had lasted about 40 years and prevented South African blacks from fairly participating in the political, economic, and social affairs of the country. The United Nations had routinely denounced apartheid, and many countries pressured South Africa to eliminate apartheid by imposing trade embargoes, investment restrictions, and cultural prohibitions (e.g., banning its sports teams from international competition). Anti-apartheid protests increasingly paralyzed the South African economy. South Africa ended apartheid and held democratic elections in 1994. South Africans overwhelmingly elected Nelson Mandela, a leading opponent of apartheid, as their president.

Many businesspersons within and outside South Africa predicted that the 1994 changeover would lead to political instability and an antibusiness government. They speculated that newly elected politicians would take revenge against the whites who had oppressed them and against businesses that had been their collaborators. Instead, the political changeover went smoothly, as did the 1998 election of Mandela's successor, Thabo Mbeki.

Mandela, Mbeki, and their party, the African National Congress, have had a positive attitude toward business, especially toward foreign companies. So, in the post-apartheid euphoria, the new political leaders awaited the increasing flow of FDI. They reasoned that the end of external sanctions and internal protests would encourage foreign businesses to develop local opportunities. They also hoped that MNEs that had left South Africa during the apartheid era would return—for example, between 1986 and 1991, 235 of the 360 U.S. MNEs in South Africa left the country.

Why would the South African government seek FDI? Unquestionably, jobs are a compelling reason. For more than a decade, South Africa has had one of the highest jobless rates in the world, with an official unemployment estimate of 26 percent. Growth is another reason. South Africa's savings and investment rates have been too low to finance sufficient business expansion, especially given that the population has been growing more than 2 percent per year. A third reason is that foreign investment in state-owned companies usually improves the quality of their goods and services. Finally, competition from foreign investment can spur local companies to innovate; South Africa used this rationale to justify opening its banking and telecom sectors

to foreign investors. Boosting competitive rivalry is important in South Africa because its market had been dominated by quasi-monopolistic conglomerates that were set up during the apartheid era. Finally, as a leading exporter of various commodities, South Africa is vulnerable to prolonged market downturns in industrialized countries. FDI would help diversify its economy.

No one questioned the enormous opportunities within South Africa. It has more than 43 million people, an improving logistics infrastructure, an advanced financial sector, a GDP per capita just under $3,000, vast mineral wealth, and good access to more than 100 million people in southern Africa. (Map 11.2 shows South Africa's location.) Since 1994, conservative public spending and a market-based fiscal policy promoted macroeconomic stability. The IMF described South Africa's macroeconomic framework as the best among developing countries around the world. South Africa seemingly had built the foundation for sustainable business development within a stabilizing democracy—an ideal place for FDI.

However, FDI trickled into South Africa from 1994 onward. In absolute terms, FDI totaled $18.4 billion in the 1994-to-2000 period. It peaked in 1999—at $4.12 billion—and has since declined to $2–$3 billion per year, which was far below the country's productive capacity. In relative terms, South Africa lags other major developing countries in attracting FDI, especially given its market potential. The United Nations World Investment Report noted that the total FDI stock in South Africa in 2000 was $52.6 billion—versus, for example, $197.6 billion in

MAP 11.2   South Africa and Its Location

South Africa's location is advantageous for serving the high-population market of southern Africa. However, South Africa is far from the markets of industrial countries.

Source: CIA Yearbook, 2002. http://www.cia.gov/cia/publications/factbook/index.html

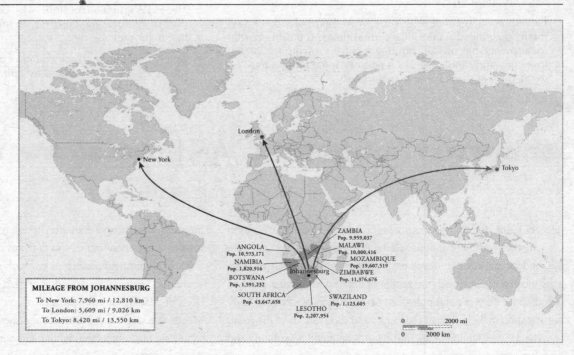

MILEAGE FROM JOHANNESBURG
To New York: 7,960 mi / 12,810 km
To London: 5,609 mi / 9,026 km
To Tokyo: 8,420 mi / 13,550 km

ANGOLA Pop. 10,593,171
NAMIBIA Pop. 1,820,916
BOTSWANA Pop. 1,591,232
SOUTH AFRICA Pop. 43,647,658
LESOTHO Pop. 2,207,954
ZAMBIA Pop. 9,959,037
MALAWI Pop. 10,000,416
MOZAMBIQUE Pop. 19,607,519
ZIMBABWE Pop. 11,376,676
SWAZILAND Pop. 1,123,605
Johannesburg

Brazil. The amount and makeup of FDI was disappointing given the expectations of post-apartheid South Africa. The problem appeared to be a mix of economic, risk, operational, incentive, image, and geographical factors. We look at each one in turn.

Generally, investors go where they see large markets and a history of sustainable growth. The former is evident in South Africa but the latter is not. South Africa has a poor growth record, expensive and inflexible labor markets, and a shortage of investor confidence. Worse still, economists estimate that South Africa requires an annual growth of around 6 percent if it is to begin reducing its unemployment. Complications arise from civil unrest and slow economic growth in much of southern Africa. These countries are important export markets. Turmoil there reduces earnings for South African export industries, thereby slowing the savings and investment cycle needed to fund growth. The ongoing depreciation in the South African currency, the rand, reflected this situation—it depreciated more than 600 percent against the U.S. dollar from 1981 through 2000. This bleak economic situation led South African companies to funnel more FDI abroad from 1991 through 2001 than their non-South African counterparts invested in South Africa. Finally, health-care and social problems have been escalating. South Africa has one of the highest rates of AIDS in the world, with an estimate one in five persons HIV positive.

South Africa has enjoyed political stability since the fall of apartheid. Still, other political problems created risks. The Corruption Perceptions Index rated South Africa as the fourth-least corrupt country in Africa but 38th out of the 91 countries ranked in 2001. (See Table 11.1.) As the former South African president of the Associated Chambers of Commerce noted, "In the case of South Africa, the extent of perceived corruption makes for a lack of confidence which, in turn, has led to a sluggish rate of fixed investment in both the public and private sectors." There were also personal safety issues. South Africa has one of the highest crime rates in the world. The World Economic Forum ranks countries by surveying the views of international business managers on various competitive factors. South Africa placed lowest on protection provided by local police of the 59 countries ranked in 1999. Protecting people and property adds a great deal of cost; firms typically spent between 5 to 10 percent of their budgets on additional security. Finally, instability in the region, particularly in Zimbabwe and Angola, threatened South Africa.

Foreign companies have run into troubles in South Africa. Staffing is a recurring problem. The exodus of young, highly qualified whites has created shortages of skilled executives and labor. Xerox, which left South Africa in 1989 but returned in 1997, said the scarcity of qualified staff is its biggest problem. It has opened and operated a training program for technical and sales staff and has adopted a school in the predominantly black township of Thembisa. A survey asked international managers about the factors that most discouraged FDI in South Africa. They noted extortion, bribery, and the difficulty in accessing global markets from South Africa, followed by poor access to capital, high administrative costs, and defective physical infrastructure. Overall, some companies reasoned that effectively running a South African operation would demand more management time than was justified by the potential returns.

The image of South Africa creates other problems. Trying to convince an executive to leave the comparatively safer haven of London to manage a new subsidiary in unruly Johannesburg is hard. In addition, the financial emigration of many of South Africa's corporate giants—switching their home stock market listings to foreign bourses in an effort to distance themselves from the negative perceptions of corruption and crime in South Africa—fanned suspicions. Some officials condemned white South Africans for unduly criticizing their country and warned that doing so jeopardized foreign investments.

Geography adds a final hurdle. South Africa is so distant from most industrial countries that potential investors sometimes did not evaluate opportunities impartially. Compounding physical distance are popular misconceptions. For example, a survey of corporate executives from around the world by South African officials concluded that one U.S. executive's remark, "We still see South Africa as one big game reserve," typified its challenge to attract foreign investment. In addition, people abroad often assume that mining dominates South Africa's economy; actually, it accounts for less than 10 percent of GDP. Similarly, people think that most of the world's diamonds come from South Africa; actually, it is the world's fifth largest producer.

The government of South Africa announced plans to create a better environment for foreign investment through job creation, increased spending on infrastructure, new capital depreciation allowances, tax cuts for lower- and middle-income groups, and a reduction in the national debt through privatization. Not everyone in South Africa agreed that the country should invest so much time and effort to attract FDI. Critics charged that a lot of the recent FDI into South Africa had been foreign acquisitions of South African companies and that this development had provided scant local benefit. Also, rather than trying to lure outsiders, some thought it more important to concentrate on "internal threats to democracy: threats from poverty, from joblessness, from lack of education, from crimes, from AIDS." The next few years is a crucial time for South Africa. It has a maturing democracy, a growing market economy, and an expanding police force. Foreigners had to determine if these changes created a sufficiently favorable investment environment.

QUESTIONS

1. What are the costs and benefits to South Africa of having more foreign direct investment? Of having less?
2. How might a company try to weigh fairly the opportunities and threats of investing in South Africa?

3. If South Africa is to receive more foreign direct investment, how should it prioritize policies to attract it?

4. Assume you work for a non-South African company and are in charge of identifying countries where your company might

expand. What factors would you consider when comparing South Africa with other developing countries? What about in terms of developed markets?

Culture Quest

VIDEO: UNDERSTANDING FOREIGN DIRECT INVESTMENTS: SPOTLIGHT ON SOUTH AFRICA

This chapter highlighted how government policies directly encourage or restrict multinational enterprise operations and their global investments. Based on viewing the accompanying video, and materials in this chapter, please answer the following questions:

1. What factors challenge the South African government's efforts to attract and retain foreign direct investment?

2. What are the key risks and opportunities for a foreign firm considering investment in South Africa? What factors would you assess? How would you prioritize them?

3. How have government attitudes toward foreign investment evolved over the past 10 or so years, specifically in developing markets like South Africa?

Chapter Notes

1 The data for this case were taken from: The Monsanto quotation is from Jonathan Kwitny, "U.S. Concerns Export Mainland-Bound Goods as Embargo Loosens," *Wall Street Journal* (March 11, 1971): 1. Ian Johnson, "China Makes Cutbacks in Industrial Investment," *Wall Street Journal* (February 4, 1999): A17; Colm Foy and Angus Madison, "China: A World Economic Leader?" *Observer*, no. 215 (January 1999): 39–42; Paulus Chan, "Doing Business in China: Trade, Legal and Cultural Considerations," *Nonwovens Industry* (February 1996); Robert F. Dodds, Jr., "Offsets in Chinese Government Procurement: The Partially Open Door," *Law and Policy in International Business* 26, no. 4 (June 22, 1995): 1119; Aimin Yan and Barbara Gray, "Bargaining Power, Management Control, and Performance in U.S.-China Joint Ventures: A Comparative Case Study," *Academy of Management Journal* 37 (December 1994): 1478; Stanely Lubman, "What Dispute? Conflicts Between Chinese and Foreign Partners in Joint Ventures," *China Business Review* 22, no. 3 (May 1995): 46; "Guangzhou Evaluates Foreign Investment," Xinhua News Agency (February 17, 1995); Gregory E. Osland and Tamer S. Cavusgil, "Performance Issues in U.S.-China Joint Ventures," *California Management Review* (January 1996): 106; Nicholas Reynolds, "End of an Era Flagged as Garment Giant Crosses the Border," *South China Morning Post* (May 29, 1995): Business section, 3; Kevin Honglin Zhang, "What Attracts Foreign Multinational Corporations to China?" *Contemporary Economic Policy* (July 2001): 336; Ping Deng, "WFOEs: The Most Popular Entry Mode into China," *Business Horizons* (July 2001): 63; Jiang Xueqin, "Letter from China," *The Nation* (March 4, 2002): 23; Quote from "Observer" is by Guang Anping as reported in "China: Special Report: Just One Way Out," *AsiaWeek* (October 19, 2001): 1; "Nanjing—Fiat Motors Ahead," *China Economic Review* (July 1, 2002): 23; and Kirby Chien,

"Taiwan Firms Speed Up Move into China," *New York Times* (August 4, 2002).

2 Maiko Miyake and Magdolna Sass, "Recent Trends in Foreign Direct Investment," *Financial Market Trends* (June 2000): 23.

3 *The World Investment Report 2001: Promoting Linkages* (Geneva: UNCTAD, 2001).

4 See Gavin Boyd and John Dunning, eds., *Structural Change and Cooperation in the Global Economy* (Northampton, MA: Edward Elgar, 1999); and Joseph E. Stiglitz, *Globalization and Its Discontents* (New York: W. W. Norton, 2002).

5 Louis Uchitelle, "Foreign Investors Turning Cautious on Spending in U.S.," *New York Times* (August 4, 2002): A1.

6 Ashish Arora, Andrea Fosfuri, and Alfonso Gambardella, "Markets For Technology in the Knowledge Economy," *International Social Science Journal* (March 2002): 3–18.

7 Jean J. Boddewyn and Thomas L. Brewer, "International-Business Political Behavior: New Theoretical Directions," *Academy of Management Review* 19 (1994): 119–43.

8 Mohsin Habib and Leon Zurawicki, "Corruption and Foreign Direct Investment," *Journal of International Business Studies* 33 (Summer 2002): 291–308.

9 John H. Dunning, "The Future of Multinational Enterprise," *Lloyds Bank Review* (July 1974): 16.

10 *World Investment Report 1999: Foreign Direct Investment and the Challenge of Development* (Geneva: UNCTAD, 1999).

11 Paul Krugman, "A Country Is not a Company," *Harvard Business Review* (January–February 1996): 40–51.

12 See William Easterly, "The Cartel of Good Intentions," *Foreign Policy* (July–August 2002): 40–50; and Peter S. Heller and Sanjeev Gupta, "Challenges in Expanding Aid Flows," *Finance & Development* 39 (June 2002): 40–44.

13 John Schauble, "China's Growth Ahead of Government Hopes," *Sydney Morning Herald* (July 16, 2002): 22.

14 Evan Osborne, "Financial Crashes in the Globalization Era," *Independent Review* 6 (Fall 2001): 165–85.

15 John Motala, "Statistical Discrepancies in the World Current Account," *Finance & Development* 34 (March 1997): 24–26.

16 Peter J. Buckley and Jane Hughes, "Incentives to Transfer Profits: A Japanese Perspective," *Applied Economics* 33 (December 2001): 2009–16.

17 Ravi Ramamurti, "The Obsolescing 'Bargaining Model'? MNC-Host Developing Country Relations Revisited," *Journal of International Business Studies* 32 (Spring 2001): 23.

18 George G. Kaufman, "Banking and Currency Crises and Systemic Risk: Lessons from Recent Events," *Economic Perspectives* 24 (Fall 2000): 9.

19 Peter Wilamoski and Sarah Tinkler, "The Trade Balance Effects of U.S. Foreign Direct Investment in Mexico," *Atlantic Economic Journal* 27, no. 1 (March 1999): 24–37.

20 See Jeff Cole, Marcus W. Brauchli, and Craig S. Smith, "Orient Express," *Wall Street Journal* (October 13, 1995): A1; and Stanley Holmes, Chester Dawson, and Carol Matlack, "Rumble Over Tokyo," *Business Week* (April 2, 2001): 80.

21 Jonathon Guthrie, "Indian Rivals Threaten Call Centre Industry," *Financial Times* (February 16, 2001): 4.

22 Robert Feenstra and Gordon Hanson, "Foreign Investment, Outsourcing, and Relative Wages," Working Paper No. 5121 (Cambridge, MA: National Bureau of Economic Research, 1995); See also Fred R. Bleakley, "U.S. Firms Shift More Office Jobs Abroad," *Wall Street Journal* (April 22, 1996): A2.

23 Vinish Kathuria, "Foreign Firms, Technology Transfer and Knowledge Spillovers to Indian

Manufacturing Firms: A Stochastic Frontier Analysis," *Applied Economics* 33 (April 2001): 625.

24 Sally Bowen, "Developing a Refined Atmosphere," *Financial Times* (April 19, 1999): 12.

25 See Bayan Rahman and Mariko Sanchanta, "Wal-Mart Develops a Taste for Japan," *Financial Times* (May 3, 2002): 13; Peter Smith, "Food Retailers Group Says Wal-Mart–Owned Chain is 'Breathing Down Our Necks,'" *Financial Times* (April 13, 2002): 13; and Peter Montagnon and Michiyo Nakamoto, "Tokyo Gives Blessing to Foreign Takeovers," *Financial Times* (June 17, 1998): 6. However, evidence is inconclusive on the extent that local companies benefit from efficiencies that foreign companies bring in. See Brian J. Aitken and Ann E. Harrison, "Do Domestic Firms Benefit from Direct Foreign Investment? Evidence from Venezuela," *American Economic Review* 89, no. 3, (June 1999): 605–18.

26 Timothy Aeppel, "Scaling the Ladder," *Wall Street Journal* (April 6, 1999): A1.

27 For support, see William Keng and Mun Lee, "Foreign Investment, Industrial Restructuring and Dependent Development in Singapore," *Journal of Contemporary Asia* 27 (March 1997): 58–71. For a refutation, see Brian J. Aitken and Ann E. Harrison, op. cit., 605.

28 Haishun Sun, "Macroeconomic Impact of DFI in China: 1979–96," *The World Economy* 21, no. 5 (July 1998): 675–94.

29 Wilbur Chung, "Identifying Technology Transfer in Foreign Direct Investment: Influence of Industry Conditions and Investing Firm Motives," *Journal of International Business Studies* 32 (Summer 2001): 211.

30 Susan E. Feinberg and Sumit K. Majumdar, "Technology Spillovers from Foreign Direct Investment in the Indian Pharmaceutical Industry," *Journal of International Business Studies* 32 (Fall 2001): 421.

31 Theodore H. Moran, *Foreign Direct Investment and Development: The New Policy Agenda for Developing Countries and Economies in Transition* (Washington, DC: Institute for International Economics, 1998).

32 David J. Teece, "Foreign Investment and Technological Development in Silicon Valley," *California Management Review* 34, no. 2 (Winter 1992): 88–106.

33 Manuel G. Serapio and Donald H. Dalton, "Globalization of Industrial R&D: An Examination of Foreign Direct Investments in R&D in the United States," *Research Policy*, no. 28 (1999): 303–16.

34 Martin Feldstein, "Outbound FDI Increases National Income," *NBER Digest* (August 1994): 4.

35 For example, see Tryphon Kollintzas and Vanghelis Vassilatos, "A Small Open Economy Model with Transaction Costs in Foreign Capital," *European Economic Review* 44 (August 2000): 1515–42.

36 Barry P. Bosworth and Susan M. Collins, "Capital Flows to Developing Economies: Implications for Saving and Investment," *Brookings Papers on Economic Activity* (Washington, DC: Brookings Institution Press, 1999): 143–64.

37 See Alan M. Rugman and Alain Verbeke, "Multinational Enterprises and Public Policy," *Journal of International Business Studies* 29, no. 1 (1998): 115–36; and David A. Lake, "Global Governance: A Relational Contracting Approach," in Aseem Prakash and Jeffrey A. Hart, eds., *Globalization and Governance* (London: Routledge, 1999): 31–53.

38 Winfried Ruigrok, "Why Nationality Is Still Important," *Financial Times* (January 5, 1996): 8.

39 See Joaquín Roy, *Cuba, the United States and the Helms-Burton Doctrine: International Reactions* (Gainesville, FL: University of Florida Press, 2000); and "Lima Declaration to Urge U.S. to Abandon Helms-Burton Law," Xinhua News Agency (November 24, 2001).

40 These are but a few of the types of antitrust actions. See J. Townsend, "Extraterritorial Antitrust Revisited—Half a Century of Change," paper presented at the Academy of International Business (San Francisco, December 1983); "U.S. Seeks to Block Gillette's Purchase of Wilkinson Assets," *Wall Street Journal* (January 11, 1990): B6; "U.S. Wins Accord with British on Glass Factories," *Wall Street Journal* (May 27, 1994): A12; and Kevin Done and Mark Odell, "BA and American Try to Revive Alliance Plans," *Financial Times* (August 4, 2001): 1.

41 "U.S. and Japan Sign Antitrust Cooperation Agreement." *International Law Update* 5 (October 1999): 10.

42 Yao-Su Hu, "Global or Stateless Corporations are National Firms with International Operations," *California Management Review* 34, no. 2 (Winter 1992): 107–26.

43 Hisu-Ling Wu and Chien-Hsun Chen, "An Assessment of Outward Foreign Direct Investment from China's Transitional Economy," *Europe-Asia Studies* 53 (December 2001): 1235–55.

44 Edward Luce and Ted Bardacke, "Thailand and Philippines Compete for $1bn Car Plant," *Financial Times* (December 5, 1995): 1.

45 Paul Peralte, "Out-of-State Car Plants Have Ripple Effect," *Atlanta Journal and Constitution* (April 8, 2001): 4E.

46 Richard Waters, "U.S. Big Business Fears Sanctions," *Financial Times* (May 16, 1996): 4.

47 Dana Milbank and Marcus W. Brauchli, "Greasing Wheels," *Wall Street Journal* (September 29, 1995): A1.

48 David Rudnick, "Pay Up, Pay Up and Play the Game," *Daily Telegraph* London (July 12, 2001): 72.

49 "Mexico Asks IBM for Proof of Alleged Bribe Request," *Wall Street Journal* (February 8, 1993). For the means-versus-end discussion, see Kent Hodgson, "Adapting Ethical Decisions to a Global Marketplace," *Management Review* (May 1992): 53–57.

50 Nancy Dunne, "Bribery Helps Win Contracts in Developing World," *Financial Times* (January 21, 2000): 6. Dunne refers to a Gallup Poll survey of almost 800 executives.

51 Milbank and Brauchli, op. cit.

52 See Marcus W. Brauchli, Matthew Rose, and Jonathan Friedland, "Foreign Donors: We Have a Stake in America, Too," *Wall Street Journal* (October 31, 1996): A19; Fran Abrams and Chris Brown, "British Firms Gave US Politicians Pounds 3m," *The Independent* (April 17, 1998): 1; and Jane Martinson. "Republican Convention: UK Firms in Party Funding Dispute," *The Guardian* (August 3, 2000): 3.

53 "The Short Arm of the Law—Bribery and Business," *The Economist* (March 2, 2002): 78.

54 See The World Bank, "World Development Report 2002: Building Institutions for Markets," World Bank Report (2001) Habib and Zurawicki, op cit.

55 Rudnick, op. cit.

56 See Jack G. Kaikati et al., "The Price of International Business Morality: Twenty Years Under the Foreign Corrupt Practices Act," *Journal of Business Ethics* 26 (August 2000): 213–23; and Macleans A. Geo-Ja Ja, and Garth L. Mangum, "The Foreign Corrupt Practices Act's Consequences for U.S. Trade: The Nigerian Example," *Journal of Business Ethics* 24 (April 2000): 245–56.

57 "The Short Arm of the Law," *The Economist*, op. cit.

58 Nelson Antosh, "Baker Hughes Offers to Settle Bribe Charge," *Houston Chronicle* (July 7, 2001): C1.

59 The OECD Convention on Combating Bribery of Foreign Public Officials in International Business Transactions specifically decrees that "enterprises should not, directly or indirectly, offer, promise, give, or demand a bribe or other undue advantage to obtain or retain business." Policy Development and Review Department, OECD.

60 Juliette Bennett, "Multinational Corporations, Social Responsibility and Conflict," *Journal of International Affairs* 55 (Spring 2002): 393–413.

61 William J. Holstein et al., "The Stateless Corporation," *Business Week* (May 14, 1990): 103.

62 Carol Graham, "Winners and Losers: Perspectives on Globalization from the Emerging Market Economies," *Brookings Review* 19 (Fall 2001): 22–26.

63 Data for this case were taken from: Carolyn Southey, "Investors Seek More Incentives," *Financial Times* (March 23, 1999): Survey section, 1; Jon Jeter, "South Africa's Image Problem Deters Investors," *Washington Post* (October 17, 1999): A21; Ben Laurance, "South Africa: Down but Not Out," *The Observer* (February 14, 1999): 4; "Foreign Banks Move In," *The Banker* 147, no. 858 (August 1997): 50–52; "Governor Goes for Gradualism," *The Banker* 147, no. 858 (August 1997): 54–56; Bernard Simon, "Shopping with Precision: Defense Offset," *Financial Times* (March 23, 1999): 4; Adrienne Roberts, "Overseas Interest Hard to Pin Down," *Financial Times* (September 20, 1999): Survey section, 4; "Business: VeldCom," *The Economist* 347 (May 16, 1998): 64; South African Press Association, "Corruption a Factor in Offshore Listings," Global News Wire (July 20, 2001); South African Press Association "FDI Revival Begins at Home," Global News Wire (January 31, 2001); James Lamont, "South Africa Sees Rise in Investment," *Financial Times* (August 3, 2001): 7; South African Press Association, Foreign Investment to South Africa Slumps," Global News Wire (September 18, 2001); "Country Profile: South Africa," *African Review of Business and Technology* (January 2, 2002); Wyndham Hartley, Farouk Chothia, and Jonathan Katzenellenbogen, "Minister Accuses South Africans of Jeopardizing Foreign Investment," *Business Day* (January 11, 2001): 1; http://www.cia.gov/cia/publications/factbook/geos/sf.html; http://lcweb2.loc.gov/frd/cs/zatoc.html.

12

INTERNATIONAL BUSINESS
NEGOTIATIONS AND DIPLOMACY

Without trouble there is no profit.

—AFRICAN (HAUSA) PROVERB

OBJECTIVES

- To show the common and conflicting interests between countries and MNEs

- To illustrate negotiations between business and government in an international context

- To trace the changing roles of home-country governments in settling MNEs' disputes with host governments

- To clarify the role of companies' public affairs and political behavior in international business

- To profile the major types of intellectual property

- To explain the position of companies and governments in the uneven global enforcement of intellectual property rights

CASE

Saudi Aramco[1]

State-owned companies control the largest oil reserves in the world. The biggest of these companies is Saudi Aramco. It ranks first in global sales, production, and reserves as well as third in refining. The economics of oil are straightforward. Tight oil supplies give Saudi Aramco immense influence to prod other oil producer countries to cut production and raise prices. However, faltering oil demand makes those petroleum producers without integrated refining and marketing operations—like Saudi Aramco—price takers.

Because the Saudi Arabian government owns Saudi Aramco, it is difficult to separate company policies from those of the government. Further, Saudi Aramco often deals directly with other state-owned oil companies. Reviewing some events that preceded and followed Aramco's first oil output in 1939 spotlight the Saudi-U.S. relationship, the activities of the international oil companies (IOCs), and the evolving negotiating strategy of Saudi Aramco.

Historically, the oil policy of the United States has tried to safeguard sufficient and cheap supplies for domestic needs as well as strengthen the country's political position internationally. In the 1920s, the United States realized that it had limited oil reserves. It then supported the moves of U.S. oil companies to acquire oil concessions in the Middle East to ensure long-term supply. (The Middle East accounts for about two-thirds of the world's oil reserves. Map 12.1 shows the world's top 12 countries in terms of proven oil reserves; the largest reserves are in the Middle East.)

The Saudi oil industry, in contrast to others in the Middle East, was developed entirely by oil companies from the United States. First movers SOCAL (Standard Oil of California) and Texaco formed a joint venture and negotiated concessions from Saudi Arabia in the 1930s. Over the next few decades, they helped build Saudi Arabia's infrastructure (such as the country's first schools and construction of a pipeline to the Mediterranean in 1945) and organized the administration of the kingdom (such as compiling its first historical records and census). At some points, the United States had no official representatives to Saudi Arabia. In its place, SOCAL and Texaco conducted some quasi-official diplomacy that continued throughout World War II. In 1948, Exxon and Mobil joined SOCAL and Texaco; this new company became Aramco. Mobil owned 10 percent, whereas the others each had a 30-percent share. Until the mid-1970s, Aramco was the largest single U.S. investment in any foreign country.

On the global stage, Exxon, Mobil, SOCAL, and Texaco, along with Gulf, Shell, and BP, were known as the "Seven Sisters." Before the 1970s, their collective control of the exploration, production, refining, and distribution of the world's oil made them nearly impervious to the policies of any single country. The Cold War put a premium on preserving relations with strategic countries. So when Saudi Arabia's King Ibn-Saud demanded more revenue from Aramco, the U.S. government got directly involved in the negotiations. In 1951, the Saudi government allowed the oil companies to maintain their ownership of Aramco in exchange for a payment of 50 percent of their profits as taxes. The U. S. government then let the companies deduct this Saudi surcharge from their U.S. tax bills.

In 1952, Saudi Arabia observed Iran's experience and recognized the possible penalty of escalating demands. Specifically, Iran had just expelled the ruling leader, Shah Reza Pahlavi, and nationalized (took ownership of) British oil holdings. The Seven Sisters then boycotted Iranian oil and brought its government to the brink of economic collapse. With the support of the CIA, the Shah returned to power and formed an Iranian oil company, one in which the Seven Sisters shared 95 percent ownership. The

MAP 12.1   The Top Countries in Oil Reserves, 2002

About two-thirds of the world's known on reserves are in the Middle East, and the top five countries in terms of reserves are in the Middle East. Also, OPEC's share of total known oil reserves is 78 percent.

Sources: BP Statistical Review of World Energy, 2002 (December 29, 2002): http://www.bp.com/centres/energy2002/oil/reserves.asp.

[a]Reserves: Generally taken to be those quantities that can likely be recovered in the future under existing conditions.

[b]R/P Ratio: "Reserves/Production Ratio"—The length of time that remaining reserves would last if current annual production were to continue at that level.

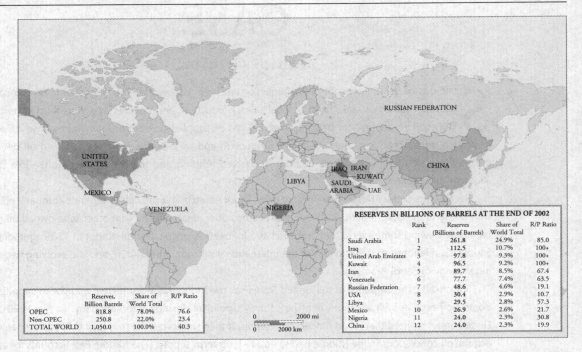

RESERVES IN BILLIONS OF BARRELS AT THE END OF 2002

	Rank	Reserves (Billions of Barrels)	Share of World Total	R/P Ratio
Saudi Arabia	1	261.8	24.9%	85.0
Iraq	2	112.5	10.7%	100+
United Arab Emirates	3	97.8	9.3%	100+
Kuwait	4	96.5	9.2%	100+
Iran	5	89.7	8.5%	67.4
Venezuela	6	77.7	7.4%	63.5
Russian Federation	7	48.6	4.6%	19.1
USA	8	30.4	2.9%	10.7
Libya	9	29.5	2.8%	57.3
Mexico	10	26.9	2.6%	21.7
Nigeria	11	24.0	2.3%	30.8
China	12	24.0	2.3%	19.9

	Reserves, Billion Barrels	Share of World Total	R/P Ratio
OPEC	818.8	78.0%	76.6
Non-OPEC	250.8	22.0%	23.4
TOTAL WORLD	1,050.0	100.0%	40.3

remaining 5 percent went to smaller, independent U.S. companies that previously had depended on the Seven Sisters for crude oil supplies.

As late as 1960, producing countries were unable to prevent the IOCs from unilaterally repealing concessions by reducing the price they paid for their oil. This pricing dilemma led first to a meeting of officials from the oil-producing countries of Iran, Iraq, Kuwait, Saudi Arabia, and Venezuela and then to the ensuing formation of the Organization of Petroleum Exporting Countries (OPEC). OPEC aimed to prevent the IOCs from lowering the prices they paid them, to boost their share of oil revenues, and to take back ownership of their domestic assets. At the time, however, OPEC lacked the power to achieve its goals.

Events in the 1960s weakened the Seven Sisters, strengthened Saudi Arabia's position in Aramco, and empowered OPEC. First, other oil companies emerged and gained concessions from countries previously not among the major suppliers—for example, Occidental in Libya and ENI in the former Soviet Union. These smaller companies lacked the Seven Sisters' diversification of supplies and were less able to move to other supply sources if a host country unilaterally changed an agreement. Second, industrial countries' growth led to oil shortages. No longer could even the Seven Sisters boycott major supplier countries, as they had with Iran, and still supply their customers. Third, the threat of military intervention to protect oil investors was decreasing. The U.S. failure to support the unsuccessful efforts of the British, French, and Israelis to prevent the Egyptian takeover of the Suez Canal in 1956 spotlighted cracks in the armor. In addition, the growing strength of the Soviet Union raised the risk of any war that resulted from such intervention.

In the 1970s, Arab nationalism changed the rules of the game. Muammar al-Gaddafi of Libya demanded higher prices from Occidental—and given its dependence on Libya for crude oil, it conceded. Gaddafi successfully reapplied this strategy to other IOCs operating in Libya. Other countries noted Libya's success; they also used OPEC to bolster their negotiating positions. During the 1970s, virtually all oil resources outside of North America passed from the control of IOCs to host governments and their national oil companies. Renegotiated agreements blocked foreign investors from exploration activities and restricted them to downstream operations, such as refining and distribution.

OPEC's Teheran Agreement of 1971 officially increased oil prices. The 1973 embargo on oil shipments to the United States in retaliation for its support of Israel during the just-completed Arab-Israeli war confirmed the cartel's market power. By then, OPEC's 11 members controlled about 93 percent the world's oil exports. In 1975, Saudi Arabia unilaterally ended concessions run by Chevron (formerly SOCAL), Mobil, Texaco, and Exxon; changed the company's name to Saudi Aramco; discontinued the practice of selling oil only to its former partners; and nationalized its oil industry.

How did Exxon, Texaco, SOCAL, and Mobil fare in Saudi Arabia after the buyout? Initially, they helped manage the Saudi oil industry by selling services that the Saudis could not obtain easily from other sources, such as training Saudis and recruiting qualified personnel from abroad. As Saudi Aramco expanded, the four exchanged technical assistance in both the exploration and extraction of oil for lucrative contract arrangements.

After the Saudi government took full ownership of Aramco, it began replacing foreign management with Saudi nationals. Eventually, Saudis held all top positions in the company. Several factors helped Saudi Aramco reduce its dependence on the former U.S. owners. The number of oil companies worldwide had steadily grown, giving the Saudis more choices when contracting services and selling crude oil. Second, engineering giants, such as Bechtel and Fluor, began selling management and engineering services that once were available only from IOCs. In addition, global market growth was shifting toward Asia, where there were government-owned companies to whom Saudi Aramco could sell directly.

In the mid-1980s, Saudi Aramco grew less confident about OPEC's power to stabilize world oil supplies and prices. Increasing output by non-OPEC countries was aggravated by the reluctance of some OPEC countries to cut production to honor quotas. Saudi Aramco soon saw international vertical integration as the best way to ensure a market for its crude oil. In 1988, it joint-ventured with Texaco's U.S. refining and marketing system; this was followed by a joint venture in South Korea with Ssangyong in 1991, the purchase of a 40-percent stake in Petron (the largest refiner and distributor in the Philippines) in 1994, and the purchase of a 45-percent interest in Petrogal of Portugal (a refiner and gas station operator) in 1996. Saudi Aramco also bought a half-share in the Greek Vardinoyannis oil group and announced joint ventures in India with Hindustan Petroleum Oil and the Indian Oil Corporation. In 1998, it joint-ventured with Shell and Texaco to create the largest refiner and marketer of petroleum products in the United States. Steadily, Saudi Aramco moved closer to its stated strategy of developing a "global presence in the refining and retail sectors."

Several factors, many of which were unexpected, came together in late 1997 and early 1998 to reduce oil prices to levels not seen since the 1970s. An economic crisis in Asia, unusually warm weather in North America and Europe, and OPEC's decision, initiated by Saudi Arabia, to increase production in late 1997 led to low consumer demand and high oil supply. Crude prices dropped more than 30 percent, falling to their lowest price, in real terms, since before the first oil shock of 1973. Falling revenues pushed Saudi Aramco to cut spending on upgrade and expansion projects, delay downstream expansion overseas, take the rare step of trimming 8,000 workers, and offer Saudi Arabian employees 45 and older an early retirement package.

In September 1998, Saudi Crown Prince Abdullah reversed the 25-year-old policy that prohibited foreign ownership and invited the IOCs back into Saudi Arabia. Saudi Aramco would no longer have a monopoly over Saudi petroleum development. The Saudi government ruled that wholly owned foreign businesses would have the right to own land and sponsor their own employees. It reduced the tax rate on company profits from 45 to 30 percent and set up the General Investment Authority (SAGIA) as a "one-stop shop" for foreign investors. In 2000, the Supreme Council for Petroleum and Minerals of Saudi Arabia began to oversee oil and gas policies in the country, thereby taking responsibility for business strategy from Saudi Aramco. In 2001, Saudi Aramco invited the IOCs to develop the Saudi gas sector. Saudi Aramco initially declared that it had more than enough money and technology to do the job. Nonetheless, the gas initiative further opened the kingdom to FDI. Then, in 2002, Saudi Minister of Petroleum Ali al-Nu'aymi stated that the kingdom was looking to privatize some of the operations of Saudi Aramco.

These dramatic policies, although anchored in the changing economics of the global oil industry, were also shaped by larger events. One, growing exploration in the Caspian Basin, offshore West Africa, and the Gulf of Mexico attracted increasing financial and technological resources from the IOCs. Two, greater investment in Saudi Arabia by U.S. companies would strengthen Saudi Arabia's "special relationship" and security ties with the United States. Three, the Saudi GDP growth rate had averaged only 0.2 percent since the early 1980s; FDI promised economic reform and business innovation. In addition, Saudi Arabia's real economic growth continued to fall behind its population growth. Per capita oil export revenues (in inflation-adjusted dollars) were $2,563 per person in 2001 versus $23,820 in 1980. Increasingly, there were too few jobs for the hundreds of thousands of politically restive young people—more than 50 percent of the Saudi population of 22.7 million is under 18. This situation took on much greater significance in the aftermath of the September 11, 2001, terrorist attack on the United States; 15 of the 19 the terrorists that hijacked the four commercial flights were Saudi citizens.

IOCs were wary about reentering Saudi Arabia. Still, none could afford to turn their backs on the opportunity presented by the reopening of the kingdom's upstream oil sector to foreign investors. Since 1999, Texaco, Chevron, Arco, Phillips, Elf, Shell, and others have submitted wide-ranging bids that detail their financial positions and technical capabilities as well as the training and job opportunities that they can offer Saudi citizens. In 2001, SAGIA reported that foreign investment commitments had reached $1.6 billion and included 53 licenses.

Saudi Arabia expected to earn about $49.6 billion in crude oil export revenues for 2002, versus $58.2 billion in 2001 and $67.3 billion in 2000. Concurrently, Saudi Arabia reevaluated its negotiating position. In November 1999, the head of state, King Fahd ibn Abd al-Aziz al-Sa'ud, stated that "the world is heading for . . . globalization" and that "it is no longer possible for [Saudi Arabia] to make slow progress." In 2002, Saudi Aramco CEO Abdullah Jumah added, "We are covering the bases right now. The ball is in the court of the foreign companies to bring innovative ideas that we haven't thought of. . . . We want to see the name of Saudi Aramco in global markets. The realities of the business world have changed and we have to adjust."

INTRODUCTION

Chapter 11 discussed how home and host countries evaluate MNEs. Evaluation is only the first part of the job. Negotiations often follow, and that is where business-government relationships get much more complicated. Governments may refuse companies original or ongoing operating permission. Governments may also impose constraints on an MNE's operations within the host country. At the same time, companies will not operate unless the terms of business are beneficial. Nevertheless, countries and companies do reach agreements that, although not usually ideal for either party, are sufficient for an evolving

FIGURE 12.1   Business-Government Negotiations in International Operations

Negotiations between businesses and governments influence government enhancements and restrictions that determine companies' operating terms.

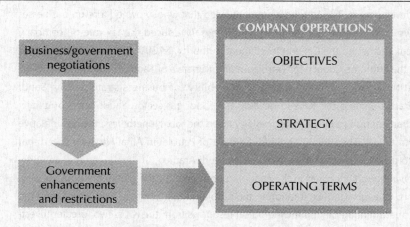

Local stakeholders sometimes fear company takeovers by foreign-owned MNEs, primarily because they may reduce the number of workers to gain efficiences. The photo shows Daewoo workers in South Korea protesting the possible sale of the company to a foreign company.

relationship. The business negotiations and diplomacy between companies and governments determine the terms of international business operations. Figure 12.1 shows the relationships.

GOVERNMENT VERSUS COMPANY STRENGTH IN NEGOTIATIONS

Both home- and host-country policies greatly influence the terms under which companies operate abroad. The strengths of the parties depend on such factors as the resources that each side has at its disposal, competitive changes, validation by public opinion, and joint efforts with other parties. However, companies have different viewpoints on how much they can influence operating terms—notably, the degree of government intervention does vary from one MNC to another within the same host country or even within the same industry. Governments also have different viewpoints on how much power they can exert over international companies.

The operating terms of international companies

- Are influenced by governments of home and host countries
- Shift as priorities shift and as the strengths of parties change

Hierarchical View of Government Authority

Governments install rules to regulate international business. In a hierarchical view of government authority, companies accept regulations as "givens," in which case they choose to comply, circumvent, or avoid. Companies will comply when the regulations do not unduly constrain their preferred mode of operations, when benefits are sufficiently attractive despite the regulations, or when they cannot alter the regulations to their advantage. Companies will circumvent regulations they find unacceptable through loopholes, either legal or illegal. For example, a firm's ability to control a foreign subsidiary in spite of a country's requirement for shared ownership might be possible if the company makes a side agreement with a local partner not to vote its shares of stock. Avoidance is simply the reverse of compliance, as a company decides not to operate in a given locale because of its onerous regulations.[2]

Bargaining View

MNEs and host countries have mutually useful assets.

As discussed in Chapter 11, the host country and the MNE control assets that may be useful to the other. **Bargaining school theory** states that the negotiated terms for a foreign investor's operations depend on how much the investor and host country need the other's assets.[3] If either a company or a country has assets that the other strongly desires and if there are few (or no) alternatives for acquiring them, negotiation will likely be one-sided. For example, the Saudi Aramco case illustrated that when a few large companies dominated the extraction, processing, shipment, and final sale of an oversupply of oil, developing countries with petroleum deposits could do little but accept the terms they were offered because they lacked alternatives for exploiting their oil. If a government refused the terms, a company could find another country that would accept its terms. As the supply of oil diminished and petroleum-producing countries found alternatives, oil-rich countries commanded stronger negotiation positions. Then again, the ensuing glut of oil and slower worldwide economies pushed oil-exporting countries to attract more FDI by offering more concessions to oil companies.

Alternative sources for acquiring resources affect company and country bargaining strengths.

There are vast differences in bargaining strength among countries, among industries, and among companies. The bargaining relationships between companies and governments depends on whether the parties see agreements as zero-sum (one party's gain equals the other party's loss) or positive-sum (both parties have net benefits) gains. In the former case, relationships may conflict because the adversarial parties both believe they will lose by making any concessions. In the latter case, the relationship may be seen as a mutually beneficial partnership of cooperation and interdependence.[4]

The biggest bargaining strengths for countries are
• Large markets
• Less business risk
• Political stability

Country Bargaining Strength   Companies typically prefer to invest in developed countries because those countries offer large markets, less business risk, and greater political stability. Because countries like the United States, China, and Germany are such attractive countries to invest in, they need not make many concessions to MNEs. Throughout these countries, however, regional areas compete for investments by offering incentives to potential investors. For example, several U.S. states vied for the first U.S. auto-manufacturing factory of Hyundai; Alabama won after offering more than $250 million in public and private incentives.[5] If incentives are used, they are most appealing when they fit closely with companies' corporate strategies and when companies believe that the government has the credibility to fulfill its promises.

Company bargaining strengths include
• Technology
• Marketing expertise
• The ability to export output
• Local product diversity
• The value of FDI

Company Bargaining Strength   MNEs experience varying degrees of host government intervention, reflecting differences in their ability to influence host governments. Companies in some industries, like life sciences or microelectronics, have traditionally commanded strong bargaining positions. Others companies may start in defensive positions. Foreign ownership in such areas as agriculture and extractive industries is often unwelcome in many countries because of the historical foreign domination of these sectors and the belief that the land and subsoil are public resources. Absent a strong welcome, foreign companies must find ways to overcome weak bargaining positions.

Generally, companies have differing abilities to influence host governments—that is, MNEs with greater bargaining power are likely to obtain more favorable terms in negotiations with host governments. At the minimum, the bargain struck between the foreign investor and the host country depends on the number of companies offering similar resources. Foreign investors are more likely to command a strong bargaining position in foreign operations when they have few competitors and when they control certain types of assets. These assets include:[6]

1. *Technology*. Governments tend to be less demanding of those companies that have technologies deemed critical to their countries' economic development. For example, governments in many countries accommodated IBM's demand for 100-percent ownership of local operations because of their need for its instrumental technology.

2. *Marketing expertise*. MNEs that have products with global brand recognition—and are thus beyond the immediate control of host government intervention—tend to have strong bargaining power. Coca-Cola, for example, has been able to gain local consumer allies who perceive its differentiated products as superior.

3. *Export performance*. The ability to export output from the foreign investment, especially when exports go to other units controlled by the parent company, fortifies a company's negotiating position. Besides earning foreign exchange, such investments help build the export capabilities of the host country. In addition, a local operation that exports a few input factors to another subsidiary in another country can indirectly create bargaining power by reducing its strategic value to the host country.

4. *Product diversity*. Governments may allow more foreign ownership when a company provides greater product diversity. MNEs that make a variety of products locally can support import substitution and boost local employment.

5. *The value of FDI*. In the past, the amount of capital that a company offered to invest did not usually affect its bargaining power. Fierce competition among countries to attract FDI, as we saw in the opening case on Saudi Aramco, gives MNEs stronger bargaining positions.

Joint Company Activities

Preventing extreme dependence on foreign companies often prompts countries to encourage their own manufacturers to consolidate operations. Officials have granted government assistance for R&D and given preference to their own companies when awarding government contracts. A notable effort has been Airbus Industrie, a consortium in Europe to compete against Boeing in commercial aircraft.[7] Other European cross-national efforts have occurred in such fields as consumer appliances, medical electronics, telecommunications, and television. For example, EUREKA, a pan-European network for market-oriented, industrial R&D, includes about 7,000 companies from 33 countries that are engaged in more than 700 projects to develop a range of technologies.[8]

Sometimes, two or more companies from different countries invest jointly abroad, not so much to strengthen the initial negotiating terms as to improve their positions in later negotiations. Investing a smaller amount in a given locality permits each company to invest in more countries, thereby reducing the impact of loss in one. Further, in the event of conflict, a host government may be more hesitant to deal simultaneously with more than one home government.

Host governments encourage joint company activities so as

- To strengthen national capabilities
- To lessen dependence on foreign companies
- To spread risk
- To deal more strongly with other governments

Home-Country Needs

The interplay between an MNE's needs and those of the host country is not the only bargaining factor in negotiations. The home-country government seldom takes a neutral position in the relationship. Like the host-country government, the home-country government aims to achieve certain economic objectives, such as increased tax revenues and full employment. It may give incentives to or place constraints on the foreign expansion of home-based companies in order to gain what it sees as its rightful share of the rewards from their transactions. Recall from the Saudi Aramco case that the U.S. government gave tax concessions to oil companies so they could develop foreign opportunities. However, the influence of the home or host government on MNEs is moderated by the political interests and relations of the two governments. When economic and political stakes are high, companies' home governments often help them negotiate. For example, when Poland announced plans to replace its aging fleet of MIG-21 fighter-aircraft, the governments of the United States, Britain, France, and Sweden lobbied Polish officials on behalf of their respective companies, Lockheed Martin, BAE, Dassault Aviation, and Saab.[9]

Other External Pressures on Negotiation Outcomes

The complementary nature of the assets that MNEs and countries control would seem, at first glance, to indicate a mutual interest in doing business. Although there are incentives to find mutual interests, there are also constraints, particularly on government decision makers. Constraints may come from local companies that the foreign investor presently or will potentially compete against, from political opponents who seize the issue of an "external" threat to incite voters against the current political leadership, or from critics who reason that the country may capture more benefits if the government takes a tougher negotiating stance. Similarly, home-country governments may respond to local pressure groups in ways that affect relationships with other governments, causing unexpected repercussions for MNEs. Companies also may face conflicting demands from stockholders, workers, consumers, suppliers, and nongovernmental organizations (NGOs). These demands may result in a relationship between the company and host country that is quite different from original expectations or intentions. Managers and government officials should understand the types, strengths, and goals of these external groups because such groups may affect the bargaining flexibility of each side.

NEGOTIATIONS IN INTERNATIONAL BUSINESS

Negotiations are the means by which a company may initiate, conduct, or terminate operations in a foreign country. At one time, negotiations were prevalent only for direct investments. However, today they play a part in other operating arrangements, such as licensing agreements, debt repayment, and technology transfer. The negotiation process often leads to multitiered bargaining: An MNE may need to reach an agreement with a local company to purchase an interest in it, to sell technology or products to it, or to loan money to it. Sometimes that agreement is presented to a host-country agency that may approve or disapprove—or may propose new terms. The MNE may need to negotiate with its home government for permission to transfer technology or for approval to borrow funds. The home and host governments may negotiate loans, investment guarantees, and overall economic and political relationships. Figure 12.2 shows these multiple relationships. Even when some of these parties do not directly take part in the negotiations, the participants may consider their needs.

FIGURE 12.2 Interrelated Negotiations

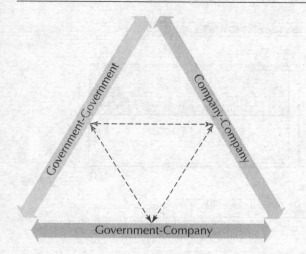

Interrelated negotiations may be necessary to reach agreement for foreign operating terms.

Source: Reprinted with permission of the Cambridge University Press.

Bargaining Process

Comprehensive bargaining among companies and governments may begin long before they agree (if, in fact, they ever do) on MNEs' terms of operations. Beside the preceding economic conditions, behavioral factors affect the bargaining process and agreement terms. Often, the parties renegotiate these terms as their relationship evolves.

Acceptance Zones   Before beginning negotiations with host nationals, a manager probably has gained some experience with a domestic bargaining process similar to that in the foreign market. For example, collective bargaining with labor as well as agreements to acquire or merge facilities with another company usually start with an array of proposals, just like negotiations with foreign organizations. The proposals undoubtedly include provisions that one side or the other is willing either to forsake entirely or to compromise on. These provisions are used as bargaining tokens, permitting each side to claim that it is reluctantly conceding some point in exchange for compromise on another point. They also serve as face-saving devices, allowing either side to report to interested parties that it had bargained sensibly and won some concessions. On fundamental points, however, there is little area for compromise.

In the bargaining process, agreement occurs only if there are overlapping acceptance zones.

As in domestic negotiations, the outcome of foreign negotiations will depend partly on other recent negotiations or events. What has taken place between other companies and a host-country government abroad or between similar types of companies or the same company in similar countries may serve as a common reference or bargaining model. Usually, negotiations do not stray far from that precedent.

Finally, there are zones of acceptance and nonacceptance for the proposals presented. If the acceptance zones overlap, an agreement is possible. If zones have no overlap, positive negotiations are not possible. For example, assume that GM insisted on 51-percent ownership of an Indian facility but would accept up to 100 percent. Assume also that the Indian government or partner insisted on 51-percent local ownership but would accept up to 75 percent. In this scenario, there is no overlap of acceptance zones in which to negotiate. However, if Toyota insisted on a "significant" interest in an Indian facility (say, 25 percent) but would take as much as it could get and if the Indian government, in turn, or a partner required 51-percent local ownership and wanted to maximize it, there would be a wide zone acceptable to both parties—for instance, 25 to 49 percent for Toyota's ownership. (See Figure 12.3.) The final agreement would depend on each party's negotiating proficiency and strengths and on the

FIGURE 12.3   Acceptance Zones in Negotiating

The lined section on the top bars reading from left to right is the company's acceptance zone, and the lined section on the bottom bars from right to left is the government's. In (a), there is no overlap, but in (b) the overlap is substantial. Although this figure illustrates ownership, the same technique may be used for other points of negotiation.

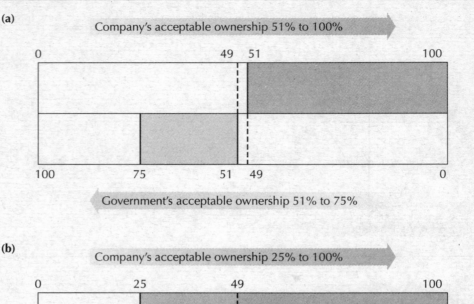

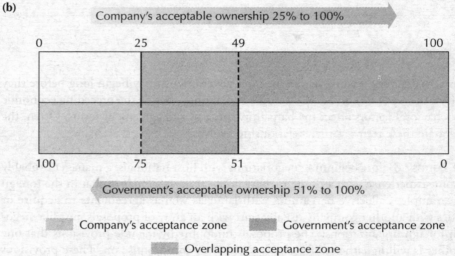

concessions made by each side. Because each side could only hypothesize on how much the other was willing to concede, the exact amount of ownership allowed might fall anywhere within the overlapping acceptance zones.

Range of Provisions   The major difference between domestic and foreign negotiations is a matter of degree. International negotiations may take much longer and may include provisions unheard of in the home country, such as a negotiated tax rate. Further, governments vary in their attitudes toward foreign investors, so their negotiating agendas also vary.[10]

Most countries offer investment incentives to attract MNEs. Direct incentives include such things as tax holidays, employee training, R&D grants, accelerated depreciation, low-interest loans, loan guarantees, subsidized energy and transportation, and exemption of import duties. Countries also provide indirect incentives, such as a trained labor force and labor laws that prevent work disruptions.

When managers negotiate to gain concessions from a foreign government, they should understand that concessions might create direct and indirect problems. For example:

- Companies may face more domestic labor problems because of claims that they are exporting jobs to gain access to cheaper labor.

- The foreign facility may be accused of dumping because of the subsidies given by the host government. For this reason, Toyota refused to accept the British government's assistance for fear that other EU countries might interfere with its sales.

- It may be more difficult to evaluate management performance in the subsidized operation because much of the profits may be due to the incentives rather than to management performance.

- There is always the risk that promises will be broken.

Negotiations are seldom a one-way street. Companies agree to performance requirements designed to help host countries attain economic and noneconomic objectives, such as a favorable balance of payments or local control over important decisions. These performance requirements include:

- Foreign-exchange deposits to cover the cost of imports and foreign-exchange payments on loans and dividends.

- Limits on payments to the parent for services it provides to its host-country subsidiary.

- Requirements to create a certain number of jobs or a certain amount of exports.

- Provisions to reduce the amount of equity held in subsidiaries.

- Maximum prices on goods sold locally.

- Obligatory levels of local input into the products manufactured.

- Limits on the number, type, and duration of expatriate assignments.

- Restrictions on the use of old or reconditioned equipment.

- Control of prices on goods the MNE imports from or exports to the host-country subsidiary.

- Demands to enter into joint ventures.

Renegotiations

It was common for companies making foreign investments early on in developing countries to obtain concessions on fixed terms for long periods or to expect that the original terms would not change. Generally, these early investments were in the commodity—like oil—and utility sectors. Those days are gone, as we saw in our opening case on Saudi Aramco. Not only may the terms of operations be negotiated before any operations begin, but also the same terms may be renegotiated anytime during start-up or after operations are under-way. For example, three U.S. MNEs—Enron, Bechtel, and GE—reached an agreement with the state of Maharastra in India to build a $2.8 billion power plant in which Enron would own 80 percent and Bechtel Enterprises and GE would each own 10 percent. After these companies had already invested $300 million, the government halted additional work, disputing the amount it owed the plant. During renegotiations of the agreement, the companies lost about $250,000 per day. Eventually, the parties agreed (1) to use more Indian naphtha (a fuel) rather than Qataran natural gas to generate electricity, (2) to allow the state of Maharastra to own 30 percent of the facility, (3) to reduce Enron's ownership to 50 percent, and (4) to reduce the price of power by 22.2 percent. Since then, the project itself has been marred by controversies involving payoffs to various officials by the now-defunct Enron. The ultimate collapse of Enron halted construction of the facility pending further renegotiations.[11]

Generally, a company's best bargaining position exists before it invests in a foreign country. Once a company transfers capital and technology abroad and trains local nationals to direct operations, the parent company is needed much less than before. Further, the company now has assets that are not easily moved to more favorable locales. The result is that the host country may be in a better position to extract additional concessions from the company. This erosion of an MNEs' bargaining strength as a host country gradually gains assets from it is known as the **theory of the obsolescing bargain**.

Agreements evolve after operations begin; the company position is usually, but not always, stronger before entering a country.

A company that is responsive to the local economy's changing needs and desires, however, can maintain or even improve its bargaining position by offering (or withholding) additional resources to the host country. One tactic is to bring in the latest production technologies. Another tactic is to use plant expansion or export markets as bargaining weapons. A company and country may often trade benefits—for example, a company may cede part of its ownership to local interests in exchange for guarantees on remission of its earnings.[12] A host government also may restrain from pushing companies too hard once they are up and running to avoid making the country less attractive to potential foreign investors.

Behavioral Characteristics Affecting Negotiations

In international negotiations, misunderstandings are a strong possibility because of cultural differences as well as possible language differences.[13] Further, the background and expertise of government officials may be quite distinct from those of businesspeople and their superiors may use different criteria to evaluate their performance.

Misunderstandings may result
from differences in

• Cultures
• Nationalities
• Languages
• Professions

Some cultural differences among
negotiators are evident

• Some negotiators are decision
  makers; some are not
• Some take a pragmatic view;
  others take a holistic view
• Some expressions do not
  translate well

Cultural Factors   In the 1930s, the humorist Will Rogers quipped, "America has never lost a war and never won a conference." Some apply this assessment to U.S. performance in business negotiations abroad. Nonetheless, companies from other countries run into problems as well. Most of the difficulty stems from cultural differences that lead to misunderstandings and mistrust between negotiating parties. Among the many possible cultural misunderstandings, the cultural framework specified in Chapter 2 identifies several:

• Individual negotiators from some countries are more likely to have the power to make decisions than are their counterparts from some other countries in part because of differences between individualist and collectivist societies. Negotiators who have the power to make decisions may lose confidence when their counterparts must reach a group decision or continually confer with their head office.

• Negotiators from low-context cultures want to get to the heart of the matter quickly. Negotiators from high-context cultures want to spend time developing general rapport and trust before addressing business details.

• Negotiators from pragmatist cultures attempt to disaggregate the issues into small categories (getting closure on specific items in a linear fashion), whereas negotiators from idealistic cultures view negotiations more holistically.

• Negotiators from cultures with high trust are less prone to try to cover every possible contingency in a contract than are negotiators from cultures with low trust.

• Negotiators from monochronic cultures prefer to give their undivided attention to one issue at a time. However, negotiators from polychronic cultures feel uncomfortable if they do not simultaneously discuss related business matters.

• Negotiators from cultures that place a high importance on punctuality and schedules are more prone to set deadlines and then make concessions at the last minute to meet the schedules than are negotiators from cultures that place less importance on punctuality and schedules. Further, they may underestimate the importance their counterparts place on the negotiations if their counterparts arrive late and do not adhere to schedules.

The importance of cultural factors may change during renegotiations because the parties already know each other. If the relationship was amicable in the original negotiations, that outlook is likely to carry over. However, if the past relationship was hostile, then the renegotiations may be marked by suspicion and stubbornness.

Language Factors   It is often difficult for negotiators to find words in another language that exactly express the intended meaning of the original statement. This difficulty can result in occasional pauses while translators consult dictionaries and thesauri. The pauses can cause negotiations to take longer than if they were among people from the same country. Moreover, if negotiations must pause while an interpreter translates, the process takes even longer. In addition, negotiators may struggle to read facial expressions because of cultural differences and the time lag caused by translation. Because English is understood worldwide, people with a different native language may understand quite well most of what is said in English; this can allow them to eavesdrop on confidential comments and form responses while remarks are being translated into their own language.

Cultural factors influence whether interpreters are acceptable. For example, Saudi managers generally prefer to negotiate in English even if they must make a great effort to speak it. When negotiators do use interpreters, each side should have its own. Seasoned interpreters brief their teams on cultural factors affecting the negotiation process. However, even with interpreters, negotiators cannot be certain that their statements are fully understood, especially if they use slang or attempt humor that is culture specific. Consider, for example, the experience of a U.S. politician who spoke through an interpreter in China.

> With typical American forthrightness, [the politician] said, "I'm going to tell you where I'm coming from." The interpreter said, "He'll now give you the name of his home town." Then he said, "I'm going to lay all my cards on the table." The interpreter said, "He'll play cards now." Then, making a joke, he said, "I'm not a member of any organized political party; I'm a Democrat." The interpreter said, "I think he just made a joke. Please laugh." The audience laughed and the politician "knew" he had their rapt attention.[14]

Culturally Responsive Strategies[15]   The fact that managers' counterparts in negotiations come from countries with different cultures does not necessarily mean they will behave according to their culture's norm.[16] First, a counterpart may be an exception to the cultural norm. Second, a counterpart may understand and be adaptive to the other's culture. Therefore, managers should determine at the start whether they will adjust to their counterparts, help their counterparts adjust to them, or follow some form of hybrid adjustment.

Figure 12.4 shows five strategic responses you might have if you were an international business manager engaged in a negotiation. The choice of response is highly dependent on how well you and your counterpart understand each other's culture. At one extreme, if you try to get your counterpart to adapt to you (Response 1), you need to convey that it is because of expediency rather than through lack of appreciation for the other's culture. For example, when ITT conducted merger talks with CGE of France, it did so in English and along ITT's style because the speed and success of starting operations were dependent on U.S. law and investment firms. At the other extreme, you may immerse yourself in your counterpart's culture, as in Response 2. For example, Coca-Cola sent personnel to Cambridge University to study the Chinese language and culture for a year before beginning a 10-year negotiation with a Chinese state-run organization. In Response 3, both you and your counterpart agree on go-betweens, brokers, or other intermediaries to simplify negotiations because neither of you is familiar with the other's culture. Response 4 is a hybrid of approaches, such as having both parties speak in their own language or moving negotiations between the two countries. Finally, Response 5 is the conduct of negotiations different from what one might find in either culture. It might occur when both parties have such extensive global experience that they have discarded many elements of their home cultures.

Professional Conflict   Government and business negotiators may begin with mutual mistrust due to historic animosity or to differences in their professional status. Businesspeople may come armed with market and economic data that government officials do not fully appreciate or accept. Officials may counter with sovereignty considerations that puzzle the businesspeople. It may take a long time before each side understands the other's point of view. Even then, it is possible that neither will try to develop a relationship that is suitable for

Negotiations may be based on

- One's own culture
- The counterpart's culture
- Some hybrid of cultures

Business and government officials may mistrust each other and may not understand each other's objectives.

FIGURE 12.4   Culturally Responsive Strategies and Their Feasibility

At each level of familiarity, a negotiator can consider feasible the strategies designated at that level and any lower level.

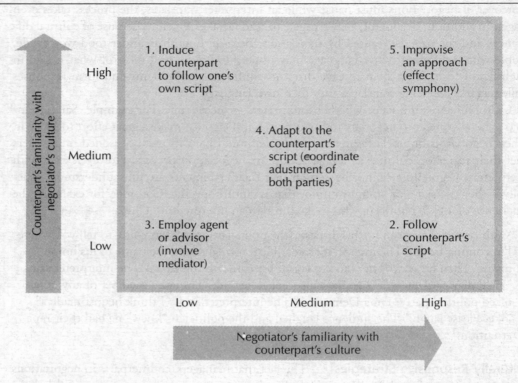

long-term objectives. Negotiators may see their rewards, such as new assignments in other countries, as dependent on immediate results and perhaps expect not to be around to face longer-term issues. Professional conflict has been particularly evident as shown by the many developing countries that have attempted to sell state-owned enterprises to foreign investors. The managers within these enterprises are often suspicious of MNEs, fearful of foreign domination, and worried about job security after privatization.[17]

> Negotiators should find some means to reinstitute future contacts.

Termination of Negotiations   When one or both parties want to terminate consideration of proposals, the method of cessation can be extremely important.[18] It may affect the negotiators' positions with their superiors, who may wonder why their appointed negotiators spent so much time and money on an effort that led to no agreement. Also, the way negotiations end likely will affect future transactions between the parties and their dealings with other organizations, both in that country and elsewhere in the world. Because termination is a tacit admission of failure, negotiators are prone to blame others publicly to save face. Such accusations may complicate future dealings that the country or the company may have with other parties. Fearing adverse consequences from termination, negotiators sometimes drag out the process until a proposal eventually dies unnoticed. When termination is necessary, the parties should find means that allow each to minimize stress, save face, and avoid publicity.

> Role-playing can be used to anticipate others' approaches, but it is hard to simulate stress situations.

Preparation for Negotiations   Role-playing is a valuable technique for projects requiring approval by a foreign government or an agreement with a foreign company. By practicing their own roles and those of the rival negotiators—and by researching the country's culture and history to determine attitudes toward foreign companies—negotiators may be much better able to anticipate responses and plan their own actions.[19]

Role-playing presupposes that the company knows who will negotiate for the other side. Usually, MNEs use a team approach so that people with the necessary range of functional expertise contribute to the negotiations. It is also common to use people at different organizational levels at different points in the negotiations.

One factor not easily simulated is the stress of being away from family and coworkers for an extended period. Because of this factor, the location of negotiations may give one side a significant bargaining advantage. Negotiating in the "home field" helps those managers who can go home at night, eat customary food, and tend to routine office matters. If managers must travel abroad for negotiations, they should budget sufficient time to adjust for jet lag—if not, they increase the risk of making mistakes.[20]

HOME-COUNTRY INVOLVEMENT IN ASSET PROTECTION

Companies fear that foreign countries will appropriate their assets without paying them adequate compensation—as we saw in the matter of Iran's nationalization of its oil industry in the opening profile of Saudi Aramco. These assets include the value of their FDIs as well as intangible assets like patents, trademarks, and copyrights. Consequently, companies press their home-country governments to deal directly with other governments to protect these assets.

Historical Background of Home-Country Protection

Historically, most foreign investment disputes concerned expropriation, particularly in developing countries.[21] As late as the period between the two world wars, home countries used military force and coercion to ensure that host governments gave foreign investors prompt, adequate, and effective compensation in cases of expropriation—this principle is known as the **international standard of fair dealing**.[22] Host countries had little to say about this standard. In conferences attended by developing countries at The Hague in 1930 and at Montevideo in 1933, participants established a treaty stating that, "foreigners may not claim rights other or more extensive than nationals."[23] On the basis of this doctrine, Mexico used its own courts in 1938 to settle disputes arising from expropriation of foreign agricultural properties in 1915.[24] This same treaty formed the precedent for later settlements and—in the absence of specific treaties—still remains in effect.

Two factors have reinforced the principle that home-countries should not intervene militarily to protect investments. The first is a series of supporting UN resolutions. The second is the fact that most expropriations have been selective rather than general; that is, a country may have expropriated the assets of only some companies and, in some cases, not even all of those assets. In these cases, intervention might lead to additional takeovers and jeopardize payment settlements for the companies. As host countries' priorities have shifted toward attracting FDI rather than expropriating it, there has been less concern about home-country intervention to protect investors. Instead, home governments have become more concerned that companies' FDI proposals receive prompt review and fair treatment.[25]

Nevertheless, **dependencia theory** holds that developing countries have practically no power in their dealings with MNEs. This theory contends that forceful, well-run MNEs systematically erode the bargaining power of host countries. When the host country tries to challenge the MNE, the latter calls upon the support of its home governments and local elites to protect its privileged position. Although home-country governments are less apt to provide military intervention, they sometimes use other means to support MNEs, such as trade pressures, aid, and influence with international lending agencies. Although popular in the 1970s and 1980s, dependencia theory is largely out of vogue today.[26] However, the leaders and political parties of some developing countries still endorse those views and use them to delay or prevent MNEs' investments.[27]

The Use of Bilateral Agreements

To improve foreign-investment climates for their MNEs, many industrial countries established bilateral treaties with other countries.[28] Although these agreements differ in detail, they generally provide home-country insurance to investors that allows them to cover losses from expropriation, political violence, government contract cancellation, and currency control—and also to exporters for losses from nonpayment in a convertible currency. For example, the United States offers policies for small companies through the a Small Business Administration (SBA) and for companies in general through the Overseas Private Investment Corporation (OPIC) and Ex-Im Bank. Coverage also is available through private insurers, international agencies such as the World Bank's Multilateral Investment Guarantee Agency (MIGA), and some host-country governments.

The home country, by approving an insurance contract, agrees to settle investors' losses on a government-to-government basis. For example, OPIC provides more than $280 million in political risk insurance coverage to U.S. companies that are engaged in more than 100 projects in the Russian manufacturing, communications, oil field development, and mining sectors.[29] If any of these companies suffer losses because of political risk in Russia, OPIC would reimburse them, and then the U.S. government would seek settlement from Russia. Other types of bilateral agreements include treaties of friendship, commerce, and navigation as well as the prevention of double taxation.

Multilateral Agreements and Settlements: FDI and Trade

When MNEs cannot reach agreement with organizations in a host country, they may agree to have a third party settle the dispute. The International Chamber of Commerce in Paris, the Swedish Chamber of Commerce, and specialized commodity associations in London frequently mediate trade disputes. Because trade transactions are generally between private companies, these disputes do not generate the same publicity as government-to-government or foreign-investment disputes. Government-to-government trade disputes are now largely the domain of the WTO. However, our earlier case on trade relations between the United States and the EU showed that allegations about unfair trade practices are first lodged with a company's home government, which then officially submits the allegations to the WTO.

A notable case of a multilateral settlement on foreign investment took place between the United States and Iran. This case differed from other attempted settlements because each country had large investments in the other's territory. When the two governments froze each other's assets because of political hostilities, Iran had substantially more invested in the United States than the United States had in Iran. The two countries agreed to appoint three arbitrators each to an international tribunal at The Hague, and those six selected three more. Part of the assets the United States had held were set aside for the payment of arbitrated claims, and amounts have been relinquished as Iran has settled with U.S. investors on a case-by-case basis.[30]

The International Center for Settlement of Investment Disputes (ICSID) operates under the auspices of the World Bank and provides parties a forum to submit their disputes. Most bilateral investment treaties designate the ICSID as the arbitration center for disputes or indicate that its rules would be applicable in ad hoc arbitrations.[31] MIGA, of the World Bank, offers insurance against losses from expropriations, war, civil disturbances, currency convertibility, and breach of contract.

Bilateral agreements improve climates for investments abroad.

Multilateral settlements of disputes may be handled by a neutral country or by a group of countries that are not involved.

The WTO is considering expanding its mandate from matters of trade to aspects of investment issues and dispute settlement. Presently, investment disputes can be linked to trade disputes, such as the prohibition of FDI that is necessary to be able to export into a market. However, the WTO is reviewing a parallel program to settle investment disputes that are unrelated to trade. Some developing countries oppose this proposal because of a belief that any such agreement would compromise their ability to determine their development strategy and industrial policy. Resistance may fade, however, if the WTO can link its investor-state dispute settlement procedures to the ICSID.[32]

Multinational Agreements: IPRs

The poet and essayist Ralph Waldo Emerson said, "If a man can write a better book, preach a better sermon, or make a better mousetrap than his neighbor, though he builds his house in the woods, the world will make a beaten path to his door." But if someone else can easily copy the better book, sermon, or mousetrap, the number of people beating a path to the door of the inventor will fall. Thus far, much of this chapter has looked at the bargaining relationship between governments and MNEs over the terms of FDI. However, business-government and government-to-government conflicts increasingly arise over the idea of intellectual property (IP) and the rights to its use, or intellectual property rights (IPRs).[33]

IP is the creative ideas, innovative expertise, and intangible insights that give an individual, company, or country a competitive advantage. An IPR is the legal right granted to persons that allows them to determine the use of their ideas and creations. Thus, for example, the registered owner of a copyright has the right to say who gets to copy it or who gets to use it for what purpose. IPRs are a legally enforceable but limited monopoly, granted by a country to an innovator. An IPR specifies the period during which others may not copy the innovator's idea, thereby allowing him or her to commercialize it in order to recoup initial investments and capture potential profits.

IPRs cover both industrial property, such as inventions and distinctive identifications of companies and products, as well as artistic property, such as books, recordings, films, and computer programs. Companies that own intangible assets want protection through enforceable patents, trademarks, and copyrights so that they may gain potential sales and profits. They argue that the social benefit of IPRs is positive because otherwise there would be little incentive to develop new industrial and artistic property. Others counter that IPRs hurt the welfare of society; they reason that unrestricted access to an innovation would greatly benefit all countries. Critics add that protecting IP lets owners charge monopoly prices that impose high costs on society. Some developing countries use these arguments to restrict the patent rights of products, like pharmaceuticals and software, so that they can make more affordable copies.[34]

Countries differ substantially in the laws that they pass and enforce to protect IP. Generally, developing countries offer weaker legal protection than do industrial countries.[35] Historically, few of their companies have created substantial intangible assets. Consequently, most developing countries have little to gain if their governments protect IPRs vigorously. In addition, the weak protection of IP lets local companies make low-price copies of products without making payments to companies that own the IPR.

Even when two countries institute similar levels of legal protection, they may use different methods to enforce their policies.[36] For example, U.S. patent applications are strictly confidential and are usually granted within two years. In contrast, Japanese applications are public and are granted in four-to-six years. Because of different national approaches to IPRs, both companies and countries have stakes in any international agreement. The GATT agreement from the Uruguay Round provides for IPR reciprocity—a country must grant to foreigners the same property rights available to its own citizens.

International treaties and agreements help safeguard patents, trademarks, and copyrights.

Pharmaceuticals and Intellectual Property Rights

Illegal copying of pharmaceutical products has been rampant for decades around the world. Local manufacturers routinely copy and market medicines that MNEs have invented, such as antibiotics and cancer drugs. They then sell these copies at steeply discounted prices because they do not need to recoup the high costs of research and development.

Although companies lose millions of dollars in revenues from counterfeit medicines, many people argue that copying is justified in some circumstances because it gives poor people access to vital medicines—indeed, in most low-income countries, health spending is often less than $10 per person per year.[37] For example, at the start of 2003, an estimated 42 million people worldwide—38.6 million adults and 3.2 million children younger than 15 years—were living with HIV/AIDS. The developing world is home to more than 90 percent of the global total. A growing number of activists, charities, and governments are challenging pharmaceutical companies over the high cost of their AIDS drugs in the developing world.[38] Current treatment of this disease relies on a triple drug combination therapy that costs about $10,000 a year in the United States. The same drugs can be obtained from generic producers in developing countries for as little as $300.[39]

The terms of patent and intellectual property laws on patented medicines authorizes governments and organizations like the WTO to sanction countries that permit local companies to make unlicensed copies of the patented drugs. However, the growing number of ill people in need of medicine in developing countries puts an increasingly brighter spotlight on the ethical implications of the right of drug companies to determine the distribution and price of their products.

As the AIDS crisis grows, developing countries have put more pressure on the WTO to modify its Trade-Related Aspects of Intellectual Property Rights (TRIPS) accord—the primary source of intellectual property protection for MNEs. Presently, TRIPS states that the production of cheaper, generic versions of a patented drug can take place without the prior consent of the patent holder only "in national emergencies or other circumstances of extreme urgency." However, developing countries want the WTO to relax this condition to let them to buy drugs for greatly reduced prices or simply manufacture cheaper, generic versions themselves.[40]

Relaxing TRIPS would weaken the intellectual property rights of pharmaceutical companies. These companies have replied that accepting this proposal would deprive them the revenues they need to support research and development to combat disease—as their managers point out, medicines do not invent themselves. Some commentators have proposed that consumers in industrial countries pay higher prices for medicines in order to finance lower priced medicines in poorer countries. Drug companies, however, worry about "parallel trade," whereby drugs sold cheaply in developing countries would make their way back to higher-priced markets through back channels. In either case, the threat of weaker protection of their intellectual property has led some drug companies to warn that developing countries—not the pharmaceutical companies—could be the biggest losers if TRIPS is changed. Observed the director-general of the International Federation of Pharmaceutical Manufacturers Associations, "The world needs to decide where it wants pharmaceutical companies to put their R&D. There are lots of diseases with currently ineffective treatments where they could put their money instead."[41]

Patents   The first major attempt to achieve cross-national cooperation in the protection of patents, trademarks, and other property rights was the Paris Convention of 1883 for the Protection of Industrial Property. Since then, the Paris Convention has been periodically revised.[42] This convention led to the International Bureau for the Protection of Industrial Property Rights (BIRPI). BIRPI grants reciprocity to foreigners whose countries are Convention members. A second major provision of the Paris Convention is that a patent registration in one country entitles the company to a grace period of protection before it registers it in other member countries. After registration, there is a transition period, during which the patent holder must use the patent within the market. If the patent holder fails to use it, then the country may grant the patent rights to another party.[43]

Three important contemporary cross-national patent agreements are the Patent Cooperation Treaty (PCT) of the World Intellectual Property Organization (WIPO), the European Patent Convention (EPC), and the EEC Patent Convention. The PCT and EPC allow companies first to make a uniform patent search and application, and then to apply for patents in all signatory countries.

Patent-infringement battles are both costly and complex and may take years to settle. For example, Gemstar-TV Guide International hired more than 170 lawyers from 18 firms to present its patent dispute to the International Trade Commission.[44] Internationally, the rapid development of technology coupled with varying patent regulations in different countries make it difficult to manage patent rights.[45] Companies usually change their patents from country to country to meet local needs, and patent infringement is often hard to prove. For example, a company in one country, where there is no patent protection on pharmaceuticals, could manufacture a drug patented by a company in the United States and sell it anywhere in the world. If the U.S. company were to file suit, it must then prove patent infringement in that particular country. Despite the challenge of finding proof in the country where the alleged infringement occurred, the company may run into unbeatable exceptions. For example, Indian patent law regarding pharmaceuticals protects only the processes by which drugs are made, not the drugs themselves. Therefore, Indian companies can make drugs that are under patent in other countries, provided they use a process that is different from the original.[46]

Trademarks   Companies invest huge sums to develop brand names. If a trademark is unable to protect the brand name, then other companies may sell similar products with the same brand name. For example, New Zealand growers began marketing what they called Chinese gooseberries as kiwifruit in the 1960s, but they neglected to register the trademark. Now companies from many countries market "kiwifruit."[47]

Even if a brand name has a trademark, it may become generic in some countries because it takes on the name of a product rather than a brand. The name then enters the public domain. For example, the name Swiss army knife is actually a foreign trademark that has become a generic term in the United States. Similarly, because the Japanese have no name for vulcanized rubber, they call it "goodyear," a name derived from the "Goodyear Tire & Rubber Company." Sometimes the issue of what is generic is decided in bilateral agreements. For example, the United States and the EU agreed that bourbon and Tennessee whiskey were names that only U.S. distillers could use, whereas Scotch whiskey, Irish whiskey, Cognac, Armagnac, Calvados, and Brandy de Jerez belong to regions of Europe.[48] Novel trademark disputes also emerge. For example, MNEs like Wal-Mart and Yahoo! ran into trademark problems in Canada, Mexico, and Puerto Rico with cybersquatting—the preemptive registration of Internet domain names that use other parties' trademarks with the intent of selling the domain name back to the trademark owner or to others.[49]

Cross-national cooperation for trademark protection is exemplified in the Trademark Registration Treaty.[50] Commonly known as the Vienna Convention, this treaty states that a company must use a trademark within three years of registering it internationally. Once the trademark has been registered internationally, each country in the treaty must accept it or provide grounds for refusal within 15 months after its registration so that the company will have time to act before the three-year period expires. Between the time a company registers a trademark and the time it enters a foreign country, another company may begin to use the trademark in that country. The first company using it can then delay or prevent entry of the original trademark holder.

Copyrights   Most large publishing and recording companies have extensive interests in foreign competitive markets. Without international copyright laws, a foreign producer could copy a book, software, CD, DVD, or film and then distribute it at cut-rate prices in the country in which it was first produced. The Universal Copyright Convention (UCC) and the Berne Convention, the major cross-national agreements, honor the copyright laws of their signatory countries. Member of WIPO now extend copyright coverage to material on the Internet.

Not all countries offer effective protection to IPRs.

Piracy   Not all countries formally support the various conventions that protect IPRs. Moreover, some countries enforce the agreements arbitrarily. Even if the rules are enforced, the penalties may be too trivial to deter violations. For example, a repeat trademark counterfeiter in the United Kingdom, whose illicit profits were estimated at $5 million, received a three-month jail sentence.[51] Technically, the terms *piracy* and *counterfeiting* describe the production of a product without the formal consent of the company that holds the patent, trademark, or copyright. The price of piracy is enormous. This chapter's closing case on global software piracy notes the exorbitant costs of piracy within just one industry. More generally, the International Anti-Counterfeiting Coalition estimates that international trade in counterfeit products runs as high as $500 billion a year—or about 9 percent of the value of all world trade.[52]

Several conditions promote piracy. Operationally, various technologies allow copyrighted material to be reproduced cheaply and without loss of quality. National attitudes can encourage piracy. Some countries offer little protection for certain products. For example, Microsoft took over the National Theater in Bucharest one evening to launch Office 2000 Professional, which had gone on sale that day in Romanian stores for $300 to $400. As the audience watched a big-screen video sales presentation by Microsoft CEO Bill Gates, hawkers on the street in front of the theater were selling counterfeit copies of Office 2000 for $2 to $3.[53] Finally, many people have few moral qualms about pirating a product or buying counterfeit goods. Observed the executive director of the Software Publishers Association, "It's ironic that people who would never think about stealing a candy bar from a drugstore seem to have no qualms about copying a $500 software package."[54]

Consumers can gain and lose from counterfeiting. Sometimes they get good-quality merchandise with a prestige label for a fraction of the price of the legitimate product. Also, counterfeit goods enable some consumers to flaunt a fake product—even if it fools few as being genuine, such as a $15 counterfeit Rolex watch.[55] However, piracy has high costs and extreme risks. Shoddy or even dangerous merchandise is frequently substituted for the original goods. For example, the World Health Organization counted 771 cases of counterfeit medicines, most of which contained little or none of the active ingredients; in fact, in some cases, the active ingredients had been replaced by lethal poisons.[56] Ultimately, if quality brands are routinely undersold by their faked counterparts, there is little incentive for companies to innovate or nurture brand recognition.

Various manufacturers' associations have emerged around the world to combat piracy. These associations propose greater border surveillance, stiffer penalties for dealing in counterfeit goods, and cessation of aid to countries that do not join and adhere to international agreements. The WTO has taken over the international property rights administration from WIPO, making enforcement more effective. It allows countries to impose trade sanctions on countries that do not protect IPRs. Many companies successfully track down violators and initiate legal actions. Still, companies struggle to prove infringement when the violations are slight changes on trademarks or product models. In response, more companies protect their products through high-tech devices, using deterrents like holographic images or microchip tags.[57] Some take even more aggressive approaches. Vuitton, a French luggage manufacturer plagued by counterfeiters, uses a withdrawal strategy. It originally sold its products through independent retailers, but now it sells registered and numbered goods only in company-owned stores. Other companies vigorously warn the public of imitations and advise consumers on how to discern the genuine product—for example, Microsoft set up an antipiracy Web site.[58]

LOOKING TO THE FUTURE

New Roles for Diplomacy in the New Century

Probably the most significant factor influencing possible change in business-government diplomacy is the end of the Cold War, which pitted the communist and noncommunist blocs against each other for nearly half a century. During that period, governments tended to influence business activities because of political-military objectives, sometimes protecting their home-based companies to gain or maintain spheres of influence abroad and sometimes withholding support for fear it might lead an otherwise neutral country to support its foe. But political schisms are not yet a thing of the past, so managers must continue to contend with government-to-government animosities when planning international expansion strategies.

New alignments of countries based on economic factors may well replace some of the political-military rivalries of the recent past. For example, a new economic rivalry between North America and Asia may become as intense as the old political rivalry between the communist and noncommunist blocs. Companies may still have to satisfy national interests in their operations to the same degree as before. In the short term, it appears as if most countries will welcome foreign companies' operations or at least take a laissez-faire attitude toward them because of a belief that, on balance, foreign investment serves the countries' national economic interests. However, there are likely to be many exceptions; for example, India and South Korea traditionally have not welcomed wholly owned foreign operations. Another exception centers on the privatization of state-owned enterprises, for which prospective buyers must negotiate on much more than the price.

Historically, there have been broad swings in host-country attitudes toward private ownership, especially foreign ownership. The present appreciation for FDI could easily reverse, particularly if governments feel their own stakeholders are receiving an unfair share of global economic benefits. For example, Sri Lanka has passed legislation to allow the renationalization of privatized companies in cases in which new owners fail to manage them successfully.[59] Regardless of the direction national policies take, companies are likely to face ever more informed and experienced government officials whenever those companies negotiate their operating terms.

Government-to-government cooperation in the effort to regulate MNEs is apt to develop slowly, at least on a global scale. There are simply too many competing interests among countries that tend to divide them on issues of economic development, product-specific agendas, and regional viewpoints. One such issue is the protection of intellectual property—such protection pits the interests of industrial countries, which create most of the products that can be patented, trademarked, or copyrighted, against the interests of many developing countries, which feel they are overcharged for their use and constrained in their application. Countries may collectively cease trade with countries that do not protect IPRs.

COLLECTIVE ACTIONS TO DEAL WITH INTERNATIONAL COMPANIES

Collective attitudes toward MNE activities

- Are clarified by a number of organizations
- Are usually fairly vague
- Involve voluntary compliance
- May make it easier for countries to legislate policies

The preceding discussion dealt primarily with companies' concerns about governments' actions (or lack of actions) to protect their tangible and intangible assets. Likewise, governments are apprehensive about MNEs' actions. Collectively, they have tried to regulate them as well as issue guidelines of expected behavior.

The League of Nations made the first widespread attempt to regulate international companies on a multilateral basis in 1929. Then the attention focused on foreign exploitation of the tropical commodities industry. However, the Great Depression derailed this effort. There have been several more attempts since World War II to regulate companies. Among them were the International Trade Organization (ITO) of 1948, which never became operative, the attempts in 1951 by the UN Economic and Social Council (ECOSOC) to regulate antitrust, and the 1961 Code for Liberalization of Capital Movements established by the OECD. The different interests of industrial and developing countries prevented most of these attempts from significantly affecting MNEs' operations.

In 1975, the United Nations created the Center on Transnational Corporations to address the concerns of many developing countries. The Center collects information on MNEs' activities, represents a forum for publicizing common grievances, and has proposed several codes of conduct for MNEs. The OECD, which is composed of industrial countries, approved its own code in 1976. The codes of both organizations are necessarily vague in order to accommodate the various interests of the different countries as well as groups within them. Similarly, the United States issued a voluntary code for foreign operations of U.S. companies. This code calls for companies operating abroad to provide a safe workplace, recognize the rights of workers to organize, and not manufacture with either forced or child labor. It also directs companies to document their positive achievements in the workplace.[60]

NGOs and industry associations have instituted a number of codes dealing with specific practices (e.g., infant formula sales and environmental practices), with specific areas of the world (e.g., employment practices in northern Mexico and Northern Ireland), or with specific industries (e.g., the International Council of Toy Makers' code to provide good working conditions and avoid the use of child labor[61]). These codes are voluntary; adoption does not guarantee enforcement. However, they symbolize a collective attitude toward specific business practices that helps governments regulate the local activities of MNEs.

CORPORATE CITIZENSHIP AND PUBLIC RELATIONS

Companies publicize good-citizenship activities, pointing out when

- Business conduct satisfies social objectives
- Nonbusiness functions help society

Many companies believe that behaving as good corporate citizens abroad will reduce local animosities and defuse concerns that might affect their short- or long-term competitiveness. Figure 12.5 illustrates this belief humorously. Some companies, like Shell, General Electric, and Sony, have published their own codes of conduct. These actions may prove insufficient, however, because employees, government officials, consumers, and other groups may overlook or misunderstand the positive effects of the company's international operations.

Because of conflicting pressures from different groups, someone can always accuse an MNE of questionable behavior. For instance, if an MNE offers higher wages, someone may accuse it of stimulating inflation and of raiding workers from rivals. If an MNE pays only the going wage, someone may accuse it of exploiting workers. Therefore, understanding the power of the competing groups that it serves in a country prepares the MNE to practice policies that benefit those groups. Within any given economy, there is usually a range of prices the market will pay, wages that workers will accept, and returns that companies normally earn on investments. An MNE may, for example, offer premium wage rates or earn superior

FIGURE 12.5 Improving Performance Through Socially Responsible Behavior

Doonesbury

BY GARRY TRUDEAU

Critics have staged protests against Nike's use of contractors in foreign countries who pay their employees low wages. The Doonesbury cartoon parodies the good performance that can result from such protests.

Source: DOONESBURY © G.B. Trudeau. Reprinted with permission of UNIVERSAL PRESS SYNDICATE. All rights reserved.

investment returns that are comparable to other prominent companies in the country without leading to accusations that it is guilty of disruptive practices—and it can still satisfy workers, stockholders, communities, and markets.

The theologian Saint Augustine recounted in the fifth century that in his youth, he used to pray, "Give me chastity and continence, but not yet." Like Saint Augustine, many companies try to postpone public relations efforts as long as possible. Often a company's public relations efforts are defensive; it simply reacts to public criticism. Once a company appears defensive, however, these efforts may prove to be too little, too late. The CEO of Levi-Strauss explained, "In today's world, an exposé on working conditions on *60 Minutes* can undo years of effort to build brand loyalty." To head off possible criticism about its suppliers' labor practices, Levi-Strauss terminated contracts in China and Peru and worked with suppliers to improve their practices in Turkey and Bangladesh. Not only did Levi-Strauss prevent criticism, but the publicity about its revised policies also earned it goodwill.[62]

Most companies work to attract supporters and preempt potential criticism. They survey customers and workers to allay misconceptions and anticipate criticism, thereby preempting more damaging accusations. Many MNEs use advocacy publicity at home and abroad to win support for their activities. For example, the pharmaceutical industry is waging a worldwide advocacy campaign, trying to convince people that any weakening of patent rights will harm the research and development of new medicines.[63] Such publicity may take the form of newspaper and magazine ads, reports, and films showing the positive effects a company's activities have had on home- and host-country societies.

Although not always possible to dispel criticism from abroad, an MNE can do several things to mitigate it. One may be as fundamental as having the managers from the parent company continue an existing policy. On the question of what to centralize and what to decentralize, there is much to be said for authorizing local managers to decide policies concerning local customs and social matters. On such sensitive issues as employment and worker output, changes should be made after consulting stakeholders. Headquarters personnel also may serve a useful public relations function locally. Their higher professional status, relative to local managers, may lead to better reception by government authorities.

An MNE also may encourage local participation in order both to reduce its image of foreignness and to develop local proponents whose personal objectives may be enriched by the company's continued operations. The parent company can assist the development of local suppliers, establish stock option plans, and gradually replace home-country personnel with local nationals. Taken to an extreme, however, local participation can result in the host country's becoming less dependent on the foreign company. Therefore, the company's strategy might be to reserve some resources so that the company remains essential to the host country.

The MNE might increase the number of local proponents by

- Sharing ownership
- Avoiding direct confrontation
- Local management
- Local R&D

For instance, a home-country R&D laboratory could direct new-product development, whereas the host-country R&D facility could supervise adaptations for the local market.

Some companies have taken on additional social functions to build local support and enhance their performance.[64] For example, Xerox supported a school in South Africa, Citibank participated in a reforestation program in the Philippines, and McDonald's sponsored a telethon in Australia to raise funds for disabled children. Merck, Novartis, and Pfizer donated drugs to fight river blindness, leprosy, and trachoma in Africa. Volvo awards an annual prize for the outstanding global innovation or discovery in the environmental field. GM publishes a public-interest report to highlight its efforts in a wide array of activities, such as environmental cleanup programs in Mexico and Eastern Europe, cancer research, AIDS education, and the global celebration of Earth Day.[65]

Good corporate citizenship and corporate publicity may not be enough to guarantee successful business practices. If public opinion is against foreign private ownership in general, all foreign companies lose. For a company doing business as a key firm in a key sector, criticisms may come from so many directions that the company's defense gradually weaken. Even in these extreme cases, a company's public affairs department may begin by identifying the worst problem areas. Advance planning can lead the company to establish policies that prevent or minimize losses, including reducing reinvestment, selling ownership to local governments or another company, and shifting into less salient local businesses.

Occasionally, an MNE may need to be resolute in its dealings with a government, even when its adversarial position becomes public. It may have a strong bargaining position, or it may perceive that compromises will weaken its bargaining relationship with other governments. Even in these instances, however, the MNE should try to preserve the legitimacy of the government, ensuring that it does not lose face over the outcome. Over time, as our opening case on Saudi Aramco showed, negotiating advantages ebb and flow between countries and companies.

Summary

- Although host countries and MNEs may hold resources that, if combined, could achieve objectives for both, conflict may cause one or both parties to regulate those resources, preventing the optimal performance of international business activities.

- Both MNE managers and host-country government officials must respond to interest groups that may perceive different advantages or no advantage at all to the business-government relationship. Therefore, the relationship's outcome may not be the one expected from a purely economic viewpoint.

- Negotiations play a more important role in determining the terms under which a company may enter and operate in a foreign country. This negotiating process is similar to the domestic processes of company acquisition and collective bargaining.

- The major differences in the international sphere are the much larger number of provisions, the general lack of fixed time duration for an agreement, and cultural differences among negotiators.

- The terms under which an MNE may operate in a given country will depend on how much the company needs the country and vice versa. As needs evolve over time, new terms of operation might alter an MNE's bargaining strength.

- Generally, a company's best bargaining position is before it makes an investment. Once it commits resources to the foreign operation, the company may not be able to move elsewhere easily.

- Often, host countries and MNEs renegotiate the terms of operations after the latter has begun local operations. A typical cause for renegotiations is the gradual shift of bargaining power from the MNE to the host country, a shift that is known as the theory of the obsolescing bargain.

- Because international negotiations occur largely between parties whose cultures, educational backgrounds, and expectations differ, it may be difficult for these negotiators to understand each other's sentiments and present convincing arguments. Role-playing offers negotiators a means of anticipating responses and planning an approach to the actual bargaining.

- Historically, industrial countries have used military intervention and coercion to ensure that host countries honored the terms it had negotiated with their investors. A series of international resolutions have replaced these methods for settling disputes. Recently, developed countries have used the promise of giving or withholding loans and aid and the threat of trade sanctions.

- Most countries have established bilateral treaties in which host countries agree to compensate investors for losses from expropriation and civil disturbances.

- Independent international organizations frequently arbitrate trade disputes. These organizations rarely settle investment disputes, however, because governments like to control what occurs within their borders.

- International agreements seek to protect important intangible property such as patents, trademarks, and copyrights. Because companies often spend millions of dollars to develop this property, worldwide protection is crucial to them.

- A big problem for companies has been the pirating of intangible assets in countries that have not signed international agreements or that do not actively enforce their own laws on the protection of IPRs.

- Companies use public relations to develop a good image, overcome a bad one, and create useful proponents for their positions.

CASE

Global Software Piracy[66]

I prowl the aisles of the software piracy mother lode, the Golden Shopping Arcade in Hong Kong's Sham Shui Po district. All around me in the basement of this dingy, block-long urban warehouse, eager shoppers paw through the bins and tables of the densely packed stalls. Inside a stall called the Everything CD shop, I buy the first of my installer discs, Volume 2. This tribute to pirate technology costs the same as all the other CD-ROMs at Golden Arcade, about 9 bucks or three for US$25. Incredibly, this disc has 86 programs on it, each compressed with a self-extracting installation utility. Volume 2 has a beta copy of Windows 95 as well as OS/2 Warp, CorelDraw! 5, Quicken 4.0, Atari Action Pack for Windows, Norton Commander, KeyCad, Adobe Premier, Microsoft Office, and dozens of other applications, including a handful written in Chinese.

Connoisseurs of the genre compare the different versions of the installer discs like fine wines. Someone from Microsoft later tells me that the retail value of the disc is between US$20,000 and US$35,000.[67]

As this account dramatizes, software technology is dogged by the problem of digital piracy—the illegal distribution and/or copying of software for personal or business use. Software piracy can range from an individual making an unauthorized copy of a software product for use, sale, or free distribution to a company's mismanagement of its software licenses. Technically, the standards of software piracy are clear. The United States, for example, stipulates that software is automatically protected by federal copyright law from the moment of its creation. Officially, Title 17 of the U.S. Copyright Act

grants the owner of the copyright "the exclusive rights" to "reproduce the copyrighted work" and "to distribute copies . . . of the copyrighted work" (Section 106). It also states that "anyone who violates any of the exclusive rights of the copyright owner . . . is an infringer of the copyright" (Section 501), and the statute sets forth several penalties for violations.

Ignorance of the law is no excuse for piracy; copiers are liable for the resulting copyright infringement whether or not they knew their conduct violated federal law. Thus, a software user who has purchased a license has the right to load the product onto a single computer and to make another copy for "archival purposes only."

The predicament of software is that, like any 'digital' product, it is extraordinarily easy to duplicate into a copy that is usually as good as the original. Consequently, piracy and counterfeiting plague the global software industry. The Business Software Alliance (BSA) and Software Publishers Association estimated that approximately 45 percent of new business software was pirated worldwide from 1994 through 1997. This piracy cost the software industry almost $50 billion in lost revenue. Table 12.1 reports the worldwide software piracy rate for the past several years.

Companies, industry associations, and governments have tried to negotiate practical solutions. Until recently, combating piracy problems was normally done by first relying on software companies to develop technical and business measures to thwart counterfeiters. Governments would then support these efforts by passing laws to specify punishments for lawbreakers.

● TABLE 12.1

WORLDWIDE SOFTWARE PIRACY RATE (PERCENT OF SOFTWARE THAT IS COPIED ILLEGALLY)

WORLDWIDE SOFTWARE PIRACY RATES, 1994–2000	
1994	49 percent
1995	46 percent
1996	43 percent
1997	40 percent
1998	38 percent
1999	36 percent
2000	37 percent

Source: Business Software Alliance, "2000 Global Software Piracy Study" (November 6, 2002): http://www.bsa.org/resources/2001-05-21.55.pdf.

For example, in the 1980s, many software companies incorporated anticopying mechanisms into their products. Although these aggressive mechanisms were largely effective, consumers complained that they made the software unduly difficult to use. Consumer objections led the software industry to discontinue these sorts of anticopying technologies. In response, software companies developed other means to protect against piracy, such as distribution business models (i.e., site-licenses and shrink-wrap licenses) and technological protections (i.e., passwords, registration numbers, encryption, and dongles). Although somewhat annoyed, customers generally accepted these methods.

Software companies successfully lobbied governments to pass and enforce supportive laws. For example, in 1993, the United States elevated software piracy from a misdemeanor to a felony if 10 or more illegal copies of software were made within a six-month period and if the copies were worth a total value of over $2,500. The United States also got more vigorous in its enforcement efforts. The United States has threatened China with trade sanctions based on findings of especially "onerous and egregious" intellectual property practices in China.

Industry associations, notably the BSA, Software and Information Industry Association (SIIA), and the International Anti-Counterfeiting Coalition (IACC), are multinational organizations that provide global services in government relations, business development, corporate education, and intellectual property protection. BSA, for example, formed in 1988, has members in more than 70 nations. Each national unit works to promote a legal online world by negotiating with governments and consumers in the international software and Internet markets. BSA members include companies like Microsoft, Adobe, Dell, IBM, Intel, Apple Computer, Intuit, and Macromedia.

Companies, governments, and associations, singly and jointly, successfully lobbied transnational institutions to help police piracy. The 170 member nations of WIPO pledged to protect intellectual property worldwide and administer several intellectual property treaties. WIPO continued to lobby members to ratify antipiracy treaties—the World Copyright Treaty (WCT) and the WIPO Performances and Phonograms Treaty (WPPT). Similarly, the WTO enacted the agreement on TRIPS to end copyright violations and counterfeiting by requiring all member nations to protect and enforce intellectual property rights. Enacted in 1995, TRIPS was at the time most comprehensive agreement on intellectual property.

Collectively, actions by companies, association, governments, and institutions testified to the usefulness of market-based solutions to software piracy. Most important, from the view of entrepreneurial software companies, practical solutions developed by them preempted the need for governments to formulate and enforce antipiracy standards and technologies.

GROWING SUCCESS

Indications from the mid-1990s testified to the effectiveness of these approaches. In 1994, the global piracy rate for PC business software was 49 percent—essentially, one of every two software applications installed in the world was pirated. Some regions, notably Asia, Eastern Europe, and the Middle East, reported piracy rates between 70 and 85 percent. However, the global piracy rate by 1999 had fallen to 36 percent. Software piracy in the Middle East, in Latin America, and in the Asia/Pacific region had declined 20 percentage points between 1994 and 1999. Western Europe saw an almost equally dramatic reduction in piracy rates, going from 52 percent in 1994 to 34 percent in 1999. North America, the leading software consumer, reported a piracy rate of 25 percent; this rate had declined six percentage points since 1994. Map 12.2 reports regional software piracy rates.

Several reasons suggested continuing decline in global software piracy. At the very least, it looked as if piracy rates were directly related to market growth. The large and mature U.S. and Canadian software market had the lowest rate of piracy, thereby implying that as software markets in other regions matured, piracy rates would also decline. Also, concerted political and company action seem to make a big difference. Specifically, many linked declining software piracy to many factors, including:

- the growing global reach of software companies.
- high profile legal proceedings against companies using illegal software.
- increased government cooperation in providing legal protection for intellectual property and in criminalizing software piracy.
- the narrowing gap between the price of legal and illegal versions as the legal prices of software declined significantly.

MAP 12.2 Worldwide Software Piracy Rates in 2000 by Region

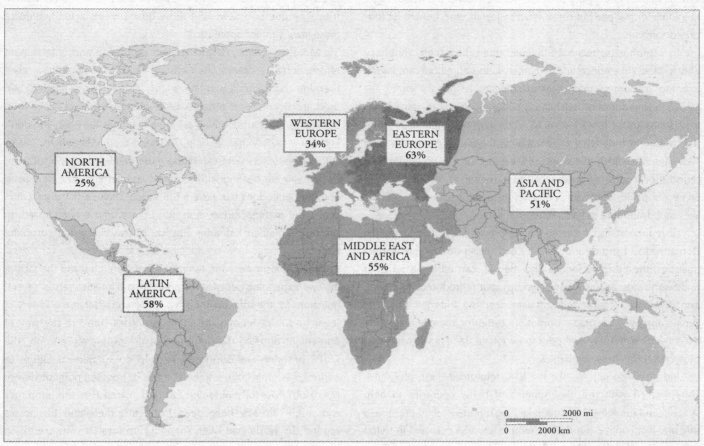

Software piracy is a significant problem around the world at the start of the twenty-first century. Regional piracy rates show high rates of software theft in all regions of the world.

Source: Business Software Alliance, 2000 Global Software Piracy Study (November 6, 2002): http://www.bsa.org/resources/2001-05-21.55.pdf.

- the increased availability of user support for software products in more foreign markets.
- the efforts of the leading software associations to negotiate trade agreements that were tougher on piracy.

Stakeholders in the software industry pushed for better protection and enforcement. In 1998, the U.S. government, assisted by various software industry associations, launched a new initiative to fight global piracy. The Office of the U.S. Trade Representative notified all countries of its mission to ensure both the legitimate use of software and adherence to international agreements. Similarly, the U.S. Congress passed the Digital Millennium Copyright Act (DMCA) in 1998; this act was the most comprehensive reform of the copyright law in the United States in a generation. The DMCA made it a criminal offense to circumvent antipiracy measures built into most commercial software; it also outlawed the manufacture, sale, or distribution of licensing code-cracking devices.

THE UPTICK

In 2001, industry groups reported that software piracy had increased in 2000—worldwide software piracy rate rose to 37 percent from 36 percent in 1999. The rise was systemic—software counterfeiting worsened from Asia to South America to Eastern Europe. Piracy now cost software companies $12 billion in annual revenue, roughly 15 percent of the software industry's $80 billion in worldwide sales.

The unexpected uptick in software piracy was alarming, given the recent push for more vigilance, tougher laws and treaties, and aggressive protection and enforcement. Some linked the uptick to market conditions—the hectic growth of the global economy spurred demand for business and consumer software, whether genuine or fake. Others linked it to the fact that organized software piracy—fueled by the Internet, organized crime, and rampant corruption—had become a multibillion-dollar industry. Whatever the cause, few thought this was temporary uptick. High-tech and law enforcement experts warned of growing piracy as people around the world, eager to join the digital age but constrained by low income, hunted for low-priced software.

In response, software companies intensified their antipiracy efforts. Many, like Adobe and Symantec, launched global campaigns, warning consumers that copying software is illegal. Some, like Microsoft, hired former federal and police investigators, staged software stings, relayed information to prosecutors on hundreds of criminal cases, and took legal action against thousands of law-breaking Web sites. Most firms added security features, such as holograms and registration codes, to document the authenticity of the software. Some companies used search engines to prowl the Internet, seeking sites that distributed or sold pirated software.

Governments also increased their efforts. In the United States, the Departments of Justice and Treasury and their primary investigative agencies, the Customs Service and the FBI, carried out a series of raids worldwide against "warez" groups that reproduced, modified, and distributed counterfeit software over the Internet. The U.S. Senate approved the Trade Promotion Authority, thereby giving the Executive Branch more authority to negotiate trade agreements that protected technology companies.

Industry associations, like the BSA, reinforced these programs. They worked with the governments of many countries to help develop and implement the necessary legal framework to promote a safe and legal online world. For example, the BSA persisted in trying to persuade officials in Mexico, Italy, and Hong Kong, among others, to get tougher on piracy. In addition, several software associations recommended that the United States place 58 countries on a "Special 301" list because of their lack of rules protecting intellectual property rights, their failure to follow vigorous enforcement actions against software theft, and their noncompliance with the WTO's TRIPS agreement.

These harder-hitting programs did show elements of success. For example, China, in connection with its accession to the WTO, amended its patent law in 2000 and its trademark and copyright laws in 2001 to make them more compliant with the TRIPS agreement. Officials in other countries, such as Costa Rica, Korea, Oman, and the Philippines, initiated or expanded antipiracy programs.

Nonetheless, observers saw that the global cat-and-mouse contest between software companies and pirates could potentially spiral out of control. Skeptics said that good intentions only went so far. That is, China had vowed to protect intellectual property, while other countries, such as Hong Kong, Malaysia, and Korea, had signed major copyright treaties. However, the president of the IACC observed, "On paper, the laws and penalties are stiffer in many countries. The question now: Will those governments actually enforce those laws? I'm not optimistic."

More worrisome, despite greater protection and enforcement efforts, software pirates often evaded capture. They easily cracked licensing codes, duplicated holograms, falsified e-mail headers, and used anonymous post office boxes. Noted an observer, "Like drug trafficking, the counterfeiting problem is so massive [that] you don't know how to get a handle on it. The bandits are everywhere." Worse still, counterfeiters were exhibiting more managerial sophistication, "When you are dealing with high-end counterfeits, you are talking about organizations that have a full supply chain, a full distribution chain, full manufacturing tools all in place, and it is all based on profits," explained Katharine Bostick, Microsoft's senior corporate attorney.

The pervasiveness and tenacity of software piracy in the face of an ever-expanding set of laws, policies, and treaties raised several questions for the software industry. Some worried that the variety of legal traditions among the many countries stood in the way of agreement on even the definition of the problem. Certainly, the TRIPS program was supposed to help do so. But its failure to address the impact of the Internet made it, from the point of view of Microsoft, "woefully outdated." Others feared that the antipiracy war might already have been lost; consumers and businesses around the world had been snapping up pirated software for so long that they might not see anything wrong with it. Similarly, others thought that millions of software users saw piracy as simply their only way to deal with Western corporations that charged exorbitant prices for an instrumental means of economic development. All in all, software makers found it increasingly difficult to stay ahead of software piracy.

QUESTIONS

1. What has been the relationship among the various organizations combating software piracy?
2. In your opinion, should software companies, industry associations, home governments, or transnational institutions take the lead in negotiating with the governments of countries with high piracy rates? Why?
3. Can the software industry expect to move forward without resorting to government-devised standards in the area of antipiracy technologies?
4. What sorts of solutions can the software industry plan to apply to the piracy problem if the problem steadily worsens?

CultureQuest™

VIDEO: GLOBAL BUSINESS AND ETHICS

This chapter discussed how ethics and diplomacy impact global business. Based on viewing the accompanying video, and materials in the chapter, please answer the following questions:

1. How does the local culture in a country influence business negotiations and ethical standards?
2. What strategies have companies developed and adopted to perform as good global corporate citizens? Do these strategies differ from country to country?
3. What is the impact of corruption on global business? How do countries and companies address this issue? What strategies might they also consider to deal with corruption?

Chapter Notes

1 Data for the case were taken from Louis Morano, "Multinationals and Nation-States: The Case of Aramco," *Orbis* (Summer 1979): 447–68; "Aramco Has Been the Bridge Between Two Nations," *The Oil Daily* (September 18, 1989): B19; Richard J. Barnet and John Cavanaugh, *Global Dreams: Imperil Corporations and the New World Order* (New York: Simon & Schuster, 1994); Mark Emond, "FTC Okays Biggest R&M Merger," *National Petroleum News* (February 1998): 13; Anthony Cave Brown, *A History of Aramco and the Royal House of Saud* (Boston: Houghton Mifflin, 1999); "Saudis Weighing Partial Privatizing of Aramco," *Los Angeles Times* (April 29, 2002): 2; Robin Allen, "Oil Companies Kept Waiting at Saudi Door," *The Financial Times* (May 1, 2002): 9; "Strategic Partners: Aramco Offers Foreign Oil Companies a Chance to Return to Saudi Arabia," *Time International* (April 12, 1999): 52; "Aramco Faces Big Challenge Integrating Majors into Saudi," *The Oil Daily* (August 17, 2001): 59; Anthony McMillan, Mamoun Fandy Cordesman, and Mohamedi Fareed, "The United States and Saudi Arabia: American Interests and Challenges to the Kingdom in 2002," *Middle East Policy* (March 2002): 1–29; EIA-Country Information on Saudi Arabia (November 2, 2002): http://www.eia.doe.gov/emeu/international/saudi.html; 2001 CIA World Factbook—Saudi Arabia (November 2, 2002): http://www.odci.gov/cia/publications/factbook/geos/sa.html; U.S. Department of Energy's Office of Fossil Energy's International Section—Saudi Arabia (November 2, 2002): http://www.fe.doe.gov/international/saudiarabia.html; U.S. State Department's Consular Information Sheet—Saudi Arabia (November 2, 2002); http://travel.state.gov/saudi.html; Library of Congress Country Study on Saudi Arabia (November 2, 2002): http://lcweb2.loc.gov/frd/cs/satoc.html; Saudi Aramco homepage (November 2, 2002): http://www.saudiaramco.com; Saudi Arabian embassy in the U.S. (November 2, 2002): http://www.saudiembassy.net/.

2 See Jean J. Boddewyn and Thomas L. Brewer, "International-Business Political Behavior: New Theoretical Directions," *Academy of Management Review* 19 (1994): 119–43; and Raymond Vernon, "Big Business and National Governments: Reshaping the Compact in a Globalizing Economy," *Journal of International Business Studies* 32 (Fall 2001): 509.

3 See Ravi Ramamurti, "The Obsolescing 'Bargaining Model'? MNC-Host Developing Country Relations Revisited," *Journal of International Business Studies* 32 (Spring 2001): 23; and Yadong Luo, "Toward a Cooperative View of MNC-Host Government Relations: Building Blocks and Performance Implication," *Journal of International Business Studies* 32 (Fall 2001): 401.

4 Boddewyn and Brewer, op. cit.

5 "Daily Briefing: Benefits to Hyundai Total $252.8 Million," *Atlanta Journal and Constitution* (April 5, 2002): 2F.

6 See Sushil Vachani, "Enhancing the Obsolescing Bargain Theory: A Longitudinal Study of Foreign Ownership of U.S. and European Multinationals," *Journal of International Business Studies* 6 (1995): 159; and Chul W. Moon and Augustine A. Lado, "MNC-Host Government Bargaining Power Relationship: A Critique and Extension Within the Resource-Based View," *Journal of Management* 26 (January–February 2000): 85.

7 See "Rumble Over Tokyo: Competition Between Boeing and Airbus," *Business Week* (April 2, 2001): 80; and John Olienyk and Robert Carbaugh, "Competition in the World Jetliner Industry," *Challenge* 42 (July–August 1999): 60.

8 See Caroline Mothe and Bertrand Quelin, "Creating New Resources Through European Contracts," *Technology Analysis and Strategic Management* (March 1999): 31–43; and "Research: EUREKA Ministerial Conference Gives Blessing for 171 New Projects," *European Report* (July 6, 2002): 462.

9 "Jochum to Visit Poland to Give Final F-16 Pitch," *Defense Daily* (March 18, 2002): 12.

10 Xinping Shi, "Antecedent Factors of International Business Negotiations in the China Context," *Management International Review* 41 (April 2001): 163.

11 See Miriam Jordan, "Enron of U.S. Settles Indian Power Dispute," *Wall Street Journal* (January 9, 1996): A10; "Enron to Drop Case Against India," *Wall Street Journal* (July 26, 1996): A8; and Saritha Rai, "Seeking Ways to Sell Enron's Plant in India," *New York Times* (April 11, 2002): W1.

12 Vachani, op. cit.

13 See Roger Volkema and Maria Fleury, "Alternative Negotiating Conditions and the Choice of Negotiation Tactics: A Cross-Cultural Comparison," *Journal of Business Ethics* 36 (April 2002): 381–97; and Ji Li and Chalmer E. Labig, Jr., "Negotiating With China: Exploratory Study of Relationship-Building," *Journal of Managerial Issues* 13 (Fall 2001): 345.

14 L. James, "Don't Think About Winning," *Across the Board* (April 1992): 49–51.

15 For an elaboration of this subject, see Stephen E. Weiss, "Negotiations with 'Romans'—Part 1," *Sloan Management Review* 35, no. 2 (1994): 51–61; and Stephen E. Weiss, "Negotiations with 'Romans'–Part 2," *Sloan Management Review* 35, no. 3 (1994): 85–99.

16 See Nancy J. Adler, Richard Brahm, and John L. Graham, "Strategy Implementation: A Comparison of Face-to-Face Negotiations in the People's Republic of China and the United States," *Strategic Management Journal* 13, no. 6 (September 1992): 463; and Richard D. Babcock and Bertha Du-Babcock, "Language-Based Communication Zones in International Business Communication," *The Journal of Business Communication* 38 (October 2001): 372.

17 See Michael W. Peng, *Business Strategies in Transition Economies* (Thousand Oaks, CA: Sage, 2000); and Patrick Arens and Keith D. Brouthers,

"Key Stakeholder Theory and State Owned Versus Privatized Firm," *Management International Review* 41 (October 2001): 377–95.

18 Klaus Macharzina, "Mediation in International Negotiations," *Management International Review* 41 (January 2001): 3.

19 Pervez Ghauri and Tony Fang, "Negotiating with the Chinese: A Socio-Cultural Analysis," *Journal of World Business* 36 (Fall 2001): 303.

20 Richard S. DeFrank, Robert Konopaske, and John M. Ivancevich, "Executive Travel Stress: Perils of the Road Warrior," *The Academy of Management Executive* 14 (May 2000): 58.

21 Thomas L. Brewer, "International Investment Dispute Settlement Procedures: The Evolving Regime for Foreign Direct Investment," *Law & Policy in International Business* 26, no. 2 (1995): 633–72.

22 See George Schwarzenberger, "The Protection of British Property Abroad," *Current Legal Problems* 5 (1952): 295–99; Oliver J. Lissitzyn, *International Law Today and Tomorrow* (Dobbs Ferry, NY: Oceana Publications, 1965), 77; and Gillis Wetter, "Diplomatic Assistance to Private Investment," *University of Chicago Law Review* 29 (1962): 275.

23 Ian Brownlie, *Principles of Public International Law* (Oxford, UK: Oxford University Press, 1966), 435–36.

24 Green H. Hackworth, *Digest of International Law* (Washington, DC: U.S. Government Printing Office, 1942), 655–61.

25 See Michael A. Geist, "Toward a General Agreement on the Regulation of Foreign Direct Investment," *Law & Policy in International Business* 26, no. 3 (Spring 1995): 673–717; and Flemming Larsen, "The Global Financial Architecture in Transition," *OECD Observer* (January 2002): 10–13.

26 For an extensive treatise on the theory, see Robert A. Packenham, *The Dependency Movement: Scholarship and Politics in Development Studies* (Cambridge, MA: Harvard University Press, 1992). For some different national views of its validity, see Ndiva Kofele-Kale, "The Political Economy of Foreign Direct Investment: A Framework for Analyzing Investment Laws and Regulations in Developing Countries," *Law & Policy in International Business* 23, no. 2–3 (1992): 619–71; and Stanley K. Sheinbaum, "Very Recent History Has Absolved Socialism," *New Perspectives Quarterly* 13, no. 1 (January 1996).

27 Jack Kemp, "Nuevo Dependencia and World Government?" Copley News Service (March 27, 2002).

28 John Linarelli, "The Role of Dispute Settlement in World Trade Law: Some Lessons from the Kodak-Fuji Dispute," *Law and Policy in International Business* 31 (Winter 2000): 263.

29 "White House Fact Sheet on Overseas Private Investment Corporation of the United States Activity in Russia," U.S. Newswire (November 14, 2001).

30 See Richard B. Lillich and Daniel B. McGraw, eds., *The Iran-United States Claims Tribunal: Its Contribution to the Law of State Responsibility* (Irvington-on-Hudson, NY: Transnational Publishers, 1998); and Neely Tucker, "In Lawsuit Against Iran, Former Hostages Fight U.S." *The Washington Post* (December 13, 2001).

31 Brewer, op. cit.

32 Andrew Walter, "NGOs, Business, and International Investment: The Multilateral Agreement on Investment, Seattle, and Beyond," *Global Governance* 7 (January 2001): 51.

33 See Amy Jocelyn Glass and Kamal Saggi, "Intellectual Property Rights and Foreign Direct Investment," *Journal of International Economics* 56 (March 2002): 387–411; and Keith Maskus, *Intellectual Property Rights in the Global Economy* (Washington, DC: Institute for International Economics, 2000).

34 Sally Goodman, "Poor Nations Push for Right to Produce Cheap Medicines," *Nature* 411 (June 2001): 982.

35 Robert L. Ostergard, Jr., "The Measurement of intellectual Property Rights Protection," *Journal of International Business Studies* 31 (Summer 2000): 349.

36 Cecile W. Garmon, "Intellectual Property Rights: Protecting the Creation of New Knowledge Across Cultural Boundaries," *American Behavioral Scientist* 45 (March 2002): 1145–59.

37 "Allying for Health," *UN Chronicle* 37 (Spring 2000): 58.

38 Salim S. Abdool Karim, "Globalization, Ethics, and AIDS Vaccines," *Science* 288 (June 2000): 2129.

39 Patricia Reaney, "South Africa Deal May Spark Global Change in Drug Access," *Reuters AlertNet* (April 19, 2001).

40 Carla Power, "Paying for AIDS," *Newsweek International* (March 19, 2001): 16.

41 Goodman, op. cit.

42 Specifically, the Paris Convention for the Protection of Industrial Property of 1883 has been revised at Brussels (1900), Washington (1911), The Hague (1925), London (1934), Lisbon (1958), and Stockholm (1967), and Amended in 1979.

43 Peggy Chaudhry and Michael Walsh, "Intellectual Property Rights," *Columbia Journal of World Business* 30 (Summer 1995): 80–92.

44 Tatiana Boncompagni, "All Hail the Gemstar Army," *American Lawyer* 24 (March 2002): 22–24.

45 Paul A. David and Dominique Foray, "An Introduction to the Economy of the Knowledge Society," *International Social Science Journal* (March 2002): 1–17.

46 "India: Cipla Launches 3-In-1 AIDS Pill," *Clinical Infectious Diseases* 33 (September 15, 2001): ii.

47 "Jeu Zespri," *The Economist* (August 10, 1996): 48.

48 EU and U.S. End Drink Dispute," *Wall Street Journal* (March 29, 1994): A10.

49 Lisa Sharrock, "The Future of Domain Name Dispute Resolution: Crafting Practical International Legal Solutions from Within the UDRP Framework," *Duke Law Journal* 51 (November 2001): 817–50.

50 Timothy W. Blakely, "Beyond the International Harmonization of Trademark Law: The Community Trade Mark as a Model of Unitary Transnational Trademark Protection," *University of Pennsylvania Law Review* 149 (November 2000): 309.

51 Alfred T. Checkett, "Can We Do More to Fight Counterfeiting?" *Security Management* (February 1999): 129–30.

52 See Nejdet Delener, "International Counterfeit Marketing: Success Without Risk," *Review of Business* 21 (Spring 2000): 16; and "Countering Counterfeiting," *Business Europe* (July 28, 1999): 5–6.

53 Richard Ernsberger, Jr. and Tony Emerson, "Software Pirates, Beware Microsoft: Nobody Has More to Lose from Bootleg Software Than the U.S. Giant," *Newsweek* (October 29, 2001): 68.

54 Peter H. Lewis, "As Piracy Grows, the Software Industry Counterattacks," *New York Times* (November 8, 1992): 12F.

55 For specific descriptions, see David H. Freedman, "Faker's Paradise," *Forbes* (April 5, 1999): 48–54.

56 "Big Jump in Seizures of Counterfeit Goods for 2001," *European Report* (July 27, 2002): 490.

57 Hallie Forcinio, "Technology Advances Anticounterfeiting Options," *Pharmaceutical Technology* 26 (June 2002): 26–31.

58 See http://www.microsoft.com/piracy/default.asp, retrieved December 18, 2002.

59 Amal Jayasinghe, "Sri Lanka May Reclaim Companies," *Financial Times* (August 8, 1996): 6.

60 Robert S. Greenberger, "Clinton to Unveil Voluntary Business Code," *Asian Wall Street Journal* (March 27, 1995): 12.

61 Shada Islam, "If It's Broke, Fix It; New Code of Conduct Will Help Regulate Toy Industry," *Far Eastern Economic Review* (June 20, 1996): 67.

62 See Karl Schoenberger, *Levi's Children: Coming to Terms with Human Rights in the Global Marketplace* (New York, N.Y.: Grove Press, 2000); and Robert D. Haas, "Ethics in the Third World," *Across the Board* (May 1994): 12–13.

63 H. David Banta, "Worldwide Interest in Global Access to Drugs," *JAMA* 285 (June 13, 2001): 2844.

64 Gary A. Weaver, Linda Klebe Trevino, and Philip L. Cochran, "Integrated and Decoupled Corporate Social Performance: Management Commitments, External Pressures, and Corporate Ethics Practices," *Academy of Management Journal* 42 (1999): 539–52.

65 "Companies and Markets," *Africa News Service* (January 31, 2002). See also http://www.environment-prize.com/about.html (October 21, 2002); http://www.gm.com/company/gmability/environment/achievements_recognition/achievements.html (October 21, 2002).

66 Data for the case were taken from Business Software Alliance (November 25, 2002): http://bsa.org/; International Anti-Counterfeiting Coalition Recording Industry (November 25,

2002): http://www.iacc.org/; Association of America (November 25, 2002): http://www.riaa. com/; Motion Picture Association of America (November 25, 2002): http://www.mpaa.org/ home.htm; Bryan W. Husted, "The Impact of National Culture on Software Piracy," *Journal of Business Ethics* 26 (August 2000): 197–211; Carol Noonan and Jeffery Raskin, "Intellectual Property Crimes," *Criminal Law Review* 38 (Summer 2001): 971; Trevor Moores and Gurpreet Dhillon, "Software Piracy: A View from

Hong Kong." *Communications of the ACM* 43 (December 2000): 88; Edward Iwata, "Software Piracy Takes Toll on Global Scale," *USA Today* (August 1, 2001): C1; Jennifer Lee, "Pirates on the Web, Spoils on the Street; Cracking Codes of Popular Software, A Small Group Can Wreak Havoc," *New York Times* (July 11, 2002): E1; Suzanne Wagner and G. Lawrence Sanders, "Considerations in Ethical Decision-Making and Software Piracy," *Journal of Business Ethics* (January 2001): 161; Donald B. Marron and

David G. Steel, "Which Countries Protect Intellectual Property? The Case of Software Piracy," *Economic Inquiry* 38 (April, 2000): 159; and Wong Choon Mei, "Microsoft Cites Software Piracy Hotspots," *Reuters Technology* (October 23, 2002).

67 A. Lin Neumann, "Information Wants to be Free—But this is Ridiculous," *Wired* (November 22, 2002). www.wired.com/wired/archive/ 3.10/piracy-pr.html

PART SIX

Operations: Overlaying Tactical Alternatives

CHAPTER 13

COUNTRY EVALUATION AND SELECTION

If the profits are great, the risks are great.

—CHINESE PROVERB

OBJECTIVES

- To discuss company strategies for sequencing the penetration of countries and for committing resources

- To explain how clues from the environmental climate can help managers limit geographic alternatives

- To examine the major variables a company should consider when deciding whether and where to expand abroad

- To provide an overview of methods and problems when collecting and comparing information internationally

- To describe some simplifying tools for determining a global geographic strategy

- To introduce how managers make final investment, reinvestment, and divestment decisions

CASE

Carrefour[1]

Carrefour, which opened its first store in 1960, is now the largest retailer in Europe and Latin America and the second largest worldwide. Its stores depend on food for about 60 percent of its sales and on a wide variety of nonfood items for the rest. In 2001, Carrefour derived 51 percent of its sales and 33 percent of its profits outside France, its home country. The Institute of Grocery Distribution ranks Carrefour as the world's most global retailer, based on foreign sales, number of countries with operations, and ratio of foreign sales to total sales. As of June 2002, Carrefour owned 5,341 stores and franchised another 4,064; of which only 3,389—a little over a third—were in France. Nevertheless, France accounted for 49 percent of its sales and 67 percent of its operating profit.

In the near future, Carrefour plans to open more than 400 new stores a year and spend nearly $3 billion per year on new stores, remodeling, and expansion. Thus, its management must decide in what countries to open these stores and where in each country to locate them. (Recently, Carrefour has placed about three-quarters of capital expenditures outside France.) Management also must decide where to buy the merchandise its stores sell.

Carrefour sells in five types of stores: hypermarkets, supermarkets, hard discount stores, cash-and-carry stores, and convenience stores. For 2001, it made 59.2 percent of its sales in hypermarkets, which are in more countries than are Carrefour's other types of retail operations. In 1963, Carrefour invented and opened the first hypermarket, an enormous commercial establishment that combines a department store and a supermarket. Whereas a typical supermarket might have 40,000 square feet, a hypermarket might have 330,000. A vice president of *Progressive Grocer* magazine explained the size difference: "A grocery store is like a family farm, a supermarket is like a big corporate farm, and a hypermarket is like the whole state of Iowa." As a rule of thumb, a hypermarket requires 500,000 households within a 20-minute drive to derive sufficient business. Carrefour's supermarkets carry less variety than its hypermarkets and accounted in 2001 for 19.8 percent of sales. Its hard discount stores, cash-and-carry stores, and convenience stores collectively accounted for 21 percent of sales. The hard discount stores sell fewer different items than supermarkets sell—mainly food products in fairly austere stores at discounted prices. The cash-and-carry stores cater strictly to the trade, such as restaurant owners and hoteliers. Its convenience stores (more than 95 percent are franchise operations) are still smaller and carry fewer items. One of Carrefour's key contributions to franchisees is selecting locations for their stores.

Carrefour's French hypermarket operation was a success from the beginning, and by 2002, Carrefour operated 177 hypermarkets in France. The timing for introducing the hypermarket concept was perfect. Supermarket operations were not yet well developed in France, and French consumers generally shopped for food items in different outlets—for example, bread, meat, fish, cheese, and fresh vegetables in different specialty stores or open markets. Few retailers had convenient or free parking, so customers had to shop long hours and make frequent trips to stores. However, by 1963, more French families had cars, more had refrigerators large enough to store a week's supply of fresh products, and more had high disposable incomes that they could spend on nonfood items. Further, more women were working, and they wanted one-stop shopping. Thus, French consumers flocked to Carrefour's suburban hypermarkets, which offered free parking and discounted prices on a very wide selection of merchandise.

However, Carrefour and other hypermarket operators have faced obstacles to French expansion. Government authorities at times have restricted new hypermarket permits to safeguard town centers, protect small businesses, and prevent visual despoliation of the countryside. As a consequence, Carrefour decided early on to expand internationally. Figure 13.1 shows both the countries where it now operates and when it entered those countries. Its first two foreign entries, both with hypermarkets, were to neighboring countries, Belgium and Spain. Carrefour managed these ventures without difficulty because its French suppliers initially provided much of the stores' stock and because its managers from France could travel easily to Belgium and Spain to oversee the operations. When Carrefour entered Belgium and Spain, the consumers of those two countries were going through lifestyle changes similar to those that helped assure the company's earlier success in France. Since then, one of the principal factors guiding Carrefour's international expansion has been countries' economic evolution. Its CEO, Daniel Bernard said, "We can start with a developing country at the bottom of the economic curve and grow within the country to the top of the curve."

Nevertheless, Carrefour has not always followed this location strategy, and the deviation has influenced its failure in some markets. It expanded into the United States and the United Kingdom in the mid-1980s after both of these countries had gone through the economic transitions that helped assure success in other locales and after other distributors had satisfied the changed consumer needs. Carrefour later pulled out of both markets. Bernard said later, "There is a race and a lot of companies are qualified for the race. To go global, you need to be early enough. Generally, in new countries you need to be the first in for the first win. When you arrive as number three or four, it is too late." However, some additional factors caused problems for Carrefour in the United States and the United Kingdom. In the United States distributors have had scant success with hypermarkets. Their introduction came well after the growth of supermarkets and smaller-scale mixed merchandise retailers, such as a typical Wal-Mart store. U.S. customers have simply not wanted to spend the time it takes to shop in a hypermarket. For example, Carrefour's Philadelphia store had 61 checkout counters, and customers had to pass all of them before they even reached the first aisle. In the United Kingdom Carrefour did well on sales of food items but not on durables; consumers preferred to shop for these in city centers where they could compare the products offered by different distributors.

Another factor influencing the choice for country expansion has been the ability to find a viable partner familiar with local operating needs. Carrefour has teamed with the Maus group in Switzerland, President Enterprise in Taiwan, the Sabanci group in Turkey, and Harbor Power Equipment in China. Such partnering has enabled Carrefour to avoid some of the errors Wal-Mart made when entering markets alone, such as stocking American footballs at its Brazilian stores (even though Brazilians play soccer instead) and introducing a stock-handling system in Brazil that did not fit Brazilian pallet sizes. However, Wal-Mart entered Mexico well before Carrefour and teamed with the best local partner, Cifra. A few years later, Carrefour partnered with Gigante, but the latter lacked sufficient resources to expand as rapidly as Carrefour desired, so Carrefour ultimately had to buy Gigante's interest in the joint operation. In Japan, Carrefour established operations in 2001 without a partner. In essence, management felt no need for a partner because tradi-

---

FIGURE 13.1   Carrefour's Store Locations by Country and Dates of Entering Those Markets

Carrefour also entered three other countries during that period from which it withdrew. These were Hong Kong, the United Kingdom, and the United States. The list of countries does not include some that became Carrefour operations through Carrefour's purchase of Promodès.

Source: Information is taken from the Carrefour Web site (September 26, 2002): http://www.carrefour.com/english.

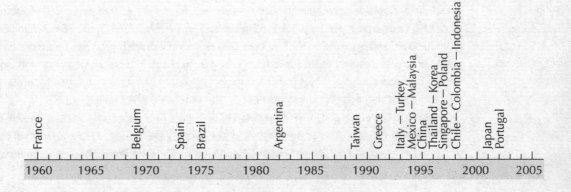

tional operating costs were so much lower than those of Carrefour's Japanese rivals. Time will tell if Carrefour can succeed in Japan without a partner; however, a retail analyst has said, "Their [Carrefour's] chances of success are zero."

Why would another company want to partner with Carrefour? Aside from financial resources, Carrefour brings to a partnership expertise on store layout, clout in dealing with global suppliers (for example, it runs a global sales campaign, "Most Awaited Month," in which the largest manufacturers of global consumer goods provide its stores worldwide with lower prices for a one-month sale), direct e-mail links with suppliers that substantially reduce buying personnel and inventories, and the ability to export unique bargain items from one country to another.

Carrefour also considers whether a country or regional location within a country can justify sufficient additional store expansion to gain economies of scale in buying and distribution. To help gain these economies, Carrefour and some of its competitors have recently been on acquisition sprees. For example, Carrefour bought Promodès, Montlaur, Euromarche, and Comptoirs stores in France, Supermercados Norte in Argentina, and a stake in Super Stock in Spain. It entered Hong Kong in 1996, but it closed operations four years later because it could not secure enough suitable sites for expansion. It also sold three hypermarkets in northern Mexico to a Mexican retailer, Soriana, because it lacked the opportunity to amass enough retail operations in the area to justify investing in a large distribution center. Likewise, some analysts feel that Carrefour may be expanding retail operations to too many countries and will not be able to build sufficient presence in each to gain necessary economies of scale. For example, Tesco, a British retailer, is expanding to fewer countries but is building a large presence in each one. In the six countries where both Tesco and Carrefour operate, Tesco is bigger in four of them. Map 13.1 shows the countries where Carrefour operates and the number of stores in each country.

MAP 13.1 **Number of Carrefour Retailers by Country, 2002**

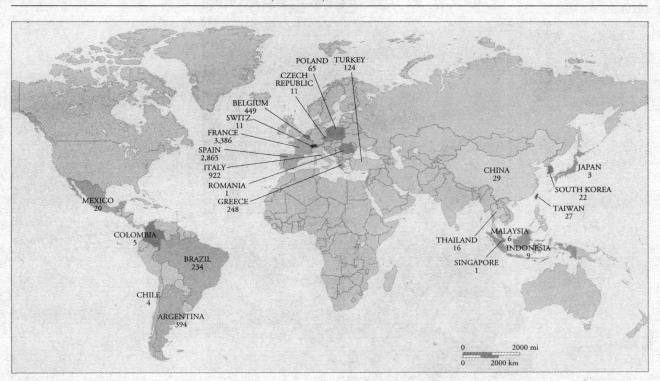

The figures show the number of Carrefour retailers per country as of June 2002 and include franchise operations. The figures do not include 57 franchise operations in Europe that are not specified on the Carrefour Web site.

Source: Information is taken from the Carrefour Web site (September 26, 2002): http://www.carrefour.com/english.

Carrefour depends primarily on locally produced goods, using manufacturers' trademarks or no trademarks at all. This strategy contrasts with such retailers as Tesco and Marks & Spencer, another British retailer, which depend heavily on own-label products. Thus, consumers can easily compare prices of most Carrefour products with those of competitors because few of its products have unique labels. Nevertheless, Carrefour has recently been pushing global purchasing. For example, much of the merchandise it sells in its Chilean stores is duty-free from Brazil because of Chile's associate membership in MERCOSUR. Further, when stores in one country find an exceptional supplier, the management passes on the information to Carrefour's merchandising group in Brussels, which then seeks markets within Carrefour stores in other countries. The Malaysian operation, for example, found a good local supplier of disposable gloves, and Carrefour now sells them in its stores worldwide.

Although mass retailers sell most of the consumer goods in industrial countries, they sell much less in most developing countries. For example, chain stores probably account for less than 3 percent of retail sales in China and India. On the one hand, this might indicate that Carrefour should be putting most of its expansion efforts into developing countries. On the other hand, some analysts feel that Carrefour will never become the world's largest retailer without a significant presence in the United States and the United Kingdom. In fact, newspapers have reported rumors that Carrefour is looking for acquisitions to penetrate those markets. These rumors for the United States have included Kmart, Target, and Costco. Carrefour actually has a minority interest in Costco.

Companies must consider both opportunity and risk when deciding whether and where to operate abroad. The photo shows a guard with Ronald McDonald protecting a McDonald's facility from rioting and looting in Jakarta, Indonesia.

INTRODUCTION

Companies seldom have enough resources to take advantage of all international opportunities. Committing human, technical, and financial resources to one locale may mean forgoing projects in other areas. So managers must be choosy. They must know how to pick the best location for their business interests.

Figure 13.2 repeats the framework introduced in Chapter 1 and highlights the fact that the choice of where to operate is a big part of carrying out a business strategy. The figure also shows that external factors influence country selection. A company should look to those countries with economic, political, cultural, and geographic conditions that mesh with its strengths. Managers might ask, "Where can we best leverage our already developed competencies?" and "Where can we go to best sustain, improve, or extend our competencies?" A company needs to determine the order of entry into potential countries and to set the allocation of resources and rate of expansion among them.

CHOOSING MARKETING AND PRODUCTION SITES, AND GEOGRAPHIC STRATEGY

Companies must determine where to sell and where to produce. In so doing, managers will need to answer two basic questions: "Which markets should we serve?" and "Where should we place production to serve those markets?" The answers to these questions can be one and the same, particularly if transport costs or government regulations mean that local production is

Companies lack resources to take advantage of all international opportunities.

Companies need to
- Determine the order of country entry
- Set the rates of resource allocation among countries

In choosing geographic sites, a company must decide
- Where to sell
- Where to produce

FIGURE 13.2 Place of Location Decisions in International Business Operations

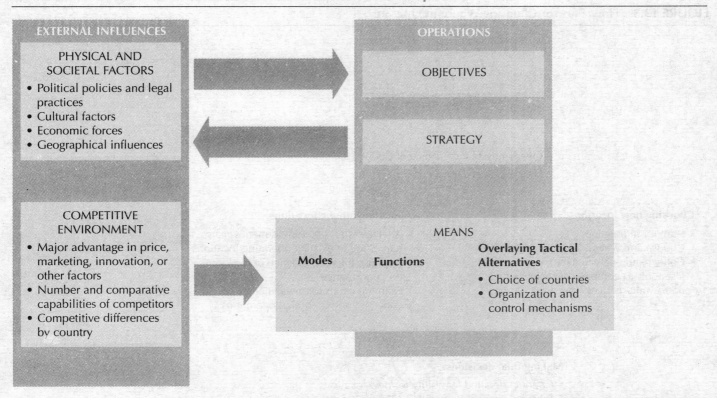

A company's choice of countries for its operations should be determined by the interaction of its objectives, competencies, and comparative environmental fit with conditions within different countries.

necessary for serving the chosen market. Many service industries, such as hotels, construction, and retailing (recall the Carrefour case), must locate facilities near their foreign customers, so decisions on market and production location are connected. If a company develops a product that consumers find attractive, it must still find means to produce and transport the product cheaply enough so that consumers will buy it. Finding the right production location, which may be abroad, allows the company to sustain a long-term competitive edge.

Decisions on market and production locations may be highly interdependent for other reasons. A company may have excess production capacity already in place that will influence its ability to serve markets in different countries. Or it may find a given market very attractive but it will forgo sales there because it is unwilling to invest in needed production locations.

The process of determining an overall geographic strategy must be flexible because country conditions change. A plan must let a company both respond to new opportunities in different locations and withdraw from less profitable ones. Unfortunately, there is little agreement on a comprehensive theory or technique for choosing the best location, one that helps companies get the most out of their resources. Further, it is hard for companies to formulate strategies when they have to make assumptions about factors in the foreign environment, such as future costs and prices, competitors' reactions, and technology.

Nevertheless, managers can use several geographic strategies. A company may expand its international sales by marketing more of its existing product line, by adding products to its line, or by some combination of these two. Most companies begin by asking, "Where can we sell more of our products?" Alternatively, they can ask, "What new product can we make to maximize sales in a given market?" In this chapter, we assume that for the most part, the company has pursued the first question. In essence, a company needs to decide where to operate and what portion of operations to place within each location. Figure 13.3 shows the

FIGURE 13.3   Flowchart for Choosing Where to Operate

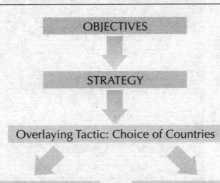

OBJECTIVES

STRATEGY

Overlaying Tactic: Choice of Countries

Choosing new locations
- Scan for alternatives
- Choose and weight variables
- Collect and analyze data for variables
- Use tools to compare variables and narrow alternatives

Allocating among locations
- Analyze effects of reinvestment versus harvesting in existing operating locations
- Appraise interdependence of locations on performance
- Examine needs for diversification versus concentration of foreign operations

Making final decisions
- Conduct detailed feasibility for new locations
- Estimate expected outcome for reinvestments
- Make location and allocation decisions based on company's financial decision-making tools

major steps international business managers must take in making these decisions. The following discussion examines these steps in depth.

SCAN FOR ALTERNATIVE LOCATIONS

To compare countries, managers use scanning techniques based on broad variables that indicate opportunities and risks. That way, decision makers can perform a detailed analysis of a manageable number of geographic locations. Scanning is like weeding out—it is useful insofar as a company might otherwise consider too few or too many possibilities.

A company can easily overlook or disregard some promising options. Some locations may be skipped rather than rejected, simply because managers either never think of them or because they eliminate consideration of a whole region without considering differences within the region. Or a company may decide to go where "everyone else has gone." For example, the former vice chairman of Chrysler said, "The chief executive who gets asked repeatedly by the press and Wall Street analysts the same question—'Why are you so slow on your China strategy?'—quickly gets the idea he's missing something and orders a China strategy. These 'forced' actions, taken because of 'peer pressure,' almost always result in disaster."[2]

A detailed analysis of every alternative might result in maximized sales or a least-cost production location, but the cost of so many studies would erode profits. A company with 1,000 products that might locate in any of 150 countries would need 150,000 different studies. Plus, other alternatives must be considered as well, such as whether to export or to set up a foreign production unit. Companies should examine any conditions that would enhance the weeding out process before they perform a more detailed feasibility study.

CHOOSE AND WEIGHT VARIABLES

When scanning, managers will take the environmental climate into consideration. The environmental climate is the external conditions in a host country that could significantly affect the success or failure of a foreign business enterprise. It can determine whether a company will make a detailed study as well as the terms under which it will initiate a project. The environmental climate reveals both opportunities and risks.

Opportunities

Managers make investment decisions after weighing opportunities against risks. Opportunities are determined by revenues less costs. From a broad scanning perspective, there are variables that indicate the amount of revenue, cost factors, and risk that might be forthcoming from one country to another.

The factors that have the most influence on the placement of marketing and production emphasis are market size, ease and compatibility of operations, costs, resource availability, and red tape. Some of these variables are more important for the market-location decision; others are more important for the production-location decision. Some variables affect both.

Market Size Sales potential is probably the most important variable managers use when determining where and whether to make an investment. The assumption, of course, is that sales will occur at a price above cost, so that where there are sales, there are profits.

In some cases, a company can obtain past and current sales figures on a country-by-country basis for the type of product it wants to sell. In many cases, however, such figures are unavailable. Nevertheless, management must make projections about what will happen to future sales.[3] Often, data such as GNP, per capita income, growth rates, population, and level of industrialization are also good indicators of market size and future sales. Of course, managers should examine how incomes and wealth are distributed. For example, Indonesia's per

Without scanning, a company may

- *Overlook opportunities and risks*
- *Examine too many or too few possibilities*

Expectation of a large market and sales growth is probably a potential location's major attraction.

capita income is low; however, there are enough millionaires to buy luxury sports cars.[4] Further, demographic factors other than income influence potential demand, such as age, gender, religion, and ethnic background. For example, Pollo Campero, a Guatemalan-based fast-food chain, successfully entered the United States by going to cities with large Central American populations.[5] Another technique for making rough estimates of market size is to base projections on a similar or complementary product for which sales figures *are* available, such as projections of flat screen television sales potential based on DVD sales data.

Ease and Compatibility of Operations   Managers prefer to go where they perceive it's easier to operate. Thus, Carrefour's managers chose their first international expansions in neighboring Belgium and Spain. Likewise, U.S. companies put earlier and more emphasis on Canada, the United Kingdom, and Mexico than would be indicated by those countries' economic sizes. These companies rank Canada and Mexico high because of geographic proximity, which makes it easier and cheaper for the companies to ship merchandise to and to control their foreign subsidiaries. Moreover, since the advent of NAFTA, U.S. companies encounter fewer border restrictions for their operations in Canada and Mexico than they do for most other locales. Also, at the early stages of international expansion, managers feel uncomfortable doing business in a dissimilar language, culture, and legal system, and this helps explain why U.S. companies' prefer to operate in Canada and the United Kingdom as opposed to, say, Russia.[6] Language and cultural similarities may also keep operating costs and risks low because of greater ease in understanding employees and customers. Finally, economic similarity influences where initial foreign operations will reside. Both Canada and the United Kingdom have high per capita incomes that are similar to those in the United States.

After companies pare alternatives to a reasonable number, they must prepare much more detailed feasibility studies. These studies can be expensive. The more time and money companies invest in examining an alternative, the more likely they are to accept it regardless of its merits, a situation known as an *escalation of commitment*. A feasibility study should have clear-cut decision points, points at which managers can cut the commitment before it escalates.

Proposals for expansion may originate almost anywhere within a company, but top-level managers should have the final say in whether they are approved because a company needs to put its limited resources to the best possible use. To this end, Eastman Kodak now has head-quarters approve projects that used to be handled by overseas managers.[7] They should give precedence to those that fit the organization's motives, limitations, and policies. For example, Blockbuster failed in Germany because it could not duplicate the successful formula it uses elsewhere. In the United States, Blockbuster depends on evening, Sunday, and holiday rentals, when people decide at the last minute to fill their leisure time. But laws in Germany prevented Blockbuster from operating at these times. Further, Blockbuster creates a store environment in the United States that attracts the whole family. However, consumers in Germany prefer to see family entertainment in a movie house and seek pornographic films from video stores.[8]

Companies may limit consideration of proposals to locales that will permit them to operate with product types and plant sizes familiar to the managers. From a policy standpoint, management may find it useful to ensure that its proposal group includes personnel with backgrounds in each functional area—marketing, finance, personnel, engineering, and production. From a policy standpoint, many companies further limit consideration of proposals to only those countries that permit them to own an acceptable percentage of operations and that allow sufficient remittance of profits.

Companies also consider local availability of resources in relation to their needs. Many foreign operations require local resources, a requirement that may severely restrict the feasibility of given locales. For example, the company may need to find local personnel or a viable local partner who understand its type of business and technology. Or it may need to add local

Companies are highly attracted to countries that

- Are located nearby
- Share the same language
- Have market conditions similar to those in their home countries

Companies often pare proposals to those countries that

- Offer size, technology, and other advantages familiar to company personnel
- Allow an acceptable percentage of ownership
- Permit sufficient profits to be easily remitted

capital to what it is willing to bring in. If local equity markets are poorly developed and if local borrowing is expensive, the company may consider locating in a different country.

Costs and Resource Availability   So far, we have discussed market-seeking operations. However, companies also go abroad to secure resources that are either unavailable or expensive in their home countries. Often, a company considers making a product or component abroad for sale where it produces that item or for export into other markets. It must examine labor costs, raw material inputs, capital requirements, utilities, real estate costs, taxes, and transportation costs in relation to productivity. Before collecting all this information in a final feasibility study, the company can narrow the alternative locations by examining a few key indicators.

Labor compensation is an important cost of manufacturing for most companies. Thus, Figure 13.4 illustrates companies' continual search for cheaper labor. However, capital intensity is growing in most industries, which reduces labor costs as a percentage of total costs and reduces the differences in production costs from one location to another. At any rate, companies can examine current labor market size, labor costs, trends in those costs, and unemployment rates to approximate labor availability and cost differences among countries. Labor, however, is not homogeneous. If a country's labor force lacks the specific skill levels required, a company may have to train, redesign production, or add supervision—all of which are expensive. In the case of specialized units, such as an R&D lab, the existing availability of specific skills is almost essential. Further, there may be sector differences in wage rates. For example, Mexican tire wages are twice those of Mexican auto wages and five times the Mexican industrial wage. This has caused tire companies, such as Goodyear and Michelin, to shift much of their tire production from Mexico to Brazil.[9] Further, labor availability and cost may change rapidly. For example, about a quarter of the labor force in South Africa is infected with HIV, which may drastically reduce the labor force over the next 10 to 15 years.[10] Travel restrictions because of the Asian SARS outbreak limited MNEs' ability to send management from headquarters to control Asian operations.

When companies move into emerging economies because of labor-cost differences, their advantages may be short-lived because:

- Competitors follow leaders into low-wage areas.
- There is little first-in advantage for this type of production migration.
- Foreign costs rise quickly as a result of pressure on wage or exchange rates.

> Costs—especially labor costs—are an important factor in companies' production-location decisions.

FIGURE 13.4

Will Companies Keep Finding New Sources of Cheap Labor?

Source: 1997 Joel Pett, *Lexington Herald-Leader.* All Rights Reserved.

As a result, some companies, especially those with rapidly evolving technologies, seek to locate production close to product-development activities. Doing this allows for a tight link between product and process technologies (for example, making smaller disk drives is as much a manufacturing problem as it is a technical one), a faster market entry with new products, and unique production technologies that cannot be easily copied by competitors.[11] These factors tend to push more of a company's production into industrial countries, in which most R&D occurs. However, a geographically isolated country, such as New Zealand, does not fit as easily into a company's global process-product integration strategy because of transportation time and cost.[12] At the same time, companies seeking to integrate different parts of their production—for example, by producing components in different countries to save on labor rates—prefer to locate activities in countries with few trade restrictions so that they are better assured of having a continuous flow of components where they need them.[13]

Increasingly, companies need to be near suppliers and customers in an area where the infrastructure will allow them to move supplies and finished products efficiently. Regional headquarters should reside near specialized private and public institutions such as banks, financing firms, insurance groups, public accountants, freight forwarders, customs brokers, and consular offices, all of which handle international functions. If a company is looking for a production location that will serve sales in more than one country, the ease of moving goods into and out of the country is very important. The company may compare countries in terms of their port facilities and trade liberalization agreements with other countries.[14] The company may also compare alternative transportation costs from production to market locations in case the usual transport means becomes unavailable. For example, U.S. toy companies such as Hasbro and Mattel depend on Asian production and ocean freight. However, they cannot afford to use air freight in the event of a prolonged shipping strike.[15]

Corporate tax rates on income also affect location decisions by MNEs, especially within regional trading groups because in such groups, companies can serve the entire region from any of several countries.

Companies should add any other important costs specific to their own operations into their analysis. If precise data are unavailable, companies may use proxies on operating conditions. For example, if a country's infrastructure is well developed and components can be easily imported, operating costs are likely to be low. If the country already turns out competitive products containing inputs similar to those required for the production being considered, management can conclude that labor costs will be sufficiently low.

The continuous development of new production technologies makes cost comparisons among countries more difficult. As the number of ways in which the same product can be made increases, a company must compare the cost of producing with a large labor input in a low-wage country with that of producing with capital intensity in a high-wage country. For example, Volkswagen moved production of its Golf Syncro from Germany to Slovakia and switched from a highly automated, capital-intensive assembly line to a labor-intensive plant because the low Slovakian wages and high productivity cut costs from those in Germany.[16] A company might have to compare large-scale production with reducing fixed costs per unit by serving multicountry markets and the latter has the advantage of multiple smaller-scale production units; the former has the advantage of reducing transport and inventory costs.

Because of other considerations, a company may not necessarily opt for the least-cost production location. For example, BMW calculated that Mexico would be the least-cost location for North American production. However, the company chose a U.S. location because it feared that a Mexican-made vehicle would lack the same luxury image. Similarly, BMW feared for many years that foreign consumers would balk at buying vehicles made in its South African plants, but it is now successfully exporting its 3-series sedans from South Africa to Japan and the United States.[17] However, in a sense, the decisions based on product image are least cost, because a company may have to incur high marketing expenses to convince consumers of quality.

Companies should consider different ways to produce the same product.

Red Tape Companies frequently compare the degrees of red tape needed to operate in given countries because red tape increases their operating costs. Red tape includes the difficulty of getting permission to operate; bringing in expatriate personnel; obtaining licenses to produce and sell certain goods; and satisfying government agencies on such matters as taxes, labor conditions, and environmental compliance. For example, Vietnam has thousands of government employees who have the power to cause trouble for foreign businesses. Their actions reflect not only what they think is the national interest, but also their desire to protect friends and state companies from competition and to receive bribes for favors. As a result, such companies as Raytheon and Sheraton Hotels have closed their Vietnamese operations.[18] The degree of red tape is not directly measurable, so companies commonly rate countries subjectively on this factor.

The degree of red tape is not directly measurable.

Risks

Is a projected rate of return of 9 percent in Bolivia the same as a projected rate of 9 percent in France? Should a company calculate return on investment (ROI) on the entire earnings of a foreign subsidiary or just on the earnings that can be remitted to the parent? Does it make sense for a company to accept a low return in one country if doing so will help the company's competitive position elsewhere? Is it ever rational for a company to invest in a country that has an uncertain political and economic future? These are but a few of the unresolved questions that companies must consider when making international capital-investment decisions.

Risk and Uncertainty Companies use a variety of financial techniques to compare potential projects, including discounted cash flow, economic value added, payback period, net present value, return on sales, return on assets employed, internal rate of return, accounting rate of return, and return on equity. The differences among these techniques is best explained in a finance course; however, the international implications of all of them are roughly the same. We will refer only to ROI as a means of explaining risk considerations in international business.

Most investors prefer certainty to uncertainty.

Given the same expected return, most decision makers prefer a more certain outcome to a less certain one. To calculate an estimated ROI, a company averages the various returns it deems possible for investments. Table 13.1 shows that two identical projected ROIs may have very different certainties of achievement as well as different probabilities. In the table, the certainty of a 10 percent projected ROI is higher for investment B than for investment A (40 percent versus 30 percent). Further, the probability of earning *at least* 10 percent is also higher for B (.40 + .30 = .70 or 70 percent) than for A (.30 + .20 + .15 = .65 or 65 percent).

● **TABLE 13.1**

COMPARISON OF ROI CERTAINTY

To determine the estimated return on investment, (1) multiply each ROI as a percentage by its probability to derive a weighted value and (2) add the weighted values. (The weighted value is probability × percentage.)

ROI AS PERCENTAGE	INVESTMENT A		INVESTMENT B	
	PROBABILITY	WEIGHTED VALUE	PROBABILITY	WEIGHTED VALUE
0	.15	0	0	0
5	.20	1.0	.30	1.5
10	.30	3.0	.40	4.0
15	.20	3.0	.30	4.5
20	.15	3.0	0	0.0
Estimated ROI		10.0%		10.0%

Experience shows that most, but not all, investors will choose alternative B over alternative A. In fact, as uncertainty increases, investors may require a higher estimated ROI.

Often, companies may reduce risk or uncertainty by insuring. However, insuring against nonconvertibility of funds or expropriation is apt to be costly. In the initial process of scanning to develop a manageable number of alternatives, the company should give some weight to the elements of risk and uncertainty. At the later and more detailed stage of the feasibility study, management should determine whether the degree of risk is acceptable so that it does not incur additional costs. If it is not, management needs to calculate an ROI that includes expenditures—for example, for insurance—to increase the outcome certainty of the operation.

When a company operates abroad, it usually has higher uncertainty than at home because the foreign operations are in environments with which it is less familiar. As a company gains experience in operating in a particular country or in similar countries, it improves its assessments of consumer, competitor, and government actions—thereby reducing its uncertainty. In fact, foreign companies have a lower survival rate than local companies for many years after they begin operations, a situation known as the **liability of foreignness**. However, those foreign companies that learn about their new environments and manage to overcome their early problems have survival rates comparable to those of local companies in later years.[19] The learning process also helps explain why companies often evaluate reinvestments or expanded investments within a country very differently from investments in a country where they lack experience. (We will discuss reinvestment decisions later in this chapter.)

Competitive Risk   A company's innovative advantage may be short-lived. Even when it has a substantial competitive lead time, the time may vary among markets. One strategy for exploiting temporary innovative advantages is known as the *imitation lag*. To pursue this strategy, a company moves first to those countries most likely to adapt and catch up to the innovative advantage, and later to other countries.[20] Those countries apt to catch up more rapidly are the ones whose companies invest a great deal in technology and whose governments offer little protection for the innovator's intellectual property rights. If the country also offers import protection, a local producer can, despite inefficiencies, gain a cost advantage over imported goods.

Companies also may develop strategies to find countries in which there is least likely to be significant competition. For example, in the opening case, we illustrated how Carrefour tries to gain first-entry advantage in markets likely to grow. By being the first major competitor in a market, it can gain the best partners, best locations, and best suppliers. Similarly, a company may reduce risk by avoiding overcrowded markets. For example, by 2002, 10 foreign automobile companies had invested in Chinese production. Although GM estimates that by 2025, China will be the world's third largest automobile market, analysts agree that the market cannot sustain 10 manufacturers.[21]

However, companies may gain advantages in locating where competitors are. To begin with, the competitors may have performed the costly task of evaluating locations, so a follower may get a "free ride." Moreover, there are clusters of competitors (sometimes called agglomeration) in various locations—think of all the computer firms in California's Silicon Valley. More recently, hundreds of high-tech computer companies from all over the world have located in Dubai.[22] These clusters attract multiple suppliers and personnel with specialized skills. They also attract buyers who want to compare potential suppliers but don't want to travel great distances between them. Companies operating in the cluster area may also gain better access to information about new developments because they frequently come in contact with personnel from the other companies.[23]

Monetary Risk   If a company's expansion occurs through direct investment abroad, exchange rates on and access to the invested capital and earnings are key considerations. The concept of *liquidity preference* is a common theory that helps explain companies' capital budgeting decisions in general and can be applied to their international expansion decisions.

Liquidity preference is the theory that investors usually want some of their holdings to be in highly liquid assets, on which they are willing to take a lower return. Liquidity is needed in part to make near-term payments, such as paying out dividends; in part to cover unexpected contingencies, such as stockpiling materials if a strike threatens supply; and in part to be able to shift funds to even more profitable opportunities, such as purchasing materials at a discount during a temporary price depression.[24]

Sometimes companies want to sell all or part of their equity in a foreign facility so that the funds may be used for other types of expansion endeavors. However, the ability to find local buyers varies substantially among countries and among industries, depending largely on the existence of a local capital market and on the potential for the operation being sold. For example, the Mexican conglomerate, Grupo Carso, spun off its stake in CompUSA, a process facilitated by CompUSA's potential profits and the developed U.S. capital market.[25] However, when Nike canceled a contract with an Indonesian-Korean joint venture in Indonesia, the partners simply had to close the operation.[26]

Assuming a company does find a purchaser for its foreign facility, chances are that it intends to use the funds in another country. If the funds are not convertible, the selling company will be forced to spend them in the host country. Of more pressing concern for most investors is both the ability to convert earnings from operations abroad and the cost of doing so. It is not surprising that investors may be willing to accept a lower projected ROI for projects in countries with strong currencies than for those in countries with weak currencies.

Present capital controls and recent exchange-rate stability are useful indicators of countries' monetary situation. Additionally, companies need to predict countries' likely future exchange rate deterioration and exchange controls. Some indicators of future problems are countries' negative trade balances, declining official reserves, high inflation, and government budget deficits.

Political Risk In Chapter 3, we discussed the consequences of political risk and explained that it occurs because of changes in political leaders' opinions and policies, civil disorder, and animosity between the host and other countries—particularly with the company's home country. It may cause property takeovers as well as damage property, disrupt operations, and cause a change in the rules governing business. Further, it may create expensive operational adjustments. Recently, for example, Unilever has encountered difficulty in attracting foreign executives to work in Pakistan because of security concerns, Occidental Petroleum has had to dedicate funds to protect its Colombian pipeline from rebel attacks, and Coca-Cola has had interrupted services (police protection of its trucks and telephone connections) in Angola because of its policy against paying bribes.[27] Managers use three approaches to predict political risk: analyzing past patterns, using expert opinion, and examining the social and economic conditions that might lead to such risk.

Political risk may come from wars and insurrections, takeover of property, and/or changes in rules.

Companies cannot help but be influenced by past patterns of political risk. However, predicting the risk on that basis holds many dangers. Political situations may change rapidly for better or worse as far as foreign companies are concerned. For example, foreign direct investment into the United States fell sharply after the 2001 terrorist attack in New York because foreign firms saw the United States as less safe than before. In a broader sense, expropriation of property occurred frequently in the 1970s and early 1980s, but it has been negligible in recent years. Nevertheless, companies continue to worry sufficiently about takeovers so that many still seek insurance against them.

Management can make predictions based on past patterns.

Substantial variations in political risk frequently exist within countries as well. With the exception of a few countries, government takeovers of companies have been highly selective. Similarly, unrest that leads to property damage and disruption of supplies or sales may not endanger the operations of all foreign companies. This may be because of the limited geographic focus of the unrest. For example, companies suffered no property damage or business disruption in Slovenia after the breakup of Yugoslavia; however, they did experience problems in other areas in the former Yugoslavia.

Asset takeover or property damage does not necessarily mean a full loss to investors. Governments have preceded most takeovers with a formal declaration of intent and have followed with legal processes to determine the foreign investor's compensation. Companies may examine past settlement patterns as an indicator of whether and how they may be compensated. In addition to the asset's book value, other factors may determine the adequacy of compensation. First, the compensation may earn a different return elsewhere. Second, other agreements (such as purchase and management contracts) may create additional benefits for the former investor. In analyzing political risk, managers should predict the likely loss if political problems occur.

Companies may also rely on experts' opinions about a country's political situation, with the purpose of ascertaining how influential people may sway future political events affecting business. The first step is reading statements made by political leaders both in and out of office to determine their philosophies on business in general, foreign input to business, the means of effecting economic changes, and their feelings toward given foreign countries. Modern technology has improved access to press reports in foreign countries. Online services include full-text reports from newspapers and television from major parts of the world, and reports are sometimes available within hours of the original publication or broadcast. However, published statements may appear too late for a company to react. The second step is for managers to visit the country and "listen" to a cross-section of opinions. Embassy officials and foreign and local businesspeople are useful sources of opinions about the probability and direction of change. Journalists, academicians, middle-level local government authorities, and labor leaders usually reveal their own attitudes, which often reflect changing political conditions that may affect the business sector. These attitudes are particularly important in countries without a well-defined and transparent legal system. For example, many U.S. companies have shied away from making investments in Russia because Russian tax and regulatory laws are so unstable and unpredictable.[28]

Companies may determine opinions more systematically by relying on analysts with experience in a country. These analysts might rate a country on specific political conditions that could lead to problems for foreign businesses, such as the fractionalization of political parties that could cause disruptive changes in government. A company also may rely on commercial risk-assessment services, such as those published by Business International, Economist Intelligence Unit, Euromoney, Political Risk Services (PRS), Bank of America World Information Services, Control Risks Information Services (CRIS), Institutional Investor, Moody's Investors Service, S. J. Rundt & Associates, Standard & Poor's Ratings Group, and Business Environment Risk Information (BERI). In fact, companies have been relying more on these services rather than on their internal generation of risk analyses. In essence, their reports generated internally are often too lengthy or abstract to be useful. Further, they are often not seen as credible by management decision makers.[29]

Finally, companies may examine countries' social and economic conditions that could lead to political instability. However, there is no general consensus as to what constitutes dangerous instability or how such instability can be predicted. The lack of consensus is illustrated by the diverse reactions of companies to the same political situations. For example, before the coalition forces defeated Iraq's Hussein government in 2003 most MNEs shunned investing in Iraq because of political uncertainty—U.S. companies were not allowed to invest—but some companies made large foreign investments there.[30] Further, different nationalities of companies may perceive risks to be different for the same locales, generally because of differences in their familiarity with the locales.[31] Other uncertainties include the time lag between a political event and an investor's ability to react. However, similar symptoms of political instability may result in different consequences for business in different countries. At times, political parties may change rapidly with little effect on business; at other times, sweeping changes for business

Companies should

• Examine views of government decision makers
• Get a cross-section of opinions
• Use expert analysts

Political instability does not always affect all foreign businesses in a country.

ETHICAL DILEMMA

Economic Efficiency, Noneconomic Concerns, and Competitive Strategies: Are They Compatible?

MNEs are frequently criticized when they shift geographic emphasis in response to legal, political, and economic changes. Some have been criticized for promoting potentially dangerous products more heavily abroad when their domestic laws dampen domestic demand. For example, the U.S. government restricts certain advertising of tobacco products, and companies have countered with heavy cigarette promotion in emerging economies where markets are growing. At the end of the Cold War, U.S. defense spending declined, and defense contractors turned more attention to foreign countries, many of which had either repressive regimes or conflicts that might escalate substantially. Relativists maintain it would be unethical to prohibit foreign sales because the sales are considered ethical where they are made. Normativists maintain that it is unethical for a government to permit its companies to do abroad what it prohibits them from doing domestically.

MNEs sometimes have been criticized for doing any business in countries with repressive regimes on the grounds that their presence strengthens those regimes. In fact, MNEs favor locations in which there is a nonbelligerent workforce, and such regimes often foster this characteristic; thus, FDI often increases when a dictatorship, especially a military one, is in power. However, even if FDI doesn't increase, MNEs may be criticized for operating in these countries. For example, Unocal was convicted in the United States of "aiding and abetting" human rights abuses in Myanmar because it paid taxes to a regime that abused those rights.[32] Once again, relativist versus normativist viewpoints come into play.

MNEs have justified their foreign investments largely on the grounds that those investments promote global efficiencies through low-cost production and high sales. But they sometimes make moves into foreign markets to counteract what would otherwise be a competitor's advantage. For example, a company may enter a potential global competitor's home market simply to prevent the competitor from amassing sufficient capital to expand worldwide. Such a move can be justified on competitive grounds but perhaps not on global efficiency grounds. Is it ethical? Would it make any difference if the foreign investor made no profit in the other company's home country? What if such an action led to reduced worldwide competition?

Similarly, MNEs often respond to countries' trade restrictions by locating behind their tariff walls, or they make location decisions based at least in part on the incentives governments give them. For example, Toyota and Peugeot-Citroen negotiated with the governments of Poland and the Czech Republic to determine which would give their joint venture more favorable operating conditions before deciding on a Czech location.[33] In fact, companies sometimes negotiate a monopoly position behind such walls in developing countries. The MNEs argue that such moves are necessary because markets would otherwise be lost; however, it is hard to justify these moves on global efficiency grounds. This brings up the dilemma of whether countries should work toward regulating FDI with global efficiency as their objective or whether each country should continue to be allowed to serve its own interests by competing for FDI.

may occur without a change in government. Rather than political stability itself, the direction of change in government seems to be very important. But even if a company accurately predicts the direction of change in government that will affect business, it will still be uncertain as to the time lag between the change and its effect.

Frustration occurs when there is a difference between a country's level of aspirations and its level of welfare and expectations—the higher the difference, the higher the level of frustration. If there is a great deal of frustration in a country, groups may disrupt business by calling general strikes and destroying property and supply lines. They might also replace government leaders. Moreover, frustrated groups and political leaders might try to blame problems on foreigners and make threats against foreign governments as well as expropriate foreign properties or change the rules for foreign-owned companies. But what is frustration? It is dissatisfaction as a result of unfulfilled needs. One cannot measure frustration directly. Nor can it be said that one country has higher frustration than another simply because it is poorer. People in the poorer country may either be aspiring for less, or they may expect their aspirations to be fulfilled with present political directions. Companies may examine growth in urbanization, literacy, televisions per capita, advertising expenditures, and labor unionization as indicators of growing aspirations. Such companies may examine infant survival rates, caloric consumption, hospital beds per capita, piped water supply per capita, and income per capita as indicators of welfare. They may then compare the indicators of aspirations with indicators of welfare to gain a sense of frustration levels.

COLLECT AND ANALYZE DATA

Companies undertake business research to reduce uncertainties in their decision process, to expand or narrow the alternatives they consider, and to assess the merits of their existing programs. Efforts to reduce uncertainties include attempts to answer such questions as these: "Can qualified personnel be hired?" "Will the economic and political climate allow for a reasonable certainty of operations?" Alternatives may be expanded by asking, "Where are possible new sources of funds or sales?" Or they may be narrowed by querying, "Where among the alternatives would operating costs be lowest?" Evaluation and control are improved by assessing present and past performance: "Is the distributor servicing sufficient accounts?" "What is our market share?" Clearly, there are numerous details that, if a company ascertains them, can be useful to it in its efforts to achieve its objectives.

A company can seldom, if ever, gain all the information its managers would like. This is because of time constraints and the cost of collecting information. Managers should estimate the costs of data collection and compare them with the probable payoff from the data in terms of revenue gains or cost savings.

Problems with Research Results and Data

The lack, obsolescence, and inaccuracy of data on many countries make much research difficult and expensive to undertake. Data discrepancies sometimes create uncertainties about location decisions. In most industrial countries, such as the United States, governments collect very detailed demographic and purchasing data, which are available cheaply to any company or individual. (But even in the United States, the Census Bureau first announced it had undercounted 3 million people and later that it had overcounted 1.3 million in the 2000 census.[34])

Using samples based on available information, a company can draw fairly accurate inferences concerning market-segment sizes and locations, at least within broad categories. In the United States, the fact that so many companies are publicly owned and are required to disclose much operating information enables a company to learn competitors' strengths and weaknesses. Further, companies may rely on a multitude of behavioral studies dealing with

Information is needed at all levels of control.

Companies should compare the cost of information with its value.

U.S. consumer preferences and experience. With this available information, a company can devise questionnaires or do some test marketing using a selected sample so that responses reflect the behavior of the larger target group to whom the company plans to sell. Contrast this situation to that of a country whose basic census, national income accounts, and foreign-trade figures are suspect and where no data are collected on consumer expenditures. In many countries, business is conducted under a veil of secrecy, consumers' buying behavior is a matter of speculation, market intermediaries are reluctant to answer questions, and expensive primary research may be required before meaningful samples and questions can be developed.

Many countries have agreed to standards for collecting and publishing various categories of data on the Internet. This agreement through the IMF came about because of a belief that the Mexican financial crisis of 1994 may have been averted had international financial authorities had better and more timely information about Mexico's trade, debt, and foreign-exchange reserves.[35]

Reasons for Inaccuracies   For the most part, incomplete or inaccurate published data result from the inability of many governments to collect the needed information. Poor countries may have such limited resources that other projects necessarily receive priority in the national budget. Why collect precise figures on the literacy rate, the leaders of a poor country might reason, when the same outlay can be used to build schools to improve that rate?

Education affects the competence of government officials to maintain and analyze accurate records. Economic factors also hamper record retrieval and analysis, because hand calculations may be used instead of costly electronic data-processing systems. The result may be information that is years old before it is made public. Finally, cultural factors affect responses. Mistrust of how the data will be used may lead respondents to answer incorrectly, particularly if questions probe financial details.

Of equal concern to the researcher is the publication of false or purposely misleading information designed to mislead government superiors, the country's rank and file, or companies and institutions abroad. For example, an in-house investigation in China's National Bureau of Statistics found over 60,000 cases of statistical misrepresentations that distorted such important figures as GNP, economic growth, and energy use.[36] Even if government and private organizations do not purposely publish false statements, many organizations may be so selective in the data they include that they create false impressions. Therefore, it is useful for managers to consider carefully the source of such material in light of possible motives or biases.

However, not all inaccuracies are due to government collection and dissemination procedures. Many studies by academicians describing international business practices are based on broad generalizations that may be drawn from too few observations, on nonrepresentative samples, and on poorly designed questionnaires.

People's desire and ability to cover up data on themselves—such as unreported income to avoid taxes—may distort published figures substantially. In the United States, illegal income from such activities as the drug trade, theft, bribery, and prostitution is not included in GNP figures. Worldwide, income from organized crime is substantial, but it does not appear in national income accounts, or it appears in other economic sectors because of money laundering.

Comparability Problems   Countries publish censuses, output figures, trade statistics, and base-year calculations for different time periods. So companies need to compare country figures by extrapolating from those different periods.

There also are numerous definitional differences among countries. For example, a category as seemingly basic as "family income" may include only the nuclear family—parents and children—in some countries, but it may include the extended family—the nuclear family plus

Information inaccuracies result from

- *Inability to collect data*
- *Purposeful misleading*

Problems in information comparability arise from

- *Differences in definitions and base years*
- *Distortions in currency conversions*

grandparents, uncles, and cousins—elsewhere. Similarly, some countries define literacy as some minimum level of formal schooling, others as attainment of certain specified standards, and still others as simply the ability to read and write one's name. Further, percentages may be published in terms of either adult population (with different ages used for adulthood) or total population. The definitions of accounting rules such as depreciation also differ, resulting in noncomparable net national product figures.

Countries vary in how they measure investment inflows. They might record the total value of the project (regardless of what portion may be locally owned or financed), the value of foreign capital invested, or the percentage of the project owned by foreign interests.[37]

Figures on national income and per capita income are particularly difficult to compare because of differences in activities taking place outside the market economy—for example, within the home, which do not, therefore, show up in income figures. The extent to which people in one country produce for their own consumption (for example, grow vegetables, bake bread, sew clothes, or cut hair) will distort comparisons with other countries where different portions of people buy these products and services.

Another comparability problem concerns exchange rates, which must be used to convert countries' financial data to some common currency. A 10-percent appreciation of the Japanese yen in relation to the U.S. dollar will result in a 10-percent increase in the per capita income of Japanese residents when figures are reported in dollars. Does this mean that the Japanese are suddenly 10 percent richer? Obviously not, because their yen income, which they use for about 85 percent of their purchase in the Japanese economy, is unchanged and buys no more. Even if changes in exchange rates are ignored, purchasing power and living standards are difficult to compare, because costs are so affected by climate and habit. Exchange rates, even when using PPP, are a very imperfect means of comparing national data.

External Sources of Information

Specificity and cost of information vary by source.

Although we have indicated variables that may be useful for making locational decisions, it is impossible to include a comprehensive list of information sources. There are simply too many. A routine search on the Internet often yields thousands of sources, and Lexis/Nexis gives full-text citations from thousands of sources. The following discussion highlights the major types of information sources in terms of their completeness, reliability, and cost.

Individualized Reports   Market research and business consulting companies will conduct studies for a fee in most countries. Naturally, the quality and the cost of these studies vary widely. They generally are the most costly information source because the individualized nature restricts prorating among a number of companies. However, the fact that a company can specify what information it wants often makes the expense worthwhile.

Specialized Studies   Some research organizations prepare fairly specific studies that they sell to any interested company at costs much lower than those for individualized studies. These specialized studies sometimes are printed as directories of companies that operate in a given locale, perhaps with financial or other information about the companies. They also may be about business in certain locales, forms of business, or specific products. They may combine any of these elements as well. For example, a study could deal with the market for imported auto parts in Germany.

Service Companies   Most companies that provide services to international clients—for example, banks, transportation agencies, and accounting firms—publish reports. These reports usually are geared toward either the conduct of business in a given area or some specific subject of general interest, such as tax or trademark legislation. Because the service firms intend to reach a wide market of companies, their reports usually lack the specificity a company may want for making a final decision. However, much of the data give useful background information. Some service firms also offer informal opinions about such things as the reputations of possible business associates and the names of people to contact in a company.

Government Agencies   Governments and their agencies are another source of information. Different countries' statistical reports vary in subject matter, quantity, and quality. When a government or government agency wants to stimulate foreign business activity, the amount and type of information it makes available may be substantial. For example, the U.S. Department of Commerce not only compiles such basic data as news about and regulations in individual foreign countries and product-location-specific information in the National Trade Data Bank, but it will also help set up appointments with businesspeople abroad.

International Organizations and Agencies   Numerous organizations and agencies are supported by more than one country. These include the UN, the WTO, the IMF, the OECD, and the EU. All of these organizations have large research staffs that compile basic statistics as well as prepare reports and recommendations concerning common trends and problems. Many of the international development banks even help finance investment-feasibility studies.

Trade Associations   Trade associations connected to various product lines collect, evaluate, and disseminate a wide variety of data dealing with technical and competitive factors in their industries. Many of these data are available in the trade journals published by such associations; others may or may not be available to nonmembers.

Information Service Companies   A number of companies have information-retrieval services that maintain databases from hundreds of different sources, including many of those already described. For a fee, or sometimes for free at public libraries, a company can obtain access to such computerized data and arrange for an immediate printout of studies of interest.

The Internet   Printed publications are quickly being transformed into archives that are older than information one may find on the Internet. This is because Internet changes appear immediately, whereas changes for periodicals must be printed, disseminated, cataloged, and shelved before they are available. The amount of materials available on the Internet and World Wide Web is expanding very rapidly; however, finding these materials is still somewhat haphazard because of cataloging methods. As with other sources, one must be concerned about the reliability of information gathered from Internet sources.

Internal Generation of Data

MNEs may have to conduct many studies abroad themselves. Sometimes the research process may consist of no more than observing keenly and asking many questions. Investigators can see what kind of merchandise is available, can see who is buying and where, and can uncover the hidden distribution points and competition. In some countries, for example, the competition for ready-made clothes may be from seamstresses working in private homes rather than from retailers. The competition for vacuum cleaners may be from servants who clean with mops rather than from other electrical-appliance manufacturers. Surreptitiously sold contraband may compete with locally produced goods. Traditional analysis methods would not reveal such facts. In many countries, even bankers have to rely more on clients' reputations than on their financial statements. Shrewd questioning may yield very interesting results. But such questioning is not always feasible. For example, Bass thinks that women consume most of its Barbicon Malt with Lemon, which sells well in Saudi Arabia. But it cannot be sure because in that country it cannot hold focus groups to discuss products, rely on phone books for random surveys, stop strangers on the street, or knock on the door of someone's house.[38]

Often a company must be extremely imaginative, extremely observant, or both. For example, one soft-drink manufacturer wanted to determine its Mexican market share relative to that of its competitors. Management could not make reliable estimates from the final points of distribution because sales were so widespread. So the company hit on two alternatives, both of which turned out to be feasible: The bottle cap manufacturer revealed how many caps it sold to each of its clients, and customs supplied data on each competitor's soft drink concentrate imports.

COUNTRY COMPARISON TOOLS

Once companies collect information on possible locations through scanning, they need to analyze the information. Two common tools for analysis are *grids* and *matrices*. However, once companies commit to locations, they need continuous updates, which they commonly make through environmental scanning. We shall now discuss grids, matrices, and environmental scanning.

Grids

Grids are tools that

- May depict acceptable or unacceptable conditions
- Rank countries by important variables

A company may use a grid to compare countries on whatever factors it deems important. Table 13.2 is an example of a grid with information placed into three categories. The company may eliminate certain countries immediately from consideration because of characteristics it finds unacceptable. These factors are in the first category of variables, in which country I is eliminated. The company assigns values and weights to other variables so that it ranks each country according to attributes it considers important. For example, the table graphically pinpoints country II as high return–low risk, country III as low return–low risk, country IV as high return–high risk, and country V as low return–high risk.

Both the variables and the weights will differ by product and company depending on the company's internal situation and its objectives. The grid technique is useful even when a company does not compare countries because it can set the minimum score needed for either investing additional resources or committing further funds to a more detailed feasibility study. Grids do tend to get cumbersome, however, as the number of variables increases. Although they are useful in ranking countries, they often obscure interrelationships among countries.

Matrices

Generally, managers may use two matrices when comparing countries: *opportunity-risk matrices* and *country attractiveness–company strength matrices*.

Opportunity-Risk Matrix   To show more clearly the summary of data, we can plot risk on one axis and opportunity on the other, a technique many companies use. Figure 13.5 is a simplified example that includes only six countries. The matrix shows that the company has current operations in four of the countries (all except countries A and E). Of the two nonexploited countries, A has low risk but low opportunity and E has low risk and high opportunity. If resources are to be spent in a new area, E appears to be a better bet than A. Of the other four countries, there are large commitments in D and F, medium ones in C, and a small one in B. In the future time horizon being examined, it appears that F will have low risk and high opportunity. D's situation is expected to improve during the studied period, C's

With an opportunity-risk matrix, a company can

- Decide on indicators and weight them
- Evaluate each country on the weighted indicators
- Plot to see relative placements

⬤ **TABLE 13.2**

SIMPLIFIED GRID TO COMPARE COUNTRIES FOR MARKET PENETRATION

Managers may choose which variables to include in the grid; this table is merely an example. Note also that managers may weight some variables as more important than others. Here, country I is immediately eliminated because the company will go only where 100-percent ownership is permitted. Countries II and IV are estimated to have the highest return; and countries II and III are estimated to have the lowest risk.

VARIABLE	WEIGHT	I	II	III	IV	V
				COUNTRY		
1. Acceptable (A), Unacceptable (U) factors						
a. Allows 100-percent ownership	—	U	A	A	A	A
b. Allows licensing to majority-owned subsidiary	—	A	A	A	A	A
2. Return (higher number = preferred rating)						
a. Size of investment needed	0–5	—	4	3	3	3
b. Direct costs	0–3	—	3	1	2	2
c. Tax rate	0–2	—	2	1	2	2
d. Market size, present	0–4	—	3	2	4	1
e. Market size, 3–10 years	0–3	—	2	1	3	1
f. Market share, immediate potential, 0–2 years	0–2	—	2	1	2	1
g. Market share, 3–10 years	0–2	—	2	1	2	0
Total			18	10	18	10
3. Risk (lower number = preferred rating)						
a. Market loss, 3–10 years (if no present penetration)	0–4	—	2	1	3	2
b. Exchange problems	0–3	—	0	0	3	3
c. Political-unrest potential	0–3	—	0	1	2	3
d. Business laws, present	0–4	—	1	0	4	3
e. Business laws, 3–10 years	0–2	—	0	1	2	2
Total			3	3	14	13

situation is deteriorating, and B's appears mixed (it will have better opportunity but more risk). Note that the world averages being used for comparison also shift during the period under consideration. The matrix is important as a reflection of the placement of a country in comparison to other countries.

But how are values plotted on such a matrix? The company must determine which factors are good indicators of its risk and opportunity and weight them to reflect their importance. For instance, on the risk axis, a company might give 40 percent (0.4) of the weight to expropriation risk, 25 percent (0.25) to foreign-exchange controls, 20 percent (0.2) to civil disturbances and terrorism, and 15 percent (0.15) to exchange-rate change, for a total allocation of 100 percent. It would then rate each country on a scale, such as 1 to 10, for each variable (with 10 indicating the best score and 1 the worst) and multiply each variable by the weight it allocates to it. For instance, if the company gives country A a rating of 8 on the expropriation-risk variable, the 8 would be multiplied by 0.4 for a score of 3.2. The company would then sum all of country A's risk-variable scores to place it on the risk axis. The company would use a similar procedure to plot the location of country A on the opportunity axis. Once the scores are determined for each country, management can determine the average scores for all countries' risks and opportunities and divide the matrix into quadrants.

A key element of this kind of matrix—and one that is not always included in practice—is the projection of the future country location. Such a placement's usefulness is obvious if the projections are realistic. Therefore, it is helpful to have forecasters who are knowledgeable not only about the countries but also about forecasting methods.

FIGURE 13.5 Opportunity-Risk Matrix

Countries above the horizontal dashed line have less risk and those to the right of the vertical dashed line have greater opportunity than the current world average. The dotted lines represent a projection of the world average for these variables in the future.

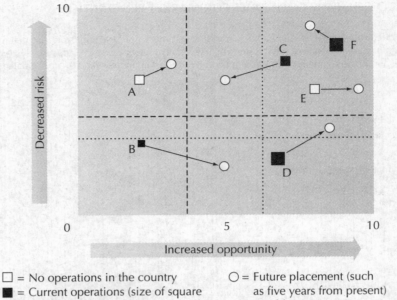

☐ = No operations in the country

■ = Current operations (size of square represents size of company operations in the country)

○ = Future placement (such as five years from present)

‐ ‐ ‐ = World average rating, present

······ = World average rating, future

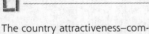

The country attractiveness–company strength matrix highlights the fit of a company's product to the country.

Country Attractiveness–Company Strength Matrix   Another matrix highlights a company's specific product advantage on a country-by-country basis. Figure 13.6 illustrates this type of matrix for market expansion before countries are plotted. The company should attempt to concentrate its activities in the countries that appear in the top left corner of the matrix and to take as much equity as possible in investments there. In this position, country attractiveness is the highest, and the company has the best competitive capabilities to exploit the opportunities. In the top right corner, the country attractiveness is also high, but the company has a weak competitive strength for those markets, perhaps because it lacks the right product. If the cost is not too high, the company might attempt to gain greater domination in those markets by remedying its competitive weakness. Otherwise, it might consider either divestment (reducing its investment) or strengthening its position through joint-venture operations with another company whose assets are complementary. A company might divest in countries in the bottom right corner or "harvest" by pulling out all possible cash it could generate while at the same time not replacing depreciated facilities. It could also license, thereby generating some income without needing to make investment outlays. In other areas, the company must analyze situations individually in order to decide which approach to take. These are marginal areas that require specific judgment.

Although this type of matrix may serve to guide decision making, managers must use it with caution. First, it is often difficult to separate the attractiveness of a country from a company's position. In other words, the country may seem attractive because of the company's fit with it. Second, some of the recommended actions take a defeatist attitude with regard to a company's competitive position. There are simply many examples of companies that built competitive strength in markets that competitors had previously dominated or that built profitable positions without being the competitive leader. Third, a company may choose to stay in a market to prevent competitors from using their dominance there to fund expansion elsewhere.

FIGURE 13.6 Country Attractiveness–Company Strength Matrix

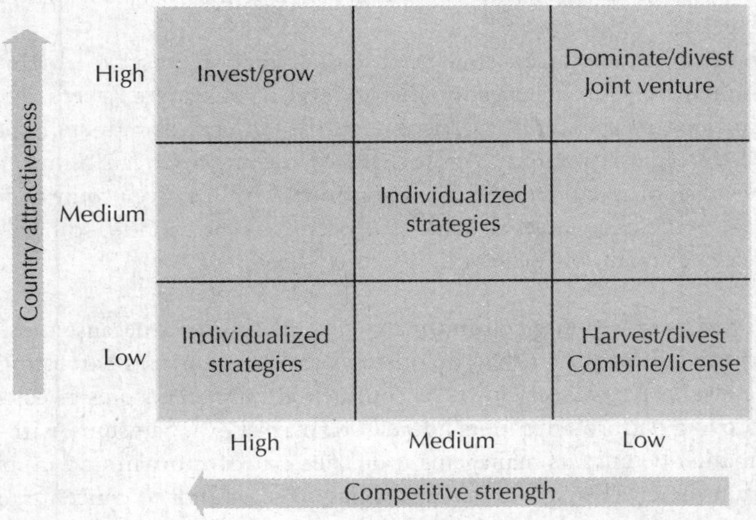

Although countries are not plotted on this matrix, those that would appear closest to the top left-hand corner are the most desirable for operations, and those that would be closest to the bottom right-hand corner are the least desirable.

Environmental Scanning

International companies rely on environmental scanning, which is the systematic assessment of external conditions that might affect their operations.[39] For example, a company might assess societal attitudes that could foreshadow legal changes. Most MNEs employ at least one executive to conduct environmental scanning continuously. The most sophisticated of these companies tie the scanning to the planning process and integrate information on a worldwide basis. Companies are most likely to seek economic and competitive information in their scanning process, and they depend heavily on managers based abroad to supply them with information.

ALLOCATING AMONG LOCATIONS

The scanning tools we have just discussed are useful for narrowing alternatives among countries. They are also useful in allocating operational emphasis among countries, but there are other factors companies need to consider. We shall now discuss three of them: reinvestment versus harvesting, the interdependence of locations, and diversification versus concentration.

Reinvestment Versus Harvesting

A company usually makes new foreign investments by transferring capital abroad. If the investment is successful, the company will earn money that it may remit back to headquarters or reinvest to increase the value of the investment. Over time, most of the value of a company's foreign investment comes from reinvestment. If the investment is unsuccessful or if its outlook is less favorable than possible investments in other countries, the company may consider harvesting the earnings to use elsewhere or even to discontinue the investment.

A company may have to make new commitments to maintain competitiveness abroad.

Reinvestment Decisions   Companies treat decisions to replace depreciated assets or to add to the existing stock of capital from retained earnings in a foreign country somewhat differently from original investment decisions. Once committed to a given locale, a company may find it doesn't have the option of moving a substantial portion of the earnings elsewhere—to do so would endanger the continued successful operation of the given foreign facility. The failure to expand might result in a falling market share and a higher unit cost than that of competitors.

Aside from competitive factors, a company may need several years of almost total reinvestment and allocation of new funds in one area in order to meet its objectives. Over time, a company may use the earnings to expand the product line further, integrate production, or expand the market served from present output. Another reason a company treats reinvestment decisions differently is that once it has experienced personnel within a given country, it may believe those workers are the best judges of what is needed for that country, so headquarters managers may delegate certain investment decisions to them.

Harvesting   Companies commonly reduce commitments in some countries because those countries have poorer performance prospects than do others, a process known as **harvesting** or **divesting**. For example, Marks & Spencer closed its continental European stores to concentrate its efforts on improving performance in its home U.K. market.[40] J. Sainsbury withdrew from the Egyptian market because its management did not expect a turnaround in its poorly performing operation there.[41] Dana sold its U.K. facility to use funds to concentrate on developing different automotive technologies.[42] When Carrefour bought Gigante's Mexican joint-venture interest, Gigante used the proceeds to build U.S. supermarkets primarily to serve Hispanic population clusters.[43]

Some indications suggest that companies might benefit by planning divestments better and by developing divestment specialists. Companies have tended to wait too long before divesting, trying instead expensive means of improving performance. Local managers, who fear losing their positions if the company abandons an operation, propose additional capital expenditures. In fact, this question of who has something to gain or lose is a factor that sets decisions to invest apart from decisions to divest. Both types of decisions should be highly interrelated and geared to the company's strategic thrust. Ideas for investment projects typically originate with middle managers or with managers in foreign subsidiaries who are enthusiastic about collecting information to accompany a proposal as it moves upward in the organization. After all, the evaluation and employment of these people depend on growth. They have no such incentive to propose divestments. These proposals typically originate at the top of the organization after upper management has tried most remedies for saving the operation.[44]

Companies may divest by selling or closing facilities. They usually prefer selling because they receive some compensation. A company that considers divesting because of a country's political or economic situation may find few potential buyers except at very low prices. In such situations, the company may try to delay divestment, hoping the situation will improve. If it does, the firm that waits out the situation generally is in a better position to regain markets and profits than one that forsakes its operation.

A company cannot always simply abandon an investment either. Governments frequently require performance contracts, such as substantial severance packages to employees, that make a loss from divestment greater than the direct investment's net value. Further, many large MNEs fear adverse international publicity and difficulty in reentering a market if they do not sever relations with a foreign government on amicable terms. Occidental Petroleum and Email and Elders decided to take losses and leave the Chinese market, but the Chinese government made their departures slow and expensive.[45]

Interdependence of Locations

The derivation of meaningful financial figures is not easy when foreign operations are concerned. Profit figures from individual operations may obscure the real impact those operations have on overall company activities. For example, if a U.S. company were to establish an assembly operation in Australia, the operation could either increase or reduce exports from the

United States. Alternatively, the same company might build a plant in Malaysia to produce a product using cheaper labor; however, doing that would necessitate more coordination costs at headquarters. Or perhaps by building a plant in Brazil to supply components to Volkswagen of Brazil, the company may increase the possibility of selling to Volkswagen in other countries. As a result of the Australian, Malaysian, or Brazilian projects, management would have to make assumptions about the changed profits in the United States and elsewhere.

The preceding discussion assumes that although overall company returns are difficult to calculate, those for the operating subsidiary are fairly easily ascertained. However, this is not always the case. Much of the sales and purchases of foreign subsidiaries may be made from and to units of the same parent company. The prices the company charges on these transactions will affect the relative profitability of one unit compared to another. Further, a company may not set the net value of a foreign investment realistically, particularly if it bases part of the net value on exported capital equipment that is obsolete at home and useless except in the country where it is being shipped. By stating a high value, a government may permit the company to repatriate a larger portion of its earnings.

Geographic Diversification Versus Concentration

Ultimately, a company may gain a sizable presence and commitment in most countries; however, there are different paths to that position. Although any move abroad means some geographic diversification, the term **diversification strategy** describes when the company moves rapidly into many foreign markets, gradually increasing its commitments within each one. A company can do this, for example, through a liberal licensing policy to ensure sufficient resources for the initial widespread expansion. The company eventually will increase its involvement by taking on activities that it first contracted to other companies. At the other extreme, with a **concentration strategy**, the company will move to only one or a few foreign countries until it develops a very strong involvement and competitive position there. There are, of course, hybrids of these two strategies—for example, moving rapidly to most markets but increasing the commitment in only a few. The following subsections discuss major variables a company should consider when deciding which strategy to use.[46] (See Table 13.3.)

Strategies for ultimately reaching a high level of commitment in many countries are

- Diversification—go to many fast and then build up slowly in each
- Concentration—go to one or a few and build up fast before going to others
- A hybrid of the two

● TABLE 13.3

PRODUCT AND MARKET FACTORS AFFECTING CHOICE BETWEEN DIVERSIFICATION AND CONCENTRATION STRATEGIES

If the conditions under "prefer diversification" exist, a company is likely to benefit by moving rapidly into many countries simultaneously; otherwise, the company might move to just one or a few foreign countries until a substantial presence is developed there.

PRODUCT OR MARKET FACTOR	PREFER DIVERSIFICATION IF:	PREFER CONCENTRATION IF:
1. Growth rate of each market	Low	High
2. Sales stability in each market	Low	High
3. Competitive lead time	Short	Long
4. Spillover effects	High	Low
5. Need for product adaptation	Low	High
6. Need for communication and distribution adaptation	Low	High
7. Program control requirements	Low	High
8. Extent of constraints	Low	High

Source: "Marketing Expansion Strategies in Multinational Marketing," from *Journal of Marketing,* Vol. 43, Spring 1979, p. 89. Reprinted by permission of the American Marketing Association.

Growth Rate in Each Market   When the growth rate in each market is high, a company usually should concentrate on a few markets because it will cost a great deal to expand output sufficiently in each market. Further, costs per unit are typically lower for the market-share leader. Slower growth in each market may result in the company's having enough resources to build and maintain a market share in several different countries.

Sales Stability in Each Market   A company may smooth its earnings and sales because of operations in various parts of the world. This smoothing results from the leads and lags in the business cycles. In addition, a company whose assets and earnings base are in a variety of countries will be less affected by occurrences within a single one; for example, a strike or expropriation will affect earnings from only a small portion of total corporate assets. Further, currency appreciation in some countries may offset depreciation in others.[47] Although diversification is usually of secondary importance as a motive for foreign expansion, it is nevertheless an added advantage from operating abroad. Further, a company may be leery of depending too much on too few foreign locations.[48]

The more stable that sales and profits are within a single market, the less advantage there is from a diversification strategy. Similarly, the more interrelated markets are, the less smoothing is achieved by selling in each.

Competitive Lead Time   We have discussed why Carrefour has wanted to gain first-in advantages. However, so many resources may be needed to capitalize on the first-in advantage that companies may be unable to move quickly into many markets. Of course, an alternative is to share ownership abroad, which Carrefour usually does. However, sequential entry into multiple markets is more common than simultaneous entry. If a company determines that it has a long lead time before competitors are likely to be able to copy or supersede its advantages, then it may be able to follow a concentration strategy and still beat competitors into other markets.

Spillover Effects   Spillover effects are situations in which the marketing program in one country results in awareness of the product in other countries. These effects are advantageous because additional customers may be reached with little additional cost. This can happen if the product is advertised through media sent cross-nationally, such as U.S. television ads that reached Canadians. When marketing programs reach many countries, such as by cable television or the Internet, a diversification strategy has advantages.

Need for Product, Communication, and Distribution Adaptation   Companies may have to alter products and their marketing to sell in foreign markets, a process that, because of cost, favors a concentration strategy. The adaptation cost may limit the resources the company has for expanding in many different markets. Further, if the adaptations are unique to each country, the company cannot easily spread the costs over sales in other countries to reduce total unit costs. For example, Ben & Jerry's took a concentration strategy by moving into the British market with as rapid an increase in distribution as possible so that it could cover the high fixed costs of its local adaptations in ice cream production and advertising.[49]

Program Control Requirements   The more a company needs to control its operations in a foreign country, the more it should develop a concentration strategy. This is because the company will need to use more of its resources to maintain that control. Its need for more control could result from various reasons, including the fear that collaboration with a partner will create a competitor or the need for highly technical assistance for customers.

Extent of Constraints   If a company is constrained by the resources it needs to expand internationally compared to the resources it can muster, it will likely follow a concentration strategy. For example, Ben & Jerry's first tried to enter the United Kingdom and Russian markets almost simultaneously but quickly dissolved its Russian operation. A company manager explained the decision by saying, "We simply don't have the people and resources. We're a small company. You tie up two or three senior managers and you have a measurable effect on the company's performance."[50]

MAKING FINAL COUNTRY SELECTIONS

Thus far, we have examined comparative opportunities on a very broad basis. At some point, a company must perform a much more detailed analysis of specific projects and proposals in order to make allocation decisions. For new investments, companies need to make on-site visits and detailed estimates of all costs and expenses. They will need to evaluate whether they should enter the market alone or with a partner. For acquisitions, they will need to examine financial statements in detail. For expansion within countries where they are already operating, managers within those countries will most likely submit capital budget requests that include details of expected returns. As we indicated earlier, companies use a variety of financial criteria to evaluate foreign investments. In addition, they rely on qualitative analysis that includes such factors as expected competitive response and the fit of new activities with existing ones. If, for example, a company's large industrial customer decides to produce in a particular country, the company's decision may be one of "how to enter" rather than "whether to enter" that country as well.

Because companies have limited resources at their disposal, it might seem that they maintain a storehouse of foreign investment proposals that they may rank by some predetermined criteria. If this were so, management could simply start allocating resources to the top-ranked proposal and continue down the list until it could make no further investments. This is often not the case, however. Companies tend to evaluate and decide on investment proposals separately. One factor is that some overriding consideration may cause one location to be considered above all others. For example, the Swiss pharmaceutical company Novartis wanted a research lab in the midst of the major portion of gene research. This research was in only one place; Boston in the United States.[51] In contrast, the U.S. pharmaceutical company Eli Lilly decided to set up research laboratories in both Europe and Asia and to hire scientists who did not want to work in the Midwest of the United States. It then compared locations in both regions.[52] When a company does not compare different locations, a positive decision usually means the project meets some minimum-threshold criteria. Of course, before a company makes a final decision, it has approved the project at various levels of increased detail.

Two major factors restricting companies from comparing investment opportunities are cost and time. Clearly, some companies cannot afford to conduct very many investigations simultaneously. If these investigations are conducted simultaneously, they are apt to be in various stages of completion at a given time. For example, suppose a company completes its investigation for a possible project in Australia but is still researching projects in New Zealand, Japan, and Indonesia. Can the company afford to wait for the results from all the surveys before deciding on a location? Probably not. The time interval between completions probably would invalidate much of the earlier results and necessitate updating, added expense, and further delays. Other time-inhibiting problems are government regulations that require a decision within a given period and changes in government regulations that impel companies to react before their competitors react. For example, when the government of India announced that foreign companies could invest in Indian newspapers, foreign publishers had to react quickly.[53] Also, other companies may impose time limits on partnership proposals.

During all of this evaluating and selecting, companies still have the pressure of satisfying stockholders and employees. Few companies can afford to let resources lie idle or be employed for a low rate of return during a waiting period. This rule of thumb applies not only to financial resources but also to such resources as technical competence, because the companies reduce their lead time over competitors when they make decisions slowly.

Most companies examine proposals one at a time and accept them if they meet minimum-threshold criteria.

LOOKING TO THE FUTURE

Will Locations and Location-Models Change?

International geographic expansion is a two-tiered consideration: How much of a company's sales and production should be outside its home country? And how should outside sales and production be allocated among countries? As yet, no comprehensive model exists to answer these questions, and perhaps differences among companies and dynamic environmental conditions make such a model impractical. Meanwhile, companies are apt simply to place more emphasis on certain locales than on others as they see opportunities evolving. Typical of this tendency was a greater emphasis on Asia by Royal Dutch Shell. By increasing the portion of its capital budget on Asia, its management expected Asia to grow from 20 percent of its business to 30 to 35 percent of its business over a 25 year period.[54]

The need for companies to allocate among opportunities because of insufficient resources is liable to play an even more important role in the near future. The receptiveness of more countries to FDI and the global move toward privatization have combined to create more opportunities from which companies may choose. At the same time, companies may not have increased their resource bases concomitantly to enable them to take advantage of all these new opportunities.

Because data availability should continue to improve, global environmental scanning will assume greater importance. Companies will continue to need information because of the global strategies of competitors and because of economic and political volatility. However, the information explosion will present new challenges as timely analysis may necessitate even greater reliance on tools that reduce the number of alternatives under consideration.

An intriguing future possibility is the near officeless headquarters for international companies. Technology may permit managers to work from anywhere as they e-mail and teleconference with their colleagues, customers, and suppliers elsewhere. Thus, managers could live anywhere in the world and work from their homes. The use of offices at home is already occurring for companies' domestic operations.[55] However, we are not convinced of this possibility. The same technology should enable managers to travel less, but business travel has soared along with advances in communications.

Summary

- Because companies seldom have sufficient resources to exploit all opportunities, two major considerations facing managers are which markets to serve and where to locate the production to serve those markets.

- Companies' decisions on market and production location are highly interdependent because companies often need to serve markets from local production, because they want to use existing production capacity, and because they may be unwilling to invest in those production locations needed to serve a desired market.

- Scanning techniques aid managers in considering alternatives that might otherwise be overlooked. They also help limit the final detailed feasibility studies to a manageable number of those that appear most promising.

- The ranking of countries is useful for determining the order of entry into potential markets and for setting the allocation of resources and rate of expansion to different markets.

- Because each company has unique competitive capabilities and objectives, the factors affecting the geographic expansion pattern will be slightly different for each. Nevertheless, companies take the environmental climate into consideration. Most companies are influenced by the relative size of country markets, the ease of operating in the specific countries, the availability and cost of resources, and the perceived relative risk and uncertainty of operations in one country versus another.

- The amount, accuracy, and timeliness of published data vary substantially among countries. Managers should be particularly aware of different definitions of terms, different collection methods, and different base years for reports, as well as misleading responses.

- Sources of published data on international business include consulting firms, government agencies, international agencies, trade associations, the Internet, and organizations that serve international businesses. The cost and specificity of these publications vary widely.

- Companies frequently use several tools to compare opportunities in various countries: *grids* that rate country projects according to a number of separate dimensions and *matrices* on which companies may plot one attribute on a vertical axis and another on the horizontal axis (e.g., opportunity and risk or country attractiveness and company strength).

- Because of the interdependence of operations in different countries, it is difficult to derive meaningful financial figures to evaluate the effects or return from operations in a single country.

- Companies normally treat reinvestment decisions separately from new investment decisions because a reinvestment may be needed to protect existing resources' viability and because there are people on location who can better judge the worthiness of proposals.

- Using a similar amount of internal resources, a company may choose initially to move rapidly into many foreign markets with only a small commitment in each (a diversification strategy) or to pursue a strong involvement and commitment in one or a few locations (a concentration strategy).

- The major variables a company should consider when deciding whether to diversify or concentrate are the growth rate and sales stability in each market, the expected lead time over competitors, the spillover effects, the degree of need for product and marketing (communication and distribution) adaptation in different countries, the need to maintain control of the expansion program, and the constraints the company faces.

- Companies must develop location strategies for new investments and devise means of deemphasizing certain areas and divesting if necessary.

- Once a feasibility study is complete, most companies do not rank investment alternatives but rather set some minimum-threshold criteria and either accept or reject a foreign project based on those criteria. This type of decision results because multiple feasibility studies seldom are finished simultaneously and there are pressures to act quickly.

CASE

Royal Dutch Shell/Nigeria[56]

In 2002, Royal Dutch/Shell (Shell) announced a $7.5 billion oil and gas investment in Nigeria over five years, the biggest industrial investment ever made in sub-Saharan Africa. A few months after the announcement, hundreds of women blocked Shell's facilities in southern Nigeria and kept workers from entering or leaving the premises. These women were protesting against their region's poverty amidst the wealth that they expected Shell to extract from that region. In effect, this protest was simply a new episode in a long-running saga. Shell had invested in and become highly dependent on Nigeria for many years because Nigeria offers low-cost petroleum extraction. At the same time, Shell has faced high political risk because of its Nigerian operations.

NIGERIAN SITUATION

Nigeria, a British colony until 1960, has a population of over 126 million, making it by far the most populous country in Africa. The country is organized into fairly autonomous states, and the government has the challenge of trying to unite 250 different ethnic and linguistic groups. At times, ethnic conflict has been severe, especially in the 1966–1970 period during a civil war between the predominantly Moslem Hausas and the predominantly Christian Ibos, who seceded unsuccessfully to form the Republic of Biafra. During that period, oil companies received demands for royalty payments on Biafran oil from the governments of both Nigeria and Biafra.

Nigeria has had a series of military coups, and military rule has existed more years than civilian rule since Nigeria gained its independence. In 1998, an elected civilian government replaced a Hausa-speaking military junta, which sought to quell, sometimes brutally, any moves by minority groups for more autonomy.

The Nigerian National Petroleum Corporation (NNPC), a government-owned company, is a joint-venture partner in all Nigerian petroleum projects. Nigeria has more foreign direct investment than any other country in Africa.

SHELL IN NIGERIA

Shell has long considered political risk in its decision making. In the early 1970s, Shell's planners realized that technical tools for predicting where oil might be found had become quite sophisticated; however, they reasoned that they should not make exploration-location decisions based only on the likelihood of finding oil at a given cost. There were many political factors that could affect the security of their ownership and of getting oil to market. They developed rating schemes to examine the underlying conditions within and between countries that could affect the security of assets and the ability to export them to their markets. Shell hired political specialists to rate these conditions in a uniform manner so that company planners could plot on one axis the technical feasibility (opportunity) of securing oil and on the second axis the political risk of securing that oil. This tool served to help in the planning of a portfolio of countries to serve as suppliers.

Shell also perfected scenario analysis to help understand conditions that might affect future global demands and supplies of petroleum and to prepare for different contingencies. One of the factors it noted was that the size of a country's oil reserves did not necessarily correspond with the country's eagerness to sell the oil. For example, a country might wish to hold back supplies because it was already running a balance-of-payments surplus, because it could not absorb increased income efficiently into its economy, or because it expected future prices to exceed the present value of investing oil income. In this analysis, Nigeria has consistently shown up as a country willing to sell almost unlimited supplies, even though its reserves are not nearly as ample as countries such as Saudi Arabia, which is more apt to limit supplies.

However, Shell began selling in Nigeria in the late 1920s, before it developed its sophisticated tools to help deal with risk and uncertainty. In 1937, it formed a joint venture with British authorities that gave it exclusive rights to explore for oil. The joint venture found oil for the first time in 1956 in Ogoniland and later in other areas of Nigeria. Map 13.2 shows Nigeria and Ogoniland, the latter a small 404-square-mile area of Nigeria at the delta of the Niger River. Subsequently, this joint venture sold exploration rights to other oil companies; however, Shell's operations control about half of Nigeria's oil output. Although Shell procures oil in a large portfolio of countries, the Nigerian operations are significant, accounting for about 10 percent of the company's petroleum sources.

THE OGONI SITUATION

The Shell joint venture includes oil wells, refineries, and a fertilizer plant in Ogoniland. The Nigerian government's revenues from these operations have traditionally gone to the country's central government, and very little has been redistributed back to Ogoniland. Beginning in 1992, a group of Ogonis, led by the

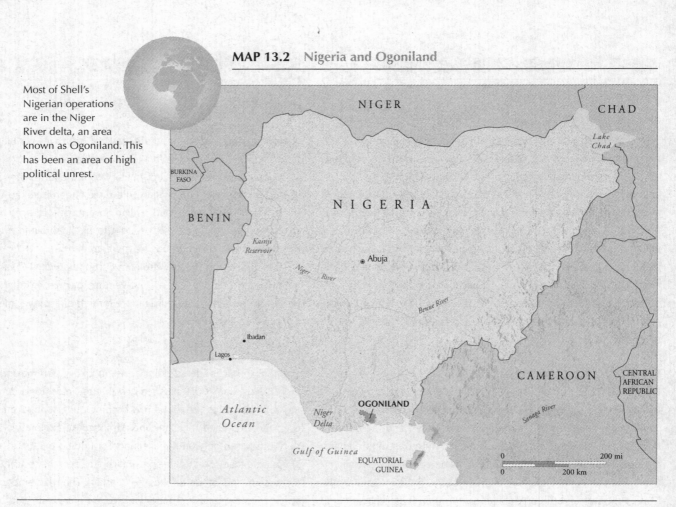

Most of Shell's Nigerian operations are in the Niger River delta, an area known as Ogoniland. This has been an area of high political unrest.

MAP 13.2   Nigeria and Ogoniland

author Kenule Saro-Wiwa, formed the Movement for the Survival of Ogoni People (MOSOP). MOSOP began campaigning for political self-determination, a greater share of oil revenues, compensation for losses from Shell's activities, and restoration of the environment in Ogoniland. Some specific charges have been that Shell oil spills have despoiled farmlands and fishing areas, that oil flares have affected health, and that the laying of pipes destroyed freshly planted crops. Saro-Wiwa accused Shell of waging an ecological war against the Ogoni people to complete a genocide. MOSOP demonstrations resulted in violence as the Nigerian army, using troops from other ethnic groups, opened fire on crowds and attacked Ogoni villages. Ogonis began sabotaging Shell facilities, and the situation became so severe that Shell suspended operations in that part of Nigeria in early 1993. The Nigerian government arrested Saro-Wiwa and eight others for inciting and directing supporters to violence, held them in jail nearly a year, and then hanged them in 1995. Shortly before his arrest, Saro-Wiwa said, "They are going to arrest us all and execute us. All for Shell."

Although Shell publicly opposed the executions and had written a letter to the Nigerian head of state requesting clemency for Saro-Wiwa, the company has been accused of not doing enough. A representative from Greenpeace, one of Shell's major critics, said, "Shell is the most powerful political actor on the Nigerian stage—both historically and currently. In Nigeria, the power doesn't come from the people, it comes from Shell. If Shell wanted to make a difference, [it] would." But the managing director of Shell's operation in Nigeria said, "We did not negotiate. We were not in a position to negotiate his release. We had no power to do so."

After the executions, Shell faced many, sometimes conflicting, pressures outside of Nigeria. It was under pressure to divest all Nigerian operations, to avoid investing in new Nigerian projects, to forgo trying to reopen operations in Ogoniland, and to pay all environmental and other costs in Ogoniland.

In 1997, Shell faced the first shareholder resolution presented to any company in the United Kingdom. The resolution called for more public accountability of the company's Nigerian operations. The shareholder group supporting the resolution included 18 public and private pension funds, 5 religious institutions, and an academic fund. At about the same time, protesters marched in Washington to urge a boycott of the purchase of Nigerian oil; the European Union froze $295 million in aid to Nigeria while considering an arms sales or full embargo on business with Nigeria; the World Bank announced it would not go forward with a $100 million investment in a gas plant in which Shell planned to participate; various organizations in South Africa called for Shell to divest its Nigerian operations; and pressures mounted in the United Kingdom for a consumer boycott of Shell.

AFTERMATH OF THE RESOLUTION

At Shell's 1998 annual meeting, groups that had criticized Shell a year earlier congratulated the company on its efforts to seek independent verification of the environmental and social impact of its global operations. However, attendees asked many questions about the Nigerian operation, indicating that Nigeria continues to be a problem for Shell. Shell's chairman said, "Nigeria is very difficult to solve . . . we'll be working on this for many years to come." One of the things Shell has done is to institute community development programs in the Niger delta region; Shell's annual budget is more than $50 million, and it employs about 130 social workers.

Meanwhile, two ethnic groups—the Ijaw and the Akassas—in addition to the Ogonis, have stepped up their complaints about the lack of economic benefits going to the people where oil fields are located. Shell has faced sabotage of its pipeline, work-stopping occupation of facilities by protesters, kidnapping of employees, and the hijacking of expensive equipment for ransom. The company even put some Ijaw youth on its payroll and asked them to stay at home and out of trouble.

Shell reasons that its announcement of massive expansion will demonstrate its support of a civilian democratic government, thus helping to reduce criticism of its earlier handling of the Ogoni problems. Next, the company believes the best way to get funds to the neglected regions is by increasing Nigerian oil revenues, which by yielding billions of dollars to the government of Nigeria will give the government more funds to spend. Finally, much of the investment will go toward natural gas production, thus keeping the environmental problem from flaring. However, if the government does not address the development problems adequately, groups in the oil-producing areas will likely put pressure on the company to provide infrastructure and social services. Not only will this reduce profits, but it will also put Shell into activities for which it lacks expertise. In the meantime, the new leader of MOSOP said, "People in Ogoni and most other places in the delta think of Shell as a company that is insensitive to people and their environment. They see it as an ally to oppression. The challenge in the rhetoric from Shell over the years has not been matched by a change in actions in Nigeria. Shell is excellent at public relations but is terrible at turning words into reality."

QUESTIONS

1. What specific political risk problems does Shell face in Nigeria? What are the underlying reasons for these problems?
2. Given the high political risk in Nigeria, why doesn't Shell go somewhere else?
3. What actions can Shell take to quell criticism about its operations in Nigeria?

Chapter Notes

1   Data for this case were taken from: www.carrefour.com/; Eirmalasare Bani, "Carrefour Gives Priority to Locally-Made Products," *Business Times* [Malaysia] (November 9, 1998): 3; "Carrefour Globalizes Sales," *Gazeta Mercantil Online* (October 13, 1998): Business & Company News, n.p.; Michiyo Nakamoto, "Carrefour Sounds Alarm for Japan's Ailing Retail Market," *Financial Times* (December 8, 2000): 36; Jo Johnson, "Carrefour Chief Has No Regrets About Promodès Takeover," *Financial Times* (April 25, 2001): 32; Rosabeth Moss Kanter, "Global Competitiveness Revisited," *Washington Quarterly* 22, no. 2 (Spring 1999): 39–58; "Report: Carrefour Plans Expansion," *HFN* 75, no. 50 (December 10, 2001): 3; "Global Strategy—Why Tesco Will Beat Carrefour," *Retail Week* (April 6, 2001): 14; "Carrefour Closes Hong Kong Chain After Site Pitfalls," *Retail Week* (September 1, 2000): 3; "Carrefour Beats Wal-Mart to Global Crown," *Retail Week* (December 15, 2000): 5; "Carrefour Aims to Win Global Retail Battle," *MMR* 17, no. 12 (June 26, 2000): 60; Lisa Vincenti, "Carrefour to Enter Wal-Mart's Turf?" *HFN* 74, no. 4 (January 24, 2000): 8; "Hypermarkets for Britain," *The Economist* (July 3, 1976): 77; "French Retailer Abandons 'Hypermarkets' in U.S." *New York Times* (September 8, 1993): D4; "Strategies for Retail Globalisation," *Financial Times* (March 13, 1998): 4; "Carrefour Opens Three Supermarkets in Chile," *Gazeta Mercantil Online* (August 29, 1997): front page section; "Gigante Quits Joint Venture," *Financial Times* (February 3, 1998): 26; Mark Albright, "This Is Just Way Too Big': European-style Hypermarkets Not as Hot in U.S.," *St. Petersburg Times* (February 12, 1990): 7; and Anthony Ramirez, "Will American Shoppers Think Bigger Is Really Better?" *New York Times* (April 1, 1990): Section 3, 11.

2   Bob Lutz, *GUTS: The Seven Laws of Business That Made Chrysler the World's Hottest Car Company* (New York: Wiley, 1998).

3   Philip Parker, "Choosing Where to Go Global: How to Prioritise Markets," *Financial Times* (November 16, 1998): mastering marketing section, 7–8.

4   Joe Leahy, "Ferrari Sales Roar Ahead in Poor, Troubled Indonesia," *Financial Times* (April 7–8, 2001): 4.

5   David Gonzalez, "Fried Chicken Takes Flight, Happily Nesting in U.S.," *New York Times* (September 20, 2002): A4.

6   Mikhail V. Gratchev, "Making the Most of Cultural Differences," *Harvard Business Review* 79, no. 96 (October 2001): 28–30.

7   Rodney L. Russell and Robert P. Jones, "Estimating for a Worldwide Company," *AACE International Transactions* (2001): IN51–IN53.

8   Khanh T. L. Tran, "Blockbuster Finds Success in Japan" *Wall Street Journal* (August 19, 1998): A14; and Cecile Rohwedder, "Blockbuster Hits Eject Button as Stores in Germany See Video-Rental Sales Sag," *Wall Street Journal* (January 16, 1998): B9A.

9   David Luchnow, "Missing Piece of the Mexican Success Story," *Wall Street Journal* (March 4, 2002): A11+.

10 See James Lamont, "South African Companies May Have to Report AIDS Rates," *Financial Times* (August 15, 2002): 1; and James Lamont,

"Investors in South Africa 'Bewildered by Action on AIDS,'" *Financial Times* (September 12, 2002): 9.

11 Andrew Bartmess and Keith Cerny, "Building Competitive Advantage Through a Global Network of Capabilities," *California Management Review* (Winter 1993): 78–103.

12 G. Bruce Knecht, "Going the Wrong Way Down a One-Way Street," *Wall Street Journal* (March 18, 2002): A1.

13 Alfredo J. Mauri and Arvind V. Phatak, "Global Integration as Inter-Area Product Flows: The Internationalization of Ownership and Location Factors Influencing Product Flows Across MNC Units," *Management International Review* 41, no. 3, (Third Quarter 2001): 233–49.

14 Nagesh Kumar, "Multinational Enterprises, Regional Economic Integration, and Export-Platform Production in the Host Countries: An Empirical Analysis for the U.S. and Japanese Corporations," *Weltwirtschaftliches Archive* 134, no. 3 (1998): 450–83.

15 Lisa Bannon, "As Holiday Season Approaches, Toy Shipments Are Imperiled," *Wall Street Journal* (October 4, 2002): A9.

16 "Volkswagen Switches Work to Low-Cost Unit in Slovakia," *Financial Times*, December 19, 1995, 4.

17 Henri E. Cauvin, "A Quest to Promote the Quality of Cars Made in South Africa," *New York Times* (November 24, 2001): C1+.

18 Sheri Prasso and Paul Magnusson, "Welcome Back?" *Business Week* (August 16, 1999): 54.

19 See Srilata Zaheer and Elaine Mosakowski, "The Dynamics of the Liability of Foreignness: A Global Study of Survival in Financial Services," *Strategic Management Journal* 18, no. 6 (June 1997): 439–64; and Stewart R. Miller and Arvind Parkhe, "Is There a Liability of Foreignness in Global Banking? An Empirical Test of Banks' X-Efficiency," *Strategic Management Journal* 23, no. 1 (January 2002): 55–75.

20 Philip Parker, "Choosing Where to Go Global: How to Prioritise Markets," *Financial Times* (November 16, 1998): mastering marketing section, 7–8.

21 David Murphy and David Lague, "As China's Car Market Takes Off, the Party Grows a Bit Crowded," *Wall Street Journal* (July 3, 2002): A8.

22 Hugh Pope, "Q: Why Are the World's IBMs Putting Down Roots in the Desert? A: Dubai," *Wall Street Journal* (January 23, 2001): A18.

23 See J. Myles Shaver and Fredrick Flyer, "Agglomeration Economies, Firm Heterogeneity, and Foreign Direct Investment in the United States," *Strategic Management Journal* 21, no. 12 (December 2000): 1175–93; Philippe Martin and Gianmarco I. P. Ottaviano, "Growth and Agglomeration," *International Economic Review* 42, no. 4 (November 2001): 947–68; and Edward E. Leamer and Michael Storper, "The Economic Geography of the Internet Age," *Journal of International Business Studies* 32, no. 4 (Fourth Quarter 2001): 641–65.

24 Liquidity preference is much like options theory, associated with the work of Robert C. Merton, Myron S. Scholes, and Fisher Black. For a good, terse coverage, see John Krainer, "The 1997 Nobel Prize in Economics," *FRBSF Economic Letter*, no. 98–05 (February 13, 1998).

25 Andrea Mendel-Campbell and Robin Emmott, "Carso to Spin Off US Holding," *Financial Times* (September 15, 2001): 18.

26 Sadanand Dhume and Maureen Tkacik, "Footwear Is Fleeing Indonesia," *Wall Street Journal* (September 9, 2002): A12+.

27 See Farhan Bokhari, "Western Expatriates Give Way to Local Heroes," *Financial Times* (August 30, 2002): 8; Alexi Barrionuevo, "Wages of Terror," *Wall Street Journal* (February 7, 2002): A1; and Henri E. Cauvin, "Braving War and Graft, Coke Goes Back to Angola," *New York Times* (April 22, 2001): Section 3, 1+.

28 Thaddeus Herrick and Alexi Barrionuevo, "U.S. Oil Firms Shy Away from Russia," *Wall Street Journal* (October 3, 2002): A10.

29 Marvin Zonis and Sam Wilkin, "Driving Defensively Through a Minefield of Political Risk," *Financial Times* (May 30, 2000): Mastering Risk section, 8–10.

30 Andrew Buncombe, "Iraq, the Threat of War," *The Independent* [London] (September 26, 2002): 7.

31 Stewart Dalby, "Political Worries Hit Investors," *Financial Times* (December 18, 1995): 4. Dalby quotes data collected by the Control Risk Group.

32 Pui-Wing Tam, "Myanmar Human-Rights Suit Against Unocal is Reinstated," *Wall Street Journal* (September 19, 2002): A10.

33 John Reed, "Poland in Slow Lane," *Financial Times* (February 26, 2002): 1.

34 "Census Bureau Issues Data on Accuracy of 2000 Count." *New York Times* (April 16, 2003): A13.

35 Robert Chote, "Nations Rally to IMF's Statistics Standards," *Financial Times* (July 30, 1996): 4.

36 James Kynge, "Pyramid of Power Behind Numbers Game," *Financial Times* (February 28, 2002): 6.

37 Michael Stephan and Eric Pfaffmann, "Detecting the Pitfalls of Data on Foreign Direct Investment: Scope and Limits of FDI," *Management International Review* 41, no. 2 (Second Quarter 2001): 189–218.

38 Tara Parker-Pope, "Nonalcoholic Beer Hits the Spot in Mideast," *Wall Street Journal* (December 6, 1995): B1.

39 Chun Wei Choo, "The Art of Scanning the Environment," *Bulletin of the American Society for Information Science* (February–March 1999): 21–24.

40 Erin White, "Marks & Spencer CEO to Step Down," *Wall Street Journal* (July 11, 2002): B8.

41 Susanna Voyle and James Drummond, "J. Sainsbury to Withdraw from Egypt," *Financial Times* (April 10, 2001): 23.

42 Nikki Tait, "Dana Set to Sell UK-Based Components Arm," *Financial Times* (November 29, 2000): 22.

43 Joel Millman, "California City Fends Off Arrival of Mexican Supermarket," *Wall Street Journal* (August 7, 2002): B1+.

44 See Jean J. Boddewyn, "Foreign and Domestic Divestment and Investment Decisions: Like or Unlike?" *Journal of International Business Studies* 14, no. 3 (Winter 1983): 28; Michelle Haynes, Steve Thompson, and Mike Wright, "The Determinants of Corporate Divestment in the U.K.," *Journal of Industrial Organization* 18, no. 8 (December 2000): 1201–22; and Jose Mata and Pedro Portugal, "Closure and Divestiture by

Foreign Entrants: The Impact of Entry and Post-entry Strategies," *Strategic Management Journal* 21, no. 5 (May 2000): 549–62.

45 Julia Leung, "For China's Foreign Investors, the Door Marked 'Exit' Can Be a Tight Squeeze," *Wall Street Journal* (March 12, 1991): A14.

46 Igal Ayal and Jehiel Zif, "Marketing Expansion Strategies in Multinational Marketing," *Journal of Marketing* 43 (Spring 1979): 84–94.

47 Rory Knight and Deborah Pretty, "The Real Benefits of Corporate Diversification," *Financial Times* (March 9, 2000): Mastering Risk section, 14–16.

48 Woo Wing Thye, "Malaysia Still Attracts FDIs as Firms Diversify," *Business Times* [Kuala Lumpur] (September 12, 2002): 6.

49 Diane Summers, "Chunky Monkey Invasion," *Financial Times* (August 11, 1994): 7.

50 See Neela Banerjee, "Ben & Jerry's Is Discovering That It's No Joke to Sell Ice Cream to Russians," *Wall Street Journal* (September 9, 1995). The quotation comes from Betsy McKay, "Ben & Jerry's Post-Cold War Venture Ends in Russia with Ice Cream Melting," *Wall Street Journal* (February 7, 1997): A12.

51 Vanessa Fuhrmans and Rachel Zimmerman, "Swiss Drug Giant Joins Exodus to U.S. with New Global Lab," *Wall Street Journal* (May 7, 2002): A1.

52 Adrian Michels, "Eli Lilly Set to Expand in Europe and Asia," *Financial Times* (December 7, 2000): 6.

53 Edna Fernandes, "India to Let Foreigners Invest in Newspapers," *Financial Times* (June 26, 2002): 6.

54 Richard Borsuk and Sharon Lim, "Asia May Gain One-Third Share of Shell's Business in 25 Years," *Wall Street Journal* (May 8, 2002): B9.

55 Deborah Hargreaves, "'Virtual' Staff Make Themselves at Home in Offices of the Future," *Financial Times* (May 14, 1999): 8.

56 Data for the case were taken from Paul Adams, Robert Corzine, William Lewis, and Roger Matthews, "Shell Facing New Onslaught over Nigeria," *Financial Times* (December 15, 1995): 3; Tony Hawkins and Simon Kuper, "Foreign Investors Are in No Hurry to Divest," *Financial Times* (November 14, 1995): 9; David Lascelles, "Shell Under Pressure as EU Toughens Stance on Nigeria," *Financial Times* (November 14, 1995): 18; Richard Hudson and Matthew Rose, "Shell Is Pressured to Scrap Its Plans for New Plant in Nigeria Amid Protests," *Wall Street Journal* (November 14, 1995): A10; Simon Kuper and David Lascelles, "ANC Sanctions Threat to Shell over Nigeria," *Financial Times* (November 18–19, 1995): 1; Pierre Wack, "Scenarios: Uncharted Waters Ahead," *Harvard Business Review* (September–October 1985): 73–89; Steve Kretzmann, "Nigeria's 'Drilling Fields,'" *Multi-national Monitor* (January–February 1995): 8–11; Simon Kuper, "Shell 'Ignored' Warnings on Nigerian Pollution," *Financial Times* (May 14, 1996): 4; William Lewis, "Shell Faces UK First in Investors' Resolution on Ethics," *Financial Times* (February 24, 1997): 1; William Wallis and Robert Corzine, "An Unhappy History of Neglect," *Financial Times* (February 23, 1999): Nigeria section, 5; William Wallis, "Ethnic Fighting Flares in Nigerian Oil Delta," *Financial Times* (June 2, 1999): 6; Robert Corzine, "Shell Calms Fears on Environment," *Financial Times* (May 9–10, 1998): 22; Robert Corzine and William Wallis, "Risk of More Disruption for Oil Companies," *Financial Times* (February 2, 1999): 8, John Bray, "Petroleum and Human Rights: The New Frontiers of Debate," *Oil & Gas Journal* (November 1, 1999): 65–69; David Buchan and Patti Waldmeir, "Shell Fails to Prevent Trial on Abuses in Nigeria," *Financial Times* (March 27, 2001): 10; John Vidal, "Branded: When Disaster Strikes," *Guardian* [London] (July 9, 2001): 10; "Shell to Invest Pounds 5.2 billion in Nigeria," *The Independent* [London] (January 9, 2002): 14; Sara McConnell, "Ethical Business: Pouring Oil on Troubled Waters," *Guardian* [London] (July 20, 2002): 22; and "Women Block Chevron and Shell Offices in Nigeria," *New York Times* (August 10, 2002): A2. For up-to-date information on Shell's situation in Nigeria from the Internet, see www.shellnigeria.com/.

14

COLLABORATIVE STRATEGIES

When one party is willing, the match is half made.

—AMERICAN PROVERB

OBJECTIVES

- To explain the major motives that guide managers when they choose a collaborative arrangement for international business
- To define the major types of collaborative arrangements
- To describe some considerations for not entering into arrangements with other companies
- To discuss what makes collaborative arrangements succeed or fail
- To discuss how companies can manage diverse collaborative arrangements

CASE

Cisco Systems[1]

Collaboration can take many forms. Companies collaborate to link with other companies in the supply chain and to gain synergy by combining complementary resources. The U.S. company Cisco, like some of its counterparts in other countries (e.g., Philips in the Netherlands and Samsung in Korea), sees its ability to ally effectively with other companies as a distinctive strength. Cisco collaborates in many ways. It has entered into joint ownership arrangements with other companies to share production, distribution, and technology-development facilities. It contracts with other companies to it share technology and it relies on other companies to produce and distribute goods and components.

Cisco Systems is the world's largest supplier of data networking equipment and the leading global supplier of computer networking solutions. In 2001, it supported its sales in 75 countries through technical centers in Australia, Belgium, Canada, India, and the United States. International sales accounted for 42 percent of its revenues. Cisco sees partnerships as the third pillar in its growth strategy, along with internal development and acquisitions. The company's official Strategic Alliances Team manages crucial partnerships with industry-leading technology and integrator companies, and it is the driving force behind the collaborative-development effort whose purpose is to accelerate new market opportunities. Implementing this strategy has led Cisco to develop a range of alliance and partnership programs with U.S. and non-U.S companies that help it compete better both domestically and internationally. Map 14.1 shows a sample of these collaborations.

Cisco's worldwide alliances help it achieve many objectives. These alliances spur the company to continue learning and to refine its competencies. They enable it to meet customer needs that fall outside its area of core competencies, while simultaneously permitting it and its partners to enhance their competitiveness

MAP 14.1 Sample of Cisco's International Collaborations

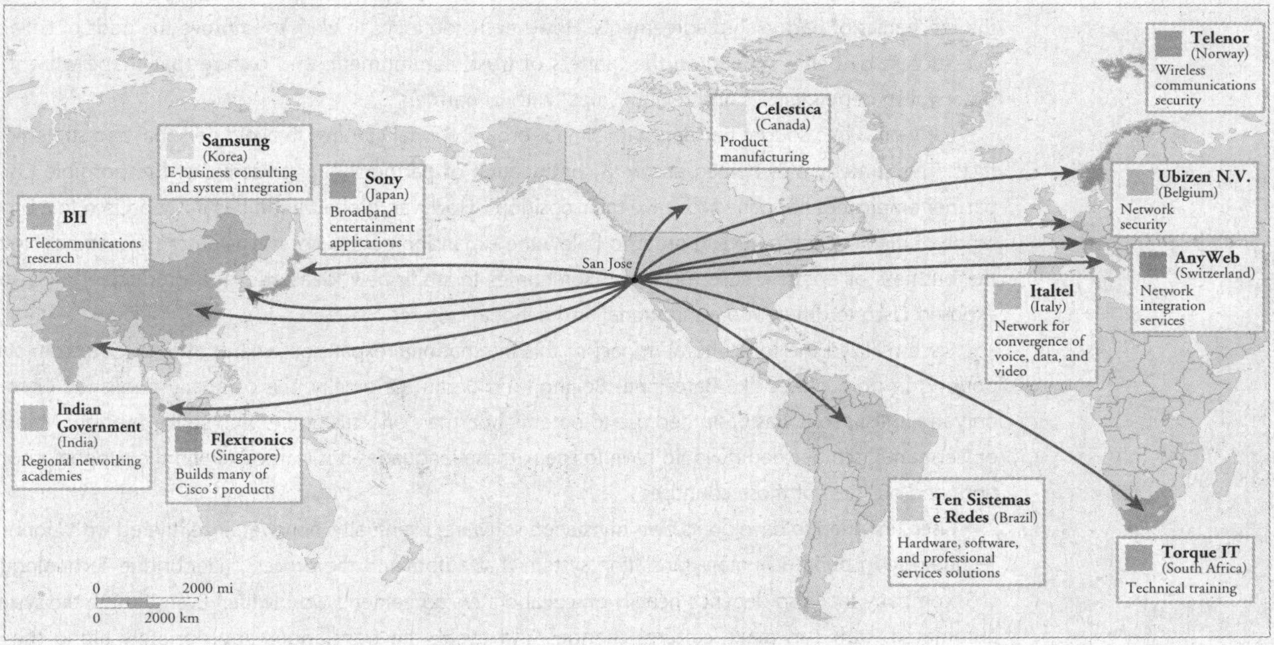

The map shows merely a small sample of Cisco's vast network of global collaborations.

by focusing them on their respective core competencies. For example, Cisco established a joint venture with the Singaporean company ePic, thus enabling the two to use their complementary technology for an Internet video monitoring service. Cisco's global alliances vice president, Charles Giancarlo, observed, "If there's technology outside Cisco that works well, we acquire it. And if we feel that we don't need it internally, we'll partner with an organization to help get it to our customers."

Alliances have also permitted Cisco to limit its capital outlays in potentially lucrative but risky ventures. For example, Cisco partnered with Motorola in 1999 in a joint venture, Spectrapoint Wireless, by spending $300 million to acquire the wireless assets of German-based Bosch Telecom. The two partners pledged to spend $1 billion more on the venture over the next five years in order to become leaders in this market. One year later, Motorola and Cisco called off the partnership because the projected market did not materialize.

Cisco believes that alliances improve its processes, reduce its costs, and expose it to the best competitive practices. Finally, collaboration provides Cisco with a cost-effective way to expand into new markets. Consequently, Steve Steinhilber, vice president of strategic alliances, said, "The number of alliances we are doing is picking up. Given the current economic climate, partnering is more appealing than acquisitions. The investments are more affordable, and you can still speed up time to market."

Cisco relies on about 150 employees to oversee its many alliances. To manage these alliances, the employees depend on the technology that has made Cisco successful—technology that facilitates communications. Thus, these employees rely on the World Wide Web, e-mail, file sharing, and conferencing to provide a network that efficiently links partners across corporate and national boundaries. These linkages have demonstrated and made available to its partners such Cisco capabilities as the Cisco Connection and Cisco Internet Business Roadmap. The Cisco Connection provides online information and interactive services worldwide, including software upgrades, technical assistance, order status, seminar registration, documentation, and training. The Cisco Internet Business Roadmap adds information on solutions, programs, tools, and sales resources. Both programs provide Cisco and its partners instant global communications, enhanced productivity, consistent business systems and lower business costs. "For many established companies, the Web has legitimized alliances," noted the director of Accenture's global alliance practice, a Cisco partner in wireless communications security.

Managing collaborative agreements poses challenges. Not all agreements lead companies to realize the value of or to achieve the business objectives they had initially expected. Cisco has generally standardized the mechanics of partnership agreements. However, it continues to work to improve the odds of collaborative success by better managing the matters of trust, commitment, and culture that shape what it calls "interwoven dependencies and relationships" with its partners.

Early on, Cisco sought partners with similar organizational cultures to avoid personal and strategic conflicts. This strategy also helped ensure a continuation of partnership arrangements if responsible Cisco or partner employees happened to leave their positions. However, globalization has pushed Cisco to a broader range of markets, sometimes in order to follow the expansion patterns of its customers, sometimes to solicit the business of possible customers, and sometimes to study new ideas and new products. Doing so has exposed Cisco to different organizational and national cultures.

Cisco realized the full cultural impact of this international expansion when traffic to Cisco.com started pouring in from places like Barcelona, Beijing, and Berlin. Originally, the company published Cisco.com only in English, so it was of limited use to potential partners and customers who spoke Spanish, Mandarin, or German. Cisco decided it would have to speak those languages if it wanted to win the support, cooperation, and business of those countries.

Cisco first tried to develop its own translation software; eventually, however, it partnered with Lionbridge Technology to build a human-translation system that automated the process. (Lionbridge Technology is a U.S. company that also depends heavily on collaborative agreements worldwide.) Even though the system is automated, staff can make cultural changes and tweak the translations appropriately along the way. Cisco.com is now published in many languages. Moreover, although Cisco manages the site's back-end systems centrally, it relies on its nearly 70 local sales and support offices around the world to maintain language-specific pages and to ensure that documents are relevant to partners within various countries.

Despite occasional problems, alliances are an important aspect of Cisco's international strategy. Cisco started early and has continued strongly to use partnerships to extend its ability to service customers in more markets around the world. Its philosophy of mutually beneficial partnerships (in whatever nation they happen to call home) and its efforts to improve partners' performance have boosted Cisco's competitiveness through innovative products, strong distribution, and a global service network. Concomitantly, its partners enhance their business credibility and gain greater market penetration.

INTRODUCTION

Figure 14.1 shows that companies must choose an international operating mode to fulfill their objectives and carry out their strategies. Many of the modes from which they may choose involve collaboration with other companies. In addition, a company may produce at home or abroad. In Chapter 8, we explained the reasons for producing abroad rather than exporting, and we discussed why (appropriability and internalization theories) companies would want to control foreign production through direct investment. Nevertheless, companies frequently handle much of their international operations through collaborative forms that lessen their control. Figure 14.2 shows the types of collaborative modes (highlighted in purple). The truly experienced MNE with a fully global orientation usually uses most of the operational modes available, selecting them according to specific product or foreign operating characteristics. Further, those modes may be combined. For example, Wendy's from the United States formed a joint venture in Canada with IAWS from Ireland to make par-baked (half-baked, then frozen for shipment) bread to ship to Wendy's Tim Hortons franchises in Canada and to an IAWS Cuisine de France subsidiary in the United States.[2] When collaboration is of strategic importance (having a large impact on total performance) to one or more of the companies, it is known as a strategic alliance. In reality, the term *strategic alliance* often describes a wide variety of collaborations, whether or not they are of real strategic importance. Collaborations provide opportunities and problems that are different from those provided by trade or wholly owned direct investment.

This chapter discusses the motives for and types of collaborative arrangements as well as the problems and methods of managing these arrangements.

FIGURE 14.1   Collaborative Arrangements as International Business Operating Modes

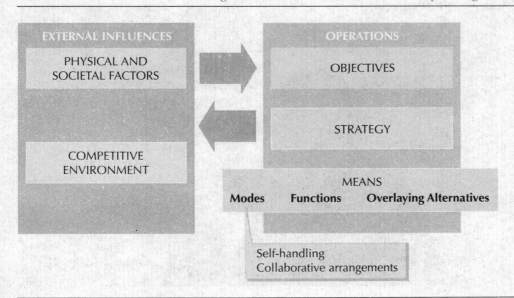

Companies must handle international business operations on their own or collaborate with other companies. Their choice is influenced externally by physical and societal factors and by their competitive environment. Their choice is also influenced by their objectives and strategies.

FIGURE 14.2   Alternative Operating Modes for Foreign Market Expansion

A company may use more than one operating mode within the same location. Those shaded in purple are collaborative arrangements. Note that exporting is the only mode for market expansion in which production is in the home country.

PRODUCTION OWNERSHIP	PRODUCTION LOCATION	
	Home country	Foreign country
Equity arrangements	a. Exporting	a. Wholly owned operations b. Partially owned with remainder widely held c. Joint ventures d. Equity alliances
Nonequity arrangements		a. Licensing b. Franchising c. Management contracts d. Turnkey operations

MOTIVES FOR COLLABORATIVE ARRANGEMENTS

The reasons that lead companies to establish collaborative arrangements for domestic operations carry over to their international operations as well. For example, a company such as McDonald's that franchises most of its operations in the United States also franchises most of its operations in foreign countries—for the same reasons, which we'll discuss in the next section. Companies also establish collaborative arrangements abroad for reasons that differ from the reasons that lie behind their domestic collaborations. For example, one of the reasons that Cisco established a joint venture in India was because Indian laws prohibited its gaining 100-percent ownership. Figure 14.3 shows both the general and internationally specific reasons for collaborative arrangements. This figure also refers back to the three objectives of international business introduced in Chapter 1.

Who says that people from an Anglo culture are undemonstrative? The photo shows the CEO and COO in London (United Kingdom) after the cross-national merger creating Time Warner EMI.

FIGURE 14.3   Relationship of Strategic Alliances to Companies' International Objectives

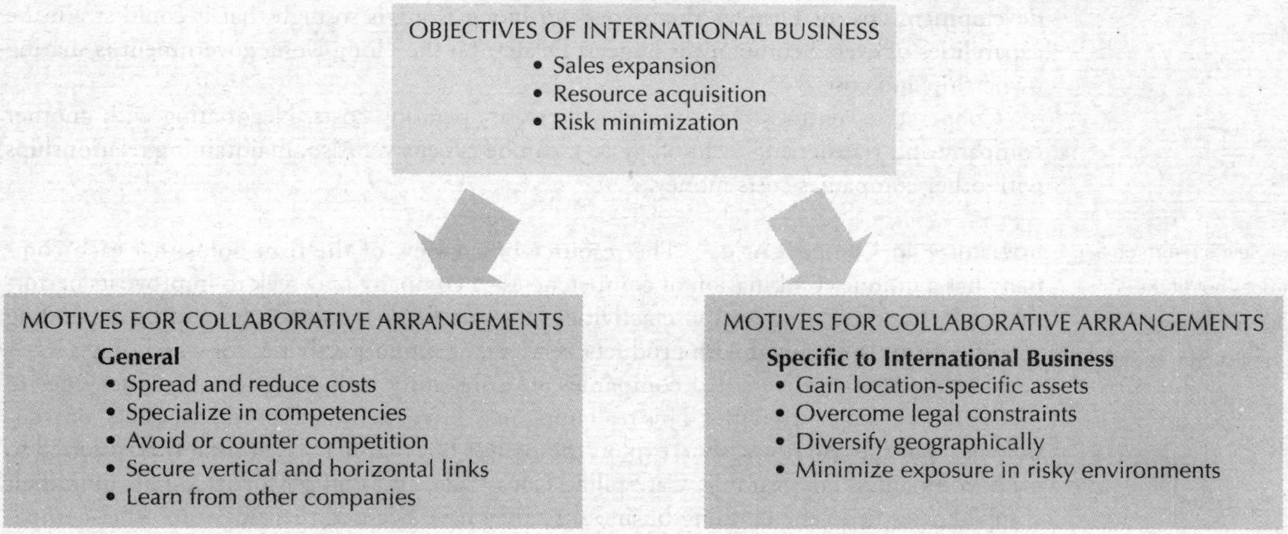

OBJECTIVES OF INTERNATIONAL BUSINESS
- Sales expansion
- Resource acquisition
- Risk minimization

MOTIVES FOR COLLABORATIVE ARRANGEMENTS

General
- Spread and reduce costs
- Specialize in competencies
- Avoid or counter competition
- Secure vertical and horizontal links
- Learn from other companies

MOTIVES FOR COLLABORATIVE ARRANGEMENTS

Specific to International Business
- Gain location-specific assets
- Overcome legal constraints
- Diversify geographically
- Minimize exposure in risky environments

Collaborative arrangements may serve companies' goals, regardless of whether they operate internationally. In addition, there are gains from collaborative arrangements that are specific to companies' international operations.

Keep in mind that each participant in a collaborative arrangement has its own primary objective for operating internationally and its own motive for collaborating. For example, GM entered a joint venture with Russian Avtovaz. GM wanted production of Avtovaz's low-priced vehicle to sell in developing countries, and Avtovaz wanted GM's financial and technical resources to make sport utility vehicles in Russia.[3]

Motives for Collaborative Arrangements: General

In this section, we'll explain the reasons why companies collaborate with other companies in either domestic or foreign operations: to spread and reduce costs, to allow them to specialize in their competencies, to avoid or counter competition, to secure vertical and horizontal links, and to learn from other companies.

Spread and Reduce Costs   To produce or sell abroad, a company must incur certain fixed costs. At a small volume of business, it may be cheaper for it to contract the work to a specialist rather than handle it internally. A specialist can spread the fixed costs to more than one company. If business increases enough, the contracting company then may be able to handle the business more cheaply itself. Companies should periodically reappraise the question of internal versus external handling of their operations.

A company may have excess production or sales capacity that it can use to produce or sell for another company. The company handling the production or sales may lower its average costs by covering its fixed costs more fully. Likewise, the company contracting out its production or sales (outsourcing) will not have to incur fixed costs that may have to be charged to a small amount of production or sales. Using this capacity also may reduce start-up time for the outsourcing company, providing earlier cash flow. Further, the contracted company may have environment-specific knowledge, such as how to deal with regulations and labor, that would be expensive for the contracting company to gain on its own. Also, contracting companies may lack the resources to "go it alone." By pooling their efforts, such contracting companies may be able to undertake activities that otherwise would be beyond their means.

Sometimes it's cheaper to get another company to handle work, especially

- At small volume
- When the other company has excess capacity

This is especially important for small and young companies.[4] But it is important for large companies when the cost of development and/or investment is very high. For example, the development cost of Disney's theme park in Hong Kong is so high that it could strain the capabilities of even a company as large as Disney. So the Hong Kong government is sharing ownership and costs.[5]

Cooperative ventures may, however, increase operating costs. Negotiating with another company and transferring technology to it can be expensive. Also, maintaining relationships with other companies costs money.

Specialize in Competencies   The **resource-based view of the firm** holds that each company has a unique combination of competencies. A company may seek to improve its performance by concentrating on those activities that best fit its competencies and by depending on other firms to supply it with products, services, or support activities for which it has lesser competency. Large, diversified companies are constantly realigning their product lines to focus on their major strengths. This realigning may leave them with products, assets, or technologies that they do not wish to exploit themselves but that may be profitably transferred to other companies. For example, Caterpillar, Coca-Cola, and Philip Morris do not think their competencies lie in the clothing business, so they have licensed their logos to other companies to put them on clothing.[6] In addition, companies may be able to pool their competencies through collaboration so that they realize greater gains than they could realize by acting alone.[7] However, a collaborative arrangement has a limited time frame, which may allow a company to exploit a particular product, asset, or technology itself if, at a later date, it gains the needed core competencies.

Avoid or Counter Competition   Sometimes markets are not large enough to hold many competitors. Companies may then band together so that they do not have to compete with one another. For example, approximately 30 communications carriers, including GTE, MCI, AT&T, and Cable and Wireless have teamed to form New World, a broadband fiber optic network connecting the United States with Latin America and the Caribbean.[8] Companies may also combine resources to fight a leader in the market. For example, Coca-Cola and Danone formed a joint venture to market bottled water in the United States so that they would be large enough to challenge PepsiCo and Nestlé, the two companies with the largest market shares.[9] Or companies may simply collude to raise everyone's profits. Only a few countries, mainly English-speaking ones, make and enforce laws against collusion.[10]

Another example of avoiding competition involves the major aluminum producers, which have developed swap contracts that allow them to save transport costs. These companies are all vertically integrated, but not in each country in which they operate. Alcan has smeltering, manufacturing, and sales in Canada, but only manufacturing and sales in France. Pechiney has smeltering, manufacturing, and sales in France, but only manufacturing and sales in Canada. Alcan might give Pechiney smeltered output in Canada in exchange for the same amount of smeltered output delivered to Alcan in France. Thus, the companies continue to compete for sales in each market without having to be as vertically integrated in each. Similarly, Ford's European plants make cars for Mazda, which it sells in Europe, and Mazda's Japanese factories make vehicles for Ford, which it sells in Japan.[11]

Secure Vertical and Horizontal Links   There are potential cost savings and supply assurances from vertical integration. However, companies may lack the competence or resources needed to own and manage the full value-chain of activities. For example, recall the LUKoil case in Chapter 8. LUKoil has abundant oil reserves but lacks final distribution skills so, in addition to picking up acquisitions abroad, it has established collaborative arrangements in countries that assure markets for its petroleum.

Licensing can yield a return on a product that does not fit the company's strategic priority based on its best competencies.

Horizontal links may provide finished products or components. For finished products, there may be economies of scope in distribution—for example, sales reps may be able to offer a full line of products, thereby increasing the sales per fixed cost for a visit to potential customers. For example, Duracell, the biggest maker of consumer batteries, and Gillette, the biggest maker of razor blades, combine their sales forces in many parts of the world to gain economies of scope.[12] There may also be a better smoothing of earnings through diversification into products with sales fluctuations at different times.

One of the fastest growth areas for collaborative arrangements has been in industries with projects that were too large for any single company to handle—for example, new aircraft and communications systems. From such an arrangement's inception, different companies (sometimes from different countries) agree to take on the high cost and high risk of development work for the different components that are needed in the final product. Then a lead company buys the components from the companies that did parts of the developmental work.

Learn from Other Companies Many companies pursue collaborative arrangements to learn about a partner's technology, operating methods, or home market so that their own competencies will broaden or deepen, making them more competitive in the future. Recall Chapter 11's case on FDI in China: Chinese government authorities allow foreign companies to tap the Chinese market in exchange for their transference of technology to Chinese partners. Sometimes each partner can learn from the other, a motive driving joint ventures between U.S. and European wine makers, such as the Opus One Winery owned by Robert Mondavi from the United States and Baron Philippe de Rothschild from France.[13]

Motives for Collaborative Arrangements: International

In this section, we'll continue discussing the reasons why companies enter into collaborative arrangements, covering those reasons that apply only to international operations. Specifically, these reasons are to gain location-specific assets, overcome governments' legal constraints, diversify geographically, and minimize exposure in risky environments.

Gain Location-Specific Assets Cultural, political, competitive, and economic differences among countries create barriers for companies that want to operate abroad. When they feel ill-equipped to handle these differences, such companies may seek to collaborate with local companies that will help manage local operations. For example, Wal-Mart first tried to enter the Japanese market on its own, but it gave up after having disappointing sales. It has since returned with a Japanese partner, Seiyu, that is more familiar with Japanese tastes and rules for opening new stores.[14] In fact, most foreign companies in Japan need to collaborate with Japanese companies that can help in securing distribution and a competent workforce—two assets that are difficult for foreign companies to gain on their own there. This has been especially true in pharmaceuticals. The top 10 Western pharmaceutical companies have about 45 percent of the global drug market but only about one-quarter of the Japanese market.[15] Access to distribution was the primary reason that Merck entered into a joint venture with Chugai in Japan for the development and marketing of over-the-counter drugs.[16]

Overcome Governmental Constraints Many countries limit foreign ownership. For example, the United States limits foreign ownership in airlines that service the domestic market and in sensitive defense manufacturers. Mexico limits ownership in the oil industry. China and India are particularly restrictive, often requiring foreign companies either to share ownership or make numerous concessions to help them meet their economic and sovereignty goals. Thus, companies may have to collaborate if they are to serve certain foreign markets.

Legal factors may be

- Direct prohibitions against certain operating forms
- Indirect (for example, regulations affecting profitability)

Other legal factors may influence the company's choice. These include differences in tax rates and in the maximum funds it can remit to its home country.

Government procurement, particularly military procurement, is another area that may force companies to collaborate. In effect, governments give preference to bids that include national companies. For example, Northrop Grumman from the United States teamed with Rolls-Royce in the United Kingdom to supply marine engines for both the British and U.S. navies.[17]

Collaboration can be a means of protecting an asset. Many countries provide little de facto protection for intellectual property rights (e.g., trademarks, patents, and copyrights) unless authorities are prodded consistently. To prevent pirating of these proprietary assets, companies sometimes have entered into collaborative agreements with local companies, which then monitor their local partners to make sure that no one else uses the asset locally. Also, some countries provide protection only if the internationally registered asset is exploited locally within a specified period. If a company does not use the asset within the country during that specified period, then whatever entity first does so gains the right to it. For example, Burger King did not use its name in time within the Australian market. Another company now uses it there, and Burger King sells its fares in Hungry Jack restaurants.[18]

> Collaboration hinders nonassociated companies from pirating the asset.

Diversify Geographically

By operating in a variety of countries (geographic diversification), a company can smooth its sales and earnings because business cycles occur at different times within the different countries. Collaborative arrangements offer a faster initial means of entering multiple markets. Moreover, if product conditions favor a diversification rather than a concentration strategy (recall the discussion in Chapter 13), there are more compelling reasons to establish foreign collaborative arrangements. However, these arrangements will be less appealing for companies whose activities are already widely extended or those that have ample resources for such extension.

Minimize Exposure in Risky Environments

Companies worry that political or economic changes will affect the safety of assets and their earnings in their foreign operations. One way to minimize loss from foreign political occurrences is to minimize the base of assets located abroad—or to share them. A government may be less willing to move against a shared operation for fear of encountering opposition from more than one company, especially if they are from different countries and can potentially elicit support from their home governments. Another way to spread risk is to place operations in a number of different countries. This strategy reduces the chance that all foreign assets will encounter adversity at the same time.

> The higher the risk managers perceive in a foreign market, the greater their desire to form collaborative arrangements in that market.

TYPES OF COLLABORATIVE ARRANGEMENTS

The forms of foreign operations differ in the amount of resources a company commits to foreign operations and the proportion of the resources located at home rather than abroad. Licensing, for example, may result in a lower additional capital commitment than a foreign joint venture will.

Throughout this discussion, keep in mind that there are always trade-offs. For example, a decision to take on no ownership stake in foreign production—for example, by licensing production to a foreign company—may reduce exposure to political risk. However, learning about that environment will be slow, delaying (perhaps permanently) your reaping the full profits from producing and selling your product abroad.

Keep in mind also that when a company has a desired, unique, difficult-to-duplicate resource, it is in a good position to choose the operating form it would most like to use. The preferred form may be exporting, selling from a wholly owned direct investment, or participating in a collaborative arrangement. However, when a company lacks this bargaining

> Collaborative arrangements allow for a greater spreading of assets among countries.

> The type of collaborative arrangement managers choose may necessitate trade-offs among objectives.

> Companies have a wider choice of operating form when there is less likelihood of competition.

When What's Right for One Partner Isn't Right for the Other Partner

One potential ethical problem arising from collaborative arrangements is a company's skirting of unethical practices by having a partner handle them. A second problem is that a company might treat its partner unethically.

How should a company deal with foreign partners whose practices on pollution, labor relations, and bribery are very different from those in its home country? On the one hand, the company might take an arm's length approach and simply transact business on the basis of quality, delivery time, and price—leaving the supplier or licensee to operate the way it is accustomed to. On the other hand, it may try to interfere with those practices.[19] Increasingly, NGOs criticize companies for what their suppliers do—or even the suppliers of their suppliers. This creates a dilemma. If a company does try to influence these practices—for example, by including operating provisions in its contracts—it may still be very difficult and costly to monitor compliance with the provisions. For example, Nike was criticized for using suppliers in Cambodia that employed underage workers despite signing a contract with Nike that they would not do so. Nike reviewed the records of all 3,800 workers but could still not be sure of ages because many birth records either didn't exist or were unreliable. To help control against supplier abuses, Nike, like some other companies, has contracted an NGO to help monitor activities of partners.[20]

All partners put resources into collaborative arrangements. The question is whether any partner should take resources from the operation that are not specified in the agreement. For example, one partner in a joint venture may transfer a scientist to the operation, who, in addition to working on the venture's R&D, learns about breakthroughs that would be useful to that partner. Would it be ethical to pass this information along? Or a highly qualified manager may be hired by a joint venture. After the manager gains experience, would it be ethical for one of the partners in the venture to hire him or her away? Would the ethical issues be any different if one partner felt it was contributing more than the other compared to its income from the venture?

strength, it faces the possibility of competition. It may have to settle on a form that is lower on its priority list; otherwise, a competitor may preempt the market.

A further constraint facing managers is finding a desirable collaboration partner. For example, if the collaboration includes a transfer of technology, it may be impossible to find a local company familiar enough with the technology or having sufficiently similar values and priorities as the company transferring technology.[21] In effect, there are costs associated with transferring technology to another entity. Usually, it is cheaper to transfer within the existing corporate family, such as from parent to subsidiary, than to transfer to another company. The cost difference is especially important when the technology is complex because a subsidiary's personnel are more likely to be familiar with the approaches the parent uses.

Some Considerations in Collaborative Arrangements

We have just discussed the reasons why companies enter into collaborative arrangements. Before explaining the types of arrangements, we shall discuss two variables that influence managers' choice of one type of arrangement over another: their desire for control over foreign operations and their companies' prior foreign expansion.

Control   The more a company depends on collaborative arrangements, the more likely it is to lose control over decisions, including those regarding quality, new product directions, and where to expand output. This is because each collaborative partner has a say in these decisions, and the global performance of each one may be improved differently. External arrangements also imply the sharing of revenues, a serious consideration for undertakings with high potential profits because a company may want to keep them all for itself. Such arrangements also risk allowing information to pass more rapidly to potential competitors. The loss of control over flexibility, revenues, and competition is an important variable that guides a company's selection of forms of foreign operation.

Prior Expansion of the Company.   When a company already has operations (especially wholly owned ones) in place in a foreign country, some of the advantages of contracting with another company to handle production or sales are no longer as prevalent. The company knows how to operate within the foreign country and may have excess capacity it can use for new production or sales. However, much depends on whether the existing foreign operation is in a line of business or performs a function that is closely related to the new product, service, or activity being initiated abroad. When there is similarity—for example, when a company that already produces office equipment decides to produce a new type of office equipment— it is likely that the new production will be handled internally. In highly diversified companies or in cases when operations are limited (such as when subsidiaries produce components only for the parent), the existing foreign facility may be handling goods or functions so dissimilar to what is being planned that it is easier to deal with an experienced external company instead.

Licensing

Under a licensing agreement, a company (the licensor) grants rights to intangible property to another company (the licensee) to use in a specified geographic area for a specified period. In exchange, the licensee ordinarily pays a royalty to the licensor. The rights may be exclusive (the licensor can give rights to no other company) or nonexclusive (it can give away rights). The U.S. Internal Revenue Service classifies intangible property into five categories.

1. Patents, inventions, formulas, processes, designs, patterns
2. Copyrights for literary, musical, or artistic compositions
3. Trademarks, trade names, brand names
4. Franchises, licenses, contracts
5. Methods, programs, procedures, systems

Usually, the licensor is obliged to furnish technical information and assistance, and the licensee is obliged to exploit the rights effectively and to pay compensation to the licensor.

Major Motives for Licensing   Frequently, a new product or process may affect only part of a company's total output and then only for a limited time. The sales volume may not be large enough to warrant establishing overseas manufacturing and sales facilities. A company that is already operating abroad may be able to produce and sell at a lower cost and with a shorter start-up time, thus preventing competitors from entering the market. For the licensor, the risk of operating facilities and holding inventories lessens. The licensee may find that the cost of the arrangement is less than if it developed the new product or process on its own.

For industries in which technological changes are frequent and affect many products, companies in various countries often exchange technology rather than compete with each other on every product in every market. Such an arrangement is known as *cross-licensing*. For example, Fujitsu from Japan, Saifun Semiconductors from Israel, and Advanced Micron

---

Internal handling of foreign operations usually means more control and no sharing of profits.

MNEs want returns from their intangible assets.

Licensing agreements may be
- *Exclusive or nonexclusive*
- *Used for patents, copyrights, trademarks, franchises, and other intangible property*

Licensing often has an economic motive, such as the desire for faster start-up, lower costs, or access to additional property rights, such as technology.

Devices from the United States entered a technology-sharing, cross-licensing agreement for complementary nonvolatile memory technology.[22]

Payment   The amount and type of payment for licensing arrangements vary. Each contract tends to be negotiated on its own merits. Figure 14.4 shows the major factors that determine

FIGURE 14.4   Determinants of Compensation for International Licensing of Technology

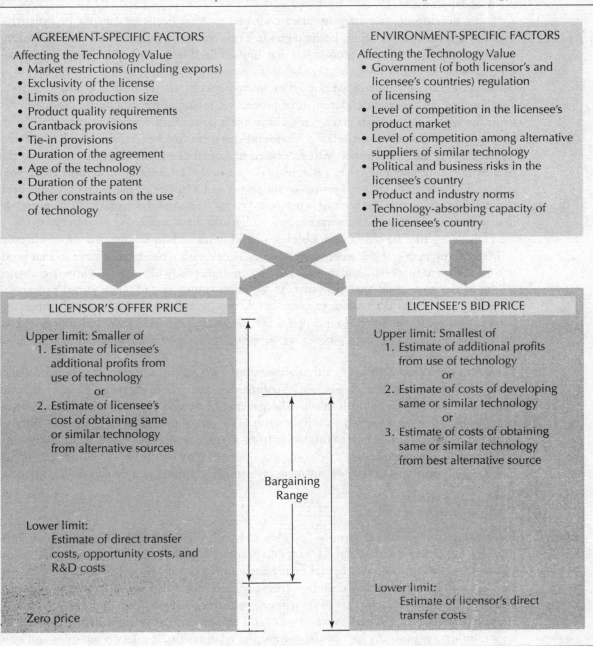

The upper left-hand box lists factors in the licensing agreement that can affect the technology's value to the licensee. The upper right-hand box gives factors external to the negotiating companies that can affect pricing. The bottom portion shows how the bargaining range derives from the licensor's and the licensee's estimates of profits and costs.

Source: Reprinted from Kang Rae Cho. "Issues of Compensation in International Technology Licensing" *Management International Review* 28, no. 2 (1988): 76, as adapted from Franklin R. Root and Farok I. Contractor, "Negotiating Compensation in International Licensing Agreements," *Sloan Management Review* (Winter 1981): 25, by permission of the publisher. Copyright © 1981 by Sloan Management Review Association. All rights reserved.

the payment amount. In the upper left-hand box, agreement-specific factors underlie negotiated clauses that may affect the value to the licensee. For example, the value will be greater if potential sales are high. The upper right-hand box in the figure lists environment-specific factors that may affect the license's value. For example, the licensee might pay a low amount if its government sets upper limits on payment or if other companies are vying to sell similar technology. Because neither the licensor nor the licensee can be sure of the price the other is willing to accept, the bottom of the figure illustrates how the bargaining range is based on the dual expectations.

Some developing countries set price controls on what licensees can pay or insist that licensees be permitted to export licensed goods. Their reasoning is that selling only to the local market results in small-scale production that spreads fixed costs inadequately and raises consumer prices. Licensors have countered that if licensees export, they should pay higher royalties because the companies could not sell exclusive rights to parties in other countries. MNEs also have argued that the development of process technologies for small-scale production in countries with small markets is often too costly but is done when economically feasible.

Companies commonly negotiate a "front-end" payment to cover transfer costs when licensing technology and then follow with fees based on actual or projected use. Licensors do this because it usually takes more than a transfer of documents when attempting to move technology abroad. The move requires engineering, consultation, and adaptation. The licensee usually bears the transfer costs so that the licensor is motivated to assure a smooth adaptation. Of course, the license of some assets, such as copyrights and trademarks, have much lower transfer costs.

Technology may be old or new, obsolete or still in use at home, when a company licenses it. Many companies transfer technology at an early or even a development stage so that products hit different markets simultaneously. This simultaneous market entry is important when selling to the same industrial customers in different countries and when global promotion campaigns can be effective. On the one hand, new technology may be worth more to a licensee because it may have a longer useful life. On the other hand, newer technology, particularly that in the development phase, may be worth less because of its uncertain market value.

Sales to Controlled Entities   Although we think of licensing agreements as being collaborative arrangements among unassociated companies, many licenses are given to companies owned in whole or part by the licensor. A license may be needed to transfer technology abroad because operations in a foreign country, even if 100-percent owned by the parent, usually are subsidiaries, which are separate companies from a legal standpoint. When a company owns less than 100 percent, a separate licensing arrangement may be a means of compensating the licensor for contributions beyond the mere investment in capital and managerial resources.

Franchising

Franchising includes providing an intangible asset (usually a trademark) and continually infusing necessary assets.

Franchising is a specialized form of licensing in which the franchisor not only sells an independent franchisee the use of the intangible property (usually a trademark) essential to the franchisee's business but also operationally assists the business on a continuing basis (e.g., through sales promotion and training). In many cases, the franchisor provides supplies. For example, Domino's Pizza grants to franchisees both the goodwill of the Domino's name and support services to get started, such as store and equipment layout information and a manager training program. As part of the continuing relationship, it offers economies and standardization through central purchasing, such as centrally purchasing mozzarella cheese in New Zealand to use worldwide.[23] In a sense, a franchisor and a franchisee act almost like a vertically integrated company because the parties are interdependent and each produces part of the product or service that ultimately reaches the consumer.

Franchisors once depended on trade shows a few times a year and costly visits to foreign countries to promote their expansion. However, because of the Internet, they now receive e-mailed requests for information around the clock, seven days a week.[24] Nevertheless, the acceptance of the franchising concept depends very much on the existence of high levels of income, education, mass media, and an entrepreneurial spirit.[25] For example, China has been slow to accept franchises (out of 625 KFC stores, only 26 are run by franchisees), but conditions are becoming much more favorable for franchise growth there.[26]

Franchising is said to have originated when King John of England granted tax-collecting franchises. In the eighteenth century, German brewers franchised beer halls as distributors.[27] Today, franchising is most associated with the United States, although many international franchisors are from outside the United States. The fastest growth businesses of U.S. foreign franchising have been food and business services because the U.S. market for these businesses is fairly mature. U.S. companies can find more growth abroad than at home.

Organization of Franchising A franchisor may penetrate a foreign country by dealing directly with franchisees or by setting up a master franchise and giving that organization (usually a local one) the rights to open outlets on its own or develop subfranchisees in the country or region. In the latter case, subfranchisees pay royalties to the master franchisee, which then remits some predetermined percentage to the franchisor. McDonald's handles its Japanese operations this way. Companies are most apt to use a master franchise system when they are not confident about evaluating potential franchisees and when it would be expensive to oversee and control franchisees' operations directly.[28]

If the franchisor is not well known to many local people, it may find it difficult to convince them to make investments. People are usually willing to make investments in known franchises because the name is a guarantee of quality that can attract customers. It is common, therefore, for lessor-known franchisors to enter foreign markets with some company-owned outlets that serve as a showcase to attract franchisees.

Operational Modifications Securing good locations for franchises can be a major problem. Finding suppliers can add difficulties and expense. For example, McDonald's had to build a plant to make hamburger buns in the United Kingdom, and it had to help farmers develop potato production in Thailand.[29] Another concern for foreign franchise expansion has been government or legal restrictions that make it difficult to gain satisfactory operating permission.

Many franchise failures abroad result from the franchisor's not developing enough domestic penetration first. Franchisors need to develop sufficient cash and management depth before considering foreign expansion. However, even a franchisor that is well established domestically may have difficulty in attaining foreign penetration, as evidenced by problems of Burger King in the United Kingdom, Wendy's in Australia, and Long John Silver's in Japan. A dilemma for successful domestic franchisors is that their success comes from three factors: product and service standardization, high identification through promotion, and effective cost controls. When entering many foreign countries, franchisors may encounter difficulties in transferring these success factors. At the same time, the more adjustments made to the host country's different conditions, the less a franchisor has to offer a potential franchisee. U.S. franchisors' success in Japan is mostly due to that country's enthusiastic assimilation of Western products. Even so, franchisors have had to make adjustments there. Wendy's sells a teriyaki burger, and Little Caesars has asparagus, potatoes, squid, and seaweed as pizza toppings.[30] McDonald's changed the pronunciation of its name in Japan to "MaKudonaldo" and substituted *Donald* for *Ronald McDonald* because of pronunciation difficulties.[31] However, the more adjustments franchisors make, the less they have to sell to potential franchisees.

Management Contracts

One of the most important assets a company may have at its disposal is management talent, which it can transfer internationally, primarily to its own foreign investments. Management contracts are means by which a company may transfer such talent—by using part of its management personnel to assist a foreign company for a specified period for a fee. The company

Many types of products and many countries participate in franchising.

Franchisors face a dilemma

- The more global standardization, the potentially lower acceptance in the foreign country.
- The more adjustment to the foreign country, the less the franchisor can offer a potential franchisee.

Management contracts are used primarily when the foreign company can manage better than the owners.

may gain income with little capital outlay. Contracts usually cover three-to-five years, and fixed fees or fees based on volume rather than profits are most common.

A company usually pursues management contracts when it believes that a foreign company can manage its existing or new operation more efficiently than it can. For example, the British Airport Authority (BAA) has contracts to manage airports in Indianapolis (United States), Naples (Italy), and Melbourne (Australia) because it had developed successful airport management skills.[32]

With management contracts, the host country gets the assistance it wants without needing foreign direct investment. In turn, the management company receives income without having to make a capital outlay. This pattern has been important in Middle East hotel operations because governments there have restricted foreign ownership. However, the operating fees have been declining and contract terms have been shortening for many of the international hotel operators because of the development of more local expertise and greater competition. This has led such companies as Six Continents, Le Meridien, and Hilton to seek more properties that they could manage in order to maintain former income levels.[33]

Turnkey Operations

Turnkey operations are

- **Most commonly performed by construction and industrial equipment companies**
- **Often performed for a government agency**

Turnkey operations are a type of collaborative arrangement in which one company contracts another to build complete, ready-to-operate facilities. Companies building turnkey operations are frequently industrial-equipment manufacturers and construction companies. They also may be consulting firms and manufacturers that decide an investment on their own behalf in the country is infeasible.

The customer for a turnkey operation is often a government agency. Many companies have chosen to perform design and construction duties, particularly in places where there are restrictions on private or foreign ownership, such as highways and ports. At this writing, some of the largest projects are for reconstruction of Iraq after the war in 2003, which is estimated to cost between $25 billion and $100 billion.[34]

One characteristic that sets the turnkey business apart from most other international business operations is the size of the contracts. Most contracts are for hundreds of millions of dollars, and many are for billions, which means that only a few very large companies—such as Bechtel, Fluor, Halliburton, Parsons, and Rust International—account for most of the international market. For example, Bechtel built a semiconductor plant for Motorola in China and a pipeline for BP in Algeria. Smaller firms often serve as subcontractors for primary turnkey suppliers. However, large companies are vulnerable to economic downturns when governments cancel big contracts.

The nature of these contracts places a great deal of importance on the hiring of executives with top-level contacts abroad as well as on ceremony and building goodwill, such as opening a facility on a country's independence day or getting a head of state to inaugurate a facility. For example, the Swiss company ABB and Brazil's Companhia Brasileira de Projectos e Obras formed a joint venture to construct a dam for the government of Malaysia. They timed the signing of the contract so that the Malaysian premier could be present for the ceremony.[35] Although public relations is an important way to gain turnkey contracts, other factors—such as price, export financing, managerial and technological quality, experience, and reputation—are needed to sell contracts of such magnitude.

Payment for a turnkey operation usually occurs in stages as a project develops. Commonly, 10 to 25 percent comprises the down payment, with another 50 to 65 percent paid as the contract progresses, and the remainder paid once the facility is operating in accordance with the contract. Because of the long time frame between conception and completion, the company performing turnkey operations can encounter currency fluctuations and should cover itself through escalation clauses or cost-plus contracts. Because the final payment is usually made only if the facility is operating satisfactorily, it is important to specify in a contract what constitutes "satisfactorily." For this reason, many companies insist on performing a feasibility study as part of the turnkey contract so they don't build something that, although desired by a local government, may be too large or inefficient. Inefficiency could create legal problems that hold up final payment—such as determining who caused the problem.

Many turnkey contracts are for construction in remote areas, necessitating massive housing construction and importation of personnel. Projects may involve building an entire infrastructure under the most adverse conditions, such as Bechtel's complex for Minera Escondida, which is high in the Andes. So turnkey operators must have expertise both in hiring workers who are willing to work in remote areas for extended periods and in transporting and using supplies under very adverse conditions.

If a company holds a monopoly on certain assets or resources, such as the latest refining technology, other companies will find it difficult to compete to secure a turnkey contract. As the production process becomes known, however, the number of competitors for such contracts increases. Companies from industrial countries have moved largely toward projects involving high technology, whereas companies from such countries as India, Korea, and Turkey can compete better for conventional projects for which low labor costs are important.

Joint Ventures

A type of ownership sharing popular among international companies is the joint venture, in which more than one organization owns a company. Recall from the opening case that Cisco participates in numerous joint ventures. Although companies usually form a joint venture to achieve particular objectives, such a joint venture may continue to operate indefinitely as the objective is redefined. Joint ventures are sometimes thought of as 50-50 companies, but more than two organizations often participate in the ownership. Further, one organization frequently controls more than 50 percent of the venture. The type of legal organization may be a partnership, a corporation, or some other form permitted in the country of operation. When more than two organizations participate, the joint venture is sometimes called a **consortium**.

Almost every conceivable combination of partners may exist in a joint venture, including

- Two companies from the same country joining together in a foreign market, such as NEC and Mitsubishi (Japan) in the United Kingdom.
- A foreign company joining with a local company, such as Great Lakes Chemical (United States) and A. H. Al Zamil in Saudi Arabia.
- Companies from two or more countries that establish a joint venture in a third country, such as that of Diamond Shamrock (United States) and Sol Petroleo (Argentina) in Bolivia.
- A private company and a local government that form a joint venture (sometimes called a mixed venture), such as that of Philips (Dutch) with the Indonesian government.
- A private company joining a government-owned company in a third country, such as BP Amoco (private British-U.S.) and Eni (government-owned Italian) in Egypt.

The more companies in the joint venture, the more complex the management of the arrangement will be. For example, when the Australian government privatized Hazelwood Power Station, a British company (National Power), an Australian company (the Commonwealth Bank Group), and two U.S. companies (PacifiCorp and Destec Energy) bought the electric utility company. This partnership meant that four companies were involved in the decision making.[36] Figure 14.5 shows that as a company increases the number of partners and reduces the amount of equity it owns in a foreign operation, its ability to control that operation declines.

Certain types of companies favor joint ventures more than others do. Companies that like joint ventures are usually new at foreign operations or have decentralized domestic decision making. Because these companies are used to extending control downward in their organizations, it is easier for them to do the same thing internationally.

Joint ventures may have various combinations of ownership.

FIGURE 14.5   Control Complexity Related to Collaborative Strategy

The more equity and the fewer partners, the more easily a company can usually control its foreign operations. Note that the nonequity arrangements may take one or many partners.

Source: The figure was adapted from *European Management Journal* 12, no. 1, Shaker Zahra and Galal Elhagrasey, "Strategic Management of International Joint Ventures," March 1994, pp. 83–93, with permission from Elsevier Science.

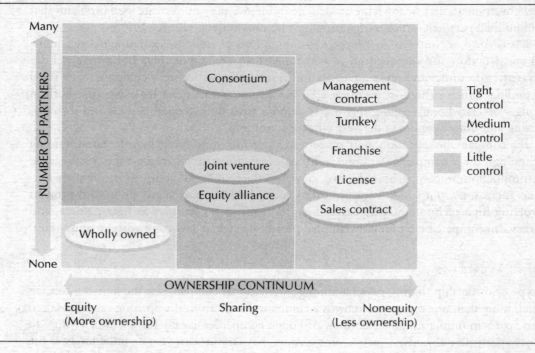

 Equity alliances help solidify collaboration.

Equity Alliances

An equity alliance is a collaborative arrangement in which at least one of the collaborating companies takes an ownership position (almost always minority) in the other(s). In some cases, each party takes an ownership, such as by buying part of each other's shares or by swapping some shares with each other. For instance, General Motors took a 20 percent interest in Fiat and Fiat took a 5 percent interest in General Motors.[37] The purpose of the equity ownership is to solidify a collaborating contract, such as a supplier-buyer contract, so that it is more difficult to break—particularly if the ownership is large enough to secure a board membership for the investing company. The airline industry epitomizes the use of equity alliances. We will discuss the airline industry in the ending case of this chapter.

 Many collaborative arrangements break down, primarily because partners

- View the arrangements' importance differently
- Have different objectives for the arrangement
- Disagree on control issues or fail to provide sufficient direction
- Perceive they contribute more than their counterparts do
- Have incompatible operating cultures

PROBLEMS OF COLLABORATIVE ARRANGEMENTS

Although collaborative arrangements have many advantages, some companies avoid them. Many arrangements develop problems that lead partners to renegotiate their relationships. Partners might renegotiate responsibilities, ownership, or management structure. In spite of new relationships, many arrangements break down or are not renewed at the end of an initial contract period. In joint ventures, one partner often buys out the other's interest so that the operation continues as a wholly owned foreign subsidiary. In other breakups, companies agree to dissolve the arrangement or they restructure their alliance.

Figure 14.6 shows that joint-venture divorce (and divorce from other collaborative arrangements) can be planned or unplanned, friendly or unfriendly, mutual or nonmutual. The major strains on collaborative arrangements are due to five factors: the importance to the partners, differing objectives, control problems, comparative contributions and appropriations, and differences in culture.[38] In spite of our focus on these problems, we do not mean to imply that there are no success stories. There are. For example, the joint venture between Xerox (United States) and Rank (United Kingdom) has performed well for a long period of time, and it even has a joint venture itself in Japan with Fuji Photo, which has also performed well.

FIGURE 14.6 Alternative Dissolution of Joint Ventures

DIVORCE SCENARIOS	EXAMPLES	OUTCOMES	EXAMPLES
Planned vs. Unplanned	General Motors (U.S.) and Toyota (Japan)	Termination by Acquisition	Daewoo Motors (South Korea) and General Motors (U.S.)
	AT&T (U.S.) and Olivetti (Italy)		
Friendly vs. Unfriendly	Vitro (Mexico) and Corning (U.S.)	Termination by Dissolution	Meiji Milk (Japan) and Borden (U.S.)
	Coors Brewing Co. (U.S.) and Molson Breweries (Canada)	Termination by Reorganization/ Restructuring of the Alliance	Matsushita Electric Industries Co. (Japan) and Solbourne Computer (U.S.)
Both agree vs. One Partner Refuses to Agree	Ralston Purina (U.S.) and Taiyo Fishery (Japan)		
	Sover S.P.A. (Italy) and Suzhou Spectacles No. 1 Factory (China)		

There is considerable variation in both the way that joint ventures dissolve and the outcome of the operation after the dissolution. Any of the scenarios might have any of the outcomes.

Source: Adapted from Manuel G. Serapio, Jr. and Wayne F. Cascio, "End Games in International Alliances," *Academy of Management Executive* (May 1996): 67.

Collaboration's Importance to Partners

One partner may give more management attention to a collaborative arrangement than the other does. If things go wrong, the active partner blames the less active partner for its lack of attention, and the less active partner blames the more active partner for making poor decisions. The difference in attention may be due to the different sizes of partners. For example, if the arrangement is between a large and a small company, the collaboration comprises a larger portion of operations for the small company than for the large one, so the small company may take more interest in it. Further, if there are disagreements, the smaller firm may be at a disadvantage because it lacks the resources to fight the larger company. For example, Igen, a small U.S. firm, licensed its technology to Boehringer Mannheim of Germany, a company whose sales are more than 100 times those of Igen. When the two companies disagreed over royalty payments, Igen fought for four years and spent $40 million in legal fees (equivalent to about one year of its sales) to win a settlement of over a half billion dollars.[39] However, this example is unusual because most small companies cannot or will not fight a larger company so effectively.

Differing Objectives

Although companies enter into collaborative arrangements because they have complementary capabilities, their objectives may evolve differently over time. For instance, one partner may want to reinvest earnings for growth and the other may want to receive dividends. One partner may want to expand the product line and sales territory, and the other may see this as competition with its wholly owned operations. A partner may wish to sell or buy from the venture, and the other partner may disagree with the prices. Or there may be different views about performance standards. For example, GM is part of a joint venture in Thailand with Fuji Heavy Industries in which it exports vehicles to Opel in Germany and Subaru in Japan. Because of disagreements over quality, both companies perform inspections, an arrangement which is both time-consuming and expensive. They have even argued over standards for paint jobs.[40]

Control Problems

By sharing the assets with another company, one company may lose some control on the extent or quality of the assets' use. For example, Calvin Klein licensed Warnaco to make its jeans and underwear, which accounted for about 40 percent of Calvin Klein's sales. Although both companies were based in the United States, Calvin Klein claimed that Warnaco sales through unauthorized retailers such as Costco and B.J.'s Wholesale Club and unauthorized design changes were diluting the image of its products worldwide. Yet to break the contract took long and expensive litigation.[41]

Some companies have well-known trademarked names that they license abroad for the production of some products that they have never produced or had expertise with. For example, Pierre Cardin has licensed its label to hundreds of licensees in scores of countries. These licensees put the label on hundreds of products—from clothing to sheets and from clocks to deodorants. Monitoring and maintaining control of so much diversity was so difficult that poor-quality Pierre Cardin–labeled products hurt the image of high-quality Pierre Cardin–labeled products. Pierre Cardin had to restructure its agreements and advertise heavily to reestablish the cachet of its name.[42] In today's world, problems in one country are quickly communicated to consumers in other countries.

In collaborative arrangements, even though control is ceded to one of the partners, both may be held responsible for problems. For example, in KFC's joint venture in China, the burden of all financial reporting to Chinese authorities fell on the Chinese partner. However, China held both partners liable for tax evasion as a result of the underreporting of income.[43] Moreover, in joint ventures and management contracts, there are gray areas as to who controls employees. For example, in Holiday Inn's 10-year management contract in Tibet, the company couldn't give incentives to or discipline its staff. Consequently, there was little it could do when waiters and waitresses took their lunch breaks at the same time guests were showing up for lunch.[44] Further, employees may have anxieties about who is in charge. For example, in a proposed joint venture between Merrill Lynch (from the United States) and UFJ (from Japan), a Japanese senior manager queried, "Who is going to be in charge—a Japanese or an American, or both?"[45]

When no single company has control of a collaborative arrangement, the operation may lack direction. At the same time, if one partner dominates, it must still consider the other company's interests.

Partners' Contributions and Appropriations

One partner's ability to contribute technology, capital, or some other asset may diminish over time compared to its partner's ability. For example, in P&G's joint venture with Phuong Dong Soap & Detergent in Vietnam, P&G wanted to expand, but Phuong had neither the funds to expand nor the willingness to allow P&G to gain a larger ownership.[46] The weak link may cause a drag on the collaborative arrangement, resulting in dissension between the partners. Further, one partner may be suspicious that the other is taking more from the operation (particularly knowledge-based assets) than it is. In almost all collaborative arrangements, there is a danger that one partner will use the other partner's contributed assets, enabling it to become a competitor. (Probably the only exception would be turnkey projects to build infrastructure.) In fact, there are many examples of companies going it alone after they no longer needed their partner, particularly if the purpose of the collaboration is to gain knowledge. For example, Abbott Laboratories bought Hokuriku Seiyaku's interest in their Japanese joint venture after gaining sufficient experience in Japan.[47] It is difficult for companies that compete head-on within their core businesses in some markets to cooperate fully for the same core business in another market. In the case of joint ventures, both partners are apt to see substantial gains when each partner offers market expansion and technology to the other.

Differences in Culture

Companies differ by nationality in how they evaluate the success of their operations. For example, U.S. companies tend to evaluate performance on the basis of profit, market share, and specific financial benefits. Japanese companies tend to evaluate primarily on how an operation helps build its strategic position, particularly by improving its skills. European companies rely more on a balance between profitability and achieving social objectives.[48] These differences can mean that one partner is satisfied while the other is not. Anheuser-Busch attributed its joint-venture breakup with Modelo (Mexican) to the fact that Modelo was run like a family business and was reluctant to share control.[49] Moreover, some companies don't like to collaborate with companies that have very different cultures. For example, British companies would least like to partner with Japanese companies, primarily because of language difficulties.[50] In spite of these potential problems, joint ventures from culturally distant countries survive at least as well as those between partners from similar cultures.[51]

In addition to national culture, differences in corporate cultures may also create problems within joint ventures. For example, one company may be accustomed to promoting managers from within the organization, whereas the other opens its searches to outsiders. One may use a participatory management style, and the other an authoritarian style. One may be entrepreneurial and the other risk averse. For this reason, many companies will develop joint ventures only after they have had long-term positive experiences with each other as a result of distributorship, licensing, or other contractual arrangements. However, as is the case with marriage, a positive prior relationship between two companies does not guarantee that partners will be well matched in a joint venture. Compatibility of corporate cultures also is important in cementing relationships.[52]

MANAGING FOREIGN ARRANGEMENTS

If collaboration can better achieve the company's strategic objectives than "going it alone" can, the company should give little consideration to taking on duties itself. However, as the arrangement evolves, partners will need to reassess certain decisions. For example, a company's resource base may change compared to that of other companies, making collaboration either more or less advantageous. Further, the external environment changes. Perhaps a certain location becomes economically risky, or its host government forbids foreign ownership in areas where the partnership would like to do future business. Because of these changes, a company needs continually to reexamine the fit between collaboration and its strategy. We shall now discuss how companies change their operating forms, how they may find and negotiate with potential partners, what contractual provisions are most important in arrangements, and how they need to assess performance of collaborative arrangements.

Dynamics of Collaborative Arrangements

In Chapter 1, we discussed how companies typically move from external to internal handling of foreign operations and how they deepen their mode of commitment over time. However, the cost of switching from one form to another—for example, from licensing to wholly owned facilities—may be very high because of the need to gain expertise from and possibly pay termination fees to another company.

Collaboration with a local company provides the opportunity to learn from the local partner, enabling the company to confidently make a deeper commitment. At the same time, the learning in one market may enable a company to enter another market at a higher level of commitment. However, the ability to carry over learning from one market to another is enhanced by cultural similarity among markets.[53]

The evolution to a different operating mode may

- Be the result of experience
- Necessitate costly termination fees
- Create organizational tensions

Organizational tension may develop internally as a company's international operations change and grow. For example, moving from exporting to foreign production may reduce the size of a domestic product division. Various profit centers all may perceive they have rights to the sales in a country that the company is about to penetrate. Legal, technical, and marketing personnel may have entirely different perspectives on contracts. Under these circumstances, a team approach to evaluating decisions and performance may work. A company also must develop means of evaluating performance by separating those things that are controllable and noncontrollable by personnel in different profit centers.

At the same time, there is evidence that as companies enter more collaborative arrangements, they get better performance from them.[54] In essence, they may choose partners better and learn how to get better synergies as a result of the link between their partners and their own operations.

Finding Compatible Partners

A company can seek out a partner for its foreign operations, or it can react to a proposal from another company to collaborate with it. In either case, it is necessary to evaluate the potential partner not only for the resources it can supply but also for its motivation and compatibility to work with the other company. A company can identify potential partners by monitoring journals and technical conferences. Partners can also be found through social activities. After a company makes contact and builds rapport with managers of one local firm, those managers may offer introductions to managers in other firms.[55] A company can increase its own visibility by participating in trade fairs, distributing brochures, and nurturing contacts in the locale of potential collaboration—thus increasing the probability that companies will be considered a partner by other companies. The proven ability to handle similar types of collaboration is a key professional qualification. For example, Cisco's track record has undoubtedly influenced other companies to consider Cisco as a collaboration partner. Because of a good track record, a partner may be able to depend more on trust rather than on expensive control mechanisms to ensure that its interests will not be usurped. Once in a collaboration arrangement, partners may also be able to build partner trust through their actions in the collaborative arrangement.[56] But every company has to start somewhere. Without a proven track record, a company may have to negotiate harder with and make more concessions to a partner.

Negotiating Process

In addition to the points discussed in Chapter 12 about cross-national negotiations, some technology transfer considerations are unique to collaborative arrangements. The value of many technologies would diminish if they were widely used or understood. Contracts historically have included provisions that the recipient will not divulge this information. In addition, some sellers have held onto the ownership and production of specific components so that recipients will not have the full knowledge of the product or the capability to produce an exact copy of it. Often, a company wants to sell techniques it has not yet used commercially. A buyer is reluctant to buy what it has not seen or evaluated, but a seller that shows the process to the potential buyer risks divulging the process technology. It has become common to set up pre-agreements that protect all parties.

Another controversial area of negotiation is the secrecy surrounding arrangements' financial terms. In some countries, for example, government agencies must approve licensing contracts. Sometimes these authorities consult their counterparts in other countries regarding similar agreements to improve their negotiating position with MNEs. Many MNEs object to this procedure because they believe that contract terms between two companies are proprietary information with competitive importance and that market conditions usually dictate the need for very different terms in different countries.

In technology agreements

- Seller does not want to give information without assurance of payment
- Buyer does not want to pay without evaluating information

LOOKING TO THE FUTURE

Why Innovation Breeds Collaboration

A half century ago, John Kenneth Galbraith wrote that the era of cheap invention was over and, "because development is costly, it follows that it can be carried out only by a firm that has the resources associated with considerable size."[57] The statement seems prophetic in terms of the estimated billions of investment dollars needed to bring a new commercial aircraft to market, eliminate death from diseases, develop defenses against unfriendly countries and terrorists, guard against cyberspace intrusions, and commercialize energy substitutes for petroleum. Moreover, markets must be truly global if high development costs are to be recouped. The sums companies need for developing and marketing these new inventions are out of reach of most companies acting alone. Of course, companies might become ever larger through internal growth or through mergers and acquisitions. Although we have seen some examples of such growth, governments have, nevertheless, established limits because of antitrust concerns. Further, companies realize that the cost of integrating a merged or acquired company can be very high.[58] Therefore, collaborative arrangements will likely become even more important in the future. They are likely to involve both horizontal and vertical linkages among companies from many industries in many countries. However, there is evidence that collaborative arrangements slow the speed of innovation.[59] Thus, large companies that have resources to go it alone may have advantages over small companies that do not.

Although some product developments require huge sums, most are much more modest. Nevertheless, companies lack all the product- and market-specific resources to go it alone everywhere in the world, especially if national differences dictate operating changes on a country-to-country basis. These situations present opportunities for alliances that employ complementary resources from different companies.

Collaborative arrangements will bring both opportunities and problems as companies move simultaneously to new countries and to contractual arrangements with new companies. For example, collaborations must overcome differences in a number of areas:

- Country cultures that may cause partners to obtain and evaluate information differently
- National differences in government policies, institutions, and industry structures that constrain companies from operating as they would prefer
- Corporate cultures that influence ideologies as well as values underlying company practices that strain relationships among companies
- Different strategic directions resulting from partners' interests that cause companies to disagree on objectives and contributions
- Different management styles and organizational structures that cause partners to interact ineffectively[60]

The more partners there are in an alliance, the more strained the decision-making and control processes will be.

Contractual Provisions

By transferring assets to a joint venture or intangible property rights to another company in a licensing agreement, a company undoubtedly loses some control over the asset or intangible property. A host of potential problems attend this lack of control and should be settled in the original agreement. Although it is impossible to anticipate all points of future disagreement and include coverage of them in a contract, provisions should outline

Transferring rights to an asset can create control problems, such as poor product quality.

- How to terminate the agreement if the parties do not adhere to the directives.
- Methods of testing for quality.
- Geographical limitations on the asset's use.
- Which company will manage which parts of the operation outlined in the agreement.
- What each company's future commitments will be.
- How each company will buy from, sell to, or use intangible assets that come from the collaborative arrangement.

Contracts should be spelled out in detail, but if courts must rule on disagreements, both parties are apt to lose something in the settlement. Contract termination and formal settlement of disputes are costly and cumbersome. If possible, it is much better for parties to settle disagreements on a personal basis. The ability to develop a rapport with the management of another company is an important consideration in choosing a partner.

Performance Assessment

When collaborating with another company, managers must

- Continue to monitor performance
- Assess whether to take over operations

Management also should estimate potential sales, determine whether the arrangement is meeting quality standards, and assess servicing requirements to check whether the other company is doing an adequate job. Mutual goals should be set so that both parties understand what is expected, and the expectations should be spelled out in the contract.

In addition to the continuing assessment of the partner's performance in collaborative arrangements, a company also needs to assess periodically whether the type of collaboration should change. For example, a joint venture may replace a licensing agreement. In some cases, even though a partner is doing what is expected, a company may assess that collaboration is no longer in its best interest. For instance, the company may decide that it wants a wholly owned FDI so that it has greater freedom.

Summary

- Some advantages of collaborative arrangements, whether a company is operating domestically or internationally, are to spread and reduce costs, allow a company to specialize in its primary competencies, avoid or counter certain competition, secure vertical and horizontal links, and learn from other companies.

- Some motivations for collaborative arrangements that are specific to international operations are to gain location-specific assets, overcome governments' legal constraints, diversify among countries, and minimize exposure in risky environments.

- The forms of foreign operations differ in how much resources a company commits and the proportion of resources committed at home rather than abroad. Collaborative arrangements reduce a company's commitment.

- Although the type of collaborative arrangement a company chooses should match its strategic objectives, the choice often will mean a trade-off among objectives.

- Licensing is granting another company the use of some rights, such as patents, copyrights, or trademarks, usually for a fee. It is a means of establishing foreign production and reaching foreign markets that may minimize capital outlays, prevent the free use of assets by other companies, allow the receipt of assets from other companies in return, and allow

for income in some markets in which exportation or investment is not feasible.

- Franchising differs from licensing in that granting the use of intangible property (usually a trademark) is an essential asset for the franchisee's business and the franchisor assists in the operation of the business on a continuing basis.

- Management contracts are a means of securing income by managing a foreign operation while providing little capital outlay. This sometimes helps the supplier to gain foreign experience, increasing its capacity to internationalize.

- Turnkey projects are contracts for construction of another company's operating facilities. These projects have been large and diverse, necessitating specialized skills and abilities to deal with top-level government authorities.

- Joint ventures are a special type of collaborative arrangement in which two or more organizations have equity in the venture. There are various combinations of owners, including local governments and private companies and two or more companies from the same or different countries.

- Equity alliances occur when a company takes an equity position in the company with which it has a collaborative arrangement so as to solidify the collaborating contract.

- Problems occur in collaborative arrangements because partners place different levels of importance on and have different objectives for the venture, find a shared ownership arrangement difficult to control, worry that their partner is putting in too little or taking out too much from the operation, and misunderstand each other because of their different country or company cultures.

- Contracting for the outside management of a company's foreign business does not negate management's responsibility to ensure that company resources are working. Management constantly needs to assess the other company's work.

CASE

International Airline Alliances[61]

Map 14.2 shows the world's 25 largest airlines and the countries where they have their headquarters. Most of the world's major airlines are in or have announced they will join an alliance whereby they combine routes, sales, airline terminal services, and frequent-flier programs. For example, by 2003, Air Canada, Air New Zealand, All Nippon Airways (ANA), Asiana, Austrian Airlines, Lauda, LOT, Lufthansa, Mexicana, Scandinavian Airlines System (SAS), Singapore Airlines, Spanair, Thai Airlines, Tyrolean, United Airlines, and Varig were in the Star Alliance.

In addition, many airlines hold ownership in other airlines. For example, KLM from the Netherlands has partial ownership of Northwest Airlines in the United States and Alitalia in Italy.

MAP 14.2   The Top 25 Passenger Airline Companies

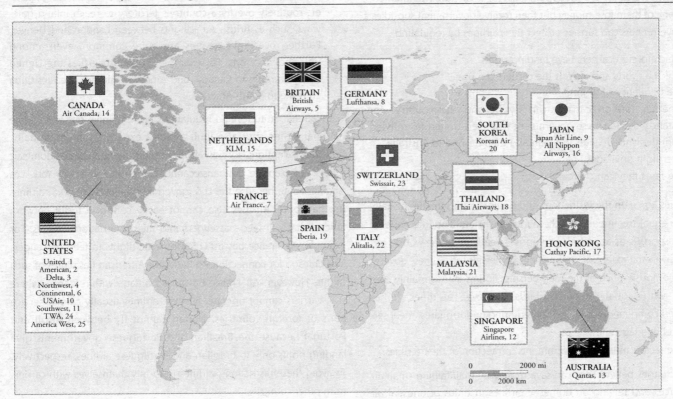

Note the preponderance of airlines in Europe and the United States. The rankings are based on revenue passenger kilometers flown (the number of paid passengers multiplied by the distance that each paid passenger flies). Airlines are sometimes measured, instead, by operating revenue, operating profit, net profit, passengers flown, and fleet size. These measures result in different rankings.

Source: ATW's World Airline Report. The information is based on 2001 operations (January 22, 2003): http://www.atwonline.com/Pdf/tables.pdf

Singapore Airlines owns 49 percent of Virgin Airlines in the United Kingdom.

These alliances have blurred the competitive distinctions among the major international carriers. However, the airline industry is unique insofar as its need to form collaborative arrangements has been important almost from the start of international air travel because of regulatory, cost, and competitive factors. In recent years, this need has accelerated because of airlines' poor profit performance, due in part to a global economic downturn and concern about international terrorism.

REGULATORY FACTORS

Countries have seen airlines as part of a key industry in which they want domestic service that is controlled by domestically owned companies. For example, the United States grants U.S.-based airlines the right to carry all passengers between domestic points, and it limits foreign ownership in U.S.-based airlines to 25 percent of voting stock and 49 percent of total equity. Many countries have ensured national control through whole or partial government ownership of airlines. Examples are Iberia, KLM, Lufthansa, and Thai Airways. Many government-owned airlines are monopolies within their domestic markets, and many of them lose money but then receive government subsidies.

Governments can further protect their airlines by regulating

- Which foreign carriers have landing rights.
- Which airports and aircraft the carriers can use.
- The frequency of flights.
- Whether foreign carriers can fly beyond the country—for instance, the Japanese government restricted United from flying from the United States to Japan and then beyond to Australia.
- Overflight privileges.
- The fares they can charge.

Countries agree on the restrictions and rights through treaties, usually to give equal treatment to each country's carriers. The International Air Transport Association (IATA) comprises nearly all of the world's airlines. Given the extent of government ownership of airlines, governments comprise much of the membership. Today, IATA is mainly concerned with global safety standards. However, at times, it has restricted competition on routes by requiring uniform fares, meal service, and baggage allowances.

Five factors influence governments' protection of their airlines.

1. Countries believe they can save money by maintaining small air forces and relying on domestic airlines in times of unusual air transport needs. For example, the U.S. government used U.S. commercial carriers to help carry troops to Somalia in 1992.

2. In aviation's early days, airlines were heavily subsidized in order to enable them to carry mail overseas, and governments wanted to support their own fledgling companies rather than foreign

ones. This consideration has shifted somewhat because mail subsidies no longer are very important internationally. For example, revenues from mail account for less than 0.5 percent of revenues for U.S. airlines.

3. Public opinion favors spending "at home," especially for government-paid travel. The public sees the maintenance of national airlines and the requirement that government employees fly on those airlines as foreign-exchange savings. (For example, when a U.S. resident uses a foreign airline internationally—say, Air France from New York to Paris—this is a service import for the United States.)

4. Airlines are a source of national pride, and aircraft (sporting their national flags) symbolize a country's sovereignty and technical competence. This national identification has been especially important for developing countries, whose airlines once were largely foreign owned—for example, the former PanAm controlled airlines in Brazil, Colombia, Mexico, Panama, and Venezuela. As soon as countries were technically and financially capable, they developed national airlines and prohibited foreign ownership.

5. Countries have worried about protecting their airspace for security reasons. This is less of a concern today because foreign carriers routinely overfly a country's territory to reach inland gateways, such as British Air's flights between London and Denver. Further, overflight treaties are quite common, even among unfriendly nations. For example, Cubana overflies the United States en route to Canada, and American Airlines overflies Cuba en route to South America.

National attitudes and regulations not only give rise to separate national airlines but also limit airlines' expansion internationally. With few exceptions, foreign airlines cannot fly on lucrative domestic routes. For example, Lufthansa cannot compete on the New York–Los Angeles route because the U.S. government allows only U.S. airlines on that route. Airlines also cannot easily control a flight network abroad that will feed passengers into their international flights. For example, Air France has no U.S. domestic flights to feed passengers into Chicago for connections to Paris, but American has scores of such flights. However, Air France has an advantage within France, where U.S. carriers cannot operate. Further, airlines usually cannot service pairs of foreign countries. United cannot fly between Brazil and Portugal because the Brazilian and Portuguese governments give landing rights only to Brazilian and Portuguese airlines, respectively. To avoid these restrictions, airlines must ally themselves with carriers from other countries.

Airlines have sought cooperative agreements to complement their route structures and capabilities. Privatization has been a recent impetus to forming alliances. For example, privatized airlines, such as British Airways and Air Canada, can no longer look to their governments for support. Instead, they must find new means to be competitive internationally. Similarly, privatization in Eastern Europe and Latin America has enabled foreign carriers to take stakes in countries' airlines in those regions. Further, deregulation of airlines in the United States and the EU has forced airlines to find new means to compete.

COST FACTORS

Certain airlines have always dominated certain international airports. They have amassed critical capabilities in those airports, such as baggage handlers and baggage handling equipment. Sharing these capabilities with other airlines may spread costs. For example, KLM has long handled passenger check-in, baggage loading, and maintenance for a number of other airlines that fly into and out of Amsterdam. Other contracts commonly cover the use of airport gates, ground equipment such as generators, and commissary services. Airlines also sometimes sublease aircraft to each other. When traffic on a route is low, airlines sometimes make market agreements to fly on alternate days. Or they may agree to share service in the same aircraft, which then has a dual flight designation.

The high cost of maintenance and reservations systems has led to recent joint ventures. Swissair, Lufthansa, and Guiness Peat Aviation are partners in a maintenance center in Ireland. United, British Airways, US Airways, Swissair, Alitalia, and Air Canada share ownership in Covia, which operates and delivers the Apollo reservation system. United, US Airways, British Air, Alitalia, Swissair, KLM, Olympic, Austrian Airlines, Aer Lingus, Sabena, and TAP Air Portugal founded another reservation system, Galileo.

COMPETITIVE FACTORS

A number of airlines have established marketing agreements to complement their route structures. For example, Northwest handles KLM's operations in its Detroit facilities, and a high portion of KLM's traffic from Detroit to the Netherlands comes from Northwest's connections. The joint use of facilities within alliances may be the wave of the future because it is nearly impossible to add gates at the largest airports and existing airlines already own all the gates.

A problem with these marketing agreements is that the connections from one airline to another show up as separate route codes in reservations systems. These displays come up last on the screens of travel agents, and the agents tend to recommend the first scheduled flights they see. Further, when passengers see that they must change airlines, they worry about making those connections across great distances within ever-larger airline terminals. This worry factor puts connections between two different airlines at a disadvantage to connections on the same airline. When KLM bought an interest in Northwest, the two airlines were able to secure the same route codes

on their connecting flights. Northwest's ticket counters show KLM's logo as well. The alliance gives Northwest service to about 80 European cities. The two airlines have come as close as possible to a merger without actually making one.

MANAGEMENT OF ALLIANCES

A problem in the proliferation of alliances is that relationships are intertwined among so many airlines that it's difficult to determine whether companies are competing, cooperating, or colluding. Management may find it increasingly hard to be cooperative, say, in joint maintenance agreements while trying to compete directly on some routes.

Government restrictions to prevent full mergers among airlines from different countries may be a blessing in some ways because corporate and national cultures may be difficult to mesh. For example, pilots at Air Canada are unionized, but those at Continental are not. Analysts conclude that the problems of combining unions after PanAm's acquisition of National was a major contribution to PanAm's eventual demise.

Other things simply may not mesh well in alliances. In the now-defunct US Airways–British Airways agreement, British Airways was strong in connections from London to Europe and Asia. But US Airway's strength was at New York's LaGuardia Airport, which is purely domestic—most connecting passengers had to change airports, not just planes. When Northwest and KLM allied, it was expected that KLM would help Northwest improve its service; however, entrenched Northwest employees would not cooperate.

QUESTIONS

1. Discuss a question raised by the manager of route strategy at American Airlines: Why should an airline not be able to establish service anywhere in the world simply by demonstrating that it can and will comply with the local labor and business laws of the host country?
2. The president of Japan Air Lines has claimed that U.S. airlines are dumping air services on routes between the United States and Europe, meaning they are selling below their costs because of the money they are losing. Should governments set prices so that carriers make money on routes?
3. What will be the consequences if a few large airlines or networks come to dominate global air service?
4. Some airlines, such as Southwest and Alaska Air, have survived as niche players without going international or developing alliances with international airlines. Can they continue this strategy?

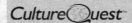

VIDEO: UNDERSTANDING ENTRY MODES INTO THE CHINESE MARKET

This chapter profiled the different types of collabrations that companies may consider when setting up global operations. Based on viewing the accompanying video, and materials in the chapter, please answer the following questions:

1. What factors do companies consider when determining the best form of operation to use when entering a new market?
2. What have been the challenges and opportunities for foreign companies in establishing collaborative arrangements in China?
3. How have Chinese government policies and attitudes toward foreign businesses evolved? How have these changes affected foreign companies' forms of operations in China?

Chapter Notes

1   Data for the case were drawn from company information retrieved from www.cisco.com; http://newsroom.cisco.com/dlls/partners/success_stories/index.html; http://www.cisco.com/public/countries_languages.shtml; http://www.cisco.com/warp/public/756/partnership/; Cisco Systems, Company's Form 10K, period ending 7/27/02 and posted at http://investor.cisco.com/ireye/ir_site.zhtml?ticker=csco&script=2100&layout=7; and from Tim McCollum, "Foreign Affairs," *The Industry Standard* (August 2, 2000); Edward B. Roberts and Wenyun Kathy Liu, "Ally or Acquire? How Technology Leaders Decide," *MIT Sloan Management Review* 43, no. 1 (Fall 2001): 26–34; Arvind Parkhe, "Interfirm Diversity in Global Alliances," *Business Horizons* 44, no. 6 (November–December 2001): 2–5; Nikhil Hutheesing, "Marital Blisters," *Forbes* (May 21, 2001): 30; Danny Ertel, "Alliance Management: A Blueprint for Success," *Financial Executive* 17, no. 9 (December 2001): 36–41; Debra Rankin and Michael Parent, "Cisco Systems Inc.," *Ivey Business Journal* 65, no. 3 (January–February 2001): 54–60; David Ticoll, "Learning from Cisco," *Tele.com* (April 17, 2000): 62; "Cisco to Set Up 34 Academies in India," *Business Line* (January 16, 2001); and "First Speaker-cum-MP3 Player," *Business Times* [Singapore] (September 2, 2002): Section ITSHELF.

2   Richard Gibson, "Wendy's Teams Up with Irish Baker in Joint Venture," *Wall Street Journal* (March 9, 2001): n.p.

3   Gregory L. White, "GM Board Approves Joint-Venture Plan with Russian Auto Maker AO Avtovaz," *Wall Street Journal* (February 8, 2001): A14.

4   See A. L. Zacharakis, "Entrepreneurial Entry into Foreign Markets: A Transaction Cost Perspective," *Entrepreneurship Theory & Practice* 22, no. 2 (1998): 23–39; and Rodney C. Shrader, "Collaboration and Performance in Foreign Markets: The Case of Young High-Technology Manufacturing Firms," *Academy of Management Journal* 44, no. 1 (February 2001): 45–60.

5   Rahul Jacob, "Hong Kong Banks on New Disney Park for Boost," *Financial Times* (August 31, 2001): 6.

6   John Wilman, "Coca-Cola Aims to Put Fizz into Fashion," *Financial Times* (January 2, 1999): 1.

7   T. K. Das and Bing-Sheng Teng, "A Resource-Based Theory of Strategic Alliances," *Journal of Management* 26, no. 1 (2000): 31–61.

8   "New World Ready to Build Caribbean Fiber System," *Fiber-Optics News* 20, no. 26 (June 26, 2000): 1.

9   Betsy McKay and Robert Frank, "Coke, Danone Discuss Joint Venture," *Wall Street Journal* (June 17, 2002): B5.

10 Philip Parker, "How Do Companies Collude?" *Financial Times* (September 28, 1998): Mastering Marketing section, 10–11.

11 Tim Burt and John Griffiths, "Ford May Use Excess Capacity in Europe to Produce Mazdas," *Financial Times* (March 3, 2000): 17.

12 Peter Marsh, "Profile Duracell," *Financial Times* (May 10, 1999): 27.

13 Jason Wilson, "Best of Both Worlds," *Continental* (April 1999): 49–51.

14 Yumiko Ono and Ann Zimmerman, "Wal-Mart Enters Japan with Seiyu Stake," *Wall Street Journal* (March 15, 2002): B5.

15 Michiyo Nakamoto, "Global Reach Through Tie-Ups," *Financial Times* (April 30, 2002): Healthcare section, 3.

16 "Merck and Chugai Form OTC Venture," *Financial Times* (September 19, 1996): 17.

17 "Northrop Grumman, Rolls-Royce Awarded Type 45 Destroyer Engine Contract," *Defense Daily International* 2, no. 11 (March 16, 2001): 1.

18 Julie Bennett, "Road to Foreign Franchises Is Paved with New Problems," *Wall Street Journal* (May 14, 2001): B10.

19 Philip Rosenzweig, "How Should Multinationals Set Global Workplace Standards?" *Financial Times* (March 27, 1998): Mastering Global Business section, 11–12.

20 Michael Skapinker, "Why Nike Has Broken into a Sweat," *Financial Times* (March 7, 2002): 8.

21 Peter J. Lane, Jane E. Salk, and Marjorie A. Lyles, "Absorptive Capacity, Learning, and Performance in International Joint Ventures," *Strategic Management Journal* 22 (2001): 1139–61.

22 Don Clark, "AMD, Fujitsu Join Israel; Concern in Bid To Shift Chip Technology," *Woll Street Journal Abstracts* (July 31, 2002): B4.

23 Pierre Dussauge, "Domino's Pizza International, Inc.," Case #398-048-1 (Jouy-en-Josas, France: H.E.C., 1998).

24 Bennett, op. cit.

25 Richard C. Hoffman and John F. Preble, "Global Diffusion of Franchising: A Country Level Examination," *Multinational Business Review* 9, no. 1 (Spring 2001): 66–76.

26 Leslie Chang, "From KFC to Beauty Spas, Chinese Are Embracing Franchises," *Wall Street Journal* (April 18, 2002).

27 John F. Preble, "Global Expansion: The Case of U.S. Fast-Food Franchisors," *Journal of Global Marketing* 6, nos. 1–2 (1992): 186, citing D. Ayling, "Franchising in the U.K.," *The Quarterly Review of Marketing* (Summer 1988): 19–24.

28 Fred Burton, Adam R. Cross, and Mark Rhodes, "Foreign Market Servicing Strategies of UK Franchisors: An Empirical Enquiry from a Transactions Cost Perspective," *Management International Review* 40, no. 4 (Fourth Quarter 2000): 373–400.

29 John K. Ryans, Jr., Sherry Lotz, and Robert Krampf, "Do Master Franchisors Drive Global Franchising?" *Marketing Management* 8, no. 2 (Summer 1999): 33–38.

30 Julie Bennett, "Product Pitfalls Proliferate in a Global Cultural Maze," *Wall Street Journal* (May 14, 2001): B11.

31 Peng S. Chan and Robert T. Justis, "Franchise Management in East Asia," *Academy of Management Executive* 4, no. 2 (May 1990): 75–85. For other changes by McDonald's in Europe, see Heather Ogilvie, "Welcome to McEurope: An Interview with Tom Allin, President of McDonald's Development Co.," *Journal of European Business* 2, no. 67 (July–August 1991): 5–12.

32 Bertrand Benoit, "BAA Wins License to Run Chinese Airports," *Financial Times* (August 30, 1999): 13.

33 Peter Goddard and Guy Standish-Wilkinson, "Hotel Management Contract Trends in the Middle East," *Journal of Leisure Property* 2, no. 1 (January 2002): 66–80.

34 Elizabeth Becker and Richard A. Oppel Jr. "U.S. Gives Bechtel a Major Contract in Rebuilding Iraq," *New York Times* (April 18, 2003): A1+.

35 See "Signing of ABB Deal for Malaysia's Bakun Dam on September 30," *Agence France Presse* (September 21, 1996); and "Malaysia Signs Dam Contract," *Financial Times* (October 3, 1996): 7.

36 Benjamin A. Holden and Nicholas Bray, "British, Australian and Two American Firms to Purchase Utility in Australia," *Wall Street Journal* (August 5, 1996): A4.

37 Paul Betts and Tim Burt, "General Motors and Fiat Close to Signing Strategic Alliance," *Financial Times* (March 13, 2000): 1.

38 There are many different ways of classifying the problems. Two useful ways are found in Manuel G. Serapio, Jr. and Wayne F. Cascio, "End Games in International Alliances," *Academy of Management Executive* 10, no. 1 (May 1996): 62–73; and Joel Bleeke and David Ernst, "Is Your Strategic Alliance Really a Sale?" *Harvard Business Review* (January–February 1995): 97–105.

39 Terrence Chea, "No Perfect Partnership," *Washington Post* (June 3, 2002): E1.

40 Gregory L. White, "In Asia, GM Pins Hope on a Delicate Web of Alliances," *Wall Street Journal* (October 23, 2002): A23.

41 Leslie Kaufman, "New Front in Calvin Klein vs. Warnaco Fight," *New York Times*, (January 17, 2001): C4.

42 See William H. Meyers, "Maxim's Name Is the Game," *New York Times Magazine* (May 3, 1987): 33–35; and Keith W. Strandberg, "EganaGoldpfeil Group Moves Forward with Pierre Cardin Watches," *National Jeweler* 96, no. 19 (October 1, 2002): 36.

43 Marcus W. Brauchli, "PepsiCo's KFC Venture in China Is Fined for Allegedly False Financial Reporting," *Wall Street Journal* (July 27, 1994): A10.

44 See Nicholas D. Kristof, "A Not-So-Grand Hotel: A Tibet Horror Story," *New York Times* (September 25, 1990): A4; and Alec Le Sueur, *Running a Hotel on the Roof of the World: Five Years in Tibet* (Chichester, UK: Summersdale, 1999).

45 David Ibison, "Culture Clashes Prove Biggest Hurdle to International Links," *Financial Times* (January 24, 2002): 17.

46 Samantha Marshall, "P&G Squabbles with Vietnamese Partner," *Wall Street Journal* (February 27, 1998): A14.

47 Ken Belson, "Abbott to Buy Full Ownership of Japan Ally," *New York Times* (April 23, 2002): W1. For factors that appear to influence the ability of foreign companies to gain knowledge about local operating conditions, see Andrew C. Inkpen and Paul Beamish, "Knowledge, Bargaining Power, and the Instability of International Joint Ventures," *Academy of Management Review* 22, no. 1 (1997): 177–202. For evidence on the buyout and dissolution of joint ventures after one party learns from the other, see Jean-François Hennart, Thomas Roehl, and Dixie S. Zietlow, "'Trojan Horse' or 'Workhorse'? The Evolution of U.S.-Japanese Joint Ventures in the United States," *Strategic Management Journal* 20, no. 1 (January 1999): 15–29. For information on the competition between collaborators, see Tarun Khanna, Ranjay Gulati, and Nitin Nohria, "The Dynamics of

Learning Alliances: Competition, Cooperation, and Relative Scope," *Strategic Management Journal* 19, no. xx (March 1998): 193–210.

48 Joel Bleeke and David Ernst, "The Way to Win in Cross-Border Alliances" *Harvard Business Review* (November-December 1991): 127–135.

49 Leslie Crawford, "Anheuser's Cross-Border Marriage on the Rocks," *Financial Times* (March 18, 1998): 16.

50 Sue Cartwright and Cary Cooper, "Why Suitors Should Consider Culture," *Financial Times* (September 1, 1995): 6.

51 Seung Ho Park and Gerardo R. Ungson, "The Effect of National Culture, Organizational Complementarity, and Economic Motivation on Joint Venture Dissolution," *Academy of Management Journal* 40, no, 2 (April 1997): 279–307. Harry G. Barkema et al., "Working Abroad, Working with Others: How Firms Learn to Operate International Joint Ventures," *Academy of Management Journal* 40, no. 2 (April 1997): 426–42, found survival differences only for differences in uncertainty avoidance.

52 Mike W. Peng and Oded Shenkar, "Joint Venture Dissolution as Corporate Divorce," *Academy of Management Executive* 16, no. 2 (May 2002): 92–105; C. F. Fey and P.W. Beamish, "Organizational Climate Similarity and Performance: International Joint Ventures in Russia," *Organizational Studies* 22, no. 5 (2001): 853–883.

53 Harry G. Barkema, John H. J. Bell, and Johannes M. Pennings, "Foreign Entry, Cultural Barriers, and Learning," *Strategic Management Journal* 17, (1996): 151–66.

54 Bharat Anand and Tarun Khanna, "Do Firms Learn to Create Value? The Case of Alliances," *Strategic Management Journal* 21, no. 3 (March 2000): 295–315.

55 Anne Smith and Marie-Claude Reney, "The Mating Dance: A Case Study of Local Partnering Processes in Developing Countries," *European Management Journal* 15, no. 2 (1997): 174–82.

56 See Sanjiv Kumar and Anju Seth, "The Design of Coordination and Control Mechanisms for Managing Joint Venture-Parent Relationships," *Strategic Management Journal* 19, no. 6 (June 1998): 579–99; T. K. Das and Bing-Sheng Teng, "Between Trust and Control: Developing Confidence in Partner Cooperation in Alliances," *Academy of Management Journal* 23, no. 3 (July 1998): 491–512; Arvind Parkhe, "Building Trust in International Alliances," *Journal of World Business* 33, no. 4 (1998): 417–37; and Prashant Kale, Harbir Singh, and Howard Perlmutter, "Learning and Protection of Proprietary Assets in Strategic Alliances: Building Relational Capital," *Strategic Management Journal* 21, no. 3 (March 2000): 217–37.

57 John Kenneth Galbraith, *American Capitalism* (Boston: Houghton Mifflin, 1952), 91–92.

58 Jeffrey Reuer, "Collaborative Strategy: The Logic of Alliances," *Financial Times* (October 4, 1999): Mastering Strategy section, 12–13.

59 Eric H. Kessler, Paul E. Bierly, and Shanthi Gopalakrishnan, "Internal vs. External Learning in New Product Development: Effects of Speed, Costs and Competitive Advantage," *R & D Management* 30, no. 3 (July 2000): 213–23.

60 These are adapted from Arvind Parkhe, "Interfirm Diversity, Organizational Learning, and Longevity

in Global Strategic Alliances," *Journal of International Business Studies* 22, no. 4 (Fourth Quarter 1991): 579–601.

61 Data for the case were taken from Andrea Rothman, "U.S. to World: Airline Deals Hinge on Open Skies,'" *Business Week* (January 11, 1992): 46; Andrea Rothman, Seth Payne, and Paula Dwyer, "One World, One Giant Airline Market?" *Business Week* (October 5, 1992): 56; "All Aboard," *The Economist* (February 29, 1992): 78; "Wings Across the Water," *The Economist* (July 25, 1992): 62; Agis Salpukas, "Europe's Small Airlines Shelter Under Bigger Wings," *New York Times* (November 8, 1992): E4; "Code Breakers," *The Economist* (November 21, 1992): 78–79; Bridget O'Brian and Laurie McGinley, "Mixing of U.S., Foreign Carriers Alters Market," *Wall Street Journal* (December 21, 1992): B1; Bill Poling, "United, American Spar with USAir, BA over Proposed Deal," *Travel Weekly* (November 12, 1992): 49; Joan M. Feldman, "The Dilemma of 'Open Skies,'" *New York Times Magazine* (April 2, 1989): 31; Philippe Gugler, "Strategic Alliances in Services: Some Theoretical Issues and the Case of Air-Transport Services," paper prepared for the Danish Summer Research Institute (DSRI) (Denmark, August 1992); Martin Tolchin, "Shift Urged on Foreign Stakes in Airlines," *New York Times* (January 9, 1993): 17; Agis Salpukas, "The Big Foreign Push to Buy into U.S. Airlines," *New York Times* (October 11, 1992): F11; Robert Crandell, "When Less Really Means More," *Financial Times* (September 17, 1996): 17; Emma Tucker, "Commission to Approve Lufthansa-SAS Venture," *Financial Times* (January 16, 1996): 3; Scott McCartney et al., "U.S. Airlines' Prospects Are Grim on Expanding Access to Asian Skies," *Wall Street Journal* (September 25, 1996): A1; Michael Skapinker, "Austrian Air Switches Allegiance to Star Alliance," *Financial Times* (September 22, 1999): 9; Edward Alden and Michael Skapinker, "United Airlines-Lufthansa Join Battle for Air Canada," *Financial Times* (October 20, 1999): 1; Michael Skapinker, "Continental Chairman Calls for Creation of Third Air Alliance," *Financial Times* (October 5, 1998): 20; Michael Skapinker, "Passengers Not Convinced," *Financial Times* (November 19, 1998): Business of Travel section, iii; Michael Skapinker, "Boarding Business Class Now," *Financial Times* (July 9, 1998): 13; J. A. Donoghue, "Network Is Everything," *Air Transport World* 36, no. 8 (August 1999): 9; Leonard Hill, "Global Challenger," *Air Transport World* 36, no. 12 (December 1999): 52–54; Robert Gribben, "City," *The Daily Telegraph* [London] (December 21, 1999): 29; Michael A. Taverna and John D. Morrocco, "Airlines Play Catch-Up in Partnership Game," *Aviation Week and Space Technology* 150, no. 12 (March 22, 1999): 70; Leonard Hill, "80 Years Young," *Air Transport World* 36, no. 10 (October 1999): 44–47; "Star Alliance Welcomes Asiana, Lot and Spanair to Its Roster of World Class Airlines," *PR Newswire* (June 1, 2002); Shirene Shan, "Alliances Bring Benefit to Passengers," *New Straits Times Press* [Malaysia] (May 14, 2002): Industry Aviation section, 24; and "Global Alliances Vulnerable to Shakeups in Four Areas," *Airline Financial News* 20, no. 23 (June 10, 2002).

CHAPTER 15

CONTROL STRATEGIES

Form your plans before sunrise.

—INDIAN-TAMIL PROVERB

OBJECTIVES

- To explain the special challenges that confront MNEs trying to control foreign operations

- To describe organizational structures for international operations

- To show the advantages and disadvantages of decision making at headquarters and at foreign subsidiary locations

- To highlight both the importance of and the methods for global planning, reporting, and evaluating

- To give an overview of some specific control considerations affecting MNEs, such as the handling of acquisitions and the dynamics of control needs

- To summarize major means of control

- To introduce the differences between a branch and a subsidiary

CASE

Johnson & Johnson[1]

Since Johnson & Johnson (J&J) began U.S. operations in 1886, it has evolved into the most broadly based health-care company in the world. International activity started in 1919 with J&J Canada; J&J now sells in more than 175 countries, generates annual global revenues of more than $36 billion, and employs 108,300 people, of whom more than 65,000 are outside the United States. Its steady success is renowned. Through 2002, the company increased annual sales for 70 consecutive years and earned money every year since going public in 1944. It regularly ranks on lists of the most admired companies and best companies to work for.

J&J's business strategy aims for leadership in its three core areas: pharmaceuticals, medical devices, and consumer products. Although this is a straightforward mission, J&J carries it out by using a complex structure that combines responsibility between 37 product groups and 14 health-care areas, known as platforms. For example, its product groups include Centocor, Neutrogena, and Ethicon Endo-Surgery. They develop, manufacture, and market products to consumers and health-care professionals worldwide. Its health-care platforms, called "platforms for growth," include biotechnology, gastrointestinals, and wound care. These are distinct health-care platforms that contain a related group of products, technologies, pathologies, modalities, and/or customers. They act as staging areas from which J&J leverages its knowledge, development skills, marketing expertise, and global reach.

J&J organizes by operating units. Map 15.1 shows the worldwide span of these operating units. Each unit has remarkable autonomy and is explicitly accountable for its individual performance. J&J tries to combine the entrepreneurial opportunities of a small company with the unique advantages of a big one. Such autonomy (decentralization), explained Ralph Larsen, CEO from 1989 to 2002, "gives people a sense of ownership and control—and the freedom to act more rapidly." His successor, Paul Weldon, concurred, adding, "The magic around J&J is decentralization." Essentially, this policy enables J&J to behave like more than 200 innovative, entrepreneurial small firms.

Nevertheless, J&J's operating units enjoyed more autonomy before the company encountered a series of financial setbacks in the late 1990s. Traditionally, J&J did not enter new markets with sweeping armies of home-office managers directed by headquarters-based generals; rather, it added another small company to its roster. J&J advised the president of the new company to call home if he or she needed help, and then it waited for superior results. Basically, headquarters believed that people who understood the business and were close to the market (philosophically, culturally, and physically) ought to be running the businesses. Thus, for example, the baby oil managers in Italy ran their own factory and got to decide how big a bottle to put the baby oil in—even if that bottle differed from the one sold in Germany, Japan, or Mexico. Historically, noted one observer, the heads of J&J's foreign subsidiaries enjoyed so much autonomy that they were called "kings of their own countries." Still, there were some procedural limits. Headquarters negotiated financial targets with the heads of the separate business units and then let them figure out the best way to meet them. Overall, J&J's executives conceded that there was often friction between operating units and headquarters, but they believed this was a reasonable price to pay for entrepreneurial operations.

J&J also maintains control through what Mr. Larsen calls the "glue that binds this company together." Specifically, for more than 50 years, J&J has used a one-page ethical code of conduct, "Our Credo," to guide how it fulfills its business responsibilities. The Credo tells all managers, worldwide, who and what to

MAP 15.1   Johnson & Johnsons's Worldwide Operations, 2002

Johnson & Johnson sells in virtually every part of the world. The map indicates where J&J has operations. The numbers indicate the number of operating units per country.

Source: http://www.jnj.com/ investor/annual_reports/2001/ family_companies.htm;jsessionid= E33PB5MFZTO14CQPCCGSU0A.

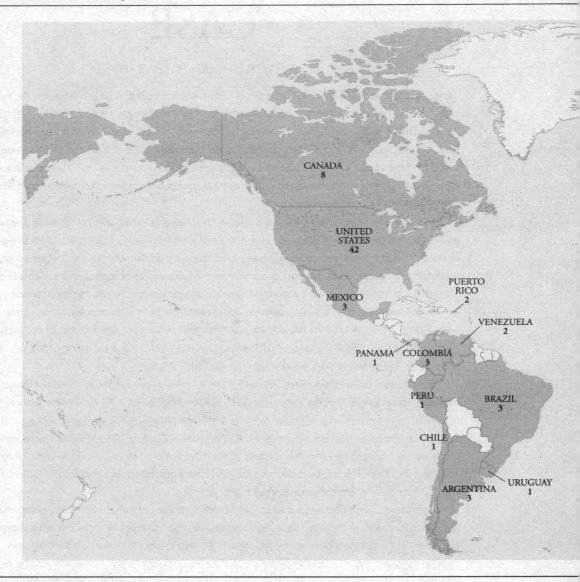

care about—and in what specific order. The Credo begins, "We believe our first responsibility is to the doctors, nurses, patients, mothers and fathers who use our products and services." Continuing on, it addresses both the communities where J&J operates and the roles and duties of J&J employees. Shareholders come last, long after suppliers and distributors. The Credo declares that shareholders will get a fair return if those other constituents get first priority. J&J has translated its Credo into 36 languages.

Decentralization has created some costs, such as inconsistent market development. For example, J&J launched Tylenol in 1960 as an over-the-counter pain reliever in the United States. Although it was available to local operating units shortly thereafter, the Japanese unit did not commence sales until 2000. In essence, decentralization enabled J&J to respond quickly to local needs, but it slowed diffusion of products and programs globally.

In the late 1990s, J&J streamlined global operations by closing 36 plants and cutting 4,100 jobs. It also aimed to improve the global perspective of its local decision making. Specifically, it placed headquarters managers in charge of the job of coordinating product production and marketing around the world. Granted, they

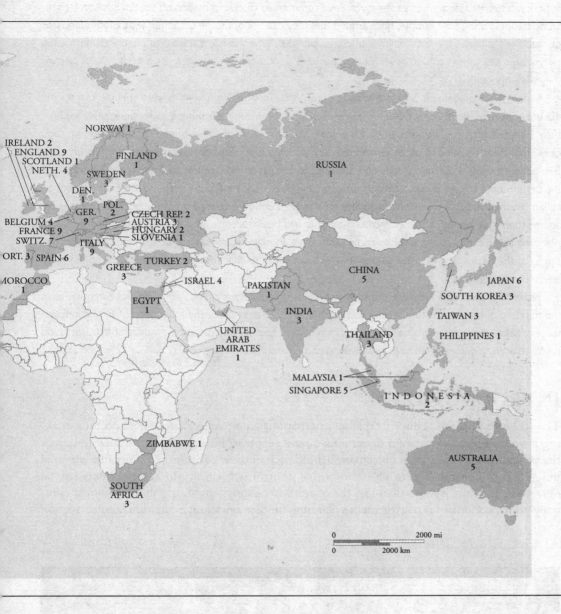

still collect lots of input from the local managers and meet with them to thrash out a unified marketing strategy; for example, they may debate whether cleanliness or beauty is the better promotion theme. Ultimately, though, when J&J rolls out a product, country managers no longer have the option to reject it.

Similarly, J&J has moved control of various activities from the operating units to headquarters, including human resources, finance, science and technology, government affairs, corporate advertising, corporate communications, and quality management. Groups at headquarters now deal with many issues that are common to many or all operating units. Management reasons that this approach lets it use its global perspective to develop cost-effective and consistent standards. Moreover, centralizing these functions frees operating units to concentrate on issues that most affect their day-to-day business performance.

Centralization, even of nonstrategic activities, has not always been readily accepted. There have certainly been successes; for example, implementing Windows 2000 in a more centralized way than before saved J&J an estimated $80 million. Still, years after starting to integrate information technologies at J&J, headquarters still finds it hard to get all of its business units to go along with even the most benign changes in policy. "I get 190 land mines in any given day," commented chief information officer (CIO) JoAnn Heisen. Some business units, for example, have argued that they can't adopt some corporate technology standards or bear their share of the cost for infrastructure upgrades. When she first started to integrate information technology, Ms. Heisen couldn't even get the business units to answer the surveys on what type of systems they were operating.

Senior J&J management is trying to build an organizational environment in which people can openly discuss important ideas. To that end, it has developed programs that encourage its far-flung units to share their expertise with counterparts around the world. Self-directed councils—of research, engineering, and operations directors, among others—meet regularly to swap ideas. Successful employees are speedily shuffled between various operating units and affiliates, leading to eclectic career paths. Managers benchmark the performance of operating companies against competitors and each other. J&J also developed a process called "FrameworkS," one in which it rotates employees through a continuing dialogue with senior management on strategic topics that cut across the company's business units. Similarly, J&J elaborated its formal planning at the business-unit level by adding initiatives on major issues such as biotechnology, the restructuring of the health-care industry, and globalization in order to challenge assumptions and to open managers to new thinking.

No matter what structures are changed or what programs are adopted, senior management believes the standard of success is plain: Decentralization has been, is, and will be the foundation of J&J's continued success. More pointedly, explained the CEO, "I am here to passionately protect the values of J&J. Our credo is value-based. It comes down to people, values, and environment."

Control questions facing all companies:

- Where should decision-making power reside?
- How should foreign operations report to headquarters?
- How can the company ensure that it meets its global objectives?

INTRODUCTION

The J&J case illustrates concerns that all international companies share: where decision-making power resides, how foreign operations should report to headquarters, and how to ensure the company meets its global objectives. Behind each of these concerns is a more fundamental one—that of control. Figure 15.1 shows that control is necessary to achieve international objectives. It is much more than just the ownership of sufficient voting shares to direct company policies. **Control** is management's planning, implementation, evaluation, and correction

Technical advances are enabling managers in different countries to communicate with each other more quickly and effectively. The photo shows a teleconference between executives of Telefonica in Madrid, Spain, and Endomol in Amsterdam, Netherlands. Nevertheless, face-to-face contact is often necessary.

FIGURE 15.1 Control in International Business

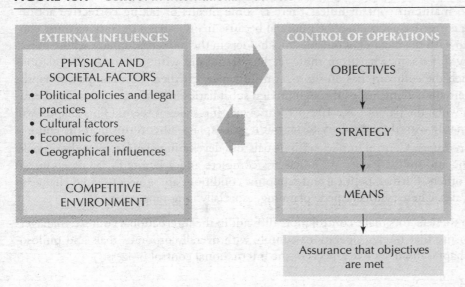

Control is the assurance that the company's objectives are met. The process involves setting objectives, a strategy to achieve them, and the means to carry out the strategy.

of performance to ensure that the organization meets its objectives. Top management's toughest challenge is to balance the company's global needs with its need to adapt to country-level differences.

Control keeps a company's direction or strategy on track. For example, J&J managers know that although cost and innovation are important, the company's major competitive advantage lies in developing, producing, and marketing personal and health-care products. Headquarters managers allocate resources to emphasize those product and geographic markets in which they prefer to grow more rapidly. It would be almost inconceivable for a manager in, say, Colombia to launch a new product there or build a plant in Ecuador (J&J has no operating unit in Ecuador) without considerable scrutiny and approval from corporate management in the United States. Further, J&J allows its country-level managers to adjust to specific environmental and competitive conditions in their countries of operation. At the same time, the subsidiaries share information, fixed costs from new product development, and spillover advantages, making it easier for J&J to sell to international distributors. In contrast, before J&J revamped its global operating structure in the late 1990s, there was little synergy among its operating units in different countries.

Control is also needed so that individuals cannot make decisions that endanger the entire company. For example, Allied Irish Banks (AIB) allowed its Allfirst Bank in the United States to operate independently, with hardly any control from headquarters in Ireland. One of its foreign exchange traders at Allfirst lost $730 million before AIB became aware of it.[2]

Several factors make control more difficult internationally than it is domestically.

1. *Distance*. In spite of the growth in e-mail and fax transmissions, many communications are still best handled through face-to-face or voice-to-voice contact. The geographic distance (especially when operations span multiple time zones) and cultural disparity separating countries increase the time, expense, and possibility of error in cross-national communications.

2. *Diversity*. This book has emphasized the need for an MNE to adjust to each country in which it operates. When market size, type of competition, nature of the product, labor cost, the currency, and a host of other factors differentiate operations among countries, the task of evaluating performance or setting standards to correct or improve business functions is extremely complicated.

Foreign control is usually more difficult than domestic control because of

- Distance—it takes more time and expense to communicate
- Diversity—country differences make it hard to compare operations
- Uncontrollables—there are more dissimilar outside stockholders and government influences
- Degree of certainty—there often are data problems and rapid changes in the environment

3. *Uncontrollables*. Evaluating employees' and subsidiaries' performance is of little help in trying to maintain control unless there is some means of taking corrective action. Effective corrective action may be minimal because many foreign operations must contend both with the dictates of outside stockholders in the foreign company, whose objectives may differ somewhat from those of the parent, and with government regulations over which the company has no short-term influence. Further, most companies handle their international operations through foreign subsidiaries, which are separate legal entities even when the parent has a 100-percent ownership stake in them. (This chapter will deal primarily with the subsidiary form, but it will explain other forms near the end.)

4. *Degree of certainty*. Control implies setting goals and developing plans to meet those goals. Economic and industry data are much less complete and accurate for some countries than for others. Further, political and economic conditions are subject to rapid change in some locales. These factors impede planning, especially long-range planning.

Although these factors make control more difficult in the international context, managers still try to ensure that foreign operations comply with overall corporate goals and philosophies. This chapter discusses five aspects of the international control process.

1. Planning
2. Organizational structure
3. Location of decision making
4. Control mechanisms
5. Special situations including the dynamics of control

PLANNING

Planning is an essential element of managerial control. A company must adapt its resources and objectives to different and changing international markets, and this takes planning. Because planning has been both implicitly and explicitly discussed already, this section presents an overview of the process.

In planning, companies must mesh objectives with internal resources and external environments and set means to implement, report, analyze, and correct.

The Planning Loop

As Figure 15.2 shows, planning must mesh a company's objectives and capabilities with its internal and external environments. It must also involve continuing reassessment—thus the concept of a loop back to early steps in the planning process. The first step (A) is to develop a long-range **strategic intent**, an objective or mission that will hold the organization together over a long period while it builds global competitive viability. Companies sometimes call this by different names, such as J&J's "Credo." Although few companies start with such an intent, most develop one as they progress toward significant international positions. Some, such as Honda and Canon, developed strategic intents to become major global competitors while they were still small domestic firms. The strategic intent may encompass whether and where a company wants to be a leader—for example, dominating its domestic market, dominating a regional or global market, or attaining profit results without being the market leader. The strategic intent may also help the company to set priorities. Most large companies publish their strategic intents (on their Web sites, for example), not only to guide their employees, but also to inform other stakeholders, such as suppliers and shareholders.[3]

The next planning step (B) is to analyze internal resources, along with environmental factors in the home country. These resources and factors affect and constrain each company differently and sometimes each product differently for the same company. Basically, the most

FIGURE 15.2 International Planning Process

A. Set long-range strategic intent

B. Analyze internal corporate resources
- I. Financial resources
  - a. Immediate and future cash flow and needs
  - b. Capital availability, including borrowing
  - c. Ability to transfer funds
  - d. Profit and dividend targets
- II. Human resources
  - a. General versus product skills
  - b. Specific functional skills
  - c. Transferability of people
  - d. Capacity use
  - e. Ability to acquire additional resources
  - f. Attitudes toward foreign activity
- III. Product resources
  - a. Capacity use and bottlenecks
  - b. Monopolistic characteristics
  - c. Adaptations needed for foreign sales
  - d. Primary versus derived demand
  - e. Transport practicality
  - f. Cost savings through scale and scope
- IV. Environmental effects
  - a. Supply and cost changes, including foreign trade
  - b. Long-run and cyclical changes in demand
  - c. Comparison with competition
  - d. Societal attitudes

C. Set international corporate objectives (based on analysis in B)
- I. Sales objectives
  - a. Maintain volume
  - b. Expand volume
  - c. Increase markup
  - d. Spread fixed costs
- II. Resource acquisition objectives
  - a. Reduce direct costs
  - b. Gain tax advantages
  - c. Gain complementary resources
- III. Diversification objectives
  - a. Diversify markets
  - b. Diversify supplies
- IV. Competitive risk minimization objectives
  - a. Acquire scarce resources
  - b. Prevent competitors' advantages

D. Analyze local conditions (in current or prospective host countries)
- I. Same factors as in B, plus
- II. Financial factors
  - a. Local evaluation methods
  - b. De facto and de jure tax systems
  - c. Timing of receivables and payables
  - d. Needs for financing suppliers and customers
  - e. Governmental priorities for funds' use
- III. Marketing factors
  - a. Cost and availability of market data
  - b. Distribution methods and costs
  - c. Nature of competition
  - d. Government regulation of price, advertising, etc.
- IV. Other factors
  - a. Attitudes toward business in general
  - b. Attitudes toward foreign business
  - c. Political and economic stability

E. Select alternatives and priorities (based on objectives in C and conditions in D)
- I. Alternatives
  - a. Location of value-added activities
  - b. Location of sales targets
  - c. Level of involvement
  - d. Product/services strategy
  - e. Global versus multidomestic marketing
  - f. Country moves as part of global strategy
  - g. Factor movement and start-up strategy
- II. Setting priorities among alternatives

F. Implement strategy
- I. Set target results/goals
  - a. Production amount
  - b. Costs
  - c. Sales
- II. Do reports showing deviations from target
- III. Do environmental analysis that might change results
- IV. Make corrections if possible
- V. Move to contingency plan

The initial step in planning is setting the company's long-range strategic intent, followed by a loop from Step F to Step B in which short- and medium-term steps are taken to achieve the intent.

successful companies internationally are those that find the right fit between what they need and what they are good at.[4] For example, a small firm inexperienced in foreign operations may lack financial and human resources, even though it may have unique product capabilities. Unlike a larger counterpart, it may have to collaborate with another company, perhaps by licensing foreign production rather than owning facilities abroad. But it still will need to control its foreign operations through a contract with the licensee that stipulates sales targets, product characteristics, and so on.

Only by making an internal analysis (step B) can a company set the overall objectives for its international activities (step C). Managers must examine these activities in conjunction with the means of competing, such as by keeping prices low or differentiating through brand recognition. For instance, a company competing largely on price and faced with rising domestic costs may pursue one of several means for cost reduction, such as locating production where costs are lower or expanding exports to spread fixed costs.

Because each country in which the company is operating or contemplating operating is unique, managers must do a local analysis (step D) before examining the final alternatives (step E).

The selection among the alternatives in step E determines the extent to which a company follows a global, transnational, or multidomestic strategy. These alternatives include

- *The location of value-added functions*—the choice of where to locate each of the functions that comprise the entire value-added chain, from research to production to after-sales servicing.
- *The location of sales targets*—the allocation of sales among countries and the level of activity in each one, particularly in terms of market share.
- *The level of involvement*—the choice of operating through wholly owned facilities, through partially owned facilities, or through contract arrangements, and whether the choice varies among countries.
- *The product/services strategy*—the extent to which a worldwide business offers the same or different products in different countries.
- *Marketing*—the extent to which a company uses the same brand names, advertising, and other marketing elements in different countries.
- *Competitive moves*—the extent to which a company makes competitive moves in individual countries as part of a global competitive strategy.
- *Factor movement and start-up strategy*—whether production factors are acquired locally or brought in by the company, and whether the operation begins through an acquisition or start-up.[5]

Managers must rank alternatives so they can easily modify (step F) as resource availability changes. A parent company may, for example, plan to remit dividends from one of its foreign subsidiaries back to itself. However, this may become impossible if a government puts foreign-exchange controls into effect. Management must then decide among its alternatives, such as borrowing more at home, remitting more from other subsidiaries, or forgoing domestic expansion or dividends. Without priorities, the company may have to make hurried decisions to accomplish its objectives even partially.

Finally, headquarters and subsidiary management should agree on specific objectives for each subsidiary and devise ways to measure both deviations from the plan and conditions that may cause such deviations. Through timely evaluation, the company can take corrective actions. There must be a constant loop from step F to step B in Figure 15.1.[6] We'll discuss evaluation methods later in this chapter.

We must make a distinction between operating plans and strategic plans. Strategic plans are longer term and similar to step A. They outline major commitments, such as what businesses the company will be in and where, and they are less subject to reevaluation.

Operating plans formulate short-term objectives and the means to carry them out. Although input for a strategic plan may come from all parts of the organization, only upper-level management can plan changes in international policies because they can see all the company's worldwide activities.

Uncertainty and Planning

The more uncertainty there is, the harder it is to plan. It is generally agreed that conditions in the international sphere are more uncertain than those in the domestic sphere because international operations are complex. International managers have to monitor many subsidiaries—many with different products—in different foreign markets.

> A company's international operations have more complexity and uncertainty than its domestic ones.

ORGANIZATIONAL STRUCTURE

No matter how good a plan is, it will achieve little unless there is an appropriate means of implementing it. International companies try to set up organizational structures (the formal patterns of their lines of communication and responsibilities) that group individuals and operational units in strategic ways. The structure depends on many factors, including

- The degree of multidomestic, global, and transnational policies that are employed.
- The location and type of foreign facilities.
- The impact of international operations on total corporate performance.

The form, method, and location of operational units at home and abroad will affect taxes, expenses—and control. Consequently, organizational structure has an important effect on the fulfillment of corporate objectives. We shall now examine the major structures of companies' international operations.

Separate Versus Integrated International Structures

All of a company's foreign subsidiaries may report to the same department or division of headquarters because that department or division is responsible for all of the company's international business. This is an international division structure. But different subsidiaries may report to different departments or divisions of headquarters because responsibility is split at headquarters by function (such as production and marketing), by product lines (such as consumer products and industrial products), or by geographic area (such as Asia and Europe). These are functional, product, and geographic structures, respectively. Figure 15.3 shows simplified organizational structures of international businesses. Most companies basically use one of these structures. Note that no structure is without drawbacks.

International Division Structure Grouping each international business activity into its own division—Figure 15.3(a)—puts internationally specialized personnel together to handle such diverse matters as export documentation, foreign-exchange transactions, and relations with foreign governments. This strategy prevents duplication of these activities in more than one place in the organization. It also creates a critical mass that is large enough to enable personnel within the division to wield power within the organization so that they can push for international expansion. However, an international division might have to depend on the domestic divisions for products to sell, personnel, technology, and other resources. Because domestic division managers are usually evaluated on the basis of performance within the domestic divisions for which they are responsible, they may withhold their best resources from the international division to improve their own performances. Given the separation between domestic and foreign operations, this structure is probably

> An international division
> - Creates a critical mass of international expertise
> - May have problems getting resources from domestic divisions

FIGURE 15.3   Placement of International Activities Within the Organizational Structures for International Businesses

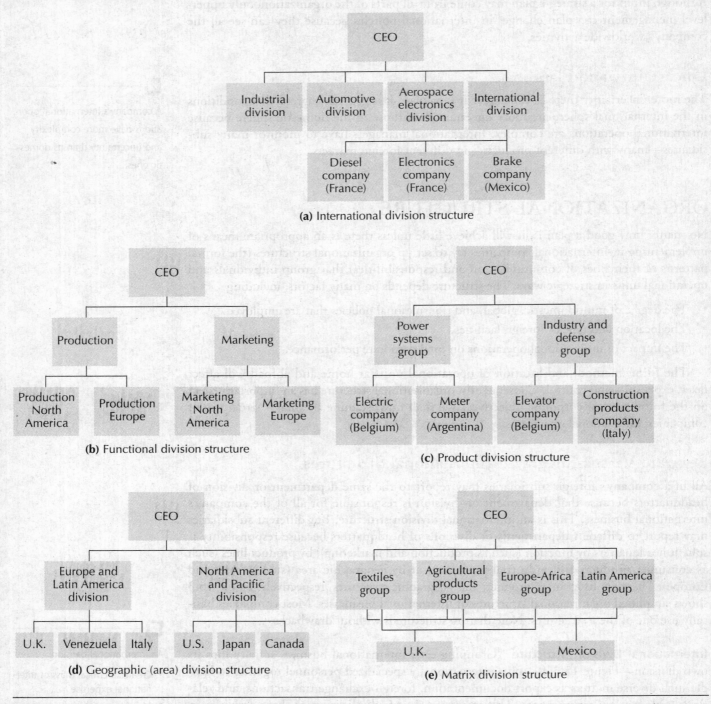

(a) International division structure

(b) Functional division structure

(c) Product division structure

(d) Geographic (area) division structure

(e) Matrix division structure

Although most companies have mixed structures, these five examples are simplified versions of the most common organizational structures for international businesses.

best suited for multidomestic strategies, those in which there is little integration and standardization between domestic and foreign operations.

Although the international division structure is not popular among European MNEs, it *is* popular among U.S. MNEs. One apparent reason for this difference is that U.S. companies depend much more on the domestic market than do European companies.

Functional Division Structure   Parts (b), (c), and (d) in Figure 15.3 show organizational structures that integrate international operations. Functional divisions, like those shown in Figure 15.3(b), group personnel organizationally so that marketing people report to other marketing people, finance to other finance people, and so on. Functional divisions are popular among companies with a narrow range of products, particularly if the production and marketing methods are undifferentiated among them. However, as new and different products are added, this structure becomes cumbersome. In a company such as General Electric (whose business spans thousands of products and services in such diverse areas as aircraft engines, a television network, plastics, home appliances, and insurance), it is hard to imagine that a head of production could understand how to produce all these products. But many oil and mineral extraction companies, such as ExxonMobil, use this structure, which is ideal when products and production methods are basically undifferentiated among countries.

> Functional divisions are popular among companies with narrow product lines.

Product Division Structure   Product divisions, as Figure 15.3(c) illustrates, are probably the most popular among international companies today, because most companies' businesses involve a variety of diverse products.[7] Because these divisions may have little in common, they may be highly independent of each other. As is true for the functional structure, the product division structure is well suited for a global strategy because both the foreign and domestic operations for a given product report to the same manager, who can find synergies between the two (e.g., by sharing information on the successes and failures of each one). Further, a separate product group structure enhances a company's ability to sell or spin off certain product lines because they are not as interwoven with its other lines. Most likely, there will be duplicated functions and international activities among the product divisions. Moreover, there is no formal means by which one product division can learn from another's international experience. Finally, different subsidiaries from different product divisions within the same foreign country will report to different groups at headquarters. For example, Figure 15.3(c) illustrates that the Belgian electric and elevator subsidiaries report to different headquarters divisions. So synergy could be lost within countries if different subsidiaries don't communicate with each other or with a common manager. For example, at one time in Westinghouse, one subsidiary was borrowing funds locally at an exorbitant rate, while another in the same country had excess cash.

> Product divisions are popular among international companies with diverse products.

Geographic (Area) Division Structure   Companies use geographic divisions, as in Figure 15.3(d), if they have large foreign operations that are not dominated by a single country or region (including the home country). This structure is more common to European MNEs, such as Nestlé, than to U.S. MNEs, which tend to be dominated by the strong domestic market. The structure is useful when maximum economies in production can be gained on a regional rather than on a global basis because of market size or the production technologies for the industry. A drawback is the possible costly duplication of work among areas.

> Geographic divisions are popular when foreign operations are large and are not dominated by a single country or region.

Matrix Division Structure   Because of the problems inherent in either integrating or separating foreign operations, some companies are moving toward matrix organizations, illustrated in Figure 15.3(e). In this organizational structure, a subsidiary reports to more than one group (functional, product, or geographic). The structure is based on the theory that because each group shares responsibility over foreign operations, the groups will become more interdependent, exchange information, and exchange resources with each other.[8] For example, product-group managers must compete among themselves to ensure that R&D personnel responsible to a functional group, such as production, develop technologies for their product groups. These product-group managers also must compete to ensure that geographic-group managers emphasize their lines sufficiently. Not only product groups, but also functional and geographic groups must compete among themselves to obtain resources held

> A matrix organization gives functional, product, and geographic groups a common focus.

by others in the matrix. For example, as Figure 15.3(e) shows, the amount of resources needed to develop textile products in Mexico depends partly on the competition between the Europe-Africa group and the Latin America group and partly on the competition between the textiles group and the agricultural products group for resources.

A matrix organization does have drawbacks. One drawback concerns how groups compete for scarce resources and how they enact their preferred operating methods. When lower-level managers fail to agree, upper management must decide which operating method to follow and how to allocate the resources, and this takes time. Further, for whatever reasons, upper management may favor a specific executive or group. As others in the organization see this occurring, they may think that the locus of power lies with a certain individual or group. Consequently, other group managers may think that pushing their own group's unique needs is futile, thus eliminating the multiple viewpoints that a matrix is supposed to bring. Or a superior may neglect to control his or her subordinates because he or she assumes (wrongly) that someone else is overseeing them. In Figure 15.3(e), for example, managers in the Latin America group might not pay close attention to day-to-day Mexican textile operations because they assume that managers in the textile division are doing this. Meanwhile, managers in the textile division may wrongly assume that managers in the Latin America group are overseeing the textile operation in Mexico closely. The false assumption that someone else was handling the responsibility was a factor in the loss of control and the demise of Barings.[9] For these reasons, some companies that adopted dual-reporting systems have gone back to conventional structures that have clear lines of responsibility, including Dow Chemical, ABB, and Citibank.[10]

Dynamic Nature of Structures

A company's structure can evolve as its business evolves. When a company is only exporting, an export department attached to a product or functional division may suffice. (In most companies, departments are within divisions.) But if international operations continue to grow—say, the company starts overseas production in addition to exporting—an export department may no longer be sufficient. Perhaps an international division replaces the department, or perhaps each product division takes on worldwide responsibility for its own products. Or if the international division becomes very large, the company may split it into geographic divisions.

Mixed Nature of Structures

Because of growth dynamics, companies seldom, if ever, get all of their activities to correspond to the simplified organizational structures described here; most have a mixed structure. For example, a recent acquisition might report to headquarters until it can be consolidated efficiently within existing divisions. Or circumstances regarding a particular country, product, or function might necessitate that it be handled separately—that is, apart from the overall structure. Some operations may be wholly owned, thus enabling a denser network of communications to develop than in other operations, where there is only partial or no ownership of the foreign operations. Further, the overall structure gives an incomplete picture of divisions in the organization. PepsiCo is organized by product lines (soft drinks and snacks), which would seem to imply that each line is integrated globally; however, each line has its own international division, which separates it from domestic operations.

Nontraditional Structures

As companies grow in size, as their product lines increase in number, and as they grow more dependent on foreign operations, control becomes more complex. New structures continue to evolve to deal with this complexity.

Network Organizations   No company is fully independent. Each is a supplier to and customer of other companies. Such interdependence is known as a **network alliance**. Each company must decide what products, functions, and geographic areas it will own and handle itself and what it will outsource to others. A company can control what it handles itself with clear superior-subordinate relationships, known as hierarchies. However, when it depends on another company—say, as an essential supplier—which one is superior and which is subordinate is not clear. Therefore, the location of control in a network alliance is ambiguous and is known as a **heterarchy**.[11] Decisions must come from negotiation and persuasion, rather than from formal authority. Likewise, when a company shares ownership with another—for example, in a joint venture—there is usually a heterarchical relationship.

Many Japanese companies are linked similarly in *keiretsus,* networks in which each company owns a small percentage of others in the network. (Many German companies are similarly intertwined, but there is no term to describe them.[12]) There are long-term strong personal relationships among high-level managers in the different companies, and the same directors often serve on more than one board. Sometimes *keiretsus* are vertical—for example, the one between Toyota and its parts suppliers. Sometimes they are horizontal. The Mitsubishi *keiretsu* consists of core companies in which no single company dominates. The businesses are extremely diverse, and they include mining, real estate, credit cards, and tuna canning. Typically, the core companies within a *keiretsu* buy and sell with each other only if it makes business sense. In Mitsubishi's case, it is hard to understand why a real estate company would need to do business with, or invest in, a tuna canning company. However, managers can exchange information that is useful to more than one company, can underwrite each other's financing, and can gain more clout when lobbying for government legislation. Strong, long-term personal relationships among managers in the companies build common interests that do not depend on formal controls. Nevertheless, this cushioning from stand-alone competition may retard a company's attainment of optimum efficiency.[13] And many of the relationships appear to be weakening during Japan's long recession.[14]

Lead Subsidiary Organizations   The major competency for designing, producing, and selling a product does not necessarily lie in the company's home country. As a result, some companies have moved the headquarters of certain divisions to foreign countries. For instance, AT&T moved its corded telephone division from the United States to France, Siemens moved its air-traffic management division from Germany to the United Kingdom, Hyundai shifted its personal computer division from Korea to the United States, and the Finnish company Nokia built its capabilities for a telecommunications product in the United Kingdom. Although these divisional headquarters are still accountable to corporate headquarters, other global operations, including those in the home country, must report to them.[15]

LOCATION OF DECISION MAKING

You might think that organizational structures tell us who makes decisions in a company, but that is not always the case. The higher the managerial level at which managers make decisions, the more they are centralized; the lower the level, the more they are decentralized. Whether decision making should be centralized or decentralized depends on whether we're talking about the company as a whole or some part of it, such as a particular subsidiary. For purposes of this discussion, decisions made at the foreign-subsidiary level are considered decentralized, whereas those made above the foreign-subsidiary level are considered centralized.

The location of decision making may vary within the same company over time as well as by product, function, and country. In addition, actual decision making is seldom as one-sided as it may appear. A manager who has decision-making authority may consult other managers before exercising that authority. Putting these exceptions aside, this section

Because of the increase in alliances among companies, control increasingly must come from negotiation and persuasion rather than from authority of superiors over subordinates.

Some divisions may be headquartered in a foreign country.

Centralization implies higher-level decision making, usually above the country level.

discusses why companies would place decision control at either the corporate or the subsidiary level. We usually associate centralized decision making with a global strategy, decentralized decision making with a multidomestic strategy, and a combination of the two with a transnational strategy. The reason for choosing one over the other is partly a function of companies' attitudes. For example, an ethnocentric attitude would influence a company to develop competencies, such as knowledge and technology, in its home country and control how they are transferred aboard. A polycentric attitude would cause the company to delegate decisions to foreign subsidiaries because headquarters personnel believe that only people on the spot know best what to do. A geocentric attitude would permit more openness to capabilities either at home or abroad, and it would be conducive to a transnational strategy.

Some conditions favor the location of decisions in one place or the other. Basically, companies should choose the location based on a combination of the following three trade-offs:

- Balancing pressures for global integration versus pressures for local responsiveness
- Balancing the capabilities of headquarters versus subsidiary personnel
- Balancing the expediency versus the quality of decisions

Pressures for Global Integration Versus Local Responsiveness

The higher the pressure for global integration, the greater the need to centralize decision making. The higher the pressure for responsiveness to local conditions, the greater the need to decentralize decision making. We shall now discuss the reasons for pressures one way or the other.

Resource Transference   A company may want to move its resources—capital, personnel, or technology—from its facilities in one country to its facilities in another. For example, it may decide to move capital to a country where the projected return is higher, hurting the performance in the other country but improving its global or overall performance. Decisions about these moves usually occur centrally because making them requires information from all operating units. Such information is often available only at headquarters. Otherwise, every unit would have to disseminate reports to every other unit, and there would be no clear-cut way to determine whether and how a resource from one locale would be used elsewhere. Further, a subsidiary will likely favor its own projects and performance—the major factor that influenced Royal Dutch/Shell to centralize financial control of U.S. operations that were once handled autonomously by its subsidiary, Shell Oil, in the United States.[16] Similarly, if the company needs to export output from its operations in one country to its operations in another (such as with vertical integration or when interdependent components make up the company's final product), centralized control may help assure this flow. However, if a subsidiary is not part of a company's integrated operation—say, because it operates in a highly protected market—there is little need for centralized control. But the subsidiary's strategies and importance to global operations may shift.[17]

Another centralized decision in resource transference may concern jurisdiction over exports. For example, if a company manufacturers the same product in the United States and Germany, which facility will export to South Africa? By answering that question centrally, the company may avoid price competition among the subsidiaries and take into consideration production costs, transportation costs, tax rates, foreign-exchange controls, and where there is excess production capacity.

Standardization   Worldwide uniformity of an MNE's products, purchases, methods, and policies may reduce its global costs substantially, even if some costs increase for a particular

Decisions on moving goods or other resources internationally are more likely to be made centrally.

Global standardization usually reduces costs, but some revenue may be lost in the process.

subsidiary. Such standardization is highly unlikely if each subsidiary makes its own decisions. For example, if an MNE standardizes machinery in its production process, it may see savings from quantity discounts on purchases, the consolidation of mechanics' training, the maintenance of manuals, and the stockpiling of spare parts inventories. The company may realize economies, not only through scale of production, but also in such activities as advertising, R&D, and the purchase of group insurance. Product uniformity gives a company greater flexibility in filling orders when supply problems arise because of strikes, disasters, or sudden increases in demand. Production can simply expand in one country to meet shortages elsewhere. However, the downside of standardization is that revenue losses may exceed the gains from cost savings—for example, because some subsidiaries end up with products that do not quite fit demand. Of course, some products are more suitable to global standardization than are others. GE's jet engines require no local adaptation, whereas Nestlé's food products do. The food industry usually does not need to integrate operations across countries because transportation costs offset savings from scale economies. At the same time, Nestlé has a need to adapt to local conditions because tastes, competitors, and distributors differ at the local level. Thus, Nestlé's products pressure it to decentralize.

However, the distinction between the need for standardization and local adaptation is not so clear-cut. For example, the pharmaceutical industry has a strong need for integration because it depends on the sale of undifferentiated products for which scale of production is important to cover the high cost of product development. Pharmaceutical companies also face most of the same competitors everywhere they sell, so (as we'll see in the next section) there are advantages to dealing with these competitors on a global basis. Nevertheless, these same companies need high local responsiveness both because different government authorities must approve each product in each country where those companies sell and because sales and distribution differ substantially from place to place. In such a situation, the location of decision making is apt to be very mixed among functions between headquarters and the subsidiaries.

The more the foreign environment requires adaptations, the more pressure there is to decentralize.

Systematic Dealings with Stakeholders   Increasingly, the people with whom a company must deal—government officials, employees, suppliers, consumers, and the general public—are aware of what that company does in other countries of operation. Concessions the company grants to stakeholders in one country may then be demanded in other countries. The company may face a dilemma if it can't afford the same concessions elsewhere. Suppose that for public relations purposes, company management in Finland decided to give preferential prices to the Finnish government and established a profit-sharing plan for employees. Profits in Finland allowed the company to give such concessions. If government officials and employees in, say, Norway—where profits aren't quite as high—asked for similar treatment, the result may be even lower profits if the company complies or poor public relations if it does not.

Even pricing and product decisions in one country can affect demand in others. With the growing mobility of consumers, especially industrial consumers, a good or bad experience with a product in one country may eventually affect sales elsewhere. This is especially true if industrial consumers themselves want uniformity in their end products. If prices differ substantially among countries, consumers may even find that they can import more cheaply than they can buy locally. Centralized decision making is necessary to ensure that operations in different countries operate toward achieving global objectives.

Global competition also may cause a company to make decisions in one country to improve performance elsewhere. For example, if a supplier gives price concessions to an automaker in Brazil, that supplier may more easily gain business in other countries in which the automaker manufactures because the automaker may prefer to deal with the same supplier worldwide. Usually, such dealings with potential global customers or competitors need centralized decision making because headquarters personnel are the only ones with information on all the countries where the company operates, such as information on what a global competitor is doing in one country that may have an impact elsewhere. However, in some cases, the subsidiary may be the best place to make decisions on how to deal with the customer or competitor once headquarters has established objectives and guidelines.

Transnational strategies imply

• Gaining knowledge and capabilities from anywhere in the organization

• Two-way information flows both horizontally and vertically

Transnational Strategies   Chapter 1 defined the transnational company as one whose strategy takes advantage of different competencies and contributions that may emanate from any part of the world by integrating them into its worldwide operations. Recently, the term *metanational* has been used to describe a company that thrives on the process of seeking out uniqueness that it might exploit elsewhere or that might complement its own existing operations. For example, high-tech firms find it advantageous to locate in Silicon Valley, but they get even more advantages by additionally gaining technology from other parts of the world.[18] To gain such benefits, a company needs a two-way flow of information between headquarters and subsidiaries and mutual evaluation of that information.

MNEs are attempting to weaken decision-making partitions so that more and better information flows through the organization (e.g., horizontally and vertically). In so doing, headquarters can better use subsidiaries' unique knowledge, and subsidiaries can better understand headquarters' global needs and pertinent conditions in other subsidiaries. In fact, if headquarters ignores subsidiaries' viewpoints, the company suffers. Companies have established various practices to improve this flow of information, such as bringing headquarters and subsidiary managers together for meetings, providing incentives to subsidiaries to work together, and linking groups through videoconferencing and computer networks. However, Oracle's experience is probably typical in that headquarters can more expeditiously request and receive information from different countries than can managers from those countries.[19]

As subsidiaries have become more interdependent, for example, because of rationalized or vertically integrated production or because they deal with common competitors and customers, managers have tended to initiate informal contact with their peers in the other subsidiaries. Such companies as Digital have established cross-cultural teams to tackle issues common to different country operations. These teams generally are composed of people chosen because of their skills and expertise, not because of their positions, and they are made up of equals, not of a superior and subordinates. The ability to reach consensus is dependent on the group members' enthusiasm as well as peer pressure within the groups, rather than on formal procedures. The advantage is the generation of more and perhaps better ideas. The disadvantages are the time it takes to decide on the cross-unit issues and the increased potential for conflict. Further, companies such as Citibank have encountered cultural conflicts that prevent cross-national teams from always working well together. For instance, the U.S. managers complained that the U.K. managers were too bureaucratic, and the U.K. managers complained that the U.S. managers would try to reach decisions without a thorough analysis.[20] In fact, there is evidence that mixing cultures on teams does not necessarily improve performance.[21]

Capabilities of Headquarters Versus Subsidiary Personnel

The more confidence there is in foreign managers, the more delegation occurs.

Upper management's perception of the competence of corporate versus local managers will influence the location of decision making. There are differences in capabilities between headquarters and local management. Decentralization may seem called for when the local management team is large rather than lean, when local managers have worked for a long time with the company, and when local managers have developed successful track records. However, the subsidiary's ability may increase or decrease over time, and this change may be caused by subsidiary managers' initiatives.[22]

Although some decisions are better left to corporate management, doing so may cause morale problems among local managers who perceive that their responsibility has been taken away. When local managers are prevented from acting in the best interest of their own operation, they tend to think, "I could have done better, but corporate management would not let me." If local managers cannot participate in the process of developing global strategies, they may lack the positive attitude to work hard to implement global strategic decisions. These managers also may not gain the experience needed to advance within the company. The head of Dow Europe has stated that more centralization reduces the chances for foreign nationals to reach upper level headquarters positions.[23]

Centralization may hurt local managers because they

- Cannot perform as well
- Do not acquire training through increased responsibility

Decision Expediency and Quality

A poor decision may be better than a good one that comes too late. However, a poor decision with major consequences should usually be avoided if possible. The following discussion highlights these points.

Cost and Expediency   Athough corporate management may be more experienced in advising or making certain decisions, the time and expense in centralization may not always justify the better advice. For example, corporate managers may need to visit a foreign subsidiary to see conditions firsthand before rendering their judgment. But many decisions cannot wait. Bringing in corporate personnel may not be warranted unless the decision has large ramifications for the company. Although meetings through digital communication links (teleconferencing, Web conferencing, video conferencing) offer hope of eliminating the need to travel as much, there are still technical and behavioral barriers to their use.[24]

Companies must consider how long it takes to get help from headquarters in relation to how rapidly a decision must be made.

Importance of the Decision   Any discussion of the location of decision making must consider the importance of the particular decisions. Sometimes a company asks, "How much can we lose through a bad decision?" The greater the potential loss and the more important the issue, the higher in the organization the level of control usually is. In the case of marketing decisions, for example, local autonomy is not nearly as prevalent for product design as it is for advertising, pricing, and distribution. Product design generally necessitates a considerably larger capital outlay than other functions; consequently, the potential loss from a wrong decision is higher. Moreover, advertising, pricing, and distribution decisions may be more easily reversed if an error in judgment occurs. Rather than telling local managers what decisions they can make, the company can set limits on expenditure amounts, thus allowing local autonomy for small outlays and requiring corporate approval on larger ones.

More important decisions are made at higher organization levels.

CONTROL IN THE INTERNATIONALIZATION PROCESS

Various factors influence how much control a company needs at different stages of internationalization. We discuss those factors below.

Level of Importance

The more important the specific foreign operations are to total corporate performance, the higher the corporate level to which those units should report. The organizational structure or reporting system, therefore, should change over time to parallel the company's increased involvement in foreign activities.

The more important the foreign operations, the higher in the organizational structure they report.

At one end of the spectrum is the company that merely exports temporary surpluses through an intermediary that takes title and handles all the export details. This entire operation is apt to be so insignificant to total corporate performance that top-level management is little concerned with it. In this case, the foreign activities should be handled at a low level in the corporate hierarchy. Anyone in the organization who knows enough about inventories and has time to discern whether orders can be filled could handle the operation.

At the other end of the spectrum is the company that has passed through intermediate stages and now owns and manages foreign manufacturing and sales facilities. Every functional and advisory group within the company undoubtedly will be involved in the facilities' establishment and direction. Because the sales, investments, and profits of the foreign operations are now a more significant part of the corporate total, people very high in the corporate hierarchy are involved.

Changes in Competencies

The larger the total foreign operations, the more likely that headquarters has specialized staff with international expertise. The larger the operations in a given country, the more likely that country unit has specialized staff.

Small companies, especially those that are fairly new to international operations, may have little if any staff in foreign countries. Further, because they typically have narrow product lines and lean structures, they are able to get key headquarters players in different functions to work closely, both together and with foreign customers or suppliers. Such headquarters involvement helped Cisco, when it was a small U.S. manufacturer of networking gear, to gain contracts with Japan's Nippon Telegraph & Telephone, and it also helped Pall, a small U.S.-based maker of filters, to develop extensive offshore manufacturing.[25] However, as a company's operations grow abroad, it develops a foreign management group that is more experienced and, therefore, more capable of operating more independently of headquarters in the overseas markets. Simultaneously, corporate managers may no longer be able to deal effectively with all international business operations because the company has entered so many different foreign markets; thus, foreign operations tend to become more decentralized. This creates a dilemma. The subsidiary in this situation has its own capabilities, but its importance to total global performance because of its size may dictate a greater need for headquarters to intervene.[26] Nevertheless, as foreign operations continue to grow, people with foreign experience move into headquarters positions, and headquarters can afford staff specialists to deal with the company's multiple international operations. At that point, recentralization becomes feasible.

Changes in Operating Forms

As the operating form evolves, so must the organizational structure.

The use of multiple operating forms, such as exporting, licensing, and joint venture, and the move from one to another may create the need to change areas of responsibility in the organization. Or it may mean that departments in the organization are not equally involved with all forms. For example, the legal department may have little day-to-day responsibility regarding exports but a great deal for licensing to the countries in which the exports are sold. Organizational mechanisms, such as joint committees and the planned sharing of information, are useful to ensure that activities complement each other. It also is useful for the company to plan organizational change so as to minimize obstacles when responsibilities shift from one group to another.

A further consideration is how important the nonequity operation is to the company's overall operations. For example, if a company contracts with only one supplier for an essential component, it is likely to control that contract more closely and from higher in the organization than it would a contract of less strategic importance.

When Push Comes to Shove, Just Who's in Control?

A corporate policy on ethics requires a control system to ensure compliance, one which should be compatible with managerial reward systems. The essential problem is that when managers are prodded to improve their performance, they may violate the ethical policy, unless they are not held responsible for performance that suffers through pursuit of the policy.

For headquarters management to control a worldwide organization, it needs information from and about all of its operating units. However, concerns about employee and consumer privacy have led to numerous restrictions on data flows among countries by international companies. These restrictions have even extended to the Internet.[27] On the one hand, the information flows could hurt individuals—for example, by affecting their credit ratings. On the other hand, restrictions not only limit companies' ability to control their foreign operations, but they also limit the ability to assess whether managers in foreign locations have the promise and track records to take on additional international responsibilities.

Developing countries are concerned about control that moves management and technical functions to the home country, leaving the menial and low-skilled jobs in the developing country. Critics recall colonial eras during which people from the colonies were forbidden responsible positions and were dependent on the colonial powers that controlled their destinies. These critics have been particularly concerned that almost all R&D takes place in industrial countries, a situation that presents dilemmas for MNEs. There are some potent arguments for centralizing most R&D in home countries. These include the availability of many people to work directly for the company, the proximity to private research organizations and universities doing related work, and the general advantages of centralized authority in reducing duplication of efforts. Companies may partially address this concern by allowing subsidiaries in developing countries to do adaptive R&D. However, MNEs with considerable R&D outside the home country seldom allow the foreign operations complete autonomy.[28] Corporate management may allocate budgets, approve plans, and offer suggestions. Therefore, because of centralized R&D, developing countries may continually be at the mercy of industrial country interests.

Although emerging economies complain that MNEs control practices from abroad, those economies, nevertheless, want companies to prevent dire effects locally. For example, Union Carbide delegated almost all decision making and day-to-day control in the management of its joint venture in Bhopal, India; however, the Indian government blamed the parent company for the deaths that resulted from a chemical leak. Although an Indian government agency was responsible for making safety inspections at the facility, it was widely known that the agency was inadequately staffed. This brought up ethical questions (as well as legal ones) concerning responsibility. The Indian government, which owned 49.1 percent of the joint venture, denied responsibility because of its lack of a controlling interest and its delegation of management to Union Carbide. Union Carbide, in turn, initially claimed that responsibility rested in the joint venture. The ethical question is whether headquarters should be responsible for actions taken at the subsidiary level and whether minority stockholders should be responsible for what majority stockholders do.

CONTROL MECHANISMS

Thus far, we have discussed how companies group their operations for the purpose of communications and control and what companies should consider when deciding where control should be located. We shall now move to the subject of the mechanisms they can use to help ensure that control is implemented.

Corporate Culture

People trained at headquarters are more likely to think like headquarters personnel.

Every company has certain common values its employees share. These constitute its **corporate culture** and form a control mechanism that is implicit and helps enforce the company's explicit bureaucratic control mechanisms. For example, without setting explicit rules, managers may conform to company tradition in terms of how they dress, how late they work, whether they socialize with other managers, and whether they go to others in the company for advice. MNEs have more difficulty relying on a global corporate culture for control because managers from different countries may have different norms and little exposure to the values prevalent at corporate headquarters. The incompatibility of organizational cultures is a detriment to the acceptance of knowledge, which MNEs need to transfer from operations in one country to operations in another to gain competitive advantage.[29] To try to overcome this problem, many companies encourage a worldwide corporate culture by promoting closer contact among managers from different countries. The aim is to convey a shared understanding of global goals and norms for reaching those goals, along with the transference of "best practices" from one country to another.[30] Frequent transfers of managers among operations in different countries help develop increased knowledge of and commitment to a common set of values and objectives; fewer procedures, less hierarchical communication, and less surveillance are thus needed.

The degree of control that corporate headquarters imposes on the selection of top managers for foreign subsidiaries may dictate to a great extent how much formal control over the subsidiaries' operations corporate personnel feel is necessary. Using home-country nationals in subsidiaries' management will likely result in subsidiary managers who think like headquarters personnel. Even having headquarters set the standards for local managers' selection and training may be perceived by local managers as a means of ensuring primary loyalty to the corporate culture rather than to the subsidiary culture. Corporate culture may be effective even if the operations are only partially owned or when the parent requires long-range planning assistance from the subsidiaries.

Coordinating Methods

Rather than changing overall structure, many companies are finding mechanisms to pull product, function, and area together.

Because each type of organizational structure has advantages and disadvantages, companies have developed mechanisms to pull together some of the diverse functional, geographic (including international), and product perspectives without abandoning their existing structures. Some of these mechanisms are

- Developing teams with members from different countries for planning, by building scenarios on how the future may evolve.[31]
- Strengthening corporate staffs (adding or creating groups of advisory personnel) so that headquarters and subsidiary managers with line responsibilities (decision-making authority) must listen to different viewpoints—whether or not they take the advice.
- Using more management rotation—for example, between domestic and international positions—to break down parochial views.
- Keeping international and domestic personnel in closer proximity to each other—for example, by placing the international division in the same building or city as the product divisions.

- Establishing liaisons among subsidiaries within the same country so that different product groups can get combined action on a given issue.
- Developing teams from different countries to work on special projects of cross-national importance so that they share viewpoints.
- Placing foreign personnel on the board of directors and top-level committees to bring foreign viewpoints into top-level decisions.
- Giving all divisions and subsidiaries credit for business resulting from cooperative efforts so that they are encouraged to view activities broadly.
- Basing reward systems partially on global results so that managers are committed to global as well as local performance.

Companies also use staff departments (such as legal or personnel) to centralize activities common to more than one subsidiary. For instance, all the geographic divisions at Heinz use one expatriate-transfer-and-compensation policy in order to minimize duplicated effort.

Reports

Reports are another control mechanism. Headquarters needs timely reports to allocate resources, correct plans, and reward personnel. Decisions on how to use capital, personnel, and technology continue without interruption, so reports must be frequent, accurate, and up-to-date to ensure meeting the MNE's objectives. Headquarters uses reports to evaluate the performance of subsidiary personnel in order to reward and motivate them. These personnel adhere to reports and try to perform well on the tasks that are reported in them so that they receive more rewards. They also seek feedback so they will know how well they are performing and can alter their performance accordingly.[32]

Written reports are more important in an international setting than in a domestic one because subsidiaries' managers have much less personal contact with managers above them. Corporate managers miss out on much of the informal communication that could tell them about the performance of the foreign operations. The following discussion highlights the content and evaluation of reports that headquarters would use to control international operations.

Types of Reports Most MNEs use reports for foreign operations that resemble those they use domestically. There are several reasons for this.

1. If reports have been effective domestically, management often believes they will also be effective internationally.
2. There are economies from carrying over the same types of reports. The need to establish new types of reporting mechanisms is eliminated, and corporate management is already familiar with the system.
3. Reports with similar formats presumably allow management to better compare one operation with another.

MNEs use reports to identify deviations from plans that could indicate problem areas. The focus of the reports may be to monitor short-term performance or longer-term indicators that match the organization's strategy. Usually, the emphasis is on evaluating the subsidiary rather than the subsidiary manager, although the subsidiary's profitability is an important ingredient in the managerial evaluation.

Visits to Subsidiaries Not all information exchange occurs through formalized written reports. Within many MNEs, certain members of the corporate staff spend much time visiting subsidiaries. Although this attention may alleviate misunderstandings, there are some

Reports must be timely in order to allow managers to respond to their information.

Reports are intended first to evaluate operating units and second to evaluate management in those units.

"rules" for conducting visits properly. On the one hand, if corporate personnel visit the tropical subsidiaries only when there are blizzards at home, the personnel abroad may perceive the trips as mere boondoggles. On the other hand, if a subsidiary's managers offer too many social activities and not enough analysis of operations, corporate personnel may consider the trip a waste of time. Further, if visitors arrive only when the corporate level is upset about foreign operations, local managers may always be overly defensive. Nevertheless, visits can serve the goal of controlling foreign operations because they enable the visitors to collect information and offer advice and directives.

Management Performance Evaluation   MNEs should evaluate subsidiary managers separately from their subsidiary's performance so as not to penalize or reward them for conditions beyond their control. For example, a company may decide not to expand further in a country because of its slow growth and risky economic and political environment, but it should still reward that country's managers for doing a good job under adverse conditions.

However, what is within a subsidiary manager's control varies from company to company (because of decision-making authority differences) and from subsidiary to subsidiary (because of local conditions). Take currency gains or losses. Who is responsible depends on whether working capital management decisions occur at headquarters or at the subsidiary level—and on whether there are instruments such as forward markets in a particular country that allow for hedging against currency value changes.

Another uncontrollable area is when headquarters managers make decisions that will optimize the entire company's performance, perhaps at the expense of a particular subsidiary. In addition, the normal profit-center records may well obscure the importance the subsidiary has within the total corporate entity.

One way to overcome the problems of evaluating performance is to look at a budget agreed upon by headquarters and subsidiary managers. Doing this can help the MNE differentiate between a subsidiary's worth and its management's performance. The budget should cover the goals for each subsidiary that will help the MNE achieve an overall objective.

Cost and Accounting Comparability   Different costs among subsidiaries may prevent a meaningful comparison of their operating performance. For example, the ratio of labor to sales for a subsidiary in one country may be much higher than that for a subsidiary in another country, even though unit production costs may not differ substantially. So management must ensure that it is comparing relevant costs. Chapter 19 will show that different accounting practices can also create reporting and accountability problems. Most MNEs keep one set of books that are consistent with home-country principles and another to meet local reporting requirements. Clearly, headquarters needs to use considerable discretion in interpreting the data it uses to evaluate and change subsidiary performance, especially if it is comparing performance with competitors from other countries whose accounting methods are different from its own.

Evaluative Measurements   Headquarters should evaluate subsidiaries and their managers on a number of indicators rather than relying too heavily on one. Financial criteria tend to dominate the evaluation of foreign operations and their managers.

Although many different criteria are important, the most important for evaluating both the operation and its management are "budget compared with profit" and "budget compared with sales value," because these immediately affect consolidated corporate figures. Many nonfinancial criteria are also important, such as market-share increase, quality control, and managers' relationship with host governments.

Information Systems   This discussion has centered on the information that managers at headquarters need to evaluate the performance of subsidiaries and their managers. Although

---

Companies should evaluate managers on things they can control, but there is disagreement concerning what is within their control.

Companies must evaluate results in comparison to budgets.

It is hard to compare countries using standard operating ratios.

A system that relies on a combination of measurements is more reliable than one that doesn't.

this information is crucial, corporate management requires additional data to plan, take action, and share to improve performance.[33] This might include

- Information generated for centralized coordination, such as subsidiary cash balances and needs, so that headquarters can move funds effectively.
- Information on external conditions, such as analyses of local political and economic conditions, so that headquarters can plan where to expand and constrict operations.
- Information that can be used as feedback from parent to subsidiaries, such as R&D breakthroughs, so that subsidiaries can compete more effectively.
- Information that subsidiaries can share so that they can learn from each other and be motivated to perform as well as other subsidiaries.
- Information for external reporting needs, such as to stakeholders and tax authorities

Companies face three problems in acquiring information: (1) the cost of information compared to its value, (2) redundant information, and (3) information that is irrelevant. For example, much of the information that is useful to a subsidiary, such as whom to contact to clear items at customs, is irrelevant to headquarters and should not be transmitted. To cope, companies should periodically reevaluate the information sources they use.

With expanding global telecommunications and computer links—especially the World Wide Web and e-mail—managers throughout the world can share information more quickly and easily than ever before. On the one hand, this technology may permit more centralization, because corporate management can more easily examine the global conditions and performance. On the other hand, managers in foreign locations may become more autonomous because they have more information at their disposal.

> Management should reevaluate information needs periodically to keep costs down, and it should ensure that information is being used effectively.

CONTROL IN SPECIAL SITUATIONS

Acquisitions, shared ownership, and changes in strategies create control problems. We shall now discuss each of them in turn.

Acquisitions

A policy of expansion through acquisition can create some specific control problems. Acquisitions can lead to overlapping geographic responsibilities and markets as well as new lines of business with which corporate management has no experience. Another control problem occurs when the acquiring company's culture is very different from that of the acquired one. These differences may be due not only to company practices but also to national practices—for example, British managers may have trouble adjusting to U.S. companies' more short-term perspectives and to Japanese companies' decision-making processes.[34] Still another problem is that existing management in an acquired firm is probably accustomed to considerable autonomy. When existing managers in the acquired company resist new control, there is some tendency to replace them with managers from headquarters, who may perform poorly because they don't know the acquired company's competitive situation well enough.[35]

Attempts to centralize certain decision making or to change operating methods may result in distrust, apprehension, and resistance to change on the part of the acquired company. Moreover, resistance may come not only from the personnel but also from government authorities who want to protect their domestic economies. These authorities may use a variety of means to ensure that decision making remains vested within the country. Of course, there are many success stories with acquisitions. For example, Siemens has done well with its acquisition of Westinghouse's fossil-fuel power plant operations. Siemens starts planning the integration process when considering an acquisition and then puts an integration manager in charge.[36]

> An acquired company usually does not achieve a complete fit with the existing organization.

Shared Ownership

Ownership sharing limits the flexibility of corporate decision making. For example, Nestlé shares ownership with Coca-Cola in a joint venture for the production and sale of canned coffee and tea drinks, and Nestlé has less autonomy for this operation than for those it owns wholly because Coca-Cola has an equal voice in decision making. Nevertheless, there are administrative mechanisms that enable a company to gain control even with a minority equity interest. These mechanisms include spreading the remaining ownership among many shareholders, contract stipulations that board decisions require more than a majority (giving veto power to minority stockholders), dividing equity into voting and nonvoting stock, and side agreements on who will control decision making. A company can also maintain control over some asset the subsidiary needs, such as a patent, a brand name, or a raw material. In fact, maintaining control is a motive for having separate licensing or franchising agreements or management contracts with a foreign subsidiary.

When a joint venture is with a competitor, control issues transcend the joint venture itself. Employees in the partner's organization may have been conditioned over the years to conspire against the other. It becomes difficult to get them to cooperate for the success of the joint venture.

Changes in Strategies

Most recent changes in strategies have involved movements from multidomestic to transnational or global operations or to shift control from subsidiary to headquarters or vice versa. But regardless of the type of change, there will be a need for new reporting relationships, changes in the type of information collected, and a need for new performance appraisal systems. When Citibank moved from a multidomestic to a regional strategy within Europe, it needed to create interdependence among operations and collect results not only on a country-by-country basis, but also by product and customer.[37] In addition to the practical problems of changing systems, there are human resource problems as well.

It is difficult to remove control from operations when managers are accustomed to much autonomy. Within Europe, for example, many U.S. companies owned very independent operations for decades in the United Kingdom, France, and Germany. These companies have often faced difficult obstacles when integrating these operations because the country managers perceive that integration brings personal and operating disadvantages. Managers who fear losses through a changed strategy continue to guard their autonomy and functional specialties and maintain existing allegiances.

THE ROLE OF LEGAL STRUCTURES IN CONTROL STRATEGIES

When operating abroad, companies may choose among legal forms that affect their decision making, taxes, maintenance of secrecy, and legal liability. Most choose a subsidiary form for which there are additional legal alternatives that vary by country.

Branch and Subsidiary Structures

When establishing a foreign operation, a company often must decide between making that operation a branch or a subsidiary. A foreign branch is a foreign operation not legally separate from the parent company. Branch operations are possible only if the parent holds 100 percent ownership. A subsidiary, however, is an FDI that is legally a separate company, even if the parent owns all of the voting stock. The parent controls a subsidiary through its voting stock and through the control mechanisms we have discussed. Because a subsidiary is

LOOKING TO THE FUTURE

Control/No Control— the Constant Balancing Act

Technological factors and government-to-government agreements tend to favor more global integration and standardization. But the legal, cultural, economic, and political differences in norms among countries are not about to be eliminated. Therefore, the balancing act to satisfy the needs for global integration and national responsiveness will continue. Companies will continue to experiment with mechanisms to handle these opposing forces. These mechanisms will be further complicated by ever-changing individual and operating unit capabilities.

As overseas sales and profits as a percentage of total sales and profits increase, headquarters is likely to pay more attention to foreign operations. Similarly, there will be pressures to centralize control to deal with the growing number of global competitors and the more homogenized needs of global consumers. However, managers in foreign subsidiaries may see the erosion of their autonomy over marketing, production, and financial decisions. To keep those managers motivated, the company may need to give them opportunities to work at corporate headquarters and in cross-national management teams so that they share in global responsibilities and understand the need for headquarters control. But with such cross-national fertilization comes the risk of clashes between cultural traditions. The lesson is that the human side of the organization may keep companies from developing global practices as rapidly as top headquarters management would like.

Conversely, MNEs might push decentralization because of their size. A number of them already have sales larger than many countries' GDPs. To manage such large organizations may require even greater decentralization and more horizontal communication among subsidiaries in different countries that are mutually dependent on parts, products, and resources. This mutual dependence among subsidiaries may, in turn, require new heterarchical relationships within the organizational structure.

legally separate from its parent, legal authorities in each country generally limit liability to the subsidiary's assets. Creditors or winners of legal suits against the subsidiary do not usually have access to the parent's other resources. This concept of limited liability is a major factor in the choice of the subsidiary form. With few exceptions, claims against a company for its actions are settled by courts either where the actions occur or where the subsidiary is legally domiciled.

Because subsidiaries are separate companies, a question arises concerning which decisions the parent may be allowed to make. Generally, this does not present a problem because there have been few limiting situations. However, court cases in several countries—for example, France and the United States—have ruled that companies were conspiring to prevent competition when the parent dictated which markets its subsidiary could serve. Another factor of control is public disclosure. Generally, the greater the control the owner has, the greater the secrecy it can maintain. In this respect, branches are usually subject to less public disclosure because they are covered by tight corporate restrictions.

From these examples, it should be clear that there are control advantages to either the branch or the subsidiary form. Each form also has different tax advantages and implications and may have different initiation and operating costs as well as abilities to raise capital. A company must consider its objectives for control, liability, secrecy, and taxes when deciding whether to use a branch or subsidiary to operate abroad.

Each legal form has different
operating restrictions.

Types of Subsidiaries and How They Affect Control Strategies

A company establishing a subsidiary in a foreign country can usually choose from a number of alternative legal forms. There are too many forms to list here; however, some distinctions between them are worth mentioning so that you understand there are many considerations. In addition to differences in liability, forms vary in terms of

- The ability of the parent to sell its ownership.
- The number of stockholders required to establish the subsidiary.
- The percentage of foreigners who can serve on the board of directors.
- The amount of required public disclosure.
- Whether equity may be acquired by noncapital contributions, such as goodwill.
- The types of businesses (products) that are eligible.
- The minimum capital required for establishing the subsidiary.

Before making a decision on a legal operating form, an MNE should analyze all of these differences in terms of its corporate objectives.

Summary

- Control of MNEs is difficult because of the geographic and cultural distances separating countries, the need to operate differently among countries, the large number of uncontrollables abroad, and the high uncertainty resulting from rapid change in the international environment and problems in gathering reliable data in many places.

- Good planning should include the establishment of a long-range strategic intent, analysis of internal corporate resources, setting of international corporate objectives, analysis of local conditions abroad, selection of alternatives and priorities, and implementation of a strategy.

- As a company expands internationally, the corporate structure must include a means by which foreign operations report. The more important the foreign operations, the higher up in the hierarchy they should report.

- Whether a company separates or integrates international operations, it usually needs to develop some control mechanism/structure to prevent costly duplication of efforts, to ensure that headquarters managers do not withhold the best resources from the international operations, and to include insights from anywhere in the organization that can benefit performance.

- The level at which decisions are made should depend on the pressures for global integration versus local responsiveness, the competence of headquarters versus subsidiary personnel, and the expediency needs that are weighed against decision quality.

- Even though worldwide uniformity of policies and centralization of decision making may not be best for a particular foreign subsidiary, overall company gains may be more than enough to overcome the individual country losses. When top management prevents subsidiaries' managers from doing their best job, however, there may be a negative effect on employee morale.

- Transnational strategies attempt to use competencies from everywhere in the MNE's worldwide organization.

- The corporate culture is an implicit control mechanism. It is more difficult to establish and maintain in MNEs because values differ among countries, but bringing managers together enhances the common culture.

- Timely reports are essential for control so that corporate/headquarters management can allocate resources properly, correct plans, and evaluate and reward personnel.

- Many MNEs use international reporting systems similar to their domestic ones because home-country management is familiar with them and because uniformity makes it easier to compare different operations.

- Generally, MNEs evaluate their subsidiaries and their subsidiary managers separately. However, MNEs may use some of the same criteria, including financial and nonfinancial performance, for both.

- Special control problems arise for acquired operations, operations that have historical autonomy, operations that are not wholly owned, and operations resulting from changes in companies' strategies. The legal structure of foreign operations may also raise control problems.

CASE

GE Hungary*

General Electric is the world's largest company in terms of market capitalization (number of shares times share price). Between 1989 and 2002, GE invested $1 billion in Tungsram and, in the process, gained 100 percent of its shares. Founded in Hungary in 1896, Tungsram is one of the world's oldest lighting companies. With this and other acquisitions, GE became the world's largest lightbulb company. (The Big Three—GE, Dutch-based Philips, and German-based Siemens—collectively control about 75 percent of the world's lighting market.)

Between 1995 and 2001, GE expanded its Hungarian operations in other businesses as well. It acquired 98 percent of Budapest Bank (BB), one of Hungary's largest banks, and an interest in Medicor, a medical equipment and instrument manufacturer. In addition, GE made greenfield investments in the manufacturing of industrial equipment and electrical switches and in an operation to repair airplane engines. In 2001, all of these except BB, a subsidiary of GE Capital, were combined into a new holding company, GE Hungary Inc. The purpose of the holding is to allow GE's manufacturing operations to negotiate with the government of Hungary with a single voice; to centralize and standardize purchasing, accounting, human resource management, and legal representation, thereby generating cost savings; and to assist in the establishment of new GE businesses in the country. Nevertheless, the five combined businesses—Lighting (employing 11,000 persons), Power Controls (1,000 employees), Engine Services (100), Medical Systems (300), and Power Systems (500)—report separately to GE's product divisions, which are headquartered in the United States. Because the lighting group, Tungsram, is by far the largest of GE's Hungarian businesses, we'll concentrate most of our discussion on that group.

From a control standpoint, GE has relied on corporate reorganization, restructuring of operations, infusion of its corporate culture, and the implementation of a standardized reporting system.

Tungsram has developed important lighting source innovations and has traditionally sold most of its production outside of Hungary. Its market position eroded during the closing era of communist rule in Hungary, and the government hired the consulting firm Arthur D. Little (ADL) to assess the situation. ADL concluded that Tungsram's cost levels were too high and its exploitation of marketing opportunities too weak. Further, it was investing less and spending less on R&D as a percent of sales compared to its competitors. Nevertheless, Tungsram could be turned around, ADL concluded, with restructur-

ing help from a strategic investor if the investor would provide capital, production technology, and management know-how. GE became that strategic investor.

CORPORATE REORGANIZATION

During the early 1990s, GE managed its European lighting acquisitions on a multidomestic basis, meaning it allowed them to operate quite autonomously. GEL, the company's lighting division, believed this autonomy was necessary because each country's operations differed significantly in terms of R&D, production capability, product structure, and market characteristics. However, in 1992, GE decided to move rapidly toward more centralized control, believing that, regionally and globally, such a move would facilitate the transfer of experience from one subsidiary to another, especially through the standardization of operations, functions, products, and culture. In addition, GE wanted to gain a common image within and among its different product groups so that it could introduce new products more effectively into foreign markets. GEL established its European headquarters in London (GE Lighting Europe, or GELE), and Tungsram lost much of the autonomy it had enjoyed until then. Figure 15.4 shows GE-Tungram's place in a simplified GE organization structure.

GELE-London decided (1) to introduce in Europe the GE brand lightbulbs as a high-priced "quality" product by using the yellow and blue GE logo, which was well known and carried a quality image in the United States, and (2) to continue selling under the Tungsram name, but to position it as a low-priced (value for money) brand, to be promoted less than the GE brand, even though the products were identical, except for the packaging. This has been a sensitive issue among Hungarians, who are proud of Tungsram's century-old tradition, scientific achievements, global reach, and name recognition in Europe.

To understand the rationales of the next two major reorganizations involving the company, we must get ahead of our story about the Tungsram restructuring. Throughout the 1990s, U.S. manufacturing productivity improvements in lighting sources slowed, and lighting competition intensified in the United States and in global markets, especially from low-cost Chinese firms. GEL's response was to close U.S. and west European plants and to transfer production to lower-cost locations, particularly in Mexico and Hungary. The choice of Hungary has been supported by the successful restructuring of Tungsram, by the sophisticated quality assurance systems required in lighting, and by the country's central location in Europe. In 2002, GE-Tungsram became GEL's new Center for Europe, the Middle East, and

*By Paul Marer, Professor and Academic Director, CEU Graduate School of Business, Budapest (draft dated October 15, 2002).

FIGURE 15.4   GE-Tungsram in GE's Organization Structure

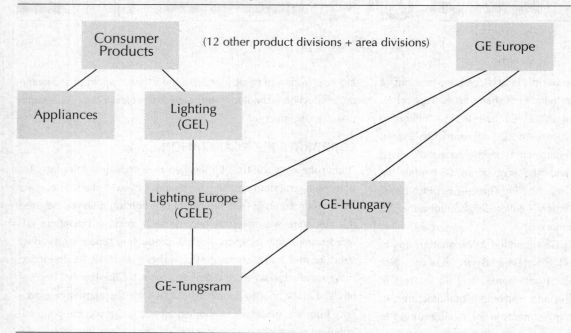

This simplified drawing shows that GE operates with a matrix structure, although the product groups have traditionally had much more power than the areas groups. Therefore, GE-Tungsram reports to both an àrea (country) group and to a product group.

Africa. The increased concentration of GEL's production and R&D in Hungary made this a logical move.

RESTRUCTURING

The Tungsram acquisition was a strategic investment for GE, made quickly to take advantage of the opportunity; however, subsequent audits showed that many costly changes were needed to make Tungsram competitive. Labor productivity was low due to over-staffing, bureaucratic administrative structures, and insufficient automation. GE reduced the labor force from nearly 20,000 in early 1990 to about 9,500 in 1993 (subsequently increased to 11,000). The acquired production facilities could not reach the quality standards demanded in Western markets, so GE bought new equipment; upgraded the telecommunications system; installed personal computers; refurbished buildings; and improved health, safety and environmental standards.

GEL consolidated its R&D, so that more than half of it now takes place in Hungary and much of the rest in the United States. A team representing all of GE's major business units makes decisions on GE's R&D priorities. Once GEL gains approval from this team for its projects, it appoints a program manager for each project. The program manager chooses team members from a large "GEL talent pool" located in different countries and made up of functional specialists, such as marketing and accounting personnel, as well as scientists and

engineers. Task-oriented teams form and disband as needs change. GEL informs the entire talent pool of planned programs and projects, encouraging individuals to volunteer as team members, though the selection is up to the program manager. The company demotes individuals who, over a period of time, are not chosen as team members and convinces them to leave the company. GEL rewards not only technical competence but also initiative, business sense, and the ability and willingness to work constructively as a member of a team.

CULTURE AS CONTROL AT TUNGSRAM

GE's corporate culture is strong, and it helps unify behavior among company personnel. The culture is based partly on U.S. norms, such as pride and optimism, and partly on the styles and practices of GE's top managers, notably that of its former CEO, Jack Welch, who believed in the quick sale of underperforming units or massive layoffs to improve those units' performance.

Initially, GEL proceeded cautiously with changing the inherited culture at Tungsram. However, in 1992, following the appointment of a new CEO at Tungsram, GEL decided to introduce the GE corporate culture more decisively and quickly. As is customary in all GE operations worldwide, GE translated its 95-page manual, *Integrity: The Spirit and Letter of our Commitment*, into Hungarian and required all Tungsram employees (as it does everywhere it operates) to pledge observance of its contents. The manual describes behavior to eliminate corruption, instructs that one must deal fairly with coworkers (regardless of gender, nationality, or creed), and requires absolute fairness in dealing with competitors and suppliers.

Many aspects of GE's culture ran counter to those at Tungsram. For example, the norm in the United States is to be inner-directed—believing that it is up to each individual to succeed and that outside constraints can be overcome if only one tries hard enough. However, the norm in Hungary used to be outer-directed—believing that uncontrollable outside forces, rather than the will of the individual, are decisive in determining outcomes (perhaps brought about by decades of Soviet rule, when there was little self-determination). In addition, GE's use of layoffs and selloffs to improve performance contrasted sharply with the experience at Tungsram, where there was a history of paternalism. For example, many Tungsram employees received company subsidies to buy apartments and vacationed at company resorts. Their children attended company kindergartens and their families rooted for Tungsram-sponsored sports teams. The best way to get a job at Tungsram was recommendation by a current employee; however, once employed, satisfactory work performance led to lifetime job security. Personal relationships and reciprocal favors were much more important than formal rules. Thus, GE faced the task of trying to enforce a universal code in a paternalistic national and corporate culture.

Initially, the going was not easy for GEL. Resentment, fed by early layoffs, the shedding of noncore businesses, and uncertainty about what GE had in store for Tungsram, led to lots of complaints by employees and by the labor unions representing them, resulting in a spate of unfavorable publicity in the Hungarian press. Gradually, however, GE succeeded in making its norms and practices accepted by a large majority of the workforce. The stabilization and eventual increase in employment certainly helped, as did the continuous substantial improvements in productivity and quality, and the resulting expansion of production and R&D.

CAMPAIGNS TO CHANGE CULTURE

One distinctive feature of GE's culture under Jack Welch was that corporate strategic initiatives were applied, with strength and fervor, in every one of GE's diverse businesses and in each of its subsidiaries, whether in the United States, Hungary, or Japan. In Welch's two decades as CEO (1981–2001), he introduced major strategic initiatives that have all been continued, becoming routine after a while.[38] These were required throughout the GE organization, Tungsram being no exception. One of these initiatives was Internet digitalization, which aims to eliminate the use of paper while generating three kinds of profit opportunities: buying inputs, marketing products, and reducing overhead. GE labels them "e-buy," "e-sell," and "e-make." For example, GE buys in excess of $50 billion in goods and services each year. Transferring some of this to online auctions has given GE access to more suppliers and lower costs, generating net savings in the 5 to 10 percent range.

The greatest hurdle to the implementation of initiatives, says Welch, was not technology but culture. For example, in Internet digitalization, salespeople worried that they might be destroying their jobs, so GE offered them bonuses to get them to help customers use GE Web sites when ordering. Separate teams, again comprised of some of the best managers, were put together to come up with potential Internet-based strategies for different businesses and products. To make sure executives would become willing agents of change in the campaign, Welch "suggested" that each of GE's top 3,000 managers should get Internet mentors, preferably under the age of 30, as he himself had done. "It is a great way to turn the organization upside down," he said.

How do such strategic initiatives play out "down in the trenches"? Miklos Csapody, former vice president and director of GE-Tungsram and director of GEL's Technology Development and R&D, said,

The changeover [to digitalized workflows] is taking place at an amazing pace. For example, [in] the beginning, no one at Tungsram was allowed to turn on a printer or to copy anything on certain days. And the idea was not to postpone the printing or copying until later. The boss stood at the door asking, "Why do you have to print or copy?" If the explanation seemed reasonable, then an independent digitization team was called in to discover the source of the problem and to eliminate it.[39]

CONTROL BY REPORTS

When Hungary had central planning, the government set costs and prices. It also owned companies, which faced no domestic competition and could not go bankrupt. The purpose of companies' reporting systems was to check plan fulfillment, not to control costs or improve profits. Under GE, all units must prepare standard reports on just about all aspects of costs and operations. Everyone faces a great deal of pressure to improve performance. Benchmarking—comparing performance indicators at one plant with those achieved by other plants that manufacture similar products, or with industry standards—has become an important tool of management control.

Improvement, then, has become the key word at Tungsram. Reducing labor, inventory, and scrap costs are critical to profitability. Initially, GEL compared Tungsram's performance against its U.S. counterparts within the GE lighting division. But this was difficult because of different operating methods. GEL invested to make Tungsram technically equivalent to facilities in the United States. GEL also implemented enterprise resource planning (ERP) modules, which standardize business practices everywhere. For example, under ERP, GEL's order processing is uniform throughout the company. Standardization of equipment and business practices eases GEL's ability to compare performance through benchmarking. Apparently, the standardization, benchmarking, and reporting have been helping to improve performance, inasmuch as Tungsram has continuously reduced its scrap rate, material content, and unit labor costs.

However, making Tungsram as good as other GEL units is not GE's ultimate aim. GE compares its managers and its operations against the best in the industry. The reporting system measures performance against stated goals.

FUTURE NEED FOR CONTROL

Today, a growing concern of GEL and of the management and employees of Tungsram is that competition from China is getting rapidly more intense. The technology of manufacturing light sources is pretty standard, except for the newest products. As China is improving quality and as its plants are receiving subsidies from local governments, the long-term strategic concern is how long GE will be willing and able to remain in the business of manufacturing light sources. In this business, foreign companies did not have much of a chance to invest in China because scores of municipal and regional governments decided to establish and subsidize light-source factories, thus generating employment through import substitution policies. As the production capacity being built is getting to be more than suffi-cient to meet domestic demand, China's firms are rapidly penetrating foreign markets. Jeff Immelt, Jack Welch's successor as GE's CEO, says, "Either you'll be a big investor in China or your biggest competitors will come from China."[40]

QUESTIONS

1. Define national and corporate cultures. How did GE's and Tungsram's cultures differ? How did GE attempt to use its culture as a control mechanism in Hungary and elsewhere?
2. What were the pros and cons of changing GEL's European operations from multidomestic to regional or global? Would such a change work the same for all of GE's product divisions?
3. What factors might account for (a) GE's initial acquisition and subsequent expansion of light-source manufacturing and R&D in Hungary? and (b) GE's establishing new types of businesses in Hungary?
4. In what ways does GE attempt to gain synergy among its operations in different countries and among its different businesses?

Chapter Notes

1 Case developed from information reported at www.jnj.com/2002AnnualReport/index.htm (April 22, 2003); www.jnj.com/; www.investor.jnj.com/ Brian O'Reilly, "J&J is on a Roll," *Fortune* (December 26, 1994): 178–85; Howard Rudnitsky, "One Hundred Sixty Companies for the Price of One," *Forbes* (February, 26, 1996): 56–60; "Can J&J Keep the Magic Going?" *Fortune* (May 27, 2002): 117; "J&J Stops Babying Itself," *Business Week* (September 13, 1999): 95; Geoff Dyer, "Hoping for a Ride as Smooth as a Baby's Bottom: Interview with Bill Weldon, Johnson & Johnson," *Financial Times* (September 20, 2002): 15; Tsun-yan Hsieh, Johanne Lavoie, and Robert A. P. Samek, "Think Global, Hire Local," *McKinsey Quarterly* (Autumn 1999): 92; Robert Scheier, "Central Intelligence: Johnson & Johnson," *CIO Insight* (December 1, 2001): Melody Petersen, "From the Ranks, Unassumingly," *New York Times* (February 24, 2002): Section 3, 2; "Going Beyond Band-Aids: Akira Matsumoto," *Japan Today* (September 21, 2002).

2 "AIB Left US Subsidiary to Act Independently," *Financial Times* (February 8, 2002): 1.

3 Barbara Bartkus, Myron Glassman, and Bruce McAfee, "Do Large European, US and Japanese Firms Use Their Web Sites to Communicate Their Mission?" *European Management Journal* 20, no. 4, (August 2002): 423–29.

4 Geert Duysters and John Hagedoorn, "Core Competence and Company Performance in the World-Wide Computer Industry," *Journal of High Technology Management Research* 11, no. 1 (Spring 2000): 75–91.

5 Part of the explanation is adapted from George S. Yip, *Total Global Strategy* (Upper Saddle River, NJ: Prentice Hall, 2003), 11–12.

6 Kimberly M. Ellis, "Strategic Contexts, Knowledge Flows, and the Competitiveness of MNCs: A Procedural Justice Approach," *Competitiveness Review* 10, no. 1 (2000): 9–24.

7 Julian Birkinshaw, "The Structures Behind Global Companies," *Financial Times* (December 4, 2000): Mastering Management section, 2–4.

8 John W. Hunt, "Is Matrix Management a Recipe for Chaos?" *Financial Times* (January 12, 1998): 10.

9 John Gapper and Nicholas Denton, "The Barings Report," *Financial Times* (October 18, 1995): 8.

10 Julian Birkinshaw, "The Structures Behind Global Companies," *Financial Times* (December 4, 2000): Mastering Management section, 2–4.

11 See Ian D. Turner, "Strategy and Organization," Management Update: Supplement to the *Journal of General Management* (Summer 1989): 1–8; and Gunnar Hedlund, "The Hypermodern MNC—A Heterarchy?" *Human Resource Management* (Spring 1986): 9–35.

12 "A Tangled Web," *Financial Times* (June 12, 2001): Germany section, 7.

13 See Brian Bremner and Emily Thornton, "Fall of a Keiretsu," *Business Week* (March 15, 1999): 34; and Greg Hundley and Carol K. Jacobson, "The Effects of the Keiretsu on the Export Performance of Japanese: Help or Hindrance?" *Strategic Management Journal* (October 1998): 927–37.

14 Vagelis Dedoussis, "Keiretsu and Management Practices in Japan—Resilience Amid Change," *Journal of Managerial Psychology* 16, no. 2 (2001): 173–88.

15 See Pervez Ghauri, "New Structures in MNCs Based in Small Countries: A Network Approach," *European Management Journal* 10, no. 3 (September 1992): 357–64; and Karl Moore, "How Subsidiaries Can Be More Than Bit Players," *Financial Times* (February 20, 1998): Mastering Global Business section, 14–15.

16 Robert Corzine and Hillary Durgin, "Shell Oil Stripped of Independence Over Investment," *Financial Times* (March 12, 1999): 15.

17 See James H. Taggart, "Strategy Shifts in MNC Subsidiaries," *Strategic Management Journal* 19 (1998): 663–81; and Nagesh Kumar, "Multinational Enterprises, Regional Economic Integration, and Export-Platform Production in the Host Countries: An Empirical Analysis for the US and Japanese Corporations," *Weltwirtschaftliches Archiv* 134, no. 3 (1998): 450–83.

18 Yves Doz, José Santos, and Peter Williamson, *From Global to Metanational* (Boston: Harvard Business School Press, 2001).

19 "Country Managers: From Baron to Hotelier," *The Economist* (May 11, 2002): 55–56.

20 Alison Maitland, "Bridging the Culture Gap," *Financial Times* (January 28, 2002): 8.

21 P. Christopher Early and Elaine Mosakowski, "Creating Hybrid Team Cultures: An Empirical Test of Transnational Team Functioning," *Academy of Management Journal* 43, no. 1 (2000): 26–49.

22 See Julian Birkinshaw and Neil Hood, "Multinational Subsidiary Evolution: Capability and Charter Change in Foreign-Owned Subsidiary Companies," *Academy of Management Review* 23, no. 4 (1998): 773–95; and Julian Birkinshaw, Neil Hood, and Stefan Jonsson, "Building Firm-Specific Advantage in Multinational Corporations: The Role of Subsidiary Initiative," *Strategic Management Journal* 19 (March 1998): 221–41.

23 "Country Managers," op. cit., 55–56.

24 Paul Taylor, "Corporate High Flyers Still Take to the Skies," *Financial Times* (April 4, 2002): 25.

25 Stephen Baker et al., "Mini-Nationals Are Making Maximum Impact," *Business Week* (September 6, 1993): 66–69.

26 Nitin Nohria and Sumantra Ghoshal, "Differentiated Fit and Shared Values: Alternatives for Managing Headquarters-Subsidiary Relations," *Strategic Management Journal* 15 (July 1994): 491–502. For a discussion of how capabilities improve with experience, see Andrew Delios and Paul Beamish, "Survival and Profitability: The Roles of Experience and Intangible Assets in Foreign Subsidiary Performance," *Academy of Management Journal* 44, no. 5 (2001): 1028–38.

27 See Leslie Chang, "China Restricts News Further Over Internet," *Wall Street Journal* (February 22, 2000); Thomas Catán, "Secrets and Spies," *Financial Times* (May 21, 2000): 12; and Brandon Mitchener and David Wessel, "U.S. in Tentative Pact Protecting Europeans' Privacy," *Wall Street Journal* (February 24, 2000): B11.

28 Robert Nobel and Julian Birkinshaw, "Innovation in Multinational Corporations: Control and Communication Patterns in International R&D Operations," *Strategic Management Journal* 19, (May 1998): 479–96.

29 Tatiana Kostova, "Transnational Transfer of Strategic Organizational Practices: A Contextual Perspective," *Academy of Management Review* 24, no. 2 (1999): 308–24.

30 See Nohria and Ghoshal, loc. cit., and Anne-Wil K. Harzing, *Managing the Multinationals* (Cheltenham, UK: Edward Elgar, 1999).

31 Daniel Erasmus, "A Common Language for Strategy," *Financial Times* (April 5, 1999): Mastering Information Management section, 7–8.

32 Anil K. Gupta, Vijay Govindarajan, and Ayesha Malhotra, "Feedback-Seeking Behavior Within Multinational Corporations," *Strategic Management Journal* 20, no. 3 (March 1999): 205–22.

33 For a good discussion of information flows in MNEs, see Anil K. Gupta and Vijay Govindarjan, "Knowledge Flows Within Multinational Corporations," *Strategic Management Journal* 21, no. 4, (April 2000): 473–96.

34 John Child, *The Management of International Acquisitions* (Oxford: Oxford University Press, 2001).

35 Peter Martin, "A Clash of Corporate Cultures," *Financial Times* (June 2–3, 2001): weekend section, xxiv.

36 Mansour Javidan, "Siemens CEO Heinrich Von Pierer on Cross-border Acquisitions," *Academy of Management Executive* 16, no. 1 (February 2002): 13–15.

37 Thomas W. Malnight, "The Transition from Decentralized to Network-Based MNC Structures: An Evolutionary Perspective," *Journal of International Business Studies* 27, no. 1 (First Quarter 1996): 43–65.

38 Jack Welch, *Jack: Straight from the Gut* (New York: Warner Books, 2001).

39 "Interview with Miklos Csapody," *Magyar Tudomany* [Hungarian Science] (June 2001).

40 Jeff Immelt, presentation before the American-Hungarian Chamber of Commerce (Budapest, June 20, 2002).

PART SEVEN

Operations: Managing Business Functions Internationally

CHAPTER 16

MARKETING

May both seller and buyer see the benefit.

—TURKISH PROVERB

OBJECTIVES

- To introduce techniques for assessing market sizes for given countries
- To describe a range of product policies and the circumstances in which they are appropriate
- To contrast practices of standardized versus differentiated marketing programs for each country in which sales are made
- To emphasize how environmental differences complicate the management of marketing worldwide
- To discuss the major international considerations within the marketing mix: product, pricing, promotion, branding, and distribution

CASE

Avon[1]

Avon, founded in 1886, is one of the world's largest manufacturers and marketers of beauty and related products. The company is headquartered in the United States, but about 62 percent of its sales are outside the country. It has direct investments in 58 countries and sells in some others through licensing, franchising, and distributor arrangements. Map 16.1 shows the location of Avon's direct investments and its breakdown of sales by region.

Avon moved into the Canadian market in 1914. Its next foreign market entry was 40 years later—into Venezuela. Avon's recent emphasis on foreign operations is due to a slowed U.S. growth potential. First, there is little or no usage gap (untapped market) in the United States for cosmetics, fragrances, and toiletries. Even if there were, only about 5 percent of the world's women live in the United States and Canada. Second, Avon's U.S. sales rely heavily on independent salespersons (almost always women working part time and known as "Avon ladies" or "Avon representatives"), who make direct sales to households by demonstrating products and giving beauty advice. They then place sales orders with Avon and deliver

MAP 16.1   Avon's Direct Investment Locations and Percentage of Sales by Region

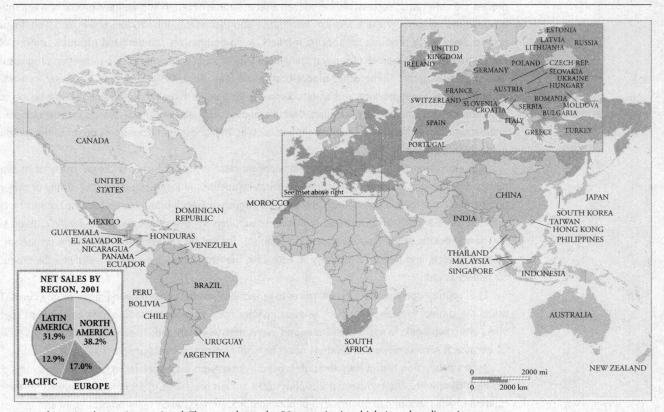

Most of Avon's sales are international. The map shows the 58 countries in which Avon has direct investments.

Source: Avon *Annual Report* (2001), 18.

orders to the customers once they receive them. But Avon now sells in J.C. Penney and Sears stores as well. As more U.S. women have entered the workforce full time, they have become less receptive to door-to-door salespersons, have less time to spend on makeup demonstrations, want to receive their purchases immediately, and are less willing to work as Avon ladies.

Concomitantly, many foreign markets have been ideal for Avon's growth. For example, the lack of developed infrastructure in the rural areas of such countries as Brazil, China, and the Philippines deters women from leaving their homes to shop for cosmetics. But in these countries, Avon ladies reach consumers in some of the most remote areas—for example, by canoe in the Amazon region of Brazil. (Avon has 700,000 representatives in Brazil, about 3.7 per thousand inhabitants.) In transitional economies, Avon's market entry has coincided with pent-up demand from the period of centrally planned economic policies. For example, Avon entered Ukraine with free makeovers at meeting halls in nine major cities, which 240,000 people attended. In rapid-growth economies, such as Chile and Malaysia, Avon taps a growing middle-class market that can afford its products. In all of the aforementioned countries, there are ample labor supplies of potential Avon ladies.

Avon gears product lines to the needs of specific markets, such as selling a skin cream, Sol & Cor, in the Brazilian market; this product combines a moisturizer, sunscreen, and insect repellent. The company also sells creams in parts of Asia to lighten the complexion, but the desire for skin lightening is too small elsewhere to justify marketing efforts.

When Avon develops new products for a given country, it disseminates the information to its facilities elsewhere. For example, Avon-Japan developed emulsion technologies to produce lotions and creams with lighter textures and higher hydration levels, and many Avon operations in other countries now use the process too. After Avon successfully introduced a separate line of health and wellness products in Argentina, it next launched them in Spain, Mexico, and Brazil—and then in the United States and Puerto Rico. In addition to developing products for specific markets, Avon emphasizes standardized products using global brands that appeal to women of many nationalities. One of them is a family of skin-protection products that uses the Anew brand. Some other global brands are Rare Gold, beComing, and Far Away fragrances. Through standardized products and brands, Avon creates a uniform global quality image while saving costs from uniform ingredients and packaging. Global branding also helps inform consumers that the company is international. This effort helps sales in countries such as Thailand, where consumers prefer to buy products made by foreign companies.

Although Avon prominently displays its name on most of its products worldwide, many of its brand names differ among countries. The company prints instructions in local languages, but it may or may not put the brand names in that language. It often uses English or French brand names because consumers consider the United States and France as high-quality suppliers for beauty products. For example, Avon sells skin care products called Rosa Mosqueta (in Spanish), Revival (in English), and Renaissage (in French) in Chile, Argentina, and Japan, respectively. In each case, the Avon logo appears prominently on the products' containers as well.

Each country operation sets its own prices to reflect local market conditions and strategic objectives. The prices are subject to change for each sales campaign. Avon runs a new campaign with different special offers every two weeks in the United States and every three weeks abroad. The brevity of campaigns is helpful because it allows companies to adjust prices in highly inflationary economies.

Avon's promotion is primarily through brochures that Avon ladies deliver to potential customers during each campaign. The company prints about 600 million brochures in 15 languages, dwarfing the circulation of any magazine or commercial publication. Additionally, Avon relies on both print and television advertising.

The basic aim of Avon's campaign is the same throughout the world—to promote its products and image, increase the number of customers served, and recruit new representatives. However, Avon has traditionally altered the execution of promotions to meet the specific needs of different markets. For example, it used the theme "Just Another Avon Lady" in the United States and Canada to show that women in all walks of life use Avon. In Germany, the ads sought to change Avon's image of being old-fashioned. In Japan, where more than 2,000 cosmetic companies compete and Avon is not a leading competitor, the company sought consumer awareness of its name. However, in 2000, it launched its first global ad campaign, "Let's Talk," with print and television ads in 25 countries.

Avon seeks to develop a global image of being a company that supports women and their needs. Avon publicizes how being an Avon lady heightens the role of women. For example, its publicity has shown how civil war in El Salvador caused casualties and disabled men, leaving women with little education to head households; however, by becoming Avon ladies, women can earn an income while continuing their duties at home. The company also gives annual Women of Enterprise Awards to leading women entrepreneurs. Avon's activities have generated additional favorable publicity in media reports, such as a 20-page article in *Veja*, a weekly Brazilian magazine. Perhaps Avon's biggest social responsibility project is its work internationally in fighting breast cancer. Avon ladies disseminate information about breast cancer along with their promotion brochures and sell pins to raise money for local needs. Avon is the largest corporate donor to breast cancer research.

Avon basically duplicates its distribution method in foreign countries, which means it sells to independent representatives who have taken orders from customers they have visited. However, it varies aspects of its distribution among countries. To begin with, not all of Avon's distribution abroad is door to door. In Russia, during the many decades of communist rule, women became wary of knocks on the door—a discomfort that persists—so representatives sell at work or through personal networks. Such selling is similar in India because women associate door-to-door transactions with old-newspaper and old-clothes buyers. In parts of Brazil, many upscale customers are cloistered in apartments that are virtually inaccessible to salespeople because of security entrances. Avon-Brazil advertises on television and offers an 800 number to reach that clientele. In response to a changed Chinese law prohibiting house-to-house sales, Avon quickly opened 2,400 beauty boutiques, lined up 9,000 independent stores to carry Avon, and opened 1,000 beauty counters. Thus, Avon made its products available in virtually every corner of the country.

A drawback of direct selling is that customers cannot obtain a product whenever they want it. They must wait until a representative visits them to place an order and then wait again to receive it. In response to this drawback, Avon-Malaysia opened a retail outlet called a beauty boutique, where customers can go to buy Avon products and receive as much personal attention as when they buy at home. Moreover, representatives can go to the boutique to obtain products immediately rather than wait for Avon to fill their orders. The concept proved so successful that Avon opened additional beauty boutiques in Malaysia and duplicated the concept in Chile.

In an interesting departure from the Malaysian experience, Avon-Argentina opened a "Beauty Center" in an upscale suburb of Buenos Aires. In addition to selling products, as in Malaysia, this center provides customers with a wide variety of services, such as hairstyling and manicures. The center also serves to build an upscale image among customers who would normally shop at retail outlets and buy imported products. Avon now follows this same approach in Mexico and Venezuela.

In some countries, particularly emerging economies, getting merchandise to consumers in rural areas is a major challenge. Mail systems are unreliable, and personal delivery to representatives is expensive. Because of this problem, Avon-Philippines pioneered a system of branch selling. Instead of delivering orders to the homes of district managers, who in turn would arrange delivery to representatives as in the United States, Avon-Philippines has established franchise centers that stock merchandise. Franchise managers visit the centers and pick up merchandise for the representatives in their district. This saves the representatives from making arduous treks, sometimes two hours by bus. The centers have experimented with more retail-like services, such as wide aisles, shopping carts, and scanners at checkout, so that the franchise managers can fill and pay for their orders quickly. Avon has since adopted the franchise center concept in other countries, such as Indonesia.

In the preceding discussion, Avon transferred successful practices in one country to other countries. To encourage the transfer of know-how, Avon brings marketing personnel from different countries together to share what are called "best practices." The company also promotes competition among countries, such as chairman's awards for country-level initiatives to improve sales, quality, and efficiency.

Avon anticipates that international operations will account for the bulk of its growth in the foreseeable future because its products are still not available to more than half the world's women.

Domestic and international marketing principles are the same, but environmental differences require managers to apply these principles differently.

INTRODUCTION

The Avon case points out that similar marketing principles are at work in domestic and foreign markets. However, environmental differences often cause managers to apply these principles differently abroad.

This chapter begins our discussion of international operating functions. Figure 16.1 shows the place of functions in international business. Specifically, we will examine how managers analyze market potential in different countries and apply international product, pricing, promotion, branding, and distribution strategies—the marketing mix—to those countries. We will also discuss whether companies should follow globally integrated or nationally responsive marketing strategies.

MARKET SIZE ANALYSIS

Chapter 13 explained the importance of market potential when trying to determine company's allocation of efforts among different countries, it discussed some common variables used as broad indicators for comparing countries' market potentials, and it briefly introduced types of sources of and problems for collecting information on international markets. Once companies decide to enter markets, they must then analyze data to determine their market

Increasingly we see advertisements for the same companies all over the world. The backdrop from the river in Shanghai, China, shows billboards advertising products from companies headquartered in Japan (TDK and Maxell), France (L'Oreal), Germany (VW), and China (Zhongwang Group).

FIGURE 16.1   Marketing in International Business

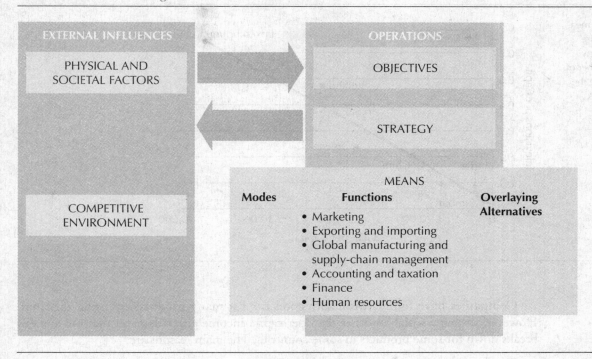

EXTERNAL INFLUENCES

PHYSICAL AND
SOCIETAL FACTORS

COMPETITIVE
ENVIRONMENT

OPERATIONS

OBJECTIVES

STRATEGY

MEANS

| Modes | Functions | Overlaying Alternatives |

- Marketing
- Exporting and importing
- Global manufacturing and supply-chain management
- Accounting and taxation
- Finance
- Human resources

Marketing is one of the necessary functions for implementing companies' international strategies.

potential in each country and their marketing mix to meet the potential. This section covers some techniques that estimate the potential size of markets as well as gap analysis—a tool to help managers decide what part of the marketing mix to emphasize most.

Total Market Potential

To determine potential demand, managers first estimate the possible sales of the category of products for all companies and then estimate their own market-share potential. For the most part, companies use the same techniques to determine market size in foreign countries that they use domestically. Therefore, we will concentrate on those techniques and nuances that apply specifically to international markets.

Domestically or internationally, the major indicators for potential sales of most products are present income and population, plus the growth in each. Managers may examine countries at different average income levels because, as incomes change, product demand may change. For example, Korean demand for apparel, cosmetics, and automobiles has grown with increased per capita income—a trend that closely parallels the experience of industrial countries in earlier years. In fact, companies expand heavily into high-growth markets because they expect that the demand for their products will increase as economies grow. Management may collect data on the consumption of a given product in countries with different per capita incomes and then project sales or numbers of the given product at different income levels by plotting a path through which average demand changes as incomes change (see Figure 16.2). In other words, a company can estimate that a country's per capita consumption of a product will move along the trend line as its per capita income increases. By multiplying the country's expected per capita consumption by its population, a company can estimate the potential demand.

Companies find income and population to be the most important determinants of a country's market size.

FIGURE 16.2   Per Capita Televisions and Per Capita GDP at PPP

As per capita GDP rises as measured by PPP, people acquire more televisions. A company may estimate that the number of televisions will move along the trend line.

Source: Figures were taken from www.geographyIQ.com (January 22, 2003).

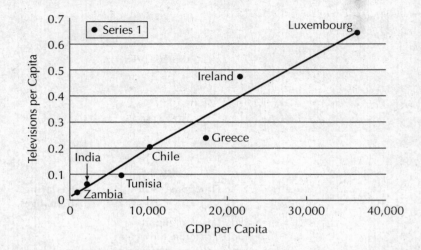

Companies must consider variables other than income and population when estimating potential demand for their products in different countries.

Companies have found reasonably good fits for many products by using this tool. However, so many variables other than per capita income affect demand that the analysis breaks down for some products in some countries. The main reasons are:

- *Obsolescence and leapfrogging of products.* Consumers in emerging economies do not necessarily follow the same patterns as those in higher-income countries. In China, for example, consumers have leapfrogged the use of traditional telephones by jumping from having no telephones to using cellular phones almost exclusively.[2]

- *Costs.* If costs of essential products are high, consumers may spend more than what one would expect based on per capita income. The expenditures on food in Japan are higher than would be predicted by either population or income level because food is expensive and work habits promote eating out. However, if costs are high for a nonnecessity, expenditures will likely be lower. For example, Norwegians spend less than one might expect on fresh fruit because the costs are high.

- *Income elasticity.* A common tool for predicting total market potential is to divide the percentage of change in product demand by the percentage of change in income in a given country. The more that demand increases, the more elastic is the demand in response to income change. Income elasticity varies by product and by income level. Demand for necessities, such as food, is usually less elastic than is demand for discretionary products, such as automobiles. Because a large portion of people in emerging economies are poor, a change in income level affects food consumption there much more than it would in a higher-income country.

- *Substitution.* Consumers in a given country may more conveniently substitute products or services than consumers in some other countries. For example, there are fewer automobiles in Hong Kong than one would expect based on income and population because the crowded conditions make the efficient mass transit system a desirable alternative to automobiles.

- *Income inequality.* Where income inequality is high, the per capita income figures are usually low because many people have little income. This masks the fact that there are middle- and upper-income people who have substantial income to spend. In Brazil and India, for example, the sale of luxury products is higher than one would expect by looking at per capita income figures. For example, LVMH, which has such luxury brands as Louis Vuitton and Christian Dior, has opened boutiques in India.[3]

- *Cultural factors and taste*. Countries with similar per capita incomes may have different preferences for products and services because of values or tastes. For example, Denmark and Switzerland have very similar per capita incomes, but per capita consumption of frozen food is much higher in Denmark because of Danes' penchant for convenience.

Given all of the above factors, managers cannot project potential demand perfectly. However, by considering all the factors that may influence the sale of their products, they can make workable estimates.

Gap Analysis

Once a company is operating in a country and estimates that country's market potential, it must calculate how well it is doing there. A useful tool in this respect is **gap analysis**, a method for estimating a company's potential sales by identifying market segments it is not serving adequately.[4] When sales are lower than the estimated market potential for a given type of product, the company has potential for increased sales. Figure 16.3 is a bar showing four types of gaps: usage, competitive, product line, and distribution. To construct such a bar, a company first needs to estimate the potential demand for all competitors in the country for a relevant period—say, for the next year or the next five years. This figure is the height of the bar. Second, a company needs to estimate current sales by all competitors, which is point *A*. The space between point *A* and the top of the bar is a usage gap, meaning that this is the growth potential for all competitors in the market for the relevant period. Third, a company needs to plot its own current sales of the product, point *B*. Finally, the company divides the difference between point *A* and point *B* into three types of gaps based on its estimate of sales lost to competitors. The distribution gap represents sales lost to competitors who distribute where the company does not. The product line gap represents sales lost to competitors who have product variations the company does not have. The competitive gap is the remaining unexplained sales lost to competitors who may have a better image or lower prices.

Companies may have different-size gaps in different markets. The large chocolate companies have altered their marketing programs among countries because of their different gaps.[5]

The difference between total market potential and companies' sales is due to gaps in:

- Usage—less product sold by all competitors than potential
- Product line—company lacks some product variations
- Distribution—company misses geographic or intensity coverage
- Competitive—competitors' sales not explained by product line and distribution gaps, such as image or price difference

FIGURE 16.3 Gap Analysis

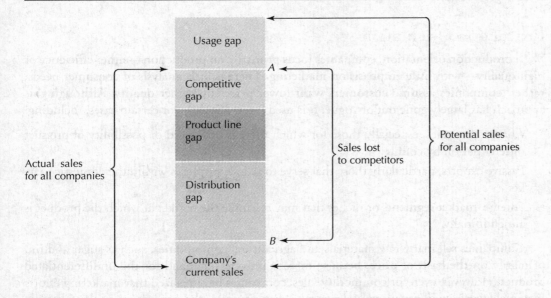

Gap analysis is a tool to help managers estimate why sales are less than the potential. The top of the bar represents total sales potential for a given period. Point A is the total of sales for all companies. The difference between A and the top of the bar is a usage gap. From the bottom of the usage gap bar to B are competitors' current sales. The company loses to competitors who distribute where the company does not, have product variations the company lacks, or are doing a better job of marketing. The bar sizes vary overall and by country because gap sizes vary.

In some markets, they have found substantial usage gaps—that is, less chocolate is being consumed than would be expected on the basis of population and income levels. Industry specialists estimate that in many countries, more than 80 percent of the population has never tasted a chocolate bar. They project that if more people in those countries could be persuaded to try chocolate bars, the companies' sales should increase with the market increase. This assumption has led companies to promote sales in those areas for chocolate in general.

The U.S. market shows another type of usage gap. Nearly everyone in this market has tried most chocolate products, but per capita consumption has fallen because of growing concern about weight. To increase chocolate consumption in general, Nestlé for a short time promoted chocolate as an energy source for the sports minded. Note, however, that building general consumption is most useful to the market leader. Nestlé, with U.S. chocolate sales below those of Mars and Hershey, actually benefited its competitors during the short-lived campaign.

Chocolate companies also have found that they have product line gaps in some hot climates in the market for sweetened products. By developing new products, such as chocolate products that melt less easily, they have been able to garner a larger share of that market. In some markets, such as Japan, they have not yet achieved sufficient distribution to reach their sales potentials. Nestlé formed a joint venture with a Japanese cake and candy maker, Fujiya, in order to make Kit Kat Bars and increase its distribution.

Finally, there are competitive gaps—sales by competitors that cannot be explained by differences between one's own product line and distribution and those of the competitors. That is, competitors are making additional sales because of their prices, advertising campaigns, goodwill, or any of a host of other factors. In markets in which per capita chocolate consumption is high, companies exert most of their efforts to gain sales at the expense of competitors.

PRODUCT POLICY

Most marketing texts categorize companies' product policies, although there is some variation in the categories they use. The treatment of these policies tends to be domestically focused. This section highlights the international application of five common product policies: production orientation, sales orientation, customer orientation, strategic market orientation, and societal marketing orientation.

Production Orientation

With production orientation, companies focus primarily on production—either efficiency or high quality—with little emphasis on marketing. There is little analysis of consumer needs; rather, companies assume customers want lower prices or higher quality. Although this approach has largely gone out of vogue, it is used internationally for certain cases, including:

- Commodity sales, especially those for which there is little need or possibility of product differentiation by country.
- Passive exports, particularly those that serve to reduce surpluses within the domestic market.
- Foreign-market segments or niches that may resemble the market at which the product is aimed initially.

Companies sell many raw materials and agricultural commodities, such as sugar and tin, primarily on the basis of price, because there is universal demand for the undifferentiated product. However, even for commodity sales, companies have realized that marketing efforts may yield positive international sales results. For example, the promotion of the Chiquita

Price is the most important factor in selling many commodities.

brand of bananas has helped increase its global supermarket distribution in a glutted market. In addition, oil producers, such as Petroven, LUKoil, and Aramco, have bought branded gasoline-distribution operations abroad to help them sell an otherwise undifferentiated product. Commodity producers also put effort into business-to-business marketing by providing innovative financing and by assuring timely, high-quality supplies.

Many companies begin exporting very passively by filling unsolicited requests from abroad. At this point, companies adapt their products very little, if at all, to foreign consumers' preferences. This practice suffices for many companies that view foreign sales as an appendage to domestic sales. In this situation, companies frequently export only if they have excess inventory for their domestic markets. In fact, fixed costs are sometimes covered from domestic sales so that companies quote lower prices on exports as a means of liquidating inventories without disrupting the domestic market.

A company may develop a product aimed at achieving a large share of its domestic market and then find there are market segments abroad willing to buy that product. Sometimes the product, such as French champagne, may have universal appeal. Other times, a company may target a mass market at home as well as niche markets in foreign locations; one example is U.S. bourbon producers that sell to niche markets worldwide. A company may also use a production orientation when selling in countries with only a small market potential. For example, in small developing countries, MNEs may make few product alterations because the market size does not justify the expense to them and because competitors are apt to be other MNEs that also make few product alterations. Companies may not even adjust the voltage requirements and plugs of electrical products to local standards, leaving the job of conversion to local purchasers instead.

Sales Orientation

Internationally, sales orientation means a company tries to sell abroad what it can sell domestically on the assumption that consumers are sufficiently similar globally. A company may make this assumption because of its ethnocentricity or because it lacks sufficient information about the foreign market it wishes to serve. This orientation differs from the production orientation because of its active rather than passive approach to promoting sales. However, there is much anecdotal evidence of foreign product failures because of assumptions that product acceptance will be the same as at home or that heavy sales efforts abroad can overcome negative foreign attitudes toward the product. Yet there also are examples of companies that have successfully transferred products abroad with little or no research on what foreign consumers want.

A company with a sales orientation is better able to sell the same product in multiple countries when consumer characteristics are similar and when there is a great deal of spillover in product information (e.g., between the United States and Canada). A company may first develop the product for its home market. It may develop a new product to launch almost simultaneously in multiple countries, as Whirlpool did for high-capacity front-loading washing machines.[6] Or it may develop the product abroad and introduce it later to its home market, as Mars did with Whiskas, a cat food.

Customer Orientation

In a company that operates according to sales orientation, management usually is guided by answers to questions such as these: "Should the company send some exports abroad?" "Where can the company sell more of product X?" That is, the product is held constant and the sales location is varied. In contrast, a customer orientation asks this question: "What can the company sell in country A?" In this case, the country is held constant and the product is varied.

Passive sales occur when

- Advertising spills over
- Foreign buyers seek new products

The unaltered domestic product may have appeal abroad.

A company may develop a product with an appeal in more than one country

- Because of spillover in product information from its home country
- Through a simultaneous multicountry launch
- By developing the product abroad

A customer orientation takes geographic areas as given.

Sometimes a company wants to penetrate markets in a given country because of the country's size, growth potential, proximity to home operations, currency or political stability, or any of a host of other reasons. In the extreme of this approach, a company would move to products completely unrelated to its existing product lines. Though an uncommon strategy, some companies have adopted it. For example, Chilena de Fosforos, a Chilean match producer, wanted to tap the Japanese market because of Japanese growth and size, because of competition within the Chilean market, and because of the promotional appeal of being able to say, "We supply Japan." However, because the company was not price competitive in Japan for matches, it successfully entered the Japanese market by making chopsticks—a product that would use its poplar forest resources and wood-processing capabilities.[7]

As with a production orientation, a company using a customer orientation may do so passively. Increasingly, purchasing agents are setting product specifications and then seeking out contracts for the foreign manufacture of components or finished products. For example, the Hong Kong company Yue Yuen Industrial Holdings produces about 14 percent of the world's footwear, mainly to specification for companies such as Nike.[8] In such cases, the supplier depends on the buyer to determine what final customers want. The supplier is primarily concerned with pricing and delivering what it is selling abroad.

The most common strategy is product changes as adaptations, done by degree.

Strategic Marketing Orientation

Most companies committed to continuous rather than sporadic foreign sales adopt a strategy that combines production, sales, and customer orientations. Companies that don't make changes to accommodate the needs of foreign markets may lose too many sales, especially if aggressive competitors are willing to make desired adaptations. Yet expertise concerning a type of product may be important, and companies want the products they sell abroad to be compatible with their expertise and with their means of dealing with competitors. Companies, therefore, tend to make product variations abroad without deviating very far from their experience. For example, breweries such as Heineken, Stroh's, Bass, and Lion, when faced with restrictions against alcoholic beverages in Saudi Arabia, have turned to sales of nonalcoholic beer (marketed as malt rather than beer).[9] Products such as computers or even coffee or tea would probably be too far from managers' areas of expertise. The U.S. home builder Pulte Homes, when entering the Argentine market, kept the same floor plans and exterior look of its U.S. homes to gain economies of standardization, but it added bidets in the bathrooms and large rear patios to fit Argentine preferences.[10]

Societal Marketing Orientation

Companies with societal marketing orientations realize that successful international marketing requires serious consideration of potential environmental, health, social, and work-related problems that may arise when selling or making their products abroad. Such groups as consumer associations, political parties, and labor unions are becoming more globally aware—and vocal. Companies must increasingly consider not only how a product is purchased but also how it is disposed of and how it might be changed to be more socially desirable. Such considerations have led Coca-Cola to develop a vitamin-enriched beverage for Botswana and returnable glass containers for Argentina and Brazil.[11]

Reasons for Product Alteration

Now that we have discussed companies' product orientations, we shall examine the legal, cultural, and economic reasons behind the tendency of companies to alter their products to fit the needs of customers in different countries.

Legal Reasons   Explicit legal requirements are the most obvious reason for altering products for foreign markets. If you don't meet the requirements, you won't be allowed to sell. The exact requirements vary widely by country but are usually meant to protect consumers. Pharmaceuticals and foods are particularly subject to regulations concerning purity, testing, and labeling. Automobiles sold in the United States must conform to safety and pollution standards not found in some other countries. However, Europe imposes stricter roof-strength standards than the United States does.[12]

When foreign legal requirements are less stringent than domestic ones, a company may not be legally compelled to alter its products for foreign sale. However, the company will have to weigh such decisions as to whether following high domestic standards abroad will raise prices and whether domestic or foreign ill will may result. Some companies have met home-country criticism for selling abroad—especially in developing countries—such products as toys, automobiles, contraceptives, and pharmaceuticals that did not meet home-country safety or quality standards.

One of the more cumbersome product alterations for companies is adjusting to different laws on packaging that protect the environment. Some countries prohibit certain types of containers, such as Denmark's ban on aluminum cans. Other countries restrict the volume of packaging materials to save resources and reduce trash. There also are differences in national requirements as to whether containers must be reusable and whether companies must use packaging materials that must be recycled, incinerated, or composted.

A recurring issue is the need to arrive at international product standards and to eliminate some of the wasteful product requirements which lead to alterations among countries. Although countries have reached agreement on some products (sprocket dimensions on movie film, technical standards on mobile phones, bar codes to identify products), other products (railroad gauges, power supplies, and electrical socket shapes) continue to vary. In reality, there is both consumer and economic resistance to standardization, such as U.S. consumers' reluctance to adapt the metric system. Economically, a complete changeover would be more costly than simply educating people and relabeling. Containers would have to be redesigned and production retooled so that sizes would be in even numbers. (Would American football have first down with 9.144 meters to go?) Even for new products or those still under development, companies and countries are slow to reach agreement because they want to protect the investments they've already made. At best, international standards will come very slowly.

Marketing managers must also watch for the indirect legal requirements that may affect product content or demand. In some countries, companies cannot easily import certain raw materials or components, forcing them to construct an end product with local substitutes that may alter the final result substantially. Legal requirements such as high taxes on heavy automobiles also shift companies' sales to smaller models, thus indirectly altering demand for tire sales and grades of gasoline.

Cultural Reasons   Religious differences obviously limit the standardization of product offerings on a global basis; thus, food franchise companies eschew sales of pork products in Islamic countries and meat of any kind in India. However, cultural differences affecting product demand are often not so easily discerned. For example, Toyota was initially unsuccessful in selling pickup trucks in the United States until it redesigned the interior with enough headroom for drivers to wear 10-gallon (37.85 liter) cowboy hats.[13] In some cases, the differences work to the advantage of producers. Tyson Foods capitalizes on taste differences by selling white meat from chicken in the United States and dark meat from chicken in Mexico at premium prices.[14] The U.S. winery Kendall-Jackson found that the British and Japanese have a preference for a blend of grapes, such as cabernet with shiraz, rather than the single varietal of grapes preferred in the United States. Thus, by blending, Kendall-Jackson

Legal factors are usually related to safety or health protection.

Examination of cultural differences may pinpoint possible problem areas.

can not only gain sales but also lower production costs because it has a greater variety of grape growers from which to choose.[15]

Economic Reasons   If foreign consumers lack sufficient income, they may not be able to buy the product the MNE sells domestically. The company may, therefore, have to design a cheaper model. Mattel was unable to sell enough Holiday Barbie dolls in some foreign countries because prices were too high, so it developed lower-priced dolls for those markets.[16] Where consumers buy personal items in small quantities, such as one aspirin, one piece of chewing gum, or one cigarette, the company usually needs new types of packaging.

Even if a market segment has sufficient income to purchase the same product the company sells at home, differences in infrastructure may require product alterations. Developing countries generally have poorer infrastructures, and companies may gain advantages by selling products that will withstand rough terrain and utility outages. The Japanese infrastructure for automobiles reflects crowded conditions and high land prices. Some U.S. automobile models are too wide to fit into elevators that carry cars to upper floors to be parked, and they cannot make narrow turns on back streets.

Finally, differences in income distribution may affect demand for certain products. In countries where people with purchasing power typically have household servants, they may forgo purchasing labor saving products. Whirlpool discovered this when trying to sell automatic washing machines in some markets. It bought seemingly obsolete technology from Korea in order to be able to sell less automated, two-tub machines in those markets.[17]

Alteration Costs

Some product alterations are cheap to make yet have an important influence on demand. One such area is packaging, which is a common alteration exporters make because of legal and climatic requirements. Before making a decision, marketing managers should always compare the cost of an alteration with the cost of lost sales from no alterations.

One cost-saving strategy a company can use to compromise between uniformity and diversity is to standardize a great deal while altering some end characteristics. Whirlpool puts the same basic compressor, casing, evaporator, and sealant system in its refrigerators for all countries, but it changes such features as doors and shelves for different countries.[18]

Extent and Mix of the Product Line

Most companies produce multiple products. It is doubtful that all of these products could generate sufficient sales in a given foreign market to justify the cost of penetrating that market. Even if they could, a company might offer only a portion of its product line, perhaps as an entry strategy.

In reaching product line decisions, marketing managers should consider the possible effects on sales and the cost of having one product as opposed to a family of products. Sometimes a company finds it must produce and sell some less lucrative products if it is to sell the more popular ones, such as sherry glasses to match crystal wine and water glasses. Or a company may be forced into a few short production runs in order to gain the mass market on other products. A company that must set up some foreign production to sell in the foreign market may be able to produce locally those products in its line that have longer production runs and import the other products needed to help sell the local production.

If the foreign market is small compared to the domestic market, selling costs per unit may be high because of the fixed costs associated with selling. In such a case, the company can broaden the product line to be handled, either by grouping sales of several manufacturers or by developing new products for the local market that the same salesperson can handle. For example, Avon sells products in some countries that it does not handle in the United States

Personal incomes and infrastructures affect product demand.

Some alterations cost less than others.

Narrowing the product line allows for concentration of efforts.

Broadening the product line may gain distribution economies.

in order to increase the average order per household—for example, Crayola products in Brazil, Disney products in Mexico, and the *Reader's Digest* in Canada, Brazil, Australia, France, and New Zealand.

Product Life-Cycle Considerations

There may be differences among countries when a product is introduced as well as in the graphed shape and the length of a product's life cycle. A product facing declining sales in one country may have growing or sustained sales in another. For example, cars are a mature product in Western Europe, the United States, and Japan. They are in the late-growth stage in South Korea and in the early growth stage in India. In Europe, automobile companies emphasize lifestyle appeals to sell cars with speed and accessories. In India, they emphasize fuel consumption, low consumer prices, and low-production cost.[19]

Product life cycles may differ by country

- At the time of introduction
- In the shape of the curve

PRICING

Within the marketing mix, companies place much importance on price. A price must be low enough to gain sales but high enough to guarantee the flow of funds required to carry on other activities, such as R&D, production, and distribution. The proper price will not only assure short-term profits but also give the company the resources needed to achieve long-term competitive viability. Pricing is more complex internationally than domestically because of the following factors:

- Different degrees of government intervention
- Greater diversity of markets
- Price escalation for exports
- Changing values of currencies
- Differences in fixed versus variable pricing practices
- Retailers' strength with suppliers in company to company sales

Let's examine each of these factors.

Government Intervention

Every country has laws that affect the prices of goods at the consumer level. A government's price controls may set either maximum or minimum prices. Controls against lowering prices usually prevent companies from eliminating competitors in order to gain monopoly positions. Many countries also set maximum prices for numerous products, which can lower companies' profits.

Government price controls may

- Set minimum or maximum prices
- Prohibit certain competitive pricing practices

The WTO permits countries to establish restrictions against any import that comes in at a price below that charged to consumers in the exporting country. Although countries may not establish restrictions, the possibility that they will makes it more difficult for companies to differentiate markets through pricing. A company might want to export at a lower price than that charged at home for several reasons. One reason might be to test sales in the foreign market. For example, a company may find it cannot export to a given country because tariffs or transportation costs make the price to foreign consumers prohibitively high. Yet its preliminary calculations show that by establishing foreign production, it may be able to reduce the price to the foreign consumer substantially. Before committing resources to produce overseas, the company may want to test the market by exporting so as to sell the product at the price it would charge if it produced locally. A company may be able to complete this test marketing before companies in the importing country can persuade their government to restrict imports. Nestlé tested the U.K. market in this way by exporting for a year from Canada to see if enough of a market would develop to justify completing a frozen-food plant to make Lean Cuisine products. Shipping such dishes as spaghetti bolognese in refrigerated ships and paying customs duties made the costs of the exported products much higher than their U.K. selling prices. However, the cost of this test was small compared to the value of the information gained and the amount of Nestlé's eventual commitment.

A company may also charge different prices in different countries because of competitive and demand factors. It may feel that prices can be kept high in the domestic market by restricting supply to that market. Excess production then can be sold abroad at a lower price, as long as that price covers variable costs and contributes to overhead.

Greater Market Diversity

Although there are numerous ways a company can segment the domestic market and charge different prices in each segment, country-to-country variations create even more natural segments. For example, companies can sell few sea urchins or tuna eyeballs in the United States at any price, but they can export them to Japan, where they are delicacies. Levi's jeans often cost twice as much in the United Kingdom than in the United States.[20] In some countries, a company may have many competitors and thus little discretion in setting its prices. In other countries, it may have a near monopoly due either to the stage in the product life cycle or to government-granted manufacturing rights not held by competitors. In near-monopoly markets, a company may exercise considerable pricing discretion, using any of the following:

- *A skimming strategy*—charging a high price for a new product by aiming first at consumers willing to pay the price and then progressively lowering the price
- *A penetration strategy*—introducing a product at a low price to induce a maximum number of consumers to try it
- *A cost-plus strategy*—pricing at a desired margin over cost

Country-of-origin stereotypes also limit pricing possibilities. For example, exporters in developing countries often must compete primarily through low prices because of negative perceptions about their products' quality. But there are dangers in lowering prices in response to adverse stereotypes because a lower price may reduce the product image even further.

Diversity in buying on credit affects sales. Credit buying increases costs, which consumers in some countries are more willing to pay than consumers in other countries. For example, the Japanese are more reluctant than Americans to rely on consumer credit. Thus, using credit payments as a means of inducing the sale of goods is less likely in Japan than in the United States. The tax treatment of interest payments also affects whether consumers will pay in cash or by credit.

Price Escalation in Exporting

Another reason pricing is complex internationally is price escalation. If standard markups occur within distribution channels, lengthening the channels or adding expenses somewhere within the system will further increase the price to the consumer. For example, assume the markup is 50 percent and the product costs $1.00 to produce. The price to the consumer would be $1.50. However, if production costs were to increase to $1.20, the 50-percent markup would make the price $1.80, not $1.70 as might be expected. Figure 16.4 shows price escalation in export sales, which occurs for two reasons.

1. Channels of distribution usually span greater distances, and so exporters need to contract with organizations that know how to sell in foreign markets.
2. Tariffs are an additional cost that may be passed on to consumers.

FIGURE 16.4   Price Escalation in Exporting if Companies Use Cost-Plus Pricing

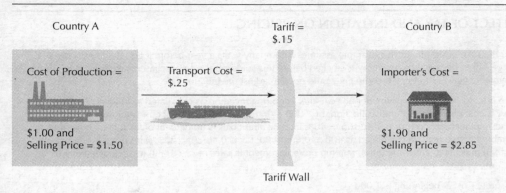

If both the producer/exporter and the importer/distributor charge 50 percent more than their costs, the added $.40 of transport and tariff costs actually increase the price to consumers in country B to $1.35 more than in country A because of markups. This may prevent the product from selling competitively.

There are two main implications of price escalation. Seemingly exportable products may turn out to be noncompetitive abroad if companies use cost-plus pricing—which many do.[21] To become competitive in exporting, a company may have to sell its product to intermediaries at a lower price to lessen the amount of escalation. It should determine what price will maximize profits.

Currency Value and Price Changes

Pricing decisions must consider replacement costs.

For companies accustomed to operating with one (relatively) stable currency, pricing in case of highly volatile currencies can be extremely troublesome. Marketing managers should make pricing decisions to assure the company of enough funds to replenish its inventory and still make a profit. Otherwise, it may be making a paper profit while liquidating itself—that is, what shows on paper as a profit may result from the company's failure to adjust for inflation while the merchandise is in stock. The company must consider not only inflation's effect on prices but also the possibility its income taxes will be based on the paper profits rather than on real profits. Table 16.1 illustrates a pricing plan to make a target profit (after taxes) of 30 percent on the cost of replacing inventory when the company collects from its sale (replacement cost). The company that does not use a similar plan may soon lack sufficient funds to operate because it receives too little to have enough merchandise to sell later. The longer the company waits to receive payment for its merchandise, the more important it becomes for it to use a graduated pricing model. For example, during high inflationary periods within various Latin American countries, companies have to raise prices very frequently.[22]

Two other pricing problems occur because of inflationary conditions.

1. The receipt of funds in a foreign currency that, when converted, buy less of the company's own currency than had been expected

2. The frequent readjustment of prices necessary to compensate for continuing cost increases

In the first case, the company sometimes (depending on competitive factors and government regulations) can specify in sales contracts an equivalency in some hard currency. For example, a U.S. manufacturer's sale of equipment to a company in Uruguay may specify that payment be made in dollars or in pesos at an equivalent price (in terms of dollars) at the time payment is made. In the second case, frequent price increases make it more difficult for the company to quote prices in letters or catalogs. Perpetual price increases may even hamper a company from distributing what it would otherwise prefer to distribute. For example, price

● TABLE 16.1

EFFECT OF TAX AND INFLATION ON PRICING

For the sake of simplicity, this example assumes a company waits a year before it gets paid for its inventory—either because the inventory is stocked before it is sold or because purchasers take time to pay. If the payment cycle is shorter, the company would need to adjust the inflation rate.

The pricing structure for payment one year after acquiring inventory is calculated as follows: Replacement cost is cost plus inflation until collection, or $1,000 + 0.36(1,000) = 1,360$; income after taxes is profit goal times replacement cost, or $0.30(1,360) = 408$. Income after taxes is 60 percent of taxable income; thus, taxable income may be calculated as $408 \div 0.6$, or 680; tax is $0.4(680) = 272$; sales price is original cost (1,000) plus taxable income (680); markup on replacement is sales price (1,680) less replacement cost (1,360), or 320.

Assume: Cost at beginning is 1,000

36% inflation

40% tax rate

30% profit goal on replacement cost after taxes

IF SOLD AND COLLECTED AS SOON AS INVENTORY IS ACQUIRED		IF SOLD AND COLLECTED A YEAR AFTER INVENTORY IS ACQUIRED	
Cost	1,000	Replacement cost	1,360
Markup	500	Markup on replacement	320
Sales price	1,500	Sales price	1,680
Minus Cost	1,000	Minus original cost	1,000
Taxable income	500	Taxable income	680
Tax @ 40%	200	Tax @ 40%	272
Income after taxes	300	Income after taxes	408

increases in vending machine sales are frequently difficult because of the need to change machines and to come up with coins or tokens that correspond to the desired percentage increase in price.

Currency-value changes also affect pricing decisions for any product that has potential foreign competition. For example, when the U.S. dollar is strong, companies can sell non–U.S.-made goods more cheaply in the U.S. market because their price in dollars declines. In such a situation, U.S. producers may have to accept a lower profit margin to be competitive. When the dollar is weak, however, foreign producers may have to adjust their margins downward.

When companies sell similar goods in multiple countries, price differences among the goods must not exceed by much the cost of bringing them in from a lower-priced country, or spillover in buying will occur. Ice cream manufacturers can vary their prices by a large percentage from country to country because the transportation costs compared to the product's price render large-scale movements across borders impractical. However, if the transportation costs compared to the product's price are low, consumers can feasibly buy abroad and import when prices vary substantially from country to country. For example, automobile prices in Canada are typically lower than those in the United States—they can be about $12,000 lower on some light GM trucks—so some Canadian distributors have been selling to U.S. customers in places where GM has not authorized them to sell. The selling or handling of goods through unofficial distributors, the *gray market*, can undermine the longer-term viability of the distributorship system, cause a company's plants in different countries to compete with each other, and make it harder for companies to spot counterfeit goods. Therefore, GM has sought to prevent this gray market activity by disallowing warranty work on these vehicles by U.S. dealers and curtailing vehicle allocations to dealers involved in the gray market.[23] Some other companies try to keep prices fairly close among countries to prevent such movements. The courts in some countries uphold the right of companies to maintain prices through distributor agreements, but companies have to monitor compliance and can find enforcement difficult.[24]

Fixed Versus Variable Pricing

MNEs often negotiate export prices, particularly to foreign distributors. Small companies, especially those from emerging economies, frequently give price concessions too quickly, limiting their ability to negotiate on a range of marketing factors that affect their costs. Such consessions include

- Discounts for quantity or repeat orders.
- Deadlines that increase production or transportation costs.
- Credit and payment terms.
- Service.
- Supply of promotional materials.
- Training of sales personnel or customers.

Table 16.2 shows ways in which an exporter (or other marketers as well) may deal more effectively in price negotiations.

There are country-to-country differences in

- Whether manufacturers set prices
- Whether prices are fixed or bargained in stores
- Where bargaining occurs
- How sale prices can be used

● TABLE 16.2

IMPORT-EXPORT PRICE NEGOTIATIONS

The goal is to delay a pricing commitment while discussing a whole package of other commitments.

IMPORTER'S REACTION TO PRICE OFFER	EXPORTER'S RESPONSE
1. Your offer is too expensive.	- Ask what is meant by too expensive.
	- Find out what is considered acceptable and on what basis.
	- Respond by providing justification.
	- Avoid lowering your price until you learn more about what the other party is looking for.
	- Find out if the objection is due to your price offer or if it reflects other factors.
	- Ask yourself, "If I'm too expensive, why are they negotiating with me?"
2. We don't have that kind of budget.	- Find out how large the budget is, and for what time frame.
	- Explore whether your offer can fit within the overall budget by combining several budget lines.
	- Propose deferred payment schedules.
	- Confirm the order and postpone deliveries until a new budget is allocated.
	- Split your order into smaller units or miniorders to meet current budget limitations.
3. That's not what we are looking for.	- Ask what they are looking for, and insist on specifics.
	- Keep questioning until you understand the real needs.
	- Repackage your offer in light of the new information received.
4. Your offer is not competitive.	- Ask what "not competitive" means.
	- Find out if competitors' offers are comparable to yours.
	- Find weaknesses in other offers and emphasize your strengths.
	- Reformulate your offer by avoiding direct comparison with competition. Stress the unique features of your products/services.

Source: Copyright 2000 from "Business Negotiations: Making the First Offer" from the *International Trade Journal*, no. 2 (2000): 12–16, by Claude Cellich. Reproduced by permission of Taylor & Fracis, Inc., http://www.routlege-ny.com.

The extent to which manufacturers can or must set prices at the retail level varies substantially by country. There is also substantial variation in whether, where, and for what products consumers bargain in order to settle on an agreed price. For instance, in the United States, consumers commonly bargain for automobiles, real estate, and large orders of industrial supplies—but not for grocery items. However, some automobile dealerships sell only on a fixed price basis, and bargaining for smaller items is increasing because of Internet transactions.[25] In contrast, consumers in most developing countries commonly bargain for both large and small items—but more likely in markets than in retail stores.[26]

Company to Company Pricing

Dominant retailers with clout can get suppliers to offer them lower prices, in turn enabling them to compete on being the lowest cost retailer. But these retailers have this clout only in markets where they dominate. For example, Wal-Mart, Marks & Spencer, and Carrefour have such clout in their domestic U.S., U.K., and French markets, respectively. However, they have been hard-pressed to gain the same advantage when entering each other's home markets.

The Internet is also causing more companies to compete for the same business, especially when there are sales of largely undifferentiated materials. Thus, many industrial buyers are claiming large price reductions through Internet buying. However, sellers can improve their positions by negotiating and by combining Internet communications with face-to-face communications.[27]

PROMOTION

Promotion is the presentation of messages intended to help sell a product or service. The types and direction of messages and the method of presentation may be extremely diverse, depending on the company, product, and country of operation.

The Push-Pull Mix

Promotion may be categorized as push, which uses direct selling techniques, or pull, which relies on mass media. An example of push is Avon's door-to-door selling of cosmetics; an example of pull is magazine advertisements for a brand of cigarettes. Most companies use combinations of both marketing strategies. For each product in each country, a company must determine its total promotional budget as well as the mix of the budget between push and pull.

Several factors help determine the mix of push and pull among countries

- Type of distribution system
- Cost and availability of media to reach target markets
- Consumer attitudes toward sources of information
- Price of the product compared to incomes

Push is more likely when
- Self-service is not predominant
- Advertising is restricted
- Product price is a high portion of income

Generally, the more tightly controlled the distribution system, the more likely a company is to emphasize a push strategy because it requires a greater effort to get distributors to handle a product. This is true, for example, in Belgium, where distributors are small and highly fragmented, forcing companies to concentrate on making their goods available. Also affecting the push-pull mix is the amount of contact between salespeople and consumers. In a self-service situation, in which there are no salespersons to whom customers can turn for opinions on products, it is more important for the company to use a pull strategy by advertising through mass media or at the point of purchase.

Because of diverse national environments, promotional problems are extremely varied. For example, about 70 percent of India's population is rural, and many people in rural areas are illiterate, poor, and without access to televisions and radios. Some mass consumer merchandisers such as Colgate-Palmolive, Unilever, Coca-Cola, and Pepsi provide samples at religious pilgrimages that millions attend in the expectation that their subsequent word-of-mouth promotions will yield sales.[28]

In many countries, government regulations pose an even greater barrier. For example, Scandinavian television has long refused to accept commercials. Other countries may put legal constraints on what a company says, thus affecting the push-pull mix. For example, in the United States, pharmaceutical companies have been using more pull promotions even for prescription drugs. They talk about the product and brand in television ads and tell the viewer to ask their physicians about it. European countries are more restrictive. Thus, in Europe, Pfizer's advertisements talk about the symptoms of erectile dysfunction and tell TV viewers to speak with their physicians about it; however, Pfizer never mentions its drug, Viagra, in these ads.[29]

Finally, the amount of consumer involvement in making a purchase decision varies by country because of income levels. When a product's price compared to consumer income is high, consumers usually will want more time and information before making a purchase decision. Information is best conveyed in a personal selling situation, which fosters two-way communication. In developing countries, MNEs usually have to use more push strategies for mass consumer products because incomes are low compared to price.

Standardization of Advertising Programs

The savings that result from using the same advertising programs as much as possible—on a global basis or among countries with shared consumer attributes—are not as great as those from product standardization. Nevertheless, they can be significant.

In addition to reducing costs, advertising standardization may improve the quality of advertising at the local level (because local agencies may lack expertise), prevent internationally mobile consumers from being confused by different images, and speed the entry of products into different countries. For example, Sony's "My first Sony" was aimed at young consumers all over the world. However, standardized advertising usually means a program that is *similar* from market to market rather than one that is *identical* in each one. For example, Pepsi had Tina Turner sing the Pepsi-Cola theme song with local bands in different countries.[30] Some of the problems that hinder complete standardization of advertising relate to translation, legality, and message needs.

Standardization usually implies using the same advertising agency globally. However, companies may differentiate campaigns among countries even if they use the same agency everywhere. By using the same agency, companies such as IBM, Colgate, and Tambrands have found that they can take good ideas in one market and quickly introduce them into other markets because they need not worry about legal and ethical problems from having one agency copy what another has done. However, some companies, such as Procter & Gamble, prefer to use more than one agency to keep the agencies in a state of perpetual competition and to cover one agency's weak spots by drawing on the ideas of another agency.

Translation   When media reach audiences in multiple countries, such as MTV programs aired throughout most of Europe, ads in those media cannot be translated because viewers watch the same transmission. However, when a company is going to sell in a country with a different language, translation is usually necessary unless the advertiser is trying to communicate an aura of foreignness. Toyota used this tactic in ads in the United States that were done completely in French and Italian with subtitles.[31] The most audible problem in commercial translation is dubbing, because words on an added sound track never quite

> Advantages of standardized advertising include
> - Some cost savings
> - Better quality at local level
> - Rapid entry into different countries

correspond to lip movements. Marketing managers can avoid dubbing problems by creating commercials in which actors do not speak, along with a voice or print overlay in the appropriate language. Pillsbury does this in India, a country with multiple languages, where its Doughboy ads are in six languages.[32]

On the surface, translating a message would seem to be easy. However, some messages, particularly plays on words, simply don't translate—even between countries that have the same language. The number of ludicrous but costly mistakes companies have made attest to translation difficulties. Sometimes what is an acceptable word or direct translation in one place is obscene, misleading, or meaningless in another. For example, the Milk Board's "Got milk?" ad comes out as "Are you lactating?" in Spanish.[33] Another problem is choosing the language when a country has more than one. For example, in Haiti, a company might use Creole to reach the general population but French to reach the upper class.

Legality   What is legal advertising in one country may be illegal elsewhere. The differences result mainly from varying national views on consumer protection, competitive protection, promotion of civil rights, standards of morality, and nationalism. In terms of consumer protection, policies differ on the amount of deception permitted, what can be advertised to children, whether companies must list warnings on products that cite possible harmful effects, and the extent to which they must list ingredients. The United Kingdom and the United States allow direct comparisons with competitive brands (such as Pepsi versus Coca-Cola), whereas the Philippines prohibits them. Only a few countries regulate sexism in advertising.

Some governments restrict the advertising of some products (such as contraceptives and feminine hygiene products) because they feel they are in bad taste. Elsewhere, governments restrict ads that might prompt children to misbehave or people to break laws (such as advertising automobile speeds that exceed the speed limit) and those that show scantily clad women. New Zealand banned a Nike ad in which a rugby team tackles the coach, as well as a Chanel ad in which the model said to her male lover before kissing him, "I hate you. I hate you so much I think I'm going to die from it darling." In both cases, the ads were deemed to threaten violence.[34]

Message Needs   An advertising theme may not be appropriate everywhere because of national differences in how well consumers know the product and how they perceive it, who will make the purchasing decision, and what appeals are most important. Recall from the discussions of gap analysis and product life cycles how product-knowledge conditions vary. For example, few Japanese own dishwashers even though they own most other appliances. In addition to size-constraints, which some manufacturers have overcome with new designs, Japanese housewives feel guilty about buying for the sake of convenience. Matsushita, which promotes convenience elsewhere, has shifted its Japanese ads to hot water conservation and hygiene.[35] The reaction to how messages are presented may also vary. For example, Leo Burnett Worldwide produced a public service advertisement to promote checkups for breast cancer. It showed an attractive woman being admired in a sundress with a voice-over message, "If only women paid as much attention to their breasts as men do . . ." Japanese viewers found it a humorous way to draw attention to an important health issue, but French viewers found it offensive because there is nothing humorous about the issue.[36]

BRANDING

A brand is an identifying mark for products or services. When a company registers a brand legally, it is a trademark. A brand gives a product or service instant recognition and may save promotional costs. MNEs must make four major branding decisions:

1. Brand versus no brand
2. Manufacturer's brand versus private brand
3. One brand versus multiple brands
4. Worldwide brand versus local brands

The international environment substantially affects only the last of these branding decisions.

Some companies, such as Coca-Cola, have opted to use the same brand and logo globally. Other companies, such as Nestlé, associate many of their products under the same family of brands, such as the Nestea and Nescafé brands, in order to make sure that these brands all share in the companies' goodwill. Nevertheless, there are a number of problems in trying to use uniform brands internationally.

Language Factors

One problem is that brand names may carry a different association in another language. For example, GM thought its Nova model could easily be called the same in Latin America, because the name means "star" in Spanish. However, people started pronouncing it "no va," which is Spanish for "it does not go." Coca-Cola tries to use global branding wherever possible but discovered that the word *diet* in *Diet Coke* had a connotation of illness in Germany and Italy. The brand is called Coca-Cola Light outside the United States.

Unilever has successfully translated the brand name for its fabric softener, while leaving its brand symbol, a baby bear, intact on the packaging. The U.S. name *Snuggle* is *Kuschelweich* in Germany, *Cajoline* in France, *Coccolino* in Italy, and *Mimosin* in Spain. But *Snuggle* did not quite convey the same meaning in English-speaking Australia, where Unilever uses *Huggy*. However, brand symbols don't necessarily work everywhere either. Big Boy put its customary statue (a boy with checkered overalls and cowlick curl) outside its restaurant in Thailand, and many Thais placed offerings at his feet because they thought it was a Buddha.[37]

Pronunciation presents other problems, because a foreign language may lack some of the sounds of a brand name or the pronunciation of the name may be a word with a meaning that is different from the original. For example, McDonald's uses Donald McDonald, not *Ronald* McDonald, in Japan because the Japanese have difficulty pronouncing the letter *R*. Marcel Bich dropped the *H* from his name when branding Bic pens because of the fear of mispronunciation in English. Some locally popular soft drinks have unappetizing meanings when pronounced in English—Mucos (from Japan), Pipi (from Serbia), Pshitt (from France), and Zit (from Greece).

Different alphabets present still other problems. For example, consumers judge English brand names by whether the name sounds appealing, whereas brand names in Mandarin and Cantonese need to have visual appeal as well because the Mandarin and Cantonese alphabets are pictograms. Such companies as Coca-Cola, Mercedes-Benz, and Boeing have taken great pains to assure not only that the translation of their names is pronounced roughly the same as in English but also that the brand name is meaningful. For example, Coca-Cola is pronounced *Ke-kou-ke-le* in Mandarin and means tasty and happy. Further, companies have sought names that are considered lucky in China, such as a name with eight strokes in it and displayed in red rather than blue.[38]

Brand Acquisitions

Much international expansion takes place through the acquisition of companies in foreign countries that already have branded products. For example, when Avon acquired Justine in South Africa, it kept the Justine name because the brand was well known and respected. However, Sara Lee acquired various Brazilian coffee roasters and is now trying to consolidate them into Brazil's first national brand because stretching the promotional budget over so many brands means that promotions are not as effective as they might be given that less is spent on any one brand to build significant positive recognition.[39]

Country-of-Origin Images

Companies should consider whether to create a local or a foreign image for their products. The products of some countries, particularly developed countries, tend to have a higher-quality image than do those from other countries.[40] For example, Czechs associate locally made products with poor quality, so P&G has added German words to the labels of detergents it makes in the Czech Republic.[41] There are also image differences concerning specific products from specific countries. For example, the British have a positive image of Australian wine; thus, a young Australian winery sought a very Australian name, Barramundi, for its wine exports to the United Kingdom.[42]

But images can change. Consider that for many years, various Korean companies sold abroad under private labels or under contract with well-known companies. Some of these Korean companies, such as Samsung, now emphasize their own trade names and the quality of Korean products.

In an innovative effort to create a British ice cream flavor along the lines of its American Cherry Garcia, Ben & Jerry's ran a contest for the best name and flavor. The flavor name *Cool Britannia* won out over such entrants as *Minty Python, Grape Expectations, Choc Ness Monster*, and *The Rolling Scones*.[43]

Generic and Near-Generic Names

Companies want their product names to become household words, but not so much that competitors can use trademarked brand names to describe their similar products. In the United States, the brand names Xerox and Kleenex are nearly synonymous with copiers and paper tissues, but they have, nevertheless, remained proprietary brands. Some other names that were once proprietary, such as cellophane, linoleum, and Cornish hens, have become *generic*—available for anyone to use.

In this context, companies sometimes face substantial differences among countries that may either stimulate or frustrate their sales. For example, aspirin and Swiss army knives are proprietary names in Europe but generic in the United States, a situation that impairs European export sales of those products to the United States because U.S. companies can produce aspirin and Swiss army knives.

DISTRIBUTION

A company may accurately assess market potential, design goods or services for that market, price them appropriately, and promote them to probable consumers. However, it's unlikely the company will reach its sales potential if it doesn't make the goods or services conveniently available to customers. Companies need to place their goods where people want to buy them. For example, does a man prefer to buy shampoo in a grocery store, barber shop, drugstore, or some other type of outlet?

Distribution is the course—physical path or legal title—that goods take between production and consumption. In international marketing, a company must decide on the method of distribution among countries as well as the method within the country where final sale occurs.

Companies may limit early distribution in given foreign countries by attempting to sell regionally before moving nationally. Many products and markets lend themselves to this sort

What Products Should Companies Market Internationally?

Critics complain that MNEs pay too little attention to the needs of developing countries. For example, they chide pharmaceutical companies for spending less on antimalarial research than on research for diseases more prevalent in industrial countries, even though malaria results in more fatalities.[44] At the same time, these critics have encouraged developing countries not to use DDT, although malaria deaths increased with the nonuse.[45] They criticize so-called superfluous products and luxury goods because they shift spending away from necessities and contribute to the enhancement of elitist class distinctions. For instance, they question making soft drinks available to consumers who lack funds for pharmaceuticals. Soft drink companies have responded that consumers should make their own choices, that introducing sanitary bottling operations has aided other industries (including pharmaceuticals), and that attempts to add vitamins or nutrition to tasty food has failed in the marketplace.[46] Nevertheless, critics question whether this is sufficient justification for continuing to sell the soft drinks. Even if products reach only affluent customers, companies may be criticized. For example, Benetton has been taken to task for opening hard-currency-only shops for tourists in Cuba and North Korea because the shops are an affront to the local population—that is, to people who are economically and legally prohibited from buying the merchandise.

Critics have also complained that MNEs promote products to people who do not understand the products' negative consequences. The most famous case involved infant formula sales in developing countries, where infant mortality increased when bottle-feeding supplanted breast-feeding. Because of low incomes and poor education, mothers frequently overdiluted formula and gave it to their babies in unhygienic conditions. Critics argued that promoting formula increased bottle-feeding. Infant formula manufacturers claimed that other factors increased bottle-feeding—specifically, more working mothers and fewer products and services being made in the home. The promotion, they argued, persuaded people to give up their "home brews" in favor of the most nutritious breast milk substitute available. Regardless, the World Health Organization passed a voluntary code to restrict formula promotion in developing countries. Critics hit Nestlé hardest because it had the largest share of infant formula sales in developing countries and because its name-identified products facilitated the organization of a boycott. The company ceased advertising that could discourage breast-feeding, limited free formula supplies at hospitals, and banned personal gifts to health officials.[47] Despite these events, few governments have prohibited infant formula sales or promotion. In the absence of regulations (for infant formula and other products), how far companies should go to protect consumers is unclear. The controversy has been compounded by the transmission of HIV virus through breast milk, a particular problem in Africa, where many women are HIV/AIDS infected.[48] At the same time, pharmaceutical companies have responded to the pressure by offering AIDS drugs to African consumers at prices substantially below those in their home countries.[49] However, is it ethical to sell at a low price in some markets but not to consumers in their home markets?

Is it unethical for a company to give in to the pressure groups that organize a boycott? A French company, Roussel Uclaf, developed the abortion pill RU-486, now called mifepristone. A German company, Hoechst, then acquired Roussel Uclaf. Hoechst, fearful of adverse publicity, initially forbade the sale of mifepristone except in the three countries (the United Kingdom, France, and

Switzerland) where Roussel Uclaf had already begun selling it. The French health ministry has insisted that the product remain on sale because it is "the moral property of women." Yet U.S. antiabortion activists took out full-page newspaper ads urging U.S. consumers not to use Allegra, a Hoechst anti-hay fever treatment, because Hoechst continued to sell mifepristone outside the United States.[50] Thus, Hoechst faced ethical criticism whether it marketed the abortion pill in the United States or not. Subsequently, it donated its U.S. mifepristone patent rights to the Population Council, a nonprofit research organization.[51]

of gradual development. In many cases, geographic barriers and poor internal transportation systems divide countries into very distinct markets. In other countries, very little wealth or few potential sales may lie outside the large metropolitan areas. In still others, advertising and distribution may be handled effectively on a regional basis.

We have already discussed operating forms for foreign-market penetration. In Chapter 17, we shall discuss both distribution channels that move goods among countries and how the title to goods gets transferred. This section does not review these aspects of distribution; it discusses distributional differences and conditions within foreign countries that an international marketer should understand.

Distribution reflects different country environments:

- It may vary substantially among countries.
- It is difficult to change.

Difficulty of Standardization

Within the marketing mix, MNEs find distribution one of the most difficult functions to standardize internationally for several reasons. Each country has its own distribution system, which an MNE finds difficult to modify because it is entwined with the country's cultural, economic, and legal environments. Nevertheless, many retailers are successfully moving internationally.

Some of the factors that influence how goods will be distributed in a given country are citizens' attitudes toward owning their own store, the cost of paying retail workers, labor legislation differentially affecting chain stores and individually owned stores, legislation restricting the operating hours and size of stores, the trust that owners have in their employees, the efficacy of the postal system, and the financial ability to carry large inventories. For example, in comparison to those in the United States, Hong Kong supermarkets carry a higher proportion of fresh goods, are smaller, sell smaller quantities per customer, and are located closer to each other. This means that companies selling canned, boxed, or frozen foods will encounter less per capita demand in Hong Kong than in the United States. They would also have to make smaller deliveries because of store sizes and would have a harder time fighting for shelf space.

A few other examples should illustrate how distribution norms differ. Finland has few stores per capita because general-line retailers predominate there, whereas Italian distribution has a fragmented retail and wholesale structure. In the Netherlands, buyers' cooperatives deal directly with manufacturers. Japan has cash-and-carry wholesalers for retailers that do not need financing or delivery services. In Germany, mail-order sales are very important; this is not the case in Italy, however, because of the country's unreliable postal system.[52]

How do these differences affect companies' marketing activities? One soft drink company, for example, has targeted most of its European sales through grocery stores. However, the method for getting its soft drinks to those stores varies. In the United Kingdom, one national distributor has been able to gain sufficient coverage and shelf space to enable the soft drink company to concentrate on other aspects of its marketing mix. In France, a single distributor has been able to get good coverage in the larger supermarkets but not in the smaller ones; consequently, the soft drink company has been exploring how to get secondary distribution without upsetting its relationship with the primary distributor. In Norway, regional distributors predominate, so a soft drink company has found it difficult to launch national promotion campaigns. In Belgium, the company could find no acceptable distributor, so it has had to assume that function itself.

Choosing Distributors and Channels

We will now compare why companies self-handle their distribution or contract with other companies to do it for them, and we will discuss how they should choose outside distributors.

Internal Handling When sales volume is low, it is usually more economical for a company to handle distribution by contracting with an external distributor. By doing so, however, it may lose a certain amount of control. However, small companies may lack the resources needed to handle their own distribution.[53] Managers should reassess periodically whether sales and resources have grown to the point that they can handle distribution internally.

Circumstances conducive to the internal handling of distribution include not only high sales volume but also several other factors, including

- When a product has the characteristic of high price or high technology, or the need for complex after-sales servicing (such as aircraft), the producer probably will have to deal directly with the buyer. The producer may simultaneously use a distributor within the foreign country that will serve to identify sales leads.
- When the company deals with global customers, especially in business-to-business sales—such as an auto-parts manufacturer that sells original equipment to the same automakers in multiple countries—such sales may go directly from the producer to the global customer.
- When the company, such as some food franchisors, views its main competitive advantage to be its distribution methods, it eventually may franchise abroad but maintain its own distribution outlet to serve as a flagship. Amway, Avon, and Tupperware are examples of companies that have successfully transferred their house-to-house distribution methods from the United States to their operations abroad. Dell Computer has successfully handled its own mail-order sales in Europe.

Distributor Qualifications A company usually can choose from a number of potential distributors. Common criteria for selecting a distributor include:

- Its financial strength.
- Its good connections with customers.
- The extent of its other business commitments.
- The current status of its personnel, facilities, and equipment.

The distributor's financial strength is important because of the potential long-term relationship between company and distributor and because of the assurance that money will be available for such things as maintaining sufficient inventory. Good connections are particularly important if sales must be directed to certain types of buyers, such as government procurement agencies. The number of other business commitments can indicate whether the distributor has time for the company's product and whether it currently handles competitive

Distribution may be handled internally

- When volume is high
- When companies have sufficient resources
- When prices or technology are high or when there is complex after-sales servicing
- When there is a need to deal directly with the customer due to the nature of the product
- When the customer is global
- To enable the company to gain a competitive advantage

Some evaluation criteria for distributors include their

- Financial strength
- Connections with customers
- Other business commitments
- Other resources

or complementary products. Finally, the current status of the distributor's personnel, facilities, and equipment indicates not only its ability to deal with the product but also how quickly start-up can occur.

Spare Parts and Repair   Consumers are reluctant to buy products that may require spare parts and service in the future unless they feel assured they will be readily available in good quality and at reasonable prices. The more complex and expensive the product, the more important after-sales servicing is. When after-sales servicing is important, companies may need to invest in service centers for groups of distributors that serve as intermediaries between producers and consumers. Earnings from sales of parts and after-sales service sometimes may match that of the original product.

Gaining Distribution   Companies must evaluate potential distributors, but distributors must choose which companies and products to represent and emphasize. Both wholesalers and retailers have limited storage facilities, display space, money to pay for inventories, and transportation and personnel to move and sell merchandise, so they try to carry only those products that have the greatest profit potential.

In many cases, distributors are tied into exclusive arrangements with manufacturers that prevent new competitive entries. For example, there are about 25,000 Japanese outlets that sell only Shiseido's cosmetics, 13,000 that sell only Toshiba products, and 11,000 that sell only Hitachi products.[54] A company that is new to a country and wants to introduce products that some competitors are already selling may find it impossible to find distributors to handle its brands. Even established companies sometimes find it hard to gain distribution for their new products, although they have the dual advantage of being known and of being able to offer existing profitable lines only if distributors accept the new unproven products.

A company wanting to use existing distribution channels may need to analyze competitive conditions carefully before offering effective incentives for those distributors to handle the product. It may need to identify problems that distributors experience and offer assistance in order to gain their loyalty. Companies alternatively may offer other incentives, such as higher profit margins, after-sales servicing, and promotional support—any of which may be offered on either a permanent or introductory basis. The type of incentive should also depend on the comparative costs within each market. In the final analysis, however, incentives will be of little help unless the distributors believe a company's products are viable. The company must sell the distributors on its products as well as on itself as a reliable company.

Hidden Costs in Foreign Distribution

When companies consider launching products in foreign markets, they must determine what final consumer prices will be in order to estimate sales potential. Because of different national distribution systems, the cost of getting products to consumers varies widely from one country to another. Five factors that often contribute to cost differences in distribution are (1) infrastructure conditions, (2) the number of levels in the distribution system, (3) retail inefficiencies, (4) size and operating-hours restrictions, and (5) inventory stock-outs.

Infrastructure   In many countries, the roads and warehousing facilities are so poor that getting goods to consumers quickly, at a low cost, and with minimum damage or loss en route is problematic. In Nigeria, for example Nestlé has had to build small warehouses across the country because it could not depend on a central warehouse that one would normally expect based on the country's area. Roads are in such poor condition that travel is slow and trucks are prone to breakdowns. Further, because of crime, Nestlé uses armed guards on its trucks and allows them to travel only during daylight hours.[55]

Levels in distribution system   Many countries have multitiered wholesalers that sell to each other before the product reaches the retail level. For example, national wholesalers sell to regional ones, who sell to local ones, and so on. This sometimes occurs because wholesalers are too small to cover more than a small geographic area. Japan typifies such a market. There are, on average, 2.21 wholesale steps between producer and retailer in Japan, compared with 1.0 in the United States and 0.73 in France. Because each intermediary adds a markup, product prices are driven up. However, such overall figures obscure differences by product. For example, fresh food passes through much longer and complex channels than such products as electronic goods.[56]

Retail inefficiencies   In some countries, particularly developing countries, low labor costs and a basic distrust by owners of all but family members result in retail practices that raise consumer prices. This distrust is evident in companies' preference for counter service rather than self-service. In the former case, customers wait to be served and shown merchandise. A customer who decides to purchase something gets an invoice which is taken to a cashier's line for payment. Once the invoice is stamped as paid, the customer must go to another line to pick up the merchandise after presenting the stamped invoice. Some retailers have counter service for purchases as small as a pencil. The additional personnel add to retailing costs, and the added time people must be in the store means fewer people can be served in the given space. In contrast, most retailers in some (mainly industrialized) countries have equipment that improves the efficiency of handling customers and reports—for example, electronic scanners, cash registers linked to inventory control records, and machines connecting purchases to credit-card companies.

Restrictions   Many countries, such as France, Germany, and Japan, have laws to protect small retailers. These laws effectively limit the number of large retail establishments and the efficiencies they bring to sales. Many countries also limit operating hours as a means of protecting employees from having to work late at night or on weekends. At the same time, the limit keeps retailers from covering the fixed cost of their space over more hours, so these costs are passed on to consumers. In Sweden, 7-Eleven stores cannot use longer open-for-business hours as a competitive advantage because Swedish law prohibits sales of a full range of goods between midnight and 6 A.M.[57]

Stock-outs   Where retailers are small, as is true of grocers in many developing countries, there is little space for storing inventory. Wholesalers must incur the cost of making small deliveries to many more establishments and sometimes may have to visit each retailer more frequently because of stock outages.

The Internet and Electronic Commerce

Estimates vary widely on the current and future number of worldwide online households and the electronic commerce generated through online sales. Nevertheless, they all indicate substantial growth. Table 16.3 shows some comparative estimates of growth. As electronic commerce increases, customers worldwide can quickly compare prices from different distributors, and this development should drive prices down.

Electronic commerce offers companies an opportunity to promote their products globally. It also permits suppliers to deal more quickly with their customers. For example, Lee Hung Fat Garment Factory of Hong Kong supplies apparel to about 60 companies in

The growth in online households creates new distribution opportunities and challenges when selling globally over the Internet.

● **TABLE 16.3**

COMPARATIVE ESTIMATES: INTERNET USERS WORLDWIDE, 2000–2006 (IN MILLIONS)

	2000	2001	2002	2003	2004	2005	2006
Computer Industry Almanac (CIA)	413.6	538.5	673.0	825.4	—	—	—
eMarketer*	352.2	445.9	529.9	622.9	709.1	—	—
eTForecasts	414.0	—	673.0	—	—	1,174.0	—
Gartner Dataquest	330.4	403.9	480.3	549.4	604.7	—	—
International Data Corporation (IDC)	400.0	—	—	—	—	977.0	—
Ipsos-Read	—	400.0	—	—	—	—	—
Morgan Stanley Dean Witter	—	—	449.0	536.0	—	—	—
Nielsen//Netratings	—	426.5	—	—	—	—	—
Ovum	—	—	—	—	—	—	923.0
Pegasus Research International	252.0	—	—	—	—	—	—

Note: *eMarketer's year 2000 baseline is from the international Telecommunication Union's estimate of Internet users aged two years and older, who have accessed the Internet within the previous 30 days.

Source: eMarketer, "Charting the Future of Business," (January 22, 2003): www.emarketer.com/products/report.php?eglobal/welcome.html. Reprinted by permission of eMarketer, Inc.

Europe and now flashes picture samples of merchandise to them over the Web. Customers, such as Kingfisher of the United Kingdom, can tinker with the samples and transmit new versions back to Hong Kong so that Lee Hung Fat produces exactly what the distributors want.[58]

Global Internet sales are not without problems. Many households, especially in emerging economies, lack access to Internet connections.[59] Therefore, if a company wants to reach mass global markets, it will need to supplement its Internet sales with sales that use other means of promotion and distribution. A company also needs to set up and promote its Internet sales, which can be very expensive. Royal Bank of Canada is spending about $75 million up-front to promote Internet sales in the United States.[60]

A company cannot easily differentiate its marketing program for each country where it operates. The same Web advertisements and prices reach customers everywhere, even though different appeals and prices for different countries might yield more sales and profits. If the company makes international sales over the Internet, it must deliver what it sells expeditiously. This may necessitate placing warehouses and service facilities abroad, which the company may or may not own and manage itself.[61]

Finally, the company's Internet ads and prices must comply with the laws of each country where the company makes sales. This is a challenge because a company's Web page reaches Internet users everywhere. For example, Land's End, a U.S. merchandiser, has long depended on its unconditional lifetime guarantee to help sell its merchandise. But German law prohibits such a guarantee on the grounds that it is a gimmick hidden in the sales price. Land's End may have to exclude Germany from its Internet sales.[62] Clearly, although the Internet creates new opportunities for companies to sell internationally, it also creates new challenges for them.

LOOKING TO THE FUTURE

Will the "Haves" and the "Have-Nots" Meet the "Have-Somes"?

Most projections are that disparities between the "haves" and "have-nots" will grow in the foreseeable future, both within and among countries. Further, because the "haves" will have greater access to the Internet, they will be better able to search globally for lower prices for what they buy. Therefore, globally, the affluent segment will have more purchasing power and will not likely forgo buying because of antimaterialistic sentiments. As people's discretionary income increases, what are now luxury products become more commonplace (partly because it takes fewer hours of work to purchase them), and seemingly dissimilar products and services (such as cars, travel, jewelry, and furniture) compete with each other for the same discretionary spending. Because of better communications and rising educational levels of the haves, they will want more choices. However, these choices may not fall primarily along national lines. Rather, companies will identify consumer niches that cut across country lines.

At the other extreme, because of growing numbers of poor people with little disposable income, companies will have opportunities to develop low-cost standardized products to fit the needs of the have-nots. Thus, companies will have conflicting opportunities—to develop luxury items to serve the haves and to cut costs to serve the have-nots.

Despite the growing proportions of haves and have-nots, demographers project that the actual numbers of people moving out of poverty levels and into middle-income levels will increase. This is largely because of population and income growth in many developing countries, especially in Asia. Such a shift will likely mean that companies' sales growth in developing countries will mainly be for products that are mature in industrial countries, such as telephones and household appliances. Further, with increased access to the Internet and lower barriers to trade, customers will be able to purchase goods from anywhere in the world. In the process, companies will find it more difficult to charge different prices in different countries. But they will more effectively be able to cut out middlemen in the distribution of their products.

What products and services are likely to enjoy the major growth markets? It is probable that data generation and storage will continue to be a major growth area during the next few decades. It also is probable that among the market-growth leaders will be companies making breakthroughs in process technologies that improve productivity (e.g., lasers, optics, and robotics) and those making breakthroughs in energy conservation (e.g., solar photovoltaics, fuel cells, and coal conversion).

Summary

- Although the principles for selling abroad are the same as those for selling domestically, the international businessperson must deal with a less familiar environment, which may change rapidly.

- Tools for assessing foreign demand for products include estimates based on what has happened in other countries and studies of historical trends. Some problems with the results from these tools include country differences in product obsolescence and leapfrogging, income elasticities, product substitution, income inequality, and cultural factors and tastes.

- Gap analysis is a tool that helps companies determine why they have not met their market potentials for given countries.

- A standardized approach to marketing means maximum uniformity in products and programs among the countries in which sales occur. Although this approach minimizes expenses, most companies make changes to fit country needs in order to increase sales volume.

- A variety of legal and other environmental conditions may call for altering products in order to capture foreign demand. In addition to determining when to alter products, companies also must decide how many and which products to sell abroad.

- Because of different demand characteristics, a product may be in a growth stage in one country and in a mature, or declining, stage in another.

- Government regulations may directly or indirectly affect the prices companies charge. International pricing is further complicated because of market diversity, price escalation for exports, fluctuations in currency values, variations in fixed versus variable pricing practices, and relative strengths in company to company sales,

- For each product in each country, a company must determine not only its promotional budget but also the mix between push and pull strategies and promotions. The relationship between push and pull should depend on the distribution system, cost and availability of media, consumer attitudes, and the product's price compared to incomes.

- Major problems for standardizing advertising in different countries are translation, legality, and message needs.

- Global branding is hampered by language differences, expansion by acquisition, nationality images, and laws concerning generic names.

- Distribution channels vary substantially among countries. The differences may affect not only the relative costs of operating but also the ease of making initial sales.

CASE

Dental News and Hotresponse*

In 1987, John Schwartz, an American living in Hong Kong, founded the family-owned *Dental News*, a quarterly magazine circulating to people interested in dental equipment, supplies, and technical developments. Medi Media Pacific, a Hong Kong–based company specializing in medical publications, bought *Dental News* from the Schwartz family in 1993. Subsequently, Havas, a French multimedia company, acquired Medi Media Pacific and then sold it to another French multimedia company, Vivendi. Logan Media International, owned by the Schwartz family and headed by Allen Logan Schwartz, the son of *Dental News*'s founder, has a contract to handle *Dental News*'s print activity. Allen, collaborating closely with his brother, also named John Schwartz, also conceived and developed Hotresponse under another company, Dissemination Inc., which their father had recently established to exploit market synergies between print and the Internet. Hotresponse is an online service that connects magazine subscribers with magazine advertisers. The first client for Hotresponse was *Dental News* in 1998. Since then, Hotresponse has obtained other clients, such as *Esquire, Maxim, Outside*, and Penton Media.

Initially, *Dental News* circulated only to Asia-Pacific countries, until its founders envisioned expansion into other emerging markets. In the early 1990s, Charles Buckwalter, president of Conexion International in Miami, Florida (United States), a publishing service for international markets, collaborated with Logan Media International to help publish Latin American *Dental News* editions. Logan Media and Conexion launched a Spanish edition (*América Latina Noticias Dentales*) in 1994 and a Portuguese edition (*Brasil Dental News*) in 1995. Subsequently, *Dental News* introduced a fourth edition for Russia and the Commonwealth of Independent States (CIS)— countries that were once part of the Soviet Union—and in 2001, a fifth edition for Poland.

Dental News is free to subscribers, which means the magazine must sell enough advertising to pay for all publication and distribution costs. Companies will advertise where they believe enough potential customers will see their ads and where they have evidence that the ads generate substantial interest in their products. *Dental News* targets non-triad markets (those outside Western Europe, Japan, and English-speaking North America). The *Dental News* management is convinced and has persuaded advertisers that potential dental product customers (such as dentists, public health officials, lab technicians, dental hygienists, and dental school professors) are inundated with product information in the triad countries. But potential customers elsewhere have too little access to information and would like more. Still, companies will advertise in *Dental News* only if the magazine has a subscription base large enough to reach enough potential dental product customers.

Dental News elicits subscriptions from exhibition booths it places at both dental trade shows and dental conferences held all over the world. The largest of the conferences is the annual meeting of the Fédération Dentaire Internationale (FDI). *Dental News* arranges for its magazine to be placed in registration packets at these dental conferences. In exchange, *Dental News* provides advertising for upcoming meetings and lists these meetings in the calendar that appears in each of its magazine issues. Increasingly, word of mouth is important in adding new circulation as existing subscribers tell their colleagues about the publication.

Yet *Dental News* is concerned that the subscription base does not become too large. Otherwise, the cost of publishing and distributing would exceed advertising revenues. Raising advertising prices to compensate for added distribution might not be feasible. Although the magazines are free, subscribers must renew their subscriptions once a year so that *Dental News* knows that subscribers are alive, interested in

*We appreciate the time and efforts of Charles Buckwalter and Allen Logan Schwartz, who provided data for the case preparation.

the magazine, and receive publications at correct addresses. By the year 2002, *Dental News*'s Asia-Pacific and Spanish-Latin American circulations were a little over 50,000 each, the Russian and CIS circulations about 15,000, and the Polish circulations about 20,000. *Dental News* terminated the Brazilian edition in 2001 for two reasons: (1) There was a decline in the Brazilian economy, and (2) tough competition from a strong dental association that had lower advertising rates and a higher circulation resulted in insufficient advertising support.

The format for the different editions is identical. The articles are in English on the left-hand side of the pages and in Mandarin, Spanish, Polish, or Russian on the right-hand side. The content is the same except for advertisements and calendars of coming events. In terms of the calendars, all four editions include information on the world meetings, but each edition includes information only on those national and regional meetings that will take place within its circulation area. In terms of advertisements, one edition may have ads that another edition doesn't have because companies may advertise in one, two, three, or

all four regions depending on where they want to distribute. However, *Dental News* gives companies discounts for advertising in multiple editions. Further, the language of ads may vary by edition. Most companies place their advertisements in Spanish for *América Latina Noticias Dentales*. However, they put them in English for the Asia-Pacific *Dental News* because that edition reaches so many different language groups.

Dental News sells ads through both its marketing staff and contractors who are responsible for different parts of the world. For example, Japan Advertising Communications sells advertising in Japan, and the Division Manager's office in Clark, South Dakota (United States), sells advertising in Europe. Once a company signs a contract to advertise, it sends materials to *Dental News* in Hong Kong, and that office prepares page films that it ships to printers in each region. For example, the office sends page films to Carvajal in Cali, Colombia, which prints the Spanish edition. Map 16.2 shows the flow from sales to advertiser, to compiler, to printer for an advertiser in Germany. Each magazine's content is primarily advertisements.

MAP 16.2   *Dental News*: **Connecting Advertisers to Subscribers Internationally**

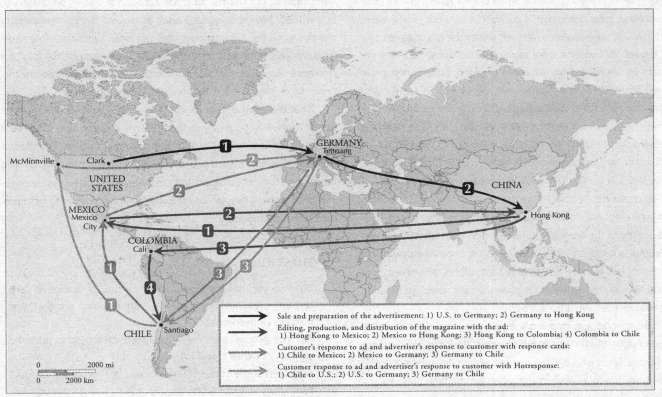

Supplying dental products is an international enterprise, so companies need to advertise in media that reach target customers in many countries. *Dental News* has four editions that go to four different regions of emerging markets, and its production, advertising, and subscriptions are all international. This map shows what happens when *Dental News* sells an ad to a supplier in Germany for its edition going to Spanish-speaking Latin America, to which a potential customer in Chile responds. The black arrow shows the international flow of selling and preparing advertisements for the publication. The red arrow shows the international flow of editing the magazine's content, preparing page sheets, printing, and distributing. The purple arrow shows the customer's and advertiser's responses through response cards. The green arrow shows the customer's and advertiser's responses when using the Web connection from Hotresponse, a process that takes minutes, whereas the response card may take more than two months.

The magazine also includes product profiles (usually from information supplied by advertisers), reprints from dental newsletters, and reports on conferences. The technical updates and practice-management articles are edited in English and sent to translators in Beijing, Mexico City, Moscow, and Warsaw for translation into Mandarin, Spanish, Russian, and Polish. The translators return them to Hong Kong, and this office then prepares page films that it also sends to regional printers. Once the regional edition is printed, it must be distributed to subscribers. For example, after Carvajal prints the Spanish language edition, it ships the magazines to each country where there are subscribers. Once they reach each country, Carvajal arranges for them to be mailed or delivered by courier, depending on the reliability of the mail service. Map 16.2 shows the distribution from the printer in Colombia to a subscriber in Chile. But this is not the end of the flow.

Dental News provides another service to bring advertisers and subscribers together. Each edition contains a response card for readers to tear out, complete, and send to their *Dental News* regional office. Respondents complete the cards by entering codes for those advertisers from whom they want more information, and they check off categories of demographic information, such as whether they have a private practice or work in a clinic. Let's say a subscriber in Santiago, Chile, wants more information from several advertisers. He or she can complete one card to request information from multiple advertisers, such as from Franz Sachs in Germany, NSK Nakanishi in Japan, Sultan Chemists in the United States, Bien-Air in Switzerland, Dentalwerk in Austria, and BJM Laboratories in Israel. This is much easier for the subscriber than writing separately to each of the companies. The subscriber mails the preaddressed card to *Dental News*'s office in Mexico City, and it is here that staff collate and forward responses for each advertiser. The Mexico City office typically gets 6,000 to 8,000 company requests per issue of *América Latina Noticias Dentales*. Once the advertiser, say Franz Sachs in Germany, receives the information from Mexico City, it can then respond directly to the interested subscribers or indirectly through distributors in the subscribers' areas. Map 16.2 also shows the flow of this process. A problem with the system is that subscribers may have to wait more than two months between the time they requested information and the time they receive it from advertisers.

In 1998, in addition to using the response card system, *Dental News* began using the services of Hotresponse. Basically, Hotresponse provides *Dental News* with a Web page (www.dentalnewsrequest.com) for subscribers. When a subscriber registers on the Web page for the first time, he or she must provide a name, contact information, and demographic details. Interestingly, subscribers have been more willing to provide complete demographic details through the Web response than through the card response. When subscribers register, they get a password for future log-ons. Thereafter, when they log on, they can access advertisers' brochures directly, find out the names

and addresses of distributors, and e-mail the manufacturers directly. What takes weeks or months in the card response system takes only a few seconds electronically.

When subscribers log on, the electronic system records what product information they access, along with the name, location, and demographic profile of subscribers. Once a week, the system merges the accesses for each advertiser with the demographic profiles of the subscribers. It places the data in an Excel spreadsheet, prepares a summary demographic profile of people accessing each advertiser's information, and forwards reports via e-mail to all the advertisers. During 2001, subscribers to *América Latina Noticias Dentales* were accessing between 1,800 and 2,000 product requests via Web page per issue. At the same time, card responses did not decline. *Dental News* estimates that there are about 150,000 dentists in Spanish-speaking Latin America, but it does not know how many of them are online.

If subscribers use the *Dental News* Web page to connect directly to manufacturers via e-mail, they may even place orders directly. Some companies forward the orders to their warehouses and distributors to fill. Others fill orders directly. Three developments have enhanced this latter option: (1) The rise in credit-card usage allows purchasers to buy without having to go to a bank to request foreign exchange to transfer to sellers; (2) intermediaries will now consolidate shipments from various suppliers, send the orders, and arrange for customs clearance on arrival; and (3) governments have lowered trade restrictions, which allows orders to more easily enter countries.

What is the advantage of contacting an advertiser through the *Dental News* Web page rather than directly through the advertiser's Web page? Subscribers can log on just once to access information from multiple advertisers. Advertisers can receive information on who is accessing their information and pass sales leads to their salespeople and distributors. They can use the demographic profiles to help prepare future promotions.

QUESTIONS

1. Why do you believe *Dental News* continues to receive card responses even though people can respond on the Web through Hotresponse?
2. As more people come online, will there be a need to print the editions of *Dental News*? Why or why not?
3. As more people come online, do you believe dental product companies will sell more directly rather than go through distributors? Do you think this may vary by type of dental product and by company? If so, why?
4. Within the marketing mix (product, price, promotion, branding, and distribution), which are most important when *Dental News* tries to sell advertising to companies producing dental products?

Chapter Notes

1   Information for this case came from Avon *Annual Reports* from 1995 to 2001; and *Outlook* (Avon's monthly in-house magazine) from 1995 to 2002.

2   Don E. Schultz, "China May Leapfrog the West in Marketing," *Marketing News* 36, no. 17 (August 19, 2002): 8–9.

3   Ravi Thakran, "LVMH Enters Indian Market," *Businessline* (July 17, 2002): 1.

4   The information in this case is from the following sources: J. A. Weber, "Comparing Growth Opportunities in the International Marketplace," *Management International Review*, no. 1 (1979): 47–54; and Van R. Wood, John R. Darling, and Mark Siders, "Consumer Desire to Buy and Use Products in International Markets: How to Capture It, How to Sustain It," *International Marketing Review* 16, no. 3 (1999): 231–42.

5   See "Chocolate Makers in Switzerland Try to Melt Resistance," *Wall Street Journal* (January 5, 1981): 14; William Hall, "Swiss Chocolate Groups Aim to Keep Outlook Sweet," *Financial Times* (April 11–12, 1998): 23; William Hall, "Wraps Come Off Chocolate's Best-Kept Secret," *Financial Times* (June 5, 1998): 20; and Stephanie Thompson, "Chocolate Gets Boost," *Advertising Age* 73, no. 30 (July 29, 2002): 12.

6   "The World's Wash Day," *Financial Times* (April 29, 2002): 6.

7   Matt Moffett, "Learning to Adapt to a Tough Market, Chilean Firms Pry Open Door to Japan," *Wall Street Journal* (June 7, 1994): A10.

8   Jon E. Hilsenrath, "Overseas Suppliers to U.S. Brands Thrive," *Wall Street Journal* (March 10, 2000): A13.

9   Tara Parker-Pope, "Nonalcoholic Beer Hits the Spot in Mideast," *Wall Street Journal* (December 6, 1995): B1.

10   Evan Pérez, "A Bit of America Rises Near Old-World Buenos Aires," *Wall Street Journal* (January 16, 2002): B1.

11   See Betsy McKay, "Drinks for Developing Countries," *Wall Street Journal* (November 27, 2001): B1+; and Betsy McKay, "Coke's Heyer Finds Test in Latin America," *Wall Street Journal* (October 15, 2002): B4.

12   Milo Geyelin and Jeffrey Ball, "How Rugged Is Your Car's Roof?" *Wall Street Journal* (March 4, 2000): B1.

13   Norihiko Shirouzu, "Tailoring World's Cars to U.S. Taste," *Wall Street Journal* (January 15, 2001): B1.

14   Joel Millman, "Illegal U.S. Chickens Pour into Mexico," *Wall Street Journal* (June 24, 1998): A15.

15   Alan Krauss, "Winery Hopes Its Blends Will Travel Well Abroad," *New York Times on the Web* (November 5, 2000).

16   Lisa Bannon, "Mattel Plans to Double Sales Abroad," *Wall Street Journal* (February 11, 1998): A3.

17   Niraj Dawar and Amitava Chattopadhyay, "The New Language of Emerging Markets," *Financial Times* (November 11, 2000): Mastering Management section, 6.

18   "The World's Wash Day," *Financial Times* (April 29, 2002): 6.

19   Arvind Sahay, "Finding the Right International Mix," *Financial Times* (November 16, 1998): Mastering Marketing section, 2–3.

20   Brandon Mitchener, "Inexpensive Levi's May Soon Be Easier to Find in Britain," *Wall Street Journal* (April 6, 2001): A13.

21   Matthew B. Myers, "The Pricing of Export Products: Why Aren't Managers Satisfied with the Results?" *Journal of World Business* 32, no. 3 (1997): 277–89.

22   Peter Rosenwald, "Surveying the Latin American Landscape," *Catalog Age* 18, no. 2 (February 2001): 67–69.

23   Dave Guilford, "GM Takes Hard Line on Gray Market," *Automotive News* 76, no. 5994 (July 22, 2002): 4.

24   Elin Dugan, "United States of America, Home of the Cheap and the Gray: A Comparison of Recent Court Decisions Affecting the U.S. and European Gray Markets," *The George Washington International Law Review* 33, no. 2 (2001): 397–418.

25   See Elliot King, "The End of Fixed Prices?" *Enterprise Systems Journal* 14, no. 12 (December 1999): 25–26; and Jerry Edgerton, "Hard Bargaining Still Pays," *Money* 28, no. 4 (April 1999): 188.

26   C. Gopinath, "Fixed Price and Bargaining," *Businessline* (July 15, 2002): p. 1.

27   Claude Cellich, "FAQ . . . About Business Negotiations on the Internet," *International Trade Forum*, no. 1 (2001): 10–11.

28   Rasul Bailay, "A Hindu Festival Attracts the Faithful and U.S. Marketers—Target Millions of Worshippers in India, Hoping to Expand Reach," *Wall Street Journal* (February 12, 2001): A18.

29   See David Pilling, "Direct Promotion of Brands Gives Power to the Patients," *Financial Times* (April 30, 2001): iii; and Sarah Ellison, "Viagra Europe Ads to Focus on Symptoms," (March 22, 2000): B10.

30   Dana L. Alden, Jan-Benedict, E. M. Steenkamp, and Rajeev Batra, "Brand Positioning through Advertising in Asia, North America, and Europe: The Role of Global Consumer Culture," *Journal of Marketing* 63, no. 1 (January 1999): 75–87.

31   Eleftheria Parpis, "Say What?" *Adweek* 42, no. 32 (August 6, 2001): 16.

32   Miriam Jordan, "Pillsbury Presses Flour Power in India," *Wall Street Journal* (May 5, 1999): B1.

33   Rick Wartzman, "Read Their Lips," *Wall Street Journal* (June 3, 1999): A1.

34   Sally D. Goll, "New Zealand Bans Reebok, Other Ads It Deems Politically Incorrect for TV," *Wall Street Journal* (July 25, 1995): A12.

35   Yumiko Ono, "Overcoming the Stigma of Dishwashers in Japan," *Wall Street Journal* (May 19, 2000): B1+.

36   Sarah Ellison, "Sex-Themed Ads Often Don't Travel Well," *Wall Street Journal* (March 31, 2000): B7.

37   See Robert Frank, "Big Boy's Adventures in Thailand," *Wall Street Journal* (April 12, 2000): B1; and Julie Bennett, "Product Pitfalls Proliferate in a Global Cultural Maze," *Wall Street Journal* (May 14, 2001): B11.

38   Bernd H. Schmitt, "Language and Visual Imagery: Issues of Corporate Identity in East Asia," *Columbia Journal of World Business* (Winter 1995): 28–36.

39   Miriam Jordan, "Sara Lee Wants to Percolate Through All of Brazil," *Wall Street Journal* (May 8, 2002): A14+.

40   See Philip Kotler and David Gertner, "Country as Brand, Product, and Beyond: A Place Marketing and Brand Management Perspective," *Journal of Brand Management* 9, no. 4–5 (April 2002):

249–61; and Keith Dinnie, "National Image and Competitive Advantage: The Theory and Practice of Country-of-Origin Effect," *Journal of Brand Management* 9, no. 4–5 (April 2002): 396–98.

41   E. S. Browning, "Eastern Europe Poses Obstacles for Ads," *Wall Street Journal* (July 30, 1992): B6.

42   Gideon Rachman, "Christmas Survey: The Brand's the Thing," *The Economist* (December 18, 1999): 97–99.

43   Tara Parker-Pope, "Minty Python and Cream Victoria? Ice Creams Leave Some Groaning," *Wall Street Journal* (July 3, 1996): B1.

44   "Limited Imagination," *The Economist* (September 28, 1996): 80–85.

45   Roger Thurow, "Choice of Evils," *Wall Street Journal* (July 16, 2001): A1+.

46   Mark Turner, "Feasting on Famine Food," *Financial Times* (November 24, 1998): 6.

47   "Cause for Concern; with Nestlé in the Spotlight Again over Its Advertising Tactics," *Marketing Week* (February 11, 1999): 28–31.

48   Michael Waldholz, "Sparks Fly at AIDS Meeting Over Breast-Feeding," *Wall Street Journal* (July 12, 2000): B2.

49   Rachel Zimmerman and Michael Waldholz, "Abbott to Cut African AIDS-Drug Prices," *Wall Street Journal* (March 27, 2001): A3+.

50   Andrew Jack, Bruce Clark, and Daniel Green, "Boycott Forces Hoechst to Drop Abortion Pill," *Financial Times* (April 9, 1997): 1.

51   Annette Fuentes, *In These Times* (March 21, 1999): 10.

52   Cecilie Rohwedder, "U.S. Firms Go After Europeans," *Wall Street Journal* (January 6, 1998): A15.

53   Oliver Burgel and Gordon C. Murray, "The International Market Entry Choices of Start-up Companies in High-Technology," *Journal of International Marketing* 8, no. 2 (2000): 33–62.

54   See "Taking Aim," *The Economist* (April 24, 1993): 74; and John Fahy and Fuyuki Taguchi, "Reassessing the Japanese Distribution System," *Sloan Management Review* (Winter 1995): 49–61.

55   Greg Steinmetz and Tara Parker-Pope, "All Over the Map," *Wall Street Journal* (September 26, 1996): R4.

56   John Fahy and Fuyuki Taguchi, "Reassessing the Japanese Distribution System," *Sloan Management Review* (Winter 1995): 49–61.

57   Hugh Carnegy, "Swedish 7-Eleven Stores Lose Some of Their Convenience," *Financial Times* (March 29, 1996): 1.

58   Karen Witcher, "Family Garment Business in Hong Kong Uses Internet to Gain Access to Global Customer Pool," *Wall Street Journal* (November 24, 1999): B15.

59   Priscilla Awde, "The Internet in Developing Countries," *Financial Times* (November 24, 1999): section 2, 1.

60   Larry M. Greenberg, "Canada Banks Try Web to Win U.S. Customers," *Wall Street Journal* (October 28, 1999): A18.

61   Scott Thurm, "Getting the Goods," *Wall Street Journal* (November 22, 1999): R39.

62   Brandon Mitchener, "Border Crossings," *Wall Street Journal* (November 22, 1999): R41.

CHAPTER 17

EXPORT AND IMPORT STRATEGIES

There may be trade and none able to do it.

—CHINESE PROVERB

OBJECTIVES

- To identify the key elements of export and import strategies
- To compare direct and indirect selling of exports
- To identify the key elements of import strategies and importing
- To discuss the role of several types of third-party intermediaries and trading companies in exporting
- To show how freight forwarders help exporters with the movement of goods
- To identify the methods of receiving payment for exports and the financing of receivables
- To discuss the role of countertrade in international business

CASE

Grieve Corporation:
A Small-Business Export Strategy[1]

It is not always easy to engage in trade, especially for small companies. The top U.S. exporters generate about 30 percent of U.S. merchandise exports, and their shipments are bigger on average than are the shipments of smaller exporters. However, most U.S. companies engaged in export activity are small, as is Grieve Corporation of Round Lake, Illinois, near Chicago.

Grieve Corporation manufactures laboratory and industrial ovens, furnaces, and heat processing systems. Before Grieve Corporation got involved in exporting, it experienced problems when one of its customers would move its manufacturing facilities overseas. Initially, Grieve Corporation would continue to supply that customer with furnaces, but this market would eventually begin to erode as the customer would source locally. The company had not considered exports proactively for three main reasons.

1. *The nature of its product.* Industrial ovens and furnaces are rather large and bulky, and they are also relatively expensive. Top management assumed the product's size would make shipping costs so high that Grieve would price itself out of the market. For example, one overseas shipment of a fully automated system to the Philippines entailed shipping costs of $40,999.

2. *Doubts about its success abroad.* Grieve is a small business, and top management assumed it could not be successful internationally. Its managers were so busy doing all that needed to be done in the domestic market with a relatively thin management structure that they just didn't have time to think strategically about the international market.

3. *Concern about competition.* More seasoned exporters from Germany, Japan, and the United Kingdom offered relatively fierce competition. Even within the United States, the company had strong competition from local producers in markets outside the Chicago area.

However, Grieve realized that something had to be done. Not only was it losing customers overseas to local suppliers, but it was also beginning to experience competition from abroad. Top management realized it needed to combat the competition or lose the market entirely. In addition, Grieve Corporation had to make shipments to both California and Connecticut, its number-one and number-two markets, and it had to contend with location competition and high transportation costs, so it decided that the international market might not be so bad. Patrick J. Calabrese, Grieve's president, attended a one-day seminar featuring the U.S. ambassadors to the ASEAN countries to determine whether or not it made sense to enter the Asian market. He left that seminar convinced there might be strong market opportunities in one of the world's fastest-growing regions. However, he was not familiar with the market, and the company had no sales offices or representatives in the ASEAN countries. He was also concerned about the British, German, and Japanese competition already entrenched in that market.

Grieve's marketing staff decided to sample potential interest in Asia by advertising in trade publications circulating in Southeast Asia, such as *Asian Industrial Reporter, Asian Literature Showcase,* and *World Industrial Reporter.* To learn more about the market, Calabrese worked with a representative from the International Trade Administration of the Chicago Export Assistance Center. This office helped him plan a trip to Asia by arranging for interpreters at each stop on his itinerary and by arranging meetings with U.S. embassy personnel. His trip was intended primarily to determine market potential and to identify possible agents. Calabrese had received inquiries from some distributors that were familiar with Grieve's product line, but he had not pursued them. However, Calabrese's staff had begun filing correspondence by country rather than by company name, so it was relatively easy to locate potential distributors and customers along with the leads provided by the U.S. Department of Commerce. In addition to these distributors, Calabrese used the U.S. Department of Commerce's Agent/Distributor Search to identify several other possible distributors. The trip was a big success for Grieve. Interviews were held with 28 potential agents over 28 days, and exclusive agents were signed up in each country.

Calabrese quickly learned that he had to cut shipping costs. So Grieve redesigned its packaging to be more compact. In addition, it began shopping among freight forwarders to find the best rates, which varied depending on the forwarder's experience and its relationship with a particular steamship company.

Calabrese also learned how important it was for him to visit potential customers in Asia personally rather than to rely on a sales manager. He said,

> The one thing that I found is that almost to an individual, [Asian customers] are very keen on a personal association. If I were to give anybody advice, I would never send a second-level individual. Never send a marketing manager or sales manager; I would send a top manager. If your company isn't too large to prohibit it, I would send the president or chairman. On the other end, you are talking to the owner of a small distributor or the president of a small manufacturing company, and you've got to meet [that person] on an equal level. My limited experience is [these people] are very cognizant of this; in other words, they are pretty much attuned to a president talking to a president. They also like to feel secure that they are dealing with someone who can make decisions.
>
> Another thing I found is that potential customers want to feel that you are financially secure and that you have sufficient funding to continue to work with them for a period of years, because it takes some time and some money on our end to get these people going.
>
> Follow-up is incredibly important. I heard all kinds of stories about American [businesspeople] who would come over and spend a day and talk to potential customers and leave [catalogs]. Then the first time the potential customers would send a fax asking for information, they didn't hear from them for two weeks, and that just turns them right off.

Although Grieve faces high transport costs and significant competition from foreign companies as it works to penetrate foreign markets, top management is optimistic. The company has a good product. As Calabrese pointed out, "Our strength is that we are selling engineered products, using our 45 years of expertise to build something for them." Through his experiences in Southeast Asia, Calabrese learned some valuable lessons about exporting successfully.

1. Know your products well. Many people who go to Asia from the United States know very little about their own products. In some cases, potential agents who have studied company brochures know more about the products than the company representative.
2. Learn about the competition in the foreign market and the potential sale for your products.
3. Advertise in the local market before going there to determine the interest level and to build contacts.
4. Work hard. Too many foreign visitors want to spend a lot of time playing golf or seeing the sights.
5. Build a strong response base back home. Most foreigners complain about poor factory backup, lengthy delays in getting correspondence answered, and delays in getting quotations.
6. Arrange for your own transportation, and don't rely on the potential representative to solve your problems for you. That shows a lack of understanding of the local environment.
7. Make someone at the home office the principal contact for the representative. People need someone who will answer questions and provide assistance.
8. Learn the customs and business etiquette of the countries you visit. Once again, the U.S. Department of Commerce can provide assistance in this area.
9. Have the authority to make decisions and commit the company. If you are going to meet with the top person in the representative organization, be responsible yourself.

Calabrese obviously learned a great deal from his initial foray overseas. Once he gained experience in Asian markets, he expanded his export activity to other countries. This new way of doing business has created some challenges, but it also has helped Grieve be more successful and profitable.

The photo shows one of the world's largest container ships, owned by the Danish company Maersk, approaching the harbor in Singapore.

INTRODUCTION

As the Grieve case demonstrates, successful exporting is a complex process. Once a company has identified the good or service it wants to sell, it must explore market opportunities, a process that entails a significant amount of market research. Next, it must develop a production or service development strategy, prepare the goods or services for market, determine the best means for transporting the goods or services to the market, sell the goods or services, and receive payment. All of these steps require careful planning and preparation. Without a separate export staff, a company must rely on specialists to move goods and services from one country to another, agents or distributors to sell the goods or services, and banks to collect payment.

As noted in Chapter 14, companies can have many strategies when entering foreign markets. In this chapter, we will focus primarily on the export strategy (see Figure 17.1), drawing from strategic concepts discussed in Chapter 14. This chapter flows logically from Chapter 16 (on marketing), because much of what we will discuss deals with elements in the marketing mix, especially channels of distribution.

As noted in Chapter 1, exporting is sending goods and services from one country to another, and importing is bringing goods and services into one country from another. Exports result in the receipt of money or claims on money, and imports result in the payment of money or claims on money. Typically, we focus on the export and import of goods, but services are becoming increasingly important in the global economy. The United States is the largest exporter of services in the world, with a 19 percent share; and the services trade worldwide constituted about $1.4 trillion in 1998, 18.6 percent of the total world trade.[2] For the remainder of the chapter, we will discuss export and import strategies, third-party intermediaries used to facilitate exports and imports, export financing, and countertrade.

FIGURE 17.1   Exporting & Importing in International Business

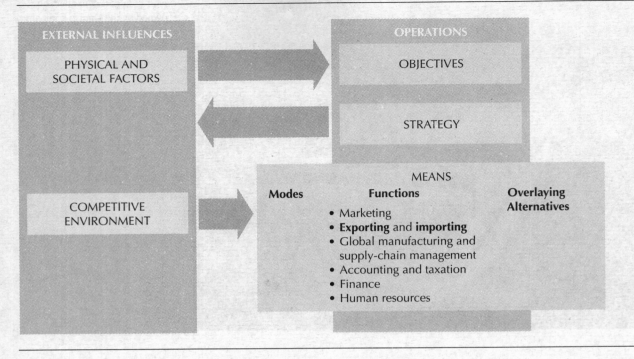

Exporting and importing are necessary functions for implementing companies' international strategies.

Entry mode depends on ownership advantages of the company, location advantages of the market, and internalization advantages that result from integrating transactions within the company.

Companies that have lower levels of ownership advantages either do not enter foreign markets or use low-risk strategies such as exporting.

Strategic considerations affect the choice of exporting as an entry mode.

EXPORT STRATEGY

A company's choice of entry mode to a foreign market depends on different factors, such as the ownership advantages of the company, the location advantages of the market, and the internalization advantages that result from integrating transactions within the company.[3] Ownership advantages are specific assets, international experience, and the ability to develop differentiated products. For example, Boeing capitalizes on its ownership advantage through the development of sophisticated aircraft; doing the same would be difficult for a new entrant to the market. Location advantages of the market are a combination of market potential (its size and growth potential) and investment risk. Internalization advantages are the benefits of holding on to specific assets or skills within the company and integrating them into its activities rather than licensing or selling them. For example, Grieve Corporation could have explored licensing its technology to manufacturers in Southeast Asia but preferred to maintain control over its technology and serve Southeast Asia through exports from its own U.S. plants.

In general, companies that have low levels of ownership advantages either do not enter foreign markets or use low-risk entry modes such as exporting. Exporting requires a lower level of investment than other modes, such as FDI, but it also offers a lower risk/return on sales, meaning the return on sales may not be as great, but neither is the risk. Exporting allows significant management operational control but does not provide as much marketing control, because the exporter is farther from the final consumer and often must deal with independent distributors abroad that control many of the marketing functions.[4]

However, the choice of exporting as an entry mode is not just a function of these ownership, location, and internalization advantages. It also must fit the company's overall strategy. Companies consider these questions before deciding to export.

- What does the company want to gain from exporting?
- Is exporting consistent with other company goals?
- What demands will exporting place on its key resources—management and personnel, production capacity, and financing—and how will these demands be met?
- Are the expected benefits worth the costs, or would company resources be better used for developing new domestic business?[5]

These are strategic questions that must take into account global concentration, synergies, and strategic motivations. Global concentration means that many global industries have only a few major players, and a company's strategy for penetrating a particular market might depend on the competition. If the competition is servicing markets by exporting, the company might be able to do okay with the same strategy. However, if the competition is servicing the local market through foreign direct investment, the company might not be as successful in the future if it only exports to the market. Global synergies arise when the company can share its expertise in areas such as R&D, marketing, and manufacturing with its operations abroad. Global strategic motivations are the reasons why a company might want to enter a market. For example, it might export to or invest in a market in a specific country as a means of combating a competitor in that market, not just because of specific market or profit potential.[6]

Exporting occurs for several good reasons. A company can export goods and services to related companies such as branches and subsidiaries, or it can export to independent customers. Sometimes a company exports final goods to its related companies overseas, which then sell the goods to consumers. Other times, a company exports semifinished goods that are used by its related companies in the manufacturing process. In many cases, however, the sale is to an outsider, and the exporter may sell directly to the buyer or indirectly through an intermediary.

Characteristics of Exporters

Research conducted on the characteristics of exporters has resulted in two basic conclusions.

1. The *probability* of being an exporter increases with company size, as defined by revenues.
2. Export *intensity*, the percentage of total revenues coming from exports, is not positively correlated with company size. The greater the percentage of exports to total revenues, the greater the intensity.

The first conclusion is based on the idea that small companies can grow in the domestic market without having to export, but large companies must export if they are to increase sales.[7] The exceptions are small high-tech or highly specialized companies that operate in market niches with a global demand as well as small companies that sell expensive capital equipment. In a study of Canadian companies, the two conclusions above were confirmed, but the author found that firm size was not the most important factor in determining the propensity to export, the number of countries served, and export intensity. Factors such as the risk profile of management and industry factors were as important as size. In other words, managers who were more likely to take a risk were also more likely to engage in exporting, and companies were more likely to engage in exporting if they were operating in industries in which the leading companies were exporters.[8]

The largest companies, such as General Electric, Boeing, and General Motors, are still the biggest exporters. But small companies are expanding their export capability. Small business now makes up 88 percent of U.S. exporters, and it accounts for one-fifth of the value of U.S. exports.[9]

Grieve is a perfect example that illustrates these concepts. Although considered a small company in terms of total sales, its export revenues are significant and are the key to its survival. It must export to maintain its market share abroad and its competitive position in the United States.

The probability of a company's being an exporter increases with the size of the company. Export intensity is not positively correlated with company size.

The largest companies are the biggest exporters, but small companies are expanding their export capability.

Exporting
- Expands sales
- Achieves economies of scale in production
- Is less risky than FDI
- Allows the company to diversify sales locations

Why Companies Export

Companies export primarily to increase sales revenues. This is true for service companies as well as manufacturers. Many of the former, such as accountants, advertisers, lawyers, and consultants, export their services to meet the needs of clients working abroad. Grieve exported products to clients that had moved abroad. Companies that are capital and research intensive, such as biotechnology and pharmaceutical companies, must export to achieve economies of scale by spreading their R&D expenditures over a larger sales area. R&D expenditures for those industries are so high as a percentage of sales that the companies have to increase revenues worldwide to be able to support the R&D efforts. Export sales can be a means of alleviating excess capacity in the domestic market. In addition, some companies export rather than invest abroad because of the perceived high risk of operating in foreign environments. Finally, many companies export to a variety of markets as a diversification strategy. For example, Grieve developed markets in Southeast Asia to expand its sales base and to diversify its markets from strictly U.S. sales. Because economic growth is not the same in every market, export diversification can allow a company to take advantage of strong growth in one market to offset weak growth in another.

Stages of Export Development

Many companies begin exporting by accident rather than by design. Consequently, they tend to encounter a number of unforeseen problems. They also may never get a chance to see how important exports can be. For these reasons, developing a good export strategy is important. As Figure 17.2 shows, export development has three broad phases.[10]

As companies move from initial to advanced exporting, they tend to export to more countries and expect exports as a percentage of total sales to grow.

These phases have less to do with company size than with degree of export development—both large and small companies can be at any stage. In fact, more new companies are exporting sooner in their own life cycle because there is a new generation of entrepreneurs and managers with a keen awareness of international business. In addition, the ability to generate sales on the Internet is one reason why companies are exporting faster. As a company establishes a homepage, Internet surfers from all over the world can have instant access to the company's product line and even initiate sales directly. A small U.S. company called Evertek Computer Corporation sells new and refurbished computers and parts. Evertek recently pur-

---

FIGURE 17.2   Phases of Export Development

As companies gain greater expertise and experience in exporting, they diversify their markets to countries that are farther away or have business environments that differ from that of their home country.

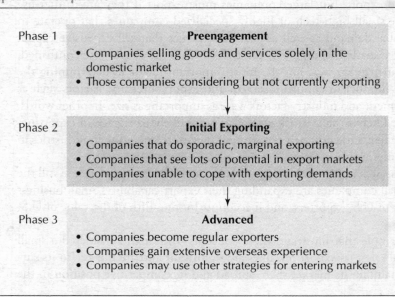

Phase 1   **Preengagement**
- Companies selling goods and services solely in the domestic market
- Those companies considering but not currently exporting

Phase 2   **Initial Exporting**
- Companies that do sporadic, marginal exporting
- Companies that see lots of potential in export markets
- Companies unable to cope with exporting demands

Phase 3   **Advanced**
- Companies become regular exporters
- Companies gain extensive overseas experience
- Companies may use other strategies for entering markets

chased an Internet-based program from the U.S. Commerce Department called BuyUSA.com, which helps Evertek find buyers around the world. Within one year of starting to use BuyUSA.com, Evertek began selling in 10 new countries, with single purchases reaching up to $75,000.[11]

Potential Pitfalls of Exporting

To understand the elements in an export strategy, let's first identify the major problems that exporters often face. The attacks of September 11 have reminded traders how risky exporting can be. In the days following the attacks, it was nearly impossible for traders to send or receive goods. Traffic eventually began flowing again, but many managers were forced to put things on hold, such as essential sales trips to countries they were exporting to. Aside from problems that are common to international business in general and not unique to exporting, such as language and other cultural factors, the following are mistakes companies new to exporting most frequently make.

1. Failure to obtain qualified export counseling and to develop a master international marketing plan before starting an export business
2. Insufficient commitment by top management to overcome the initial difficulties and financial requirements of exporting
3. Insufficient care in selecting overseas agents or distributors
4. Chasing orders from around the world instead of establishing a base of profitable operations and orderly growth
5. Neglecting the export business when the domestic market booms
6. Failure to treat international distributors on an equal basis with their domestic counterparts
7. Unwillingness to modify products to meet other countries' regulations or cultural preferences
8. Failure to print service, sales, and warranty messages in locally understood languages
9. Failure to consider use of an export management company or other marketing intermediary when the company does not have the personnel to handle specialized export functions[12]

Designing an Export Strategy

Designing an export strategy can help managers avoid making the costly mistakes mentioned above. Figure 17.3 shows an international business transaction chain, which we'll discuss in the remainder of the chapter. A successful export (and import) strategy must take each element of the transaction chain into consideration.

To establish a successful export strategy, management must

1. *Assess the company's export potential by examining its opportunities and resources.* First of all, the company needs to determine if there is a market for its goods and services. Next, it needs to make sure it has enough production capacity to deliver the goods or services to foreign customers.

2. *Obtain expert counseling on exporting* Most governments provide assistance for their domestic companies, although the extent of commitment varies by country. For U.S. companies, the best place to start is with the nearest Export Assistance Center of the International Trade Administration (ITA) of the U.S. Department of Commerce. Such assistance is invaluable in helping an exporter get started. In the Grieve case, for example, Calabrese used a lot of information provided by the U.S. government to learn about Asian markets. Other government agencies also assist exporters. As a company's export plan increases in

In designing an export strategy, managers must

- Assess export potential
- Get expert counseling
- Select a market or markets
- Formulate and implement an export strategy

FIGURE 17.3   International Business Transaction Chain

In between negotiating a sale and delivering/receiving the goods and services, both the exporter and the importer need to consider a variety of shipping and financial issues.

*Financial transactions occur at every stage of this process.

Source: Export America, Vol. 1, November 1999, 17. Magazine Published by the International Trade Administration of the U.S. Dept. of Commerce

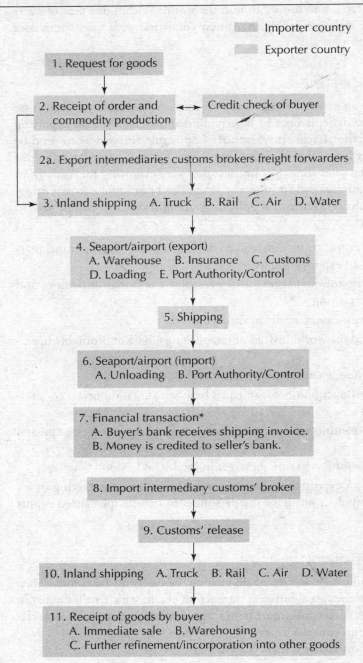

Importer country

Exporter country

1. Request for goods

2. Receipt of order and commodity production ←→ Credit check of buyer

2a. Export intermediaries customs brokers freight forwarders

3. Inland shipping   A. Truck   B. Rail   C. Air   D. Water

4. Seaport/airport (export)
   A. Warehouse   B. Insurance   C. Customs
   D. Loading   E. Port Authority/Control

5. Shipping

6. Seaport/airport (import)
   A. Unloading   B. Port Authority/Control

7. Financial transaction*
   A. Buyer's bank receives shipping invoice.
   B. Money is credited to seller's bank.

8. Import intermediary customs' broker

9. Customs' release

10. Inland shipping   A. Truck   B. Rail   C. Air   D. Water

11. Receipt of goods by buyer
    A. Immediate sale   B. Warehousing
    C. Further refinement/incorporation into other goods

scope, it probably will want to secure specialized assistance from banks, lawyers, freight forwarders, export management companies, export trading companies, and others.

3. *Select a market or markets.* This key part of the export strategy may be done passively or actively. In the former, the company learns of markets by responding to requests from abroad that result from trade shows, advertisements, or articles in trade publications. Grieve's Calabrese took a more active approach by selecting Southeast Asia as an area for export development as a result of a seminar he attended featuring the U.S. ambassadors to the ASEAN countries. A company also can determine the markets to which products like its own are currently being exported. For example, in the U.S. setting, U.S. Census foreign trade statistics identify the markets for different classifications of exports, and the

National Trade Data Bank (NTDB) provides specific industry reports for different countries. The NTDB is updated monthly, so potential exporters can get the most recent studies. Similar forms of assistance are found in other countries.

4. *Formulate and implement an export strategy.* In this step, a company considers its export objectives (immediate and long term), the specific tactics it will use, a schedule of activities and deadlines that enable it to achieve its objectives, and the allocation of resources that allows it to accomplish the different activities. Then it implements the strategy by getting the goods and services to foreign consumers.

A detailed export business plan is an essential element in the implemention of an effective export strategy. Table 17.1 provides a sample of such a plan. The development of the plan

---

● **TABLE 17.1**

AN EXPORT BUSINESS PLAN

A detailed export business plan is an essential element in the implementation of an effective export strategy. The plan must consider company resources, identify specific markets, and establish specific plans for dealing with marketing, legal, manufacturing, personnel, and financial elements. Finally, it must include a schedule for implementing the plan.

I. Executive summary
  A. Key elements of the plan
  B. Description of business and target markets
  C. Brief description of management team
  D. Summary of financial projections

II. Business history
  A. History of company
  B. Products-services offered and their unique advantages
  C. Domestic-market experience
  D. Foreign-market experience
  E. Production facilities
  F. Personnel—international experience and expertise
  G. Industry structure, competition

III. Market research
  A. Target countries
    1. Primary
    2. Secondary
    3. Tertiary
  B. Market conditions in target countries
    1. Existing demand
    2. Competition
    3. Strengths and weaknesses of the economy— barriers to entry, etc.

IV. Marketing decisions
  A. Distribution strategies
    1. Indirect exporting
    2. Direct exporting
    3. Documentation
    4. Direct investment, strategic alliances
  B. Pricing strategy
  C. Promotion strategy
  D. Product strategy

V. Legal decisions
  A. Agent/distributor agreements
  B. Patent, trademark, copyright protection
  C. Export/import regulations
  D. ISO 9000
  E. Dispute resolution

VI. Manufacturing and operations
  A. Location of production facilities for exports
  B. Capacity of existing facilities
  C. Plans for expansion
  D. Product modification necessary to adapt to local environment

VII. Personnel strategies
  A. Personnel needed to manage exports
  B. Experience and expertise of existing personnel
  C. Training needs of existing personnel
  D. Hiring needs in the short term and long term

VIII. Financial decisions
  A. Pro forma financial statements and projected cash flows assuming export activity
  B. Identification of key assumptions
  C. Current sources of funding—private and bank funding
  D. Financial needs and future sources of funding
  E. Tax consequences of export activity
  F. Potential risk and sources of protection

IX. Implementation schedule

depends on the nature of the company. For a small or medium-size company, the plan usually gets the attention of the top levels of management, as was the case with Grieve Corporation. Larger companies might establish a separate export department to deal with the export of all products. Research has shown that commitment precedes success in exporting, and the development of an export department is one indicator of commitment by top management.[13] In Chapter 15, we discussed several different organizational forms that MNEs might adopt, so the export function might be allocated to an international division, the different lines of business, or the regional-national organizations. But whether the company is large or small—or whether the export function is centralized into an export department or diffused into different product or regional organizations—it is important to follow the steps outlined in Table 17.1 so that an effective strategy is carried out.

IMPORT STRATEGY

Thus far, we've talked mostly about exporters and exporting. Importing is the bringing of goods and services into a country and results in the importer paying money to the exporter in the foreign country. Traditional goods imports are fairly easy to understand. When Nissan North America brings the Infinity I45 sedan from Nissan Japan to the U.S. market, it creates an import for the United States. In addition to merchandise imports, such as the Infinity I45 sedan, there are a variety of service imports. SAP software, from the German software company of the same name, is a service (even though it comes in a package, software *is* considered to be a service). Foreign banks, such as Deutsche Bank, that provide financial services to U.S. customers also create service imports.

> **Two basic types of imports**
>
> - Industrial and consumer goods to independent individuals and companies
> - Intermediate goods and services that are part of the firm's global supply chain

There are two basic types of imports: (1) those that provide industrial and consumer goods and services to individuals and companies that are not related to the foreign exporter, and (2) those that provide intermediate goods and services to companies that are part of the firm's global supply chain. Why import in the first place? Companies import goods and services because they can be supplied to the domestic market at a cheaper price and better quality than competing goods manufactured in the domestic market. In the case of the Infinity I45 sedan, Nissan manufactures some of its product line in the United States, but some of its product line is manufactured in Japan and exported to the United States. The Infinity I45 fits into the latter category. As we will see in Chapter 18, there are strategic reasons to manufacture some products in one location and others in another location. Specialization of production and export to markets around the world is more efficient than manufacturing every product in every market. Nike buys shoes manufactured in several Asian countries, including Korea, Taiwan, China, Thailand, Indonesia, and Vietnam, because of the cheaper cost. It would be impossible to manufacture the same product in an industrial country and be able to sell it at a reasonable price because of the relatively high labor costs. Finally, companies import products that are not available in the local market. For example, North America imports bananas from tropical climates because the climate of North America is not suitable for growing bananas. Were it not for imports, nobody in North America could consume fresh bananas.

There is not as much research done on import strategies as is the case for export strategies. However, there are three broad types of importers.

> **Three broad types of importers**
>
> - Looking for any product around the world to import and sell
> - Looking for foreign sourcing to get their products at the cheapest price
> - Using foreign sourcing as part of their global supply chain

1. Those that are looking for any product around the world that they can import. They might specialize in certain types of products—such as sports equipment or household items—but they are simply scanning the globe and looking for any product that will generate positive cash flow for them.

2. Those that are looking at foreign sourcing to get their products at the cheapest price. A small Utah-based company called ForEveryBody (www.foreverybody.com) started out

selling a variety of bath and body products. Soon, however, it began to branch out into decorative products for homes, so it identified manufacturers in China that could supply it with specific products for its stores.

3. Those that use foreign sourcing as part of their global supply chain. This strategy will be discussed in Chapter 18.

The import process is also illustrated in Figure 17.3, and it basically mirrors the export process. It involves both strategic and procedural issues. In fact, the export business plan in Table 17.1 could easily be adapted to make it an import business plan. Managers need to research potential markets, both in terms of the countries themselves and the suppliers. Then they need to determine the legal ramifications of importing the products, both in terms of the products themselves and the countries from which they come. Managers also need to deal with third-party intermediates, such as freight forwarders and customs agents, and they need to arrange financing for the purchase.

Importing requires a certain degree of expertise in dealing with institutions and documentation, but not every company may have this skill. Consequently, a company may elect to work through an **import broker**. The import broker obtains various government permissions and other clearances before forwarding necessary paperwork to the carrier that is to deliver the goods to the importer. Import brokers in the United States are certified as such by the U.S. Customs Service to perform the functions needed to bring products into the country.

> An import broker is an intermediary who helps an importer clear customs.

The Role of Customs Agencies

When importing goods into any country, a company must be totally familiar with the customs operations of the importing country. In this context, "customs" are the country's import and export procedures and restrictions, not its cultural aspects. The primary duties of the U.S. Customs Service (www.customs.ustreas.gov) are the assessment and collection of all duties, taxes, and fees on imported merchandise, the enforcement of customs and related laws, and the administration of certain navigation laws and treaties. As a major enforcement organization, it also deals with smuggling operations and is increasingly involved in helping protect against foreign terrorist attacks.[14]

> Customs agencies assess and collect duties and ensure that import regulations are adhered to.

An importer needs to know how to clear goods, what duties to pay, and what special laws exist regarding the importation of products. On the procedural side, when merchandise reaches the port of entry, the importer must file documents with customs officials, who assign a tentative value and tariff classification to the merchandise. The U.S. government has over 10,000 tariff classifications, and approximately 60 percent of them are subject to interpretation—that is, a particular product could fit more than one classification. It is almost an art form for companies to figure out the tariff classification that will give them the lowest possible tariff. Then customs officials examine the goods to determine whether there are any restrictions on their importation. If there are restrictions, the goods may be rejected and be prevented from entering the country. If the goods are allowed to enter, the importer pays the duty and the goods are released. The amount of the duty depends on the product's country of origin, the type of product, and other factors.

> Ways a customs broker can help
> - Value products to help them qualify for more favorable duty treatment
> - Qualify for duty refunds through drawback provisions
> - Defer duties by using bonded warehouses and foreign trade zones
> - Limit liability by properly marking an import's country of origin

A broker or other import consultant can help an importer minimize import duties by

- *Valuing products in such a way that they qualify for more favorable duty treatment.* Different product categories have different duties. For example, finished goods typically have a higher duty than do parts and components.
- *Qualifying for duty refunds through drawback provisions.* Some exporters use in their manufacturing process imported parts and components on which they paid a duty. In the United States, the drawback provision allows domestic exporters to apply for a 99-percent

> Drawback provisions allow U.S. exporters to apply for a refund of 99 percent of the duty paid on imported components, provided they are used in the manufacture of goods that are exported.

refund of the duty paid on the imported goods, as long as they become part of the exporter's product.

- *Deferring duties by using bonded warehouses and foreign trade zones*. Companies do not have to pay duties on imports stored in bonded warehouses and foreign trade zones until the goods are removed for sale or used in a manufacturing process.
- *Limiting liability by properly marking an import's country of origin*. Because governments assess duties on imports based in part on the country of origin, a mistake in marking the country of origin could result in a higher import duty. For example, in the United States, if a product or its container is not properly marked when it enters the country, the product could be assigned a marking duty equal to 10 percent of the customs value. This would be in addition to the normal tariff.[15]

Import Documentation

Importers must submit documents to customs that determine whether the shipment is released and what duties are assessed.

When a shipment arrives at a port, the importer must file specific documents with the port director in order to *take title* to the shipment. (*Take title* means the importer receives the products without purchasing them—that is, without laying out any money.) These documents are of two different types: (1) those that determine whether customs will release the shipment, and (2) those that contain information for *duty assessment* and statistical purposes. The specific documents that customs requires vary by country but include an entry manifest, a commercial invoice, and a packing list. For example, the exporter's commercial invoice contains information such as the port of entry to which the merchandise is destined; information on the importer and exporter; a detailed description of the merchandise, including its purchase price; the currency used for the sale; and the country of origin.

THIRD-PARTY INTERMEDIARIES

Third-party intermediaries—companies that facilitate the trade of goods but that are not related to either the exporter or the importer

As noted in Figure 17.3, both exporters and importers use a variety of third-party intermediaries—companies that facilitate the trade of goods but that are not related to either the exporter or the importer. A company that either exports or is planning to export must decide whether its internal staff will handle certain essential activities or if it will contract with other companies. Regardless, the following functions must occur:

Companies use external specialists for exporting before developing internal capabilities.

1. Stimulate sales, obtain orders, and do market research
2. Make credit investigations and perform payment-collection activities
3. Handle foreign traffic and shipping
4. Act as support for the company's overall sales, distribution, and advertising staff

Direct exports—goods and services are sold to an independent party outside of the exporter's home country

Indirect exports—goods and services are sold to an intermediary in the domestic market, which then sells the goods in the export market

Handling these functions internally can be costly and can require expertise a company doesn't have. Most companies initially use external specialists and intermediary organizations to assume some or all of these functions, although a company later may develop in-house capabilities to perform them. Specialists are useful for such duties as preparing export documents, preparing customs documents in the importing country, and identifying the best means of transportation. Most companies can benefit at some time from the use of an intermediary organization. Some of them act as agents on behalf of the exporter, and some take title to the goods and sell them abroad. Others perform certain specialized aspects of the export process. For example, a freight forwarder is responsible for moving the products from domestic to foreign markets.

Exporting may be either direct or indirect. Direct exports are goods and services sold to an independent party outside of the exporter's home country. Indirect exports are sold to an intermediary in the domestic market, which then sells the goods in the export market. Services are more likely to be sold in a direct basis, but goods are exported both directly and indirectly.

Direct Selling

Exporters undertake direct selling to give them greater control over the marketing function and to earn higher profits. **Direct selling** is when an exporter sells through sales representatives, to distributors, to foreign retailers, or to final end users. A **sales representative** sells products in foreign markets on a commission basis, without assuming risk or responsibility.

The sales representative may have exclusive rights to sell in a particular geographic area or may have to compete with other sales representatives that represent the firm. It is more common for sales representatives to have exclusive rights to a territory. For example, Grieve's sales representatives operated on an exclusive basis in their respective markets.

A **distributor** in a foreign country is a merchant who purchases the products from the manufacturer and sells them at a profit. Distributors usually carry a stock of inventory and service the product. They also usually deal with retailers rather than end users in the market.

Companies should consider the following points about each potential foreign sales representative or distributor:

The size and capabilities of its sales force

Its sales record

An analysis of its territory

Its current product mix

Its facilities and equipment

Its marketing policies

Its customer profile

The principles it represents and the importance of the inquiring company to its overall business

Its promotional strategies[16]

A company that has sufficient financial and managerial resources and decides to export directly rather than working through an intermediary must set up a solid organization. This organization may take any number of forms, ranging from a separate international division, to a separate international company, to full integration of international and domestic activities. Whatever the form, there commonly is an international sales force that is separate from the domestic sales force because of the different types of expertise required in dealing in foreign markets.

Exporters can also sell directly to foreign retailers. Usually, these products are limited to consumer lines, but the growth of large retail chains around the world has facilitated the export of products to the large chains, which gives the exporter instant coverage to a wide area. Exporters can also sell directly to end users. A good way to generate such sales is by printing up catalogs or by going to trade shows, or such sales can be generated when foreign buyers either get company brochures or respond to advertisements in trade publications.

An example of a company that sells directly to buyers is Cooley Distillery, the sole Irish-owned distiller of Irish whiskey. Cooley exports 81.5 percent of its production, up from 23.4 percent in 1990. Cooley has a powerful customer list and sells in over 40 countries, including the top 25 retailers in Europe. In spite of this situation, Cooley has elected to sell ex-distillery,

Direct selling involves sales representatives, distributors, or retailers.

A sales representative usually operates on a commission basis.

A distributor is a merchant who purchases the products from the manufacturer and sells them at a profit.

which means that the customer takes title directly from Cooley's distillery and handles all of the shipments. Cooley maintains a small bonded warehouse in the United Kingdom to handle just-in-time shipments to supermarket chains that order small quantities, but it generally lets the buyer handle shipping and storage in foreign markets.[17]

Direct Exporting Through the Internet and Electronic Commerce

Internet marketing allows all companies—both large and small—to engage in direct marketing quickly, easily, and cheaply.

Electronic commerce is an important way for companies to export their products to end users. A study conducted by Forrester Research found that 7 percent of revenues from worldwide trade in 2002 was from e-commerce. Forrester estimates that by 2007, e-commerce will produce 20 percent of revenues in world trade.[18] E-commerce will be especially important for SMEs (small and medium-size enterprises) that can't afford to establish an elaborate sales network internationally. E-commerce is easy to start, it provides faster and cheaper delivery of information, it provides quick feedback on new products, it helps to improve customer service, it is available to a global audience, it helps to level the field of competition, it can be a strategic tool to access different markets, it's cheaper than a phone call, and it helps establish electronic data interchange (EDI) with both suppliers and customers.[19]

Through Internet exporting, companies can establish homepages in different languages to target different audiences. In the case of industrial products, they can install software to track hits to their homepage and then send sales reps to potential customers or have local distributors contact them. In the case of consumer products, companies such as J. Crew can sell their products directly to consumers all over the world. Internet marketing is a direct form of marketing that is exploding in importance.

Indirect Selling

In **Indirect selling**, the exporter sells goods directly to or through an independent domestic intermediary in the exporter's home country that exports the products to foreign markets. The major types of indirect intermediaries are the **export management company (EMC)**; the **export trading company (ETC)**; and export agents, merchants, or remarketers. EMCs and ETCs sometimes act as agents operating on a commission and sometimes take title to the merchandise. The terms *EMC* and *ETC* are sometimes used interchangeably, especially for the smaller intermediaries. The larger intermediaries, however, are almost always referred to as export trading companies or simply trading companies, because they typically deal with both exports and imports. We will discuss both types of intermediaries.

Export Management Companies

An EMC acts as the export arm of a manufacturer.

An EMC usually acts as the export arm of a manufacturer—although it can also deal in imports—and often uses the manufacturer's own letterhead in communicating with foreign sales representatives and distributors. The EMC primarily obtains orders for its clients' products through the selection of appropriate markets, distribution channels, and promotion campaigns. It collects, analyzes, and furnishes credit information and advice regarding foreign accounts and payment terms. The EMC may also take care of export documents, arrange transportation (including the consolidation of shipments among multiple clients to reduce costs), set up patent and trademark protection in foreign countries, and assist in establishing alternative forms of doing business, such as licensing or joint ventures.[20]

EMCs operate on a contractual basis, usually as an agent of the exporter.

EMCs operate on a contractual basis, often as the agent for an exporter, and provide exclusive representation in a well-defined foreign territory. The contract specifies pricing, credit and financial policies, promotional services, and basis for payment. An EMC might operate on a commission basis for sales (unless it takes title to the merchandise) and take a retainer for other services. EMCs usually concentrate on complementary and noncompetitive products so that they can present a more complete product line to a limited number of foreign importers.

In the United States, most EMCs are small, entrepreneurial ventures that tend to specialize by product, function, or market area. The Federation of International Trade Associations (FITA) estimates that there are around 600 EMCs in the United States and that each represents about 10 suppliers. This means that only 6,000 U.S. companies are using EMCs, although FITA believes that thousands more would benefit from using EMCs.[21] Although EMCs perform an important function for companies that need their expertise, a manufacturer that uses an EMC may lose control over foreign sales because it is passing off that responsibility to an independent party. If the EMC does not actively promote the product, the company will not generate many exports. The manufacturer needs to balance the desire for control with the cost of performing the export functions directly.[22]

Most EMCs are small, entrepreneurial ventures that specialize by product, function, or market area.

Export Trading Companies

ETCs resemble EMCs, and the terms are often used interchangeably. ETCs operate more on the basis of demand than of supply. ETCs are like independent distributors that match up buyers and sellers. ETCs find out what foreign customers want and then identify different domestic suppliers for the products. Rather than representing a manufacturer, an ETC looks for as many manufacturers as it can find to supply overseas customers. Because ETCs could control the foreign distribution of products and collaborate with producers of competing products, they could be open to antitrust allegations.

In 1982, the U.S. government enacted the Export Trading Company Act, which removed some of the antitrust obstacles to the creation of ETCs in the United States. It was hoped that ETCs would lead to greater exports of U.S. goods and services. The legislation allows banks to make equity investments in commercial ventures that qualify as ETCs, something that would not be possible in the absence of the legislation. The Federal Reserve Board must approve these applications before the bank can start export operations. Many of the banks concentrate on customers in their geographical market and in parts of the world in which they already have a good banking network. ETCs are important to banks, because banks provide the financial side of the export business, so being able to invest in an ETC gives the banks access to more of the business than just the financing side.

ETCs are like EMCs, but they tend to operate on the basis of demand rather than of supply. They identify suppliers who can fill orders in overseas markets.

ETCs in the United States are exempt from antitrust provisions in order to allow them to collaborate with other companies to penetrate foreign markets.

Non-U.S. Trading Companies

As Table 17.2 shows there are 16 trading companies in the *Fortune* Global 500 companies ranked according to revenues. Two things are interesting about Table 17.2. One is that there are no U.S. trading companies on the list. In fact, only four countries are represented: Japan (9 companies), South Korea (4 companies), Germany (1 company), and China (2 companies). The second interesting point is that several of the trading companies suffered losses in 2001. In fact, in 1995, the four biggest companies on the cummulative Global 500 list were Mitsubishi, Mitsui, Itochu, and Sumitomo. Since then they have lost rank, and not one of them is listed in the top 10 in 2001. (Mitsubishi, the largest trading company, ranks number 12 on the Global 500 list.) In the United States, there is a large number of small trading companies, while the trading companies from other countries are among the biggest companies in their respective countries and in the world. Of the top 20 largest companies in the world in terms of revenues, 3 are Japanese trading companies.[23] Let's see why Japan dominates the trading company industry.

The largest trading companies in the world are from Japan, South Korea, Germany, and China, not the United States.

● TABLE 17.2

TOP GLOBAL TRADING COMPANIES, 2001

GLOBAL 500 RANK*	COMPANY	COUNTRY	2001 REVENUE ($ MILLIONS)	2001 PROFITS ($ MILLIONS)	PROFIT % OF REVENUE	RANK
12	Mitsubishi	Japan	105,814	482	0	5
13	Mitsui	Japan	101,206	443	0	6
17	Itochu	Japan	91,177	242	0	8
23	Sumitomo	Japan	77,140	362	0	4
25	Marubeni	Japan	71,757	−931	(1)	16
28	E.ON	Germany	66,453	1,834	3	1
74	Nissho Iwai	Japan	43,703	10	0	13
118	Samsung	South Korea	33,212	32	0	11
219	Hyundai	South Korea	21,702	−186	(1)	15
248	LG International	South Korea	19,516	26	0	10
255	Tomen	Japan	19,073	38	0	9
273	Toyota Tsusho	Japan	18,040	70	0	7
289	SK Global	South Korea	17,214	−95	(1)	14
305	Nichimen	Japan	16,437	11	0	12
311	Sinochem	China	16,164	82	1	3
392	COFCO	China	13,004	131	1	2

*These numbers represented the ranking of each trading company in the Global 500 List.

Source: From *Fortune* (July 22, 2002). ©2002 TIME, INC. http://www.fortune.com/lists/G500/indsnap_76.htm. Reprinted by permission of Time, Inc.

Japanese trading companies are known as *sogo shoshas*; they are the trading arms of the large *keiretsus*—Japanese business groups that are networks of manufacturing, service, and financial companies.

The **sogo shosha**, the Japanese equivalent word for *trading company*, can trace its roots back to the late nineteenth century, when Japan embarked on an aggressive modernization process. At that time, the trading companies were called **zaibatsu**—large, family-owned businesses composed of financial and manufacturing companies usually held together by a large holding company. These companies were very powerful, so U.S. General Douglas MacArthur (sent to Japan to institute New Deal reforms after WWII) broke them up and made many of their activities illegal. However, the families and relationships did not go away, so the *zaibatsu* reformed into the *keiretsu* organizations, meeting the letter of the law even if they didn't exactly meet the spirit of the law. However, there was greater concern after World War II about the reconstruction of Japan than of eliminating all vestiges of the past, so the *keiretsus* linking financial, manufacturing, and trading companies started up again.

When these trading companies were first organized after World War II, their primary functions became handling paperwork for import and export transactions, financing imports and exports, and providing transportation and storage services. However, their operations expanded significantly beyond exporting to include investing in production and processing facilities, establishing fully integrated sales systems for certain products, expanding marketing activities, and developing large bases for the integrated processing of raw materials.[24]

An example of the type of activities that the Japanese trading companies pursue is the joint purchase by Itochu Corporation and Arco of the western U.S. coal operations of Coastal States Energy Company. Although Itochu holds a 35-percent equity interest in the coal operations, located primarily in Utah, it uses its marketing expertise in Japan and elsewhere in the Pacific Rim to sell the coal.[25] Just as the Japanese trading companies are part of the larger corporate relationships known as *keiretsu*, so too are Korean trading companies part of the large Korean business groups called *chaebol*. Although the Korean trading companies modeled themselves after their Japanese counterparts, there are some differences. The *sogo shoshas* are loosely linked to the rest of the *keiretsu*, while the companies in the *chaebol* are tightly linked to each other, with a high degree of intercompany transactions with each other and with the trading companies. The *sogo shoshas* are not only more loosely linked to their *keiretsus* but also more professionally managed, whereas the *chaebol* are still very dependent on family patriarchs. The Japanese trading companies are big in commodities and are heavily involved in triangular trading. For example, a Japanese company may sell Latin American commodities to the United States, whereas the Korean companies derive about 70 percent of their revenues from Korean exports.[26] However, the *chaebol* are trying hard to challenge the *sogo shoshas* in the trading company market. Because of the Japanese recession, the Internet, and increased competition, the *sogo shoshas*, particularly the smaller ones, are struggling to remain profitable. The larger ones (those listed in the top five trading companies of the *Fortune* Global 500) have enough capital to close down or restructure unprofitable businesses. It may not be long before the Korean *chaebol* catch up to the smaller Japanese *sogo shoshas*.[27]

Chaebol—Korean business groups that are similar to *keiretsu* and also contain a trading company as part of the group

Foreign Freight Forwarders

To assist in the transport of goods from one country to another, companies usually employ the services of a **freight forwarder**, known as the travel agents of cargo. A freight forwarder is an agent for the exporter in moving cargo to an overseas destination.[28] The freight forwarder is used for both imports and exports, because one company's exports is another company's imports. Even export management companies and other types of trading companies often use the specialized services of foreign freight forwarders.

A foreign freight forwarder is an export or import specialist dealing in the movement of goods from producer to consumer.

The foreign freight forwarder is the largest export intermediary in terms of value and weight of products managed. However, the services it offers are more limited than those of an EMC. Once an exporter makes a foreign sale, it hires the freight forwarder to obtain the best routing and means of transportation based on space availability, speed, and cost. The freight forwarder will get the products from the manufacturing facility to the air or ocean terminal and then overseas. The forwarder secures space on planes or ships and necessary storage prior to shipment, reviews the letter of credit, obtains export licenses, and prepares necessary shipping documents. It also may advise on packing and labeling, purchase transportation insurance, repack shipments damaged en route, and warehouse products, which saves the exporter the capital investment of warehousing. However, the freight forwarder does not take title to the goods or act as a sales representative in a foreign market. It simply deals with the preparation and transportation of goods.

The typical freight forwarder is the largest export intermediary in terms of value and weight handled.

The freight forwarder usually charges the exporter a percentage of the shipment value, plus a minimum charge dependent on the number of services provided. The forwarder also receives a brokerage fee from the carrier. Despite these costs, using a freight forwarder is usually less costly for an exporter than providing the service internally, because most companies, especially the SMEs, find it difficult to set up a full-time department to deal with freight issues and keep up with shipping regulations. The forwarder also can get exporters shipping space more easily (because of its close relationship with carriers) and consolidate shipments to obtain lower rates.

Freight forwarders, especially the smaller ones, sometimes specialize in the mode used—such as surface freight, ocean freight, and airfreight—and the geographical area served. Increasingly, however, the freight forwarders handle many modes—truck, rail, and airfreight, for example.[29] The movement of goods across different modes from origin to destination is known as **intermodal transportation**.

Different transportation modes—surface freight (truck and rail), ocean freight, airfreight

Intermodal transportation—the movement across different modes from origin to destination

Ocean freight is the cheapest way to move merchandise, but it also is the slowest. Even though it still dominates global trade, its position is eroding somewhat. Ocean freight rates are based on space first and weight second. Rate schedules also differ depending on the ports and the direction the goods travel. For example, different rates apply to shipments from the United States to Germany and to shipments from Germany to the United States. Forwarders help manufacturers get the best contract and help prepare the products for export. Exporters can load merchandise in a container for shipment overseas, or they can rely on a freight forwarder to consolidate their shipments with others. As mentioned in the opening case, Grieve's president believes in getting quotes from different freight forwarders when booking space on cargo ships. Even large companies compare rates. The person who handles the export of Shell Oil Company's nonhazardous lubricating oils and greases negotiates rates with the steamship lines himself, but if the forwarders' steamship line rates are lower, he will use the forwarders instead.[30]

Since the terrorist attacks of September 11, more security measures have been put into place to protect international shipping. The president of the World Shipping Council warns that the possibility of terrorist intervention is high, particularly for container trade. The explosion on the French tanker *Limburg* off the coast of Yemen in October 2002 brings this threat to light.[31]

Three trends favor the airfreight business over ocean freight: more frequent shipments, lighter-weight shipments, and higher-value shipments. The trend toward global manufacturing, which we will discuss in Chapter 18, and shrinking product life cycles have created a boom in airfreight traffic. Airfreight is much more effective in accomplishing these trends than is ocean freight. Higher-value shipments are more likely to use airfreight as long as they are not too bulky, because the exporter wants to get the product into the hands of the importer as soon as possible and collect on the sale. In most cases, the exporter cannot get paid for the sale until delivery is completed. Federal Express and United Parcel Service have launched ad campaigns targeted at small businesses to promote their shipping services. In UPS's new campaign, it announces that it can provide services to small companies in logistics, freight forwarding, customs clearance, technology, and finance.[32]

Factors favoring airfreight over ocean freight: more frequent shipments, lighter-weight shipments, higher-value shipments

Export Documentation

Freight forwarders also can help exporters fill out exporting documents. One of these documents is an **export license**. Each country determines whether domestic products or products transshipped through its borders can be exported to certain countries. In the United States, an exporter needs to check with the U.S. Department of Commerce to determine if its products can be shipped under a general license or if they must be exported under an individually validated license (IVL). For example, exports of certain high-tech products might be restricted for national security reasons, so an exporter must apply for an IVL to determine whether the exportation is permitted.

An export license allows products to be shipped to specific countries.

Of the many documents that must be completed, some of the most important (excluding financial documents, which we discuss in the next section) follow.

Key export documents are pro forma invoice, commercial invoice, bill of lading, consular invoice, certificate of origin, shipper's export declaration, and export packing list.

A *pro forma invoice* is an invoice, like a letter of intent, from the exporter to the importer that outlines the selling terms, price, and delivery if the goods are actually shipped. If the importer likes the terms and conditions, it will send a purchase order and arrange for payment. At that point, the exporter can issue a commercial invoice.

A *commercial invoice* is a bill for the goods from the buyer to the seller. It contains a description of the goods, the address of buyer and seller, and delivery and payment terms. Many governments use this form to assess duties.

A *bill of lading* is a receipt for goods delivered to the common carrier for transportation, a contract for the services rendered by the carrier, and a document of title.

A *consular invoice* is sometimes required by countries as a means of monitoring imports. Governments can use the consular invoice to monitor prices of imports and to generate revenue for the embassies that issue the consular invoice.

A *certificate of origin* indicates where the products originate and usually is validated by an external source, such as the chamber of commerce. It helps countries determine the specific tariff schedule for imports.

A *shipper's export declaration* is used by the exporter's government to monitor exports and to compile trade statistics.

An *export packing list* itemizes the material in each individual package, indicates the type of package, and is attached to the outside of the package. The shipper or freight forwarder, and sometimes customs officials, use the packing list to determine the nature of the cargo and whether the correct cargo is being shipped.

EXPORT FINANCING

From the exporter's point of view, there are four major issues that relate to the financial aspects of exporting: (1) the price of the product, (2) the method of payment, (3) the financing of receivables, and (4) insurance.

Product Price

Product pricing of exports entails many of the same factors that managers consider in pricing their products for domestic markets. But as we saw in Chapter 16, there also are differences, such as taking exchange rates into consideration. If the exporter bills in its own home-country currency, the importer absorbs the foreign-exchange risk and must decide whether to pass on any possible exchange-rate differences to the consumer. If the exporter bills in the currency of the importer's country, the foreign-exchange risk falls on the exporter. For example, Cooley Distillery of Ireland prices in euros in Europe, British pounds in the United Kingdom, and U.S. dollars elsewhere. It absorbs all of the exchange risk itself, although it has some expenses in British pounds and U.S. dollars that it can use to offset its revenues in pounds and dollars. Another difference between domestic and export pricing is that export prices tend to escalate from transportation costs, duties, multiple wholesale channels in the importing countries, the cost of insurance, and banking costs.

Finally, the export's price may depend on dumping laws in the importing country. Recall from Chapter 6 that dumping is the sale of exports below cost or below what they sell for in the domestic market. Developing countries, led by China and India, are increasingly filing antidumping charges against bigger nations, particularly the United States. Whereas only a handful of cases were filed in the 1980s, over 700 cases were filed in the last half of the 1990s. In mid-2002, U.S. exporters had 90 active investigations and 89 penalty tariffs. Among companies under scrutiny by developing countries in 2002 were Amana, International Paper, Dow Chemical, 3M, and Bristol-Myers Squibb.[33] An exporter must be aware of the dumping laws in each foreign market and the degree to which these laws are enforced.

Method of Payment

The flow of money across national borders is complex and requires the use of special documents. Exporters and importers must deal in foreign exchange, and the transfer of funds from one bank to another across national borders can be complicated and can take time.

Financial issues related to exporting:

- Product price
- Method of payment
- Financing of receivables
- Insurance

Export pricing is influenced by

- Exchange rates
- Transportation costs
- Duties
- Multiple wholesale channels
- Insurance costs
- Banking costs
- Antidumping laws

Methods of payments are

- Cash in advance
- Letter of credit
- Draft or bill of exchange
- Open account

In descending order in terms of security to the exporter, the basic methods of payment for exports are

Cash in advance
Letter of credit
Draft or bill of exchange
Open account

When an individual or a company pays a bill in a domestic setting, it typically uses a check. This is also known as a *draft* or a commercial *bill of exchange*. A draft is an instrument in which one party (the drawer) directs another party (the drawee) to make a payment. The drawee can either be a company like the importer or a bank. In the latter case, the draft would be considered a bank draft. Documentary drafts and documentary letters of credit are often used to protect both the buyer and the seller. They require that payment be made based on the presentation of documents conveying the title. If the exporter requests payment to be made immediately, the draft is called a *sight draft*. If the payment is to be made later—for example, 30 days after delivery—the instrument is called a *time draft*. A time draft is more flexible to the importer and more risky to the exporter because the longer the exporter has to wait for the money, the more likely something could go wrong, making it difficult or impossible for the importer to pay. In addition, if the exporter is assuming the foreign-exchange risk, the risk increases as the time increases. A time draft drawn on a bank and bearing the bank's promise to pay at a future date is known as a *banker's acceptance*. Banks assist in establishing and collecting a draft and usually charge the exporter a modest fee that ranges from about one-eighth to one-quarter percent of the value of the draft, with a minimum of $35 to $75 and a maximum of $150 to $200.

Documentary draft—an instrument instructing the importer to pay the exporter if certain documents are presented

Sight draft—payments must be made immediately

Time draft—payment is to be made at a future date

With a bill of exchange, it is always possible the importer will not be able to make payment to the exporter at the agreed-upon time. A **letter of credit** (**L/C**), however, obligates the buyer's bank in the importing country to honor a draft presented to it, provided the draft is accompanied by the prescribed documents. However, the exporter still needs to be sure that the bank's credit is valid as well. The letter of credit can be a forgery, issued by a "nonexistent bank." The exporter, even with the added security of the bank, still needs to rely on the importer's credit because of possible discrepancies that could arise in the transaction. A letter of credit does not eliminate foreign-exchange risk if the sale is denominated in a currency other than that of the exporter's country. However, a letter of credit denominated in the exporter's currency means the exporter incurs no risk of loss as a result of possible exchange-rate fluctuations. As with a draft, a letter of credit may be issued at sight or time. Even in the case of a letter of credit drawn with a sight draft, it may take two or three days for the cash to clear, so the exporter's collecting bank might be able to extend immediate credit to the exporter. In addition, the exporter might try to discount the letter of credit (sell it to someone else at less than face value) to get instant access to cash.

A letter of credit obligates the buyer's bank to pay the exporter.

When an exporter requires a letter of credit, the importer is responsible for arranging for it at the importer's bank. Figure 17.4 explains the relationships among the parties to a letter of credit. A letter of credit can be revocable or irrevocable. A revocable letter of credit is one that can be changed by any of the parties. However, both exporter and importer may prefer an irrevocable letter of credit (see Figure 17.5), which is a letter that cannot be canceled or changed in any way without the consent of all parties to the transaction. With this type of L/C, the importer's bank is obligated to pay and is willing to accept any drafts (bills of exchange) at sight, meaning these drafts will be paid as soon as the correct documents are presented to the bank. As noted earlier, an L/C can also be issued at time. The exporter must adhere precisely to all of the conditions on the letter of credit—such as the method of transportation and the description of the merchandise—otherwise, the letter of credit will not be paid without approval of all parties to an elimination of the discrepancies. The L/C

A revocable letter of credit may be changed by any of the parties to the agreement. An irrevocable letter of credit requires all parties to agree to a change in the documents.

FIGURE 17.4   Letter-of-Credit Relationships

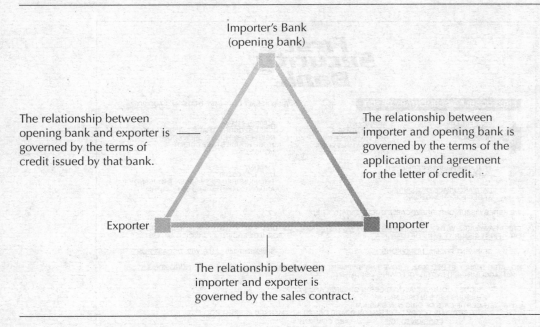

Importer's Bank
(opening bank)

The relationship between opening bank and exporter is governed by the terms of credit issued by that bank.

The relationship between importer and opening bank is governed by the terms of the application and agreement for the letter of credit.

Exporter

Importer

The relationship between importer and exporter is governed by the sales contract.

A letter of credit guarantees the exporter that the importer's bank will pay for the imports. The credit relationship exists between the importer and the importer's bank (the opening bank). A confirmed letter of credit has an added guarantee from the exporter's bank: If the importer's bank defaults, the exporter's bank must pay.

Source: Adapted from *Export and Import Financing Procedures* (Chicago: The First National Bank of Chicago), 22.

in Figure 17.5 is a hard-copy, typed L/C, but First Security Bank and many other banks are now issuing L/Cs electronically. They can establish an L/C system template on the customer's system that allows them to submit the L/C to the bank, and the bank can then transfer the L/C electronically to the overseas supplier—which is faster than filling out a paper copy, taking it to the bank, and mailing it to the overseas supplier.

A letter of credit transaction may include a confirming bank in addition to the parties mentioned previously. With a **confirmed letter of credit**, the exporter has the guarantee of an additional bank, sometimes in the exporter's home country, sometimes in a third country. It rarely happens that the exporter establishes the confirming relationship. Usually, the opening bank seeks the confirmation of the L/C with a bank with which it already has a credit relationship. If this letter of credit is irrevocable, none of the conditions can be changed unless all four parties to it agree in advance.

An exporter occasionally may sell on **open account**. The necessary shipping documents are mailed to the importer before any payment from or definite obligation on the part of the buyer. Releasing goods in this manner is somewhat unusual because the exporter risks default by the buyer. An exporter ordinarily sells under such conditions only if it has successfully conducted business with the importer for an extended time. This is generally the arrangement when the importer and exporter are members of the same corporate group.

A confirmed irrevocable letter of credit adds an obligation to pay for the exporter's bank.

Open account—the exporter bills the importer but does not require formal payment documents; usually for members of the same corporate group

Financing Receivables

The increased distances and time of exporting can create cash flow problems for the exporter. This is especially true if the exporter extends payment through a time draft.

Because exporting is risky, banks often are unwilling to provide funding for it. This is a major problem for small exporters that do not have the working capital to sustain themselves between production and payment. These companies complain that banks will not fund small needs for working capital arising from exporting but provide funding readily to domestic clients that are greater credit risks. Small exporters need to find a way to access funds or guarantee their export revenues so that banks will lend them working capital.

FIGURE 17.5   An Irrevocable Export Letter of Credit

A letter of credit is a precisely worded document whose terms must be adhered to in order for the exporter to receive payment.

Source: First Security Bank, N.A. Reprinted with permission.

First Security Bank®

| **IRREVOCABLE DOCUMENTARY CREDIT** | ISSUED IN SALT LAKE CITY, UTAH ON 1 AUG 2002 |

MAIL TO

BENEFICIARY
XYZ COMPANY
HONG KONG

APPLICANT
ABC COMPANY
123 ANY STREET
ANY TOWN, UT 99999

ADVISING BANK
FIRST SECURITY TRADE SERVICES LTD.
NEW HENRY HOUSE, 3RD FLOOR
10 ICE HOUSE STREET CENTRAL
HONG KONG

TRANSSHIPMENTS PERMITTED
PARTIAL SHIPMENTS PERMITTED

AMOUNT
USD $257,000.00
TWO HUNDRED FIFTY SEVEN THOUSAND
AND 00/100 UNITED STATES DOLLARS

DATE AND PLACE OF EXPIRY
31 DEC 2002, HONG KONG

WE HEREBY ISSUE OUR IRREVOCABLE DOCUMENTARY CREDIT

CREDIT AVAILABLE WITH ___ANY BANK___ BY _NEGOTIATION_ OF DRAFT AT ___30 DAYS B/L DATE___ DRAWN ON __FIRST SECURITY BANK OF UTAH, N.A.__ FOR 100 PERCENT OF INVOICE AMOUNT.

SHIPMENT FROM: __HONG KONG__   SHIPMENT TO: __U.S. WEST COAST PORT__

NO LATER THAN: __01 DEC 2002__ COVERING SHIPMENT OF __GENERAL MERCHANDISE__ FOB __HONG KONG__
WHEN ACCOMPANIED BY THE FOLLOWING DOCUMENTS:

- 2 SIGNED COMMERCIAL INVOICES IN ORIGINAL AND 1 COPY
- 2 PACKING LISTS IN ORIGINAL
- 1 CERTIFICATE OF ORIGIN IN ORIGINAL
- FULL SET PLUS 1 COPY OF CLEAN ON BOARD OCEAN B/L'S MARKED FREIGHT COLLECT

CONSIGNED TO:
ABC COMPANY
1234 SOUTHWEST LANE
SALT LAKE CITY, UT 84111

NOTIFY:
FORWARDING COMPANY, INC.
AMELIA EARHART DRIVE
SALT LAKE CITY, UT 84101

SPECIAL CONDITIONS:
- DOCUMENTS MUST BE PRESENTED TO PAYING/NEGOTIATING BANK WITHIN 21 DAYS AFTER THE DATE OF SHIPMENT HOWEVER WITHIN VALIDITY OF LETTER OF CREDIT.
- DOCUMENTS MUST BE PRESENTED IN ONE MAIL.
- INSURANCE COVERED BY BUYER.
ALL CHARGES EXCEPT THE OPENING BANK'S CHARGES ARE FOR THE ACCOUNT OF THE BENEFICIARY.

NOTE THAT WE WILL ASSESS A DISCREPANCY FEE OF USD40.00 ON EACH PRESENTATION OF DOCUMENTS CONTAINING DISCREPANCIES.

REIMBURSEMENT INSTRUCTIONS:
VIA REGISTERED MAIL TO:
FIRST SECURITY BANK OF UTAH, N.A.
INTERNATIONAL DEPARTMENT
41 EAST 100 SOUTH
P.O. BOX 30004
SALT LAKE CITY, UT 84130

CONFIRMATION INSTRUCTIONS:
WITHOUT ADDING YOUR CONFIRMATION.

WE HEREBY ENGAGE WITH DRAWERS, ENDORSERS, AND BONA FIDE HOLDERS THAT DRAFTS DRAWN AND NEGOTIATED IN CONFORMITY WITH THE TERMS OF THIS CREDIT WILL BE DULY HONORED ON PRESENTATION AND THAT DRAFTS ACCEPTED WITHIN THE TERMS OF THIS CREDIT WILL BE DULY HONORED AT MATURITY. EACH DRAFT MUST BE ENDORSED ON THE REVERSE THEREOF BY THE NEGOTIATING BANK. THE AMOUNT OF EACH DRAFT MUST BE ENDORSED ON THE REVERSE OF THIS CREDIT BY THE NEGOTIATING BANK.

THE NUMBER OF THE CREDIT AND THE NAME OF OUR BANK MUST BE QUOTED ON ALL DRAFTS REQUIRED. IF THE CREDIT IS AVAILABLE BY NEGOTIATION, THE AMOUNT OF EACH DRAWING MUST BE ENTERED ON THE REVERSE OF THIS CREDIT BY THE NEGOTIATING BANK.

THIS CREDIT IS SUBJECT TO THE UNIFORM CUSTOMS AND PRACTICE FOR DOCUMENTARY CREDITS, 1993 REVISION, INTERNATIONAL CHAMBER OF COMMERCE, PUBLICATION NO. 500.

AUTHORIZED SIGNATURE(S)

First Security Bank - Financial Services Division - 41 East 100 South - Salt Lake City, Utah 84111
Telephone (801) 246-5334 - SWIFT Address: FSBUUS55

Exporters can get financing from banks and through factoring or forfaiting.

Factoring—the discounting of a foreign account receivable

However, there are many other funding sources that exporters can access, both public and private.[34] Exporters can get access to funds through **factoring** and **forfaiting**. Factoring is the discounting of a foreign account receivable. Basically, the factoring company is a finance provider in situations in which a bank may be hesitant to lend money to the exporter. The exporter turns over its export receivables, sometimes for a small administrative fee, to the factor. In return, the factor gives the exporter about 80 to 85 percent of value of the receivables up front and then collects the debt itself, paying the balance to the exporter after collecting the debt.[35] Pinnacle Display, a British start-up printer company, accessed funds this way. When Pinnacle first started, it desperately needed working capital, but the banks wouldn't lend it any money, even though it had a lot of firm orders from reputable clients. A factoring company bought Pinnacle's high-end receivables (those from the best customers) and advanced the company some funds to help it out of its desperate situation. It worked out fine, and Pinnacle Display has been growing strongly ever since.[36]

Forfaiting is similar to factoring. Typically, a forfaiter buys from an exporter the debt due from its customer, usually in the form of a promissory note or bill of exchange. A bank in the importer's country usually guarantees these instruments. This allows the exporter to get paid immediately and is usually a cheaper form of payment for the importer than if it had to borrow from a bank or get credit extended to it by the exporter. An example of forfaiting involves International Remote Imaging Systems (IRIS), a U.S.-based manufacturer of medical equipment. The company sold $750,000 worth of equipment to medical labs in Turkey. However, IRIS needed to extend credit to the importer for two years because of the order's size. To receive payment sooner, IRIS found a Turkish bank willing to guarantee the note receivable from the Turkish importer and then sold the receivable to a forfaiter, thus allowing it to get paid right away.

> Forfaiting—similar to factoring but usually for longer time periods and with a guarantee from a bank in the importer's country.

In addition, exporters can apply for guarantees from government agencies, such as the Small Business Association (SBA) (www.sba.gov) and the Export-Import Bank of the United States, in order to get banks to loan them money while waiting for receivables. The Ex-Im Bank is an independent federal agency that supports the export of U.S. goods and services through loan guarantees and insurance programs. In 2001, Ex-Im Bank supported $12.5 billion of U.S. exports and more than 2,000 U.S. companies. Ex-Im Bank offers four programs. (1) working capital guarantees, (2) export credit insurance, (3) guarantees of commercial loans to foreign buyers, and (4) direct loans to foreign buyers.[37] The bank does not compete with commercial lenders, but it assumes the risks they cannot accept. It always must have a reasonable assurance of repayment. The programs are open to companies of all sizes, and enhancements have been made in some programs to support environmental goods and services. However, the Ex-Im Bank has favored the large exporters, such as Boeing, even though it tries to help out the little exporter too.

> Government agencies, such as the Export-Import Bank in the United States, can provide direct loans to exporters or guarantee foreign receivables so that exporters can get bank financing of receivables.

Ex-Im Bank's working capital guarantees cover 90 percent of the principal and interest on commercial loans to creditworthy small and medium-size companies. With the guarantees, lenders can provide funds on a single project or revolving-credit basis. Export credit insurance policies protect against both political and commercial risks, thus keeping a foreign buyer from defaulting on payment. The insurance helps exporters finance receivables more easily by assigning the policy's proceeds to the lender. Guarantees of commercial loans to foreign buyers of U.S. goods or services cover 100 percent of principal and interest against political and commercial risks of nonpayment. Direct loans can also be made to foreign buyers of U.S. goods. The bank was reauthorized by President Bush in June 2002 to remain open until September 2006, when authorization will be reviewed again.[38]

Insurance

There are two kinds of insurance that are used most often in exports. The first kind of insurance covers the transportation of products. Damaging weather conditions, rough handling by carriers, and other hazards to cargo make insurance an important protection for exporters.[39] The terms of sale determine whether the exporter or the importer is responsible for the insurance, and that should affect the cost of the export. Marine cargo insurance and air carrier insurance should be purchased to protect against damage or loss.

> Two types of export insurance
> - Insurance on transportation risks, such as weather or rough handling by carriers
> - Political, commercial, and foreign-exchange risk that might keep the exporter from collecting from the importer

The second type of insurance covers political, commercial, and foreign-exchange risk. Some private sector insurance companies will cover these types of risks for established exporters with a proven track record, but government agencies tend to be the most important insurer for these risks. In the United States, for example, the Ex-Im Bank offers commercial and political risk insurance. Political risks include war and expropriation. Commercial risks arise from buyer default and insolvency. Foreign-exchange risk arises when a fall in the value of the foreign currency results in the exporter receiving less of their own currency. Insurance premiums are based on the risk of the transaction, including the country where the risk has been incurred. The Ex-Im Bank awarded insurance to Environmental Dynamics Inc. (EDI), a small U.S. company, so that EDI could expand its business internationally. The insurance enabled EDI to offer competitive credit terms to a large customer base while minimizing foreign risk. In 2000, EDI increased foreign sales by 200 percent in over 30 countries.[40]

COUNTERTRADE

Countertrade is when goods and services are traded for each other.

Countries sometimes have so much difficulty generating enough foreign exchange to pay for imports that they need to devise creative ways to get the products they want. Reasons for not generating enough foreign exchange could be that the country's currency is nonconvertible, the country doesn't have enough cash, or it doesn't have sufficient lines of credit. Both companies and governments often must find creative ways of settling payment, such as trading goods for goods as part of the transaction. Countertrade is any one of several different arrangements by which goods and services are traded for each other. Countertrade can be divided into two basic types: barter based on clearing arrangements used to avoid money-based exchange; and buybacks, offsets, and counterpurchase, which are used to impose reciprocal commitments.[41] Countertrade has also been called a hostage exchange, as opposed to a contract exchange, because it creates artificial bonds and dependencies specific to transactions.[42]

It is difficult to know how big the countertrade market is. Estimates in the past have ranged from 10 to 40 percent of total exports, but that figure is difficult to verify. Countertrade generally increases in economies that are experiencing economic fallouts. Countertrade increased in Asia in 1997 as a result of the Asian financial crisis. In Argentina, countertrade among common citizens has increased due to a severe shortage of cash.[43] There are several types of countertrade, but the three most common are barter, buybacks, and offset.

Barter

Barter occurs when goods or services are traded for goods or services.

Barter, the oldest form of countertrade, is a transaction in which goods or services are traded for goods or services of equal value without any flow of cash. In 2002, Thailand and Indonesia signed a $40 million deal in which Indonesia would supply Thailand with an agricultural aircraft, train carriages, and fertilizer in exchange for Thai rice.[44] There are barter firms that act as an intermediary between the exporter and importer, often taking title to the goods received by the exporter for a price or selling the goods for a fee and a percentage of the sales value.

Buybacks—products the exporter receives as payment that are related to or originate from the original export

Buybacks are products the exporter receives as payment that are related to or originate from the original export. An example would be one in which a company exports capital equipment for a country's mining operation and receives as payment minerals that it can sell on world markets. Consider a specific example: PepsiCo provided Pepsi syrup to state-owned bottling plants in Russia and received Stolichnya vodka, which it marketed in the West.

Offset Trade

Another type of countertrade, called **offset trade**, is becoming increasingly important. Offset trade occurs when an exporter sells products for cash and then helps the importer find opportunities to earn hard currency. Offsets are most often used for big-ticket items, such as military sales. The Czech government recently announced that in competition for its jet fighter procurement, offset would be the deciding factor as opposed to technical and performance criteria and price.[45] Offset arrangements are usually one of two types.

1. Direct offsets include any business that relates directly to the export. Generally, the exporter seeks contractors in the importer's country to joint-venture or coproduce certain parts if applicable. For example, an aircraft exporter could partner with a company in the importer's country to manufacture components that would be used in the manufacture of the aircraft.

2. Indirect offsets include all business unrelated to the export. Generally, the exporter is asked by the importer's government to buy a country's goods or invest in an unrelated business.[46] Some of the most common direct offset practices in military sales include coproduction, licensed production, subcontractor production, overseas investment, and technology transfer. Examples of indirect offsets might include assisting in the export of unrelated products from the host country or generating tourist revenues for the host country.

Figure 17.6 shows how a complex transaction might be structured. As noted in the figure, the transaction involves the primary exporter, the importing government, and other secondary exporters and importers.

Whether companies get into the complexities of offset trade depends mainly on the demand for their products, whether they have alternative sources of supply, and the extent of foreign-exchange problems in the buying country. In any case, offset trade results primarily from foreign-exchange shortages and is a good example of how companies and governments can compensate for such a shortage through creative business transactions.

> In offset trade, the exporter sells goods for cash but then undertakes to promote exports from the importing country in order to help it earn foreign exchange.

FIGURE 17.6 An Offset Transaction

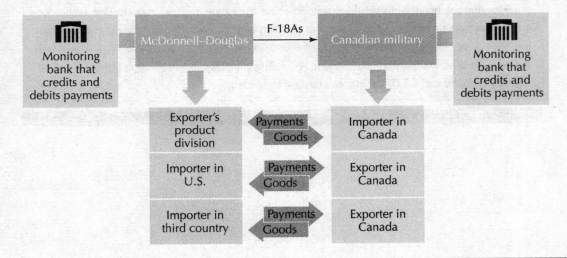

In this form of countertrade, the exporter is required to find ways for the importing country to earn foreign exchange to pay for the exports.

Source: From Pompiliu Verzariu, *Countertrade, Barter, Offsets,* ©1985, New York: McGraw-Hill. Reprinted by permission of The McGraw-Hill Companies.

ETHICAL DILEMMA

Is Demand Always Just Cause to Export?

There are several ethical issues in exporting. Two of them are the exportation of hazardous substances and whether or not to sell sensitive technology to countries that could be or are enemies to the exporter's domestic country. Concerning the exportation of hazardous substances, especially pesticides and chemicals, most people feel that exporting companies should accept the ethical norms of a host country. However, regulations concerning pesticides are more lax in many developing countries than they are in industrial countries. So exporting pesticides or harmful chemicals that are illegal in a company's home country but not in the host country leads to an ethical dilemma. There is a major argument over the concept of prior informed consent (PIC), which would require each exporter of a banned or restricted chemical to obtain through its home-country government the express consent of the importing country to receive the banned or restricted substance. Countries favoring the PIC concept argue that many developing countries are not adequately informed of the danger of certain chemicals and, therefore, need the assistance of industrial countries. Those against PIC argue that this principle infringes on the national sovereignty of importing countries and replaces their ethical norms with those of the exporting country.[47]

Second, governments often control the export of so-called sensitive technology to certain countries, but there are a number of companies that try to bypass the controls and sell the technology to whomever will buy it. Before the Iron Curtain fell in 1989, Toshiba shipped to the former Soviet Union sensitive technology that could be used in submarine warfare. The company transshipped products through different ports in order to disguise the sale and shield itself from prosecution. However, this illegal activity was eventually uncovered. Another example of the exportation of sensitive technology involves the arming of Saddam Hussein prior to the Persian Gulf War. A British company was found guilty of exporting a large gun, disguised as industrial pipes, that could be used as an offensive weapon. The company lied about the nature of the export but eventually was found out. In addition, German companies were guilty of selling to Libya chemicals that could be used in chemical warfare. In these cases, documents were falsified to keep the authorities from finding out about the transactions' true nature.

Sometimes shippers lie to freight forwarders about the nature of their products. One freight forwarder was working with a company that was shipping large drums to Sweden by air. The forwarder asked the shipper if the drums contained hazardous materials, and the shipper said no. In fact, unfortunately, the drums contained a very toxic material. This substance leaked through the drum and ate through the bottom of a 747 just as it was landing in Sweden.

LOOKING TO THE FUTURE

How Will Technology Affect Exporting?

Exporting continues to differ among countries in terms of its importance in generating GDP and, therefore, jobs. When the global economy is growing and barriers come down, exports tend to increase. When the world is in an economic slowdown, nontariff barriers to trade combine with low demand to slow the rate of export growth. Predictions of export activity are directly tied to predictions of economic growth. Future economic growth is tied to efforts to reduce trade barriers. Examples of these efforts are the EU and NAFTA. When barriers to trade rise, exporters from large countries such as the United States pull back their exporting efforts and focus on domestic markets.

Advances in transportation and communications will continue to facilitate export growth and make it easier for companies to reach international markets. One example of advances in communication is electronic data interchange, the electronic movement of information. As freight forwarders continue to automate, they become better able to transmit documents electronically, which will reduce border delays in getting goods to market. Also, advances in communications will allow shippers to track shipments more accurately so that they can predict when the shipments will arrive in port to be claimed by the importer.

An area in which companies probably will receive little relief in the next few years is government assistance, especially in the financial area. Most industrial countries have serious federal budget deficits, a result of the economic slowdown and reduced tax receipts, and so they have been forced to privatize and cut government services. One of those areas affected will be exports. In the United States, cutbacks in funding to the Department of Commerce, the SBA, and the Ex-Im Bank have made it more difficult for exporters to get assistance—especially access to loan guarantees. Predictions say this situation will not improve soon; the pressure to penetrate markets alone will continue on the small exporter.

One of the major developments in the future will be the use of the Internet, which will allow companies to engage in direct exporting. E-commerce will bring together producers and consumers from all over the world in ways and at a level never before seen. Small and medium-size companies that cannot afford to have a large export staff will be able to generate Internet sales relatively easily and cheaply. This will be one of the major developments in exporting and importing.

Summary

- The probability of a company's becoming an exporter increases with company size, but the extent of exporting does not directly correlate with size.

- Companies export to increase sales revenues, use excess capacity, and diversify markets.

- Companies new to exporting (and also some experienced exporters) often make many mistakes. One way to avoid mistakes is to develop a comprehensive export strategy that includes an analysis of the company's resources as well as its export potential.

- As a company establishes its export business plan, it must assess export potential, obtain expert counseling, select a country or countries where it will focus its exports, formulate its strategy, and determine how to get its goods to market.

- Importers need to be concerned with strategic issues (why import rather than buy domestically) and procedural issues (what are the steps that need to be followed to get goods into the country).

- Customs agencies assess and collect duties, as well as ensure that import regulations are adhered to.

- Exporters may deal directly with agents or distributors in a foreign country or indirectly through third-party intermediaries, such as export management companies or other types of trading companies. Internet marketing is a new form of direct exporting that is allowing many small and medium-size companies to access export markets as never before.

- Trading companies, can perform many of the functions for which manufacturers lack the expertise. In addition, exporters can use the services of other specialists, such as freight forwarders, to facilitate exporting. These specialists can help an exporter with the complex documentation that accompanies exports.

- There are four major issues in the financial aspects of exporting—the price of the product, the method of payment, the financing of receivables, and insurance.

- Export prices are a function of domestic pricing pressures, the impact of exchange rates, price escalation due to longer channels of distribution, duties, multiple wholesale channels, cost of insurance, banking costs, and antidumping laws.

- In descending order in terms of security, the basic methods of payment for exports are cash in advance, letter of credit, draft, and open account.

- A letter of credit is a financial document that obligates the importer's bank to pay the exporter.

- Government agencies in some countries, such as the Ex-Im Bank in the United States, provide assistance in terms of direct loans to importers, bank guarantees to fund exporters' working capital needs, and insurance against commercial and political risk.

- Countertrade is any one of several different arrangements by which goods and services are traded for each other, on either a bilateral or a multilateral basis. Barter means trading goods or services for goods or services. Offsets are agreements by which the exporter helps the importer earn foreign exchange or the transfer of technology or production to the importing country.

CASE

Sunset Flowers of New Zealand, Ltd.[48]

After 18 months of residing in the United States, John Robertson, a New Zealander, glances frequently at a map of the United States on his wall, wondering when he will get the time and resources to travel into the various metropolitan areas of the central, southern, and eastern states. Through such travel, he believes, he can gain an improved appreciation of the characteristics of the markets for fresh-cut flowers, an item that he began importing into the United States from New Zealand during his summer "vacation" from school.

In August, Robertson and his family left New Zealand for Seattle so that he could study for his MBA degree at the University of Washington. A month earlier, he had resigned from his job and leased the family house and small farm. On completion of the degree, the Robertsons intended to return to New Zealand, where John would seek employment in a senior management position with a company involved in exporting.

New Zealand is a country the size of Oregon, with a population of nearly four million in 2002. The relatively small size of its population base coupled with its distance from world markets (see Map 17.1) inhibits its ability to establish an industrial base competitive with those of the world's leading industrial countries. Therefore, New Zealand depends heavily on world trade, importing fuel and manufacturing products and gaining most of its foreign exchange through exports of agricultural produce. Its f.o.b. exports average around 22 percent of its GDP, compared with the U.S. figure of 12 percent. (The letters *f.o.b.* stand for "free on board," which includes the cost of the product to the city of export but excludes international shipping costs.) To hold its place in the world economy, New Zealand lobbies hard to remove the restrictions imposed on imported agricultural products by the EU, Japan, and the United States. Along with this campaign, efforts are being made to diversify into horticultural products such as fresh flowers and fruit.

Immediately prior to leaving New Zealand, Robertson had worked for almost four years as the financial manager of a company involved in growing, wholesaling, and exporting live ornamental trees and shrubs. To sell its products on world markets, the company used agents, including two who were based in the United States, one in Japan, and one in Europe. The agents were paid retainers and typically provided services for several exporters. The experience gained from working for this company provided Robertson with a background in the procedures necessary for exporting. It also gave him insight into the problems that exporters face when trying to compete in foreign markets, where control over representation is hindered by distance and lack of knowledge of business procedures.

It was while working for this company that Robertson was introduced to cut-flower products. The Robertsons raised enough money to purchase a farm and then became acquainted with their neighbors, the Pratts, who were first-class horticulturists. The Pratts had developed a new variety of the Leucadendron plant that yielded a beautiful, red leaflike flower, which the Robertsons and Pratts felt they could export successfully.

During their first year of production, the Robertsons and Pratts formed a new entrepreneurial venture. They exported their yield through an established export company whose principal line of business was exporting fresh fruit and vegetables. The company had a large market share of this business and also had assumed a significant share of the exports of cut flowers from New Zealand. The New Zealand cut-flower export industry was small and, with the exception of trade in orchids, immature. Export companies provided the many part-time cut-flower growers with the marketing infrastructure that the growers themselves were unable to put together.

As the harvesting season progressed, the returns paid to the venture by the exporter declined until they reached a point at which production levels of 10,000 stems or fewer became only marginally profitable. Gary Pratt and John Robertson met with the exporter to discuss the trends. The exporter explained that price was a function of volume and that the lower prices resulted from the increased volumes of cut flowers being placed on world markets. Export market returns were substantiated by documentation.

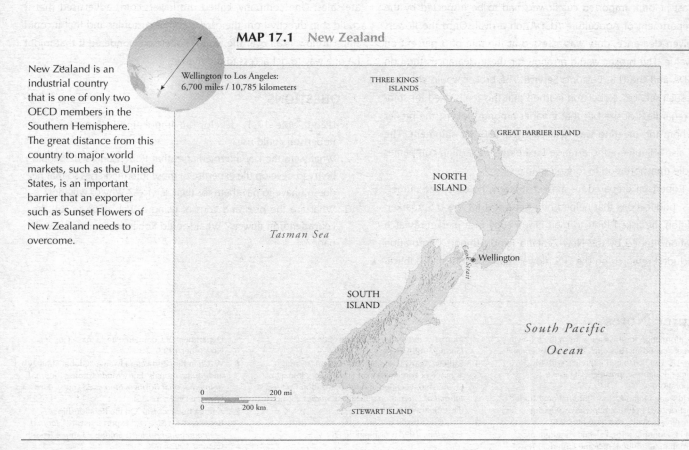

MAP 17.1 New Zealand

New Zealand is an industrial country that is one of only two OECD members in the Southern Hemisphere. The great distance from this country to major world markets, such as the United States, is an important barrier that an exporter such as Sunset Flowers of New Zealand needs to overcome.

Wellington to Los Angeles:
6,700 miles / 10,785 kilometers

THREE KINGS ISLANDS

GREAT BARRIER ISLAND

NORTH ISLAND

Tasman Sea

Cook Strait

● Wellington

SOUTH ISLAND

South Pacific Ocean

0   200 mi
0   200 km

STEWART ISLAND

Pratt and Robertson were not convinced by the explanation. However, they knew little about world markets for fresh-cut flowers, and they could only speculate as to the reasons for the price movements. As there were no other established cut-flower export companies to turn to, the only way to research the matter seemed to be to do so themselves. Robertson's move to the United States to get his MBA degree presented the opportunity to carry out some research there.

During his first semester of school, Robertson had little time to do research. At the end of the winter quarter, when he picked up a sample cart of Leucadendron flowers consigned by Pratt to him at Sea-Tac Airport, his ideas on how to approach the market were not yet defined. He took the flowers home and, on inspection, found that they had kept well in transit and that their quality was good.

In the six days remaining before school began again, Robertson decided to concentrate on researching the production and shipping costs associated with the product, production forecasts, import procedures, the basic structure of the U.S. cut-flower industry, and market reaction to the Leucadendron.

When he had picked up the samples from the airport, Robertson was told by airline officials that if he were going to undertake imports of invoice value greater than $250, he would have to engage the services of a customs broker. Presuming such brokers to be the experts on import procedures, he made an appointment with one. The broker was most helpful. Imported cut flowers had to be inspected by the U.S. Department of Agriculture (USDA) on arrival. Once the flowers were given clearance, duty was assessed at the rate of 8 percent on f.o.b. value. The broker would arrange for these clearances through the USDA and the U.S. Customs Service. The broker would charge a fee for such services. Robertson learned that this fee is fixed for shipments regardless of size but that it varies among brokers; the broker with whom the meeting was held charged $50 per shipment. The broker also volunteered to arrange for freight forwarding companies to handle transportation to foreign markets.

As Robertson prepared his market strategy, he consulted numerous U.S. publications that helped him get a feel for the U.S. market. In addition, he asked Pratt to mail him a copy of a market-research publication funded by the New Zealand Export-Import Corporation that included research on the U.S. flower market. From that publica-

tion, he learned that the major agricultural exports from New Zealand in order of importance were kiwifruit, apples, berryfruit, processed kiwifruit, flowers and plants, squash, frozen vegetables, and onions. So he knew that there were experienced cut-flower exporters and third-party intermediaries in New Zealand and that the world market for cut flowers was used to seeing New Zealand products. Robertson finally contacted a Seattle wholesaler who was willing to place a large order for flowers, provided he was given exclusive rights to distribute the flowers in Washington State. Robertson was pleased with the reaction from the wholesaler but wondered if he had made the approach after insufficient preparation. Had he underpriced the product? Was the wholesaler's credit sound? Were exclusive rights typically given in this industry, and should he have conceded them? Was the reaction one that is normal when a new product is shown to a market? Would repeat orders be placed? In addition to these market-related issues, there were administrative and organizational issues to consider. What should be his role in the marketing chain? Should he act as an agent taking a commission or buy from Pratt and resell the product? What form of organization should he establish?

Robertson also checked out some Web sites on cut flowers and noticed that several companies had great Web sites on cut flowers—that is, they had pictures of the products and used the site to generate sales. One company, called proflowers.com, advertised that it could ship directly from the grower to the customer and that it could ship cut flowers all over the world. Robertson wondered if that might be one way to get access to the market.

QUESTIONS

1. Using Table 17.1, develop an import-marketing plan that Robertson could use.
2. What were the key intermediaries that Robertson used? Should he try to develop the expertise of those intermediaries so that he doesn't have to pay them for their services? Why or why not?
3. What are the pros and cons of using a Web page to sell the Leucadendron flowers? What should Robertson put on his Web page?

Chapter Notes

1 The information for this case is from the following source: "Exporting Pays Off," *Business America* (May 17, 1993): 19; and interview with Mr. Patrick J. Calabrese, president of Grieve Corporation.
2 World Trade Organization, "International Trade Statistics 2001" (2001): http://www.wto.org/english/res_e/statis_e/statis_e.htm, 23.
3 John H. Dunning, "The Eclectic Paradigm of International Production: Some Empirical Tests,"

Journal of International Business Studies 19 (Spring 1988): 1–31.
4 Sanjeev Agarwal and Sridhar N. Ramaswami, "Choice of Foreign Market Entry Mode: Impact of Ownership, Location and Internalization Factors," *Journal of International Business Studies* 23, no. 1 (First Quarter 1992): 2–5.
5 U.S. Department of Commerce, *Guide to Exporting, 1998* (Washington, DC: U.S.

Department of Commerce and Unz & Co., Inc., November 1997), 3.
6 W. Chan Kim and Peter Hwang, "Global Strategy and Multinationals' Entry Mode Choice," *Journal of International Business Studies* 23, no. 1 (First Quarter 1992): 32–35.
7 Andrea Bonaccorsi, "On the Relationship Between Firm Size and Export Intensity," *Journal of International Business Studies* 23, no. 4 (Fourth Quarter 1992): 606.

8 Jonathan L. Calof, "The Relationship Between Firm Size and Export Behavior Revisited," *Journal of International Business Studies* 25, no. 2 (Second Quarter 1994): 367–87.

9 Paul Magnusson, "The Split-Up That's Slanting the Trade Deficit," *Business Week* (June 7, 1999): 38.

10 Leonidas C. Leonidou and Constantine S. Katsikeas, "The Export Development Process: An Integrative Review of Empirical Models," *Journal of International Business Studies* 27, no. 3 (Third Quarter 1996): 524–25.

11 "A San Diego Company Uses the Internet to Go Global," news on U.S. Department of Commerce Web site (August 18, 2002): http://www.usatrade.gov/website/website.nsf/WebBySubj/Main_WhatsNew081802.

12 "Most Common Mistakes of New-to-Export Ventures," *Business America* (April 16, 1984): 9.

13 Paul Beamish et al., "The Relationship Between Organizational Structure and Export Performance," *Management International Review* 39 (First Quarter 1999): 51.

14 See the homepage of U.S. Customs for an organizational chart and of specific responsibilities. See also "Mission Statement, Organizational Chart" (2002): www.customs.ustreas.gov/about/about.htm.

15 Ibid.; and U.S. Department of the Treasury, U.S. Customs Service, *Importing into the United States* (Washington, DC: U.S. Government Printing Office, September 1991), 41.

16 U.S. Department of Commerce, *A Basic Guide to Exporting, 1998,* op. cit., 19–25.

17 Interview with John Teeling, Executive Chairman of Cooley Distillery (2002).

18 Julie Meringer, "E-Commerce Next Wave: Productivity and Innovation," Forrester Research in a speech to the World Trade Organization in Geneva (April 22, 2002): http://www.wto.org/wto/english/tratop_e/devel_e/sem05_e/sem05_prog_e.htm.

19 A. J. Campbell, "Ten Reasons Why Your Business Should Use Electronic Commerce," *Business America* (May 1998): 12–14.

20 See U.S. Department of Commerce, *Guide to Exporting, 1998,* op. cit., 20; and Philip MacDonald, *Practical Exporting and Importing,* 2nd ed. (New York: Ronald Press, 1959), 30–40.

21 Courtney Fingar, "ABCs of EMCs," The Federation of International Trade Associations (July 2001): http://fita.org/emc.html.

22 "Basic Question: To Export Yourself or to Hire Someone to Do It for You?" *Business America* (April 27, 1987): 14–17.

23 Paola Hjelt, "The Fortune Global 500: The World's Largest Corporations," *Fortune* (July 22, 2002): http://www.fortune.com.

24 "Arco, Itochu Units to Purchase Coastal's Utah Coal Operations," PR Newswire (October 24, 1996). Available in LEXIS/NEXIS NEWS: CURNWS.

25 Ibid.

26 Assif Shameen, "Playing Korea's Recovery: The Trading Companies May Be One Way to Do It," *Asiaweek* (September 20, 1996): 66. Available in LEXIS/NEXIS NEWS: CURNWS.

27 "Middlemen in a Muddle," *The Economist* (May 23, 2002): www.economist.com.

28 U.S. Department of Commerce, *Guide to Exporting, 1998,* op. cit., 63.

29 Helen Richardson, "Freight Forwarder Basics: Contract Negotiation," *Transportation & Distribution* (May 1996). Available in LEXIS/NEXIS NEWS: CURNWS.

30 Ibid.

31 "In Peril on the Sea," *The Economist* (October 9, 2002): www.economist.com.

32 "UPS Unveils 'What Can Brown Do for You?' Ad Campaign," *Business First* (February 7, 2002): http://louisville.bizjoumals.com/louisville/stories/2002/02/04/daily35.html.

33 Paul Magnusson, "Commentary: A U.S. Trade Ploy That Is Starting to Boomerang," *Business Week* (July 29, 2002): www.businessweek.com.

34 See "Obtaining Financing," *Tradeport* (January 2000): www.tradeport.org/ts/financing/index.html.

35 Steve Marsh, "Factoring for the Millennium," *Credit Management* (December 1999): 34–35.

36 Ibid.

37 www.exim.gov (2002).

38 Ibid.

39 U.S. Department of Commerce, *Guide to Exporting, 1998,* op. cit., 66.

40 "Environmental Dynamics Inc. Is Ex-Im Bank Small Business Exporter of the Year," press release for Environmental Dynamics Inc. (April 5, 2001): http://www.wastewater.com/awards.html.

41 J. F. Hennart, "Some Empirical Dimensions of Countertrade," *Journal of International Business Studies,* 21 (1990): 243–70.

42 Chong Ju Choi, Soo Hee Lee, and Jai Boem Kim, "A Note on Countertrade: Contractual Uncertainty and Transaction Governance in Emerging Economies," *Journal of International Business Studies* 30, no. 1 (First Quarter 1999): 196.

43 See Jonathon Bell, "Plane Trading," *Airfinance Journal* (June 1998): 34–36; and Elizabeth Love/Quilmes, "Argentina: The Post-Money Economy," *Time* (February 5, 2002): http://www.time.com/time/world/article/0,8599,199474,00.html.

44 "Commodities: Thai Countertrade Deal Signed," Laksamana.net (June 10, 2002): http://www.laksamana.net/printcfm?id=2893.

45 Ross Davies, "A Deal with Strings Attached," *Financial Times* (July 17, 2002): www.ft.com.

46 American Countertrade Association, "Forms of Countertrade" (2002): www.countertrade.org/index.html.

47 Tom L. Beauchamp and Norman E. Bowie, *Ethical Theory and Business,* 4th ed. (Upper Saddle River, NJ: Prentice Hall, 1993), 514–15.

48 Adapted from Harry R. Knudson, "Sunset Flowers of New Zealand, Ltd.," *Journal of Management Case Studies* 1, no. 4 (Winter 1985). Reprinted with permission.

CHAPTER 18

GLOBAL MANUFACTURING AND SUPPLY CHAIN MANAGEMENT

Right mixture makes good mortar.

—ENGLISH PROVERB

OBJECTIVES

- To describe different dimensions of global manufacturing strategy
- To examine the elements of global supply chain management
- To show how quality affects the global supply chain
- To illustrate how supplier networks function
- To explain how inventory management is a key dimension of the global supply chain
- To present different alternatives for transporting products along the supply chain from suppliers to customers

CASE

Samsonite's Global Supply Chain[1]

Samsonite Corporation is a U.S.-based company that manufactures and distributes luggage all over the world. In fiscal year 2002, Samsonite generated $736.3 billion in revenues but incurred losses equal to $3.59 per share in 2002, $2.01 in 2001, and $2.53 in 2000. Samsonite was listed on the NASDAQ stock market, but it was delisted in January 2002 for failing to meet NASDAQ standards. Although Samsonite began in 1910 in Denver, Colorado, it took many years for it to become a global company. In 1963, Samsonite set up its first European operation in the Netherlands and later, in 1965, began production in Belgium. Shortly thereafter, it erected a joint-venture plant in Mexico to service the growing but highly protected Mexican market. By the end of the 1960s, Samsonite was manufacturing luggage in Spain and Japan as well. In addition to its manufacturing operations, Samsonite was selling luggage worldwide through a variety of distributors.

In the 1970s, business began to take off in Europe. In 1974, Samsonite developed its first real European product, called the Prestige Attaché, and business began to expand in Italy, causing it to rival Germany as Samsonite's biggest market in Europe. Although the U.S. market began to turn to softside luggage in the 1980s, the European market still demanded hardside luggage, so Samsonite developed a new hardside suitcase for Europe called the Oyster case. Then softside luggage began to increase in importance, although Europe was still considered a hardside market. In the 1980s, Samsonite opened a new plant in France to manufacture the Prestige Attaché and other key products.

With the fall of the Iron Curtain in the early 1990s, Samsonite purchased a Hungarian luggage manufacturer and began to expand throughout Eastern Europe. During this same time period, Samsonite established several joint-venture companies throughout Asia, including China, to extend its reach there.

To establish products of high quality, Samsonite embarked on two different programs. The first was an internal program in which Samsonite conducted a drop test, a tumble test, a wheel test, and a handle test to determine if its products were strong enough and of sufficient quality for customers. The second program was two different, independent quality-assurance tests.

1. The European-based ISO 9002 certification demonstrates how companies implement quality in their operations, discussed later in this chapter.
2. The GS Mark is the number-one government-regulated third-party product test market of Germany.

The GS Mark, Gepruefte Sicherheit (translated "Tested for Safety"), is designed to help companies comply with European product liability laws as well as other areas of quality and safety. To enhance quality, Samsonite introduced state-of-the art CAD-CAM machinery in its plants. Samsonite also introduced a manufacturing technique in which autonomous cells of about a dozen employees assembled a product from start to finish.

As noted in Map 18.1, Samsonite had six company-owned production facilities and one joint-venture production facility in Europe in 2002. In addition, it has subsidiaries, joint ventures, retail franchises, distributors, and agents set up to service the European market. Although Samsonite initially serviced the European markets through exports, the transportation costs were high, and the demand for luggage soared in Europe, so Samsonite decided to begin production in Belgium in 1965. In the early years, Samsonite had a decentralized supply chain, as illustrated in Figure 18.1, whereby it operated through different wholesale layers before it finally got the product to the retailers. As Samsonite's business grew, management decided to centralize its supply chain so that products were manufactured and shipped to a

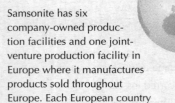

MAP 18.1   Samsonite's Production Facilities in Europe

Samsonite has six company-owned production facilities and one joint-venture production facility in Europe where it manufactures products sold throughout Europe. Each European country of operations is labeled here with Samsonite's corporate logo.

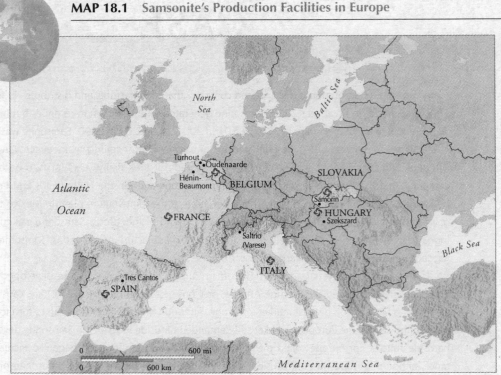

FIGURE 18.1   Samsonite's Decentralized Supply Chain (1965–1974)

In the early years of market penetration in Europe, Samsonite shipped luggage from its factories in Europe to factory warehouses, then to national warehouses. From there, luggage was shipped to wholesalers, who sold to retailers. This cumbersome distribution system lengthened the time it took to get product to retailers and increased the cost.

Source: F. De Beule and D. Van Den Bulcke, "The International Supply Chain Management of Samsonite Europe," Discussion Paper 1998/E/34, Centre for International Management and Development, University of Antwerp, p. 13.

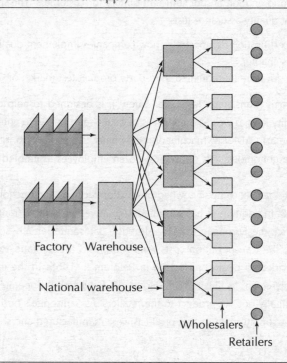

FIGURE 18.2   Samsonite's Centralized Supply Chain (1975–mid-1980s)

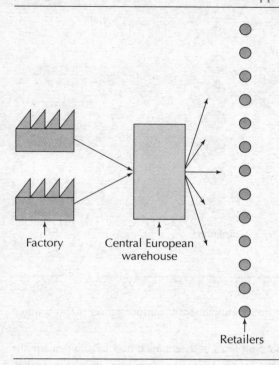

Factory   Central European
                   warehouse

Retailers

Samsonite decided to supply the European market by shipping products directly from the factory to a centralized European warehouse and from there to the retailers upon request.

Source: F. De Beule and D. Van Den Bulcke, "The International Supply Chain Management of Samsonite Europe." Discussion Paper No. 1998/E/34, Centre for International Management and Development, University of Antwerp, p. 14.

central European warehouse, which then directly supplied retailers upon request (see Figure 18.2). This centralized structure was put into place to eliminate the need to rely on wholesalers. Samsonite had to worry about transporting manufactured products to the warehouse, storing them, and transporting them to the retailers in the different European markets. Samsonite invested heavily in information technology to link the retailers to the warehouse and thereby manage its European distribution system more effectively. Retailers would place an order with a salesperson or the local Samsonite office in their area, and the order would be transmitted to the warehouse and shipping company by modem. The retail market in Europe began shifting at the turn of the century, so Samsonite responded by opening franchised retail outlets in October 2002 beginning in Antwerp and spreading to other areas. As the V.P. of marketing and sales put it, "We are anticipating a shift in the market, in which the traditional luggage channel will no longer be at the forefront and a wide new retail opportunity will emerge."

As noted earlier, Samsonite sold two basic types of suitcases: hardside and softside. Most of the R&D was initially done in the United States, but the need to develop products for the European market led the company to establish R&D facilities in Europe. Samsonite invested heavily in R&D and in the manufacture of specialized machinery to help keep a competitive edge. To facilitate the transportation and storage of suitcases, Samsonite located its production facilities close to the centralized warehouse. Softside luggage is less complex technologically, and Samsonite purchased Oda, the Belgium softside luggage company, to enter that market. Then it licensed its technology to other European companies. By the mid-1990s, 48 percent of Samsonite's sales came from hardside luggage, 22 percent from softside, and 30 percent from attaché cases and travel bags, some of which were hardside and some softside. However, the trend for hardside luggage in Europe is changing. By fiscal 2000, softside luggage comprised 51 percent of European sales. In 2001 and 2002, sales of softside luggage continued to increase as a percentage, and hardside luggage sales declined.

As Samsonite expanded throughout the world, it continued to manufacture its own products and license production to other manufacturers. Then Samsonite entered into subcontract arrangements in Asia and Eastern Europe. In Europe, the subcontractors provide final goods as well as the subassemblies used in

FIGURE 18.3   Samsonite's Global Supply Chain (1996–Present)

As Samsonite expanded production throughout Europe, it had to deal with subcontractors as well as its own factories. Its success in Europe was due to its ability to manage the supply chain from supplier to factory to warehouse to consumer.

Source: F. De Beule and D. Van Den Bulcke. "The International Supply Chain Management of Samsonite Europe," Discussion Paper No. 1998/E/34. Centre for International Management and Development. University of Antwerp, p. 21.

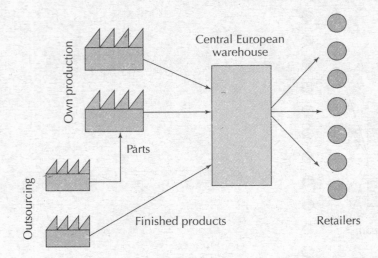

Samsonite factories. Figure 18.3 illustrates Samsonite's coordination of outsourced parts and finished goods, along with its own production.

Samsonite is a good example of the challenges a firm faces in determining how best to manage the supply chain from supplier to consumer. The greater the geographic spread of the company, the more challenging the management of the supply chain becomes.

INTRODUCTION

The Samsonite case illustrates a number of dimensions of the supply chain networks that link suppliers with manufacturers and customers. The objective of this chapter is to examine

The photo shows a worker in the foreign trade zone in Panama, a country that depends heavily on the international transshipment of goods and on international banking operations.

FIGURE 18.4   Global Manufacturing and Supply Chain Management in International Business

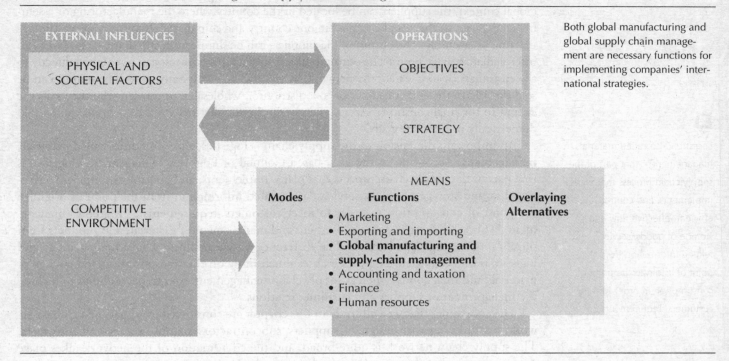

Both global manufacturing and global supply chain management are necessary functions for implementing companies' international strategies.

these different networks and how a company can manage the links most effectively to reach customers. As Figure 18.4 shows, global manufacturing and supply chain management is important in companies' international business strategies. We will start by discussing global manufacturing strategy and then move to supply chain management issues. In terms of global supply chain management, we will look at supplier networks, inventory management, and transportation networks.

A company's **supply chain** encompasses the coordination of materials, information, and funds from the initial raw material supplier to the ultimate customer.[2] It is the management of the value-added process from the suppliers' supplier to the customers' customer.[3]

Figure 18.5 illustrates the concept of a global supply chain. Suppliers can be part of the manufacturer's organizational structure, as would be the case in a vertically integrated company,

Supply chain—the coordination of materials, information, and funds from the initial raw material supplier to the ultimate customer

FIGURE 18.5   The Global Supply Chain

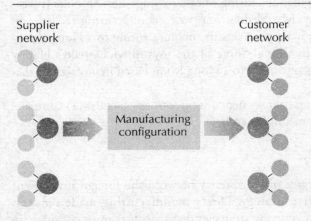

The global supply chain links the suppliers' supplier with the customers' customer, accounting for every step of the process between the raw material and the final consumer of the good or service.

or they can be independent of the company. The direct suppliers also have their networks. In a global context, the suppliers can be located in the country where the manufacturing or assembly takes place, or they can be located in one country and ship materials to the country of manufacture or assembly. The output of the suppliers can be shipped directly to the factory or to an intermediate storage point. The output of the manufacturing process can be shipped directly to the customers or to a warehouse network, as was the case with Samsonite. The output can be sold directly to the end consumer or to a distributor, wholesaler, or retailer, who then sells the output to the final consumer. As was the case in the supplier network, the output can be sold domestically or internationally.

An important dimension of the supply chain is **logistics**, also sometimes called **materials management**. According to the U.S.-based Council of Logistics Management, "logistics is that part of the supply chain process that plans, implements, and controls the efficient, effective flow and storage of goods, services, and related information from the point of origin to the point of consumption in order to meet customers' requirements."[4] Materials management is inbound logistics or the movement and management of materials and products from purchasing through production. The difference between supply chain management and logistics is one of degree. Logistics focuses much more on the transportation and storage of materials and final goods, whereas supply chain management extends beyond that to include the management of supplier and customer relations.

The companies that we will study in this chapter are considered to be part of a global network that links together designers, suppliers, subcontractors, manufacturers, and customers. The supply chain network is quite broad, and the coordination of the network takes place through interactions between firms in the networks.[5]

GLOBAL MANUFACTURING STRATEGIES

In the opening case, Samsonite initially exported to Europe, but it eventually set up Samsonite-Europe and established manufacturing facilities in different countries. Samsonite invested in Europe because of the location-specific advantages of the European market (big demand). It entered through foreign direct investment because it wanted to take advantage of the firm-specific assets that it possessed (an excellent product line and a solid manufacturing process) and internalize those advantages rather than sell them to an outside manufacturer.[6] Although Samsonite entered into some licensing agreements and subcontracted some manufacturing, the majority of its production, especially of its high-end hardside luggage, was kept under control of the company's network.

Although Samsonite engaged in its own manufacturing for the most part, it also subcontracted, or outsourced, manufacturing to other firms. Twenty-seven percent of *Fortune* 1000 companies outsource logistics and distribution.[7] Nike, for example, does not own any manufacturing facilities, but it subcontracts manufacturing to other companies. So Nike is basically a design and marketing company. Mattel does not own manufacturing facilities in China to manufacture Barbie dolls, but it subcontracts the manufacturing to a Hong Kong-based company that has investments in China. Some of the toys in McDonald's Happy Meals or Burger King meals are also subcontracted to a Hong Kong-based manufacturer that produces the toys in China.

The success of a global manufacturing strategy depends on four key factors: (1) compatibility, (2) configuration, (3) coordination, and (4) control.[8]

Manufacturing Compatibility

Compatibility in this context is the degree of consistency between the foreign investment decision and the company's competitive strategy. Direct manufacturing made sense in Samsonite's case but not in Nike's case. Company strategies that managers must consider are

---

Logistics (also called materials management)—that part of the supply chain process that plans, implements, and controls the efficient, effective flow and storage of goods, services, and related information from the point of origin to the point of consumption in order to meet customers' requirements

---

Compatibility—the degree of consistency between FDI decisions and a company's competitive strategy

- *Efficiency/cost*—reduction of manufacturing costs.
- *Dependability*—degree of trust in a company's products, its delivery, and price promises.
- *Quality*—performance reliability, service quality, speed of delivery, and maintenance quality of the product(s).
- *Flexibility*—ability of the production process to make different kinds of products and to adjust the volume of output.
- *Innovation*—ability to develop new products and ideas.[9]

Cost-minimization strategies and the drive for global efficiencies force MNEs to establish economies of scale in manufacturing, often by producing in areas with low-cost labor. This is one of the major reasons why many MNEs established manufacturing facilities in Asia, Mexico, and Eastern Europe. This type of foreign direct investment is known as offshore manufacturing, but clearly any manufacturing that takes place outside of a company's home country is considered "offshore." Offshore manufacturing escalated sharply in the 1960s and 1970s in the electronics industry as one company after another set up production facilities in the Far East, mostly in Taiwan and Singapore. Those locations were attractive because of low labor costs, the availability of cheap materials and components, and the proximity to markets. Even the athletic shoe market left the United States for Taiwan and Korea. As wages rose in Korea, however, manufacturing began to shift to other low-cost countries—China, Indonesia, Malaysia, Thailand, and Vietnam.

China particularly has become the hot spot for manufacturing and has even been termed by the *Wall Street Journal* as "the world's factory floor." It's output is so large and wide-ranging that it exerts deflationary pressure around the world on products such as textiles, TVs, and mobile phones. China is now the world's fourth largest industrial base behind the United States, Japan, and Germany. Many MNEs set up operations in China in the 1980s to capitalize on China's huge population and growing demand. Companies have now found that it is more cost-effective for them to manufacture products in China, not just for the local market but also for export to the rest of the world. Foreign companies with manufacturing facilities in China, such as General Electric, Toshiba, Siemens, Samsung, and General Motors, have expanded their focus from the local market to exports. Philips Electronics produces some of its products solely in China and plans to make China its global supply base, from which it will export its products around the world.[10]

Despite the popularity of manufacturing in one low-cost location, the need for responsiveness or *flexibility* because of differences in national markets may result in regional manufacturing to service local markets. As a company's competitive strategies change, so too do its manufacturing strategies. In addition, MNEs may adopt different strategies for different product lines, depending on the competitive priorities of those products.

Manufacturing Configuration

Next, the company's managers need to determine the configuration of manufacturing facilities. There are three basic configurations that MNEs consider as they establish a global manufacturing strategy. The first is to have centralized manufacturing and to offer a selection of standard, lower-priced products to different markets. That is basically a manufacture-and-export strategy. It is common for new-to-export companies to use this strategy, typically through their home-country manufacturing facilities. The second configuration is the use of regional manufacturing facilities to serve customers within a specific region. That is what Samsonite did initially in Europe with its production facilities in Belgium. Third, market expansion in individual countries, especially when the demand in those countries becomes significant, might argue for a multidomestic approach in which companies manufacture products close to their customers, using country-specific manufacturing facilities to meet local needs.[11] Although Samsonite did not manufacture in every country where it sold its

Key company strategies:

- Efficiency/cost
- Dependability
- Quality
- Flexibility
- Innovation

Cost-minimization strategies— economies of scale, low-cost labor areas

Offshore manufacturing—any investment that takes place in a country different from the home country

Manufacturing configuration

- Centralized manufacturing in one country
- Manufacturing facilities in specific regions to service those regions
- Multidomestic—facilities in each country

products, it divided its broad European regional strategy into smaller areas, setting up seven factories to manufacture products for the European market. Unless the company has manufacturing facilities in every country where it is doing business, it must combine exporting with manufacturing. In reality, MNEs choose a combination of these approaches depending on their product strategies.

Often, countries will also specialize in the production of parts or final goods, a process described in Chapter 8 as rationalization. When Samsonite opened a new factory in Hénin-Beaumont, France, in the 1980s, it manufactured the Prestige Attaché case and the Beauty case. Doing so allowed it to stop production of those products in Oudenaarde, Belgium, so that it could focus on the new Oyster product line there. That allowed Samsonite to specialize in the manufacture of certain products in certain plants. It then exported its production to the centralized European warehouse for distribution to retailers all over Europe.

Some companies specialize in manufacturing according to product or process.

Coordination and Control

Coordination—linking or integrating activities into a unified system

Control—systems, such as organizational structure and performance measurement systems, to ensure that managers implement company strategies

Coordination and control fit well together. Coordinating is the linking or integrating of activities into a unified system.[12] The activities include everything along the global supply chain from purchasing to warehousing to shipment. It is hard to coordinate supplier relations and logistics activities if those issues are not considered when the manufacturing configuration is set up. Samsonite took configuration and coordination into account when it set up its second manufacturing facility in Europe. As demand increased in Europe and as new product lines were added, Samsonite knew that it needed to open up a second plant. However, it wanted to maintain the central European warehouse concept, so it identified a location that would allow it to coordinate transportation and storage relatively easily and quickly.

Once the company determines the manufacturing configuration that it will use, it must adopt a control system to ensure that company strategies are carried out. Control can be the measuring of performance so that companies can respond appropriately to changing conditions. Another aspect of control structure is the organizational structure, and Samsonite established a European headquarters in Oudenaarde, Belgium, to coordinate all of its activities in Europe.

GLOBAL SUPPLY CHAIN MANAGEMENT

Earlier in the chapter, we defined global supply chain management and provided a simplified view of a global supply chain in Figure 18.5. A comprehensive supply chain strategy should include the following elements: (1) customer service requirements, (2) plant and distribution center network design, (3) inventory management, (4) outsourcing and third-party logistics relationships, (5) key customer and supplier relationships, (6) business processes, (7) information systems, (8) organizational design and training requirements, (9) performance metrics, and (10) performance goals.[13] In this section, we will discuss information systems as a key part of the global supply chain management system. In the remainder of the chapter, we will discuss total quality management, inventory management, and two key networks: supplier networks and transportation networks. Global supply chain management integrates these networks beyond the firm itself to improve customer satisfaction levels and enhance profitability.

A key to making the global supply chain work is a good information system.

The key to making a global information system work is information. As noted earlier in the chapter, Samsonite invested heavily in information technology that allowed it to speed up the delivery time to retailers. Information could be transmitted to the warehouse directly by the retailer or through a salesperson, which triggered an order to ship immediately. Many companies use electronic data interchange (EDI) to link suppliers, manufacturers, and customers, and intermediaries, especially in the food manufacturing and carmaking industries, in which suppliers replenish in high volumes. In a global context, EDI has been used to link exporters with customs to facilitate the quick processing of customs forms, thus speeding up the delivery of products across borders. Wal-Mart is known for its revolutionary use of EDI to connect its suppliers to its inventory ordering system. Wal-Mart has 14,000 suppliers throughout the world that process $217 billion worth of transactions annually.[14] However, EDI has some drawbacks. It is relatively limited and inflexible. It provides basic information but does not adapt easily to rapidly changing market conditions, a necessary condition in the global marketplace. It is relatively expensive to implement, so many small and medium-size companies find it difficult to afford. Also, it is based on proprietary rather than on widely accepted standards, so systems tend only to be able to link together suppliers and their customers. In addition, it focuses more on the business-to-business value chain and does not deal effectively with end-use customers.[15]

The next wave of technology affecting the global supply chain was the implementation of information technology packages known as enterprise resource planning (ERP). Companies such as the German software giant SAP, Oracle, Baan, and PeopleSoft introduced software to integrate everything in the back office of the firm—the part of the business that dealt with the firm itself but not with the customer (known as the front office). Around 67 percent of large and midsize companies in the United States use some form of ERP, with 15 percent more planning to implement ERP by 2004.[16] ERP is essential for bringing together the information inside the firm and from different geographic areas, but its inability to tie in to the customer and take advantage of e-commerce has been a problem.

The next technological wave linking together the parts of the global supply chain is e-commerce. As an example, Dell Computer Corporation has a factory in Ireland that supplies custom-built PCs all over Europe. Customers can transmit orders to Dell via call centers or Dell's Web site. The company relays the demand for components to its suppliers. Trucks deliver the components to the factory and haul off the completed computers within a few hours. Dell has established an **extranet** for its suppliers—a linkage to Dell's information system via the Internet—so that they can organize production and delivery of parts to Dell when they need it. Dell uses the Internet to plug its suppliers into its customer database so that it can keep track of changes in demand. It also uses the Internet to plug customers into the ordering process and allows them to track the progress of their order from the factory to their doorstep.[17] Wal-Mart announced in October 2002 that it was moving its EDI-based infrastructure from traditional but expensive value-added networks (VAN) to the Internet. This is good news for many of its 14,000 vendors which transact, via EDI, more than $217 billion a year with Wal-Mart. All of their transactions with Wal-Mart will now be on the Web—a substantial cost savings over VANs for Wal-Mart and its vendors.[18]

Despite the bursting of the dot-com bubble in 2000, most experts agree that the Internet will revolutionize communications across all levels of the global supply chain, but it will occur at different speeds in different areas. The number of worldwide Internet users is rising—by 48 percent in 2000 and 27 percent in 2001, Internet trade between businesses rose 73 percent in 2001, and online retail spending rose by 56 percent.[19] The real attraction of the Internet in global supply chain management is that it not only helps to automate and speed up internal processes in a company through the intranet but also spreads efficiency gains to the business systems of its customers and suppliers.[20] The new technology wave using the Internet is that of private technology exchange (PTX), which is an online collaboration model that brings manufacturers, distributors, value-added resellers, and customers together to execute trading transactions and to share information about demand, production, availability, and more. PTXs will increase the efficiency of the supply chain and reduce costs for participants. Some of the front-running companies participating in PTXs are Ace Hardware, Cisco, and the Ford Motor Company. The technology is still new, so not many companies have adopted the model.[21]

EDI (electronic data interchange)—the electronic linkage of suppliers, customers, and third-party intermediaries to expedite documents and financial flows

ERP (enterprise resource planning)—software that can link information flows from different parts of a business and from different geographic areas

E-commerce—the use of the Internet to join together suppliers with companies and companies with customers

Extranet—the use of the Internet to link a company with outsiders

Private Technology Exchange (PTX)—an online collaboration model that brings manufacturers, distributors, value-added resellers, and customers together to execute trading transactions

The challenge in global supply chain management is that some networks can be managed through the Internet, but others—especially in emerging markets—cannot because of the lack of technology. Even though the Internet growth numbers are impressive, e-commerce still only accounts for 2 percent of all trade. The use of the Internet varies by location and by industry. North America is at least five years ahead of some countries in Europe, especially Eastern Europe. Industries such as computing and electronics, aerospace and defense, and motor vehicles are blasting ahead, while industrial equipment, food and agriculture, heavy industries, and consumer goods are lagging behind.[22] It is no coincidence that the leaders in e-commerce are those that have invested significant amounts of money over the years in information technology—notably in the defense and motor vehicles industries.

QUALITY

Quality—meeting or exceeding the expectations of a customer

An important aspect of all levels of the global supply chain is total quality management. **Quality** is defined as meeting or exceeding the expectations of the customer. More specifically, it is the conformance to specifications, value, fitness for use, support (provided by the company), and psychological impressions (image).[23] For example, no one wants to buy computer software that has a lot of bugs. However, the need to get software to market quickly may mean getting the product to market as soon as possible and correcting errors later. In the airline industry, service is a key. Some airlines, such as Singapore Air, have developed a worldwide reputation for excellence in service. That is a distinct competitive advantage, especially when trying to attract the business traveler.

Quality—or lack thereof—can have serious ramifications for a company. Ford Motor Company lost around $1 billion in 2001 because of faulty Firestone tires placed on its Ford Explorers. Because of this and other quality problems, Ford, along with General Motors and DaimlerChrysler are taking a hard look at the way Japanese carmakers manufacture their cars with higher efficiency and fewer defects. As DaimlerChrysler puts it, we're "raiding Toyota Motor Corporation for quality expertise." *Consumer Reports* puts the quality of American cars in 2002 at about the level of Japanese cars in 1985. The American car companies are learning to root out problems before assembly and bring each supplier into the design process earlier, hoping to spot component problems early. They are finding some success, particularly in their international plants. Ford's Brazil plant produces some of the best-quality results of any of its factories.[24]

Quality can mean zero defects, an idea perfected by Japanese manufacturers who refuse to tolerate defects of any kind. Before the strong emphasis on zero defects, U.S. companies operated according to the premise of **acceptable quality level (AQL)**. This premise allowed an acceptable level of poor quality. It held that unacceptable products would be dealt with through repair facilities and service warranties. This type of manufacturing/operating environment required buffer inventories, rework stations, and expediting. The goal was to push through products as fast as possible and then deal with the mistakes later. However, it is increasingly evident that AQL is inferior to zero defects, and global companies that take quality more seriously will beat the competition.[25]

Zero defects—the refusal to tolerate defects of any kind

Acceptable quality level—there is a tolerable level of defects, and defects can be corrected through repair and service warranties

Total Quality Management

TQM (total quality management)—a process whose goal is to eliminate all defects

The Japanese approach to quality is **total quality management (TQM)**. TQM is a process that stresses three principles: (1) customer satisfaction, (2) employee involvement, and (3) continuous improvements in quality.[26] The goal of TQM is to eliminate all defects. TQM often focuses on benchmarking world-class standards, product and service design, process design, and purchasing.[27]

The center of the entire process, however, is customer satisfaction, which to achieve may raise production costs. The difference between AQL and TQM centers on the attitude toward quality. In AQL, quality is a characteristic of a product that meets or exceeds engineering standards. In TQM, quality means that a product is "so good that the customer wouldn't think of buying from anyone else."

TQM is a process of continuous improvement at every level of the organization—from the mailroom to the boardroom. It implies that the company is doing everything it can to achieve quality at all stages of the process, from customer demands, to product design, to engineering. For example, if management accounting systems are focused strictly on cost, they will preclude measures that could lead to higher quality. The key is to understand the company's overall strategy. TQM does not use any specific production philosophy or require the use of other techniques, such as a just-in-time system for inventory delivery. TQM is a proactive strategy. Although benchmarking—determining the best processes used by the best companies—is an important part of TQM, using the best practices of other companies is not intended to be a goal. TQM means that a company will try to be better than the best.

Executives who have adopted the zero-defects philosophy of TQM claim that long-run production costs decline as defects decline. The continuous improvement process is also known as *kaizen*, which means identifying problems and enlisting employees at all levels of the organization to help eliminate the problems. The key is to make continuous improvement a part of the daily work of every employee. TQM in a global setting is challenging because of cultural and environmental differences. In 1987, Samsonite entered into a cooperation agreement with a Hungarian luggage manufacturer to produce and supply low-end softside luggage for Samsonite, but it did not produce enough quality products due to the lack of advanced technology. Samsonite was forced to invest heavily in the Hungarian partner to get it up to world-class standards. Eventually, its efforts were successful.

Kaizen—the Japanese process of continuous improvement, the cornerstone of TQM

A new management tool, Six Sigma, is starting to displace TQM as the corporate-reengineering tool of choice. Six Sigma is a highly-focused system of quality control that scrutinizes a company's entire production system. It aims to eliminate defects, slash product cycle times, and cut costs across the board. It was introduced by Motorola in the 1980s and has been adopted by many MNEs, including General Electric, GlaxoSmithKline, and Lockheed Martin. It is unknown whether Six Sigma will eliminate the use of TQM, but for now, it is important for companies to explore both tools to determine the one that will better improve quality in the organization.[28]

Six Sigma—a quality control system aimed at eliminating defects, slashing product cycle times, and cutting costs across the board.

Quality Standards

There are three different levels of quality standards: (1) a general level, (2) an industry-specific level, and (3) a company level. The first level is a general standard, such as the Deming Award, which is presented to firms that demonstrate excellence in quality, and the Malcolm Baldrige National Quality Award, which is presented annually to companies that demonstrate quality strategies and achievements. However, even more important than awards is certification of quality. As part of the effort to establish the single European market, the EU, through the International Standards Organization (ISO) in Geneva, established the ISO 9000 certification, which became effective in 1987. ISO 9000 is a set of five universal standards for a Quality Assurance system that is accepted around the world. The standards apply uniformly to companies in any industry and of any size. ISO 9000 is intended to promote the idea of quality at every level of an organization. Initially, it was designed to harmonize technical norms within the EU. Now it is an important part of business operations throughout Europe and has been adopted in 161 countries throughout the world. In 2000, the ISO revised the standards and refer to them now as the ISO 9000:2000.

Levels of quality standards

- General level—ISO 9000, Malcolm Baldrige National Quality Award
- Industry-specific level
- Company level

Basically, under ISO 9000:2000, companies must document how workers perform every function that affects quality and install mechanisms to ensure that they follow through on the documented routine. ISO 9000:2000 certification entails a complex analysis of management systems and procedures, not just quality-control standards. Rather than judging the

ISO 9000—a European set of quality standards intended to promote quality at every level of an organization

FIGURE 18.6   ISO 9000 Certification: An Important Edge?

Source: DILBERT reprinted by permission of United Feature Syndicate, Inc.

quality of a particular product, ISO 9000:2000 evaluates the management of the manufacturing process according to standards it has created in 20 domains—from purchasing to design to training. A company that wants to be ISO certified must fill out a report and then be certified by a team of independent auditors.[29] The process can be expensive and time-consuming. Each site of a company must be separately certified. The certification of one site cannot cover the entire company. Although ISO certification is becoming an important consideration for companies expecting to do business in the EU, it is not the solution to all quality issues, as noted in Figure 18.6. However, ISO certification of suppliers will help them to get more business, especially with European companies. When companies, especially European companies, are choosing among different suppliers, it would be very beneficial for the supplier to have ISO certification.

U.S. companies that operate in Europe are becoming ISO certified to maintain access to the European market. When DuPont lost a major European contract to an ISO-certified European company, it decided to become certified. By doing so, not only was DuPont able to position itself better in the European market, but it also benefited from the experience of going through ISO certification and focusing on quality in the organization. Some European companies are so fanatical about ISO certification that they will not do business with a supplier that is certified if its suppliers are not also ISO certified. They want to be sure that quality flows back to every level of the supply chain.

In addition to the general standards described earlier, there are industry-specific standards for quality, especially for suppliers to follow. In addition, individual companies set their own standards for suppliers to meet if they are going to continue to supply them. Samsonite's concerns in Eastern Europe and its subsequent work with Eastern European suppliers to meet its quality requirements are an example of how companies set their own standards and work with suppliers.

> Non-European companies operating in Europe need to become ISO certified in order to maintain access to that market.

SUPPLIER NETWORKS

> Sourcing—the process of a firm having inputs supplied to it from outside suppliers (both domestic and foreign) for the production process

Global sourcing and production strategies can be better understood by looking at Figure 18.7. **Sourcing** is the firm's process of having inputs (raw materials and parts) supplied to it for the production process. Figure 18.7 illustrates the basic operating environment choices (the home country or any foreign country) by stage in the production process (sourcing of raw materials and parts and the manufacture and assembly of final products). Global sourcing is the first step in the process of materials management, also called logistics, which includes sourcing, inventory management, and transportation between suppliers, manufacturers, and customers.

FIGURE 18.7   Global Sourcing and Production Strategy

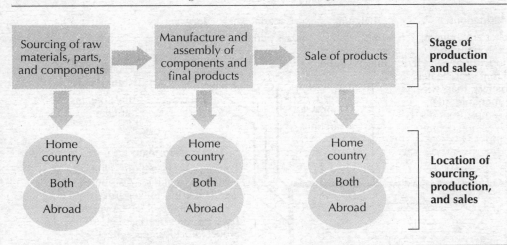

Companies confront many possibilities when sourcing raw materials, parts, and components, and assembling them into final goods to serve worldwide markets. For example, a U.S. company could source components in the United States, assemble them in Mexico, and export the final product back to the United States or to other countries. To be global, a company must choose "abroad" at least once.

For example, Ford assembles cars in Hermosillo, Mexico, and ships them into the United States for end-use consumers. The cars are designed by Mazda, a Japanese company, and use some Japanese parts. Ford can purchase parts manufactured in Japan and ship them to the United States for final assembly and sale in the U.S. market, or it can have Japanese- and U.S.-made parts shipped to Mexico for final assembly and sale in the United States and Mexico. For Mexican assembly, some of the parts come from the United States, some from Japan, and a small percentage from Mexico. When Ford decided to manufacture the Escort in Europe, it used the global sourcing of parts from plants in 15 different countries for final assembly in the United Kingdom and Germany, as Figure 18.8 illustrates.

Companies can manufacture parts internally or purchase them from external (unrelated) manufacturers. Samsonite manufactured most of the parts that went into its luggage, but it sourced some of its parts from unrelated suppliers—such as wheels for suitcases from Czech suppliers. As mentioned earlier, Samsonite sourced semifinished, softside parts from East European subcontractors to use in its own factories. Companies can also assemble their own products internally or subcontract to external companies, as noted earlier in the examples of Nike, Mattel, and McDonald's Happy Meals toys. Manufacture of parts and final assembly may take place in the company's home country, the country in which it is trying to sell the product, or a third country.[30]

Sourcing in the home country enables companies to avoid numerous problems, including those connected with language differences, long distances and lengthy supply lines, exchange-rate fluctuations, wars and insurrections, strikes, politics, tariffs, and complex transportation channels. However, for many companies, domestic sources may be unavailable or may be more expensive than foreign sources. In Japan, foreign procurement is critical, because nearly all of that country's uranium, bauxite, nickel, crude oil, iron ore, copper, coking coal and approximately 30 percent of its agricultural products are imported. Japanese trading companies came into being expressly to acquire the raw materials needed to fuel Japan's manufacturing.

Companies pursue global sourcing strategies for a number of reasons.

1. To reduce costs—due to less expensive labor, less restrictive work rules, and lower land and facilities costs
2. To improve quality

Companies can manufacture parts internally or purchase them from external manufacturers.

Using domestic sources for raw materials and components allows a company to avoid problems with language differences, distance, currency, politics, and tariffs, as well as other problems.

Companies outsource abroad to lower costs and improve quality, among other reasons.

FIGURE 18.8   The Global Component Network for Ford's European Manufacturing of the Escort

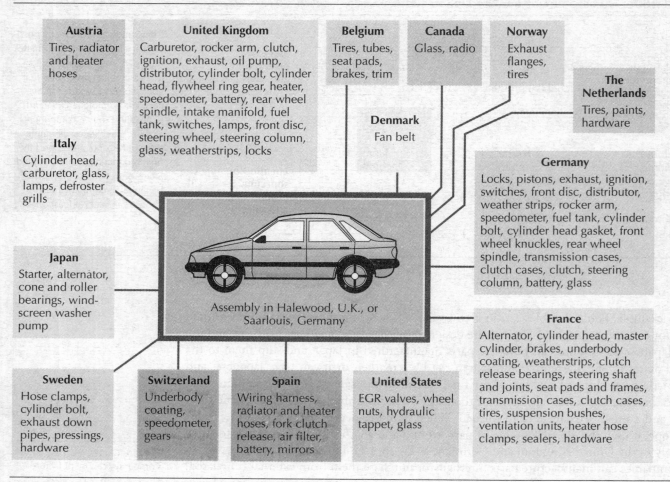

Austria
Tires, radiator and heater hoses

United Kingdom
Carburetor, rocker arm, clutch, ignition, exhaust, oil pump, distributor, cylinder bolt, cylinder head, flywheel ring gear, heater, speedometer, battery, rear wheel spindle, intake manifold, fuel tank, switches, lamps, front disc, steering wheel, steering column, glass, weatherstrips, locks

Belgium
Tires, tubes, seat pads, brakes, trim

Canada
Glass, radio

Norway
Exhaust flanges, tires

The Netherlands
Tires, paints, hardware

Denmark
Fan belt

Italy
Cylinder head, carburetor, glass, lamps, defroster grills

Germany
Locks, pistons, exhaust, ignition, switches, front disc, distributor, weather strips, rocker arm, speedometer, fuel tank, cylinder bolt, cylinder head gasket, front wheel knuckles, rear wheel spindle, transmission cases, clutch cases, clutch, steering column, battery, glass

Japan
Starter, alternator, cone and roller bearings, windscreen washer pump

Assembly in Halewood, U.K., or Saarlouis, Germany

France
Alternator, cylinder head, master cylinder, brakes, underbody coating, weatherstrips, clutch release bearings, steering shaft and joints, seat pads and frames, transmission cases, clutch cases, tires, suspension bushes, ventilation units, heater hose clamps, sealers, hardware

Sweden
Hose clamps, cylinder bolt, exhaust down pipes, pressings, hardware

Switzerland
Underbody coating, speedometer, gears

Spain
Wiring harness, radiator and heater hoses, fork clutch release, air filter, battery, mirrors

United States
EGR valves, wheel nuts, hydraulic tappet, glass

Ford assembles Escorts in only two facilities in Europe, but parts and components used in the automobiles come from all over the world.
Source: From *World Development Report 1987* by World Bank, copyright 1984 by the World Bank. Used by permission of Oxford University Press, Inc.

3. To increase exposure to worldwide technology
4. To improve the delivery-of-supplies process
5. To strengthen the reliability of supply by supplementing domestic with foreign suppliers
6. To gain access to materials that are only available abroad, possibly because of technical specifications or product capabilities
7. To establish a presence in a foreign market
8. To satisfy offset requirements (as discussed in Chapter 17)
9. To react to competitors' offshore sourcing practices[31]

In some ways, global sourcing is more expensive than domestic sourcing. For example, transportation and communications are more expensive, and companies may have to pay brokers and agent fees. Given the longer length of supply lines, it often takes more time to get components from abroad, and lead times are less certain. This problem increases the inventory carrying costs and makes it more difficult to get parts to the production site in a timely manner. If imported components come in with errors and need to be reworked, the cost per unit will rise, and some components may have to be shipped back to the supplier.

Three major configurations of outsourcing have emerged.

1. Vertical integration
2. Arm's-length purchases from outside suppliers
3. Japanese *keiretsu* relationships with suppliers

Vertical integration occurs when the company owns the entire supplier network or at least a significant part of it. The company may have to purchase raw materials from outside suppliers, but it produces the most expensive parts itself. Arm's-length purchases are the same as outsourcing. The Japanese *keiretsus*, as discussed in Chapter 15, are a group of independent companies that work together to manage the flow of goods and services along the entire value-added chain.[32]

Make or Buy Decision

MNE managers struggle with a dilemma: Which production activities should be performed internally and which ones could be subcontracted to independent companies, a process also sometimes called **outsourcing**. That is the make or buy decision. In the latter case, they also need to decide whether the activities should be carried on in the home market or abroad. A recent survey of the use of outsourcing by businesses reveals the importance of control measures. Accenture conducted a survey in 2002, questioning 150 executives from *Fortune* 1000 companies about the biggest barriers to expanding their use of outsourcing. Nearly one half (48 percent) reported that loss of operational control was the biggest barrier. Other barriers were cultural barriers in the organization (19 percent), costs (14 percent), and long-term dependency on an external organization (11 percent).[33]

In deciding whether to make or buy, MNEs could focus on those parts that are critical to the product and that they are distinctively good at making. They could outsource parts when suppliers have a distinct comparative advantage, such as greater scale, lower-cost structure, or stronger performance incentives. They also could use outsourcing as an implied threat to underperforming employees that if they don't improve, the companies will move their business elsewhere.[34]

In determining whether to make or buy, the MNE needs to determine the design and manufacturing capabilities of potential suppliers compared to its own capabilities. If the supplier has a clear advantage, management needs to decide what it would cost to catch up to the best suppliers and whether it would make sense to do so.

Supplier Relations

Ford Motor Company's Web site states,

> We are working more closely [with our suppliers] on product manufacturing and assembly. For example, at Ford's new Northeast Industrial Complex in Bahia, Brazil, 29 suppliers will be working with Ford to launch an innovative process later this year that will take Ford and its suppliers to new levels of cooperation. Suppliers are providing higher levels of value-added [activities] including design expertise and value-chain management. Ford and its suppliers will be sharing the site, services, and management of the plant.[35]

If an MNE decides it must outsource rather than integrate vertically, it must determine how to work with suppliers. Toyota pioneered the Toyota Production System in order to work with unrelated suppliers. Toyota sends a team of manufacturing experts to each of its key suppliers to observe how the supplier organizes its factory and makes its parts. Then the team advises on how to cut costs and boost quality. For example, Toyota approached Bumper Works, a small 100-person factory in Illinois, and asked its management to design

---

Major outsourcing configurations
- Vertical integration
- Arm's-length purchases from outside suppliers
- Japanese *keiretsu* relationships with suppliers

Outsourcing—purchasing inputs from outside suppliers not related to the company

Make or buy—outsource or supply parts from internal production

If MNEs outsource instead of source parts from internal production, they need to determine the degree of involvement with suppliers.

and manufacture a bumper that would meet Toyota's rigid specifications. After demonstrating that it could satisfy Toyota, Bumper Works became the sole supplier for that company's U.S. facilities. However, Toyota expected annual price reductions, higher-quality bumpers, and on-time deliveries. Toyota helped Bumper Works determine how to change the dies in its metal-stamping process so that it could provide the flexibility that Toyota required for different types of bumpers.

It is also common for Toyota to identify two suppliers for each part and have the suppliers compete aggressively with each other. The supplier that performs the best gets the most business. However, both suppliers know that they will have an ongoing relationship with Toyota and will not be dumped easily.[36]

This is a good example of the close relationships that Japanese companies develop with their suppliers. It is very different from the arm's-length relationship that U.S. companies tend to have with their suppliers. Further, Toyota has been able to reduce the number of supplier relationships it develops, which allows it to focus on a few key suppliers, promising to give them a lot of business if they perform up to Toyota standards. For example, for its British operations, Toyota relies on about 150 parts suppliers, compared with the 500 to 1,000 suppliers typical for other European automakers.[37]

The Purchasing Function

The purchasing agent is the link between the company's outsourcing decision and its supplier relationships. Just as companies go through stages of globalization, so does the purchasing agent's scope of responsibilities. Typically, purchasing goes through four phases before becoming "global."

1. Domestic purchasing only
2. Foreign buying based on need
3. Foreign buying as part of procurement strategy
4. Integration of global procurement strategy[38]

Phase 4 occurs when the company realizes the benefits that result from the integration and coordination of purchasing on a global basis and is most applicable to the MNE as opposed to, say, the exporter. When purchasing becomes this global, MNEs often face the centralization/decentralization dilemma. Should they allow each subsidiary to make all purchasing decisions, or should they centralize all or some of the purchasing decisions? The primary benefits of decentralization include increased production facility control over purchases, better responsiveness to facility needs, and more effective use of local suppliers. The primary benefits of centralization are increased leverage with suppliers, getting better prices, eliminating administrative duplication, allowing purchasers to develop specialized knowledge in purchasing techniques, reducing the number of orders processed, and enabling purchasing to build solid supplier relationships.[39]

Companies pursue five major sourcing strategies as they move into phases 3 and 4 in the preceding list (foreign buying as part of procurement strategy and integration of global procurement strategy).

1. Assign domestic buyer(s) for international purchasing
2. Use foreign subsidiaries or business agents
3. Establish international purchasing offices
4. Assign the responsibility for global sourcing to a specific business unit or units
5. Integrate and coordinate worldwide sourcing[40]

These strategies move from the simple to the more complex, similar to the concept illustrated in Figure 1.7 on the usual patterns of internationalization. Companies start by using a domestic buyer and progress all the way to integrating and coordinating worldwide sourcing into the company's purchasing decisions so that there is no difference between domestic and foreign sources. Some companies are going even further than the last step and are coordinating worldwide purchasing with competitor companies. In June 2003, Hyundai Motor Co., DaimlerChrysler AG, and Mitsubishi Motors Corp. will begin joint worldwide purchases of car parts to the tune of $13 billion. The joint purchases will help the companies cut procurement costs and establish localized car-part supply chains in the global market.[41]

Figure 18.9 summarizes some of the key concepts in the preceding discussion in terms of selecting the best supplier. The key is for managers to select the best supplier, establish a solid relationship, and continuously evaluate the supplier's performance to ensure the best price, quality, and on-time delivery possible.

The use of the Internet in purchasing (termed e-sourcing) is growing in popularity. A study based on the responses of U.S. and European companies found that those that use e-sourcing

FIGURE 18.9 Assessing the Organization's Global Sourcing Needs and Strategy

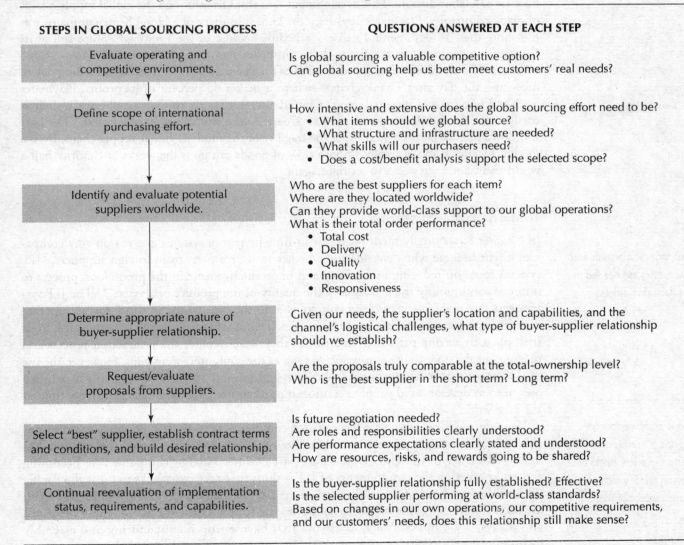

STEPS IN GLOBAL SOURCING PROCESS	QUESTIONS ANSWERED AT EACH STEP
Evaluate operating and competitive environments.	Is global sourcing a valuable competitive option? Can global sourcing help us better meet customers' real needs?
Define scope of international purchasing effort.	How intensive and extensive does the global sourcing effort need to be? • What items should we global source? • What structure and infrastructure are needed? • What skills will our purchasers need? • Does a cost/benefit analysis support the selected scope?
Identify and evaluate potential suppliers worldwide.	Who are the best suppliers for each item? Where are they located worldwide? Can they provide world-class support to our global operations? What is their total order performance? • Total cost • Delivery • Quality • Innovation • Responsiveness
Determine appropriate nature of buyer-supplier relationship.	Given our needs, the supplier's location and capabilities, and the channel's logistical challenges, what type of buyer-supplier relationship should we establish?
Request/evaluate proposals from suppliers.	Are the proposals truly comparable at the total-ownership level? Who is the best supplier in the short term? Long term?
Select "best" supplier, establish contract terms and conditions, and build desired relationship.	Is future negotiation needed? Are roles and responsibilities clearly understood? Are performance expectations clearly stated and understood? How are resources, risks, and rewards going to be shared?
Continual reevaluation of implementation status, requirements, and capabilities.	Is the buyer-supplier relationship fully established? Effective? Is the selected supplier performing at world-class standards? Based on changes in our own operations, our competitive requirements, and our customers' needs, does this relationship still make sense?

Source: Reprinted with permission from the publisher, the Institute for Supply Management, Inc. TM, "The Globalization of the Supply Environment." *The Supply Management Environment,* by Stanley E. Fawcett, 2000, Vol. 2, p. 53.

negotiate a 14.3 percent reduction in goods and services costs, cut sourcing cycles in half, reduce sourcing administrative costs by 60 percent, and shorten time-to-market cycles by 10 to 15 percent.[42]

INVENTORY MANAGEMENT

Whether a company decides to source parts from inside or outside the company or from domestic or foreign sources, it needs to manage the flow and storage of inventory. This is true of raw materials and parts sourced from suppliers, work in process and finished-goods inventory inside the manufacturing plant, and finished goods stored at a distribution center, such as the centralized European warehouse for Samsonite.

If the company sources parts from a variety of suppliers from around the world, distance, time, and the uncertainty of the international political and economic environment can make it difficult for managers to determine correct reorder points for the manufacturing process. For example, in October 2002, the United State's West Coast ports closed for 10 days because of a labor dispute. This development sent shudders through the global supply chains of many companies. Playmates Toys Inc., the U.S. subsidiary of a Hong Kong company, was put more than 14 days behind delivery schedule because of the shutdown. Ships full of its Christmas inventory—from Disney dolls, Simpsons figures, and Water Babies toys—lined up at sea. The shutdown dampened retail sales for Playmates Toys on its largest selling day of the year—the day after Thanksgiving—where it makes 45 percent of its profits. Playmates Toys and hundreds of other companies found alternate routes to their retail buyers, such as costly airfreight and shipments to the East Coast. As the *Wall Street Journal* stated, "The port shutdown offers a clear illustration of the fragility of the modern global-supply chain. Even a modest hiccup in the normally smooth flow of goods can gum the works at factories half a world away, and take weeks to set right again."[43]

Just-in-Time Systems

In Chapter 8, we briefly mentioned just-in-time inventory systems as a reason why companies might hesitate when considering whether to source parts from foreign suppliers. "JIT systems focus on reducing inefficiency and unproductive time in the production process to improve continuously the process and the quality of the product or service."[44] The JIT system gets raw materials, parts, and components to the buyer "just in time" for use, sparing companies the cost of storing large inventories. That is what Dell hoped to accomplish in its Irish plant by having parts delivered just as they were to enter the production process and then go out the door to the consumers as soon as the computers were built. However, the use of JIT means that parts must have few defects and must arrive on time. That is why companies need to develop solid supplier relationships to ensure good quality and delivery times if JIT is to work.

Foreign sourcing can create big risks for companies that use JIT, because interruptions in the supply line can cause havoc. Many retail companies experienced this firsthand as described earlier in the U.S. West Coast port closure. Foreign companies are becoming experts at meeting the requirements of JIT—ships that take two weeks to cross the Pacific dock within an hour of scheduled arrival, and factories are able to more easily fill small orders. However, because of distances alone, the supply chain is open to more problems and delays.[45] Companies such as Toyota that have set up manufacturing and assembly facilities overseas to service local markets have practically forced their domestic parts suppliers to move overseas as well in order to allow Toyota to continue with JIT manufacturing. That is why so many Japanese parts suppliers, such as DENSO, a major Toyota

Distance, time, and uncertainty in foreign environments cause foreign sourcing to complicate inventory management.

JIT—sourcing raw materials and parts just as they are needed in the manufacturing process

It is hard to combine foreign sourcing and JIT production without having safety stocks of inventory on hand, which defeats the concept of JIT.

supplier, have moved to the United States and Mexico to be near their major customers. (See case on page 559.)

A company's inventory management strategy—especially in terms of stock sizes and whether or not JIT will be used—determines frequency of needed shipments. The less frequent the delivery, the more likely the need to store inventory somewhere. Because JIT requires delivery just as the inventory is to be used, some concession must be made for inventory arriving from foreign suppliers. Sometimes that means adjusting the arrival time to a few days before use rather than a few hours. Kawasaki Motors Corp., U.S.A. carries a minimum of three days' inventory on parts coming from Japan, with an average inventory of five days.[46]

Quality of inventory is important, because inventory with significant amounts of defects will create problems for JIT. If the buyer has to purchase more because of expected defects, there will be not only wasted inventory but also higher carrying costs. Nike contracts out the manufacture of shoes to China, but it also has a Nike team on hand at the factories in China to ensure high-quality manufacturing. The geographic distance between buyer and supplier, language differences, and cultural differences can increase the time it takes to educate suppliers on how to supply products of high quality.[47]

JIT typically implies sole sourcing for specific parts in order to get the supplier to commit to the stringent delivery and quality requirements inherent in JIT. However, if the only supplier is a foreign supplier, it would be too risky to permit just one supplier. That means cultivating multiple suppliers, at least one of which may be a foreign supplier. The problem is that using multiple suppliers may preclude the buyer from getting volume pricing from the supplier. One strategy is that buyers may use a sole supplier for all but critical inputs. Then it is best to cultivate solid secondary suppliers.[48]

Foreign Trade Zones

In recent years, **foreign trade zones (FTZs)** have become more popular as an intermediate step in the process between import and final use. FTZs are areas in which domestic and imported merchandise can be stored, inspected, and manufactured free from formal customs procedures until the goods leave the zones. The zones are intended to encourage companies to locate in the country by allowing them to defer duties, pay fewer duties, or avoid certain duties completely. Sometimes inventory is stored in an FTZ until it needs to be used for domestic manufacture. As noted earlier, one of the problems with JIT is the length of the supply line when relying on global sourcing, possibly causing either the buyer or the supplier to stockpile inventory somewhere until it is needed in the manufacturing process. One place to stockpile inventory is in a warehouse in an FTZ.

FTZs can be general-purpose zones or subzones. A general-purpose zone usually is established near a port of entry, such as a shipping port, a border crossing, or an airport, and it usually consists of a distribution facility or an industrial park. A subzone usually is physically separate from a general-purpose zone but is under the same administrative structure. Since 1982, the major growth in FTZs has been in subzones rather than in general-purpose zones because companies have sought to defer duties on parts that are foreign sourced until they need to be used in the production process. For example, the major growth in subzones in the United States has been in the automobile industry, especially in the Midwest. Subzone activity is spreading to other industries, especially to shipbuilding, pharmaceuticals, and home appliances, and it is becoming more heavily oriented to manufacturing and assembly than was originally envisioned.

FTZs are used worldwide. In Japan, they are being established for the benefit of foreign companies exporting products to that country. Japanese zones serve as warehousing and repackaging facilities at which companies can display consumer goods for demonstration to Japanese buyers.[49]

Foreign trade zones (FTZs)—special locations for storing domestic and imported inventory in order to avoid paying duties until the inventory is used in production or sold

In the United States, there are 50 states with FTZ projects, $240 billion a year in merchandise is handled in FTZs, and $15 billion is exported from FTZs each year.[50] FTZs in the United States have been used primarily as a means of providing greater flexibility as to when and how customs duties are paid. However, their use in the export business has been expanding. The exports for which these FTZs are used fall into one of the following categories:

Foreign goods transshipped through U.S. zones to third countries

Foreign goods processed in U.S. zones and then transshipped abroad

Foreign goods processed or assembled in U.S. zones with some domestic materials and parts, then reexported.

Goods produced wholly of foreign content in U.S. zones and then exported

Domestic goods moved into a U.S. zone to achieve export status prior to their actual exportation[51]

Transportation Networks

Transportation links together suppliers, companies, and customers.

For a firm, the transportation of goods in an international context is extremely complicated in terms of documentation, choice of carrier (air or ocean), and the decision on whether to establish its own transportation department or outsource to a third-party intermediary. Transportation is one of the key elements of a logistics system. The key is to link together suppliers and manufacturers on the one hand and manufacturers and final consumers on the other. Along the way, the company has to determine what its warehouse configuration will be. For example, McDonald's provides food items to its franchises around the world. It has warehouses in different countries to service different geographic areas. In the Samsonite case, there was no discussion of the issues surrounding transportation and warehousing from suppliers to Samsonite's factories, but the movement of goods from factories to retailers was an important issue.

Third-party intermediaries, such as Emery, are crucial in storing and transporting goods.

Third-party intermediaries are an important dimension to transportation networks. For example, Emery Worldwide is a division of Menlo Worldwide group, a company that specializes in transportation and logistics solutions for companies. It is a $2.9 billion integrated carrier providing global air and ocean freight transportation, logistics management, customs brokerage, and expedited services to manufacturing, industrial, retail, and government customers. Based in Redwood City, California, Emery provides service to 200 countries through a network of more than 600 service centers and agent locations around the world. One of Emery's customers is Iomega, the San Diego, California, company that manufactures the Zip drive, a personal storage solution that can help people protect, secure, capture, and share digital information. Iomega entered into an agreement with Emery to use its freight forwarding services and to use Emery's warehouse facilities in Singapore to store inventory and supply finished product to customers all over Asia. Iomega designs the products in its San Diego and Utah facilities and subcontracts parts to be made by suppliers all over Asia. Generally, Iomega's parts are small and made mainly out of plastic and metal. Some parts are supplied by more than one supplier. Emery handles the shipment of parts from the suppliers to its distribution center in Singapore. One section of the distribution center is dedicated to Iomega products. In this section is an assembly line on which Iomega personnel, most of whom are brought into Singapore from Sri Lanka as guest workers, can engage in "pick-n-pack," an assembly operation in which they pick parts off a conveyer belt and pack them for customers. Then the final goods are packaged and stored by Emery until they are sent by truck to the Changi Airport Airfreight Centre for shipment by plane, truck, or ship to customers in Asia. In this example, you can see all of the elements of the transportation networks that are so essential in international logistics.

Singapore has one of the largest container ports in the world. Most goods are transported internationally by container. Goods can be loaded into containers and sent to ports by rail or truck. Then they can be sent overseas by airfreight or ocean freight. The transportation company, like Emery, can try to fill up a container with just the company's products, or it can combine the products with those of another company and share container space.

The logistics management that companies like Emery engage in is very detail oriented, requiring the ability to gather, track, and process large quantities of information. To be effective, logistics companies need to implement key technologies, including communications technologies, satellite tracking systems, bar-coding applications, and automated materials handling systems.[52] Emery employs all of these technologies at its Singapore facilities to help companies like Iomega ship their goods worldwide.

ETHICAL DILEMMA

What Supplier Relations Approach Yields the Best Results?

A utilitarian view of ethical conduct argues that the worth of actions or practices is determined by their consequences. That is, an action or practice is right if it leads to the best possible balance of good consequences and bad consequences for all the parties affected.[53] How does that concept work in the case of supplier relations? When an MNE such as Toyota develops close relationships with its suppliers, both parties are exposed to risk. In working with a supplier, Toyota requires a full understanding of that supplier's manufacturing capabilities and financial position. This requirement is difficult for non-Japanese companies because they are not used to providing such detailed information to customers. Toyota takes a hard-line approach to improving quality and driving down costs, but in turn, it provides its suppliers with a stable business relationship. It shares development information with a supplier's competitors but not in such a way as to damage its relationship with the supplier. Even though it is in Toyota's self-interest to keep costs as low as possible in order to maximize its competitiveness within the industry, the company also upholds its ethical obligation to treat its suppliers fairly. As long as Toyota maintains a stable business relationship with suppliers and helps them become more competitive as manufacturers, its actions result in a positive utilitarian outcome.

In contrast, some of GM's supplier relations in the past have been far less positive. When GM requires suppliers to enter into contractual agreements and then tears up the contracts and forces the suppliers to renegotiate, it is acting in its own self-interest and to the suppliers' detriment. Given the negative impact on the suppliers, one could argue that GM's actions do not constitute positive ethical conduct according to the utilitarian view. Following the departure of its head of purchasing to Volkswagen, GM was forced to look at its past actions to determine if that is the way it wanted to act in the future. As Toyota increases its production in the United States to take advantage of currency differences and market opportunities, it will form more relationships with U.S. auto parts manufacturers—thus providing a basis for comparison with the tactics of U.S. automakers. In the face of this competition, U.S. automakers may find that they have to adjust their supplier relations or lose some suppliers to Toyota. As companies continue to outsource and deal with suppliers from different countries and cultures, they will have to adjust to different attitudes toward supplier relations.

LOOKING TO THE FUTURE

To Be Global a MNE Must Establish Strong Supply Chain Links

In establishing manufacturing facilities to serve worldwide markets, MNEs started with large home-market plants and exported to foreign markets. As the importance of those markets increased, companies needed to establish manufacturing facilities abroad, almost in a multidomestic approach. Now, however, they are finding that they need much stronger control over manufacturing operations worldwide in order to take advantage of market differences and to drive down costs.

Improvements in communications technology will continue to facilitate the flow of information worldwide. The increasing use of the Internet and wireless applications to establish extranet connections with suppliers and customers will give companies significant flexibility in establishing relationships and should improve quality, delivery time, and responsiveness to consumer demands. Companies will have available a wider array of suppliers to choose from, and suppliers can be more responsive to consumer demands by getting the right inventory to the production system at the right time.

As companies examine their core competencies, they will have to decide if they want to be in the manufacturing business (as Samsonite is) or if they want to outsource their manufacturing (as Nike does). Whichever strategy they adopt, they will certainly have to develop a stronger global supply chain management system.

Summary

- A company's supply chain encompasses the coordination of materials, information, and funds from the initial raw material supplier to the ultimate customer.

- Logistics, or materials management, is that part of the supply chain process that plans, implements, and controls the efficient, effective flow and storage of goods, services, and related information from the point of origin to the point of consumption in order to meet customers' requirements.

- The success of a global manufacturing strategy depends on compatibility, configuration, coordination, and control.

- Cost-minimization strategies and the drive for global efficiencies often force MNEs offshore to low-cost manufacturing areas, especially in Asia and Eastern Europe.

- Three broad categories of manufacturing configuration are one centralized facility, regional facilities, and multidomestic facilities.

- The key to making a global supply chain system work is information. Companies are rapidly turning to the Internet as a way to link suppliers with manufacturing and eventually with end-use customers.

- Quality is defined as meeting or exceeding the expectations of customers. Quality standards can be general (ISO 9000), and company specific (AQL, zero defects, TQM, and Six Sigma).

- Total quality management (TQM) is a process that stresses customer satisfaction, employee involvement, and continuous improvements in quality.

- Global sourcing is the process of a firm having raw materials and parts supplied to it from domestic and foreign sources.

- Domestic sourcing allows the company to avoid problems related to language, culture, currency, tariffs, and so forth. Foreign sourcing allows the company to reduce costs and improve quality, among other things.

- Under the make or buy decision, companies have to decide if they will make their own parts or buy them from an independent company.

- Companies go through different purchasing phases as they become more committed to global sourcing.

- When a company sources parts from suppliers around the world, distance, time, and the uncertainty of the international political and economic environment can make it difficult for managers to manage inventory flows accurately.

- Just-in-time focuses on reducing inefficiency and unproductive time in the production process to improve continuously the process and quality of the product or service.

- The transportation system links together suppliers with manufacturers and manufacturers with customers.

CASE

DENSO Corporation and Global Supplier Relations[54]

In 2002, DENSO Corporation, the Japanese auto parts supplier formerly known as NIPPONDENSO, was struggling to determine what strategy it should pursue to succeed and move forward into the twenty-first century. Should it continue to be tightly linked to Toyota as its major parts supplier? Or, given that it makes products other than auto parts, should it become less dependent on the automotive industry in general and on Toyota in particular? Should it continue to invest so many resources in Japan even though economic growth is next to zero and signs of recovery are minimal? And because the demand for its product varies so much from customer to customer, DENSO also wondered how it could better manage its production and inventory levels. As the CEO stated, "Component suppliers are facing ever-tougher standards as automobile manufacturers fight a global battle for survival."

BACKGROUND ON DENSO

DENSO is the third-largest auto parts supplier in the world, just behind Delphi of the United States and Bosch of Germany. Prior to 1949, it was a part of Toyota, but then it spun off into a separate company even though Toyota still retains 25 percent of DENSO's issued stock. Thus, DENSO is part of the Toyota *keiretsu* that includes companies in automotive parts, steel, precision machinery, automatic looms, textiles, household wares, office and housing units, and other products. As Map 18.2 shows, DENSO's world headquarters and most of its domestic manufacturing facilities are in Aichi prefecture on the east coast of Japan and close to Toyota City, the headquarters for Toyota Corporation. Toyota's domestic manufacturing plants are also located in Aichi prefecture, so there is a close proximity between DENSO and Toyota plants.

As illustrated in Figure 18.10, only 6.3 percent of DENSO's 2002 revenues were in nonautomotive products, mostly in telecommunications and environmental systems. The wireless technology that DENSO developed for cars is being used to bring out new forms of mobile communication for individuals, a highly competitive market. In terms of environmental systems, DENSO manufactures water purifiers, spot heaters, and biodegradation garbage disposals. However, its real strength is the automotive parts industry.

MAP 18.2   **DENSO Corporation in Japan**

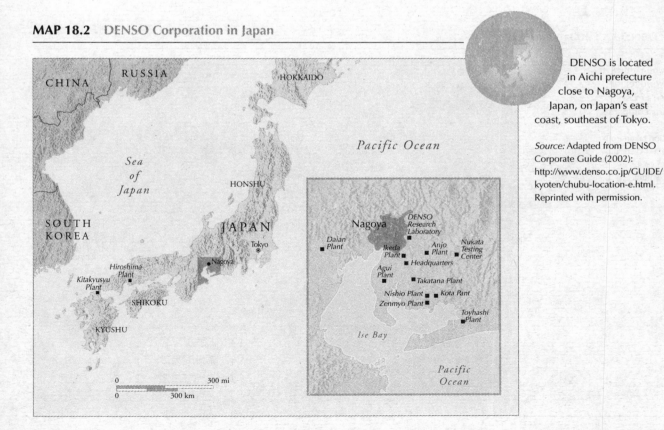

DENSO is located in Aichi prefecture close to Nagoya, Japan, on Japan's east coast, southeast of Tokyo.

Source: Adapted from DENSO Corporate Guide (2002): http://www.denso.co.jp/GUIDE/kyoten/chubu-location-e.html. Reprinted with permission.

FIGURE 18.10   DENSO Sales Breakdown, FY 2002

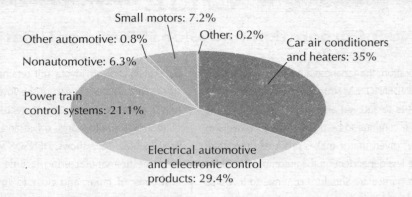

Source: DENSO Corporation FY 2002
Interim Financial Results,
http://www.denso.co.jp/index-e.htm.

Small motors: 7.2%

Other automotive: 0.8%

Nonautomotive: 6.3%

Other: 0.2%

Power train
control systems: 21.1%

Car air conditioners
and heaters: 35%

Electrical automotive
and electronic control
products: 29.4%

Although DENSO is a major supplier to Toyota, it supplies parts to all companies manufacturing automobiles in Japan. In addition, it is the most global of the Japanese auto parts companies. DENSO generated 32 percent of its fiscal 2002 revenues from overseas sales. DENSO has 11 domestic plants, 88 international companies (of which 65 are production facilities), and employs over 86,600 workers. Map 18.3 shows that DENSO has production facilities in every world region except Africa and Russia. DENSO initially expanded overseas to supply Toyota's overseas plants, but now it supplies other auto companies overseas as well. Toyota has 66 production companies in 27 countries in every region of the world.

QUALITY STANDARDS AND MANUFACTURING PRACTICES OF DENSO

DENSO has to meet tough quality standards. First, it needs to satisfy Toyota's rigid quality standards by using TQM and by striving for zero defects. Second, it complies with both ISO 9001 and QS9000 certification so that it can qualify as a supplier for auto manufacturers in

MAP 18.3   DENSO'S Global Network

With production facilities in almost every world region, DENSO is Japan's most global auto parts company.

Source: Information taken from DENSO Corporation Web site, http://www.denso.co.jp/co-INF0-e/index.html.

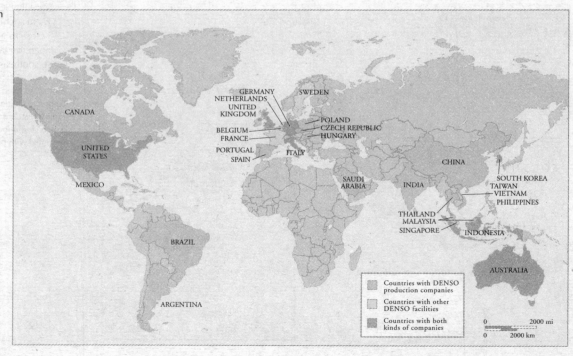

Europe and North America. QS9000 is a quality standard specifically for the auto industry. Chrysler, Ford, and General Motors established QS9000 in 1994 to provide requirements and measurables (events that can be quantified and specific measures that can be used to describe those events) for the automotive industry. QS9000 is derived from ISO 9001, but it is more specific to the auto industry. Under the guidelines, suppliers must adapt their quality systems to meet the expectations of the automakers. QS9000 is required for any supplier of Ford, General Motors, and DaimlerChrysler.

DENSO separates its production facilities into a parts manufacturing area, a subassembly area, and a final assembly area. It uses a flexible and automated assembly line with significant robotics. The Takatana Plant of DENSO assembles instrument panels for its customers. DENSO has created a "green belt" around the plant, perhaps so workers can look at trees, not factories. It also has invested heavily in an information system for production control, even though it traditionally has used and is currently using a *kanban* system. The kanban system is a JIT system pioneered by Toyota. *Kanban* literally means "card" or "visible record" in Japanese. The kanban cards are used to control the flow of production through a factory. For example, Toyota uses *kanban* in the assembly of a Lexus at its Tsutsumi assembly plant just south of Toyota City, and DENSO supplies automatic air conditioners to the plant on a JIT basis. In the *kanban* system used by Toyota, DENSO ships air conditioners to the Tsutsumi plant just before they need to go into production. They are kept in a bin that has a card attached to it identifying the number of air conditioners in the bin. When the assembly process begins, a production-order card signifies that a bin of air conditioners needs to be moved to the assembly line. When the bin is emptied, it is moved to a storage area and replaced with a full bin. The *kanban* card is removed from the empty bin and is used to order a replacement from DENSO. DENSO ships parts to Toyota approximately 8 to 10 times a day, 24 hours a day. In order to service Toyota, DENSO keeps roughly a five-day inventory of some parts.

The same process used by Toyota is also used by DENSO to manufacture the air conditioner. An air conditioner requires an electronic control unit, a cabin air temperature sensor, an ambient air temperature sensor, a solar radiation sensor, a coolant temperature sensor, an evaporator sensor, a compressor with magnetic clutch, a heater core, a condenser, expansion valves, and so on. DENSO manufactures some of these parts, and outside suppliers manufacture others. In 1999, DENSO's assembly plant for its instrument clusters (speedometer, etc.) was running on one 8-hour shift, which was at about 80 percent capacity. However, its parts production was running two shifts.

DENSO had pretty good labor relations, because its labor union is a company union. However, DENSO management still maintained that salary negotiations are pretty tough. Workers are hired for life and paid a salary, which is based on a mixture of age, expertise, and performance. There is a relatively small wage gap among DENSO employees. Employee performance is evaluated every six months, with a bonus paid every six months.

DENSO'S FUTURE

In assessing DENSO's strengths and weaknesses, management feels that its production and production training are very strong. However, it needs to further improve its R&D if it is going to continue to move forward into the future. The key is to continue to develop new products, both inside and outside of the auto industry, if it is going to continue to generate revenues. DENSO still engages in lifetime employment, and it feels that this employment system helps it to improve continuously.

Domestic demand in Japan has been relatively flat from the mid-1990s to the present, which has made it difficult for DENSO to keep generating growth in revenues. Because it is dependent on the auto industry, its fortunes rise and fall with those of Toyota and its other key customers. It is making a big push to sell to DaimlerChrysler, because it is the third-largest auto company in the world, just behind GM and Ford. Approximately 32 percent of DENSO's sales come from overseas operations. DENSO's plants in the United States and Mexico service the U.S. market. As a whole, DENSO is still growing, but demand varies for different divisions. The electronics division, for example, is growing, so DENSO management has been shifting employment to that division. Because of lifetime employment, DENSO does not want to lay off workers, so it finds new product lines to which it can shift workers. Then it retrains them for the job. Each of its plants has an on-site education facility. Usually, however, DENSO's employees stay in one division until they retire.

A major challenge DENSO faces is that Toyota is still based on a *kanban* system, even though the rest of the industry is moving away from *kanban*. Toyota uses forecasts, which can help DENSO plan its production, but the final production cycle is based on *kanban*. Mitsubishi and Honda, however, request products based on a forecast of demand and do not use *kanban*. Their final orders are placed three days in advance, and they have much more fluctuation in demand than does Toyota. Toyota tries to schedule a relatively flat production schedule, meaning that there is not a great deal of fluctuation in its demand, whereas the demand from Mitsubishi and Honda fluctuates a great deal. Even though DENSO supplies all major auto companies in Japan, it relies on Toyota for 56 percent of its revenues. It needs to figure out how to diversify its revenue base more without losing Toyota's business.

The U.S. subsidiary of DENSO purchased supply chain management software in 2002 to help it in demand planning, forecasting and scheduling, order management, and shipping control. This purchase will help DENSO International America to fulfill the needs of all its customers, not just Toyota. An alternative to *kanban* is MRP—material requirements planning. MRP is a computerized information system that addresses complex inventory situations like DENSO's (manufacturing parts for its own use as well as for several different auto companies). MRP calculates the demand for parts from the production schedules of the companies that use the parts. DENSO's dilemma is that some of its customers forecast demand, but Toyota uses *kanban* and requires delivery of parts when it empties its bins. DENSO is hoping that it can establish a good MRP or similar computer-based information system to solve the complexity of producing so many parts for so many different companies.

QUESTIONS

1. How has DENSO's relationship with Toyota affected its international strategy?
2. What types of quality programs has DENSO adopted, and how do you think they will affect DENSO's future as a global supplier?
3. Why does it make a difference whether DENSO uses *kanban* or MRP?
4. What challenges will DENSO face as it diversifies its customers and its product lines?
5. What do you notice in the layout of the Takatana plant that demonstrates DENSO's commitment to its employees?

Chapter Notes

1   The information in this case is from the following sources: F. De Beule and D. Van Den Bulcke, "The International Supply Chain Management of Samsonite Europe," Discussion Paper No. 1998/E/34, Centre for International Management and Development, University of Antwerp (1998); "Samsonite History" (2002): www.samsonite.com; "Company Briefing Book," *Wall Street Journal*, www.wsj.com (January 27, 2000); "Tüv Essen" http://tuvessen.com/; Samsonite Quarterly Report, SEC form 10-Q (2002); and "Samsonite Introduces POINT A Franchise Concept," Samsonite Web site (October 1, 2002): www.samsonite.com.

2   Deloitte & Touche, "Energizing the Supply Chain," *The Review* (January 17, 2000): 1.

3   Stanley Fawcett, "Supply Chain Management: Competing Through Integration," in Tom L. Beauchamp and Norman E. Bowie, eds., *Ethical Theory and Business* (Upper Saddle River, NJ: Prentice Hall, 1993), 514.

4   "Council of Logistics Management," http://www.clm1.org (2002).

5   Homin Chen and Tain-Jy Chen, "Network Linkages and Location Choice in Foreign Direct Investment," *Journal of International Business Studies* 29, no. 3 (Third Quarter 1998): 447.

6   For a discussion of firm-specific advantages, location-specific advantages, and internalization, see the following: John H. Dunning, *International Production and the Multinational Enterprise* (London: Allen & Unwin, 1981); Peter Buckley & Mark Casson, *The Future of the Multinational Enterprise* (London: Macmillan Press, 1976); and Peter Caves, "International Corporations: The Industrial Economics of Foreign Investment," *Economica* 56 (1971): 279–93.

7   "Few Companies Use Outsourcing as Strategic Business Imperative," *Supply Chain Brain's e-Insider* Newsletter (July 10, 2002): http://www.supplychainbrain.com/news/e07.10.02.newsletter.htm.

8   Stanley E. Fawcett and Anthony S. Roath, "The Viability of Mexican Production Sharing: Assessing the Four Cs of Strategic Fit," *Urbana* 3, no. 1 (1996): 29.

9   See S. C. Wheelwright, "Reflecting Corporate Strategy in Manufacturing Decisions," *Business*

Horizons 21, (February 1978); S. C. Wheelwright, "Manufacturing Strategy: Defining the Missing Link, *Strategic Management Journal* 5 (1984): 77–91; Frank DuBois, Brian Toyne, and Michael D. Oliff, "International Manufacturing Strategies of U.S. Multinationals: A Conceptual Framework Based on a Four-Industry Study," *Journal of International Business Studies* 24, no. 2 (Second Quarter 1993): 313–14; and Robert H. Hayes, Steven C. Wheelwright, and Kim B. Clark, *Dynamic Manufacturing* (New York: Free Press, 1988), 10–11.

10 Karby Leggett and Peter Wonacott, "Surge in Exports from China Gives a Jolt to Global Industry," *Wall Street Journal* (October 10, 2002): www.wsj.com.

11 Michael E. McGrath and Richard W. Hoole, "Manufacturing's New Economies of Scale," *Harvard Business Review* (May–June 1992): 94.

12 Fawcett and Roath, op. cit., 29.

13 Deloitte Counseling, "Energizing the Supply Chain: Trends and Issues in Supply Chain Management," (2000): www.dc.com.

14 Richard Karpinski, "Wal-Mart Mandates Secure, Internet-Based EDI for Suppliers," *Internetweek.com* (September 12, 2002): http://www.internetweek.com/supplyChain/INW20020912S0011.

15 "You'll Never Walk Alone," in "Business and the Internet: A Survey," *The Economist* (June 26, 1999): 11–12.

16 Fenella Scott and Jim Shepherd, "The Steady Stream of ERP Investments," AMR Research (August 26, 2002): www.amrreaserch.com.

17 www.dell.com (2002).

18 Karpinski, op. cit.

19 "How E-Biz Rose, Fell, and Will Rise Anew," *Business Week* (May 13, 2002): http://www.businessweek.com.

20 "You'll Never Walk Alone," op. cit., 17.

21 Cindy Cronin, "Five Success Factors for Private Trading Exchanges," *e-Business Advisor Magazine* (August 2001): http://businessadvisor.us/Articles.nsf/aid/CRONC01

22 Ibid., 17, 20.

23 Lee J. Krajewski and Larry P. Ritzman, *Operations Management: Strategy and Analysis*, 4th ed.

(Reading, MA: Addison-Wesley, 1996), 141–42.

24 See "Detroit Is Cruising for Quality," *Business Week* (September 3, 2001): www.businessweek.com; and Todd Zaun et al., "Auto Makers Get More Mileage from Low-Cost Plants Abroad," *Wall Street Journal* (July 31, 2002): www.wsj.com.

25 Hayes, Wheelwright, and Clark, op. cit., 17.

26 Krajewski and Ritzman, op. cit., 140.

27 Ibid., 156.

28 PricewaterhouseCoopers, "Six Sigma and Internal Control," (2002): http://www.pwcglobal.com/extweb/manissue.nsf/DocID/A09497E3D72ABCD085256B92005E627D.

29 See Jonathan B. Levine, "Want EC Business? You Have Two Choices," *Business Week* (October 19, 1992):58; and The International Organization for Standardization homepage (2002): http://www.iso.ch/iso/en/ISOOnline.frontpage, 2002.

30 Masaaki Kotabe and Glen S. Omura, "Sourcing Strategies of European and Japanese Multinationals: A Comparison," *Journal of International Business Studies* (Spring 1989): 120–22.

31 Robert M. Monczka and Robert J. Trent, "Global Sourcing: A Development Approach," *International Journal of Purchasing and Materials Management* (Spring 1991): 3.

32 Russell Johnston and Paul R. Lawrence, "Beyond Vertical Integration—The Rise of the Value-Adding Partnership," *Harvard Business Review* (July–August 1988): 98.

33 "Few Companies Use Outsourcing as Strategic Business Imperative," *Supply Chain Brain* (2002): www.supplychainbrain.com.

34 John McMillan, "Managing Suppliers: Incentive Systems in Japanese and U.S. Industry," *California Management Review* (Summer 1990): 38.

35 Ford Motor Company (2000): http://www.ford.com/ "Building Relationships (2000 Report)"

36 Joseph B. White, "Japanese Auto Makers Help Parts Suppliers Become More Efficient," *Wall Street Journal* (September 10, 1991): 1.

37 Ibid.

38 Monczka and Trent, op. cit., 4–5.

39 Stanley E. Fawcett, "The Globalization of the Supply Environment." *The Supply Environment* 2 (Tempe, AZ: NAPM, 2000).

40 Robert M. Monczka and Robert J. Trent, "Worldwide Sourcing: Assessment and Execution," *International Journal of Purchasing and Materials Management* (Fall 1992): 17–18.

41 "Auto Makers Team Up to Buy $13 Billion in Parts," *Wall Street Journal* (October 11, 2002): www.wsj.com.

42 Tim Minahan, "Making E-Sourcing Strategic," The Aberdeen Group (September 2002): http://www.aberdeen.com/ab_company/hottopics/esourcing2002/default.htm.

43 Gabriel Kahn, Trish Saywell, and Queena Sook Kim, "Backlog at West Coast Docks Keeps Christmas Toys at Sea," *Wall Street Journal* (October 21, 2002): www.wsj.com.

44 Krajewski and Ritzman, op. cit., 732.

45 Kahn, Saywell, and Kim, op. cit.

46 Shawnee K. Vickery, "International Sourcing: Implications for Just-in-Time Manufacturing," *Production and Inventory Management Journal* (Third Quarter 1989): 67.

47 Ibid., p. 69.

48 Ibid., p. 70.

49 "World Becomes Smaller as Japan, Central Europe Catch Zone Fever," *The Journal of Commerce and Commercial* (October 1991): 6B.

50 "Information Summary," Foreign-Trade Zones Board (February 2002): http://ia.ita.doc.gov/ftzpage/ftzinfo.html.

51 John J. DaPonte Jr., "Foreign-Trade Zones and Exports," *American Export Bulletin* (April 1978)

52 Fawcett, "The Globalization of the Supply Environment," op. cit., 11.

53 Tom L. Beauchamp and Norman E. Bowie, *Ethical Theory and Business*, 4th ed. (Upper Saddle River, NJ: Prentice Hall), 21–22.

54 Company reports from Toyota and DENSO; interviews with DENSO management; "DENSO International America Selects Future Three for E-Commerce Initiative," Future Three press release (August 6, 2002): http://www.future3.com/denso.htm.

CHAPTER 19

MULTINATIONAL ACCOUNTING AND TAX FUNCTIONS

Even between parents and children, money matters make strangers.

—JAPANESE PROVERB

OBJECTIVES

- To examine the major factors influencing the development of accounting practices in different countries and the worldwide harmonization of accounting principles
- To explain how companies account for foreign-currency transactions and translate foreign-currency financial statements
- To illustrate how companies report their impact on the environment
- To investigate the U.S. taxation of foreign-source income
- To examine some of the major non-U.S. tax practices and to show how international tax treaties can alleviate some of the impact of double taxation

CASE

Enron and International Accounting Harmonization[1]

The discovery of Enron's inflated earnings and underreported liabilities caused ripples throughout the global economy and accounting profession that couldn't be explained in 10 textbooks this size. Enron, an energy trading company based in Houston, Texas, was famous for posting huge profits in the newly deregulated electricity and natural gas industries. It specialized in creating contracts for companies that allowed them to hedge their exposure to fluctuations in energy prices and supply. By the end of 2000, Enron was a participant in one-quarter of all the electricity and gas deals done by energy producers, traders, and utilities. *Fortune* magazine called it the most innovative company in America, and it ranked number seven on the *Fortune* 500. It participated in trading weather derivatives and used its money to invest in foreign utilities, and CEO Jeffrey Skilling considered analysts, questioning of the company's business practices an act of heresy.

However, there was a dark side to Enron's success. Enron was not only innovative in the energy trading business, but it borrowed heavily to support its growth into emerging markets throughout the world. Using unusual accounting methods, Enron was able to hide most of these liabilities in separate operations off its balance sheets through partnerships and other special purpose entities. Over 3,000 companies were created, which issued bonds secured by Enron stock. However, since at least 3 percent of the stock of the companies was owned by outsiders, Enron didn't have to disclose their existence to shareholders. And most of these companies existed to manipulate Enron's quarterly earnings rather than to have a real business purpose. Investors had no idea of the risks involved with these off-balance-sheet companies. With the help of its auditor, Arthur Andersen, Enron was also able to inflate its earnings in a way that was invisible to the average investor. Enron's collapse was huge—at the time, the largest bankruptcy to ever be filed in the United States. Enron's stock price dropped from $90 to $0.36 per share in less than two years. The same "innovative" accounting structure that brought success to the company ultimately contributed to its untimely demise. Arthur Andersen was then faced with questions from the general public and the SEC about its auditing capabilities and the role it played in the Enron debacle. The questions and subpoenas would eventually cause the collapse of what was at the time the largest U.S. accounting firm. Andersen was eventually indicted, not because of accounting irregularities, but because it had shredded Enron-related documents and as a result of an obstruction of justice charge brought by the U.S. government.

Other major accounting crises developed in the cases of MCI WorldCom, Tyco International, Vivendi Universal, Global Crossing, and others. If there is a silver lining in these crises of confidence in the accounting system, it is that the need for harmonized, understandable accounting regulations is now emphasized around the world. The United States, including the Securities and Exchange Commission (SEC) and the Financial Accounting Standards Board (FASB), recognizes the need for reform of its accounting and auditing practices.

Even before Enron's collapse, the European Union announced that all EU firms will have to follow the International Accounting Standards by 2005. In September 2002, the FASB agreed to join with the International Accounting Standards Board (IASB) in the effort to eliminate the differences between their two standards. Both boards have a tentative goal to complete the first set of consistent standards by 2005. Bob Herz, a former member of the IASB, resigned from his IASB post to become the chairman of the U.S. FASB. Considering his past, he is thought to be the right man to serve as the catalyst who will harmonize the accounting standards of all nations, especially those of the United States. Before his new appointment to the FASB, Herz indicated that he was hopeful the FASB and the SEC would move away from their rules-based approach and move toward the IASB's principles-based approach. Accountants in the United States are wary of the legal liability that a principals-based approach might pose, because it relies more on judgment than on complying with specific accounting standards as is the case in the United States. The question is whether the political pressures of his new post will keep Herz from accomplishing what he indicated is needed for accounting standards.

The key, according to Herz, is the need of both sides to make concessions. Whether this sudden change in the U.S. perspective with respect to international accounting standards has resulted from the problems experienced with Enron and Andersen would be complete speculation. However, the flexibility of International Accounting Standards (IAS) is being applauded after the Enron scandal, with some saying that the scandal could have been avoided if the reporting had been based on IAS. This sudden change in opinion by the United States could create a globally understandable set of accounting standards that could increase the efficiency of the capital markets globally. As Bob Herz put it,

> U.S. GAAP has always been held up as the highest quality standard in the world, and if you measure quality by the number of rules you have, then [that standard is]. But the Enron collapse showed that prescriptive rules aren't the answer to everything.

The United States has promised in the past to allow foreign-based companies into its capital markets—without reconciliation—if foreign companies prepared their accounts according to international rules. However, this has yet to happen. Foreign companies that list their shares on the New York Stock Exchange, the world's largest and strongest capital market, still need to produce a reconciliation to U.S. generally accepted accounting principles (GAAP). Some analysts say the IASB's strength was weakened when Senator Carl Levin produced an e-mail from Enron suggesting that its executives would be able to pay for influence over the IASB's standards. However, many more analysts believe the bankruptcy of Enron should give the IASB more credibility in America. Partly because it shows the cracks in the so-called infallible U.S. standards and, more important, if international rules had been applied, Enron would have been forced to report more about its special-purpose vehicles.

The simple problem is that today's capital markets are global, and the existing auditing and accounting regulations are not. Accounting origins and traditions are as individual as the languages of the nations that produce them. This inconsistency is causing global investors and auditors headaches and raising the cost of capital for corporations worldwide. However, adopting global accounting standards is not the only important issue confronting those who want to reduce the cost of raising capital globally. Accounting standards are established for the purpose of providing relevant and reliable information, and there must be appropriate monitoring and enforcement infrastructure in place worldwide. Protecting the integrity of U.S. markets is the reason the SEC has remained reluctant to adopt standards that are too broad or allow too many optional treatments.

In order to establish its credibility with the United States, the IASB appointed several influential U.S. officials to the board of trustees. Arthur Levitt, former chairman of the SEC, was appointed as head of the group that chose the initial trustees. Because the European Union and United States comprise the world's largest capital markets, the IASB ended up with an unbalanced board. Europe and the United States account for 13 of the 19 International Accounting Standards Committee (IASC) foundation trustees and 10 out of the 14 IASB board members. Developing countries fare much worse, with only Brazil making the list. Nevertheless, many of these developing countries have adopted IASB standards to increase their access to the world's capital markets. The FASB, in an announcement in October 2002, said that it will issue a final statement by the end of 2003, one that will set forth those differences with IASB standards that will be eliminated. However, much remains to be done in the ongoing effort to harmonize and merge the world's accounting standards. What form will international accounting standards (IASs) take? Will enough countries adopt IASs completely to allow comparability between financial statements? What cultural, economic, and institutional factors will have to be overcome for worldwide adoption of these international accounting standards?

Bank secrecy laws are often associated with Switzerland, although a number of countries offer secrecy and havens from tax payments. The photo shows the safe deposit in Zurich Kantonalbank in Zurich, Switzerland.

INTRODUCTION

International business managers cannot make good decisions without relevant and reliable information about accounting and taxation (Figure 19.1). Although accounting and information systems specialists provide such information, managers must also understand which data they need and the problems specialists face in gathering it from different accounting systems around the world. The accounting and finance functions of any MNE are closely related. Each relies on the other to fulfill its own responsibilities.

The financial manager of any company—domestic or international—is responsible for procuring and managing the company's financial resources. This individual is usually one of the members of the top management team of a company. For example, Manfred Gentz, one of the 13 members of the board of management of DaimlerChrysler, is the head of Finance and Controlling. John Connors was the Chief Financial Officer (CFO) for Microsoft in 2002, and he was also senior vice president of Finance and Administration, serving as one of only 15 executive officers of the firm. The controller, or chief accountant, of Microsoft would report to Mr. Connors. The CFO relies on the accountant to provide the right information. Jacques

The accountant is essential in providing information to financial decision makers.

FIGURE 19.1   Accounting in International Business

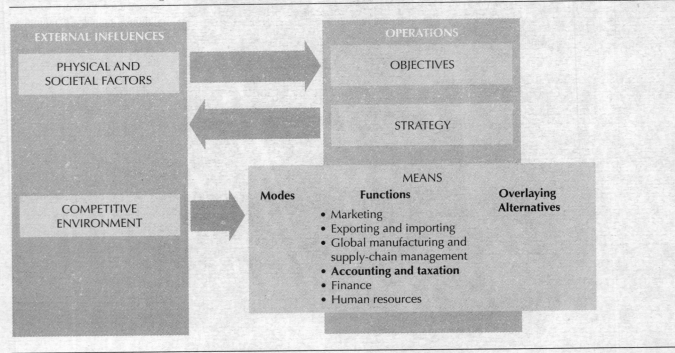

EXTERNAL INFLUENCES

PHYSICAL AND
SOCIETAL FACTORS

COMPETITIVE
ENVIRONMENT

OPERATIONS

OBJECTIVES

STRATEGY

MEANS

Modes   Functions   Overlaying
                                      Alternatives
• Marketing
• Exporting and importing
• Global manufacturing and
  supply-chain management
• **Accounting and taxation**
• Finance
• Human resources

Accounting is one of the necessary functions for implementing companies' international strategies.

Espinasse, who takes over for Guilluame Hannezo as senior vice president and CFO of Vivendi Universal in mid-2002, holds an MBA. from the University of Michigan. He has the responsibility, along with the CEO, for the reorganization of Vivendi Universal as the result of a massive acquisition campaign during the past few years, which transformed the company from a water and waste management company into a media giant.

The actual and potential flow of assets across national boundaries complicates the finance and accounting functions. The MNE must learn to cope with differing inflation rates, exchange-rate changes, currency controls, expropriation risks, customs duties, tax rates and

FIGURE 19.2

The role of the corporate controller has expanded beyond the traditional roles of management accounting.

Source: From *the Wall Street Journal*—Permission, Cartoon Features Syndicate.

methods of determining taxable income, levels of sophistication of local accounting personnel, and local as well as home-country reporting requirements.

A company's controllership (accounting) function collects and analyzes data for internal and external users. The traditional responsibilities of the controller are

> the process of identification, measurement, accumulation, analysis, preparation, interpretation, and communication of financial information used by management to plan, evaluate, and control [activities] within an organization and to assure [the] appropriate use of accountability for [the organization's] resources. Management accounting also comprises the preparation of financial reports for nonmanagement groups such as shareholders, auditors, regulatory agencies, and tax authorities.[2]

However, the role of the corporate controller has expanded beyond the traditional roles of management accounting. Today's controller is engaged in other activities in the international arena, such as evaluating potential acquisitions abroad, disposing of a subsidiary or a division, managing cash flow, seeking new sources of financing, hedging currency and interest rate risks, tax planning, and helping in the planning of corporate strategy.[3] Today's accountant must have a much broader perspective of business in general—and international business in particular for the purposes of this book—than was the case even as recently as a decade ago.

As Chapter 15 noted, foreign managers and subsidiaries are usually evaluated on the basis of data from the controller's office. The controller generates reports for internal consideration, local government needs, creditors, employees, stockholders, and prospective investors. The controller handles the impact of many different currencies and inflation rates on the statements and should be familiar with different countries' accounting systems.

This chapter discusses some key accounting and tax issues facing companies that do business abroad. Initially, we will examine how accounting differs around the world and how global capital markets are forcing countries to consider harmonizing their accounting and reporting standards. Then we will examine some unique issues facing MNEs, such as accounting for foreign-currency transactions, translating foreign-currency financial statements, reporting on foreign operations to shareholders and potential investors, and dealing with tax issues. Although the focus will be on problems of MNEs, many of these issues affect any company doing business overseas, even a small importer or exporter. Foreign-currency transactions, such as denominating a sale or purchase in a foreign currency, must be accounted for in dollars, and this is true of both large and small firms. In addition, even small companies have to figure out how to tax the earnings on foreign revenues.

The controller of an international company must be concerned about different currencies and accounting systems.

FACTORS INFLUENCING THE DEVELOPMENT OF ACCOUNTING AROUND THE WORLD

One problem that an MNE faces is that accounting standards and practices vary around the world. Financial statements in different countries even look different from each other in both form (or format) and content (or substance). To illustrate that substance (the content and quality of information in the financial statements), let's compare the balance sheet of France-based Vivendi Universal from Table 19.1 with those of companies from two other countries. Table 19.2 contains the balance sheet for Intel, the U.S.-based microcomputer components company, and Table 19.3 contains the balance sheet for Marks & Spencer, the U.K.-based retail company. The balance sheets for Vivendi Universal and Intel are in the format of

Both the form and the content of financial statements are different in different countries.

$$\text{Assets} = \text{Liabilities} + \text{Shareholders' equity}$$

The major difference between Vivendi Universal and Intel is the order of liquidity. Vivendi Universal starts with the least liquid assets and goes to the most liquid assets, whereas Intel starts with the most liquid assets and moves to the least liquid.

● TABLE 19.1

VIVENDI UNIVERSAL BALANCE SHEET (IN € MILLIONS)

	2001	2000
ASSETS		
Goodwill, net	€37,617	€47,133
Other intangible assets, net	23,302	20,180
Property, plant and equipment, net	23,396	19,989
Investments accounted for using the equity method	9,176	9,177
Seagram's spirit and wine net assets held for sale	—	8,759
Other investments	5,583	7,342
Total long-term assets	**99,074**	**112,580**
Inventories & work in progress	3,163	3,219
Accounts receivable	21,094	19,242
Deferred tax assets	4,225	3,908
Short-term loans receivable	2,948	1,171
Cash and cash equivalents	4,725	3,271
Other marketable securities	3,773	7,347
Total current assets	**39,928**	**38,158**
TOTAL ASSETS	**€139,002**	**€150,738**
SHAREHOLDERS' EQUITY AND LIABILITIES		
Share capital	€5,972	€5,945
Additional paid-in capital	28,837	27,913
Retained earnings	1,939	22,817
Total shareholders' equity	**36,748**	**56,675**
Minority interest	10,208	9,787
Deferred income	1,856	1,560
Provisions and allowances	6,331	5,946
Long-term debt	27,777	23,954
Other long-term liabilities and accrued expenses	5,688	6,337
Total long-term liabilities	**88,608**	**104,259**
Accounts payable	26,414	23,497
Deferred taxes	9,977	8,130
Bank overdrafts and other short-term borrowings	14,003	14,852
Total current liabilities	**50,394**	**46,479**
TOTAL LIABILITIES AND SHAREHOLDERS' EQUITY	**€139,002**	**€150,738**

Source: Courtesy of Vivendi Universal Corporation, FY2001 Balance Sheet (2001): www.vivendiuniversal.com.

● TABLE 19.2

INTEL CORPORATION BALANCE SHEET, IN MILLIONS—EXCEPT PAR VALUE, DECEMBER 29, 2001 AND DECEMBER 30, 2000

	2001	2000
Assets		
Current assets:		
Cash and cash equivalents	$7,970	$2,976
Short-term investments	2,356	10,497
Trading assets	1,224	350

	2001	2000
Assets		
Accounts receivable, net of allowance for doubtful accounts of $68 ($84 in 2000)	2,607	4,129
Inventories	2,253	2,241
Deferred tax assets	958	721
Other current assets	265	236
Total current assets	**17,633**	**21,150**
Property, plant and equipment:		
Land and buildings	10,709	7,416
Machinery and equipment	21,605	15,994
Construction in progress	2,042	4,843
	34,356	28,253
Less accumulated depreciation	16,235	13,240
Property, plant and equipment, net	**18,121**	**15,013**
Marketable strategic equity securities	**155**	**1,915**
Other long-term investments	**1,319**	**1,797**
Goodwill, net	**4,330**	**4,977**
Acquisition-related intangibles, net	**797**	**964**
Other assets	**2,040**	**2,129**
Total assets	**$44,395**	**$47,945**
Liabilities and stockholders' equity		
Current liabilities:		
Short-term debt	$409	$378
Accounts payable	1,769	2,387
Accrued compensation and benefits	1,179	1,696
Accrued advertising	560	782
Deferred income on shipments to distributors	418	674
Other accrued liabilities	1,247	1,440
Income taxes payable	988	1,293
Total current liabilities	**6,570**	**8,650**
Long-term debt	**1,050**	**707**
Deferred tax liabilities	**945**	**1,266**
Commitments and contingencies		
Stockholders' equity:		
Preferred stock, $0.001 par value, 50 shares authorized; none issued	–	–
Common stock, $0.001 par value, 10,000 shares authorized; 6,690 issued and outstanding (6,721 in 2000) and capital in excess of par value	8,833	8,486
Acquisition-related unearned stock compensation	(178)	(97)
Accumulated other comprehensive income	25	195
Retained earnings	27,150	28,738
Total stockholders' equity	**35,830**	**37,322**
Total liabilities and stockholders' equity	**$44,395**	**$47,945**

Source: The Consolidated Balance Sheet reprinted from the 2001 Annual Report of Intel Corporation is courtesy of Intel Corporation, copyright © 2002, all rights reserved.

● **TABLE 19.3**

MARKS & SPENCER BALANCE SHEET

	NOTES	THE GROUP 2001 £M	THE GROUP 2000 £M	THE COMPANY 2001 £M	THE COMPANY 2000 £M
Fixed Assets					
Goodwill	12	–	1.3	–	–
Tangible Assets					
Land and buildings		**2,735.2**	2,774.1	**2,430.4**	2,458.5
Fit out, fixtures, fittings and equipment		**1,291.9**	1,386.7	**1,056.2**	1,145.3
Assets in the course of construction		**91.8**	81.3	**51.2**	44.8
	13	**4,118.9**	4,242.1	**3,537.8**	3,648.6
Investments	14	**58.3**	55.0	**445.8**	450.4
		4,177.2	4,297.1	**3,983.6**	4,099.0
Current Assets					
Stocks		**472.5**	474.4	**299.7**	315.1
Debtors					
Receivable within one year	15A	**917.2**	988.3	**642.7**	795.2
Receivable after more than one year	15B	**1,712.1**	1,566.9	**72.9**	80.3
Investments	16	**260.0**	386.4	–	–
Cash at Bank and In Hand	17	**154.4**	301.1	**82.0**	89.8
		3,516.2	3,717.1	**1,097.3**	1,280.4
Current Liabilities					
Creditors amounts falling due within one year	19	**(1,981.6)**	(2,162.8)	**(729.1)**	(736.0)
Net Current Assets		**1,534.6**	1,554.3	**368.2**	544.4
Total Assets Less Current Liabilities		**5,711.8**	5,851.4	**4,351.8**	4,643.4
Creditors amounts falling due after more than one year	20	**(735.1)**	(804.3)	–	–
Provisions for liabilities and charges	22	**(315.7)**	(126.6)	**(119.2)**	(113.0)
Net Assets		**4,661.0**	4,920.5	**4,232.6**	4,530.4
Capital and Reserves					
Called up share capital	24,25	**716.9**	718.6	**716.9**	718.6
Share premium account	25	**375.6**	369.4	**375.6**	369.4
Revaluation reserve	25	**455.6**	457.9	**454.0**	458.9
Capital redemption reserve	25	**2.6**	–	**2.6**	–
Profit and loss account	25	**3,094.7**	3,359.4	**2,683.5**	2,983.5
Shareholders Funds (All Equity)	25	**4,645.4**	4,905.3	**4,232.6**	4,530.4
Minority interests (all equity)		**15.6**	16.5	–	–
Total Capital Employed		**4,661.0**	4,921.8	**4,232.6**	4,530.4

Source: From Marks & Spencer Balance Sheet, 31 March 2001. Reprinted by permission.

The balance sheet for Marks & Spencer is in the analytical format of

fixed assets + current assets − current liabilities − noncurrent liabilities = capital and reserves

In the case of Marks & Spencer, "creditors amounts falling due after more than one year" is the same as noncurrent liabilities. Some terms are different, such as *inventories* under the current assets section of Intel's report and *stocks* in the Marks & Spencer report, and *receivables* and *payables* or *liabilities* for Intel and Vivendi Universal and *debtors* and *creditors* for Marks

& Spencer. In addition, Intel presents only a set of consolidated financial statements, whereas Marks & Spencer presents both company (meaning "parent company") and group ("consolidated") financial statements. Some observers argue that differences in format are a minor matter, a problem of form rather than substance. In fact, however, the substance also differs, because companies can measure assets and determine income differently in different countries. This concept was illustrated in the case of Vivendi Universal when it reported different income numbers in 2001 under French GAAP and U.S. GAAP. In 2001, Vivendi Universal reported a net loss of € −13,597, million in accordance with the French GAAP, but it reported a net loss of € −1,172 million under U.S. GAAP, a difference of € 12,425 million, or approximately $12.6 billion.

Accounting Objectives

Accounting is defined as "a service activity whose function is to provide quantitative information, primarily financial in nature, about economic entities that is intended to be useful in making economic decisions and in making reasoned choices among alternative courses of action."[4] It is important for the accounting process to identify, record, and interpret economic events. Every country needs to determine what objectives of the accounting system it has put into place.

> Accounting provides information for decision making.

According to the **Financial Accounting Standards Board**, the private sector body that establishes accounting standards in the United States, financial reporting, the external reporting of accounting information, should provide information for the purposes of

> The Financial Accounting Standards Board (FASB) sets accounting standards in the United States.

- Investment and credit decisions.
- Assessment of cash flow prospects.
- Evaluation of enterprise resources, claims to those resources, and changes in them.[5]

To establish objectives, managers have to determine who are the major users of financial information. The International Accounting Standards Board (IASB) and its predecessor, the International Accounting Standards Committee, identify the following key users:

> The IASB is an international private sector organization that sets accounting standards.

- Investors
- Employees
- Lenders
- Suppliers and other trade creditors
- Customers
- Governments and their agencies
- The public[6]

> Critical users of accounting information are investors, employees, lenders, suppliers and other trade creditors, customers, governments and their agencies, and the public.

It is important to identify users, because a focus on different users might result in different financial information being reported. For example, Germany's major users have historically been creditors, so accounting has focused more on the balance sheet, which contains a description of the company's assets. In the United States, however, the major users are investors, so accounting has focused more on the income statement. Investors see the income statement as an indication of the future success of the company, which affects the company's stock and its flow of dividends. There is no consensus on whether there should be a uniform set of accounting standards and practices for all classes of users worldwide—or even for one class of users—but the general movement seems to be toward investors.

In Figure 19.3, we identify some of the forces leading to the development of accounting practices internationally. Although all of the factors shown in the figure are significant, their importance varies by country. For example, investors are an influence in the United States and the United Kingdom, but creditors—primarily banks—are more of an influence in Germany and Switzerland.

> Equity markets are an important source of influence on accounting in the United States and the United Kingdom. Banks are influential in Germany and Switzerland, and taxation is a major influence in Japan and France.

FIGURE 19.3   Environmental Influences on Accounting Practices

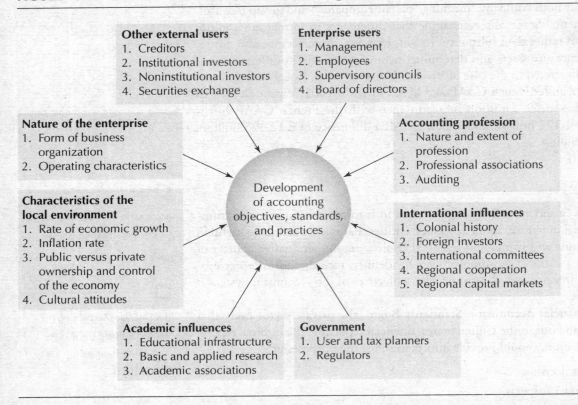

Other external users
1. Creditors
2. Institutional investors
3. Noninstitutional investors
4. Securities exchange

Enterprise users
1. Management
2. Employees
3. Supervisory councils
4. Board of directors

Nature of the enterprise
1. Form of business organization
2. Operating characteristics

Accounting profession
1. Nature and extent of profession
2. Professional associations
3. Auditing

Characteristics of the local environment
1. Rate of economic growth
2. Inflation rate
3. Public versus private ownership and control of the economy
4. Cultural attitudes

International influences
1. Colonial history
2. Foreign investors
3. International committees
4. Regional cooperation
5. Regional capital markets

Development of accounting objectives, standards, and practices

Academic influences
1. Educational infrastructure
2. Basic and applied research
3. Academic associations

Government
1. User and tax planners
2. Regulators

The importance of any of these environmental influences on accounting practices varies by country.

Source: Reprinted from *The International Journal of Accounting,* Fall 1975, by Lee H. Radebaugh, "Environmental Factors Influencing the Development of Accounting Objectives, Standards and Practices—The Peruvian Case," p. 41, with permission from Elsevier Science.

Generally accepted accounting principles (GAAP) are those established in each country that must be followed by companies when generating their financial statements.

Culture influences measurement and disclosure practices.

Measurement—how to value assets.

Disclosure—the presentation of information and discussion of results.

Taxation has a big influence on accounting standards and practices in Japan and France, but it is less important in the United States. Certain international factors also have weight, such as former colonial influence and foreign investment. For example, most countries that are current or former members of the British Commonwealth have accounting systems similar to the United Kingdom's. Former French colonies use the French model, and so forth. Thus, companies from those countries use standards and practices that are similar to companies from other countries in the same group. These differences in accounting influences have resulted in differences in accounting standards and practices. As we saw in the opening case, the differences complicate things for MNEs, because they need to prepare and understand reports generated according to local **generally accepted accounting principles** as well as prepare financial statements consistent with the GAAP in the home country. Each country may have its own GAAP, which are the accounting standards recognized by the profession as being required in the preparation of financial statements by external users.

Cultural Differences in Accounting

A major source of influence on accounting standards and practices is culture. Of special interest to international investors are the differences in measurement and disclosure practices among countries—*measurement* meaning "how companies value assets, including inventory and fixed assets"; *disclosure* meaning "how and what information companies provide and discuss in their annual and interim reports for external users of financial data."

Figure 19.4 depicts the accounting practices of various groupings of countries within a matrix of the cultural values of secrecy-transparency and optimism-conservatism. With respect to accounting, secrecy and transparency indicate the degree to which companies disclose information to the public. Countries such as Germany, Switzerland, and Japan tend to have less disclosure (illustrating the cultural value of secrecy) than do the United States and the United Kingdom—both are Anglo-Saxon countries—which are more transparent or open with respect to disclosure. This is illustrated by the more extensive footnote disclosures in reports of the Anglo-Saxon countries than is the case elsewhere. However, the Enron scandal illustrates that companies from supposedly open and transparent countries can also be secretive.

Optimism and conservatism (in an accounting, not a political sense) are the degree of caution companies exhibit in valuing assets and recognizing income—an illustration of the measurement issues mentioned earlier. Countries more conservative from an accounting point of view tend to understate assets and income, while optimistic countries tend to be more liberal in their recognition of income. As noted earlier in the chapter, banks primarily fund French companies, which is true also in Germany and Japan, and banks are concerned with liquidity. So French companies tend to be very conservative both when recording profits that keep them from paying taxes and when declaring dividends in order to pile up cash reserves to service their bank debt. In contrast, U.S. companies want to show earnings power to impress and attract investors. British companies tend to be more optimistic in earnings recognition than are U.S. companies, but U.S. companies are much more optimistic than continental European and Japanese companies. The Asian financial crisis demonstrated that most Asian countries still fit squarely in the upper-right quadrant of measurement and disclosure. In particular, companies from Korea and Southeast Asia were guilty of a lack of transparency, which made it difficult for banks and investors to know where to lend and invest their money. They often put their money in Asian companies on the basis of relationships and reputation instead of good financial information. One of the reforms the IMF strongly recommended was for Asian countries to improve transparency in the financial reporting of their companies so that the capital markets could operate more efficiently.

In spite of the differences shown in Figure 19.4, there is clear evidence that countries in the upper-right quadrant, especially the Germanic and Latin European countries, are moving

Secrecy and transparency refer to the degree to which corporations disclose information to the public. Optimism and conservatism refer to the degree of caution companies display in valuing assets and recognizing income.

British companies are optimistic when recognizing income, and U.S. companies are slightly less optimistic. Japanese and continental European companies are even less optimistic than U.S. ones.

FIGURE 19.4 Cultural Differences in Measurement and Disclosure for Accounting Systems

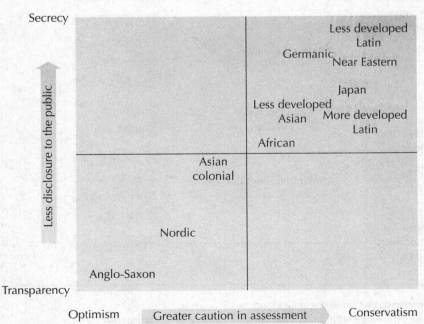

Anglo-Saxon countries (such as the United Kingdom and the United States) have accounting systems that tend to be transparent and optimistic. Systems in Germanic countries, for example, tend to be secretive and conservative.

Source: International Accounting and Multinational Enterprises, 5th edition, by Lee H. Radebaugh and Sidney J. Gray, Copyright © 2002, John Wiley & Sons, Inc. This material is used by permmission of John Wiley & Sons, Inc.

toward more optimism and transparency due to the influence of capital markets, which require disclosures more in line with the Anglo-Saxon model.

Classification of Accounting Systems

Although accounting standards and practices differ significantly worldwide, we can still group systems used in various countries according to common characteristics. Figure 19.5 illustrates one approach to classifying accounting systems. It does not attempt to classify all countries, but it simply illustrates the concept using several developed Western countries.

The authors used the concept of natural science to classify countries. As you move from left to right, you move from the general to the specific. Macro-uniform systems are shaped more by government influence than are micro-based systems. The major accounting influences on countries that fit into the macro-uniform category are a strong legal system, especially a codified legal system rather than a common law system, and tax law. These systems also tend to be more conservative and secretive about disclosure. Japan and Germany are legal-based systems, and Spain and France are tax-based systems. The former Soviet-bloc countries would also fit in the macro category. However, China is trying to adopt international accounting standards that are more in line with capital markets, thus being more micro than macro in orientation.

Micro-based systems include features that support pragmatic business practice and have evolved from the British system. The United States is an example of a country that

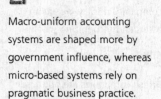

Macro-uniform accounting systems are shaped more by government influence, whereas micro-based systems rely on pragmatic business practice.

FIGURE 19.5   Classification of Accounting Systems of Developed Western Countries

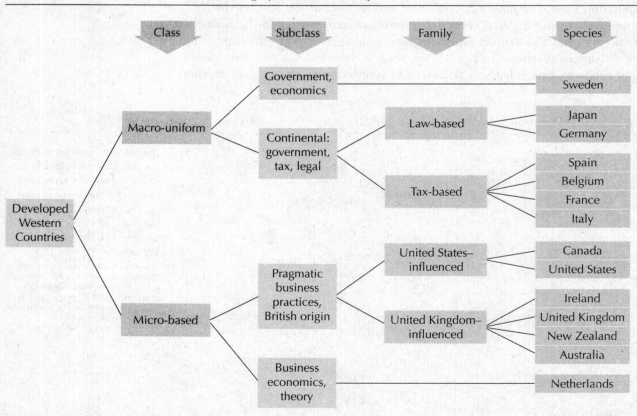

Accounting systems can be macro-uniform or micro-based depending on how important government influence is.

Source: From C. W. Nobes, "A Judgmental International Classification of Financial Reporting Practices," *Journal of Business Finance and Accounting* (Spring 1983): Reprinted by permission of Blackwell Publishing Ltd.

fits in the micro category. It exhibits more optimism and transparency than countries in the macro category, and it also relies less on legal and tax requirements than do Germany, France, and Japan. The focus tends to be more on capital markets and less on banks and tax authorities. Other countries that closely model the United States are Mexico and Canada, two members of NAFTA. The British model is also a micro-based model, but it relies even less on legal and tax influences than does the United States. Current and former members of the British Commonwealth, such as the Bahamas, Australia, and New Zealand, also fit into this category.

International Accounting Standards (IAS) more closely approximate the standards used in micro-based systems. Companies in countries belonging to the European Union are required to adopt IAS by the year 2005. Also, many countries throughout the world have adopted IAS as their reporting standard. Stock exchanges in 52 countries allow IAS at least as an allowable alternative to their country GAAP. More countries are expected to follow this trend to harmonization, which is discussed in a later section of this chapter.

The bottom line is that MNEs need to adjust to different accounting systems around the world, thus making the accounting function more complex and costly. The financial statements of a company include not only the statements themselves but also the accompanying footnotes. Companies that list on stock exchanges usually provide an income statement, a balance sheet, a statement of stockholder's equity, and a cash flow statement. In addition, they provide extensive footnotes, depending on the country where they list. The financial statements of one country differ from those in another country in six major ways:

1. Language
2. Currency
3. Type of statements (income statement, balance sheet, etc.)
4. Financial statement format
5. Extent of footnote disclosures
6. Underlying GAAP on which the financial statements are based

Major reporting issues:
- Language
- Currency
- Type of statements (income statement, etc.)
- Financial statement format
- Extent of footnote disclosures
- Underlying GAAP on which the financial statements are based

A company wishing to provide financial information for investors throughout the world needs to deal with all six issues. As far as language goes, English tends to be the first choice of companies choosing to raise capital abroad, but other languages do appear. For example, in its 2001 annual report, DaimlerChrysler lists the languages available for the following publications:[7]

DOCUMENT	EDITION (LANGUAGE)
Interim Report 2nd Quarter 2002	English German
Interim Report 1st Quarter 2002	English German
Annual Report 2001 DaimlerChrysler	English German
Annual Report on Form 20-F 2001 Report	English

Intel and Marks & Spencer also provide their information in English, although Intel uses American English and Marks & Spencer uses British English. Many companies also provide a significant amount of information on their homepages on the Internet in different languages. Managers can just click on the desired language button, and all the information is provided in that language. For example, Ericsson, the Swedish telecommunications company, has a homepage full of information for people all over the world. The company even has a link, www.ericsson.com.br, which gives financial information, as well as general information, in Portuguese.

A second issue in classifying systems is currency. As we saw in Vivendi Universal's case, the financial statements are provided in euros, although the 2001 figures are provided in dollars in the English version of the 20-F reconciliation (Table 19.8). Intel's financial statements are in U.S. dollars, and Marks & Spencer's reports are in British pounds. Not only does Ericsson provide its balance sheet and income statement in Portuguese to Brazilian readers, but it also provides the information in reals, Brazil's currency.

As noted earlier, a company can issue several major financial statements. Most countries require the balance sheet and income statement. Not all require a statement of cash flows, but such a statement is becoming more common. Foreign corporations that want to list their securities on the New York Stock Exchange must provide a statement of cash flows because that is required for U.S. companies as well. One of the few international standards allowed by the U.S. SEC is IAS 7, which requires a cash flow statement that is essentially the same as FASB Statement 95.

Financial statement format is not a big issue, but it can be confusing for a manager to read a balance sheet prepared in an analytical format, as is the case with Marks & Spencer, when the manager is used to seeing it in the balance format, as is the case with Intel. A major area of difference is the use of footnotes. Footnote disclosures in the United States tend to be the most comprehensive in the world. For example, U.S. companies go into great detail describing the way certain information is determined as well as the detail behind the numbers. Greater transparency is synonymous with more extensive footnote disclosures.

Finally, the most problematic area is that of differences in underlying GAAP. A major hurdle in raising capital in different countries is dealing with widely varying accounting and disclosure requirements. Although this problem is decreasing as more stock exchanges allow the use of IAS, some countries care more about those differences than others. In Germany and the Netherlands, for example, the principle of *mutual recognition* applies. That means that a foreign registrant that wants to list and have its securities traded on the Frankfurt or Amsterdam stock exchange need only provide information prepared according to the GAAP of the home country. However, other exchanges, like the New York Stock Exchange and NASDAQ, require foreign registrants either to *reconcile* their home-country financial statements with the local GAAP or to *recast* their financial statements in accordance with local GAAP. In the United States, this information is provided in a document called Form 20-F, which companies must file with the SEC. That is what Vivendi Universal does for its financial statements registered in the United States.

Major approaches to dealing with accounting and reporting differences:

- Mutual recognition
- Reconciliation to local GAAP
- Recast financial statements in terms of local GAAP

HARMONIZATION OF DIFFERENCES IN ACCOUNTING STANDARDS

Despite the many differences in accounting standards and practices, a number of forces are leading to harmonization, such as

- A movement to provide information compatible with the needs of investors.
- The global integration of capital markets, which means that investors have easier and faster access to investment opportunities around the world and, therefore, need financial information that is more comparable.
- The need of MNEs to raise capital outside of their home-country capital markets while generating as few different financial statements as possible.
- Regional political and economic harmonization, such as the efforts of the EU, which affects accounting as well as trade and investment issues.
- Pressure from MNEs for more uniform standards to allow greater ease and reduced costs in general reporting in each country.

Major forces leading to harmonization:

- Investor orientation
- Global integration of capital markets
- MNEs' need for foreign capital
- Regional political and economic harmonization
- MNEs' desire to reduce accounting and reporting costs

Spurred by these developments, some countries and organizations are working to harmonize accounting standards on a regional as well as an international level. Regionally, the most ambitious effort is taking place in the EU, which is interested in promoting the free flow of capital throughout Europe. The European Commission is empowered to set directives, which are orders to member countries to bring their laws into line with EU requirements within a certain transition period. The EU's initial accounting directives identified the type and format of financial statements that European companies have to use, the measurement bases on which they should prepare financial statements, and the importance of consolidated financial statements. It also required auditors to ensure that financial statements reflect a true and fair view of the operations of the company being audited instead of just adhering to the national laws of the different countries. The EU's influence is spreading beyond its members. Other countries in Europe, both Eastern and Western, are in the process of adopting EU accounting directives in preparation for becoming members.

The EU's directives improved the comparability of financial statements, but member countries can still interpret the directives differently. Thus, EU companies listing outside of their home countries must still provide two sets of financial statements—the home-country statements and reconciliation. To enhance the harmonization process, the EU has decided to support the harmonization efforts of the IASB. In the spring of 2002, the EU directed its member countries to adopt International Accounting Standards, as set forth by the IASB, by 2005. The reason for choosing the IASB is that the EU can influence standards because it is represented on the IASB, and it also avoids funding and developing a competing standards-setting body.[8]

The IASC, the forerunner of the IASB, was organized in 1973 by the professional accounting bodies of Australia, Canada, France, Germany, Japan, Mexico, the Netherlands, the United Kingdom and Ireland, and the United States, has worked toward harmonizing accounting standards. Initially, the IASC wanted to develop standards that would have rapid and broad acceptance, focusing mostly on improved disclosure. However, it became obvious that the major stock exchanges of the world would never accept such loose standards for companies that wanted to list on the exchanges. There were too few standards and too many alternatives permitted for the standards that had been issued. In addition, there was no enforcement mechanism other than the best efforts of the member organizations to ensure that the standards would be adhered to in the individual countries.

The turning point in the significance of IASC standards came in 1995 when the International Organization of Securities Commissions (IOSCO) announced publicly that it would endorse IASC standards if the IASC developed a set of core standards acceptable to IOSCO. IOSCO is significant because it is comprised of the stock market regulators of most of the stock markets in the world, including the SEC in the United States. Once IASC completed its work, IOSCO would permit foreign companies to list on their exchanges using IASC standards without having to reconcile to local GAAP.

Another major factor affecting the harmonization of accounting standards worldwide was the reorganization of the IASC in 2000. The international professional activities of the accountancy bodies were organized under the International Federation of Accountants (IFAC) in 1977. IFAC comprises 156 professional accounting organizations representing 114 countries and over two million accountants. Map 19.1 identifies IFAC member countries. In 1981, IASC and IFAC agreed that IASC would have full and complete autonomy in the setting of international accounting standards and in the issue of discussion documents on international accounting issues. At the same time, all members of IFAC became members of IASC. This relationship continued until the IASC's constitution was changed in May 2000 as part of the reorganization of the IASC.

Trustees for the IASC foundation searched for and appointed members of the IASB, the new international standards-setting body. In order to ensure a broad international basis, the trustees of the foundation came from North America (6 trustees), Europe (6), Asia/Pacific (4), and at-large (3). The IASB consists of 14 members, appointed by the trustees, from 9 countries primarily in Europe and North America. The trustees brought the new structure into effect on April 1, 2001.[9]

Before the Enron scandal and the collapse of Arthur Andersen, the major challenge to the supremacy of the IASB's GAAP was the United States. Because the U.S. stock market is the largest stock market in the world, hosting about half of the world's stock market capitalization

The EU is harmonizing accounting to promote the free flow of capital.

Other countries in Europe, including those of Eastern Europe and the former Soviet Union, are following the lead of the EU.

The International Organization of Securities Commissions wants the IASC to develop a core set of accounting standards that securities regulators can have confidence in.

The IASB comprises professional accounting bodies and is attempting to harmonize accounting standards.

MAP 19.1   Membership of the International Federation of Accountancy and International Accounting Standards Board

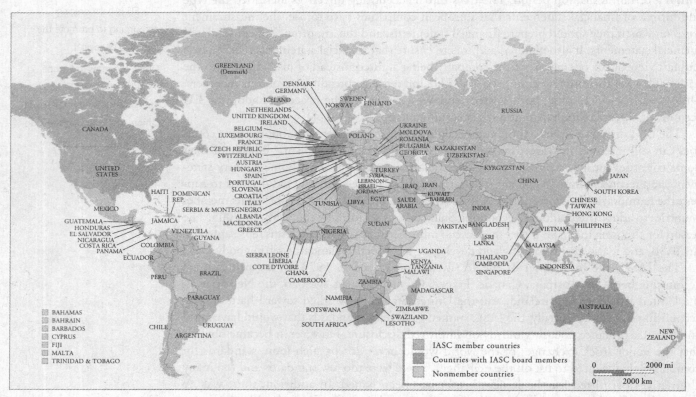

The IFAC membership consists of 156 accountancy organizations from 114 countries. The members from the United States are the American Institute of Certified Public Accountants, the Institute of Management of Accountants, the National Association of State Boards of Accountancy, Information Systems Audit and Control Association, and the Institute of Internal Auditors. The IASB's 14 board members come from 9 countries.

Source: See http://www.ifac.org/MemberBodies.html for list of member countries of IFAC.

(the number of shares of stock traded times the market price of the shares), U.S. accounting standards dominate. For IASB standards to have universal acceptance, the U.S. SEC will have to accept the standards. There are still many differences between IASB GAAP and U.S. GAAP. However, those differences should disappear as the U.S. and the IASB work to combine their standards rather than to compete against one another for supremacy.

TRANSACTIONS IN FOREIGN CURRENCIES

In addition to eliminating or minimizing foreign-exchange risk, a company must concern itself with the proper recording and subsequent accounting of assets, liabilities, revenues, and expenses that are measured or denominated in foreign currencies. These transactions can result from the purchase and sale of goods and services as well as the borrowing and lending of foreign currency.

Recording of Transactions

Any time an importer has to pay for equipment or merchandise in a foreign currency, it must trade its own currency for that of the exporter to make the payment. Assume Sundance Ski Lodge, a U.S. company, buys skis from a French supplier for 28,000 euros when the exchange rate is 1.1000 dollars per euro. Sundance records the following in its books:

Purchases	5,500	
Accounts payable		5,500

€ 5,000 @ 1.1000

If Sundance pays immediately, there is no problem. But what happens if the exporter extends 30-days' credit to Sundance? The original entry would be the same as the one here, but during the next 30 days, anything could happen. If the rate changed to 1.1500 dollar per euro by the time the payment was due, Sundance would record a final settlement as

Accounts payable	5,500	
Loss on foreign exchange	250	
Cash		5,750

The merchandise stays at the original value of $5,500, but there is a difference between the dollar value of the account payable to the exporter ($5,500) and the actual number of dollars that the importer must come up with to purchase the euros to pay the exporter ($5,750). The difference between the two accounts ($250) is the loss on foreign exchange and is always recognized in the income statement.

The company that denominates the sale or purchase in the foreign currency (the importer in the current case) must recognize the gains and losses arising from foreign-currency transactions at the end of each accounting period, usually monthly. In the example here, assume the end of the month has arrived and Sundance still has not paid the French exporter. The skis continue to be valued at $5,500, but the payable has to be updated to the new exchange rate of $1.1500 per euro. The journal entry would be

Loss on foreign exchange	250	
Accounts payable		250

The liability now would be worth $5,750. If settlement were to be made at the end of the next month and the exchange rate were to remain the same, the final entry would be

Accounts payable	5,750	
Cash		5,750

If the U.S. company were an exporter and anticipated receiving foreign currency, the corresponding entries (using the same information as in the example here) would be

Accounts receivable	5,500	
Sales		5,500
Cash	5,750	
Gain on foreign exchange		250
Accounts receivable		5,500

In this case, a gain results because the company received more cash than if it had collected its money immediately.

Correct Procedures for U.S. Companies

The procedures that U.S. companies must follow to account for foreign-currency transactions are found in Financial Accounting Standards Board Statement No. 52, "Foreign Currency Translation." Statement No. 52 requires companies to record the initial transaction at the spot exchange rate in effect on the transaction date and to record receivables and payables at subsequent balance sheet dates at the spot exchange rate on those dates. Any foreign-exchange gains and losses that arise from carrying receivables or payables during a period in which the exchange rate changes are taken directly to the income statement.[10]

Procedures vary in other countries, however. Some countries recognize transaction losses but not gains in their income statements. That means that a loss reduces income and a gain

Foreign-currency receivables and payables give rise to gains and losses whenever the exchange rate changes. Transaction gains and losses must be included in the income statement in the accounting period in which they arise.

The FASB requires that U.S. companies report foreign-currency transactions at the original spot exchange rate. It also requires that subsequent gains and losses on foreign-currency receivables or payables be put on the income statement.

increases income. Other countries allow a loss that results from a major devaluation to adjust the value of the underlying asset rather than be taken directly to income. The IASB pretty much follows the procedure required in the United States, but it allows a company to write up (increase) the value of an asset by the amount of foreign-exchange loss resulting from a one-time devaluation of the currency. That increase would then be written off over the useful life of the asset as a higher depreciation charge rather than be taken directly to the income statement as a one-time loss. As an example, assume that a company from South Korea purchases from a German supplier a large piece of equipment used in manufacturing textiles and has to pay the supplier in euros. Shortly after purchasing the equipment but before payment is made, the Korean won devalues against the euro by 10 percent. According to the IASB standard, the Korean company could increase the value of the asset by 10 percent and write off that increase as a higher depreciation expense over the life of the asset. As more countries move to a freely floating exchange-rate system, as discussed in Chapter 10, there are fewer examples of major devaluations occurring. However, countries that have a soft peg to another currency (meaning that they peg the value of their currency to something else, such as the U.S. dollar, but allow changes to occur against the dollar) could still experience a devaluation of their currency.

TRANSLATION OF FOREIGN-CURRENCY FINANCIAL STATEMENTS

Translation—the process of restating foreign-currency financial statements.

Consolidation—the process of combining the translated. financial statements of a parent and its subsidiaries into one set of financial statements.

Even though U.S.-based MNEs receive reports originally developed in a variety of different currencies, they eventually must end up with one set of financial statements in U.S. dollars to help management and investors understand their worldwide activities in a common currency. The process of restating foreign-currency financial statements into U.S. dollars is **translation**. The combination of all of these translated financial statements into one is **consolidation**, as illustrated in the financial statements of Vivendi Universal, Intel, and Marks & Spencer.

Translation in the United States is a two-step process.

1. Companies recast foreign-currency financial statements into statements consistent with U.S. GAAP. This occurs because a U.S. company with a subsidiary in Brazil must keep the books and records in Brazil according to Brazilian GAAP. For consolidation purposes, however, the resulting financial statements have to be issued according to U.S. GAAP in format as well as content. As an example of content, Brazil might require that inventories be valued a certain way. For the U.S. consolidated financial statements, however, inventories must be valued according to U.S., not Brazilian, standards.

2. Companies translate all foreign-currency amounts into U.S. dollars.

FASB Statement No. 52 describes how companies must translate their foreign-currency financial statements into dollars. All U.S. companies, as well as foreign companies that list on a U.S. exchange, must use Statement No. 52.

Translation Methods

The functional currency is the currency of the primary economic environment in which the entity operates.

Statement No. 52 allows companies to use either of two methods when translating foreign-currency financial statements into dollars: the current-rate method or the temporal method. The method the company chooses depends on the **functional currency** of the foreign operation, which is the currency of the primary economic environment in which that entity operates. For example, one of Coca-Cola's largest operations outside the United States is in Japan. The primary economic environment of the Japanese subsidiary is Japan, and the functional currency is the Japanese yen. The FASB identifies several factors that can help management determine the functional currency. Among the major factors are cash flows, sales prices, sales market data, expenses, financing, and intercompany transactions. For example, if the cash flows and expenses are primarily in the foreign operation's currency, that is the functional currency. If they are in the parent's currency, that is the functional currency.

If the functional currency is that of the local operating environment, the company must use the **current-rate method**. The current-rate method provides that companies translate all assets and liabilities at the current exchange rate, which is the spot exchange rate on the balance sheet date. All income statement items are translated at the average exchange rate, and owners' equity is translated at the rates in effect when the company issued capital stock and accumulated retained earnings.

If the functional currency is the parent's currency, the MNE must use the temporal method. The **temporal method** provides that only monetary assets (cash, marketable securities, and receivables) and liabilities are translated at the current exchange rate. The company translates inventory and property, plant, and equipment at the historical exchange rates, the exchange rates in effect when the assets were acquired. In general, the company translates most income statement accounts at the average exchange rate, but it translates cost of goods sold and depreciation expenses at the appropriate historical exchange rates.

Companies can choose the translation method—current rate or temporal rate—that is most appropriate for a particular foreign subsidiary, so they don't have to use one or the other for all subsidiaries. Vivendi Universal, with manufacturing and sales offices in many locations all around the world, uses the current rate for some and temporal for others. Historically some of its most important functional currencies were the French franc, British pound, Italian lira, Spanish peseta, and U.S. dollar. The euro has now replaced the franc, lira and peseta and is the key functional currency for Vivendi Universal. Coca-Cola operates in 200 countries and uses 59 different functional currencies. This is typical of most MNEs.

Figure 19.6 summarizes the selection of translation method, depending on the choice of functional currency. As in the preceding explanation, if the functional currency is the currency of the country where the foreign subsidiary is located, the current-rate method applies. If the functional currency is the reporting currency of the parent company, the temporal method applies.

Tables 19.4 and 19.5 show a balance sheet and income statement developed under both approaches in order to compare the differences in translation methodologies. Some of the key assumptions are

$1.5000	Historical exchange rate when fixed assets were acquired and capital stock was issued
$1.6980	Current exchange rate on December 31, 2002
$1.5617	Average exchange rate during 2002
$1.5606	Exchange rate during which ending inventory was acquired
$1.5600	Historical exchange rate for cost of goods sold

The current-rate method applies when the local currency is the functional currency.

The temporal method applies when the parent's reporting currency is the functional currency.

FIGURE 19.6 Selection of Translation Method

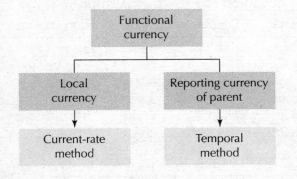

According to FASB Statement No. 52, management can choose either the current-rate method or the temporal method to translate the financial statements of a foreign subsidiary or branch from the foreign currency to the parent currency (the U.S. dollar for a U.S. firm). The choice of translation method depends on the choice of functional currency.

Also, the beginning balance in retained earnings for both methods is assumed to be $40,000. The British pound was rising in value (strengthening) between the time when the capital stock was issued ($1.500) and the end of the year ($1.6980), so the balance sheet reflects a positive accumulated translation adjustment under the current-rate method. This is consistent with the idea that assets were gaining value in a strong currency.

Disclosure of Foreign-Exchange Gains and Losses

With the current-rate method, the translation gain or loss is recognized in owners' equity. With the temporal method, the translation gain or loss is recognized in the income statement.

A major difference between the two translation methods is in the recognition of foreign-exchange gains and losses. Under the current-rate method, the gain or loss is called an accumulated translation adjustment and is taken directly to the balance sheet as a separate line item in owners' equity. Under the temporal method, the gain or loss is taken directly to the income statement and thus affects earnings per share.

● TABLE 19.4

BALANCE SHEET, DECEMBER 31, 2002

	POUNDS	TEMPORAL METHOD RATE	TEMPORAL METHOD DOLLARS	CURRENT-RATE METHOD RATE	CURRENT-RATE METHOD DOLLARS
Cash	20,000	1.6980	33,960	1.6980	33,960
Accounts receivable	40,000	1.6980	67,920	1.6980	67,920
Inventories	40,000	1.5606	62,424	1.6980	67,920
Fixed Assets	100,000	1.5000	150,000	1.6980	169,800
Accumulated depreciation	(20,000)	1.5000	(30,000)	1.6980	(33,960)
Total	180,000		284,304		305,960
Accounts payable	30,000	1.6980	50,940	1.6980	50,940
Long-term debt	44,000	1.6980	74,712	1.6980	74,712
Capital stock	60,000	1.5000	90,000	1.5000	90,000
Retained earnings	46,000	*	68,652	*	77,481
Accumulated translation adjustment					12,507
Total	180,000		284,304		305,640

*Retained earnings is the sum of all income earned in prior years and translated into dollars and this year's income. There is no single exchange rate used to translate retained earnings into dollars.

● TABLE 19.5

INCOME STATEMENT, 2002

	POUNDS	TEMPORAL METHOD RATE	TEMPORAL METHOD DOLLARS	CURRENT-RATE METHOD RATE	CURRENT-RATE METHOD DOLLARS
Sales	230,000	1.5617	359,191	1.5617	359,191
Expenses:					
Cost of goods sold	(110,000)	1.5600	(171,600)	1.5617	(171,787)
Depreciation	(10,000)	1.5000	(15,000)	1.5617	(15,617)
Other	(80,000)	1.5617	(124,936)	1.5617	(124,936)
Taxes	(6,000)	1.5617	(9,370)	1.5617	(9,370)
Translation gain (loss)	24,000		(9,633)		37,481
Net Income	24,000		28,652		37,481

ENVIRONMENTAL REPORTS

Earlier in the chapter, we discussed the major financial statements companies must present in order to list on stock exchanges in the United States and elsewhere. One report that is not required but is often presented by companies is an environmental report. Typically, the environmental report is separate from the annual report and is not part of the financial statements or footnotes. One of Vivendi Universal's largest segments is Environmental Services. Vivendi Universal devotes several pages to the operating results of this business segment as well as a page in its annual report dealing with environmental liability issues. Although it provides a general statement on its environmental programs, it does not provide a significant amount of quantitative information. There are over 295,000 employees working in the Environment Services segment out of a total of 380,000+ in the whole company.[11]

The SKF Group, headquartered in Sweden, is one of the world's leading producers of rolling bearings and bearing steel. It is a huge company, with over 45,400 employees and 80 manufacturing sites around the world. Table 19.6 illustrates some of the information in SKF's environmental report, including raw material and energy usage.

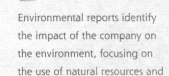

Environmental reports identify the impact of the company on the environment, focusing on the use of natural resources and efforts to recycle waste.

● TABLE 19.6

KEY ENVIRONMENTAL PERFORMANCE DATA FOR SKF GROUP

The SKF Group is a Swedish company that manufactures rolling bearings, bearing steel, and industrial precision components at around 80 manufacturing sites throughout the world. It provides a separate environmental report to show what it is doing to comply with environmental standards.

PARAMETER COUNTRY MAIN PRODUCT	UNITS	CAJAMAR BRAZIL BEARINGS	SCHWEINFURT GERMANY BEARINGS	HOFORS SWEDEN STEEL	ELGIN U.S. SEALS	VEENENDAAL HOLLAND COMPONENT	VARESE ITALY SEALS
Raw material—metal and rubber	Tons	4,839	31,200	419,500	43	11,765	9,594
	Tons	1,650	6,253	0	165	0	776
Turning chips	Tons	1,768	9,020	2,300	0	0	10.6
	% recycled	100	100	100	N/A	N/A	100
Other metal scrap	Tons	1,460	5,800	116,100	34.7	4,626	58
	% recycled	100	100	100	100	100	100
Grinding swarf	Tons	763	3,000	644	0	797	0
	% recycled	100	100	83	N/A	0	N/A
Used oil	Tons	461	558	70	63	19.4	1.3
	% recycled	100	100	100	100	100	100
Paper and carton	Tons	131	350	53	87	23.1	5.2
	% recycled	100	100	100	100	100	100
Water	1,000 m\fs^3	41.6	895	238	86.7	247	18.52
Heating energy	GWh	0	90	40	0	0	0
Electric energy	GWh	29.3	115	370	15.6	15.1	17.6
Electricity—Co\fs7 2 \fs14 equiv.	Tons	24,000	8.3	12,200	12,800	9,830	1.2
Fuel oil	Tons	28.1	185	7,000	0	0	0
Natural gas	1,000 Nm^3	0	2,181	0	26	1,852	736
Coal	Tons	0	0	10,200	0	0	0
LPG	Tons	27.7	79	9,800	15.3	8.5	0
Alcohols	Tons	1.1	203	0.5	16.6	0.2	8.8
Solvents	Tons	0.3	175	9	2.7	43.7	6.1
Oils	Tons	324	807	270	33	219	0.8
Grease	Tons	23	6.8	34	1.2	0	4.1
PCB on site	Yes/No	No	No	No	No	No	No
Ozone depleters—Class I	Kg	0	0	0	0	0	0
Ozone depleters—Class II	Kg	0	0	0	0	0	0

N/A = not applicable

Source: From SKF Environmental Report (2001).

Although there are no mandatory environmental disclosure requirements comparable to the financial reporting requirements, Vivendi Universal refers to the certification of its environmental operations in Europe according to the European Eco Audit Ordinance, and SKF included a compliance statement by Lloyd's Register Quality Assurance Limited. Lloyd's audited SKF's sites and the health, safety, and environmental information in the SKF Environmental Report. However, environmental reporting varies a lot from company to company and country to country, especially because it is voluntary information.

TAXATION

Tax planning influences profitability and cash flow.

Tax planning is crucial for any business because taxes can profoundly affect profitability and cash flow. This is especially true in international business. As complex as domestic taxation seems, it is simple compared to the intricacies of international taxation. The international tax specialist must be familiar with both the home country's tax policy on foreign operations and the tax laws of each country in which the international company operates.

Taxation has a strong impact on several choices.

- Location of the initial investment
- Choice of operating form, such as export or import, licensing agreement, overseas investment
- Legal form of the new enterprise, such as branch or subsidiary
- Method of financing, such as internal or external sourcing and debt or equity
- Method of setting transfer prices

This section examines taxation for the company with international operations, using U.S. tax policy because of the nature and extent of U.S. FDI. However, as any country finds domestic companies generating more and more foreign-source income, it must decide on the principles of accounting for that income. Principles of taxation that U.S.-based MNEs face at home and abroad are—or could be—applicable to companies domiciled in other countries.

Exports of Goods and Services

Many manufacturers find it easier and more profitable to sell expertise, such as patents or management services, than to export goods or to invest abroad. Generally, payment comes from royalties and fees, and the foreign government usually taxes this payment. Because the parent makes the sale of services, the sale also must be included in the parent's taxable income.

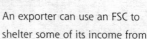

An exporter can use an FSC to shelter some of its income from taxation. The FSC must be engaged in substantial business activity.

To gain tax advantages from exporting, a U.S. company can set up a **foreign sales corporation (FSC)** according to strict IRS guidelines. To qualify as an FSC, a company must be engaged in the exporting of either merchandise or services, such as engineering or architectural services. Substantial economic activity must also occur outside the United States. An FSC cannot be a mailbox company in Switzerland that simply passes documents from the United States to the importing country. It must

- Maintain a foreign office.
- Operate under foreign management.
- Keep a permanent set of books at the foreign office.
- Conduct foreign economic processes (such as selling activities).
- Be a foreign corporation.[12]

If a foreign corporation qualifies as an FSC, a portion of its income is exempt from U.S. corporate income tax. Also, any dividends that the FSC gives to its parent company are eligible for an exemption of up to 15 percent of export earnings from U.S. income taxation as long as the income is foreign trade income.

It is estimated that some 6,000 corporations are taking advantage of FSC provisions, resulting in tax breaks worth billions of dollars. In 1999, the World Trade Organization, at the request of the European Union, investigated the 14-year-old FSC provision and ruled that it was an illegal export subsidy. In 2002, the WTO rejected the U.S. appeal and authorized the EU to slap $4 billion in tariffs on U. S. goods unless the United States restored the FSC to comply with WTO guidelines. However, that does not seem likely, as any changes would significantly harm huge U.S. exporters, such as Boeing, General Electric, Walt Disney Company, and Microsoft.[13]

Foreign Branch

A foreign branch is an extension of the parent company rather than an enterprise incorporated in a foreign country. Any income the branch generates is taxable immediately to the parent, whether or not cash is remitted by the branch to the parent as a distribution of earnings. However, if the branch suffers a loss, the parent is allowed to deduct that loss from its taxable income, reducing its overall tax liability.

> Foreign branch income (or loss) is directly included in the parent's taxable income.

Foreign Subsidiary

While a branch is a legal extension of a parent company, a foreign corporation is an independent legal entity set up in a country (incorporated) according to the laws of incorporation of that country. When an MNE purchases a foreign corporation or sets up a new corporation in a foreign country, that corporation is called a subsidiary of the parent. Income that is earned by the subsidiary is either reinvested in the subsidiary or remitted as a dividend to the parent company. Subsidiary income is either taxable to the parent or tax deferred—that is, it is not taxed until it is remitted as a dividend to the parent. Which tax status applies depends on whether the foreign subsidiary is a controlled foreign corporation—CFC (a technical term in the U.S. tax code)—and whether the income is active or passive.

> Tax deferral means that income is not taxed until it is remitted to the parent company as a dividend.

A **controlled foreign corporation (CFC)**, from the standpoint of the U.S. tax code, is any foreign corporation that meets this condition: more than 50 percent of its voting stock is held by "U.S. shareholders." A U.S. shareholder is any U.S. person or company that holds 10 percent or more of the CFC's voting stock. Any foreign subsidiary of an MNE would automatically be considered a CFC from the standpoint of the tax code. However, a joint-venture company abroad that is partly owned by the U.S.-based MNE and partly by local investors might not be a CFC if the U.S. MNE does not own more than 50 percent of the stock of the joint-venture company. Table 19.7 shows how this might work. Foreign corporation A is a CFC because it is a wholly owned subsidiary of a U.S. parent company (U.S. person V). Foreign corporation B also is a CFC because U.S. persons V, W, and X each own 10 percent or more of the voting stock, which means they qualify as U.S. shareholders and their combined voting stock is more than 50 percent of the total. This situation might exist if three U.S. companies partnered together with a foreign partner to establish a joint venture overseas. Such collaborative arrangements are not uncommon, especially in telecommunications and high-tech industries. Foreign corporation C is not a CFC because even though U.S. persons V and W qualify as U.S. shareholders, their combined stock ownership is only 40 percent. U.S. persons X and Y do not qualify as U.S. shareholders because their individual ownership shares are only 8 percent each.

> In a CFC, U.S. shareholders hold more than 50 percent of the voting stock.

If a foreign subsidiary qualifies as a CFC, the U.S. tax law requires the U.S. investor to classify the foreign-source income as active income or Subpart F (or passive) income. **Active income** is derived from the direct conduct of a trade or business, such as from sales of products manufactured in the foreign country. **Subpart F income**, or passive income, which is specifically defined in Subpart F of the U.S. Internal Revenue Code, comes from sources other than those connected with the direct conduct of a trade or business, generally in tax-haven countries. Subpart F income includes

> Active income is that derived from the direct conduct of a trade or business. Passive income (also rolled Subpart-F income) usually is derived from operations in a tax-haven country.

● TABLE 19.7

DETERMINATION OF CONTROLLED FOREIGN CORPORATIONS

A controlled foreign corporation must have U.S. shareholders holding more than 50 percent of the voting shares.

| | PERCENTAGES OF THE VOTING STOCK | | |
SHAREHOLDER	FOREIGN CORPORATION A	FOREIGN CORPORATION B	FOREIGN CORPORATION C
U.S. person V	100%	45%	30%
U.S. person W		10	10
U.S. person X		20	8
U.S. person Y			8
Foreign person Z		25	44
Total	100%	100%	100%

- *Holding company income*—primarily dividends, interest, rents, royalties, and gains on sale of stocks.
- *Sales income*—from foreign sales corporations that are separately incorporated from their manufacturing operations. The product of such entities is manufactured outside of and sold for use outside of the CFC's country of incorporation, and the CFC has not performed significant operations on the product.
- *Service income*—from the performance of technical, managerial, or similar services for a company in the same corporate family as the CFC and outside the country in which the CFC resides.

Subpart F income usually derives from the activities of subsidiaries in tax-haven countries such as the Bahamas, the Netherlands Antilles, Panama, and Switzerland. The U.S. government treats any country whose income tax is lower than that of the United States as a tax-haven country. The tax-haven subsidiary may act as an investment company, a sales agent or distributor, an agent for the parent in licensing agreements, or a holding company of stock in other foreign subsidiaries that are called grandchild—or second-tier—subsidiaries. This setup is illustrated in Figure 19.7. In the role of holding company, its purpose is to concentrate cash from the parent's foreign operations into the low-tax country and to use the cash for global expansion.

FIGURE 19.7   A Tax-Haven Subsidiary as a Holding Company

A parent company can shelter income from U.S. income taxation by using a tax-haven subsidiary located in a low-tax country.

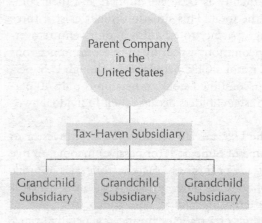

FIGURE 19.8 Tax Status of Active and Subpart F Income from Foreign Subsidiaries of U.S. Companies

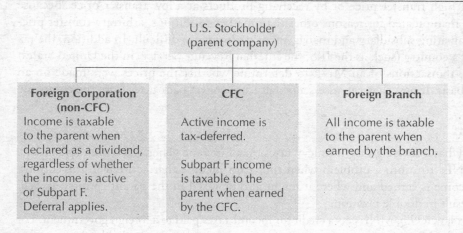

U.S. Stockholder
(parent company)

Foreign Corporation (non-CFC)	**CFC**	**Foreign Branch**
Income is taxable to the parent when declared as a dividend, regardless of whether the income is active or Subpart F. Deferral applies.	Active income is tax-deferred. Subpart F income is taxable to the parent when earned by the CFC.	All income is taxable to the parent when earned by the branch.

Different rules regarding the tax status and deferability of income are in effect for non-CFCs, CFCs, and foreign branches.

Figure 19.8 illustrates how the tax status of a subsidiary's income is determined. All non-CFC income—active and Subpart F—earned by the foreign corporation is deferred until remitted as a dividend to the U.S. shareholder (the parent company in this example). In contrast, a CFC's active income is tax deferred to the parent, but its Subpart F income is taxable immediately to the parent as soon as the CFC earns it. If a foreign branch earns the income, it is immediately taxable to the parent company, whether it is active or Subpart F. There is an exception, however. If the foreign-source income is the lower of $1 million or 5 percent of the CFC's gross income, none of it is treated as Subpart F income. At the other extreme, if the foreign-source income is more than 70 percent of total gross income, all of the corporation's gross income for the tax year is treated as Subpart F income. Also, foreign-source income subject to high foreign taxes is not considered Subpart F income if the foreign tax rate is more than 90 percent of the maximum U.S. corporate income tax rate. Assuming a corporate tax rate of 35 percent in the United States, that means that a parent would not have to consider any income as Subpart F income that is earned in a country with a corporate tax rate greater than 31.5 percent (90% × 35%).[14]

Transfer Prices

A major tax challenge as well as an impediment to performance evaluation is the extensive use of transfer pricing in international operations. A **transfer price** is a price on goods and services sold by one member of a corporate family to another, such as from a parent to its subsidiary in a foreign country. Because the price is between related entities, it is not necessarily an **arm's-length price**—that is, a price between two companies that do not have an ownership interest in each other. The assumption is that an arm's-length price is more likely than a transfer price to reflect the market accurately.

Companies establish arbitrary transfer prices primarily because of differences in taxation between countries. For example, if the corporate tax rate is higher in the parent company's country than in the subsidiary's country, the parent could set a low transfer price on products it sells the subsidiary in order to keep taxable profits low in its country and high in the subsidiary's country. The parent also could set a high transfer price on products sold to it by the subsidiary.

Companies also may set arbitrary transfer prices for competitive reasons or because of restrictions on currency flows. In the former case, if the parent ships products or materials at a low transfer price to the subsidiary, the subsidiary would be able to sell the products to local consumers for less. In the latter case, if the subsidiary's country has currency controls on

A transfer price is a price on goods and services one member of a corporate family sells to another.

Arbitrary transfer pricing affects performance evaluation.

dividend flows, the parent could get more hard currency out of the country by shipping in products at a high transfer price or by receiving products at a low transfer price. Because prices can be manipulated for reasons other than market conditions, arbitrary transfer pricing makes evaluating subsidiary and management performance difficult. In addition, the tax authorities of a country (such as the IRS, the Internal Revenue Service, in the United States) can audit the transactions of an MNE to determine whether the prices were made on an arm's-length basis. If not, they can assess a penalty and collect back taxes from the company.

Tax Credit

Every country has a sovereign right to levy taxes on all income generated within its borders. However, MNEs run into a problem when they earn income that is taxed in the country where the income is earned and where it might also be taxed in the parent country as well. This could result in double taxation.

In U.S. tax law, a U.S. MNE gets a credit for income taxes paid to a foreign government. For example, when a U.S. parent recognizes foreign-source income (such as a dividend from a foreign subsidiary) in its taxable income, it must pay U.S. tax on that income. However, the U.S. IRS allows the parent company to reduce its tax liability by the amount of foreign income tax already paid. However, it is limited by the amount it would have had to pay in the United States on that income. For example, assume that U.S. MNE A earns $100,000 of foreign-source income on which it paid $40,000 (40 percent tax rate) on that income. If that income is considered taxable in the United States, A would have to pay $35,000 in income taxes (35 percent tax rate). In the absence of a tax credit, A would have paid a total of $75,000 in income tax on the $100,000 of income, a 75 percent tax rate. However, the IRS allows A to reduce its U.S. tax liability by a maximum of $35,000—what it would have paid in the United States if the income had been earned there. If A's subsidiary had paid $20,000 in foreign income tax (a 20 percent tax rate), it would have been able to claim the entire $20,000 as a credit because it was less than the U.S. liability of $35,000. A will pay a total of $35,000 in corporate income tax on its foreign source income—$20,000 to the foreign government and $15,000 to the U.S. government.

The IRS allows a tax credit for corporate income tax U.S. companies pay to another country. A tax credit is a dollar-for-dollar reduction of tax liability and must coincide with the recognition of income.

NON-U.S. TAX PRACTICES

Differences in tax practices around the world often cause problems for MNEs. Lack of familiarity with laws and customs can create confusion. In some countries, tax laws are loosely enforced. In others, taxes generally may be negotiated between the tax collector and the taxpayer—if they are ever paid at all.

Variations among countries in GAAP can lead to differences in the determination of taxable income. This, in turn, may affect the cash flow required to settle tax obligations. For example, companies in France can depreciate assets faster than would be the case in the United States, which means that they can write off their value against income, thus lowering taxable income. In Sweden, companies can reduce the value of inventories, which increases their cost of goods sold and lowers taxable income.

Problems with different countries, tax practices arise from
• Lack of familiarity with laws
• Loose enforcement

Taxation of corporate income is accomplished through one of two approaches in most countries: the separate entity approach, also known as the classical approach, or the integrated system approach. In the **separate entity approach**, which the United States uses, each separate unit—company or individual—is taxed when it earns income. For example, a corporation is taxed on its earnings, and stockholders are taxed on the distribution of earnings (dividends). The result is double taxation. However, in January 2003, the U.S. Congress was considering proposals to eliminate taxes on dividends which would eliminate double taxation of corporate earnings in the United States.

In the separate entity approach, governments tax each taxable entity when it earns income.

Most other developed countries use an **integrated system** to eliminate double taxation. The British give a dividend credit to shareholders to shelter them from double taxation. That means that when shareholders report the dividends in their taxable income, they also get a credit for taxes paid on that income by the company that issued the dividend. That keeps the shareholder from paying tax on the dividend because the company had already paid a tax on it. In Germany, a split-rate system means that two different tax rates are levied on corporate earnings. Because shareholders have to pay tax on dividends, the corporation pays a low tax on income that is distributed as a dividend and a higher tax on income that is retained in the business and is not distributed as a dividend. In addition, the shareholder gets a credit for taxes paid by the corporation on that dividend.

Countries also have unique systems for taxing the earnings of the foreign subsidiaries of their domestic companies. Some, such as France, use a territorial approach and tax only domestic-source income. Others, such as Germany and the United Kingdom, use a global approach, taxing the profits of foreign branches and the dividends received from foreign subsidiaries. The United States is the only country to tax unremitted earnings in the form of Subpart F income.

> An integrated system tries to avoid double taxation of corporate income through split tax rates or tax credits.

Value-Added Tax

A **value-added tax** has been around since 1967 in most Western European countries and is used in other countries as well. A VAT is computed by applying a VAT tax rate on total sales. However, any company that purchased materials or other inputs into its manufacturing process from companies that might have already paid a VAT on their sales needs to pay the tax only on the difference between its sales and inputs that have already been taxed. As the name implies, VAT means that each independent company is taxed only on the value it adds at each stage in the production process. For a company that is fully integrated vertically, the tax rate applies to its net sales because it owned everything from raw materials to finished product.

Despite efforts by the EU toward harmonization among its members, the VAT rates vary significantly among European countries. However, the EU is narrowing differences in rates for like categories of goods. The VAT does not apply to exports, because the tax is rebated (or returned) to the exporter and is not included in the final price to the consumer. This practice results in an effective stimulus for exports. In addition, it is considered by U.S. tax officials and MNEs to be a subsidy to European exports, because the export price can be lower than the domestic price of goods by the amount of the VAT.

> With a value-added tax, each company pays a percentage of the value added to a product at each stage of the business process.

Tax Treaties: The Elimination of Double Taxation

The primary purpose of tax treaties is to prevent international double taxation or to provide remedies when it occurs. The United States has active tax treaties with more than 48 countries. The general pattern between two treaty countries is to grant reciprocal reductions on dividend withholding and to exempt royalties and sometimes interest payments from any withholding tax.

The United States has a withholding tax of 30 percent for owners (individuals and corporations) of U.S. securities that are issued in countries with which it has no tax treaty. However, interest on portfolio obligations and on bank deposits is normally exempted from withholding. When a tax treaty is in effect, the U.S. rate on dividends generally is reduced to 15 percent, and the tax on interest and royalties is either eliminated or is reduced to a very low level.

An example is a protocol to the 1980 tax treaty between the United States and Canada. It took effect on January 1, 1996, and it

> The purpose of tax treaties is to prevent double taxation or to provide remedies when it occurs.

1. Reduces the withholding rate on dividends paid to a corporation owning 10 percent or more of the voting stock of the payer. The withholding rate amounted to 6 percent for payments in 1996, and 5 percent thereafter.
2. Reduces the withholding rate on interest to 10 percent.
3. Reduces the tax resulting from the imposition of both U.S. estate tax and Canadian income tax on transfers at death.[15]

In Transfer Pricing, "Legal" Doesn't Always Mean "Ethical"

Arbitrary transfer pricing can create legal and ethical problems. In the United States and many other countries, companies are expected to establish transfer prices on an arm's-length basis. Doing this ensures that companies pay taxes on profits based on market decisions. However, when companies manipulate profits to minimize global tax payments and to maximize cash flows, they may be breaking the law. Laws in this regard are much more rigid in Canada, France, Germany, the United Kingdom, and the United States than elsewhere. The U.S. government, for example, requires that companies use an arm's-length price on intracompany transactions between the United States and foreign countries; otherwise, the IRS will allocate profits between the two taxing jurisdictions. Sometimes foreign companies underinvoice shipments to the United States to minimize customs payments. The U.S. Customs Service can fine them and force them to correct the invoice and to pay the proper duty.

Some countries, such as Italy, Japan, and Korea, are less interested in rigid transfer-pricing policies. Others, such as Ireland, Puerto Rico, and a few other tax-haven countries, have no transfer-pricing policies. So an MNE needs to determine whether it is ethical to transfer profits to low-tax countries through arbitrary transfer-pricing policies. By shifting profits to a low-tax country, the MNE is not harming tax collection in that country, but it is harming tax collection in the country from which the profits are shifted. In trying to maximize cash flows, management of an MNE is likely to assume that "legal" means "ethical." If there are no legal requirements for transfer-pricing policies in a particular country, management is likely to assume that the absence of law implies permission to pursue the company's self-interest.

In some cases, an MNE might take advantage of transfer-pricing policies to transfer cash out of weak-currency developing countries. If a developing country has currency controls and does not allow cash to be shipped out in the form of dividends, a company might be tempted to charge a high transfer price on a product shipped to the country as a way of getting cash out. Doing this also results in lower taxable income in the developing countries and lower tax payments, which create a problem for developing countries that desperately need hard currency. Such behavior by MNEs could be construed as unethical. Further, if a country has laws that establish the need for market-based transfer prices, the actions could be construed as illegal. It is doubtful that an MNE's home country would encourage the use of market-based transfer prices, because a high price on exports to developing countries would result in greater taxable income in the home country.

Several treaties and protocols were signed between the United States and foreign countries with an effective date of January 1, 1996, and they were very similar. In those treaties involving the reduction of withholding rates on dividends, the rate was typically 5 percent, although the rate for Portugal was 15 percent in some cases, 10 percent in others.

Companies should set up

- Branches in early years to recognize losses
- Subsidiaries in later years to shield profits

PLANNING THE TAX FUNCTION

Because taxes affect both profits and cash flow, they are a consideration in MNEs' investment decision process. If a U.S. MNE decides to generate revenues through exports, it can set up an FSC to reduce its tax bill—assuming that the FSC survives the WTO process or that the United States can come up with something else if the FSC has to be eliminated. When a U.S. parent company decides to set up operations in a foreign country, it can do so through a

LOOKING TO THE FUTURE

What Will Become the Coca-Cola of Accounting Standards?

There are two parts to this chapter—accounting and taxation. From an accounting standpoint, the key question is this: "What will become the Coca-Cola of accounting standards—U.S. GAAP or IASB GAAP?" In other words, which will have the most recognized brand name in accounting standards? IASB GAAP has a lot going for it. It is being set by most of the major countries in the world, so it is the product of a great deal of negotiation, compromise, and broad-based input. It is appealing to the Europeans, because they have a lot of influence in the development of its standards. In addition, it has the backing of the EU. It is also modeled after the capital-markets orientation of the United Kingdom and the United States.

However, IASB GAAP also has some shortcomings. It lacks an effective enforcement mechanism; it deals with a narrow, although important, range of issues; and it has been criticized for having developed standards that have too many alternatives and that are too much a product of compromise rather than principle.

U.S. GAAP's major criticism is that it is set only by the United States—why should the United States be able to dictate accounting standards for the rest of the world? That is a valid criticism, but the major vote in favor of U.S. GAAP is that half of the world's stock market capitalization is located in the United States and that companies that want access to U.S. capital must play by U.S. rules. However, as noted earlier, the Enron scandal and subsequent scandals in corporate America have cast doubt on the credibility of the application of U.S. accounting practices. In the future, U.S. accounting standards will become even more international as the FASB cooperates with standard-setters from around the world, including the IASB, to establish new accounting standards. More likely than not, the SEC will allow certain IASB standards to be used for foreign companies, as it has already done with cash flow statements and consolidation accounting, while reserving the right to keep U.S. GAAP for the majority of the reporting. As IASB GAAP and U.S. GAAP converge, some of the concerns may disappear.

It is hard to predict what will happen in taxation, because tax policy is subject to the whim of governments. Certainly, tax differences among countries in the EU will narrow in the years to come. Harmonization should take place in the determination of taxable income and in the tax rates themselves. MNEs will need to be more creative in their tax planning worldwide as they seek to minimize their tax liabilities.

---

branch or a foreign subsidiary. If the parent expects the foreign operations to show a loss for the initial years of operation, it should begin with a branch, because the parent can deduct branch losses against its current year's income.

Tied in with the initial investment decision as well as with continuing operations is the financing decision. Both debt and equity financing affect taxation. If loans from the parent finance foreign operations, the repayment of principal is not taxable, but the interest income to the parent is taxable. Also, the interest that the subsidiary pays is generally a business expense for that entity, which reduces taxable income in the foreign country. Dividends are taxable to the parent and are not a deductible business expense for the subsidiary. One reason why international finance subsidiaries are set up outside the United States is to escape withholding tax requirements.

An MNE aiming to maximize its cash flow worldwide should concentrate profits in tax-haven or low-tax countries. This can be accomplished by carefully selecting a low-tax country for the initial investment, setting up companies in tax-haven countries to receive dividends, and carrying out judicious transfer pricing. For example, because of its low-tax status and

Debt and equity financing both have tax ramifications.

membership in the EU, Ireland can be both a manufacturing center that supplies the EU with goods and a tax-haven country. The Subpart F income provisions require complicated tax planning, but opportunities still exist. Tax law is very complex, and a company needs the counsel of an experienced tax specialist.

Summary

- The MNE must learn to cope with differing inflation rates, exchange-rate changes, currency controls, expropriation risks, customs duties, tax rates and methods of determining taxable income, levels of sophistication of local accounting personnel, and local as well as home-country reporting requirements.

- A company's accounting or controllership function is responsible for collecting and analyzing data for internal and external users.

- Culture can have a strong influence on the accounting dimensions of measurement and disclosure. The cultural values of secrecy and transparency refer to the degree of disclosure of information. The cultural values of optimism and conservatism refer to the valuation of assets and the recognition of income. Conservatism results in the undervaluation of both assets and income.

- Financial statements differ in terms of language, currency, type of statements (income statement, balance sheet, etc.), financial statement format, extent of footnote disclosures, and the underlying GAAP on which the financial statements are based.

- The IASB, an independent, privately-funded accounting standard setter, is charged with developing a single set of high quality, understandable and enforceable global accounting standards. Standards developed by the IASB require transparent and comparable information in general purpose financial statements. In cooperation with national accounting standard setters around the world, the IASB hopes to achieve convergence in accounting standards. The major competitor is U.S. GAAP, although the FASB and IASB are working together to eliminate major differences in the two standards.

- When transactions denominated in a foreign currency are translated into dollars, all accounts are recorded initially at the exchange rate in effect at the time of the transaction. At each subsequent balance sheet date, recorded dollar balances representing amounts owed by or to the company that are denominated in a foreign currency are adjusted to reflect the current rate.

- Companies enter foreign-exchange gains and losses arising from foreign-currency transactions on the income statement during the period in which they occur. Companies enter gains and losses arising from translating financial statements by the current-rate method as a separate component of owners' equity. Companies enter gains and losses arising from translating according to the temporal method directly on the income statement.

- International tax planning has a strong impact on the choice of location for the initial investment, the legal form of the new enterprise, the method of financing, and the method of setting transfer prices.

- Tax deferral means that the income a subsidiary incorporated outside the home country earns is taxed only when it is remitted to the parent as a dividend, not when it is earned.

- A controlled foreign corporation (CFC) must declare its Subpart F income as taxable to the parent in the year it is earned, whether or not it is remitted as a dividend.

- A transfer price is a price on goods and services sold by one member of a corporate family to another and thus tends to be set in an arbitrary rather than arm's-length fashion.

- A tax credit allows a parent company to reduce its tax liability by the direct amount its subsidiary pays a foreign government on income that must also be taxed by the parent company's government.

- Countries' policies vary as to what is taxable income and how they assess taxes. The United States taxes each separate unit (the separate entity approach), while most other developed countries use an integrated system that minimizes or eliminates double taxation.

- The purpose of tax treaties is to prevent international double taxation or to provide remedies when it occurs.

- MNEs attempt to establish an organizational structure that allows them to minimize their overall tax payments.

 # CASE

Vivendi Universal[16]

In December of 2000 French-based Vivendi's merger with France's Canal+ and Canada's Seagram Co. Ltd. created a global communications giant with diverse products in many countries throughout the world. This merger of French and Canadian companies brought together two organizations with different cultures and accounting standards. The merger was overwhelmingly approved by the shareholders of Vivendi, Seagram, and Canal+ with votes in favor of the merger of 96.6 percent, 90.4 percent, and 98.6 percent respectively. Following the merger, Vivendi Universal, as it is now called, began its battle with the conflicting French and U.S. GAAPs and made a serious attempt to inform its millions of global shareholders of the many differences between them. (Although Seagram was based in Canada, it prepared its financial statements in accordance with U.S. GAAP because over 50 percent of its shareholders were U.S. residents.)

COMPANY STATISTICS AND INFORMATION

In 2002, French-based Vivendi Universal (VU) employed more than 381,000 people worldwide, 86,200 of which were in Media and Communications. VU's Music Group (UMG) is considered to be the world's No. 1 music company, with a 22.7 percent share of the market in 2001 and wholly-owned, joint-venture, or licensed operations in 63 countries. One of every four albums sold worldwide in 2001 was a Universal album.

Vivendi Universal Publishing (VUP) is the third-largest publisher worldwide and a major international brand name in the industry, with strong local brands in four language areas (English, French, Spanish, and Portuguese). VUP held leading positions in all sectors of content creation: literature, reference, school, college, and kids, as well as games and consumer press. VUP was responsible for publishing *American Heritage Dictionaries* and Houghton Mifflin textbooks, and it is No. 2 in the world at producing PC games.

Vivendi Universal Entertainment, including such divisions as Universal Studios, Canal +, and StudioCanal, is a major global force in film and television production. Universal operates the world's second-largest studio with a 16.3 percent market share outside the United States and 11.75 percent in the United States in 2001. In the same year, Universal Studios was the only studio to release five films which grossed over $100 million outside the United States. Canal + is the European leader in pay television and is No. 1 in Europe in digital television. Together, Universal Studios and StudioCanal own the world's second-largest audio visual rights library, which includes more than 9,000 feature films and 40,000 hours of television programming. A natural extension of its film and television businesses, Universal Studios theme parks are renowned for their themed entertainment. Universal theme parks are located in the United States, Europe, and Japan, and together they welcomed more than 28 million visitors in 2001. VU is also the world's No.1 Internet music service provider, with over 50 million registered users worldwide in May 2002.

Given the public attention received by VU's media and communications businesses they may seem to be the most important part of its operations; however, this is not the case. Vivendi Environment, by far the largest part of VU and probably the part of VU that most people don't know about, provides substantial strength and stability to aid the company in overcoming its huge dependence on fluctuations of taste in the audio and visual entertainment market. Vivendi Environment (VE) employs 295,000 people worldwide and provides environmental services to municipalities and corporations. VE is the world leader in water services (USFilter and Culligan), with over 110 million customers in more than 100 countries. It is No. 1 in Europe and No. 3 worldwide in waste management, providing services to 70 million people throughout the world. Additionally, VE is No. 1 in Europe in energy services, and is the No. 1 private operator in transportation. See Figure 19.9 for Vivendi's business segment breakdown and Figure 19.10 for a regional revenue breakdown.

ACCOUNTING DIFFERENCES

European companies tend to be more conservative than their U.S. counterparts in most areas of operations, including accounting. This is largely a culture issue, but it is also a necessity because of the need to conform to their countries' various accounting regulations. In VU's case there are several differences between the accounting practices of the French and U.S. GAAPs that need to be addressed.

The French accounting system is very rigid as a result of misappropriation of funds by officials dating back to Louis X and Louis XIV. The origins of France's accounting practices can be traced back to the PCG, a general chart of accounts explaining each account's function, which spells out the use of an account in relation to financial statements and explanatory notes. The French believe that the chart of accounts enables French accountants to easily adapt to the variety of industries in all sectors of the economy. The PCG can also be used as an easy tool for teaching accounting and is essential at every level

FIGURE 19.9   Vivendi Universal's Revenue Breakdown by Business Segment, 2001 Pro forma Revenue (in € millions)

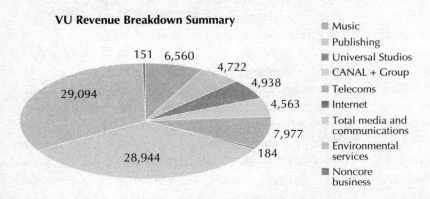

VU Revenue Breakdown Summary

- Music
- Publishing
- Universal Studios
- CANAL + Group
- Telecoms
- Internet
- Total media and communications
- Environmental services
- Noncore business

Source: Vivendi Universal Corporation, FY 2001 Key Data by Business, 2001, www.vivendiuniversal.com.

FIGURE 19.10   Vivendi Revenue Breakdown Geographically 2001 Revenue by Region (%)

Source: Vivendi Universal Corporation, FY2001 Key Data by Business, 2001, www.vivendiuniversal.com.

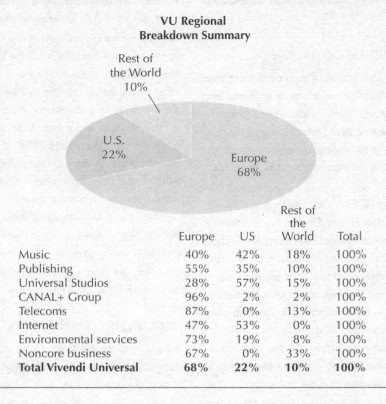

VU Regional Breakdown Summary

	Europe	US	Rest of the World	Total
Music	40%	42%	18%	100%
Publishing	55%	35%	10%	100%
Universal Studios	28%	57%	15%	100%
CANAL+ Group	96%	2%	2%	100%
Telecoms	87%	0%	13%	100%
Internet	47%	53%	0%	100%
Environmental services	73%	19%	8%	100%
Noncore business	67%	0%	33%	100%
Total Vivendi Universal	**68%**	**22%**	**10%**	**100%**

of accounting education. There are also several benefits to using the PCG. It is the universal language of accountants and bookkeepers in France; and because of the PCG's uniform numbering system and classification of accounts, the cost of making entries, training, and software programs is drastically reduced. Additionally, tax authorities require a business to use the PCG for preparation of their taxes, thus eliminating huge discrepancies between the tax and public financial statements.

The Commission des Operations de Bourse (COB) was created in 1967 to supervise published financial reports, France's financial markets, and the information that companies who raise capital on public markets provide. The COB is modeled after the SEC in the United States and its powers include (1) issuing regulations for all those who operate in the financial markets, (2) conducting inquiries, making searches, verifying, and informing the public as well as bringing matters to the courts, (3) ratifying the choices of auditors made by a public company.

Regardless of the historical divergences of countries' accounting systems, there are going to be similarities and differences. Table 19.8 is a 20-F reconciliation of Vivendi Universal's 2001 financial statements. As the reconciliation shows, there are three primary differences in VU's statements between French and U.S. GAAP. First, accounting for proportionate ownership is different under U.S. and French GAAP. Proportionate ownership under

French GAAP is changed to full consolidation for an entity controlled or more than 50 percent owned by the parent company under U.S. GAAP, and the equity method is used for those between 20 percent and 50 percent owned. No proportionate ownership is allowed under U.S. GAAP.

Second, certain transactions are recoded using different line items in the financial statements using U.S. GAAP versus French GAAP. These are reclassifications only. There is no number change, only movement among line items in which reconciliation is required. For example, French GAAP treats gains and losses on foreign exchange as part of the financing cost of the business, and these gains and losses are grouped with interest costs in "financing charges." Therefore, this represents a minor change to the EBITDA and EBIT presentation.

Third, the adjustments column represents a difference in accounting conventions between French and U.S. GAAP. These transactions are common because of the many differences between the two. The differences between the French and U.S. balance sheets are significant, but not nearly to the extent evident in the Income Statement. As the 20-F reconciliation shows, Assets (as well as Liabilities and Stockholders' Equity) in U.S. GAAP are roughly 109 percent of assets according to French GAAP. The following paragraph was included in VU's 2001 financial statements and demonstrates the huge impact French GAAP can make on the Income Statement.

TABLE 19.8

ILLUSTRATION OF FRENCH GAAP TO U.S. GAAP BALANCE SHEET RECONCILIATION, DECEMBER 31, 2001 IN €BILLIONS

ASSETS	FRENCH GAAP	ELIMINATION OF PROPORTION (1)	RECLASSIFI-CATIONS (2)	ADJUST-MENTS (3)	US GAAP	PRIMARY EXPLANATIONS OF RECLASSIFICATIONS AND ADJUSTMENTS
Cash and cash equivalents	4.72	−0.28			4.45	
Other marketable securities	3.77	−0.04	−3.73		0.00	**Reclassified** to Investments, Treasury Shares and Retained Earnings.
Receivables net	24.04	−2.41	−1.11	−0.01	20.51	**Reclassified** to Investments.
Accounts receivable	21.09	−2.11	−0.40	0.90	19.49	**Adjusted** to account for VE's Receivable Sales program.
Short-term loans receivable	2.95	−0.30	−0.71	−0.92	1.02	**Adjusted** to eliminate BSkyB.
Inventories	3.16	−0.32		−0.20	2.64	
Deferred taxes	4.22	−0.14	−4.09		0.00	**Reclassified** to Other Current Assets and Other Assets.
Other current assets			0.80		0.80	**Reclassified** from Deferred Taxes.
Total Current Assets	**39.93**	**−3.18**	**−8.13**	**−0.21**	**28.40**	
Investments	14.76	0.18	2.57	−0.28	17.23	**Reclassified** from GW net, ST loans and Other marketable securities.
Investment accounted for using the equity method	9.18	0.26	3.26	1.50	14.20	**Adjusted** to reverse French GAAP impairment charge impact.
Other investments	5.58	−0.08	−0.69	−1.78	3.03	**Adjusted** to eliminate BSkyB.
Property, plant & equipment	23.40	−4.68	0.48	0.06	19.26	
GW net	37.62	−0.02	−0.72	21.05	57.94	**Reclassified** to Investments & from Intangible Assets. **Adjusted** to add back the French GAAP impairment charge and GW registered against shareholders' equity under French GAAP.
Intangible assets	23.30	−0.29	−2.76	−0.33	19.91	**Reclassified** to GW net and Other Assets.
Other assets			715	124	840	**Reclassified** from Deferred Taxes, Intangible Assets and Other Investments. **Adjusted** for BSkyB, deceased properties, VE public service contracts, etc.
Total Noncurrent Assets	**99.07**	**−4.82**	**6.73**	**21.75**	**122.73**	
TOTAL ASSETS	**139.00**	**−8.01**	**−1.40**	**21.54**	**151.14**	

LIABILITIES & STOCKHOLDERS' EQUITY	FRENCH GAAP	ELIMINATION OF PROPORTION (1)	RECLASSIFI-CATIONS (2)	ADJUST-MENTS (3)	US GAAP	PRIMARY EXPLANATIONS OF RECLASSIFICATIONS AND ADJUSTMENTS
Short-term debt and current, portion of long-term debt	14.00	−0.65	0.47	1.23	15.05	**Adjusted** to reconsolidate VE's Receivable Sales program.
Deferred taxes	9.98	−0.19	−9.79		0.00	**Reclassified** to Deferred Income Taxes.
Accounts payable	26.41	−2.20		−0.05	24.16	
Payables and accrued liabilities	23.37	−2.20		−0.05	21.12	
Accrued royalties and participations	3.05				3.05	
Total Current Liabilities	**50.39**	**−3.04**	**−9.32**	**1.18**	**39.21**	
Long-Term debt	27.78	−2.56	1.63	−2.22	24.61	**Reclassified** from Other Liabilities. **Adjusted** for BSkyB
Accrued royalties and participations long-term			0.49		0.49	
Deferred income taxes			9.79	2.38	12.17	**Adjusted** for U.S. GAAP deferred tax treatment.

● **TABLE 19.8**

ILLUSTRATION OF FRENCH GAAP TO U.S. GAAP BALANCE SHEET RECONCILIATION, DECEMBER 31, 2001 IN €BILLIONS (continued)

LIABILITIES & STOCKHOLDERS' EQUITY	FRENCH GAAP	ELIMINATION OF PROPORTION (1)	RECLASSIFI-CATIONS (2)	ADJUST-MENTS (3)	US GAAP	PRIMARY EXPLANATIONS OF RECLASSIFICATIONS AND ADJUSTMENTS
Other liabilities	13.88	−1.14	−2.42	−0.94	9.39	**Reclassified** to long-term debt and accrued royalties and participations Long-Term. **Adjusted** for deceased real estate and VE's public service contracts.
Provisions and allowances (other long-term liabilities)	6.33	−0.62	−0.33	−1.05	4.32	
Other long-term liabilities	5.69	−0.06	−1.22	0.40	4.80	
Deferred income	1.86	−0.45	−0.86	−0.28	0.26	
Total Liabilities	**92.05**	**−6.74**	**0.17**	**0.40**	**85.87**	
Minority interest	10.21	−1.23	−0.30	0.42	9.10	
TSAR			0.30		0.30	
Put Options				1.60	1.60	**Adjusted** for U.S. GAAP recognition. Not recognized under French GAAP.
Shareholders' equity						
Common shares	5.97		0.00	0.00	5.97	
Additional paid-in capital	28.84		0.00	4.16	33.00	
Retained earnings	7.46	−0.04	−0.86	15.27	21.82	
Accumulated other comprehensive income			0.96	−0.30	0.65	
Treasury shares at cost	−5.52		−1.66		−7.18	
Total Shareholders' Equity	**36.75**	**−0.04**	**−1.56**	**19.12**	**54.27**	
TOTAL LIABILITIES AND SHAREHOLDERS' EQUITY	**139.00**	**−8.01**	**−1.40**	**21.54**	**151.14**	

Source: http://finance.vivendiuniversal.com/finance/, accessed on October 15, 2002.

For the year ended December 31, 2001, the net loss under U.S. GAAP was €1,135 million compared to a net loss of €13,597 million under French GAAP. The most significant reconciling item was the reversal of the goodwill impairment charge, which increased net income by approximately 12.6 billion. Other reconciling items, specific to 2001, resulted from the differential accounting treatment for the sale of our investment in BSkyB, which increased net income by approximately 110 million, and the adoption of Statement of Financial Accounting Standards (SFAS) No. 133, "Accounting for Derivative Instruments and Hedging Activities," which increased net income by approximately 74 million. The most significant reconciling item impacting all periods presented relates to business combination accounting, as described in Note 14 to our Consolidated Financial Statements. As permitted under French GAAP prior to December 31, 1999, goodwill could be recorded as a reduction of shareholders' equity when the acquisition was paid for with equity securities, whereas under U.S. GAAP goodwill is always recognized as an asset. The reconciliation impact is that French GAAP potentially results in a lower net asset value being assigned to acquisitions, which results in higher gains on the sales of businesses as compared to U.S. GAAP. Additionally, the amortization of goodwill charged to earnings is lower under French GAAP than under U.S. GAAP.

The adjustment of a net loss of €1.135 billion under U.S. GAAP and €13.597 billion under French GAAP is a change of 1,198 percent. The difference to the millions of VU shareholders and investors throughout the world on this change in accounting loss is huge. The paragraph cited here also suggests the major differences between U.S. GAAP and French GAAP on income statements. These include but are not limited to accounting for goodwill, business combination (acquisition) accounting, and accounting for derivative and hedging activities.

ACCOUNTING ISSUES ARISE

Vivendi Universal's organization can be traced back to a French imperial decree enabling the company, then called CGE, to supply water in Lyons, France. CGE exceled in "Environmental" operations and expand their water operations with waste management, energy, and transportation operations. In 1998, CGE changed its name to Vivendi. Vivendi proposed a merger with Canal + (Europe's first pay-TV provider and a company it helped create) and Seagram (best known for its Absolut Vodka and the owner of Universal Studios) in June 2000, which was really when investors and media around the world started to take notice. In September 2000, Vivendi began its accounting saga by being listed on the New York Stock Exchange under the symbol "V," thereby agreeing to provide its financial statements in terms of U.S. GAAP through Form 20-F reconciliations and hiring Arthur Andersen as their U.S. auditor. In December 2000, the successful merger with Canal + and Seagram created a new company, known as Vivendi Universal.

As part of the merger VU was forced to sell its stake in British Sky Broadcasting Group PLC (BSkyB), but since it could not find a buyer, VU transferred the stake to Deutsche Bank in exchange for cash. Under French GAAP, the proportion of BSkyB debt carried by these shares should have stayed on Vivendi's books. However, VU's auditor, Andersen, argued that under U.S. securities law, this debt could be removed from the balance sheet, allowing the media group to post a profit, something it was doing with another company it audited named Enron. It seems that VU successfully disguised these accounts from the firm's liabilities, though the measures were against French GAAP according to findings of an investigation published by *Le Monde,* a French newspaper. A COB investigation also discovered letters and e-mails that showed how VU's management, led by Chairman Jean-Marie Messier, attempted to discourage its French auditor, Salustro-Reydel, from applying French GAAP to VU's BSkyB shares. Chairman Jean-Marie Messier resigned as chairman in July 2002, and in September 2002, the board of directors refused to give him severance pay because VU's stock began to plummet under his reign. Jean-Marie Messier's successor, Jean-Rene Fourtou announced in a September 25, 2002, board meeting that he plans to sell off about $10 billion of assets that Messier acquired, hoping to cure the financing problems pursuant to the $19 billion dollars worth of debt Messier created in his acquisitions. In a statement in March 2003, Fourtou said, "2002 has been an extremely difficult year for Vivendi Universal. 2003 will be a year of transition and of financial and economic progress." Among business units that Fourtou is considering selling are Universal Studios, Universal Music, and two of its U.S. cable TV channels.

QUESTIONS

1. Based on this short description, do you agree with Vivendi Universal's acquisition and diversification strategy?

2. If you were to sell off $10 billion of Vivendi Universal's assets, which divisions would you keep and which would you eliminate?

3. Using the 20-F reconciliation, what is the most common type of reconciliation? What impact does this have on current and future financial statements under U.S. and French GAAP?

4. What do you see as the key accounting issues facing Vivendi Universal's board of directors? How might these be resolved through the use of International Accounting Standards?

Chapter Notes

1   The information in this case is from the following sources: Michael Peel, "Big Win Hangs in the Balance for Accountants," *Comment & Analysis* (June 5, 2000): 25; "The Impossible Dream," *The Economist* (March 2, 2002); John House, "Financial Reporting: IASB Meeting—A Difficult Balancing Act," *Accountancy* (February 1, 2002); "Rulemakers Move Closer to Global Accounting Standards," *Washington Post* (September 19, 2002): E04; IASC Web site (2002): http://www.iasc.org.uk/; and Edward Helmore, "Towers of Steel, Feet of Clay," *The Observer* (December 2, 2001): 5.

2   "Statement on Management Accounting, No. 1A," *Institute of Management Accountants* (1981), as quoted in Paul J. Wendell, *Corporate Controller's Manual* (New York: Warham, Gorham & Lamont, 1998), A1–A3.

3   Ibid.

4   "Basic Concepts and Accounting Principles Underlying Financial Statements of Business Enterprises," *Statement of the Accounting Principles Board No. 4* (New York: American Institute of Certified Public Accountants, 1970), paragraph 40.

5   Financial Accounting Standards Board, "Objectives of Financial Reporting by Business Enterprises," *Statement of Financial Accounting Concepts No. 1* (Stamford, CT: FASB, 1979), paragraphs 34–54.

6   International Accounting Standards Committee, *International Accounting Standards 1998* (London: IASC, 1998), paragraph 9, pp. 36–37.

7   DaimlerChrysler Investor Relations Internet Web site: http://www.daimlerchrysler.com/index_e.htm.

8   "Uniform Rules for International Accounting Standards from 2005 Onwards," *European Parliament Daily Notebook* (March 12, 2002).

9   www.iasc.org.uk (2002).

10   Financial Accounting Standards Board, "Foreign Currency Translation," *Statement of Financial Accounting Standards No. 52* (Stamford, CT: FASB, December 1981), 6–7.

11   *Vivendi Universal Annual Report,* 20-F (2001): 88.

12   William H. Hoffman et al., *West Federal Taxation: Corporations, Partnerships, Estates, and Trusts,* 2000 ed. (Cincinnati: South-Western, 2000), Section 9, p. 33.

13   Geoff Winestock and John McKinnon, "EU Gets Approval to Impose Tariffs on U.S. Products," *Wall Street Journal* (September 3, 2002): A3

14   Hoffman et al., op. cit., Chapter 9, p. 30.

15   "U.S. Tax Treaty Developments," *Deloitte & Touche Review* (February 5, 1996): 5.

16   Sources for the case were various issues of the annual report of the Vivendi Universal Corporation (FY 2001); "Universal Issues Statement In Response to Inquiries Regarding Published News Articles," *Business Wire* (July 2, 2002); http://finance.vivendiuniversal.com/finance/ (2002); Corie Brown, "Vivendi to Sell Water Business," *Los Angeles Times* (September 25, 2002): Business section, 2; "French Auditors to Investigate Vivendi," *Los Angeles Times* (September 14, 2002): Business section, 3; Carol Matlack, "What Will Happen to Vivendi's Goodies?" *BusinessWeek* (July, 15, 2002): 44; Phyllis Furman, "French Regulators Commence Probe of Vivendi Universal at Paris Headquarters," *Daily News, L.P.* (July 10, 2002): www.nydailynews.com; Malcom Warner, *International Encyclopedia of Business and Accounting,* vol. 1 (London: Routledge, 1996).

20

THE MULTINATIONAL
FINANCE FUNCTION

To have money is a good thing; to have a say over the money is even better.

—YIDDISH PROVERB

OBJECTIVES

- To describe the multinational finance function and how it fits in the MNE's organizational structure
- To show how companies can acquire outside funds for normal operations and expansion
- To discuss the major internal sources of funds available to the MNE and to show how these funds are managed globally
- To explain how companies protect against the major financial risks of inflation and exchange-rate movements
- To highlight some of the financial aspects of the investment decision

CASE

Nu Skin Enterprises[1]

Nu Skin Enterprises, a U.S.-based network-marketing company, operates in 34 countries throughout Asia, the Americas, and Europe. It now generates most of its income from Asia. Nu Skin's primary market in Asia is Japan, followed by Taiwan and Korea. Because Nu Skin operates in so many countries, exchange rate volatility has always affected its bottom line. Rate volatility became even more important, however, once Japan displaced the United States as Nu Skin's leading market. After Nu Skin began operations in Japan in 1993 and up until mid-2002, the yen continued to weaken while fluctuating against the dollar and this translated into millions of dollars of losses for Nu Skin in exchange rate exposure despite huge gains in local revenues.

Nu Skin, a leader in multilevel marketing, was founded in 1984 in Provo, Utah. Blake Roney, a young entrepreneur, envisioned the development and distribution of personal care products through direct selling. His idea was to organize a sales force of independent, self-motivated entrepreneurs who would build their own organizations supported by Nu Skin products and marketing materials. As sales started increasing, Roney expanded the product line to include premium items like shampoos, lotions, makeup, skin care products, and nutritional products. A few years later, Nu Skin expanded its nutritional line with the acquisition of Pharmanex and created a technology division called Big Planet.

Nu Skin's international strategy was to open one new market per year. It opened its first international office in Canada in 1990. Its exposure to the Asian market started in Hong Kong in 1991. In 1993, Nu Skin opened an office in Japan, the world's largest direct-sales market. Nu Skin saw great opportunity in Japan because other direct-sales companies had proven successful in the Asian market. Asians, particularly the Japanese, enjoy direct selling, door-to-door selling, and the personal contacts acquired using this model of selling. As a result, network marketing companies have flourished in Japan.

Nu Skin does not outlay a large capital investment when opening a new market. It generally starts with one office, one warehouse, and up to 60 employees with one expatriate (U.S. manager). Nu Skin financed its entry into Japan the same way it financed its entry in other markets—with internal sources of funds. The U.S. corporate office allocates internal funds for the opening of new markets. Nu Skin finances its growth in each market mainly with its retained earnings. In 1996, Nu Skin management created a holding company called Nu Skin Asia Pacific (NSAP) to manage the financials of Nu Skin's Asia Pacific markets. Nu Skin then went through a public offering in order to be listed on the New York Stock Exchange, and in 2002, Nu Skin issued a second public offering, which helped it to raise money for expansion in China planned for 2003.

It didn't take long for Nu Skin, in its operations abroad, to realize the impact of foreign exchange rates on net income. In 1993, when Nu Skin Japan (NSJ) began operations, the dollar/yen exchange rate was very volatile, fluctuating from 125 yen/dollar at the beginning of the year to the yen strengthening to 109 by the end of the year. The yen strengthened again in 1995 when it hit 80.63 to the dollar. However, the situation changed in mid-1995, and the dollar began to strengthen against the yen. From an average low of 84.33 yen in 1995, the yen weakened in value to over 110 to the dollar by the end of 1996. The Asian financial crisis hit Japan from 1997 to 1998, and the exchange rate fluctuated drastically while the economy hit rock bottom. Fortunately for Nu Skin, direct-sales businesses typically do well in depressed economies with high unemployment because such firms, like Nu Skin, provide a way for people to begin their own businesses. Sales continued to climb despite the economic woes in Japan.

Nu Skin has used hedging strategies to reduce the risk of currency fluctuations involved in its international operations. To understand how the volatility in exchange rates affects Nu Skin, it is necessary to view an example of how Nu Skin uses dollars and yen. NSJ earns profits in Japan, denominated in yen, which are translated into dollars for the financial reports; the subsequent dividends are then converted into dollars and deposited into dollar-based bank accounts. When the value of the yen was weak compared to the dollar (as it was in 1997 versus the previous years), that translated into fewer dollars. In 1998, the yen weakened even further against the dollar, translating into millions in lost dollar-based revenues for Nu Skin. The futures market showed doubt in the yen strengthening against the dollar. Because of the futures outlook and the general fluctuation of the market, Nu Skin sought to reduce its exposure to the exchange-rate market. It increased its hedging activities by entering into forward contracts, which guaranteed receivables at certain dollar/yen exchange rates. Although exchange-rate losses amounted to $5.5 million in 1997, this hedging policy helped minimize the losses on its books.

The trend changed in 2002, when the dollar weakened against the yen from a high in February 2002 of 134.77 yen/dollar to a low in July of 115.71. This helped Nu Skin's dollar-based revenues because such a large portion of its income is from Japan. Third quarter earnings in Japan and Korea were up 7 percent from 2001 in constant currency terms, but they were up 9 percent when taking the new exchange rate into account.

Nu Skin chose another strategy to minimize exchange-rate risk—borrowing in local currencies. Exchange-rate differentials from its debt offset the differentials from its assets. Nu Skin assumed a loan in Japanese yen. When the yen strengthens against the dollar, the loan translates into a higher amount in dollars, and when the yen weakens against the dollar, the loan translates into a lower amount in dollars. This offsets the exchange-rate gains and losses from Nu Skin's revenues in Japan. Nu Skin lowers the possibility of peak profits it may make from exchange rate translations, but it also lowers the possibility of valleys. Although Nu Skin does not eliminate the risk in foreign-exchange transactions from its international operations, it significantly lowers that risk, thus helping to stabilize its revenues in the long run.

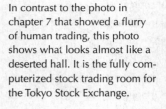

In contrast to the photo in chapter 7 that showed a flurry of human trading, this photo shows what looks almost like a deserted hall. It is the fully computerized stock trading room for the Tokyo Stock Exchange.

FIGURE 20.1   Finance in International Business

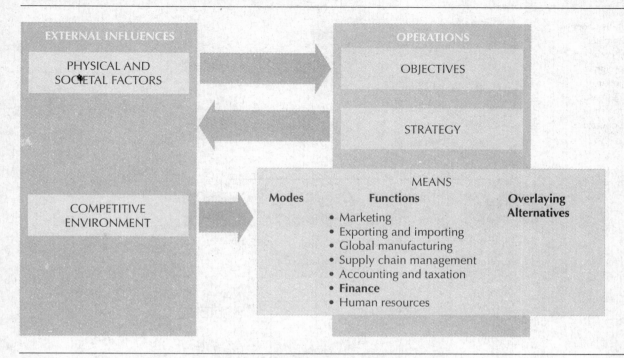

Finance is one of the necessary functions for implementing companies' international strategies.

INTRODUCTION

Why do you need to understand capital markets, cash management, and financial risk? Having a good product idea is not sufficient for success. MNEs need to get access to capital markets in different countries in order to finance expansion. Indeed, finance is integral to firms' international strategies, as Figure 20.1 shows. The small company involved only tangentially in international business may be concerned primarily about the foreign-exchange function of its commercial bank and not global capital markets. It may use the bank to buy and sell foreign exchange and to hedge foreign-exchange risk, but it probably doesn't think about borrowing money or issuing stock on foreign capital markets. However, the MNE investing and operating abroad usually is concerned about access to capital in local markets as well as in large global markets. This chapter examines external sources of funds available to companies operating abroad and internal sources of funds that arise from intercompany links. Nu Skin's intercompany lending in Japan illustrates that point. The chapter also examines global cash management, risk-management strategies, and international dimensions of the capital investment decision.

THE FINANCE AND TREASURY FUNCTIONS IN THE INTERNATIONALIZATION PROCESS

One of the most important people on the management team is the chief financial officer. This chapter focuses on the CFO's most important global treasury responsibilities. Figure 20.2 illustrates how the CFO's responsbilities fit into the organizational structure of the firm and how global finance fits into the treasury function.

The finance function in the firm focuses on cash flows. The management activities related to cash flows can be divided into four major areas.

The corporate finance function acquires and allocates financial resources among the company's activities and projects. Four key functions are

- Capital structure
- Capital budgeting
- Long-term financing
- Working capital management

FIGURE 20.2   Location of Treasury Function in the Corporate Organizational Structure

The treasury function falls under the responsibility of the chief financial officer, and it comprises domestic and foreign responsibilities. The global finance function within treasury is a resource to all of the strategic business units of a company.

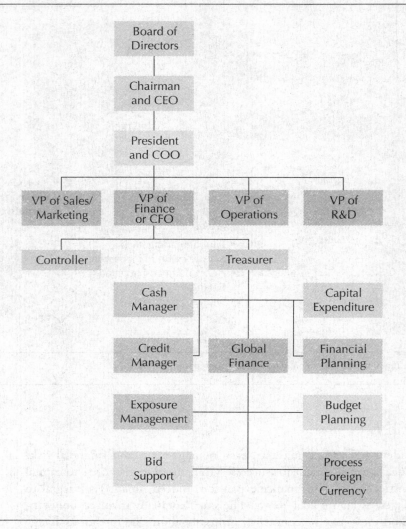

1. *Capital structure*—determining the proper mix of debt and equity
2. *Capital budgeting*—analyzing investment opportunities
3. *Long-term financing*—selection, issuance, and management of long-term debt and equity capital, including location (in the company's home country or elsewhere) and currency (the company's home currency or a foreign currency)
4. *Working capital management*—proper management of the company's currency assets and liabilities (cash, receivables, marketable securities, inventory, trade receivables, short-term bank debt)[2]

The CFO acquires financial resources and allocates them among the company's activities and projects. Acquiring resources (financing) means generating funds either internally (within the company) or from sources external to the company at the lowest possible cost. When Nu Skin needed funds to expand, it issued stock and borrowed money in the U.S. market, but it also did both of these activities in Japan and the rest of Asia. Allocating resources (investing) means increasing stockholders' wealth through the allocation of funds to different projects and investment opportunities.[3]

The CFO's job is more complex in a global environment than in the domestic setting because of forces such as foreign-exchange risk, currency flows and restrictions, different tax rates and laws pertaining to the determination of taxable income, and regulations on access to capital in different markets. In the remainder of the chapter, we will examine the following six areas: (1) global debt markets, (2) global equity markets, (3) offshore financial centers, (4) internal sources of funds, (5) foreign-exchange risk management, and (6) capital budgeting in an international context.

GLOBAL DEBT MARKETS

The CFO must determine the degree to which a firm funds the growth of the business by debt, which is known as **leverage.** The degree to which companies use leverage instead of equity capital—known as stocks or shares—varies from country to country. Country-specific factors are a more important determinant of a company's capital structure than is any other factor, because companies tend to follow the financing trends in their own country and their particular industry within their country. Japanese companies, for example, are more likely to follow the capital structure of other Japanese companies than they are of U.S. or European companies. Leveraging is often perceived as the most cost-effective route to capitalization, because the interest companies pay on debt is a tax-deductible expense, whereas the dividends paid to investors are not.

However, leveraging may not be the best approach in all countries for two major reasons. First, excessive reliance on long-term debt increases financial risk and thus requires a higher return for investors. Second, foreign subsidiaries of an MNE may have limited access to local capital markets, making it difficult for the MNE to rely on debt to fund asset acquisition.[4] In a study of foreign subsidiaries of U.S. MNEs, it was found that the debt/asset of those studied averaged 0.54, which means that 54 percent of assets were funded by debt and 46 percent were funded by equity. The debt/asset ratio on average for companies in a few countries was as follows: the Netherlands (0.32), Brazil (0.37), Australia (0.49), Mexico (0.51), Canada (0.52), England (0.64), Japan (0.65), and Germany (0.69).[5]

In addition, different tax rates, dividend remission policies, and exchange controls may cause a company to rely more on debt in some situations and more on equity in others. It is important to understand that the different debt and equity markets discussed in this chapter have different levels of importance for companies worldwide.

One of the major causes of the Asian financial crisis in 1997 was that Asian companies relied too much on debt to fund their growth, especially bank debt. The lack of development of bond and equity markets forced companies to rely on bank debt for growth. Many of the Asian banks borrowed dollars from international banks and lent the money to local companies in local currencies, not dollars. When the Asian currencies fell against the dollar, many of the banks could not service their loans and went into bankruptcy. Some of the Asian companies that borrowed dollars directly from foreign banks couldn't generate enough local currency to pay off the debt, and they were brought close to bankruptcy. As a result, many have been forced to exchange debt for equity, thereby losing some of their control or selling themselves outright to foreign investors who could pay off their dollar debt.[6] Argentine companies and banks also had a large amount of foreign debt, a factor which helped escalate its monetary crisis in 2002. Companies are renegotiating contracts with their foreign lenders in an attempt to repay some of their loans.

An MNE that needs to raise capital through debt markets has a number of options. The local domestic debt market is the first source that a company will tap. This means Japan for Japanese companies, but it could also mean Japan for the Japanese subsidiary of a U.S. company. Nissan lists several types of long-term debt in its annual report. In its 2000 *Annual Report*, it listed bonds in Japanese yen, Australian dollars, U.S. dollars, and euros.[7] So companies can tap international banks for local currency borrowings or Eurodollar borrowings as well as the longer-term bond markets.

Companies can use local and international debt markets to raise funds.

A Eurocurrency is any currency banked outside of its country of origin.

Eurocurrencies

The **Eurocurrency market** is an important source of debt financing for the MNEs to complement what they can find in their domestic markets. A **Eurocurrency** is any currency that is banked outside of its country of origin. Currencies banked inside of their country of origin are also known as onshore currencies, and currencies banked outside of their country of origin are also known as offshore currencies. In essence, the Eurocurrency market is an offshore market. The Eurocurrency market started with the deposit of U.S. dollars in London banks, and it was called the Eurodollar market. As other currencies entered the offshore market, the broader *eurocurrency* name was adopted for use for the market. Given the introduction of the euro as the new currency in Europe, the term *Eurocurrency* is confusing, but the Eurocurrency market predates the euro, and the confusion will probably not go away. Eurocurrencies could be dollars or yen in London, euros in the Bahamas, or British pounds in New York City. **Eurodollars**, which constitute a fairly consistent 65 to 80 percent of the Eurocurrency market, are dollars banked outside of the United States. Dollars held by foreigners on deposit in the United States are not Eurodollars, but dollars held at branches of U.S. or other banks outside of the United States are.

The major sources of Eurocurrencies are

Major sources of Eurocurrencies

- Foreign governments or individuals
- MNEs
- Foreign banks
- Countries with large balance-of-payments surpluses

- Foreign governments or individuals who want to hold dollars outside of the United States.
- Multinational corporations that have cash in excess of current needs.
- European banks with foreign currency in excess of current needs.
- Countries such as Germany, Japan, and Taiwan that have large balance-of-trade surpluses held as reserves.

The demand for Eurocurrencies comes from sovereign governments, supranational agencies such as the World Bank, companies, and individuals. Eurocurrencies exist partly for the convenience and security of the user and partly because of cheaper lending rates for the borrower and better yield for the lender.

The Eurocurrency market is a wholesale (companies and other institutions) rather than a retail (individuals) market, so transactions are very large. Public borrowers such as governments, central banks, and public sector corporations are the major players. MNEs are involved in the Eurodollar market; however, nearly four-fifths of the Eurodollar market is in the interbank market.

A Eurocredit is a type of loan that matures in one to five years.

Syndication occurs when several banks pool resources to make a large loan in order to spread the risk.

The Eurocurrency market is both short and medium term. Short-term borrowing has maturities of less than one year. Anything from one to five years is considered a **Eurocredit**, which may be a loan, line of credit, or other form of medium- and long-term credit, including **syndication**, in which several banks pool resources to extend credit to a borrower and spread the risk.

A major attraction of the Eurocurrency market is the difference in interest rates compared with those in domestic markets. Because of the large transactions and the lack of controls and their attendant costs, Eurocurrency deposits tend to yield more than domestic deposits do, and loans tend to be cheaper than they are in domestic markets. Traditionally, loans are made at a certain percentage above the **London Inter-Bank Offered Rate (LIBOR)**, which is the deposit rate that applies to interbank loans within London. The LIBOR rates quoted on October 16, 2002, were

LIBOR is the interest rate that banks charge each other on Eurocurrency loans.

3.3200 percent one month; 3.30038 percent three months; 3.22156 percent six months; 3.22500 percent one year. British Bankers' Association average of interbank offered rates for dollar deposits in the London market based on quotations at 16 major banks.[8]

At the same time, the prime rate in the United States was 4.75 percent, based on the best rate on corporate loans posted by 75 percent of the nation's 30 largest banks. In addition, prime rates were listed as 4.5 percent for Canada, 3.25 percent for Germany, 2.75 percent for Switzerland, 4.00 percent for Britain, and 1.375 percent for Japan. However, the *Wall Street Journal* noted that it is very difficult to compare prime rates and the LIBOR rate because lending practices vary so much from country to country.

How much above LIBOR the interest rate that a borrower is charged all depends on the creditworthiness of the customer, and it must be large enough to cover expenses and build reserves against possible losses. The Eurocurrency market's unique characteristics mean that the borrowing rate usually is less than it would be in the domestic market. Most loans are variable rate, and the rate-fixing period generally is six months, although it may be one or three months. Another unique characteristic of the Eurocurrency market is that it is completely unregulated. No single country or agency, not even the Bank for International Settlements, regulates Eurocurrency transactions.

International Bonds: Foreign, Euro, and Global

Many countries have active bond markets available to domestic and foreign investors. The earlier long-term debt example of Nissan involves bonds issued in Japan, Australia, the United States, and Europe. The bonds issued in yen are for ¥557 billion and matures (must be paid back) in 2007 at interest rates of 1.7 to 3.6 percent. The bonds issued in euro are for ¥162 billion and mature in 2009 at interest rates of 0.2 to 9.6 percent. Even though the domestic bond market dominates total bond issues, with the U.S. market offering the best opportunities, the international bond market still fills an important niche in financing. One of the reasons why the U.S. bond (and stock) markets in the United States are so influential is because the companies of continental Europe and Japan still rely disproportionately on banks for finance—on average, banks constitute about 75 percent of corporate funding. That figure varies across Europe—from 70 percent in Germany and France to 80 percent in Spain, but it is much lower in Britain.[9] This may change, however, because banks across the world are tightening their loan outflows as a result of emerging market collapses like the ones in Asia in 1997 and Argentina in 2002. Emerging bond markets have been growing more quickly than developed markets, but they are still only 5.6 percent of the total global bond market. Investors generally focus on purchasing foreign currency from emerging markets, but the bond market is four times as large as the currency market (i.e., $1,645 billion versus $432 billion). Emerging bond markets are gradually becoming an alternative source of funding for governments, corporations, and global fixed-income investors.[10]

The international bond market can be divided into foreign bonds, Eurobonds, and global bonds. **Foreign bonds** are sold outside of the borrower's country but are denominated in the currency of the country of issue. For example, a French company floating a bond issue in Swiss francs in Switzerland would be selling a foreign bond. Foreign bonds typically make up about 18 percent of the international bond market. They also have creative names, such as Yankee bond (issued in the United States), Samurai bond (issued in Japan), and Bulldog bond (issued in England).

A **Eurobond** is usually underwritten (placed in the market for the borrower) by a syndicate of banks from different countries and sold in a currency other than that of the country of issue. A bond issue floated by a U.S. company in dollars in London, Luxembourg, and Switzerland is a Eurobond. Eurobonds make up approximately 75 percent of the international bond market.

The **global bond**, introduced by the World Bank in 1989, is a combination of a domestic bond and a Eurobond—that is, it must be registered in each national market according to that market's registration requirements. It also is issued simultaneously in several markets, usually those in Asia, Europe, and North America. Global bonds are a small but growing segment of the international bond market.

Foreign bonds are sold outside of the country of the borrower but in the currency of the country of issue.

Eurobonds are sold in countries other than the one in whose currency the bond is denominated.

A global bond is registered in different national markets according to the registration requirements of each market.

The international bond market is an attractive place to borrow money. For one thing, it allows a company to diversify its funding sources from the local banks and the domestic bond market and borrow in maturities that might not be available in the domestic markets. In addition, the international bond markets tend to be less expensive than local bond markets. However, not all companies are interested in global bonds or Eurobonds. Before the Asian financial crisis hit, Asian companies relied on their domestic banks more because of the ready availability of cheap loans. In addition, the companies and banks tended to develop a cozier relationship than might be the case with Western companies and banks.[11] However, the Asian financial crisis demonstrated the fundamental flaws in this strategy as banks went bankrupt and as companies were forced to face the fact that they couldn't generate enough funds to pay back the loans.

Although the Eurobond market is centered in Europe, it has no national boundaries. In contrast to most conventional bonds, Eurobonds are sold simultaneously in several financial centers through multinational underwriting syndicates and are purchased by an international investing public that extends far beyond the confines of the countries of issue.

U.S. companies first issued Eurobonds in 1963 as a means of avoiding U.S. tax and disclosure regulations. They are typically issued in denominations of $5,000 or $10,000, pay interest annually, are held in bearer form, and are traded over the counter (OTC), most frequently in London.[12] Any investor who holds a bearer bond is entitled to receive the principal and interest payments. In contrast, for a registered bond, which is more typical in the United States, the investor is required to be registered as the bond's owner in order to receive payments. An OTC bond is traded with or through an investment bank rather than on a securities exchange, such as the London Stock Exchange.

An example of a non–U.S. dollar Eurobond issue is found in the 2002 annual report of Marks & Spencer, the British retail company. In 2002, Marks & Spencer issued a £368.2 million Eurobond at 6⅜ percent fixed rate, which was stated to mature in 2011. Marks & Spencer then entered into an interest rate swap with another company in which it agreed to exchange its fixed rate obligation with a floating rate obligation.[13] An investment bank would have facilitated the swap. Marks & Spencer probably got a reasonably good Eurobond fixed interest rate because it is a British company and was issuing the bond in Eurosterling. The counterparty (the other company in the swap agreement) might have wanted a fixed rate obligation in sterling initially but couldn't get it for whatever reason, so it had to settle for a floating rate obligation. As interest rates in Britain began to come down, it made sense for Marks & Spencer to enter into the swap to lower its overall interest charge. In a floating rate bond, the interest rate changes every six months, so as interest rates come down, the holder of the floating rate bond would end up paying lower interest to the bondholders. The holder of the floating rate bond might have wanted to trade to a fixed rate bond to eliminate the uncertainty of future interest rates and to lock in an interest rate that was attractive to it.

The top five investment banks in the world that deal in the Eurobond market are Deutsche Bank (Germany), Morgan Stanley Dean Witter (United States), UBS Warburg (Switzerland), ABN Amro (the Netherlands), and Merrill Lynch (United States).[14] The ranking varies a little depending on the specific currency being issued, but these are the top banks.

Occasionally, Eurobonds may provide currency options, which enable the creditor to demand repayment in one of several currencies, thus reducing the exchange risk inherent in single-currency foreign bonds. More frequently, however, both interest and principal on Eurobonds are payable to the creditor in U.S. dollars. It is also possible to issue a Eurobond in one currency—say, the U.S. dollar—and then swap the obligation to another currency. (The process is similar to the interest-rate swap just described.) For example, a U.S. company with a subsidiary in Britain would generate lots of British pounds through normal operations, and it could use the pounds to pay off a British pound bond. If the U.S. company had

Eurobonds are typically issued in denominations of $5,000 or $10,000, pay interest annually, are held in bearer form, and are traded over the counter.

Some Eurobonds have currency options, which allow the creditor to demand repayment in one of several currencies.

issued Eurobonds in dollars in London, it could enter into a swap agreement through an investment bank to exchange its future dollar obligations with a British pound obligation and use the pound revenues to pay off the swapped obligation.

EQUITY SECURITIES AND THE EUROEQUITY MARKET

Another source of financing is equity securities, where an investor takes an ownership position in return for shares of stock in the company and the promises of capital gains—an appreciation in the value of the stock—and maybe dividends. One way a company can easily and inexpensively get access to capital is through a private placement with a venture capitalist. In this case, a wealthy venture capitalist (or perhaps a venture-capital firm investing the money of one or several wealthy individuals) will invest money in a new venture in exchange for stock. As shown in Table 20.1, the amount of venture capital decreased from 2000 to 2001 by 50 percent due to the global economic slowdown.[15] Another source of demand for private placements is the corporate restructuring market in Europe. In recent years, European mergers have primarily taken place between firms in the same country, but mergers are now crossing national borders. Cross-European mergers have increased the demand for cash, and private placements have helped to fill that demand.[16]

In addition to private placements, companies can access the equity-capital market, more commonly known as the stock market. Companies can raise new capital by listing their stocks (also known as shares) on a stock exchange, and they can list on their home-country exchange or on a foreign exchange. Nu Skin Asia Pacific raised money through an initial public offering (IPO) in 1996 by listing on the New York Stock Exchange. The growth in globalization has forced companies to look at equity markets as an alternative to debt markets and banks as a source of funds. As in Map 20.1 notes, the 10 largest stock markets in the world in terms of **market capitalization** (the total number of shares of stock listed times the market price per share) are in the developed countries.

It has been interesting to track the development of the emerging stock markets, as Figure 20.3 shows. The emerging markets grew steadily as a percentage of total stock market capitalization until the end of 1994. They dipped a little bit as a percentage of total in 1995 but recovered in 1996 to 11.1 percent of total. By 1998, however, the Asian financial crisis had clobbered the emerging stock markets, and they plunged to only 6.9 percent of total. Emerging stock

Many companies around the world are using private placements to raise equity capital because it is easier and cheaper.

Stock markets are another source of equity capital.

The three largest stock markets in the world are in New York, Tokyo, and London.

⬤ **TABLE 20.1**

TOTAL WORLDWIDE VENTURE CAPITAL

AMOUNTS INVESTED (DOLLARS IN BILLIONS)	1998	1999	2000	2001	PERCENT CHANGE 2000 TO 2001
Total World	82.0	155.0	199.0	100.0	−50%
North America	56.4	116.3	145.5	62.8	−57%
Western Europe	16.2	26.8	32.0	21.5	−33%
Asia Pacific	4.9	9.1	12.3	11.9	−3%
Middle East & Africa	1.0	1.4	3.7	1.9	−49%
Central & South America	2.7	0.7	3.7	1.3	−65%
Central & Eastern Europe	0.2	0.2	0.4	0.3	−25%

Source: VC Opportunities in Europe. Adapted from study by Price Waterhouse Coopers (September 2002): http://www.europeanvc.com/figures.htm.

MAP 20.1   Market Capitalization, 2001 (in billions of U.S. dollars)

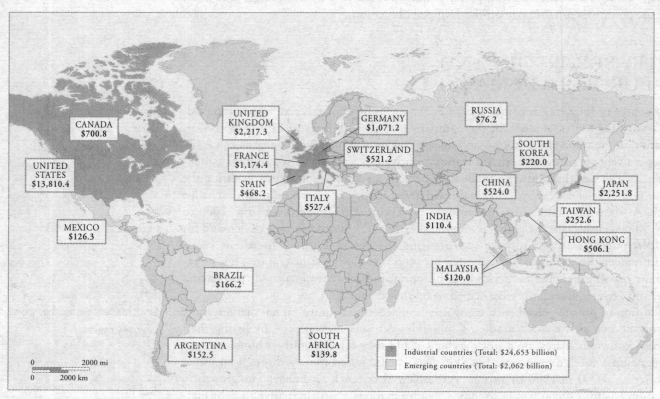

Stock markets in the developed countries far surpass those in emerging countries in terms of market capitalization (a measure of the size of a stock market: total number of shares listed times the price per share). Fifty percent of the world's market capitalization is in the U.S. market, which is comprised of the New York Stock Exchange, the American Stock Exchange, and the NASDAQ. The map illustrates the top 10 industrial markets and the top 10 emerging markets. Totals include all markets worldwide, not just the industrial and emerging countries shown on the map.

Source: Standard & Poor's, *Standard & Poor's Emerging Stock Markets Factbook 2002* (New York: McGraw-Hill, 2002).

markets have slowly recovered from the Asian crisis and Russian crisis of 1998. In 2000, the stock markets of developed countries, beginning with the ones in the United States, began falling. Then in 2002, the United States, in its first recession in 10 years, led the rest of the world into a global recession. Investors have increasingly turned their money from the United States and other major stock markets to emerging markets. Emerging stock markets weathered the global recession better than markets in developed countries.

From 1993 to 1998, the total world market capitalization nearly doubled, and from 1998 to 2002, it leveled off, which means that companies might be having difficulties raising cash by issuing stock. Some of the explosion in market activity in the mid-1990s was the result of privatizations taking place in emerging markets, and some was general economic growth in the world. Yet the stock market was clearly becoming a more significant force in raising new capital for expansion and as a way to facilitate mergers and acquisitions. However, the softening of the market in 2001 and 2002 was clearly a blow to companies that needed to raise cash for expansion.

Another significant event in the past decade is the creation of the **Euroequity market**, the market for shares sold outside the boundaries of the issuing company's home country. Prior to 1980, few companies thought about offering stock outside the national boundaries of their headquarters country. Since then, hundreds of companies worldwide have issued stock simultaneously in two or more countries in order to attract more capital from a wider variety of shareholders.

The Euroequity market is the market for shares sold outside the boundaries of the issuing company's home country.

FIGURE 20.3   Growth of Emerging Stock Markets

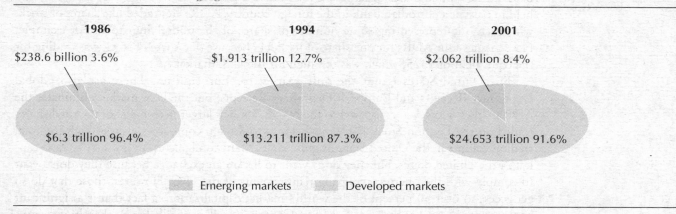

The market capitalization of emerging stock markets rose from 3.6 percent of the world's total in 1986 to 12.7 percent in 1994, and back to 8.4 percent in 2001. The Asian and Russian financial crises devastated emerging stock markets, and they only started to recover in 1999.

Source: Standard & Poor's, *Standard & Poor's Emerging Stock Markets Factbook 2002* (New York: McGraw-Hill, 2002).

In some cases, companies list on only one foreign exchange. It is expensive to list on foreign exchanges and so companies often list on one big one, such as the New York Stock Exchange or the London Stock Exchange. However, some companies list on different exchanges, especially if they have foreign investments in several countries and are trying to raise capital in those countries. For example, when Daimler and Chrysler merged and issued global shares around the world, it did so on 21 different markets in eight different countries: Germany, the United States, Austria, Canada, France, Britain, Japan, and Switzerland. However, the U.S. and German markets were the most important ones. The U.S. market is important for U.S. and foreign companies looking for equity capital and is popular for Euroequity issues partly because of the market size and the speed with which offerings are completed. The large pension funds in the United States can buy big blocks of stock at low transaction costs. Pension fund managers regard foreign stocks as a good form of portfolio diversification.

The New York Stock Exchange identifies four major reasons why a foreign company should list on the NYSE (and these reasons could apply to U.S. companies trying to determine the benefits of listing on a foreign exchange).

1. The NYSE provides opportunities to develop a broad shareholder constituency in the United States through exposure to the widest possible range of individual and institutional investors.
2. The NYSE facilitates U.S. mergers and acquisitions through the use of an NYSE-listed security as acquisition currency.
3. The NYSE increases the visibility of a company, its products and services, and the trading of its shares in the United States.
4. The NYSE supports a company's incentive program for its U.S. employees by providing a liquid market in the United States for its shares.[17]

There are 471 foreign companies that list on the New York Stock Exchange, more than triple the number of companies that listed in 1993. The countries with the most companies listed on the NYSE are Canada (81), the United Kingdom (65), Brazil (36), Mexico (25), and France (22). By October 2002, 907 foreign companies were listed on one of the three big U.S. exchanges, with most listed on the NYSE (471).

The most popular way for a Euroequity to get a listing in the United States is to issue an **American Depository Receipt (ADR).** An ADR is a negotiable certificate issued by a U.S.

An ADR is a negotiable certificate issued by a U.S. bank that represents shares of stock of a foreign corporation.

bank in the United States to represent the underlying shares of a foreign corporation's stock held in trust at a custodian bank in the foreign country. ADRs are traded like shares of stock, with each one representing some number of shares of the underlying stock. For example, Nestlé issues four ADRs for one share of its stock, because one share of stock was trading for the equivalent of $325, which was too high for the U.S. market.

The United States is not the only market for Euroequities. There are also Global Depositary Receipts and European Depositary Receipts, but the U.S. market dominates the ADR market. However, compared to the NYSE, a much larger percentage of the total shares traded on the London Stock Exchange belongs to foreign companies even though the total trading volume in the United States is quite large. Many foreign corporations try to raise capital in the United States, but they don't want to list on an exchange because they don't want to comply with the onerous reporting requirements of the SEC. However, those that do so get access to over 50 percent of the world's market capitalization, a fact that is a significant advantage to those that have a U.S. listing. Companies will generally list on their home country's exchange first and then venture into the international exchanges with depository receipts. Throughout the 1990s, funds raised from ADRs in developing countries averaged around $7 billion per year. Since the turn of the century, that figure has jumped to around $22 billion per year, peaking in 2000.[18]

The global share offering by DaimlerChrysler is the first of its kind in the world. Other companies with global share offerings listed on the NYSE are Celanese AG, UBS Warburg, and Deutsche Bank. It is important for MNEs to list their securities on foreign exchanges as mentioned earlier in the NYSE example. As MNEs generate more of their revenues outside of their home country, it is easier to attract investors from the countries where they are operating. As global stock markets continue to grow, especially in the emerging markets, it will be even easier for companies to raise equity capital outside of their home markets.

Some ADRs will list for the same price in the home country and foreign country exchange, but as seen in the Nestlé example, some companies list for different prices in different countries. Taiwan Semiconductor shares were worth 70 percent more in New York than they were in Taiwan in January 2000. Also, the ADRs of Infosys, an Indian software contractor, traded at nearly two-and-a-half times their value in India. At the same time, ADRs for Singapore, Japanese, and British companies were trading at the same value as in their home markets. There are a couple of reasons why that is the case. The latter countries are relatively open to the outside world, so traders spotting price differences in two markets can buy or sell securities until the price differences disappear. However, Taiwan and India have regulated markets in which foreigners are allowed to own only a certain percentage of the shares and in which currency controls make it difficult to buy and sell assets. In addition, the ADRs represent only a small percentage of the companies' shares. As the Asian markets begin to recover, the demand for high-tech stocks is pushing up the prices for ADRs. As markets open up, these price differences should eventually disappear.[19]

There are a number of movements to improve stock market activity around the world. Europe's plan was to introduce a unified stock exchange once the euro was introduced. However, that remains one of the EU's unfinished projects. Now that the euro is in use and the capital markets are flowing more freely, Europe is one step closer to a unified stock exchange.[20] The major innovation in share trading around the world is Internet trading. U.S. electronic trading companies such as E*Trade and Charles Schwab & Company are now doing business in Europe and competing with local e-trade companies. Some of the large investment banks, such as J. P. Morgan; Morgan Stanley Dean Witter, and UBS Warburg, have joined together to strengthen Tradepoint, a British-based electronic exchange. More than 20 European fund managers, led by Merrill Lynch Mercury Asset Management and Barclays Global Investors, are building their own electronic network, called E-Crossnet, which will help reduce the broker's role and the cost of making trades. A NASDAQ-type

A global share offering, such as the one issued by Daimler-Chrysler, is the simultaneous offering of actual shares on different exchanges.

A major source of competition to the stock exchanges will be the electronic trading of stocks through companies such as E*Trade.

exchange called Easdaq has been established in Brussels and is concentrating on high-tech European stocks. The whole world of e-trade could provide strong competition to stock exchanges in European as well as developing countries, just as it is beginning to put pressure on the major exchanges in the United States.[21]

OFFSHORE FINANCIAL CENTERS

Offshore financial centers are cities or countries that provide large amounts of funds in currencies other than their own and are used as locations in which to raise and accumulate cash. Usually, the financial transactions are conducted in currencies other than the currency of the country and are thus the centers for the Eurocurrency market. Generally, the markets in these centers are regulated differently—and usually more flexibly—than domestic markets. These centers provide an alternative, (usually) cheaper source of funding for MNEs so that they don't have to rely strictly on their own national markets. Offshore financial centers have one or more of the following characteristics:

- large foreign-currency (Eurocurrency) market for deposits and loans (in London, for example)
- market that is a large net supplier of funds to the world financial markets (in Switzerland, for example)
- market that is an intermediary or pass-through for international loan funds (in the Bahamas and the Cayman Islands, for example)
- economic and political stability
- efficient and experienced financial community
- good communications and supportive services
- official regulatory climate favorable to the financial industry, in the sense that it protects investors without unduly restricting financial institutions[22]

These centers are either operational centers, with extensive banking activities involving short-term financial transactions, or booking centers, in which little actual banking activity takes place but in which transactions are recorded to take advantage of secrecy and low (or no) tax rates. In the latter case, individuals may deposit money offshore to hide it from their home-country tax authorities, either because the money was earned illegally—such as in the drug trade—or because the individual or company does not want to pay tax. London is an example of an operational center; the Cayman Islands is an example of a booking center. Although there are many offshore financial centers, the most important are Bahrain (for the Middle East), Brussels, the Caribbean (servicing mainly Canadian and U.S. banks), Dublin, Hong Kong, London, New York, Singapore, and Switzerland. London is a crucial center because it offers a variety of financial services in both debt and equity transactions and has a large domestic market; it also serves the offshore market. The Caribbean centers (primarily the Bahamas, the Cayman Islands, and the Netherlands Antilles) are essentially offshore locations for New York banks. Switzerland has been a primary source of funds for decades, offering stability, integrity, discretion, and low costs. Singapore has been the center for the Eurodollar market in Asia (sometimes called the Asiadollar market) since 1968, thanks to its strategic geographic location, its strong worldwide telecommunications links, and government regulations that have facilitated the flow of funds. Hong Kong is critical because of its unique status with respect to China and the United Kingdom and its geographic proximity to the rest of the Pacific Rim. Bahrain, an island country in the Persian Gulf, is the financial center of petrodollars (dollars generated from the sale of oil) in the Middle East.

Offshore financial centers are good locations for establishing finance subsidiaries that can raise capital for the parent company or its other subsidiaries. They allow the finance

Offshore financial centers provide large amounts of funds in currencies other than their own.

Offshore financial centers can be operational centers or booking centers.

Key offshore financial centers are in Bahrain, the Caribbean, Hong Kong, Ireland, London, New York, Singapore, and Switzerland, among other locations.

FIGURE 20.4   Internal Sources of Working Capital for MNEs

There are many ways in which MNEs can use internal cash flow to fund worldwide operations.

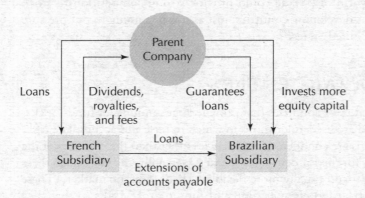

subsidiaries to take advantage of lower borrowing costs and tax rates. However, the U.S. Congress is proposing legislation to halt the reincorporation of companies to offshore locations because of the loss in tax revenues.[23]

INTERNAL SOURCES OF FUNDS

Funds are working capital, or current assets minus current liabilities.

Although the term *funds* usually means "cash," it is used in a much broader sense in business and generally refers to working capital—that is, the difference between current assets and current liabilities. A company that wants to expand operations or needs additional capital can look not only to the debt and equity markets but also to sources within itself. For an MNE, the complexity of internal sources is magnified because of the number of its subsidiaries and the diverse environments in which they operate. Figure 20.4 shows a parent company that has two foreign subsidiaries. The parent, as well as the two subsidiaries, may be increasing funds through normal operations. These funds may be used on a companywide basis, perhaps through loans. The parent can loan funds directly to one subsidiary or guarantee an outside loan to the other. Equity capital from the parent is another source of funds for the subsidiary.

Sources of internal funds:
- Loans
- Investments through equity capital
- Intercompany receivables and payables
- Dividends

Funds also can go from subsidiary to parent. The subsidiary could declare a dividend to the parent as a return on capital or could loan cash directly to the parent. If the subsidiary declared a dividend to the parent, the parent could lend the funds back to the subsidiary. The dividend would not be tax deductible to the subsidiary, but it would be included as income to the parent, and the parent would have to pay tax on the dividend. If the subsidiary loaned money to the parent, the interest paid by the parent would be tax deductible to the parent and would be taxable income to the subsidiary.

Intercompany financial links become extremely important as MNEs increase in size and complexity. In 2002, the energy giant Enron was forced to declare bankruptcy partially due to an enormous amount of debt hidden in its web of complex subsidiaries, many of which were offshore. Goods as well as loans can travel between subsidiaries, giving rise to receivables and payables. Companies can move money between and among related entities by paying quickly (leading payments), or they can accumulate funds by deferring payment (lagging payments). They also can adjust the size of the payment by arbitrarily raising or lowering the price of intercompany transactions in comparison with the market price, a transfer pricing strategy. For example, Nu Skin Enterprises charges a transfer price to its subsidiaries when it transfers product to them.

Thus, cash comes from debt and equity markets both domestically and overseas and from internal sources. In addition, companies can generate cash from normal operations—from selling cars if it is DaimlerChrysler to selling personal care items if it is Nu Skin Enterprises. The problems of managing cash globally are complex. International cash management is complicated by differing inflation rates, changes in exchange rates, and government restrictions on the flow of funds. To understand how companies can utilize their internal sources of funds more effectively in a global setting, we need to discuss global cash management and the multilateral netting of funds.

Global Cash Management

Effective cash management is a chief concern of the CFO, who must answer the following three questions to ensure effective cash management:

1. What are the local and corporate system needs for cash?
2. How can the cash be withdrawn from subsidiaries and centralized?
3. Once the cash has been centralized, what should be done with it?

The cash manager, who reports to the treasurer (as illustrated in Figure 20.1), must collect and pay cash in the company's normal operational cycle and then must deal with financial institutions, such as commercial and investment banks, when generating and investing cash. Before the cash manager remits any cash into the MNE's control center—whether at regional or headquarters level—he or she must first assess local cash needs through cash budgets and forecasts. Because the cash forecast projects the excess cash that will be available, the cash manager will know how much cash can be invested for short-term profits.

Cash budgets and forecasts are essential in assessing a company's cash needs.

Once local cash needs are met; the cash manager must decide whether to allow the local manager to invest any excess cash or to have it remitted to a central cash pool. If the cash is centralized, the manager must find a way of making the transfer. A cash dividend is the easiest way to distribute cash, but government restrictions may interfere. For example, foreign-exchange controls may prevent the company from remitting as large a dividend as it would like. Cash also can be remitted through royalties, management fees, and repayment of principal and interest on loans.

Dividends are a good source of intercompany transfers, but governments often restrict their free movement.

Many developing countries with large foreign debt, such as Brazil, have made transferring money abroad difficult for companies operating within them because they want to curtail the outflow of foreign exchange. For example, one U.S. company with large operations in Brazil used dividends, loan repayments, and sales commissions to transfer funds out of Brazil. The Brazilian operation was treated as a manufacturing facility, and all export sales were made by a sales subsidiary of the U.S. parent. When the manufacturing facility was established in Brazil, it was financed primarily through debt rather than equity. The parent could get more cash out of Brazil by paying off principal and interest than it could by paying a dividend, which was subject to large taxes. When the Brazilian manufacturer made foreign sales, it could pay a commission to the sales company in the United States, which allowed it to transmit more funds abroad. However, the Brazilian government constantly tried to lower the amount of the commission, while the parent company tried to increase it.

FOREIGN-EXCHANGE RISK MANAGEMENT

As illustrated earlier, global cash-management strategy focuses on the flow of money for specific operating objectives. Another important objective of an MNE's financial strategy is to protect against the foreign-exchange risks of investing abroad. The strategies that an MNE adopts to do

Major financial risks arise from exchange-rate changes.

this may mean the internal movement of funds as well as the use of one or more of the foreign-exchange instruments described in Chapter 9, such as options and forward contracts.

If all exchange rates were fixed in relation to one another, there would be no foreign-exchange risk. However, rates are not fixed, and currency values change frequently. Instead of infrequent one-way changes, currencies fluctuate often and both up and down. A change in the exchange rate can result in three different exposures for a company: **translation exposure**, **transaction exposure**, and **economic or operational exposure**.

□──────
Three types of foreign-exchange exposure—translation, transaction, economic or operational.

Translation Exposure

□──────
Translation exposure arises because the dollar value of the exposed asset or liability changes as the exchange rate changes.

Foreign-currency financial statements are translated into the reporting currency of the parent company (assumed to be U.S. dollars for U.S. companies) so that they can be combined with financial statements of other companies in the corporate group to form the consolidated financial statements. Exposed accounts—those translated at the balance sheet rate or current exchange rate—either gain or lose value in dollars when the exchange rate changes. For example, assume a subsidiary of a U.S. company operates in Mexico and has 900,000 pesos in a bank account there. If the Mexican peso were to depreciate in relation to the dollar from 9.5 pesos per dollar to 10 pesos per dollar, the subsidiary's bank account would drop in value from $94,737 (900,000/9.5) to $90,000 (900,000/10) as a result of the depreciation. However, the subsidiary still has pesos in the bank account; it's just that the dollar equivalent of the pesos has fallen, resulting in a loss.

The combined effect of the exchange-rate change on all assets and liabilities is either a net gain or loss. However, the gain or loss does not represent an actual cash flow effect because the cash, in the example here, is only *translated* into dollars, not *converted* into dollars. The problem is that reported earnings can either rise or fall against the dollar because of the translation effect, and this can affect earnings per share and stock prices. A good example is Nu Skin Enterprises. In 2001, when most foreign currencies were falling against the dollar, its annual report stated that earnings would have been higher if the dollar had not been so strong. When Nu Skin translated its foreign earnings into dollars, they were lower than they would have been if the dollar had remained at the same level as the previous year.

Transaction Exposure

□──────
Transaction exposure arises because the receivable or payable changes in value as the exchange rate changes.

Denominating a transaction in a foreign currency represents foreign-exchange risk because the company has accounts receivable or payable in foreign currency that must be settled eventually. For example, assume a U.S. exporter delivers merchandise to a British importer for a total price of $500,000 when the exchange rate is 1.5000 dollars per pound, or £ 333,333 ($500,000/1.5000). If the exporter were to receive payment in dollars, there would be no immediate impact on the exporter if the dollar/pound exchange rate changed. If payment were to be received in pounds, however, the exporter might incur a foreign-exchange gain or loss. For example, with the exchange rate at 1.5000 dollars per pound, the sale would be carried on the exporter's books at $500,000, but the underlying value in which the sale is denominated would be £ 333,333. If the rate moved to 1.4000 dollars per pound by the time the receivable was collected, the exporter would receive 333,333 pounds, but that payment would be worth $466,666 (the 333,333 × 1.4000), a loss of $33,334. This would be an actual cash flow loss to the exporter.

□──────
Economic, or operating, exposure arises from effects of exchange-rate changes on
• Future cash flows
• The sourcing of parts and components
• The location of investments
• The competitive position of the company in different markets

Economic Exposure

Economic exposure, also known as operating exposure, is the potential for change in expected cash flows. Economic exposure arises from the pricing of products, the sourcing and cost of inputs, and the location of investments. Pricing strategies have both an immediate and a long-term impact on cash flows. For example, the inventory sold to the British importer probably was sold to final users before the exchange rate changed, but future sales would be affected by the rate change. Assume the exporter sold its most recent shipment of $500,000 at an exchange rate of 1.5000 dollars per pound for a cost to the importer of 333,333 pounds. If the British pound were to weaken to 1.4000 dollars per pound, the exporter would have two choices. The first choice is to continue to sell the product to the British importer for $500,000, which would now cost the importer 357,143 pounds. At the higher price, the importer might lose market share if consumers were not willing to pay the higher price. Or the importer could absorb the cost increase in its profit margin and continue to sell the product for a total of 333,333 pounds. The exporter's second choice is to sell the inventory to the importer for fewer dollars so that the pound equivalent is still 333,333 pounds. At the new exchange rate of 1.4000, the sale price would have to be $466,666. The exporter would end up with lower revenues and thus a lower profit margin. Exporters and importers must always determine the impact of a price change on volume. This example illustrates the impact of an exchange-rate change on any cash flows. If a U.S. parent were to receive a dividend, royalty, or management fee in foreign currency, a drop in the foreign currency would result in weaker dollars when the foreign currency amount is converted into dollars.

Exposure-Management Strategy

To protect assets adequately against risks from translation, transaction, and economic exposure of exchange-rate fluctuations, management must

- Define and measure exposure.
- Organize and implement a reporting system that monitors exposure and exchange-rate movements.
- Adopt a policy assigning responsibility for minimizing—or *hedging*—exposure.
- Formulate strategies for hedging exposure

Defining and Measuring Exposure   Most MNEs will see all three types of exposure: translation, transaction, and economic. To develop a viable hedging strategy, an MNE must forecast the degree of exposure in each major currency in which it operates. Because the types of exposure differ, the actual exposure by currency must be kept track of separately. For example, the translation exposure in Brazilian reals should be kept track of separately from the transaction exposure because the transaction exposure will result in an actual cash flow, while the translation exposure may not. Thus, the company generates one report on translation exposure and another on transaction exposure. The company may adopt different hedging strategies for the different types of exposure.

A key aspect of measuring exposure is forecasting exchange rates. Estimating exchange rates is similar to fortunetelling: Approaches range from gut feelings to sophisticated economic models, each having varying degrees of success. Whatever the approach, a company should estimate and use ranges within which it expects a currency to vary over the forecasting period. Some companies develop in-house capabilities to monitor exchange rates, using economists who also try to obtain a consensus of exchange-rate movements from the banks with whom they deal. Their concern is to forecast the direction, magnitude, and timing of an exchange-rate change. Other companies contract out this work.

A Reporting System   Once the company has decided how to define and measure exposure and estimate future exchange rates, it must create a reporting system that will assist in protecting it against risk. To achieve this goal, substantial participation from foreign operations

---

To protect assets from exchange-rate risk, management needs to

- *Define and measure exposure*
- *Establish a reporting system*
- *Adopt an overall policy on exposure management*
- *Formulate hedging strategies*

All three types of exposure must be monitored and measured separately.

Exchange-rate movements are forecasted using in-house or external experts.

The reporting system should use both central control and input from foreign operations.

must be combined with effective central control. Foreign input is important to ensure that the information, the company uses in forecasting is effective. Because exchange rates move frequently, the company must obtain input from those who are attuned to the foreign country's economy. Central control of exposure protects resources more efficiently than letting each subsidiary and branch manage its own exposure. Each organizational unit may be able to define its own exposure, but the company also has an overall exposure. AT&T, for example, requires its strategic business units (SBUs) to coordinate foreign-currency transactions with corporate treasury so that its foreign-exchange hedging unit can undertake the most cost-effective hedging strategy possible. To set hedging policies on a separate-entity basis might not take into account the fact that exposures of several entities (that is, branches, subsidiaries, affiliates, and so on) could offset one another. For example, one SBU of AT&T might have an exposed asset position in yen, and another might have an exposed liability position in yen. Without central control, both SBUs might incur hedging costs to protect their exposed positions. However, AT&T's central foreign-exchange unit in corporate treasury could offset the exposed asset position with the exposed liability position and not have to incur hedging costs.

Management of an MNE should devise a uniform reporting system for all of its subsidiaries. The report should identify the exposed accounts the company wants to monitor, the amount of exposure by currency of each account, and the different time periods under consideration. Exposure should be separated into translation, transaction, and economic components, with the transaction exposure identified by cash inflows and outflows over time.

The time periods on the report depend on the company. Companies can identify their exposure positions for different periods into the future, such as 30, 60, and 90 days; 6, 9, and 12 months; or 2, 3, and 4 years. The reason for the longer time frame is that operating commitments, such as plant construction and production runs, are fairly long term.[24]

Once each basic reporting unit has identified its exposure, the data should be sent to the next organizational level for preliminary consolidation. That level may be a regional headquarters (for Latin America or Europe, for example) or a product division, depending on the company's organizational structure. The preliminary consolidation enables the region or division to determine exposure by account and by currency for each time period. The resulting reports should be routine, periodic, and standardized to ensure comparability and timeliness in formulating strategies. Final reporting should be at the corporate level, where top management can see the amount of foreign-exchange exposure. Specific hedging strategies can be taken at any level, but each level of management must be aware of the size of the exposure and the potential impact on the company.

A Centralized Policy   It is important for management to decide at what level hedging strategies will be determined and implemented. Several hedging strategies will be discussed in the next section. To achieve maximum effectiveness in hedging, top management should determine hedging policy. Having an overview of corporate exposure and the cost and feasibility of different strategies at different levels in the company, the corporate treasurer should be able to design and implement a cost-effective program for exposure management. However, the company may have to decentralize some exposure management decisions so it can react quickly to a more rapidly changing international monetary environment. However, such decentralization should stay within a well-defined policy established at the corporate level. Some companies run their hedging operations more as profit centers and nurture in-house trading desks. Those working at the trading desks actually buy and sell foreign exchange in the market rather than have the trader at a commercial bank effect the trades for the company. Most MNEs, however, are traditional and conservative in their approach, preferring to cover exposure (enter into a hedging strategy that minimizes losses due to exposed positions) rather than to extract huge profits or risk huge losses.

Formulating Hedging Strategies   Once a company has identified its level of exposure and determined which exposure is critical, it can hedge its position by adopting operational and/or financial strategies, each with cost/benefit implications as well as operational implications. The safest position is a balanced position in which exposed assets equal exposed liabilities.

Nu Skin uses operational and financial strategies to reduce exposure. Operational strategies involve adjusting the flow of money and resources in normal operations in order to reduce foreign-exchange risk. First, management must determine the working capital needs of a subsidiary. Then it needs to adjust the flows of receivables, payables, and inventory. Although it may be wise to collect receivables as fast as possible in a country in which the local currency is expected to depreciate, the company must consider the competitive implications of doing so. If it tries to collect receivables too fast and does not give the buyer proper time to make payment, the buyer may go to another seller that is willing to offer better credit terms.

The use of debt to balance exposure is an interesting strategy. Many companies "borrow locally," especially in weak-currency countries, because that helps them to avoid foreign-exchange risk from borrowing in a foreign currency.

Companies in Argentina that borrowed dollars found themselves in serious trouble when the peso devalued against the dollar, because they couldn't generate enough local currency revenues to pay off the higher debt. If they had borrowed in local currency, they would not have had the same problem. One problem with this strategy is that interest rates in weak-currency countries tend to be high, so there must be a trade-off between the cost of borrowing and the potential loss from exchange-rate variations. Protecting against loss from transaction exposure becomes complex. In dealing with foreign customers, it is always safest for the company to denominate the transaction in its own currency because it won't have any foreign-exchange exposure. The risk shifts to the foreign customer that has to come up with your currency. Or the company could denominate purchases in a weaker currency and sales in a stronger currency. If forced to make purchases in a strong currency and sales in a weak currency, it could resort to contractual measures such as forward contracts or options, or it could try to balance its inflows and outflows through astute sales and purchasing strategies.

Another operational strategy—leads and lags—protects cash flows among related entities, such as a parent and subsidiaries. A **lead strategy** means either collecting foreign-currency receivables before they are due when the foreign currency is expected to weaken or paying foreign-currency payables before they are due when the foreign currency is expected to strengthen. With a **lag strategy**, a company either delays collection of foreign-currency receivables if that currency is expected to strengthen or delays payables when the currency is expected to weaken. In other words, a company usually leads into and lags out of a hard currency and leads out of and lags into a weak currency.

There are two problems with a lead and lag strategy. First, it may not be useful for the movement of large blocks of funds. If there are infrequent decisions over small amounts of money, it is easy to manage the system, but as the number, frequency, and size of transactions increase, the system becomes difficult to manage. Second, leads and lags are often subject to government control, and it may be difficult to get permission to move currency.

Sometimes an operational strategy means shifting assets overseas to take advantage of currency changes. When the yen strengthened against the U.S. dollar, for example, Toyota shifted more of its manufacturing into the United States to take advantage of the cheaper dollar. As long as the yen was strong, it was difficult to export from Japan to the United States, so companies could service U.S. demand through production in the United States.

In addition to the operational strategies just mentioned, a company may hedge exposure through financial contracts such as forward contracts and options, also known as derivatives. The most common hedge is a forward contract. For example, assume a U.S. exporter sells

---

Hedging strategies can be operational or financial.

Operational strategies include

- Using local debt to balance local assets
- Taking advantage of leads and lags for intercompany payments

---

A lead strategy means collecting or paying early.

A lag strategy means collecting or paying late.

Forward contracts can establish a fixed exchange rate for future transactions.

Currency options can assure access to foreign currency at a fixed exchange rate for a specific period of time.

goods to a British manufacturer for £1 million, with payment due in 90 days. The spot exchange rate is 1.5000 dollars per pound, and the forward rate is 1.4500 dollars per pound. At the time of the sale, the transaction is recorded on the exporter's books at $1.5 million, and a corresponding receivable is set up for the same amount. However, the exporter is concerned about the exchange risk. The exporter can enter into a forward contract, which will guarantee that the receivables convert into dollars at a rate of 1.4500 dollars per pound, no matter what the actual future exchange rate is. This move will yield $1.45 million. Even though the company gets $50,000 less than it could have at the initial spot rate, it has eliminated any risk for the future. Or the exporter could wait until it collects the receivable in 90 days and gamble on a better rate in the spot market. If the actual rate at that time is 1.4700 dollars per pound, the exporter will receive $1.47 million, which is not as good as the initial receivable of $1.5 million but is better than the forward yield of $1.45 million. But if the dollar strengthens to 1.4000 dollars per pound, the exporter would be much better off with the forward contract.

A foreign-currency option is more flexible than a forward contract because it gives its purchaser the right, but not the obligation, to buy or sell a certain amount of foreign currency at a set exchange rate within a specified amount of time. For example, assume a U.S. exporter decides to sell merchandise to a British manufacturer for £1 million when the exchange rate is $1.5000 per pound. At the same time, the exporter goes to Goldman Sachs, its investment banker, and enters into an option to deliver pounds for dollars at an exchange rate of $1.5000 per pound at an option cost of $25,000. When the exporter receives the £1 million from the manufacturer, it must decide whether to exercise the option. If the exchange rate is above $1.5000, it will not exercise the option, because it can get a better yield by converting pounds at the market rate. The only thing lost is the $25,000 cost of the option, which is like insurance. However, if the exchange rate is below $1.5000—say, $1.4500—the exporter will exercise the option and trade pounds at the rate of $1.5000. The proceeds will be $1.5 million less the option cost of $25,000.

A good example of how companies use operational and financial hedging strategies is Coca-Cola. Because approximately 77 percent of Coke's operating income in 2001 came from outside of the United States, foreign-currency changes can have a major impact on reported earnings. Coke manages its foreign-currency exposures on a consolidated basis, which allows it to net certain exposures from different operations around the world and also allows it to take advantage of natural offsets—for example, cases in which British pound receivables offset British pound payables. It also uses derivative financial instruments to further reduce its net exposure to currency fluctuations. Coke enters into forward-exchange contracts and purchases currency options in several currencies, most notably the euro and Japanese yen, to hedge firm sales commitments. It also purchases currency options to hedge certain anticipated sales.[25]

THE CAPITAL BUDGETING DECISION IN AN INTERNATIONAL CONTEXT

The parent company needs to compare the net present value or internal rate of return of a foreign project with that of its other projects and with that of others available in the host country.

The last international dimension of the treasury function that we will discuss in the chapter is the capital budgeting decision whereby the MNE needs to determine which projects and countries will receive its capital investment funds. The parent company must compare the net present value or internal rate of return of a potential foreign project with that of its other projects around the world to determine the best place to invest its resources. The technique used to compare different projects is capital budgeting. Several aspects of capital budgeting are unique to foreign project assessment.

- Parent cash flows must be distinguished from project cash flows. Parent cash flows refer to cash flows from the project back to the parent in the parent's currency. Project cash flows refer to the cash flows in local currency from the sale of goods and services.

- Remittance of funds to the parent, such as dividends, interest on loans, and payment of intracompany receivables and payables, is affected by differing tax systems, legal and political constraints on the movement of funds, local business norms, and differences in how financial markets and institutions function.

- Differing rates of inflation must be anticipated by both the parent and subsidiary because of their importance in causing changes in competitive position and in cash flows over time.

- The parent must consider the possibility of unanticipated exchange-rate changes because of both their direct effects on the value of cash flows as well as their indirect effects on the foreign subsidiary's competitive position.

- The parent company must evaluate political risk in a target market because political events can drastically reduce the value or availability of expected cash flows.

- The terminal value (the value of the project at the end of the budgeting period) is difficult to estimate because potential purchasers from host, home, or third countries—or from the private or public sector—may have widely divergent perspectives on the value of the project. The terminal value is critical in determining the total cash flows from the project. The total cash outlay for the project is partially offset by the terminal value—the amount of cash the parent company can get from the subsidiary or project if it sells it eventually.[26]

Because of all the forces listed here, it is very difficult to estimate future cash flows, both to the subsidiary and to the parent company. There are two ways to deal with the variations in future cash flows. One is to determine several different scenarios and then determine the net present value or internal rate of return (IRR) of the project. The other is to adjust the hurdle rate, which is the minimum rate of return that the project must achieve in order for it to receive capital. The adjustment is usually made by increasing the hurdle rate above its minimal level.

Once the budget·is complete, the MNE must examine both the return in local currency and the return to the parent in dollars from cash flows to the parent. Examining the return in local currency will give management a chance to compare the project with other investment alternatives in the country. However, cash flows to the parent are important, because it is from these cash flows that dividends are paid to shareholders. If the MNE cannot generate sufficient return to the parent in the parent's currency, it will eventually fall behind in its ability to pay shareholders and pay off corporate debt.

ETHICAL DILEMMA

What's Wrong with Banking in a Tax-Haven Country?

Cash flow management gives rise to numerous ethical dilemmas. Many critics question the practice of setting up subsidiaries in tax-haven countries such as the Cayman Islands in order to take advantage of lower tax rates and the secrecy there. MNEs have been known to transfer money illegally into tax-haven countries to pay bribes. This practice became common knowledge in the United States when President Nixon ran for reelection in the early 1970s, and it was later found out that his reelection committee had obtained illegal campaign contributions and kept the money in offshore bank accounts so that they wouldn't be discovered.

The secrecy possible in tax-haven countries makes them natural locations in which to hide cash. However, not all use of tax havens is illegal. Although the governments of high-tax countries may criticize domestic companies that shelter income in tax-haven countries, those companies may simply be taking advantage of differences in tax rates and may not necessarily be acting unethically.

As noted in Chapter 19, the EU went to the WTO with complaints against a particular U.S. tax law, the Foreign Sales Corporation (FSC). The FSC was set up under the Nixon administration and was originally designed to provide taxpayer subsidies to U.S. exporting companies. The subsidies help companies lower prices on goods sold abroad, thus enabling them to sell more goods and also helping them to reduce the U.S. trade deficit. With this law, it is legal for U.S. exporters to set up branch offices in tax-haven countries, usually the Cayman Islands, thus allowing them to deduct 15 percent of their export earnings from their income taxes. The foreign office is usually just a front that allows companies, on paper, to show that the foreign office bought and sold the goods that are to be exported. The U.S. deficit continued to grow larger, and the U.S. exporting companies enjoyed the effect of the tax break on their bottom line.

Many countries questioned whether the tax laws were ethical or even legal. Later, the U.S. government justified the income tax break law because Europeans and many other countries rebate sales tax on their exports. In August 2002, the WTO ruled in favor of the Europeans—the U.S. tax-haven laws are considered an illegal tax break because of the lack of real business purpose of the operations in the tax-haven countries. Europeans can now impose penalty tariffs on U.S. goods to Europe of up to $4 billion a year, or Europe can demand that the United States remove tariffs on European goods of up to the same amount.[27]

LOOKING TO THE FUTURE

Capital Markets and the Information Explosion

It is difficult to forecast trends in global capital markets because of rapid economic changes worldwide. As world trade increases and as global interdependence rises, the velocity of financial transactions also must increase. Financial markets will continue to be dominated by the world's largest—New York, Tokyo, and London. However, action increasingly will take place in the developing nations within Eastern Europe as its countries align more closely with the EU; Latin America as its countries recover from the Argentine crisis; and Southeast Asia. As fund managers continue to diversify their portfolios to include securities of developing countries and as investment advisors continue to recommend that their clients diversify their portfolios away from domestic to global funds, the interest in developing country markets will continue to rise. However, the sharp drop in global stock markets after September 11 will continue to put pressure on fund managers to manage resources wisely. This pressure will clearly benefit investors by producing high returns, and it will also help the developing nations in capital formation. However, a key consideration for the future is the impact of e-trades on securities trading. As electronic trading increases in Europe, share trading will be greatly affected in Europe.

Two events will significantly influence the cash-management and hedging strategies of MNEs in the future: information and technology growth, and the growing number and sophistication of hedging instruments (financial derivatives such as options and forwards). Information growth will continue to enable companies to get information more quickly and cheaply. In addition, electronic data interchange (EDI) will allow them to transfer information and money instantaneously worldwide. Companies will significantly reduce paper flow and increase the speed of delivery of information and funds, enabling them to manage cash and to use intercompany resources much more effectively than before. Consequently, companies will reduce not only the cost of producing information but also interest and other borrowing costs.

Summary

- The corporate finance function deals with the acquisition of financial resources and their allocation among the company's present and potential activities and projects.

- CFOs need to be concerned with the international dimensions of the company's capital structure, capital budgeting decisions, long-term financing, and working capital management.

- Country-specific factors are the most important determination of a company's capital structure.

- Two major sources of funds external to the MNE's normal operations are debt markets and equity markets.

- A Eurocurrency is any currency banked outside of its country of origin, but it is primarily dollars banked outside the United States.

- A foreign bond is one sold outside the country of the borrower but denominated in the currency of the country of issue. A Eurobond is a bond issue sold in a currency other than that of the country of issue. A global bond is one issued simultaneously in North America, Asia, and Europe according to the listing requirements of each market.

- The three largest stock markets in the world are in New York, Tokyo, and London, with the U.S. markets controlling nearly half of the world's stock market capitalization.

- Euroequities are shares listed on stock exchanges in countries other than the home country of the issuing company. Most foreign companies that list on the U.S. stock exchanges do so through American Depositary Receipts, which are financial documents that represent a share or part of a share of stock in the foreign company. ADRs are easier to trade on the U.S. exchanges than are foreign shares.

- Offshore financial centers such as Bahrain, the Caribbean, Hong Kong, London, New York, Singapore, and Switzerland deal in large amounts of foreign currency and enable companies to take advantage of favorable tax rates.

- The major sources of internal funds for an MNE are dividends, royalties, management fees, loans from parent to subsidiaries and vice versa, purchases and sales of inventory, and equity flows from parent to subsidiaries.

- Global cash management is complicated by differing inflation rates, changes in exchange rates, and government restrictions on the flow of funds. A sound cash-management system for an MNE requires timely reports from affiliates worldwide.

- Management must protect corporate assets from losses due to exchange-rate changes. Exchange rates can influence the dollar equivalent of foreign-currency financial statements, the amount of cash that can be earned from foreign-currency transactions, and a company's production and marketing decisions.

- Foreign-exchange risk management involves defining and measuring exposure, setting up a good monitoring and reporting system, adopting a policy to assign responsibility for exposure management, and formulating strategies for hedging exposure.

- Companies can enter into operational or financial strategies for hedging exposures. Operational strategies include balancing exposed assets with exposed liabilities, using leads and lags in cash flows, and balancing revenues in one currency with expenses in the same currency. Financial strategies involve using forward contracts, options, or other financial instruments to hedge an exposed position.

- When deciding to invest abroad, MNE management must evaluate the cash flows from the local operation as well as the cash flows from the project to the parent. The former allows management to determine how the project stacks up with other opportunities in the foreign country, and the latter allows management to compare projects from different countries.

CASE

Dell Mercosur[28]

Todd Pickett, CFO of Dell Mercosur, was facing the end of 2002 with conflicting predictions of the value of the Brazilian currency, the real, and what to do to hedge Dell's operation in Brazil. Although Pickett was concerned about Dell's exposure in the other Mercosur countries, especially Argentina, Brazil is clearly the largest concern. The year 2002 began with the shocks resulting from the Argentine financial crisis that started at the end of 2001, and it ended with the election in October of Luiz Inácio Lula da Silva, known simply as Lula, as the president of Brazil. Lula, the leader of the Worker's Party and long-time leftist politician, had held the lead throughout the year. The markets were skeptical of Lula's potential leadership, a factor which caused the real to fall from 2.312 reals per U.S. dollar at the end of 2001 to a record 4 reals to one U.S. dollar at one point just prior to the election. After the election, the real began to strengthen somewhat, as noted in Figure 20.5, but Pickett had to base his strategies on whether the real would continue to strengthen or would weaken again.

FIGURE 20.5   Exchange Rates for Brazilian Real and U.S. Dollar

Source: www.x-rates.com (2002).

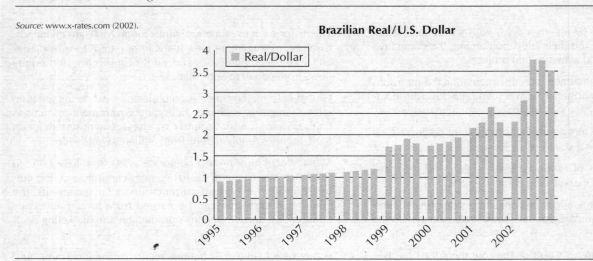

DELL'S HISTORY

Founded in 1984 by Michael Dell, the computer company operates in 34 countries with 36,000 employees, of which about 14,400 are outside the United States, and recorded $32 billion in sales for 2002. In the last five years, Dell has expanded beyond PCs to servers, storage, and communications equipment. Most PC manufacturers have claimed poor results since the technology bubble burst in 2000—IBM left the industry in 2000 and Compaq and HP merged in 2001 in hopes of boosting their competitive position. Unlike its competitors, Dell has thrived in the past few years, moving from a market share of 12 percent to 15 percent in 2001, the number-one spot in the industry. Fiscal 2002 was one of the toughest years to date in the PC industry. Because of the softening of the global economy and the events of September 11, demand for PCs was down sharply. Dell responded with an aggressive price strategy and reduced costs through workforce reductions and facility consolidations. Although global industry shipments fell in 2002 by 5 percent, Dell's unit shipments increased by 15 percent, thus enabling Dell to retain its number-one position.

Dell bases its success on its build-to-order, direct sales model. Dell has eliminated resellers and retailers and sells directly to the customer by phone or over the Internet. Dell customizes every computer to the customer's needs and waits to build the computer until it is ordered. As a result, Dell requires little inventory (4 days on average) and is able to deliver the newest technology to its customers. Costs are kept to a minimum compared to its competitors because it has no costly retail outlets and little inventory.

Dell began assembling computers in Round Rock, Texas, in 1985 and moved to global production in the following order:

1990: Opened manufacturing plant in Ireland
1996: Opened manufacturing plant in Malaysia
1998: Opened manufacturing plant in China
1999: Opened manufacturing plants in Tennessee and Brazil

Dell's 2002 Form 10K reports,

Sales outside the United States accounted for approximately 35% of the Company's revenues in fiscal year 2002. The Company's future growth rates and success are dependent on continued growth and success in international markets. As is the case with most international operations, the success and profitability of the Company's international operations are subject to numerous risks and uncertainties, including local economic and labor conditions, political instability, unexpected changes in the regulatory environment, trade protection measures, tax laws (including U.S. taxes on foreign operations), and foreign currency exchange rates.

DELL IN BRAZIL

Dell's production facility in Brazil is in Eldorado do Sul, close to Porto Alegre, the capital of Rio Grande do Sul, the southern-most state in Brazil. In addition, its call center in Brazil, similar to the one in the photo of Dell's call center in Bray, Ireland, services both Brazil and Argentina. Its Brazilian facility, which consists of 100,000 square feet of leased property, is the smallest of its facilities outside the United States, but the potential in Brazil and Argentina is huge, and Dell is planning further expansion. Because of the tariff-free provisions of Mercosur and the close proximity of Dell's manufacturing facilities in the south of Brazil, Dell is well positioned to service all of Mercosur with its Brazilian manufacturing operations. In FY 2002, it held a 4½

Dell's call center in Bray, Ireland.

Source: Courtesy of Dell Computer Corp.; http://www.dell.com/ downloads/us/corporate/ image_bank_locations/ bray_call_ctr_300.jpg (November 5, 2002).

percent market share in Brazil, behind HP/Compaq, IBM, and a Brazilian company. However, it was rapidly moving up to third place in the market and growing quickly.

Although Dell is divided into products and customers, it is managed generally on a geographic basis. Terry Kahler, the general manager of Dell Mercosur, reports to the head of the Americas/ International Group, who in turn reports to Rosendo Parra, the vice president of the Americas/International Group in Austin, Texas. Pickett works very closely with Kahler but reports directly to the CFO staff in Austin.

Dell's revenues in Brazil are denominated in reals, and most of its operating costs are also denominated in reals. However, about 97 percent of Dell's manufacturing costs in Brazil are denominated in U.S. dollars since Dell imports parts and components from the United States. It translates its financial statements according to the current rate method, which means that assets and liabilities are translated into dollars at the current exchange rate, and revenues and expenses are translated at the average exchange rate for the period. Because of business development loans from the Brazilian government, Dell's net exposed asset position in Brazil is quite small, but it is subject to foreign-exchange gains and losses as the rate changes.

HEDGING STRATEGY

In its Form 10K for FY 2002, Dell states its foreign currency hedging strategy as follows:

> The Company's objective in managing its exposure to foreign currency exchange rate fluctuations is to reduce the impact of adverse fluctuations on earnings and cash flows associated with

foreign currency exchange rate changes. Accordingly, the Company utilizes foreign currency option contracts and forward contracts to hedge its exposure on forecasted transactions and firm commitments in most of the foreign countries in which the Company operates. The principal currencies hedged during fiscal 2002 were the British pound, Japanese yen, euro, and Canadian dollar. The Company monitors its foreign currency exchange exposures to ensure the overall effectiveness of its foreign currency hedge positions. However, there can be no assurance the Company's foreign currency hedging activities will substantially offset the impact of fluctuations in currency exchange rates on its results of operations and financial position.

The Company uses purchased option contracts and forward contracts designated as cash flow hedges to protect against the foreign currency exchange risk inherent in its forecasted transactions denominated in currencies other than [the] U.S. dollar. Hedged transactions include international sales by U.S. dollar functional currency entities, foreign currency denominated purchases of certain components, and intercompany shipments to certain international subsidiaries. The risk of loss associated with purchased options is limited to premium amounts paid for the option contracts. The risk of loss associated with forward contracts is equal to the exchange rate differential from the time the contract is entered into until the time it is settled. These contracts generally expire in [12] months or less.

The company also uses forward contracts to economically hedge monetary assets and liabilities, primarily receivables and payables that are denominated in a foreign currency. These contracts are not designated as hedging instruments under generally accepted accounting principles, and, therefore, the change in the instrument's fair value is recognized currently in earnings and is reported as a component of investment and other income (loss), net. The change in the fair value of these instruments represents a natural hedge as their gains and losses offset the changes in the underlying fair value of the monetary assets and liabilities due to movements in currency exchange rates. These contracts generally expire in three months or less.

Based on these general statements of principle, Dell's strategy is to hedge all foreign-exchange risk, which is a very aggressive hedging strategy. Since there is no options market for Brazilian reals, Pickett uses forward contracts to hedge the foreign exchange risks in Brazil.

Corporate treasury monitors currency movements worldwide and provides support to Pickett's Brazilian treasury group in terms of currency forecasts and hedging strategies. Within the broad strategy approved by corporate treasury, the Brazilian group establishes a strategy and then works with corporate on specific execution of the strategy.

There are two key parts to the strategy. One has to do with forecasting exposure, and the other has to do with designing and executing the strategy to hedge the exposure. Although the balance sheet exposure is not material, it still must be forecast and is partly a function of the cash flows generated by revenues. The revenue side is more difficult to forecast, so Pickett hedges about 80 percent of forecasted revenues. However, the Dell team in Brazil has become very adept at forecasting revenues and in executing a strategy in order to reach its target forecast. The team works hard on identifying the challenges in reaching its target and in devising policies to overcome those challenges. Its execution strategies vary widely quarter by quarter, and the management team has become very good at meeting its targets by working closely together and being flexible. Pickett and Kahler work closely together on a daily basis to execute their strategy.

The second key to the strategy is designing and executing the hedging strategy. Since revenues vary on a daily basis, Pickett does not enter into contracts all at once. Instead, he works with corporate treasury to enter into contracts in different amounts and different maturities depending on when it expects to generate the operating revenues. Revenues are generally lower at the beginning of the quarter and are always higher in the last week or two of the quarter, so

he enters into contracts accordingly. Timing is a crucial issue. The gain or loss on a forward contract is the difference in exchange rates between when the contract is entered into and when it is settled. The key is to unwind (or settle) the contracts while the rate is still favorable. Pickett noted that if Dell began to unwind the contracts in the last week or two of the quarter instead of the last day or two of the quarter, it could get much more favorable foreign-exchange gains. His strategy was so successful that in some quarters, Dell was generating more financial income than operating income. Although Pickett and his treasury team have some flexibility in designing and implementing strategy, corporate treasury keeps in close touch, depending on their forecasts of the exchange rate and the strategy that Dell Brazil is following. Corporate treasury uses a consensus forecast of exchange rates that is provided by a group of banks, but banks have different scenarios. For example, in the last quarter of 2002, corporate was relying on bank forecasts that the real would revalue even more by the end of the year.

Pickett's dilemma was that his gut feel was that the real would actually fall instead of rise. That would indicate a different hedging strategy. He was resisting entering into hedges while corporate was pressuring him to do just that. But he was closely watching the forward market, and when it began to move, he decided it was time to enter into the contracts. But who knows what will happen to Brazil if Lula, Brazil's new president, loses fiscal control of the ninth largest economy in the world, resulting in another round of inflation and a falling currency. Dell has significant market opportunities in Mercosur, but the financial risks will make for exciting times in the years to come.

QUESTIONS

1. Given how Dell translates its foreign currency financial statements into dollars, how would a falling Brazilian real affect Dell Mercosur's financial statements?

2. Dell imports about 97 percent of its manufacturing costs. What type of exposure does that create for it? What are its options to reduce that exposure?

3. Describe and evaluate Dell's exposure management strategy.

4. What are the costs and benefits of hedging all foreign exchange risk?

Chapter Notes

1 Information for the case is taken from the Nu Skin Enterprise annual reports (1997, 1998) and personal interviews (2002).

2 David K. Eiteman, Arthur I. Stonehill, and Michael H. Moffett, *Multinational Business Finance*, 8th ed. (Reading, MA: Addison-Wesley, 1998), 3.

3 Alan C. Shapiro, *Modern Corporate Finance* (New York: Macmillan, 1988), 1.

4 "Theory Versus the Real World," *Finance & Treasury* (April 26, 1993): 1.

5 Ibid., 2.

6 Henry Sender, "Financial Musical Chairs," *Far Eastern Economic Review* (July 29, 1999): 30–36.

7 "Long-Term Debt," *Nissan Annual Report* (2000), 49.

8 "Money Rates," *Wall Street Journal* (October 16, 2002): www.wsj.com.

9 "Europe's American Dream," *The Economist* (November 21, 1998): 71.

10 "Global Financial Stability Report," *International Monetary Fund* (September 2002): 48.

11 "An Offer They Can Refuse," *Euromoney* (February 1995): 76.

12 Anant Sundaram, "International Financial Markets," *Handbook of Modern Finance*, ed. Dennis E. Logue, (New York: Warren, Gorham, Lamont, 1994), F3–F4.

13 "Financial Review," *Marks & Spencer Annual Report* and Financial Statements (2002): http://www2.marksandspencer.com/thecompany/investorrelations/annualreport/fin_review.shtml.

14 "EMU Shuffles the Rankings," *Euromoney* (May 1999): 106.

15 "VC Opportunities in Europe," adapted from a study by PriceWaterhouseCoopers (September 2002): http://www.europeanvc.com/figures.htm.

16 "Private Equity Stirs Up the Pot," *Euroweek* (October 1999): 27–34.

17 "Non-U.S. Listed Companies" (2002): www.nyse.com/international/international.html.

18 "Global Financial Stability Report," International Monetary Fund, 2002, www.imf.org: 56.

19 "American Depositary Receipts: Over the Odds," *The Economist* (January 15, 2000): 77.

20 The Center for European Reform, "The Euro: The Future of European Stock Markets" (2002): http://www.cer.org.uk/nr_03/euro.html.

21 Stanley Reed, "Bourse Busters," *Business Week* (August 16, 1999): 52–53.

22 "How the Heavyweights Shape Up," *Euromoney* (May 1990): 56.

23 "Bermuda-Bound?" *Business Week* (June 3, 2002): 14.

24 Helmut Hagemann, "Anticipate Your Long-Term Foreign Exchange Risks," *Harvard Business Review* (March–April 1977): 82.

25 "Financial Risk Management," *Coca-Cola Annual Report* (2001).

26 Eiteman et al., op. cit., 584–85.

27 "The WTO Kibosh on a U.S. Tax Break," *Business Week* (September 3, 2002): www.businessweek.com.

28 Interview with Todd Pickett (2002); www.dell.com (2002); Dell's 2002 10Ks (2002), www.dell.com; Michael Schrage, "The Dell Curve," *Wired Magazine*, issue 10.7 (July 2002): http://www.wired.com/wired/archive/10.07/dell.html.

CHAPTER 21

HUMAN RESOURCE MANAGEMENT

If the leader is good, the followers will be good.

—PHILIPPINE PROVERB

OBJECTIVES

- To illustrate the importance of human resources in international business
- To explain the unique qualifications of international managers
- To evaluate issues that arise when companies transfer managers abroad
- To examine companies' alternatives for recruitment, selection, compensation, development, and retention of international managers
- To discuss how national labor markets can affect companies' optimum methods of production
- To describe country differences in labor policies and practices
- To highlight international pressures on MNEs' relations with labor worldwide
- To examine the effect of international operations on collective bargaining

CASE

Dow's International Management Development[1]

Dow Chemical, founded in 1897 in Midlands, Michigan, is a global science and technology-based company that develops and manufactures chemical, plastic, and agricultural products and services for customers in 170 countries. More than half of its nearly $28 billion in annual sales come from foreign markets. Dow's operations include eight global businesses that rely on 208 manufacturing sites located in 38 countries. Dow's workforce of nearly 50,000 employees is spread across 168 countries. Map 21.1 shows the regional distribution of Dow's workforce.

The need to run these far-flung operations has led Dow to develop a decidedly international management group. Specifically, nearly three-quarters of Dow's top management committee are managers who either were non-U.S. born or have had considerable foreign experience. Its CEO, for example, was born in Liverpool, England, and had held previous positions with Dow U.K, Dow Europe, Dow Hong Kong, Dow Asia, and Dow North America.

This placement of foreign-born and/or internationally experienced persons in Dow's leadership is suggestive of general processes of internationalization. Specifically, Peter Drucker, a leading management scholar, reasoned that a truly multinational company "demands of its management people that

MAP 21.1   The Worldwide Distribution of Dow's Workforce

NORTH AMERICA
29,000 Employees

EUROPE
9,500 Employees

ASIA
3,000 Employees

CENTRAL AND
SOUTH AMERICA
4,000 Employees

AFRICAN CONTINENT
2,400 Employees

MIDDLE EAST AND
INDIAN SUBCONTINENT
2,000 Employees

0   2000 mi
0   2000 km

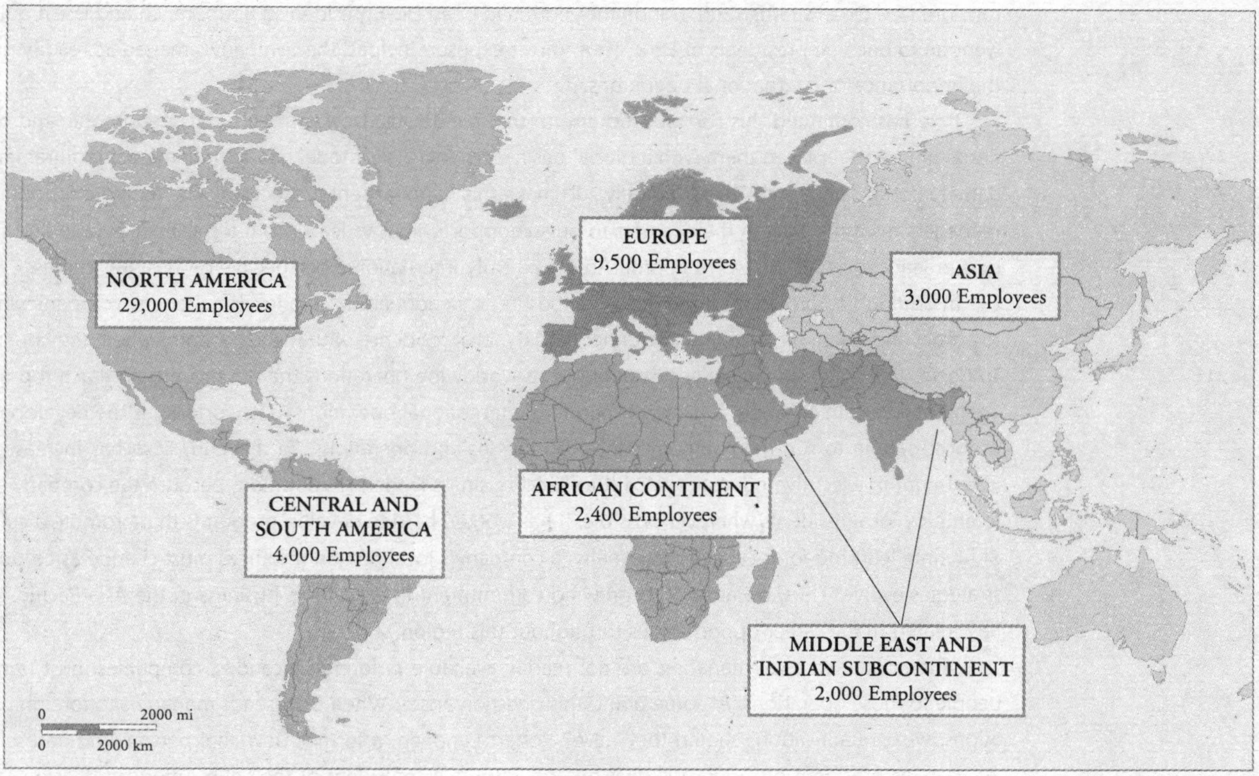

Source: www.dow.com (September 24, 2002).

they think and act as international businessmen [and businesswomen] in a world in which national passions are as strong as ever." A company whose top management includes people from various countries with varied country experiences presumably is less likely to place the interests of one country above those of others and arguably will have a worldwide outlook. While some may debate the strength of this relationship, few question that the experience of working abroad under different environmental and company conditions helps managers grasp some of the challenges that are not as prevalent in a purely domestic context.

Although a global outlook pervades Dow today, it neither naturally nor quickly emerged—that is, making international operations an integral part of the company's commitment required Dow seek a commitment to international business from a broad spectrum of managers. The company estimates that it took about 20 years to bring about this change in outlook. Until 1954, just over 6 percent of Dow's business took place outside of the United States. Moreover, over 80 percent of that amount was generated by its foreign subsidiary in Canada. A company historian recounted this attitude in the late 1950s, observing:

> As for the overseas operations, a majority of the veterans regarded them as a sideline. The foreign market was all right as a place for getting rid of surplus products, but the only truly promising market was in the United States. They questioned the idea of the company becoming too deeply involved in countries whose politics, language, culture, monetary controls, and ways of doing business were strange to them.

While some of Dow's younger managers did not share this ethnocentric attitude, Dow still needed to take dramatic steps to convert the majority of its managers to an international outlook. One method the company's president employed in 1958 was to give international responsibilities to people who were widely perceived to be destined for top-level positions in the company. For example, the company appointed C. B. Branch, manager of Dow's fastest-growing department, to be head of foreign operations. It assigned Herbert "Ted" Dow Doan, a 31-year-old member of the board of directors, to visit Europe on a fact-finding mission. (Ted Doan's father and grandfather both had been Dow presidents.) Both Branch and Doan quickly went on to become presidents of Dow. Thus, direct exposure helped the company's managers readily grasp the importance of international operations.

Dow has continued this sort of program. In the mid-1990s, Dow dismantled its geographic and functional units and replaced them with a global business model. This model had a fundamental requirement— namely getting people to "think globally." To make this happen, senior executives increasingly encouraged managers from the start of their careers to pursue opportunities to learn from top-caliber people and from best practices around the world in order to gain a truly international perspective on business success.

In addition to providing international exposure to headquarters' top-level managers, companies need to attract and retain high-quality personnel (largely local residents) within each country where they operate. To do so, Dow gives its executives throughout its worldwide operations the opportunity to reach top management levels. In addition, in Dow's expanding international operations, a key priority is the development of local people to run the company's local businesses and operations. To this end, Dow has increased its investment in executive education for future local business leaders. In addition, because the company aims to employ local residents wherever possible, it has worked hard to develop programs that promote a culture of lifetime learning for local workers. Finally, a company's local human resources must change as corporate strategies evolve. Thus, because of its growing commitment to expand its business in the Asia Pacific, Dow has created many career opportunities throughout this region.

When qualified local managers are not readily available in foreign locations, companies must transfer people to those operations. At some point, this question arises: When Dow sends managers to foreign operations, what qualifications should they have? Robert Lundeen, a former Dow chairperson who had served 12 years as president of the Pacific division and 3 years as president of the Latin American division, gave some indication of his philosophy. After endorsing the crucial need for technical expertise, he said, "When I worked in Asia, I observed that many Americans seemed to delight in their insularity, and that attitude hurts the ability . . . [to] do business in foreign countries."

This drawback, along with the difficulty that some managers have in adjusting to foreign locations, led Dow to brief all prospective transferees on company transfer policies. In addition, they are given information about the country where they will be assigned, as compiled by personnel in the host country. Dow follows this procedure with a meeting between transferees and their spouses and recently repatriated employees and their spouses to explain the emotional issues involved in the move's early stages. Couples are also given the option of attending a two-week language and orientation program.

For many years, Dow had difficulty convincing people to accept foreign assignments because of the difficult experiences associated with repatriating them to acceptable positions. Dow has tried to correct this problem by

- Sending some of its best people abroad so that "everybody will want them when they come back."
- Assigning higher-level supervisors to serve as "godfathers" who look after the transferred employees' home-career interests and keep them up-to-date on organizational activities.
- Providing each transferee with a written guarantee of a job at the same or higher level upon returning from the foreign assignment.

Finally, one may question whether these outlooks and programs directly affect those U.S. workers who do not plan to go abroad. Certainly, the global nature of its business leads Dow to encourage employees to consider traveling or living and working internationally. Those who do not plan to do so still must think globally—that is, even in the event that certain domestic positions may not require international travel or relocation, those home-country managers often work as part of global teams on projects with a global scope. The company has supported this collaboration with communications technology that networks every desktop. Senior executives believe this capability lets people seamlessly support one another around the globe as they work on team projects. Indeed, as Dow formally declared, geography does not limit any employee's career. No matter where a manager happens to call home, he or she is a part of a global team who has opportunities to work on projects and take on responsibilities with a scope that transcends national borders.

It's hard to imagine that the housing development in this photo is outside Beijing, China. A South African resident walks within the Western style development built to house business expatriates working in the area.

INTRODUCTION

Our opening case highlights one company's efforts to deal with international human resources, efforts which are more comprehensive than those of most MNEs. In addition, Dow Chemical invests in developing its global intellectual assets, which include human capital (the knowledge that each individual has and generates) and organizational capital (the knowledge that has been institutionalized within the structure, processes, and culture of the organization).

Most international companies agree on the importance of qualified personnel in the effort to achieve foreign growth and operational objectives. For instance, at a roundtable discussion of chief executives on how the world is changing and what management can do to respond, the chairman of Unilever said, "The single most important issue for us has been, and will continue to be, organization and people."[2] Figure 21.1 shows the importance of international human resources in international business.

The need for highly qualified people is crucial. Any company must determine its human resource needs, hire people to meet those needs, motivate them to perform well, upgrade their skills so that they can move onto more challenging tasks, and ultimately retain them. Several factors make international human resource management different from domestic management.

- *Different labor markets.* Each country has a different mix of available workers and a different mix of labor costs. MNEs can gain advantages by accessing these various human resource capabilities.[3] For example, GM's Mexican upholstery operation employs low-cost production workers, and IBM's Swiss R&D facility hires skilled physicists. Whether companies seek resources or markets abroad, they may make the same product differently in different countries—for example, by substituting hand labor for machines because of diverse labor markets.

FIGURE 21.1   Human Resources in International Business

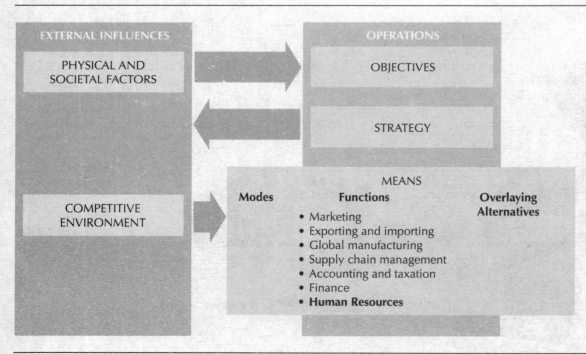

Human resource management is one of the necessary functions for implementing companies' international strategies.

- *International worker mobility problems.* There are legal, economic, physical, and cultural barriers to overcome when transferring workers to a foreign country.[4] Yet MNEs benefit from moving people, especially when there are shortages of people with needed skills in a particular country. In such situations, companies often must develop special recruitment, training, compensation, transfer, and retention practices.

- *National management styles and practices.* Employees' attitudes toward different management styles vary from country to country, and so do prevailing leadership practices and labor-management relations.[5] These differences may strain relations between headquarters and subsidiary personnel or make a manager less effective when working abroad than when working at home. At the same time, the experience of working with different national practices gives companies opportunities to transfer successful practices from one country to another.

- *National orientations.* Although a company's goals may include attaining global efficiencies and competitiveness, its personnel (both labor and management) may emphasize national rather than global interests. Certain human resource practices can alleviate extreme national partiality.[6]

- *Strategy and control.* Companies find that some country operations are more important to global success than others. Further, country operations differ in cross-national integration, dependence on headquarters for resources, and need for national responsiveness. These differences may change over time. Management qualifications and styles need to parallel the needs of these different national operations in order to achieve the company's worldwide strategy.[7]

This chapter develops these points by discussing the implications for managerial personnel and then examining labor personnel issues.

MANAGEMENT QUALIFICATIONS AND CHARACTERISTICS

We begin our discussion of international human resource management by examining the relationships between headquarters and subsidiaries, national variations in managerial styles, and management qualifications and characteristics for headquarters and subsidiaries.

Headquarters-Subsidiary Relationship

International staffing is two tiered. First, subsidiaries need people who can manage well locally. Second, headquarters needs people who can coordinate and control worldwide and regional operations. These two staffing needs are closely related because headquarters managers typically select and evaluate subsidiary managers. Both sides must be sufficiently aware of and willing to trade-off the competing requirements of global integration and national responsiveness.

These trade-offs are complex and depend on the company's philosophy (for example, ethnocentric, polycentric, or geocentric) and on the countries' operational benefits from independence versus interdependence. There is much less need to impose standard human resource practices—such as hiring qualifications and training programs—or a corporate culture abroad when a company has a multidomestic strategy than when it has a global or transnational strategy.[8] Regardless of where the company lies between these extremes, it may face dilemmas because the technology, policy, and managerial style it has developed in one locale may be only somewhat suitable elsewhere. International managers, at headquarters and in subsidiaries, must recognize when to introduce and when not to introduce practices to a country.

Headquarters and subsidiary managers must communicate well to ensure that they understand each other. Because geographic distance constrains travel for face-to-face meetings and different time zones complicate voice-to-voice exchange, much of the communication between

Headquarters and subsidiary management must consider country and global needs.

Headquarters-subsidiary relationships are affected by

- Company philosophy (ethnocentric or polycentric)
- Benefits of independence or interdependence

International communications are complex and more likely to be misunderstood than domestic ones are.

headquarters and subsidiaries is written and sent by e-mail, faxes, and letters. However, these written contacts are imperfect substitutes for face-to-face and voice-to-voice communications, which allow immediate questions and clarifications when managers are unsure they understand exactly what others mean. Nevertheless, companies have been able to reduce the number of international trips by bringing groups together electronically.[9] Indeed, the challenges of international travel, made worse by the events and oucomes of September 11, 2001, have spurred international managers to devise ways to manage the relationship between headquarters and subsidiaries. For example, more managers utilize online collaboration technologies, such as web, video, and voice conferencing. While these technologies do not substitute for in-person interaction, they help create an organizational setting that is as close as possible to being there and enable people to work and communicate effectively over distances. In addition, some companies report that virtual mettings, besides reducing travel costs and risks, boost productivity by building better relationships with more frequent contact, more responsive customer service, and faster decision-making cycles. For example, Bristol-Myers Squibb uses video communications systems to help its scientists collaborate globally so they can identify and make available pharmaceutical therapies more quickly.

Communication difficulties, no matter through what sort of medium, arise when managers' native languages differ. Corporate communications, directives, and manuals may require translation, which takes time and money. If they are not, the content may be understood perfectly abroad, but the comprehension time may be longer because people read more slowly in a second language. Likewise, in order to do the same quality work as home-country counterparts, communication problems may force a manager working abroad to spend more time on a project. Although headquarters managers often overlook or downplay these inherent inefficiencies, they still hold subsidiary management responsible for meeting the company's objectives. Cultural differences color the intents and perceptions of what is communicated. Managers mistakenly may assume that foreigners will react the same way as their colleagues to decision making and leadership styles—a particular problem with team projects that include various nationalities. The problem is amplified in cooperative arrangements when business activities include not just different nationalities but also different companies.[10]

Communication between headquarters and subsidiary management is eased somewhat because English has become the international language of business.[11] Managers cannot learn all the languages in every country in which their companies operate. So business between, say, Italy and Saudi Arabia, may be conducted in English. Even some MNEs from non–English-speaking countries, such as ABB of Switzerland, have adopted English as their official office language. A working knowledge of the subsidiary country's language can, nevertheless, help headquarters managers gain acceptance by subsidiary personnel as well as better understand local events.[12]

The aftermath of the terrorist attacks of September 11, 2001 have constrained the mobility of international businesspersons—both at headquarters and subsidiaries—to manage their relationship. Most notably, foreign travel has seen increased difficulty and danger. In recourse, managers and companies have adopted various precautions. Some avoid flying U.S. flag carriers overseas, opting for lower-profile airlines. Others have applied stringent safeguards. Black & Decker, for example, asked employees to reconsider plans for overseas trips. Novartis went a step farther, placing restrictions on its 9,000 North American employees who travel for the company to about ten countries. While it declined to identify these ten nations, Novartis banned travel to some of them, limited travel to essential purposes only for others, and, for the remainder, required the employee notify the company's corporate security department before departure. Operationally, many companies now routinely purchase trip cancellation insurance. In addition, more companies instruct employees to order tickets only through the company's official travel agency in order to avoid the confusion that followed 9/11; in the resulting turmoil, many companies had trouble finding employees who had bought tickets from other sources. Procedurally, companies now advise workers to put together a communication system with friends, family, and business associates so that somebody is familiar with their plans. Similarly, companies advise personnel to register with American embassies overseas upon arrival and, in some situations, supplement a cell phone with a short-wave radio.

Matching Style to Operations

Where there is a need for cross-border integration, whether between headquarters and subsidiaries or among subsidiaries, humanist, feeling-type managers (those concerned with how their decisions will affect others, particularly others' feelings) are apt to be more effective than scientific, thinking-type managers (those concerned with processing information analytically and objectively). The reason this is so is that the collaborative nature of cross-border integration requires a high level of cross-personal cooperation. Cooperation is enhanced when managers take into account the outlooks of people who can expedite or impede integration.[13]

Similarly, the MNEs that follow a multidomestic strategy do not need to transfer human resource competencies from one unit to another; in fact, this is not generally possible. The operation in Singapore might work independently to develop human resource practices that deal effectively with labor shortages and high worker mobility in its market without transferring information on such practices to units of the company in other countries. The MNEs that follow a global strategy would attempt to transfer their home-country policies and practices to their foreign units because they feel that such policies are valid outside the parent country. The MNEs that follow a transnational strategy would attempt to transfer their best practices to all operations in all countries, regardless of where they happened to originate.[14]

There is also a need to manage in a style that motivates and engages subordinates. Recall from Chapter 2 that there are different national norms in terms of employee preference, such as between authoritarian and participatory styles of leadership and individualism versus collectivism in the workplace. Although any country has successful managers whose styles vary, there is substantial anecdotal evidence of greater success when managerial actions are congruent with subordinates' preferences and expectations.[15] Thus, managers may improve their performance by adjusting to the preferred management styles of the people with whom they are working.

Qualifications Specific to Headquarters and Subsidiaries

Thus far, we have emphasized managerial qualifications that apply to the relationship between headquarters and subsidiaries. In addition, headquarters managers who are responsible for international operations have duties that differ from those of their domestic counterparts. Similarly, foreign subsidiary managers have responsibilities that generally differ from those of home-country managers at similar organizational levels. We now discuss these topics.

Headquarters Management Headquarters managers who are responsible for international business must interact frequently with high-level authorities in foreign countries to negotiate investments, sell technology, evaluate new market opportunities, assess monetary conditions, and so on.[16] Their tasks are even more difficult than those faced by subsidiary managers because they must be away from home for extended and indefinite periods. Their international trips are stressful before, during, and afterwards.[17] Before, they must make arrangements while trying to complete pending work and to spend time with their families. During their trip, they eat, sleep, and move in unfamiliar places while seeking the confidence of and rapport with people in many different foreign countries. Upon their return, they face the work that has piled up in their absence, the preparation of expense reports, and the guilt from being away from family. Further, they may suffer jet lag, a condition in which one's biological clock tells the body the wrong time to sleep, eat, and feel alert or drowsy; under the best circumstances, this clock can adjust by only one or two hours a day.[18] However, frequent moves between time zones may also have long-term adverse physical and mental effects, such

Corporate managers abroad

- Deal at top levels in many countries
- Experience the rigors of foreign travel
- Face difficulties if they have risen entirely through domestic divisions

as slower reactions and poorer performance.[19] Figure 21.2 satirizes the problem of jet lag. Even if headquarters personnel can reduce the rigors of foreign travel, they may be ill at ease with the foreign aspects of their responsibilities if their rise to the corporate level has been entirely through their performance in domestic divisions.

Headquarters staff traveling abroad can also face problems of loneliness, particularly in their personal lives.[20] Such staff people are apt to miss family events and the celebrations that take place during their home country's holidays. International trips tend to be longer and farther away than domestic ones, making it difficult to return home on weekends. As one international executive commented,

> Often you won't be able to plan in advance when you are leaving on business or when you will return. Being present at birthdays, school plays, anniversaries, family reunions, and other events may become the exception instead of the rule. While you're away, mortgage payments will probably be due, the MasterCard bill will arrive, the furnace will fail, your child will get chicken pox, the IRS will schedule a full audit, the family car will be totaled, and your spouse will sue for divorce.[21]

In summary, it takes a distinctive type of individual to adjust to extensive travel to many different environments. Moreover, this individual also needs an exceptional family to accept the frequent absences and recovery periods from travel fatigue.

Subsidiary Management   Although foreign subsidiaries usually are much smaller than the parent, their senior managers often must perform top-level management duties. This may mean taking responsibility for a variety of business functions and spending time on external relations with the community, government, and public. Managers with comparable profit or cost responsibility in the home country may perform middle-management tasks; as such, they may lack the breadth of experience necessary for a top management position in a foreign subsidiary. A subsidiary manager also must work independently because most subsidiary operations lack many staff functions, such as market research. At headquarters, a manager can get advice from specialists by walking to the next office or floor or by making a few telephone calls. The subsidiary manager, however, often must rely on his or her own personal judgment.

Top managers in subsidiaries usually have broader duties than do managers of similar-sized home-country operations.

FIGURE 21.2

The travel required to oversee international operations is stressful.

Source: From *Punch Magazine.* Reprinted by permission.

"I've never actually met him—as soon as he's over the jet lag, it's time for another trip in search of overseas markets."

INTERNATIONAL MANAGERIAL TRANSFERS

Managers are either **locals**, citizens of the countries in which they are working, or **expatriates**, noncitizens. Expatriates are either **home-country nationals**, citizens of the country in which the company is headquartered, or **third-country nationals**, citizens of neither the country in which they are working nor the headquarters country. Locals or expatriates may be employed in the company's home country or in its foreign operations. Most managerial positions in both headquarters and foreign subsidiaries are filled by locals rather than expatriates. The one exception is for project management in some developing countries, such as Saudi Arabia, in which there is an acute shortage of qualified local candidates. Nevertheless, expatriates play an important role in the international business of most companies. We now discuss the reasons companies use locals and expatriates, as well as companies' human resource practices for expatriates.

Reasons for Staffing with Locals

Many people enjoy the excitement of living and working abroad. Others, however, prefer not to work in a foreign country, particularly if they perceive an assignment as long term or permanent. Nationality can moderate this disposition; some nationalities (notably, U.S., Australian, British, and Dutch) are more willing to accept foreign assignments than are others (notably, French, Germans, Italians, Spanish, and Swiss).[22] The most common reason why managers reject a foreign assignment is their perception that the assignment will negatively affect their family's lifestyle due to unacceptable living conditions, inadequate educational opportunities for their children, and the inability to be near aging parents. Career considerations are also important; the foreign assignment may take the manager outside the corporate mainstream for advancement and because the spouse can rarely get a permit to work in a comparable job abroad.[23] If the couple is unmarried, the "significant other" may not even be able to get permission to live in the foreign location. A distinction is made between a foreign assignment of fixed duration and one that is open-ended. Many more people can cope with a position abroad if they know that they will return home after a specific period.

There are also legal impediments to using expatriates, such as licensing requirements that prevent companies from using expatriate accountants and lawyers. In many cases, companies have established offices to employ people who cannot or will not work where a company would prefer. For example, they have established local R&D labs and regional staff offices when personnel declined to move to the country where global headquarters is located.

The greater the need for local adaptations, the more advantageous it is for companies to use local managers. Normally, they have a better understanding of local conditions than do expatriates. The need to adapt may arise because of unique environmental conditions, barriers to imports, or the existence of strong local competitors or large local customers.

When the host country is suspicious of foreign-controlled operations, local managers may be perceived locally as "better citizens" because they presumably put local interests ahead of the company's global objectives. This local image may play a role in employee morale as well. Many subsidiary employees prefer to work for someone from their own country.[24] Similarly, if a company reserves most top jobs for expatriates, it may struggle to attract and retain qualified locals. The possibility of advancement motivates local employees to perform well. Without this incentive, they may seek employment elsewhere.

Finally, a compelling reason to staff with locals is that they usually cost far less than do expatriates. At the very least, companies must pay moving expenses for expatriates as well as adjust their salary for local conditions. For example, U.S. firms spend, on average, $1.3 million for each expatriate during the course of a typical three-year foreign assignment.[25] Most human resource managers face growing pressure to control the cost of expatriate assignments. Some have responded by hiring more locals.[26]

International managers are isolated and have less access to staff specialists.

Foreign managerial slots are difficult to fill because
- Many people prefer not to move
- There are legal impediments to using expatriates

Managers view fixed-term and open-ended assignments differently.

Local managers may help sales and morale.

What Are Fair Labor Practices Anyway?

Critics argue that MNEs often set up capital-intensive rather than labor-intensive production methods, which contribute less to creating jobs in developing countries.[27] Ethical dilemmas arise over whether a laborsaving production method is truly more economical given larger societal circumstances. For example, machine-made textiles are cheaper to manufacture than are hand-woven ones. However, hand-woven textiles employ millions in India, and their production is a strong cultural value of self-reliance. As India's production of machine-made textiles has increased (some directed by MNEs), the number of unemployed weavers have increased. Critics argue that the hand-loom industry should be subsidized and that, on ethical grounds, companies should not establish production that will cause unemployment. Some critics argue that perpetuating inefficient production condemns workers and their descendants to lifetimes of low-paid drudgery.

The evidence is mixed on whether MNEs modify manufacturing methods simply to minimize costs. There are undoubtedly biases toward replicating facilities that had been engineered to reduce the amount of high-priced labor in industrialized countries. Also, production needs in industrialized countries spur management to design control systems that emphasize output per person as a measure of efficiency. Further, many governments want to showcase modern plants as symbols of economic development. However, case studies point to substantial alterations by MNEs, such as using human labor instead of mechanized loading equipment, because of local costs and availabilities.

When labor is substituted for capital, its comparatively lower productivity leads to low wages. Some companies, nevertheless, have been disparaged for their labor rates given the price of their end products and what they pay celebrities to advertise them. For example, protests have pushed Nike to notify its contract manufacturers that it does not support sweatshop conditions.[28] Still, critics complain that Nike's suppliers pay workers only a few dollars a day while Nike sells many of its shoes for more than $100 and pays prominent sports figures, such as Tiger Woods, millions of dollars to advertise them.[29] Many also condemn companies for making products in so-called sweatshops. However, there is disagreement among companies, unions, and human rights groups that have tried to develop a voluntary code of conduct for the apparel industry on what constitutes a sweatshop.[30] For example, some contend that it is sufficient for companies to pay the local minimum or prevailing wage, but others argue for paying wages high enough to meet a universal standard of needs. Some contend that employees should work no more than 48 hours per week, and others argue for a 60-hour standard. Companies have replied to these concerns by adopting codes of conduct and by monitoring worker conditions in foreign factories that serve as suppliers. However, they have struggled to effect changes in the foreign factories and even more difficult to quell criticism of their practices.

MNEs also are scorned for exploiting women in many developing countries, in which they have had less formal education than men have, have been trained since childhood in tasks requiring manual dexterity, and are willing to accept lower wages than men will. Their qualifications are thus ideal for certain labor-intensive activities. Without the constraints of sex discrimination legislation, companies advertise openly that they prefer to hire females. Governments even encourage the practice. For example, Malaysia's investment-promotion programs advertised "the manual dexterity of the Oriental female."

Similarly, some critics contend that the hiring of children by MNEs in developing countries is unethical because the practice denies children access to the education needed for their future development. For the record, the International Labor Organization (ILO) estimates that there are nearly 250 million children between ages 5 and 17 who work; about half of them work full-time.[31] But what if the choice is not between working and education? For many poor children in these countries, there is little or no opportunity for education. Without the prospect for work, many may join the legions of abandoned street children, such as those in Guatemala City who sniff glue to suppress hunger pains and steal barely enough to subsist. Bangladesh likewise criticized a proposed U.S. law that would restrict the importation of child-made products, arguing that it could force thousands of children into begging or prostitution. The ILO agrees that the threat of trade sanctions might endanger rather than protect children. Pragmatically, UNICEF concedes the unfortunate need for children to work in poverty situations, but it urges eliminating child labor that is hazardous or exploitative.

Reasons for Using Expatriates

Although expatriate managers comprise a minority of total managers within MNEs, companies use expatriates because of their competence to fill positions, their need to gain foreign experience, the need to refine their business skills, and their ability to control operations according to headquarters' preferences.

Generally, companies use expatriate managers when they cannot find qualified local candidates. This is partly determined by a country's level of development; expatriates represent a much smaller portion of subsidiary managers in industrial than in developing countries. This also is determined by the need to transfer technologies abroad; a company that transfers new products or production methods, especially in start-up operations, usually needs to transfer personnel to or from subsidiaries until the operation runs smoothly.

MNEs transfer people abroad so that they may understand the overall corporate system. In companies that have specialized activities in certain countries (such as extraction separated from manufacturing or basic R&D separated from applied R&D), long-term foreign assignments may be the only means to develop a manager's breadth. When there are cross-national mergers, such as when Daimler-Benz and Chrysler formed DaimlerChrysler, international transfers between the two companies prevented the newly merged company from operating as two separate companies.[32] These assignments also enhance a manager's ability to work in a variety of social systems.

Foreign assignments, in principle, are valuable educational experiences that prepare managers for greater corporate responsibility that spans both domestic and foreign operations. Historically, however, companies have been slow to reward people who have international experience with top-level corporate positions. For example, few CEOs at the largest U.S. companies have worked outside the United States, and few large U.S. companies have foreigners either as board members or in high corporate positions. Some data suggest this situation is changing. Many CEOs assert that international experience will be more important in the future.[33]

MNEs use home-country expatriates to control foreign operations because they are accustomed to doing things the "headquarters way."[34] Often, MNEs rotate foreign nationals though headquarters positions so that they also learn the way people at headquarters do their jobs. Rotating many home- and host-country nationals through different locales enables a company to begin developing a hybrid corporate culture that understands the demands of both global integration and national responsiveness. There is growing evidence of a new cadre of expatriates who neither carry their home-country values everywhere they go nor go native wherever they happen to be stationed. Instead, they adopt a global management mindset.[35]

The type of ownership of foreign operations influences how companies use expatriates for control. For example, expatriates transferred abroad to a joint venture may be in an ambiguous situation, unsure of who they represent and uncertain of whether they should report to

The most qualified person may be an expatriate.

Multicountry experience gives upward-moving managers new perspectives.

People transferred from headquarters are more likely to know corporate policies. People transferred to headquarters learn the headquarters way.

both partners or just the partner that transferred them. Nevertheless, many companies with local partners insist on using their own personnel for positions in which they fear local personnel will make decisions in their own, rather than in the joint venture's, best interest. For example, foreign partners commonly transfer expatriates to their Chinese joint ventures to ensure that money is spent only on business-related items.[36]

Home-Country Versus Third-Country Nationals

Most companies' innovations in technology, product, and operating procedures originate in their home countries. Companies normally transfer such innovations to their foreign operations later. Because they use expatriates to pass on new methods, personnel with recent home-country experience (usually home-country nationals) are more likely to have the preferred qualifications.

However, third-country nationals sometimes have more compatible technical and adaptive qualifications than do home-country expatriates.[37] For example, a U.S. company used U.S. personnel to design and manage a Peruvian plant until it could train local managers. Years later, the company decided to manufacture in Mexico using a plant that more closely resembled the Peruvian operations than its U.S. operations in terms of size, product qualities, and factor inputs. The company used its Spanish-speaking Peruvian managers to plan and start up the Mexican facility because these managers knew the technical needs and could easily adapt to living in Mexico. When companies establish lead operations abroad, such as headquarters for a product division or a country operation that is larger than that in the home country, third-country nationals are more likely to have the competencies needed for the foreign assignments.

Some Individual Considerations for Transfers

We have discussed the importance of nationality when deciding who to transfer to which foreign assignment. But who among the home-country nationals or among the foreign nationals should the company transfer? We now discuss individual attributes that companies consider.

Technical Competence   Unless a foreign assignment is plainly intended to train and develop an expatriate, local employees will often resent someone coming in from a foreign country (usually at higher compensation) who they feel is no more qualified than they are. Corporate decision makers, expatriate managers, and local managers agree that technical competence, usually indicated by past performance, is the biggest determinant of success in foreign assignments.[38] The expatriate must know the technical necessities of the position and, if necessary, how to adapt to foreign variations, such as scaled-down plants and equipment, varying productivity standards, less efficient infrastructure, limited credit supply, and restrictions on available mass media.[39] Because of the need for technical competence, managers commonly have several years' worth of work experience behind them before a company offers them a foreign assignment.

Adaptiveness   Some companies rely only on technical competence to select expatriates. Still, three types of adaptive characteristics influence an expatriate's success when entering a new culture.

1. Those needed for self-maintenance, such as self-confidence and personal resourcefulness
2. Those related to the development of satisfactory relationships with host nationals, such as flexibility and tolerance
3. Cognitive skills and sensitivities that help one to perceive accurately what is occurring within the host society[40]

The expatriate who lacks any of these qualities may be unable to function effectively in the host country. If the expatriate cannot adapt, he or she may leave the foreign assignment—

Third-country nationals may know more about

- Language
- Operating adjustments

Technical competence factors are a necessary attribute.

either by choice or by company decision. Unfortunately, companies struggle to assess these adaptability characteristics.

Recent surveys indicate that less than 10 percent of expatriates fail to complete their assignments abroad—a much lower rate than had been found in earlier studies and one that is no higher than the domestic assignments rate.[41] Nevertheless, the direct relocation cost for an expatriate is high, running, on average, about $60,000.[42] In addition, the company incurs a high cost in lost performance if the expatriate is ineffective due to adjustment difficulties. We have discussed how some managers decline expatriate positions because of their negative perceptions about the assignment. For some of those managers who do accept positions, this perception becomes a harsh reality.

A frequent reason for failure in a foreign assignment is the inability of the members of the expatriate's family to adjust to their new home.[43] A move abroad means new living and shopping habits, new school systems, and unfamiliar social and commercial practices. In addition, close friends and relatives—the personal support system—are left behind. However, some individuals do enjoy and adapt easily to a foreign way of life; MNEs should use them if possible. Some companies even maintain a core international group of employees who are the only ones assigned abroad. Other employees can do a number of things to help themselves adjust to foreign locations, including learning the local language and associating with local support groups such as religious groups and expatriate associations.[44] In addition, the employees can seek information from people who have positive memories of their expatriate experiences.

> Family adaptation is important.

Local Acceptance Expatriates may encounter some acceptance problems regardless of who they are or where they come from. It usually takes time before employees view managers as legitimate, and expatriates may not be there long enough to achieve this status. Local employees may feel that the best jobs go to overpaid, undermotivated foreigners, especially because companies sometimes send managers abroad to reward or find a place for them rather than for their potential performance.[45] Expatriates commonly make unpopular local decisions in order to meet global objectives. Alternatively, local management may have had experiences with expatriates who made short-term decisions and then departed before dealing with the longer-term implications. If negative stereotypes are added to these attitudes, an expatriate may struggle to succeed. Certain individuals may encounter insurmountable problems when dealing as an expatriate with employees, suppliers, and customers—for example, a Jewish manager in Libya, a very young manager in Japan, or a female manager in Saudi Arabia. The U.S. Civil Rights Act extends the nondiscrimination provisions of civil rights law to cover U.S. citizens' employment abroad, except where foreign law prohibits the employment of a certain class of individual.[46] However, because most discrimination problems abroad are cultural rather than legal, companies find it difficult to administer this act.[47]

> Expatriates may meet with local prejudice.

Some wonder if companies overreact to these sorts of acceptance problems. Consider various negative characterizations of women: They should not give orders to men, they are temperamental, clients will neither respect nor accept them, employees will not take them seriously, they do not have the stamina to work in harsh areas, and they do not want to upset their husbands' careers.[48] Partly because of these stereotypes, MNEs have assigned few women to expatriate positions, especially to foreign women in the companies' home countries.[49] Nonetheless, women have succeeded as expatriates in such male-dominated places as India, Japan, and Thailand because they were seen in the workplace first as foreigners and then as women. This should not imply that successful female expatriates confronted few challenges. Typically, they faced discrimination outside the workplace, such as in banks and immigration offices, and they encountered sexist remarks that, although deemed inoffensive locally, would be unacceptable elsewhere. They used such coping devices as giving off the "right signals" through attire and demeanor, adapted communication styles that would not seem abrasive, and simply accepted that cultural norms are different.[50] Suggestions for companies to improve the acceptability of women as expatriates may be applied to other groups as well. These include selecting well-qualified women who command authority, specifying a clear title and job position, disseminating in advance information about the person's high qualifications, posting expatriate women to locations where there are already local women in management positions who might serve as mentors, and establishing longer than normal assignments to develop role models.[51]

Securing a Successful Foreign Assignment   Although the preceding discussion highlights difficulties with foreign assignments, most expatriate assignments are successful. Indeed, many students seem more intrigued about getting foreign assignments than avoiding them. In reality, the chances of being offered a foreign assignment soon after graduation are small. Companies generally want people to prove themselves domestically before transferring them abroad. Therefore, demonstrating a good work record is probably the major prerequisite to becoming an expatriate. Once this prerequisite is met, an employee may gain an edge over other candidates by additionally demonstrating knowledge of the language and environment of a foreign assignment. Of course, an individual who simply wants the experience of living and working abroad may set off to a foreign country and work at temporary jobs—with or without government work permits—to earn enough to survive. Many young people do this to help them determine their career goals, and the experience helps them become valuable employees later on.[52]

Post-Expatriate Situations

Up to a third of returning expatriates typically leave their companies within one year of repatriation and nearly half within two years of returning home.[53] Problems with repatriation arise in three general areas: personal finances, readjustment to the home-country work environment, and readjustment to the home-country social life.

Coming home can require adaptation in many areas, including
- Financial
- Work
- Social

Companies give expatriates many financial benefits to encourage them to accept a foreign assignment. While abroad, expatriates may live in the finest neighborhoods, send their children to prestigious schools, employ domestic help, socialize with elites, and still save more money than before the move. They immediately lose this lifestyle upon returning home. Further, returning expatriates often find that some of their former peers were promoted while they were abroad, that they now have less authority, that they are now "little fish in a big pond," and that they now have less in common with their friends than before the foreign assignments began. Some human resource practices for smoothing repatriation include providing expatriates with advance notice of when they will return, more information about their new jobs, placement in jobs that leverage their foreign experiences, housing assistance, reorientation programs, periodic visits to headquarters, and enlisting a formal headquarters mentor to watch over their interests while they are abroad.[54]

The significance of an overseas assignment to one's career may be positive, neutral, or negative. The outcome generally depends on individual differences, the company's commitment to foreign operations, and the communication links between headquarters and expatriates.

Companies with a high commitment to global operations, such as Dow Chemical, see multicountry experience just as essential as multifunctional and multiproduct experience in reaching the upper echelons of the company. Nevertheless, some companies with a strong international commitment effectively segregate foreign and domestic operations so that they function almost as two separate companies. If the domestic business dominates, there may be little exchange of personnel between domestic and foreign operations as well as little advancement of personnel with international experience to top-level positions.

With or without foreign work experience, few people reach the top rungs of companies. Some companies, particularly those with international divisions, depend heavily on a cadre of highly qualified specialists who may either rotate between foreign locations and international headquarters assignments or spend most of their careers abroad. Although most do not reach the top management levels of the parent, they can reach plateaus above most domestic managers in terms of compensation, responsibility, and prestige. Further, many people just have a penchant for international living. For example, after stints in Singapore and London, a Morgan Stanley expatriate in India said, "I still don't want to go back to the United States. It's a big world—lots of things to see."[55]

In some companies, foreign assignments carry a high career risk, regardless of corporate executives' statements to the contrary.[56] This risk may arise for two reasons. First, there may be little provision to fit someone into the domestic or headquarters organization upon repatriation. An office does not sit vacant while one is abroad for several years; the repatriated employee also cannot easily bump his or her replacement. Holding a position available while an employee is abroad is particularly difficult when the foreign assignment is of indefinite length. Such open-ended assignments are a significant portion of the total. Second, some "out of sight, out of mind" issues may occur. Expatriates may never know about promotion opportunities in the home country unless colleagues inform them.

When repatriated employees have career problems, it becomes more difficult to convince other people to take foreign assignments.[57] A few companies, like Dow Chemical, make written guarantees that repatriated employees will return to jobs at least as good as those they left behind. Some companies simply explain the career risk and compensate employees so highly that they are enticed to become expatriates. Other companies integrate foreign assignments into career planning and develop mentor programs to look after the expatriates' domestic interests.

Foreign nationals who are transferred to headquarters sometimes confront a different problem. If the assignment is a promotion from a manager's subsidiary post rather than part of a planned rotation, then the move to headquarters may be permanent. For example, the Brazilian head of a Brazilian subsidiary may have performed so well that the MNE wants to give that manager multicountry responsibility at the corporate office in New York. Because the manager would not be able to return to Brazil without taking a demotion, he or she might decline the transfer.

Expatriate Compensation

If a U.S. company transfers its British finance manager, who is making $150,000 per year, to Italy, where the going rate is $100,000 per year, what should the manager's salary be? Or if the Italian financial manager is transferred to the United Kingdom, what pay should the company offer? Should it compensate in dollars, pounds, or euros? Whose holidays should apply? Which set of fringe benefits should apply? These are but a few of the many questions a company must resolve when it posts people abroad. MNEs developing an international workforce frequently run into problems in dealing with differing pay levels, benefits, and perquisites. On the one hand, the company must control costs; on the other, it must maintain high employee morale.

The amount and type of compensation needed to entice a person to move to another country vary widely by individual and locale. Company practices also vary widely in terms of compensation for differences. Companies with few expatriate employees may work out foreign compensation packages on a case-by-case basis. As international activities grow, however, it becomes cumbersome to administer individual packages. In addition, if consistency is sought in transfer policy, some people will receive more than would be necessary to persuade them to go abroad given the unequal conditions among countries. Overall, the package may multiply the compensation cost in comparison with what the expatriate had been making domestically. Table 21.1 illustrates a typical expatriate compensation package.

Cost of Living Most expatriates encounter cost-of-living increases, primarily because their accustomed way of living is expensive to replicate in a new environment. Generally, personal habits are difficult to change. For example, Westerners pay steep premiums in some parts of Asia to rent accommodations with Western-styled bathrooms and kitchens.[58] Knowledge of the local country is a second consideration. Expatriates may obtain food and housing at higher than the local rate because they do not know the language well, where to buy, or how to bargain. For example, a U.S. family based in China commonly spends more money on buying the same goods than they would back home because they often prefer to buy many

MNEs must pay enough to entice people to move but must not overpay.

Living is more expensive abroad because
- Habits change slowly
- People often don't know how and where to buy

● **TABLE 21.1**

TYPICAL FIRST-YEAR COST FOR A U.S. EXPATRIATE (MARRIED, TWO CHILDREN) IN TOKYO, JAPAN

The difference in the compensation of chief executive officers and that of the typical hourly employee is significant to extreme in various countries.

Direct compensation costs	
Base salary	$100,000
Foreign-service premium	15,000
Goods and services differential	73,600
Less: U.S. housing norm*	(15,400)
U.S. hypothetical taxes	(17,200)
Company-paid costs	
Schooling (two children)	15,000
Annual home leave	4,800
Housing*	150,000
Japanese income taxes†	84,000
Transfer/moving costs	38,000
Total company costs	$447,800

*Assumes company rents housing in its name and provides to expatriate. If company pays housing allowance instead, Japaneese income taxes (and total costs) will be about $65,000 higher.
†Note that Japanese income taxes will increase each year as some company reimbursements, most notably for taxes, become taxable.

Source: Organization Resources Counselors, Inc.

Western items that must be imported and thus have been charged high tariffs.[59] Housing costs also vary substantially because of crowded conditions that raise land prices as well as shortages of domiciles that are acceptable to expatriates.[60]

Most companies raise salaries (sometimes called a "goods-and-services differential") to offset the higher costs in a foreign country. A few companies reduce the cost-of-living differential over time, reasoning that as expatriates adapt to their new environment, they should adjust to local purchasing habits—for example, by buying vegetables from a neighborhood market instead of using imported packaged goods. When moves are to countries with a lower cost of living, however, few companies reduce an employee's pay because doing so might adversely affect the employee's morale. These postings may then give expatriates a windfall gain. In any event, companies remove the differential when the expatriate returns home.

Companies compare their expatriate compensation packages with those offered by other companies, often with information from consulting firms such as Towers Perrin or CIGNA that specialize in international compensation.[61] In addition, companies rely on estimates of cost-of-living differences—even if the estimates are imperfect. MNEs commonly use such sources as the U.S. State Department's cost-of-living index published yearly in *Labor Developments Abroad*, the *U.N. Monthly Bulletin of Statistics*, and surveys by the *Financial Times, P-E International, Business International*, and the *International Monetary Fund's Staff Papers*. In using any of these sources, companies must determine which items are included in order to adjust for those that have been omitted. Some items commonly omitted are housing, schooling, and taxes. Differences in inflation and exchange rates may quickly render surveys and indexes obsolete, so companies need to make cost-of-living adjustments frequently.

The ultimate objective of cost-of-living adjustments is to ensure that expatriates' after-tax income and, presumably, their job motivation will not suffer because of a foreign assignment.

MNEs use various cost-of-living indexes and

- Increase compensation when the foreign cost is higher
- Do not reduce compensation when the foreign cost is lower
- Remove the differential when the manager is repatriated

Because taxes are usually assessed on the adjustments companies make to the base salaries, companies have to adjust even further upward if the foreign tax rate is higher than the home country's.

Foreign-Service Premiums and Hardship Allowances There are bound to be goods and services that expatriates must do without when living abroad. Consequently, companies frequently give expatriates foreign-service premiums just for accepting a foreign assignment. This practice appears to be fading, however, especially for assignments in so-called world capitals like New York, London, and Tokyo, in which companies assume there is little deprivation and many interested executives.[62] Further, the hardships from foreign assignments are declining as advances in transportation and communications enable expatriates to keep in closer contact with people in their home countries; as the openness of economies allows them to buy familiar goods and services; and as the general level of housing, schooling, and medical services increasingly meet their needs.

Few, however, deny that living conditions in certain settings pose particularly severe hardships, such as harsh climatic or health conditions, or expose the expatriate family to political unrest that places everyone in danger.[63] For instance, expatriate personnel in such MNEs as Goodyear, Eastman Kodak, and Sanyo have been targeted for kidnapping and armed assault. Figure 21.3 shows attacks against U.S. citizens and U.S. facilities abroad. Companies have had to not only rethink their hardship allowances but also purchase ransom insurance, provide training programs on safety for expatriates and families, pay for home alarm systems and security guards, and assess their legal liability regarding employee safety.[64] Yet even where conditions are less severe, expatriates may encounter living conditions that are substandard (or superior) when compared to those at home. Thus, companies need to compensate an expatriate in ways that reflect his or her local environment. It may make sense, for example, for companies to offer expatriates in Switzerland a different set of rewards than those offered to their counterparts in Indonesia.[65]

Employees may encounter living problems for which the company pays extra compensation.

FIGURE 21.3 Attacks on U.S. Citizens and Facilities, 1995–2001

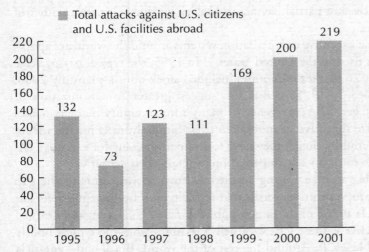

Total attacks against U.S. citizens and U.S. facilities abroad

Year	Attacks
1995	132
1996	73
1997	123
1998	111
1999	169
2000	200
2001	219

Location of Attacks	
North America	9
Eurasia	22
Africa	40
Western Europe	104
Asia	29
Middle East	33
Latin America*	877

The number of attacks included attacks against U.S. facilities and attacks in which U.S. citizens suffered casualties. They indicate the widespread nature of violence that can threaten expatriates.

Source: Various Reports, *Patterns of Global Terrorism,* The Office of the Coordinator for Counterterrorism, Department of State, United States.

*The main reason for the high number of attacks in Latin America is the number of terrorist bombings of the Cano Limon-Covenas oil pipeline in Colombia. For instance, the 483-mile pipeline was bombed 152 times in 2000. The pipeline is jointly owned by the Colombian government, Occidental Petroleum Corp, and Respol-YPF.

Finally, hardship may occur because of potential changes in total family income and status. In the home country, all members of the family may be able to work. About a quarter of companies provide spouses of expatriates with job-search assistance, often through networks with other companies.[66] For example, Eastman Kodak tries to find employment for spouses; when it cannot, it pays for a partial loss in income.[67] However, host governments seldom grant people other than the transferred employee permission to work. Therefore, the spouse or companion of an expatriate may have to either give up well-paying and satisfying employment or be separated from the partner for long periods. Some companies increase the expatriate's compensation, and about one-third of large U.S. companies assist couples with commuter marriages.[68]

Remote Areas   Many international projects are in areas so remote that companies would get few people to transfer there if those companies did not find ways to improve their quality of life. For example, Lockheed Aircraft set up its own color TV broadcasting station in Saudi Arabia for its expatriates there. Also, INCO built schools, hospitals, churches, supermarkets, a golf course, a yacht club, a motel, and a restaurant for its expatriates in Indonesia.

Expatriates in remote areas are often handled differently from employees elsewhere. To attract the large number of people needed for construction and start-up, MNEs usually will offer fixed-term contract assignments at high salaries and hire most people from outside the company. For example, in the remote oil fields of southern Chad, a trailer compound houses about 55 highly paid expatriates of ExxonMobil who sign on for eight-week tours of duty.[69] The people typically attracted to these assignments are willing to undergo difficult living conditions because they can save money at a rate far greater than at home.

Complications of Nationality Differences   As companies employ expatriates from home and third countries, compensation issues grow more complicated. Worse still, there is no consensus among companies on how to deal with most of these issues. For example, salaries for similar jobs vary substantially among countries, as do the relationships of salaries within the corporate hierarchy. Figure 21.4 shows the disparity of annual pay packages for CEOs by company nationality. The method of payment also varies substantially. For example, long-term incentives, such as options on restricted stock, are popular in the United States but not in Germany. However, German managers often receive compensation that U.S. managers do not, such as housing allowances and partial payment of salary outside Germany, neither of which is taxable.

Some evidence suggests that executive compensation systems around the world are adopting many of the pay practices used in the United States.[70] In 1995, the typical pay package for CEOs in 10 of the largest 26 market economies included stock-option plans; by 2000, the number had nearly doubled, to 19. Several factors suggest greater 'Americanization' of executive compensation packages. The emergence of many foreign equity markets makes stock options a more attractive incentive in more countries. Similarly, as companies from more countries become more multinational, they have to compete globally for executive talent. Likewise, local firms often must boost compensation to retain their executives.

There is still considerable variance among countries, however, in terms of the gap between the compensation of top executives versus that of the typical hourly employee. For example, on average, the CEOs at 365 of the largest publicly traded U.S. companies earned $13.1 million in 2000—effectively, these CEOs earned 531 times what the typical hourly employee took home (see Table 21.2). Around the rest of the world, Brazil and Venezuela are leaders in pay disparity—though they are still fall far short of the U.S. multiple. In contrast, Japan has the smallest gap between the CEO and average-worker pay. Interestingly, some debate whether U.S.-style executive pay practices can eventually set global standards when they apparently promote wider compensation inequality between managers and workers.

FIGURE 21.4   Variance in CEO Pay Packages Among Countries

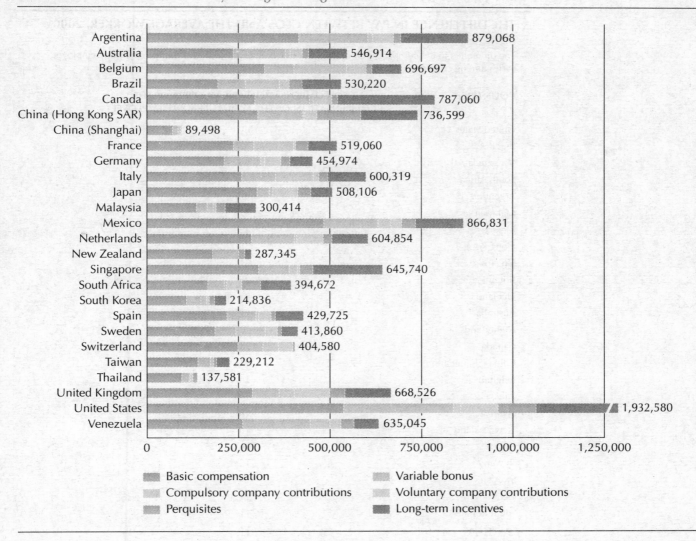

Country	Amount
Argentina	879,068
Australia	546,914
Belgium	696,697
Brazil	530,220
Canada	787,060
China (Hong Kong SAR)	736,599
China (Shanghai)	89,498
France	519,060
Germany	454,974
Italy	600,319
Japan	508,106
Malaysia	300,414
Mexico	866,831
Netherlands	604,854
New Zealand	287,345
Singapore	645,740
South Africa	394,672
South Korea	214,836
Spain	429,725
Sweden	413,860
Switzerland	404,580
Taiwan	229,212
Thailand	137,581
United Kingdom	668,526
United States	1,932,580
Venezuela	635,045

Legend:
- Basic compensation
- Variable bonus
- Compulsory company contributions
- Voluntary company contributions
- Perquisites
- Long-term incentives

The average annual pay package of the chief executive of an industrial company with annual revenues of approximately US$500 million in annual sales in 26 countries. The figures from April 1, 2001, are expressed in U.S. dollars converted at then prevailing exchange rates, and are not weighted to compensate for different costs of living or levels of taxation.

Source: "Exhibit 1, Total Remuneration—Chief Executive Officer," *Worldwide Total Remuneration 2001–2002*, Towers Perrin, http://www.towers.com/towers/default.asp.

MANAGEMENT RECRUITMENT AND SELECTION

Many companies have personnel record systems that include data on home- and foreign-country nationals. These data include not only the usual technical and demographic data but also—if the company has international activities—information on such adaptive capabilities as foreign-language qualifications, willingness to accept foreign assignments, and results of company-administered tests.[71] However, a company may encounter problems in bringing foreign managers into the system; if the company owns less than 100 percent of the foreign facility, the other stockholders may object. To the extent that companies have detailed personnel records, they can compare employees to gauge which ones may be best suited for positions with international responsibility.

Companies typically know more about their employees' technical capabilities than their adaptive ones. Still, improving the selection of expatriates pushes them to measure personal

Foreign personnel are not easily encompassed in information inventories because foreign operations may not be wholly owned.

● **TABLE 21.2**

THE DIFFERENCE IN PAY BETWEEN CEOS AND THE AVERAGE WORKER, 2000

The difference in the compensation of chief executive officers and that of the typical hourly employee varies among countries.

COUNTRY	CEO COMPENSATION AS A MULTIPLE OF THE COMPENSATION OF THE TYPICAL HOURLY EMPLOYEE
United States	531
Brazil	57
Venezuela	54
South Africa	51
Argentina	48
Malaysia	47
Mexico	45
Hong Kong	38
Singapore	37
Britain	25
Thailand	23
Australia	22
Netherlands	22
Canada	21
China (Shanghai)	21
Belgium	19
Italy	19
Spain	18
New Zealand	16
France	16
Taiwan	15
Sweden	14
Germany	11
South Korea	11
Switzerland	11
Japan	10

Average employees were assumed to work in industrial companies with about $500 million in annual sales. Estimates provided by *Worldwide Total Remuneration 2001–2002*. Towers Perrin.

Source: Eric Wahlgren, "Pay and Perks," *Business Week* (April 18, 2001).

adaptability for foreign transfer. For example, people who have successfully adjusted to domestic transfers or have previous international experience are more likely to adapt abroad. In addition, some companies use a variety of personality testing mechanisms as assessment aids. Companies are increasingly including spouses and children in tests and extensive interviews because a foreign assignment is usually more stressful for the family than for the transferred employee. For example, a survey of prominent multinationals found most expatriate assignments fail because of family difficulties.[72] Problems arise because the expatriate employees generally receive advanced training, but the spouses must start at the bottom in developing new social relations and in learning how to carry out the day-to-day management of the home. The separation from friends, family, and career often make the nonworking spouses lonely, and so they increasingly look to their working spouses for more companionship. Typically, the working spouses have less time because of the demands of their new jobs. This situation can provoke marital stress, which, in turn, affects work performance. As a result, interviewers look not only at likely adaptiveness but also at whether marriages can weather the stress of a foreign assignment.

One way a company can bypass some of these problems is to acquire a foreign company and, hence, its personnel. Companies may also form joint ventures with companies abroad so that the partner will contribute personnel to the operation as well as take responsibility for hiring new personnel. In Japan, where the labor market is tight and people are reluctant to move to new companies, foreign firms use Japanese partners extensively. However, relying on a partner to manage local human resources creates the risk that employees may see their primary allegiance to that partner rather than to the foreign investor.

Acquisitions and joint ventures secure staff but the staff may be

- *Inefficient*
- *Hard to control*

INTERNATIONAL DEVELOPMENT OF MANAGERS

Companies need people with a variety of specialized skills to carry out global operations. Therefore, programs to develop managers internationally must be tailored, to some degree, to specific individuals and situations.[73] There are three principle developmental needs.

1. Top executives must have a global mindset that is free of national prejudices. They must understand the global environment so that they can provide the leadership needed to attain a global mission.
2. Managers with direct international responsibility must be able to balance the well-being of corporate and national operations.
3. Managers without direct international responsibility must understand the importance of international competition on the company's performance.

Managers can gain these perspectives and knowledge before they join or after they begin working for a company.

To help meet these developmental needs, business schools are expanding their international offerings and requirements. Still, there is little agreement as to what students should study to help prepare them for international responsibilities. Two popular approaches are (1) to transfer specific knowledge about foreign environments and international operation and (2) to develop interpersonal awareness and adaptability. The former may tend to remove some of the fear and aggression that emerge when dealing with the unknown, whereas the latter approach tends to make people more receptive to foreign environments. However, the awareness of a difference does not necessarily imply a willingness to adapt to it, particularly to a cultural variation. Although either approach generally helps a person adjust better than those who lack training, there appears to be no significant difference in the effectiveness of the two approaches.[74]

Companies continue the international development of employees after they hire them. Such companies must also develop employees because many of them feel ill equipped to manage growing worldwide responsibilities as they move up in their organizations. To counter this tendency, a company can train those people who are about to take a foreign assignment, such as through language and orientation programs. Alternatively, it could include international business components in external or internal programs for all employees—irrespective of whether the person plans to work abroad. Examples of internal programs are those at PepsiCo and Raychem, which bring foreign nationals to U.S. divisions for six months to a year; IBM's regional training centers, in which managers from several countries convene for specific topics; P&G's training on globalization issues; and programs at GE, Motorola, and Honda of America to teach foreign languages and cultural sensitivity.

The most common predeparture training is an informational briefing. Topics typically include cultural differences, political structures, job design, compensation, housing, climate,

There is an increase in international studies in universities.

Postemployment training may include

- *Environment-specific information*
- *Adaptiveness training*
- *Training by an unaffiliated company abroad*

education, health conditions, home sales, taxes, transport of goods, job openings after repatriation, and salary distribution.[75] Companies sometimes follow predeparture training with cultural training about six months after expatriates arrive in a foreign country in the belief that they can then better engage these topics.

While working in foreign countries, managers strive to break down nationalistic barriers that impair companies' development of global corporate cultures and achievement of integrated global strategies. To balance a company's global and national needs, managers must be neither too ethnocentric nor too polycentric. Therefore, MNEs aim to develop managers who are committed to the subsidiary at which they work and also to the parent company's global well-being. However, companies rarely find such a dual allegiance.

Figure 21.5 shows four types of expatriate managers: (1) *free agent*, (2) *heart at home*, (3) *going native*, and (4) *dual citizen*.[76] There are two types of free agent. The first includes people who put their careers above either the parent company or the foreign operation where they are working. They often are highly effective, but they will move with little warning from one company to another, may serve their own short-term interests at the expense of the company's long-term ones, and do not plan to return to their home country. The second type of free agent includes people whose careers have plateaued at home and who take a foreign assignment only for the bigger paycheck. The heart at home type is overly ethnocentric and is usually eager to return home. When the company wants strong headquarters control, this type of person may be quite effective. The going native type learns and accepts the local way of doing business, wants to stay in the foreign location, and prefers not to consult headquarters. This type of person may be appropriate for situations in which the company follows multidomestic practices. The dual citizen type has a clear understanding of global needs, why he or she is needed at the foreign subsidiary, and local realities that may necessitate national responsiveness. This person usually finds methods to align the interests of headquarters and the subsidiary; overall, this is the most effective type of expatriate manager.

To counterbalance the heart at home type, the company may send younger managers abroad and go to great length to facilitate their cultural adjustment. To counterbalance the going native effect, the company may send people abroad who have strong ties to the company, limit their time away from headquarters, keep in close contact with them (perhaps through a mentor program), and assist their repatriation. In either situation, the company

FIGURE 21.5   Allegiance of Expatriate Managers

The "dual citizen" type of manager is most effective at balancing global and local needs. However, each of the other types can be very effective for specific types of foreign operations.

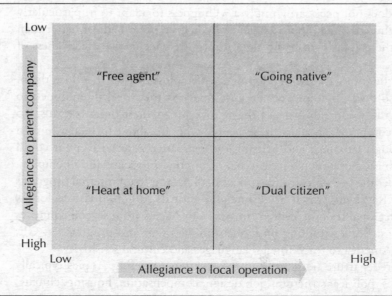

should handle the international transfer so that the expatriate understands why he or she has been selected for the post, how performance will be measured, the objectives of the parent company and local unit, and the location of control. These recommendations also may apply to other than expatriate employees. For example, local managers in foreign subsidiaries may be less apt to be a heart at home type if they have closer contact with headquarters and believe their future is tied more to global than to local interests.

The degree to which companies develop the international capabilities of their managers depends on the importance of their international operations. The MNE that is highly dependent on and committed to international operations has more extensive international human resource needs than those of a company that exports or imports a small share of its output. The latter type of company mostly needs personnel who are technically trained or knowledgeable about trade documentation, foreign-exchange risk, and political-economic conditions.

LABOR-MARKET DIFFERENCES

As a company moves onto foreign production, it must consider how to staff, motivate, compensate, and retain its foreign workforce. The norms in these human resource activities vary substantially from one country to another. Thus, there is some danger in a company's effort to replicate home-office organizational structures, office routines, and job descriptions abroad, particularly in developing countries. In addition, laborsaving devices that are economically justifiable at home, where wage rates are high, may be more costly than labor-intensive types of production in a country with high unemployment rates and low wages. Because of differences in labor skills and attitudes, the company also may find it beneficial to simplify tasks and use equipment that would be considered obsolete in an industrial economy. Finally, using labor-intensive methods may gain the favor of government officials who are combating local unemployment.

MNEs may shift labor or capital intensities if costs differ in foreign labor markets.

INTERNATIONAL LABOR MOBILITY

People often try to emigrate from countries with high unemployment and low wages to countries with labor shortages and high wages. Migration flows are shaped by the type of legal entry restrictions that a country uses to minimize the economic and social problems of absorbing large numbers of immigrants. Because of these restrictions, companies depend less today on imported labor than in earlier generations, despite the presence of sizable numbers of legal and illegal workers in industrial countries.

There is pressure for labor to move from high-unemployment and low-wage areas to places of perceived opportunities.

The incentive to hire immigrant workers is straightforward: They often work for a fraction of what domestic workers with comparable skills demand. This is especially true of illegal immigrants who cannot afford—or prefer not—to return to their home countries. It is also true within the European Union, where workers may move legally from one country to another in response to wage rate differences. For example, construction workers from other EU countries (mainly Britain, Ireland, and Portugal) work in Germany for considerably less than the wages paid to German laborers. In other cases, companies have sought specialists from abroad. Shared Resources, a small U.S.-based computer system company, recruits employees in India to work on contracts in Columbus, Ohio.[77] Critics usually accuse companies of behaving unethically when they hire foreign employees at lower wages than domestic workers.[78]

Companies are less certain of labor supply when they depend on foreign laborers because

- *Countries become restrictive*
- *Workers return home*
- *Turnover necessitates more training*

Migrant workers in many countries have permission to stay for only short periods, such as three to six months for New Zealand's workers from Fiji and Tonga. In many other cases, workers leave their families behind in the hope of returning home after saving enough money while working in the foreign country. This creates workforce uncertainty for employers.

Another uncertainty is the extent to which government authorities will restrict the number of foreign workers because of pressures both from domestic laborers who want to protect their job opportunities and from groups prejudiced against foreigners.

The influx and use of foreign workers create additional workplace problems. For example, in parts of Western Europe, companies relegate certain nationality groups to less complex jobs because their native language complicates training them. One result has been the development of homogeneous ethnic work groups at cross-purposes with other groups in the organization, as well as the emergence of go-betweens who can communicate with management and labor.

Since September 11, 2001, entering and residing in many countries, particularly the United States, has become more difficult. Prior to September 11, the United States relied on its Visa Waiver Program, established in 1986, to permit the citizens of 28 participating countries to travel to the United States for business visits, temporary local assignments, or tourism for 90 days or less without first obtaining a visa from U.S. embassies abroad. Travelers from visa waiver countries to the United States totaled approximately 17.6 million in 2000 and 14.7 million in 2001. The events preceding 9/11—many of the terrorists who hijacked the commercial flights had fabricated visa applications—led many to question the effectiveness of U.S. visa programs. Some worried that terrorists could again exploit these programs to enter the United States. Consequently, in 2002, the U.S. Congress passed the Border Security Act, which mandated a registration system that would allow authorities to track all incoming visa holders by 2005. The U.S. Justice Department widened the new law's instructions, setting up a special program to register visa holders already living in the United States—regardless of how long they had lived in the country. Increased visa security has also impeded the international mobility of businesspeople. For example, in 2003, several hundred international passengers a day were missing connecting flights at Bush Intercontinental Airport in Texas because of delays at the immigration counter. Revised visa regulations now required virtually all international travelers arriving on direct flights from other countries to appear before an immigration inspector before catching a connecting flight to other U.S. cities. Motions for more detailed visa processing requirements along with pending calls for biometric collection threatened to further complicate international labor mobility.

LABOR COMPENSATION DIFFERENCES

Companies can gain competitive advantages by establishing production facilities where they can pay labor less than their competitors pay. We now examine national differences in the amount and method of paying workers, along with the dynamics of comparative labor costs.

Reasons for Country Differences in Labor Compensation

The compensation that companies pay depends on workers' contributions to the business, the supply of and demand for particular skills (the so-called going wage) in the area, the cost of living, government legislation, and collective-bargaining ability. Companies' methods of payment (salaries, wages, commissions, bonuses, and fringe benefits) depend on local customs, feelings of security, taxes, and government requirements. Both the amount and method of payment are affected by a country's culture. For example, within a highly individualistic, meritocratic society such as the United States, there is a preference for compensation based on proportional contribution—the result being a heavy reliance on bonuses and a high disparity in incomes within the organization. In a collectivist society, such as Japan, there is a preference for more egalitarian allocations, regardless of contributions.[79] In an economy in which people have a high need to avoid risk, workers prefer job security and income preservation rather than income growth.[80]

MNEs usually pay slightly better than their local counterparts do in lower-wage countries (although they still pay less than what they do in higher-wage countries). They typically pay more because of their management philosophies and structures. An MNE's usual management philosophy, particularly in contrast to that of a local, family-run company, is to attract higher skilled workers by offering higher relative wages. In addition, the higher productivity of its product and process technologies may allow it to compensate employees more than local companies do. Further, when a company enters a country, experienced workers may demand higher compensation purely because they expect foreign companies to pay higher wages.

Differing Costs of Benefits

Fringe benefits differ radically from one country to another. Consequently, direct-compensation figures do not accurately reflect the amount a company must pay for a given job in a given country. The types of benefits that are either customary or have been required also vary. In Japan, for example, large companies commonly give workers such benefits as family allowances, housing loans and subsidies, lunches, children's education, and subsidized vacations. As a result, fringe benefits make up a much higher portion of total compensation in Japan than in the United States. Moreover, in many countries, companies give end-of-the-year bonuses, housing allowances, long vacations, profit sharing, and payment supplements based on the number of children the worker has.[81]

In many countries, firing or laying off an employee may be either expensive or nearly impossible, resulting in unexpectedly higher costs for a company accustomed to the efficient economies of regulating its workforce. In the United States, for example, companies expect to lay off workers when demand falls seasonally or cyclically. In many countries, however, a company has no legal recourse except to fire workers—and then perhaps only if it is permanently closing down its operations, at which time it must pay high severance compensation.[82] To halt operations in such countries, a company must come to an agreement with its unions and the government on such issues as extended benefits and the retraining and relocation of workers. At the same time, unemployment benefits are low in the United States compared with those in Western Europe, so there is more incentive for unemployed U.S. workers to find new jobs.

Too often, companies compare compensation expenses on a per-worker basis, which may bear little relationship to the total expenditure for employees. Workers' abilities and motivations vary widely. Consequently, it is the output associated with labor cost, or labor productivity, which is important. Seemingly cheap labor actually may raise the total compensation expenditure because of the need for more supervision, added training expenses, and adjustments in production methods. For example, Quality Coils, a small U.S. company, moved some operations to Mexico because hourly wages were only about one-third of what the company paid in Connecticut. However, the company later returned to Connecticut because of high absenteeism and low productivity in Mexico.[83] Further, if labor turnover is high, there is an ongoing, continuing need to hire and train workers.

Differences among countries in the amount and type of compensation continually change. Salaries and wages (as well as other expenditures) may rise more rapidly in one locale than in another. Therefore, the competitiveness of operations in different countries may shift. For example, in the 1980s, Korean workers made millions of shoes for Nike and Reebok; however, as Korean labor costs grew, most of these jobs shifted to China and Indonesia, which eventually saw some of these jobs move onto lower-cost producers in Vietnam.[84]

The process of comparing costs is difficult due to shifting capabilities. An example illustrates this idea. Assume U.S. productivity per worker in manufacturing increased by 2.8 percent (or 1.028 of what it was before), and hourly compensation rates went up by 10.2 percent (or 1.102) of what they were before. The result was a unit labor-cost increase of 7.2

MNEs may need to pay more than local companies to entice workers from existing jobs.

Fringe benefits vary substantially among countries.

In many countries, it is nearly impossible or expensive to lay off workers.

Relative costs change, so MNEs must consider

- Productivity change
- Labor-rate change
- Conversion of labor rate to competitor's currency

percent (1.102 divided by 1.028). Meanwhile, in the United Kingdom, productivity increased by 5.9 percent (or 1.059 of what it was before) and hourly compensation rates by 16.2 percent (or 1.162 of what they were before), amounting to a unit labor-cost increase of 9.7 percent (1.162 divided by 1.059). This meant that labor costs adjusted to productivity were rising more rapidly in the United Kingdom than in the United States in terms of local currencies. However, if the pound depreciated substantially in relation to the dollar, the labor cost measured in dollars could actually have become more favorable in the United Kingdom than in the United States.

COMPARATIVE LABOR RELATIONS

In each country in which an MNE operates, it must deal with groups of workers whose approach to the workplace reflects the sociopolitical environment of the country. This environment affects whether they join labor unions, how they bargain, and what they want from companies.

Sociopolitical Environment

There are striking international differences in how labor and management view each other. When there is little mobility between the two groups (generally, children of laborers become laborers, and children of managers become managers), a marked class difference exists. Companies may face considerable labor tension in such situations. Labor may perceive itself in a class struggle, even in the face of shrinking wage gaps. In such countries as Brazil, Switzerland, and the United States, labor and management tend to be adversaries in a zero-sum game.[85] In contrast, labor groups in many countries vote the way their labor leaders instruct them to vote; typically, they rely on national legislation rather than on collective bargaining to negotiate with management. Such mechanisms as strikes or slowdowns to effect changes also may be national in scope. In these situations, a company's production or ability to distribute its product may be much more dependent on the way labor perceives general work conditions in the whole country rather than on how it perceives specific conditions in the company where it works.

Approaches to reconcile labor tension differ by country. The use of mediation by an impartial party is mandatory in Israel but voluntary in the United States and the United Kingdom. Among countries that have mediation practices, attitudes toward it are diverse. For example, there is much less enthusiasm for it in India than in the United States. Not all differences are settled through changes either in legislation or through collective bargaining. Other means are the labor court and the government-chosen arbitrator. For example, wages in many Austrian industries are arbitrated semiannually.

Union membership as a portion of the total workforce has been falling in most countries. This is illustrated in Figure 21.6. There are several reasons for this decline.

- *Increase in white-collar workers as a percentage of total workers.* White-collar workers see themselves more as managers than as laborers.
- *Increase in service employment in relation to manufacturing employment.* There is more variation in service assignments than in manufacturing, so many workers believe their situations differ from that of their coworkers.
- *Rising portion of women in the workforce.* Traditionally, women have been less apt to join unions.
- *Rising portion of part-time and temporary workers.* Workers do not see themselves in the job long enough for a union to help them much.
- *Trend toward smaller average plant size.* More direct interactions between workers and managers align their interests, thereby harmonizing outlooks.

Overall attitude in a country affects how labor and management view each other and how labor will try to improve its lot.

FIGURE 21.6 Trade Union Decline in Industrialized Countries

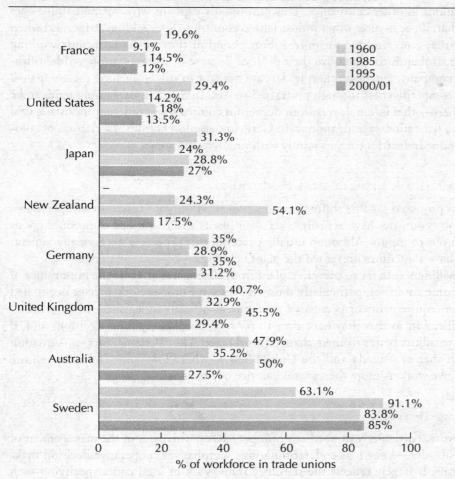

Various factors have influenced the general decline of trade union membership in select industrialized countries.
Compiled From Various Sources.

- *Decline in the belief in collectivism among younger workers.* Few of today's younger workers have suffered economic deprivation; hence, they question the value of collective solutions.[86]

The overall decline in union membership is a long-running trend. Still, there are exceptions. Unions in Sweden, for instance, have maintained their strength because they have forged cooperative relationships with large companies (such as Electrolux and Volvo) to improve corporate competitiveness and to share the rewards from the results.

Union Structure

Companies in a given country may deal with one or several unions that, depending on the situation, may represent workers in many industries, in many companies within the same industry, or in only one company. If it represents only one company, the union may represent all plants or just one plant. Although there are variations within countries, one type of relationship typically predominates within most countries. For example, unions in the United States tend to be national, representing certain types of workers (for example, airline pilots, coal miners, truck drivers, or university professors). Thus, a company may deal with several different national unions. Each collective-bargaining process usually is characterized by a single company on one side rather than an association of different companies that deals with one of the unions representing a certain type of worker in all of the companies' plants. In

Union structure can be

- National or local
- Industry or company
- One or several for the same company

Japan, one union typically represents all workers in a given company and has informal affiliations with unions in other companies. This purportedly explains why Japanese unions are less militant than those in most other industrialized countries. They seldom strike, and when they do, they may stop working for only a short period of time or may continue working while wearing armbands to symbolize their protest. Because of workers' stronger identification with the company, Japanese union leaders are hesitant to risk weakening the company's international competitiveness through protracted strikes. In Sweden, bargaining tends to be highly centralized—that is, employers from numerous companies in different industries deal together with a federation of trade unions. In Germany, employers from associations of companies in the same industries bargain jointly with union federations.

Protection from Closures and Redundancy

Workers' takeover of plants has been done to publicize their plight.

In response to proposed layoffs, shifts in production location, and cessation of operations, workers in many countries have actually taken over plants and continued to produce goods until they ran out of inputs. Although usually peaceful, this process is occasionally violent. These efforts have sometimes prevented the plant's closing.

Prior notification of plant closings has been legislated in some countries.

Workers' willingness to try to prevent a plant from closing underscores the importance of this issue. In some countries, particularly those in Western Europe, workers have negotiated prenotification requirements or persuaded government officials to legislate them. Workers prefer prenotification so that they have time to try to counter companies' decisions and, if unsuccessful, to adjust better to their changed workplace. The Western European situation contrasts with that of Canada and the United States, where few labor contracts require employers to give workers more than a week's notice of closure.

Codetermination

Some MNEs seek labor-management cooperation through the sharing of leadership.

In some countries, particularly in northern Europe, labor participates in the management of companies. This idea—known as **codetermination**—emphasizes cooperative decision making within firms. It largely reflects the statutory framework of legal codes specifying such behavior as well as the cultural orientation toward a "works community" that involves the entire workforce. Procedurally, labor is represented on the board of directors, either with or without veto power.

Despite some voluntary moves toward codetermination, most existing examples have been mandated by legislation, such as that in Germany.[87] These moves have been dictated by employee pressures because of the employees' belief that, like stockholders, they also bear risks and have stakes in the success of the company. Although there are some early examples of workers deterring investment outflows, acquisitions, and plant closures, codetermination has had little effect on companies' international business decisions or on the speed with which companies reach those decisions. One reason for this weak effect is that workers' broad range of goals prevents their representatives from taking strong stances on particular issues.

TEAM EFFORTS

In some countries, companies emphasize work teams to foster group cohesiveness and to involve workers in multiple, rather than in a limited, number of tasks. It is common for companies to compensate employees partly on group output so that their peers will exert pressure to reduce absenteeism and to increase work effort. Involving workers in multiple tasks by rotating their jobs within work groups improves motivation and develops replacement skills that are useful when someone is absent. Companies have also instituted practices that allow workers' groups to control their own quality procedures and repair their own equipment. Although the team efforts have worked well in some places, such as Sweden, they have occasionally failed. For example, Levi-Strauss introduced the team concept to its U.S. factories but got poor results because its workers wanted to be paid on an individual incentive system.[88] Generally, MNEs have adapted the team concept to national cultures. For example, in Japanese quality circles, small groups of workers concentrate on precise problems. GE tried transferring this concept to work groups in the United States, but workers found it too constricting. GE then adopted large-group meetings on ill-structured issues called "Work-Out," during which workers could legitimately debate managers about tactical and strategic matters.[89]

INTERNATIONAL PRESSURES ON NATIONAL PRACTICES

The International Labor Organization (ILO) dates back to 1919. It was founded on the premise that the failure of any country to adopt humane labor conditions impedes other countries' efforts to improve their own conditions. Several associations of unions from different countries also support similar ideals. These associations include various international trade secretariats representing workers in specific industries—for example, the International Confederation of Free Trade Unions (ICFTU), the World Federation of Trade Unions (WFTU), and the World Confederation of Labour (WCL). These organizations' activities, along with the general enhancement of worldwide communications, increasingly publicize the different labor conditions among countries. Among the newsworthy reports have been legal proscriptions against collective bargaining in Malaysia, wages below minimum standards in Indonesia, and the use of forced labor and child labor in developing countries. Upon publicizing such conditions, these organizations then champion economic and political sanctions to provoke change.[90]

Similarly, various codes of conduct on industrial relations, such as those issued by the OECD, ILO, and EU, influence MNE labor practices. Although the codes are voluntary, they may signal future transnational regulations of MNE activities. Trade unions have been anxious for clarifications of the guidelines and want to make them legally enforceable because the typical vagueness of the content creates considerable room for interpretation.

The ILO monitors labor conditions worldwide.

MULTINATIONAL OWNERSHIP AND COLLECTIVE BARGAINING

An unresolved debate is whether companies systematically weaken labor, especially collective bargaining procedures, by having multinational operations. We now examine this issue along with labor union responses to companies' multinationality.

MNE ADVANTAGES

Critics argue that MNE weaken labor because their product and resource flows let them hold out longer before settling a strike, their multiple operations let them switch production to another country where labor conditions are more favorable, and their size and complexity prevent unions from determining their capacity to meet their demands. We review each rationale.

Product and Resource Flows Presumably, the MNE that can divert output from its facilities in different countries and sell it to the consumers in the country where a strike is occurring has little incentive to settle a strike. Moreover, because each country may comprise only a small percentage of an MNE's total worldwide sales, profits, and cash flows, a strike in one country may minimally affect its global performance. Again, an MNE faces slight pressure to

Labor may be at a disadvantage in MNE negotiations because

- *Lesser resources*
- *The country bargaining unit is only a small part of MNE activities*
- *MNE may continue serving customers with foreign production or resources*
- *The size and complexity of MNEs*

MNE limitations come from capacity, legal restrictions, shared ownership, integrated production, and differentiated products.

resolve labor tensions. Therefore, an MNE's ability to hold out longer may give it an advantage over labor in collective bargaining that a domestic company does not have.

Operationally, an MNE can continue to supply customers in the strike-afflicted country only if it has excess capacity and produces an identical product in more than one country. Even if it meets these preconditions, an MNE would still confront the transport and tariff costs that led it to establish multiple production facilities in the first place. If the MNE partially owns the struck operation, partners or even minority stockholders may balk at financing a lengthy work stoppage. Further, if the idle facilities normally produce components needed for integrated production in other countries, then a strike may have far-reaching effects. For example, a strike at one GM facility in the United States prevented GM's Mexican plants from getting parts needed for assembly operations. Moreover, Mexican laws against layoffs meant GM had to maintain its Mexican workers on the payroll, thus adding pressure on GM to settle the strike.[91] In summary, there appear to be advantages of international diversification for collective bargaining, but only in limited circumstances.

MNEs may threaten workers with the prospect of moving production abroad.

Production Switching   Companies sometimes threaten to move production to other countries to extract wage reductions from their workers. This tactic presses unions to demand less compensation in favor of more job security. For example, Daimler-Benz's German workers agreed to accept lower wages after the company procured agreements from French, Czech, and British labor to work for less.

Although production shifts would seem plausible when a company has manufacturing facilities in more than one country, at other times they would seem more plausible when different companies own facilities in different countries. For example, suppose a Canadian company competes with Brazilian imports. If Canadian workers demand and get substantial wage increases that result in higher product prices, the Brazilian competitor will likely seize the opportunity to build Canadian market share at the expense of the Canadian company and its workers. However, suppose the Brazilian company also owns the facility in Canada. The Brazilian management would have to weigh the cost-saving advantages of moving its production from Canada to Brazil against the losses it would incur in Canada by discarding its facilities there.

Labor claims it is disadvantaged in dealing with MNEs because

• Decision making is far away
• It is hard to get full data on MNEs' global operations

Size and Complexity of MNEs   Observers claim it is difficult for labor unions to deal with MNEs because of the complexities in the location of their decision making and the difficulties in interpreting their financial data. Essentially, critics reason that when the ultimate decision makers are far removed from the bargaining location, such as home-country headquarters, arbitrarily stringent management decisions are more likely. Conceivably, the opposite might happen, particularly if the demands abroad seem low in comparison with those being made at home. In reality, labor relations usually are delegated to subsidiary management.

Unions regularly examine MNEs' financial data to determine MNEs' ability to meet their demands. Interpreting these data is complex because of disparities among managerial, tax, and disclosure requirements in home and host countries. Labor has been particularly leery of the possibility that MNEs might manipulate transfer prices (recall the discussion in Chapter 19) to give the appearance that a given subsidiary cannot meet labor demands. However, these concerns overemphasize a company's ability to increase compensation and deemphasize the seemingly more important issue of going-wage rates in both the industry and geographic area. Although MNEs may report many complex data, at least one set of financial statements must satisfy local authorities. This set should be no more difficult to interpret than that of a purely local company. In terms of transfer pricing, it is doubtful that MNEs set artificial levels to aid in collective bargaining situations since doing so simply creates problems elsewhere. Specifically, if an MNE understates profits in one country, it would have to overstate them elsewhere, which would then put it at a disadvantage in collective bargaining in that country.

LOOKING TO THE FUTURE

Which Countries Will Have the Jobs of the Future?

As capital, technology, and information grow more mobile among countries and companies, human resource development should account increasingly for competitive differences. Consequently, companies' access to and retention of more qualified personnel should grow more important. This will be a challenge because companies will run into greater difficulty retaining highly skilled, highly valued workers in the future.

Demographers are nearly unanimous in projecting that populations will grow much faster in developing countries (China being an exception) than in industrial countries—at least up to the year 2030. At the same time, the number of retirees as a percentage of the population in industrial countries will grow as people live longer and retire earlier. People will also need to be educated for more years to get the so-called better jobs. Overall, these industrial-country trends indicate that there will be fewer people to do the productive work within society. Industrial countries may adjust in any of several ways or combinations of them.[92] Each way has a number of social and economic consequences to which MNEs must adapt.

One adjustment might be for industrial countries to encourage emigration from developing countries, which do not generate enough jobs for their potential workers. In Canada, the United States, and parts of Western Europe, there has been a long-term entry of foreign workers, both legally and illegally, from developing countries. This entry generates assimilation costs within industrial countries and a brain drain from developing countries when highly qualified people leave for other countries. Some, however, suggest that emigration benefits everyone by encouraging brain circulation among industrial and developing countries.[93] Specifically, an increasing number of Taiwan's, China's, Korea's, and India's biggest U.S. success stories, lives that become firmly rooted in that country, are returning to their native homes to start companies. Nonetheless, times of economic downturns will likely see unemployed industrial-country citizens blame foreign workers for their plight. Under this scenario, companies will have to spend more time getting work permits and integrating different nationalities into their workforces.

Another potential adjustment in industrial countries is the continued push toward adopting robotics and other laborsaving equipment.[94] Although this may help solve some of the employee shortages in industrial countries, it will escalate companies' need for workers with higher skill levels. In fact, less educated members of the workforce may be either unemployable, forced to take lesser-paying jobs in the service sector, or compete with immigrants for less appealing jobs. Gaps between haves and have-nots may thus widen within industrial countries as well as between those countries and developing countries. In this scenario, have-nots may pressure governments to push companies to shift technological development away from laborsaving priorities.

A third possible adjustment is the acceleration of industry migration to developing countries to tap supplies of productive labor. At the same time, developing countries may devise ways to support brain circulation or, if unsuccessful, halt the process of brain drain. Either approach will shift more entry-level production jobs away from industrial countries.[95] If successful, businesspersons who return to their countries will likely shift many low-skilled jobs to their home market. Industrial-country governments will then face the tough problem of what to do with underqualified workers who face deteriorating job prospects.[96]

Labor Initiatives

Unions can engage several tactics to counter the power of MNEs. Internationally, they can share information, assist bargaining units in other countries, and deal simultaneously with MNEs.[97] Nationally, they can pressure for laws that restrict the mobility and methods of MNEs.

Labor might strengthen its position relative to MNEs through cross-national cooperation.

Information Sharing   The most common international cooperation among unions is exchanging information. This sort of collaboration helps them to determine the validity of a company's claims as well as to reference precedents from other countries on bargaining issues. International confederations of unions, trade secretariats composed of unions in a single industry or a complex of related industries, and company councils that include representatives from an MNE's plants around the world all participate in the exchange of information. European work councils (EWCs) represent a company's employees throughout the European Union. Through an EWC, a company informs and consults with employees on such issues as its corporate strategies so that the employees can prepare for possible product and market changes.

Assistance to Foreign Bargaining Units   Labor groups in one country may support their counterparts in other countries. Popular measures include refusing to work overtime to supply a market normally served by striking workers' production, sending financial aid to workers in other countries, and disrupting work in their own countries. For example, French workers pledged to disrupt work at Pechiney in support of striking workers in the company's U.S. facilities. However, this type of support is still extremely rare.

Simultaneous Actions   There have been few examples of simultaneous negotiations and strikes. Labor's cooperation across borders is difficult due to national differences in union structures and workers' objectives. The percentage of workers in unions is much higher in some countries than in others—for example, it is much higher in Germany than in neighboring France. Many organized workers in France and Portugal belong to communist unions that clash with unions representing the bulk of workers elsewhere in Europe. In addition, wage rates and workers' preferences differ from country to country. For instance, Spanish workers are more willing to work on weekends than are German workers. Further, there has been growing nationalism among workers in the face of increasing foreign competition.

National Approaches   Unions' efforts to counter MNEs' power have taken place primarily on a national basis. Usually, there is little enthusiasm among workers to support their counterparts in another country, largely because workers tend to view each other as competitors. Even when labor in one country helps labor in another, it likely is trying to achieve its own specific goals. For example, a union representing U.S. tomato pickers helped its Mexican counterpart win a stronger contract—thus dissuading the Campbell Soup Company from moving operations to Mexico. Even in Canada and the United States, which have long shared a common union membership, there has been a move among Canadian workers to form unions independent of those in the United States. One Canadian organizer summed up much of the attitude by saying, "An American union is not going to fight to protect Canadian jobs at the expense of American jobs." The logic is that international unions will adopt policies favoring the bulk of their membership, which in any joint Canadian-U.S. relationship is bound to be American.

National legislation in some countries has provided for worker representation on boards of directors, has regulated the entry of foreign workers, and has limited imports and foreign investment outflows. Most future initiatives will likely take place at the national rather than at the international level.

Summary

- The tasks of international managers differ from those of purely domestic managers in several ways, including knowing how to adapt home-country practices to foreign locales and dealing with high-level government officials.

- The top-level managers of foreign subsidiaries normally perform much broader duties than do domestic managers with similar cost or profit responsibilities. They must resolve communications problems, usually with less staff support, between corporate headquarters and subsidiaries.

- MNEs employ more locals than expatriate managers because the former understand local operating conditions and may focus more on long-term goals.

- Hiring locals rather than expatriates demonstrates that opportunities are available for local citizens, shows consideration for local interests, avoids the red tape of cross-national transfers, and is usually materially cheaper.

- MNEs transfer people abroad to infuse technical competence and home-country business practices, to control foreign operations, and to develop managers' business skills.

- MNEs that transfer personnel abroad should consider their technical competencies, how well the people will be accepted, how well they will adapt to local conditions, and how to treat them when they return home from their foreign assignment.

- When transferred abroad, an expatriate's compensation usually is increased because of hardship and differences in cost of living. Transfers to remote areas typically carry higher premiums.

- Salaries for similar jobs vary substantially among countries, both in terms of the composition of pay-packages for top managers as well as the compensation gap between top managers and hourly workers.

- Companies frequently acquire personnel abroad by buying existing companies. They also may go into business with local companies, which then assume most staffing responsibilities.

- Many companies maintain personnel record systems that include data on home and foreign-country nationals, including information on their technical skills and adaptive capabilities.

- Two major international training functions are building a global awareness among managers in general and equipping managers to handle the specific challenges of a foreign assignment.

- When setting up a new operation in a foreign country, a company may use existing facilities as guides for determining labor needs. However, it should adjust its compensation scheme to reflect different labor skills, costs, and availabilities.

- When companies depend on an imported labor supply, they often run into special stability, supervision, and training challenges.

- Because of national variations in fringe benefits, direct-compensation figures do not accurately reflect the amount a company must pay for a given job. In addition, job-security benefits (no layoffs, severance pay, etc.) add substantially to compensation costs.

- Although per-worker comparisons are useful indicators of labor-cost differences, the output associated with total costs is relevant for international competitiveness. These costs may shift over time, thus changing international competitive positions.

- A country's sociopolitical environment will largely determine the type of relationship between labor and management and affect the number, representation, and organization of unions.

- Employees in the local market may resort to aggressive actions to protect their jobs and preserve the local operation.

- Codetermination is a type of labor participation in a company's management and usually is intended to cultivate a cooperative rather than an adversarial environment.

- International organizations pressure companies to follow internationally accepted labor practices wherever they operate, regardless of whether the practices conflict with the norms and laws of the host countries.

- MNEs are often blamed for weakening the position of labor in the collective-bargaining process because of those companies' international diversification, threats to export jobs, and complex structures and reporting mechanisms.

- International cooperation among labor groups in a concerted effort to confront MNEs is minimal. Labor groups' initiatives include information exchanges, simultaneous negotiations or strikes, and refusals to work overtime to supply the market in a struck country.

CASE

Tel-Comm-Tek (TCT)[98]

In January 2003, Steven Jones, a U.S. national and managing director of the Indian subsidiary of Tel-Comm-Tek (TCT), a U.S.-headquartered company, announced his resignation and intention to return to the United States within a month. TCT immediately began a search for his replacement.

TCT manufactures a variety of small office equipment (primarily copying machines, dictation units, laser printers, and paper shredders) in nine different countries. It distributes and sells these products worldwide, most recently reporting sales in more than 70 countries. Although it had no manufacturing facility in India, it had sold

MAP 21.2   India

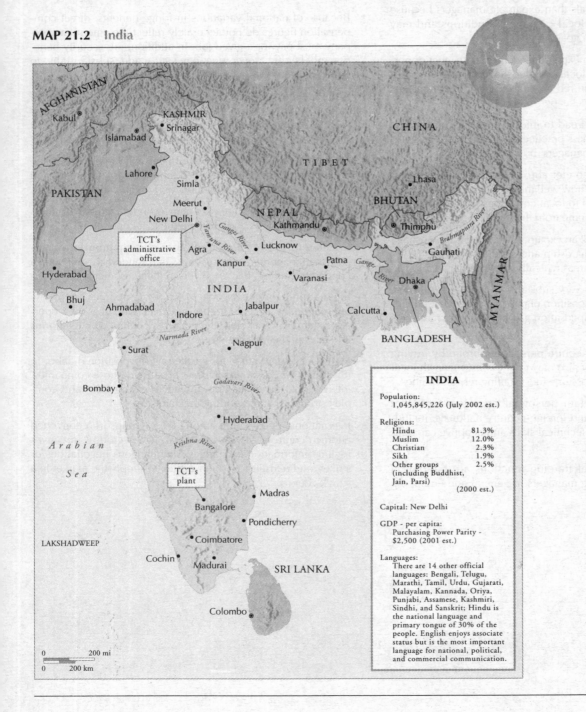

INDIA

Population:
1,045,845,226 (July 2002 est.)

Religions:
Hindu	81.3%
Muslim	12.0%
Christian	2.3%
Sikh	1.9%
Other groups	2.5%
(including Buddhist, Jain, Parsi)	
	(2000 est.)

Capital: New Delhi

GDP - per capita:
Purchasing Power Parity - $2,500 (2001 est.)

Languages:
There are 14 other official languages: Bengali, Telugu, Marathi, Tamil, Urdu, Gujarati, Malayalam, Kannada, Oriya, Punjabi, Assamese, Kashmiri, Sindhi, and Sanskrit; Hindu is the national language and primary tongue of 30% of the people. English enjoys associate status but is the most important language for national, political, and commercial communication.

and serviced products there since the early 1980s. Originally, it hired independent importers to sell its products. It soon realized that generating higher sales required setting up its own operations. In 1985, it opened a sales office in New Delhi. Map 21.2 profiles India and identifies its major cities.

By 2000, several factors spurred TCT to expand its Indian operations. TCT's Indian sales operation (with about 100 employees) had consistently reported higher sales and profitability. However, its growing success was not without some worries. Specifically, TCT feared that local trade restrictions, then under discussion by government officials, would eventually ban the import of the sorts of small office equipment that it made.

Country conditions in India made greater investment appealing. India had stable democratic institutions and corporate laws; a large English-speaking population; and productive, economical workers. Already, several foreign and Indian multinationals designed and manufactured office equipment locally.

In the fall of 2002, TCT had begun constructing its first factory in Bangalore, the center of India's Silicon Valley (see Map 21.1). The first production run was set for June 2003. Logistically, TCT planned to supply the factory with imported components for laser printers and then hire about 150 production-line workers to assemble them. TCT's managers believed that local assembly of laser printers would give the company the most leverage to continue importing other parts of its product line.

TCT enlisted a U.S. engineering firm to supervise construction of its plant in Bangalore. Upon completion, TCT would "turn over the key" to the on-site factory director, a recently arrived U.S. expatriate sent specifically to run the completed plant. This director reported directly to TCT's U.S. headquarters on production and quality control matters. He or she would report to TCT India's managing director, the now vacant position, in New Delhi on all other matters, such as accounting, supply-chain logistics, finance, and labor relations. The managing director of TCT India, in turn, reported to the Asian Regional Office at TCT's U.S. headquarters.

TCT preferred to fill executive vacancies by promotion from within. In addition, TCT used a mix of home-, host-, and third-country nationals to staff management positions in foreign countries. TCT often rotated its managers among its foreign and U.S. locations. Increasingly, headquarters saw international experience as an important factor in determining whom to promote. Following procedure, the Asian Regional Office charged a selection committee to nominate the new managing director for TCT India. The committee identified six candidates.

Tom Wallace   A 30-year TCT veteran, Wallace is knowledgeable and experienced in the technical and sales aspects of the job. Although he has never worked abroad, he has regularly toured the company's foreign operations and always expressed interest in an expatriate position. His superiors regularly rate his performance as proficient. He will retire in about four-and-a-half-years. He and his wife speak only English. Their children are grown and live with their own children in the United States. Presently, Wallace supervises a U.S.-based operation that is about the size of that in India—once the new factory goes on line there. However, the merger of Wallace's unit with another TCT division will eliminate his current position within six months.

Brett Harrison   Harrison, 40, has spent 15 years with TCT. His superiors consider him highly competent and poised to move into upper-level management within the next few years. He has never been posted to an overseas position. Still, for the past three years, he has worked in the Asian Regional Office and has frequently visited Southeast Asian operations. Both he and his wife have traveled to India several times in the last 20 years and are well acquainted with its geography, politics, customs, and outlooks. The Harrisons personally know some U.S. expatriates in the Bangalore region. Their children, ages 14 and 16, have also vacationed in India with their parents. Mrs. Harrison is a mid-level executive with a multinational pharmaceutical company that does not have an Indian operation.

Atasi Das   Born in the United States, Das joined TCT 12 years ago after earning her MBA from a university in Pennsylvania. At 37, she has successfully moved between staff and line positions with broader responsibilities. For two years, she was the second in command of a product group that was about half the size of the expanding Indian operations. Her performance regularly earns ratings of excellent. Currently, she works on a planning staff team based at TCT headquarters. When she originally joined TCT, she noted that her goal was to be assigned international responsibilities, and she pointed to her undergraduate major in international affairs as evidence of her long-term plan. She recently reiterated her interest in international responsibilities, believing it to be an essential career step. She speaks Hindi and is unmarried. Her parents, who now live in the United States, are first-generation immigrants from India. Several family members and relatives live in Kashmir and Punjab, northern states of India.

Ravi Desai   Desai, 33, currently is an assistant managing director in the larger Asian operation. He helps oversee production and sales for the Southeast Asian markets in Singapore, Malaysia, and China. A citizen of India, he has spent his 10 years with TCT working in Southeast Asia. He holds an MBA from the prestigious Indian Institute of Management. Some in TCT see him as a likely candidate to direct the Indian operation eventually. He is married with four children (ages two to seven) and speaks English and Hindi well. His wife, also a native Indian, neither works outside the home nor speaks English.

Jalan Bukit Seng   Seng, 38, is the managing director of TCT's assembly operation in Malaysia. A citizen of Singapore, Seng has worked in either Singapore or Malaysia his entire life. However, he earned university and MBA degrees from leading universities in the United States. He is fluent in Singapore's four official languages—Malay, English, Mandarin, and Tamil—and sees himself learning other languages as needed. His performance reviews, both with respect to the Malaysia plant and other TCT plant operations around the world, have consistently been positive, with an occasional ranking of excellent. While Seng is unmarried, he is close to his extended family, which lives in Singapore and Malaysia.

Saumitra Chakraborty At 27, Chakraborty is an assistant to the departing managing director in India. He has held that position since joining TCT upon graduating from a small, private university in Europe four years earlier. Unmarried, he consistently earns a job performance rating of competent. While he excels in employee relations, he lacks any line experience. Still, he has successfully increased TCT India's sales, largely owing to his personal connections with prominent Indian families and government officials and to his skillfulness with the ways of the Indian business environment. Besides speaking India's main languages of English and Hindi fluently, Chakraborty speaks Kannada (the local language of Bangalore).

QUESTIONS

1. Which candidate should the committee nominate for the assignment? Why?
2. What challenges might each candidate encounter in the position?
3. How might TCT go about minimizing these challenges facing each candidate?
4. Should all candidates receive the same compensation package? If not, what factors should influence each package?
5. What recommendations can you offer to help a company facing this sort of decision that will enable it to balance professional and personal concerns?

Chapter Notes

1 The data for the case were taken from Edwin McDowell, "Making It in America: The Foreign-Born Executive," *New York Times* (June 1, 1980): Section 3, p. 11; Don Whitehead, *The Dow Story* (New York: McGraw-Hill, 1968); Paul L. Blocklyn, "Developing the International Executive," *Personnel* 66 (March 1989): 44–47; "Globesmanship," *Across the Board* 27 (January–February 1990): 24–34; "Popoff on Challenges for Dow and for the Industry," *Chemical Week* (May 18, 1994): 26–28; Susan J. Sinsworth, "Issues Management Is Central to Frank Popoff's Globalization Strategy," *Chemical Engineering News* 72, no. 21 (May 23, 1994): 25–29; Gordon Petrash, "Dow's Journey to a Knowledge Value Management Culture," *European Management Journal* 14, no. 4 (August 1996): 365–73; Vijay Govindarajan and Anil K. Gupta, "Building an Effective Global Business Team," *Sloan Management Review* 42 (Summer 2001): 63; "Expat Spouses: It Takes Two," *Financial Times* (March 1, 2002) and www.dow.com (December 12, 2002).

2 "Globesmanship," *Across the Board* 27 (January–February 1990): 26, quoting Michael Angus.

3 Janamitra Devan and Parth Tewari, "Brains Abroad," *The McKinsey Quarterly* (Autumn 2001): 51.

4 Henk Overbeek, "Neoliberalism and the Regulation of Global Labor Mobility," *The Annals of the American Academy of Political and Social Science* (May 2002): 74–91.

5 William Q. Judge, "Is a Leader's Character Culture-Bound or Culture-Free? An Empirical Comparison of the Character Traits of American and Taiwanese CEOs," *Journal of Leadership Studies* 8 (Fall 2001): 63–79.

6 Varinder M. Sharma, "Entry into Latin America BEMs: High or Low Resource Commitment Modes?" *International Journal of Commerce and Management* 12 (Spring 2002): 41–68.

7 See Montserrat Entrialgo, "The Impact of the Alignment of Strategy and Managerial Characteristics on Spanish SMEs," *Journal of Small Business Management* 40 (July 2002): 260–71; and Keith D. Brouthers, "Institutional,

Cultural and Transaction Cost Influences on Entry Mode Choice and Performance," *Journal of International Business Studies* 33 (Summer 2002): 203–22.

8 See Ben L. Kedia, Richard Nordtvedt, and Liliana M. Perez, "International Business Strategies, Decision-Making Theories, and Leadership Styles: An Integrated Framework," *Competitiveness Review* 12 (Winter–Spring 2002): 38–53; and "The New Teamwork," *Business Week* (February 18, 2002): EB12.

9 Matt Hamblen, "NetMeeting Cuts Dow's Travel Expenses," *Computerworld* (March 9, 1998): 20.

10 Anthony Ferner, Javier Quintanilla, and Matthias Z. Varul, "Country-of-Origin Effects, Host-Country Effects, and the Management of HR in Multinationals: German Companies in Britain and Spain," *Journal of World Business* 36 (Summer 2001): 107.

11 Amy Sitze, "Language of Business: Can E-Learning Help International Companies Speak a Common Language?" *Online Learning* 6 (March 2002): 19–23.

12 Stephen Baker, "Catching the Continental Drift: These Days, English Will Suffice for Americans Working in Europe. To Be a Player, However, the Smart Expatriate Needs the Gift of Tongues," *Business Week* (August 14, 2001).

13 See Maddy Janssens, "Developing a Culturally Synergistic Approach to International Human Resource Management," *Journal of World Business* 36 (Winter 2001): 429–51; and Nicholas Athanassiou and Douglas Nigh, "Internationalization, Tacit Knowledge and the Top Management Teams of MNCs," *Journal of International Business Studies* 31 (Fall 2000): 471.

14 Sully Taylor, Schon Beechler, and Nancy Napier, "Toward an Integrative Model of Strategic International Resource Management," *Academy of Management Review* 21 (1996): 959–85, discusses these in the context of multidomestic and a combination of global and transnational strategies.

15 Terri A. Scandura, Mary Ann Von Glinow, and Kevin B. Lowe, "When East Meets West: Leadership 'Best Practices' in the United States

and the Middle East," *Advances in Global Leadership* 1 (1999): 233–46.

16 Tsun-yan Hsieh, Johanne Lavoie, and Robert Samek, "Are You Taking Your Expatriate Talent Seriously?" *The McKinsey Quarterly* (Summer 1999): 71.

17 Ricahrd DeFrank, Robert Konopaske, and John Ivancevich, "Executive Travel Stress: Perils of the Road Warrior," *Academy of Management Executive* 14 (May 2000): 58–71.

18 For a discussion of the adjustment problem, see Joann S. Lublin, "More Toasts, Less Sleep: The Globe-Trotting CEO," *Wall Street Journal* (November 19, 1998): B1.

19 Raj Persaud, "Too Much Jetlag Can Damage Your Mind," *Business Traveler* (May 2000): 21.

20 See Margaret Shaffer et al., "Struggling for Balance Amid Turbulence on International Assignments: Work-Family Conflict, Support and Commitment," *Journal of Management* 27 (January–February 2001): 99; and Chris Moss, "Expats: Thinking of Living and Working Abroad?" *The Guardian* (October 19, 2000): 4.

21 David C. Waring, "Doing Business Overseas," *Cornell Enterprise* (Fall–Winter 1988): 29.

22 Robert Taylor, "Companies Cut Back Overseas Transfer Benefits," *Financial Times* (July 18, 1996): 1, reporting a survey by Monks advisor.

23 See Iris I. Varner and Teresa M. Palmer, "Successful Expatriation and Organizational Strategies," *Review of Business* 23 (Spring 2002): 8–12; and Jan Selmer, "Practice Makes Perfect? International Experience and Expatriate Adjustment," *Management International Review* 42 (January 2002): 71–88.

24 Vijay Pothukuchi et al., "National and Organizational Culture Differences and International Joint Venture Performance," *Journal of International Business Studies* 33 (Summer 2002): 243–66.

25 Estimates reported in the second annual study of expatriate issues, conducted from January through March 2002 and sponsored by CIGNA International Expatriate Benefits; the National Foreign Trade Council; trade and investment; and WorldatWork (November 11, 2002): http://www.prnewswire.com/micro/CI9.

26 Valerie Frazee, "Relo Administrators Believe Expats Are Overpaid," *Business and Management Practices* 3 (July 1998): 4, quoting a survey by Runzheimer International of 103 international relocation administrators from U.S.-based companies showing that 72 percent feel pressure to cut the costs and that 52 percent are responding by hiring locals.

27 Harris Dellas and Vally Koubi, "Industrial Employment, Investment Equipment, and Economic Growth," *Economic Development & Cultural Change* 49 (July 2001): 867.

28 Rebecca De Winter, "The Anti-Sweatshop Movement: Constructing Corporate Moral Agency in the Global Apparel Industry," *Ethics & International Affairs* 15 (October 2001): 99–117.

29 Thad Williamson, "Who Wants to Be a Cheerleader for a Sweatshop?" *Dollars & Sense* (July–August 2002): 24–27.

30 David Weil, "Regulating Noncompliance to Labor Standards: New Tools for an Old Problem," *Challenge* 45 (January–February 2002): 47–75.

31 See http://www.ilo.org/public/english/comp/child for full report. Also see http://www.stopchildlabor.org/pressroom/childpr0509.html, retrieved November 11, 2002.

32 Jeffrey Ball, "DaimlerChrysler's Transfer Woes," *Wall Street Journal* (August 24, 1999): B1.

33 See Paula Caligiuri and Victoria Di Santo, "Global Competence: What Is It, and Can It Be Developed Through Global Assignments?" *Human Resource Planning* 24 (September 2001): 27–36; and Mark Morgan, "Career-Building," *Strategic Finance* 83 (June 2002): 38–44.

34 Chi-fai Chan and Neil Holbert, "Marketing Home and Away: Perceptions of Managers in Headquarters and Subsidiaries," *Journal of World Business* 36 (Summer 2001): 205.

35 See "High-Tech Nomads: These Engineers Work as Temps on Wireless Projects All Over the World," *Time* (November 26, 2001): B20; and Ben L. Kedia and Ananda Mukherji, "Global Managers: Developing a Mindset for Global Competitiveness," *Journal of World Business* 34 (Fall 1999): 230.

36 David Ahlstrom, Garry Bruton, and Eunice S. Chan, "HRM of Foreign Firms in China: The Challenge of Managing Host Country Personnel," *Business Horizons* 44 (May 2001): 59.

37 Calvin Reynolds, "Strategic Employment of Third Country Nationals: Keys to Sustaining the Transformation of HR Functions," *Human Resource Planning* 20 (March 1997): 33–50.

38 Susan Schneider and Rosalie Tung, "Introduction to the International Human Resource Management Special Issue," *Journal of World Business* 36 (Winter 2001): 341–46.

39 See Caligiuri and Di Santo, op. cit., and Hsieh, Lavoie, and Samek, op. cit.

40 See Sunkyu Jun, James Gentry, and Yong Hyun, "Cultural Adaptation of Business Expatriates in the Host Marketplace," *Journal of International Business Studies* 32 (Summer 2001): 369; and J. Stewart Black and Mark Mendenhall, "Cross-Cultural Training Effectiveness: A Review and a Theoretical Framework for Future Research," *Academy of Management Review* 15 (January 1990): 117.

41 John D. Daniels and Gary Insch, "Why Are Early Departure Rates from Foreign Assignments Lower Than Historically Reported?" *Multinational Business Review* VI, no. 1 (Spring 1998): 13–23.

42 Data provided by National Foreign Trade Council (www.nftc.org) and by Maria L. Kraimer, Sandy Wayne, and Renata Jaworski, "Sources of Support and Expatriate Performance: The Mediating Role of Expatriate Adjustment," *Personnel Psychology* 54 (Spring 2001): 71.

43 See "Expat Spouses: It Takes Two," *Financial Times* (March 1, 2002); and Margaret Shaffer and David Harrison, "Forgotten Partners of International Assignments: Development and Test of a Model of Spouse Adjustment," *Journal of Applied Psychology* 86 (April 2001): 238.

44 Christopher Cole, "Bridging the Language Gap: Expatriates Find Learning Korean Key to Enjoying a More Satisfying Life," *The Korea Herald* (August 16, 2002).

45 J. Stewart Black and Hal B. Gregersen, "The Right Way to Manage Expats," *Harvard Business Review* (March–April 1999): 52–61.

46 Eric A. Savage and Kenneth J. Rose, "At Home Abroad: Americans Working Outside the Country Often Benefit from the Extraterritorial Application of U.S. Anti-Discrimination Laws," *New Jersey Law Journal* 168 (June 3, 2002): 28–31.

47 Patricia Feltes, Robert K. Robinson, and Ross L. Fink, "American Female Expatriates and the Civil Rights Act of 1991: Balancing Legal and Business Interests," *Business Horizons* (March–April 1993): 82–86.

48 Virginia E. Schein, "A Global Look at Psychological Barriers to Women's Progress in Management," *Journal of Social Issues* 57 (Winter 2001): 675–89.

49 Linda Stroh, Arup Varma, and Stacey Valy-Durbin, "Why Are Women Left at Home: Are They Unwilling to Go on International Assignments?" *Journal of World Business* 35 (Fall 2000): 241.

50 See M. Linehan and Hugh Scullion, "Factors Influencing Participation of Female Executives in International Assignments," *Comportamento Organizacional e Gestao* 6 (2001): 213–26; and Sully Taylor and Nancy Napier, "Working in Japan: Lessons from Women Expatriates," *Sloan Management Review* (Spring 1996): 76–84.

51 Paula M. Caligiuri and Wayne F. Cascio, "Can We Send Her There? Maximizing the Success of Western Women in Global Assignments," *Journal of World Business* 33 (1998): 394–416.

52 See Chris Brewster, "Making Their Own Way: International Experience Through Self-Initiated Foreign Assignments," *Journal of World Business* 35 (Winter 2000): 417; and Vesa Suutari et al., "Expatriate Assignment Versus Overseas Experience: Contrasting Models of International Human Resource Development," *Journal of World Business* 32 (1997): 351–68.

53 "New Survey Suggests Ways to Maximize Expatriate Performance and Loyalty," *Internet Wire* (March 27, 2001). Estimates reported at 2001 National Foreign Trade Council's International HR Management Symposium. See also Leslie Gross Klaff, "The Right Way to Bring Expats Home," *Workforce* 81 (July 2002): 40–44; and Jeff Barbian, "Return to Sender: Companies That Fail to Effectively Manage Employees Returning from a Foreign Assignment May Find Their Investments Permanently Hitting the Road," *Training* 39 (January 2002): 40–43.

54 Linda K. Stroh, Hal B. Gregersen, and J. Stewart Black, "Closing the Gap: Expectations Versus Reality Among Repatriates," *Journal of World Business* 33 (1998): 111–24. See also Klaff, op. cit.

55 Barry Newman, "Expat Archipelago," *Wall Street Journal* (December 12, 1995): A1.

56 Mila Lazarova and Paula Caligiuri, "Retaining Repatriates: The Role of Organizational Support Practices," *Journal of World Business* 36 (Winter 2001): 389–402.

57 Meredith Downes and Anisya Thomas, "Managing Overseas Assignments to Build Organizational Knowledge," *Human Resource Planning* 22 (December 1999): 33.

58 "Tokyo Tops in H.K. Survey on Living Cost for Expatriates," *Japan Economic Newswire* (January 24, 2002).

59 "Expatriate Life; Cost of Living Report," *China Economic Review* (March 12, 2001).

60 "Home Away from Home: Expatriate Housing in Asia," *The Korea Herald* (May 2, 2002).

61 Robert Taylor, "Recruitment: World of Difference in Human Resources," *Financial Times* (January 7, 2000): 11.

62 Carolyn Gould, "Expat Pay Plans Suffer Cutbacks," *Workforce* 78 (September 1999): 40–45.

63 Judy Clark, "Added Global Risks Impact Security Planning for Oil, Gas Expat Workers," *The Oil and Gas Journal* 100 (April 2002): 32–37.

64 Roberto Ceniceros, "Precautions, Training Can Lessen Risk of Kidnapping," *Business Insurance* 35 (May 14, 2001): 26.

65 George T. Milkovich and George T. Bloom, "Rethinking International Compensation," *Compensation and Benefits Review* (January 1998): 15–23.

66 Geoffrey W. Latta, "Expatriate Policy and Practice: A Ten-Year Comparison of Trends," *Compensation and Benefits Review* 31, no. 4 (July–August 1999): 35–39, quoting studies by Organization Resources Counselors.

67 Alison Maitland, "A Hard Balancing Act: Management of Dual Careers," *Financial Times* (May 10, 1999): 11.

68 Valerie Frazee, "Expert Help for Dual-Career Spouses," *Workforce* 78 (March 1999): S18.

69 Jerry Useem, "Exxon's African Adventure: How to Build a $3.5 Billion Pipeline—with the 'Help' of NGOs, the World Bank, and Yes, Chicken Sacrifices," *Fortune* (April 15, 2002): 102.

70 Towers Perrin, *2001–2002 Worldwide Total Remuneration.*, http://www.towers.com/TOWERS/services_products/TowersPerrin/wwtr01/wwtr01htm.

71 D. Ones and C. Viswesvaran, "Relative Importance of Personality Dimensions for Expatriate Selection: A Policy Capturing Study," *Human Performance*, 12 (1999) 275–294.

72 Diane E. Lewis, "Families Make, Break Overseas Moves," *Boston Globe*, (October 4, 1998): 5D; "Expat Spouses: It Takes Two," *Financial Times* (March 1, 2002). Notably, companies are increasingly addressing the concerns of expatriate spouses. Some MNEs, like AstraZeneca, PricewaterhouseCoopers, and Unilever formed the Permits Foundation to lobby governments worldwide to develop better laws on expatriate spouse employment. This foundation argues that discriminatory employment laws against expatriates spouses are ultimately harmful to a country's economy.

73 Christopher A. Bartlett and Sumantra Ghoshal, "What Is a Global Manager?" *Harvard Business Review*, September–October 1992, 124–132.

74 P. Christopher Earley, "Intercultural Training for Managers: A Comparison of Documentary and Interpersonal Methods," *Academy of Management Journal*, 30, no. 4 (December 1987). 685–698; Sharon Leiba-O'Sullivan, "The Distinction Between Stable and Dynamic Cross-cultural Competencies: Implications for Expatriate Trainability," *Journal of International Business Studies* 30 (Winter 1999): 709.

75 Valerie Frazee, "Send Your Expats Prepared for Success," *Workforce* 78 (March 1999): S6.

76 J. Stewart Black and Hal B. Gregersen, "Serving Two Masters: Managing the Dual Allegiance of Expatriate Employees," *Sloan Management Review* (Summer 1992): 61–71, covers the typologies of expatriates.

77 Timothy Aeppel, "A Passage to India Eases a Worker Scarcity in Ohio," *Wall Street Journal* (October 5, 1999): B1.

78 Michael Massing, "From Protest to Program," *The American Prospect* 12 (July 2, 2001): S2.

79 Chao C. Chen, "New Trends in Rewards Allocation Preferences: A Sino-U.S. Comparison," *Academy of Management Journal* 38 (1995): 408–428.

80 Paul S. Hempel, "Designing Multinational Benefits Programs: The Role of National Culture," *Journal of World Business* 33 (1998): 277–294.

81 Alberto Alesina, Edward Glaeser, and Bruce Sacerdote, "Why Doesn't the United States Have an European-Style Welfare State? *Brookings*

Papers on Economic Activity (Fall 2001): 187–276.

82 Christine Evans-Klock, Peggy Kelly, Peter Richards, and Corinne Vargha, "Worker Retrenchment: Preventive and Remedial Measures," *International Labour Review* 138 (Spring 1999): 47.

83 Bob Davis, "Illusory Bargain," *Wall Street Journal* (September 15, 1993): A11.

84 Tim Larimer, "Sneaker Gulag: Are Asian Workers Really Exploited?," *Time International* (May 11, 1998): 30.

85 Bruce E. Kaufman, "Reflections on Six Decades in Industrial Relations: An Interview with John Dunlop," *Industrial and Labor Relations Review* 55 (January 2002): 324–349.

86 Nancy Mills, "New Strategies for Union Survival and Revival," *Journal of Labor Research* 22 (Summer 2001): 599.

87 John Addison, "Nonunion Representation in Germany," *Journal of Labor Research* 20 (Winter 1999): 73–91.

88 Ralph T. King, Jr., "Jeans Therapy," *Wall Street Journal* (May 20, 1998): A1.

89 Dave Ulrich, Steve Kerr, and Ron Ashkenas, *The GE Work-Out: How to Implement GE's Revolutionary Method for Busting Bureaucracy and Attacking Organizational Problems—Fast!* (New York: McGraw-Hill, 2002).

90 Ans Kolk and Rob van Tulder, "Child Labor and Multinational Conduct: A Comparison of International Business and Stakeholder Codes," *Journal of Business Ethics* 36 (March 15, 2002): 291–302.

91 Neil Templin, "GM Strike Hits Mexican Output as Talks on Settlement Resume," *Wall Street Journal* (March 20, 1996): A3.

92 The Annecy Symposium, "The Future of Work, Employment and Social Protection," *International Labour Review* 140 (Winter 2001): 453–475.

93 AnnaLee Saxenian, "Brain Circulation: How High-Skill Immigration Makes Everyone Better Off," *Brookings Review* 20 (Winter 2002): 28–32; Moises Naim, "The New Diaspora: New Links Between Émigrés and their Home Countries Can Become a Powerful Force for Economic Development," *Foreign Policy* (July–August 2002): 96–98.

94 Mark Poster, "Workers as Cyborgs: Labor and Networked Computers," *Journal of Labor Research* 23 (Summer 2002): 339–354.

95 "We Must Halt the Brain-Drain," *Africa News Service* (December 17, 2001).

96 "The Poorest Are Again Losing Ground," *Business Week* (April 23, 2001): 130.

97 Robert A. Senser, "Workers of the World: It's Time to Unite," *Commonweal* 127 (September 22, 2000): 13; Julie Kosterlitz, "Unions of The World Unite: European and American Unions Working Together," *National Journal* 30 (May 16, 1998): 1134.

98 Based on information reported in "India," *CIA World Handbook 2002*; http://www.cia.gov/publications/factbook/geos/in.html; "India: A Country Study," *Library of Congress*, http://memory.loc.gov/frd/cs/intoc.html; India, Country Profile, *BBCi*, http://news.bbc.co.uk/1/hi/world/south_asia/country_profiles/1154019.stm; and various publications of the *United Nations*, http://www.un.org/.

Glossary

Absolute advantage: A theory first presented by Adam Smith, which holds that because certain countries can produce some goods more efficiently than other countries, they should specialize in and export those things they can produce more efficiently and trade for other things they need.

Acceptable quality level (AQL): A concept of quality control whereby managers are willing to accept a certain level of production defects, which are dealt with through repair facilities and service centers.

Accounting: The process of identifying, recording, and interpreting economic events.

Acquired advantage: A form of trade advantage due to technology rather than due to the availability of natural resources, climate, etc.

Acquired group memberships: Affiliations not determined by birth, such as religions, political affiliations, and professional and other associations.

Acquisition: The purchase of one company by another company.

Active income: Income of a CFC that is derived from the active conduct of a trade or business, as specified by the U.S. Internal Revenue Code.

Ad valorem duty: A duty (tariff) assessed as a percentage of the value of the item.

ADR: *See* American Depositary Receipt.

Advance import deposit: A deposit prior to the release of foreign exchange, required by some governments.

AFTA: *See* ASEAN Free Trade Area.

ALADI: *See* Latin American Integration Association.

American Depositary Receipt (ADR): A negotiable certificate issued by a U.S. bank in the United States to represent the underlying shares of a foreign corporation's stock held in trust at a custodian bank in the foreign country.

American terms: *See* U.S. terms.

Andean Group (ANCOM): A South American form of economic integration involving Bolivia, Colombia, Ecuador, Peru, and Venezuela.

APEC: *See* Asia Pacific Economic Cooperation.

Appropriability theory: The theory that companies will favor foreign direct investment over such nonequity operating forms as licensing arrangements so that potential competitors will be less likely to gain access to proprietary information.

Arbitrage: The process of buying and selling foreign currency at a profit that results from price discrepancies between or among markets.

Area division: *See* Geographic division.

Arm's-length price: A price between two companies that do not have an ownership interest in each other.

Ascribed group memberships: Affiliations determined by birth, such as those based on gender, family, age, caste, and ethnic, racial, or national origin.

ASEAN: *See* Association of South East Asian Nations.

ASEAN Free Trade Area (AFTA): A free-trade area formed by the ASEAN countries on January 1, 1993, with the goal of cutting tariffs on all intrazonal trade to a maximum of 5 percent by January 1, 2008.

Asia Pacific Economic Cooperation (APEC): A cooperation formed by 21 countries that border the Pacific Rim to promote multilateral economic cooperation in trade and investment in the Pacific Rim.

Association of South East Asian Nations (ASEAN): A free-trade area involving the Asian countries of Brunei, Indonesia, Malaysia, the Philippines, Singapore, and Thailand.

Back-to-back loan: A loan that involves a company in Country A with a subsidiary in Country B, and a bank in Country B with a branch in Country A.

Balance of payments: Statement that summarizes all economic transactions between a country and the rest of the world during a given period of time.

Balance-of-payments deficit: An imbalance of some specific component within the balance of payments, such as merchandise trade or current account, that implies that a country is importing more than it exports.

Balance-of-payments surplus: An imbalance in the balance of payments that exists when a country exports more than it imports.

Balance of trade: The value of a country's exports less the value of its imports ("trade" can be defined as merchandise trade, services, unilateral transfers, or some combination of these three).

Balance on goods and services: The value of a country's exports of merchandise trade and services minus imports.

Bank for International Settlements (BIS): A bank in Basel, Switzerland, that facilitates transactions among central banks; it is effectively the central banks' central bank.

Bargaining school theory: A theory holding that the negotiated terms for foreign investors depend on how much investors and host countries need each other's assets.

Barter: The exchange of goods for goods or services instead of for money.

Base currency: The currency whose value is implicitly 1 when a quote is made between two currencies; for example, if the cruzeiro is trading at 2,962.5 cruzeiros per dollar, the dollar is the base currency and the cruzeiro is the quoted currency.

Basic balance: The net current account plus long-term capital within a country's balance of payments.

Bid (buy): The amount a trader is willing to pay for foreign exchange.

Bill of exchange: *See* Commercial bill of exchange.

Bill of lading: A document that is issued to a shipper by a carrier, listing the goods received for shipment.

BIRPI: *See* International Bureau for the Protection of Industrial Property Rights.

BIS: *See* Bank for International Settlements.

Black market: The foreign-exchange market that lies outside the official market.

Body language: The way people move their bodies, gesture, position themselves, etc., to convey meaning to others.

Bonded warehouse: A building or part of a building used for the storage of imported merchandise under supervision of the U.S. Customs Service and for the purpose of deferring payment of customs duties.

Booking center: An offshore financial center whose main function is to act as an accounting center in order to minimize the payment of taxes.

Branch (foreign): A foreign operation of a company that is not a separate entity from the parent that owns it.

Brand: A particular good identified with a company by means of name, logo, or other method, usually protected with a trademark registration.

Bretton Woods Agreement: An agreement among IMF countries to promote exchange-rate stability and to facilitate the international flow of currencies.

Broker (in foreign exchange): Specialists who facilitate transactions in the interbank market.

Buffer-stock system: A partially managed system that utilizes stocks of commodities to regulate their prices.

Bundesbank: The German central bank.

Buy local legislation: Laws that are intended to favor the purchase of domestically sourced goods or services over imported ones, even though the imports may be a better buy.

Buybacks: Counterdeliveries related to, or originating from, an original export.

CACM: *See* Central American Common Market.

Canada-U.S. Free Trade Agreement: An agreement, enacted in 1989, establishing a free-trade area involving the United States and Canada.

Capital account: A measure of transactions involving previously existing rather than currently produced assets.

Capital market: The market for stocks and long-term debt instruments.

Capitalism: An economic system characterized by private ownership, pricing, production, and distribution of goods.

Caribbean Community and Common Market (CARICOM): A customs union in the Caribbean region.

Caribbean Free Trade Association (CARIFTA): *See* Caribbean Community and Common Market.

CARICOM: *See* Caribbean Community and Common Market.

Caste: A social class separated from others by heredity.

CEFTA: *See* Central European Free Trade Association.

Central American Common Market (CACM): A customs union in Central America.

Central bank: A government "bank for banks," customarily responsible for a country's monetary policy.

Central European Free Trade Association (CEFTA): An association which went into effect on July 1, 1992, with an initial membership of the Czech Republic, Slovakia, Hungary, and Poland, and whose goal was to establish a free trade area that includes the basic trade structure of the EU by the year 2000.

Centralization: The situation in which decision making is done at the home office rather than at the country level.

Centrally planned economy (CPE): *See* Command economy.

Certificate of origin: A shipping document that determines the origin of products and is usually validated by an external source, such as a chamber of commerce; it helps countries determine the specific tariff schedule for imports.

CFC: *See* Controlled foreign corporation.

Chaebol: Korean business groups that are similar to *keiretsu* and also contain a trading company as part of the group.

Chicago Mercantile Exchange (CME): The largest commodity exchange in the world, dealing primarily in agricultural products, U.S. treasury bills, coins, and some metals.

CIA: The Central Intelligence Agency, a U.S. government agency charged with gathering intelligence information abroad.

Civil law system: A legal system based on a very detailed set of laws that are organized into a code; countries with a civil law system, also called a codified legal system, include Germany, France, and Japan.

Civil liberties: The freedom to develop one's own views and attitudes.

COCOM: *See* Coordinating Committee on Multilateral Exports.

Code of conduct: A set of principles guiding the actions of MNEs in their contacts with societies.

Codetermination: A process by which both labor and management participate in the management of a company.

Codified legal system: *See* Civil law system.

Collaborative arrangement: A formal, long-term contractual agreement among companies.

COMECON: *See* Council for Mutual Economic Assistance.

Command economy: An economic system in which resources are allocated and controlled by government decision.

Commercial bill of exchange: An instrument of payment in international business that instructs the importer to forward payment to the exporter.

Commercial invoice: A bill for goods from the buyer to the seller.

Commission on Transnational Corporations: A United Nations agency that deals with multinational enterprises.

Commodities: Basic raw materials or agricultural products.

Commodity agreement: A form of economic cooperation designed to stabilize and raise the price of a commodity.

Common law system: A legal system based on tradition, precedent, and custom and usage, in which the courts interpret the law based on those conventions; found in the United Kingdom and former British colonies.

Common market: A form of regional economic integration in which countries abolish internal tariffs, use a common external tariff, and abolish restrictions on factor mobility.

Communism: A form of totalitarianism initially theorized by Karl Marx in which the political and economic systems are virtually inseparable.

Communitarian paradigm: The government defines needs and priorities and partners with business in a major way.

Comparable access: A protectionist argument that companies and industries should have the same access to foreign markets as foreign industries and companies have to their markets.

Comparative advantage: The theory that there may still be global efficiency gains from trade if a country specializes in those products that it can produce more efficiently than other products.

Compound duty: A tax placed on goods traded internationally, based on value plus units.

Concentration strategy: A strategy by which an international company builds up operations quickly in one or a few countries before going to another.

Confirmed letter of credit: A letter of credit to which a bank in the exporter's country adds its guarantee of payment.

Conservatism: A characteristic of accounting systems that implies that companies are hesitant to disclose high profits or profits that are consistent with their actual operating results; more common in Germanic countries.

Consolidation: An accounting process in which financial statements of related entities, such as a parent and its subsidiaries, are combined to yield a unified set of financial statements; in the process, transactions among the related enterprises are eliminated so that the statements reflect transactions with outside parties.

Consortium: The joining together of several entities, such as companies or governments, in order to strengthen the possibility of achieving some objective.

Consular invoice: A document that covers all the usual details of the commercial invoice and packing list, prepared in the language of the foreign country for which the goods are destined, on special forms obtainable from the consulate or authorized commercial printers.

Consumer-directed market economy: An economy in which there is minimal government participation while growth is promoted through the mobility of production factors, including high labor turnover.

Consumer price index (CPI): A measure of the cost of typical wage-earner purchases of goods and services expressed as a percentage of the cost of these same goods and services in some base period.

Consumer sovereignty: The freedom of consumers to influence production through the choices they make.

Continental terms: *See* European terms.

Control: The planning, implementation, evaluation, and correction of performance to ensure that organizational objectives are achieved.

Controlled foreign corporation (CFC): A foreign corporation of which more than 50 percent of the voting stock is owned by U.S. shareholders (taxable entities that own at least 10 percent of the voting stock of the corporation).

Convertibility: The ability to exchange one currency for another currency without restrictions.

Coordination: Linking or integrating activities into a unified system.

Copyright: The right to reproduce, publish, and sell literary, musical, or artistic works.

Corporate culture: The common values shared by employees in a corporation, which form a control mechanism that is implicit and helps enforce other explicit control mechanisms.

Correspondent (bank): A bank in which funds are kept by another, usually foreign, bank to facilitate check clearing and other business relationships.

Cost-of-living adjustment: An increase in compensation given to an expatriate employee when foreign living costs are more expensive than those in the home country.

Cost-plus strategy: The strategy of pricing at a desired margin over cost.

Council for Mutual Economic Assistance (CMEA or COMECON): A regional form of economic integration that involved essentially those communist countries considered to be within the Soviet bloc; terminated in 1991.

Council of Ministers: One of the five major institutions of the EU; composed of one member from each country in the EU and entrusted with making major policy decisions.

Countertrade: A reciprocal flow of goods or services valued and settled in monetary terms.

Country analysis: A process of examining the economic strategy of a nation state, taking a holistic approach to understanding how a country, and in particular its government, has behaved, is behaving, and may behave.

Country-similarity theory: The theory that a producer, having developed a new product in response to observed market conditions in the home market, will turn to markets that are most similar to those at home.

Country size theory: The theory that larger countries are generally more self-sufficient than smaller countries.

Court of Justice: One of the five major institutions of the EU; composed of one member from each country in the EU and serves as a supreme appeals court for EU law.

CPE (centrally planned economy): *See* Command economy.

Creolization: The process by which elements of an outside culture are introduced.

Cross-licensing: The exchange of technology by different companies.

Cross rate: An exchange rate between two currencies used in the spot market and computed from the exchange rate of each currency in relation to the U.S. dollar.

Cultural imperialism: Change by imposition.

Cultural relativism: The belief that behavior has meaning and can be judged only in its specific cultural context.

Culture: The specific learned norms of a society, based on attitudes, values, and beliefs.

Culture shock: A generalized trauma one experiences in a new and different culture because of having to learn and cope with a vast array of new cues and expectations.

Currency swaps: The exchange of principal and interest payments.

Current-account balance: Exports minus imports of goods, services, and unilateral transfers.

Current-rate method: A method of translating foreign-currency financial statements that is used when the functional currency is that of the local operating environment.

Customs duties: Taxes imposed on imported goods.

Customs union: A form of regional economic integration that eliminates internal tariffs among member nations and establishes common external tariffs.

Customs valuation: The value of goods on which customs authorities charge tariffs.

Debt-service ratio: The ratio of interest payments plus principal amortization to exports.

Decentralization: The situation in which decisions tend to be made at lower levels in a company or at the country-operating level rather than at headquarters.

Deferral: The postponing of taxation of foreign-source income until it is remitted to the parent company.

Demand conditions: Includes three dimensions: the composition of home demand (or the nature of buyer needs), the size and pattern of growth of home demand, and the internationalization of demand.

Democracy: A political system that relies on citizens' participation in the decision-making process.

Dependencia theory: The theory holding that LDCs have practically no power when dealing with MNEs as host countries.

Dependency: A state in which a country is too dependent on the sale of one primary commodity and/or too dependent on one country as a customer and supplier.

Derivative: A foreign-exchange instrument such as an option or futures contract that derives its value from some underlying financial instrument.

Derivatives market: Market in which forward contracts, futures, options, and swaps are traded in order to hedge or protect foreign-exchange transactions.

Devaluation: A formal reduction in the value of a currency in relation to another currency; the foreign-currency equivalent of the devalued currency falls.

Developed country: High-income country. Also called industrial country.

Developing country: A poor country. Also known as an emerging country.

Direct foreign investment: *See* Foreign direct investment.

Direct identification drawback: A provision that allows U.S. firms to use imported components in the manufacturing process without having to include the duty paid on the imported goods in costs and sales prices.

Direct investment: *See* Foreign direct investment.

Direct quote: A quote expressed in terms of the number of units of the domestic currency given for one unit of a foreign currency.

Direct selling: A sale of goods by an exporter directly to distributors or final consumers rather than to trading companies or other intermediaries in order to achieve greater control over the marketing function and to earn higher profits.

Directive: A proposed form of legislation in the EU.

Disclosure: The presentation of information and discussion of results.

Discount (in foreign exchange): A situation in which the forward rate for a foreign currency is less than the spot rate, assuming that the domestic currency is quoted on a direct basis.

Distribution: The course—physical path or legal title—that goods take between production and consumption.

Distributor: A merchant in a foreign country that purchases products from the manufacturer and sells them at a profit.

Diversification: A process of becoming less dependent on one or a few customers or suppliers.

Diversification strategy: A strategy by which an international company produces or sells in many countries to avoid relying on one particular market.

Divestment: Reduction in the amount of investment.

Documentary draft: An instrument instructing the importer to pay the exporter if certain documents are presented.

Draft: An instrument of payment in international business that instructs the importer to forward payment to the exporter.

Drawback: A provision allowing U.S. exporters to apply for refunds of 99 percent of the duty paid on imported components, provided they are used in the manufacture of goods that are exported.

Dumping: The underpricing of exports, usually below cost or below the home-country price.

Duty: A government tax (tariff) levied on goods shipped internationally. Also called tariff.

Dynamic effects of integration: The overall growth in the market and the impact on a company of expanding production and achieving greater economies of scale.

EC: *See* European Community.

E-commerce: The use of the Internet to join together suppliers with companies and companies with customers.

Economic Community of West African States (ECOWAS): A form of economic integration among certain countries in West Africa.

Economic exposure: The foreign-exchange risk that international businesses face in the pricing of products, the source and cost of inputs, and the location of investments.

Economic integration: The abolition of economic discrimination between national economies, such as within the EU.

Economic system: The system concerned with the allocation of scarce resources.

Economics: A social science concerned chiefly with the description and analysis of the production, distribution, and consumption of goods and services.

Economies of scale: The lowering of cost per unit as output increases because of allocation of fixed costs over more units produced.

ECOWAS: *See* Economic Community of West African States.

ECU: *See* European Currency Unit.

EEC: *See* European Economic Community.

EEC Patent Convention (EPC): An important cross-national patent convention that involves the members of the EU.

Effective tariff: The real tariff on the manufactured portion of developing countries' exports, which is higher than indicated by the published rates because the ad valorem tariff is based on the total value of the products, which includes raw materials that would have had duty-free entry.

EFTA: *See* European Free Trade Association.

Elastic (product demand): A condition in which sales are likely to increase or decrease by a percentage that is more than the percentage change in income.

Electronic data interchange (EDI): The electronic movement of money and information via computers and telecommunications equipment.

Embargo: A specific type of quota that prohibits all trade.

EMC: *See* Export management company.

Emerging country: Low- and middle-income country. Also known as developing country.

EMS: *See* European Monetary System.

Enterprise resource planning (ERP): Software that can link information flows from different parts of a business and from different geographic areas.

Entrepôt: A country that is an import/export intermediary; for example, Hong Kong is an entrepôt for trade between China and the rest of the world.

Environmental climate: The external conditions in host countries that could significantly affect the success of a foreign business enterprise.

Environmental scanning: The systematic assessment of external conditions that might affect a company's operations.

EPC: *See* European Patent Convention.

Equity alliance: A situation in which a cooperating company takes an equity position (almost always a minority) in the company with which it has a collaborative arrangement.

ERP: *See* Enterprise resource planning.

Essential-industry argument: The argument holding that certain domestic industries need protection for national security purposes.

ETC: *See* Export trading company.

Ethnocentrism: A belief that one's own group is superior to others; also used to describe a company's belief that what worked at home should work abroad.

Eurobond: A bond sold in a country other than the one in whose currency it is denominated.

Eurocredit: A loan, line of credit, or other form of medium- or long-term credit on the Eurocurrency market that has a maturity of more than one year.

Eurocurrency: Any currency that is banked outside of its country of origin.

Eurocurrency market: An international wholesale market that deals in Eurocurrencies.

Eurodollars: Dollars banked outside of the United States.

Euroequity market: The market for shares sold outside the boundaries of the issuing company's home country.

European Central Bank (ECB): Established July 1, 1998, the ECB is responsible for setting the monetary policy and for managing the exchange-rate system for all of Europe since January 1, 1999.

European Commission: One of the five major institutions of the EU; composed of a president, six vice presidents, and 10 other members whose allegiance is to the EU and serving as an executive branch for the EU.

European Community (EC): The predecessor of the European Union.

European Council: One of the five major institutions of the European Union; made up of the heads of state of each of the EU members.

European Currency Unit (ECU): A unit of account based on a currency basket composed of the currencies of the members of the EU.

European Economic Community (EEC): The predecessor of the European Community.

European Free Trade Association (EFTA): A free-trade area among a group of European countries that are not members of the EU.

European Monetary System (EMS): A cooperative foreign-exchange agreement involving most of the members of the EU and designed to promote exchange-rate stability within the EU.

European Parliament: One of the five major institutions of the EU; its representatives are elected directly in each member country.

European Patent Convention (EPC): A European agreement allowing companies to make a uniform patent search and application, which is then passed on to all signatory countries.

European terms: The practice of using the indirect quote for exchange rates.

European Union (EU): A form of regional economic integration among countries in Europe that involves a free-trade area, a customs union, and the free mobility of factors of production that is working toward political and economic union.

Exchange rate: The price of one currency in terms of another currency.

Eximbank: *See* Export-Import Bank.

Exotic currencies: The currencies of developing countries. Also called exotics.

Expatriates: Noncitizens of the country in which they are working.

Experience curve: The relationship of production-cost reductions to increases in output.

Export-Import Bank (Eximbank): A U.S. federal agency specializing in foreign lending to support exports.

Export-led development: An industrialization policy emphasizing industries that will have export capabilities.

Export license: A document that grants a government permission to ship certain products to a specific country.

Export management company (EMC): A company that buys merchandise from manufacturers for international distribution or sometimes acts as an agent for manufacturers.

Export packing list: A shipping document that itemizes the material in each individual package and indicates the type of package.

Export tariff: A tax on goods leaving a country.

Export trading company (ETC): A form of trading company sanctioned by U.S. law to become involved in international commerce as independent distributors to

match up foreign buyers with domestic sellers.

Exports: Goods or services leaving a country.

Exposure: A situation in which a foreign-exchange account is subject to a gain or loss if the exchange rate changes.

Exposure draft: The first draft of an accounting standard, which is open to comment by parties other than the IASC.

Expropriation: The taking over of ownership of private property by a country's government.

Externalities: External economic costs related to a business activity.

Extranet: The use of the Internet to link a company with outsiders.

Extraterritoriality: The extension by a government of the application of its laws to foreign operations of companies.

Factor conditions: Inputs to the production process, such as human, physical, knowledge, and capital resources, and also infrastructure.

Factoring: The discounting of a foreign account receivable.

Factor mobility: The free movement of factors of production, such as labor and capital, across national borders.

Factor-proportions theory: The theory that differences in a country's proportionate holdings of factors of production (land, labor, and capital) explain differences in the costs of the factors and that export advantages lie in the production of goods that use the most abundant factors.

FASB: *See* Financial Accounting Standards Board.

Fatalism: A belief that events are fixed in advance and that human beings are powerless to change them.

Favorable balance of trade: An indication that a country is exporting more than it imports.

FCPA: *See* Foreign Corrupt Practices Act.

FDI: *See* Foreign direct investment.

Fees: Payments for the performance of certain activities abroad.

Financial Accounting Standards Board (FASB): The private-sector organization that sets financial accounting standards in the United States.

FIRA: *See* Foreign Investment Review Act.

First-in advantage: Any benefit gained in terms of brand recognition and the lining up of the best suppliers, distributors, and local partners as a result of entering a market before competitors do.

First-mover advantage: A cost-reduction advantage due to economies of scale attained through moving into a foreign market ahead of competitors.

Fisher Effect: The theory about the relationship between inflation and interest rates; for example, if the nominal interest rate in one country is lower than that in another, the first country's inflation should be lower so that the real interest rates will be equal.

Fixed price: A method of pricing in which bargaining does not take place.

Floating currency: A currency whose value responds to the supply of and demand for that currency.

Floating exchange rate: An exchange rate determined by the laws of supply and demand and with minimal government interference.

Foreign bond: A bond sold outside of the borrower's country but denominated in the currency of the country of issue.

Foreign Corrupt Practices Act (FCPA): A law that criminalizes certain types of payments by U.S. companies, such as bribes to foreign government officials.

Foreign direct investment (FDI): An investment that gives the investor a controlling interest in a foreign company.

Foreign exchange: Checks and other instruments for making payments in another country's currency.

Foreign-exchange control: A requirement that an importer of a product must apply to government authorities for permission to buy foreign currency to pay for the product.

Foreign freight forwarder: A company that facilitates the movement of goods from one country to another.

Foreign investment: Direct or portfolio ownership of assets in another country.

Foreign Investment Review Act (FIRA): A Canadian law intended to limit foreign control of that country's economy.

Foreign sales corporation (FSC): A special type of corporation established by U.S. tax law that can be used by a U.S. exporter to shelter some of its income from taxation.

Foreign trade zone (FTZ): A government-designated area in which goods can be stored, inspected, or manufactured without being subject to formal customs procedures until they leave the zone.

Forfaiting: Similar to factoring but usually for longer time periods and with a guarantee from a bank in the importer's country.

Forward contract: A contract between a company or individual and a bank to deliver foreign currency at a specific exchange rate on a future date.

Forward discount: *See* Discount.

Forward premium: *See* Premium.

Forward rate: A contractually established exchange rate between a foreign-exchange trader and the trader's client for delivery of foreign currency on a specific date.

Franchising: A specialized form of licensing in which one party (the franchisor) sells to an independent party (the franchi*see*) the use of a trademark that is an essential asset for the franchi*see*'s business and also gives continual assistance in the operation of the business.

Freely convertible currency: *See* Hard currency.

Free trade area (FTA): A form of regional economic integration in which internal tariffs are abolished, but member countries set their own external tariffs.

Freight forwarder: *See* Foreign freight forwarder.

Fringe benefit: Any employee benefit other than salary, wages, and cash bonuses.

FSC: *See* Foreign sales corporation.

FTZ: *See* Foreign trade zone.

Functional currency: The currency of the primary economic environment in which an entity operates.

Functional division: An organizational structure in which each function in foreign countries (e.g., marketing or production) reports separately to a counterpart functional group at headquarters.

Futures contract: An agreement between two parties to buy or sell a particular currency at a particular price on a particular future date, as specified in a standardized contract to all participants in that currency futures exchange.

FX swap: A simultaneous spot and forward transaction.

G7 countries: *See* Group of 7.

GAAP: *See* Generally accepted accounting principles.

Gap analysis: A tool used to discover why a company's sales of a given product are less than the market potential in a country; the reason may be a usage, competition, product line, or distribution gap.

GATT: *See* General Agreement on Tariffs and Trade.

General Agreement on Tariffs and Trade (GATT): A multilateral arrangement aimed at reducing barriers to trade, both tariff and nontariff ones; at the signing of the Uruguay round, the GATT was designated to become the World Trade Organization (WTO).

Generalized System of Preferences (GSP): Preferential import restrictions extended by industrial countries to developing countries.

Generally accepted accounting principles (GAAP): The accounting standards accepted by the accounting profession in each country as required for the preparation of financial statements for external users.

Generic: Any of a class of products, rather than the brand of a particular company.

Geocentric: Operations based on an informed knowledge of both home and host country needs.

Geographic division: An organizational structure in which a company's operations are separated for reporting purposes into regional areas.

Geography: A science dealing with the earth and its life, especially with the description of land, sea, air, and the distribution of plant and animal life.

Global bond: A combination of domestic bond and Eurobond that is issued simultaneously in several markets and that must be registered in each national market according to that market's registration requirements.

Global company: A company that integrates operations located in different countries.

Globally integrated company: *See* Global company.

Global sourcing: The acquisition on a worldwide basis of raw materials, parts, and subassemblies for the manufacturing process.

Go–no-go decision: A decision, such as on foreign investments, that is based on minimum-threshold criteria and does not compare different opportunities.

Grandchild subsidiary: An operation that is under a tax-haven subsidiary. Also called a second-tier subsidiary.

Grantback provisions: Stipulations requiring that licen*see*s provide licensors with the use of improvements made on the technology originally licensed.

Gray market: The handling of goods through unofficial distributors.

Gross domestic product (GDP): The total of all economic activity in a country, regardless of who owns the productive assets.

Gross national income (GNI): Formerly referred to as Gross National Product.

Gross national product (GNP): The total of incomes earned by residents of a country, regardless of where the productive assets are located.

Group of 7 (G7): A group of developed countries that periodically meets to make economic decisions; this group consists of Canada, France, Germany, Italy, Japan, the United Kingdom, and the United States.

GSP: *See* Generalized System of Preferences.

Hard currency: A currency that is freely traded without many restrictions and for which there is usually strong external demand; often called a freely convertible currency.

Hardship allowance: A supplement to compensate expatriates for working in dangerous or adverse conditions.

Harvesting: Reduction in the amount of investment. Also known as divestment.

Hedge: To attempt to protect foreign-currency holdings against an adverse movement of an exchange rate.

Heterarchy: An organizational structure in which management of an alliance of companies is shared by so-called equals rather than being set up in a superior-subordinate relationship.

Hierarchy of needs: A well-known motivation theory stating that there is a hierarchy of needs and that people must fulfill the lower-order needs sufficiently before they will be motivated by the higher-order ones.

High-context culture: A culture in which most people consider that peripheral and hearsay information is necessary for decision making because such information bears on the context of the situation.

High-need achiever: One who will work very hard to achieve material or career success, sometimes to the detriment of social relationships or spiritual achievements.

High-value activities: Activities that either produce high profits or are done by high-salaried employees such as managers.

Historically planned economy (HPE): The World Bank's term for Second-World countries in transition to market economies.

History: A branch of knowledge that records and explains past events.

Home country: The country in which an international company is headquartered.

Home-country nationals: Expatriate employees who are citizens of the country in which the company is headquartered.

Horizontal expansion: Any foreign direct investment by which a company produces the same product it produces at home.

Host country: Any foreign country in which an international company operates.

HPE: *See* Historically planned economy.

Hyperinflation: A rapid increase (at least 1 percent per day) in general price levels for a sustained period of time.

IASC: *See* International Accounting Standards Committee.

Idealism: Trying to determine principles before settling small issues.

Ideology: The systematic and integrated body of constructs, theories, and aims that constitute a society.

IFE: *See* International Fisher Effect.

ILO: *See* International Labor Organization.

IMF: *See* International Monetary Fund.

Imitation lag: A strategy for exploiting temporary monopoly advantages by moving first to those countries most likely to develop local production.

Import broker: An individual who obtains various government permissions and other clearances before forwarding necessary paperwork to the carrier that will deliver the goods from the dock to the importer.

Import deposit requirement: Government requirement of a deposit prior to the release of foreign exchange.

Import licensing: A method of government control of the exchange rate whereby all recipients, exporters, and others who receive foreign exchange are required to sell to the central bank at the official buying rate.

Import substitution: An industrialization policy whereby new industrial development emphasizes products that would otherwise be imported.

Import tariff: A tax placed on goods entering a country.

Imports: Goods or services entering a country.

In-bond industry: Any industry that is allowed to import components free of duty, provided that the components will be reexported after processing.

Independence: An extreme situation in which a country would not rely on other countries at all.

Indigenization: The process of introducing elements of an outside culture.

Indirect quote: An exchange rate given in terms of the number of units of the foreign currency for one unit of the domestic currency.

Indirect selling: A sale of goods by an exporter through another domestic company as an intermediary.

Individualistic paradigm: Minimal government intervention in the economy.

Individually validated license (IVL): A special export license under which certain restricted products need to be shipped.

Industrial country: High-income country. Also known as developed country.

Industrialization argument: A rationale for protectionism that argues that the development of industrial output should come about even though domestic prices may not become competitive on the world market.

Inelastic (product demand): A condition in which sales are likely to increase or decline by a percentage that is less than the percentage change in income.

Infant-industry argument: The position that holds that an emerging industry should be guaranteed a large share of the domestic market until it becomes efficient enough to compete against imports.

Inflation: A condition where prices are going up.

Infrastructure: The underlying foundation of a society, such as roads, schools, and so forth, that allows it to function effectively.

Input-output table: A tool used widely in national economic planning to show the resources utilized by different industries for a given output as well as the interdependence of economic sectors.

Intangible property: *See* Intellectual property rights.

Integrated system: A system for taxation of corporate income aimed at preventing double taxation through the use of split rates or tax credits.

Intellectual property rights: Ownership rights to intangible assets, such as patents, trademarks, copyrights, and know-how.

Interbank market: The market for foreign-exchange transactions among commercial banks.

Interbank transactions: Foreign-exchange transactions that take place between commercial banks.

Interdependence: The existence of mutually necessary economic relations among countries.

Interest arbitrage: Investing in debt instruments in different countries and earning a profit due to interest-rate and exchange-rate differentials.

Interest rate differential: An indicator of future changes in the spot exchange rate.

Intermodal transportation: The movement across different modes from origin to destination.

Internalization: Control through self-handling of foreign operations, primarily because such control is less expensive to deal within the same corporate family than to contract with an external organization.

International Accounting Standards Committee (IASC): The international private-sector organization that sets financial accounting standards for worldwide use.

International Bureau for the Protection of Industrial Property Rights (BIRPI): A multilateral agreement to protect patents, trademarks, and other property rights.

International business: All business transactions involving private companies or governments of two or more countries.

International division: An organizational structure in which virtually all foreign operations are handled within the same division.

International Fisher Effect (IFE): The theory that the relationship between interest rates and exchange rates implies that the currency of the country with the lower interest rate will strengthen in the future.

International Labor Organization (ILO): A multilateral organization promoting the adoption of humane labor conditions.

International Monetary Fund (IMF): A multigovernmental association organized in 1945 to promote exchange-rate stability and to facilitate the international flow of currencies.

International Monetary Market (IMM): A specialized market located in Chicago and dealing in select foreign-currency futures.

International Organization of Securities Commissions (IOSCO): An international organization of securities regulators that wants the IASC to establish more comprehensive accounting standards.

International standard of fair dealing: The concept that investors should receive prompt, adequate, and effective compensation in cases of expropriation.

International Trade Administration (ITA): A branch of the U.S. Department of Commerce offering a variety of services to U.S. exporting companies.

Intervention currencies: The currencies in which a particular country trades the most.

Intranet: The use of the Internet to link together the different divisions and functions inside a company.

Intrazonal trade: Trade among countries that are part of a trade agreement, such as the EU.

Investment Canada: A Canadian act whose intent is to persuade foreign companies to invest in Canada.

Invisibles: *See* Services.

IOSCO: *See* International Organization of Securities Commissions.

Irrevocable letter of credit (L/C): A letter of credit that cannot be canceled or changed without the consent of all parties involved.

Islamic law: A system of theocratic law based on the religious teachings of Islam. Also called Muslim law.

ISO 9000: A quality standard developed by the International Standards Organization in Geneva that requires companies to document their commitment to quality at all levels of the organization.

IVL: *See* Individually validated license.

Jamaica Agreement: A 1976 agreement among countries that permitted greater flexibility of exchange rates, basically formalizing the break from fixed exchange rates.

JIT: *See* Just-in-time manufacturing.

Joint venture: A direct investment of which two or more companies share the ownership.

Just-in-time (JIT) manufacturing: A system that reduces inventory costs by having components and parts delivered as they are needed in production.

Kaizen: The Japanese process of continuous improvement, the cornerstone of TQM.

Keiretsu: A corporate relationship linking certain Japanese companies, usually involving a noncontrolling interest in each other, strong high-level personal relationships among managers in the different companies, and interlocking directorships.

Key industry: Any industry that might affect a very large segment of a country's economy or population by virtue of its size or influence on other sectors.

Labor market: The mix of available workers and labor costs available to companies.

Labor union: An association of workers intended to promote and protect the welfare, interests, and rights of its members, primarily by collective bargaining.

LAFTA: *See* Latin American Free Trade Association.

Lag strategy: An operational strategy that involves either delaying collection of foreign-currency receivables if the currency is expected to strengthen or delaying payment of foreign-currency payables when the currency is expected to weaken; the opposite of a lead strategy.

Laissez-faire: The concept of minimal government intervention in a society's economic activity.

Latin American Free Trade Association (LAFTA): A free-trade area formed by Mexico and the South American countries in 1960; it was replaced by ALADI in 1980.

Latin American Integration Association (ALADI): A form of regional economic integration involving most of the Latin American countries.

Law: A binding custom or practice of a community.

Lead country strategy: A strategy of introducing a product on a test basis in a small-country market that is considered representative of a region before investing to serve larger-country markets.

Lead strategy: An operational strategy that involves either collecting foreign-currency receivables before they are due when the currency is expected to weaken or paying foreign-currency payables before they are due when the currency is expected to strengthen; the opposite of a lag strategy.

Lead subsidiary organization: A foreign subsidiary that has global responsibility (serves as corporate headquarters) for one of a company's products or functions.

Learning curve: A concept used to support the infant-industry argument for protection; it assumes that costs will decline as workers and managers gain more experience.

Letter of credit (L/C): A precise document by which the importer's bank extends credit to the importer and agrees to pay the exporter.

Leverage: The degree to which a firm funds the growth of the business debt.

Liability of foreignness: Foreign companies' lower survival rate in comparison to local companies for many years after they begin operations.

LIBOR: *See* London Inter-Bank Offered Rate.

License: Formal or legal permission to do some specified action; a government method of fixing the exchange rate by requiring all recipients, exporters, and others that receive foreign exchange to sell it to the central bank at the official buying rate.

Licensing agreement: Agreement whereby one company gives rights to another for the use, usually for a fee, of such assets as trademarks, patents, copyrights, or other know-how.

Licensing arrangement: A procedure that requires potential importers or exporters to secure permission from government authorities before they conduct trade transactions.

Lifetime employment: The Japanese custom that workers are effectively guaranteed employment with the company for their working lifetimes and that workers seldom leave for employment opportunities with other companies.

LIFFE: *See* London International Financial Futures Exchange.

Liquidity preference: A theory that helps explain capital budgeting and, when applied to international operations, means that investors are willing to take less return in order to be able to shift the resources to alternative uses.

Lobbyist: An individual who participates in advancing or otherwise securing passage of legislation by influencing public officials before and during the legislative process.

Local content: Costs incurred within a given country, usually as a percentage of total costs.

Locally responsive company: Synonym for multidomestic company.

Locals: Citizens of the country in which they are working.

Location-specific advantage: A combination of factor and demand conditions, along with other qualities, that a country has to offer domestic and foreign investors.

Logistics: That part of the supply chain process that plans, implements, and controls the efficient, effective flow and storage of goods, services, and related information from the point of origin to the point of consumption, to meet customers' requirements; sometimes called materials management.

London Inter-Bank Offered Rate (LIBOR): The interest rate for large interbank loans of Eurocurrencies.

London International Financial Futures Exchange (LIFFE): An exchange dealing in futures contracts for several major currencies.

London Stock Exchange (LSE): A stock exchange located in London and dealing in Euroequities.

Low-context culture: A culture in which most people consider relevant only information that they receive firsthand and that bears very directly on the decision they need to make.

Maastricht (Treaty of): The treaty approved in December 1991 that was designed to bring the EU to a higher level of integration and is divided into the Economic Monetary Union (EMU) and political union.

Macro political risk: Negative political actions affecting a broad spectrum of foreign investors.

Management contract: An arrangement whereby one company provides management personnel, who perform general or specialized management functions to another company for a fee.

Manufacturing interchange: A process by which various plants produce a range of components and exchange them so that all plants assemble the finished product for the local market.

Maquiladora: An industrial operation developed by the Mexican and U.S. governments in which U.S.-sourced components are shipped to Mexico duty-free, assembled into final products, and reexported to the United States.

Marginal propensity to import: The tendency to purchase imports with incremental income.

Market capitalization: A common measure of the size of a stock market, which is computed by multiplying the total number of shares of stock listed on the exchange by the market price per share.

Market economy: An economic system in which resources are allocated and controlled by consumers who "vote" by buying goods.

Market environment: The environment that involves the interactions between households (or individuals) and companies in the allocation of resources, free from government ownership or control.

Market socialism: The state owns significant resources, but allocation comes from the market price mechanism.

Materials management: *See* Logistics.

Matrix: A method of plotting data on a set of vertical and horizontal axes in order to compare countries in terms of risk and opportunity.

Matrix division structure: An organizational structure in which foreign units report (by product, function, or area) to more than one group, each of which shares responsibility over the foreign unit.

Measurement: How to value assets.

Mentor: A person at headquarters who looks after the interests of an expatriate employee.

Mercantilism: An economic philosophy based on the beliefs that a country's wealth is dependent on its holdings of treasure, usually in the form of gold, and that countries should export more than they import in order to increase wealth.

Merchandise exports: Goods sent out of a country.

Merchandise imports: Goods brought into a country.

Merchandise trade balance: The part of a country's current account that measures the trade deficit or surplus; its balance is the net of merchandise imports and exports.

MERCOSUR: A major subregional group established by Argentina, Brazil, Paraguay, and Uruguay, which spun off from

ALADI in 1991 with the goal of setting up a customs union and common market.

MFA: *See* Multifibre Arrangement.

MFN: *See* Most-favored-nation.

Micro political risk: Negative political actions aimed at specific, rather than most, foreign investors.

Middle East: The countries on the Arabian peninsula plus those bordering the eastern end of the Mediterranean; sometimes also including other adjacent countries, particularly Jordan, Iraq, Iran, and Kuwait.

Ministry of International Trade and Industry (MITI): The Japanese government agency responsible for coordinating overall business direction and helping individual companies take advantage of global business opportunities.

Mission: What the company will *seek* to do and become over the long term.

Mission statement: A long-range strategic intent.

Mixed economy: An economic system characterized by some mixture of market and command economies and public and private ownership.

Mixed venture: A special type of joint venture in which a government is in partnership with a private company.

MNE: *See* Multinational enterprise.

Monochronic culture: A culture in which most people prefer to deal with situations sequentially (especially those involving other people), such as finishing with one customer before dealing with another.

Monopoly advantage: The perceived supremacy of foreign investors in relation to local companies, which is necessary to overcome the perceived greater risk of operating in a different environment.

Most-favored-nation (MFN): A GATT requirement that a trade concession that is given to one country must be given to all other countries.

Multidomestic company: A company with international operations that allows operations in one country to be relatively independent of those in other countries.

Multilateral agreement: An agreement involving more than two governments.

Multilateral Investment Guarantee Agency (MIGA): A member of the World Bank Group that encourages equity investment and other direct investment flows to developing countries by offering investors a variety of different services.

Multinational corporation (MNC): A synonym for multinational enterprise.

Multinational enterprise (MNE): A company that has an integrated global philosophy encompassing both domestic and overseas operations; sometimes used synonymously with multinational corporation or transnational corporation.

Multiple exchange-rate system: A means of foreign-exchange control whereby the government sets different exchange rates for different transactions.

Muslim law: *See* Islamic law.

National responsiveness: Readiness to implement operating adjustments in foreign countries in order to reach a satisfactory level of performance.

Nationalism: The feeling of pride and/or ethnocentrism that focuses on an individual's home country or nation.

Nationalization: The transfer of ownership to the state.

Natural advantage: Climatic conditions, access to certain natural resources, or availability of labor, which gives a country an advantage in producing some product.

Need hierarchy: *See* Hierarchy of needs.

Neomercantilism: The approach of countries that apparently try to run favorable balances of trade in an attempt to achieve some social or political objective.

Net capital flow: Capital inflow minus capital outflow, for other than import and export payment.

Net export effect: Export stimulus minus export reduction.

Net import change: Import displacement minus import stimulus.

Netting: The transfer of funds from subsidiaries in a net payable position to a central clearing account and from there to the accounts of the net receiver subsidiaries.

Network alliance: Interdependence of countries; each company is a customer of and a supplier to other companies.

Network organization: A situation in which a group of companies is interrelated and in which the management of the interrelation is shared among so-called equals.

Newly industrializing country (NIC): A developing country in which the cultural and economic climate has led to a rapid rate of industrialization and growth since the 1960s.

Nonmarket economy: *See* Command economy.

Nonmarket environment: Public institutions (such as government, government agencies, and government-owned businesses) and nonpublic institutions (such as environmental and other special-interest groups).

Nonpublic institutions: Special-interest groups, such as environmentalists.

Nonresident convertibility: The ability of a nonresident of a country to convert deposits in a bank to the currency of any other country; also known as external convertibility.

Nontariff barriers: Barriers to imports that are not tariffs; examples include administrative controls, "Buy America" policies, and so forth.

Normal quote: Synonym for direct quote.

North American Free Trade Agreement (NAFTA): A free-trade agreement involving the United States, Canada, and Mexico that went into effect on January 1, 1994, and will be phased in over a period of 15 years.

OAU: *See* Organization of African Unity.

Objectives: Specific performance targets to fulfill a company's mission.

Obsolescing bargain (theory of): The premise that a company's bargaining strength with a host government diminishes after the company transfers assets to the host country.

OECD: *See* Organization for Economic Cooperation and Development.

OEEC: *See* Organization for European Economic Cooperation.

Offer rate: The amount for which a foreign-exchange trader is willing to sell a currency.

Official reserves: A country's holdings of monetary gold, Special Drawing Rights, and internationally acceptable currencies.

Offset: A form of barter transaction in which an export is paid for with other merchandise.

Offset trade: A form of countertrade in which an exporter sells goods for cash but then helps businesses in the importing country to find opportunities to earn hard currency.

Offshore financial centers: Cities or countries that provide large amounts of funds in currencies other than their own and are used as locations in which to raise and accumulate cash.

Offshore manufacturing: Manufacturing outside the borders of a particular country.

Oligopoly: An industry in which there are few producers or sellers.

OPEC: *See* Organization of Petroleum Exporting Countries.

Open account: Conditions of sale under which the exporter extends credit directly to the importer.

Operational centers: Offshore financial centers that perform specific functions, such as the sale and servicing of goods.

OPIC: *See* Overseas Private Investment Corporation.

Opinion leader: One whose acceptance of some concept is apt to be emulated by others.

Optimism: A characteristic of an accounting system that implies that companies are more liberal in recognition of income.

Optimum-tariff theory: The argument that a foreign producer will lower its prices if an import tax is placed on its products.

Option: A foreign-exchange instrument that gives the purchaser the right, but not the obligation, to buy or sell a certain amount of foreign currency at a set exchange rate within a specified amount of time.

Organization of African Unity (OAU): An organization of African nations that is more concerned with political than economic objectives.

Organization for Economic Cooperation and Development (OECD): A multilateral organization of industrialized and semi-industrialized countries that helps to formulate social and economic policies.

Organization for European Economic Cooperation (OEEC): A 16-nation organization established in 1948 to facilitate the utilization of aid from the Marshall Plan; it evolved into the EU and EFTA.

Organization of Petroleum Exporting Countries (OPEC): A producers' alliance among 12 petroleum-exporting countries that attempt to agree on oil production and pricing policies.

Organizational structure: The reporting relationships within an organization.

Outright forward: A forward contract that is not connected to a spot transaction.

Outsourcing: The use by a domestic company of foreign suppliers for components or finished products.

Overseas Private Investment Corporation (OPIC): A U.S. government agency that provides insurance for companies involved in international business.

Over-the-counter (OTC) market: Trading in stocks, usually of smaller companies, that are not listed on one of the stock exchanges; also refers to how government and corporate bonds are traded, through dealers who quote bids and offers to buy and to sell "over the counter."

Par value: The benchmark value of a currency, originally quoted in terms of gold or the U.S. dollar and now quoted in terms of Special Drawing Rights.

Parliamentary system: A form of government that involves the election of representatives to form the executive branch.

Passive income: Income from investments in tax-haven countries or sales and services income that involves buyers and sellers in other than the tax-haven country, where either the buyer or the seller must be part of the same organizational structure as the corporation that earns the income; also known as Subpart F income.

Patent: A right granted by a sovereign power or state for the protection of an invention or discovery against infringement.

Patent Cooperation Treaty (PCT): A multilateral agreement to protect patents.

PCT: *See* Patent Cooperation Treaty.

Peg: To fix a currency's exchange rate to some benchmark, such as another currency.

Penetration strategy: A strategy of introducing a product at a low price to induce a maximum number of consumers to try it.

Philadelphia Stock Exchange (PSE): A specialized market dealing in select foreign-currency options.

Piggyback exporting: Use by an exporter of another exporter as an intermediary.

Piracy: The unauthorized use of property rights that are protected by patents, trademarks, or copyrights.

Planning: The meshing of objectives with internal and external constraints in order

to set means to implement, monitor, and correct operations.

Plant layout: Decisions about the physical arrangement of economic activity centers within a manufacturing facility.

PLC: *See* Product life cycle theory.

Pluralistic societies: Societies in which different ideologies are held by various segments rather than one ideology being adhered to by all.

Political freedom: The right to participate freely in the political process.

Political ideology: The body of constructs (complex ideas), theories, and aims that constitute a sociopolitical program.

Political risk: Potential changes in political conditions that may cause a company's operating positions to deteriorate.

Political science: A discipline that helps explain the patterns of governments and their actions.

Political system: The system designed to integrate a society into a viable, functioning unit.

Polycentrism: Characteristic of an individual or organization that feels that differences in a foreign country, real and imaginary, great and small, need to be accounted for in management decisions.

Polychronic culture: A culture in which most people are more comfortable dealing simultaneously with all the situations facing them.

Porter diamond: A diagram showing four conditions—demand (conditions); factor endowments (conditions); related and supporting industries; and firm strategy, structure, and rivalry—that usually must all be favorable for an industry in a country to develop and sustain a global competitive advantage.

Portfolio investment: An investment in the form of either debt or equity that does not give the investor a controlling interest.

Positive-sum gain: A situation in which the sums of gains and losses, if added together among participants, is positive, especially if all parties gain from a relationship.

Power distance: A measurement of preference for consultative or autocratic styles of management.

PPP: *See* Purchasing-power parity.

Pragmatism: Settling small issues before deciding on principles.

Premium (in foreign exchange): The difference between the spot and forward exchange rates in the forward market; a foreign currency sells at a premium when the forward rate exceeds the spot rate and when the domestic currency is quoted on a direct basis.

Pressure group: A group that tries to influence legislation or practices to foster its objectives.

Price escalation: The process by which the lengthening of distribution channels increases a product's price by more than the direct added costs, such as transportation, insurance, and tariffs.

Prior informed consent (PIC): The concept of requiring each exporter of a banned or restricted chemical to obtain, through the home-country government, the expressed consent of the importing country to receive the banned or restricted substance.

Privatization: Selling of government-owned assets to private individuals or companies.

Product division: An organizational structure in which different foreign operations report to different product groups at headquarters.

Product life cycle (PLC) theory: The theory that certain kinds of products go through a cycle consisting of four stages (introduction, growth, maturity, and decline) and that the location of production will shift internationally depending on the stage of the cycle.

Production switching: The movement of production from one country to another in response to changes in cost.

Promotion: The process of presenting messages intended to help sell a product or service.

Protectionism: Government restrictions on imports and occasionally on exports that frequently give direct or indirect subsidies to industries to enable them to compete with foreign production either at home or abroad.

Protestant ethic: A theory that there is more economic growth when work is viewed as a means of salvation and when people prefer to transform productivity gains into additional output rather than into additional leisure.

Pull: A promotion strategy that sells consumers before they reach the point of purchase, usually by relying on mass media.

Purchasing power: What a sum of money actually can buy.

Purchasing-power parity (PPP): A theory that explains exchange-rate changes as

being based on differences in price levels in different countries. Also, the number of units of a country's currency to buy the same products or services in the domestic market that $1 U.S. would buy in the United States.

Push: A promotion strategy that involves direct selling techniques.

Quality: Meeting or exceeding the expectations of a customer.

Quantity controls: Government limitations on the amount of foreign currency that can be used for specific purposes.

Quota: A limit on the quantitative amount of a product allowed to be imported into or exported out of a country in a year.

Quota system: A commodity agreement whereby producing and/or consuming countries divide total output and sales in order to stabilize the price of a particular product.

Quoted currency: The currency whose value is not 1 when an exchange rate is quoted for two currencies.

Rationalization: *See* Rationalized production.

Rationalized production: The specialization of production by product or process in different parts of the world to take advantage of varying costs of labor, capital, and raw materials.

Reciprocal quote: The reciprocal of the direct quote. Also known as the indirect quote.

Regression: A statistical method showing relationships among variables.

Reinvestment: The use of retained earnings to replace depreciated assets or to add to the existing stock of capital.

Relationship enterprises: Networks of strategic alliances among big companies, spanning different industries and countries.

Renegotiation: A process by which international companies and governments decide on a change in terms for operations.

Repatriation: An expatriate's return to his or her home country.

Representative democracy: A type of government in which individual citizens elect representatives to make decisions governing the society.

Resource-based view of the firm: A perspective that holds that each company has a unique combination of competencies.

Return on investment (ROI): The amount of profit, sometimes measured before and sometimes after the payment of taxes, divided by the amount of investment.

Revaluation: A formal change in an exchange rate by which the foreign-currency value of the reference currency rises, resulting in a strengthening of the reference currency.

Reverse culture shock: The experience of culture shock when returning to one's own country that is caused by having accepted what was experienced abroad.

Revocable letter of credit: A letter of credit that can be changed by any of the parties involved.

Rio Declaration: The result of the Rio Earth Summit, which sets out fundamental principles of environmentally responsive behavior.

Rio Earth Summit: A meeting held in Rio de Janeiro in June 1992 that brought together people from around the world to discuss major environmental issues.

ROI: *See* Return on investment.

Rounds: Conferences held by GATT to establish multilateral agreements to liberalize trade.

Royalties: Payments for the use of intangible assets abroad.

SADC: *See* Southern African Development Community.

SADCC: *See* Southern African Development Co-ordination Conference.

Sales representative (foreign): A representative that usually operates either exclusively or nonexclusively within an assigned market and on a commission basis, without assuming risk or responsibility.

Sales response function: The amount of sales created at different levels of marketing expenditures.

SDR: *See* Special Drawing Right.

Second-tier subsidiaries: Subsidiaries that report to a tax-haven subsidiary.

Secondary boycott: The boycotting of a company that does business with a company being boycotted.

Secrecy: A characteristic of an accounting system that implies that companies do not disclose much information about accounting practices; more common in Germanic countries.

Secular totalitarianism: A dictatorship not affiliated with any religious group or system of beliefs.

Securities and Exchange Commission (SEC): A U.S. government agency that regulates securities brokers, dealers, and markets.

Separate entity approach: A system for taxation of corporate income in which each unit is taxed when it receives income, with the result being double taxation.

Service exports: International received earnings other than those derived from the exporting of tangible goods.

Service imports: International paid earnings other than those derived from the importing of tangible goods.

Services: International earnings other than those on goods sent to another country. Also referred to as invisibles.

Services account: The part of a country's current account that measures travel and transportation, tourism, and fees and royalties.

Settlement: The actual payment of currency in a foreign-exchange transaction.

Shipper's export declaration: A shipping document that controls exports and is used to compile trade statistics.

Sight draft: A commercial bill of exchange that requires payment to be made as soon as it is presented to the party obligated to pay.

Silent language: The wide variety of cues other than formal language by which messages can be sent.

Single European Act: A 1987 act of the EU (then the EC) allowing all proposals except those relating to taxation, workers' rights, and immigration to be adopted by a weighted majority of member countries.

Skimming strategy: The strategy of charging a high price for a new product by aiming first at consumers willing to pay the price and then progressively lower the price.

Smithsonian Agreement: A 1971 agreement among countries that resulted in the devaluation of the U.S. dollar, revaluation of other world currencies, a widening of exchange-rate flexibility, and a commitment on the part of all participating countries to reduce trade restrictions; superseded by the Jamaica Agreement of 1976.

Society: A broad grouping of people having common traditions, institutions, and collective activities and interests; the term nation-state is often used in international business to denote a society.

Soft budget: A financial condition in which an enterprise's excess of expenditures over earnings is compensated for by some other institution, typically a government or a state-controlled financial institution.

Soft currency: *See* Weak currency.

Sogo shosha: Japanese trading companies that import and export merchandise.

Sourcing strategy: The strategy that a company pursues in purchasing materials, components, and final products; sourcing can be from domestic and foreign locations and from inside and outside the company.

Southern African Development Community (SADC): An organization endeavoring to counter the economic influence of South Africa in the region by focusing on economic objectives, such as regional cooperation in attracting investment.

Sovereignty: Freedom from external control, especially when applied to a body politic.

Special Drawing Right (SDR): A unit of account issued to countries by the International Monetary Fund to expand their official reserves bases.

Specific duty: A duty (tariff) assessed on a per-unit basis.

Speculation: The buying or selling of foreign currency with the prospect of great risk and high return.

Speculator: A person who takes positions in foreign exchange with the objective of earning a profit.

Spillover effects: Situations in which the marketing program in one country results in awareness of the product in other countries.

Spin-off organization: A company now operating almost independently of the parent because its activities do not fit easily with the parent's existing competencies.

Spot market: The market in which an asset is traded for immediate delivery, as opposed to a market for forward or future deliveries.

Spot rate: An exchange rate quoted for immediate delivery of foreign currency, usually within two business days.

Spread: In the forward market, the difference between the spot rate and the forward rate; in the spot market, the difference between the bid (buy) and offer (sell) rates quoted by a foreign-exchange trader.

Stakeholders: The collection of groups, including stockholders, employees, customers, and society at large, that a company must satisfy to survive.

State capitalism: A condition in which some developed countries, such as Japan and Korea, have intervened in the economy to direct the allocation and control of resources.

Static effects of integration: The shifting of resources from inefficient to efficient companies as trade barriers fall.

Stereotype: A standardized and oversimplified mental picture of a group.

Strategic alliance: An agreement between companies that is of strategic importance to one or both companies' competitive viability.

Strategic intent: An objective that gives an organization cohesion over the long term while it builds global competitive viability.

Strategic plan: A long-term plan involving major commitments.

Strategy: The means companies select to achieve their objectives.

Subpart F income: Income of a CFC that comes from sources other than those connected with the active conduct of a trade or business, such as holding company income.

Subsidiarity: A principle that implies that EU interference should take place only in areas of common concern and that most policies should be set at the national level.

Subsidiary: A foreign operation that is legally separate from the parent company, even if wholly owned by it.

Subsidies: Direct assistance from governments to companies, making them more competitive.

Substitution drawbacks: A provision allowing domestic merchandise to be substituted for merchandise that is imported for eventual export, thus allowing the U.S. firm to exclude the duty paid on the merchandise in costs and in sales prices.

Supply chain: The coordination of materials, information, and funds from the initial raw material supplier to the ultimate customer.

Swap: A simultaneous spot and forward foreign-exchange transaction.

Syndication: Cooperation by a lead bank and several other banks to make a large loan to a public or private organization.

Tariff: A government tax levied on goods, usually imports, shipped internationally; the most common type of trade control.

Tax credit: A dollar-for-dollar reduction of tax liability that must coincide with the recognition of income.

Tax deferral: Income is not taxed until it is remitted to the parent company as a dividend.

Tax-haven countries: Countries with low income taxes or no taxes on foreign-source income.

Tax-haven subsidiary: A subsidiary of a company established in a tax-haven country for the purpose of minimizing income tax.

Tax treaty: A treaty between two countries that generally results in the reciprocal reduction on dividend withholding taxes and the exemption of taxes or royalties and sometimes interest payments.

Technology: The means employed to produce goods or services.

Technology absorbing capacity: The ability of the recipient to work effectively with technology, particularly in relation to the need for training and equity in the recipient in order to effect a transfer.

Temporal method: A method of translating foreign-currency financial statements used when the functional currency is that of the parent company.

Terms currency: Exchange rates are quoted as the number of units of the terms currency per base currency.

Terms of trade: The quantity of imports that can be bought by a given quantity of a country's exports.

Theocratic law system: A legal system based on religious precepts.

Theocratic totalitarianism: A dictatorship led by a religious group.

Theory of country size: The theory which holds that countries with large land areas are more apt to have varied climates and natural resources, and, therefore, generally are more nearly self-sufficient than smaller countries.

Theory of obsolescing bargain: The erosion of bargaining strength from a group as countries gain assets from them.

Third-country nationals: Expatriate employees who are neither citizens of the country in which they are working nor citizens of the country where the company is headquartered.

Tie-in provisions: Stipulations in licensing that require the licen*see* to purchase or sell products from/to the licensor.

Time draft: A commercial bill of exchange calling for payment to be made at some time after delivery.

Time series: A statistical method of illustrating a pattern over time, such as in demand for a particular product.

TNC: *See* Transnational company.

Tort: A civil wrong independent of a contract.

Total quality management (TQM): The process that a company uses to achieve quality, where the goal is elimination of all defects.

Totalitarianism: A political system characterized by the absence of widespread participation in decision making.

TQM: *See* Total quality management.

Trade creation: Production shifts to more efficient producers for reasons of comparative advantage, allowing consumers access to more goods at a lower price than would have been possible without integration.

Trade diversion: A situation in which exports shift to a less efficient producing country because of preferential trade barriers.

Trade Related Aspects of Intellectual Property Rights (TRIPS): A provision from the Uruguay round of trade negotiations requiring countries to agree to enforce procedures under their national laws to protect intellectual property rights.

Trademark: A name or logo distinguishing a company or product.

Transaction exposure: Foreign-exchange risk arising because a company has outstanding accounts receivable or accounts payable that are denominated in a foreign currency.

Transfer price: A price charged for goods or services between entities that are related to each other through stock ownership, such as between a parent and its subsidiaries or between subsidiaries owned by the same parent.

Transit tariff: A tax placed on goods passing through a country.

Translation: The restatement of foreign-currency financial statements into U.S. dollars.

Translation exposure: Foreign-exchange risk that occurs because the parent company must translate foreign-currency financial statements into the reporting currency of the parent company.

Transnational: (1) An organization in which different capabilities and contributions among different country-operations are shared and integrated; (2) multinational enterprise; (3) company owned and managed by nationals from different countries.

Transnational company (TNC): A company owned and managed by nationals in different countries; also may be synonymous with multinational enterprise.

Transparency: A characteristic of an accounting system that implies that companies disclose a great deal of information about accounting practices; more common in Anglo-Saxon countries (United States, United Kingdom).

Triad strategy: A strategy proposing that an MNE should have a presence in Europe, the United States, and Asia (especially Japan).

TRIPS: *See* Trade Related Aspects of Intellectual Property Rights.

Turnkey operation: An operating facility that is constructed under contract and transferred to the owner when the facility is ready to begin operations.

Underemployed: Those people who are working at less than their capacity.

Unfavorable balance of trade: An indication of a trade deficit—that is, imports are greater than exports. Also called deficit.

Unilateral transfer: A transfer of currency from one country to another for which no goods or services are received; an example is foreign aid to a country devastated by earthquake or flood.

Unit of account: A benchmark on which to base the value of payments.

United Nations (UN): An international organization of countries formed in 1945 to promote world peace and security.

United Nations Conference on Trade and Development (UNCTAD): A UN body that has been especially active in dealing with the relationships between developing and industrialized countries with respect to trade.

Universal Copyright Convention (UCC): A multilateral agreement to protect copyrights.

Unrequited transfer: *See* Unilateral transfer.

U.S.-Canada Free Trade Agreement: *See* Canada-U.S. Free Trade Agreement.

U.S. shareholder: For U.S. tax purposes, a person or company owning at least 10 percent of the voting stock of a foreign subsidiary.

U.S. terms: The practice of using the direct quote for exchange rates.

Value-added tax (VAT): A tax that is a percentage of the value added to a product at each stage of the business process.

Value chain: The collective activities that occur as a product moves from raw materials through production to final distribution.

Variable price: A method of pricing in which buyers and sellers negotiate the price.

VAT: *See* Value-added tax.

VER: *See* Voluntary export restrictions.

Vertical integration: The control of the different stages as a product moves from raw materials through production to final distribution.

Virtual manufacturing: Subcontracting the manufacturing process to another firm.

Visible exports: *See* Merchandise exports.

Visible imports: *See* Merchandise imports.

Voluntary export restraint (VER): A negotiated limitation of exports between an importing and an exporting country.

Weak currency: A currency that is not fully convertible.

West African Economic Community: A regional economic group involving Benin, Burkina Faso, Ivory Coast, Mali, Mauritania, Niger, and Senegal.

Western Hemisphere: Literally the earth's area between the zero and 180th meridian, but it usually indicates the continents of the Americas and adjacent islands, excluding Greenland.

WIPO: *See* World Intellectual Property Organization.

World Bank: A multilateral lending institution that provides investment capital to countries.

World Intellectual Property Organization (WIPO): A multilateral agreement to protect patents.

World Trade Organization (WTO): A voluntary organization through which groups of countries negotiate trading agreements and which has authority to over*see* trade disputes among countries.

WTO: *See* World Trade Organization.

Zaibatsu: Large, family-owned Japanese businesses that existed before World War II and consisted of a series of financial and manufacturing companies usually held together by a large holding company.

Zero defects: The elimination of defects, which results in the reduction of manufacturing costs and an increase in consumer satisfaction.

Zero-sum game: A situation in which one party's gain equals another party's loss.

Photo Credits

Company Index and Trademarks

Name Index

Subject Index